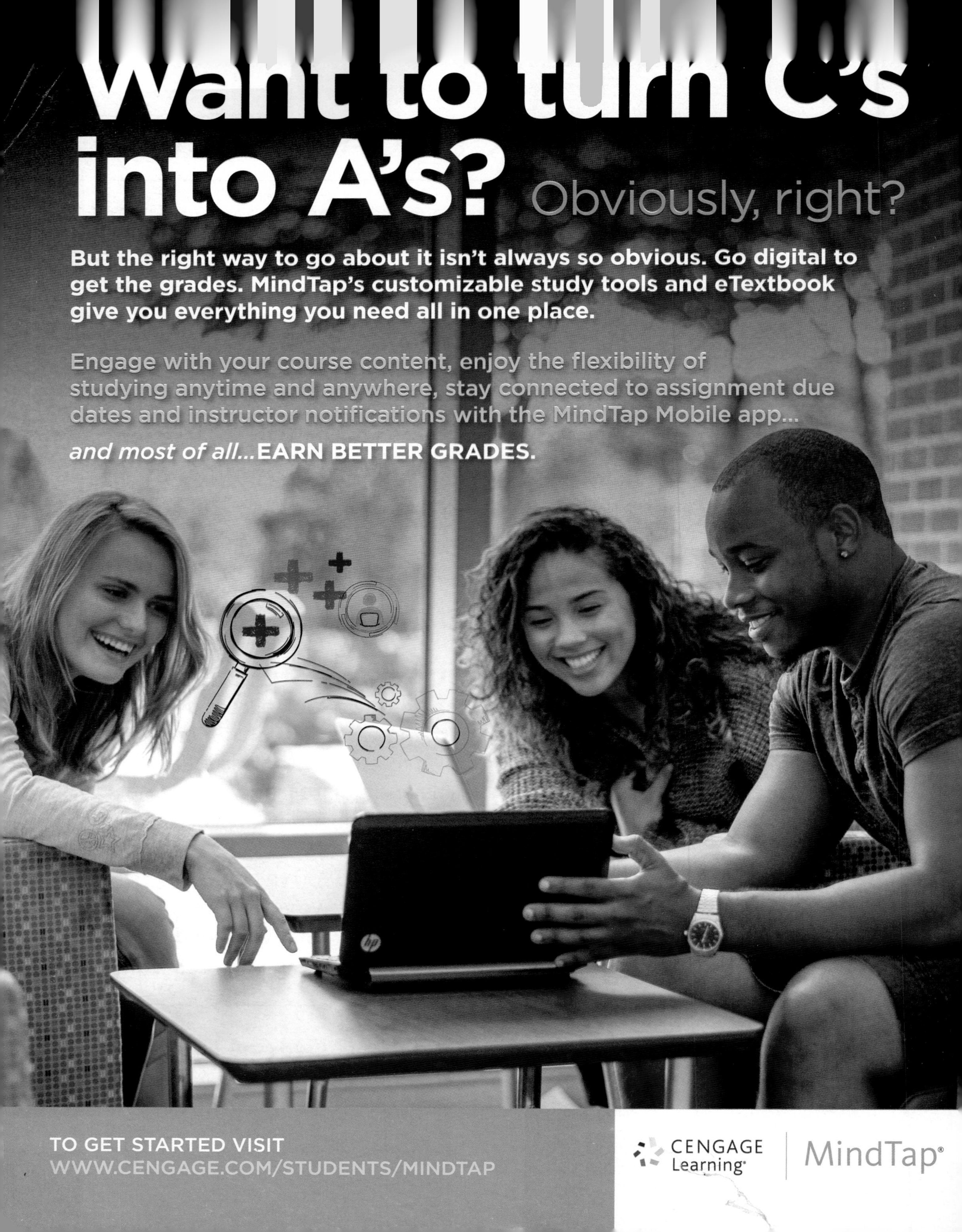
Want to turn C’s into A’s? Obviously, right?
But the right way to go about it isn’t always so obvious. Go digital to get the grades. MindTap’s customizable study tools and eTextbook give you everything you need all in one place.
Engage with your course content, enjoy the flexibility of studying anytime and anywhere, stay connected to assignment due dates and instructor notifications with the MindTap Mobile app...
and most of all...EARN BETTER GRADES.
TO GET STARTED VISIT
WWW.CENGAGE.COM/STUDENTS/MINDTAP
CENGAGE Learning
MindTap®

GLOBAL AMERICANS

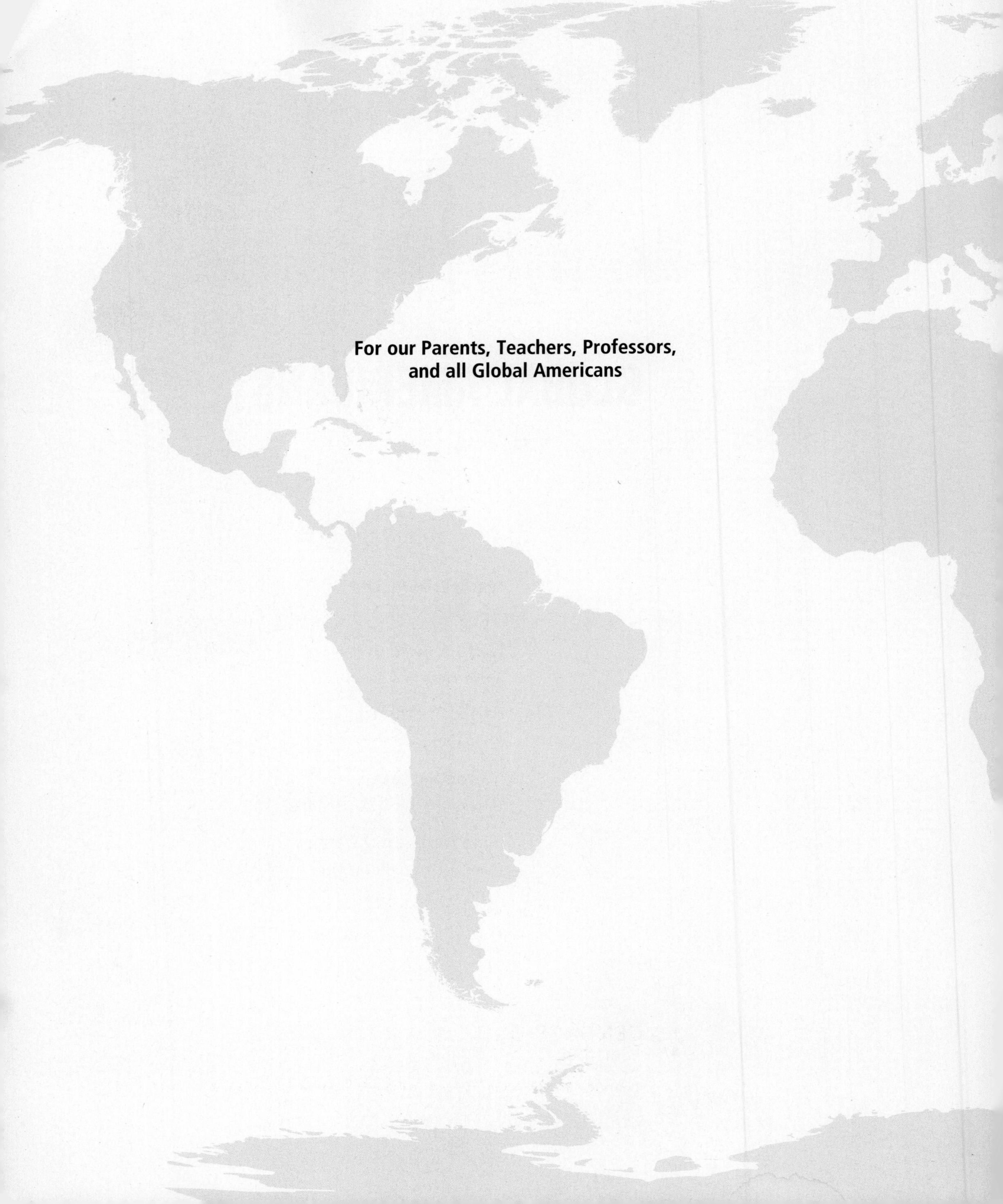

For our Parents, Teachers, Professors,
and all Global Americans

GLOBAL AMERICANS

VOL 1: to1877

A History of the United States

Maria E. Montoya
New York University

Laura A. Belmonte
Oklahoma State University

Carl J. Guarneri
Saint Mary's College of Californina

Steven W. Hackel
University of California, Riverside

Ellen Hartigan-O'Connor
University of California, Davis

Lon Kurashige
University of Southern California

CENGAGE Learning

Australia • Brazil • Mexico • Singapore • United Kingdom • United States

CENGAGE Learning

Global Americans: A History of the United States
Maria E. Montoya / Laura A. Belmonte / Carl J. Guarneri / Steven W. Hackel / Ellen Hartigan-O'Connor / Lon Kurashige

Product Director: Paul Banks

Product Manager: Joseph Potvin

Managing Content Developer: Anais Wheeler

Content Developer: Erika Hayden

Associate Content Developer: Andrew Newton

Product Assistant: Emma Guiton

Senior Marketing Manager: Valerie Hartman

Senior Content Project Manager: Carol Newman

Senior Art Director: Cate Barr

Manufacturing Planner: Fola Orekoya

IP Analyst: Alexandra Ricciardi

IP Project Manager: Erika Mugavin

Production Service / Compositor: SPi Global

Text Designer: Jeanne Calabrese

Cover Designer: Nilou Moochhala / NYM Design

Cover Image: (left to right): Joseph Brant (George Romney/Getty Images), Harriet Tubman (Library of Congress Prints and Photographs Division), Carmen Ghiradelli (National Portrait Gallery), Olaudah Equiano (*Everett Collection Inc/Alamy Stock Photo*), Clara Barton (JT Vintage/ Glasshouse Images/Alamy Stock Photo), Medicine Snake Woman (Natawista) (Montana Historical Society)

For product information and technology assistance, contact us at **Cengage Learning Customer & Sales Support, 1-800-354-9706**

For permission to use material from this text or product, submit all requests online at **www.cengage.com/permissions**.

Further permissions questions can be emailed to **permissionrequest@cengage.com**.

Library of Congress Control Number: 2016951291

Student Edition:
ISBN: 978-1-337-10111-0

Loose-leaf Edition:
ISBN: 978-1-337-10123-3

Cengage Learning
20 Channel Center Street
Boston, MA 02210
USA

Cengage Learning is a leading provider of customized learning solutions with employees residing in nearly 40 different countries and sales in more than 125 countries around the world. Find your local representative at **www.cengage.com**.

Cengage Learning products are represented in Canada by Nelson Education, Ltd.

To learn more about Cengage Learning Solutions, visit **www.cengage.com**.

Purchase any of our products at your local college store or at our preferred online store **www.cengagebrain.com**.

Printed in the United States of America
Print Number: 01 Print Year: 2016

Brief Contents

Contents

Maps & Features

History Without Borders

Global Americans

Timelines

Preface

Global Americans embodies a new, internationalized approach to American history. In their form and content, most textbooks portray the United States as a national enterprise that developed largely in isolation from the main currents of world history. In contrast, this textbook speaks to an increasingly diverse population of students and instructors who seek to understand the nation's place in a constantly changing global, social, and political landscape. It incorporates a growing body of scholarship that documents how for five centuries North America's history has been subject to transnational forces and enmeshed in overseas activities and developments.

American history was global in the beginning, and it has been ever since. We therefore present a history of the United States and its Native American and colonial antecedents in which world events and processes are central features, not just colorful but peripheral sidelights. Our narrative is meant to show how at each stage of its unfolding, the American story was shaped by exchanges of goods, people, and ideas with others, and in turn how Americans exerted growing influence abroad. This enlarged American history is intended to break down curricular walls that discourage connections between U.S. and world history. Its globally informed narrative also aims to capture more accurately how Americans have actually experienced their lives in the past as well as the present.

Students today face a world that is rapidly changing with stepped-up exchanges of ideas and goods that reshape the economy; new technologies that transform work and communication; global conflicts over ideologies and religions; and political and economic developments that challenge the United States' role in the world. We believe that history students need a narrative that recovers the global contexts of America's past and helps them understand the origins of the interconnected world in which we live. *Global Americans* weaves together stories, analysis, interpretation, and visual imagery from across time and place to craft a new American history that develops in relation to events and peoples across this continent and beyond. While integrating this enlarged geographic coverage into our narrative, we have taken care not to sacrifice the detailed coverage of domestic events that are keys to the nation's history and to include consideration of the distinctive features and ideas that have shaped that history.

World history narratives sometimes neglect the human element in favor of describing economic systems and impersonal forces. *Global Americans* instead focuses on people. Our narrative is committed to integrating the experiences of Americans whose stories are often omitted from U.S. history courses because they are somehow deemed foreign or because they represented minority voices. We also cast new light on familiar figures and events by placing them in a global or transnational context. *Global Americans* reflects our belief that different groups of people have had, and still have, claims to being American and part of U.S. history. The narrative of American history is enriched by exploring the world of Native Americans prior to their contact with Europeans and Africans, as well as examining the full range of Spanish, French, Dutch, and English colonial projects for trade and settlement. Just as we do not see global contexts as incidental to this history, we do not portray the period prior to the founding of the United States as simply a prelude to nationhood. The colonial history of North America is the story of a place laid claim to by various peoples and governments. Including its diversity of actors and aspirations adds contingency to a national story that is often told as if destined or preordained. After the United States achieved independence, its history similarly underwent a process of conflict and experiment in the context of international and local events and people. The nation's territorial spread, its mix of peoples, and its global position were forged in the crucible of powerful domestic and international influences. Today's Americans experience the effects of both the local and the global as they work, play, worship, consume, travel, and wage war or peace. We have aimed to construct a historical narrative that does justice to the dramatic conflicts, diverse peoples, and myriad connections that have created our American world.

What's New About This Textbook?

A global perspective informs the presentation of the essential social, economic, religious, and political themes of American history.

Global Context

U.S. history textbooks have traditionally conceptualized American history as distinct and standing apart from the rest of the world, with events beyond its borders acknowledged almost solely through U.S. foreign policy and wars. Yet recent scholarship has emphasized how the United States has considered global social, economic, and cultural factors, and historians have highlighted the role of the United States in the world. Engaging this expanded notion of U.S. history requires a new look at the United States as a nation with a web of worldwide connections.

We build on this scholarship by suggesting that borders have historically been porous and fluid and that demographics have constantly shifted from the precolonial era to the present. We show that the early history of North America was created by the intersections of Atlantic, Pacific, Indian, and African history, as well as one element in Europe's expansion during the early modern era. Thus, the experiences of Indians, the Spanish, the French, the Dutch, and the English all figure prominently in the early chapters. We consider transatlantic slavery and the diaspora of African peoples as part of a thousand-year saga that is not limited to the history of North America or the United States. We continue the focus on migration and diverse populations throughout the nineteenth- and twentieth-century chapters, and we give special attention to commerce and trade and the ways in which technology, culture, and ideas are transmitted across national boundaries. With a global perspective, the narrative of U.S. history connects to the rest of the world not only through the actions of presidents, generals, and diplomats, but also through the experiences of business leaders, social activists, missionaries, workers, immigrants, refugees, athletes, musicians, artists, tourists, and consumers.

At the same time, the core narrative of American political, economic, and social history constitutes the spine of *Global Americans*. Our work covers all the major domestic trends and events and highlights all the familiar players. Presidents and presidential elections serve to mark eras and change over time. Students will always know that they are situated in the broadly familiar terrain of U.S. history. But the traditional narrative looks different within a global context, and this informs the other themes that run through the book.

A Continental Nation

Global context necessitates a continental orientation. Our work takes seriously that the history of all parts of the nation and its territories matters, not just the regions formally incorporated into the United States during the Revolutionary War. What happened before the United States became a nation had important consequences for the society that would later develop. For example, we want our students to understand how California Indians experienced the Franciscan missions, how Spanish soldiers and settlers reacted to life in this distant frontier, and how North American regions settled by Spain differed from New France or British North America. We also want our students to understand how the peoples and lands of the trans-Mississippi West were and were not incorporated into the United States during the nineteenth and twentieth centuries. Our focus on the American West, on the nation's continental borderlands, and on its territories, including Alaska and Hawai'i, provides new perspectives on westward migration, the slavery controversy, railroads and industrialization, and the centrality of California to modern American culture.

One of the most important recent intellectual developments in history has been the move to view the Atlantic World as a loosely integrated region with connections that transcend nation-states and national boundaries. Just as we chronicle the integration of the Americas into an Atlantic system of politics, commerce, and culture during the Age of European Expansion, we similarly treat the Pacific Ocean and the lands adjacent to it as an integrated region that has long affected American history. Seeing the U.S. East and West coasts as elements within their respective oceanic communities reinforces our global integration framework.

Diversity in Global and Continental Contexts

Global integration and a continental orientation allow a fresh look at issues of race, class, and gender. In recent decades, historians and their textbooks have given much consideration to racial and ethnic minorities, the lives of working people, and the roles of women, yet they have been slower to advance an interpretive framework that presents U.S. history from their varying points of view and acknowledges multiple perspectives within these groups. In contrast, we examine what it looked like to live through events in U.S. history from different perspectives; we explore diversity *within* the categories of race, ethnicity, and class; and we situate movements for women's rights and LGBT rights within national and transnational contexts. For example, we discuss the very different impact the diffusion of European consumer goods in the eighteenth century had on the lives and politicization of free women, enslaved women, and Cherokee women. In an example from the nineteenth century, we describe the roles played by the *Californio*, *Tejano*, and New Mexican *Hispano* elite in the economic and political conquest of the Southwest by the United States during the 1830s and 1840s, and we examine the ways colonialism affected women and families in this region. During the twentieth century, we place World War II in the context of worldwide, concurrent racial ideologies and situate the U.S. civil rights movement in the context of global struggles for human rights. We also look at the rise of politically conservative Christian activity in light of rising religious fundamentalism worldwide.

Format for Each Chapter

Global Perspective

Each chapter deliberately embeds a global framework in the text and in the features. The opening vignette sets the focus by making global connections, and the chapter introduction deliberately surveys the global context of the chapter's time frame. This global context is reinforced in presentation of events and people throughout the chapter text and reiterated at the end of the chapter in a summary and globalized timeline. The strategy for achieving a global perspective derives from what we have come to call, during the book's development, the Five Cs: comparisons, connections, concepts, contexts, and consequences. Different national experiences are *compared. Connections* among international social movements are examined as are theories and models concerning, for example, revolutions, nation building, industrialization, imperialism, feminism, and racism. We look at the broad international *contexts* for what seem to be internal developments, such as the American Revolution and Progressivism. We track worldwide *consequences* for what seem to be American events—plantation slavery and commercial cotton, for example, or Henry Ford's moving assembly line—as well as the impacts of international ideas and events on America's history.

Opening Vignette

Each chapter opens with a story of an individual who has crossed borders—in geography, national boundaries, culture, or identity—and whose experience exemplifies the book's global integration framework.

Visual Headings

Each section within a chapter opens with an image that signals the content that follows. These photos, cartoons, paintings, and objects of material culture prompt students to connect, understand, and remember major points and ideas. An informative caption directs interpretation of the image and promotes visual learning. For example, in the book's first chapter, the "Open Hand" symbol of the Eastern Woodlands peoples can be read as either a welcome or a warning. In the chapter on the American Revolution, an eyewitness watercolor depicting four different soldiers in the Continental forces at Yorktown—a black soldier, a New England militiaman, a backcountry rifleman, and a French officer—demonstrates not only the diversity among fighting men but also the different motives for fighting the American War for Independence. Furthermore, in the chapter on the New Deal, we use an image of Franklin Roosevelt broadcasting a "fireside chat" to signal his innovations in connecting the presidency to the people through technology and his efforts to explain his administration's policies in everyday language.

Focus Questions and Subheading Clues

At the end of each visual heading is a focus question that guides students in absorbing and interpreting the information in the subsections that follow. For example, the major section on the U.S. Constitution asks:

- As you read, focus on the ways in which the relationship between local and federal power was central to the framing of the Constitution and the debates over its ratification. Which side won the debate initially? Ultimately?

Each subheading in that section is then annotated with a brief statement of core content intended both to cue understanding and aid in review.

- The Constitutional Convention rethinks the new nation's political structure.
- The new Constitution creates a stronger central government.
- The debates over ratifying the Constitution center on federal powers and the nature of a republic.
- The continuing importance of protecting individual rights against a powerful central government reflects the Revolution's legacy.

Together, these clues build toward an informed, comprehensive answer to the focus question that opened the section. In conjunction with the focus question, the clues are designed to support departmental and campuswide learning objectives and assessment programs.

Key Terms

Within each chapter, approximately forty specialized terms are boldfaced for students' attention with brief definitions appearing on the same page. Terms highlighted include concepts, laws, treaties, movements and organizations, legal cases, and battles. Unlike other textbooks, *Global Americans* also includes specialized terms relating to world events that affected Americans, such as *Revolutions of 1848* and *blitzkrieg*. The key terms thus highlight the connections between U.S. history and developments around the globe.

Global Americans Portraits

Each chapter features three portraits—brief biographies and often an image—of individuals whose lives or careers cross borders or were affected by international events. These portraits also highlight the various ways people experienced the social, economic, and political turmoil discussed in the chapter narrative. The familiar (e.g., Harriet Tubman) and less familiar (e.g., Medicine Snake Woman and Dith Pran) are both represented. Collectively, the portraits aim to challenge preconceptions and offer surprising new insights into people as diverse as Daniel Boone, who joined both sides of the American Revolution and ended up a local official in Spanish North America, and Hedy Lamarr, who is best-known as a Hollywood starlet, but who was also a self-taught inventor who made a major contribution to the wireless communication revolution.

History Without Borders

Each chapter includes a global feature highlighting an issue, idea, product, or material object that was not constrained by political borders. A brief essay, images, and a world or hemisphere map trace the global path of ideas and goods. Often this feature reveals something not well known by Americans on a topic not typically included in a U.S. history textbook, such as the Iroquois' adoption of Chinese vermilion as body paint, Japan's antinuclear movement in the 1950s, and the impact of artificially created nitrogen fertilizer on world food production. Critical thinking questions help students place American events or trends in a larger, global context. This feature is not merely global decoration but rather an extension of an already globalized text.

Summary and "Thinking Back, Looking Forward"

The core text of each chapter ends with a summary that revisits the focus questions to establish large-scale generalizations and promote a synthetic understanding of U.S. history and its connections to the world. The "Thinking Back, Looking Forward" element directs students to see long-term trends and recurring themes that appear across chapters.

Timeline

A timeline at the end of each chapter is intended to help students review by visualizing chronology and events' cause and effect. Timelines conventionally list the most important events covered in the chapter. In our chapters, timelines incorporate international events to reinforce the book's global framework and use maps to correlate the regions of the world with events in the timeline.

Resources

A list of secondary and Internet sources appears in each chapter. These are the resources that we believe are useful to both students and instructors who want to dig deeper into the content of the chapter. They are not meant to be comprehensive but rather to suggest the richness of the field.

Note on Terminology

As authors we have grappled with the challenge of finding the appropriate term for a specific ethnic or racial group during a particular period in history. These terms are not fixed, but in fact shift over historical periods, adding even more complexity. The terms we have chosen to use in each of the chapters are deliberate and reflect our understanding of both the historiography and contemporary uses. Our intention is not to make a final determination about the use of specific ethnic and racial labels, but rather to help teachers suggest that these terms can be used as a basis for discussion regarding the importance of names and who gets to decides various labels.

Note on Images

The images in *Global Americans* have been thoughtfully chosen to help students engage with the text on a visual level as well as a reading comprehension level. We encourage instructors to have their students "read" the images carefully and ask questions about each of them. We have also selected some images that are quite disturbing, such as an image of the lynching of Will Brown in Chapter 18 and the liberation of Jews from a World War II concentration camp in Chapter 21. We debated the pros and cons of using these images, deciding to do so because we believe that they reflect important historical moments with which we want students to engage and interpret.

MindTap

MindTap Instant Access Code: ISBN – 9781337114677
MindTap Printed Access Card: ISBN – 9781337116107

MindTap for *Global Americans* is a personalized, online learning platform that provides students with an immersive learning experience to build and foster critical thinking skills. Through a carefully designed chapter-based learning path, MindTap allows students to easily identify learning objectives; draw connections and improve writing skills by completing unit-level essay assignments; read short, manageable sections from the e-book; and test their content knowledge with map- and timeline-based critical thinking questions.

MindTap allows instructors to customize their content, providing tools that seamlessly integrate YouTube clips, outside Websites, and personal content directly into the learning path. Instructors can assign additional primary source content through the Instructor Resource Center and Questia primary and secondary source databases that house thousands of peer-reviewed journals, newspapers, magazines, and full-length books.

The additional content available in MindTap mirrors and complements the authors' narrative, emphasizing the global forces and dynamics that have been central to the history of the United States. It also includes primary source content and assessments not found in the printed text. To learn more, ask your Cengage Learning sales representative to demonstrate it for you—or go to www.Cengage.com/MindTap.

Instructor Resources

The Instructor's Companion Website, accessed through the Instructor Resource Center (login.cengage.com), houses all of the supplemental materials you can use for your course. This includes a Test Bank, Instructor's Manual, and PowerPoint Lecture Presentations. The Test Bank, offered in Microsoft® Word® and Cognero® formats, contains multiple-choice, identification, true or false, and essay questions for each chapter. Cognero® is a flexible, online system that allows you to author, edit, and manage test bank content for Western Civilization,10e. Create multiple test versions instantly and deliver through your LMS from your classroom, or wherever you may be, with no special installs or downloads required. The Instructor's Resource Manual includes chapter summaries, suggested lecture topics, map exercises, discussion questions for the primary sources, topics for student research, relevant websites, suggestions for additional videos, and online resources for information on historical sites. Finally, the PowerPoint Lectures are ADA-compliant slides collate the key takeaways from the chapter in concise visual formats perfect for in-class presentations or for student review.

Acknowledgements

The development and writing of *Global Americans* has taken almost a decade. Along the way, we have indebted ourselves to some very fine editors and scholars who helped us find our collective voice as well as the will to continue on what has been an enormous project. We would like to thank Irene Beiber and Sally Constable who first approached us about writing such a textbook. Along the way, we had the great fortune to work with Ann West and Jean Woy who both helped shape the book in the early stages. We were also lucky enough to have Clint Attebery guide the team through a critical juncture. Our biggest debt, however, goes to Ann Grogg, an exceptional editor, who worked closely with each of us to translate our knowledge into a readable and usable text for college students. We are all better writers from having her skillful touch on our prose.

We also owe a debt of gratitude to each other for the years of hard work as we each read and edited chapters that were often far afield from our own special area of expertise. Throughout the long process of writing and editing, we coauthors have held lively biweekly conference calls in which every stage of every chapter was discussed in detail. *Global Americans*, therefore, is the outcome of countless hours of shared discussions about American history and how it should be presented to a new generation of students.

We are also indebted to many colleagues who voiced their encouragement, read draft chapters, and provided helpful suggestions for improvement.

Alexander Haskell, *University of California, Riverside*
James Huston, *Oklahoma State University*
Ann M. Little, *Colorado State University*
Peter Mancall, *University of Southern California*
Lisa Materson, *University of California, Davis*
Andrew Needham, *New York University*
Marcy Norton, *George Washington University*
Gregory E. O'Malley, *University of California, Santa Cruz*
Lorena Oropeza, *University of California, Davis*
Thomas J. Osborne, *Santa Ana College (emeritus)*
Robert C. Ritchie, *Henry E. Huntington Library*
Susanah Shaw Romney, *New York University.*
Virginia Scharff, *University of New Mexico*
Carole Shammas, *University of Southern California*
Terri Snyder, *California State University, Fullerton*
Michael Witgen, *University of Michigan*

We want to thank all the scholars who were contracted by Cengage as expert reviewers of the text at various stages. Their critiques were thoughtful and much appreciated.

Thomas Adam, *The University of Texas at Arlington*
Ian Aebel, *University of Iowa*
Brian Alnutt, *Northampton Community College*
Rick Ascheman, *Rochester Community and Technical College*
Shelby Balik, *Metropolitan State University of Denver*
Evan Bennett, *Florida Atlantic University*
Katherine Benton-Cohen, *Georgetown University*
Angela Boswell, *Henderson State University*
Blanche Brick, *Blinn College*
Rachel Buff, *University of Wisconsin*
Brian Casserly, *Bellevue College*
Tonia Compton, *Columbia College*

Cynthia Counsil, *Florida State College at Jacksonville*
David Dalton, *College of the Ozarks*
Bruce Daniels, *The University of Texas at San Antonio*
Wendy Davis, *Campbellsville University*
Rodney Dillon, *Palm Beach State College*
Shaughnessy Doyel, *Saint Charles Community College*
Shannon Duffy, *Texas State University*
Mark Elliott, *University of North Carolina at Greensboro*
Richard Filipink, *Western Illinois University*
Kristen Foster, *Marquette University*
Jennifer Fry, *Moravian College*
Joshua Fulton, *Moraine Valley Community College*
Bryan Garrett, *The University of Texas at Arlington*
Matthew Garrett, *Bakersfield College*
Diane Gill, *North Lake College*
Aram Goudsouzian, *University of Memphis*
Larry Grubbs, *Georgia State University*
Elisa Guernsey, *Monroe Community College*
David Hamilton, *University of Kentucky*
Kristin Hargrove, *Grossmont College*
Aimee Harris-Johnson, *El Paso Community College*
Justin Hart, *Texas Tech University*
Mary Ann Heiss, *Kent State University*
Robin Henry, *Wichita State University*
Warren Hofstra, *Shenandoah University*
Thomas Humphrey, *Cleveland State University*
Matthew Hutchinson, *Kennesaw State University*
Sheyda Jahanbani, *University of Kansas*
Ely Janis, *Massachusetts College of Liberal Arts*
Volker Janssen, *California State University, Fullerton*
Patricia Knol, *Triton College*
Tim Lehman, *Rocky Mountain College*
Carmen Lopez, *Miami Dade College*
Frances M. Jacobson, *Tidewater Community College*
Eric Mayer, *Victor Valley College*
Suzanne McFadden, *Austin Community College*
Mark Mengerink, *Lamar University*
Robert O'Brien, *Lone Star College-CyFair*
Deirdre O'Shea, *University of Central Florida*
Stephen Patnode, *Farmingdale State College*
Darren Pierson, *Blinn College*
David Raley, *El Paso Community College*
Monica Rankin, *The University of Texas at Dallas*
Nik Ribianszky, *Georgia Gwinnett College*
Ayesha Shariff, *Saint Paul College*
John Smolenski, *University of California, Davis*
Diane Vecchio, *Furman University*
Felicia Viator, *University of California, Berkeley*
Elwood Watson, *East Tennessee State University*
William Whisenhunt, *College of DuPage*
Vibert White, *Bethune Cookman University*
Scott Williams, *Weatherford College*
Mary Wolf, *University of Georgia*

We are indebted to the following for creating the instructor and student resources for *Global Americans*: Elizabeth Bischof, University of Southern Maine; Christopher

Jillson, New York University; Carmen Lopez, Miami Dade College; Sarah Nytroe, DeSales University; Jacqueline Shine, University of California, Berkeley; and Mary Montgomery Wolf, University of Georgia.

We are also happy to have this opportunity to express our gratitude to the great folks at Cengage who have shepherded this project through the process that took words on a manuscript page and made them into the vibrant text and on-line resources that you see here, especially Paul Banks, product director; Joe Potvin, product manager; Carolyn Lewis, executive director of development; Anais Wheeler, content development manager; Lauren MacLachlan, production manager; Carol Newman, senior content project manager; Cate Barr, senior art director; Valerie Hartman, senior marketing manager; Erika Hayden, content developer; Andrew Newton, associate content developer; Rob Alper, senior learning design author/consultant; Charlotte Miller, art editor; Emma Guiton, product assistant; Erika Mugavin, intellectual property project manager; and Alexandra Ricciardi, intellectual property analyst.

Finally, we are so appreciative of our families who have hung in there with us as we drafted chapters, slogged through rewrites, sat through too many conference calls while on vacation, and rejoiced as it all came together. It does not go without saying that we could not have done this without all of their support. Thank you.

About the Authors

Maria E. Montoya earned her B.A at Yale University in 1986 and Ph.D. at Yale in 1993. She is Associate Professor of History at New York University as well as the Dean of Arts and Science at New York University, Shanghai. She was previously Associate Professor of History at the University of Michigan where she also served as the Director of Latina/o Studies. Her articles include works on western, labor, Latina/o, and environmental history, and they have appeared in the *Western Historical Quarterly, The Journal of Women's History*, and *American Quarterly*. She is the author of *Translating Property: The Maxwell Land Grant and the Conflict over Land in the American West, 1840-1900* (University of California Press, 2002). She has taught the U.S. History survey for more than twenty years and has worked on the AP U.S. History Development Committee and consulted with the College Board.

Laura A. Belmonte earned her B.A. at the University of Georgia and her Ph.D. at the University of Virginia in 1996. She is Department Head and Professor of History at Oklahoma State University. A specialist in the history of U.S. foreign relations, she is the author of *Selling the American Way: U.S. Propaganda and the Cold War* (University of Pennsylvania Press, 2008) and numerous articles on cultural diplomacy. Belmonte is editor of *Speaking of America: Readings in U.S. History* (Cengage, 2nd edition, 2006), and she is concurrently working on books on U.S. global policy on HIV/AIDS and the history of the international LGBT rights movement (Bloomsbury, forthcoming 2017). She is a member of the U.S. Department of State's Historical Advisory Committee on Diplomatic Documentation. After participating in the 2005 National Endowment for the Humanities summer institute "Rethinking America in Global Perspective," she began teaching undergraduate and graduate courses with a transnational focus, including "America in International Perspective" and "HIV/AIDS in Transnational Perspective."

Carl J. Guarneri earned his B.A. at the University of Pennsylvania, M.A. at the University of Michigan, and his Ph.D. at Johns Hopkins University in 1979, and he is Professor of History at Saint Mary's College of California, where he has taught since then. He has also been a visiting professor at Colgate University and the University of Paris. A historian of nineteenth-century America, Guarneri has won national fellowships for his research and published books and articles on reform movements, utopian socialism, the Civil War, and American cultural history, which include *The Utopian Alternative: Fourierism in Nineteenth-Century America* (Cornell University Press, 1991) and two edited collections: *Religion and Society in the American West* (University Press of America, 1987), and *Hanging Together: Unity and Diversity in American Culture* (Yale University Press, 2001). He is currently writing a book on the Civil War career of Charles A. Dana, an influential New York journalist and Assistant Secretary of War. Through his publications and presentations, Guarneri has also been a leading voice in the movement to globalize the study and teaching of U.S. history. He has codirected institutes for the National Endowment for the Humanities on "Rethinking America in Global Perspective." His survey-course reader, *America Compared: American History in International Perspective* (Cengage, 2nd ed., 2005), and his brief textbook, *America in the World: United States History in Global Context* (McGraw-Hill, 2007) are seminal undergraduate texts, and his anthology, *Teaching American History in a Global Context* (M.E. Sharpe, 2008), offers a globalizing "toolkit" for U.S. history instructors.

Steven W. Hackel earned his B.A. at Stanford University and his Ph.D. at Cornell University in 1994. From 1994 to 1996, he was a postdoctoral fellow at the Omohundro Institute of Early American History and Culture and a visiting Assistant Professor at the College of William and Mary. He taught at Oregon State University from 1996 to

2007 and is now Professor of History at the University of California, Riverside. Within the larger field of early American history, Hackel's research focuses on the Spanish Borderlands, colonial California, and California Indians. Hackel is especially interested in Indian responses to Spanish colonialism, the effects of disease on colonial encounters, and new ways of visualizing these processes through digital history. His first book, *Children of Coyote, Missionaries of Saint Francis: Indian-Spanish Relations in Colonial California*, 1769-1850, was published by the Omohundro Institute of Early American History and Culture (2005) and garnered numerous national prizes. His most recent book, *Junípero Serra: California's Founding Father* (Hill and Wang, a division of Farrar, Straus and Giroux, 2013), was named a top-ten book for 2013 by Zócalo Public Square and the best book of the year on early California by the Historical Society of Southern California. He has edited two volumes of essays and published nearly two dozen scholarly essays and has been awarded fellowships from the National Endowment for the Humanities and many other agencies.

Ellen Hartigan-O'Connor earned her B.A. at Yale University and Ph.D. at the University of Michigan in 2003. She is Associate Professor of History at the University of California, Davis, where she teaches courses on gender, American social and cultural history, and the histories of colonialism and capitalism. She is the author of *The Ties That Buy: Women and Commerce in Revolutionary America* (University of Pennsylvania Press, 2009) as well as articles and book chapters on gender and economy in the eighteenth and nineteenth centuries. With support from the National Endowment for the Humanities, she is currently completing a project on auctions and market culture in early America, tracing the economic and cultural power of a widespread but little-studied institution. She became interested in globalizing U.S. history through her expertise in Atlantic world and transnational women's and gender histories. She is coeditor of the *Oxford Handbook of American Women's and Gender History* (Oxford University Press, forthcoming), and a board member of Women and Social Movements. A founding and Standing Editor of *Oxford Bibliographies—Atlantic History*, Hartigan-O'Connor is also a speaker with the Organization of American Historians' Distinguished Lectureship Program.

Lon Kurashige earned his B.A. from the University of California, Santa Barbara and his Ph.D. from the University of Wisconsin-Madison in 1994. Since 1995, he has taught at the University of Southern California, where he is Associate Professor of History. He is author of *Two Faces of Exclusion: The Untold History of Anti-Asian Racism in the United States* (Chapel Hill: University of North Carolina Press, 2016) and *Japanese American Celebration and Conflict: A History of Ethnic Identity and Festival, 1934-1990* (University of California Press, 2002). He was the winner of the History Book Award from the Association for Asian American Studies in 2004. He coedited "Conversations in Transpacific History," a special edition of *Pacific Historical Review* (2014) and *Major Problems in Asian American History*, 2nd ed. (Cengage Learning, forthcoming 2017). His article "Rethinking Anti-Immigrant Racism: Lessons from the Los Angeles Vote on the 1920 Alien Land Law" won the Carl I. Wheat prize for best publication to appear in the *Southern California Quarterly* between 2012 and 2014. His other publications include articles published in the *Journal of American History, Pacific Historical Review*, and *Reviews in American History*. Kurashige has been awarded fellowships from the Fulbright Program, Social Science Research Council, Rockefeller Foundation, the National Endowment for the Humanities, and other funding agencies.

The Tewa's Mole story tells of how they came to their homeland in the Rio Grande Valley in New Mexico, emerging from a dark world into the light.

1 The First American Peoples: Migration, Settlement, and Adaptation

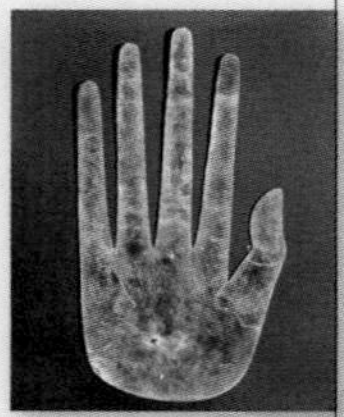

In the beginning, according to a Native American creation story, the whole world was dark. The people lived underground in blackness. They did not know that their world was dark because they had no knowledge of anything else; no one had taught them about the blue sky world. After a long time in darkness, the people began to get restless. Some asked, "Is this all the world there is? Will there never be another world?"

Ira Block/National Geographic Creative

Then Mole came to visit, digging his way through the darkness with his little paws and sharp-pointed nails. The old men asked Mole, "Is there more to the world than this, friend? You travel far and fast underground. What have you discovered? Is there anything else?"

"Follow me," said Mole. The people lined up behind Mole, and he began to dig his way upward. As Mole clawed away the earth, the people took it from his little paw-hands and passed it back along their line, from one person to the next, to get it out of their way. That is why the tunnel that Mole dug upward for the people was closed behind them. That is why they could never find their way back to their old dark world.

When at last Mole stopped digging and the people came out into their new world, light shone all round them and washed them like a blessing. The people, like Mole, were blinded by the light. They were frightened and hid their eyes with their hands to protect their sight.

While all the people were standing there, arguing about what to do, they heard a woman speaking to them. "Be patient, my children" she said, "and I will help you. . . . Take your hands away from your eyes, but do it slowly, slowly. Now wait a minute. Move them a little bit farther away. Now, do it again. And again."

Four times the people moved their hands away from their eyes. At last their eyes were freed and opened, and they could see little old Spider Woman, grandmother of the Earth and of all living things.

She showed them corn and told them to weed it and hoe it and water it. She told them to go live near the great Turtle Mountain in the south. But they were not sure where it was.

Old Spider Woman then told them, "When you find the signs of your two friends again—Mole and me—you will have found your place."

For a very long time the people wandered here and there. They endured hardships and quarreled about what they should do. Finally, only two were left, man and woman. They journeyed southward over a hard road. Then they saw a strange animal crawling along.

"Look what a strange track this thing leaves in the sand," they said, and they remembered that they had seen these tracks before. "They look like Mole's tracks," he said. She said, "Its back is as hard as stone, but it has a design carved and painted on it. Look, that design is Grandmother Spider's web!"

And at that moment, they knew they had found their home.

How is the Tewa's origin story reflective of the experiences shared among the first American peoples?

Go to MindTap® to watch a video on the Tewa's Mole story and learn how this creation myth illustrates the themes of this chapter.

This is how the Tewa—a group of Pueblo Indians of the Rio Grande Valley in New Mexico—understand how they came to their homeland. Their story, like those of so many other Indians and others who settled in America, speaks of a migration from a distant land, an uncertain fate, the importance of family, a dependence on animals, and the eventual adaptation of people to their environment with a growing sense of rootedness and history. These themes—migration, settlement, and adaptation—have been central to human history since time immemorial. In more recent times, humans across the globe have increasingly innovated, using fire, irrigation, and metallurgy to modify their homelands and create labor-saving tools while developing complex and novel social structures to organize their societies. All of these developments unfolded at different rates in different societies as diverse peoples responded to changes in their environment or envisioned new opportunities for development and advancement. The challenge for the people of ancient America—and all of those who came later—was, as they saw it, to find their proper place within nature and the larger world. For them, it is a story that unfolded over more than 15,000 years. In some places, people established empires; elsewhere they lived in smaller groups. Everywhere human society developed as people exchanged commodities and ideas across networks that fostered regionally specific cultures that together supported millions of inhabitants. By 1500 CE (in the common era), a tapestry of peoples with distinctive economic, social, political, and religious systems called America their home.

1-1 First Peoples of the Americas

Canadian Museum of Civilization

This artistic representation depicts an extended family, probably like the ones who came to the land of Beringia more than 12,000 years ago. Small groups like this were among the first inhabitants of North America, and their descendants peopled much of the Americas.

As you look at this image, what sort of technologies do you see displayed? How might they have these allowed people to survive in frigid Beringia? ▶

Go to MindTap® to practice history with the Chapter 1 **Primary Source Writing Activity: Adaptation and America's First Peoples.** Read and view primary sources and respond to a writing prompt.

Modern science offers its own story about human origins in the Americas, one that is not necessarily at odds with Indian origin stories. This chapter of human history unfolded long before there were written records and in places where the archaeological record is scant or gone. But scientific evidence has enabled scholars to describe human origins and migrations across the globe and into the Americas. The work of physical anthropologists suggests that humans first came to the Americas at least thirteen thousand years ago from the places that we know today as Siberia, Alaska, and the Yukon Territory. As the first American peoples moved south, they splintered and evolved into different groups. Over millennia, the peoples developed different cultures as they settled in different environments with different resources and challenges. Societies came and went in response to environmental changes and their own internal logic. The most prominent societies endured for centuries if not longer. Others vanished quickly, leaving no trace in the archaeological record.

☞ As you read, focus on the different understandings of Native American origins. To what degree do you think that science and Native American origin stories can be reconciled?

1-1a Scientific Evidence

Aided by modern science, scholars map the earliest migrations to the Americas.

Until about 2 million years ago, ***Homo erectus***, the distant ancestors of modern humans, lived only in Africa. Their dispersal was slow and probably caused by a change in the earth's climate and a drying out of the Sahara region. By 1.8 million years ago, these early humans had spread to western Asia and the island of Java in Indonesia, which was connected at that time to the mainland. By 500,000 years ago *Homo erectus* lived in China. About 400,000 years ago *Homo erectus* evolved into ***Homo sapiens*** and sometime around 150,000 to 100,000 years ago, anatomically modern humans known to us as ***Homo sapiens sapiens*** evolved in East Africa. Again, climate change drove humans to settle new lands. During the last worldwide glacial advance, 50,000 years ago, sea levels fell when much of the earth's moisture became trapped in the ice caps, exposing more of the earth's land to settlement by these creative and adaptive humans. The new lands and connections among them allowed humans to settle another 60 percent of the earth. People migrated into northeastern Asia; some went by boat to Australia. Later, a group ventured overland from Siberia to Alaska and ultimately southward in the Americas (see Map 1.1).

Specifically, most archaeologists believe that the earliest immigrants to the Americas came from Asia across a land bridge about 12,500 to 10,000 BCE (before the common era), but perhaps as long ago as 23,000 BCE. Nearly all ancient human skulls found in the Americas have a dental pattern that matches those of ancient human remains found in northeastern Asia. Moreover, most Native Americans today have blood type O or A as opposed to type B, which evolved after humans migrated to the Americas.

To understand events and migrations that occurred so many thousands of years ago among peoples who left no written records, scholars rely on material evidence, such as stone tools and fired pottery, burial remains, and food scraps. Stone and clay tools used to kill and cook animals predominate in the archaeological record. Organic matter, such as clothes, shelters, or foods, has only occasionally survived. Thus, scholars know something about how early humans hunted, prepared their food, and what they ate but only a little about what they wore, the homes they built, and the thoughts and behaviors that animated their lives.

Given these limits, the scientific technique known as carbon 14 (C14) dating has been extremely helpful for the study of early human history across the globe. Carbon 14, a radioactive atom produced in the upper atmosphere, is incorporated into carbon dioxide and absorbed from the air by green plants. When animals eat plants, carbon dioxide is absorbed into the animals' tissue. When a plant or animal dies, the C14 atoms within it break down at a constant rate. Therefore, by measuring the amount of C14 in anything that was once alive—seeds, cotton, bone, or wood—scientists can measure the length of time that has passed since the organism died. Carbon 14 dating has allowed archaeologists to determine with precision the antiquity of the organic matter in tools, bones, clothing, and even feces left behind by the first human inhabitants of the Americas. This has allowed scholars to map the geographic distribution and cultural evolution of ancient Americans with some authority. In the future, the study of DNA—the basic inherited genetic material that determines the makeup of human bodies—taken from ancient human, plant, and animal remains promises to increase our understanding of people who came to inhabit America long ago.

1-1b Beringia during the Pleistocene

People from Siberia move across Beringia, an arid and frigid land.

Although Alaska, Canada's Yukon Territory, and northeast Siberia are divided today by political boundaries, rugged mountains, and frigid ocean waters, they share a common history related to the Pacific Ocean and its periodic changes from dramatic fluctuations in the earth's climate. During the geologic period known as the **Pleistocene**, which stretched from roughly 2.6 million to 11,700 years ago, nearly all the northern regions of the Northern Hemisphere were covered by enormous ice sheets. Yet the lowlands of Alaska, the Yukon, and northeast Siberia remained mostly ice free because they were so **arid**. As the climate cooled, much of the earth's water was trapped in ice, lowering the level of the Pacific Ocean as much as 360 feet. During the final phase of the Pleistocene, **Beringia**, the land mass between Siberia and Alaska, was exposed (see Map 1.2), and a continuous thousand-mile wide land bridge, the **Bering land bridge**, connected Asia to North America.

Beringia was frigid. It was cold enough to grow glaciers but too dry to do so. As the earth became steadily colder, its grasslands became a refuge for large mammals, such as wooly mammoths, horses, saber-toothed cats, rhinoceros, antelope, **bison**, musk-ox, caribou, grizzly bears, wolverines, wolves, and lions. Beringia was home to such an abundance and diversity of animals that it can be likened to today's East African Savannah.

Homo erectus Meaning "upright human." Extinct species of early humans that emerged in Africa 1.9 million years ago and lived throughout much of the Pleistocene.

Homo sapiens Meaning "wise human." Human ancestor with greater intelligence and adaptability than *Homo erectus*.

Homo sapiens sapiens Anatomically modern humans. Evolved from *homo sapiens* 150,000 years ago.

Pleistocene Geological epoch that lasted from 2.6 million to 11,700 years ago covering the latest period of repeated glaciation.

arid Absence or scarcity of water to the extent that animal and plant life is hindered or prevented.

Beringia Frigid grassland that emerged between Siberia and Alaska during the Pleistocene when more of the earth's water was trapped in the polar ice caps.

Bering land bridge Thousand-mile wide bridge of land in eastern Beringia that connected Asia and North America during the Pleistocene.

bison Large grass-eating animal that inhabited much of the Northern Great Plains. Referred to as the *American Buffalo*, but buffalo and bison are not the same species.

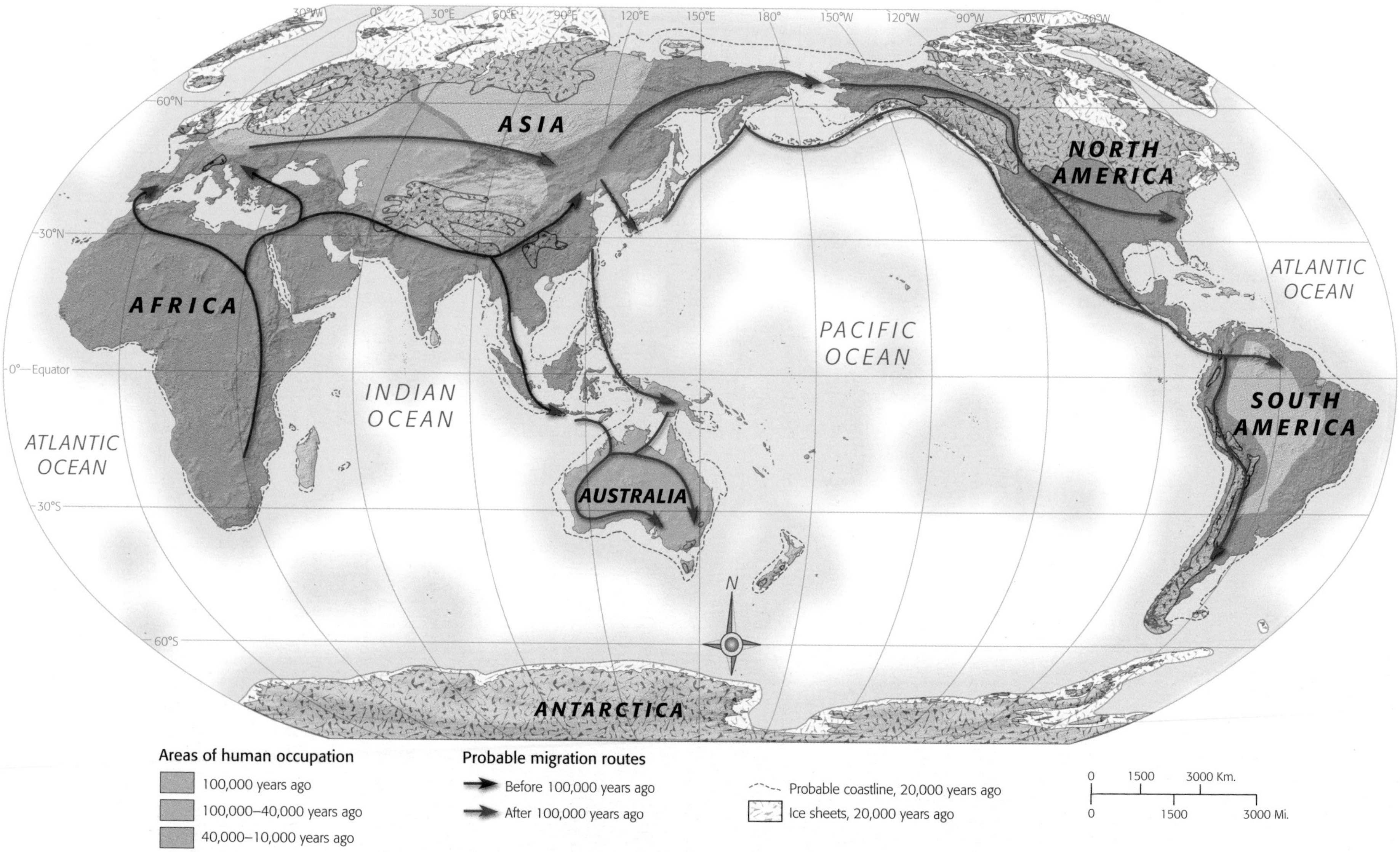

Map 1.1 Spread of Modern Humans around the Globe. In a process that unfolded over hundreds of thousands of years, human occupation of the globe spread from East Africa to the Americas. Humans took two routes from Asia to the Americas: Some traversed a land bridge across Beringia while others ventured down the Pacific Coast in small watercraft. ▲

Humans of the late Pleistocene—known to us as **Paleoindians**—probably first came to Beringia more than twelve thousand five hundred years ago. They had mastered the use of fire to survive the cold and learned to hunt large mammals for food and to make clothing of their fur or hides. Paleoindians did not completely depend upon big game. They also relied on plants and smaller animals. Women and men together gathered and prepared the daily foods.

Once Paleoindians had moved beyond the southern reaches of Beringia (south and east as far as Alaska and central Canada), they encountered ice sheets a mile high that blocked passage southward. An Arikara creation story tells of the First People encountering "wide, thick ice and deep water" on their original great journey. Other Native American oral traditions recount perilous travels through frigid or dark lands. Many describe ancestral origins in an underworld or a place of darkness, perhaps metaphorical renderings of memories of life above the Arctic Circle in the winter.

The first settlers of the Americas came from Beringia, but they took more than one route. It seems certain that about 10,500 BCE, as the climate warmed, Paleoindians moved south through an ice-free corridor east of the northern Rocky Mountains in present-day western Canada. But the discovery of human artifacts in Monte Verde, Chile, that date to the same time period suggest that by then, some groups had already come down the Pacific coast in watercraft. Rafts or boats were used at the time; fifty thousand years ago, people from Southeast Asia had used them to reach Australia. Human remains ten thousand years old have been found on an island off the California coast.

Scholars debate why Paleoindians moved south. One theory holds that as hunters, they were following large mammals. Another suggests that seasonal waterfowl migrations inspired their move. Notably, in some Native American myths, birds are often the discoverers of lands unseen to humans. In the biblical story of Noah and the great flood, a dove sent out to see whether the waters had receded returns with a fresh olive leaf to prove that they had done so. An ancient story among the Paiutes tells how humans overcame an insuperable ice barrier with the help of ravens and eventually migrated to the American West. According to the Paiutes, long ago, "Ice had formed ahead of them and it reached all the way to the sky. The people could not cross it. . . . A Raven flew up and struck the ice and cracked it. Yet the people still could not cross. Another Raven flew up again and cracked the ice again. Again Raven flew up again and broke the ice, this time allowing the people to cross."

1-1c Clovis Peoples

Although the exact date when humans came to Beringia or when they headed south is not known, they were in North America by 11,000 BCE, thereby initiating one of the final chapters in the global advance of humans that began in Africa millions of years ago. These first migrants entered a hunter's paradise—animals were abundant and not afraid of humans. The settlers would have been well nourished and increased in numbers rapidly, possibly doubling or tripling with each generation. Thus, a small band of just twenty-five Beringian Paleoindians could have initiated a population of one million across the Americas within three hundred fifty years.

Clovis people make beautifully distinctive fluted projectile points.

In 1932 in Clovis, New Mexico, archaeologists unearthed a fluted stone spear tip from these early Americans determined to be about thirteen thousand years old. These points—known as **Clovis Points**—have been found throughout much of North and South America and date to roughly the same time, suggesting that these peoples settled the Americas within about two hundred years.

At the peak of Clovis culture, most large mammals in the Americas died off. These extinctions coincided with a dramatic and sudden global warming after the Late Pleistocene. Around 8000 BCE, the enormous ice sheets that had covered much of northern North America began to melt. The runoff raised sea levels and flooded coastal regions, including much of Beringia. The melting ice sheets also led to changes in weather patterns. The cold grasslands of the Americas warmed and dried, large lakes disappeared, and forests grew in regions that had been tundra. As habitats changed, **megafauna**, large grazing animals, such as mammoths and mastodons, died out. Human hunting accelerated their extinction. As Clovis peoples overhunted large predators, such as lions and cats, populations of smaller **herbivores** that fed on plants increased, and as these herbivores overgrazed dwindling grasslands, they destroyed the habitats of megafauna, horses, and camels.

Paleoindians Earliest peoples to settle the Americas during the late Pleistocene, probably about 12,500 years ago.

Clovis Points Distinctive fluted-projectile points, typically 3 to 6 inches long, manufactured by the Paleoindians (Clovis peoples) between 13,000 to 10,000 years ago and found across North America.

megafauna Large animals, such as mastodons.

herbivores Animals that subsist by eating plant material.

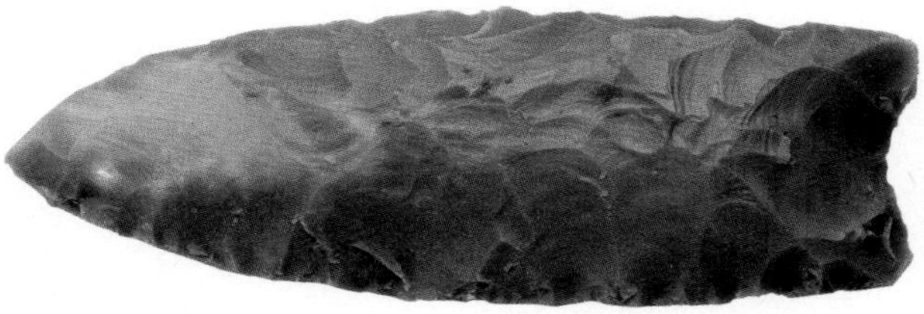

Clovis Point, Arizona, Thirteen Thousand Years Before Present (BP) Clovis points are finely worked, typically three to six inches long, and sharp enough to penetrate and kill large animals. Markings indicate that the points were bound to shafts or straight sticks. These points were exceptionally well-designed pieces of weaponry and were more advanced than any projectile produced in the world at that time. This point and others like it were most likely made by descendants of Paleoindians who came from Beringia. ▲ Brian Brockman/Getty Images

Map 1.2 The Peopling of the Americas About thirteen thousand years ago, America's earliest human inhabitants began to arrive from Beringia, a now submerged land mass that connected Siberia and Alaska. Some came over land and, in a separate migration, others came by sea, hugging the Pacific Coast all the way to the southern tip of South America. ▲

With these extinctions, Clovis peoples began to hunt bison and smaller mammals, and they made smaller projectile points. More important, they dispersed and separated, forming distinct cultures. The megafaunal extinctions also limited the ways their cultures could develop as horses and camels died out. The Clovis peoples, therefore, did not have an opportunity to domesticate these animals or to gain immunity to diseases that come from living with domesticated animals. Thus, in the distant future, they and the myriad peoples of the Americas who descended from them would be vulnerable to epidemics that originated in some domesticated animals.

1-2 From the Archaic Period to the Dawn of Agriculture

Carver Mostardi/Alamy Stock Photo

Depicted here is *Chicomecoatl*, an Aztec goddess of agriculture. She holds in her hands cobs of corn, a crop planted in Mexico more than 3,890 years before the present. Its cultivation marked a period of transition for many peoples of the Americas toward an agricultural existence.

As you look at this image of an ancient corn cob, think about how it differs from those of today. What does it suggest about plant adaptations in the wake of human settlement across North America? ▶

In the absence of megafauna and in the wake of retreating ice sheets, the first peoples of the Americas continued to disperse and form distinct cultures. As people adapted to environmental shifts after the Late Pleistocene, they depended less on migrating animals, lived more in families, and moved locally to be near seasonal food sources. Some took up agriculture, and their societies grew large and complex. Others sustained themselves in a variety of ways as hunter-gatherers.

☞ As you read, focus on the diversity of peoples and cultures across the Americas. How did this diversity come to be? In what ways was it expressed? What, if anything, did the diverse peoples of the Americas have in common?

1-2a The Archaic Period

Indians' technological advances lead to new ways of hunting and subsistence.

With global warming, the Paleoindian world gave way to the **Archaic period**, an epoch that began about 8000 BCE and lasted some seven thousand years. The Archaic period describes in general terms an Indian culture markedly different from that of the Paleoindian. Each group left the Paleoindian period and entered the Archaic at its own rate, at a different time, and on its own terms.

In the final millennia of the Archaic, many groups established year-round settlements, some of which were inhabited for decades and even centuries. This **sedentism** was in part a response to the increasing population of the Americas, which made it impossible for peoples to obtain new resources by simply moving into unoccupied regions. During the Archaic period, Indians domesticated the dog, a descendant from wild ancestors in the Eastern hemisphere. In **Mesoamerica**, dogs became a source of food, just as chickens would become later. Farther north, Indians bred dogs to carry or pull loads. In Mesoamerica, Indians raised turkeys for food, and other birds, such as macaws and parrots were raised for their plumage.

Most Archaic peoples were **hunter-gatherers**, pursuing diversified food sources. They caught fish, gathered nuts and berries, or hunted small animals, such as ducks and squirrels, and large ones such as deer, moose, and caribou. In the Late Archaic, about 3000 BCE to 1000 BCE, Indians in coastal New England built fish traps in shallow tidal backwaters. They cut small trees for stakes and drove them into the ground parallel to the shore, then heaped low brush among them. High tide brought fish and water across the traps, and when the tide receded, fish could be caught in nets and baskets.

In the plains of central North America, some hunting groups pursued bison, which they killed in great numbers either with spears or by driving them off cliffs. The primary weapon of the Archaic hunter was the spear thrower, or **atlatl**, a flexible shaft with a handle at one end and a hook at the other into which a spear was fitted.

Archaic period Stage of cultural development following the Paleoindian period and marked by sedentism. Commonly began around 8000 BCE but varied from group to group.

sedentism Society or people that remain in one place year round.

Mesoamerica Cultural region in the Americas stretching from Mexico to northern Costa Rica. Site of numerous ancient civilizations.

hunter-gatherers Society in which most food is obtained from wild plants and animals.

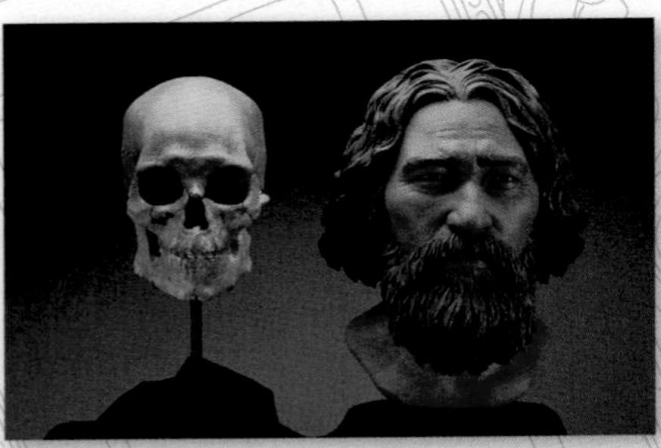

Brittney Tatchell, Smithsonian Institution

Modern recreation of the facial features of Kennewick Man

Global Americans In 1996, two college students in Kennewick, Washington, found a human skull along the Columbia River. Scientists who eventually unearthed a complete skeleton recently determined that it was from a man, known as **Kennewick Man**, who lived 9,000 years ago. He was a descendant of maritime hunters who worked their way along the shoreline of Beringia and eventually ventured down the Pacific coast to the tip of South America. Stocky and muscular when he died at age forty, Kennewick Man's right arm was overdeveloped—like a baseball pitcher's—from a lifetime of spear throwing. His hands and forearms suggest that he often pinched his fingers together, perhaps as he made spear points. The food and water that he consumed left a chemical signature in his bones that reveals an adventurous life on the road. He died 300 miles inland, yet for twenty years he had lived on marine animals, such as seals, sea lions, and fish. And the water he drank was Alaskan in origin. Thus, Kennewick Man was a traveler who died far from his home. He very well might have been a trader of projectile points, perhaps crafted from stone quarried in the north. His life speaks to the mobility of America's earliest inhabitants as they made a living across regions that were sparsely settled and rich with opportunity. Most humans are forgotten within three generations of their lives. Remarkably, Kennewick Man speaks to us 360 generations after he lived.

The weapon essentially lengthened the arm of the hunter and allowed the snap of the hand and wrist to add speed and make the spear more deadly. Some Late Archaic hunters added stone weights to atlatls to increase their force. Archaic peoples of the Upper Midwest and the Great Lakes region also made axes, harpoons, and smaller tools of copper so pure they did not need smelting, the extraction of base metal from ore.

In addition to using these advanced tools and hunting technologies, Archaic peoples modified the environment in ways unimagined by Clovis peoples. By deliberately setting fires, they created and maintained meadows favored by deer, which they then herded or killed according to their needs. As they became more sedentary, they developed heavy stone tools, food storage sites, and large-scale trade networks. Indians also began to deposit exotic stones and other items as grave goods.

1-2b Daily Life

Archaic peoples build enormous earthen mounds.

Like the Clovis peoples, Archaic peoples lived across the Americas. Most left only tools, bones, and garbage as indications of their lives. Some, however, left clues to their diet in desiccated feces. Those found in caves in Kentucky reveal that Archaic peoples drank a beverage brewed from now-extinct grasses.

One of the most enduring innovations of the Archaic period in northeastern North America was the construction of large earthen mounds. Around 5000 BCE, peoples in Beothuk Island, Newfoundland, buried an adolescent under a mound. Around the youth's neck was a whistle, and next to the body were a harpoon, knives, weapon points, and an antler used to crush minerals into paint. Around 4000 BCE, people in northeast Louisiana at a site known today as Poverty Point, began constructing a circular complex of eleven mounds, the tallest of which

atlatl Tool used by Indians to accelerate the throwing velocity of a spear.

Poverty Point Earthworks Peoples at Poverty Point, Louisiana, created a complex of nested octagonal earthworks, the largest of which is more than three-quarters of a mile across. The size and intricacy of these structures suggest a labor-intensive construction program and a complex social and political organization not possible during the nomadic days of the Clovis peoples. ▼ Richard A. Cooke/Documentary Value/Corbis

is twenty-five feet high. These mounds must have been used for food preparation, for they contain remains of mussels, snails, fish, deer, and turkeys as well as many plants. But they also presumably were important centers of rituals.

Nearly everywhere in ancient America, shamans or priests served as intermediaries between people and the gods. But individuals frequently believed that they, too, received messages from the gods or the deceased through dreams or in times of solitude with the use of hallucinogenic drugs. Sacred power was everywhere—in plants and animals, in the oceans and heavens, and in all of creation. Time passed in cycles of decades or centuries and then repeated itself. The world was thus by and large a predictable place according to the most learned leaders of these ancient societies.

1-2c Development of Agriculture and Declines in Health

Agriculture leads to increased concentrations of people and declines in their health.

Agriculture—the methodical cultivation of food crops—developed gradually in the Americas as it did elsewhere in the world. Rather than a conscious choice by Indians to put down their atlatls and take up hoes, the dawn of agriculture in the Americas came about through the coevolution of humans and plants. In the earliest phases of this process, plants that humans ate were dispersed—by excretion or spillage—and underwent genetic changes that made them more attractive to and more dependent on humans for dispersal and reproduction. This incidental domestication began with **maize** (also known as *corn* today) in Mesoamerica about 3500 BCE, although Mesoamericans did not cultivate it until about 2700 BCE. In the American Southwest, maize, squash, and beans were first domesticated about 1500 BCE, although maize did not become a staple crop for another two thousand years. Indians first began to eat sunflower, squash, and march elder in eastern North America about 5000 BCE. The incidental domestication of these plants began to occur in river floodplains around 2000 BCE. But it was another five hundred years before people cultivated these crops.

Almost certainly, maize, squash, and beans were carried north from Mesoamerica. One simple fact—the north-south orientation of the western hemisphere—dictated the pace of agricultural diffusion. As people move north or south over hundreds of miles, they pass through different climate zones. This is not so much the case when they move along an east-west axis. Thus, a crop that prospered in one region of the Americas might require generations of modification before it could survive in a region to the north or south that had a slightly different climate.

The gradual shift to agriculture involved more than simply farming crops and herding animals. It entailed major changes in residential patterns, the organization of work, and the creation of material culture. Typically, agriculture is associated with the development and use of ceramic pots for cooking or fiber baskets for gathering, and it involves clearing brush or forest and the cultivation of cereals that can be stored through the seasons.

In Western culture, agriculture is associated with progress toward more complex political, social, and economic organization and is usually associated with large populations. But analysis of ancient human bones suggests that human health and nutrition declined with the advent of agriculture. The healthiest Native Americans were the earliest who lived in small, mobile groups. They wasted no time or energy building large monuments but consumed a nutritious and varied diet. Moreover, their relative isolation from others protected them from infectious diseases, and mobility reduced their contact with germs and parasites associated with waste. As people became more agricultural and lived in larger urban settlements, they lost the health advantages of the Paleoindian and Archaic lifestyle. They spent more time acquiring food and lived fewer years.

The greatest brake on population growth in ancient America was not a shortage of food or high mortality but low **fertility** (live births per woman). Most Paleoindian and Archaic people lived into their thirties; on average, women produced only two to three children. Although estimates of the population of the Americas in 1500 range from below 10 million to above 100 million, probably about 50 million people lived in the Americas in the year 1500. The most densely populated regions were associated with the Indian empires of Mesoamerica and Central and South America. Most people lived south of Mexico; between 7 and 10 million people lived north of Mexico in 1500.

1-2d Diversity, Commonalities, and Gender

Diverse cultures understand gender in their own ways.

As people dispersed throughout the Americas, they splintered into hundreds and then thousands of separate groups, each distinct from the other, in what is known as **cultural differentiation**. These societies were built on different systems of labor, political organization, religious beliefs, and material resources. Native American peoples spoke thousands of different languages, and their economies were shaped to local environments. Some remained primarily hunter-gatherers; others turned mainly to agriculture. Some lived in brush huts; others crafted large apartment-style homes out of rock and adobe. Some lived in large towns of thousands and thousands of people, and others lived in hamlets of only a few families. Some lived in the same place year round. Others followed game across large territories throughout the year.

agriculture Cultivating the soil, producing crops, and raising livestock to enhance human life. Requires labor organization and allows food surpluses that support sedentism.

maize Grain known as *corn* in English-speaking countries, domesticated by Mesoamericans more than 5,000 years ago. An important staple and commodity in ancient America.

fertility Production of offspring as opposed to the capability to do so.

cultural differentiation Process through which cultures evolve separately and differentiate from one another.

kinship Social relationship determined by blood, marriage, or residence. Kinship categories and relationships often differ across cultures.

gender Culturally constructed category of people that varies across societies and over time and relates to nearly all aspects of social organization.

sex Category rooted in biology suggesting that one is male or female based on reproductive anatomy and other physical attributes.

Thousands of years of human experience also resulted in commonalities among people of the Americas. Nearly everywhere, people drew their identity from their family, community, or village. **Kinship**—the extended family ties that bind humans together—was basic to human society in the Americas. In fact, people were likely to have their most enduring ties with their kin, not with their spouses. Marriage was a respected institution but one that was not always lifelong. Male leaders might have more than one wife or marry sisters. Such arrangements ensured that leadership would be centralized and passed to the offspring of ruling elites and families. In most societies, men held the political power, but women held society together through their economic activities, their contributions to the household and family, and their family lineages. Indian societies were marked by inequalities, and slavery was common. Most slaves were war captives or criminals. They were more than menial laborers and on occasion played important and valued roles in village society, especially if they were adopted into a family.

Throughout human history, societies have assigned tasks and responsibilities to individuals based upon their sex and gender. But they have not always done so in the same way. **Gender** is a culturally constructed category that varies across societies and over time and relates to nearly all aspects of social organization. **Sex**, however, is rooted in biology and suggests that one is male or female based on biological characteristics. Native American societies of the past usually assigned gender roles based on sex. Typically, men hunted and held political power and women farmed and gathered fruits, nuts, and other edible vegetation that they prepared for their families. But most Indian societies also had at least one other category beyond male and female. Some individuals had within themselves both male and female spirits. As such, they occupied a third gender and were referred to as *two-spirits*.

The creation stories of some Indian groups reveal a wide spectrum of gender categories beyond the simple binary of male/female. For example, in Southern California, among the Kumeyaay, *Warharmi*, a man-woman spirit, provided seeds and culture. Among the Zunis, who lived in the Southwest, such individuals were the *two-spirit Ko'lhamana* who brought together and reconciled the warring and often incompatible lifestyles of male hunters and female farmers, thereby bringing greater harmony to society. Thus, within native society itself at the time of creation and beyond, people and beings who occupied what can be termed a third gender transcended the expectations of their biological sex and played a meaningful role in society.

1-3

Mesoamerica and Peru

The Maya book known as the *Dresden Codex* is a twelfth century copy of a text that was created three or four centuries earlier. It is the oldest surviving manuscript written in the Americas and is one of fifteen surviving pre-Columbian manuscripts. Not all of the seventy eight pages of the Codex have been deciphered, but it is known to contain almanacs, astronomical and astrological tables, and ritual schedules as well as instructions concerning New Year's ceremonies as well as descriptions of the Aztec Rain God's locations.

As you study this image, look for the dramas and emotions being played out. Can you decipher any of the codes or symbols or tools? ▶

Universal History Archive/Universal Images Group/Getty Images

☞ As you read, think about the common characteristics that marked the cultures of the Americas. What roles do ritual, ceremony, and gender play in the early civilizations of the Americas?

Throughout the Americas, as people moved from one region to another and traded and interacted with neighbors near and far, they created diverse cultures and sophisticated civilizations. Local environments and different belief systems led to a stunning array of cultures across the Americas. Some followed big game; others were agricultural or used fire to manage their environment. As trade networks evolved, diverse peoples became integrated into regional economies (see Map 1.3). Four broad cultural regions suggest the diversity of Native America in the year 1500 CE: Mesoamerica and Peru, the Agricultural Southwest and the Arid Interior, the Pacific West, and the Woodlands.

1-3a The Maya and Teotihuacán

Two monumental civilizations rise and decline.

Central America and the Mexican Highlands were to Ancient America what Mesopotamia and Egypt were to Eurasia—densely populated areas from which political, economic, and social change emanated. The Mayans created a grand, urbanized civilization that lasted from 150 BCE to 800 CE (see Map 1.4). At its peak, it had a population of 3 to 5 million. Its kings and occasional queens held religious, political, and military authority over a vast expanse of people and lands. Nobles helped control the subject peoples who, practicing intensive agriculture, produced a surplus of corn that supported urban elites and artisans.

The Mayans had an advanced understanding of the movement of the stars and planets. Their calendar was based on the solar year, and they conceived of time as cyclical. Learned men looked to the stars to understand the distant past, and they carved accounts of the events on slabs that adorned their palaces, temples, and pyramids. The Mayans built large pyramids with distinctively steep slopes that were often topped with temples. They were dedicated to their gods who, they believed, required sacrifices. In time, they began to practice human sacrifice.

Tikal was one of the most important Mayan cities. By 100 BCE, it was an important center for trade and the production of artisan goods involving flint, jade, granite, shells, and **obsidian**—a naturally occurring glass that can be fashioned into blades, arrowheads, and ornaments. Tikal's population was probably fifty thousand in 200 CE, and grew until 400 CE, when it came under the domination of its rival Teotihuacán.

obsidian Naturally occurring volcanic glass widely traded throughout ancient America and processed into projectile points and artifacts.

Map 1.3 North American Indian Peoples, ca. 1500 CE. Nearly every corner of North America was occupied by native peoples, who practiced an incredible range of diverse cultures. This map shows only the largest, most populous peoples, omitting scores of other groups and the thousands of individual villages that characterized native North America. ▼

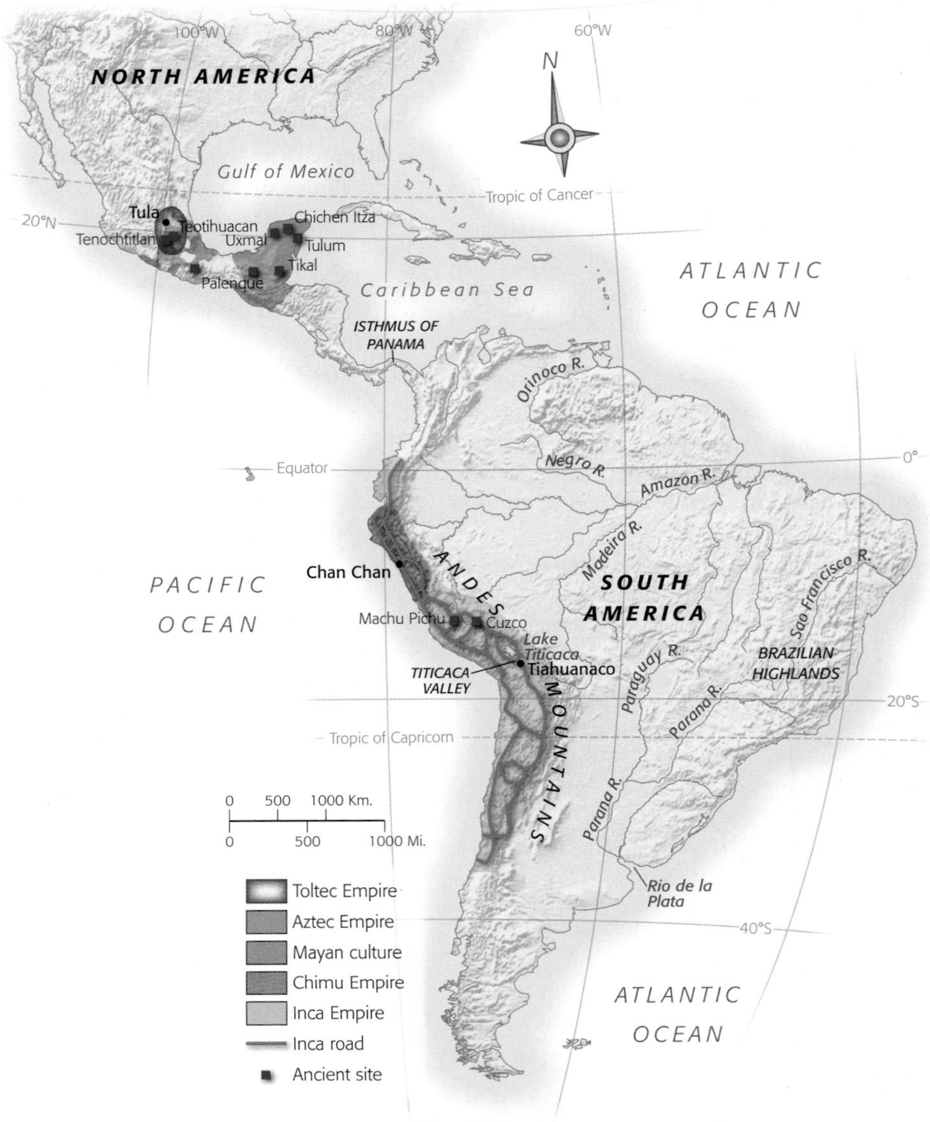

Map 1.4 South America and Mesoamerica, ca. 900–1500 CE. Mesoamerica and South America were the sites of Ancient America's most populous, wealthy, and dominant Indian empires. Their political, cultural, and economic influence stretched well beyond the territories they controlled. ▲

In conquering Tikal, the Teotihuacanos were likely attempting to control sources of obsidian and gain a monopoly over cutting tools and weaponry in Mesoamerica, but they also may have been trying to secure a reliable source of cacao, a tree that produced edible seeds. Cacao seeds were not just the main currency of Mesoamerica; they were also the basis for *Chocolatl*, a drink favored by the ruling elite.

North and west of the Mayas, near today's Mexico City, the ancient city of Teotihuacán flourished from 150 BCE to 650 CE. By 100 CE, it had a population of about eighty thousand people and was marked by grand avenues and monuments. At its peak five hundred years later, it covered twenty square miles and had two hundred thousand residents. This growth depended on good land, abundant water, intensive agriculture, and the control of important resources, such as obsidian. The city was also a center for north-south commerce and highland-lowland trade. Until about 300 CE, most of Teotihuacán's inhabitants lived in adobe structures. After that time, most lived in more permanent stone buildings with multiple apartments.

Teotihuacán controlled Mesoamerica's most important sources of obsidian. Ten percent of the city's laborers worked in the city's six hundred obsidian workshops. Teotihuacán also had a least one hundred ceramic workshops and exported clay pottery and figurines in addition to textiles, wood, and leather products. To support these nonagricultural workers, the city extracted a large surplus of food from the countryside.

Hugo Brizard/Shutterstock.com

Teotihuacán Teotihuacán was a sacred community, much like Mecca today. The construction of the huge Sun Pyramid, which would eventually be 245 feet high, began around 1 CE; at the same time, most of the population from around Teotihuacán moved into the city itself. The pyramid, one of the largest structures of ancient America, required at least three million cubic feet of earth. Twenty other pyramid complexes, as well as numerous wide avenues, were constructed in Teotihuacán. ▲

In addition to its wide trade networks and vibrant economy, the city was held together by devotion to Tlaloc, a fertility god, and to Quetzalcóatl, the "Feathered Serpent." Priests performed religious rituals that attracted thousands. The priests also governed the city, serving as clerks and administrators. Like the Maya, the priests of Teotihuacán had an advanced knowledge of astronomy and mathematics, and they kept careful records of the seasons as well as of tribute from the countryside.

For reasons that remain obscure, Teotihuacán collapsed in about 650 CE. Most likely, problems in trade and subsistence reinforced a sense that the city was no longer favored by the gods, and the ruling priests lost their authority. By 750 CE, the city was in ruins, home to only three thousand people. Most Teotihuacanos returned to the countryside from which their ancestors had come. The city's collapse dealt a devastating blow to the Maya. By 900 CE, Mayan civilization had declined, but even now it remains a vibrant and distinctive culture.

1-3b The Mexica and Tenochtitlán

The Mexica create a society based on conquest, violence, and literacy.

After the fall of the Maya and Teotihuacán, the Toltec, who migrated into Mexico's central valley from the north, achieved brief dominance in Mesoamerica through their adoption of the cult of Queztalcóatl and the formation of a loose military alliance of many Mexican peoples. But drought, war, and famine undermined the Toltec state, which collapsed in 1168 CE. In its wake rose the Mexica, or Aztecs, a Mesoamerican society famed for its militarism. The Mexica came to central Mexico from the north in the mid-1200s, and their culture and society were shaped by perpetual war and their belief that they were a chosen people. They believed their war god Huitzilopochtli had told them to build a city where they saw an eagle perched on a cactus eating a snake. When they saw such a sight in a lagoon near the ruins of Teotihuacán, they founded Tenochtitlán, "the place of the cactus." To them, the eagle represented Huitzilopochtli, and the snake it consumed their drive for conquest. The cactus on which the eagle landed was full of symbolism: Its red fruit calls to mind the human heart, the organ that would become so central to the Mexica rite of human sacrifice.

Through wars and political struggles, the Mexicas dominated Mesoamerica by 1428 CE. As their power and conquests increased, a cult arose around Huitzilopochtli. The war god became the center of a vigorously enforced state religion that was promoted through a form of centralized education. Mexica priests, like those of Teotihuacán, were clerks and administrators, but they also were responsible for the cult and for mediating between people and the gods. Mexica society was intensively militaristic; children of the elite were trained as warriors. Its laws, pronounced by kings but validated by priests and considered to be divinely inspired, were strict and feared. Drunkards were enslaved and then killed if they repeated their crime. Thieves and adulterers were executed.

Mexica society was hierarchical: At the top stood the emperor and his officials; next were the warrior-nobles, whose men, if captured by enemies, were expected to die with honor. Priests kept and prepared the sacred books. Commoners might work as artisans or farmers on land owned by nobles. The elite dined on meat, tortillas, and tamales and enjoyed drinking chocolate. Commoners rarely ate meat and subsisted on ground maize, beans, and vegetables. Elite men served the state. Elite women stayed at home until marriage and then were charged with producing children and woven goods. Women commoners often worked outside the home as vendors or midwives. Their boys went to school to learn religion and the arts of war; girls learned religion and domestic skills in preparation for marriage, which usually occurred around age sixteen.

The cult of Huitzilopochtli cannot be separated from the Mexica interest in human sacrifice. Previous Mesoamerican peoples had practiced human sacrifice on occasion, but the Mexica brought this bloody ritual to a new level. They believed it was necessary to appease an angry god and to maintain the cycle of existence. Human sacrifice kept the sun rising, the rain falling, and the seasons passing. The sacrifice itself was incidental to the central rite: the excision of the living human heart.

Humans sacrificed for Huitzilopochtli were held down over a stone slab. The priest slashed the victim's chest with an obsidian knife, removed the palpating heart, and threw it into a caldron of fire. Then the body was tossed down the temple steps, where it tumbled past victims ascending to similar deaths. The corpses were eaten or traded, and

History without Borders

Obsidian—A Mirror on the Past

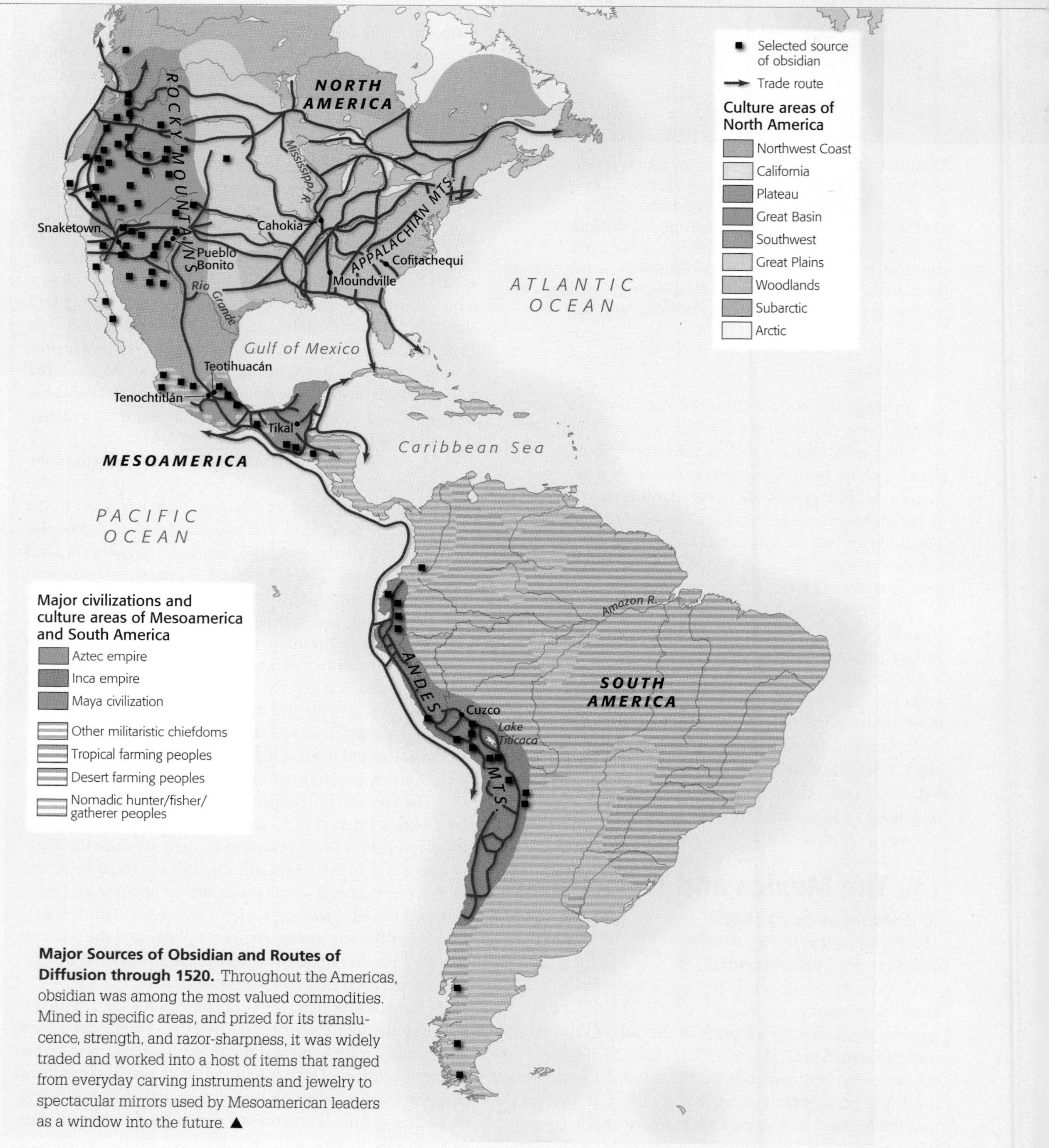

Major Sources of Obsidian and Routes of Diffusion through 1520. Throughout the Americas, obsidian was among the most valued commodities. Mined in specific areas, and prized for its translucence, strength, and razor-sharpness, it was widely traded and worked into a host of items that ranged from everyday carving instruments and jewelry to spectacular mirrors used by Mesoamerican leaders as a window into the future. ▲

The Granger Collection, New York

Aztec Warriors with Obsidian Swords In a world without steel, Mesoamerican warriors fashioned swords and clubs out of wood into which they embedded razor-sharp blades of obsidian. These weapons, known as *macuahuitl*, were deadly in close combat. Here three warriors are shown armed with *macuahuitl*; they also carry shields and regalia. ▲

Werner Forman/UIG/AGE Fotostock

Aztec Mirror, 1400–1520 In Mesoamerica, mirrors were not used to study one's own appearance but rather as divinatory aids that could provide a portal to otherworld entities and the distant future. Created by master artisans of finely worked obsidian, obsidian mirrors were prized by the elite as important symbols of their status. ▲

Before 1500, the Americas were largely without metal tools. In a world without steel, obsidian—a dark volcanic glass—was among the commodities most valued by native peoples. For thousands of years, people across the Americas used it to make cutting tools as well as ritual artifacts and everyday trinkets. Its value derived from its relative scarcity, its luminosity, and its workability. Notably, obsidian does not have a crystalline structure, so in the hands of a skilled artisan, it can be carved or knapped into deadly blades, projectile points, brilliant jewelry, and other items for domestic and ritual use. Because obsidian points can be made microscopically thin, even today the sharpest scalpels are made of obsidian rather than metal.

The molecular content of each obsidian flow is unique and thus all obsidian objects can be traced to a specific site and source. This allows scientists to determine the precise origin of the obsidian used across the Americas. As a result of their studies of how the first inhabitants of America used obsidian, scholars can glimpse the extensive trade networks that tied together the distant and disparate peoples of the Americas. It is now clear that obsidian was among the most widely circulated commodities in the Americas. Obsidian originally mined in the American West has been found by archaeologists in the Northeast, and obsidian from Mesoamerica has been found in many regions of North America, such as Oklahoma and the Southeast.

Because obsidian was often mined near active or extinct volcanoes—places Indians often associated with gods, sacred animals, and revered ancestors—many peoples believed that it was imbued with special characteristics that gave it unusual power. Some held that as a substance, it was nearer to the gods than people. Among the Aztec, the trade and veneration of obsidian reached epic proportions. It seems entirely possible that had the Aztec not had adequate sources of obsidian, its culture might not have placed such a premium on human sacrifice. Its warriors prayed for success in their wars with these words: "May he savor the fragrance, the sweetness of death by the obsidian knife. . . . May he desire the flowery death by the obsidian knife. May he savor the scent . . . the sweetness of the darkness, the din of battle."

The Aztecs believed that *Tezcatlipoca*, the Master of Fate, saw the world reflected in a magical obsidian mirror. In a sense, scholars today play a similar role. They study this beautiful, mysterious glass for insight into the ways and beliefs of the ancient peoples of the Americas who, because of the passage of hundreds and even thousands of years, can be glimpsed darkly by the scant traces of their lives that survive today.

Critical Thinking Questions

► What role did obsidian play in Mesoamerican society?

► Can you think of other goods and commodities that were similarly central to Mesoamerican society?

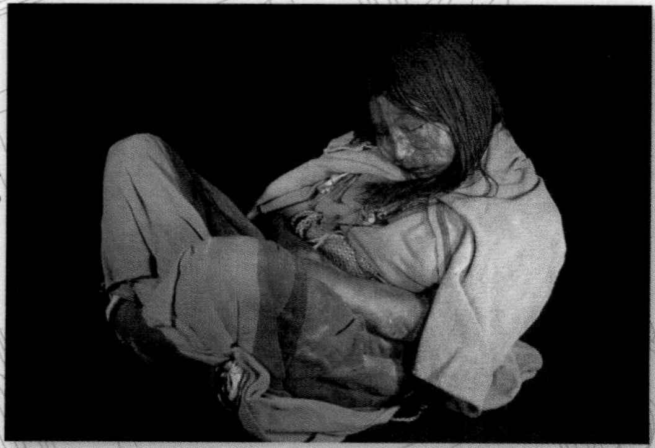

Johan Reinhard/National Geographic Creative

Global Americans In 1999, the frozen bodies of three children sacrificed more than 500 years ago were found enshrined near the 20,000-foot summit of Volcán Llullaillaco, the highest volcano in the Andes. Child sacrifice was important to the expansionist imperial Inca state and performed at pivotal moments, such as a ruler's death or a natural disaster. The eldest of the three children, likely a 13-year-old girl, known to us as the "**Llullaillaco Maiden**," was probably a peasant from the countryside selected for her beauty; the younger two were probably her attendants. A year before her death, the Maiden was taken to Cuzco where her life was transformed. She lived as an elite under the direction of priestesses and practiced the exalted feminine arts of weaving textiles and brewing *chicha*, a beer made of fermented corn. In the weeks before her death—according to a chemical analysis of her long, tightly-braided hair—she consumed increasing amounts of coca and *chicha* as she participated in sacred ceremonies along the hundreds of miles to the Volcán Llullaillaco. Heavily sedated and clenching a small clump of coca between her teeth, she succumbed to the frigid high altitude at the appointed time on Llullaillaco. She was surrounded by items from across the empire: seashells, feathers, coca, corn, and dried meat. She was far from her home and her upbringing, but the coca and the *chicha* and her tomb atop the Andes placed her in proximity to the Inca gods and perhaps even eternity.

their skulls were stored on racks in the temple. During the inauguration of the Great Temple in 1487 CE, more than twenty thousand people were sacrificed over four days. Most were conquered peoples. Some were drugged; others went calmly to their deaths as they, too, believed in the rituals that consumed them. Although the exact number of victims will never be known, it is clear that as the empire expanded, so did the practice of human sacrifice. In addition to its brutality, the empire was also noted for its literate priesthood, its monumental architecture, its finely worked gold and silver artifacts, and its unparalleled feather works.

Under Mexica rule, the Valley of Mexico had a population of at least 1 million. With 300,000 residents, the city of Tenochtitlán was the most populous in the world outside of Asia. Although the Mexica created a complex system of gardens and canals in their capital city, Tenochtitlán could supply only about 5 percent of the food it needed. The Mexica state successfully managed the redistribution of food and labor from countryside to city, but it was an unwieldy empire with thirty-eight subject provinces rendering tribute, diverse peoples and languages, and a territory half the size of Mexico today. By 1500, the empire had stalled. Its wars against rival nations had become quagmires. Soon, the empire began to collapse. It seemed the gods could no longer be appeased and the cycle of life was imperiled. Moctezuma, the ruler, became depressed, berated his troops, and worried aloud at the approach of the Mexica year *Ce Acatl* (in Europe, 1519), for it was believed that in that year, the man-god Quetzalcoatl would return.

1-3c The Inca of Peru

The Inca establish ancient America's most expansive empire.

The last and most extensive American Indian empire emerged in central Peru around 1200 CE. Like the Mexica, the Inca built an empire through con-quest and the subjugation of productive farming societies. By 1525, from their capital of Cuzco, home to tens of thousands of people, the Inca dominated nearly all of the Andes, a mountain chain running the length of South America. Each Inca king was believed to be divine, and after his death, his wealth maintained his cult and his mummified body. Thus, to secure his own legacy, every Inca king launched new wars of conquest.

The Inca conquest could be brutal—nearly all men captured in war were forced into the Inca army—but the Inca state tolerated conquered peoples' religions and brought their elites into the state. In fact, many of the Inca's greatest cultural achievements—unique stone masonry, exquisite textiles and ceramics and gold work, precise astronomical observations—were derived from earlier or conquered Andean civilizations. The Inca excelled in organizing and centralizing their sprawling empire.

Unlike in Mesoamerica where Mayan and Mexica merchants dealt independently with one another, the Inca state controlled the economy. It built a system of regional warehouses and maintained more than fourteen thousand miles of roads. An elaborate system of runners and pack trains allowed supplies and messages to reach all corners within days. The Inca were skilled in agriculture. With the development of a vast system of irrigation, they grew potatoes, maize, peanuts, and cotton. They were also skilled surgeons and unparalleled weavers. Although they had no formal writing system, they recorded trade and census data with colored and knotted strings called *quipus*. All the cords in a Quipu hung from a single string. Their positions and colors signaled what was being counted, and the type of knot indicated a number. Typically, the knot's placement signified units of 1, 10, 100, or more. Altogether, the Inca created the most efficient, integrated empire in the Americas, incorporating millions of people into their economy and culture.

1-4

The Agricultural Southwest and the Arid Interior

The Hohokam created extensive canals to irrigate their fields in the area that is now Phoenix, Arizona. These massive canals not only moved huge amounts of water but are also monuments to Hohokam engineering skill and social organization.

What does this image, which shows the size of an ancient irrigation canal from the American Southwest, tell you about how and why some early societies built such canals while others did not? ▶

Peter V. Bianchi/National Geographic Stock

A thousand miles north of the Valley of Mexico in the arid region that became the American Southwest, complex but far less populous civilizations emerged. The Hohokams and the Anasazis adopted agriculture, sedentism, and pottery making. Further east, the Numa moved into the arid Great Basin. In the prairie-grasslands of the Great Plains, where there were few streams for irrigation but vast expanses of sturdy grasses, Indian life and culture formed around vast herds of bison.

☞ As you read, think about how climate and resources shaped the cultures of the Southwest and the Great Plains. What set the cultures of the Southwest apart from others in ancient America?

1-4a The Hohokam Peoples

The Hohokam trade across great distances and create elaborate irrigation systems.

Central to the development of Hohokam communities in the Gila and Salt River valley of present-day southern Arizona was the creation of a dependable system for allocating water (see Map 1.5). Unlike Mesoamerican farmers, who had reliable water sources, the Hohokam of the arid desert dug irrigation canals that were ten feet deep, thirty feet wide, miles long, and lined in plaster to capture and divert scarce water. In the Salt River Valley, fourteen major canals distributed water through a thousand miles of smaller canals and channels. With this water, the Hohokam raised corn, beans, and squash, which they harvested twice a year. They also grew agave, cotton, tobacco, and other plants. To supplement their diet, they gathered wild plants from the desert and hunted rabbits, deer, and antelope. Befitting their desert environment, the Hohokam lived in brush-covered semisubterranean homes in towns situated beyond river floodplains to ensure their survival. They constructed large earthen mounds, produced fine pottery, and created ornaments from shells they obtained from peoples of the Pacific coast and the Gulf of California. The most important export of the Hohokam was turquoise, which Mesoamericans prized for its color and the ease with which it could be worked into jewelry. In return, the Hohokam imported copper bells and tropical macaws, which they bred in pens.

Altogether, the Hohokam numbered about fifty thousand, and Snaketown, their largest town, had several thousand inhabitants at its peak. It was sustained by canals that irrigated huge fields of maize, squash, and cotton. Among the Hohokam, ball games brought communities together. They played with a small rubber ball on slightly oval ball courts up to sixty-five yards long with large hoops or rings through which contestants sought to kick goals. The Hohokam constructed more that two hundred of these ball courts. Fans sat in earthen bleachers to watch their team play.

After the fall of the Toltec in 1168, Mesoamerican influences in the north declined. The Hohokam stopped building ball courts and abandoned their semisubterranean homes for adobe dwellings built above ground. Soon thereafter, the Hohokam abandoned their small, dispersed settlements and congregated into fewer and larger towns. At this time, the Hohokam began to construct their Great Houses, such as Casa Grande. At the center of this large walled complex was a building that was several stories high; most likely it was used for celestial observations and to survey canals. A flood, not invaders, devastated these desert-dwelling people by sweeping away most of their communities and irrigation canals in the second half of the fourteenth century. The Sonoran desert would not be inhabited again until the modern city of Phoenix was established six centuries later.

1-4b The Anasazi

The Anasazi build extensive roads and communities.

At the same time that the Hohokam emerged as an agricultural and sedentary people, the Anasazi developed a similar culture in the high desert plateau of the Southwest. The Anasazi were skilled stonemasons, and in this exceptionally arid climate, many of

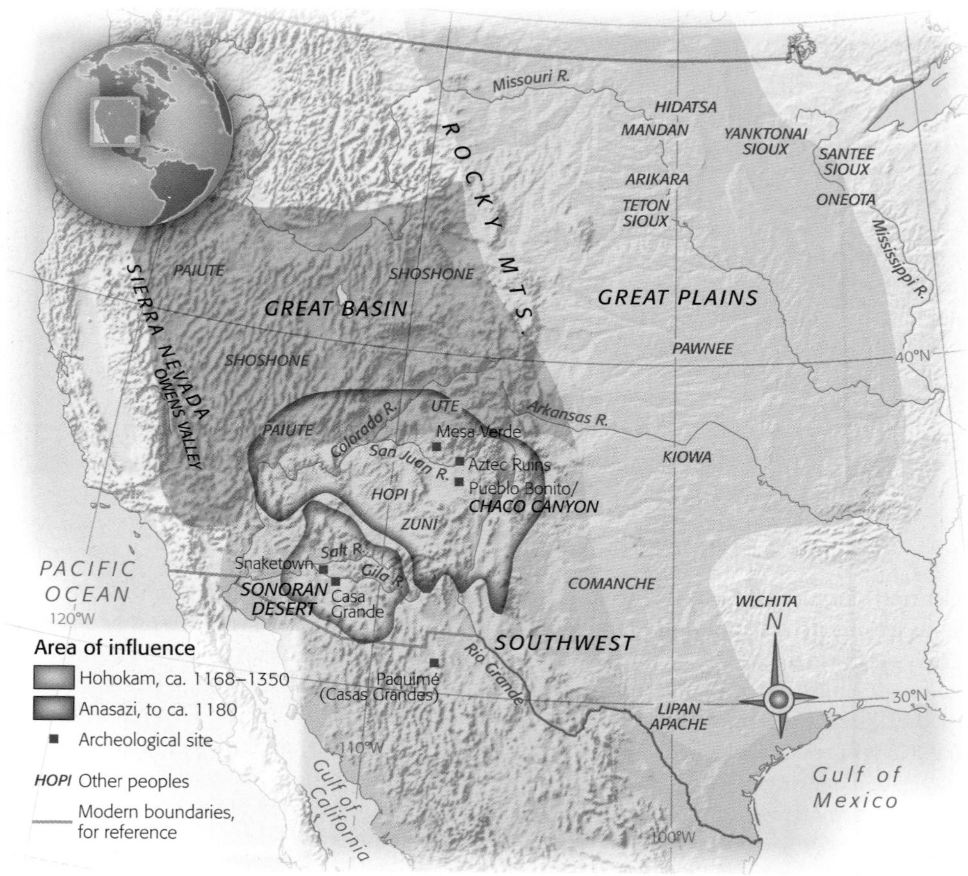

Map 1.5 The Peoples of the Great Plains and Southwest, ca. 1450. In the largely arid interior of the North American West, the Great Basin and the Great Plains were thinly settled, but in the Southwest tens of thousands of people lived in scores of permanent settlements adjacent to rivers or on the tops of highly defensible mesas. In the Southwest, irrigation and the manipulation of water were central to agriculture. ▲

their buildings survive. A thousand years ago, some five thousand Anasazi lived in Chaco Canyon in the San Juan Basin of New Mexico. Pueblo Bonito, their largest town, was at the center of a sprawling network of Anasazi communities and housed several hundred people, who worshiped their deities in semisubterranean **kivas**. To collect and transport water to their fields, the residents of Chaco Canyon built an extensive system of dams, ditches, canals, and reservoirs. The Anasazi also built cliff dwellings, and at Mesa Verde in southwestern Colorado, they built a nearly impregnable two hundred-room complex into the cliffs.

By about 1150, roads linked Pueblo Bonito to one hundred fifty smaller communities. These roads radiated out from Chaco Canyon straight as an arrow for hundreds of miles. Some were narrow; others were nearly thirty feet wide; some paralleled each other for miles. They were built by a people who had neither wheeled vehicles nor pack animals, and their use remains somewhat of a mystery. Clearly, though, the roads enabled the Anasazi to more easily transport over great distances food and the hundreds of thousands of timbers required to build their towns in Chaco Canyon and elsewhere.

kivas Semisubterranean rooms used by Puebloan and the Hohokam peoples for spiritual ceremonies.

If too much water in the form of a flood destroyed the Hohokam, not enough water doomed the Anasazi. Tree-ring studies indicate a terrible drought between 1150 and 1180 CE, forcing people to move from Chaco Canyon and related sites as food systems failed. Perhaps the people went 60 miles north, for at this time the community known today as *Aztec Ruins* emerged. When it, too, collapsed a century later, another community, Paquimé (or Casas Grandes), 390 miles south of Pueblo Bonito, became a regional center. Here Katsinas—supernatural beings associated with rain and fertility—were first depicted on walls and murals. In all likelihood, the Paquimé are the ancestors of today's Pueblo Indians of Arizona and New Mexico because Zuni and Hopi traditions tell of Chaco Canyon as a place where their ancestors lived. By 1500, around two hundred fifty thousand Puebloans lived in some 134 communities across Arizona and New Mexico.

1-4c The Great Basin

About a thousand years ago, the Numas, ancestors of the Utes and Shoshones, moved from California and Nevada into the arid Great Basin, bringing

The Numa move seasonally, skillfully taking advantage of resources.

Martin Gray/Getty Images

Pueblo Bonito, Chaco Canyon Pueblo Bonito had six hundred rooms, a central plaza, and forty "kivas," or half-underground rooms with wood roofs that were important ceremonial centers. The community's crescent shape allowed the sun to light and warm each of the town's structures. ▲

with them their techniques of food production. They set up small encampments alongside lakes, streams, and springs. Few Numa practiced agriculture but most relied on **camas**, potato-like lily bulbs, and pine nuts. These two sources of food could be processed and stored for later use. The peoples moved seasonally from encampment to encampment to be near their sources of food. Men fished and hunted, and in late spring, women dug up camas, which they pounded into meal. In the fall, family groups harvested pine nuts. The Numas were skilled basket weavers, and they wove containers that other societies might have produced out of ceramics.

Almost alone among peoples of the Great Basin, the Northern Paiutes of the Owens Valley of southeastern California practiced agriculture. They irrigated root plants that, with the region's seeds and nuts, allowed them to establish small, permanent villages. To the north, the Northern Paiutes of southern Utah and Nevada grew maize, beans, squash, and sunflowers near streams and springs; elsewhere they used irrigation to grow their crops.

1-4d The Great Plains

Indians of the Great Plains develop their culture based on bison.

Over millennia, humans and bison developed together on the Great Plains. In bison, humans had a dependable source of a lean, flavorful meat; a sweet supply of fat; thick hides for robes and covers for their homes; horns and bones to make into tools and weapons; and wool for garments and rugs. As the extent of the Great Plains shifted with the climate, so did bison ranges, and humans migrated accordingly. Bison increased in numbers when humans burned the prairie grasslands annually, an intervention into the plains ecology that stimulated the growth of the tender grasses on which bison fed.

The societies that developed alongside the bison were among the most stable in the Americas. About 2500 BCE, the plains became less arid, and bison herds increased, supporting small bands of nomadic hunter-gatherers for the next two thousand years. Around 250 CE, Plains Indians adopted the bow and arrow, which they used to kill bison at close range.

The rhythms of Plains Indian society followed those of the bison. For most of the year, bison lived in small herds composed of calves and a mature cow while bulls grazed in small numbers on their own. In late summer, bison cows and bulls came together to mate and to feed on tender grasses. As winter approached, cows with their calves separated from bulls. Similarly, plains peoples lived in small groups most of the year and came together in the summer in groups that ranged from twenty-five to one hundred individuals, the numbers required to hunt bison most efficiently. In the winter, when food was scarce, bands contracted to the size of a few families to survive. They carried their tipis, clothes, and food on their backs, or they bred dogs as beasts of burden.

In a typical hunt, Plains Indians constructed a corral at the base of a bluff or the end of a ravine. To call the bison, a young man sang a song that sounded like a distressed bison. This call attracted cows, who led the herd over the embankment or up into the ravine, where armed men slaughtered dozens of the confused and injured animals. Men and women butchered the bison and spent days celebrating the successful hunt. The meat not consumed immediately was cut into long thin strips and dried into strips or pounded and mixed with fat and berries to form **pemmican** for later use. For thousands of years, and long after 1500, peoples of the Central Plains lived in this manner.

But other Plains Indians were sedentary. About 1 CE, some began to live in villages, and some around modern Kansas City began to cultivate small amounts of maize. Others constructed burial mounds. Around 850 CE, some peoples settled as far north as central South Dakota, building homes of wooden posts and earthen roofs, which provided excellent protection from frigid winters. Although they still relied on bison, these peoples also grew maize, beans, squash, and sunflowers. For centuries, they expanded up the Missouri Valley. As their numbers grew, so did the size of their villages. Known today as the *Oneotas*, these people improved the soil with ash and planted maize in ridge-and-ditch fields, an agricultural practice that was as labor intensive as it was productive.

About the same time that the Oneotas were settling the Upper Midwest, the Wichitas, the Pawnees, and the Arikaras moved onto the Central Plains. They shared a common culture, although they developed separate polities and languages. They lived in square earth lodges in villages next to fields where they grew maize, beans, squash, and sunflowers. Their villages lasted until about 1450 when drought or a colder climate caused them to disperse.

camas Plant in the lily family with an edible bulb.

pemmican Concentrated food used by Indians consisting of lean meat dried, pounded fine, and mixed with melted fat.

1-5

The Pacific West

Some Native Americans made pots, but most in the Far West were expert basket weavers and created baskets that varied widely in shape, size, and function. California Indian basketry reveals the diversity and creativity of Native American culture.

As you look at this image, can you discover some of the uses for these baskets? Why did California Indians make baskets of such a wide range of shapes and sizes? ▶

The Granger Collection, New York

The peoples of the Pacific West, encompassing Alaska, the Northwest Coast and Columbia Plateau, California, and Hawai'i, did not adopt formal agriculture, but they did consistently modify the land to maximize food production. They had no large urban centers and lived in thousands of decentralized villages. Nowhere else in the Americas were there so many languages and different cultures.

☞ As you read, focus on the diversity of the peoples of the Pacific West. Can you discern how the peoples of the Pacific West used the sea?

1-5a Alaska

Aleuts and Eskimos build a rich culture.

Although it is widely accepted that North America was settled by Paleoindians who came south from what is now Alaska, very little is known about the peoples who took their place in Alaska. It seems that by about 3000 BCE, a new wave of immigrants—the Aleuts and the Inuits, also known as *Eskimos*—came to the area from Siberia (see Map 1.6). These people had begun to develop separate cultures before they crossed the Bering Sea by canoe, and they spoke their own languages. The Aleuts settled the Aleutian Islands, and the Inuits settled on the Alaska mainland.

Over thousands of years, the Aleuts became highly skilled maritime peoples ingenious in making watercraft and tools and in using animal hides, intestines, and bladders. They even used whale skins for clothing. With canoes, spears, and nets, Aleutian men ventured into icy waters to hunt fish, whales, porpoises, seals, sea lions, and sea otters. They built homes of drift logs and whalebone; most were about twenty feet across and oval shaped with walls sunk several feet into the ground. Mats of skin and grass provided a place for people to eat and sleep. Scholars have found evidence of permanent villages on high bluffs. Aleutian society, like that of Northwest Coast peoples, was stratified into the rich, the ordinary, and slaves, usually war captives or orphans who performed hard labor.

potlatch Ceremonial feast of Northwest Coast Indians marked by the host's distribution of gifts to demonstrate wealth and generosity with the expectation of eventual reciprocation.

Alaska's remoteness and heavy forest cover complicate archaeological work, but it is known that the Eskimos ate game and wildfowl and hunted whales. They often concentrated in large villages and spent summers along the coast where they harvested and dried salmon for later use. In other seasons, they lived in semisubterranean homes covered with sod to keep out the cold. They insulated their clothes with fur. They made blades and projectile points out of slate and pottery of local earth, and they carved ivory from walrus tusks into exquisite animal- and humanlike figures.

1-5b Northwest Coast and Columbia Plateau

The Chinook and others trade extensively and depend on salmon for their subsistence.

From Northern California through Southeast Alaska, along what is now called the *Northwest Coast*, scores of different groups developed an economy and society dependent on rivers, forests, and the sea. Persistent fogs make this area unsuited for maize agriculture, but tobacco and camas can grow. The northwestern coastal peoples also ate sea mammals, fish, deer, berries, and roots. They built multifamily houses out of enormous planks hewed from cedar trees and wore distinctive, beautiful basketry hats.

Among these Pacific Northwest peoples, the most important ceremony was the **potlatch**. Elite families held this feast to commemorate significant moments in the lives of their children, such as a naming or a marriage. The potlatch began with speeches, continued through feasting and socializing, and culminated in the giving of beads, food, artwork, and other items of great value to the guests. This generosity redistributed wealth and cemented power relationships by creating reciprocal obligations across the community.

The Chinook of the lower Columbia River were the most prominent of the Pacific Northwest peoples. Class divisions structured their daily life, and slavery was common. Those born into freedom had their foreheads cradled and shaped to be long and sloping. Slaves, by contrast, had natural, rounded heads. They performed basic labor and suffered abuse from their masters. Some were captives seized in war; others had lost everything, including their own freedom, through gambling or other misadventures.

The Chinook lived at the center of a crucial trading zone, and their language became the language of commerce across the Pacific Northwest. Salmon was the mainstay of the economy, even for those who lived far inland

Map 1.6 The Peoples of Alaska, the Pacific Northwest, and California, ca. 1450. The tremendously rich natural environments along the coast and interior river valleys of the Pacific Northwest and California contributed to a tremendous range of Indian groups and extremely dense settlements across enormous regions. In California, Indians often used fire to modify their natural environment, promoting the growth of plants and animals they valued for food and the production of cultural items. ▲

on the Columbia Plateau. The Chinook caught and processed enormous amounts of salmon, which they dried and pounded into a flour for later use. Through these and other activities, such as gathering berries, men and women contributed protein to the diet.

1-5c California

California is among the most diverse and densely settled regions in the Americas.

Around 2000 BCE, when sea levels stabilized and the Pacific Coast climate became predictable, the people in what is now California began to thrive as they learned to use a marvelous variety of plants and animals. Nowhere in North America were there more local variations in climate—even within narrow valleys, environments vary from one side to another—and people adapted to them, creating regional cultures along the wet coastal regions of the north, the desert of the southeast, the moderate climate of central California, and the Sierra Nevada mountain range.

A hallmark of ancient Native California is the seeming paradox of a very large population that was dense, diverse, and decentralized. Recent estimates suggest that some three hundred to three hundred fifty thousand people lived in California in the year 1500. Collectively, they spoke more than one hundred different languages—20 percent of all of the languages spoken in North America. Each language group was composed of an even larger number of independent peoples. The basic political unit was a central village and one or more affiliated hamlets. In some regions, groups were as small as two hundred fifty people; in others, as large as fifteen thousand people. The relatively small territories that Indian groups controlled initially led scholars to believe they were unsophisticated, but research has shown that they were as worldly as any ancient American people. They manufactured baskets of great utility and beauty. They studied the heavens as skilled astronomers and mathematicians. They relied on trade to obtain goods such as obsidian that were not locally available. And because of their small villages, they looked to their neighbors for marriage partners.

As hunter-gatherers, California peoples managed their environment and practiced intensive plant and animal husbandry. They used fire to clear fields and encourage the growth of grasses, which would provide food for deer. Coastal people tended oyster beds. Rather than developing a single crop, such as maize, California Indians profited from the diversity of edible plants that grew naturally.

California Indians relied most of all on acorns produced by the abundant oaks. Women gathered the acorns in huge baskets and crushed, soaked, and dried them several times to remove a poisonous acid. The dried meal was used year-round to make porridge or thin cakes. Protein-rich acorns supported large and dense populations; men supplemented the diet by hunting deer and other game and fish.

For gathering acorns and other purposes, California Indians made a stunning variety of baskets. Some were large for gathering grains; some were small for keeping precious items; others were so tightly woven that they could carry water. Just

tomols Plank-built boats constructed by the Chumash and other California groups to ply the coast and travel between the mainland and coastal islands.

aquaculture Cultivation of fish for food.

about every group had its own style. Some wove the fibers clockwise, others counterclockwise; some embroidered baskets with bird feathers, and others enhanced them with small shells. More than just containers, baskets were an expression of a local aesthetic that used natural resources in a way to suggest the unity of the earthly world with the supernatural.

Most of California was characterized by small semiautonomous villages. Warfare among California Indians was uncommon but erupted sporadically, prompted by competition over food sources. Unlike most California Indians, the Chumash of the Santa Barbara region, numbering about fifteen thousand people, lived in scores of related villages. The Chumash of the coast and the Channel Islands had ***tomols***, seaworthy canoes about thirty feet long. They were constructed of planks cut from driftwood or redwood and held together by a sort of glue and then reinforced by hemp cords passed through small holes. The canoes were sealed with pine tar and dried asphalt and then sanded with shark skin and painted.

Like most peoples, the Chumash had a clear division of labor. Women gathered acorns and shellfish, and men hunted seals and sea lions. The Chumash who lived in the interior drew geometric shapes and mysterious human animal figures in local caves that continue to inspire even as they confound. Like most coastal people in California, the Chumash converted local olivella shells into beads, which became a medium of exchange across California. In fact, the name *Chumash* means "bead money makers."

1-5d Hawai'i

Sixteen or seventeen hundred years ago, thousands of years after most of the Americas had been settled, perhaps a single large ocean-going canoe sewn together by cords and propelled by a woven sail, set forth from the Marquesa Islands in the South Pacific. The canoe was double hulled and contained a rich cargo: edible plants as well as breeding pairs of dogs, pigs, and fowl and stowaway rats and weeds. The crew was composed of twenty or so Lapita Polynesians, a people who for centuries had been settling the islands of the Pacific east of Samoa. They were well prepared to establish a permanent presence wherever they made landfall.

> The Hawaiian islands are among the most recently settled regions of the Pacific.

What led these Lapita explorers to sail out into the ocean is not known, but it was an epic voyage. A reconstruction of ocean currents and wind patterns reveals that the canoe sailed, rather than drifted, some two thousand miles northwest. After weeks at sea, they reached a chain of uninhabited volcanic islands ideally suited for the Polynesian lifestyles and economy. The migrants named them Hawaiki, or Hawai'i, after their homeland. For fifteen centuries, the Hawaiian islands supported a rich and flourishing society that evolved from the descendants of that single canoe.

The Lapita were wise to bring plants and animals with them, for Hawai'i had only one native mammal, a small bat, and few edible plants. Soon after their arrival, the Lapita began to cultivate taro, sweet potato, banana, breadfruit, yam, and coconut. Rainfall was adequate to support their crops, and vegetation provided cordage and thatching. They ate seabirds and native geese and derived much of their subsistence from the tropical waters, which contained hundreds of species of fish and crabs and more than 1,000 types of mollusks.

Archaeologists have discovered a great variety of hooks, sinkers, and nets used by the islands' early dwellers. They have also found that by the 1300s, Hawaiians had initiated **aquaculture**, building hundreds of shore and inland ponds that they stocked with fish to harvest. The harvest yielded more than 2 million pounds of fish per year. For their rich bounty, the Lapita thanked Lono, the god of fertility and production, to whom they dedicated an annual festival.

Early Hawaiians did not live in major population centers; rather, like most farmers, they were dispersed across the land. They built temples and shrines out of stone and adorned them with carved sculptures. They possessed no draft animals or wheeled vehicles. They used canoes to travel along the coast and walked overland on a network of trails.

In the first centuries after the Lapita arrived, the population of the islands doubled with each generation. By around 1100, it had reached about twenty thousand inhabitants. Over the next four centuries, the population increased steadily, probably exceeding two hundred thousand. Hawaiian society was hierarchical with a chief and a ruling class on top and a base of laborers at the bottom. As the population increased, so did competition for land, and by 1100, territorial boundaries were well marked and defended by local chiefs who paid tribute to a paramount chief.

Witold Skrypczak/Getty Images

Rock Art, Chumash, Painted Cave Like many Native Americans in the West, the Chumash of California adorned some of the caves in their homelands with mysteriously complex and beautiful images that most likely were the creation of their religious and spiritual leaders. It is believed that some of these drawings represented celestial bodies and others concerned themes of reproduction and animal life. ◄

1-6

The Woodlands

This open hand is an iconic image from the Eastern Woodlands peoples who lived east of the Mississippi River nearly two thousand years ago. Cut skillfully from a piece of Mica, a sheet mineral that cleaves nearly perfectly, this hand may have been worn or carried. It is just one example of the artistic accomplishments of the Woodlands peoples, who often created beautiful jewelry and decorated their everyday items with images and geometric designs.

In looking at this graceful form, do you think it draws us into Hopewell culture, or does it warn us away? ▶

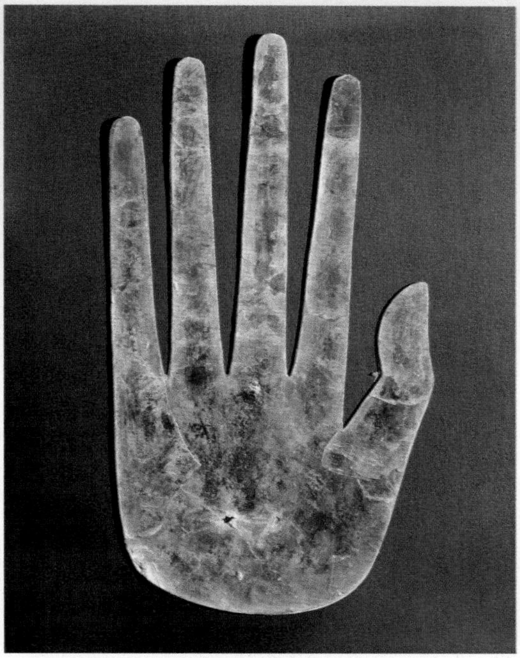

Heritage Images/Fine Art/Corbis

The Woodlands refers to both the forested eastern half of North America and the common culture of Native Americans who lived there beginning thousands of years ago. The Woodlands can be very cold in winter and very humid in the summer. The forests of the Woodlands have an abundance of streams and rivers with varied food sources, including deer in the south, caribou in the north, and fish and sea mammals along the coast. Woodlands peoples developed agriculture, extensive trade networks, and social and political systems that supported some of the largest urban centers in ancient North America.

☞ As you read, focus on the unique cultures of the peoples of the Woodlands. Can you identify the cultural characteristics shared by Woodlands peoples?

1-6a The Adenas and Hopewell

The Adena and Hopewell build earthen structures of unparalleled size.

Two thousand years ago, the Adenas and then the Hopewell of the Ohio River Valley (see Map 1.7), who lived in small agricultural settlements, built some of the largest, most exact, and numerous geometric earthen constructions ever. Remains of these huge earthworks, some of which were miles long, can still be seen in aerial photographs, although most were destroyed by twentieth-century urban development. Their purposes are uncertain but they may have functioned as burial mounds or calendrical or astronomical devices. The Adenas and Hopewell were exceptionally skilled in producing textiles and ceramics and in crafting objects of aesthetic and symbolic value—wondrous copper ear spools, breast plates, mirrors, figurines, and pipes for tobacco.

The metals, shells, and woods of which these objects were made came from great distances. The Hopewell used grizzly bear teeth from the Rockies, obsidian from Yellowstone in Wyoming, iron from Kansas, mica from North Carolina, shells and shark and alligator teeth from the Gulf of Mexico, copper from the Great Lakes, and silver from Ontario. In turn, the goods they created were carried far across eastern North America and have been recovered in burial sites throughout the Southeast. For reasons that are still unclear, the Hopewell went into decline around 400 CE and had disappeared by 800 CE, but elements of their culture had already spread through trade over much of eastern North America.

1-6b Cahokia and the Mississippians

Cahokia emerges as one of the great urban centers of ancient America.

In the region of the Mississippi Valley known as the **American Bottom**, elements of the Adena and Hopewell tradition survived among a people known as the *Mississippians*. The American Bottom is a broad floodplain of the Mississippi River in southwestern Illinois about twenty-five miles long and at most a dozen miles wide. Its swamps and small lakes were rich in game, plants, and waterfowl, and Mississippian peoples found its soil ideally suited for agriculture. By around 900 CE, its fertile lands were increasingly and intensively planted, and over the next five centuries the region experienced a remarkable cycle of rise and decline. The building of Cahokia, its largest town, coincided with the onset of a global warming trend that increased summer rainfall and improved the corn harvest. By 1050–1150 CE, the American Bottom held one of the largest populations north of Mexico—at least ten thousand people, and perhaps as many as thirty thousand.

Mississippians were like the Hopewell in that they were at the center of a wide trade network, produced beautiful artifacts, and built large mounds. But the Mississippians outstripped their predecessors in the production of maize, in their mound building, and in their social and town organization. They grew maize on raised ridge-and-ditch fields, and maize production became the key to the increasing population of the Mississippians.

Mississippian towns were marked by large mounds and plazas, and they dominated the flat river valleys of the American Bottom. Just outside modern

American Bottom Flood plain of Mississippi River near modern-day St. Louis where indigenous culture flourished a thousand years ago.

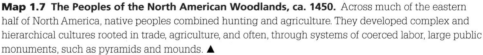

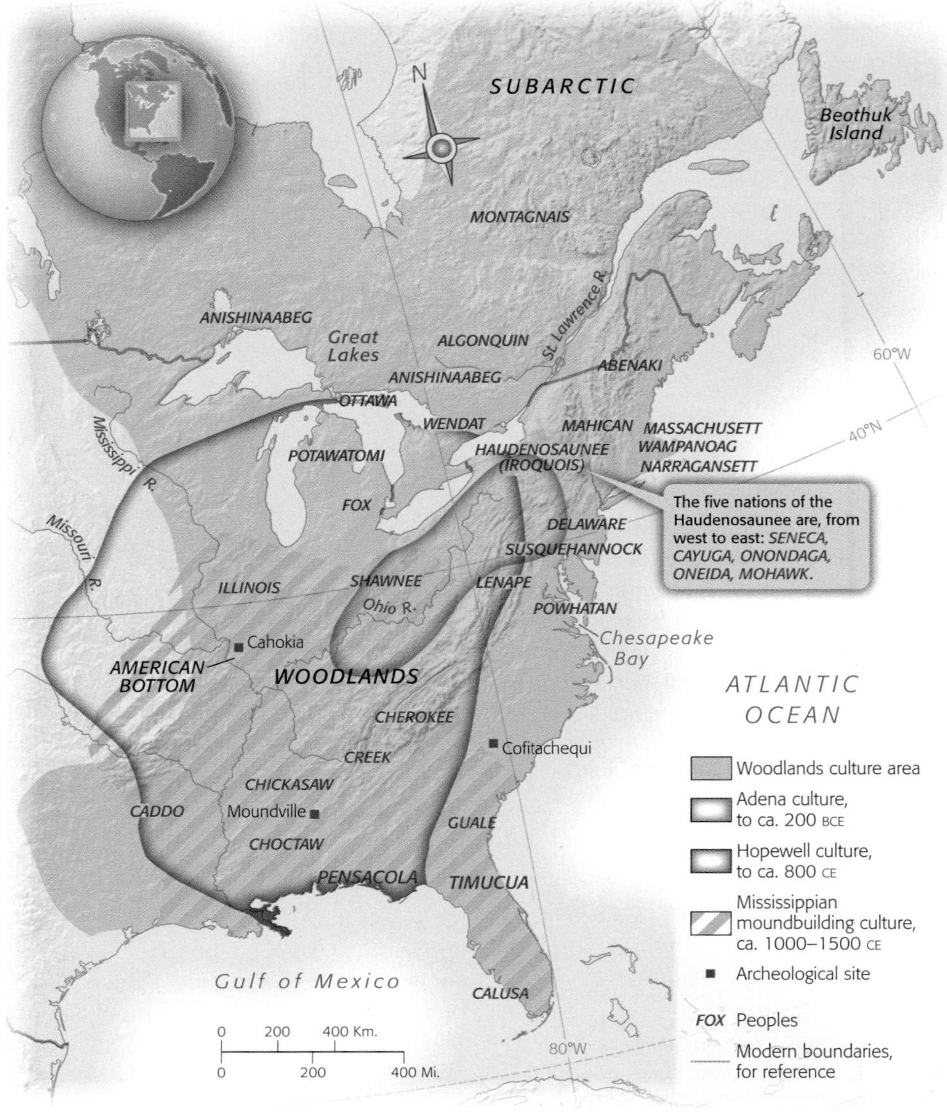

Map 1.7 The Peoples of the North American Woodlands, ca. 1450. Across much of the eastern half of North America, native peoples combined hunting and agriculture. They developed complex and hierarchical cultures rooted in trade, agriculture, and often, through systems of coerced labor, large public monuments, such as pyramids and mounds. ▲

St. Louis, Cahokia flourished from 800 to 1200 CE. It was a sacred place, just as Teotihuacán was for Mesoamerica, and it drew people from small, semi-independent communities across the area. Its urban design, monumental mounds, dependence on maize, and overall layout seem to reflect Mesoamerican influences.

Building Cahokia's mounds required a complex and coercive labor system. The greatest construction, Monks Mound, is among the largest ancient structures in the Americas. At its base, it is 330 yards by 250 yards, and it is more than 30 yards high. This massive mound composed of 22 million cubic feet of soil was built one basket of earth at a time. To prevent its erosion, Cahokian engineers used four different types of soils and installed a complicated system of drains. Monks Mound was crowned with a large wooden structure that faced south, toward the sun. It was but one of some 100 mounds the Cahokians constructed. Smaller mounds were often used as burial sites for rulers and men and women who were sacrificed at the time of their ruler's burial. In one tomb, archaeologists unearthed 260 victims, who seem to have been killed so that they could accompany their leader in the afterlife.

During its height in 1000 CE, Cahokia's residents built neighborhoods of small, rectangular houses and numerous wood buildings most likely used for rituals and astronomical observations. By 1200 CE, the central plazas and mounds were ringed with a wooden palisade. Cahokia became fragmented and declined during the 1300s. Its abandonment likely coincided with the onset of a cooler climate that reduced maize harvests and undermined its society. Nonetheless, elements of Mississippian culture survived in the American Southeast into the early eighteenth century.

1-6c Southeastern Societies

> Many Southeastern societies are hierarchical and have religious leaders as rulers.

In the centuries after Cahokia collapsed, other Mississippian societies flourished. Major cities, such as Cofitachequi in present-day South Carolina, and Moundville, south of Tuscaloosa, Alabama, were, like Cahokia, agriculturally based and relied on forced labor. These hierarchical societies with a total population of about ten thousand were organized as **chiefdoms** and overseen by a class of priests. Like other Mississippian societies, they produced many items for export and trade. They drew on Mesoamerican and Cahokian cultural traits.

Some Mississippians shared a Southeastern Ceremonial Complex centered on a trio of gods or individuals who were variously represented in stone, ceramic, shell, and copper objects. An important symbol was a man-god with hawk wings and a tobacco-moth proboscis. For the Mississippians, hawks were symbols of power, and tobacco moths were valued for pollinating tobacco, an important crop. Southeastern Ceremonial Complex personages were often depicted wearing the spiraling shell of a conch, a symbol that for Mesoamericans indicated legitimate leadership.

The Pensacola on the Gulf Coast, the Calusas in Florida, and the Guales—Southeastern Woodlands peoples who lived farther east along the Atlantic Coast—were not associated with this complex, although they were also organized into chiefdoms and had some cultural resemblance to Mississippian peoples. These peoples lived in settlements that were smaller than Cahokia and did little farming because they were surrounded by bountiful food sources. The historic peoples of the Southeast—the Caddos, Choctaws, Chickasaws, Cherokees, and the Creeks—would not emerge until the sixteenth century in the wake of collapse of the chiefdoms of the South.

1-6d Iroquoian Speakers

> Iroquoian-speaking peoples form one of North America's most important political confederacies.

Iroquoian Woodlands people lived east of the Great Lakes and in what is today upstate New York. Sometime after 500 CE, many of the people of the Northeast began to cultivate corn, which they most likely received from peoples to their west. By 1300 CE Iroquoian peoples depended on corn. As the climate cooled and became drier, competition and warfare broke out among the peoples of the Northeast. As a result, Iroquoians began to consolidate and fortify their towns against raids from their enemies, most likely the Wendat (Huron), an agricultural and hunting people who lived in the northern Great Lakes region. Iroquoians had extensive trade relations with peoples farther north. Eventually, Iroquois villages were configured into five related entities—the Mohawk, Oneida, Onondaga, Cayuga, and Seneca—and they formed the **Haudenosaunee** (whole house), **Iroquois Confederacy**, or **League of the Five Nations**. Through their league, the Five Nations would ultimately emerge as the most powerful Indians in the Northeast.

The Haudenosaunee lived in towns of about fifty residences, each occupied by several families. Most towns were made up of clans descended from a common female ancestor, and people of these **matrilineal** clans, who traced their descent through the maternal line, shared a **longhouse**. These impressive wooden structures—some more than one hundred yards long—had a central hallway, semiprivate rooms, and rooftop openings to allow smoke to escape. The Iroquois typically inhabited their town sites for about three generations and then built a new town about ten miles away where soil and timber had not been depleted.

Effigy Smoking Pipe, Second Century BCE to First Century CE This stone pipe fragment is carved in the shape of a tattooed warrior head. The surviving ear bears a large piercing. ▲ The Ohio Historical Society; Photographer

Among the Haudenosaunee and Wendat, various forms of labor were divided according to gender, which in turn shaped social organization and family relations. Women cared for the longhouses; planted and harvested village fields of corn, beans, squash, and tobacco; crafted clothes and pottery; and watched over children. Men prepared the cornfields for planting, caught fish, and hunted deer, beaver, elk, rabbit, turkeys, geese, and pigeons. Men were also responsible for external relations, namely war, trade, and diplomacy. By the nature of their work, women spent more time in and around villages than men, who were often absent fishing, hunting, and trading. This gendered division of labor led to **matrilocal** residential patterns within Iroquoian peoples. This meant that a married couple would reside with the wife's parents, not the groom's. It would have been logical for women rather than men to have lived together and formed the basis of households. Furthermore, descent, inheritance, and family ties were matrilineal in that children did not inherit their father's property but that of their mother's brother,

chiefdoms Form of social, political, and economic organization in which power is exercised by a single person, the paramount chief, over many communities.

Haudenosaunee, Iroquois Confederacy, or League of the Five Nations "Whole House," confederacy, or league formed by the five Iroquois nations: the Mohawk, Oneida, Onondaga, Cayuga, and Seneca.

matrilineal Kinship system in which ancestral descent is traced through the maternal line.

longhouse Long narrow residential building favored by Iroquoian-speaking Indians in northeastern North America.

matrilocal System in which a married couple resides with or near the wife's parents.

The Granger Collection, New York

Global Americans Iroquoian-speaking communities before 1500 were often bathed in blood as villagers fell upon one another and their neighbors in a cycle of violence and revenge. In the later decades of the 1400s, Hiawatha, a leader from Onondaga, embodied the suffering caused by these conflicts. Through the words of a stranger, **Deganawidah**, a Huron (Wendat) prophet from the north, who came to be known as the Peacemaker, Hiawatha led his people toward peace, power, and unity. Hiawatha had lost three daughters to violence. With words of condolence and gifts of beads, the Peacemaker eased Hiawatha's grief and articulated rituals that became the basis for unity among all five Iroquois Nations. Words and beads (wampum) were to replace war and weapons. Tribes were to retain control over their own villages, but a Grand Council of fifty leaders would oversee common concerns. Deganawidah charged the leaders of each of the Nations to show patience "that your skin be of a thickness of seven spreads of the hands." The words of Deganawidah preserved peace among the Haudenosaunee, but in a bitter irony, the Haudenosaunee, then freed from their own internecine conflict, turned on their enemies, in particular Deganawidah's Huron. As the life of Deganawidah suggests, Indian communities in early America were independent yet integrated into larger networks of contact and exchange. Villages might very well be ringed with palisades, but individuals and ideas moved across borders.

and in old age, individuals often counted on their nieces and nephews for support rather than their own children.

1-6e Algonquian Speakers

Autonomous Algonquian-speaking peoples inhabit much of the Northeast Woodlands.

The Haudenosaunees warred and traded with a range of Algonquian-speaking peoples who lived around them and occupied most of the Northeast from Beothuk Island south along the coast to the Chesapeake Bay. To the north were the Ottawas, Algonquins, and Montagnais; to the east were the Mahicans, Abenakis, and Wampanoags. To the south were the Delawares and Susquehannocks, and in the west were the Shawnees, Potawatomis, Anishinaabegs, Illinois, and Fox. Like the Haudenosaunees, Algonquian-speaking peoples had a vast knowledge of plants and animal behaviors that enabled them to subsist in a demanding and variable seasonal climate. They did not organize themselves into large polities like the southern Mississippians or into confederacies like the Haudenosaunee. Algonquian communities were generally small, and most people lived in dome-shaped houses made of bent saplings covered with mats of hides. Those who lived close to the sea had more food options than other peoples of the Eastern Woodlands, so Algonquians relied less on cultivated agriculture than did the Haudenosaunees or the Wendats. North of Maine the growing season was too short for agriculture.

In New England and the mid-Atlantic, the Massachusetts, Wampanoags, Narragansetts, and Lenapes built few permanent towns, relying more on more seasonal camps. In summer, coastal Algonquians hunted seals and whales, gathered shellfish, and caught fish. In the winter, northern family groups moved into the interior to hunt deer, elk, moose, bear, and beaver for food and for the raw materials for clothing and tools. This varied economy served them well for centuries, but limited food sources and harsh winters kept their numbers low.

Summary

The peopling of the Americas was a relatively recent development in a global process that has been ongoing since the emergence of humanity in Africa millions of years ago. Human migration to the Americas was the result of technological advance and changes in the earth's climate. When the earth's ocean levels fell as the earth cooled, Beringia emerged from the ocean, and skilled hunters who had harnessed fire were able to push the human frontier of settlement across this land bridge into the Americas. Others ventured down coastal waters all the way to the tip of South America.

The first peoples who settled across the Americas quickly made their homes in habitable regions, and beginning about thirteen thousand years ago, a common culture known as *Clovis* dominated much of North America. Soon after the rise of Clovis, the earth's climate changed again. This gradual global warming—the result of a slight change in the earth's axis—and the skill of Clovis hunters led to the extinction of the large mammals that had been the prey and cultural foundation of the first peoples who settled across the Americas. Predictably, humans adjusted to these changes, and as they did, they developed agriculture and other skills that allowed them to make a living just about everywhere in the Americas.

As humans came to inhabit more of the regions of the Americas, they developed diverse cultures, all in response to their needs, desires, and local environmental conditions. In South America and Mesoamerica, vast agricultural empires emerged, peopled by millions. They were united by complex cosmologies and religious beliefs and were supported by agricultural surpluses that flowed into capital cities, such as Tenochtitlán. Further north, across North America, the locus of daily life was the village, and Indians developed an enormous range of cultures and languages. Some relied on animals, such as bison, for food and clothing. Others depended on acorns or salmon for sustenance. Nearly all the peoples of the Americas traded with neighbors for commodities they could not produce. But even as they consumed goods from beyond their own region, peoples remained distinctly diverse. This diversity was the essence of America in 1500 and the product of millennia of migration, settlement, and adaptation.

Thinking Back, *Looking Forward*

As you review this chapter, think about universals in human experience. What prompted the migrations of the first American peoples before 1500? In the next chapters, look for what prompts later migrations to the Americas. Look, too, for the mechanisms of empire—how do conquests and absorptions of diverse people change across time? In what ways are family structures in Native American, European, and African societies related to economies? How does gender correlate to work? How do religious beliefs shape communities and the roles of individuals in them? These are just some of the themes from Chapter 1 that subsequent chapters will explore. To make your study concrete, review the timeline and reflect on the entries there. Think about their causes, consequences, and connections. How do they fit with global trends?

Additional Resources

Books

Calloway, Colin G. *One Vast Winter Count: The Native American West before Lewis and Clark*. Lincoln: University of Nebraska Press, 2003. ▶ Synthesis of Native American history and life in the western half of North America.

Clendinnen, Inga. *Aztecs: An Interpretation*. Cambridge, England: Cambridge University Press, 1991. ▶ Wonderfully written cultural history of the Aztecs and the rite of human sacrifice.

Fagan, Brian M. *Chaco Canyon: Archaeologists Explore the Lives of an Ancient Society*. Oxford, England: Oxford University Press, 2005. ▶ Accessible and illustrated discussion of one of the most important archaeological sites in North America.

Mann, Charles C. *1491: New Revelations of the Americas before Columbus*. New York: Vintage Books, 2006. ▶ Highly readable account of Native North America through 1491.

Richter, Daniel K. *Before the Revolution: America's Ancient Pasts*. Cambridge, MA: Harvard University Press, 2011. ▶ Masterful overview of North American Indians before contact and through the colonial period.

Snow, Dean R. *The Iroquois*. Oxford, England: Blackwell, 1994. ▶ Concise account of Iroquois history and culture through the eighteenth century.

Sturtevant, William C., ed. *Handbook of North American Indians*. Washington, D.C.: Smithsonian Institution, 1978–2008. ▶ Comprehensive multivolume work covering the history and anthropology of Native North America in totality.

Trigger, Bruce G. *North America. Cambridge History of the Native Peoples of the Americas*. Cambridge, England: Cambridge University Press, 1996. ▶ Comprehensive synthesis of discussion of American Indians before contact with Europeans.

——— *The Huron Farmers of the North*. 2nd Ed. Belmont, California: Wadsworth/Thomson Learning, 2002. ▶ Opening chapters provide best historical account of Huron culture and life.

Go to the MindTap® for **Global Americans** to access the full version of select books from this Additional Resources section.

Websites

Infinity of Nations. (http://nmai.si.edu/exhibitions/infinityofnations/california-greatbasin/134512.html). ▶ Descriptions and images of material culture from across all regions of the Americas. National Museum of the American Indian.

Chaco Canyon: History and Culture. (http://www.nps.gov/chcu/learn/historyculture/index.htm). ▶ National Park Service Website discussing the center of Chacoan culture.

MindTap®

Continue exploring online through MindTap®, where you can:
- **Assess your knowledge with the Chapter Test**
- **Watch historical videos related to the chapter**
- **Further your understanding with interactive maps and timelines**

The First American Peoples

2,600,000–50,000 BCE

Glaciers advance often covering much of the northern portions of the northern hemisphere as far south as the 40th parallel during the Pleistocene epoch.

150,000–100,000 BCE

Homo sapiens sapiens emerges in East Africa.

50,001–25,000 BCE

Climate cools and glaciers advance, exposing more land along coastal areas.

Humans travel to Australia in watercraft and settle.

25,001–10,000 BCE

Paleoindians move across Beringia overland to North America and down coastal waters of the Pacific all the way to southern South America.

11,500 BCE

Clovis culture emerges.

10,001–5000 BCE

Climate warms, melting ice sheets, submerging Beringia and the ancient coastline of Pacific Ocean. Clovis peoples disperse across much of the Americas.

Largest mammals in North America go extinct, including the horse.

Agriculture emerges in the Middle East (9000 BCE), the Sahara (8000 BCE), Asia (7000 BCE), and Mesoamerica (5000 BCE).

5001–2500 BCE

3000 BCE

Inuits settle Alaska mainland.

2500 BCE

Aleuts settle Aleutian Islands.

Bronze metallurgy emerges in Asia.

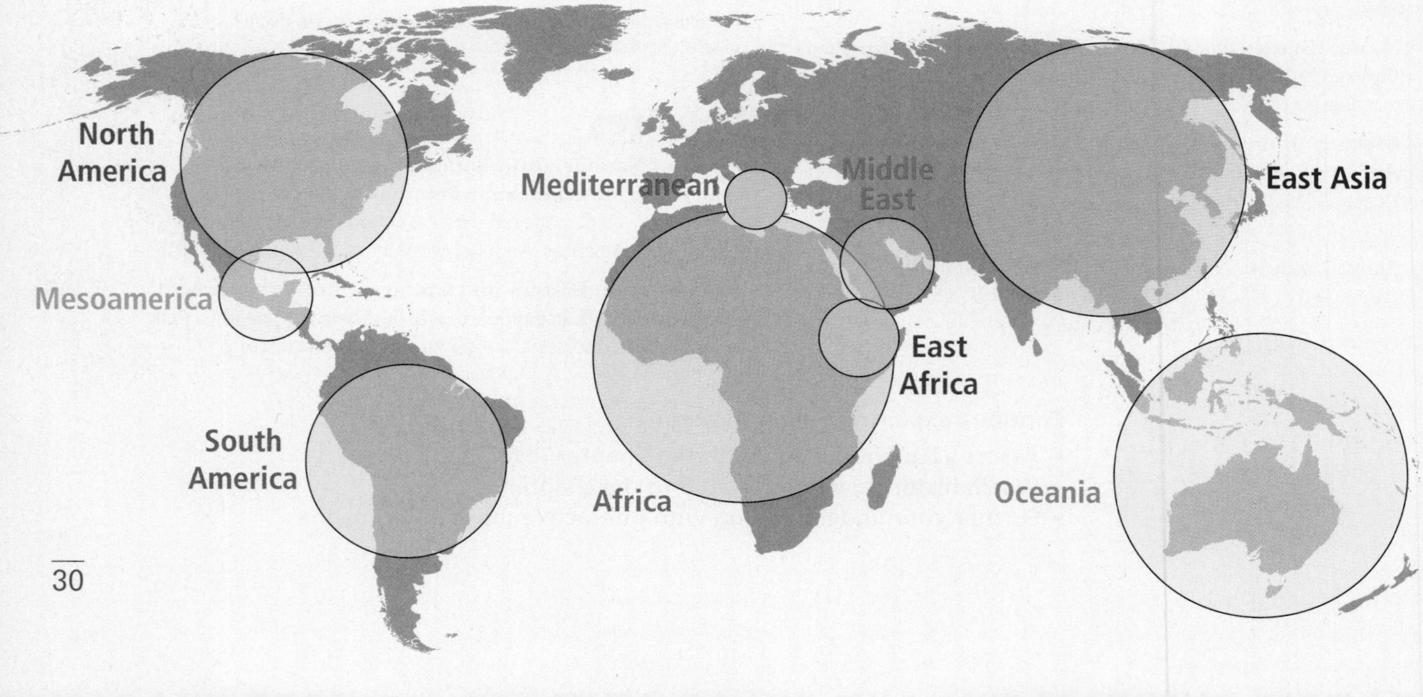

2501 BCE–1 CE

2000 BCE

Indians settle most of California and use fire to manage the environment.

1000 BCE

Iron metallurgy emerges in the Mediterranean.

Rome is founded.

600 BCE

Iron metallurgy emerges in China.

200 BCE

Adena culture declines.

150 BCE

Mayan and Teotihuacán civilizations flourish.

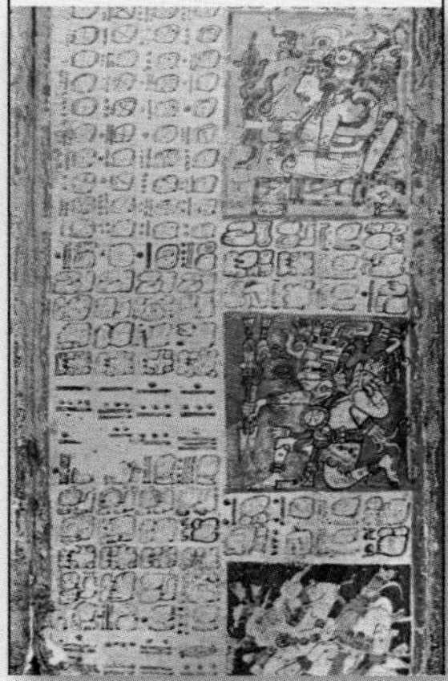

2–500 CE

Plains Indians adopt bow and arrow and develop culture around bison hunting.

300 CE

Pacific Islanders settle Hawaiian Islands.

501–1000 CE

650 CE

Teotihuacán declines.

800 CE

Hopewell culture disappears.

Cahokia emerges as an urban center.

800–900 CE

Mayan civilization declines.

1001–1275 CE

1000 CE

Numa move to Great Basin.

Mississippian chiefdoms emerge.

1100 CE

Emergence of Iroquois Confederacy.

1168–1350 CE

Hohokam peoples build Casa Grande.

1168 CE

Toltec civilization declines.

1180 CE

Drought undermines Anasazi.

1200 CE

Incan empire emerges in Peru.

1230s CE

Mali empire begins in Africa.

1300 CE

Cahokia is abandoned.

1276–1500 CE

1300 CE

Cahokia is abandoned.

1325 CE

Mexicas establish capital of Tenochtitlán.

1350 CE

Flooding destroys Hohokam fields.

1428 CE

Mexicas achieve dominance over Mesoamerica.

1438 CE

The Incan empire comes to dominance in South America.

1500 CE

Mississippian cultures decline.

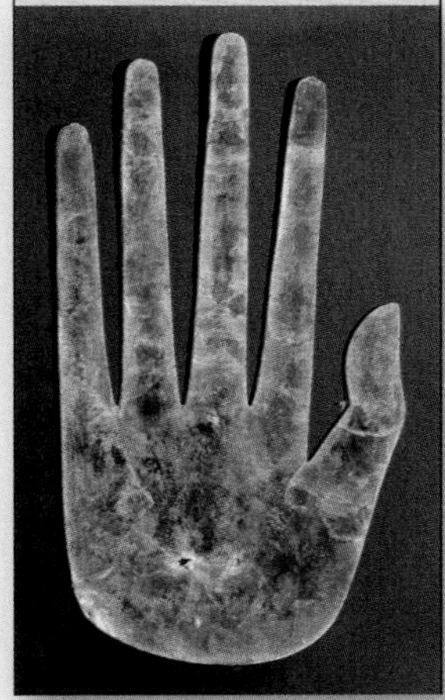

Go to MindTap® to engage with an interactive version of the timeline. Analyze events and themes with clickable content, view related videos, and respond to critical thinking questions.

2 Joining the Hemispheres: Europe, Africa, and the Americas to 1585

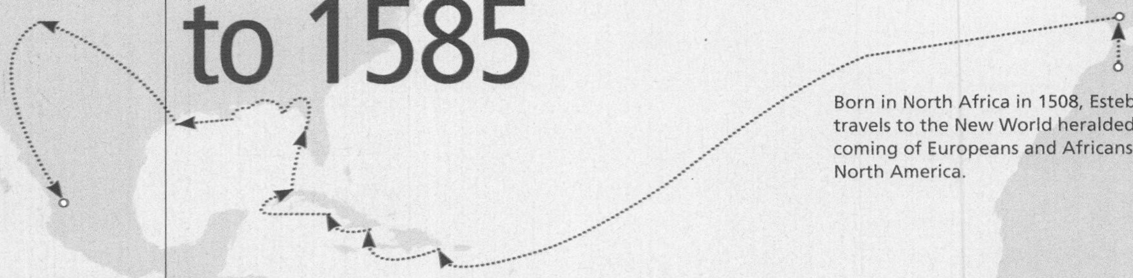

Born in North Africa in 1508, Estebanico's travels to the New World heralded the coming of Europeans and Africans to North America.

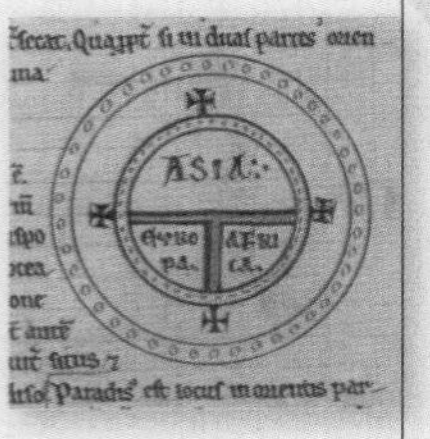

2-1 Europe, the Mediterranean World, and Africa to 1500

2-1a The Greater Mediterranean and Overland Empires
2-1b Religion and the Greater Mediterranean
2-1c Africa and Slavery in the Ancient World
2-1d Medieval Europe: Capitalism, War, and Disease
2-1e The Emergence of Early Modern Europe

2-2 Opening up the Ocean World

2-2a The Age of European Expansion
2-2b Iberian Pioneers at Sea
2-2c Colonization of the Atlantic Islands
2-2d Spain and Portugal in the Caribbean and Brazil
2-2e The World Encompassed

2-3 Spain's Empire in the Americas

2-3a Spanish Beginnings in the Caribbean and West Indies
2-3b Conquests of Mexico, Peru, and Brazil
2-3c Spanish Imperial Structures of Governance and Commerce
2-3d Spanish Exploration of Florida and the Southwest

2-4 Europe in the Americas to 1585

2-4a The French
2-4b The Spanish, the Chesapeake, and War over the Seas
2-4c The English, Ralegh, and Roanoke
2-4d Biological Consequences

Among the most important events and themes in the related histories of Europe and the Americas are the encounters between different civilizations. For thousands of years, Indians in the Americas traded and shared ideas and commodities among themselves as did the peoples of Asia, Africa, and Europe. Beginning in the late fifteenth century, Europeans crossed the Atlantic Ocean and brought the two worlds into permanent contact. Few individuals from this period more fully embody these encounters than Estebanico, a black man born in Africa, enslaved and taken to Spain, and transported to the Americas. There he embarked on a transcontinental journey—from Florida to Texas to Mexico—in one of the great odysseys in American history.

Print Collector/Getty Images

Estebanico was probably born in the early 1500s in Azemmour, a Muslim city in the province of Doukkala in the North African kingdom of Morocco. This region boasted expansive plains ideal for wheat cultivation. In the late fifteenth and early sixteenth centuries, gold and slaves attracted the Portuguese to coastal Africa. They conquered Azemmour in 1508.

Estebanico was baptized as a Christian and was given the name Stephen to honor the first Christian martyr, who in 35 CE (or common era) had been stoned to death for his beliefs. At some point early in his life, Estebanico was enslaved and most likely was taken to Spain in the early 1520s. There Andrés Dorantes de Carranza, a Spanish nobleman, purchased him. A few years later, Dorantes requested permission from the Spanish monarch to join an expedition to Florida led by the Spanish nobleman Pánfilo de Narváez. The king approved his request and appointed him a captain. In 1527, Dorantes sailed to the Caribbean, bringing Estebanico with him.

The expedition was a fiasco. Narváez disembarked with 400 men and 80 horses near present-day Tampa Bay. A local people, the Timucua, hoping to encourage the newcomers to leave their lands, assured Narváez that "gold and plenty of everything" lay just to the northwest in the Apalachee province. Before long, Narváez's overland party, which included Dorantes and Estebanico, became separated from ships trailing them along the coast. Soon, the ships returned to Spain, leaving more than 240 men on land to fend for themselves. Many became ill and died; others were cut down by Apalachee bowmen. Survivors ate their horses, made rafts from the horses' skins and sails from their own clothes, and tried to sail to Mexico. Off what is now Galveston Island, a storm destroyed their rafts and killed most of them, including Narváez. Eighty made it ashore.

For the next six years, Narváez's second in command, Álvar Núñez Cabeza de Vaca, and three others, including Estebanico, lived among the Karankawa and their neighbors, first as slaves and then as emissaries and healers. In 1534, the four set out for Mexico on foot. According to Cabeza de Vaca's narrative of the journey, "The black man always spoke to [Indians along the way] and informed himself about the roads we wished to travel and the villages that there were and about other things that we wanted to know." The four moved from one local people to another, presenting themselves as healers, using Catholic

> How does Estebanico's story herald the coming of Europeans and Africans to the Americas?
>
> Go to MindTap® to watch a video on Estebanico and learn how his odyssey relates to the themes of this chapter.

rituals, rudimentary medical knowledge, and a bit of theater. Two years later, escorted by 600 Pima Indians, the four men stumbled on a group of Spanish slave raiders several hundred miles north of central Mexico.

In 1537, after hearing the survivors' tales, Antonio Mendoza, the viceroy of New Spain—as Spain called the colony of Mexico—launched an exploration of the north. When he could not persuade any other survivors to join him, he turned to Estebanico, whose skill as both scout and mediator was well known. On his return journey to what would become the American Southwest in April 1539, Estebanico's earthly adventures ended. An Indian leader, perhaps the leader of the Zuni town of Cíbola, asked Estebanico if he had brothers. Sensing that the man was speaking metaphorically, Estebanico replied that he had an infinite number and that they were armed and nearby. Hearing that, the Indians killed him.

Estebanico's journeys heralded the coming of Europeans and Africans to the Americas: Waves of men and women would cross the Atlantic carrying with them ideas, beliefs, technologies, plants, animals, and germs that would remake the Western Hemisphere. But Estebanico's story also harkened back to the integration of Europe and Africa that had begun more than a thousand years before. His enslavement, his religion, his great travels, and his death—all were emblematic of the brutal inequalities, religious conflicts, and clashes of culture that marked the interactions of Europe, Asia, Africa and then America through the late sixteenth century.

2-1

Europe, the Mediterranean World, and Africa to 1500

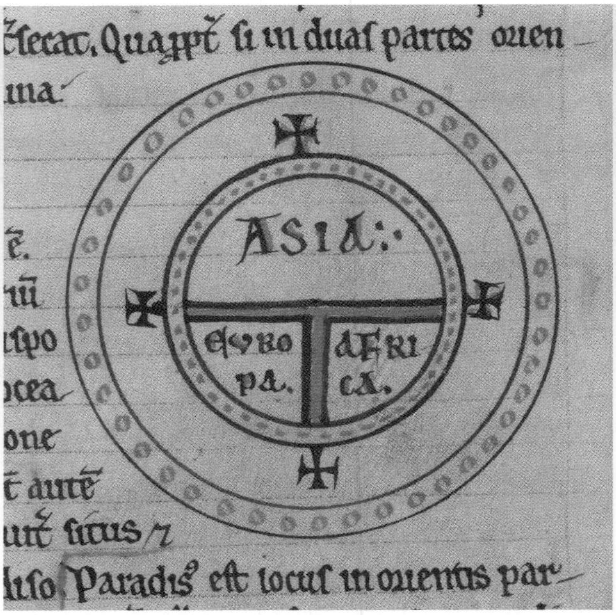

Known as a T-O map, this stylized rendering of Europe, Africa, and Asia was popular in Europe in the early Middle Ages. The T represents the Mediterranean Sea; it separates the three known continents of Asia, Europe, and Africa. All are surrounded by an O, which represents the outer sea that was believed to surround the habitable portions of the earth. Typically, T-O maps had Jerusalem at their center, suggesting the close relationship between science and religion in the Middle Ages. As people mapped, settled, and conquered the Greater Mediterranean, they believed they had conquered the world.

What does this map reveal about how Europeans understood the world and its peoples? ▶

From ancient times, the Mediterranean was a hub of trade linking Europe, Africa, and Asia. People, commodities, ideas, and disease all moved along the established trade routes. One of the oldest and most important routes carried millions of West Africans into slavery among Muslims in the east. Trade was not the only force bringing disparate peoples into close contact. In Europe at various times and in various regions, religion produced unity, polarization, and conflict. But European Christians also engaged in wars with Muslims to the east. Both trade and religion divided the Greater Mediterranean world and established patterns of conquest and dominion that would persist for centuries. During the Middle Ages and continuing through the early modern period, Europeans transformed their economic, political, and religious institutions in ways that led them to look far beyond their own borders.

☞ As you read, consider how war and conquest, religion, trade, and disease affected the Greater Mediterranean world over the course of centuries. How did these factors variously unite and divide people?

2-1a The Greater Mediterranean and Overland Empires

Expanding overland trade networks link the Mediterranean to Asia and Africa.

The peoples of Europe, Asia, the Middle East, and Africa first came into contact with one another via overland trade networks and the relatively calm waters of the Mediterranean. As peoples of the Greater Mediterranean encountered one another and traded technologies, ideologies, and even people, they created an integrated world just as Indians had done across North America. As early as 3000 BCE (before the common era), the eastern Mediterranean witnessed the emergence of some of the world's first agricultural societies. By 1500 BCE (see Map 2.1 on page 37) as a result of an emphasis on farming, which allowed for food production on a mass scale, the population of Egypt reached into the millions, and its influence extended as far as Syria to the east and Nubia, a gold-rich African province to the south. Nubians themselves established overland caravans that linked their own trade networks—and by extension, Egypt's—to the Niger and Congo basins of western Africa as well as those of Ethiopia. Traders moved goods from central and southern Africa to the Mediterranean, the Red Sea, and even to India and China.

Across the Mediterranean from Egypt, the Minoans on the isle of Crete emerged as the Mediterranean's first maritime power. By 2000 BCE, they were trading regularly with Egypt, Sicily, Greece, and the Aegean islands. The Mycenaeans of southern Greece, meanwhile, eventually conquered much of the Mediterranean, sending ships as far as the Iberian Peninsula and the Black Sea. Around 1000 BCE, the Phoenicians of the Middle East began to dominate Mediterranean trade with western Asia. To cement their presence in distant lands, they founded the city of Carthage in North Africa in 750 BCE. After the decline of the Phoenicians, the empires of Persia and Greece rose to power, leading to a fierce rivalry between them during the fifth and fourth centuries BCE.

The integration of the Mediterranean world accelerated under Alexander of Macedonia, better known today as Alexander the Great. Between 334 and 323 BCE, he defeated the Persian Empire and conquered lands stretching from Greece to India. Greek dominance lasted until the rise of Rome. By 117 CE, the Romans controlled the entire Mediterranean, binding together between 50 and 60 million people in Europe, western Asia, and North Africa by granting all conquered peoples the full privileges of Roman citizenship. During the *Pax Romana* (31 BCE to 180 CE), large fleets of ships moved enormous quantities of goods across the Mediterranean. Roman overland routes reached into east Asia and sub-Saharan Africa where merchants traded for gold and other commodities. A portion of this gold was then shipped along the **Silk Road** to East Asia in exchange for spices, jewelry, and silk. During the erosion of Roman authority by 476 CE, the eastern portion of the empire developed into Byzantium, which included the Balkans, Greece, Anatolia (modern-day Turkey), Syria, Palestine, and Egypt.

As Europeans, Asians, North Africans, and the people of the Middle East came into sustained contact, devastating epidemics started to occur more frequently. The most severe—known as a **virgin soil epidemic**—struck when a population was exposed to a disease for the first time without having been able to build up immunity. In this era, virgin soil epidemics of smallpox, measles, influenza, typhus, or bubonic plague typically claimed up to one-third of an affected population within a few months of first exposure. Epidemics coincided not only with trade but also with urbanization. Growing cities produced enormous amounts of waste and filth, attracting rats and fleas that carried disease and spread parasitic infections.

In 1260, the Mongols—a pastoral nomadic Asian people led by Genghis Khan (1206–1227) and his descendants—reached Egypt. Over the next century, they established the largest land empire in human history, ruling more than 200 million people from the Black Sea to the Pacific coasts of China and Korea. Although the Mongol Empire was relatively short lived, it represented a pivotal time in the increasing integration of East and West. People, not just goods, moved between them. Asian technologies, such as gunpowder, movable type, and the compass, flowed into Europe. The Italian explorer Marco Polo traveled the Silk Road to China, reaching the seat of the Mongol Empire in 1275. His account of his travels, the riches of the Mongols, and their innovations, such as the use of coal as a heating fuel, excited Europeans and whetted the appetites of merchants who imagined huge markets in the East.

Soon after the collapse of the Mongol Empire in the fourteenth century due to disputes among the descendants of Genghis Kahn, the Silk Road was taken over by the Ottoman Turks, a Muslim people who became, by the sixteenth century, the great rival to Christian Europe. By 1500, Istanbul, the capital of the Ottoman Empire situated on the southwestern coast of the Black Sea, had become Europe's largest city. The Ottomans conquered Greece and the Balkans, southeastern Europe, much of western Asia, and North Africa from Egypt to Persia. Although the Empire, which encompassed as many as 50 million people, was Muslim, it tolerated Christians and Jews. Under Sultan Suleiman the Magnificent (1520–1566), the Turks gained control of overland routes that linked Europe to the Indian Ocean. With the improvement of maritime technologies during the fourteenth century, European merchants and rulers began to dream about ocean routes that could bypass the Turks and link them directly with the Chinese and the Indies.

Silk Road Ancient 4,000-mile trade route from China to the Mediterranean Sea. Opened around 100 BCE and closed in 1453 when the Ottoman Turks took Constantinople.

virgin soil epidemic Virulent and often lethal epidemic caused by the introduction of a disease into a society to which the group has had no exposure and is therefore largely immunologically defenseless.

2-1b Religion and the Greater Mediterranean

Monotheistic religion expands cross the Mediterranean.

Increasingly united through trade and conquest, the Greater Mediterranean was also united through religion, but sometimes not without coercion. The ancient Hebrews, a Semitic people, played a crucial role in the acceptance throughout the Greater Mediterranean of **monotheism**, the belief that there is only one god. Around 3000 BCE, the Hebrews wrote what we know today as the Torah and the Hebrew Bible (or to Christians, the Old Testament), which became foundational not only for Judaism but also for Christianity and Islam.

Christianity emerged in ancient Palestine at the same time that the Roman Empire was expanding its reach in the region. The life and death of Jesus of Nazareth, a Jewish man who lived in Roman-ruled Palestine in the first century, inspired a group of Jews to start a new sect. These followers of Jesus considered him the divine son of God and believed that their religion should be spread to all peoples. They won converts to Christianity throughout the Mediterranean, and in 313 CE, the Roman Emperor Constantine ended the persecution of Christians in his empire. By 400, Christianity had become the official Roman religion.

Islam, the third major religion to emerge in the Greater Mediterranean, was founded by Muhammad Ibn Abdullah about two hundred years later. Muhammad was born in Mecca, a remote trading city in the Arabian desert west of the Red Sea, around 570 CE. In 610, he experienced a series of visions in which he was visited by the angel Gabriel who revealed to him a new faith and named Muhammad the last of God's messengers, the final prophet in a line that included Abraham, Moses, and Jesus. His followers compiled the Quran, a poetic account of his revelations. Like Christianity, Islam sought to convert unbelievers to the faith.

After Muhammad's death, Muslim Arab armies conquered much of the Greater Mediterranean. By 750, the Islamic world extended from Iberia and Morocco in the west to Central Asia in the east. Nonbelievers had to submit to Muslim rule. One result was that many Christians longed for the reconquest of Spain, a process that would not be completed until the late fifteenth century.

Connected to this and other struggles against Islam, Christians sponsored their own military expeditions, the **Crusades**, to take what they saw as the "Judeo-Christian" Holy Land—or Palestine—back from the Muslims. A single Crusade could be composed of as many as sixty thousand soldiers. The first Crusade, launched in 1095, succeeded in conquering Jerusalem and much of the rest of the Holy Land for a while, offering Europeans more direct access to trade routes that brought exotic textiles and spices from the East.

monotheism Belief in the existence of one transcendent god.

Crusades Medieval period military campaigns sanctioned by the Catholic Church to push Muslims out of the Holy Land and restore Christian access to sacred sites.

2-1c Africa and Slavery in the Ancient World

Sprawling trade including grain, precious metals, salt, and slaves links Africa to Europe and the Middle East.

Even before the expansion of Islam into North Africa and sub-Saharan Africa, the continent had become part of the Mediterranean world through a sprawling slave trade. By the seventh century, Africa had been connected to Eurasia through trade routes that ran across sub-Saharan Africa and into the East African coast. The Mali and Songhai Empires of the sub-Saharan Sudan had long shipped gold and salt to the east of Africa and increasingly sent enormous numbers of slaves across the continent. The Sudanese benefited most from this trade and created powerful regional empires. By the 1460s, Gao, the capital city of the Songhai Empire, had as many as 100,000 people and a large merchant class that worked closely with Mediterranean traders. The Songhai sent gold and slaves north to Mediterranean societies, and in return, they received glass, copperware, cloth, perfumes, and horses.

In many African societies, slavery was common simply because there was no other private, revenue-producing property recognized in African law. In the Sudan, some slaves were manual laborers while others were valued for their intellectual abilities. Typically, however, slaves in Africa were considered members of the household, enjoying basic rights. Notably, there was no unifying sense of Africanness across the continent, and many African peoples seem to have thought little about enslaving those who lived in neighboring kingdoms.

The ancient Mediterranean world had embraced slavery. Classical Greece and ancient Rome were both slave societies: Well over 20 percent of their populations were enslaved. Later, beginning in the seventh century, Mediterranean merchants and their leaders, as well as Arabs and their Muslim allies, promoted a slave trade that over centuries ensnared 10 to 15 million individuals from sub-Saharan Africa and delivered them as bondsmen to the Greater Mediterranean, North Africa, and the Persian Gulf states. Unlike in classical Greece and ancient Rome, where just about anyone could be enslaved, in this new system, the least respected slaves were those who were black. Thus, Europeans, Africans, and Arabs developed complex trade systems that moved African slaves across Africa and linked their enslavement with the color of their skin. The subtleties of African slave ownership were rarely recognized in the societies of the Greater Mediterranean.

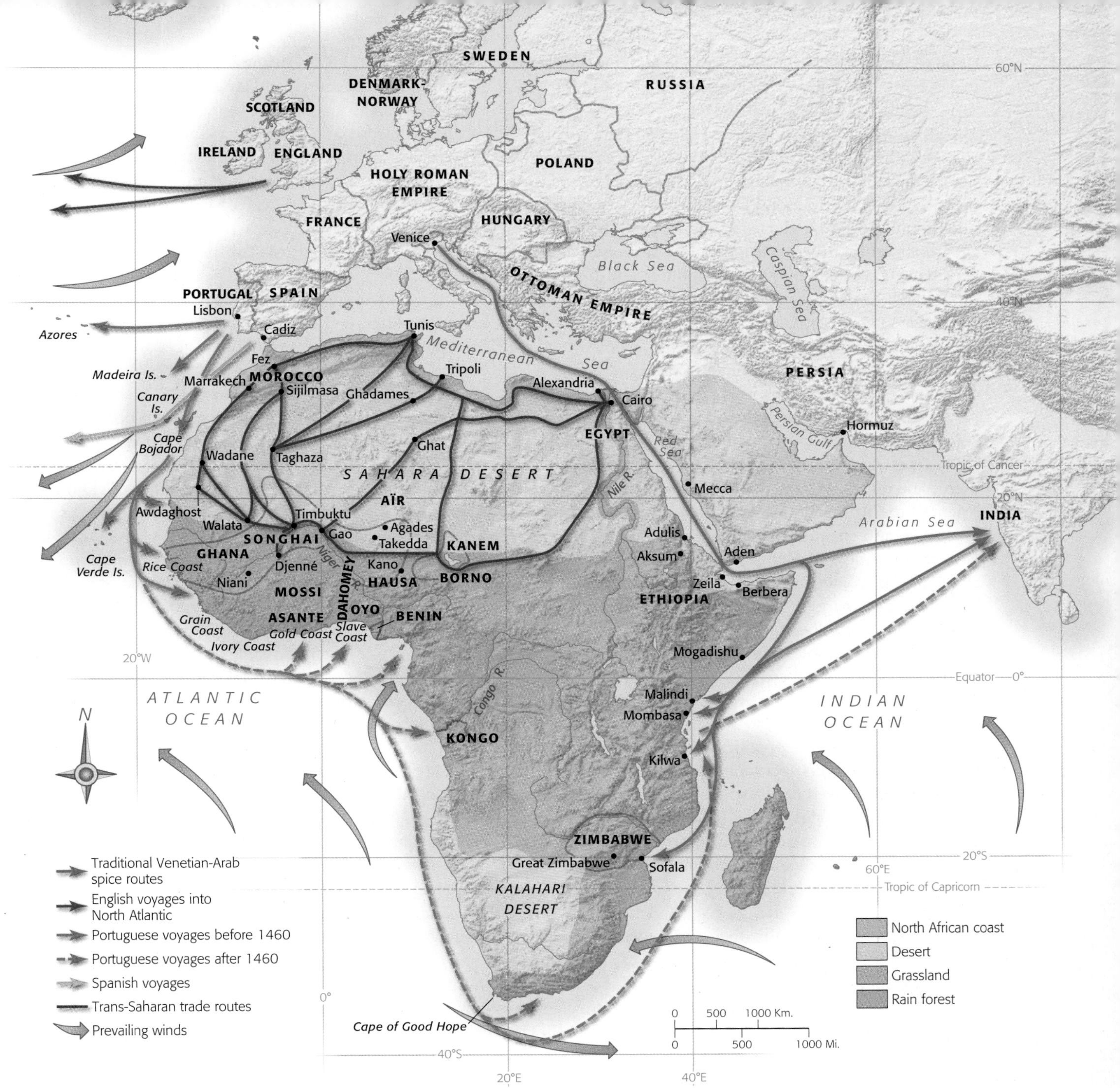

Map 2.1 Trade Routes Connecting Europe, Africa, and Asia, Fifteenth Century Beginning in 1420, Portuguese mariners explored the coast of West Africa to create direct trade with Africans. Once they had traveled south of the Sahara they began to establish more direct relationships with people of the interior. Eventually Portuguese mariners sailed all the way around Africa and into the Indian Ocean. ▲

2-1d Medieval Europe: Capitalism, War, and Disease

Medieval Europe was at once dynamic and rigid. Its dynamism lay in its growing population and its expanding commerce throughout the Greater Mediterranean; its rigidity lay in its static social structures. During the Middle Ages, the cities of northern and western Europe were small backwaters. In the year 1000, Paris and London had only about 20,000 and 10,000 residents, respectively. By comparison, Cordoba in Spain had 500,000 inhabitants and Baghdad was home to nearly 1 million people. However, between 700 and 1300, the population of Europe increased from 25 million to 70 million as a

Medieval Europe is characterized by extensive trade and a rigid social structure.

result of the general peace that prevailed and improvements in agricultural technologies. In the eleventh and twelfth centuries, cities such as Paris and Milan expanded to nearly 100,000 residents, and with this growth came other changes.

One change was that the urban poor increased in number. As a result, the Roman Catholic Church, towns, and private individuals founded **almshouses**, places where the poor could get food and shelter. The rise of cities was also accompanied by the growth of an increasingly influential merchant class that sought commodities and luxuries in distant and exotic trading centers. Between 1100 and 1350, European trade with Asia in luxury goods hit new peaks. Europeans shipped flax, wines, olive oil, woolen textiles, timber, fruit, and hemp to China. In return, they received such luxuries as perfumes, silk, gems, and spices. By the early 1200s, commerce centered on the Mediterranean began to replace agriculture as the central focus of the economy of western Europe. In the following centuries, as commerce and trade accelerated, **capitalism**—a dynamic system oriented toward economic growth and private control of resources and profits—emerged first in Venice, Genoa, Bruges, and Antwerp. But capitalism was at this time constrained by the Catholic Church's condemnation of usury—the practice of charging interest on borrowed money—and complicated by cumbersome business practices.

Merchants, nobles, and the clergy were the most outward-looking members of European society, but they constituted only about 10 percent of the population. The overwhelming majority—80 percent—of Europe's residents were peasants, trapped in a social system known as **manorialism**, in which peasants payed dues to a lord on whose land they lived in return for the lord's military protection. Also at the very bottom of society were laborers, farmhands, and shepherds who had no land and whose work and wages were less secure.

Religion also determined one's place in society. The vast majority of Europeans were Christian, and they considered local religious minorities, including Jews and Muslims, to be pagans or infidels. Non-Christians, most notably Jews, were often relegated—if not confined—to their own neighborhoods. Some countries expelled Jews altogether as did France in 1182 and Spain in 1492.

The Roman Catholic Church itself dominated medieval Europe. Priests were presumed to have enormous influence over whether an individual's soul would go to heaven after death. During the Middle Ages, the power of the Pope, the head of the Catholic Church and the ultimate authority within it, greatly increased. In some areas, the power of the papacy rivaled or exceeded that of secular rulers. Two religious orders, or formally organized communities of faith, recognized by the church and lay governments, arose at this time: the Franciscans and the Dominicans. Both espoused poverty, chastity, and obedience, and both relied on the donations of laymen. The men in these orders did not retreat from the world but ventured out to spread Catholicism through Europe and the Greater Mediterranean.

In response to increased papal power and growing national rivalries, European rulers tried to exercise more control over their lands and people. The increase in royal power was not uncontested from below. King John of England was compelled to sign the **Magna Carta** in 1215, thereby agreeing to not levy taxes without the approval of his nobles and granting all men immunity from illegal imprisonment. Yet during the Hundred Years War (1337–1453) between England and France, monarchical power in both countries increased as kings increased taxes on their constituents in order to fund their armies. The consolidation of power was most dramatic in Spain. In 1469, Queen Isabella and King Ferdinand subordinated the nobility and towns to their rule. They introduced the Inquisition in 1478 to investigate and punish religious dissidents and conquered Granada in 1492, expelling 150,000 Jews and 300,000 Muslims from Spain. After these monarchs defeated Granada, they never fully deactivated the army, forming the core of a standing army that supported their increasingly powerful state. Isabella and Ferdinand also began to regulate the domestic economy and foreign trade. For instance, they blocked the import of any commodities that might weaken home industries, promoted the export of Spanish goods, and restricted Spanish merchants' use of foreign flagged ships. By the end of the fifteenth century, Ferdinand and Isabella of Spain, Henry VII of England, and Louis XII of France presided over powerful political structures that controlled the resources necessary to put large armies in the field and ensure that their nations' economies supported the state.

Increasingly powerful monarchies could do nothing to stop the onset of climate change, which, in a phenomenon known as the **Little Ice Age**, led to a drop in temperatures in Europe and elsewhere between the fourteenth and nineteenth centuries. The coldest years were the first third of the fourteenth century. The resulting crop failures and famine killed 10 percent of Europe's population, and survivors were ravaged by epidemics. The plague that arrived in Europe in 1347 from the Black Sea on a ship carrying grain and infected rats quickly spread through crowded cities and their sewage-strewn streets. Within a few years, the Black Death killed nearly 1 in 3 Europeans; in crowded cities, 7 in 10 died during the height of the epidemic. As a result of the Black Death and other epidemics, Europe's population fell from 70 million in 1200 to 45 million in 1400. The plague was even more devastating in Egypt and other parts of Africa, and in Asia (see Map 2.2). In Egypt, it ended centuries of prosperity and stability, killing up to one-third of Egypt's population in less than two years. In North Africa, where the Black Death had the greatest impact, it led to nearly five centuries of decline.

almshouses Buildings in which poor people are allowed to live for free; originated in Europe in the Middle Ages.

capitalism Economic system in which the things that are used to make and transport products (such as land, factories, ships) are privately owned.

manorialism Social system in which people known as serfs worked and fought for and rendered tribute to nobles who gave them protection and the use of land in return.

Magna Carta Latin for *Great Charter*, which English barons forced King John of England to accept in 1215, guaranteeing English subjects fundamental rights and privileges.

Little Ice Age Period of declining global temperatures from the early fourteenth to mid-nineteenth centuries in Europe and North America.

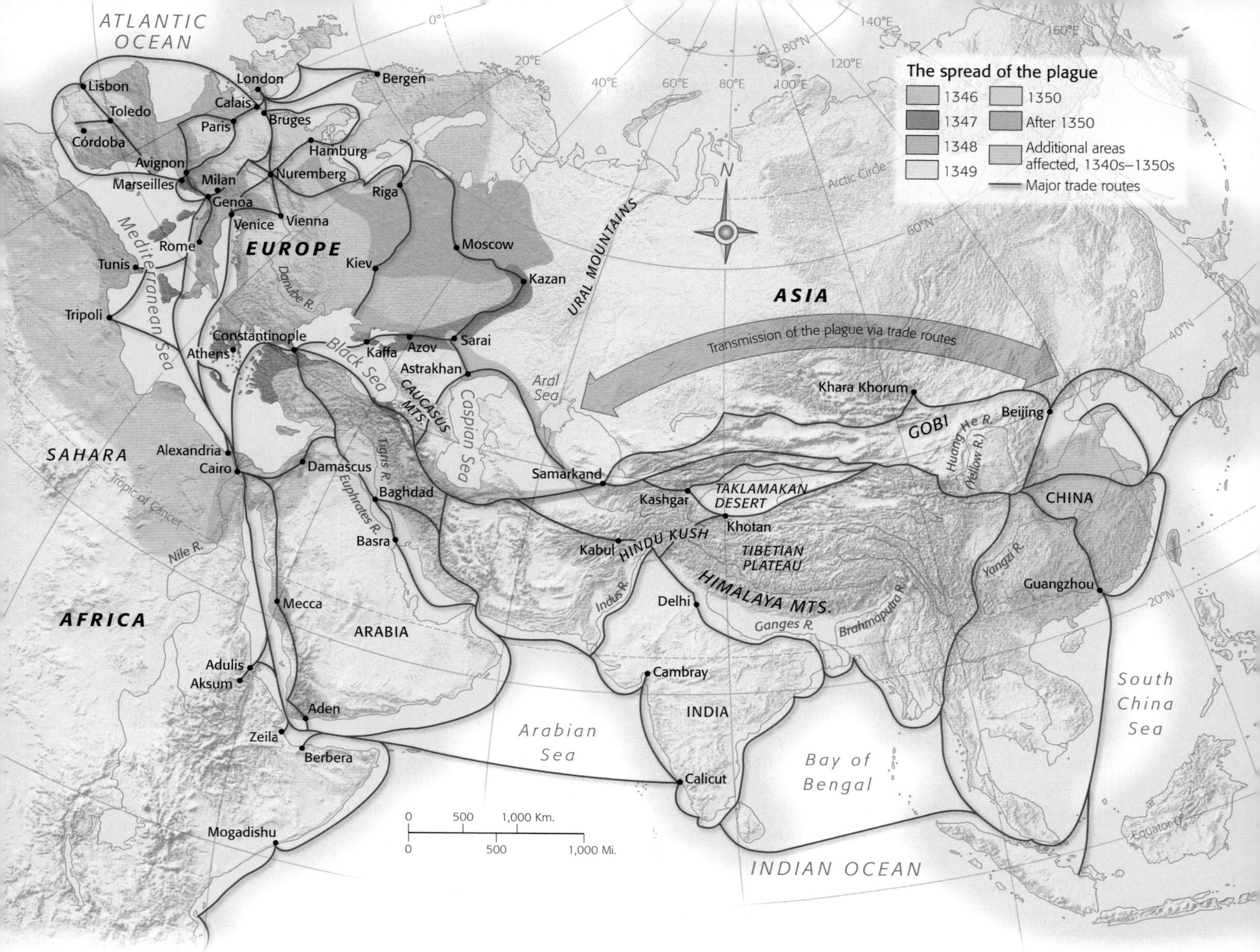

Map 2.2 The Spread of the Plague across Asia, North Africa, and Asia, Mid-Fourteenth Century
As trade networks increasingly tied together the economies of Asia, North Africa, and Asia, diseases, such as the plague, spread with devastating effect, killing millions and undermining commerce and trade. ▲

2-1e The Emergence of Early Modern Europe

European religious and national rivalries deepen.

In 1500, at the dawn of what we now call the *Early Modern Period,* western Europeans were still dominated by the Roman Catholic Church, centered on the Greater Mediterranean, and were only dimly aware of the world beyond the Mediterranean. But dramatic changes would soon reshape not only Europe but distant lands as well. A central event in western European history was the unification in 1492 of Spain under a single monarchy and the ***Reconquista***—the reconquest, or the ultimately successful war to drive Muslims from the Iberian Peninsula. The Spanish conquerors won fame, wealth, and honor. Soon they would turn their sights across the Atlantic.

While the *Reconquista* transformed the Iberian Peninsula, the **Renaissance**, a century-long efflorescence of the arts, literature, and science, redirected much of European thought and culture. The Renaissance coincided with the population rebound after the Black Death and was spurred by the patronage of great artists and scientists by the leading monarchs of Europe. By 1600, Europe's population numbered 80 million. Paris had

Reconquista Period of conflict with Muslims in Iberia for 781 years from 711 (Muslim conquest) to 1492 (their expulsion by Spanish Catholics after the fall of Granada).

Renaissance Period of European history (fourteenth and seventeenth centuries) bridging Medieval and Early Modern periods; characterized by new interest in science and ancient art and literature.

500,000 residents, London had 200,000, and Seville had 150,000. Human knowledge expanded, spurred by the movement of inventions and ideas among Europe, China, and Asia.

The Renaissance was also marked by a return to the classical texts of ancient Greece and Rome, a growing belief in the power and worth of the individual, the expansion of secularism, and the development of ideas of scientific inquiry. The foundation of many of these changes was Johannes Gutenberg's invention of movable type in 1454 (it had actually been invented by the Chinese centuries before, but Gutenberg was not aware of Chinese techniques), allowing books to be printed easily and cheaply in Europe for the first time, which led to the spread of knowledge geographically and to the lower levels of society.

At the same time that the Renaissance led many to question European institutions, the Christian Church split. Until 1517, all the followers of Christ were united under the Roman Catholic Church or the Greek Orthodox Church. That changed when the German monk-turned-professor Martin Luther (1483–1546) claimed that everyone, not just priests, was entitled to hear and interpret the word of God. He broke further from Catholicism when he argued that only faith, not specific acts, could absolve a person of sin and ensure salvation. Excommunicated from the Catholic Church, Luther led a religious revolution known as the **Protestant Reformation**. The Roman Catholic Church responded with the **Counter-Reformation**. The Pope summoned the Council of Trent (1543–1563) to affirm Catholic doctrine and expanded the Inquisition to persecute dissidents. But ultimately the Church turned from confronting Protestants to attempting to convert people outside of Europe.

Portrait of John Calvin (1509–1564) A follower of Luther, John Calvin even more forcefully rejected Catholicism by arguing for predestination, the belief that God chooses people before their birth for either heaven or hell. Both Lutherans and Calvinists disavowed the celibacy of priesthood, changed the form and content of the Mass, rejected Catholic saints and church hierarchies, and focused on the life of Christ and his teachings rather than on the Virgin Mary and the belief that one could obtain divine favors through her intercession. ▲

Beginning in the sixteenth century, this religious conflict between Protestants and Catholics heightened national rivalries. England, long a rival of Spain, became Protestant under Henry VIII (1509–1547), who left the Roman Catholic Church and became head of an independent Church of England when the Pope refused to annul his current marriage so that he could marry his mistress, Anne Boleyn. France remained divided between Catholics and French Protestants, known as *Huguenots*, and religious conflicts convulsed France from the 1560s through the 1580s, especially after Huguenot rioting in Paris in 1572 that was followed by Catholics massacring some 30,000 Huguenots.

Throughout this era, Phillip II of Spain (1556–1598) remained resolutely Catholic and saw himself as the great defender of the faith. He confronted one of his greatest challenges in what were known as the Low Countries of northern Europe—a region consisting largely of today's Netherlands and Belgium and ruled by his family, the Spanish Habsburgs. There, his attacks on Protestants angered businessmen and nobles, who increasingly demanded freedom of worship and political autonomy from Spain. These tensions led to a general revolt in the Low Countries against Spain in 1566 and Spain's sack of Antwerp in 1576. In 1581, in the **Union of Utrecht**, the seven northern Dutch provinces united to form the United Provinces of the Netherlands. In 1588, the northern provinces of the Low Countries finally separated from Spain. They became fully independent in 1609 when they formed the country known today as the Netherlands or Holland.

Amid these upheavals, a new form of capitalism rose to prominence in north and northwest Europe. Under **commercial capitalism**, money was typically invested in

Protestant Reformation Religious movement initiated by Martin Luther, John Calvin, and others in 1517 that caused a split within Christianity, dividing Catholics and Protestants.

Counter-Reformation Catholic Church response to the Protestant Reformation beginning with the Council of Trent (1545–1563) and running through the mid-seventeenth century.

Union of Utrecht Treaty signed in 1579 unifying the twelve northern and Protestant provinces of the Netherlands; independence not recognized by Spain until 1609.

commercial capitalism Preindustrial form of capitalism centered on trade rather than production.

trading enterprises. Wealthy individuals formed **joint-stock companies** and sold shares, or stocks, and in so doing raised huge amounts of capital. The English and the Dutch of the Low Countries—both rising maritime commercial empires— most vigorously promoted commercial capitalism, and the English Channel and the North Sea began to surpass the ports of the Mediterranean as the primary economic routes of Europe. Through the late 1500s, Antwerp was the hub of European commerce and at times had some 2,500 ships from distant lands in its harbor. By the 1620s, Amsterdam was the center of Europe's transatlantic capitalist commerce, and increasingly, as wealth and goods flowed into the city from overseas, it was the center of Europe's most prosperous, diverse, and tolerant society.

joint-stock companies Private business entity in which individuals purchase various shares of ownership, providing the company the equity to invest in its operations.

2-2 Opening up the Ocean World

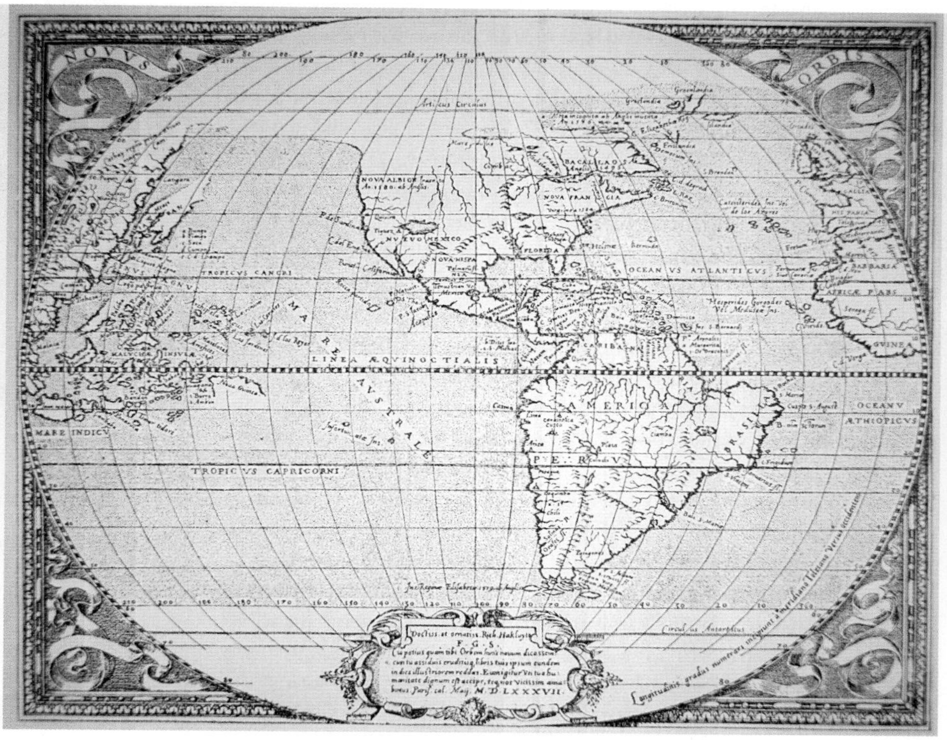

Sometimes known as the Hakluyt Martyr map because it accompanied Richard Hakluyt's translation of *Peter Martyr's De Orbe Novo (the Eight Decades)*, this map refers to Sir Francis Drake's circumnavigation of the globe and encompasses most of what Europeans knew about the world nearly a century after the voyages of Columbus. It is the first map to include the colonies of New Mexico and Virginia.

Private Collection/Peter Newark American Pictures/Bridgeman Images

How does this map compare to the T-O map presented earlier? ▶

Go to MindTap® to practice history with the Chapter 2 **Primary Source Writing Activity: The World Encompassed.** Read and view primary sources and respond to a writing prompt.

Between 1450 and 1550 as Europe and the Mediterranean world underwent many internal transformations, Europeans also began to set off across the Atlantic Ocean on voyages of exploration, conquest, and trade. With new technologies that allowed them to harness the ocean's winds and currents, the Spanish, Portuguese, Dutch, and English reached the west coast of Africa as well as what came to be known by Europeans as the *New World.* Colonists started trading with the locals, including for slaves. They also experimented with crops, such as sugar, in new forms of production that quickly proved incredibly profitable but enormously destructive to native laborers. Finally, the colonists sent back reports of opportunities for wealth and land, spurring on even greater voyages. By the early decades of the sixteenth century, European navigators had circumnavigated the globe.

☞ As you read, look for the different contributions that rival nations made to the Age of European Expansion. What motivated Europeans to move beyond the Mediterranean, and how did their understandings of the Atlantic and the world change as a result?

2-2a The Age of European Expansion

Economic goods and new technologies drive Europeans to explore far beyond the Greater Mediterranean.

Legend holds that in the fifth century CE, an Irish monk, St. Brendan, sailed out into the Atlantic and discovered enchanted islands. Five hundred years later, in the year 1001, Scandinavian seafarers sailed west from Iceland and under Eric the Red established settlements on Greenland. Soon thereafter, Leif Ericson founded a settlement in northern Newfoundland that he called *Vinland.* But Vinland was very far from Europe, and its colonization did not lead to a lasting bond between the colonists and the homeland.

Centuries later, the Chinese became the first great oceanic naval power under the leadership of Muslim Admiral Zheng He (1371–1433) who initiated voyages to the Middle East, East Africa, Southeast Asia, and India. Although the Chinese were the most advanced mariners of their day, they saw little value in trade with foreign nations.

They also lacked the economic strength or the religious zeal to follow their voyages with colonies and conversion campaigns.

Western Europeans developed their own maritime technologies, but used them to different effect. In what is known today as the Age of European Expansion (1450–1650), Italian, Portuguese, French, and Spanish mariners explored the Atlantic, hoping to reach Asia and thereby bypass overland trade routes controlled by the Ottoman Turks. These expeditions were also spurred by new technologies. They were also propelled by Europeans' desires for greater access to gold and slaves from West Africa and a militant Catholicism that wanted not only to push Islam back but also to win new converts for Rome. Other reasons included the increasingly confident and competitive European states and merchants who vied for economic supremacy in the Greater Mediterranean and the economic markets of Europe. Early explorations failed to yield a direct route to what Europeans called the *Indies,* yet they unwittingly achieved something far more influential: They encountered the people of the Americas, bringing them, mostly against their will, into the European economic system.

The ships that proved most useful for European voyages of exploration were built after centuries of innovation in ship design and construction. In the Middle Ages, Europeans constructed two basic types of ships, one propelled by oars and the other by sails. Both were suited for the Mediterranean and the waters of Europe's Atlantic coastline. The oared vessel, or galley, was long and thin. When outfitted for war, it might hold several hundred men. These ships were ill suited for long voyages because they had limited space in which to carry provisions and were not trustworthy on the open seas. The sailing ships, or round ships, depended primarily on the wind and were therefore much cheaper to operate than a galley. Early sailing ships were almost as wide as they were long and usually propelled by a single square sail. They could not sail into the wind. Thus, they too were ill suited for long voyages on the open sea.

In the fifteenth century, a revolution in ship design resulted in a new kind of ocean-going boat. The sternpost rudder replaced steering oars as standard equipment. Ships added more sails, and many gained a third mast. By using a variety of sails, mariners could take advantage of a variety of wind conditions. Although the new ships were relatively small, they could sail into the wind.

The most important navigational tool during the Age of European Expansion was the magnetic compass, an instrument developed by the Chinese, brought west by the Muslims, and adopted by Europeans in the twelfth century. For travel in the Mediterranean, pilots carried charts indicating coastlines, ports, crucial geographical features, and compass directions for sailing from port to port. Mariners who sailed in uncharted ocean waters, however, had to rely on the compass, the **mariner's astrolabe**, and their powers of observation and calculation.

mariner's astrolabe
Astrological instrument used to determine a ship's north-south location while at sea.

Mariner's Astrolabe, Thirteenth Century. Seafarers used a mariner's astrolabe—a large brass ring with a needle—that allowed the measurer to determine the height of the midday sun and therefore the ship's latitude, or north-south position. More difficult, and problematic, was the calculation of the ship's speed and east-west position, which could only be approximated. Despite these limitations, by the mid-fifteenth century, mariners had the ships and basic tools necessary to venture into the Atlantic, far beyond the sight of land. ▲

Portuguese bronze nautical astrolabe, 1608, by Francisco de Goes, diameter 19.7 cm. /Istituto e Museo di Storia della Scienza, Florence, Italy/De Agostini Picture Library/Bridgeman Images

2-2b Iberian Pioneers at Sea

Portuguese mariners venture down the coast of Africa and eventually discover a maritime route to the Far East.

The Portuguese, who lived along the western coast of the Iberian Peninsula, first explored the Atlantic by following the west coast of Africa south. Portuguese traders were frustrated with limited access to the overland routes to the Far East and angered that the city-state of Venice had monopolized the commerce of the eastern Mediterranean. Portuguese leader Prince Henry (1394–1460), who declared "if you are strong in ships, the commerce of the Indies is yours," became a leading proponent of maritime exploration. Once the Portuguese modified their ships for the high seas of the ocean, their narrow-hulled ships known as *caravels* became ideal for the exploration of the Atlantic Ocean and the shallow coastal rivers and waters of West Africa.

In 1420, the Portuguese began to explore the West African coast in search of direct access to gold and another precious commodity, salt. In the 1440s, Portuguese ships passed the southern boundary of the Sahara desert, allowing them to trade directly with Africans. In the region where the coast of Africa turns east, the Portuguese established a series of forts, and soon African gold, salt, and slaves began arriving in Portugal by sea.

Portuguese ships may have been agile, but explorations advanced slowly. Some were simply blown off course into the Atlantic. Portuguese exploration continued eastward. With the Far East as the ultimate goal, in 1487 Bartolomeu Dias sailed around the southern tip of Africa into the Indian Ocean. The Portuguese soon established trading posts on the East African coast, violently pushing aside the Muslim traders who had formerly controlled the region. A decade later, Vasco da Gama sailed from Portugal to India. Europeans had finally found a sea route from Europe to the east. Portuguese traders established posts in Kolkata (formerly known as "Calcutta") and Goa, and da Gama returned to Portugal with a fortune in cinnamon, cloves, ginger, pepper, gems, and textiles. Before long, Portugal, a small country of only 1 million people, had established a maritime empire with trading posts that stretched as far east as China and Japan.

2-2c Colonization of the Atlantic Islands

The Portuguese create slave plantations on islands off the coast of Africa.

In addition to opening up new seafaring routes down the coast of Africa and to the Far East, the Portuguese colonized islands off the coast of Africa—the Canary and the Madeira Islands. There they initiated a process of conquest and exploitation that would be repeated again and again in different ways as Europeans encountered new lands. On these islands, the Portuguese established brutal plantation systems that produced valuable staple crops for sale and export by using the labor of African slaves.

On Madeira Island, the Portuguese set fires for seven years to clear forests so that they could introduce new crops. Then, in 1425, after raising cattle, pigs, wheat, and grapes did not prove profitable enough for Portuguese merchants, they introduced sugar cane imported from Sicily. By the end of the fifteenth century, Madeira was well on the way to leading the world in sugar production. The Portuguese planters relied on slaves. Among the earliest were a small number of Jews and Muslims still remaining in Portugal as well as African slaves whom the Portuguese had purchased on their excursions down the African coast. The majority were Guanches, natives taken from the Canary Islands during the height of the Portuguese conquest.

The Guanche had settled the Canary Islands from Africa at least a thousand years before and had had no contact with Europeans until the late 1200s or early 1300s. In 1402, Spaniards first attempted to conquer the Canary Islands, and they finally succeeded in 1478. They were able to subdue the Guanches, who probably numbered about 20,000 but who were not united, had no ships, spoke different languages, and had no weapons that could match European iron. Above all, the Guanches lacked immunity to the diseases that Europeans carried to the Islands. In the mid-1490s, two virgin soil epidemics, one of them typhus, killed nearly two-thirds of the Guanches on the two largest of the Canary Islands.

As the Guanches died by the thousands, the Portuguese seized or purchased West Africans to replace them as laborers in the sugar plantations they were establishing on the Canary Islands and on those that already existed on the Madeiras. The European trafficking in slaves would prove far more disastrous to the African continent than indigenous slave systems had been. On Madeira and the Canary Islands, the Portuguese learned how to introduce valuable crops to new and promising lands, how to conquer and subdue native peoples, and how to either enslave those natives or replace them with enslaved Africans. The deadly and exploitative plantation system that the Portuguese pioneered in the islands off Africa would change the course of world history.

2-2c Spain and Portugal in the Caribbean and Brazil

Sailing for Spain, Columbus reaches the Caribbean, mistaking it for Asia.

The Portuguese voyages of exploration and colonization provided opportunities for a generation of men to find glory and riches. Among these men was Christopher Columbus, who was born in the important Italian commercial town of Genoa and lived for many years in Lisbon, the capital of Portugal, where he became steeped in maritime culture. Columbus married the daughter of a Portuguese governor of the Madeira Islands, and he visited the Canary Islands and the Azores. Most likely he sailed on Portuguese ships down the coast of West Africa.

Columbus was a devout Catholic fascinated by the writings of Marco Polo. He dreamed of sailing to China to open up a direct trade route with Asia and to introduce Christianity to the Chinese. The Portuguese believed that Columbus would fail, so Columbus sold his vision to Ferdinand and Isabella of Spain, whose recently united kingdoms had no experience with maritime exploration. Spain provided Columbus with three ships manned by eighty-seven men for what the most advanced maps of the day suggested would be a short journey to China.

In the summer of 1492, Columbus sailed west and in October made landfall at a number of Caribbean islands where he encountered the Taino, an Arawak-speaking people. He then sailed to the island of Hispaniola (today,

Tomas Abad/Alamy Stock Photo

Portrait of Christopher Columbus, 1519. Before his departure, Columbus signed contracts with the Spanish monarchs authorizing him to "discover and acquire islands and mainlands in the Ocean Sea" for Spain. Once in the Far East, Columbus planned to set up a small trading settlement for the crown. ▲

the island that Haiti and the Dominican Republic share) and back to Europe by way of Cuba. Columbus believed he had been to the outskirts of China. He brought back to Spain two very important discoveries: tobacco, which his men had acquired in Cuba, and an understanding of the winds of the Atlantic, which allowed Europeans to sail to the Western Hemisphere with the confidence that they would be able to return to Europe.

Isabella was disappointed that Columbus had not actually made contact with China and sponsored three more expeditions that he led. He returned to the Caribbean in 1493 with a fleet of seventeen ships and 1,200 men, including a priest, farmers, artisans, and laborers, in the hope of founding a colony. Not until his fourth expedition in 1504 did Columbus begin to realize that he had discovered an entirely unknown land. Eventually, he and others began to refer to the Caribbean Islands as the *West Indies* and to the native inhabitants of the Americas as *Indians*.

Less than a decade after Columbus had stumbled onto the West Indies, Portugal did the same in Brazil. Pedro Alvares Cabral, like Columbus, believed he could find a more direct route to Asia by sailing as far west as possible off the coast of Africa rather than the more southerly route taken by da Gama. His fleet left Lisbon in early March 1500 and six weeks later made landfall in a harbor of present-day Brazil, a land that at that time had between 2 and 4 million indigenous inhabitants known as the Tupi. Cabral ordered a massive cross to be raised, claimed the land for his king, and sent news to Portugal to tell the king of this new discovery.

2-2e The World Encompassed

Thirty years after Columbus's first voyage, mariners circumnavigate the globe.

Without realizing what they had done, explorers like Columbus and Cabral had initiated a revolution: They had transformed the world's oceans from barriers to seaways and in the process shifted the center of their commercial world from the Mediterranean Sea to the Atlantic Ocean. This revolution set off a scramble among European nations to sponsor their own voyages of discovery and conquest. John Cabot, an Italian, claimed the eastern coast of North America for England in 1497. Two years later, the Italian Amerigo Vespucci sailed on a Portuguese expedition to South America, where he determined that Brazil was not part of Asia but rather the edge of a continent previously unknown to Europeans. Another Italian, Giovanni Verrazano, claimed Canada for France in 1524. Both of these explorers had set out in the hope of reaching Asia directly; although they were unsuccessful, the expeditions fueled the hopes of Europeans that a sea passage could be found through the North American continent.

Spain continued to sponsor voyages of exploration, some of which probed the interior of the Americas (see Map 2.3). In 1513, Vasco Núñez de Balboa crossed the isthmus of Panama and came upon the Pacific Ocean—which he claimed for Spain. In 1519, Ferdinand Magellan, a Portuguese mariner in the employ of Spain, set out to fulfill the dream of Columbus and others by finding a western sea route to Asia from Europe. Magellan's fleet of five ships and 270 men set sail in September 1520. They wintered on the coast of present-day southeast Argentina, rounded the southern tip of the continent that November, and then sailed northwest into the Pacific. In March 1521, the expedition reached the Philippines, where Magellan was killed by locals whom he had hoped to convert to Christianity. Sixteen months later, in September 1522, the expedition's sole remaining ship dropped anchor in Spain. The surviving crew had sought a more direct route to the East, but they had accomplished something more pivotal. They were the first men to circumnavigate the earth, and their voyage greatly advanced Europeans' understanding of the world and its seas, thereby accelerating the integration of distant regions into a nascent Atlantic economy and expanding European empires.

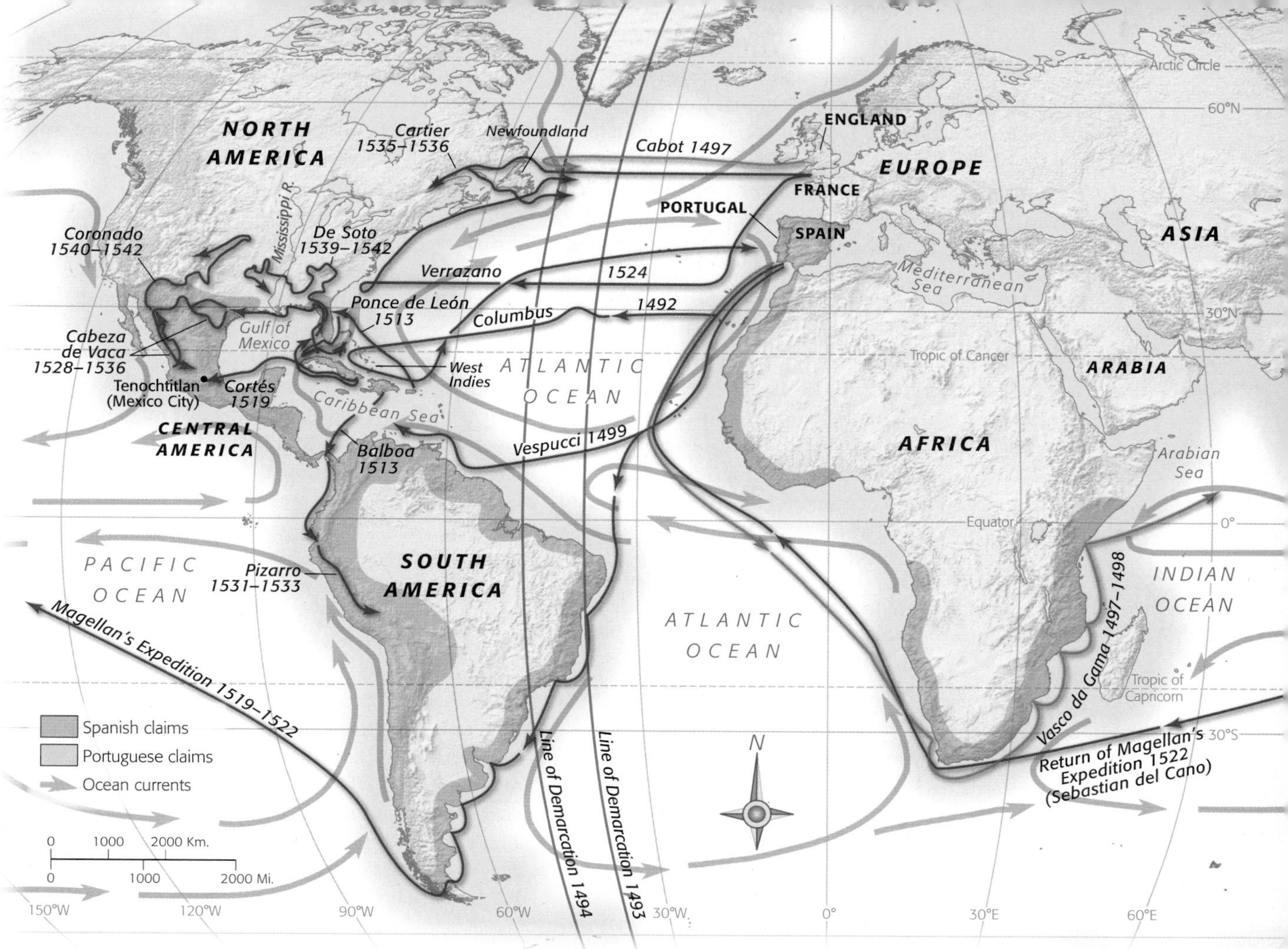

Map 2.3 European Explorations, 1492–1610 Beginning in the late fifteenth century, Spain and Portugal, followed by France and England, explored and then set out to colonize the Americas. Of the European powers, Spain claimed and controlled the greatest expanse of territory in the Americas. ▲

2-3

Spain's Empire in the Americas

This image, which shows Indians led by an Eagle Warrior attacking besieged Spaniards, illustrated a history of New Spain published in 1581 by the Spanish friar, Diego Durán (Codex Durán, folio 30a.) Durán was fluent in Nahuatl, the Aztec language, and worked with Aztec informants to write his book, which was in many ways sympathetic to Native peoples.

As you look at the contrasting weapons, postures, and clothing of these two groups, what can you deduce about their military strategies and the place of war in their societies? ▶

Codex Duran: Pedro de Alvarado (c.1485–1541) companion-at-arms of Hernando Cortes (1485–1547) besieged by Aztec warriors (vellum), Duran, Diego (16th century)/Biblioteca Nacional, Madrid, Spain/The Bridgeman Art Library

Following Columbus's expeditions, Spain explored and conquered many lands and peoples of the Americas. Spain brought the systems honed on Madeira and the Canary Islands to the West Indies, provoking a native population decline and moral outrage among some Spanish clerics. But Spain justified its colonization on religious, legal, economic, and moral grounds. Spain conquered the empires of Mexico and Peru, seizing much gold and silver and prompting Spanish conquistadores to search the Western Hemisphere for other wealthy civilizations to conquer. Once this initial period of excitement passed, Spain set out to rule its new lands and peoples by creating administrative structures designed to exploit and control native peoples. East and north of Mexico, Spain explored both Florida and what would become the American Southwest, but by the mid-sixteenth century, it had all but abandoned the dream of easy wealth in these lands.

☞ As you read, think about the motivations that lay behind the Spanish conquest. What reasons did the Spanish use to justify their control of unfamiliar lands and peoples?

2-3a Spanish Beginnings in the Caribbean and West Indies

Spain finds legal justification for its Caribbean colonies even as they prove deadly and exploitative.

Most Spaniards had little difficulty justifying their New World conquests. Like other Christians, they believed that their god had given them "dominion" over all creatures on the earth. In 1493, Pope Alexander VI—in what is known as the *Papal Donation*—decreed that he had the right to "give, grant, and assign" newly discovered lands to the Spanish and Portuguese monarchs so that they might bring the indigenous peoples to Christianity. The next year the Pope formally granted to Spain sovereignty over "all islands and mainlands, found or to be found" beyond a demarcation line negotiated by Spain and Portugal running 370 miles west of the Azores. Under the Treaty of Tordesillas (1494), Spain was granted rights to all lands to the west of the southeastern edge of South America, and Portugal to those to the east of the line. Thus, within a few years of Columbus's first voyage, the Spanish and Portuguese and the Roman Catholic Church had obtained what they understood to be exclusive control over the New World and its peoples.

Requerimiento Spanish legal document read to Indians during early phase of Spanish conquest demanding peaceful submission to Spain and Catholicism to avoid war, enslavement, or death.

encomienda System in which Spain granted an *encomendero* the right to Indian labor and tribute in a conquered community and required the *encomendero* to educate Indians in Catholicism.

In exerting authority over Indians, Spaniards relied on policies that Spanish and Muslim armies had used during their long battle for control over Iberia. The Spanish **Requerimiento** ordered Indians to "acknowledge the [Catholic] Church as the ruler and superior of the whole world, and the high priest called Pope, and in his name the king and queen [of Spain]." Indians who accepted the authority of the crown and the supremacy of Catholicism would be treated reasonably well. Those who refused to submit were informed that they would be enslaved or killed.

On the island of Hispaniola, Columbus and his countrymen faced challenges that would characterize virtually all European efforts to colonize the Americas. Europeans brought disease to the Americas, just as they had done to Madeira and the Canary Islands. Hispaniola had a native population of at least 500,000 Tainos before the arrival of Columbus. By 1496, perhaps as many as 350,000 had died, most likely from typhus, the same disease that had felled the majority of Guanche. By 1518, smallpox had further decimated a Taino population also reeling from virgin soil epidemics of measles and pneumonia. Smallpox soon spread to Puerto Rico, Jamaica, and Cuba, and by the 1550s, had reduced the population of the Caribbean by 90 percent.

Although Spain conquered Hispaniola and Santo Domingo (1508), Puerto Rico (1508), Jamaica (1509), and Cuba (1511) with relative ease thanks to superior weaponry and epidemics, it was not immediately clear whether and how the islands would generate income for Spain. In theory, Spaniards in Hispaniola would get rich by trading with the Tainos for gold. The Tainos, however, had little of the yellow metal, and what they did have had come from elsewhere. When his dreams of gold went unfulfilled, Columbus shipped Tainos to Spain to be sold as slaves. Isabella, however, ended the slave trade because she consistently affirmed that Indians, once they accepted Spanish sovereignty, were vassals of the crown and therefore free. Two loopholes, however, allowed Spanish slave-raiding expeditions to continue scouring the Caribbean in search of potential slaves: Indians who rebelled against Spanish authority were considered legitimate targets for enslavement, and Indians enslaved by other Indians could be obtained through purchase or barter.

The fact that the Spanish could not easily or legally enslave Indians presented colonizers with two problems: Who would work in the plantations and mines they planned to establish? And if those operations could not be made profitable through enslaved Indians, why should Spaniards risk life and limb to settle distant lands? The governor of Hispaniola, Nicolás de Ovando, found the answer in 1503 when he initiated in the Caribbean a system that had evolved in Spain during the long war against Islam. During the *Reconquista*, Spain had relied on a system known as the ***encomienda*** in which conquered Muslim villagers were assigned as laborers to conquering Spanish military leaders. In Hispaniola, the *encomenderos*—the men who held the grants of Tainos labor—were to look after the welfare of their Indian charges and ensure that they were instructed in the Catholic faith. Ovando also mandated that Indians be brought from the countryside into central towns where they would be easier to control and convert. Moving the surviving Tainos into towns, however, only made them more susceptible to European diseases. Forced labor, resettlement into towns, and the

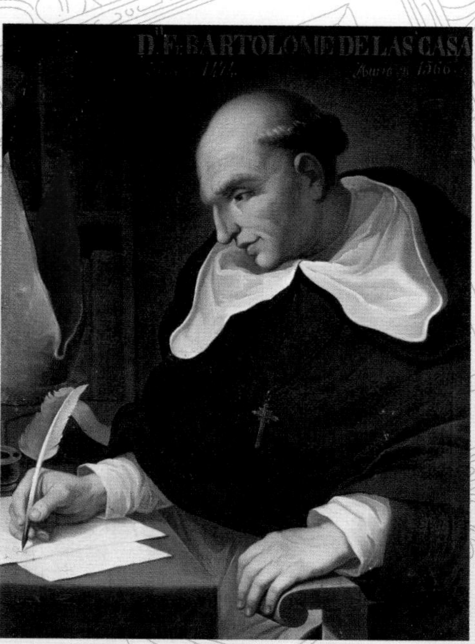

Dea Picture Library/Getty Images

Global Americans In the wake of Columbus's voyages and the Spanish conquest of the Caribbean, thousands of Spaniards crossed the Atlantic in search of their fortunes. Among those who enriched themselves was the father of **Bartolomé de las Casas** (1484–1566) who sailed with Columbus on his second voyage and settled in Hispaniola. In 1498, the father returned to Spain with a present for his son: a Taino slave. Four years later, at age twenty-eight, Bartolomé sailed for the West Indies in the footsteps of his father. There he was a conquistador: He worked to suppress Indian rebellions and was rewarded with *encomiendas* on Hispaniola and Cuba. Eventually, however, he began to see the Spaniard's treatment of Indians in the West Indies as "unjust and tyrannical" and moved from exploiting to protecting Indians. He renounced his own *encomiendas*, became a Dominican friar in 1523, and became history's most vocal and effective critic of Spanish colonialism. He always believed in converting Indians to Catholicism, and in 1540, he met with King Charles and denounced the "murder and destruction" of the Indians by *encomenderos*. Las Casas's pleas led to the New Laws of 1542, sealing his reputation as a great reformer. But his views and writings also laid the foundation for the "Black Legend," the incorrect belief that Spaniards were the cruelest of colonists. The English would embrace and popularize this idea to justify their anti-Catholicism and explain away their own treatment of Indians in North America, which at times was worse.

diseases that accompanied the Spanish invasion all but destroyed the Taino within several decades of the arrival of Columbus.

The catastrophic depopulation and ruthless exploitation of the indigenous people of Hispaniola and other Caribbean islands conquered by Spain in the early 1500s prompted moral outrage among some Spaniards. One priest and *encomendero*, Bartolomé de las Casas, surrendered his encomienda grant in 1514 and spent the next half century trying to secure the humane treatment of Indians under Spanish rule. Eventually, his efforts bore fruit. In 1542, the Spanish crown promulgated "New Laws" that reformed the *encomienda* system and abolished the enslavement of Indians in Spain's American possessions.

On Hispaniola, however, long before the New Laws curtailed the *encomienda*, Spaniards had introduced sugar cultivation and had begun to rely less on Indian laborers. In the early 1500s, they constructed a mill whose Spanish managers came from the Canary Islands, which Spain had taken from Portugal in the 1470s and where it had already cultivated sugar. By 1518, the Spanish crown had worked with the Portuguese to bring enslaved Africans to Hispaniola to work in sugar cultivation. Two decades later, more than thirty mills were on the island; they were the earliest example of plantation slavery in the Caribbean. Despite these advances, the Spanish sugar industry on Hispaniola peaked in 1570 and then declined, undone by competition from Brazil. Spanish trade to and from the West Indies also remained vulnerable to predation because ships had to travel narrow and undefended shipping lanes and negotiate the Trade Winds, which blew west most of the year and complicated sailing east across the Atlantic.

2-3b Conquests of Mexico, Peru, and Brazil

Spain conquers America's largest and wealthiest Indian empires.

With confidence in the justness of their conquests, Spanish **conquistadores** radiated out from the Caribbean to discover and conquer new territories. In 1518, Diego Velázquez, governor of Cuba, placed Hernán Cortés in charge of an expedition to explore and take control of the interior of Mexico but at the last minute revoked his commission. In an act of mutiny, Cortés stuck to his plan and in 1519 sailed from Cuba with eleven ships and more than 600 men. He soon formed an alliance with the Tlaxcala, who resented the rule of the Aztecs. Cortés then marched on the Aztec capital of Tenochtitlán and boldly seized the Aztec ruler Moctezuma, throwing the empire into chaos. Cortés had by his side an Indian woman of noble birth—baptized as Doña Marina—who was his translator and legitimator. In June 1520, Aztec warriors forced the Spanish invaders from the capital city. Velázquez sent Pánfilo de Narváez to arrest Cortés, but Cortés defeated Narváez. Soon smallpox arrived and spread quickly through the thickly settled countryside of Mexico. Within a year, the Aztecs had fallen to disease and Spanish military might as had the Guanches and Tainos. After a seventy-five-day siege in the summer of 1521, Cortés took the ruined city of Tenochtitlán, thereby giving Spain nominal control over an empire of 25 million people.

conquistadores Spanish or Portuguese soldiers or leaders who conquered much of the Americas between the sixteenth and eighteenth centuries.

Benson Collection, University of Texas, Austin

Global Americans The conquest of the Americas was anything but an exclusively male affair. Few women, however, played a more direct and controversial role in early American history than **Malintzin,** or Doña Marina. She was born in 1500 in a remote region of Mexico that stood on the periphery of the Aztec world. When she was a child, her mother sold her to Aztec traders who in turn sold her to the Maya, among whom she lived for many years. In 1519, when Cortés overwhelmed the town of Tabasco where she was enslaved, she was among twenty slave women offered to him as a gesture of submission. Baptized and renamed Marina, she was then given by Cortés to another Spaniard. Soon though, she became invaluable to Cortés, who took her back. He had with him a Spaniard who spoke Maya but not Nahuatl, so he was unable to communicate with the emissaries sent by Moctezuma, the Aztec leader. When Malintzin realized Cortés's predicament, she stepped forward and made it known that she spoke Maya and Nahuatl, her native tongue. With her assistance, Cortés built an Indian alliance that allowed him to conquer central Mexico, and for that some have judged her harshly. But she had no loyalty to the Aztecs, who had sold her into slavery, and she sensed that the powerful Cortés could best ensure her own survival. She and Cortés had a son together, the first *mestizo*, or person of Spanish and Indian ancestry. She later married a lesser conquistador and died of illness in 1529 at a young age, as did so many in colonial Mexico.

In search of gold to enrich themselves, Spaniards quickly moved to the south, west, and north of Tenochtitlán, reaching what are now Guatemala, El Salvador, Honduras, Florida, and California. As early as 1523, however, word had reached Spanish Mexico of a rich and powerful state—the Inca—somewhere to the south. The conquistadores Francisco Pizarro and Diego de Almagro set out to find it.

By 1532, when Pizarro arrived on the coast of Peru, the Inca empire was reeling from three successive virgin soil epidemics and a civil war. Pizarro, following the approach taken by Cortés, seized the Inca ruler, Atahualpa. He then demanded an enormous ransom in gold for his return. Once the Spaniards received some eleven tons of gold and thirteen tons of silver, they baptized and then murdered Atahualpa. In the wake of Atahualpa's death, civil war among the Inca continued, and the Spaniards began to fight among themselves for the riches of the Inca empire. Indian resistance continued until the Spaniards murdered Túpac Amaru, the last Inca ruler, in 1572. What remained of the Americas' greatest empire was then ruled by Spaniards.

In the same years that Spain was conquering Mexico and Peru, Portugal was beginning to settle Brazil, which it had first reached a generation earlier. The Portuguese—like the Spaniards on Hispaniola—relied on the system they had first employed on the Atlantic Islands. In 1530, the Portuguese divided Brazil into vast "captaincies," each composed of some 75 miles of coastline that stretched deep into the interior. Those Portuguese who received captaincies were expected to settle them at their own expense, and, in return, they received generous economic privileges.

The Portuguese in Brazil had trouble identifying a valuable export commodity until they settled upon dyewood, which could be used to produce a red dye of great value to European textile manufacturers. But the industry languished because the local Tupi had little need for the cheap trade goods that the Portuguese offered them in return for the wood. Some Portuguese enslaved the Tupi, many of whom fled into the interior. Countless others died of smallpox and other epidemics.

In the 1520s, a series of circumstances dictated that sugar would become the mainstay of the Brazilian export economy. Because of their experiences with plantations in Portugal and on the Atlantic islands, the Portuguese knew how to produce sugar. Coastal Brazil was suitable for the crop, and in the absence of the discovery of any precious metals in the colony, the Portuguese crown granted tax exemptions for new sugar plantations. In 1559, it authorized the opening of a slave trade between Africa and Brazil, and in 1570, the Portuguese crown abolished Indian slavery in the colony. Sugar production increased rapidly. The first mill opened in 1526. In 1576's the colony's 57 mills produced 2,500 tons for export, and a half century later 346 mills produced more than 20,000 tons.

2-3c Spanish Imperial Structures of Governance and Commerce

Spain moves quickly to organize and exploit its colonies.

Within a decade of Columbus's first voyage, Spain had in place colonial systems of exploitation and governance. To govern and make profitable their American conquests, Spaniards often worked through Indian leaders to organize labor drafts and extract tribute. They allowed Indian communities to govern themselves as

Map 2.4 The Viceroyalties of Colonial Latin America The Spanish and Portuguese monarchs delegated their authority in the Americas to viceroys, men who ruled over large administrative units. Within each viceroyalty were smaller administrative units, such as territories, which in turn were ruled by royal governors in concert with other royally appointed officials. ▲

long as they submitted to Spanish authority and met their labor and tribute obligations (see Map 2.4). In addition to the *encomienda*, the Spaniards instituted the ***repartimiento***, a forced rotational labor draft requiring Indians to work for Spaniards for a specific amount of time and for wages. After the discovery of silver in northern Mexico in 1550, silver became the most plentiful, valuable, and dependable export. Where there were no Indians to work the mines, Spaniards imported African slaves by the tens of thousands.

repartimiento Spanish labor organization system that compelled a certain number of Indians from each community to hire themselves out weekly to Spanish employers. Superseded the *encomienda*.

The Spanish crown delegated its authority in the Americas to **viceroys**, who ruled in the king's name over the expansive regions of New Spain, New Granada, Peru, and Río de la Plata. Viceroyalties were divided into smaller governmental units known as *audiencias*, which in turn were divided into *corregimientos*. At the local level, individual towns created their own municipal councils. During the first decades of the conquest, Indian leaders and nobles often staffed these councils. In the Indies, the Spanish crown followed a precedent set during the *Reconquista* and retained the power to organize the church in conquered regions. This meant that royal officials could appoint church officials such as bishops, thereby giving the crown nearly absolute religious authority in Spain's overseas territories.

The crown also funded legions of missionaries who set out to convert Indians to Catholicism. Franciscans first arrived in Mexico in 1524. By the middle of the century, a thousand missionaries were in New Spain, and the church claimed to have baptized millions of Indians. Many of the conversions were partial at best, aided by superficial similarities between Catholicism and Indian beliefs. Many Indians fused their god, Quetzalcoatl, with Saint Thomas; others likened an Indian rain god to Saint Peter. The Spanish practice of building Catholic churches above or in close proximity to Indian sacred places furthered the blending of religions.

The crown desired the natural wealth of the Americas, in particular silver, and colonists believed that they needed European commodities that they could not produce for themselves. Thus, transatlantic commercial networks developed quickly, linking Spain and its American colonies and reflecting the ascendant economic philosophy of **mercantilism**. A central tenet of mercantilism was the belief that overseas trade should be regulated in ways that supported strong national monarchies. The main goal of this system was to allow the state to amass bullion, which was equated with domestic prosperity and power at home and abroad.

Charles V, who ruled Spain's Empire from 1519 until 1556, regulated the transatlantic trade. Because it was a reliable source of taxes and he was a mercantilist, he believed that the overseas market should strengthen the central state. Charles required that all transatlantic trade be carried on Spanish ships, that only Spanish goods be shipped to the colonies, and that merchants obtain special licenses to trade certain goods. All goods—mostly precious metals, hides, cochineal, and sugar—had to travel to Spain in the *Carrera de Indias*, the heavily guarded Spanish fleet. In Spain, the *Casa de Contratación*, or House of Trade, founded in 1503 as a royal trading house, organized the fleets and collected the duties on exports and taxes on imports. Charles's successor, Phillip II (1556–1598), tightened royal control over the transatlantic trade. For instance, he restricted trade outbound from Spain to the ports of Seville and Cadiz and designated four legal ports of entry in Spanish America. He also granted trade monopolies to the leading commercial concerns in the viceregal capitals of Mexico City and Lima. In effect, these changes gave the Spanish crown the ability to carefully regulate and tax the transatlantic trade, thereby creating a Spanish mercantilist system that remained in place for more than a century.

viceroys Royal officials who manage a region or country in the name of a monarch.

mercantilism Economic theory and policy to regulate a rival nation's economy to increase the power of Spain, England, Portugal, and France.

The *Casa*, and therefore the Spanish crown, controlled immigration to the Indies. Would-be immigrants needed royal approval to emigrate, and foreigners, Jews, Muslims, and heretics were prohibited from emigrating altogether. The Spanish crown did not see a pressing need for mass immigration because the colonies could rely on Indians and African slaves for labor. Still, in the sixteenth century, about 80,000 Spaniards immigrated to New Spain. About two-thirds of the early immigrants were men, but over time, more families crossed the Atlantic. In 1570, the Spanish population in the Americas was about 150,000.

2-3d Spanish Exploration of Florida and the Southwest

> Spanish dreams of Indian cities of gold persist in Florida and the American Southwest.

Not until 1513 did Spanish explorers venture into lands that would one day be part of the United States. That year, Juan Ponce de León, the former governor of Puerto Rico and one of the richest men in the Caribbean, claimed the Atlantic Coast of North America from southern Florida to Newfoundland for Spain. Early exploration focused on Florida because it was adjacent to the Caribbean. Contrary to legend, there is no proof that Ponce de León hoped to find a fountain of youth in Florida. In reality, he was in search of gold and slaves. He died in 1521 after being wounded by an arrow shot by a Calusa Indian in Florida.

Pánfilo de Narváez ventured to Florida in 1528 at the head of the expedition that included Estebanico, who was discussed in the chapter opening. One of the other survivors of that disastrous expedition, Álvar Nuñez Cabeza de Vaca, published a narrative of his journey in 1542, writing of emeralds and the great towns in the Mexican north. Even before their publication, however, Cabeza de Vaca's tales inspired a generation of would-be conquistadors. In 1539, Viceroy Antonio Mendoza sent a small group led by a Franciscan, Fray Marcos de Niza, and Estebanico north. Before long, Niza was back in Mexico telling all who would listen of lands in the north that were even richer than Mexico. He spoke of having seen Cíbola, one of seven cities in the north rumored to hold great wealth.

To determine the veracity of Niza's claims, Mendoza commissioned an expedition led by Francisco Vázquez de Coronado. In 1540 Coronado set out with 300 Spanish soldiers, 6 Franciscans, 1,000 Indian allies, and 1,500 horses and pack animals. Niza guided the expedition. After they reached Cíbola, a village of 100 families, Coronado wrote despairingly to the viceroy, "He [Fray Marcos] has not told the truth in a single thing that he said, but everything is the opposite of what he related, except the name of the cities and the large stone houses." Coronado and his men pushed their explorations further into the northern interior (see Map 2.5), soon encountering the Pueblo Indians, a local people. Food shortages became acute in the winter of 1540–1541, and warfare broke out when the Indians tired of the Spaniards' demands for food, wood, and women.

Determined to make an example of a village he deemed uncooperative, Coronado attacked the pueblo of Arenal and burned alive its people who resisted. In the spring of 1541, Coronado gave up the dream of Cíbola and turned his considerable energies to finding Quivira, another city fabled for its riches. Coronado's Indian guide, known as the Turk because of his attire, led the Spaniards through what are now Texas, Oklahoma, and central Kansas. There, on the trackless Great Plains, Coronado's dreams died. Coronado strangled the Turk with an iron collar, having learned from him that the Pueblo Indians had asked him to "take us to a place where we and our horses would starve to death."

In Florida, another Spanish expedition grew similarly disillusioned. Hernándo de Soto arrived in Florida in the early summer of 1539 with perhaps a thousand soldiers, two hundred horses, and swine, which he planned to use to feed his men. De Soto had made a personal fortune in the conquest of Peru, but he believed that Florida held greater riches. He and his men looted Indian villages and enslaved their occupants. Casualties on both sides ran high. "At night," one Spaniard recalled, "we dressed our wounds with the fat of the dead Indians as there was no medicine left." In 1542, de Soto died of a fever, and several

Map 2.5 Spanish Exploration of New Mexico, Mid-Sixteenth Century Motivated by the erroneous belief that the region north of Mexico City contained a kingdom of unfathomable wealth, Spanish conquistadores ventured to the far north. They encountered numerous groups of sedentary Indians but not the gold and silver of their dreams. ▼

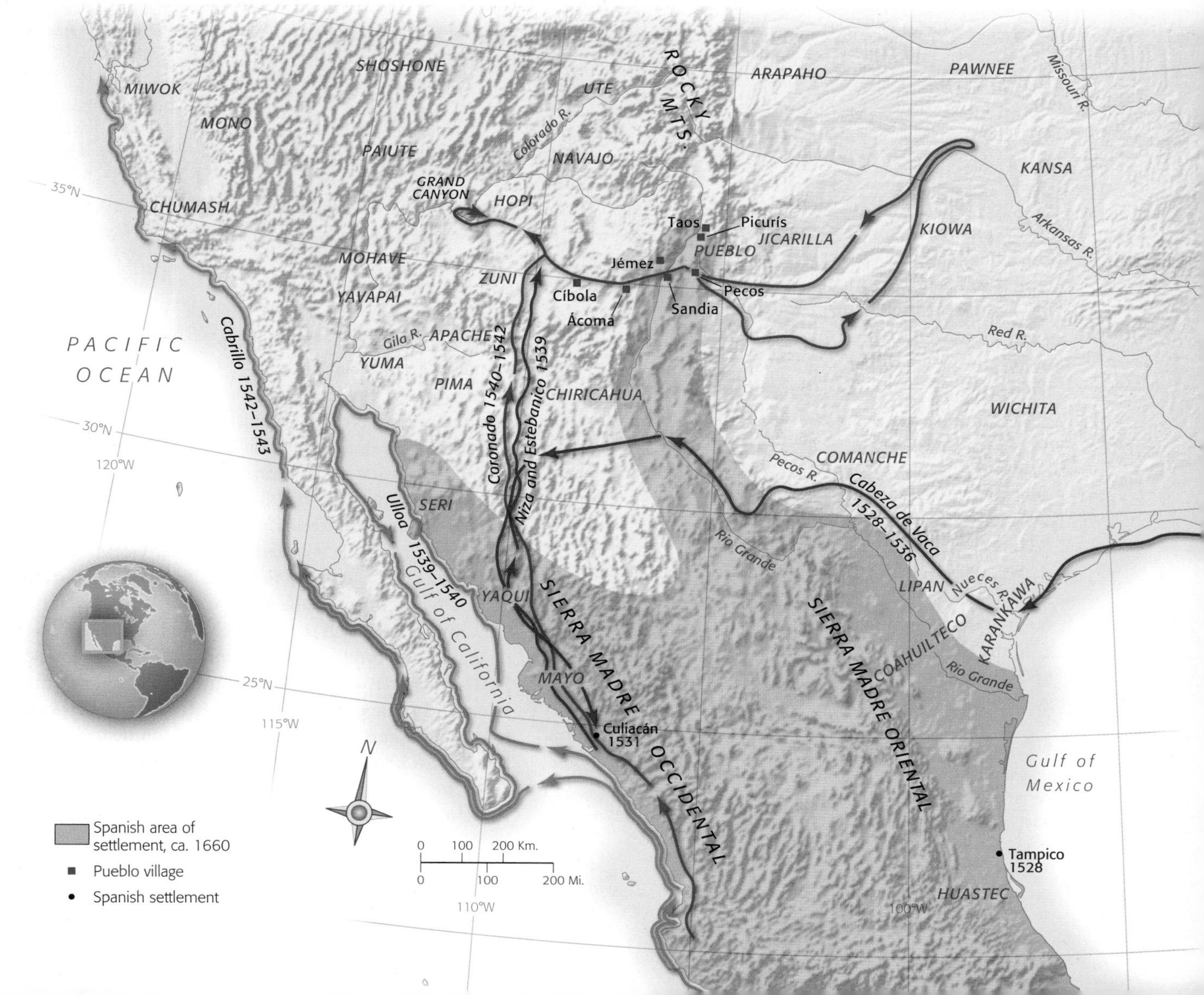

hundred of his soldiers—after three years of a fruitless search for wealth in Florida—retreated down the banks of the Mississippi and into the Gulf of Mexico.

By the 1540s, it was clear to Spaniards that northern North America was not home to rich empires comparable to those they had conquered in Mexico or Peru. When the Spanish settled the north, it was not of the monarchy's doing. Instead, the private initiative of rich men funded the settlements and to a large degree delegated the task of reorganizing Indian lives to Catholic missionaries who sought poverty and anonymity with the same zeal that men like Coronado and de Soto had craved wealth and fame. Still, the viceroy of New Spain did see a pressing need for a military presence in Florida to protect Spanish treasure fleets from pirates. A Spanish post along the southeast coast of Florida, the viceroy reasoned, would keep pirates at bay and provide sanctuary for Spanish ships that on occasion ran aground in the region. In 1557, Phillip II, on his subordinate's advice, ordered the construction of a fort on the Gulf of Mexico and another along the Atlantic Coast at the Point of Saint Elena, known today as Tybee Island, Georgia.

2-4 Europe in the Americas to 1585

The inscription of this watercolor drawing *Indian Village of Pomeiooc* by John White (created in 1585 to 1586) reads, "The towne of Pomeiock and true forme of their howses, couered | and enclosed some wth matts, and some wth barcks of trees. All compassed | abowt wth smale poles stock thick together in stedd of a wall."

Examine the architecture of these buildings and the layout of this village. What they do they reveal about Indian life in this place and time? ▶

World History Archive/Newscom

In the decades after the conquest of Mexico, other European powers launched their own expeditions of exploration and conquest, challenging Spain's dominance in the Americas. At first, such was the power of the Spanish navy that other nations largely avoided direct confrontation. France explored deep into the interior of the continent's far north, for instance. But the destruction of the Spanish Armada in 1588 opened the seas to other powers. The English joined the competition for overseas colonies, especially once Queen Elizabeth and British merchants had been swayed to the view that the English, as Protestants, would be more successful in securing the wealth of the Americas than Catholic Spain (see Table 2.1). The first attempts by England and France to colonize in North America were failures. Although many early settlements proved ephemeral, the biological consequences of European expansion and settlement were nothing short of cataclysmic for the Americas and its peoples.

☞ As you read, focus on the different national cultures of colonization and expansion that Europeans brought to America. What are the similarities and differences between early French, English, and Spanish colonies in the New World?

2-4a The French

Indians and Spaniards drive French explorers and Huguenots out of eastern North America.

In the wake of Magellan's circumnavigation, French Atlantic merchants sponsored Giovanni Verrazano's exploration between today's Georgia and Maine in an attempt to find the Northwest Passage. The French arrived in North America in 1534 when Jacques Cartier made the first of his voyages to the New World. He was in search of a passage to the Far East. To avoid lands claimed by Spain and Portugal, he sailed to the north of the continent, making landfall in Newfoundland, which he quickly dismissed as worthless. Cartier then made his way up the St. Lawrence River, where he met a group of Haudenosaunees from the village of Stadacona, which would become Quebec. Sailing further north, he concluded mistakenly that the St. Lawrence River was a path to the orient.

The following year, Cartier returned, set up a winter camp at Stadacona, and traveled up river to a much larger village, Hochelaga, the future site of Montreal. Although the Hochelagans received Cartier well, he withdrew to Stadacona fearing an attack. There he learned of the kingdom of Saguenay to the west. Indians said it was rich in gold, silver, and other precious resources. Cartier abandoned finding a passage to the Far East, but he decided that a French colony on the St. Lawrence could be used as a staging area from which to explore the interior of the continent and to conquer Saguenay. To further his plans, Cartier kidnapped the Indian leader Donnacona and his sons and took them back to France so that they could tell their stories to French officials. When Cartier returned in 1541, the now openly hostile local Indians killed more than thirty-five of his men. By 1543, the French had abandoned Stadacona and would not return until the fur trade lured them back in the following century. Canada was no longer of interest to the French, especially after Donnacona's description of Saguenay was revealed to be an invention.

The French, however, had continued to probe elsewhere for weaknesses in Spanish and Portuguese claims because they had never fully accepted the Treaty of Tordesillas. They sponsored encroachments on Portuguese Brazil. And in 1562, French explorer Jean Ribault established Charlefort in what is now South Carolina. The settlement of thirty men struggled, and the Spaniards destroyed it in 1563.

In 1564, a group of French Huguenots established Fort Caroline near the St. John's River in what is now Jacksonville, Florida, in a region previously explored by Ribault, who had intended to establish a "New France." He returned the following year with five ships and hundreds more French Huguenots who believed that by settling in the New World, they were striking a blow against Catholic Spain and securing a refuge for Protestants. The settlers also dreamed of gold, silver, and subservient Indians, none of which they found. Tensions rose with the local Indians, and the French decided to abandon the colony. Before they could, Pedro Menéndez de Avilés, a veteran of Spain's New World colonial ventures, marched five hundred soldiers and Indian allies to Fort Caroline. He found a poorly defended colony manned by a few sickly Frenchmen. Menéndez spared the women and children but hanged the men, apparently under a sign that read "I do this not as to Frenchmen, but as to Lutherans." Menéndez then headed south and killed all Frenchmen he could find. With the French Protestant threat eliminated from Florida, Menéndez established a town at Santa Elena on the site of the destroyed Charlefort and created a permanent settlement at St. Augustine in 1565. By 1567, Menéndez had established five military bases along the Atlantic coast and two forts along the Gulf coast to keep other Europeans at bay.

2-4b The Spanish, the Chesapeake, and War over the Seas

Spain establishes a mission on the Chesapeake that comes to a violent end.

In 1561, two years before Spain went to war against the French in Florida, a Spanish ship sailing north of Florida was blown off course and made landfall in the Chesapeake Bay, or what the Spanish called the *Bahía de Santa María*. There they encountered a small group of Woodlands Indians in a land the Spanish knew as Ajacán. The ship's commander, Antonio Velázquez, took two of these Indians—a leader known as Paquinquineo and his servant—back to Spain. Paquinquineo, who became known to the Spanish as Don Luís de Velasco, was presented to King Phillip II, who looked favorably on him. After years of unexpected adventures, in 1570 Don Luis led a group of Jesuits to a village near the James River where he was given a joyful greeting by friends and family who had long assumed he was dead.

But by that point, the land of plenty that Don Luís had described to Spaniards no longer existed following six years of famine. And the Jesuits' hopes that they could establish a mission and convince the Indians to plant communally were

TABLE 2.1 Major European Explorers and Conquerors of the Americas, 1492–1564

Date	Explorer/Conqueror	Sponsoring Country	Region
1492	Christopher Columbus	Spain	Caribbean and Central America
1497	John Cabot	England	Newfoundland
1500	Pedro Cabral	Portugal	Brazil
1513	Juan Ponce de León	Spain	Florida
1513	Vasco Nuñez de Balboa	Spain	Isthmus of Panama
1519–1521	Hernán Cortés	Spain	Mexico
1519–1522	Ferdinand Magellan	Spain	The world (circumnavigation)
1524	Giovanni Verrazano	Spain	Canada
1530s	Francisco Pizarro	Spain	Peru
1534–1541	Jacques Cartier	France	Canada
1539–1541	Hernando de Soto	Spain	Florida and the Southeast
1540–1541	Francisco Vazquez de Coronado	Spain	Southwest
1562–1564	Jean Ribault	France	Florida

Archive Photos/Getty Images

Global Americans It is a commonplace that during the colonial period, Europeans and Africans moved west and crossed the Atlantic to the Americas. But a number of Native Americans also went from America to Europe. Most became slaves or curiosities until they sickened and died. A surprising number, however, through luck, determination, and even cunning, returned to their homelands where they resisted colonization. Among these was **Paquinquineo**, also known as Don Luis de Velasco, whom Spaniards took from the Chesapeake in 1561. In Madrid, he became a favorite of the king, but in 1562, when Don Luis grew homesick, King Phillip supported his return to his homeland. Although he sailed for Mexico in the summer of that year, it would be many years before he reached Mexico City. He fell seriously ill and was nursed by Dominicans, who also baptized him. In 1566, Phillip II sent Don Luis and two Dominicans to explore the Chesapeake, but their ship was blown off course and landed in Seville. Don Luis lived in Spain among Jesuits for four more years. By then he spoke Spanish and understood the Spaniards, offering to help establish a mission in his homeland and lead them to "great kingdoms." In 1570, finally, he returned home accompanied by eight Jesuits. Before long, he led a bloody rebellion against the missionaries, killing many himself, and disappearing without a trace into the countryside. Years later, however, he was probably among a group of Indians who, dressed in the black robes of Jesuits, tried to lure a Spanish ship to shore so that he could attack it. And a half century later, he was almost certainly involved in an attack that nearly wiped out the Jamestown colony. Having left his own culture and learned what European settlements would mean for his people, he devoted his life to keeping them at bay.

dashed. As the mission failed and the Jesuits banned trade with the Indians, Don Luis abandoned the Spaniards to live with his uncle, a chief, in a distant village. Eventually, he led an attack on the Spaniards, all of whom except a boy, Alonso, were killed. The boy related the tragedy years later to none other than Pedro Menéndez de Aviles who had come to investigate the fate of the Jesuits. When he learned that the missionaries had been killed, Menéndez took revenge by killing nearly thirty local Indians. The Indians would not forget this violent intrusion into their homelands.

Although the French had failed to establish a settlement in Spanish Florida, they (and later, the English) turned to **privateering** in order to prey on the riches that Spain had extracted from the Americas and to deny the legitimacy of Spain's overseas possessions. Privateers were not the same as pirates; pirates stole for themselves whereas privateers were state-sponsored sailors of fortune who plundered the ships of another country. Typically, the sponsoring monarchy took one-fifth of the plunder. During the first half of the sixteenth century when Spain and France were at war almost continuously, France granted licenses to men willing to attack the Spanish treasure fleet. In the final decades of the century, when England and Spain were at war, the English did the same.

privateering Person or ship authorized by a government to attack foreign ships during wartime; in essence, a legalized pirate.

Among the most successful English privateers was Francis Drake. In 1572, he stole a fortune in Spanish gold and silver from a mule train that was traversing the Isthmus of Panama. Five years later, he set off on another voyage to attack the Spanish treasure fleet. Within three years, he had stolen 800,000 pounds in Spanish treasure and sailed around the globe. In 1579, toward the end of that voyage, Drake sailed up the Pacific Coast, claiming northern California for England.

Drake had not only challenged Spain's claim to the west coast of the continent and the Pacific Ocean but also destroyed Spanish settlements on the Atlantic Ocean. In 1586, before heading back to England laden with Spanish treasure, he sacked Spanish Florida, prompting Spain to abandon its settlement at Santa Elena and transfer its residents and the colony's capital to the sole remaining Spanish settlement in Florida, St. Augustine.

2-4c The English, Ralegh, and Roanoke

England's first attempt to plant a colony in North America ends in failure.

In 1585, to spread Protestantism and beat back Catholic Spain, England established its first outpost in North America. The settlement at Roanoke, however, was a dismal failure, undermined by the English crown's emphasis on privateering over colonization. In

British Library Board/Robana/Art Resource, NY

Watercolor drawing of *An Indian Man and Woman Eating* by John White. White's early realistic images of Indians challenged reigning European notions of Indians as naked savages cannibals. Here, a man and a woman eat maize rather than human flesh, and they appear sociable, not barbaric near-humans who live through hunting alone. ▲

1578, Queen Elizabeth had given Humphrey Gilbert a six-year grant to explore and settle unclaimed portions of North America, but he died at sea before he could carry out his expedition. In 1584, the grant passed to his half-brother, Walter Ralegh, a favorite of the queen and a militant Protestant. Ralegh imagined a vast estate for himself on Roanoke Island in a land he would name Virginia in honor of Elizabeth, known as the *Virgin Queen.* Colonists devoted to agriculture would enrich him through rents and a share of the crops they raised. The colony would also be a base for privateering expeditions, which would benefit the monarch. As preparation for this settlement, the English scouted Roanoke, situated off of today's North Carolina.

The following year, Ralegh's cousin, Richard Grenville, and some 100 settlers, including the artist John White, sailed for Roanoke. Bad weather, the captain's desire to spend weeks privateering, and the queen's decision to divert many of the ships to the war against Spain, weakened the settlement before it even began. When one of the ships ran aground off Roanoke, the 107 Englishmen of the expedition found themselves with only twenty days' provisions. Later that summer, Grenville returned to England, leaving in charge the veteran military commander Ralph Lane who expected a supply ship later that fall. Through the long winter of 1585–1586, Lane's men searched for food, gold, and a water route to Asia. They also spread disease among the native population and grew desperate for food because the Indians had no provisions for men who offered nothing in return.

To the colonists' surprise, Drake arrived in June 1586 with a fleet of twenty-three ships fresh from sacking St. Augustine. The privateer, however, had no provisions to spare. After a hurricane laid waste to Drake's fleet, Lane abandoned the colony, sailing to England with nearly all of the colonists. When Grenville arrived in July with supplies, he found a colony nearly abandoned. He too then returned to England with his ships and several hundred colonists, leaving behind fifteen Englishmen.

Despite these setbacks, Ralegh sponsored another plan for Virginia. The "Cittie of Ralegh," governed by John White and peopled by 110 recruits who had paid their way to the colony and would receive grants of hundreds of acres of land, was to be founded in the Chesapeake Bay, which Ralegh considered a better base for privateering than Roanoke Island. A second settlement was to be established in Roanoke, and it was to be run by an Indian named Manteo, whom the English had captured during their first attempt at colonization. Ralegh intended to dub him "Lord of Roanoke."

Under White's command, Ralegh's ships arrived in Roanoke in July 1587 carrying 117 colonists. They found no settlers. Just a single skeleton remained of the men whom Grenville had left. The local Croatoans refused to subject themselves to Lord Manteo's authority or provide the settlers with food. Hoping to rescue the colonists from starvation, White returned to England in late August for provisions. But in England, he encountered the hard reality of England's priorities. The war with Spain took precedence over the survival of a hundred souls on the margins of the English empire.

To punish England for its support of privateering, Phillip II of Spain in 1588 had sent his Armada to destroy the English fleet and attack the nation itself. Only after English forces under the command of Drake defeated the Armada did White make his way back across the Atlantic although as a passenger on a privateering ship that carried neither provisions nor more settlers.

Setting foot on Roanoke Island in August 1590, White discovered the settlement vacant and overgrown and the word *CROATOAN* carved in a post near an abandoned house. White could not linger in Roanoke to investigate the colony's disappearance. The privateers who carried him were eager to move on, and he soon sailed with them to the West Indies where they searched for Spanish ships to plunder.

2-4d Biological Consequences

> The opening up of the Ocean World transforms both Europe and the Americas.

Although European settlements in America from Mexico and Peru to New France and Roanoke all played out on vastly different scales and trajectories, there was one common denominator: The interactions between newcomers and Natives

History without Borders

Chocolate

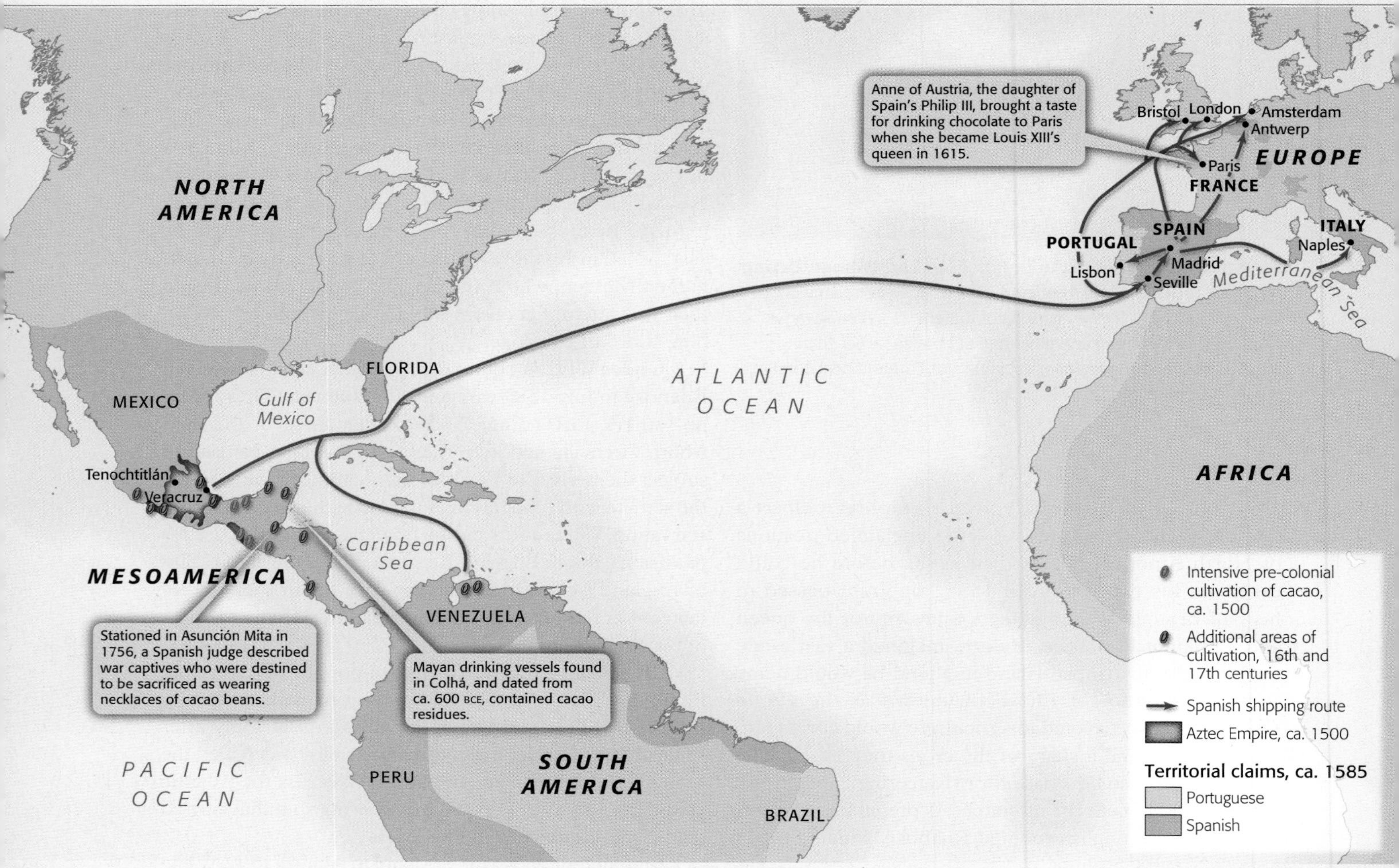

The Production and Trade of Chocolate during the Early Modern Period Chocolate was produced in specific regions of Mesoamerica and widely consumed. The Spanish carried chocolate back to Europe, where it was accepted across the continent. ▲

Europeans came to the Americas convinced in their cultural superiority over Native Americans. They believed that they were the bearers of civilization and that Indians were savages, peoples whose customs and beliefs were not only primitive but infused with idolatrous and even diabolical practices. Europeans looked at Indians' clothing, dwellings, and temples and saw the antithesis of their culture. Thus, Europeans believed that in colonizing the Americas, they would become the Indians' teachers and that Indians would adopt key elements of European culture or risk annihilation and damnation. Yet Spaniards and then most Europeans adopted intact a central Mesoamerican practice: the ritual consumption of chocolate. Europeans did not modify chocolate to suit their own tastes but learned to drink it like Mesoamericans. In a reverse of European expectations and assumptions regarding the consumption of chocolate, culture flowed from the colonized to the colonizer. Indians taught; Europeans emulated.

When Spaniards came to settle and colonize the Americas, cacao—the bean from which chocolate is produced—had long been a staple across Mesoamerica. Cacao grows best in tropical lowland regions and thus many groups obtained it through the sprawling trade networks of Mesoamerica. The Aztecs so prized cacao that they demanded it as tribute from their subject peoples. From Central America to Northwest Mexico, cacao beans functioned as a currency. Mesoamericans consumed cacao in the

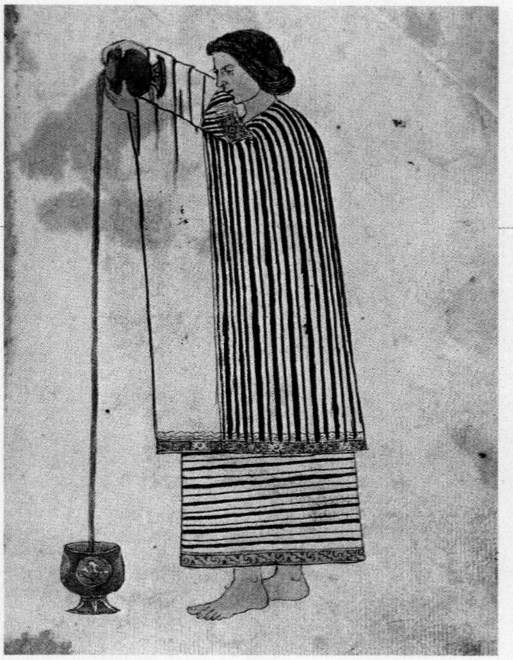

De Agostini/DEA/Getty Images

***Woman Turning Chocolate*, Codex Tudela, 1553.** As this image suggests, indigenous women produced, prepared, and served chocolate. They roasted cacao "beans" over a fire; pounded them into paste; flavored the paste with flowers, chilies, black pepper, and vanilla; diluted the mixture with water; and, in an indispensible preparation of the drink, poured the concoction between vessels until a froth formed as shown here. Finally, they served the drink in lacquered gourds or specially prepared cups. ▲

Fine Art Images/Heritage Images/Getty Images

***Still Life with an Ebony Chest*, 1652, Antonio Pereda y Salgado.** By the 1590s, chocolate had become an item of consistent trade across the Atlantic. By the 1620s, thousands of pounds were sent to Spain each year. Between 1650 and 1700, Venezuela exported more than 7 million pounds of chocolate to Spain. Shown here are the accoutrements of chocolate preparation and service, which were becoming a part of cultured life. To the right are cacao and sugar. On the cabinet and to the left are various vessels necessary to properly prepare, froth, and consume the beverage. ▲

form of chocolate as a beverage, hot or cold. The emphasis Mesoamericans placed on the color, fragrance, taste, temperature, and presentation of the drink suggests that it was designed to appeal to many senses.

Initially, Europeans found the drink disgusting. One observer concluded that it "seemed more a drink for pigs, than a drink for humanity." Another likened the froth to feces. These views faded as Spaniards, who comprised a distinct minority in Mexico in the sixteenth century, found themselves in a chocolate consumption culture. Spanish men constituted the majority of immigrants to New Spain, and many married Indian women and employed others as domestic servants who prepared and served Mexican chocolate the Mesoamerican way. Markets, villages, and town plazas abounded with the drink. And everywhere, in a continuation of pre-Hispanic practices, Indian leaders, Spanish nobles, and leading clerics served chocolate beverages as a form of sociability.

As Spaniards traveled back to Iberia, they brought chocolate with them, and they continued to consume it as a drink, accented with pepper and topped by a frothy foam. In the seventeenth century, long after the drink had become common in Spain, Europeans added sugar to their chocolate to approximate the Mesoamerican drink, which Indians had commonly flavored with honey. Similarly, when Europeans added cinnamon, black pepper, anise, and rose to their chocolate, they were replacing hard-to-find Mesoamerican fragrances and flavors. In the eighteenth century, Europeans, aware that they had assimilated Indian tastes and eager to support a Spanish ideology of conquest, claimed to have "improved" the drink and separated it from its pre-Hispanic origins when, in fact, Europeans had adopted Mesoamerican tastes and practices that were of ancient origin.

Critical Thinking Questions

► What other New World beverages and foods did Europeans add to their diets?

► In what other ways might one argue that Europeans assimilated Native American practices?

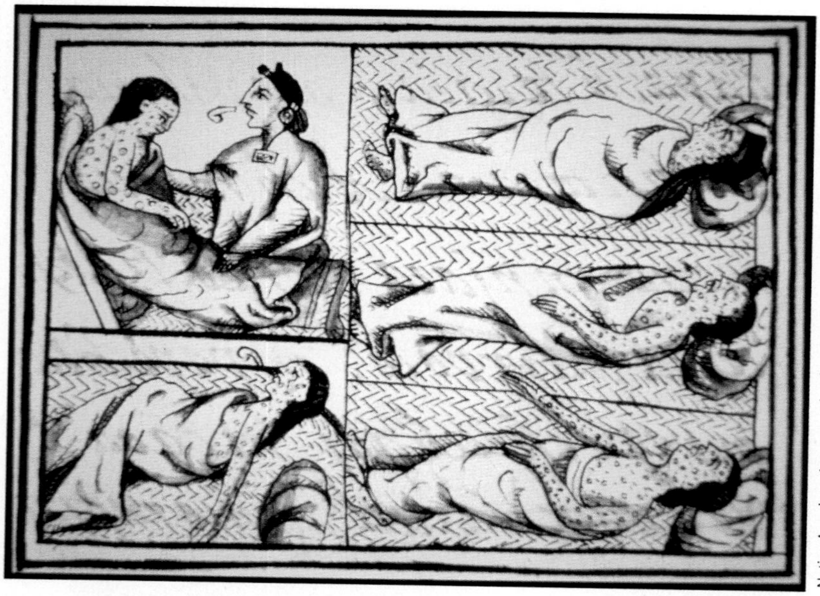

Aztec Doctor Examining Indian with Smallpox, circa 1540. This image, created by a Native American scribe or artist in sixteenth-century postconquest Mexico, indicates the rapid spread of smallpox throughout the body of a victim. ▲

Columbian Exchange Transfer of plants, animals, people, ideas, and technologies between Europe and the Americas over the centuries in the wake of Columbus's 1492 voyage.

were shaped by the diseases that Europeans introduced to the Native world. Just about everywhere in the Americas, virgin soil epidemics of smallpox, measles, influenza, and typhus were the handmaidens of European imperial expansion. Deadly diseases introduced by Europeans claimed tens of millions of Indians across the Americas in one of the most tragic chapters in human history. In Central Mexico alone, the population fell from 25 million in 1519 to less than 2 million in 1580.

The plants and animals that Europeans brought to the Americas contributed to this tragic episode as well. European crops displaced local species, altering ecological balances and upending Native American societies. At the same time, Europeans' horses, cattle, pigs, sheep, goats, and chickens thrived in the Americas, disrupting Indians' long established ways of life and putting their societies in peril.

Eventually, American plants, animals, and microbes flowed to Europe as well, although with not nearly the same dire consequences. Europeans imported avocados, cashews, coca, cocoa, maize, manioc, papayas, pecans, pineapples, potatoes, quinoa, rubber, squash, sunflowers, strawberries, sweet potatoes, tomatoes, and vanilla. They also contracted a virulent form of syphilis as well as yellow fever and yaws from the Americas. This two-way traffic across the Atlantic is known today as the **Columbian Exchange** (see Map 2.6). Its effects ensured that European expansion across the Atlantic transformed Europe, not just the Americas.

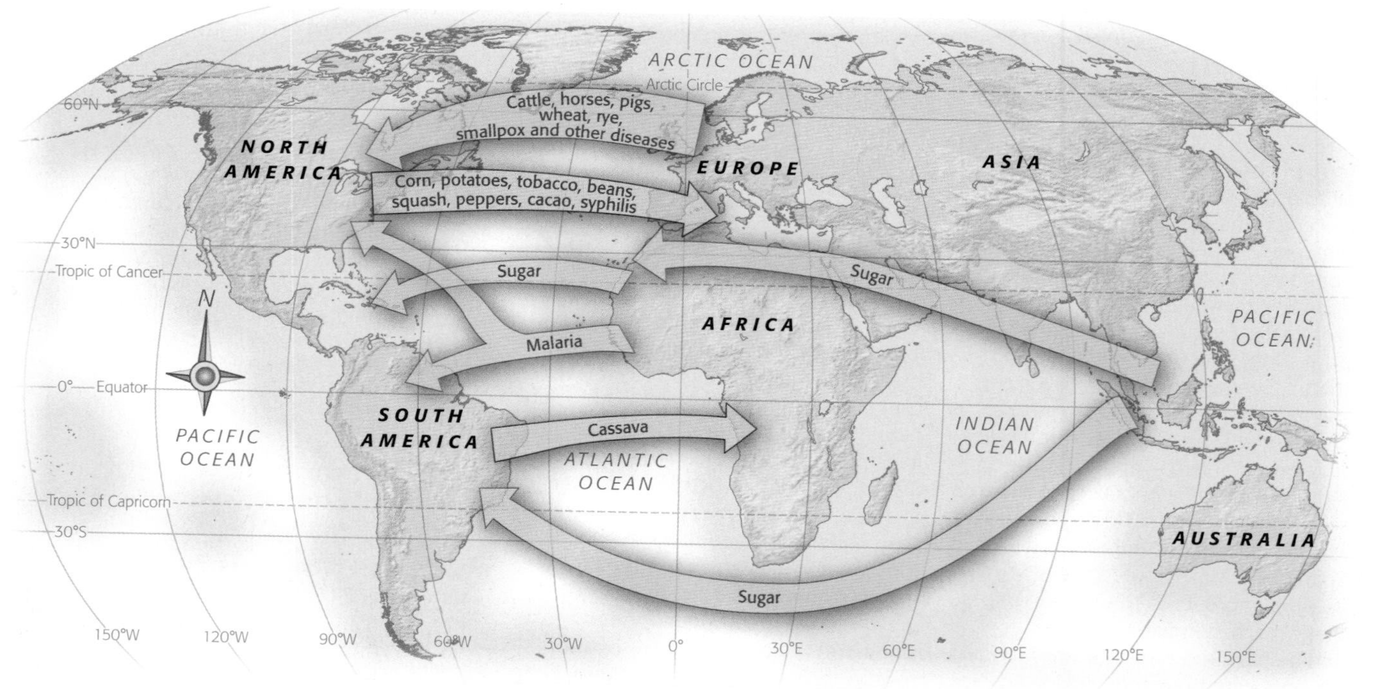

Map 2.6 Major Items of the Columbian Exchange With the linking of the Eastern and Western Hemispheres through commerce, trade carried plants, animals, people, and microbes back and forth across the Atlantic, dramatically altering the societies, economies, and ecosystems of the Americas, Europe, and Africa. ▲

Summary

In one way, at least, the sixteenth century closed much as it had begun. Because every French and English settlement along the Atlantic Coast had failed or been destroyed, Spain remained unrivaled in the New World. But in every other way, both Europe and the Americas had been transformed. In the Americas, the Spanish conquests and colonial policies killed untold millions of Indians and greatly increased Spain's power. In Europe, the discovery and conquest of the Americas reoriented commerce and intensified competition among nations. Suddenly, Europeans who had felt hemmed in by the Ottoman Turks had other avenues for trade and expansion. The most dynamic trade then proceeded across the Atlantic rather than around the Mediterranean. European powers began competing for advantage in the Americas while Indians in the Americas sought to preserve their cultures and lives under European rule.

<Thinking Back, *Looking Forward*>

As you review this chapter, think about the role that organized religion played in European society and the effects on Europe and Africa of the Age of Expansion. What drove Europeans to venture so far beyond the Mediterranean? How did Europeans justify their overseas colonies? What unintended effects did the European discovery of the New World have? Why did Europe "discover" Africa and the Americas rather than vice versa? Are the processes of exploration and expansion universal human goals? In the next chapter, look for patterns in European settlement in the Americas and think about how different nations had their own goals and strategies for colonization.

To make your study concrete, review the timeline and reflect on the entries there. Think about their causes, consequences, and connections. How do they fit with global trends?

Additional Resources

Books

Alchon, Suzanne Austin. *A Pest in the Land; New World Epidemics in Global Perspective*. Albuquerque: University of New Mexico Press, 2003. ▶ Cogent discussion of epidemic disease in a global context.

Clendinnen, Inga. *Ambivalent Conquest: Maya and Spaniard in Yucatán, 1517–1570*. Cambridge, England: Cambridge University Press, 1987. ▶ Best account of early missionary activity in colonial Mexico.

Crosby, Alfred. *The Columbian Exchange: Biological and Cultural Consequences of 1492*. Westport CT: Greenwood Press, 1972. ▶ The pioneering discussion of the movement of plants, animals, and germs across the Atlantic after Columbus.

Elliott, J. H. *The Old World and New, 1492–1650*. Cambridge, England: Cambridge University Press, 1970. ▶ Illuminating essays on what Europeans made of the discovery of the Americas.

Kupperman, Karen O. *Roanoke: The Abandoned Colony*. Totowa, NJ: Rowman & Allanheld, 1984. ▶ Excellent account of England's failed first North American colony.

Lockhart, James. *The Nahuas after the Conquest*. Stanford, CA: Stanford University Press, 1992. ▶ Brilliant exploration using the study of language to examine Indian life under Spanish rule.

Mancall, Peter C. *Hakluyt's Promise: An Elizabethan's Obsession for an English America*. New Haven, CT: Yale University Press, 2007. ▶ A penetrating examination of Hakluyt, England's most vociferous promoter of overseas colonization.

Phillips, Carla Rahn, and William Phillips. *The Worlds of Christopher Columbus*. Cambridge, England: Cambridge University Press, 1992. ▶ Brilliant and readable account of the world's most famous maritime explorer.

Reséndez, Andrés. *A Land So Strange: The Epic Journey of Cabeza de Vaca*. New York: Basic Books, 2007. ▶ Exciting account of the transcontinental journey of Cabeza de Vaca.

Townsend, Camilla. *Malintzin's Choices: An Indian Woman in the Conquest of Mexico*. Albuquerque: University of New Mexico Press, 2006. ▶ Complex and sympathetic biography of the Indian woman who helped Cortés conquer Mexico.

Go to the MindTap® for **Global Americans** to access the full version of select books from this Additional Resources section.

Websites

1492: An Ongoing Voyage. (http://www.loc.gov/exhibits/1492/) ▶ Website devoted to the Columbian voyages.

Early Canada Online. (http://eco.canadiana.ca/) ▶ Complete archive relating to most aspects of New France.

MindTap®

Continue exploring online through MindTap®, where you can:

- **Assess your knowledge with the Chapter Test**
- **Watch historical videos related to the chapter**
- **Further your understanding with interactive maps and timelines**

Joining the Hemispheres, Europe, Africa, and the Americas

3,000 BCE–1 CE

3000 BCE

Agriculture emerges in the eastern Mediterranean.

2,000 BCE

Minoans become first maritime power in the Mediterranean.

1,000 BCE

Phoenicians dominate Mediterranean trade with Asia.

323 BCE

Alexander the Great creates empire stretching from Greece to Asia.

2–999 CE

117

Romans exert control over the Mediterranean.

400

Christianity becomes official religion of Rome.

570

Muhammad is born.

1000–1249

1001

Ericson establishes Vinland in Newfoundland.

1095

Catholic Church launches first Christian Crusade to the Holy Land (Palestine).

1182

France expels Jews.

1215

King John of England signs *Magna Carta*.

1250–1349

1260

Mongols initiate the largest land empire in history, extending from the Black Sea to the Pacific coast of China and Korea.

1275

Marco Polo travels the Silk Road to China.

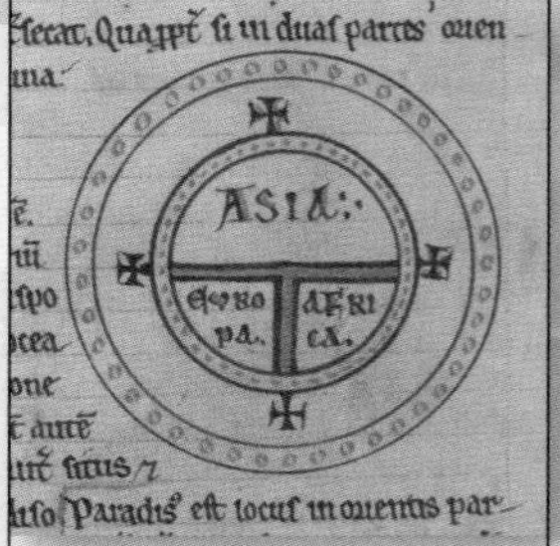

1300

Capitalism emerges

The Renaissance begins.

1347

Black Death plague devastates Europe.

1350–1499

1420s

Portuguese explore the coast of West Africa.

1425

Portuguese introduce sugar cultivation to Madeira Island.

1454

Gutenberg invents movable type.

1492

Columbus makes landfall in the Caribbean.

Spain expels Jews and Muslims and completes *Reconquista*.

1493

Papal donation grants Spain control over New World lands.

1494

Spanish and Portuguese sign Treaty of Tordesillas.

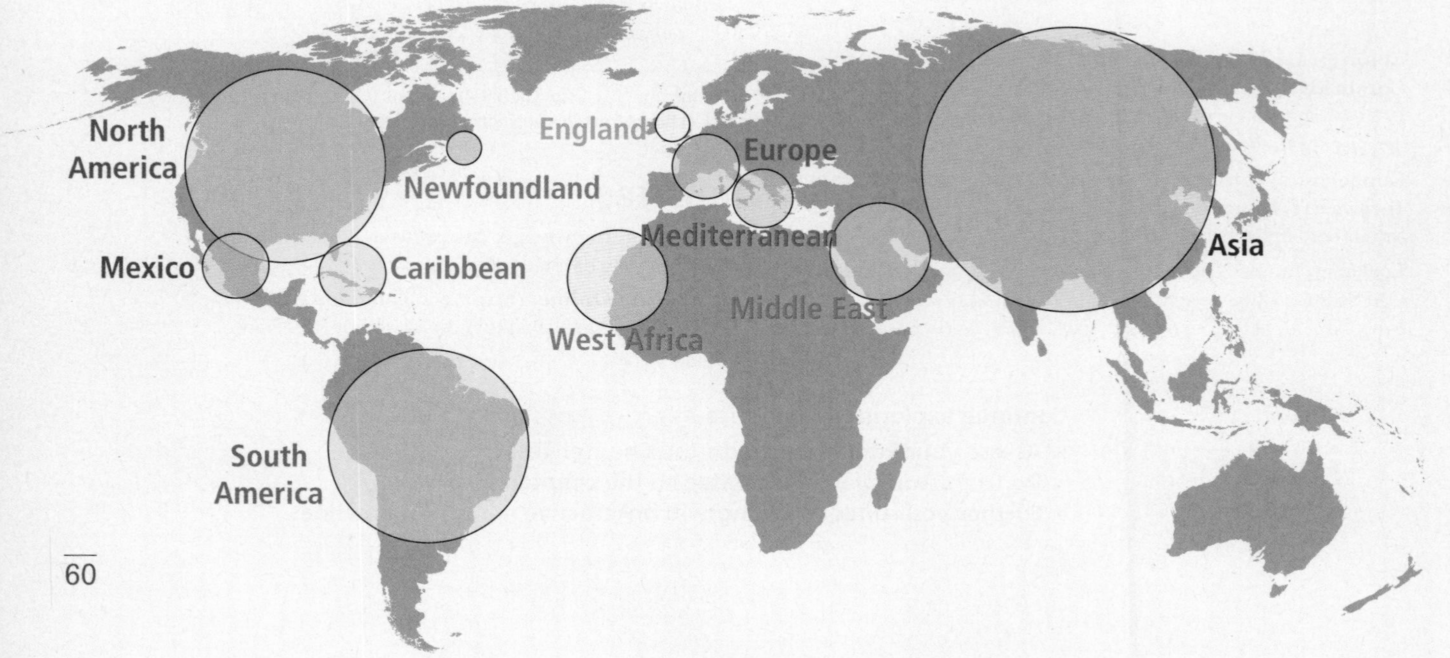

1500–1519

1500

Cabral sails to Brazil.

Istanbul becomes Europe's largest city.

1503

Spain establishes the *Casa de Contratación*.

1517

Protestant Reformation begins.

1519

Cortés sails from Cuba to mainland to begin conquest of Mexico.

1520–1539

1521

Cortés conquers Mexico.

1522

Magellan's crew completes circumnavigation of the globe.

1528

Narváez expedition ventures to Florida.

1532

Spain initiates conquest of Peru.

1534

Cartier voyages to New France.

1539

De Soto explores Florida.

1540–1559

1540

Coronado explores the American Southwest.

1542

Spain's New Laws abolish slavery in the New World.

1543

Counter-Reformation begins with Council of Trent (1563).

1560–1579

1565

Menéndez de Aviles destroys Fort Caroline and establishes St. Augustine.

1572

Spaniards murder Túpac Amaru, the last Inca ruler.

1579

Drake claims California for England.

1580–1590

1581

Union of Utrecht creates United Provinces of the Netherlands.

1585

English establish settlement on Roanoke Island.

1588

English navy destroys Spanish Armada.

1590

English find Roanoke settlement abandoned.

Go to MindTap® to engage with an interactive version of the timeline. Analyze events and themes with clickable content, view related videos, and respond to critical thinking questions.

3 Experimentation, Resistance, and Persistence

1585–1650

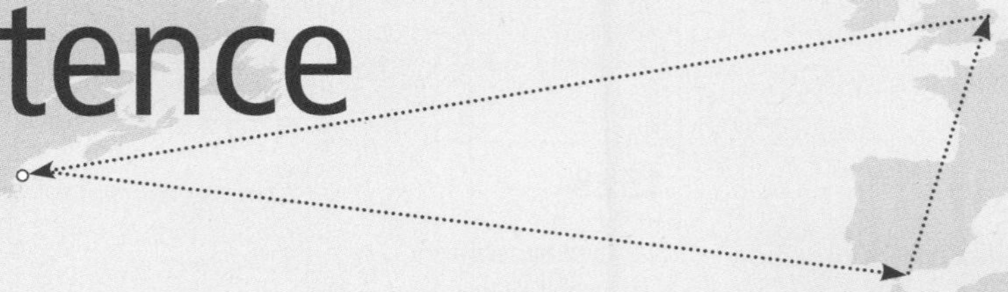

Tisquantum, who is known to most Americans as Squanto, was taken as a slave to Spain and made his way back to his village of Pawtuxet as an interpreter for a colonial English venture.

3-1
Spain and France in the Borderlands

3-1a Florida and the Timucuas and Guales
3-1b New Mexico and the Pueblo Indians
3-1c New France and the Wendats (Hurons)
3-1d Missionaries and Indians
3-1e Life in New France and New Mexico

3-2
New Netherland

3-2a Rise of the Dutch
3-2b Dutch West Indian Company
3-2c Life in New Netherland

3-3
Establishment of Virginia

3-3a Jamestown Settlement in the Shadow of Spain
3-3b Conflict in Tsenacomoco, 1609–1614
3-3c Reorganization and Tobacco
3-3d Opechancanough's Rebellions

3-4
Formation of New England

3-4a Separatists of Plymouth Plantation
3-4b Establishment of the Massachusetts Bay Colony
3-4c Dissenters in New England
3-4d Puritans and Pequots
3-4e Life in the Chesapeake and New England

3-5
African Slavery in the Americas

3-5a Sugar Revolution in the West Indies
3-5b Plantation Laborers: Servants to Slaves
3-5c Slave Life in the West Indies
3-5d African Slavery on the Mainland: The Early Years

Every Thanksgiving, Americans commemorate the American creation story. The tale goes something like this: When a handful of English settlers first arrived in 1620 in what would become New England, they were cold, tired, and hungry. Had it not been for the generosity of an Indian named Squanto who taught them how to plant corn and how to fish, these settlers, the Pilgrims, would have perished. The next fall after a bountiful harvest, the Pilgrims welcomed Squanto and other Indians to a great feast of thanksgiving to celebrate their survival. This familiar story suggests that the Indians and English formed friendships and partnerships that were at the core of the early American experience. It also suggests that the English were the first Europeans to come to America and that their early relations with Indians were peaceful.

Massachusetts Historical Society

This carved elm burl porridge bowl is a work of Wampanoag craftsmanship and may date to the 17th century. It carries an inscription that in part reads: "A Trophy from the Wigwam of King Philip When he was Slain in 1676." ▲

Although most Americans know this tale, few are familiar with the biography of Squanto and the degree to which he, like most people in colonial America, moved between worlds and crossed boundaries. Squanto's full name was Tisquantum, or "powerful other than human." In 1614, English explorers captured him and twenty-seven other Pawtuxet Indians to sell them into slavery. Transported to Spain, Tisquantum was taken in by Franciscan friars. Somehow he made his way to London by 1617. He subsequently returned to his homeland in March 1619 as an interpreter attached to an English colonial expedition.

He found that his tribe, the Pawtuxet, was gone. Between 1616 and 1618, a catastrophic epidemic, most likely transmitted by French fur traders, had devastated his people. The land that the English had once described as "the Paradise of all those parts" had become, said a later settler, "a new found Golgotha," the biblical "place of skulls." A refugee in his own homeland, Tisquantum was taken captive by the Pokonokets, a tribe within the larger group of affliated peoples known as the Wampanoag. Soon Tisquantum befriended their chief, Massasoit. Through Massasoit, Tisquantum contacted the Pilgrims, who had unknowingly founded their colony where his people had once lived. Realizing that his survival was tied to the English, Tisquantum taught the newcomers Pawtuxet methods of maize cultivation. Thus, by the time he encountered them, he was a global traveler well versed in English ways who acted as much out of self-interest as out of concern for the struggling Europeans. The colonial world he knew was not one of harmonious coexistence between Native Americans and Europeans but of conflict, enslavement, disease, and tense negotiation. Tisquantum succumbed to disease in 1622 and passed into myth as Squanto, the noble and generous Native American behind our Thanksgiving celebrations.

In Tisquantum's experiences, we can see the outlines of so many others who lived in early America. From the late sixteenth century through the middle of the seventeenth century, the Spanish, French, Dutch, and English had extensive contacts with other Native Americans as they sought to expand their existing colonies or begin new ones. With the colonization of various regions of North America (see Table 3.1), Europeans brought disease and dislocation to the local peoples. Indians

How do Tisquantum's experiences with the English and other Native American groups reflect the tensions, hardships, and opportunities of those who lived in early America?

Go to MindTap® to watch a video on Tisquantum and learn how his story relates to the themes of this chapter.

responded in creative ways, as Tisquantum had, as they tried to adjust to what was for them in many ways a vastly different world. Europeans also suffered in their early attempts to create settlements out of lands they knew poorly and came ill prepared to colonize. Just as Tisquantum had crossed the Atlantic under what were unique circumstances, great numbers of Europeans—some free, others bound laborers—voyaged across the sea, hoping to find new opportunity. Some did, but later generations of settlers would be the ones to most enjoy the fruits of the labors of the first colonists. Hardship—not bountiful feasts—was the common denominator of the first decades of intensive European settlement in North America.

3-1 Spain and France in the Borderlands

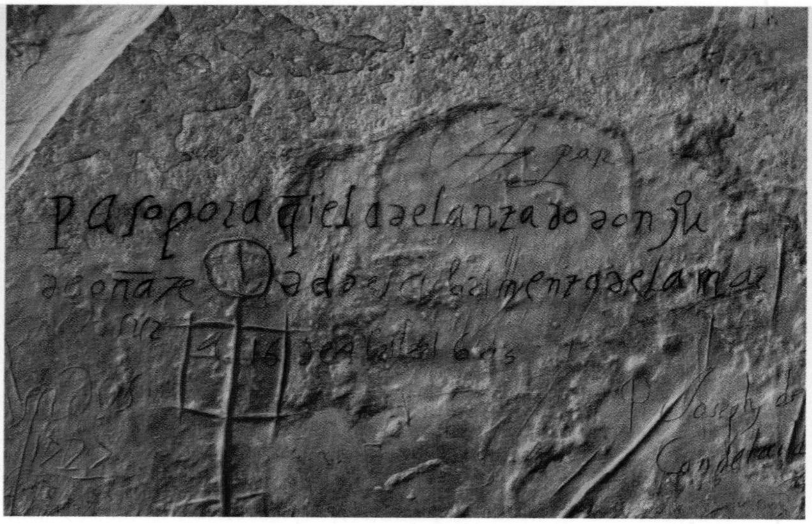

This rock carving on the El Morro National Monument is among the earliest records of the Spanish exploration and settlement in New Mexico. It reads, "The adelantado Don Juan de Oñate passed by here from the discovery of the Sea of the South [as the Spanish knew the Pacific Ocean] on April 16, 1605."

Why would Juan de Oñate carve his name into this rock? How does Oñate describe himself? ►

Witold Skrypczak/Alamy Stock Photo

In the late sixteenth century, Spain expanded existing settlements in the Caribbean and northern Mexico and founded colonies in Florida and New Mexico. In both regions, the Spanish monarchy relied on wealthy men to fund and organize the new settlements, but in both areas, the colonies struggled and were eventually taken over by the crown. Another similarity was that in both regions, the Spanish exploited native people for food and labor. In New France (present-day Eastern Canada), in contrast, the French treated Indians far better than the Spanish, relying on them for help in hunting animals for fur, which was extremely valuable in Europe. Only later did France establish full agricultural settlements in Quebec and Montreal. Life for the mostly young and male Europeans in these colonial settlements varied greatly because Spain and France administered their colonies in different ways.

adelantamiento Royal grant of economic and political privilege to a man in return for his undertaking the conquest of a frontier territory.

adelantado Person to whom an *adelantamiento* is granted.

royal colony A crown-controlled colony ruled by a governor appointed by the monarch.

situado Annual payment or expense from the Spanish crown to maintain the province of Florida.

☞ As you read, consider how the different colonial strategies of Spain and France led to remarkably varied settlements in the regions they claimed as their own. What distinguished one colonial region from another?

3-1a Florida and the Timucuas and Guales

Spain establishes a foothold in Florida through fortifications, missions, and Indian labor, seeking to protect the sea-lanes that carried treasure from New Spain to Iberia.

With the death of Menéndez de Aviles in 1574 and the abandonment of St. Elena in 1576, Spain was left with a single military outpost in Florida, St. Augustine. Well into the seventeenth century, Spanish Florida remained a defensive enterprise intended to protect the Spanish treasure fleet as it sailed for Spain. King Phillip II of Spain had offered an ***adelantamiento***, a royal concession of economic and political privilege to a wealthy man who planned to undertake, at his own expense, the conquest of a frontier territory. But defending Florida's long coastline against a French return and the potential arrival of the English required more money than any ***adelantado*** possessed. So Florida quickly became a **royal colony** for which the crown spent nearly sixty-five thousand pesos per year to defend. The bulk of the ***situado***, as the cost of sustaining Florida was called, went to support Spanish soldiers stationed at St. Augustine.

Beyond St. Augustine, the second major Spanish institution in Florida was a sprawling chain of Catholic missions. Although the Jesuits had failed to create missions among the Florida Indians, the Franciscans who began to arrive in 1573 succeeded, founding dozens of missions in the region that today encompasses Florida, Georgia, South Carolina, and Alabama. By 1655, more than forty missions in Florida manned by seventy Franciscans ministered to at least twenty-six thousand Indians. Many of these Indians were Guale, Timucua, Apalachee, and Apalachicola refugees whose tribes had been decimated by diseases introduced by De Soto in the 1530s.

The Spanish governors of Florida cultivated allies among the native elite, known to them as ***caciques***, by offering them clothing, knives, beads, cloths, scissors, and hatchets. With the support of these elites, Spanish soldiers and the Franciscans instituted the *repartimiento*, drawing laborers from Indian villages, who were compensated by their *caciques* with the gifts they received from the Spaniards.

A final pillar of Spanish colonization in Florida was the ***sabana*** system in which Indians affiliated with missions planted corn, wheat, beans, and other crops to support not only the Franciscans and themselves but also the soldiers at St. Augustine. The *repartimiento* turned Indian men into conscript laborers for only a week each year, but the *sabana* turned Indian women into peasants for months on end. Nevertheless, the Spanish system in Florida was built on well-established Indian practices. Spanish governors worked through Indian leaders who had long appropriated agricultural labor and tribute from their vassals. But the Indians did not always tolerate their Spanish overlords and rebellions became common.

3-1b New Mexico and the Pueblo Indians

In New Mexico, Juan de Oñate establishes Spanish settlements that exploit Indians.

New Mexico lacked the strategic importance of Florida, but the colony's settlement was similar: It began with a violent conquest and failed *adelantamiento*. The crown soon took over sending missionaries and soldiers. New Mexico emerged from the fantasies and treasure of Juan de Oñate, scion of one of New Spain's most successful silver mining families. Oñate won a contract from Phillip II to conquer New Mexico and promised to deliver to the king "a new world, greater than New Spain."

With such dreams dancing in his head, in 1598, Oñate crossed the Rio Grande River with 129 soldiers, a number of settlers, seven Franciscans, and several thousand sheep, horses, goats, oxen, and cattle. He asked the Pueblo Indians to "voluntarily" accept the supreme authority of the crown and the Pope. With the memory of how Coronado had burned alive villagers from Arenal, few challenged Oñate.

Oñate established his headquarters among the Tewa in the pueblo of Okhe, which he renamed San Juan. The Tewa were agricultural and lived in permanent multistory adobe and stone dwellings. Unprepared for winter in New Mexico, Oñate's soldiers and officers made increasing demands on the Tewa for food and clothing, and some even resorted to murder, torture, and rape. At the pueblo of Acoma, cultural misunderstandings and Spanish aggression led to crisis. When a Spanish soldier stole two turkeys, a bird sacred to the Acomas, and then raped an Indian woman, the Acomans attacked and killed Spaniards, including a nephew of Oñate.

In revenge, a Spanish army of 72 men destroyed Acoma, killing more than 800 men, women, and children and taking hundreds more captive. Oñate found the Indian captives guilty of murder. He sentenced those over the age of 12 to 20 years of servitude. In a bloody spectacle, Oñate's men severed one foot of all male captives over age 25.

A central institution of the colonization of New Mexico (see Map 3.1) was the *encomienda*, which the New Laws had phased out in central New Spain. But in 1601, Oñate revived the system to reward himself and his followers, requiring the dozens of pueblo communities under his jurisdiction to pay annual tribute in return for military protection, which the Indians did not need. Perhaps even more oppressive was the *repartimiento*, which was more harsh than in Florida.

Despite the wealth that he gained from the *encomienda*, Oñate was soon bankrupt, and in 1606, King Phillip replaced him with a royal governor. Oñate remained in the colony until he was finally banished for abusing Indians. But the colony survived. The 90 leading Spaniards in the region eked out a living growing corn, wheat, and vegetables, and raising cattle. They extracted what wealth and labor they could from Indians and depended on provisions from Mexico. In 1608, after Oñate's departure from the colony, the Spanish established Santa Fé, which became the capital of New Mexico in 1610.

If the Franciscans had not bestowed **baptism** on Indians in New Mexico, the crown would have abandoned the colony. But missionaries successfully argued that the crown could not forsake baptized Indians. By the late 1630s, nearly one thousand settlers controlled most of the land and water in New Mexico, and they still depended on thousands of Indians for labor and goods. This exploitative colonial system endured through the 1670s, in part because the Spanish in New Mexico, as in Florida, enriched Indian leaders with gifts.

caciques Title derived from the Taino language that the Spaniards across their possessions applied to Indians they identified as among the leadership elite.

sabana System in Florida in which Spaniards forced Indians at missions to raise agricultural products to feed the mission, missionaries, and soldiers.

baptism Christian sacramental process of formalizing admission into the Christian Church.

3-1c New France and the Wendats (Hurons)

> In New France, the French and the Wendat cooperate to create a commercial frontier centered on beaver skins.

Far to the north of Florida in what is now eastern Canada, the French developed a far less coercive colony, one based on a cooperative relationship between themselves and Indians. In the decades after Cartier abandoned his St. Lawrence River settlements, low-level trade between the French and Indians resumed in the dry fishery camps on the Atlantic Coast. There the French processed their catch from the Grand Banks. Before long, this trade became an industry of its own. The French would trade metal, glass, and cloth to Indians for food and animal skins. The French valued beaver fur above most other goods because beaver fur was scarce in Europe where the animals had been hunted to extinction. The production of fur did not require French laborers or the coercion or enslavement of Indians. Instead, Indians trapped the animals, processed the fur, and transported it to the coast for purchase by the French. When the broad-brimmed beaver felt hat became fashionable in western Europe in the early sixteenth century, the Canadian fur trade exploded.

monopoly The complete control of the entire supply of goods or a service in a certain area or market usually granted by the government.

In 1598, the French King Henry IV renewed a grant to the nobleman Troilus de Mesgouez, marquis de La Roche, giving him a **monopoly**, which granted complete control of specific goods, over trade between Canada and France. Yet neither La Roche nor his successor, Pierre Du Gua, sieur de Monts, was able to enforce the monopoly. There were simply too many places along the coast where Indians and the French could trade. In 1607, de Monts's men abandoned Canada, but the following year, one of his associates, Samuel de Champlain, ventured to a narrow point up the St. Lawrence River and established Quebec, which was his rendering of the Algonquin term for *narrow passage*.

Champlain wanted to secure furs in the interior before they could make their way to coastal trading posts frequented by rival traders. His plan was to forge trading partnerships with the local Algonquins, Algonquin-speaking Innus (Montagnais), and the Iroquois-speaking Wendats (Hurons), whose villages lay hundreds of miles farther west (see Map 3.2).

The trade at first proved beneficial to all involved. The French profited by exchanging a knife for a pelt that could later be sold for 200 times the knife's original value. The local people profited too. For millennia, the Wendats had traded with Indians beyond their own region, eager to acquire exotic goods like those the French now brought. To maintain the trade, the French had to learn the Wendats

Map 3.1 Colonial New Mexico and Its Native Peoples, Sixteenth and Seventeenth Centuries Pueblo Indian communities were concentrated along the Río Grand River more than a thousand miles north of Mexico City. ▼

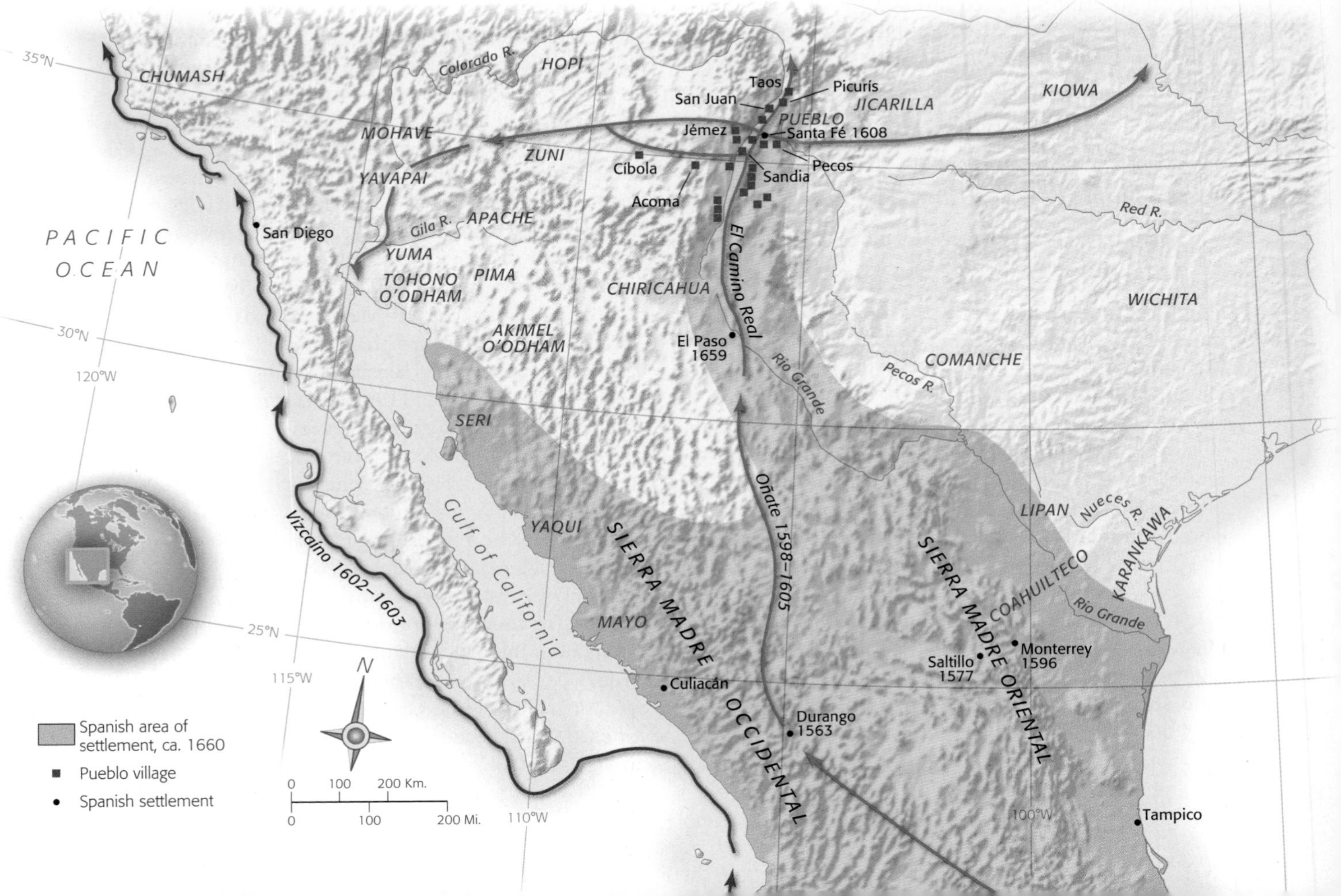

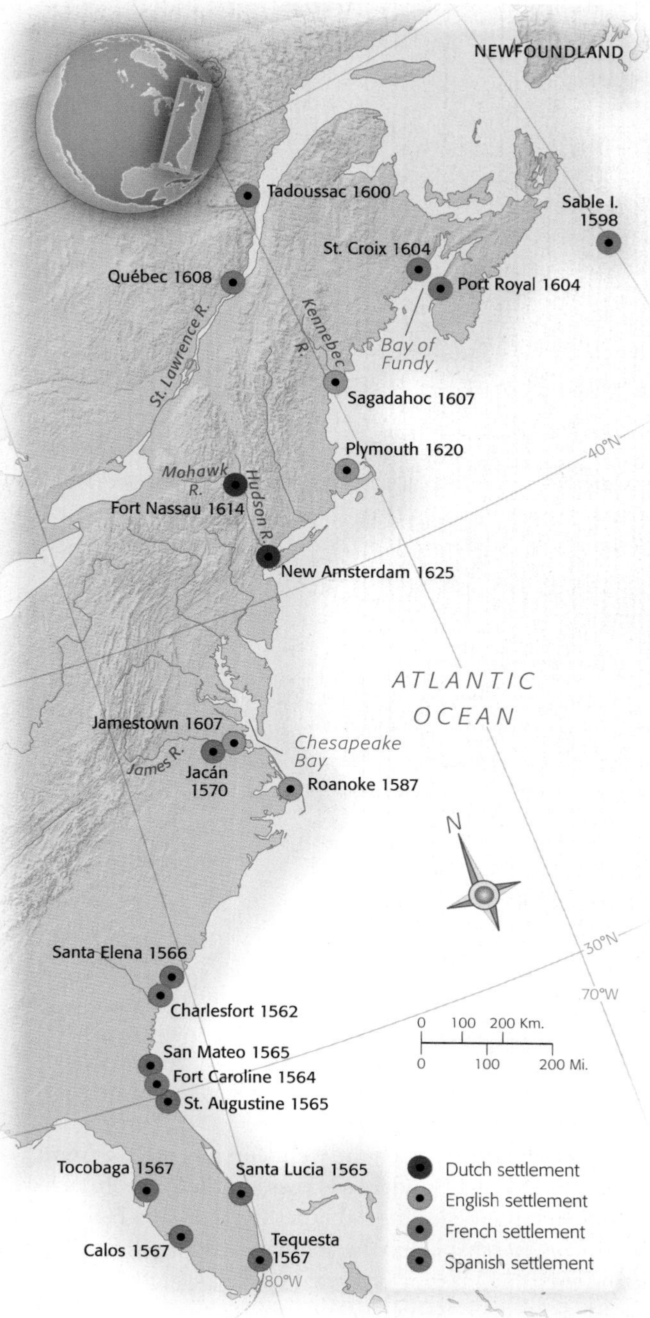

Map 3.2 European Settlements in Eastern North America, 1565–1625 Between the 1560s and the 1620s, European powers established numerous competing settlements along the coast of eastern North America as they jockeyed with one another for control over lands and native peoples. ▲

language and pledge to support the Wendats in their conflict against their traditional enemies to the south, the Haudenosaunees (Iroquois). Except for urging the Indians to collect larger numbers of furs, at first the French did not disrupt their lives. French traders often dressed like Indians, learned to paddle canoes and wear snowshoes, and joined in many ritual activities, such as hunting and steam baths. Some traders lived with Wendat women.

The French decision in 1627 to transfer de Monts's monopoly to a new group, the Company of 100 Associates, signaled a new era in New France. Composed of a large number of especially devout Catholics, the Company pressured Champlain to give Jesuit missionaries a leading role in French relations with Indian trading partners. Jesuit missionaries became most active in an area controlled by the Wendats, who accepted missionaries only after Champlain threatened them with the end of the trade. The years in which the Jesuits lived in Wendat lands coincided with devastating epidemics that reduced the Wendat's numbers, made them vulnerable to Haudenosaunee attacks, and undermined French control of the fur trade.

3-1d Missionaries and Indians

Catholic missionaries across the Americas prompt change and rebellion among Indians.

Catholic missionaries were integral to Indian–European relations in most frontier regions settled by France and Spain in the Americas. But nearly everywhere the missionaries appeared, disease, conflict, and tragedy undermined their ambitions and legacies and brought destruction and pain to Indians. The leaders of Spain and France saw it as their responsibility to bring Catholicism to Native Americans, and they concluded that Catholic missionaries, who took vows of poverty and were often funded by their own orders, were an inexpensive means of colonizing. But missionaries were not restricted to the Americas. As part of the Counter-Reformation, they also spread across Europe and Asia, attempting to bring their version of Christianity to millions of people.

In North America, the most active missionaries were **Franciscans**, whose blend of piety, poverty, and zeal made them a favorite of the Spanish crown. They came to the Americas by the thousands, establishing missions in Florida, Texas, New Mexico, Arizona, and California. Followers of the Society of Jesus, known as **Jesuits**, established missions in New France, Florida, Arizona, and Lower California.

Catholic missionaries had a common approach to Indians. Missionaries directed their efforts at children, who they believed were easier to convert than adults. They demanded that adult Indians live in sedentary communities, avoid premarital sex, practice lifelong monogamy, adopt European agricultural techniques, and attend catechism and Mass. Some Indians converted, but others rejected the missionaries and their beliefs. Most Indians were more interested in the food and trade goods the missionaries provided than the religious instruction they offered. Nearly all missionaries met with opposition and thus depended on soldiers for their survival.

Franciscans Members of a devout Roman Catholic order who adhere to teachings of Saint Francis of Assisi (1181/1182–1226), who preached poverty and the spread of the Gospel.

Jesuits Roman Catholic male religious order founded in 1540 by Francis Xavier and Ignatius of Loyola.

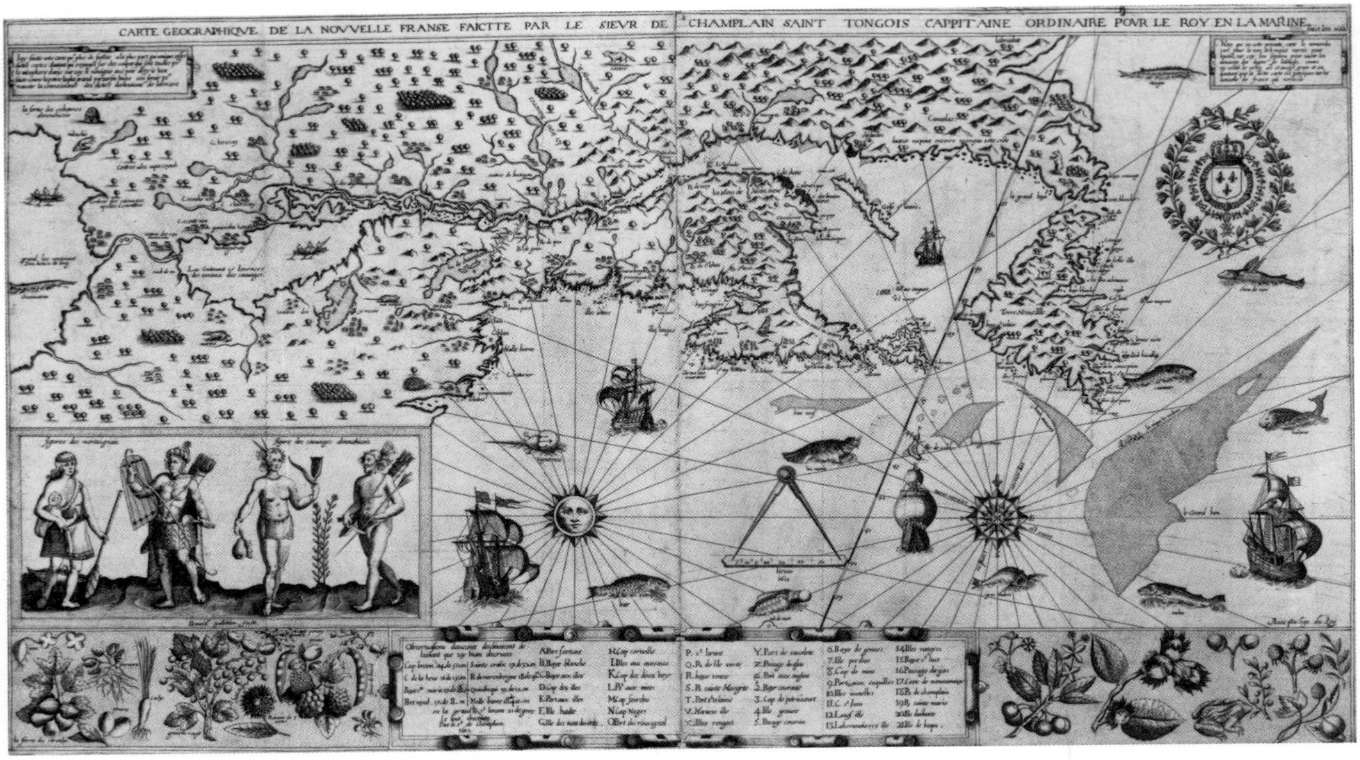

MPI/Getty Images

Detailed Portraits of Indians from Champlain's 1612 Map Archaeology suggests that the fur trade in the early sixteenth century ushered in a period of change in Wendat culture. Wendat peoples began to substitute tools of iron for those of stone. They put unfamiliar items to new uses, making arrowheads and ornaments out of copper kettles. With access to tools that simplified daily tasks, the Wendat had time for other pursuits and enjoyed a burst of creativity revealed in surviving artifacts including combs, pipes, masks, and pendants. ▲

Indians who failed to attend Mass or committed what the missionaries considered to be sexual transgressions, theft, or acts of idolatry were imprisoned or whipped. Missionaries believed that once Indians had consented to baptism, they were the missionaries' spiritual children who had agreed to live according to Catholic notions of morality, marriage, and sexuality.

Lethal epidemics that coincided with the arrival of missionaries created chaos in Native American communities. In humid Florida, where contagion spread quickly, epidemics in 1595, 1612, 1616, 1649, 1650, and 1655 wiped out entire villages. Those that survived were unable to meet Spanish demands for male laborers. In response, Indians launched coordinated attacks on the Florida missions. In 1577 and 1597, the Guales killed missionaries and burned missions. In both instances, the Spanish responded by killing hundreds of Indians and torching numerous villages. In New Mexico, Indian resentment exploded periodically, including in December 1639 when Indians at Taos and Jémez Pueblos killed their Franciscans and two soldier–settlers and then destroyed the mission church.

In New France in the 1630s, half of the thirty-five thousand Wendats died from smallpox after the arrival of the Jesuits. Some Wendats believed that the Jesuits—who remained healthy—deliberately spread disease. They saw the Jesuits' celibacy as indicative of supernatural power and came to associate baptism with death. The Wendats had relied on Jesuit assurances that they would protect them in the event of a Haudenosaunee attack. During the late 1640s, however, when the Wendats were reeling from epidemics and the Haudenosaunees attacked, the French accompanying the Jesuits did little. By 1650, the Haudenosaunees had dispersed the Wendats. Missionaries then abandoned the interior of New France and retreated to the St. Lawrence River Valley with their converts. The French fur trade also collapsed, undone by missionaries, diseases, and the Haudenosaunee onslaught.

3-1e Life in New France and New Mexico

In both New France and New Mexico, colonial society is marked by economic inequality and political instability.

As long as the fur trade had been profitable, the French had little reason to settle Canada. Thus, in the 1620s, there were only seventy French colonists in New France. Over the following decades, however, French settlement gradually expanded up the St. Lawrence River with the

Mary Evans Picture Library/Alamy Stock Photo

Global Americans **María de Jesús de Ágreda** was a Franciscan nun who lived in Spain between 1601 and 1665. Born into an exceptionally devout Catholic family, she was said to have manifested extraordinary spiritual gifts from an early age. A well-known mystic, she wrote a series of influential books in which she recounted what she claimed were revelations from the Virgin Mary. She lived at a time when exceptionally spiritual Catholics claimed to experience levitation and many other paranormal phenomena. María de Jesús claimed to have been carried to what is now present-day New Mexico and Texas on the wings of saints and to have been protected there by angels. She asserted that she had preached the Gospel to Indians in their native languages in what is now the Southwest and awakened in Indians a desire for Catholic conversion. Although no Spaniard had ever seen her in New Spain and she was said never to have left her convent, her stunningly accurate descriptions of the Indians of New Mexico won over many who had been detractors and skeptics. Franciscan missionaries found her writings deeply inspirational and took from them and her claims to have traveled to the Americas proof that God favored them in the evangelization of the New World and was aiding the spread of the Gospel in miraculous ways.

establishment of Trois-Rivieres in 1634 and Montreal in 1642. At the same time, the lower St. Lawrence increasingly became the home of displaced native peoples. Montaignais groups, having hunted the beaver to extinction in their desire to trade with the French, settled near Quebec in 1638. Algonquins fleeing the Haudenosaunees migrated to Trois-Rivieres and Montreal in the 1640s, and Wendat refugees arrived in Quebec in the early 1650s. Nearly all lived in Jesuit missions, separate from the French settlers.

Socially, the French colony strongly resembled rural France. The Company of 100 Associates granted dozens of ***seigneuries***, or tracts of land, to nobles, the Jesuits, merchants, and a few commoners. Those granted *seigneuries* were required to recruit settlers to live and work on them to make the concessions profitable or at least self-sustaining. The early *seigneuries* were long narrow lots on the St. Lawrence River encompassing hundreds of square miles. Lots such as these were common in France, particularly in Normandy, from which many early settlers recruited to live on the seigneuries came. Such lots could be easily surveyed and provided all who lived on them access to a river or a public road. In France, the families who lived on the lots were known as ***habitants*** and paid annual rents to their ***seigneur***.

To populate and work the land of the Canadian *seignuries*, the Company did not recruit French families because few would have risked the long journey to a harsh land. Nor did it look to refugee Indians. Rather, it recruited nearly two thousand penniless, male **indentured servants**, known to the French as ***engagés***. They committed themselves to three years of work in return for room and board and the promise of a small tract of land when their obligations had been fulfilled. If all went well, they became *habitants* on their own land.

In comparison, life across the continent in New Mexico was riven by conflict to a far greater degree than in New France. Pueblo Indians, Spanish Franciscans, and soldier–settlers all competed for limited resources in an exploitative and divided colony. Most of the early settlers were single men who often married Pueblo Indian women or took them as concubines. There was no *presidio*, or military garrison, in New Mexico. Rather, the king expected settlers to bear arms and defend the colony.

After the collapse of Oñate's rule, the governors who followed him viewed the office as a path to wealth. Each knew that in a land without mineral wealth, his gains would depend on the exploitation of Indians. But each successive governor was undermined by powerful Franciscans who believed that soldiers' demands on Indians threatened the Christian society they hoped to establish among the Indians. In the five decades after Oñate stepped down, seventeen men assumed the governorship, and nearly all suffered ruin as a result of Franciscan resistance.

In New Mexico, land and Indian laborers were the key to wealth, and more than sixty soldiers received *encomienda* grants. The yields of the *encomienda* grants, however, declined along with the Pueblo Indians, who suffered terribly from introduced diseases. A smallpox epidemic killed about twenty thousand Pueblo Indians in 1636, reducing their number by one-third. With the population in decline across the Rio Grande Valley, the Spanish forced the Pueblo people to congregate into some forty-three towns, and in 1643, the Spanish shifted the onus of the *encomienda* tribute from the declining communities to the surviving individuals. Each Indian was then required to provide one cotton blanket and 2.6 bushels of corn each quarter.

seigneuries Large tracts of land granted in New France.

habitants Free settlers in New France who generally farmed land they leased from a *seigneur*.

seigneur Holder of a *seigneurie*.

indentured servants Person bound by contract to work for another for a specified time, usually in return for payment of travel expenses and maintenance.

engagés French term for indentured servants.

3-2

New Netherland

Niday Picture Library/Alamy Stock Photo

View of New Amsterdam, painted by Johannes Vingboons in approximately 1664, shows the city as seen from the Hudson River. The windmill in the background and the architecture of the buildings are typically Dutch.

What does this image tell us about the nature of Dutch settlement in New Amsterdam? ▶

Long before the Haudenosaunees overran the Wendats in the 1640s, the Dutch had begun to challenge the French for dominance in the fur trade with Northeastern Woodlands peoples. In fact, the Dutch colony of New Netherland at first resembled New France in that it relied on the capital of private investors, trade with Indians, and the presence of large property holders. But the similarities largely end there. New Netherland developed along its own trajectory, which was shaped by the priorities of the Netherlands, a rising and tolerant Protestant maritime nation that devoted scant resources to the colony, offered few incentives to those who might immigrate, and was more concerned with its intense rivalry with Spain than growing this remote colony.

☞ As you read, consider how settlement and life in New Netherland compared to that in New France, New Mexico, and Florida. What was most distinctive about each colony?

3-2a Rise of the Dutch

The Dutch reject mercantilism and concentrate on trade, not the creation of overseas colonies.

During their struggle for independence from Catholic Spain in the late sixteenth century, the Dutch emerged as a great maritime power. As part of his plan to punish the Dutch for their revolt, in 1585 Phillip II imposed an embargo on all Dutch ships, forbidding them to trade directly with Spain or Portugal. Rather than breaking the Dutch merchant marine or the movement toward independence, Phillip's initiatives spurred the Dutch to new heights. Opting for the Atlantic over the continent, Dutch traders began to trade directly with merchants and producers in Africa, the Americas, and the East Indies. By the time the Spanish had lifted their ill-fated embargo, the Dutch merchant marine was the largest in Europe and had ties to traders in every corner of the known Atlantic. In 1602, the Dutch created the **Dutch East India Company (VOC)**, referred to as the *Company*, which allowed the Dutch to take the dominant position in trade with Asia from the Portuguese.

Dutch East India Company (VOC) Dutch trading company founded in 1602 and granted a twenty-one-year monopoly over trade with Asia.

Northwest Passage Passage by sea linking the Atlantic and Pacific Oceans searched for by Europeans but not discovered until the mid-twentieth century given the severity of the Arctic climate.

In 1609, the Company hired the Englishman Henry Hudson to search for a **Northwest Passage** to Asia with the aim of discovering the long-elusive direct route to the East Indies. The Company's goal was to establish a secure trading monopoly in Asia on behalf of the Netherlands. When Hudson found the northern route in the Arctic blocked by frozen seas, he sailed south along the Eastern coast of the North American continent and then inland, 160 miles up the river that was to bear his name. At present-day Albany, New York, he reached shallow water. Local Indians approached with furs they hoped to exchange for beads and other goods. In subsequent years, Dutch trading vessels returned to trade for beaver pelts with Mahicans and their neighbors to the West, the Haudenosaunee Mohawks. By 1614, the future site of Albany had become one of numerous places of annual exchange between Native American and Dutch traders, all under the direction of the New Netherlands Company. The optimistic Dutch began to refer to the whole region as New Netherland.

3-2b Dutch West India Company

To challenge the Spanish and establish overseas colonies, the Dutch create the West India Company.

Dutch exploration in New Netherland had begun during a short period of peace between the Netherlands and Spain. In 1621, however, Spain and the Netherlands slid back into war, and the Spanish attempted to destroy the Dutch trade in Europe and the Atlantic. In response, the Netherlands

National Maritime Museum, Greenwich, London, Caird Fund

A [Dutch] Ship in a Rough Sea When Spain and the Dutch signed a truce in 1609, the Dutch used the respite from hostilities to extend their power throughout the Atlantic. For the most part, the Dutch staked their prosperity on organizing and carrying the trade of other nations. ▲

immediately created the **Dutch West India Company (WIC)** to challenge the Spanish, and bolster or create Dutch settlements in Africa and North and South America. By the 1640s, the WIC had control over nearly 1,000 merchant or war ships and had captured or destroyed more than 600 Spanish vessels.

In 1624, the Dutch renamed their trading post on the Hudson Fort Orange, and, to bolster their claim to the territory and to protect the mouth of the Hudson from foreign incursions, they officially established the colony of New Netherland. The colony was bounded by the Delaware and the Connecticut Rivers and populated by several dozen French-speaking refugees from what is now Belgium. In its first decades, New Netherland subsisted through its monopoly over the beaver trade, and the WIC exported 16,300 beaver pelts in 1635. Eventually, the WIC sought to encourage people to migrate and trade at their own expense by suspending the monopoly on the trade of fur. By the mid-1650s, Dutch traders were exporting 80,000 pelts per year from New Netherland, but the WIC still struggled to make a profit from the colony.

Despite its investment in New Netherland, the WIC's main interest was in the South Atlantic and the coast of Africa. During peacetime, Dutch ships had carried large amounts of sugar directly to Amsterdam's twenty-nine sugar refineries. But in the early 1620s, when Spain and the Netherlands were again at war, Amsterdam had no supply of sugar. In 1624, Holland shocked Spain by seizing Bahia, the capital of Brazil, but a Spanish fleet carrying 12,500 soldiers forced the Dutch out within a year. Over the following two decades, the Dutch were able to conquer half of the fourteen captaincies of Brazil, naming them New Holland, and established sugar plantations. Needing a steady supply of laborers for these plantations, the Dutch through the WIC became very involved in the transatlantic slave trade. In these years, the Dutch also established a colony in Guiana along eight hundred miles of the South American coastline as well as one at the Southern Cape of Africa, known as Cape Colony or Cape Town. New Netherland, however, languished in obscurity, attracting few settlers and little interest from the Netherlands.

Dutch West India Company (WIC) Dutch trading company founded in 1621 to develop and promote Dutch trading interests in competition with Spain, Portugal, and England.

Manhattan Situated on the North River, **1639** In 1628, the WIC fortified the town that became known as New Amsterdam. By 1630, about 270 settlers, including many whole families, lived along the island's southern tip. ►

Vinckeboons, Joan/Library of Congress Geography and Map Division Washington, D.C. 20540–4650 USA dcu

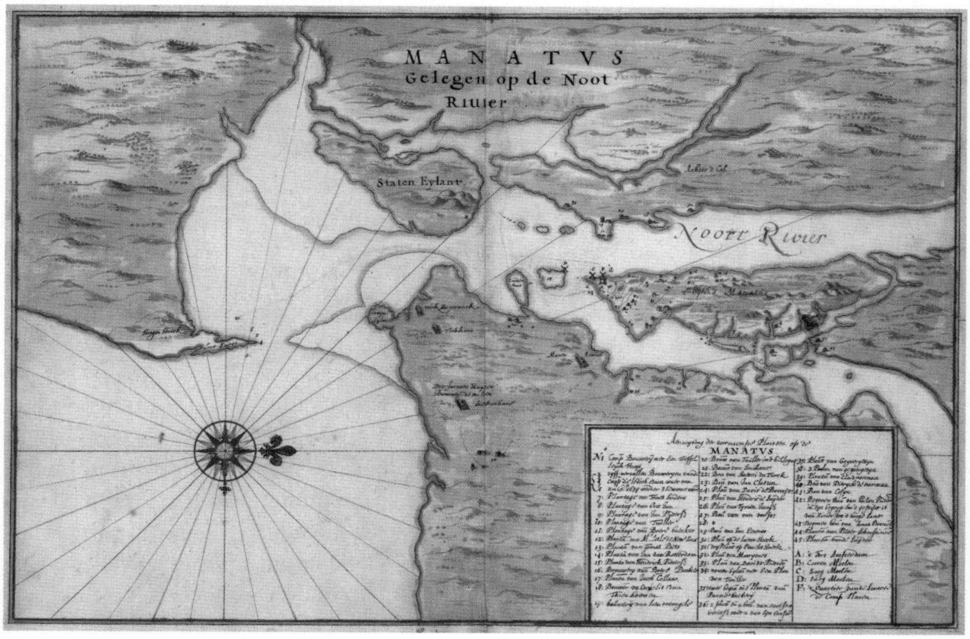

National Gallery of Art/Rembrandt van Rijn

Global Americans Born in Amsterdam in 1627, **Sara Kierstede** was the child of Scandinavian immigrants who came to the Netherlands earlier and most likely moved to New Netherland in 1630 in search of work. Her family was among the first to settle in the patroonship of Rensselaerswijk where they spent several years as tenant farmers. When her father became a member of the patroonship's governing council, the family moved to Manhattan where they became the first tenant farmers for the WIC and later farmed on their own land. Sara was likely multilingual from an early age. As a child in Rensselaerswijk, she probably learned Mahican from Indian children in the area and may have learned Scandinavian and German from her parents. Daily contact with Indians provided women like Sara with many of the foods and household items they needed. As an adult, she acquired fluency in Munsee. She became a key translator for the Dutch colony and took part in important negotiations between the Munsee and the Dutch in the lower Hudson in the late 1650s and early 1660s. Remarkably, during these years, Sara, like many Dutch housewives, gave birth to ten children. While she may have seemed an unlikely person to play a key role in the colony's intercultural relations, her mastery of the Munsee language emerged from her transatlantic background and her daily contact with Native Americans who frequented Manhattan markets and provided women like Sara with many of the foods and household items they needed.

3-2c Life in New Netherland

New Netherland emerges as a small and diverse colony with great disparities of income and privileges.

Unlike French and Spanish Catholics, the Protestant Dutch were more concerned with their own salvation than with converting Indians. They had no great plans to convert Indians and did not send missionaries to the colony. Nor did they demand that Indians be incorporated into their society and laws. Yet Dutch plans for agricultural settlements still led to tension, especially over the issue of land. On the lower Hudson, Dutch pigs, cattle, and farms encroached on Indian lands. In 1640, the colony began requiring local Munsee villagers to pay tribute in corn, furs, or beads, which provoked a bloody war that raged until 1645.

For coastal Algonquins, the arrival of the Dutch ushered in an era of transformation and hardship, but not one rooted in Spanish-style labor exploitation or the pressures of Catholic missionaries. The Algonquin-speaking peoples of Long Island Sound had traditionally crafted valuable items out of clamshells. When they acquired iron tools in trading with the Dutch, they began fashioning strings of shell beads called **wampum** that had great value to Dutch traders. In the 1620s, a representative of the WIC secured a virtual monopoly on Pequot wampum, which the Dutch in turn traded in the interior for furs. The Dutch monopoly over Pequot-produced wampum fanned rivalries among the Pequot and their Narragansett neighbors, who were soon at war.

As in New Spain and New France, the Europeans also brought disease with them, adding to the Indians' woes. In 1634, Dutch traders reported with horror that more than 950 of 1,000 Indians in one village along the Connecticut River Valley had died from smallpox.

The directors of the WIC hoped that the New Netherland and Cape Town colonies would produce valuable commodities for export. But neither did. And because the Netherlands boasted a strong economy and tolerant religious environment, the WIC had trouble recruiting settlers. Thus, in 1629, company leaders created New Netherland's original governing laws, the **Freedoms and Exemptions**, intending to build up the colony through **patroonships**—huge tracts of manorial lands similar to the French *seigneuries*—granted to influential shareholders in return for a pledge to transport laborers to the colony. **Patroons** had the right to trade in pelts and could administer their fiefdoms largely as they wished. Unlike Spanish *encomenderos*, they had no claim to Indian labor or tribute. The Freedoms and Exemptions also offered independent settlers as much land as they could cultivate but specified that if they did not occupy the land, it reverted back to the WIC. This provision denied settlers the ability to sell their property or bequeath it to their children. Over time, however, as the colony liberalized its landholding laws, its population increased to about two thousand by 1643. Over the next two decades, settlers established seventeen towns in New Netherland, and agriculture,

wampum Shell beads manufactured by Northeast Woodland peoples that served as currency and memory devices.

Freedoms and Exemptions Dutch West India Company governing document (1629) to promote settlement of the New Netherland colony; created patroonships for those who could bring over at least fifty settlers.

patroonships Large tract, as deep as sixteen miles, deeded by Dutch West India Company to investors bringing at least fifty settlers to the New Netherland colony.

Patroons Holder of a patroonship.

especially growing tobacco, became more central. By 1664, the value of tobacco exported from the colony had surpassed that of peltries.

The local authorities tightly controlled the economic and religious life of New Amsterdam. They fixed the prices for all goods and made the Calvinist Dutch Reformed Church the official church of the colony. Membership was restricted to those who showed outward signs, such as church attendance and prosperity, that they were chosen by God for salvation.

In 1654, a small group of Jews arrived in the colony from Recife, Brazil, fleeing the Portuguese conquest of the Dutch colony there. New Netherland's director, Peter Stuyvesant, wanted to bar them from settling, but he was overruled by officials in the Netherlands who knew that the Jews had supported the WIC in Brazil and had lost everything. These Jewish settlers were not allowed to open businesses and were expected to live together in an ethnic enclave on the edge of New Amsterdam. But at the same time, the Dutch authorities were tolerant of Jews and other non-Calvinist groups as long as they practiced their religion in the privacy of their homes.

In 1655, New Netherland extended its influence in the Delaware River Valley by bloodlessly conquering New Sweden, a colony sponsored by the Swedish West India Company in 1638. Hundreds of Swedish, Finnish, German, and Dutch settlers lived in the region, and they put up little resistance to the Dutch invasion. Under Dutch rule, they enjoyed local autonomy, controlling their own courts and lands. New Netherland endured as a diverse colonial region until the mid-1660s when the growing Anglo-Dutch rivalry led to warfare between the two nations.

3-3 Establishment of Virginia

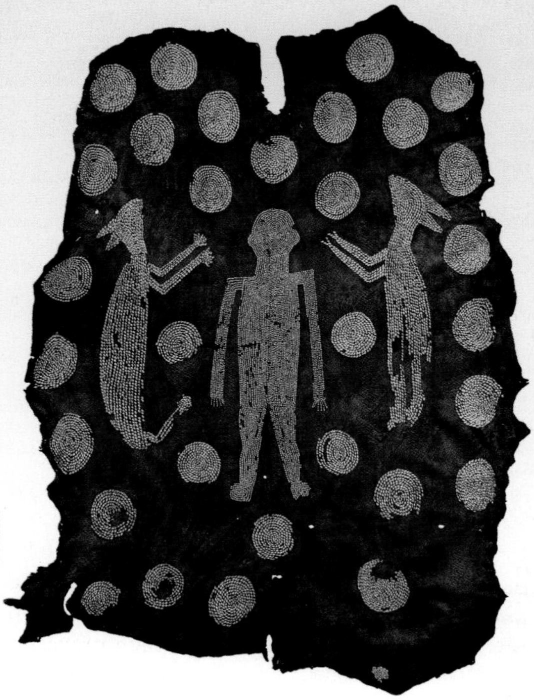

Powhatan Indians made this decorated leather tent by sewing together four white-tailed deer hides with sinew thread. The shell beadwork decoration consists of a central standing human figure flanked by two upright quadrupeds and surrounded by dozens of disks. Each of the disks most likely represents one of the communities tied together in the Powhatan chiefdom. This item is often identified as *Powhatan's mantle*. ▶ Ashmolean Museum/Mary Evans/The Image Works

What does the careful beadwork suggest about native culture and craftsmanship in early Virginia?

Go to MindTap® to practice history with the Chapter 3 **Primary Source Writing Activity: Expectations and Realities.** Read and view primary sources and respond to a writing prompt.

Although England eventually established more colonies in North America than any other European nation, it was slow to extend its influence overseas. Late sixteenth century English attempts to settle North America had met logistical challenges, poor leadership, and false expectations. Under the rule of King James I (1603–1625), England renewed its push for settlements on the mainland. Ultimately, growing tobacco brought a measure of viability to English settlements in the Chesapeake region. But as they expanded tobacco cultivation, the English encroached on Indians' land. By the middle of the seventeenth century in the wake of two major Indian rebellions, the Virginia colony had made killing Indians, or pushing them off their lands, a major goal.

☞ As you read, consider the divergent goals of Indians and the English and the evolution of their views toward the other. In what ways were English views of Indians typical of all European colonists?

3-3a Jamestown Settlement in the Shadow of Spain

In the early years of the Virginia colony, the settlement nearly collapses and has tense relations with surrounding Indians.

In the early 1600s, even after the debacle of Roanoke, the English established overseas colonies amid rising pressures to join the Spanish, French, and Dutch in the race for American colonies. Merchants wanted to exploit the fish, furs, and timber of northeast North America and grow tobacco, hops, and hemp in the Chesapeake (see Map 3.3).

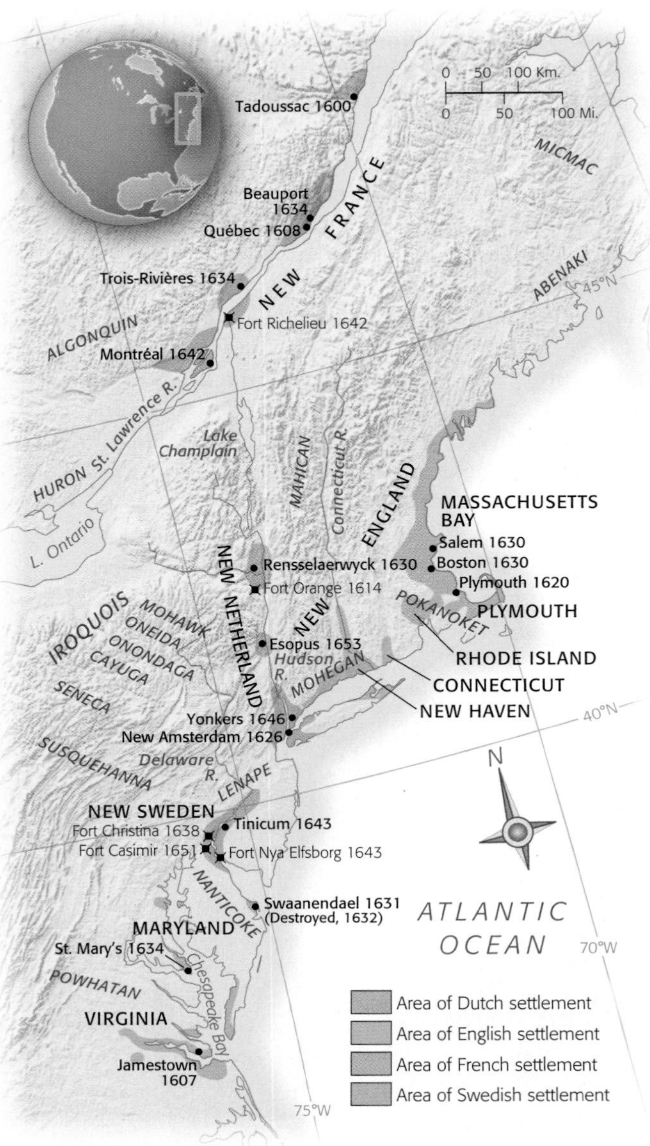

Map 3.3 European Settlements in the Chesapeake, Mid-Atlantic, and New England, 1607–1650 European settlements in eastern North America in the first half of the seventeenth century clung to the Atlantic Coast and interior rivers as commerce and connections to Europe proved vital to their survival. ▲

Many in England believed that England was overpopulated and needed colonies to alleviate this situation. England's defeat of the Spanish Armada in 1588 had opened the seas to England's ships that could provision overseas colonies. The English, in the wake of Las Casas, believed that they as Protestants could act more humanely to the New World's peoples than Spanish Catholics. And the landed gentry who invested in overseas colonization wanted to destroy the Spanish and engage in privateering. For all of these reasons, the crown in 1606 granted charters and monopoly rights to two privately funded joint-stock companies overseen by the newly created Council of Virginia. The Western Merchants' Virginia Company, based in Plymouth, funded a doomed colony at Sagadahoc (Maine) in 1606. The following year, in April 1607, the London Virginia Company established a settlement at Jamestown in a region that the local Paspahegh people called Tsenacomoco, or *densely inhabited land.*

In the early seventeenth century, Tsenacomoco was governed by a paramount chief named Powhatan. A generation earlier, Spaniards had come to the region to establish a mission, ostensibly with the support of the Algonquin known to Spaniards as Luís de Velasco, who was almost certainly a contemporary and relative of Powhatan. The Spanish attacks—and Luís's knowledge of Spain and its other colonies—prompted Indians of the region to create new alliances with one another, leading to the expansion of the Powhatan paramount chiefdom over most of the Chesapeake. By the early sixteenth century, Chief Powhatan had at his disposal a fighting force of nearly one thousand warriors and ruled over about twenty thousand villagers.

Fearful of a Spanish attack from the sea, Captain Christopher Newport founded the Jamestown colony on a small island some fifty miles up the James River. From the start, it struggled. Many of the colonists were "gentlemen" who dreamed of easy riches in the colony. They had money to invest in the colony but few skills to ensure its survival. Only

Powhatan and His Countrymen with John Smith, 1624
Powhatan, in a bid to demonstrate his power, invited Smith and his men to leave Jamestown, live under his rule, and trade "Hatchets and Copper" for food. Smith declined, but, as he later wrote, he was dragged before Powhatan, his head was placed on stones, and the Indians prepared to "beat out his braines." Yet one of Powhatan's many daughters, the 11-year old Pocahontas, "got his head in her armes, and laid her owne upon his to save him from death." With Pocahontas acting as an intermediary, the English and the Powhatan entered a period of tense coexistence. ▲

Ætatis suæ 21. A° 1616.
Matoaks als Rebecka daughter to the mighty Prince
Powhatan Emperour of Attanoughkomouck als Virginia
converted and baptized in the Christian faith, and
Wife to the wor.ll Mr Tho: Rolff.

National Portrait Gallery/Smithsonian Institution/Art Resource, New York.

Global Americans The westward crossing of the Atlantic Ocean by millions of Europeans and Africans is a central and well-known aspect of American colonial history. Less familiar are the far smaller, yet still significant, contingents of Native Americans who traveled from their homes across the Atlantic to Europe. Like Paquinquineo, **Pocahontas** was one of these travelers. She was among 175 Indians who visited England between 1500 and 1776. In 1616, two years into her marriage, Pocahontas, John Rolfe, their baby son Thomas, and perhaps ten other Indians traveled from Tsenocommah to England. Their voyage was an attempt by the Virginia Company to show off Pocahontas, who was then known to the English as Lady Rebecca, as proof of the English conquest. Powhatan, who saw the trip as a fact-finding delegation that might learn more about the English, supported it. In January 1617, King James I ceremoniously welcomed Pocahontas and the other Native Americans with her to his court where they attended a performance of a theatrical work by the noted playwright Ben Jonson. In the eyes of the English elite, the Indians were something of a sensation and became instant celebrities. Unlike Tisquantum, who had survived his trip to and from Europe, Pocahontas did not. Roughly one in four of the Indians who traveled across the Atlantic died on foreign soil. Pocahontas became sick and weak as she waited to sail home and died in England at age twenty. With her death, the dream of a long-term English-Indian alliance in Tsenacomoco died.

a dozen were skilled craftsmen. There were no missionaries among them. Their royal charter spoke of bringing Christianity to the Indians, but the colony was a profit-seeking venture.

Suffering marked the first years of the settlement. Meager rations, Indian attacks, a humid summer, and the approach of winter caused tensions to rise. The first governor of the colony, Edward Wingfield, was accused of hoarding food and plotting with the Spanish to destroy the colony. Stripped of his authority, he returned to England. Some men deserted to Indian villages in search of food. More than 100 succumbed to hunger. By January 1608, only 38 still inhabited the settlement, and they had become dependent on the Paspahegh for sustenance.

More Englishmen would have died had not John Smith, one of the colony's six "councilors," taken control. He forced the settlers to build cabins and begin the hard work of preparing the ground for crops. He used deadly force to coerce the Indians into trading corn.

In 1608, some additional one hundred settlers arrived in Jamestown. Most of them also expected easy wealth and had no interest in rebuilding the colony's fort. They sent ore back to England, but it was found to be worthless, and despair overtook the colonists. Food stores dwindled again in 1609. Powhatan told Smith that if the English provided him with a grindstone, fifty swords, some firearms, copper, and beads, he would give the colony corn, avoiding war. But the English did not have the goods Powhatan desired. As Powhatan plotted to kill the English settlers, his daughter, Pocahontas, alerted Smith to the plan, and he survived it. But he was injured in a firearm mishap, was then ousted in a coup, and was sent back to England in the fall of 1609. In Smith's absence, the starving colonists and the aggrieved Indians went to war.

3-3b Conflict in Tsenacomoco, 1609–1614

The colonists grow desperate and use all means to survive.

For five years, the English and the Powhatan Indians fought a nearly continuous battle. When the English tried to pillage Indian stores, Powhatans laid siege to Jamestown. Holed up in their fort with scant food, the settlers became desperate. Some resorted to cannibalism. Before other settlers executed him, one man confessed to having murdered his pregnant wife and "chopped" her into "pieces and salted her for his foode." When word of these horrors reached London in 1609, the Virginia Company reduced the price of its shares, promised land in Virginia to all investors, and launched a public campaign to promote interest in the colony.

By the winter of 1609–1610, more than 900 settlers had been sent to Virginia, but just 60 remained alive. Six hundred more Englishmen ended up traveling to Virginia, yet their arrival in the spring of 1610 only hastened the colony's disintegration. In June, the survivors abandoned Jamestown and set sail for England, but before they reached the open sea, they were met by three ships carrying new leaders, 400 settlers, and provisions to last a year. The arrival of Sir Thomas Dale with 300 settlers in 1611 further strengthened Jamestown, as did Dale's imposition of martial law. He put every settler to work, and those who resisted faced severe punishment.

In the spring of 1613 amid the ongoing war, the settlers kidnapped Pocahontas. The English at first hoped to ransom her but soon decided that she would be more valuable as the first Christian convert in Virginia. The English held her captive for a year in the remote outpost of Henrico. During her incarceration, a settler named John Rolfe taught her English. Rolfe believed it was God's plan for the two to marry so that he could redeem the English pledge to bring civilization to the Indians. Pocahontas's feelings for Rolfe are unclear. In 1614, when Chief Powhatan agreed to the marriage, the eighteen-year-old Pocahontas was baptized and given the name Rebecca. With the marriage, the English secured peace with the Powhatan.

3-3c Reorganization and Tobacco

Tobacco cultivation rescues the floundering colony.

After years of failure, the directors of the Virginia Company shifted their strategy again and began sending over higher numbers of men who could build a colony, not just men who dreamed of riches and a quick return to England. During the early seventeenth century, nearly 200,000 people from England, Wales, and Scotland who wanted to leave their homeland had simply gone to Ireland. Getting those who wanted more land or more freedom of religious expression to cross the Atlantic, however, was another matter. The most common inducement to get people to migrate to Virginia was indentured servitude that promised laborers free ocean passage and free land at the end of seven years of labor. As a further inducement, in 1619, the company offered one hundred acres of land to anyone willing to travel to Virginia. The company also instituted what became known as the **headright system** under which anyone who paid his or her own passage to Virginia would receive fifty acres for each additional person they brought with them. This system was intended to encourage entire families to immigrate but rarely did so. In 1619, the company also ordered Jamestown's governor to allow the election of a representative legislative assembly, the first in North America. It became known as the **House of Burgesses**. In response to these changes, 4,500 colonists, including a large number of women, arrived in Virginia between 1619 and 1624.

John Rolfe's dream of converting the Powhatan to Christianity proved impossible. But the West Indian tobacco he planted in 1612 changed Jamestown's fortunes in another way. By the early seventeenth century, England had been swept by a craze for smoking. Despite efforts, including those by the king, to dissuade people from smoking, by 1638, Virginia was exporting 3 million pounds of tobacco annually grown in fields worked largely by English indentured servants.

headright system System to promote settlement in English colonies that gave land to those who brought in new settlers, usually by paying for the transportation of settlers.

House of Burgesses Virginia's legislative body, the first in British North America; established in 1619.

proprietary colony Colony granted by a monarch to an individual with full governing rights.

3-3d Opechancanough's Rebellions

Fearing that the English will push them off all of their land, the Powhatan attack, provoking a vicious English counterattack.

The expansion of tobacco cultivation upended relations between the colony and the Powhatan. Thousands of recently arrived Englishmen ventured up the rivers that flowed into the Chesapeake, carving vast tobacco plantations out of the forest. The Powhatan realized that the English threatened to overwhelm them. With the death of Chief Powhatan in 1618, leadership passed to Opechancanough and the charismatic war leader Nemattanew. In early March 1622, two English servants claimed that Nemattanew had killed their master, and when he resisted arrest, they shot him. The murder greatly affected the Powhatan. On March 22, 1622, Opechancanough led a large-scale, well-coordinated attack on the English. The Powhatan caught the settlers by surprise, killing 347, about one-quarter of the English inhabitants. Among the dead was John Rolfe.

The slaughter provoked the collapse of the Virginia Company, and the crown took over the colony in 1624. Opechancanough's attack also fundamentally altered English–Indian relations. Those English who survived pursued a ruthless policy of extermination, seeing Indians as a savage people whose culture and values they deemed the antithesis of their own. In one 1624 battle, the Virginians massacred 800 Indians. In 1632, after a decade of war, Opechancanough sued for peace. Some English wanted to continue the war, but the Indians offered land, and a peace was made. In 1644, in their final offensive, the Powhatan killed 500 Englishmen, but this did little to slow the colony's growth. In 1646, the English captured the elderly Opechancanough. The governor hoped to ship him to London, but an English soldier shot and killed the Indian leader. Soon thereafter, a punitive peace was imposed on the Powhatan. With the threat of Indian attack no more, Jamestown prospered through the mid-1670s, a remarkable turnaround from the colony's disastrous early years.

The English established Maryland, a second colony on the Chesapeake, in 1634. Maryland was a **proprietary colony**, meaning that it was the sole property of its proprietor, George Calvert, first Lord Baltimore, who had received the grant as a gift from King Charles I. Calvert, who had previously tried to found a colony in Newfoundland and had been thrown out of Jamestown because of his Catholicism, planned the colony as a refuge for England's persecuted Catholics. He died in 1632 just as his grant was being approved. His son, Cecilius Calvert, second Lord Baltimore, governed the colony from England until his death in 1675. The family's views on religious toleration were embodied in Maryland's 1649 Act of Religious Toleration, which granted freedom of religious expression to all Christians.

The Chesapeake colonies, Maryland and Virginia, were marked by social instability. In the Chesapeake,

75 percent of the seventy-five thousand indentured servants who had arrived before 1680 were men. As a result, men outnumbered women in the region three to one. Although single women quickly found husbands, they, like the men, faced a life made difficult by heavy fieldwork and dangerous disease. Men in the colony typically lived to their mid-forties and women to their late thirties. And half of all English children born in the Chesapeake died before age twenty. Late marriage, early adult death, and high mortality of infants and children meant that English society in the Chesapeake could not reproduce itself.

3-4 Formation of New England

In this first Seal of the Massachusetts Bay Colony, an Indian man beseeches the English to "Come over and help us." The man's words were inspired by a similar passage in the Bible (Acts 16: 9) in which the apostle Paul encounters in a dream a pagan man from Macedonia, who begs him to "Come over to Macedonia and help us." ► Seal of the Massachusetts Bay Company, the first settlement, founded in 1630 (litho), American School/Private Collection/Peter Newark American Pictures/Bridgeman Images

Look at the man in the seal. How is he portrayed, and what does his image suggest about the Massachusetts Bay Colony's view of Indians?

If the Chesapeake colonies were motivated by profit and marked by death and disease, the settlements of New England (see Map 3.4) were prompted by a desire for freedom of religious expression and characterized by a healthy and stable population. Fearing oppression in England, two very different groups of Protestants had sailed to New England. One group settled in Plymouth, and the other landed in Massachusetts Bay. Each group, seeking freedom to worship as it pleased, was intolerant of others, routinely expelled dissenters, and did not attempt to evangelize among the Indians. The English in New England built a society based on family ties and religious devotion. Ultimately, they fought a war against the Indian people that was tragically similar in intent to that waged in Virginia.

☞ As you read, consider the nature of the Puritan settlements in Plymouth and Massachusetts Bay. How did colonial life in New England and the Chesapeake vary?

3-4a Separatists of Plymouth Plantation

> A small number of English colonists establish Plymouth Plantation, breaking with the Anglican Church and separating from England.

Like the Virginia settlements, Plymouth Plantation was shaped by earlier Indian–European interactions. For a century, Europeans fishing the Grand Banks of the Atlantic had come to the mainland to trade with the local population. In the early 1600s, the French had explored the Northeast in search of furs, and in 1608 the English had founded the short-lived colony at Sagadahoc. In 1614, John Smith returned to North America and thoroughly mapped the region, naming it New England, and promoting its colonization. That same year, Thomas Hunt, an associate of Smith's, took twenty-seven Indians prisoner, intending to sell them into slavery in Spain. Among them was Tisquantum, the Pawtuxet man better known today as Squanto.

Among the English who first settled in New England were radical Calvinists known as **Separatists**. These **Puritans** had broken from the Church of England because they believed it had not moved far enough from Catholicism. In 1607, these settlers had moved to the Netherlands, where they worshipped openly. But fearing that their children would grow up more Dutch than English, they sought a new home. The Virginia Company granted them the right to its northern lands in the North American continent. In 1620, thirty-five Separatists and more than sixty-five others sailed across the Atlantic on the *Mayflower*. During the voyage, non-Separatists challenged the authority of the colony's leaders after realizing that they were headed to land well north of the Company's jurisdiction. In response, men on board drafted the **Mayflower Compact**, a temporary governing charter that established a "Civil Body Politic" binding all the men of the ship together. The document provided for the election of a

Separatists Puritans who severed ties to the Anglican Church in the belief that it was hopelessly corrupt.

Puritans English Protestants who regarded the reformation of the Church of England as incomplete and sought to simplify and regulate forms of worship.

Mayflower Compact First governing document of Plymouth Plantation subjecting settlers to a government of their own making; signed on ship on November 11, 1620.

Table 3.1 North American European Settlements, 1585–1650

Year Founded	Colony/ Settlement	Founding Nation
1585	Roanoke	English
1607	Virginia	English
1608	Quebec	French
1608	Santa Fé	Spanish
1620	Plymouth	English
1624	New Netherland	Dutch
1630	Massachusettes Bay	English
1634	Maryland	English
1634	Rhode Island	English
1636	Connecticut	English
1638	New Sweden	Swedish

governor by the male colonists, regular meetings over matters of self-governance, and various laws for all to abide.

In November 1620, the colonists landed on what is now known as Cape Cod and soon relocated across the bay to the place that John Smith named Plymouth. They were not soldiers, indentured servants, or men who dreamed of gold, but families of husbands, wives, children, and servants committed to the construction of a Protestant utopia in the wilderness. They did not expect the Indians to work for them and planned instead to farm and fish—but they lacked the skills to do either. Soon, like the English at Jamestown, they starved. The Indians avoided them, appalled that the colonists had settled on the grounds of an Indian village destroyed by an earlier epidemic.

Only in the spring of 1621, after half of the colonists had died of starvation, did the Indians reach out to establish relations. Massasoit, a local chief, wanted to forge a trade and military alliance with the English that might give him leverage against his neighbors, the Narragansetts. With Tisquantum acting as an intermediary, Massasoit and the settlers agreed to a treaty of mutual defense that paved the way for trade, including Indian corn for English goods. Massasoit used the agreement to enhance his status across the region, bringing together disparate Indian groups into a new people known as the Wampanoag. They continued to rise in power under the leadership of Massasoit's sons, Wamsutta and Metacom, or as the English were to know them, Alexander and Philip.

By the late 1620s, the several hundred settlers at Plymouth enjoyed a stable existence based on subsistence agriculture and trade with the Indians. As among the English at Jamestown, the rights to own land and participate in a representative government attracted settlers. At first, the Separatists held all their land, tools, livestock, and horses in common, but few were happy with this arrangement. In 1623–1624, each family received a permanent assignment of land on which to plant corn, and in 1627, each settler was granted twenty acres. The colonists elected their own governors and in 1636 formed a legislative body composed of representatives elected by landowning males. The colony's well-governed, industrious population grew exponentially. By 1643, nearly two thousand people were living in Plymouth, and by 1675, the number neared five thousand.

3-4b Establishment of the Massachusetts Bay Colony

A large group of Englishmen establish the Massachusetts Bay Colony in the belief that their utopian society will lead to the spiritual reformation of England.

During the 1620s, Puritans, faced increasing concern for their religious expression. With the coronation of Charles I (reign from 1625 to 1629), who took a French, Catholic wife, some Puritans

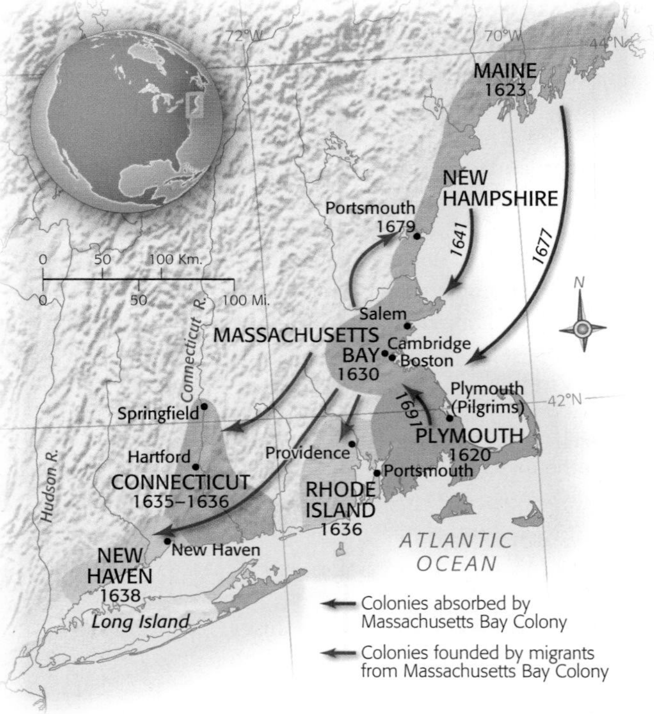

Map 3.4 Seventeenth-Century New England Settlements As the seventeenth century progressed, the initial English colonies of Massachusetts Bay and Plymouth spawned other English settlements throughout New England. ▲

John Winthrop, c.1640 (oil on canvas), Dyck, Sir Anthony van (1599–1641)/Private Collection/Peter Newark American Pictures/The Bridgeman Art Library

Portrait of John Winthrop This portrait by an anonymous painter captures John Winthrop, a wealthy English Puritan lawyer who was the leader of the Massachusetts Bay Colony. He was the colony's governor for most years between 1630 and 1649, and his son served as governor of Connecticut from 1635 to 1639. ▲

concluded that the only way to reform English society was to do so from afar, beyond the reach of a society they viewed as corrupt. They dreamed of creating a model Christian Utopia dedicated to industriousness, community, and the worship of God. After Charles appointed William Laud, an autocratic Puritan foe, to be Bishop of London in 1628 and then tried the following year to rule without Parliament, these Puritans created the Massachusetts Bay Company, securing a royal grant to settle land north and east of Plymouth. "We must consider that we shall be as a city on a hill, the eyes of all people are upon us," wrote their leader, John Winthrop. These settlers were **non-separating congregationalists** in that they did not officially break with the Anglican Church as had the Plymouth Separatists.

The first Massachusetts Bay colonists enjoyed spiritual satisfaction and political autonomy not available to them in England. The colony admitted to church and town membership only those who met high standards of spirituality and behavior; those who did meet these standards saw themselves as a select group. The colony's charter, issued in 1629, did not articulate where the company had to hold its meetings. When the principal investors decided to hold their meetings in the colony, they effectively broke free from crown oversight. The crown revoked the charter in 1637 but lacked the resources to seize the colony. By then, its leaders had turned the company's leadership council into the **Massachusetts General Court**, which soon became a colonial legislature. Men who owned property and were members of the church were considered freemen and were allowed to vote in the colony's elections.

With a clear religious vision and the prospect of autonomy awaiting them, an unprecedented number of English people sailed for Massachusetts. In 1630, one thousand made the journey. By 1635, ten thousand had come, and by 1642, twenty-one thousand. Only the outbreak of the English Civil War (see Chapter 4) ended what is known now as the *Great Migration*. Although families made up the majority of these first immigrants, one-third of those before 1650 had been single adult males, and single men outnumbered single women four to one. Eventually, nearly all the women married, and had children. They and their husbands could expect to far outlive those who settled in the Chesapeake.

In its early years, the Massachusetts Bay Colony offered Englishmen unprecedented economic opportunity. In 1629, the colony's directors enacted a policy akin to Virginia's headright system. Settlers who paid their way to the colony would receive fifty acres of land and fifty more for every servant they brought with them. There were to be no *patroons*, *seigneuries*, or peasantry in Massachusetts Bay. The colonists, convinced that in the eyes of God the Indians had no title to land that they did not enclose or use to graze domesticated animals, worried little about the morality, ethics, or legality of appropriating Indian territory.

The Puritans in the colony practiced a different form of Calvinism than did those in England. Across the colony, like-minded believers signed covenants, chose and ordained their own ministers, and determined church membership. The goal of the **New England Way** policy was to restrict membership to those who appeared predestined for salvation. After 1636, the Massachusetts Bay Company gave highly selective town proprietors the power to grant acreage to those they deemed spiritually worthy. Most of the acreage was reserved for the children and grandchildren of the colony's founders. Newcomers not related to the prominent families could hope only for small lots, meaning that many families had little to pass on to their children and grandchildren.

non-separating congregationalist Puritan who did not officially separate from the Anglican Church and hoped to lead it to reformation by modeling the life of a Christian fundamentalist.

Massachusetts General Court Governing council of the Massachusetts Bay Colony established in 1630.

New England Way Policy reflecting emphasis that the first Massachusetts Bay settlers placed on the conversion experience; restricted church membership to those deemed likely to be destined for salvation.

History without Borders

Climate Change

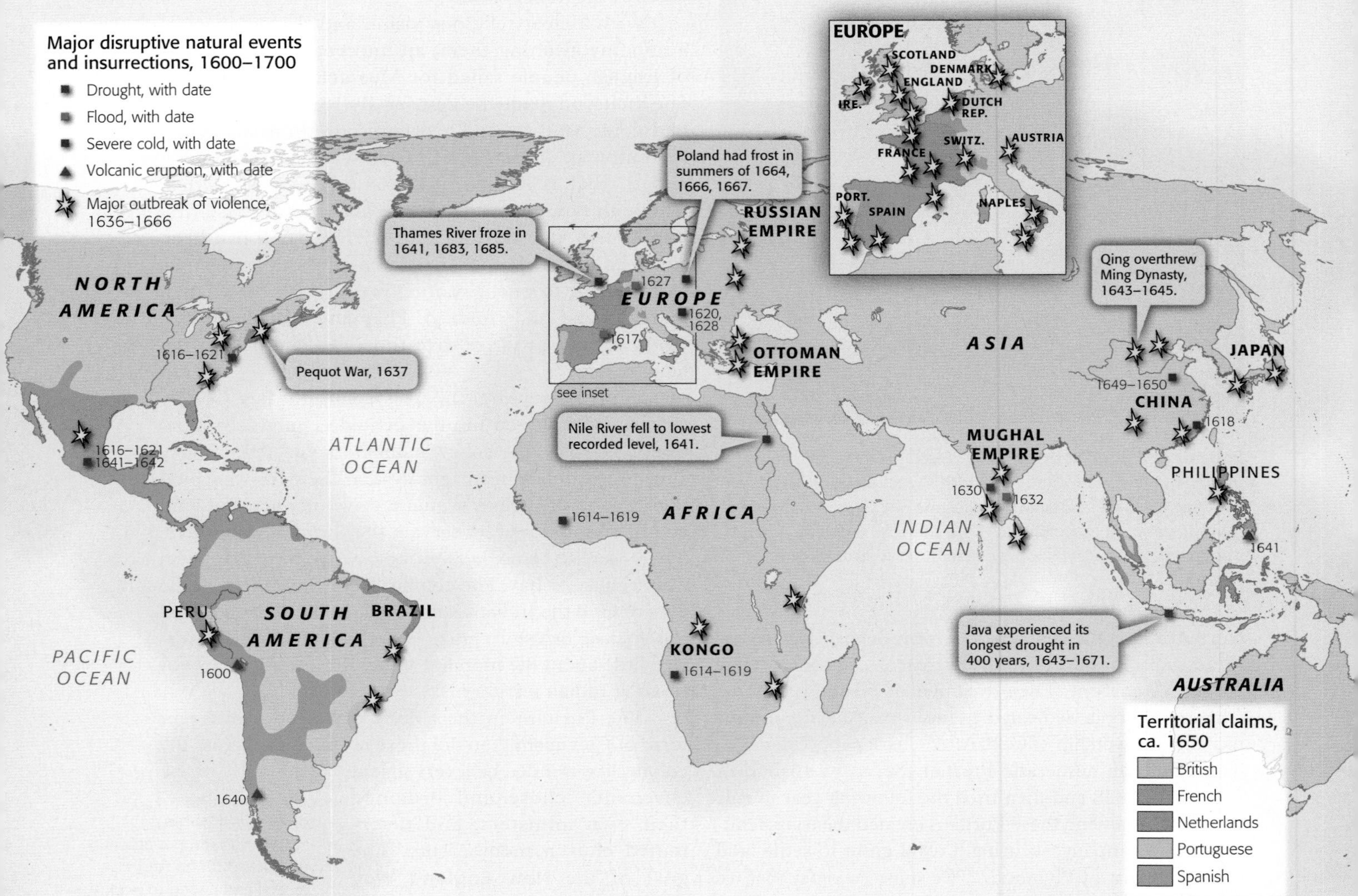

The Little Ice Age Unbeknownst to European explorers and settlers, the mid-seventeenth century was a period of unusually cold winters across much of the Northern Hemisphere. This period, known as the Little Ice Age, brought suffering and desperation to Indians and Europeans across the Americas. ▲

European settlement in the New World and Indian-European interactions often were shaped by climate and mistaken notions of geography and weather. Europeans believed that the earth's hemispheres were symmetrical, that is, that the continents of both hemispheres were mirror images. They also believed that lands situated midway between the equator and the poles would have a moderate climate similar to that of Europe. Thus, most of the settlers who came to the North American Atlantic coast in the seventeenth century arrived there expecting to find mild winters and manageable summers. Ill-prepared for extremes of weather, the settlers were baffled and then alarmed by the North American cold winters and hot summers. The Europeans did not understand that much of North America's climate was shaped by its own great landmass, which was quick to dissipate heat in the summer and slow to release it in the winter. Europeans also mistakenly believed that through their own actions—planting crops and grazing animals—they could modify the land, which would in turn modify the climate in ways that would render it more habitable for them.

The ill effects of these mistaken notions were exacerbated by dramatic climate change in the seventeenth century. Scientists have shown that

The Gallery Collection/Corbis

***The Hunters in the Snow*, Pieter Brueghel the Elder, 1565** This image shows the encroachment of winter into urban life and people frolicking on frozen ponds. ◄

Heritage Images/Hulton Fine Art Collection/Getty Images

***The Frozen Thames*, Abraham Hondius, 1677** London was particularly hard hit by blasts of cold winter air. One man in London recorded "fantastic" occurrences, and noted with surprise that "one honest woman (they say) ... had a great longing to have her husband to get her with child upon the [frozen] Thames [River]." ◄

the period in which much of North America was explored and then settled by Europeans was one of enormous, perhaps even unprecedented, environmental stress. Indeed, the Northern Hemisphere experienced such severe cold and extreme drought in the mid-seventeenth century that scientists now refer to this period as the *Little Ice Age*. Data from a variety of sources—tree-ring studies, diaries, letters, sermons, glacial activity, ice cores, and sunspot activity—demonstrate that the seventeenth century was the coldest century in the past millennium. This most likely resulted from a decline in solar activity and volcanic eruptions that created dust clouds that lowered the earth's temperature.

The Little Ice Age was global. It affected Europe as well as North America. Indian oral traditions describe the winters of the early 1600s as unusually harsh, and archaeological evidence suggests that it was a period of crisis and change for many peoples. Similarly, in major cities of Europe and Asia, temperatures plunged, harvests failed, rivers froze, and peasant rebellions erupted. Europeans could not help but comment on the unusual weather and peoples' responses to it. One man in London, for example, recorded "fantastic" occurrences, and noted with surprise that "one honest woman (they say) . . . had a great longing to have her husband to get her with child upon the [frozen] Thames [River]." In 1641, John Winthrop, governor of the Massachusetts Bay Colony, noted in his journal "that all the Bay was frozen over, so much and so long, as the like, by the Indians relations, had not been so these forty years."

In this period of unusual climate change, Europeans and Native Americans struggled not only against one another but also against a challenging and changing climate that brought upheaval to much of the world.

Critical Thinking Questions

► How might Europeans and Native Americans have sought to understand climate change?

► What aspects of climate change would have been apparent to people of the seventeenth century? What aspects would not have been visible to them?

Go to MindTap® to engage with an interactive version of **History without Borders: Climate Change.** Learn from an interactive map, view related video, and respond to critical thinking questions.

3-4c Dissenters in New England

> Heavy immigration and rapid population growth brings challenges to the Puritan elite, who banish deserters from the colony.

Puritans in Massachusetts Bay strove for homogeneity in all aspects of their society and warned those with divergent religious or political views to conform or face expulsion. The Massachusetts General Court punished civil offenders, regulated prices, and mandated church attendance. Neighbors monitored one another's behavior. But there were differences among Puritans over how best to express their religious beliefs, and these disagreements drove many to secede from the colony. In 1636, two Puritan leaders, Thomas Hooker and John Davenport, sought independence from the colony's leadership and established towns and churches at Hartford and New Haven without crown sanction. Eventually, these settlements combined with an earlier one at Saybrook founded by John Winthrop Jr. made up the colony of Connecticut.

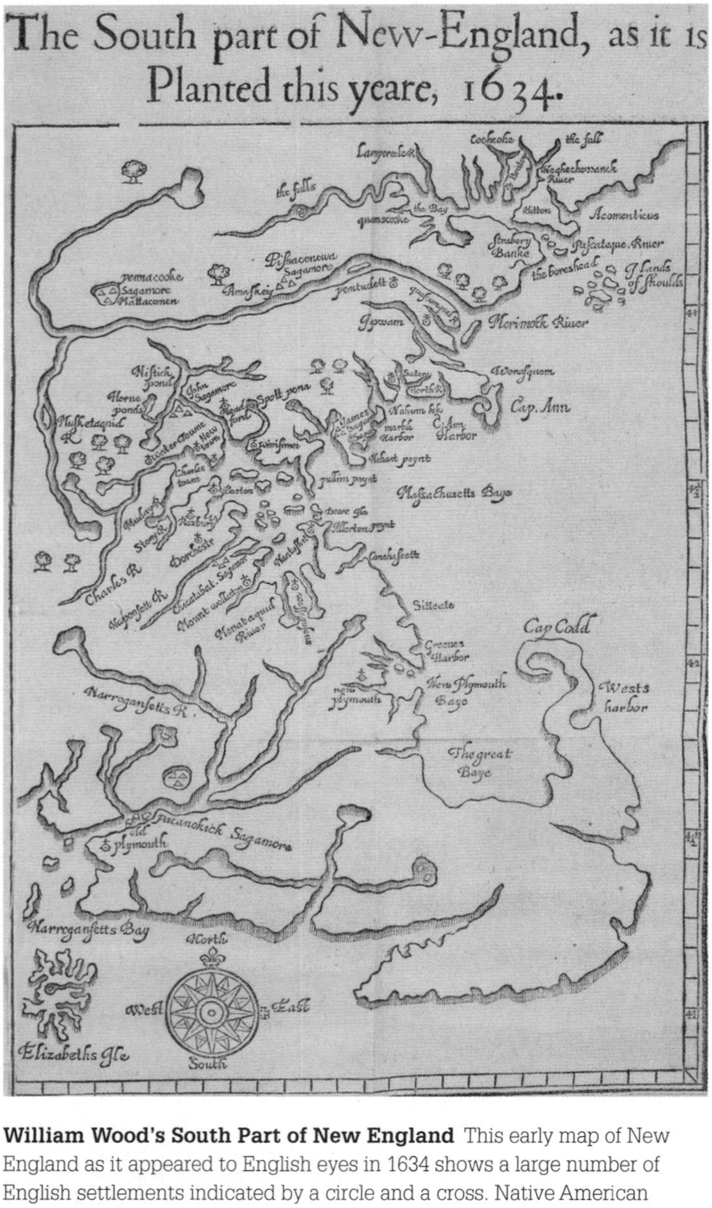

Beinecke Library, Yale University

William Wood's South Part of New England This early map of New England as it appeared to English eyes in 1634 shows a large number of English settlements indicated by a circle and a cross. Native American villages and their leaders are shown as triangles, some of which are surrounded by palisades. ▲

Not every act of secession was as peaceful. The theologian and Salem pastor Roger Williams claimed that the colonists should break with the Church of England and that nonmembers of the Congregationalist Church should not be forced to attend as the Massachusett's Bay Colony's leaders insisted. He based his claim on the ground that only God, not the colony's leaders, could articulate proper forms of worship. Williams also challenged the colony's claim to own all Indian land that fell within its grant as well as the belief that Indians had no title to their ancestral homelands. In 1635, with Williams refusing to be silenced, the General Court banished him. He eventually moved south and settled on land given to him by the Narragansetts. The town he established, Providence, became the core of the colony of Rhode Island, which received its own charter from Parliament in 1644.

Equally troubling to colony leaders was Anne Hutchinson who threatened not only the religious leadership of New England but also prevailing gender norms. Hutchinson held meetings in her home to discuss her minister's sermons, arousing concern, for women were to have no public role in religious or civil affairs. She and several others also challenged the Calvinist notion of predestination. Hutchinson was put on trial in 1637 and banished and excommunicated as a result. In 1638, she and many of her followers headed to Rhode Island, joining Roger Williams's new settlement.

In addition to independent-minded and outspoken Puritans, the colony's leadership had to contend with thousands of arriving settlers who did not share their religious convictions. Gradually, the General Court became a secular colonial legislature, and, as the colony expanded, it was no longer possible for neighbors to watch one another closely or for everyone to easily attend church. Rooted from the beginning in religious rather than economic pursuits, the colony began to leave behind its original mission as merchants gained power in the colony.

3-4d Puritans and Pequots

> Puritans defeat the Pequot in battle and find in their victory an affirmation from God.

In the midst of these emerging divisions in New England society, settlers found common cause in war against the Indians, whom they saw as savages, the opposite of civilized man (see Table 3.2). The first major conflict was the Pequot War of 1636–1638, which erupted in the Connecticut River Valley. The war's causes included the English greed for land, the Pequot's willingness to trade with the Dutch, the desire on both sides to avenge previous attacks by the other, and the English ambition to demonstrate their supremacy over Indians in New England.

Table 3.2 Major Anti-Colonial Indian Rebellions and Wars, 1585–1650

Year of Rebellion	Colony Indians Attacked
1597	Florida
1622	Virginia
1637	New England
1639	New Mexico
1644	Virginia

In 1633, the Pequot attacked a trading vessel they believed was Dutch but was in fact English. Among the nine dead was the prominent Englishman John Stone. In 1636, when another Englishman, John Oldham, was found dead in Pequot country, the Massachusetts Bay Colony's leaders decided to demonstrate their supremacy by doing "justice upon the Indians" rather than waiting for the Pequot to surrender the killers of Stone and Oldham.

Volunteers from the colony headed to Block Island, intent on killing the local men and enslaving their women and children. But the raiders found few Indians and had to settle for torching their villages. In retaliation, the Pequot attacked the English in Hartford, New Haven, and Saybrook. In May 1637, John Underhill and John Mason led a combined force of 90 Englishmen, 70 Mohegans, and 500 Narragansetts against a Pequot village of about 700 on the Mystic River. The English and their Indian allies encircled the village and set fires that burned to death nearly all of the Pequot villagers. Horrified, the Narragansetts abandoned their English allies. As the battles continued, the English killed more Pequots and sold captives into slavery in the West Indies and Bermuda. The war ended in 1638 by which time the Pequots had almost ceased to exist. Like those Powhatans who remained in Virginia, the survivors largely were excluded from English society.

To the Puritans, their victory was proof that they were still God's chosen people. They now controlled most of southeastern New England along with access to the region's valuable trade in furs and wampum. In 1643, the colonies of Massachusetts Bay, Connecticut, New Haven, and Plymouth allied themselves for a common defense against the French, Dutch, and Indians, creating the **New England Confederation**. This was the first significant effort by English colonists to form an intercolonial alliance for mutual benefit.

3-4e Life in the Chesapeake and New England

Daily life in the Chesapeake and in New England varies greatly.

Colonial life in the Chesapeake and New England diverged, largely because the regions attracted a dramatically different type of colonist. Immigrants to the Chesapeake were, for the most part, poor, unattached men who gambled that they would be able to find a better livelihood in Virginia. Immigrants to New England, by contrast, were by and large economically comfortable families who had left England out of religious conviction.

In the Chesapeake, the Virginia Company was motivated by profits, sending single male laborers to cultivate tobacco. Of the 120,000 settlers who moved to the Chesapeake in the seventeenth century, 85 percent were indentured servants, nearly all were male and single, and half were between the ages of twenty and twenty-nine. These servants worked every day but Sunday, from sunup to sundown, in an environment where malaria, typhoid, and dysentery were endemic and often lethal. With high mortality and an imbalanced ratio between the sexes, immigration was the source of the colony's population growth in the seventeenth century. In contrast, nearly 90 percent of all immigrants to New England arrived with relatives. Almost half were women or girls. Because the ratio between the sexes was roughly equal in New England, the vast majority of men and women married and had large families. The colonial population in New England not only was self-sustaining from the beginning but also its settlers found an environment conducive to agriculture and general good health. They could reasonably expect to outlive their peers in England.

In the Chesapeake, where there was no overriding imperative for literacy, schooling often completely depended on parents, who were often uneducated. In New England, childrearing was a major focus of life, particularly for women. Puritans believed that infants, as inheritors of original sin, were depraved and that baptism might grant them some measure of God's grace. However, children needed proper cultivation through strong parenting and formal education so that they could study the Bible and thereby fulfill their spiritual promise. Boys were often better educated than girls were in writing, mathematics, and Latin, the main areas of study.

The contrast between lives in the two regions was no more apparent than in the settlers' dwellings. Most dwellings in the Chesapeake were temporary because, as once the soil of a particular plot of land was exhausted, planters moved with their servants to a new area. Small planters and their servants most often lived in wood dwellings with dirt floors while poorer households in the Chesapeake lacked basic necessities, such as chairs, beds, and mattresses, and might have had only one iron pot for cooking cornmeal mush. These households were devoid of books and all other nonessential items. New Englanders, who lived on stable family plots, built wooden-frame homes that were meant to endure and furnished them with simple but sturdy furniture. In the Chesapeake, only the wealthiest planters lived like modestly prosperous New England Puritans.

In Virginia, where tobacco was cultivated across a vast landscape, settlers lived on isolated plantations. There were few communities other than Jamestown, and, therefore, the settlers had none of the bustling fairs and market days or crowded taverns and inns that were so common to the towns of colonial Massachusetts.

New England Confederation
Confederation of Puritan colonies in British North America designed to protect them against Indian or Dutch attack. In existence from 1643 to 1684.

3-5 African Slavery in the Americas

This engraving shows activities associated with sugar making in the Caribbean. Central to the scene is the sugar works. Also shown are the huts of the enslaved and the planter's home in the background.

As you look at this illustration depicting the many steps in the processing of sugar cane, what social relations do you see at work? How does the illustration reveal the sharp social divisions between slaves and planters? ▶

Sugar Refinery, Colored engraving from Jean Baptiste du Tertre, *Histoire Générale des Antilles Habitées par les Francois* (Paris, 1667), vol. 2, p. 122. Bibliotheque Nationale, Paris, France/Bridgeman Images

As important as Jamestown, Plymouth, and the Massachusetts Bay Colony were to English colonization in North America, the West Indies, because of the dramatic rise of sugar cane cultivation on those islands, became not only the crown jewel of England's overseas empire but also the most profitable of any European colonies in the Americas. In creating the modern plantation dependent on enslaved African labor, Caribbean sugar planters sparked a revolution in sugar production that had global importance. As demand for sugar increased, so did West Indies planters' demand for slaves. A highly profitable and destructive slave trade was the result. A slave-driven society, the English West Indies witnessed unparalleled tragedy in this era and instituted policies of labor exploitation that eventually spread to the English colonies on the mainland. So rich did the planters become that the mainland colonies began to emulate them. By 1650, all the English mainland colonies had slaves, and each colony began to articulate the proper place of slaves and the institution of slavery within their emerging societies. Moreover, because West Indian planters focused almost exclusively on sugar, they had to import food to sustain their slaves, much of which came from British North America. Thus, with the explosion of sugar cultivation in the Caribbean came a greater integration of the disparate parts of England's emerging transatlantic empire.

☞ As you read, think about the similarities and differences between the development of slavery in the West Indies and on the mainland of North America. What were the distinguishing features of West Indian sugar plantations?

3-5a Sugar Revolution in the West Indies

The English cultivation of sugar takes off in the West Indies where the English revolutionize the production of sugar.

First developed in the Mediterranean, Europeans carried the production of sugar to Iberia, the Atlantic islands of Madeira, the Canaries, and Sao Tome in the fifteenth century and then to the Caribbean and Brazil. By the sixteenth century, sugar was sold in all major towns and cities of western Europe. The rich used sugar to create spectacular culinary displays whereas shopkeepers, artisans, and peasants used it to preserve fruits and make jams. In the seventeenth century, as sugar became available at lower prices, its appeal broadened. Europeans used it to sweeten tea, coffee, and chocolate, and the market for sugary breads, pastries, cakes, and candies expanded.

The price of sugar dropped as its supply increased with European colonization of the West Indies (see Map 3.5). Sugar was a natural fit for the islands of the Caribbean because sugar cane grows best in the tropics where rain is frequent and heavy. The distance from Europe was not problematic because sugar can be stored a long time without spoiling. And because land on the islands was scarce and expensive to clear for agriculture, sugar was one of the few profitable crops that offered a high enough yield per acre to justify the investment.

The production of sugar was an intensive process in which Europeans came to rely almost exclusively on forced slave labor. Sugar had to be extracted from the cane, the stalk of the sugar plant, within two days of harvest or it would dry up. Thus, slaves processed the cane in mills near where it was cultivated. Slaves extracted the sugar from the cane by feeding it quickly into a mill's cylindrical rollers, which crushed it. Slaves then boiled the resulting juice in a series of large copper pots until it crystallized. Then they ladled the sugar into barrels. The **molasses** that might seep out of the barrels was processed again to produce additional crystallized sugar or rum. The harvesting, milling, boiling, curing, and distilling kept a large work force of slaves busy from January until May. The rest of the year slaves tended the cane fields or worked on other aspects of the plantation.

The English who settled the island of Barbados in 1627 had planted sugar cane, relying on a mixed labor

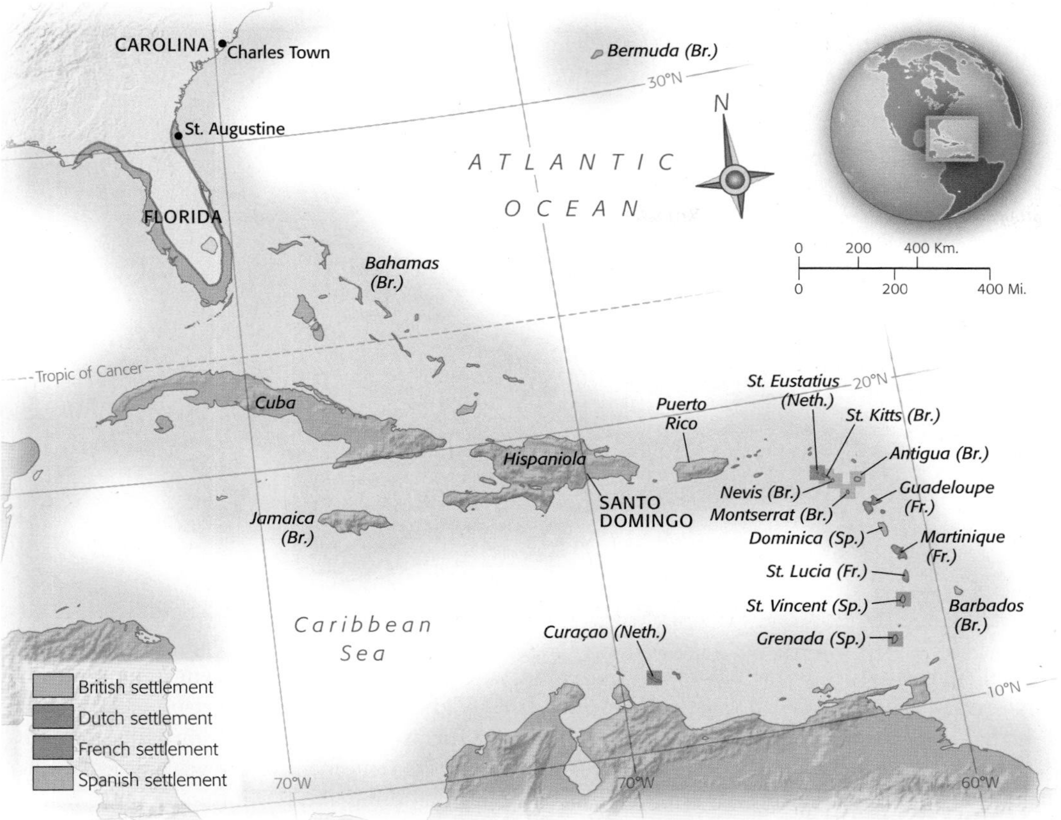

Map 3.5 Caribbean Colonies, 1660 The islands of the Caribbean, once Europeans stripped them of their native vegetation and populated with enslaved Africans, proved to be enormously profitable centers of sugar production that enriched Dutch, English, Spanish, and French planters. ◄

force of English indentured servants and African slaves. By the mid-seventeenth century, however, the planters realized that African slaves were a better investment than Englishmen who would work for only five or six years. At the same time, English merchants invested heavily in the planters, allowing them to expand their processing of cane by purchasing the necessary slaves. With Dutch ships transporting provisions to Barbados and sugar to Europe, the Barbados sugar boom began. By the 1650s, Barbados was a world leader in the production of "white gold." The planters continuously expanded their crops by destroying rainforests and planting new cane. By 1665, the island was denuded of nearly all of its native vegetation.

The English planters had achieved their success by revolutionizing the production of sugar. Previously, on the Atlantic Islands, in Brazil, and in the Spanish Caribbean, sugar cane had been grown in small quantities and brought to a mill owner whose slaves processed the sugar. On Barbados, planters owned not only the fields where the cane was grown but also their own mills and laborers. Barbadian planters also introduced **gang labor**, which involved rigid discipline and whipping to force slaves to work as hard as possible. Sugar cultivation on Barbados was a harbinger of modes of production in the mainland colonies.

The "sugar revolution" drove social, economic, and environmental change throughout the Atlantic world. The sugar industry spread across the Caribbean to French Guadeloupe in the 1650s, Martinique a decade later, and then St. Kitts, Nevis, Antigua, and Montserrat in the 1670s. With the arrival of sugar, these islands shifted from diverse agriculture to monoculture, from small-scale to large-scale cultivation, from sparse to dense settlements, and from indentured labor to slavery. English sugar production became extraordinarily profitable, rivaling silver mining in Mexico and dwarfing English exports from the mainland. In 1686, London merchants imported £674,518 worth of goods from the West Indies compared to £141,600 worth from all of the mainland colonies combined. Sugar also tied all of the English colonies together. West Indian planters devoted all their land to sugar cane, forcing them to import food and other necessities. As early as the 1640s, farmers in coastal New England exported grain and salt pork to the West Indies, which provided the colonists the ability to buy goods from England.

molasses Thick dark to light brown syrup that is separated from raw sugar in the production of sugar.

gang labor Brutal form of labor on a plantation that forced slaves to work unrelenting hours from sunup to sundown.

3-5b Plantation Laborers: Servants to Slaves

Sugar did not bring slavery to Barbados, but it accelerated a shift already underway from a reliance on predominantly male English indentured

Barbados planters shift from a reliance on servants to slaves.

"Cutting the Sugar Cane" This image shows slaves harvesting sugar cane. Note the woman and child in the foreground sorting the cane, the elderly slave in the left supervising the crew, and the English planter, the only man on horseback, which suggests his social and political power. ▶

servants to a labor force of African slaves. In the colony's earliest years, indentured servants had produced most of the sugar. Some had arrived in Barbados voluntarily, but many had been kidnapped and transported to the island against their will. Others were thieves and vagabonds sent to the island as punishment. Seeking higher and higher profits, the planters began to treat their servants like slaves. To prevent them from rebelling, the planters passed laws that restricted their movement and imposed harsh punishments for any acts of resistance. In the mid-1640s, Barbadian planters began to construct fortified homes to protect themselves from their debased English laborers. In one incident, the planters executed eighteen conspirators who they feared were plotting an islandwide rebellion.

After potential immigrants in England grew wary of the labor regime in the West Indies, their supply dried up. The planters turned to African slaves, paying £25 for a slave's entire lifetime of labor, although many slaves died long before they reached old age. In comparison, an English indentured servant cost £12 for five years of work. The English also came to believe that Africans were better laborers than English indentured servants because they were more accustomed to hot climates.

In 1640, a few hundred black slaves were on Barbados. In 1685, there were 46,000 black slaves and only 20,000 whites. In the eighteenth century, well over 1 million African slaves were sent to the English sugar islands. Most died during the first months of the **seasoning** process to their new environment as the result their exposure to new foods, new diseases, and a brutal labor regime. Slaves who did not perish in the first year endured, on average, between seven and seventeen more years of brutal labor.

The planters, meanwhile, became wealthy beyond their wildest dreams. A well-run plantation on Barbados generated up to a 200 percent annual return on investment. The planters built great houses stocked with imported furnishings, china, and silver and, despite the tropical environment, insisted on wearing fine multilayered English clothing and consuming a meat-heavy diet. Still, most planters longed to return to Europe with their wealth and health intact. Even though they held nearly absolute political and economic power, they loathed the climate and what they saw as their primitive surroundings.

seasoning Process through which immigrants to the Americas adjusted to changes in climate, food, and working conditions. Often resulted in death.

3-5c Slave Life in the West Indies

Slaves live under an oppressive regime against which they occasionally rebel.

African slaves in the West Indies led lives of nearly unending suffering. They were forbidden from marrying, tied to one plantation for life, and denied any chance of freedom. Medical care was minimal, and nutrition was grossly inadequate. Slaves lived in flimsy huts and had few possessions, nothing more than mats for sleeping, gourds for drinking, and pots for cooking. Everywhere in the West Indies, slave deaths consistently outnumbered births, and only through the continued importation of new slaves did planters maintain their labor forces of between 100 and 500 slaves per plantation.

In the cane fields, slaves worked in gangs of about twenty people supervised by a driver, usually an older slave who carried a whip to enforce discipline. Other slaves toiled by themselves as carters or wagoners and transported cane to the mills or barrels of sugar to the wharves. A small number worked as watchmen, coopers, masons, carpenters, or domestic servants, attending to the needs of planters. All worked six days a week for 10 or 11 hours per day. Children went to work at age four or five and worked until they died. Cane cutting was usually confined to daylight hours, but mills and boilers ran day and night, and some slaves worked through both.

Because slavery had all but vanished from England in the thirteenth century, English law had no precedents for the governance of slaves. Planters in Barbados developed their own slave code in 1661, which characterized Africans as savage heathens and allowed a planter to punish his slaves as he saw fit without fear of punishment. A slave guilty of a minor offense was whipped and had his nose slit. Murder, rape, arson, theft, and assault were all capital crimes for slaves. They could not leave their plantations without explicit permission from their masters.

The masters believed that if the slaves could move freely, they would plot rebellions. Masters lived in constant fear of a slave uprising and reacted with great violence to suspected plots. In 1675, after they discovered plans for a slave revolt, Barbados officials arrested the suspects, burning six alive and beheading another eleven. The following year, in response to the failed rebellion, planters further restricted slaves' activity and mobility.

Despite the punitive slave code, slaves on Barbados planned major rebellions in 1683, 1685, 1692, and 1701, only to be found out on the eve of the uprisings. In Jamaica, another English sugar colony, six major slave revolts occurred between 1673 and 1694. Throughout the West Indies, runaway slaves became common and often persisted for generations in independent settlements known as **maroon communities** in remote locations of each island.

Compared with the laws and customs of Spanish America, the English slave codes that emerged in the West Indies and later in the English mainland colonies were far more restrictive, offering no path to manumission. In New Spain, especially in urban areas, a free African labor force began to outnumber that of slaves by 1700. But in the Caribbean, slaves vastly outnumbered free blacks, and those very few who had gained manumission saw their own freedom diminish over the seventeenth century.

3-5d African Slavery on the Mainland: The Early Years

The enslavement of Africans is widespread across the European colonies in North America.

The shift in Barbados from a society with a handful of slaves to a society entirely reliant on them foreshadowed the experience of some but not all of the colonies of mainland North America. African slaves had been brought to Virginia in 1619, New Netherlands in 1628, and New England in 1638. But through 1650, English indentured servants vastly outnumbered slaves.

Far more than any other colony in eastern North America, tiny New Netherland depended on slaves in its early years. By 1640, some 100 African slaves were living in New Amsterdam, composing about 30 percent of the city's population. In contrast to those on Barbados, the New Amsterdam slaves soon were allowed to live and work on their own in return for a certain amount of labor and an annual payment to the Company. They joined the Dutch Reformed Church, served in the militia, and eventually accumulated their own property. In 1644, eleven enslaved men and their wives petitioned for and gained "half-freedom" from the WIC. They had to pay the Company an annual tribute of twenty-two bushels of grain and "one fat hog" or return to slavery.

The more densely populated New England, where large families did most of the labor, was slower to adopt slavery. Puritanism itself was not irreconcilable with slavery. In 1630, the same year of the establishment of the Massachusetts Bay Colony, Puritans founded a colony on Providence Island, off the coast of Nicaragua. Planning to grow tobacco, these colonists purchased slaves from the Dutch and later sold some of their slaves to traders who took them to New England where they became among the first slaves sold in the region. This is only one example of the trade connections between the mainland colonies and the Caribbean slave societies. Although slaves never became indispensable to the survival of Massachusetts colonies, Africans and English indentured servants were the main source of menial labor for the most affluent families. The few slaves in New England worked in households or as field hands. Notably, the Puritans also approved laws allowing the enslavement of Indians captured in a "just war," such as the Pequot War of 1637.

With its tobacco fields in need of cultivation, Virginia purchased more slaves than other mainland colonies. African slaves had been in Virginia at least since 1619. Some of these early slaves had Spanish or Portuguese names, were nominally Christian, and had grown up or lived near the commercial centers that Europeans had established in West Africa. In their dress, behavior, and familiarity with European languages, these slaves understood European ways. A few found that, through luck and industry, they could win their freedom. Yet it soon became impossible for others to follow this path. In the 1640s, the colony passed the first of many laws excluding people of African descent from entry into white society. In 1643, Virginia enacted legislation that all adult men who worked the land were tithable and thus occupied the lowest social status in society. Crucially, the law also classified "Negro" women as such, thereby placing black and white women servants in separate social categories before the law. White European servant women were considered more appropriate for domestic work, whereas, in the words of one Virginia planter, "Yet som wenches that are nasty and beastly and not fit to be employed are put [to work] in the ground."

Maryland adopted legislation similar to that of Virginia in 1654. Most important, at this time Virginia planters enshrined in law lifelong servitude for slaves. In 1646, Francis Pott sold a Negro woman and a boy to another man, "to the use of him ... forever."

maroon communities Independent communities formed by African refugees who had escaped slavery.

Six years later, William Whittington sold to Pott "one Negro girle named Jowan; aged Ten yeares and with her Issue and Produce duringe her (or either of them) for their Life tyme. And their successors forever."

African slavery was on the ascendance in the English colonies in 1650, but in New Spain, it had long since peaked. Slaves were common only in wealthy urban areas such as Mexico City where the affluent could afford them. Relative to slaves working on sugar plantations in the West Indies, these slaves lived well, although they were still always at the mercy of their masters. They had a better chance of marrying and having children. They could become artisans or skilled laborers and thereby win their freedom. Across New Spain, slaves formed lively confraternities within the Catholic Church, creating for themselves a rich religious and associational life. In New France, meanwhile, colonists held Indian slaves, but not until the establishment of the colony of Louisiana in the early eighteenth century did the French on the mainland hold African bondsmen.

Summary

Between the 1580s and the 1650s, Europeans shifted from exploring to settling North America. Their motivations were diverse, including wealth, religious expression, political freedom, and national rivalries. Most failed to find what they sought, but a few enjoyed spectacular success. Almost all Europeans who came to the Americas had incorrect notions about the geography, climate, and Indians. The immigrants optimistically imagined rivers that did not exist, a mild climate, and Indians who could easily be brought into European religions and systems of labor. Faced with repeated invasions, Indians confronted Europeans as best they could, trying variously to understand, profit from, and fend off Europeans. But to just about every corner of native North America, Europeans brought disease, depopulation, war, dispossession, and even enslavement or genocide. Although these forces raged across much of North America between 1580 and 1650, they did not completely destroy native North American peoples. Still, by the middle of the seventeenth century, a continent that had been shaped by hundreds of diverse Indian cultures was giving way to one increasingly dominated by a handful of European nations that held extremely dismissive views of Indians. In the same years that England was experimenting with diverse forms of settlements in Virginia and New England, it was causing a revolution in the organization and management of the production of sugar in the West Indies, which would have global import. By mid-century, Barbados had emerged as a world leader in the production of sugar, enriching England as Mexican silver had enriched the Spanish and knitting together Africa, the Caribbean, and North America in a web of commerce and brutality of transatlantic proportions. In these years, African slavery also began on the mainland colonies, in New England, and the Chesapeake, and New Netherland.

Thinking Back, *Looking Forward*

As you review this chapter, compare European colonization in the Americas. How many different forms of colonization can you discern during the first century and a half of European expansion in the Americas? How did different patterns of empire and immigration shape European societies in the Americas? Similarly, how many different ways did Native American peoples respond to European settlements and colonization? What made possible the intersection of European, Caribbean, and African worlds in the West Indies?

In the next chapter look for the various ways that Europeans sought to develop coordinated transatlantic empires and try to understand the origins of the rebellions that convulsed many American colonies in the late seventeenth century.

To make your study concrete, review the timeline and reflect on the entries there. Think about their causes, consequences, and connections. How do they fit with global trends?

Additional Resources

Books

Bushnell, Amy Turner. *Situado and Sabana: Spain's Support System for the Presidio and Mission Provinces of Florida*. New York: American Museum of Natural History, 1994. ▶ Careful study that captures the intersection of Spanish and Native American worlds in early Florida.

Dunn, Richard S. *Sugar and Slaves: The Rise of the Planter Class in the English West Indies, 1624–1713*. Chapel Hill: University of North Carolina Press, 1972. ▶ Classic study of the sugar revolution in the English Caribbean.

Greer, Alan. *Mohawk Saint: Catherine Tekakwitha and the Jesuits*. Oxford, England: Oxford University Press, 2005. ▶Fascinating biography of Tekakwitha and the Jesuits who saw her saintly Catholic devotion.

Gutierrez, Ramón A. *When Jesus Came, the Corn Mothers Went Away: Marriage, Sexuality, and Power in New Mexico, 1500–1846*. Stanford, CA: Stanford University Press, 1991. ▶ Stunning and controversial study of sex and power in colonial New Mexico.

Horn, James. *Land as God Made It: Jamestown and the Birth of America*. New York: Basic Books, 2005. ▶ Lively account that places Jamestown in an Atlantic context.

Morgan, Edmund S. *The Puritan Dilemma: The Story of John Winthrop*. Boston: Little, Brown. 1958. ▶ Probing biography of the tensions at the heart of the leader of New England Puritans.

Romney, Susanah Shaw. *New Netherland Connections: Intimate Networks and Atlantic Ties in Seventeenth-Century America*. Chapel Hill: University of North Carolina Press, 2014. ▶ Reconstruction of the indispensable role of women in the Dutch colony in the seventeenth century.

Rushforth, Brett. *Bonds of Alliance: Indigenous and Atlantic Slaveries in New France*. Chapel Hill: University of North Carolina Press, 2013. ▶ Path-breaking examination of Indian slavery in New France.

Townsend, Camilla. *Pocahontas and the Powhatan Dilemma*. New York: Hill and Wang, 2004. ▶ Stirring and sympathetic biography of the Indian woman whose history is intertwined with that of the Jamestown settlement.

Weber, David J. *The Spanish Frontier in North America*. New Haven, CT: Yale University Press, 1992. ▶ Magisterial overview of Spanish exploration and settlement in North America.

Go to the MindTap® for **Global Americans** to access the full version of select books from this Additional Resources section.

Websites

Virtual Jamestown. http://www.virtualjamestown.org/ ▶ Website covering most aspects of the Jamestown colony.

Plymouth Colony Archive. http://www.histarch.illinois.edu/plymouth/ ▶ Extensive online materials relating to early settlement of Plymouth.

MindTap®

Continue exploring online through MindTap®, where you can:

- **Assess your knowledge with the Chapter Test**
- **Watch historical videos related to the chapter**
- **Further your understanding with interactive maps and timelines**

Experimentation, Resistance, and Persistence

1585–1600

1573

Franciscan missionaries replace Jesuits in Florida.

1588

England destroys Spanish Armada.

1597

Guales rebel in Florida.

1598

Oñate claims New Mexico for Spain.

Spanish soldiers attack Acoma Pueblo.

1601–1609

1602

Dutch East India Company (VOC) is established.

1603

Queen Elizabeth I dies; James I (monarch1603–1625) is crowned.

1606

Oñate is ousted and replaced by a royal governor.

1607

English establish Jamestown.

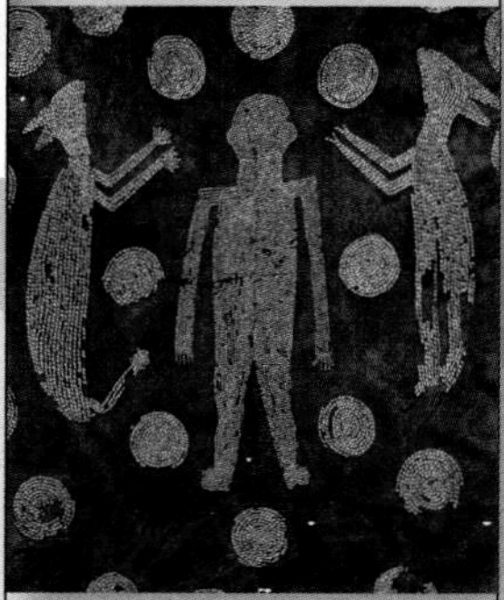

1608

Champlain establishes Quebec City.

Spain establishes Santa Fé in New Mexico.

1609

John Smith is sent back to England.

1610–1615

1610–1611

Hudson searches for Northwest Passage.

1612

Rolfe introduces tobacco to Virginia.

1613

The English kidnap Pocahontas.

1614

Pocahontas marries John Rolfe.

Tisquantum (Squanto) is kidnapped.

1616

Epidemic begins in New England, killing nearly all the Pawtuxet by 1620.

1619–1621

1619

First African slaves arrive in Virginia.

Headright system is established in Virginia.

Elected assembly is established in Virginia.

1620

Pilgrims establish Plymouth Plantation.

Pocahontas dies in England.

1621

Dutch West Indian Company (WIC) is established.

1622–1625

1622

Rebellion of Opechancanough kills 347 Englishmen in Virginia.

Tisquantum (Squanto) dies.

1624

Dutch establish New Netherland.

1625

James I dies; Charles I is crowned.

1626–1630

1628

First African slaves arrive in New Netherland.

1629

Freedoms and Exemptions becomes governing document in New Netherland.

Massachusetts Bay Colony gets charter.

Charles I dismisses Parliament.

1630

John Winthrop sails for New England with approximately 700 Puritans.

1631–1635

1630s

Jesuit missionaries begin working with Wendats.

Smallpox overwhelms Wendats.

Opechancanough sues for peace.

1632

Great Migration to New England.

1635

Massachusetts banishes Roger Williams.

1636–1640

1636

Pequot War breaks out.

1637

Massachusetts banishes Anne Hutchinson.

1638

New Sweden is established.

First African slaves arrive in New England.

1639

Indians at Taos and Jemez rebel.

1640

Dutch in New Netherland demand tribute from Munsees.

Charles I summons Parliament.

1641–1644

1642

French establish Montreal.

English Civil War begins.

1644

Indian rebellion in Virginia kills 500 Englishmen.

1645–1655

1647

Charles I is arrested.

1649

Charles I is executed for treason.

1650

Haudenosaunees defeat Wendats.

1654

Jewish settlers arrive in New Amsterdam from Brazil.

1655

Dutch conquer New Sweden.

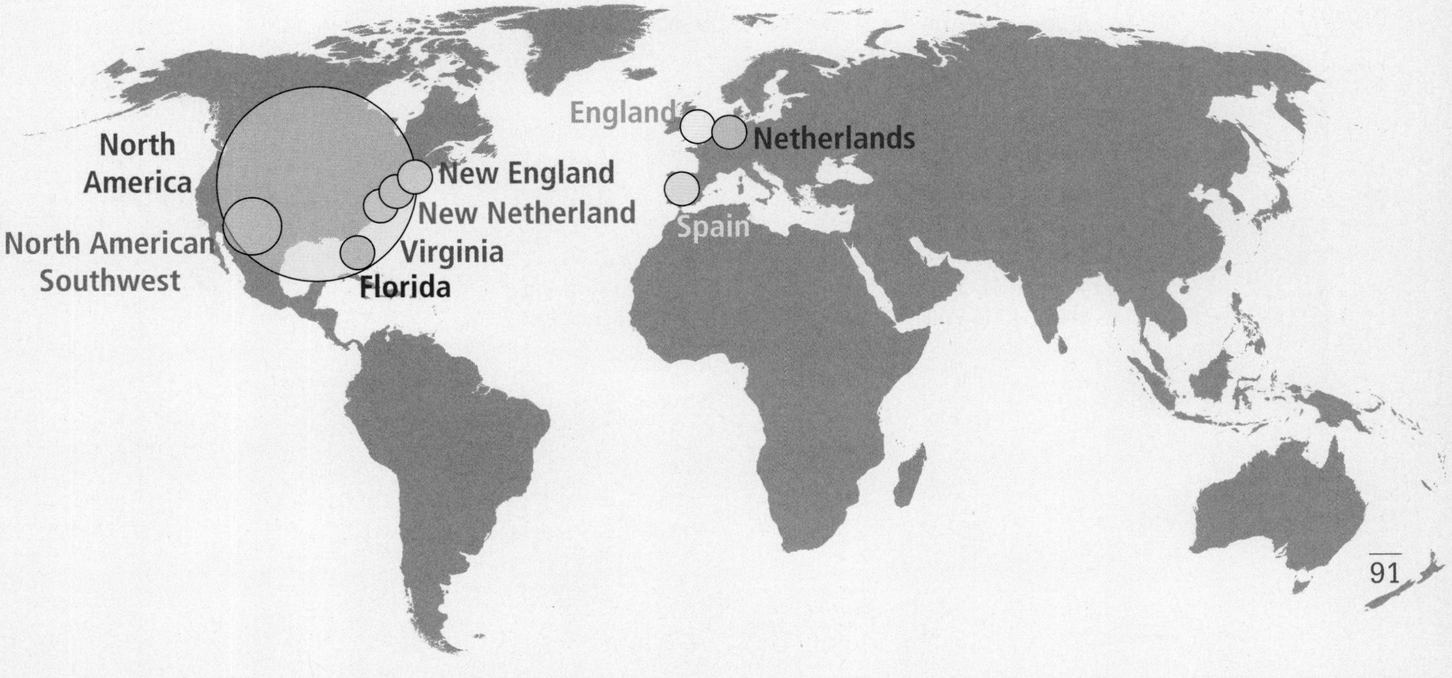

4 Empires across the Atlantic World

1650–1700

William Penn dubbed his colony, gifted by King Charles II, the "Holy Experiment" and led a group of Quakers there.

Few men have experienced the vicissitudes of fortune—or embodied the conflicts and contradictions of their age—as William Penn Jr., who went from privilege to imprisonment, from being among the world's largest landholders to being debt ridden, all in a matter of decades. Penn was born in 1644, the son of a famous naval officer during a period of English history that saw civil war, the beheading of a king, a Puritan Commonwealth, the restoration of the monarchy, and the creation of new colonies in British North America. He was raised in affluence, afforded a fine education, and groomed to take over his father's properties. As a young man, Penn was sent to Ireland to check on some of the family's estates, and there he became most interested in Quakerism, a religious sect that Anglicans, Puritans, and Penn's father considered dangerous and heretical. Members of The Society of Friends were known derisively as Quakers because of their desire to "tremble at the word of the Lord." Central to Quaker belief is the conviction that people's souls can communicate directly with God, a God that makes itself known through an "inner light." To Quakers, trained ministers and religious ceremonies are unnecessary and an impediment to spiritual enlightenment. Penn's father was so displeased with his son's beliefs that he banished him from the family home. Homeless and cut off from his family, Penn's Quaker beliefs deepened. He soon became one of the great defenders of the Quakers, and he suffered imprisonment numerous times in the 1670s for his beliefs.

The Peaceable Kingdom, 1832–34 (see also 84503)/Hicks, Edward (1780–1849)/Phaidon Press/Private Collection/Bridgeman Images

Trained as a commercial painter, Edward Hicks painted more than a hundred versions of *The Peaceable Kingdom* between 1820 and 1849. This detail shows Hicks's rendering of William Penn meeting with Native American leaders who he attempted to treat fairly and with respect. ▲

With his father's death in 1670, Penn gained a modest inheritance, and in 1677, he was among a group of Quakers who purchased land in the newly established province of West Jersey. In 1681, seemingly to repay a long-standing debt to the Penn family and rid England of its Quakers, King Charles II granted Penn some 45,000 square miles of territory west of New Jersey and north of Maryland, making him overnight the owner of an estate that dwarfed even the largest in England. In the following year, Penn led a large migration of Quakers to his colony, one that he dubbed the "Holy Experiment." He envisioned Pennsylvania as a place where colonists could worship in accordance with their beliefs and where Native Americans would be treated fairly by colonists. In 1684, he traveled back to England, and although he did not die until 1718, he would spend only two more years in Pennsylvania. Nevertheless, his vision of a colony that allowed free religious expression drew tens of thousands from across western Europe.

Although an ocean separated England from North America, Penn's life shows that political, religious, and economic events on European soil and elsewhere shaped the colonies. In England, a new king sought to reward loyal supporters like Penn with colonies in North America.

How does William Penn's founding of Pennsylvania reflect the religious and economic developments of the age in England and North America?

Go to MindTap® to watch a video on Penn and learn how his story relates to the themes of this chapter.

Later, however, a revolution in England meant that Penn's royalist contacts had become his greatest liability. He was branded a traitor, forced into hiding, and eventually imprisoned for debt. Penn's life and career were also shaped by the economic currents of his age. As proprietor of Pennsylvania, he was charged with the enforcement of the trade legislation that came to embody the imperial rivalries of Spain, England, and the Netherlands. Furthermore, his city, Philadelphia, emerged as a commercial center and became a central port for the disembarkation of slaves in the mid-Atlantic colonies. Remarkable for its scope, brutality, and widespread acceptance, the transatlantic slave trade expanded dramatically in the second half of the seventeenth century as plantation agriculture took hold, European empires solidified, and commerce quickened. Penn clearly espoused liberty for individuals, but he held a dozen slaves on Pennsbury, the estate from which he sought to administer his "Holy Experiment," and Pennsylvania itself profited by exporting food to West Indian slave plantations. Penn's life fully reflected the contradictions of the era in which he lived.

4-1 English Civil War and Restoration Colonies

This painting, titled *The Execution of Charles I*, 1649, shows the execution of Charles I by forces backed by Parliament and the Puritan general Oliver Cromwell. Charles I was found guilty of treason for fighting a war against Parliament and executed on January 30, 1649.

Consider the various scenes and people in this painting. What story or stories are being told here and from what point or points of view? ▶

Fine Art Premium/Corbis

For much of the seventeenth century, England was in political turmoil. The execution of Charles I, the Civil War, the Puritan Commonwealth, and finally, the restoration of the Stuart kings were English events that shaped politics in the colonies. The rise to power of the Puritans in England ended the Puritan migration to New England and convulsed politics in the Chesapeake. Later, a new king sought tight control over existing colonies and rewarded his most loyal followers in England by granting them five colonies in British North America: Carolina, New York, New Jersey, Pennsylvania, and Delaware. Across these colonies, political institutions developed according to local circumstances and the visions of the men who organized them.

absolute monarchy Form of monarchical rule in which the monarch, unencumbered by laws or a legislature, enjoys unrestrained power.

☞ As you read, consider how the restoration colonies were established. How did they differ from colonies that England had founded decades earlier?

4-1a English Civil War and Restoration Colonies

Violent political upheavals in England create turbulence in the colonies of British North America.

With the death of Queen Elizabeth in 1603, the English crown passed to James I (who ruled from 1603 to 1625) and then to his son Charles I (who reigned from 1625 to 1649) (see Table 4.1). James also passed to Charles his belief in the unrestricted power of **absolute monarchy**. Charles I made enemies by granting commercial monopolies to his political favorites and promoting Anglicanism as the only recognized faith, thereby antagonizing Puritans and Presbyterians alike. Starting in 1629, he tried to rule the country without parliamentary consultation, but in the late winter of 1640, a major fiscal crisis forced him to recall the governing body. Nevertheless, the monarch's relationship with the realm's legislators disintegrated soon after. In 1642,

Table 4.1 Seventeenth-Century English Rulers

Ruler	Reign
Elizabeth I	1558–1603
James I	1603–1625
Charles I	1625–1649
Oliver Cromwell	1653–1658
Richard Cromwell	1658–1659
Charles II	1660–1685
James II	1685–1688
Mary II	1689–1694
William III	1689–1702

Source: Voyages: The Trans-Atlantic Slave Trade Database. www.slavevoyages.org

Charles tried to raise an army without parliamentary support to suppress a rebellion in Ireland. An outraged Parliament raised an army against the king and began passing laws that favored Calvinism over Anglicanism. In 1645, Parliament banned the Anglican **Book of Common Prayer** and then ordered the execution of Archbishop Laud. In the ensuing **English Civil War**, 200,000 English died in battle and from disease. In 1649, the victorious Parliamentarians beheaded Charles I, and for the next decade, England was a kingless "commonwealth." In 1653, the Puritan general Oliver Cromwell staged a military coup, pledging to impose order on a war-torn society. With his army, he seized Ireland and Scotland, which by then had become largely Presbyterian, and then banned Catholicism.

The English Civil War brought trade with British North America almost to a halt, prompting an economic crisis in the colonies that led New Englanders to increased self-sufficiency and to create their own merchant fleet. The colonists began exploiting the Atlantic fisheries off Newfoundland for food and the hardwood forests near their settlements for shipbuilding. New England merchants participated in a trade of commodities that connected colonial ports in the Azores and Madeira, West Africa, and the Caribbean. This trade resembled a triangle in its overall shape, but the same ship did not complete each leg of the trade. Merchants carried timber and grains to the Azores and Madeira Island. Ships from there sailed to the coast of Africa where they bought slaves, which experienced slavers then transported to Barbados. Finally, to complete the triangular circuit, merchants returned to New England with Barbadian molasses and a handful of remaining slaves.

The English Civil War also curtailed the Great Migration because Puritans chose to stay and fight Charles and then supported the rule of Cromwell, who held the title of Lord Protector. In fact, 15 percent of Puritans and 30 percent of Puritan ministers who had left for New England in the Great Migration returned to England during the Civil War. The other English colonies were affected by the war as well. The Virginia legislature denounced the execution of the king but in return for supporting Parliament was granted the right to choose its own council and governor. In Maryland, tensions between Catholics and Protestants erupted after the assembly passed the Maryland Toleration Act of 1649, which guaranteed Puritans the right to worship in a colony that had been dominated by Catholics.

By 1654, Cromwell had triumphed over Ireland and Scotland and negotiated peace with the Dutch, one of England's bitterest rivals. The devout Puritan next plotted to conquer Catholic Spain's holdings in the West Indies through a series of military adventures known as the **Western Design**. Admiral William Penn and General Robert Venables, who had gained glory in his suppression of the Irish, assembled an armada of more than fifty ships and 9,000 men. In the spring of 1655, the fleet arrived at Hispaniola. But within three weeks, 1,700 of Venables's men were dead from disease, starvation, and Spanish ambushes. When the English attacked neighboring Jamaica, they suffered similar losses but ultimately succeeded. At the cost of 5,000 troops, Venables seized the colony's capital and renamed it Spanish Town. The English hoped to use the island as a base from which to plunder Spanish treasure fleets but did not achieve that goal because of poor military organization. Eventually, Jamaica proved profitable for the English crown through sugar cultivation. Cromwell died in 1658, and with his death ended the Western Design and Puritan rule in England.

4-1b Establishment of Carolina

England established the colony of Carolina as a buffer between Florida and the Chesapeake.

Upon Cromwell's death, Charles II, son of the beheaded Charles I and king from 1660 to 1685, reclaimed the throne in what became known as the **Stuart Restoration**. He pledged to support the Church of England, work with Parliament, expand England's territorial holdings, and continue to challenge England's main commercial rivals, the Netherlands and Spain. Over the next dozen years, the English seized New Netherland and in the formerly Dutch territory established the colonies of New York, New Jersey, Pennsylvania, and Delaware. Farther south, the English founded Carolina as a bulwark against Spanish expansion north from Florida (see Map 4.1). In what are now known as the *Restoration colonies*, proprietors of the colonies promoted religious toleration, worked toward increased governmental control, and tried to ground the social order with a landed elite in power (see Table 4.2).

Book of Common Prayer Anglican book of standardized prayers revised and republished in 1662.

English Civil War Political and military conflict pitting Parliamentarians against Monarchists over the nature of government in England between 1642 and 1651.

Western Design English attack on Spanish holdings in the West Indies to secure a Caribbean base from which the English could threaten Spanish treasure routes.

Stuart Restoration Period in England during which the monarchy was restored following civil war and Puritan rule.

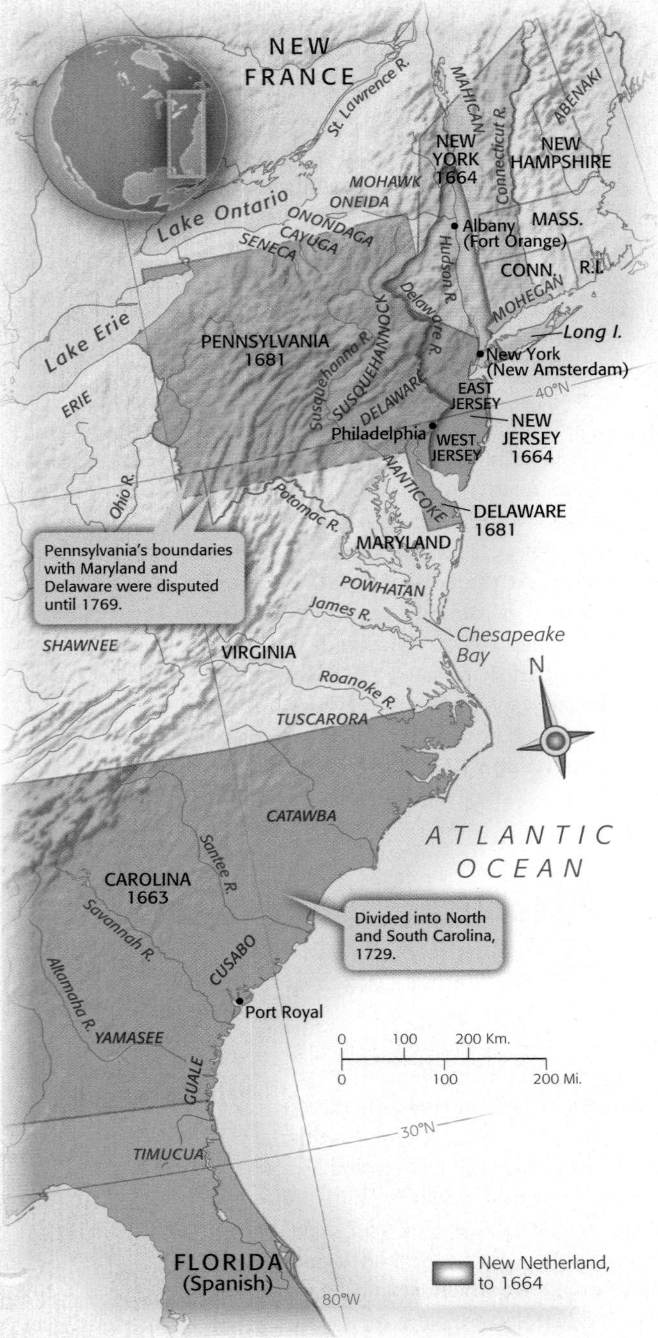

Map 4.1 The Restoration Colonies, ca. 1681 Once the Stuart's were restored to power in England, they established five new colonies in British North America: Carolina, New York, New Jersey, Pennsylvania, and Delaware. ▲

Fundamental Constitutions Outlines for the government of Carolina, written by one of the colony's proprietors and John Locke; it granted freedom of religion, upheld slavery, and proposed a feudal social order.

The first of the Restoration colonies, Carolina, was created in 1663 when Charles granted eight courtiers the vast expanse of land between Virginia and Florida. The proprietors hoped to earn money by renting land to immigrants, but few were willing to live in their new society. In 1667, one of the proprietors, Anthony Ashley-Cooper, persuaded the others to invest their own money in the colony. They sent 300 settlers, only 100 of whom were still alive when the small fleet landed at Port Royal on the Carolina coast. Nearly half were from Barbados, which had become overcrowded as a result of the sugar boom and offered little opportunity for the children of planters to advance themselves. These Barbadian migrants were rich, and many arrived with slaves. At first they attempted to grow tobacco, cotton, and silk and then turned to producing beef and naval stores, but they met with little success.

Table 4.2 Restoration Colonies and Proprietors

Year	Colony	Proprietor
1664	New York	James, Duke of York
1664	New Jersey	Sir George Carteret, John Land Berkeley
1665	North Carolina	Carolina Proprietors
1670	South Carolina	Carolina Proprietors
1681	Pennsylvania and Delaware	William Penn

Source: Voyages: The Trans-Atlantic Slave Trade Database. www.slavevoyages.org

In 1669, Carolina's proprietors issued the **Fundamental Constitutions**, a political treatise coauthored by proprietor Ashley-Cooper and his secretary, a brilliant young man named John Locke. Because the Fundamental Constitutions were based on landed nobility extracting labor from tithing serfs, they proved highly unpopular with settlers, who knew that Massachusetts, Virginia, and the other existing colonies had a social order based on settlers owning land. As a result, the colony's legislature did not ratify the Fundamental Constitutions.

By the early eighteenth century, the northern region of Carolina was oriented around tobacco cultivation. The southern region centered on a trade in deerskins, enslaved Indians, and cultivated rice, the colony's principal commercial crop. The technical knowledge to produce rice and the labor required to plant and harvest were often the province of slaves, many of whom had been brought to the colony from rice-producing regions of West Africa. In 1729, the two regions of Carolina became separate colonies both ruled by the crown.

4-1c New England, New York, and New Jersey

In the 1660s, Charles II establishes three new colonies in northern North America, cementing England's control over a large contiguous territory.

Not all of the colonies fully accepted the Stuart Restoration, and Charles II was alarmed by reports that Massachusetts magistrates had come to see their colony as a free state and refused to swear fealty to the king. Moreover, Puritans not only balked at the idea of religious tolerance but had in fact banned the Anglican Book of Common Prayer. Charles believed that part of New England's

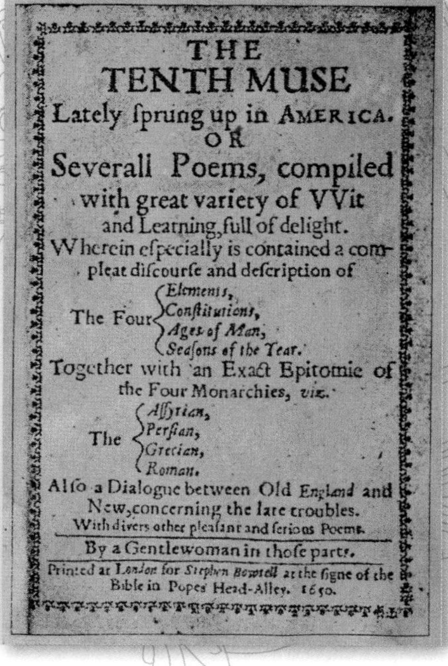
THE
TENTH MUSE
Lately ſprung up in AMERICA.
OR
Severall Poems, compiled
with great variety of VVit
and Learning, full of delight.
Wherein eſpecially is contained a com-
pleat diſcourſe and deſcription of
The Four { Elements, Conſtitutions, Ages of Man, Seaſons of the Year.
Together with an Exact Epitomie of
the Four Monarchies, viz.
The { Aſſyrian, Perſian, Grecian, Roman.
Alſo a Dialogue between Old England and
New, concerning the late troubles.
With divers other pleaſant and ſerious Poems.
By a Gentlewoman in thoſe parts.
Printed at London for Stephen Bowtell at the ſigne of the
Bible in Popes Head-Alley. 1650.

The Granger Collection, New York

Global Americans

Often overlooked because of their near invisibility in a world of letters dominated by men, women were nevertheless important readers and writers in seventeenth-century New England. Puritanism put a high priority on reading literacy because it was the way into the Bible and god's words. Some Puritan women in New England could write, but none seems to have done so with the skill and acclaim of **Anne Bradstreet**. Her collection of poetry, *The Tenth Muse*, was the first volume published by a woman in New England. Bradstreet was born in 1612 in England and came to Massachusetts in 1630 with other Puritans. Like most Puritan women, she had a large family, giving birth to eight children between 1633 and 1652. But her writing set her apart even as it focused on her role as mother and a deeply religious woman. Near the end of her life, she composed a spiritual autobiography for the benefit of her children. In typical Puritan fashion, it was filled with doubts about her own spiritual state. She advised her children to find faith in adversity: "If at any time you are chastened of God, take it as thankfully and joyfully as in greatest mercyes, for if yee bee his yee shall reap the greatest benefitt by it." She concluded with modesty and self-deprecation, traits that were typical of women of her time and place: "This was written in much sicknesses and weakness, and is very weakly and imperfectly done; but, if you can pick any Benefitt out of it, it is the marke which I aimed at." Bradstreet died in 1672.

intransigence was a result of the presence of New Netherland, which stood between Virginia and Massachusetts. The king believed that conquering New Netherland, which England had long insisted was an illegitimate encroachment on its territory, would not only strike a blow against his Dutch rivals but also help him control New England.

In England's confrontation with the Dutch in North America, the king's brother, James, the Duke of York, played a central role. Charles gave him control over virtually all unsettled land England claimed between Virginia and Nova Scotia, a region that included New Netherland. In 1664, James sent some three hundred troops commanded by Colonel Richard Nicolls, who were joined by a militia from Connecticut, to take New Amsterdam, which surrendered without a fight. Under the terms of the surrender, known as the **Articles of Capitulation**, the Dutch West India Company and the city's inhabitants, regardless of nationality, retained their property, New Amsterdam became New York City, and the trading post Fort Orange became Albany. Dutch settlers in New York City and on Long Island lived under English rule, but settlers elsewhere continued to live under Dutch law. The transfer of Albany to the English forced the Mohawks, who had lost their Dutch trading partners, into an alliance with the French to secure the trade goods and arms that they desired.

In 1665, James gave the land between the Hudson and Delaware Rivers, as well as lands farther north, to two proprietors, Sir George Carteret and Lord John Berkeley, both of whom had helped plan Nicolls's expedition. In 1676, the large grant was divided into East and West New Jersey. Presbyterians from England and Scotland came to East New Jersey and Quakers from England and Scotland immigrated to West New Jersey. But economically, both colonies struggled, and in 1702, the crown took control and united the two as a single colony, New Jersey.

The charter that the king gave James to govern New York was the briefest of any of the seventeenth-century colonial charters. It gave James nearly absolute power to control all governmental appointments in New York, set customs duties and taxes, regulate trade, direct the local militias, make the colony's laws, and adjudicate legal matters as though he were a judge. James had few opportunities to act on this power himself, however, because he never set foot in the colony, which was instead administered by a series of governors, the first of whom was Nicolls.

In writing and promulgating the **Duke's Laws**, the code that governed much of the colony, Nicolls imposed the Stuarts' vision of absolute rule on a colony that had previously enjoyed a great deal of autonomy, if not self-rule, under the Dutch. The Duke's Laws made no provision for an elected assembly or town meetings, granted religious liberty to Christians, and protected slavery, decreeing that no law prevented masters from taking "Servants for the Term of years or Life." Finally, the code decreed that no settler could purchase land from Indians without permission from the governor and that only licensed traders could engage in commerce with the Indians.

Yet Anglo-Dutch relations in New York inevitably became strained, reflecting the long rivalry between the two nations, and the larger currents of that rivalry were soon felt in the colony. New York, poorly defended by the English, was retaken by the Dutch in 1673 during the third Anglo-Dutch War. The Dutch sent Nicolls back to England and asserted their political and economic control over the region. But the Dutch once again relinquished the colony as part of the 1674 settlement that ended the war.

Articles of Capitulation Document through which the Dutch formally surrendered the colony of New Netherland to the English.

Duke's Laws Fundamental laws governing New York under the English that outlined an absolutist government but granted religious toleration to individuals.

Charter of Liberties and Privileges Fundamental laws governing New York approved by the assembly in 1683.

First Frame of Government Ideas of government set forth by William Penn in 1682 that became the original governing document of Pennsylvania,

Quakers Egalitarian and progressive religious movement that emerged in England in 1647 and challenged the fundamental tenets of Anglicanism and Puritanism.

Charter of Privileges Modification of Pennsylvania government creating an independent legislature in 1701.

The new English governor of New York, Edmund Andros, tried to thoroughly anglicize the colony, requiring all official records to be kept in English. He also made all residents of the colony take an oath of fidelity to the English king. But the people of New York—Dutch, English, and otherwise—became restless with their lack of say in these matters. In 1683, in response to popular clamoring, James allowed the election of a colonial assembly for the first time, and the assembly promptly drafted a **Charter of Liberties and Privileges**. The Charter mandated that elections be held every three years among male property owners and the freemen of New York City and granted the right of trial by jury and religious toleration for all Protestants. Suddenly, New Yorkers enjoyed greater power and autonomy than colonists elsewhere in British North America.

4-1d Pennsylvania and Delaware

William Penn establishes Pennsylvania, bringing Quakers and greater religious diversity to British North America.

In 1681, Charles II granted William Penn an extensive tract of land south and west of New York, a territory known as Pennsylvania in honor of Penn's father. In 1702, the lower half of the territory became the colony of Delaware. Given the power to create his own government, Penn set forth his ideas in a document known as the **First Frame of Government** (1682). He guaranteed settlers liberty of conscience, freedom from persecution, an elected assembly with the sole power to set taxes, and due process of law, all of which made the colony very attractive to people across western Europe, many of whom lived in countries with greater restrictions on religious expression and far fewer rights and liberties.

Penn promoted his colony throughout England, Ireland, and Germany, and in 1685 alone, about 8,000 immigrants arrived. Between 1675 and 1690, more than 10,000 **Quakers**, nearly half of the total number in England at that time, immigrated to the colony. Philadelphia, situated on the Delaware River, quickly emerged as a busy port city, and by 1690, had 3,900 residents and rivaled Boston and New York for commercial supremacy in British North America. By 1700, the colony had almost 18,000 residents and was sending large quantities of wheat and meat to the West Indies, where planters relied on the imported food to feed their slaves. In 1701, Penn further modified the colony's government, signing the **Charter of Privileges**, which created a one-house legislature and made it fully independent of his influence. Pennsylvania's relations with neighboring Indians were among the most progressive in colonial America because of Quaker pacifism and Penn's insistence on purchasing land fairly from Indians before advancing settlement. Penn's growing reputation among Native Americans for treating them justly led the colony to become a refuge for Indians who clashed with colonists in Maryland, Virginia, and Carolina.

4-2 Expansion of Imperial Rivalries for Trade and Territory

National Maritime Museum, Greenwich, London, Caird Collection

This painting, *A Dutch Merchantman Attacked by an English Privateer, off La Rochelle*, by Cornelis van Wieringen, shows two ships approaching one another. The Dutch ship is in the middle, while the English privateer is on the right. Both ships have opened fire. In the background, a French ship approaches.

As you look at the image, and the positioning of the ships, try to imagine this sort of warfare. What motivated this type of piracy and privateering, and what was its effect on colonial America? ▶

In the second half of the seventeenth century, as Spain's transatlantic trade declined, England and France created new rules of commerce designed to prevent them and others, in particular the Dutch, from profiting from their overseas colonies. English colonies resisted new commercial regulations, but this legislation eventually brought wealth to British North America and integrated its colonies into an expanding empire. The French took control of New France and embarked on further explorations and settlements in Canada's interior and in the lower Mississippi Valley. Spain, which had long pursued similar policies, expanded into the Southwest but was unable to integrate these frontiers into its empire other than as defensive peripheries. In these same years, in response to the rivalry of the French and English, the Haudenosaunees, who also had imperial and economic ambitions of their own, reached an agreement with the colony of New York, allowing them to expand their own influence in the Northeast.

☞ As you read, consider the origins and structures of European empires. What were the strengths and weaknesses of eighteenth-century transatlantic empires?

4-2a Anglo-Dutch Rivalry for Transatlantic Trade

Compared to Spain, England was slow to regulate trade between the home country and its colonies. Spain had created its House of Trade a decade after Columbus returned from his first voyage, but it was nearly half a century after the establishment of Jamestown before England regulated its overseas trade.

European imperial rivalries play out not only in the contest for territory but increasingly in the arena of trade and commerce.

In the early seventeenth century, no gold was found in Virginia, and England lacked the resources of a strong navy or a powerful monarch to tighten trade rules. But by the mid-seventeenth century, Barbados sugar and Virginia tobacco appeared profitable enough to form the basis of a very lucrative transatlantic commerce, and by then, England had the largest navy in the world. During Cromwell's rule and the Stuart Restoration, therefore, England committed not only to regulating its transatlantic trade but also to capturing an increased share of all of the commerce between Europe and the Americas (see Map 4.2).

Navigation Acts A series of English laws that mandated that trade between England and the colonies traveled in English ships and promoted specific industries through bounties and reduced tariffs.

During the English Civil War, the Dutch had so increased their dominance of trade between Europe and the New World that the Dutch shipped more than the combined total of the rest of Europe. This Dutch supremacy was seen as a mortal threat to the English government. To combat the Dutch, Parliament passed the **Navigation Acts**, mercantilist laws that greatly enhanced state control over England's portion of the transatlantic trade. In 1650, Parliament banned foreign ships from trading with English colonies. The following year, it mandated that trade between England and its colonies travel in ships owned by Englishmen and that all European goods imported to England had to be carried either by English ships or ships belonging to the country where the products originated. In effect, this law was

Map 4.2 Seventeenth-Century Transatlantic Trade Routes During the seventeenth century, the Atlantic became a veritable highway with goods and people moving quickly and regularly between Europe, Africa, South America, the Caribbean, and North America. ▼

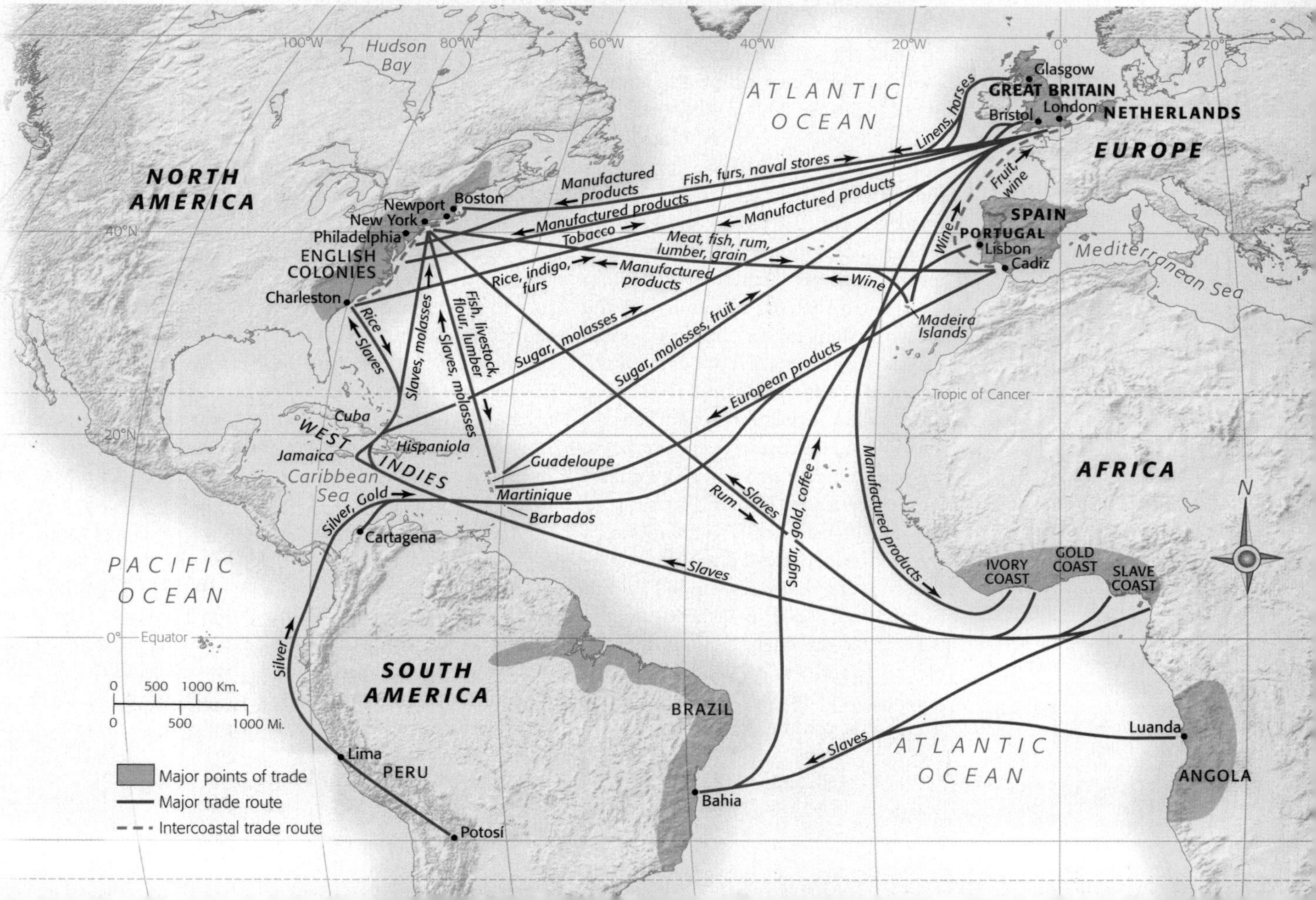

designed to cut Dutch merchants out of English commerce because the Dutch produced few if any exports. The Dutch offered the lowest shipping rates for sugar and tobacco, so planters in Barbados and the Chesapeake objected, but they capitulated when the greatly strengthened English navy approached their shores to enforce the law.

In 1651, Parliament passed the **Enumeration Act**, which required that key commodities and goods produced in English colonies—tobacco, sugar, cotton, indigo, dyewoods, and ginger—be exported only to England or an English port, where import duties would be collected. In 1663, the newly passed Staple Act mandated that European commodities destined for the English colonies be shipped through England. The Dutch saw all of these laws as part of a commercial attack on their trading empire, and to reverse these policies, they fought losing wars against England in 1652–1654, 1665–1667, and 1672–1674.

In North America, the lengthy coastline and the relative lack of English civil servants made it easy for smugglers and importers to evade the new trade regulations. Thus, in 1673, Parliament passed the Plantation Duty Act, requiring English ship captains to either post bond that they would deliver commodities to an English port or immediately pay the appropriate duties. To enforce the law, the crown initiated a colonial **customs service** that extended to British North America the corps of inspectors that had long been a presence in English ports. These inspectors boarded ships and searched for enumerated commodities and foreign manufactures. A generation later, the Navigation Act of 1696 further strengthened enforcement. Colonial governors had to swear to enforce trade laws. The crown directly paid the customs inspectors who received new tax-collecting powers. The crown also brought **vice admiralty courts** to the colonies. To the colonists' ire, judges in these courts instead of juries rendered verdicts, a process that impinged on the rights of due process long enjoyed by the English. The Navigation Act of 1696 also incentivized prosecutions by granting whistle-blowers, the governor, and the crown a share of any fines collected. Just as important, that act created the **Board of Trade** in England, which recommended legislation to Parliament and instructed royal governors in the colonies how to protect and expand legitimate trade. England's ability to enforce its new trade regulations as well as its supremacy in the Anglo-Dutch wars ultimately ended Dutch dominance of transatlantic commerce. By the early eighteenth century, England was the most important Atlantic naval power with only France as its main commercial rival.

Enumeration Act 1651 law in which England designated that high-value commodities could be exported only from colonies to England or an English port.

customs service English officials in charge of collecting import and export taxes and duties on goods shipped between the English colonies and England.

vice admiralty courts English military-style courts that oversaw the prosecution of those accused of smuggling.

Board of Trade English governmental committee established in 1696 to oversee the economic development of its colonies.

filles du roi French term, literally *daughters of the king*, referring to some eight hundred women who were transported at royal expense to provide marriage partners for the male settlers of New France.

The legislation regulating trade during this period—although controversial—brought the disparate colonies of British North America into an increasingly coherent and powerful empire. Across much of colonial America, but in particular British North America, the increased access to markets of consumer goods transformed dietary and consumption patterns of all colonists. Although the expansion and globalization of Atlantic commerce was a complicated development after 1650, the tropical items—tobacco; sugar; sugar products such as molasses and rum; and caffeinated drinks, such as chocolate, tea, and coffee—that brought energy and seemed to satisfy the appetite became paramount. By 1700, these seemingly frivolous products had altered the dietary habits of millions of people within reach of the Atlantic. Nearly 75 percent of the goods coming into Amsterdam and 85 percent coming into London from the Americas were tobacco and sugar products.

4-2b New France and Empire Building

New France grows in population and settlements.

Like the English, the French king Louis XIV (reigned from 1643 to 1715) and his chief minister, Jean-Baptiste Colbert, who served from 1665 to 1683, pursued a mercantilist strategy to combat Dutch dominance of the transatlantic trade. The French crown took control of its overseas colonies, passed laws that allowed it to directly profit from them, and tried to increase its share of transatlantic trade. In 1664, Colbert also oversaw the creation of the French East India Company, which controlled commerce between France, Africa, and the East Indies with Canada, and ensured that all trade goods were carried on French ships. Furthermore, to promote domestic industry, Colbert placed high tariffs on imported foreign goods and regulated nearly all domestic industries.

In Canada, France set out to rebuild a colony that had been nearly destroyed in the 1640s and 1650s when the Haudenosaunees overran the Wendats (Hurons) and the Jesuit missions. In 1663, the crown took over the management of the colony and increased the number of *seigneuries* granted in the St. Lawrence Valley where 75 percent of the colonial population lived. Hoping to create a feudal order in Canada, France sent thousands of *habitants* to populate the *seigneuries*. Agriculture, however, remained at the subsistence level, and fur was the principal export.

Like most militarized frontier regions, New France had far fewer women than men. And of the men who immigrated, only one in twenty was married. Royal officials scoured orphanages in France, offering women the prospect of a husband, land, and a dowry in New France. In the decade after 1663, eight hundred of these ***filles du roi*** made the journey at royal expense, and most married quickly. After 1673, female immigration to the colony virtually ceased, but with the emergence of stable families, the population grew steadily, climbing from three thousand in 1663 to fourteen thousand in 1700. Although there was no elected legislature, crown officials running the colony built schools, hospitals, and churches.

None of this expansion and development would have been possible had the crown not sent one thousand additional soldiers to Canada in 1665. Their commander, Viceroy Alexandre de Prouville, sieur de Tracy, who was fresh from a victory over the Dutch in Guiana, had orders to "exterminate" the Mohawks in revenge for their earlier attacks on French settlements. The ensuing French campaign led to few Mohawks deaths but caused widespread destruction in their communities. Weary of battle, weakened by disease, and deprived of Dutch arms after the English conquest of New Netherland, the Mohawks sued for peace in 1667.

With New France self-sufficient and secure, the French looked beyond Quebec and Montreal, hoping to spread their empire into the interior. French fur traders, known as ***coureurs de bois***, ventured into the western Great Lakes region known to the French as the *pays d'en haut*. As in the days of Champlain, these men often took Native American wives, spoke local languages, and generally lived as Indians. French explorers also headed south. In 1673, Louis Joliet and Jacques Marquette traveled down the Mississippi River to its juncture with the Arkansas River. In 1682, René Robert Cavalier, sieur de La Salle, followed the Mississippi River to the Gulf of Mexico, naming the region *Louisiane* in honor of Louis XIV and claiming coastal land with an ideal port that he called *Nouvelle Orléans*. La Salle tried to return to Canada in 1684, but having overshot the Mississippi River, he wandered for three years in Texas looking for the river until he his own men murdered him.

To counter the growing presence of the French in Canada and the interior of the continent, England's Charles II chartered the Hudson's Bay Company in 1670. The company received a monopoly over an immense territory, known as *Rupert's Land*, which encompassed one-third of today's Canada. The company established six coastal forts on Hudson Bay and began diverting valuable trade from the French. In response in 1682, the French established the Compagnie du Nord. Four years later, the governor of the company sent out various expeditions to capture the English forts, and through the 1690s, the English and French battled for control of Hudson Bay and its peltries. Among those who led the French attack on the English forts was Pierre le Moyne d'Iberville, a native of Montreal.

In 1698, Iberville began the French settlement of the lower Mississippi Valley, intending to complete what La Salle had left unfinished. In April 1699, he established Fort Maurepas on the eastern side of what is now Biloxi Bay. It was the first capital of the colony of Louisiana and served as a base for further exploration of the region. But the eighty French men posted there survived only by trading with the neighboring Biloxi Indians for provisions; disease, boredom, heat, bad water, and the failure of the settlement's crops doomed the settlement. In 1701, with England and France officially at war, the fort was moved some sixty miles east to present-day Mobile, a site that was closer to the settlements of the Spain, a French ally.

4-2c Spain's Decline

Spanish transatlantic trade declines and its frontier settlements stagnate.

In the sixteenth century, Spain had integrated its overseas commerce into an imperial system and ensured that much of the wealth from American mines and plantations flowed back to Spain and, in turn, supported colonial expansion. But in the seventeenth century, just as the Netherlands, England, and France pursued their own mercantilist agendas, Spain's system began to collapse. By 1700, it was in tatters.

The decline in Spain's revenue from transatlantic trade was a consequence of the growth of smuggling, a drop in silver production, the challenges posed by imperial rivals, and New Spain's production of items previously imported from abroad. From 1606 to 1650, the value of official trade between Spain and New Spain fell 60 percent, and from 1650 to 1699, the value of New Spain's exports dropped 75 percent. Furthermore, Spain spent more money each year on the defense of its overseas colonies, which constantly needed new fortresses, arms, garrisons, ships, and *situados* to defend against the growing Dutch and English ambitions. At the same time, foreign merchants began to use Spaniards as front men to win official Spanish trading contracts to the extent that by the turn of the eighteenth century, only 10 percent of the goods shipped to the Spanish Indies actually originated in Spain. Notably, while Spain's transatlantic system frayed, the Spanish colonies themselves moved toward self-sufficiency and an integrated economic system in which each region specialized in particular commodities.

Spain's desire to protect remote areas of New Spain from foreign encroachment had led it into new territories that had little economic value. To a large degree, these lands, north, west, and east of the silver mines of northern New Spain, remained isolated, undeveloped, poorly provisioned, and expensive to maintain. For example, on behalf of Spain, Jesuits and Franciscans explored Sonora, Baja California, and Texas, establishing isolated missions that attracted only small numbers of Indians. Florida, also a defensive periphery, probably never had more than seven hundred and fifty soldiers and settlers and rarely grabbed royal attention. That changed in 1668, when the English corsair *Robert Searles* sacked St. Augustine, ransomed its women, and sailed off with many captives. Spanish alarm increased with the English establishment of Charles Town in Carolina, which prompted

coureurs de bois French term, literally, *runners of the woods*, referring to male French fur traders in New France who traveled to the interior, often in the company of Indians.

History without Borders

The Spread of the Horse

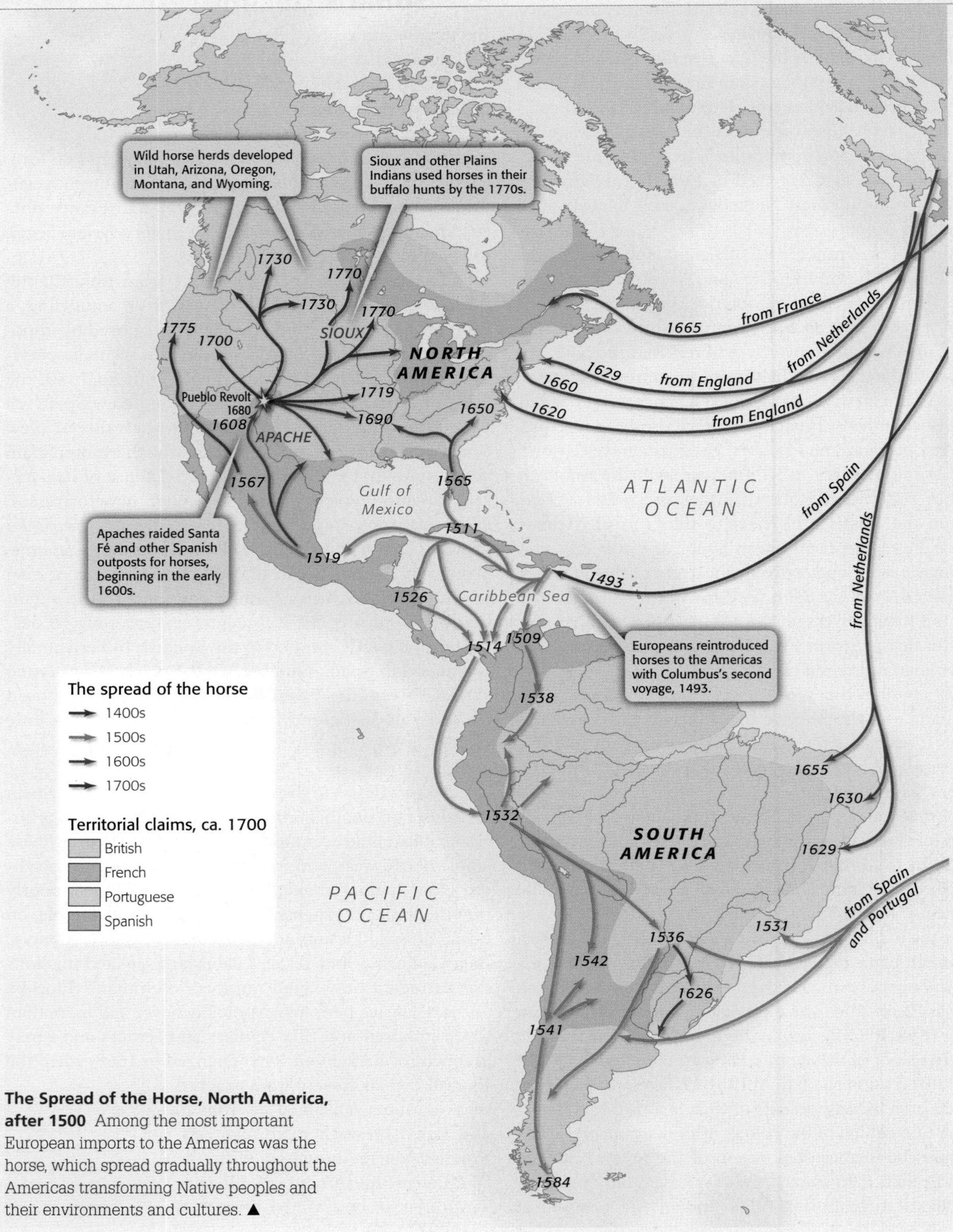

The Spread of the Horse, North America, after 1500 Among the most important European imports to the Americas was the horse, which spread gradually throughout the Americas transforming Native peoples and their environments and cultures. ▲

'Mamusse Wunneetupanatamwe up-Biblum God' ('The-Whole Holy his-Bible God'), title page from 'The Bible', also known as the 'Eliot Indian Bible', translated into the Massachusett language by the Reverend John Eliot (1604–90), published by Samuel Green and Marmaduke Johnson, 1663 (engraving), American School, (17th century)/Massachusetts Historical Society, Boston, MA, USA / Bridgeman Images

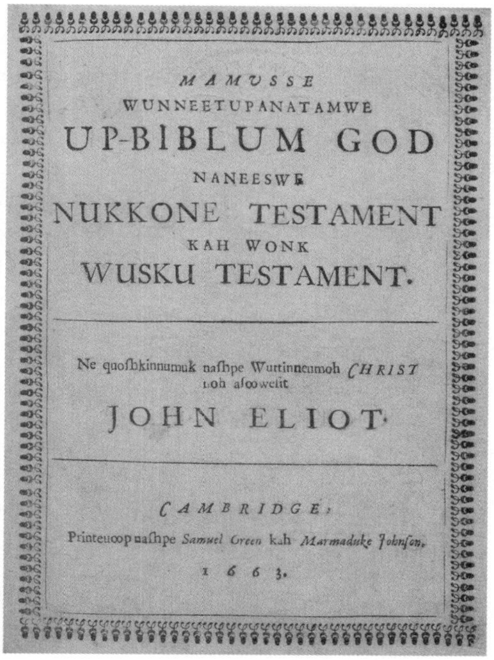
MAMUSSE
WUNNEETUPANATAMWE
UP-BIBLUM GOD
NANEESWE
NUKKONE TESTAMENT
KAH WONK
WUSKU TESTAMENT.

Ne quoshkinnumuk nashpe Wuttinneumoh CHRIST
noh asoowesit
JOHN ELIOT.

CAMBRIDGE:
Printeuoop nashpe Samuel Green kah Marmaduke Johnson.
1663.

Eliot Bible, 1663 In 1646, the Massachusetts colony banned Native American religious practices and authorized John Eliot, a Puritan minister, to "civilize" and Christianize the Massachusetts. Funded and encouraged by people in England, Eliot began working with Indians to translate the Bible into the Massachusetts' language. In 1663, he began to print and circulate the "Eliot Bible" with an initial run of one thousand copies. ▲

from one of these settlements. Kateri (Catherina) Tekakwitha's devotion to Catholicism won her the admiration of Jesuit missionaries.

In 1678, the weakened Haudenosaunees entered into the first of several agreements with the English that established what became known as the **Covenant Chain**.

In Massachusetts, Indians surrounded by English settlers and facing increasing encroachment on their lands also found temporary haven in Christian enclaves. By 1674, some 2,300 Indians resided in at least fourteen **Praying Towns**, under the Protestant missionary John Eliot. In these separate Indian Christian communities in New England, Indians lived like the English yet apart from them, electing their own magistrates, speaking English, and praying regularly. The English continued to regard these communities with suspicion and disdain and never fully accepted their presence in New England.

Covenant Chain Seventeenth-century treaties between the Haudenosaunee and the English that promoted peace and the Haudenosaunee claims to supremacy over other Indian groups.

Praying Towns A series of English mission towns established under the Protestant missionary John Eliot in Massachusetts in the mid-seventeenth century.

Creek Confederacy Confederacy of Southeastern Woodlands Indians.

In the Southeast, an infusion of English trade goods brought turmoil to Indians. In return for rum and firearms, Indians traded deerskins that were valued by the English to produce belts, gloves, and hats. More important was the swift expansion of an Indian slave trade promoted by the English. Rival Indian groups, in particular those in the **Creek Confederacy**, seized captives for sale to the English. This trade became the most profitable in Carolina in the final decades of the seventeenth century. The English put some Indian slaves to work on plantations but, because Native Americans often fled to their homelands, sent most to New York, Boston, or the West Indies. As many as fifty thousand Indian slaves—more than the number of Africans brought to the mainland colonies in the same period—were sold in Charles Town between 1670 and 1715. At the same time as this trade flourished, the growth of English settlements in Carolina put pressure on Indian landholdings, setting the stage for conflict in the following decades.

4-3 Transatlantic Slave Trade and Slavery

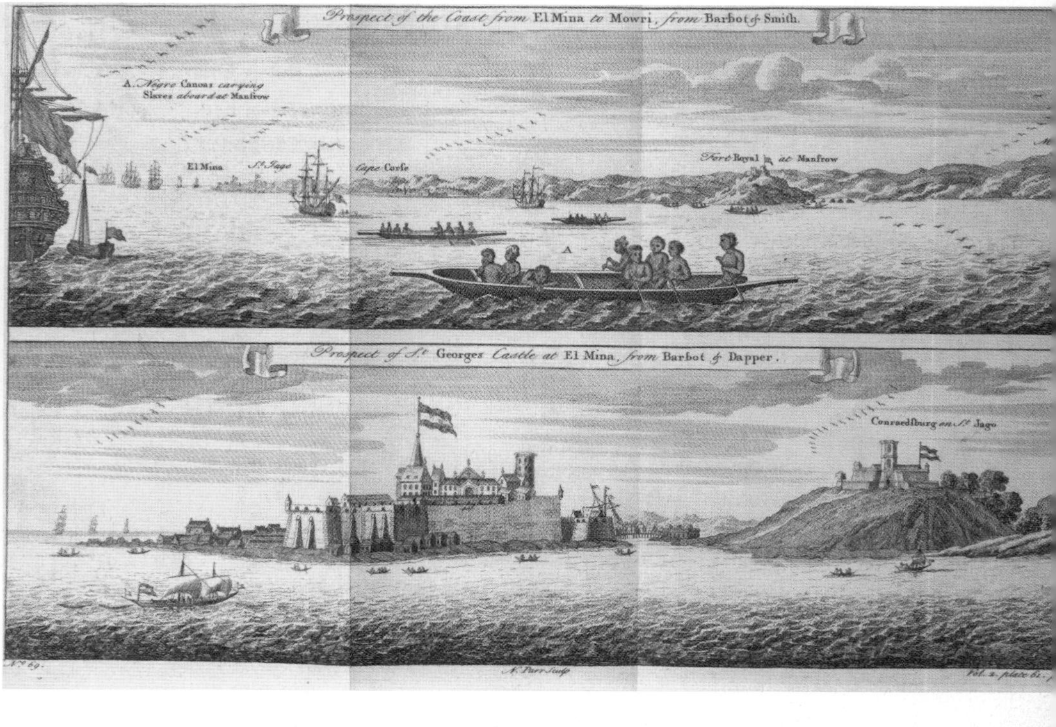

Rare Books Division, NYPL.

This engraving, created from sketches made in the late seventeenth century, depicts canoes ferrying enslaved Africans from shore to larger vessels. This was just one small part in the slaves' long journey from freedom to enslavement in the Americas.

How does this image depict a crucial moment in the transatlantic slave trade? ▶

Go to MindTap® to practice history with the Chapter 4 **Primary Source Writing Activity: The Slave Trade.** Read and view primary sources and respond to a writing prompt.

Royal African Company (RAC) English royal trading company that held a monopoly in the English slave trade from 1660 through 1689.

In the second half of the seventeenth century, the slave trade expanded and moved to the center of the transatlantic economy driven by growth in the production of sugar in the Americas. For slave traders, profits ranged from 3 percent to 30 percent per ship, and by the 1680s, half of all imports and exports to and from Africa were related to the trade. For the enslaved, the horrors began when they were taken captive in Africa, continued through a harrowing transoceanic voyage, and continued with their sale in the Caribbean or North America. The slave trade produced human suffering of unparalleled proportions as millions of Africans were taken from their homelands and scattered across the Americas. The majority of slaves were consigned to Caribbean or Brazilian sugar plantations where they endured miserable conditions until they died of disease and overwork.

☞ As you read, look for key moments in the process through which Africans were enslaved. In what different ways were slaves put to work in the Americas?

4-3a Slave Origins, Ages, and Sex

The flow of slaves from Africa is enormous and shaped by European and African priorities.

The transatlantic slave trade spanned half the globe and was well documented. European countries taxed the traders, merchants insured their ships and human cargo, and ports and customs officials recorded the comings and goings of ships brimming with slaves. The trade increased over time because slave traders became more efficient, slave ships became larger, and the sugar colonies' demand for slaves was unceasing. The trade began in earnest as early as 1500 and was not abolished until 1867. During that period, at least 12.5 million men, women, and children were taken from Africa on at least forty thousand ship voyages. About 10.7 million survived the ocean crossing to the New World. More than any other factor, the sugar boom shaped the transatlantic slave trade in the seventeenth century. All told, 90 percent of all slaves carried to the Americas were destined to labor in the production of sugar. The trade grew steadily over the centuries and increased dramatically between 1600 and 1700, more than doubling over the second half of the seventeenth century, rising from 155,687 slaves shipped in the 1650s to 339,557 in the 1690s (see Figures 4.1 and 4.2). Despite the enormity of these numbers, not until 1700 did the value of slaves from Africa surpass the value of the metals, spices, and other goods Europeans took from the African continent.

At mid-century, the Portuguese dominated the slave trade. They carried slaves to the sugar-producing colonies of the Spanish Caribbean and Portuguese Brazil. In 1660, however, King Charles II of England chartered the Company of Royal Adventurers in Africa as part of his broader strategy of challenging Dutch trade. In 1663, the company was reorganized as the **Royal African Company (RAC)**, with Charles's son James as its governor. The company held a monopoly over the English slave trade from the purchase of slaves in Africa to their sale in the New World. With the creation of the RAC, the English participation in the slave trade grew dramatically. In 1664, England for the first time shipped more slaves to the Americas than Portugal did. By the 1690s, the English were responsible for 34 percent, or 116,495 slaves, taken from Africa, up from their share of 6 percent before the RAC.

All told, the British carried about 2.5 million West Africans to the English colonies in North America and the Caribbean before 1800. They delivered 2.2 million to the Caribbean, including 925,000 to Jamaica and another 450,000 to Barbados. By comparison, about 310,000 slaves had disembarked on mainland North America before 1800 (see Map 4.3). Half of the slaves (primarily men) shipped to the British Caribbean died within three years of arrival, and the majority of survivors never had children, meaning that English sugar colonies never developed

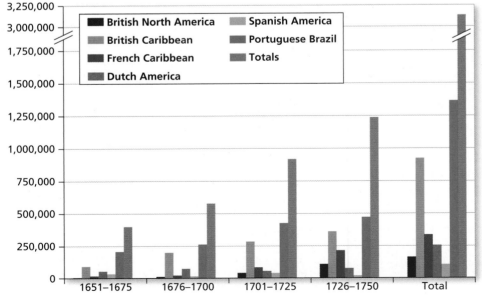

Figure 4.1 Number of Slaves Disembarking in the Americas by Region, 1651 to 1750 In the century between 1651 and 1750, some 3,131,146 slaves arrived in the Americas, with the brutal and lethal sugar colonies continuing to be the final destination of most. The overwhelming majority disembarked in Brazil (1,362,560), the British Caribbean (921,278), and the French Caribbean (332,612). Of the 3,131,146, some 161,021 slaves disembarked in mainland North America, and nearly all arrived between 1700 and 1750, a period when plantation owners had greater access to African slaves. ►

Source: Voyages: The Trans-Atlantic Slave Trade Database. www.slavevoyages.org.

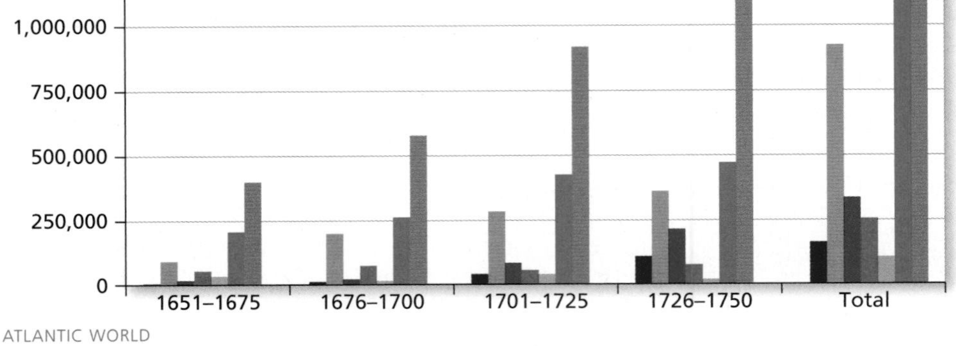

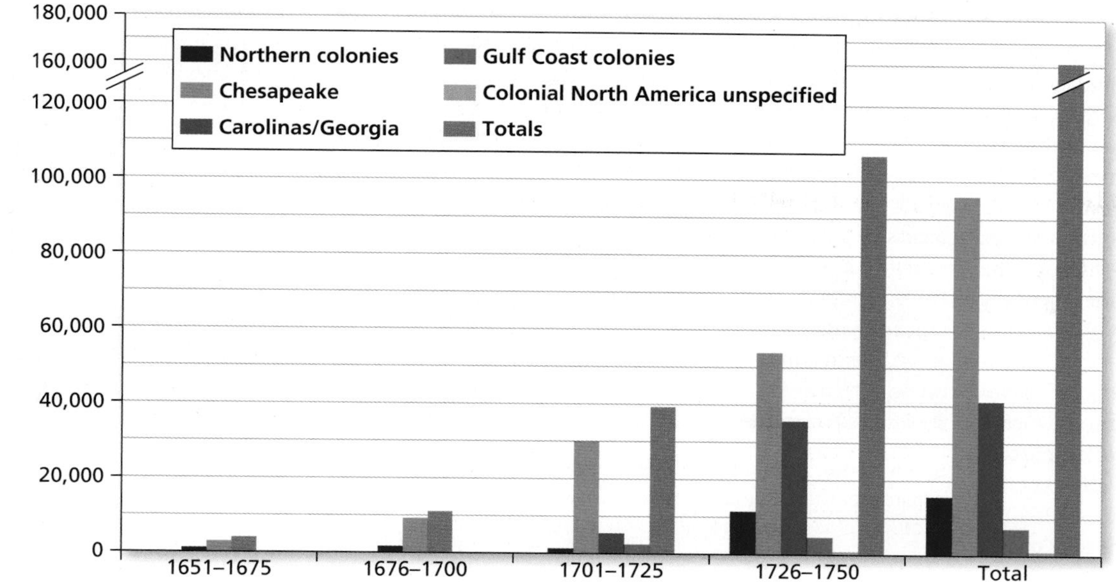

Figure 4.2 Number of Slaves Disembarking on Mainland by Region, 1651 to 1750 Some 161,021 African slaves disembarked in the North American mainland colonies between 1651 and 1750. Of these, nearly all (145,324) arrived after 1700, with 95,978 going to the Chesapeake and 41,143 to Georgia. ◀ Source: Voyages: The Trans-Atlantic Slave Trade Database. www.slavevoyages.org.

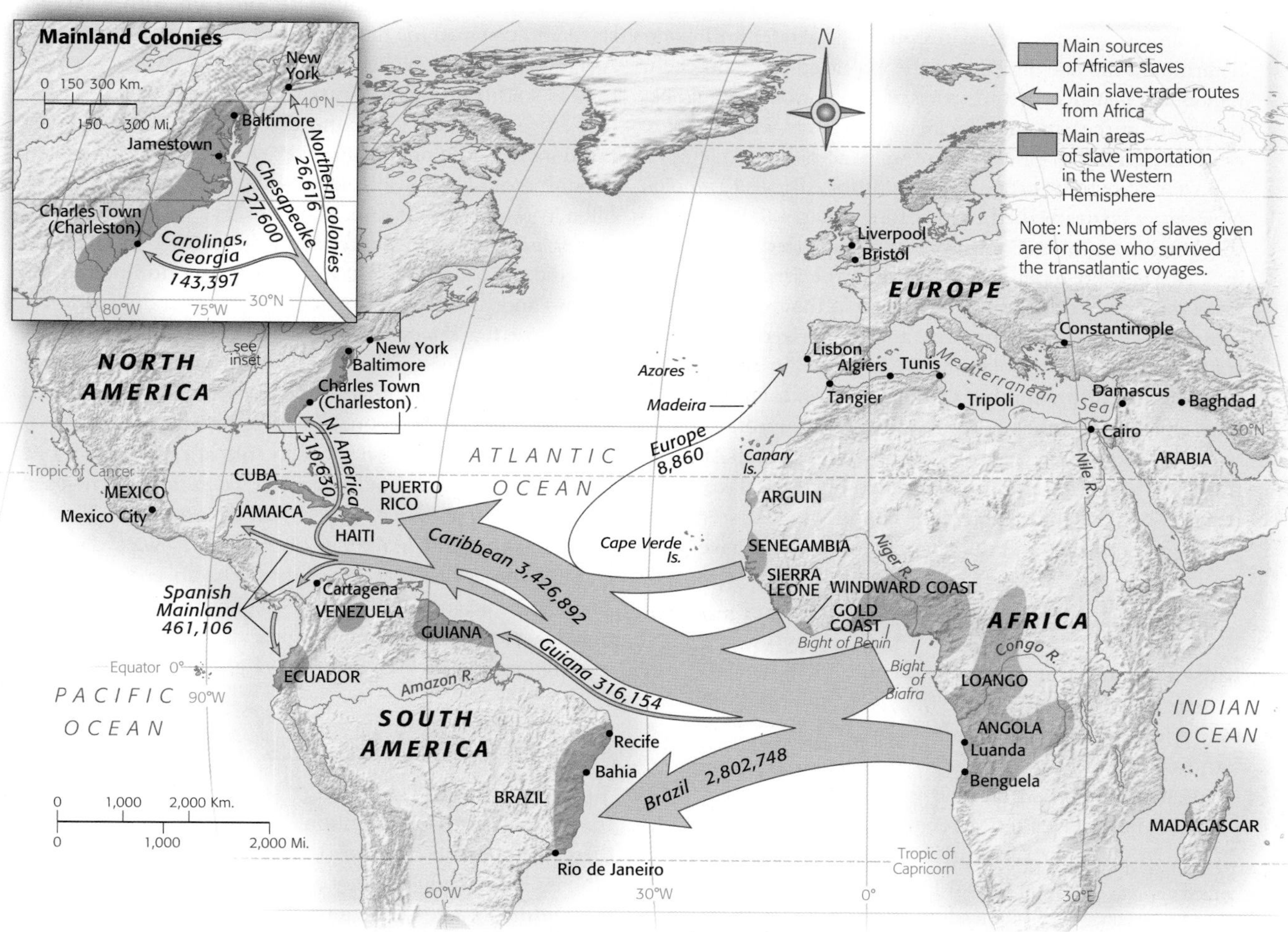

Map 4.3 African Origins and American Destinations of Enslaved Africans Europeans Brought to the Americas, Sixteenth to Eighteenth Centuries European slave ships carried millions of enslaved Africans across the Atlantic during the Early Modern period. The overwhelming majority were taken to the sugar plantations of the Caribbean and Brazil, where most died within a few years of their arrival. ▲

sustainable slave populations and thus constantly imported more slaves. In contrast, in the mainland colonies, the number of slaves increased rapidly as many took mates and produced children born into slavery. In 1800 in what had become the United States, there were 900,000 slaves while at the same time—despite the arrival of nearly nine times as many slaves—there were only 800,000 in the British Caribbean.

Overall, the majority of slaves were taken from west central Africa, a region that today includes part of Gabon, Congo, Zaire, and Angola. But between 1676 and 1725, the majority came from the **Slave Coast**, a coastline today in eastern Ghana, Togo, Benin, and western Nigeria. This shift had more to do with the rise and fall of African peoples and empires than the preferences of European slave traders. African cultures, systems, and conceptions of gender and work determined the age and sex of the exported slaves in each region. For instance, in some parts of Africa, women could be sold for more in domestic African slave markets, whereas men commanded higher prices in slave sales across the Atlantic.

National Maritime Museum, Greenwich, London

Slave Coffle, from a Slave Merchant's Journal, 1793–1794 Like other African commodities that Europeans prized, slaves were sold from one group of African traders to another as the slaves were driven from the interior in small groups bound to each other. Often they were kept in pens and fed minimally, and as a result, one in four slaves died on the journey from the interior to the coast. Some resisted but with little chance of gaining freedom. ▲

The slave trade proved disastrous for Africa as a whole. Millions of Africans died even before they could be sent to the Americas, and millions more were displaced. As slavery in Africa became a major industry after the arrival of European traders, African leaders involved in the trade became increasingly violent, oppressive, and militarized. The slave trade reduced the population of Africa and in some areas vastly reduced the number of men, leading to an increase in polygamy and other cultural transformations. Before the onset of the slave trade, Africa's share of the overall Atlantic trade was small, yet it further declined once the slave trade began. The slave trade robbed the continent of laborers and provoked enduring and devastating conflict and poverty.

4-3b African Captivity

> For millions, the horrors of slavery begin in Africa with kidnapping and forced marches.

Most slaves brought to the Americas were first captured by African slave hunters and bandits or sold into slavery by their countrymen or their families. Few slaves left a record of their captivity. One recounted how "a people came from a far and unknown country . . . and burnt all their towns." Another, Peter Kondo, stated that he was "kidnapped in the Basare country, where he had gone to buy corn." A man named Fije explained that he "was sold by his uncle because he had not presented him with a female slave and cows on his father's death." And another named Asa recounted that he had killed a man, "on which account he was sold [into slavery] by the king."

Slave Coast Coastline of West Africa from which millions of Africans were enslaved and transported across the Atlantic.

Middle Passage Transatlantic voyage between Africa and America.

Slaves who survived the forced march to the coast faced a dire situation, for they were then confined in one of the numerous large-scale prisons built by European traders, often in swampy, disease-ridden areas. For weeks or months, slaves languished in dark, stale dungeons. Untold numbers died. Corpses were unceremoniously dumped in the swamplands in such numbers that human landfills formed. Only those few slaves who had connections to the local rulers could potentially be set free. When European slave traders arrived, African and European merchants transferred the slaves by canoes or small boats to the traders' ships.

This short trip from shore to ship afforded slaves one last chance to escape, but most failed. Their final moments in Africa were terrifying. An elderly enslaved woman, doomed to a life of servitude in the Caribbean and known today only as 'Sibell, described her terror after she had been taken to the coast and sold into slavery, "me nebber see de great ships pon de water before, me nebber hear de Waves before which me frighten so much-ee dat me thought me would die."

4-3c The Middle Passage

> The Middle Passage kills many and destroys aspects of the culture of survivors.

The transatlantic crossing that 'Sibell and 12.5 million of others were forced to embark on is known today as the **Middle Passage**. The term is Eurocentric in that it describes the middle leg of the European slave trader's journey that began with a passage from Europe to Africa with trade goods, continued with a "middle" passage from Africa to America with slaves, and

National Museum of American History/Kenneth E. Behring Center/Smithsonian Institution

Restraining Irons, Eighteenth Century Slaves at every point in their descent into bondage in the Americas were bound and restrained, often with impregnable irons. ▲

concluded with a final passage from America to Europe with goods purchased in the colonies. In the seventeenth century, roughly 20 percent of slaves died on the Middle Passage, though the figure fell steadily to 10 percent by the late eighteenth century as traders paid more attention to the health and cleanliness of their human cargo. Slaves already weak from famine and disease were the most likely to die on ship, and they often did so soon after embarkation. During the voyage, dysentery, fever, measles, smallpox, and scurvy often spread, causing further deaths. Slaves were often deprived of food and water, only worsening their condition. Women suffered slightly lower mortality than average, and children had the highest mortality.

Hygiene onboard was primitive but understood as important for the survival of the cargo. Some shipmasters would smoke the ship with tobacco or wash the decks with vinegar to prevent the spread of illness. Fresh air was probably the most important factor in health, and in good weather, slaves were allowed on deck. They were usually fed twice a day. Like animals, they were placed in front of a trough of rice and beans ten at a time and given spoons to feed themselves.

In the hold, men were bound together in pairs, left leg to right leg, left wrist to right wrist. Some masters removed the chains once the ship was at sea, others removed them during the day, and some did not remove them at all until the destination had been reached. Women were rarely shackled and often held above deck, only to suffer sexual abuse at the hands of their captors. Captives were naked, without possessions, and at the mercy of men who held guns, knives, whips, and branding irons. So grim were the conditions that some slaves concluded that they had in fact died and entered an underworld.

On ships crowded with traumatized strangers, many elements of African society began to dissolve. Family, kin, lineage, social status, even names now held little or no meaning in a new society composed of people unmoored from the village and family communities that had reared them. Sometimes, however, slaves did find familiar faces or fellow countrymen or form new bonds on the ship as 'Sibell recounted, when "me go in de ship me find my country woman Mimbo, my country man Dublin, my Country woman Sally."

Enough social bonds survived the journey into slavery or were formed on ships that slaves, working together, rebelled against their captivity and the conditions of their confinement. Rebellions took place on 10 percent of all slave ships, and on average about 10 percent of rebelling slaves would be killed in each instance. In total, about 100,000 rebel slaves died on the Middle Passage. Although most rebellions never gained the slaves' freedom, they did have a significant effect on the slave trade as shipmasters, fearing insurrection, spent an additional 20 percent of their budgets on security, a sum that if used to purchase and transport more slaves would have led to the enslavement of an additional one million Africans.

Once on land, survivors of the Middle Passage were again inspected, prodded, and then sold, often in small numbers so as to erase any sort of community that might have survived the voyage or been forged in the ships' holds. Perhaps as many as 300,000 slaves who had survived the Middle Passage were shipped to other parts of the Americas. In a grim reminder of their captivity in Africa, newly arrived slaves in North America were frequently marched in chains for days or weeks from coastal ports to

The Art Archive/Alamy Stock Photo

***Slaves Below Deck*, Francis Meynell, 1846** Millions endured the horrors of the transatlantic passage but few recorded it for posterity. This rare image shows the misery and monotony of slaves held below deck. ▲

plantations, where they were again subjected to physical violence intended to render their servitude both hopeless and permanent. The lash, the stocks, dismemberment, and even death awaited those who resisted. For many, this was the final step in a tragic African diaspora as well as the beginning of another horrific ordeal, one whose legacies continue in both Africa and the Americas to this day.

4-3d Slavery in the Northern and Chesapeake Colonies

Slaves work in a variety of capacities, but most toil in agricultural pursuits.

In 1700, some 5,700 people of African descent lived in the Northern and Middle Colonies. In the agricultural areas of Pennsylvania and New Jersey, the Hudson Valley, Long Island, southern Massachusetts, Connecticut, and Rhode Island, most male slaves worked as jacks-of-all-trades on farms that raised livestock and crops destined for the West Indies. A smaller number worked in tanneries, mines, forges, and foundries. At the same time, wealthy whites in the North began buying female slaves to work in their kitchens instead of continuing to rely on white servants who were more expensive. Slaves in the North lived in whatever extra space existed in their masters' homes or estates, such as closets, backrooms, cellars, or shacks. Some raised gardens to supplement their diets and used their free time to work for other whites who would pay them for their labor. Significant numbers of slaves worked in towns and ports as either common laborers or skilled craftsmen.

The Chesapeake had by far the largest number of people of African descent with some 19,600 in 1700 and had the most laws regulating slavery. It was in the Chesapeake that elite planters became the first colonial Britons on the mainland to enshrine slavery in law. In 1655, Elizabeth Key, a mulatto woman born to a slave mother and a free white man, successfully claimed her freedom on the basis of her father's status. The county court had made the decision based on English common law, which held that "the Child of a Woman slave begott by a freeman ought to be free." But the decision was superseded in 1662 when the Virginia legislature, which was controlled by the wealthiest slave-holding planters, mandated that all children born in Virginia "shall be held bond or free only according to the condition of the mother," thereby creating a system in which slavery became self-reproducing. Under this law and a similar one adopted by Maryland the following year (see Table 4.3), the children of slaves across the Chesapeake were considered property of their parents' owner, and the paternity of the child born to a slave woman was irrelevant. This law not only relieved planters of any responsibility for children born to slave women they raped but also was a reversal of English law in which children followed the status of their father.

A 1667 Virginia law declared that the baptism of a slave did not confer freedom, thereby closing another avenue slaves had often turned to that supported the claim that their children should be free. Previously, European Christians had typically refrained from enslaving other Christians, but in Virginia, Christians then could and did enslave black Christians. In 1669, planters in the colony granted themselves nearly complete control over the management of their slaves, declaring that it was not a felony if a slave died while being "corrected" by an owner. Finally, in 1672, the colony committed itself to policing slaves and compensating owners from the public treasury if a fugitive slave was killed while being recaptured. Slaves in Virginia were whipped for minor offenses and had little freedom of movement. Furthermore, to guard against slave conspiracies, not more than four slaves were allowed to meet, and any meeting of four or fewer was allowed for only a short period of time.

Because most slaves in the Chesapeake lived on small plantations and travel among plantations was restricted, it was difficult if not impossible for them to create a settled community or social life. Because planters imported more males than females, men had little opportunity to find wives, fathered

The Granger Collection, New York

Overseer and Slaves, 1798 Everywhere male and female slaves who resisted slavery were beaten. This watercolor by Benjamin J. Latrobe depicts an overseer armed with a whip watching over enslaved women as they work. ▲

Global Americans

Like many others in the early modern period, Anthony Johnson could not sign his own name; thus in a 1666 legal proceeding, he left his own distinctive mark.

When captured in his native Angola, Antonio had no idea that he would become a prosperous slaveholder. After being sold to Arab slave traders, "Antonio a Negro" was sold to a Virginia Company representative in 1621 as a "servant" but actually was a slave. For a dozen years, Antonio worked alongside white indentured servants on Richard Bennett's tobacco plantation. There, he married "Mary a Negro woman." She and Antonio eventually farmed independently, and they had their children baptized, all actions of a couple assimilating into English society. Eventually, Antonio and Mary gained their freedom by purchasing it with funds they had saved while working for Bennett. Antonio changed his name to **Anthony Johnson** and ultimately purchased 250 acres and used black and white indentured servants on his own plantation. Anthony and Mary were part of a very small group of blacks in the Chesapeake in the mid-seventeenth century who had arrived in a period when race and slavery had not yet rigidified in the North American colonies. Africans could amass assets within a generation or two of their immigration and even purchase their own freedom. Between 1650 and 1700, however, such opportunities were numbered as planters pursued profitable and inhumane methods of extracting wealth from their imported laborers, as laws began to draw firm distinctions between African slaves and European servants in society, and as vast new systems of trade, commerce, and exploitation became central to not only the emerging colonies but also the Atlantic world that they shaped.

Table 4.3 Major Virginia Laws Related to Slavery

Year	Law
1662	Slavery inherited from mother regardless of status of father
1667	Christian baptism no longer alters status as a slave
1669	Planters who kill a slave while punishing him or her no longer guilty of a felony
1672	Colony commits to compensating owners from slaves killed while being recaptured

few children, and could not carry on their family's lineages, which were of paramount importance in Africa. Furthermore, because pregnant slave women were allowed no additional rest, they often suffered miscarriages. Planters could sustain this brutal order only with force. Maiming and beatings, sanctioned by law, became routine in the second half of the seventeenth century, as the Chesapeake transitioned from a society with slaves to a slave society.

Paradoxically, masters believed their slaves were part of their households and families. The planters were proponents and defenders of a **patriarchal** family structure in which wives, children, servants, and slaves all lived under the authority of the father. A good father provided protection and sustenance for his dependents while maintaining strict control of his household. For example, one Virginia planter told his slave that "If you will be good I shall be yr Loving Master," and at the same time threatened to have him "Slasht Severly, and pickled" if he was disobedient. In the late eighteenth century, masters began to imagine themselves as enlightened paternalists and created the fiction of the happy slave.

Because slaves were cheaper in the long run than indentured servants, planters moved away from servants and bought slaves in greater and greater numbers throughout the second half of the seventeenth century. This shift had a number of effects on slaves. First, it eroded the already minimal standards of decency and respect that they had been accorded when working alongside white servants. In the absence of white laborers, slaves were forced to work even longer hours, under tighter supervision, and with greater regimentation. They received less food, worse shelter, and poorer medical attention than white servants. Many slaves were forced to work on Sunday, and holidays were limited to Christmas, Easter, and Pentecost. As they assumed near total control over their slaves, Chesapeake planters also denied slaves the right to any sort of independent economy.

Slaves resisted this new regime. Some plotted, albeit with little success, against planters, and others feigned ignorance and incompetence. Some ran away, usually only to be recaptured. At the same time, opportunities for the dwindling number of free blacks in the Chesapeake dried up. They were denied the rights to employ white servants, to hold office, to bear arms, to participate in the militia, and to vote. And as blackness became synonymous with slavery, many free blacks were kidnapped and sold into slavery.

4-3e Slavery in the Lowcountry

The task system and the persistence of African culture characterize slavery in the Lowcountry.

In 1700, the coastal region of Carolina known as the Lowcountry or Lower South counted only about 3,400 African slaves. Slaves in the Lowcountry grew rice and indigo under the **task system**. After slaves completed a set amount of work each day or week, time was their own. Lowcountry planters offered their slaves little food, clothing, or medical attention. Although many African slaves had a sickle-cell trait that gave them some immunity against malaria, the living and working conditions in Carolina still proved fatal to many. Thus, the region's slave population increased only as planters imported them.

patriarchal Manifestation or institutionalization of male dominance over women and children in the family and in society in general.

task system Form of labor organization in which slaves were given an assignment to complete in a specific amount of time.

Slaves in this region lived together in unhealthy quarters. Yet these lodgings became the centers of their nonworking lives as well as outposts of African life and culture. Slaves built their quarters themselves, often using African construction techniques. Sitting in the shadow of the planter's mansion, these villages allowed slaves a modicum of permanence and stability. Within their villages, slaves asserted their rights to rest on Sunday and to own small plots of land where they cultivated vegetables, fowl, and rice. They spoke African languages, practiced African customs, celebrated African holidays, and kept their African names. Fewer slaves in the Lower South converted to Christianity than in the Chesapeake and the North.

As in the Chesapeake, planters used new laws and violence to support their rule. By 1690, planters in South Carolina were legally blameless if a slave died while being "corrected," even if the death was caused by a planter's "willfulness, wantonness, or bloody mindedness." As in regions to the north, slaves in the Lower South began to resist, in ways small and large, the brutal regime they found themselves living under.

4-4 Colonies in Crisis

There are no images of King Philip, Wampanoag leader, that date to the period in which he lived. In this image published in 1722, *Depiction of Metacomet, also known as King Philip of Wampanoag* by Paul Revere, note how Philip is dressed and the artifacts that are associated with him.

How is King Philip portrayed? What do his clothing and accoutrements of leadership say about him? ▶

Yale University Art Gallery

By the late seventeenth century, after decades of settlement and the integration of colonies into expanding imperial frameworks, it was evident that the European colonies in North America would endure. But, at the same time, most faced grave challenges. New Mexico weathered one of the most destructive and successful Indian counteroffensives in the history of the North American colonies. New England did as well, and was also unsettled again by political upheaval whose origins lay across the Atlantic. Virginia, meanwhile, confronted a servant rebellion that escalated into civil war. None of these crises proved fatal, but all permanently changed the colonies in which they occurred.

☞ As you read, focus on the nature of conflict and crises in specific regions. Is there a common source of the various rebellions that shook colonial America in the late seventeenth century?

4-4a The Pueblo Revolts

Indians across New Mexico rebel, expel the Spaniards, and force a lessening in the terms of Spanish rule.

After a steady accumulation of grievances, Pueblo Indians in 1680 rose against a colonial order that threatened their existence. In the previous decades, the number of Indians had declined as the result of disease, and the Spanish had raised tribute levels, compounding Indian hardship. Spanish demands disrupted the Pueblos' relations with their neighbors because the agricultural surplus that the Pueblos had long traded with the Apache on the Great Plains began instead to go to the Spanish. Viewing their own survival as imperiled, the Apache launched violent raids on Pueblo communities to take by force what they could no longer acquire through trade. The onset of drought and famine in the 1660s only led to additional violence. In 1673, Apache raiders torched the community of Hawikuh, killing 200 people and taking a thousand captive. Amid the crisis, many Pueblos who had practiced Catholicism at Spanish insistence returned to their Native religion. In 1675, New Mexico's governor responded by trying to stamp out what remained of Pueblo spirituality, taking particular aim at traditional dances. The governor had three Pueblo religious leaders hanged for sorcery and sedition and another forty-three beaten for practicing their religion.

The confrontation exploded in August 1680 with the **Pueblo Revolt**, a carefully planned rebellion by more than two dozen Indian communities. The rebellion was led by Po'pay, a religious leader from San Juan Pueblo who was one of the forty-three Indians beaten by the Spaniards. Within days, the rebels had killed a fifth of the province's 2,500 settlers, most of whom were caught off guard. Spanish survivors first took refuge in the capital of Santa Fé where they fought off an Indian siege. Eventually, the Spanish governor Antonio de Otermín led 1,500 refugees, many of whom were Indian servants, three hundred miles south to El Paso del Norte where they lived for the next twelve years.

Po'pay had his followers target all evidence of Catholicism. The rebels killed twenty-one of thirty-three missionaries in the province and destroyed most of the mission churches. A Pueblo man captured by the Spanish reported that Po'pay ordered his men to "break up and burn the images of the holy Christ, the Virgin Mary and the other saints, the crosses, and everything pertaining to Christianity." The rebels also called for male Indians to disavow the marriages that Franciscans had performed among them and to "separate from the wives" they had been forced to wed. To cleanse them of Christianity, Po'pay made all baptized Indians plunge themselves into the closest river in an attempt to have them wash away the baptism.

Po'pay's revolt succeeded because he had been able to unify many disparate groups that all shared common grievances against Spanish rule. But once the Spaniards had been driven out, the Pueblo coalition fractured. In 1692, a new Spanish governor, Diego de Vargas, led eight hundred Spaniards back into New Mexico and began exploiting divisions among the Pueblo. He quickly re-established Spanish rule, which included the economic exploitation of Indians and the prominence of Catholicism. Another Pueblo rebellion in 1696 left five Franciscans dead. In response, the Franciscans began to tolerate some aspects of Native religion and the colony's tribute system was abolished. But by that time, decades of drought and famine had reduced the Pueblo Indians' numbers to about fourteen thousand. These survivors no longer posed a serious threat to the Spaniards, and as a result, New Mexico entered a period of peace and unchallenged Spanish rule.

4-4b King Philip's War

The Puritans' religious inflexibility and continued encroachment on Indian lands prompts crises in church membership and a new Indian war.

The Puritan society that had emerged from the Great Migration of the 1630s was exclusionary, ruled largely by zealous church founders and laymen who did not fully admit settlers deemed spiritually lacking into their society. The children of the first generation of Puritan immigrants inherited property, church membership, and political power from their parents. But their children, like the mid-century immigrants to the colony, did not gain church membership and the political and economic opportunities that went with it unless they could demonstrate through a conversion experience that they indeed had saving faith. To arrest the decline in church membership, church leaders instituted the **Half-Way Covenant** (1662) under which the children and grandchildren of church members received partial church membership even if they had not had a conversion experience. Though they were granted membership, they were denied communion and a vote in church affairs. Still, church membership continued to decline. Frustrated and concerned ministers across New England subjected their congregants to angry sermons, known as **jeremiads**, in which they condemned their congregants for straying from the fundamentalism of the first generation of colonists.

If Puritan New England suffered internal turmoil because settlers found to be spiritually lacking were denied full participatory rights, it suffered nearly total ruin because most New England settlers refused to grant Indians any place at all in their world. Whereas colonists in New Mexico had attempted to exploit and convert the Pueblos, who vastly outnumbered them, New Englanders in the late 1670s sought to do away with the Native Americans in their midst whom they increasingly outnumbered. In the nearly forty years after the Pequot War, settlers and Indians had confronted one another numerous times. But the conflict that the English called **King Philip's War** (1675–1678) represented a new level of violence and hatred.

The spark for the war was the death of John Sassamon and the prosecution of three Indians for his murder. Sassamon was a longtime aide of the Wampanoag leader Metacom, or Philip, son of Massasoit, and had worked with the Puritan minister John Elliot to translate the Bible. Before his death, Sassamon had informed the Plymouth governor, Josiah Winslow, that Philip and other Indians were plotting to destroy the English and that he feared that Philip would kill him if he knew of their conversation. Soon thereafter, Sassamon was found dead in a frozen pond. Philip denied his involvement, but the Plymouth authorities arrested three of his counselors who were found guilty and executed.

A few days later, a group of Wampanoags, seemingly acting on their own, attacked the Plymouth town of Swansea, killing nine settlers. English militias supported by the governments of Plymouth, Massachusetts Bay, and Connecticut prepared a counterattack. Many were eager to push the Indians off of the

Pueblo Revolt Anticolonial rebellion of Pueblo Indians across New Mexico that temporarily forced the Spanish out of the province.

Half-Way Covenant Partial church membership in New England begun in 1662 that granted limited membership to the children and grandchildren of church members.

jeremiads Sermon full of lament and bitterness intended to provoke congregants to action; name derived from the biblical prophet Jeremiah.

King Philip's War Armed conflict (1675–1678) in New England between the Wampanoag and Narragansett Indians on one side and the English and their Indian allies on the other.

lands that remained in their control, and they feared that those Indians who had moved to Eliot's Praying Towns had become an enemy within. By the fall of 1675, the English militias had confined all of the Native Americans at the Praying Towns on an island in Boston Harbor.

As the region spiraled into war, Philip organized a large-scale attack on the English. Of the ninety towns in New England, Wampanoags and Narragansetts attacked fifty and destroyed thirteen. But the English proved more deadly. In an echo of the massacre of the Pequots decades earlier, New England militiamen surrounded a Native American village in Rhode Island, set it afire, and killed some one thousand Narragansetts. Philip and many of his followers fled south, perhaps mistakenly believing that New York's governor would aid them as New Netherland's governor once had. But Governor Edmund Andros, along with Mohawk allies he had armed, forced Philip and his people back into Massachusetts where English forces surrounded and killed Philip in the spring of 1676. By the end of the war, five thousand Indians, or half the Native American population in New England, had been murdered, killed in battle, or had died from the privations the war had brought. The English sold one thousand survivors into slavery and exiled another two thousand.

The English did not escape the war unscathed. Nearly one thousand English died in the conflict, and the cost of the war led to tax increases that sparked popular resentments. Moreover, the war so destabilized the colonies that they were unable to fend off the crown's plan to bind them more tightly into an imperial structure.

4-4c Bacon's Rebellion

Declining social mobility for an increasing number of disgruntled servants prompts a rebellion.

Virginia, too, was riven by rebellion although of a different kind. In 1676, planters allied with Governor William Berkeley confronted men who followed Nathaniel Bacon, a recently arrived planter. **Bacon's Rebellion** came without warning, but the seeds of the conflict had been planted in an earlier era. As the result of a boom in tobacco production, Virginia had grown rapidly since mid-century, and by 1670, the colony's population stood at around thirty-five thousand. But most of the profits in the tobacco economy went to the richest and most powerful planters. Small planters also suffered more than their richer counterparts under the 1660 Navigation Act, which declared that goods and commodities produced in the colonies could be sold only in English ports. The result was diminished demand for tobacco, prompting the price of the crop to drop by half.

Bacon's Rebellion Armed rebellion led in 1676 by Nathaniel Bacon against William Berkeley, governor of Virginia, primarily over the colony's Indian policy and access to land.

Bacon's wealth made him an unlikely rebel, but he and others were troubled by the declining opportunity for less wealthy men to rise, especially now that more and more indentured servants were outliving their terms of indenture. Bacon and others were especially upset with Berkeley's Indian policy, which had led to the removal of the Powhatans from the vicinity of the most settled areas of Virginia but assured them land above the York River. This area, however, was considered crucial to the economic ambitions of a frustrated generation of servants and former servants who had no land. Servants in Virginia, many of whom had gained their freedom after years of toil and could now not afford land, had little choice but to become tenants, virtually ensuring them a life of poverty. Bacon spoke to these struggling planters' fears and gave them hope that they could grow more tobacco by seizing Indian lands.

On the other side of the conflict stood Berkeley, who owned a 1,000-acre plantation and one of the colony's largest contingents of slaves at a time when there were only two thousand Africans in the colony. Berkeley and his planter friends, known as the *Green Spring faction*, used their connections and power to amass large landed estates. They imported servants and slaves and got 50 acres per head, allowing them to control virtually all of the good land suitable for tobacco cultivation, except that which was held by Indians. Berkeley, like other colonial governors of the time, favored the creation of a landed aristocracy. One of the largest slave owners in the colony, Berkeley supported the expansion of slavery. He had signed the legislation in the 1660s and 1670s that had enshrined slavery in the colony's laws. Furthermore, Berkeley was an absolutist. He called elections in 1661, just after he was appointed royal governor, but not again until 1676. Four years later, he signed legislation that denied the vote to men who did not own property.

Because there were few Indians living above York River, Bacon and his followers believed, incorrectly, that they could easily expel them (see Map 4.4). In January 1676, Chesapeake planters and militiamen marched out to the frontier, surrounded a group of Doegs and Susquehannocks, enticed their leaders to negotiate, and then murdered them. Further violence soon followed, leading to widespread fear among people in northern Virginia of a pan-Indian attack. Soon, 60 out of 71 plantations in the region were abandoned, and by March, three hundred Virginians had been killed.

To settle the dispute, Berkeley proposed a line of forts to keep Indians and settlers separate, but those who already had plantations believed that this would cost them too much in additional taxes. At this point, Bacon asked Berkeley for permission to go to war against any Indians he could find. When Berkeley refused, Bacon forced him at gunpoint to grant the requested military commission. Declaring Bacon a rebel, Berkeley went after him with three hundred planters and English soldiers. In May 1677, at the end of the conflict among Berkeley, Bacon and the local Indians, the surviving Powhatans had been

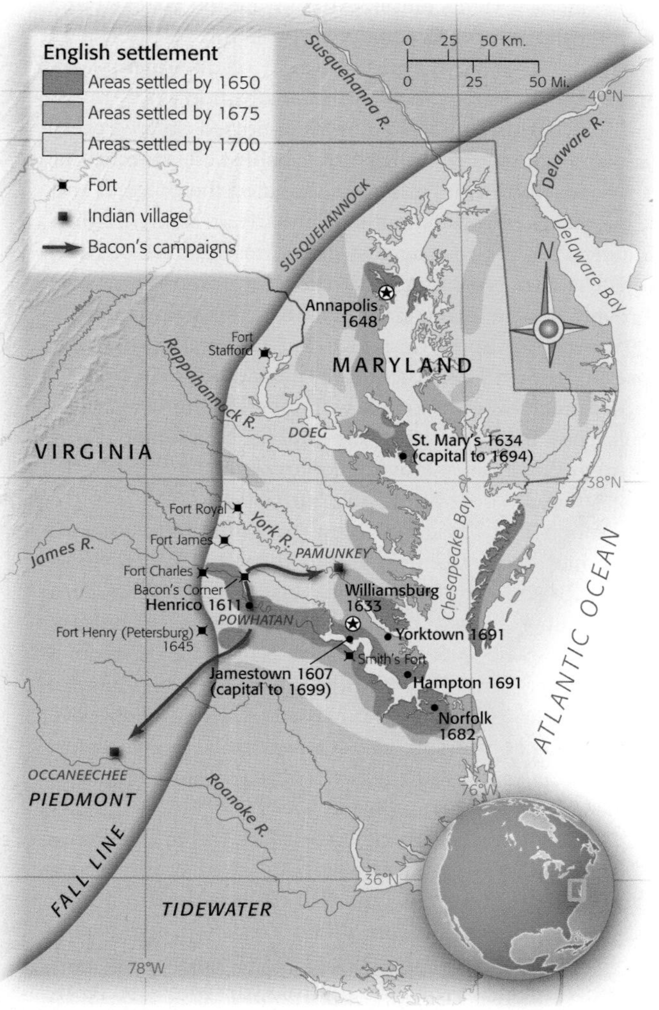

Map 4.4 Bacon's Rebellion and English Expansion in the Chesapeake to 1700 By 1700 English cultivation of tobacco in Virginia had pushed far into the interior. In the wake of Bacon's Rebellion, Indians' loss of land in the Chesapeake accelerated. ▲

defeated by Bacon's men, who had also burned the capital of Jamestown to the ground. Bacon died of a fever during the conflict, and almost two dozen of his followers were captured and executed by the Virginia authorities after the conflict ended.

Bacon's Rebellion revealed that colonial government was largely powerless to prevent murderous attacks by settlers who wanted to establish their own plantations. Although the rebellion by Bacon and his followers had been put down, the expansion of English settlement onto Indian land above the York River continued given the destruction of the Powhatans as a fighting force. The Native Americans of the region recognized that the price of their survival was submission to English society. Over the coming decades, as the Powhatans declined, new English tobacco planters profited immensely on lands that were formerly Indian.

4-4d The Glorious Revolution in British North America

A political revolution in England sparks popular rebellion across British North America.

In the late seventeenth century, many of the challenges the colonies faced originated in events in England. King Charles II attempted to establish greater control over the colonies. Most influentially, he encouraged Massachusetts leaders to make their government more secular. In response to their refusal, he revoked the colony's charter in 1684 and disbanded the General Court. He also jeopardized the colonists' landholdings, causing significant popular anger.

When Charles died in February 1685, his Catholic brother, James II, succeeded him. In England, James pushed Protestants out of government office in favor of Catholic appointees. James II imposed his authority on the colonies in 1686 by combining Plymouth, Massachusetts, Rhode Island, Connecticut, New Jersey, and New York into one colony, known as the **Dominion of New England**. He also promoted the Anglican Sir Edmund Andros to the dominion's governorship (see Map 4.5). Puritan fears about Andros were realized when he converted a Puritan church in Boston into an Anglican one. He alienated other groups in Massachusetts when he officially terminated the colony's representative assembly, imposed new taxes, and limited the power of town meetings.

Dominion of New England Administrative unit encompassing northern colonies in British North America from 1686 to 1689 that colonists bitterly opposed.

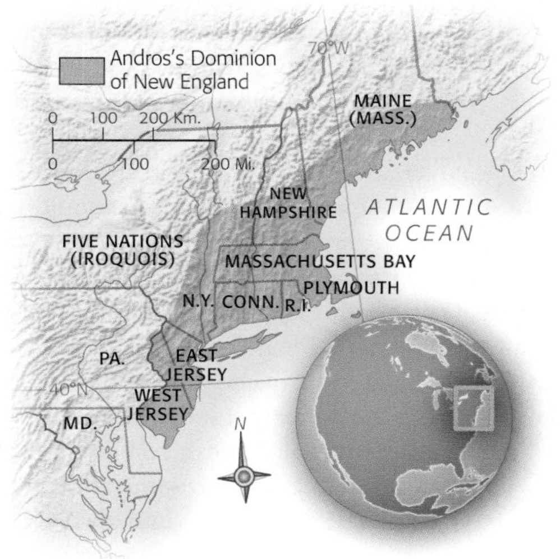

Map 4.5 The Dominion of New England, 1686 When James II became king of England, he sought to consolidate his power in the colonies by creating one large colony composed of Plymouth, Massachusetts, Rhode Island, Connecticut, New York, and New Jersey. ▲

Andros was unpopular in Massachusetts, but James was hated in England. In view of his appointment of Catholics to high office and cultivation of the Pope, many English Protestants feared that he would make England a Catholic nation again. In June 1688, James's queen, Mary of Modena, gave birth to a boy, which seemed to open the possibility of a dynasty of absolutist Catholic kings in England. The opponents of James—namely aristocrats and Anglican bishops—invited William, the Dutch Prince of the Netherlands, who was married to the king's Protestant daughter, Mary, to intervene and force James to accept a Protestant successor and recognize the authority of Parliament. In the fall of 1688, William assembled an enormous fleet of five hundred ships and forty thousand men and invaded England. He did so to pursue his own agenda: Fearing a renewed war with France, the Dutch military leader wanted to ensure that the English did not ally with France against the Netherlands. When James showed little interest in fighting for the throne, his regime collapsed, allowing William to conquer the island with little resistance. In 1689, Parliament transferred the throne to William and Mary as joint sovereigns.

Glorious Revolution Largely peaceful overthrow of James II and ascent to the throne of William and Mary who agreed to a limited monarchy.

Declaration of Rights Document crafted by English Parliament in 1689 during the Glorious Revolution that listed the wrongs committed by James II and the rights that all English citizens hold.

Bill of Rights Act of English Parliament in 1689 that essentially endorsed the Declaration of Rights and established basic civil rights for English citizens.

constitutional monarchy Governmental system in which the monarchy is constrained by a written constitution.

British Constitution Body of laws and principles that define the scope of the English government and guarantee English citizens basic rights and privileges.

Leisler's Rebellion Anti-authoritarian rebellion (1689–1691) in New York prompted by the Glorious Revolution in England.

As part of the **Glorious Revolution**, an event that shaped politics in the distant colonies, William and Mary decreed that Catholics could never hold the throne of England. They also extended religious toleration to various groups of dissenting Protestants through the Toleration Act of 1689, a law that, despite its name, denied freedom of religion to Jews and Catholics. Significantly, the new rulers assented to Parliament's **Declaration of Rights**, which amounted to a **Bill of Rights**. William and Mary disavowed absolutist rule by accepting a **constitutional monarchy** and agreeing to limits on the crown's power imposed by Parliament. The monarchs could no longer simply suspend or ignore acts of Parliament. They could not levy taxes or maintain a standing army without Parliamentary approval. Debate in Parliament was to be free. Elections were to occur regularly. Moreover, all Englishmen could now petition the crown without fear of retribution, had the right to trial by jury, were free from excessive bail or fines, and no longer subject to cruel and unusual punishment. With the overthrow of James II, Englishmen came more firmly to believe that these "ancient rights and liberties" were the birthright of all Englishmen and that the crown was forever subject to the rule of law enshrined in a series of documents and precedents known as the **British Constitution**.

The British in the colonies followed suit; Protestant denominations, mainly the established churches of Anglicans and Presbyterians, dominated the political and religious life of most colonies. Similarly, in many English colonies, settlers rose against the representatives of royal authority. In New England, the Dominion was overthrown, and the original colonial charters again became the basis of law and governance. In Maryland, Protestants rose up against Lord Baltimore, the Catholic proprietor, and defeated his government without resorting to violence. Backed by the king, the rebels established a largely Protestant government. Catholics could still practice their religion but could not vote or hold office.

When news reached New York that William and Mary had taken the throne and then that Andros had been imprisoned by his rivals in Massachusetts, New York militiamen removed Lt. Governor Francis Nicholson, and seized New York City's fort to "save" the city from a much-feared Catholic and Indian invasion from Canada. A week later—in what is known as **Leisler's Rebellion**—Jacob Leisler, the son of a German Calvinist pastor, emerged as captain of the fort and then as commander of the colony.

Leisler's proficient rule came to an end in the spring of 1691 when the new crown-appointed governor, Henry Sloughter, arrived from England. He was determined to put down's Leisler's revolt. When Leisler finally surrendered, he was arrested, charged with treason, and sentenced to death. From the scaffold, on May 16, 1691, Leisler made an eloquent plea for his life, professing that he had not been motivated by personal gain but by the cause of Protestantism. Nevertheless, Sloughter had Leisler and his assistant hanged and cut down and beheaded while still alive.

4-4e King William's War and the 1692 Witchcraft Panic

Indian warfare and religious fundamentalism lead to a witch panic in New England.

Although many English colonists cheered the bloodless assent of William to the crown, his coronation meant more bloodshed in the colonies. William quickly started a war known in Europe as the *Nine Years' War* and in the colonies as *King William's War* (1689–1697). His enemy was France, England's long-time religious, cultural, territorial, and economic rival. William built up the English navy, and his early naval victories enhanced England's position in world trade and finance. In the colonies, however, the conflict provoked devastating frontier warfare and instability. England's Indian allies attacked the French, and France's Indian allies attacked English frontier outposts across New England, causing havoc and paranoia. Unbeknownst to the colonists at the time, King William's War was the first of a series of four bloody and extraordinarily expensive intercolonial wars, whose origins lay in Europe. These wars, largely fought between the English and the French pulled in Indians along the frontier between New England and New France, and would not be concluded until the defeat of the French and their Indian allies in the Seven Years War (1754–1763).

With the outbreak of King William's War, colonists in Massachusetts and Maine feared that neither their colonial governments nor a distant England could protect them from Indian attack. To fight the war against France, England had to build a much larger navy and army, create a state bureaucracy to run them, and then increase taxes to pay for it all. England, therefore, quickly moved from the lightest-taxed nation in Europe to among the heaviest taxed. Even so, the national debt increased each year. The beefed-up army and navy did little to help the colonists. England focused on protecting itself from invasion, and any remaining resources were sent to protect the lucrative West Indies. As fear pervaded the northern colonies, English defenses on the Massachusetts frontier collapsed because of the desertion of the men whom the then-deposed Andros had pressed into military service. When Indians who were aided by the French attacked in the winter of 1689–1690, the English suffered terrible losses and hundreds, if not thousands, abandoned their frontier settlements.

Not coincidentally, at that very moment, scores of colonists across Essex County, Massachusetts, gripped by fears of an Indian attack, began to level accusations of witchcraft against their neighbors and community members. The panic started in Salem Village, a small farming community about fifteen miles north of Boston, when a group of adolescent girls began to have bizarre fits. Samuel Parris, father of one of the girls and uncle of another, called a local physician. The physician suspected the girls were "under an evil hand." In February 1692, warrants went out for the arrest of three women whom the girls claimed were their tormentors. Two of the women denied the charges, but a third, a West Indian slave named Tituba, confessed. In the early spring, numerous women were tried and sentenced to death for witchcraft. One man, Giles Cory of Salem village, was accused of being a wizard, and for this crime, he was pressed to death by heavy weights progressively piled on top of his body. As the panic spread, 150 people were formally charged. As in previous episodes in the witch hysteria that gripped Europe from 1450 to 1750, three-fourths of the accused witches in New England were women who seemed to disrupt social expectations or norms. Women who had no husband or children or who had inherited property were vulnerable to charges of witchcraft.

Illustration of a Witch from Cotton Mather Account, 1689 Witchcraft was a crime because a witch was believed to have made a pact with the devil. A large number of those seemingly tormented by the devil were refugees from various Indian attacks on the frontier and were haunted by fears and memories of violence, captivity, and murder. ▼

In late September 1692, after twenty executions and with more than one hundred suspected witches in jail, the panic came to a close when ministers from eastern Massachusetts prevented the use of "spectors," or apparitions, as evidence. From that moment, it became almost impossible to prosecute anyone for witchcraft, and the remaining suspects, including Tituba, were eventually freed. The Peace of Ryswick (1697) ended the Nine Years' War in Europe, but it was not until the Grand Settlement of 1701 that war ended in America with the Haudenosaunees pledging neutrality in future wars between England and France. By the war's end, the Haudenosaunees had lost 2,000 of their total population of 8,600 and had narrowly saved themselves from destruction.

Summary

In the second half of the seventeenth century, revolutions and rebellions shook the emerging colonies. In the Caribbean, a revolution in the production of sugar sparked not only new dietary habits in England but also more plantations in the West Indies that depended on hundreds of thousands of enslaved Africans. To supply these laborers, Europeans kidnapped or purchased and sent into captivity millions of Africans who suffered horrible violence and indignities. A smaller number of Africans were transported to the mainland colonies where they were consigned to a slaves' existence without hope of liberation as new laws remade the lives of Africans in America. In the realm of international affairs, nations battled one another not only for territory but also for commerce as mercantilist thought revolutionized the way that the English and French colonies traded with one another and their own mother countries. Overall, England was on the ascendance, having defeated the Dutch in various conflicts, and Spain's focus remained on the consolidation of its long-established colonies. Although many English colonists resisted the new regulations, they in time strengthened local economies and the ties between colonies and the homeland. The greatest threat to the colonies in the late seventeenth century resulted from internal challenges as frustrated servants, oppressed Indians, ambitious leaders, and panicked believers challenged their leaders and neighbors in their attempts to find peace and security in a world beset by change and transformation.

<Thinking Back, *Looking Forward*>

As you review this chapter, think about how events on the continent of Europe continued to shape the American colonies and locate the origins of the transatlantic slave trade in other earlier slave systems. To what extent was commerce a key factor in the integration of American colonies into larger imperial frameworks? How important were coercion and absolutism to the new societies taking root in colonial America?

To make your study concrete, review the timeline and reflect on the entries there. Think about their causes, consequences, and connections. How do they fit with global trends?

Additional Resources

Books

Berlin, Ira. *Many Thousands Gone: The First Two Centuries of Slavery in North America*. Cambridge, MA: Harvard University Press, 1998. ▶ Best single-volume study of slavery across all the regions of colonial America.

Brown, Kathleen M. *Good Wives, Nasty Wenches, and Anxious Patriarchs: Gender, Race, and Power in Colonial Virginia*. Chapel Hill: University of North Carolina Press, 1996. ▶ Rereading of early Virginia history through the intersecting axes of gender and race.

Elliot, J. H. *Empires of the Atlantic World: Britain and Spain in America, 1492–1830*. New Haven, CT: Yale University Press, 2006. ▶ Thorough and engaging exploration of the economic, political, and intellectual foundations of England and Spain's transatlantic empires.

Eltis, David. *The Rise of African Slavery in the Americas*. Cambridge, England: Cambridge University Press, 2000. ▶ Stunning quantitative study of the transatlantic slave trade based on an examination of the shipping records of the trade itself.

Morgan, Philip D. *Slave Counterpoint: Black Culture in the Eighteenth-Century Chesapeake and Lowcountry*. Chapel Hill: University of North Carolina Press, 1998. ▶ Comprehensive and comparative study of slavery across the southern colonies.

Nash, Gary B. *Quakers and Politics: Pennsylvania, 1681–1726*. Princeton, NJ: Princeton University Press. ▶ Classic study of the Penn family's colony in America.

Norton, Mary Beth. *In the Devil's Snare: The Salem Witchcraft Crisis of 1692*. New York: Alfred A. Knopf, 2002. ▶ Painstaking and evocative reconstruction of the witchcraft crisis and the larger context within which it unfolded.

O'Malley, Gregory E. *Final Passages: The Intercolonial Slave Trade of British America, 1619–1807*. Chapel Hill: University of North Carolina Press, 2014. ▶ A rediscovery of the movements of thousands of slaves between the English colonies.

Ritchie, Robert C. *Captain Kidd and the War Against the Pirates*. Cambridge, MA: Harvard University Press, 1986. ▶ Swashbuckling account of England's most famous pirate.

Smallwood, Stephanie E. *Saltwater Slavery: A Middle Passage from Africa to American Diaspora*. Cambridge, MA: Harvard University Press, 2008. ▶ Gripping study of the Middle Passage and the meaning of slavery.

Go to the MindTap® for **Global Americans** to access the full version of select books from this Additional Resources section.

Websites

Voyages: The Transatlantic Slave Trade Database. http://slavevoyages.org/tast/index.faces ▶ Easy-to-search database with stunning set of records detailing more than forty thousand slave ships and their human cargo..

Salem Witch Trials Documentary Archive and Transcription Project. http://salem.lib.virginia.edu/home.html ▶ Archive of court records and other documents related to the trials in 1692.

MindTap®

Continue exploring online through MindTap®, where you can:

- **Assess your knowledge with the Chapter Test**
- **Watch historical videos related to the chapter**
- **Further your understanding with interactive maps and timelines**

Empires across the Atlantic World

1647–1655

1647

George Fox establishes Quaker religion.

1649

Charles I is executed.

1651

Enumeration Act passes.

1653

Oliver Cromwell assumes control of England.

1654–1655

Cromwell launches the Western Design.

1656–1660

1658

Cromwell dies.

1660

Charles II assumes control of England beginning the Stuart Restoration.

1661–1664

1662

Virginia legislature rules that slavery is a status inherited from the mother.

Church leaders institute Half-Way Covenant.

1663

Royal African Company is founded.

Eliot Bible is first published.

English Parliament passes the Staple Act.

English establish Carolina.

1664

England conquers New Netherland and founds New York.

Dutch formally surrender New York under the Articles of Capitulation.

1665–1670

1665

English establish the Colony of New Jersey.

1667

Mohawks sue for peace with French.

1668

English sack Jamaica.

1669

Carolina adopts the Fundamental Constitutions.

1671–1675

1673

English Parliament passes the Plantation Duty Act.

Joliet and Marquette explore upper Mississippi River.

1675

King Philip's War breaks out.

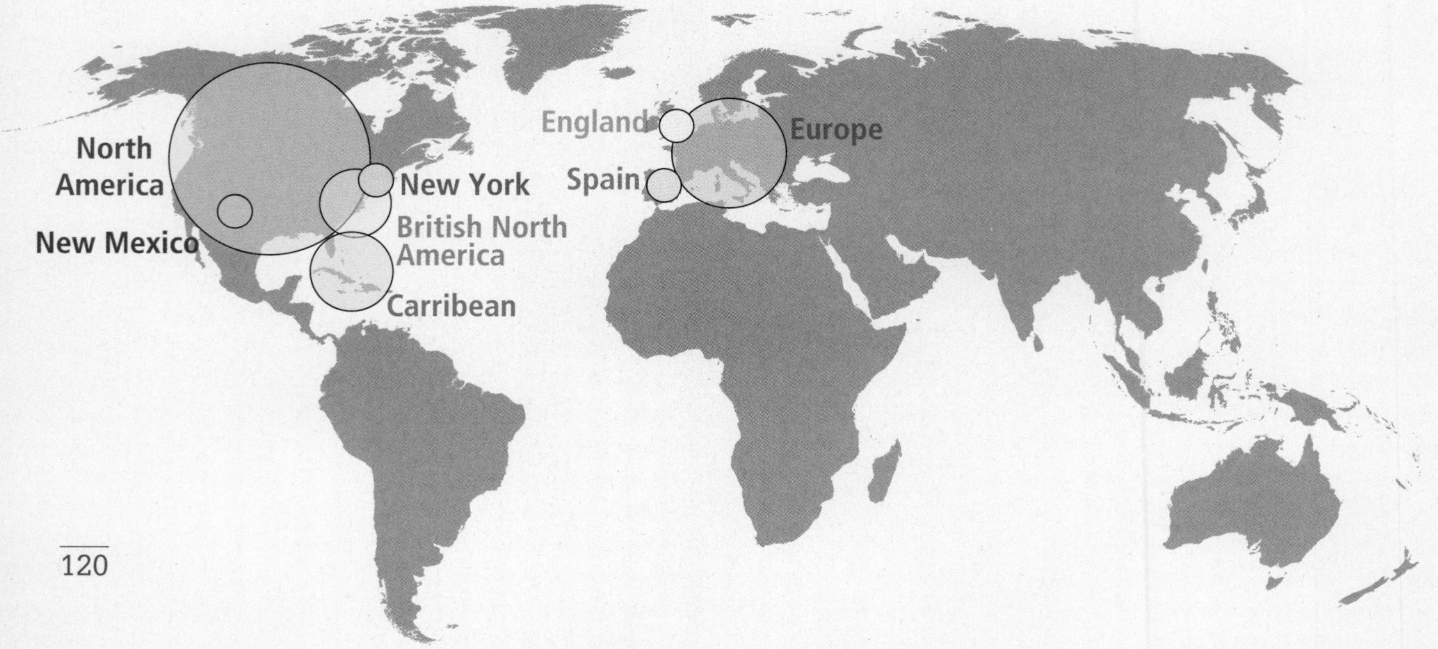

1676–1680	1681–1685	1686–1690	1691–1695	1696–1702
1676 New Jersey is divided into East and West Jersey. Kateri Tekakwitha is baptized. Bacon's Rebellion breaks out. **1678** Haudenosaunees and New York form Covenant Chain. **1680** Pueblo Revolt erupts.	**1681** Penn establishes Pennsylvania. **1682** Penn outlines his First Frame of Government. La Salle explores the Mississippi River to the Gulf of Mexico. **1683** Penn issues the Charter of Liberties. New York issues Charter of Liberties and Privileges. King Philip's War ends. **1684** Charles II revokes Massachusetts Bay Colony charter.	**1689** William and Mary ascend to the throne in the Glorious Revolution. Parliament suspends the Royal African Company's monopoly. Leisler takes over New York City's fort in Leisler's Rebellion. King William's War breaks out between the English and French. Witchcraft panic begins in Salem and spreads throughout New England.	**1692** Vargas leads reconquest of New Mexico.	**1696** Second Pueblo Revolt breaks out. Board of Trade is established in England.  **1697** Peace of Ryswick ends the Nine Years' War. **1698** French settle lower Mississippi Valley. **1701** Haudenosaunees declare neutrality. **1702** Crown unites East and West Jersey in single colony.

5 Colonial Society and the Bonds of Empire

1700–1750

Born in Africa, taken captive in his youth, and carried to British North America, Broteer Furro, also known as Venture Smith, experienced the horrors and humiliations of the transatlantic slave trade. Through luck and perseverance, he survived and purchased his own freedom after decades of hardship.

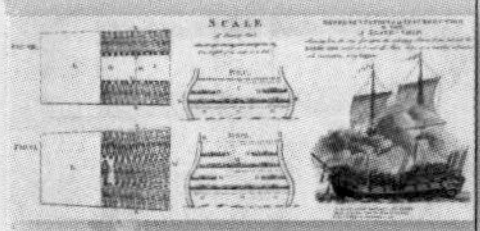

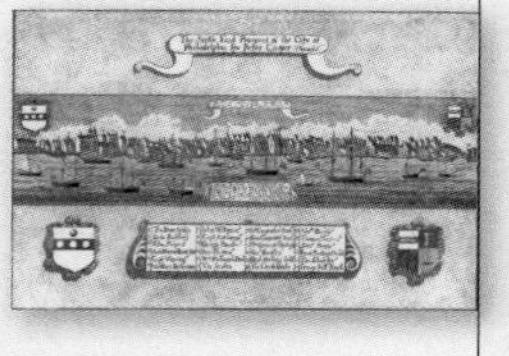

In an age defined by the exchange of commodities across the Atlantic and the movement, forced or voluntary, of hundreds of thousands of people to the Americas, the story of Broteer Furro is both distinct and emblematic. Born in 1729 in Dukandarra, Guinea, Furro lived a peaceful life until he was eight, when slave hunters raided his town. "The very first salute I had from them," Furro recalled, "was a violent blow on the head with the fore part of a gun, and at the same time a grasp around the neck." Furro then saw his father "tortured to death," a "shocking scene" that was always "fresh" in his mind.

A View Taken Near Bain, on the Coast of Guinea in Africa. Engraved by Catherine Prestell, published by J. Phillips, London, 1789, after sketches on location by Carl B. Wadstrom.

Broteer was imprisoned in a coastal slave station and eventually sold to Robertson Mumford, a Rhode Island slave trader, who purchased him "for four gallons of rum, and a piece of calico," a common form of cotton cloth. Mumford renamed the young boy Venture. After a transatlantic crossing, in which 60 of the 260 slaves on board Mumford's ship perished, Venture disembarked in Rhode Island.

Without much help, Venture fought his own battle against slavery for the remainder of his life. For refusing Mumford's son's orders, he was bound and threatened with death. Years later, Mumford beat him "with a club two feet long and as large around as a chair-post." This brutality defined slavery in America throughout the early eighteenth century, an era when slaves worked in a variety of capacities, not just on plantations. To be black, whether free or enslaved, was to be despised and treated, in Venture's words, like "the black dog." Venture was purchased by one Captain Oliver Smith, and from then on he went by the name Venture Smith. Against all odds, Smith survived decades of the humiliation and brutality of slavery and ultimately purchased his freedom and that of his family and friends.

Venture Smith's story is distinctive because it ends in his hard-won freedom. But it is also emblematic in that it reflects the terrible experiences of slaves in early America. Smith is a reminder that across the eighteenth century, slavery was expanding in colonial America. His life also suggests the challenges overcome not just by slaves but also by the great numbers of people who came to the Americas from Europe and Africa as laborers. Moreover, Smith's life demonstrates the degree to which the global trade of people and commodities had knit together African, American, and European communities. Smith, purchased as a child for four gallons of rum and a piece of calico, was not only witness to the transnational commerce that shaped colonial America but also was its tragic embodiment.

How does Venture Smith's journey from slavery to freedom reflect the realities of transnational commercial development of the colonial age?

Go to MindTap® to watch a video on Smith and learn how his story relates to the themes of this chapter.

5-1

Peoples in Motion

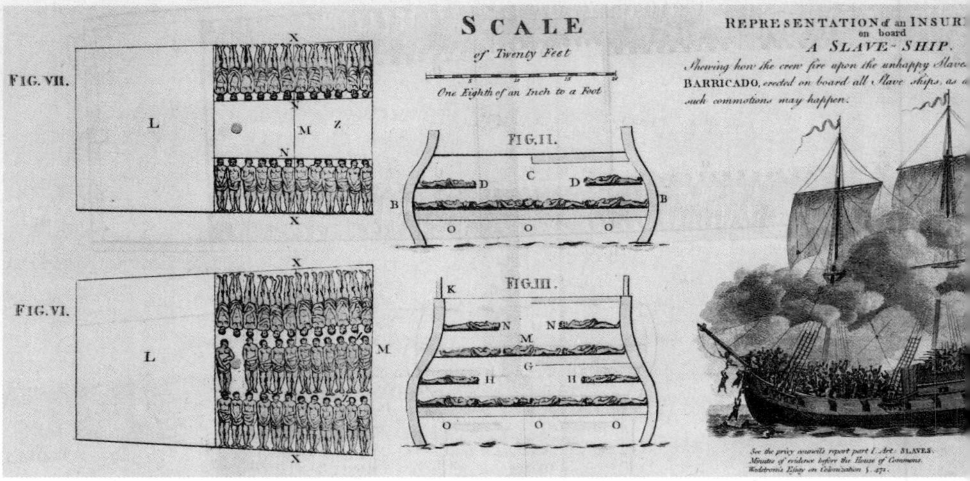

This plan for *The Brookes*, an actual slave ship, from Carl B. Wadstrom's *An Essay on Colonization, particularly applied to the Western coast of Africa... in Two Parts* (1794, 1795), shows how Africans were stowed in the holds. In an added touch of realism, the inset depicts a revolt aboard a slave ship with the crew shooting the rebels. This ship was designed to carry 609 slaves (351 men, 127 women, 90 boys, and 41 girls).

The Art Archive

Look closely at the detailed plan of this ship. How is its hold portrayed? How are slaves depicted? ▶

After the crises of the late seventeenth century, the British colonies entered a period of stability, and the transatlantic economy continued to expand. As a result, vast numbers of people came to British North America in the early eighteenth century. Some came as slaves from Africa or as convicted felons from England. Others, most notably Germans, sold themselves or their children into years of labor to gain passage across the Atlantic. Still others left increasingly impoverished homelands in Ireland or Scotland. At the same time, the birthrate in the colonies rose to new heights, and the population of much of colonial America exploded. All of these factors contributed to a population increase in eastern North America from 251,000 non-Indians in 1700 to 1,186,000 by 1750 (see Table 5.1). These swelling numbers forced Indians into migrations of their own. Many went to Detroit and the Ohio River Valley as refugees.

☞ As you read, consider the range of circumstances under which people came to colonial America. Did they in any way share a common experience?

5-1a Unwilling Voyagers: African Slaves

In comparison to New Spain or Peru, where Spaniards built colonies on the backs of large populations of indigenous laborers, England's North American colonies were sparsely populated by local peoples. When the English colonists needed laborers and indentured servants were in short supply, as they were in the first half of the eighteenth century, colonists turned to African slaves. As a consequence, in the first half of the eighteenth century, slavery dramatically expanded on the mainland.

The population of slaves continues to grow through the transatlantic trade.

In 1700, only about 28,000 blacks lived in British North America. By 1750, there were 252,000. As in earlier periods, the vast majority of slaves were taken to the Caribbean or Brazil, but now 6.5 percent of those sold in the Americas were sold on the North American mainland, up from 1.5 percent in the previous half century. Of the slaves imported to British North America in this half century, nearly 84,000 disembarked in the Chesapeake, 41,000 in the Carolinas and Georgia, 7,000 in the Gulf colonies, and 13,000 in the northern colonies. These Africans came from many different ethnic groups and regions of Africa, and buyers often selected them based on their origins. For instance, South Carolinians and Georgians expressed a preference for slaves from Senegambia, where Africans knew how to cultivate rice, the most important crop in these areas.

Although African slaves constituted about half of all new arrivals to the colonies through 1750, they represented about 80 percent of all women who sailed to North America before 1800, largely because few European women had incentives to do so of their own volition. The forced migration of enslaved African women—who performed much of the domestic work in the colonies that women in Europe did—compensated for the deficit of European women in British North America through the early decades of the eighteenth century.

The importation of African women to the colonies led to the **natural increase** of the slave population in North

Table 5.1 Population of British North America by Broad Colonial Region, 1700–1750

Across the first half of the eighteenth century the population of British North America exploded because of massive immigration and a steady natural increase.

Year	Total	New England	Middle Colonies	Chesapeake	Lowcountry
1700	251,444	92,763	53,537	88,164	16,980
1710	327,360	115,094	69,592	117,254	25,420
1720	467,465	170,893	103,084	153,890	39,598
1730	636,045	217,351	146,981	211,713	60,000
1740	912,742	289,704	220,545	296,533	105,960
1750	1,1864,08	360,011	296,459	377,754	152,184

Source: *Historical Statistics of the United States*, millennial ed. Cambridge, England: Cambridge University Press, 2006.

HANDOUT/KRT/Newscom

St. George's Castle at Elmina and St. Jago, Gold Coast, Late Seventeenth Century Slaves brought to the Americas were first imprisoned in coastal forts notorious for the miserable conditions. This engraving shows some of the European forts built for this purpose along the coast of Africa. ◄

natural increase Population growth resulting from more births than deaths.

Act of Union Act of 1707 unifying the kingdoms of Scotland and England.

Scots-Irish Person of Scottish ancestry who immigrated from Ireland to British North America.

America. The climate and work regimes on the mainland, although brutal, were never as lethal as those in the Caribbean, meaning that women on the mainland were more likely to survive and bear children. Slaveholders knew that their future wealth was tied to the reproductive capacities of slave women. Later in his life, Thomas Jefferson expressed a widely held belief when he wrote that he considered an enslaved woman "who brings a child every two years more profitable than the best man of the farm. What she produces is an addition to the capital, while his labors disappear in mere consumption."

5-1b The Irish and Scots-Irish

Very large numbers of immigrants come from Scotland and Ireland.

In England, the conditions that had prompted immigration in the seventeenth century—a weak economy and religious persecution—changed after the Glorious Revolution, and the number of immigrant English people to North American plunged. But that of the Scots and the Irish increased as a result of high rents, famine, and religious oppression in those lands. These immigrants arrived in America in large numbers, especially after the **Act of Union**, which formally allowed Scots to move to the English colonies. More than 150,000 people from Ireland or Scotland went to North America, usually in whole families. Among those who left were Ulster Scots from Northern Ireland, who as Protestants were persecuted by the dominant Catholic population. Some 70,000 Ulster Scots immigrated, often in groups organized by their Presbyterian ministers. To distinguish themselves from Irish Catholics, they called themselves the **Scots-Irish**. Overall, the majority of immigrants from Ireland and Scotland settled in western Pennsylvania because they had trouble acquiring land closer to the coast (see Map 5.1). Many took land claimed by Indians, speculators, or the colonial government; over time this became a source of conflict on the frontier.

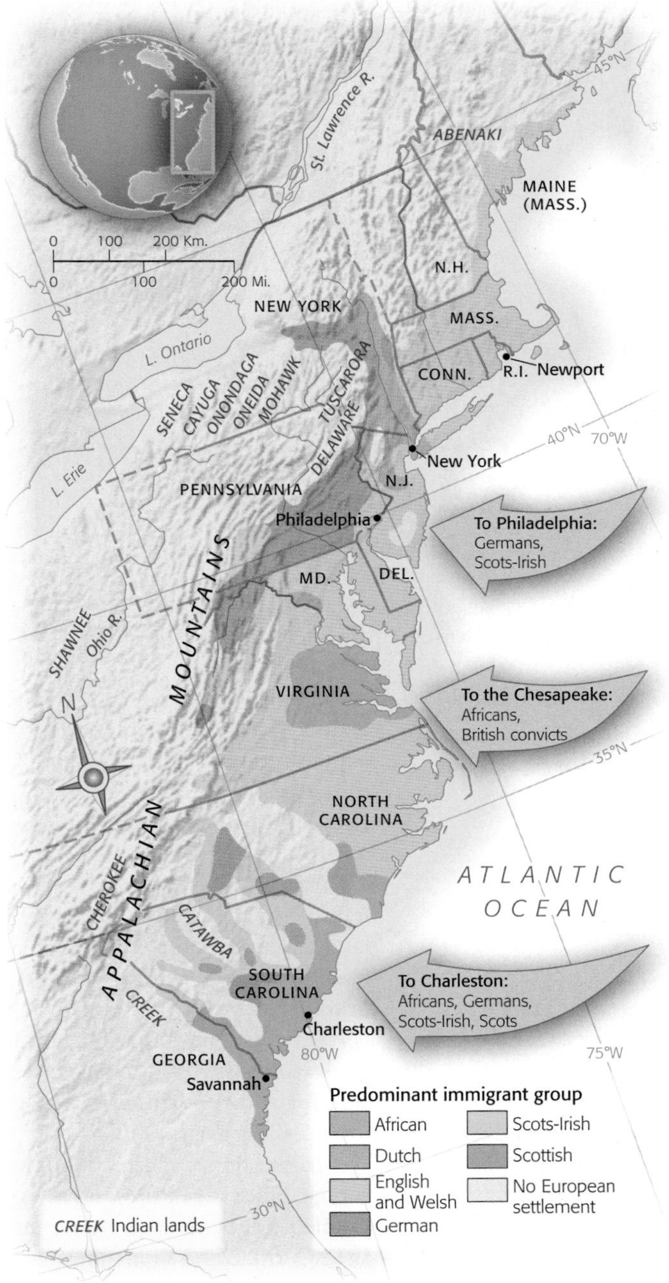

Map 5.1 European Immigration and Slave Transports to British North America, Mid-Eighteenth Century Through the eighteenth century, immigrants from western Europe and slaves from Africa swelled the population of British North America. ▲

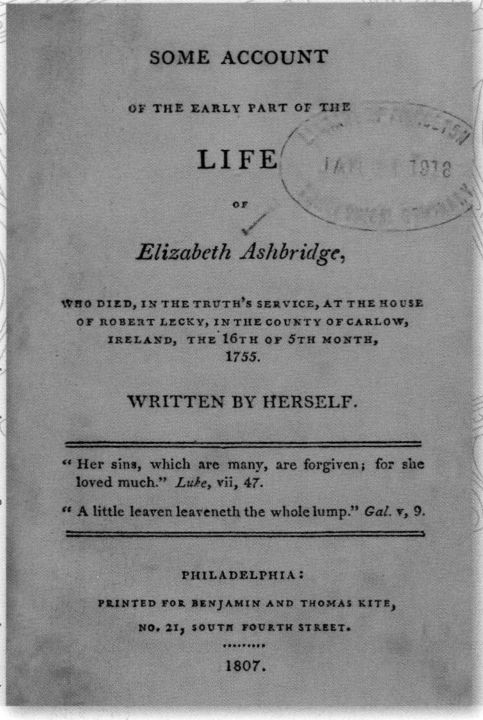

SOME ACCOUNT

OF THE EARLY PART OF THE

LIFE

OF

Elizabeth Ashbridge,

WHO DIED, IN THE TRUTH'S SERVICE, AT THE HOUSE OF ROBERT LECKY, IN THE COUNTY OF CARLOW, IRELAND, THE 16TH OF 5TH MONTH, 1755.

WRITTEN BY HERSELF.

"Her sins, which are many, are forgiven; for she loved much." *Luke*, vii, 47.

"A little leaven leaveneth the whole lump." *Gal.* v, 9.

PHILADELPHIA:

PRINTED FOR BENJAMIN AND THOMAS KITE, NO. 21, SOUTH FOURTH STREET.

1807.

OpenLibrary/Princeton Theological Seminary Library

Global Americans In an age marked by spiritual and economic uncertainly, **Elizabeth Ashbridge** led an especially tumultuous life marked by personal, economic, and spiritual travails. She was born in England in 1713. Her father, a ship's surgeon, was at sea during most of her childhood. She rebelled against her parents and eloped at age fourteen only to find herself a widow five months later. To escape her father's scorn, she moved to Ireland. Soon she became disillusioned with Catholicism. Desiring change, Ashbridge ventured to Pennsylvania in 1732, only to be forced to sign a four-year contract as an indentured servant to pay for her voyage. Like so many servants of her time, she found her master cruel, but after three years, she bought out the remainder of her contract with money she had earned doing various odd jobs. She had less luck extricating herself from a bad marriage to a schoolteacher with whom she moved frequently as he pursued one job after another. But she eventually found happiness in the Quaker faith and in her third marriage. In 1753, Ashbridge became a Quaker minister—something that would have been unimaginable to her in youth—and traveled to England and Ireland to speak about her own spiritual journey. After nearly two years, she fell ill, attributing her growing infirmities to "bodily hardship in traveling" and "spiritual exercise in mind." She died in Ireland in 1755, having completed her spiritual journey not far from where she spent much of her difficult youth chasing not only financial independence but also religious ideals.

5-1c Convicts, Redemptioners, and Huguenots

Indentured servants from many life experiences continue to arrive from western Europe.

In the early eighteenth century, English policymakers actively discouraged Englishmen and women from leaving the home country in the belief that a large population of workers in the mother country was one foundation of a mercantilist empire. These policy makers did want supposedly troublesome people—vagabonds, criminals, and supporters of the now-deposed Stuart monarchs—to leave. In the first half of the eighteenth century, England deported some 50,000 convicts, many of whom were sold into seven- or fourteen-year terms of labor. Male convicts cost one-third of the price of an African slave, and female convicts sold for two-thirds the price of their male counterparts.

In the hopes of creating a more robust labor force in the colonies, English policy makers also encouraged German and French Protestants to relocate to British North America, which was particularly attractive to Germans. Some 500,000 left the Rhineland in the eighteenth century with around 70,000 of them moving to Philadelphia (see Table 5.2). About 37,000 Germans arrived between 1749 and 1754 in one of the largest and most concentrated immigrations to North America since the Puritan migration of the 1630s. The majority of German and French immigrants were Protestants, but they came from many different denominations: Lutherans, **Moravians**, Baptists, and **Pietists**. Most were seeking affordable land, religious toleration, and low taxes—all of which could be found in Pennsylvania. Most went as families, although some entire neighborhoods and communities moved, too. The majority paid their own way across the Atlantic, yet roughly a third—known as **redemptioners**—sold their own labor, or that of their children, to pay for the transatlantic voyage. Meanwhile, in 1685, the French king Louis XIV revoked the **Edict of Nantes**, effectively outlawing the Huguenot (Protestant) faith and spurring 150,000 Huguenots to flee. French laws prohibited Protestants from moving to New France, so most resettled in Switzerland, Germany, Holland, and England. About 10,000 eventually made it to British North America.

Table 5.2 Major Sources of Immigration to British North America, 1700–1750

Africans	145,000
Ireland	80,000
Scotland	79,000
Germany	70,000
English Convicts	50,000

Moravians Protestant denomination originating in central Europe often dedicated to missionary work.

Pietism Seventeenth-century Protestant religious movement originating in Germany stressing Bible study and personal religious experience over engagement with the world.

redemptioners European immigrants who gained passage to American colonies by selling themselves or their children into indentured servitude to pay for the cost of the transatlantic voyage.

Edict of Nantes Law promulgated in France in 1598 granting Protestants (known in France as *Huguenots*) a measure of religious and civil liberties in some parts of the country but revoked by Louis XIV in 1685.

5-1d Indian Refugees

Massive population growth and increased settlement in the colonies drives Indians out of their homelands.

The expansion of the British colonies' population forced many Indians out of their homelands. Thousands abandoned the Northeast for the new French post of Detroit. Similarly, Indians fleeing New England in the wake of King Philip's War and the outbreak of King William's War in 1689 streamed into the region between New England and New France.

Colonial expansion also created conflict and refugees in the Carolinas. In South Carolina, the Shawnee Savannahs, after being attacked by the Catawbas, who had been armed by the English, fled west to live with the Creeks or north to Pennsylvania, a colony that welcomed Indians on its frontier. In North Carolina, colonists and their livestock crowded out the Iroquoian-speaking Tuscaroras. In 1711, the Tuscaroras sought to expel the colonists, killing more than a hundred settlers. But in the war that ensued, nearly fifteen hundred Tuscaroras were killed and another one thousand sold into slavery. In 1717, most survivors fled north, and in 1722, they became the sixth nation in the Haudenosaunee confederacy.

In a chaotic colonial world, rivalries and animosities between Indians persisted, and some groups worked with Europeans to dispossess other Indians. Even though the English had supported the Yamasees of South Carolina against the Tuscaroras, the Yamasees too felt the sting of encroaching settlers. In 1715, they rose in a conflict known as **The Yamasee War**, supported by Creeks, Catawbas, Cherokees, and French allies, killing hundreds of English settlers in South Carolina. In 1716, however, when the Cherokees entered the war in hope of defeating the Creeks, the Yamasees were forced to find refuge in Spanish Florida. Similarly, when Pennsylvania officials produced a blatantly forged treaty asserting that the Delawares had agreed to sell a swath of land whose size would be determined by how far a man could walk in a day and a half, the Iroquois Confederacy supported the colony in the swindle. In 1737, in what is known as the **Walking Purchase**, the colony hired two professional walkers who, after a good deal of practice, walked 64 miles in the allotted time. When the Delawares refused to vacate nearly 1,200 square miles of their land, the Haudenosaunees forced them out. Many Delawares took refuge in the Ohio Valley, where numerous other tribes had gone as well. These groups created new interethnic communities that sought political independence from France and England yet desired to trade freely with both, stoking an increasingly heated imperial rivalry for control over the Ohio Valley.

The Yamasee War Conflict in 1715–1717 between Indians and English settlers in South Carolina.

Walking Purchase Fraudulent agreement between the Penn family and Indians in Pennsylvania that dispossessed the Delawares of much of their land; supported by the Haudenosaunees.

5-2 Regional Cultures and Social Change

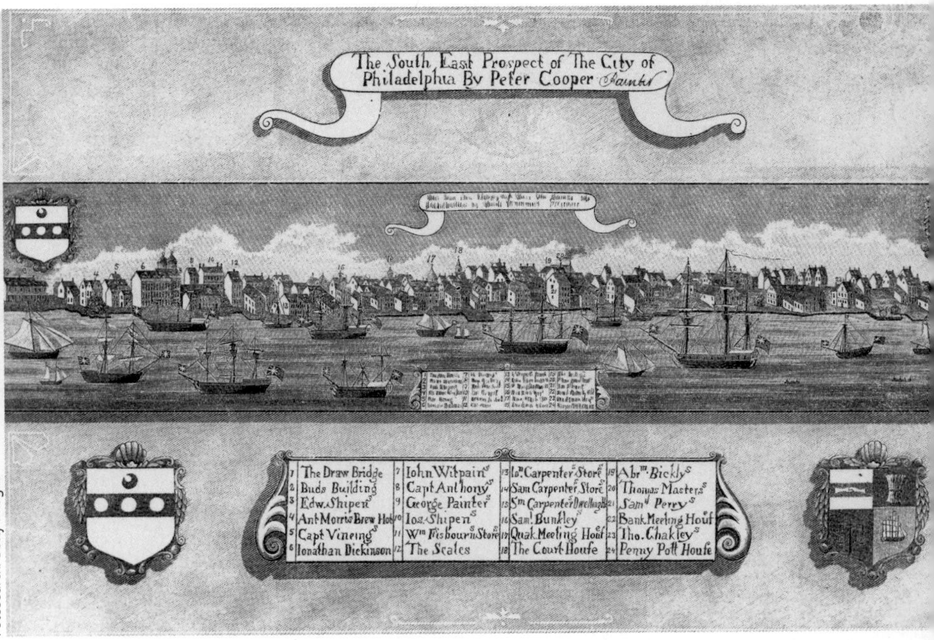

Fotosearch/Getty Images

This engraving from Peter Cooper's *The Southeast Prospect of the City of Philadelphia* (1720) shows a view from the harbor of Philadelphia, where ships wait to pick up or drop off cargo. This was a typical scene in one of the busiest commercial entrepôts in British North America.

How does the painting portray the city? What might the range of ships in the harbor suggest about commerce at the port? ▶

With the natural increase of colonial populations and the arrival of very large numbers of European immigrants and African slaves, new regional cultures emerged and old ones changed. New England's population exploded, largely through natural increase. This growth led to the establishment of new towns and far-flung settlements, further fraying bonds of community and family. The Middle Colonies received the bulk of free immigrants from Europe, and the region soon became characterized by ethnic and religious diversity and craft production. The Chesapeake's population expanded as the result of natural increase and the arrival of Europeans and tens of thousands of slaves, and towns and cities grew in a region known mostly for its isolated plantations. The populations of New France and New Spain, meanwhile, grew more slowly, and the lives of settlers in the colonies changed little over the decades. Across nearly all of colonial America, even in regions without plantations, coerced labor of Indians or Africans remained a common feature of daily life.

Table 5.3 White Population of British North America by Broad Colonial Region, 1700–1750

Year	Total Number	New England	Middle Colonies	Chesapeake	Lowcountry
1700	223,071	91,083	47,541	68,547	13,565
1710	284,662	112,509	60,229	89,959	18,820
1720	398,798	166,937	87,574	114,832	24,770
1730	538,424	211,233	126,606	157,893	34,000
1740	755,539	281,163	185,258	212,502	57,781
1750	934,340	349,029	248,515	227,204	82,384

Source: *Historical Statistics of the United States*, millennial ed. Cambridge, England: Cambridge University Press, 2006.

☞ **As you read, consider the range of regional cultures that developed across colonial America. What accounts for the differences from region to region?**

5-2a New England and the Middle Colonies

Population growth and the consumer revolution drive the growth of towns and port cities.

In New England (Massachusetts, Connecticut, Rhode Island, and New Hampshire), population growth from 93,000 in 1700 to 360,000 by 1750 meant that many people had to leave existing towns and settled areas if they hoped to establish viable farms of their own. Many in the rising generation of adults set out for the frontier, which helped accelerate the decline of local church and religious observance as the center of life in the region. As a result, the religious institutions that had differentiated New England from the rest of colonial America in the seventeenth century withered. Ports such as Boston and Salem were transformed by merchants and new patterns of consumption, and in the process became more like their cosmopolitan English counterparts than the self-contained and austere villages created by the Puritans. For many New Englanders, the pursuit of wealth became as important, if not more so, than concerns about personal salvation, and material gain trumped community and consensus.

The Middle Colonies (Delaware, Pennsylvania, New Jersey, and New York) also experienced social change driven by population growth and economic development. Largely the result of immigration, the non-Indian and non-slave population increased sixfold from 53,000 in 1700 to 296,000 in 1750 (see Table 5.1). Most immigrants were English, but 40 percent were ethnic Germans, Quakers, Jews, or Catholics, who continued to practice their beliefs in America. As a result, the Middle Colonies emerged as the most diverse region in colonial America. As in New England, settlers were increasingly devoted to economic advancement (see Map 5.2).

Slavery remained an important but not defining institution in New England and the Middle Colonies. The number of slaves imported depended on the Atlantic labor market. When the European economy was in decline and sea-lanes to colonial America were open, indentured servants immigrated. But when the European economy was

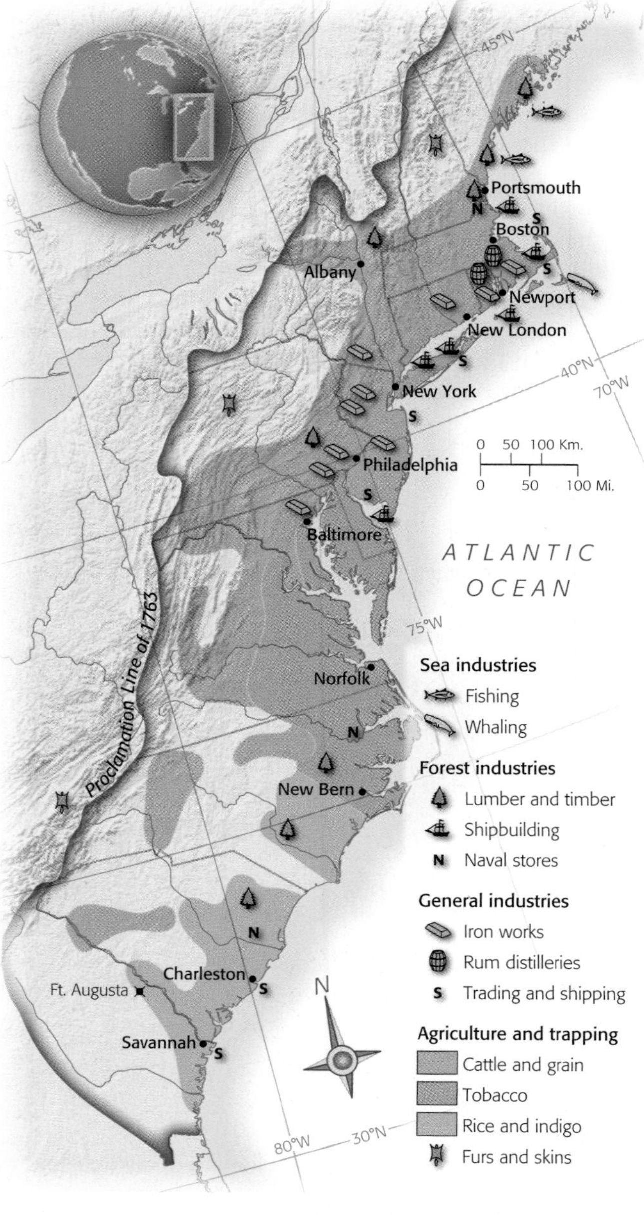

Map 5.2 Major Economic Industries, British North America, Mid-Eighteenth Century By the middle of the eighteenth century, regions continued to specialize in certain industries but overall the economy of British North America was increasingly diversified. ▲

expanding or war prevented transatlantic travel, the supply of available laborers fell and slave imports to Boston, New York, and Philadelphia rose. However, because the European population increased so quickly because of immigration, slaves constituted a large percentage of the population only in a few urban centers. By 1750, a quarter of all slaves in the colony of New York lived in New York City, and one-third of all Massachusetts slaves lived in Boston. Many urban slaves labored on wharves, in shipyards, or on ships. Nearly all worked alongside white laborers. Tradesmen and artisans owned some slaves. A few lived on their own and worked for wages that they then turned over to their masters. Most did not marry or have children because their masters did not want to be responsible for wives or offspring.

Table 5.4 Black Population of British North America by Broad Colonial Region, 1700–1750

Year	Total Number	New England	Middle Colonies	Chesapeake	Lowcountry
1700	28,373	1,680	3,661	19,617	3,415
1710	42,698	2,585	6,218	27,295	6,600
1720	68,667	3,956	10,825	39,058	14,828
1730	97,621	6,118	11,683	53,820	26,000
1740	159,224	8,541	16,452	84,031	50,200
1750	252,068	10,982	20,736	150,550	69,800

Source: *Historical Statistics of the United States*, millennial ed. Cambridge, England: Cambridge University Press, 2006.

5-2b The Chesapeake

As the white population increases, so does the demand for slaves, which creates a divided society based on ideas of free and slave as well as white and black.

The Chesapeake colonies of Virginia and Maryland also experienced social change as a result of population growth. The white population of the Chesapeake grew from 69,000 in 1700 to 227,000 in 1750, largely the result of the founding of permanent settlements, which improved life expectancy and, by extension, increased the birthrate. Soon the many new settlements were connected by an expanding and extensive system of roads, bridges, and ferries. Across the Chesapeake, life remained largely secular, even if by mid-century the Church of England had made inroads in the colony.

The racial makeup of the Chesapeake was starkly different from that of New England and the Middle Colonies. In a society dominated by plantations, slaves were the foundation of economic life. In 1700, slaves composed 22 percent of the population in Maryland and Virginia, a figure that reached 40 percent in 1750 (see Map 5.3). In 1700, 19,617 blacks were enslaved in the Chesapeake, and by 1750, there were 150,550 (see Table 5.4). By the 1760s, more than half of the households in the most prosperous areas had slaves.

The slaves came from Africa, for the most part, which represented a change from the previous century. In the mid-1600s, slaves constituted only 3 percent of the Chesapeake's population and most arrived by way of the Caribbean on the ships of the Royal Africa Company. But the company's monopoly on the shipment of slaves to the English colonies collapsed in 1689, and in 1698 Parliament suspended it. The direct shipment of slaves to the Chesapeake from Africa rose more than tenfold from fewer than 3,000 in the 1680s to nearly 35,000 in the 1730s. Between 1700 and 1750, nearly 120,000 African slaves were sold in the region, six times as many in the previous 50 years.

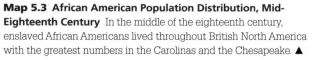

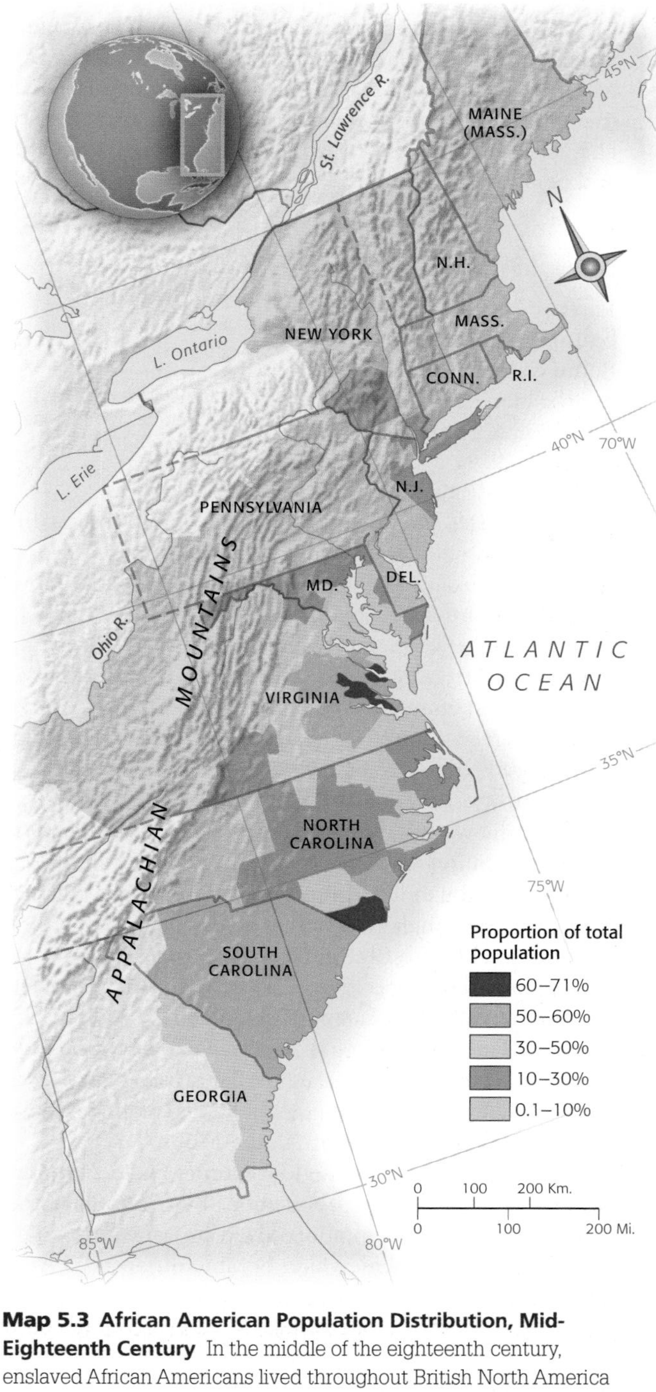

Map 5.3 African American Population Distribution, Mid-Eighteenth Century In the middle of the eighteenth century, enslaved African Americans lived throughout British North America with the greatest numbers in the Carolinas and the Chesapeake. ▲

The British viewed these newly arrived slaves direct from Africa as strange, libidinous, heathenish, and frightful, although they valued the slaves as laborers. Chesapeake masters ordered them not to converse with fellow slaves in their native languages. They were put to work weeding between rows of tobacco plants, using only their bare hands or simple tools. Planter William Tatham wrote that slaves worked "from daylight until the dusk of the evening and some part of the night, by moon or candlelight, during the winter." Under these harsh conditions, new arrivals sickened, and many died soon after coming to the Chesapeake. Children born into slavery in the Chesapeake, in contrast, were healthier than their African parents and conversant in English.

As the enslaved population in the Chesapeake increased in size, slaveholders' fears of rebellion grew. Many whites believed that their slaves were united against them when, in fact, the slaves in the Chesapeake were characterized by many variations in homeland, language, and personal experiences.

5-2c The Lowcountry

Rice and indigo production in the South drives the need for more slaves and land in Georgia, which also acts as a buffer against the Spanish.

Farther south, in the Lowcountry (North Carolina, South Carolina, and Georgia), immigration had increased the non-Indian population from 17,000 in 1700 to 147,000 by 1750, despite the ravages of various diseases, including malaria. In South Carolina, the English wars with neighboring Indians—the Tuscaroras and the Yamasees—resulted in an Indian slave labor force of about 2,000 people. But this did not satisfy planters' desires for slaves, and they started importing them from Africa at a high rate. By the 1720s, Africans outnumbered whites two to one in lowland South Carolina and three to one along the coast. By 1750, the colony had 49,000 slaves, or 66 percent of its population, the highest proportion in any colony in North America.

Georgia was established in 1732 as a utopian experiment and a buffer against Spanish Florida. It was intended for settlement by the "worthy poor" who had been released from prison in England. Because of its rules limiting private landholdings to five hundred acres, prohibiting rum, and banning the importation of slaves, the colony attracted only five thousand settlers by 1750. When Georgia's charter expired in 1753, the colony reverted to the crown. Soon thereafter, royal officials relaxed the colony's ban on slavery and loosened restrictions on landholding, creating a foundation for the colony's growth in the 1760s.

The Lowcountry had two distinct slave populations by 1750. Slaves on plantations lived in unhealthy quarters, which became outposts of African life and culture. These were often small villages where life achieved a modicum of permanence and stability. Slaves asserted their rights to Sundays free from work and to their own small plots of land, where they cultivated vegetables, fowl, and rice. Common languages and experiences rooted in memories of Africa and the Middle Passage bound many Lowcountry plantation slaves together. As in previous decades, Lowcountry rural slaves practiced African customs, celebrated African holidays, and one in five carried an African name. This cultural continuity and the lack of command of the English language meant that Christianity made little impact among these slaves.

A different slave world developed in Lowcountry urban areas where wealthy Carolina planters often maintained a second residence staffed by slaves. By 1720, Charles Town had one thousand four hundred whites and almost as many slaves. Most of these slaves lived in back rooms, basements, or attics in their master's residence. They spoke English and came into contact with large numbers of other slaves in port towns, where they worked as porters, drayers, stevedores, skilled craftsmen, seamstresses, and weavers. Highly skilled urban slaves arranged for their own employment and lodging and paid their master a portion of their wages. Some urban slaves dressed in extravagant clothing and powdered wigs, and, like their masters, scorned plantation slaves whom they viewed as wretched.

5-2d New France and New Spain

In the continent's interior, French settlers cultivate relations with their Indian neighbors and enslave those they receive in exchange for goods while Spanish settlement in northern New Spain proceeds slowly.

The population growth, expanding diversity, and social upheavals that characterized the English colonies were not fully mirrored in the French or Spanish possessions. At the turn of the eighteenth century, the bulk of French settlement in Canada was situated along the St. Lawrence River where fifteen thousand French settlers lived. Over the next half century, the population of New France grew to nearly eighty-five thousand, mostly owing to natural increase because French policies prohibited Protestants from immigrating and Catholics had little incentive to leave France. There were small minorities of Catholic Scots, Irish, Germans, Basques, and New Englanders who were taken captive or who had deserted, and ***métis***.

As in the English colonies, slavery was an important institution in the French colonies, although it was not nearly as important on the mainland as it was in the French Caribbean. Few if any of the slaves in New France came from Africa. Rather, they were captive Indians who in the early 1700s constituted about 5 percent of the population. They worked as farmhands, stevedores, domestic servants, and assistants in craft and artisanal industries. In Montreal, half of all home-owning colonists came to hold at least one slave. In Louisiana, by contrast, most Indians successfully resisted enslavement, leading French plantations to import African slaves. By the 1720s, the colony had about fourteen

métis Offspring of a Native American woman and a European man in the colonial era, most common in seventeenth-century New France.

hundred enslaved Africans compared to about one hundred sixty Indian slaves, many of whom were women.

To govern their growing number of African slaves in Louisiana, in 1724, slaveholders adopted the ***Code Noir***. This Black Code set minimum standards of conduct for masters so that slaves would have less desire to rebel. It ostensibly prevented masters from torturing their slaves, but it allowed planters to beat them with rods and whips. It prohibited intermarriage, denied slaves the right to appear in court, and mandated their instruction in Catholicism. The Black Code forbade masters from breaking up slave families by selling individuals. It also gave slaves the right to charge their masters with poor treatment. But there is no record of a slave bringing such a case. Few slaves, it seems, even knew of the Black Code's existence.

By 1731, the enslaved African population of the lower Mississippi Valley reached four thousand, meaning that there were more slaves than French colonists. Above New Orleans, slaves grew tobacco; below the city, they raised the **indigo plant** used in the production of dye. In New Orleans, slaves built levees, canals, and docks. Some became skilled artisans and dominated certain trades. Like the slaves of English Charles Town, New Orleans' slaves with free time hired themselves out as laborers. Some even bought their freedom.

In the frontier regions of New Spain, meanwhile, population growth was slow. Officials continued to rely on Catholic missions and military fortifications to secure New Spain's claims to its northern regions, where diseases eroded mission populations, and government officials increasingly saw missionaries as holdovers from the past. Remote pockets of Spanish settlement in New Mexico and parts of the Gulf Coast and Texas had no easy access to trade with the Atlantic world or even with each other and thus attracted few immigrants. News of the larger world arrived rarely and almost always in the form of government newsletters, bulletins, and edicts. The military and its forts were poorly staffed, badly organized, and inconsistently provisioned. By 1765, after eighty years of settlement, the population of New Mexico approached ten thousand, nearly a third of whom lived in and around El Paso, where they had remained after the Pueblo Revolt of 1680. Under Spanish law, slavery was illegal in New Mexico, and the colony had no African slaves. But Spanish residents throughout New Mexico often held Indian domestic servants and farmhands, whom they effectively treated as slaves.

Code Noir French code of 1724 intended to regulate slaves and masters in Louisiana; based on code issued by Louis XIV in 1685.

indigo plant Source of blue dye.

5-3

The Colonial Economy in the Atlantic Age

Joseph Van Aken, an Antwerp-born English painter, depicts here an elite family having tea in what was usually an elaborately staged social event. In this detail of the 1720 painting, *An English Family at Tea*, a servant woman pours as a manservant brings more tea and another guest to the party. In the first half of the eighteenth century, wealthy English colonists enjoyed regular tea parties, but so too did increasing numbers of the less affluent.

How does the artist portray this scene? What gender roles are demonstrated in this image? ▶

Tate, London/Art Resource, NY

A dynamic transatlantic economy widened the social gap between people at the top and at the bottom of the income scale. Planters and merchants enriched themselves, most often at the expense of common laborers and slaves. Income inequality increased as the economy grew, especially in urban areas. With their newfound wealth or because sugar- and caffeine-based commodities were so cheap, both the elite and the middling classes engaged in new forms of ritual and consumption. The wealthy enjoyed tea and liquors, clothing, and other finery. Others, in particular laborers, depended on sugar products for energy and on caffeine products in the form of tea and coffee for stimulation as they tried to keep up in an economy that demanded more work and offered less leisure time.

☞ As you read, consider not only how the economy of colonial America grew but also how it distributed wealth. What characterized the culture of the affluent in British North America in the first half of the eighteenth century?

5-3a Economic Diversification and Growth

Diverse economies develop across colonial America.

Across much of colonial America from 1700 to 1750, particularly in the English colonies, population growth accompanied the expansion of trade, and economic production became more diverse as settlers moved from subsistence farming to the production of staples and commodities for the commercial market. In New England, farmers began to produce food for large, distant markets, bringing higher profits and increasing uncertainty to their economic lives because they came to depend on overseas demand. The fish and lumber export industries employed thousands, and a large shipbuilding industry grew to supply the vessels needed to transport commodities to Europe or the Caribbean.

Wheat and other grains remained central to the society and economy of the Middle Colonies. Increased production of grain and surplus production of fish, livestock, lumber, barrel staves, and other basic goods lifted the export economy. With this economic expansion, New York and Philadelphia surpassed Boston as the largest and most important centers of economic activity in British North America.

In the Chesapeake, the economy diversified beyond tobacco, which remained profitable for the largest planters but less so for others because the price of tobacco declined from overproduction. Increasingly, small-scale planters' families turned to the production of grains and other goods that were necessary to feed the region's expanding population. In South Carolina, even though rice cultivation dominated the export trade, the economy diversified as indigo grew in importance in the 1740s. North Carolina, like the Chesapeake, exported tobacco to England; it also produced naval stores, lumber, shingles, and barrel staves.

In New France, in the far northeast of the colony, inhabitants focused on fishing, whereas along the St. Lawrence, settlers farmed their extensive riverine plots and shipped their small surpluses to Montreal and Quebec. Isolated settlements of the interior, such as St. Louis and Des Moines, sustained themselves through fur trade with Indians.

In much of northern New Spain, settlers focused on their own survival more than the search for a staple export commodity. In New Mexico, merchants traded iron goods, firearms, horses, and mules to Plains Indians, who had long exchanged buffalo robes for cotton goods and corn produced by Pueblo Indians. The most lucrative trade item on the Great Plains remained Indian captives, especially young women, who were often taken on the Plains and then sold to the settlers of New Mexico.

5-3b Colonial Regulations and International Trade

Mercantilist trade regulations shape the economy at the same time that consumer preferences remake patterns of consumption in the English colonies.

England continued to pursue mercantilist policies with its colonies in North America. By 1720, the bureaucracy in the colonies dedicated to policing transatlantic commerce had expanded to twelve thousand men, who reported to the Board of Trade. But smugglers continued to evade capture and prosecution. Meanwhile, import merchants continued to oppose the Navigation Acts, believing that the policies increased their expenses and reduced their profits. The acts, however, did benefit the economy overall. They helped sustain the English navy, which reduced the risk of piracy, thereby allowing ships to travel with more goods and fewer arms. Furthermore, in the south, the acts promoted the production of indigo. Elsewhere they supported a booming shipping industry. The acts had little effect in the Middle Colonies, which largely produced goods not protected by the acts, such as fish, flour, and meat. In the South, those who produced staples such as tobacco, which could not be sent directly to foreign markets, attacked the acts as oppressive and damaging.

Of particular frustration to colonists were English laws that prevented or curtailed the production of certain goods. The Wool Act of 1699, the Hat Act of 1732, and the Iron Act of 1750 were all designed to protect England's economy by preventing the colonists from producing those goods. The Molasses Act of 1733 imposed a heavy tax on the importation of molasses from the French West Indies, which the colonists distilled to make rum. The goal was to protect British West Indies sugarcane growers against French competition. American colonists, however, insisted that the British West Indies alone could not produce enough molasses to meet their needs. Colonists bypassed the Molasses Act through smuggling, but it remained a source of conflict.

5-3c The Consumer Revolution in British North America

The middling classes begin the consumption of imported goods.

If the latter decades of the seventeenth century were marked by the increased production and consumption of tropical goods—tobacco, tea, chocolate, and sugar—the first half of the eighteenth century was characterized by a spike in the consumption of consumer goods manufactured in England. Small manufacturers produced more and more cloth, ceramics, cutlery, glassware, paper, and textiles in response to rising demand. People increasingly purchased goods that were prominently displayed in shop windows and widely advertised in journals, magazines, and newspapers. In British North America, colonists took part in this consumer culture. Stores proliferated, and peddlers fanned out across the countryside as the simple and austere world of homespun cloth and wooden plates gave way to store-bought linens and tableware.

The goods that colonists consumed were not in themselves revolutionary, for they did not constitute technological breakthroughs in the way that the wheel, the compass, or the musket had. Rather, what was revolutionary about these goods was what they communicated about the people who purchased them.

In British North America, the traditional signs of prosperity, such as houses, land, and livestock, no longer effectively communicated social rank, especially in a society that was growing more urban and more commercial by the year. Moreover, in a society undergoing massive immigration and in which titles and ranks meant little, there was great desire for inexpensive and fashionable items that would be recognized immediately as indicators of social status. Ordinary men and women—not just the wealthy—began to buy consumer goods, including embroidered waistcoats, clay pipes, fancy snuff boxes, card tables, sets of carved chairs, china plates, and silver forks. Colonial women also bought more practical items, such as soap, cloth, candles, and clothing, which saved them the time and labor they otherwise would have devoted to producing themselves. Poorer folks, and even some slaves, tried to keep up as best they could.

To pay for what they wanted to consume, colonists produced and exported more tobacco, rice, indigo, and foodstuffs. They also took advantage of new forms of credit. For instance, the passage of the Tobacco Inspection Act of 1730 proved influential in the Chesapeake. It mandated that all tobacco exported from Virginia be inspected and stored at one of forty warehouses in the region. Planters sold their tobacco to the warehouses and in return received credits, which functioned as currency and could be used with local merchants. In the six years after the passage of the act, the quantity of British goods imported to Virginia and Maryland doubled. Similar forms of credit also emerged in the northern colonies at this time.

As this consumer revolution took hold, the value of colonial imports increased from 450,000 pounds to 1.5 million pounds per year, increasing the colonies' importance to England. In 1700, colonists consumed 10 percent of British exports, and by the 1770s, the figure was 37 percent.

Side table and pair of spindle back chairs, Lancashire (oak)/English School (18th century)/Private Collection/Bridgeman Images

Carved Chairs These carved chairs were emblematic of the fine finished goods enjoyed by the affluent in British North America. ▲

5-3d The Refinement of the Colonial Elite

> The colonial elite increasingly style themselves after the upper classes in England.

The expansion of trade increased the wealth and size of the colonial elite, and although many of these people were born in America, they started to emulate European codes of genteel behavior. For the elite, gentility was a means of asserting cultural superiority and their growing interest in establishing the legitimacy of their institutions and political power.

The richest colonists adopted ostentatious lifestyles best symbolized by their homes. At the end of the seventeenth century, a small group of merchants in Boston and Philadelphia built grand houses in the fashionable **Georgian style**. Soon, similar houses were under construction across British North America. These houses were not only very large but boasted a ballroom or parlor, whose sole purpose was entertainment. They also typically had manicured gardens, where the genteel walked and conversed.

Within their houses, the genteel tried to build a world of order and beauty. They donned ruffled shirts, dined with fine silver, and moved about with studied grace. They hired teachers and tutors for their children, hoping to send them to college, something that had formerly been the province only of those destined for careers as clergymen. Most importantly, they steeped themselves in manuals of genteel comportment. As a boy of age ten or twelve, George Washington's tutor required him to copy some "110 Rules of Civility and Decent Behavior in Company and Conversation." Washington learned, "Bedew no man's face with Spittle by approaching him when you speak" and "In the Company of those of Higher Quality than yourself Speak not ti[ll] you are ask'd a Question then Stand upright put of[f] your hat and Answer in few words." Washington's firm mouth in portraits of him later in life reflected this early study of composure.

Georgian style Architectural style popular in England and the colonies between 1720 and 1830 characterized by symmetrical two-story houses with a central entryway.

History without Borders

Piracy

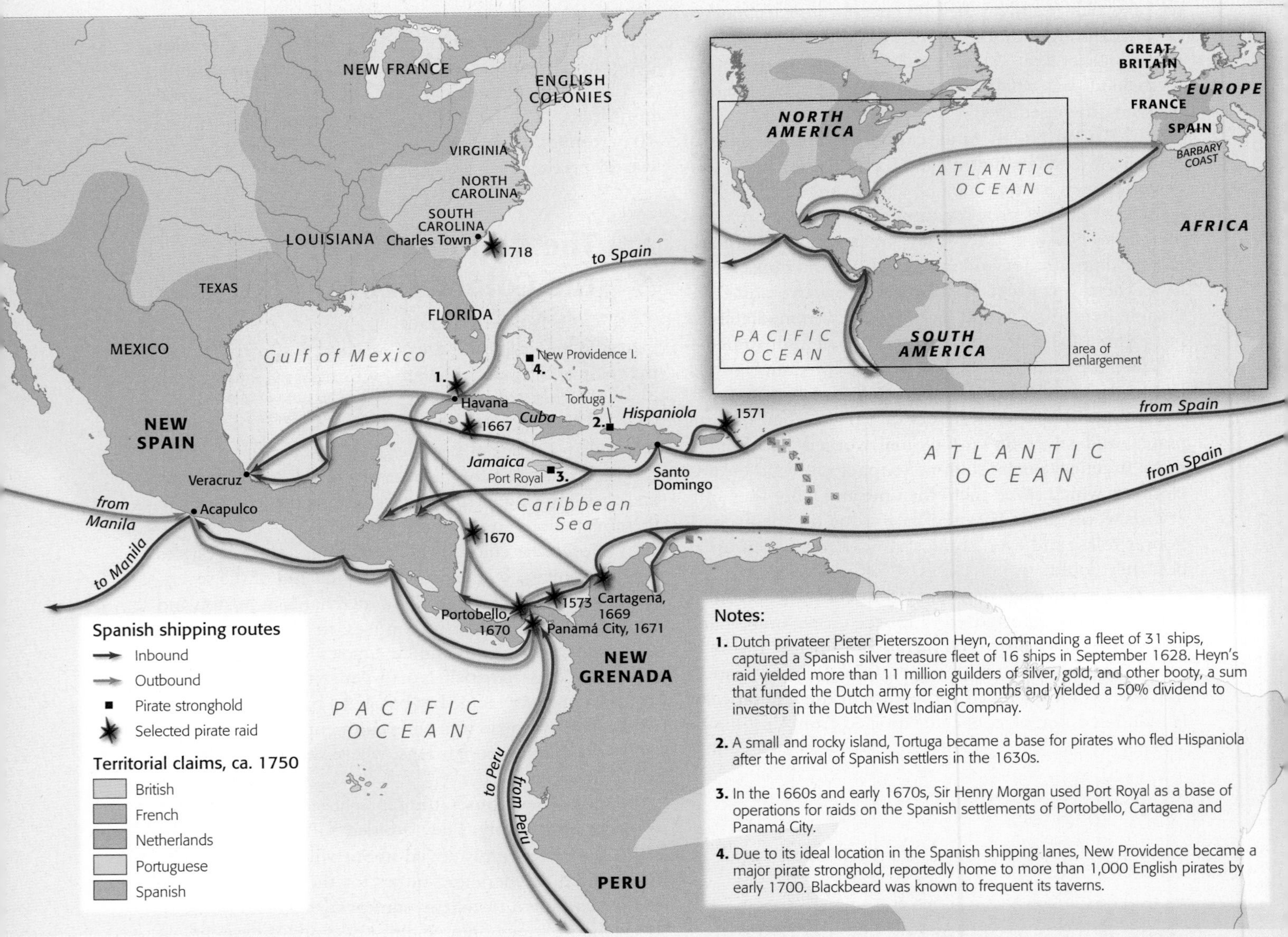

NEW FRANCE
ENGLISH COLONIES
VIRGINIA
NORTH CAROLINA
SOUTH CAROLINA
Charles Town
1718
LOUISIANA
TEXAS
FLORIDA
MEXICO
Gulf of Mexico
to Spain
New Providence I.
4.
1.
Havana
1667
Cuba
Tortuga I.
2.
Hispaniola
1571
from Spain
NEW SPAIN
Veracruz
Jamaica
Port Royal
3.
Santo Domingo
ATLANTIC OCEAN
from Spain
from Manila
Acapulco
to Manila
Caribbean Sea
1670
1573
Cartagena, 1669
Portobello, 1670
Panamá City, 1671
NEW GRENADA
PACIFIC OCEAN
to Peru
from Peru
PERU
GREAT BRITAIN
EUROPE
FRANCE
SPAIN
BARBARY COAST
NORTH AMERICA
ATLANTIC OCEAN
AFRICA
PACIFIC OCEAN
SOUTH AMERICA
area of enlargement
Spanish shipping routes
Inbound
Outbound
Pirate stronghold
Selected pirate raid
Territorial claims, ca. 1750
British
French
Netherlands
Portuguese
Spanish
Notes:
1. Dutch privateer Pieter Pieterszoon Heyn, commanding a fleet of 31 ships, captured a Spanish silver treasure fleet of 16 ships in September 1628. Heyn's raid yielded more than 11 million guilders of silver, gold, and other booty, a sum that funded the Dutch army for eight months and yielded a 50% dividend to investors in the Dutch West Indian Compnay.
2. A small and rocky island, Tortuga became a base for pirates who fled Hispaniola after the arrival of Spanish settlers in the 1630s.
3. In the 1660s and early 1670s, Sir Henry Morgan used Port Royal as a base of operations for raids on the Spanish settlements of Portobello, Cartagena and Panamá City.
4. Due to its ideal location in the Spanish shipping lanes, New Providence became a major pirate stronghold, reportedly home to more than 1,000 English pirates by early 1700. Blackbeard was known to frequent its taverns.

The Golden Age of Piracy Pirate havens and pirate attacks were concentrated around the major shipping routes to and from Spain, especially where sea lanes narrowed and ships laden with treasure and merchandise proved vulnerable. ▲

Few economic activities are more lawless than piracy, which flourishes in the interstices between nations and on the open seas. The first half of the eighteenth century is often referred to as a "Golden Age of Piracy," for between 1700 and 1730, it experienced a booming industry that extended to most of the world's oceans. In this period, the famous pirate, Edward Teach, better known as Blackbeard, was most active. With the conclusion of the Queen Anne's War in 1713 and in 1714, the wider conflict of which it was part—the War of the Spanish Succession—thousands of sailors and ship captains found themselves unemployed. Many became pirates, and piracy expanded in the coasts of the Caribbean, the Atlantic of North America, West Africa, and the Indian Ocean.

Pirates of the era preyed on the growing transatlantic trade that kept

Blackbeard the Pirate The details of Blackbeard's early life are murky. Most likely he was born into a respectable family in Bristol, England's second most important port. By the late 1690s, he was in the Caribbean and during Queen Anne's War (1701–1713) seems to have operated from Jamaica, where he served on board a ship that was engaged in "privateering," piracy sponsored by the English and against Spanish ships. ▲

Black Bart Capt. Bartholomew Roberts, also known as "Black Bart," raises his sword to his two ships after capturing a fleet of eleven English, French, and Portuguese slave ships off the coast of Africa. ▲

the sea-lanes busy between Africa, the Caribbean, North America, and western Europe. In 1718, Blackbeard and his fleet blockaded Charles Town and ransacked nine ships that were awaiting entrance to the harbor. Such activities alarmed Virginia's governor, Alexander Spotswood, who dispatched two ships to track down Blackbeard. They found him anchored in an inlet in North Carolina, overpowered his men, and killed him. They severed his head from his body and hung it from the rigging.

As piracy took its toll, more nations, especially after the signing of the Treaty of Utrecht in 1714, began to increase the size of their navies in order to protect their merchant fleets. By the 1730s, the Golden Age of Piracy in the Atlantic was over. Nevertheless, piracy continued to offer opportunities to sailors and to create problems for government officials wherever there was a valuable and unprotected maritime trade. This was especially true in the Mediterranean, where pirates from the coast of North Africa (often referred to as *Barbary Pirates*) attacked Italy, Spain, and islands in the Mediterranean. Scholars estimate that between the sixteenth and the nineteenth centuries, perhaps as many as 1 million European sailors were captured by Barbary Pirates and sold into slavery in North Africa. But after the 1720s, at least, piracy no longer hindered the expansion of global trade.

Critical Thinking Questions

- ▶ What events led to the rise and fall of piracy across the Atlantic?
- ▶ What was the life of a pirate like?

5-3e Inequality

Inequality is a defining feature of colonial America.

The benefits of the expanding economy were not shared equally. Poverty was common in cities, where urban laborers often went unemployed or moved from job to job. Indentured servants struggled, and most lived in desperation. Elizabeth Sprigs, an indentured servant in a Maryland household, wrote her father in England that she worked day and night, was fed a meager ration of salty corn, and was "tied up and whipp'd." She slept wrapped "up in a Blanket . . . on the Ground," and begged her father to send her clothing as she was "almost naked" and had "no shoes nor stockings to wear."

Elizabeth Sprigs may have suffered more than most indentured servants, but few English women held wealth of their own, and few slaves and Native Americans had an opportunity to amass wealth in the first place. But white, property-holding men had chances for a reasonable income and more opportunity to advance than in England or continental Europe. Few free settlers seem to have been poor, and at least two-thirds of rural householders owned their own land by 1750.

On the mainland, white Southerners were the richest, largely because they held nearly twice as much land as the average landowner in other colonies and because they owned laborers who reproduced themselves. The landed elite—those controlling more than a thousand acres of land and holding at least ten slaves—controlled half of the wealth in the Chesapeake. Whites who could not afford slaves or land often had no choice but to settle in the interior, where the lack of roads made tobacco cultivation far less profitable. The distribution of land in New England, by contrast, was fairly egalitarian because of the custom of dividing land among heirs.

In the Middle Colonies, wealth became less evenly distributed as a small group of merchants amassed large fortunes. Roughly 20 percent of the population—mostly widows, children, and persons with infirmities—remained mired in poverty. In response, some merchants established almshouses and workhouses to care for the growing numbers of urban poor. Pennsylvania offered easy land for those who could afford their own passage to America, but it also had the largest number of indentured servants.

In British North America outside of regions dominated by plantations, roughly 70 percent of land was worked by those who owned it. In contrast, land ownership in New France, and therefore wealth, was far less equitably distributed. Land was first granted to a *seigneur*, a lord, who then "sold" small portions of the property to settlers. Settlers, however, never truly owned the land. Rather, they had to provide roughly 8 to 10 percent of their annual income, in the form of produce, to the *seigneur*. Under this system, wealth became concentrated among a small number of *seigneurs* who spent their riches on fineries imported from France, not goods produced in the colony.

5-4 Imperial Rivalries, Territorial Expansion, and Border Warfare

This painting, attributed to José de Páez, ca. 1765, shows a Franciscan view of the 1758 destruction of Mission San Sabá, in Texas. Franciscans venerated missionaries who were killed in Indian rebellions, believing that their deaths and the miracles that might follow would attract Indian converts.

How does the artist portray the Indians' attack on the mission? What are the central images in this dramatic rendering? ▶

DeAgostini/Getty Images

Across the first half of the eighteenth century, wars over European succession and trade roiled the margins of American colonies. The War of the Spanish Succession prompted Queen Anne's War in the colonies, pitting England against Spain and France and leading to frontier warfare across northern New England. Farther south, the war sparked conflicts between English Carolinians and Spanish Floridians. Soon thereafter, the War of the Quadruple Alliance—pitting Spain against France, England, Holland, and Austria—prompted the French and Spanish to spar over Texas and the Gulf Coast. Later disputes led England to charter the colony of Georgia to protect the Carolinas from incursions from Spanish Florida. Amid all of this territorial jockeying, the French formally established

New Orleans as an anchor to their growing ambitions in the lower Mississippi River Valley. The War of the Austrian Succession brought renewed violence to some of the colonies. And later, on the other side of the continent, Russian fur hunters ventured down the Pacific Coast, one factor that led Spain to establish outposts in Alta California. More often than not, Indian peoples, who had already been pushed to the edges of European settlement, saw their own fortunes decline as they became pawns in European disputes or impoverished when trading partnerships collapsed in war.

☞ As you read, consider the relationship between European conflicts and those that erupted in the colonies. How did these wars reshape colonial America?

5-4a War on the Northern Frontier

Conflicts that begin in Europe bring violence to the northern frontier.

The peace that England and France had agreed to in 1697, ending King William's War, was brief. The eighteenth century opened with a war that quickly engulfed the colonies (see Table 5.5). The **War of the Spanish Succession** (1701–1714) began when the king of Spain, Carlos II, died heirless. Louis XIV of France put forward his own grandson, Philip, as heir to the Spanish throne. Leopold, the Holy Roman Emperor, countered with his own son, Charles. England's Queen Anne, fearing the unified might of Spain and France if Philip became king of Spain, backed Charles. The conflict that resulted was known in the colonies as **Queen Anne's War**. Unlike King William's War, which ended in a stalemate, England won, at least in Europe, seizing territory from both Spain and France and blocking the feared unification of the two monarchies.

In North America, however, the English did not fare so well. Because the British crown's priorities were in Europe, not the colonies, an English fleet intended to attack the French by

Etow Oh Koam, King of the River Nations

Sa Ga Yeath Qua Pieth Ton, King of the Maguas

No Nee Yeath Tan no Ton, King of the Generath

Tac Yec Neen Ho Gar Ton, Emperor of the Six Nations

The Four Indian Kings In 1710, leading English colonists, hoping to lure the Iroquois out of neutrality and gain added English support for the war, organized a delegation of four "Iroquois Kings," who traveled to England for an audience with Queen Anne. They were in fact not kings or even noted leaders, and one was a Mohican. But they were a sensation in London and boosted Parliamentary support for an all-out offensive against the French. ▲

Etow Oh Koam, King of the River Nations, 1710 (oil on canvas), Verelst, Johannes or Jan (b.1648–fl.1719)/Private Collection/The Bridgeman Art Library; (top left) Sa Ga Yeath Qua Pieth Ton, King of the Maguas, 1710 (oil on canvas), Verelst, Johannes or Jan (b.1648–fl.1719)/Private Collection/The Bridgeman Art Library; (top right) No Nee Yeath Tan no Ton, King of the Generath, 1710 (oil on canvas), Verelst, Johannes or Jan (b.1648–fl.1719)/Private Collection/The Bridgeman Art Library; (bottom left) Tac Yec Neen Ho Gar Ton, Emperor of the Six Nations, 1710 (oil on canvas), Verelst, Johannes or Jan (b.1648–fl.1719)/Private Collection / Bridgeman Images (bottom right)

Table 5.5 The Intercolonial Wars, 1690–1748

Across much of the late colonial period, wars on the continent sparked wars in the Americas. These related conflicts often carried different names.

War's Name in North American Colonies		Corresponding War in Europe	Nations Involved
1689–1697	King William's War	Nine Years' War	E, H vs. F, S
1702–1713	Queen Anne's War	War of the Spanish Succession	E, H, A vs. F, S
1718–1720	War of the Quadruple Alliance		S vs. F, E, H, A
1739–1748	King George's War	War of the Austrian Succession	E, H, A, vs. F, S, P

E = England; H = Holland; F = France; S = Spain; A = Austria; P = Prussia

War of the Spanish Succession European conflict of 1701–1713 triggered by the death in 1700 of the infirm and childless King Charles II of Spain. See also Queen Anne's War.

Queen Anne's War Conflict in North America that emerged from Europe's War of the Spanish Succession.

sailing up the St. Lawrence was twice diverted to other war fronts. Not until 1710 did the English send warships to Boston. Meanwhile, French troops and their Abenaki allies besieged New England frontier towns. The war led to hundreds of English captives being taken to New France, where they were adopted, sold into slavery, or used as bargaining chips in negotiations.

In the spring of 1711, England launched its largest invasion yet in the New World. It consisted of fourteen battle ships and some eight thousand men. Hundreds of Iroquois took part. Yet, as the ships made their way up the St. Lawrence River, fog obscured their passage and several ran aground, killing some nine hundred Englishmen. To the shock of the Iroquois, who had agreed to give up their neutrality to fight with them, the English abandoned the battle and sailed home.

The war ended in 1713, when the **Treaty of Utrecht** resulted in the Bourbon Philip V being crowned as king of Spain. But it also required him to renounce any claim to the French throne, thereby preserving the balance of power in Europe. In the settlement, France gave Acadia, Newfoundland, and the Hudson Bay to England, and Spain agreed to give up its monopoly over the transport and sale of slaves to Spanish colonies.

In 1740, during the **War of the Austrian Succession**, known in British North America as **King George's War**, Britain allied with Austria against much of Europe, and the English again tried to conquer New France. In 1745, with the assistance of some four thousand volunteers from New England and a British naval squadron, Massachusetts governor William Shirley took the French fort at Louisburg in the Gulf of St. Lawrence. After nearly half a century of attempting to dislodge the French from Canada, the English colonists were thrilled with their victory. They were then shocked when the English returned the fort to France in the 1748 peace of Aix la Chapelle, which ended the conflict. By relinquishing the fort, the English regained lands that the French had taken from them in India and Flanders. Once again, the English colonists realized that imperial priorities lay elsewhere.

Treaty of Utrecht Agreement concluding War of the Spanish Succession in 1713 that confirmed Philip as king of Spain with his renunciation of the French throne.

War of the Austrian Succession European conflict of 1740–1748 over the succession to the throne of the Holy Roman Empire.

King George's War Name in North America given to Europe's War of the Austrian Succession.

War of the Quadruple Alliance European conflict over terms of Treaty of Utrecht and territories in Italy.

Comanchería Region of today's New Mexico, west Texas, and adjacent areas occupied by the Comanches once they had mastered equestrianship.

5-4b Conflict on the Southern Borderlands

France and Spain jockey for territory in the South in wars originating in Europe.

Farther south, wars and new alliances repeatedly remade international boundaries along an arc of land stretching from Texas to the Carolinas (see Map 5.4). France had established forts on Biloxi Bay and the Mississippi River in 1699 and had laid claim to Louisiana, all in Spanish territory. But because of the alliance between Spain and France during Queen Anne's war, Spain did not destroy the French settlements. France did little to develop Louisiana other than establishing trade relations with the local Choctaws, Chickasaws, Alabamans, and Caddos.

After the Treaty of Utrecht, Spain remained wary of French intentions along the Gulf Coast. The arrival in 1714 of the French trader Saint-Denis at the Spanish Mission San Juan Bautista, just south of the Río Grande, prompted Spain to reoccupy Texas. Meanwhile, the French established a trading post at Natchitoches, creating a western boundary between French Louisiana and Spanish Texas. To ensure that the French would move no farther west, the Spaniards established two more missions among the Caddo tribe. In 1718, the new governor of Texas, Martín de Alarcón, established a presidio, San Antonio de Béjar (whose chapel would later be known as the *Alamo*), and the *villa* of San Antonio along the San Antonio River.

In 1718–1720, in the **War of the Quadruple Alliance**, Spain hoped to destroy Charles Town but instead lost Pensacola in a surprise attack by the French. Spain, fearing a French thrust from Louisiana into Texas, relocated soldiers and missionaries to San Antonio. And in 1721, Spanish soldiers evicted the French from east Texas and established a fort near Natchitoches. By 1727, however, the Spanish abandoned its missions in east Texas, which were difficult to provision.

Meanwhile, Spanish troubles on the southern Great Plains increased when Pawnees, Wichitas, and Comanches, who already had large supplies of Spanish horses, received guns from the French. Horses had first reached the Plains in the Spanish *entradas* of the sixteenth century, but no significant herds had remained behind after the Spaniards departed. Spanish mustangs eventually spread across northern New Spain and reached the southern Great Plains by the early eighteenth century. In the 1730s, as their horse herds grew, the Comanches made the conversion to full-blown equestrianism with remarkable speed.

In 1740, during King George's War, South Carolinians invaded Florida, taking the smaller posts of northern Spanish Florida, yet failed to conquer St. Augustine. Spain then retaliated by attacking coastal Georgia, which the English were able to defend. After the war's conclusion, Spanish missionaries abandoned Florida, unable to win converts among Indians who preferred English trade goods.

In the 1740s and 1750s, the Comanches pushed the Apaches from the Northern Great Plains. To the Spanish, the southern Great Plains became known as the ***Comanchería***. In 1757, to protect the San Antonio missions, bring the Apaches into the Spanish fold, and keep the Comanches at bay, the Spanish established another fort and mission at San Sabá in central Texas. In March 1758, Comanche raiders destroyed the mission, blocking a Spanish–Apache alliance and securing their control of the southern Great Plains.

Map 5.4 European Expansion across Colonial America to 1750 By the middle of the eighteenth century, Spain, France, and England all had extensive claims to much of North America. Spain sought to control the region stretching from Florida to Baja California with missions and forts; France maintained a sprawling fur trading empire across the American interior; and England had established populous settlements from Georgia to Maine. ▲

5-4c European Expansion and the Pacific Coast

Russian and Spanish settle on the Pacific Coast.

With the major European nations warring over territory and trade in North America, the Russian crown hoped to establish its own power in Europe through the exploration of the Northern Pacific. In 1741, Danish mariner Vitus Bering and Russian officer Alexei Chirikov led an expedition that sailed east from Siberia. After a harrowing winter that killed Bering and many of his men, the survivors returned to Russia carrying some nine hundred sea otter pelts, which commanded huge prices in China. In subsequent years, Russia launched more expeditions to hunt otter, seals, and sea lions. These voyages lasted years and often proved fatal to many of those who staffed them. Moreover, the voyages devastated the indigenous people they encountered.

In 1781, Russian merchants organized the **Russian-American Company** to establish fur-trading colonies on the North Pacific Coast. Three years later, the company founded Russia's first permanent settlement east of Siberia on Kodiak Island. A decade later, more than three hundred thirty colonists were on the island, all of them men. The Russian colonial venture remained the most limited European enterprise in North America, yet it did prompt Spain to defend Alta California against Russian encroachment.

In 1765, largely as a result of the new Russian presence to the north, José de Gálvez, a high-ranking official who King Carlos III had sent to New Spain to inspect the Spanish colonies, ordered the settlement of Alta California. In 1769, Gálvez sent five expeditions to Alta California, three by sea and two by land. They headed for the port of Monterey to take possession of the province for Spain. However, these expeditions were plagued by illness, shortages of food, and the inability to find Monterey, which they did not locate until 1770.

Russian-American Company Russian joint-stock company that received royal monopoly in 1799 to settle and hunt fur-bearing animals from the Aleutian Islands to today's Alta California.

Alta California developed along the same trajectory as other Spanish territories, with the establishment of missions serving as the foundation for later settlements. Leading

Global Americans

Missionaries embodied the international nature of the colonial encounter between Indians and Europeans, and few more than Father **Junípero Serra**. Serra was born on the Spanish Mediterranean island of Mallorca in 1713. Raised in a small agricultural village, he then studied for the priesthood in Palma, the island's capital and a center of Catholicism in the western Mediterranean. At age thirty-five, Serra gave up a professorship to become a missionary in New Spain. He worked for eight years organizing missions north of Mexico, where he also was an investigator for the Mexican Inquisition. He then spent another decade traveling around the countryside leading popular religious revivals. After a short stint as an administrator of missions in Baja California, Serra went north to Alta California in 1769 when he was 56 years old. There he spearheaded the establishment of Franciscan missions, starting at San Diego. A tireless advocate of the missions, he walked thousands of miles over frontier trails and roads seeking to spread the gospel. Serra was a staunch defender of the use of corporal punishment and believed that Indians needed to take up European modes of agriculture. His commitment to his faith was extraordinary, although the effects of his and other missionaries' actions were often disastrous for Indians. In 2015, Pope Francis canonized Junípero Serra, calling him a "founding father" and "the evangelizer of the Pacific Coast."

the missionaries into Alta California was Father Junípero Serra, a zealous Franciscan. The military, which depended on the missions for basic foodstuffs, established forts at San Diego (1769), Monterey (1770), San Francisco (1776), and Santa Barbara (1782) and the agricultural settlements of San José (1777) and Los Angeles (1781).

The missions proved as deadly to Alta California Indians as they had to the Wendats and other Indians across colonial America. In 1820, the Franciscan overseeing the Alta California missions wrote that the missionaries found themselves "with a people miserable and sick, [and] with rapid depopulation of *rancherías* [villages] which with profound horror fills the cemeteries." By the mid-1830s, the Franciscans had baptized more than eighty thousand Indians, but almost sixty thousand had died.

5-5 Politics, Religion, and Daily Life

This 1747 painting captures an elite New England family, that of the artist, John Greenwood. Note the basket of needlework and the flame stitch canvas work on the table that suggest the accomplishments of the women. The book on the middle of the table in the painting's center hints at their literacy.

As you examine this painting, what sense do you get of these women's lives, circumstances, and responsibilities? ▶

The Greenwood-Lee Family, c.1747 (oil on canvas), Greenwood, John (1727–92)/ Museum of Fine Arts, Boston, Massachusetts, USA/Bequest of Henry Lee Shattuck in memory of the late Morris Gray/Bridgeman Images

Go to MindTap® to practice history with the Chapter 5 **Primary Source Writing Activity: Daily Life in the Colonial Regions.** Read and view primary sources and respond to a writing prompt.

Colonial society in North America by 1750 was firmly rooted in beliefs and practices that were European in form but everywhere shaped by local attitudes, immigrant peoples, colonial circumstances, and new intellectual currents and religious practices. In their politics, colonists in British North America subscribed to English notions of liberty and power and deferred to their betters but enjoyed far more access to freedom and a free press than their counterparts in England. In their religious beliefs, colonists in New England looked back to an idealized Puritan past yet were at the same time changed by the circulation of contemporary religious views and practices. Women, the illiterate, and African Americans played an increasing role in affairs of religion. Yet on the whole, the patriarchal organization of society persisted, and gender roles were slow to change despite the efforts of those who challenged them. African Americans suffered enslavement and, even if free, terrible indignities. Daily life in the colonial regions of New France and New Spain continued apace but—with the exception of New Orleans—these regions were not fully integrated into the Atlantic economy. In these areas, patriarchy and Catholicism structured daily life, population increased slowly, and economies remained local.

☞ As you read, consider how gender and wealth shaped peoples' lives. How did different colonial communities reflect them?

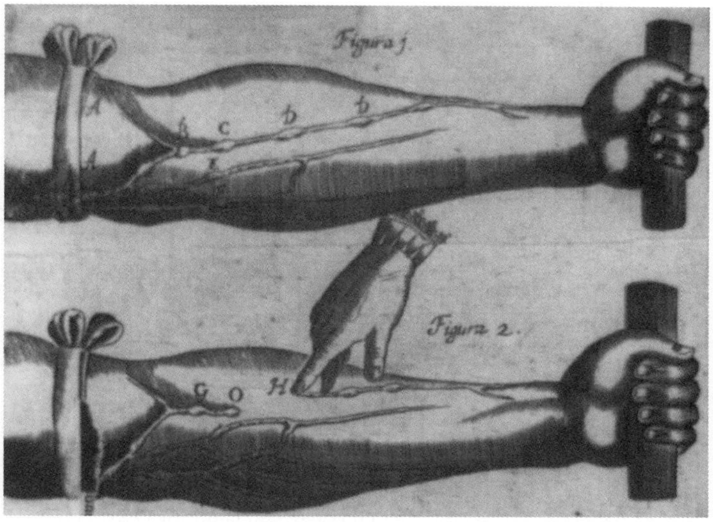

Library of Congress. William Harvey

Image of Veins from Harvey's *Exercitatio Anatomica de Motu Cordis et Sanguinis in Animalibus* By using the scientific method, William Harvey established the circulation of the blood throughout the human body. His findings were first published in an illustrated volume in 1628. ▲

5-5a The Enlightenment in Europe and America

New intellectual currents, based on previous ideas, reshape the thoughts of many colonists.

In the late seventeenth century, many vestiges of the medieval worldview gave way in the face of the Scientific Revolution. On a foundation of breakthroughs made by earlier Western, Muslim, and Asian thinkers, European scientists overturned the belief that the earth was at the center of the cosmos, discovered the fundamental laws of the universe, and developed more accurate understandings of the human body. Galileo Galilei (1564–1642) proved that the sun was the center of the solar system, which in turn was just a small part of an enormous galaxy. In his *Mathematical Principles of Natural Philosophy* (1687), Sir Isaac Newton used the scientific method and his own discovery of gravity to explain for the first time the movements of the seas, the moon, planets, and stars. William Harvey (1578–1657) discovered that blood circulates through the body and determined how the heart functions. These and other discoveries allowed Europeans in the century after 1650 to create more accurate clocks, invent the modern blast furnace, develop basic steam engines, build new and more efficient spinning machines, and take the first steps to the science of medicine.

Moreover, these developments in the natural and human sciences helped to launch a philosophical movement known as the Enlightenment, which rejected many traditional beliefs, including religious ideas, and venerated human reason as the only means to understand the world and improve society. Although they worked in many different fields, Enlightenment thinkers shared a common desire to substitute the search for objective truth for a trust in religious faith. Because of their beliefs and writings, the idea of human free will began to replace the notion that human destiny was determined by God.

In the Americas, Enlightenment ideas first gained acceptance in the British colonies. Anglicans and some other religious groups welcomed the writings of Newton and the political philosopher John Locke and attacked Puritan churches and their emphasis on Calvinist notions of predestination. Benjamin Franklin (1706–1790) was the quintessential Enlightenment figure in America. He combined an interest in science with a belief that human reason could improve the lot of mankind. Franklin was a printer, a politician, a scientific investigator, a humorist, and an autobiographer. He was also a **Deist**, believing that God had created the universe but no longer intervened in human affairs. With little more than a kite, he conducted a famous experiment proving that lightning and electricity were one in the same.

Deism Belief that a supreme being had created the world that was run by natural laws rather than supernatural interventions.

Great Awakening Mid-eighteenth century religious revival in Great Britain and British North America.

In New Spain, the Catholic Church, the Inquisition, and the universities rejected the new ways of thinking. As a result, the Enlightenment did not gain traction in the colony until the end of the century.

5-5b The Great Awakening in British North America

Religious revivals spread across British North America.

During the mid-eighteenth century, a series of religious upheavals known as the **Great Awakening** swept through England and British North America. It was a reaction to the waning of orthodox Calvinist belief in the colonies and the rise of Enlightenment rationalism and Deism. The revival spread through existing transportation and commercial networks and was

The Reverend Mr Samson Occom, engraved by Jonathan Spilsbury, 1768 (mezzotint), Chamberlin, Mason (1727–87) (after)/Private Collection/© Michael Graham-Stewart/Bridgeman Images

Global Americans During the colonial period, some Indians were brought to Europe as captives. Others, like Pocahontas, went out of curiosity and to represent their people. **Samson Occom**, a Mohegan preacher from New England, crossed the Atlantic to raise money for an Indian school in his homeland. Born in the early 1720s, Occom was exposed to Christianity during the Great Awakening, and he began to study for the ministry under the leading Protestant missionary, Eleazer Wheelock. Exceptionally gifted, Occom learned to read and write English and mastered Greek, Latin, and Hebrew. He was ordained in 1759, and in 1765, he traveled throughout the southern colonies with George Whitefield, one of the leaders of the Great Awakening who was then on his sixth preaching tour of British North America. Later that year, Occom traveled to England on his own preaching tour. Over the next two years, he delivered more than three hundred sermons in the British Isles and helped raise more than £12,000 for his cause. Occom achieved such fame on this trip that the University of Edinburgh offered him an honorary degree, which modesty led him to decline. When Occom returned home, he was shocked to learn that Wheelock had not fulfilled his promise to care for his wife and children but had abandoned them. Occom spent the remainder of his life as a teacher and preacher, and he is widely considered to be the first Native American to publish his own writings. He died in 1792, having not only straddled Indian and European worlds but also ventured across the Atlantic and throughout the colonies.

facilitated by newspapers, other printed materials, and new forms of marketing. No similar revival occurred in New France and New Spain, where Catholic missionaries and parish priests enforced the observance of Catholic rituals, and where, as a result, the Enlightenment had less impact.

The Great Awakening is most closely associated with three Protestant preachers: Jonathan Edwards (1703–1758), George Whitefield (1714–1770), and Gilbert Tennant (1703–1764). In the colonies, the revival began in the mid-1730s in Jonathan Edwards's congregation in Northampton, Massachusetts. He found it alarming that his congregants believed that humans were not innately sinful and could gain salvation by divining the will of God. In response, he preached highly emotional sermons rooted in orthodox Calvinist principles of the arbitrariness of predestination and the horrors of hell. He also urged that only by surrendering to God's will and reforming their behavior could individuals achieve salvation and heavenly joy. Edwards believed that "scarcely a single person in the whole town" was left untouched by the revival and that his emotional preaching style was the reason.

Meanwhile, George Whitefield, a traveling minister from England, became the movement's leading figure, connecting various revivals across the colonies and inspiring a truly broad religious movement. Along with John Wesley (1703–1791), Whitefield was one of the founders of Methodism, an evangelical form of Protestantism that believed in itinerant preaching by unordained ministers and was particularly devoted to salvation of the poor and common folk. Perhaps the most powerful public speaker of his day, Whitefield spoke before an estimated thirty thousand gatherings in his career, often in front of tens of thousands of people. He made fifteen tours of Scotland, three of Ireland, and seven of the North American colonies between 1739 and 1741. As the cost of printing materials dropped, Whitefield was able to publish his

Library of Congress Prints and Photographs Division[LC-USZ62-108255]

Cartoon Lampooning George Whitefield, 1763 Preacher George Whitefield was among the most recognizable figures in eighteenth-century British North America. His charismatic and dramatic preaching drew crowds, admiration, and derision, as shown in this cartoon. ▲

sermons in all the colonies and use newspapers to advertise his upcoming visits. Although he denounced the growing consumerism of his age, he advertised widely in print and offered quantity discounts, prepayment incentives, and home delivery of his materials—all inventions of the consumer revolution. Whitefield was so prolific that American printers, the most prominent of whom was Ben Franklin, produced some eighty thousand copies of Whitefield's works.

Whitefield preached discipline, morality, and social harmony, but New England preachers such as Gilbert Tennent radicalized the conservative religious movement by attacking the established clergy as passionless. Itinerant preachers such as Tennent offered alternatives to the bland palate of religion often provided by local ministers. As a result of their work, once-peaceful congregations became engulfed in disputes between "Old Lights"—orthodox clerics—and "New Lights"—evangelicals— over the religious fitness of their ministers.

The overall impact of the Great Awakening went far beyond debates over ministerial authority. Lay preachers—often women and even Native Americans—shattered elite white men's hold on religious speech. With a new set of preachers coming to the fore, many people felt liberated from the belief that their destinies were tied to the beliefs of their social superiors. The upheavals of the Great Awakening weakened and recast the bonds between individuals, families, communities, and society.

5-5c English Liberty and Liberalism in the Eighteenth Century

The English develop very precise ideas about politics and rights in the eighteenth century.

The Enlightenment influenced political theorists in England, who came to believe they had perfected the art of politics and governance. They conceived of three forms of government: monarchy (the rule of one), aristocracy (the rule of a few), and democracy (the rule of many or all). These thinkers believed that these forms could degenerate respectively into tyranny, oligarchy, or mob rule, and they argued that a stable government included elements of each form, balancing them within a single constitution. Many believed that England had achieved its great power through the establishment of a **mixed and balanced government** after the Glorious Revolution. In England, the monarchy was represented in the figure of the king, aristocracy in the House of Lords, and democracy in the House of Commons. The crown executed the law but was checked by courts and controlled by aristocratic and popular elements in Parliament that also restrained one another.

The concept of **liberty** occupied the center of English political identity during the eighteenth century even if the presence of slavery within the empire revealed that it did not extend to all. For the English, liberty meant not only the rights they enjoyed under the English Constitution but also, more generally, the right to resist arbitrary government. The English by 1700 had come to believe passionately that liberty and power were always in conflict. Thus, it was necessary, the English believed, for the rule of law to mediate between the contending forces of power and liberty and for the laws themselves to have been approved by representatives elected by the people themselves. Not all English people believed that the system worked. Many **radical Whigs**, notably John Trenchard and Thomas Gordon, asserted that the crown, through patronage, bribes, and collusion, had gained control over the English government and threatened to deny Englishmen their proper liberty. This view was widely accepted in the colonies by an elite who was suspicious of English imperial objectives and concerned about England's rising debt and costly military.

mixed and balanced government Form of government that integrates elements of democracy, aristocracy, and monarchy.

liberty Right recognized under the British Constitution to resist arbitrary government as understood by eighteenth-century Britons; the antithesis of power.

radical Whigs English political commentators who feared moral decay in English society and the royal encroachment on the powers of Parliament.

liberalism English belief that government was a social contract entered into freely between the people and their chosen representatives and rulers.

In addition to liberty, the English believed that **liberalism** was crucial to individual freedom. In this respect, no thinker was more important than John Locke, author of *Two Treatises of Government*, which was published in 1689 but did not achieve a wide readership until the first half of the eighteenth century. Locke dismissed the idea that governments were divinely sanctioned and that they, like families, had to be governed by authoritarian fathers. He argued that government existed as a social contract between the people and their rulers. Men surrendered some liberty to their rulers in return for the protections of the rule of law. But the people always retained their natural rights, and, according to Locke, a government that broke the social contract could be overthrown, by violence if necessary.

5-5d Politics and Power in the Colonies

The well-established governors and upper houses of the colonial assemblies lose power to the rising lower assemblies.

In British North America in particular, politics was the province of white men. Only those who had property could vote, but because of the widespread availability of land, between 50 and 80 percent of adult white males were eligible. This was far more than the 5 percent who held the privilege in Britain at that time. Colonial politics, however, were anything but democratic. In many of the colonies, Jews, Catholics, Baptists, and Quakers could not vote. Some free blacks who held land could vote but most lost the right as the eighteenth century progressed. A small number of women, usually propertied widows, voted in New England. Indians were denied the right to vote everywhere. And even the white men who voted often did so in ways that were not fully independent. **Deference** was common in all colonies, particularly in the South. In the Chesapeake, political power became concentrated in the elite planters, who built towns and colleges and were only marginally responsive to the people. Leading families also tended to intermarry so that an ever-smaller number of families controlled society. Over time, disadvantaged whites were cut off from power.

Throughout the first half of the eighteenth century, England was preoccupied with wars in Europe and managing its commercial empire and thus devoted little energy to governing the colonies. In this period of "salutary neglect," the colonies developed their own systems of governance. By 1700, nearly all the colonies had a governor, a lower house, and an upper house. Colonial governors, who were largely selected by officials in England, were quite powerful. They advised on judicial appointments, vetoed legislation in the upper houses, and dissolved assemblies or simply denied them the right to meet. But soon enough, colonial governors lost power to the lower assemblies as colonists fought back, inspired by England's own theories about the proper functioning of politics. New assemblies of colonists acted as if they were their own House of Commons. They asserted control over tax legislation, the militia, and, at times, the governor's salary. When the governors, their councils, and the Upper Houses objected, their opponents saw threats to liberty and the onset of tyranny, as predicted by the radical Whigs.

In New France, politics and governance reflected the institutions of the home country: an absolutist monarchy backed by an army but without a parliament. Only the king's sense of obligation to his people tempered his ultimate authority. To govern New France, the king appointed three officials. The most powerful was the governor-general, but just below him was the intendant who controlled finances and much of the daily administration of the colony. Both had to respect the bishop, who was in charge of parish priests and wielded enormous moral authority. They shared power with a crown-appointed council composed of five to seven *seigneurs*, the largest landholders.

New Spain boasted a large bureaucracy, but on the frontier, from Alta California to Florida, there was strict oversight by colonial governors but no elected legislatures. Spanish governors presented themselves as impartial judges, but most were absolutists who looked to profit from their offices. In the remote corners of northern New Spain, state authority was checked only by Catholic missionaries and their powerful leaders. The locus of local political power in New Spain's communities was the town council, which was not a democratic forum but rather an avenue for local elites to carry out their will.

deference Respect or esteem granted to an elder or a social superior.

Zenger case Landmark New York libel case of 1735 that resulted in protections for free expression in printed materials.

5-5e The Press and Political Culture

Literacy, politics, and freedom of the press emerge in the English colonies.

In the rural areas of British North America, formal politics intruded on daily life only during elections, but in cities such as Boston, New York, and Philadelphia, men interested in discussing and debating politics formed clubs and associations that met regularly. In 1727, Benjamin Franklin created a weekly club, the Junto. Wealthy men usually founded these societies, but the less affluent created their own, too, meeting in coffee houses and taverns. All of these clubs helped create an increasingly informed citizenry, a process also advanced through the creation of the first circulating libraries in colonial America and the expansion of newspaper culture. Franklin established the first of these, the Library Company of Philadelphia, in 1731. By 1740, thirteen colonial newspapers were published in the colonies, and they were increasingly affordable to an expanding literate populace.

Although the right to freely express one's ideas in most cases extended to legislators so that they could represent their constituents and express their views without fear of reprisal, this right was not afforded to ordinary citizens or publishers under the British Constitution. Similarly, freedom of the press was not guaranteed by law and was discouraged by local assemblies, who feared that the public would be swayed by printed materials, which could be inaccurate. Although the government could not censor printed materials, authors and publishers could be prosecuted for defaming government officials.

In 1734, for example, the New York government jailed newspaper editor John Peter Zenger and charged him with seditious libel for writing in his paper, *The New York Daily*, that Governor William Cosby was a corrupt tyrant. Andrew Hamilton, a lawyer from Philadelphia, rose to Zenger's defense, claiming that Zenger's allegations about Cosby were true and therefore could not constitute seditious libel. The jury sided with Zenger, declaring him not guilty and freeing him from jail. The **Zenger case** established the right of the colonial press to criticize the government, decreed that the truth cannot be considered defamatory, and suggested that future prosecutions of this sort would be hard to win.

In comparison, in neither New France nor the distant corners of Spanish America did movements for freedom of expression emerge. Spanish and French officials censored printed materials, but these mostly consisted, in the first place, of religious texts and legal manuals. The size and distance of Spain's colonial empire also worked against the spread of ideas and the creation of a shared political culture. New Spain spanned some 5 million square miles, and few of its distant colonies were connected by trade. In comparison, the thirteen English mainland colonies encompassed only about 322,000 square miles and intercolonial trade was robust.

5-5f Patriarchy and Gender Roles

> Traditional roles and institutions dominate life in colonial America.

Martin Luther, the founder of Protestantism, reflected early modern beliefs about the abilities of women when he stated that "woman is a different animal to man, not only having different members, but also being far weaker in intellect . . . she . . . does not equal the dignity and glory of the male." From these misogynistic ideas, rooted in scripture and embedded in law, flowed a set of patriarchal beliefs that shaped society and granted men formal powers over women and children. Compared to women, men were seen as more able to control themselves. Women were viewed as weak and vulnerable and thus likely to succumb to sexual or demonic temptation.

In British North America, women could not hold public office, serve in the military, or train in a profession. Unmarried white women above the age of eighteen and widowed women had a few limited rights: They could sue and be sued, transfer property, and write wills. But once married, a woman—and nearly all women in the colonies eventually married—could not transfer property, enter into a contract, initiate a lawsuit, or make a will without the consent of her husband. According to William Blackstone, the most important interpreter of English law, marriage meant that the husband and wife were considered one person. A married woman's state was called *coverture*, in that it was under the "cover" or protection of "her husband, her baron or lord," that "she performs everything."

Women's work responsibilities varied across class, region, and season, but throughout colonial America, women bore the greatest responsibility for tending the home fire, preparing meals, rearing children, baking bread, making cheese, carrying water and waste, spinning wool, sewing, cleaning and ironing clothes, slaughtering pigs and chickens, brewing beer, and working in the household garden. In urban areas, women spent more time in marketplace exchanges than in domestic production, but no matter where they lived, they were responsible for their family's medical care and basic education.

Most men, meanwhile, performed heavy domestic labor, maintaining structures and buildings, tending to animals, producing crops, and managing lands. In urban areas, some worked as artisans, craftsmen, or common laborers or as lawyers, merchants, or ministers. Men were expected to bring their sons into their line of work, teaching them their trade just as women were to teach their daughters how to serve their husbands and care for their families. In Protestant New England, girls and boys were taught to read and write so they could study the Bible. In the Chesapeake and the Carolinas, rates of literacy were lower except among the male children of planters. In Catholic New France and New Spain, where literacy and religious practice did not go hand in hand, few boys and fewer girls attained literacy.

5-5g Sexuality, Marriage, and Reproduction

> Conservative notions about marriage and sexuality structure life across colonial America.

Because there were few forms of reliable contraception and because families needed children for labor, a white woman in colonial America typically had a child every two to two-and-a-half years. Women gave birth at home under the care of female relatives and a midwife. By and large, white families were healthy and grew quickly in size with most women bearing six or seven children during their lives.

Throughout colonial America, as in Europe, infant mortality (death in the first year of life) occurred in between 15 and 25 percent of births although that figure could reach 40 percent during epidemics. Thus, parents chose not to immediately attach themselves to their children and often treated boys and girls similarly at first, waiting until they were six or seven to dress and raise them in gender-specific ways.

Across colonial America, sex between unmarried persons was forbidden by law but common in practice. In Virginia and Maryland, where laws of indentured servitude prevented women from marrying, as many as one in five servant women became pregnant out of wedlock. And in New England, one in three brides was pregnant at the time of marriage. According to the laws across the British colonies, if the offending couple did not become engaged, they could be jailed for three days, whipped, and fined. If the couple were engaged, however, the fine would be halved.

In the British colonies, adultery was seen as sinful and a threat to society and thus was grounds for divorce and punishment by death. The death sentence, however, was hardly ever imposed. Adulterers were fined, jailed, placed in the stocks, whipped, branded, or forced to wear signs indicating their crime. In Catholic New Spain, many Hispanic men believed that they could enhance their honor by protecting the sexual purity of their female relatives, especially their wives and daughters. Thus, Hispanic wives and daughters in New Spain often lived in seclusion at the insistence of their husbands, fathers, and brothers.

The response to all forms of nonheterosexual relations was general revulsion. Male homosexuality was deemed a capital offense, but female homosexuality was never even acknowledged in the criminal codes of British North America. Advice books suggested it could be fatal.

Reproductive knowledge and health were largely the concern of women because they stood to be most affected by sex. Ignorance about the biology of human sexuality was widespread, especially among men. Many people believed that sperm originated in the spinal cord, that copulation during menstruation would beget a monstrosity, and that conception was deemed impossible without simultaneous orgasm.

Couples usually delayed marriage until they had sufficient resources to live independently. Free men tended to marry in their mid-twenties and free women a few years younger. In some British colonies, women could divorce on the grounds of their husbands' desertion, adultery, bigamy, or impotence, but divorce was not common, and divorce with the right to remarry was exceptionally rare. Divorced women had no legal status and no legal right to their children or what had formerly been their property, including inheritances and their dowry. More common than divorce, especially among the lower classes, was the informal dissolution of marriage. It was also common for a spouse to die and for the widow or widower to remarry. As a result, there were many blended, sprawling families, and some mothers and fathers came to refer to children who were not their own but under their care as "sons- or daughters-in-law."

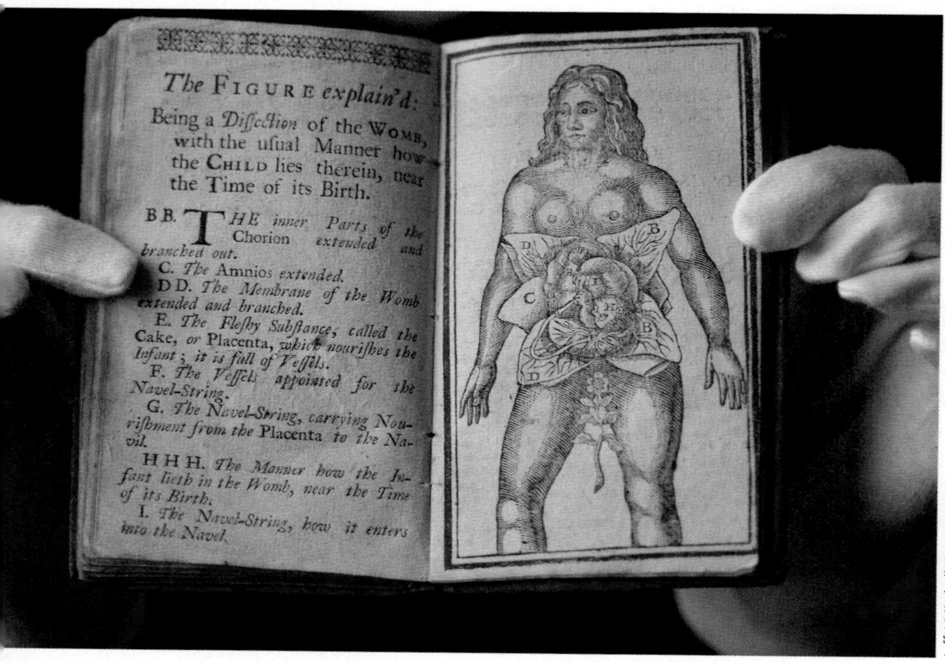

Jeff J Mitchell/Getty Images

Detail from Aristotle's *Masterpiece* The most widely circulated and printed sex and midwifery manual in the eighteenth century was published by an author who falsely claimed to have been Aristotle. The book gained popularity for the advice it dispensed as well as its illustrations of the male and female bodies. It was published in three editions and one hundred printings. ▲

Given their comparative rarity, elderly relatives were often appreciated and cared for by their family. Religion provided rituals and meaning to those in their final hours and to those who sought to comfort them. Hell, for Protestants and Catholics, was as real as heaven, and death's approach inspired terror or provided comfort to the faithful of all Christian denominations.

5-5h Slave Resistance and Rebellions

> As varied as the slaves and the conditions of slavery were across colonial America, so too was slave resistance.

In comparison to white families, the families of slaves were far more fragile in every respect. The hardships slaves faced in starting and maintaining families was just one aspect of their lives, however, that prompted them to resist their masters. Nearly every aspect of slave life—clothing, drumming, dancing, dressing, singing, eating, speaking, worshipping, and mourning—could become a form of resistance. Slaves sometimes turned to violence or to poisoning and arson. When flames destroyed Charles Town in 1740, slaveholders assumed that slaves had set fire to the city.

Slaves damaged tools, sabotaged machines, and ruined crops of tobacco, rice, or corn by harvesting it too soon or too late. Others worked slowly or lackadaisically. Still others "stole" from their masters or "stole" themselves by running away to maroon communities. Spanish Florida essentially invited runaways after 1693 when the Spanish king, Carlos II, issued a proclamation "giving liberty" to all fugitive slaves.

Slave rebellions were common in the Caribbean, where slaves often vastly outnumbered planters, but they were rare in British North America, where the chances of survival, much less success, were very low. In 1712, twenty-four Africans burned a New York building and killed nine men who sought to douse the flames. In response, civil authorities killed twenty-one suspected rebels and six others committed suicide. In 1741, when mysterious fires plagued New York City, some two hundred people including at least twenty poor whites were arrested out of fear that they and slaves were conspiring to overthrow the city government. Even with little evidence to support their fears, officials executed thirty-five slaves and four alleged white accomplices.

The largest slave uprising in British North America was small relative to those in the Caribbean. In South Carolina in 1739, one hundred armed slaves killed several whites and fled toward Florida. A white militia, aided by Indian auxiliaries, defeated the slaves in a pitched battle. This uprising, known as the **Stono Rebellion** after the river where the slaves' attack began, was put down ruthlessly and the rebels' severed heads were mounted on fence posts.

Many whites recognized that slaves toiled in subhuman conditions, yet few voiced opposition to slavery. In New England, Puritan ministers such as Cotton Mather owned slaves and argued that their conversion to Christianity and education were more important than their manumission.

Only among Quakers did arguments for the liberation of slaves advance, albeit slowly. In 1754, John Woolman, a Quaker tailor and bookkeeper from New Jersey, published *Some Considerations on the Keeping of Negroes*, the first anti-slavery tract in British North America. Four years later, Philadelphia Quakers, led by Anthony Benezet, outlawed slavery among local members. But it would be another generation until manumission became a matter of open discussion, even in the North.

The few slaves in colonial America who attained freedom lived in isolation and impoverishment. Lawmakers denied free blacks the rights associated with freedom. They were forbidden from testifying against a white person, punished more severely than whites for crimes, taxed more heavily, prevented from owning firearms, and discriminated against when they tried to purchase property, borrow money, or move from place to place. Of the several hundred free blacks living in Boston in 1742, 110 lived in a church-sponsored poor house and another 36 lived in a public workhouse.

Stono Rebellion South Carolina slave rebellion, the largest in British North America.

Summary

The first half of the eighteenth century was a period of dramatic transformation for much of colonial America. Spain, France, and England competed for territory and trade. Wars over European succession and trade roiled the edges of many colonies, leading to the destruction and seizure of some frontier settlements. Native Americans, who had already been pushed to the margins of the colonies, in many cases became pawns in European disputes. Moreover, their proportion among the overall population continued to decline because of illness and war as well as the explosion of the colonial population.

In this period, the colonies in British North America proved the most dynamic and expansive. They attracted hundreds of thousands of immigrants, nearly half of whom were, in one way or another, unwilling migrants, coming either from Africa as slaves or from western Europe as transported convicts or refugees from their homelands. With their arrival, distinctive cultures emerged in New England, the Middle Colonies, the Chesapeake, and the South. Population growth and the increasingly dynamic transatlantic economy also led to a widening of the gap between rich and poor. Yet the elite, the middling, and the poor all engaged new patterns of consumption and, at times, religious practice.

By 1750, life in the colonies of British North America had been transformed. English colonists debated notions of liberty and power in their political clubs and enjoyed far more access to the franchise and a free press than did Englishmen. The Great Awakening had remade Protestant religious views and practices and had allowed women, the unlettered, and a few free African Americans to take on roles of religious authority.

Slaves, however, experienced none of the excitement and opportunity that characterized this half century, even though their labor was in many respects the foundation of both. A small number gained a modicum of autonomy in port cities along the Atlantic Coast, both in the North and South of British North America. Although most remained enslaved, their lives were far more manageable than Africans transported to the Caribbean sugar colonies. Many married and had families, but the satisfaction they took in these accomplishments must have been tempered by the realization that the children they created were born into slavery. Finally, daily life in the frontier regions of New France and New Spain changed less in these years. as the dynamic centers of French and Spanish colonial life developed elsewhere. Nevertheless, local populations continued to shape regions and create cultures of their own.

<Thinking Back, *Looking Forward*>

As you review this chapter, think about the large-scale immigration to the Americas from the earliest days of settlement through 1750 and evaluate the roles labor, religion, and politics played in the movement of peoples across the Atlantic. To what extent did people cross the Atlantic of their own volition? Why did they do so? By and large, why did European women not immigrate in large numbers to the colonies?

In the next chapters, look for the ways in which European conflicts continued to shape life in colonial America.

To make your study concrete, review the timeline and reflect on the entries there. Think about their causes, consequences, and connections. How do they fit with global trends?

Additional Resources

Books

Bailyn, Bernard. *The Origins of American Politics*. New York: Alfred A. Knopf, 1968. ▶ Best concise discussion of politics in British North America.

Barr, Juliana. *Peace Came in the Form of a Woman: Indians and Spaniards in the Texas Borderlands*. Chapel Hill: University of North Carolina Press, 2007. ▶ Pioneering study of the role of women in Indian-Spanish relations in the Southwest.

Berkin, Carol. *First Generations: Women in Colonial America*. New York: Hill and Wang, 1996. ▶ Concise overview of women's experiences in British North America.

Bushman, Richard. *The Refinement of America: Persons, Houses, Cities*. New York: Alfred A. Knopf, 1992. ▶ Study of the evolution of an elite material culture in the eighteenth century in English colonies.

Greene, Jack P. *Pursuits of Happiness: The Social Development of Early Modern British Colonies and the Formation of American Culture*. Chapel Hill: University of North Carolina Press, 1988. ▶ Sweeping synthesis describing the evolution of a common English culture across the English colonies by 1750.

Hackel, Steven W. *Junípero Serra: California's Founding Father*. New York: Farrar, Straus, and Giroux, 2013. ▶ Penetrating biography of the Mallorcan imperial priest who founded California's missions and was canonized in 2015.

Hofstadter, Richard. *America at 1750: A Social Portrait*. New York: Alfred A. Knopf, 1971. ▶ Brief and riveting account of the English colonies' social development through 1750.

Norton, Marcy. *Sacred Gifts, Profane Pleasures: A History of Tobacco and Chocolate in the Atlantic World*. Ithaca, NY: Cornell University Press, 2008. ▶ Intellectual and economic history of Europeans' gradual reception of tobacco and chocolate in the seventeenth century.

Shammas, Carole. *The Pre-industrial Consumer in England and America*. New York: Oxford University Press, 1990. ▶ Path-breaking economic study of changing patterns of consumption in British North America.

Usner, Daniel H. Jr. *Indians, Settlers, and Slaves in a Frontier Exchange Economy: The Lower Mississippi Valley before 1783*. Chapel Hill: University of North Carolina Press, 1992. ▶ Examination of how economic exchange created points of cultural contact and understanding among blacks, Indians, and the French in Louisiana.

Go to the MindTap® for **Global Americans** to access the full version of select books from this Additional Resources section.

Websites

Early California Population Project, Huntington Library. (http://www.huntington.org/Information/ECPPmain.htm) ▶ Online and searchable database of baptisms, marriages, and burials of Indians, soldiers, and settlers in colonial California, 1769 through 1850.

Canada: The Research Program in Historical Demography. (http://www.genealogie.umontreal.ca/en/LePrdh) ▶ Online and searchable database for Quebec and French Canada, 1621 through 1849, including all baptisms, marriages, and burials.

MindTap®

Continue exploring online through MindTap®, where you can:

- **Assess your knowledge with the Chapter Test**
- **Watch historical videos related to the chapter**
- **Further your understanding with interactive maps and timelines**

Colonial Society and Bonds of Empire

1693–1711

1693
Spanish Florida offers freedom to fugitive slaves from British North America.

1698
Parliament suspends the Royal African Company's monopoly on the transport of slaves from Africa to British North America.

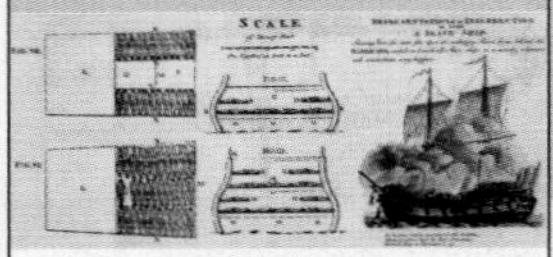

1701
Queen Anne's War/War of the Spanish Succession begins.

1702–1704
Carolinians wage attacks on Spanish Florida.

1704
French-Mohawk raid Deerfield, Connecticut.

1712–1716

1712
Slaves rebel in New York City.

1713
Treaty of Utrecht is signed, ending the War of Spanish Succession and confirming Philip as king of Spain.

1715–1716
Yamasee War breaks out in Southeast between Indians and English settlers.

1717–1720

1717
The Tuscaroras move north from North Carolina.

1718
Mission San Antonio de Béjar is established in Texas.

1718–1720
The War of Quadruple Alliance pits Spain against France, England, Holland, and Austria.

1721–1725

1722
The Tuscaroras join the Haudenosaunees.

1724
Code Noir is decreed in Louisiana.

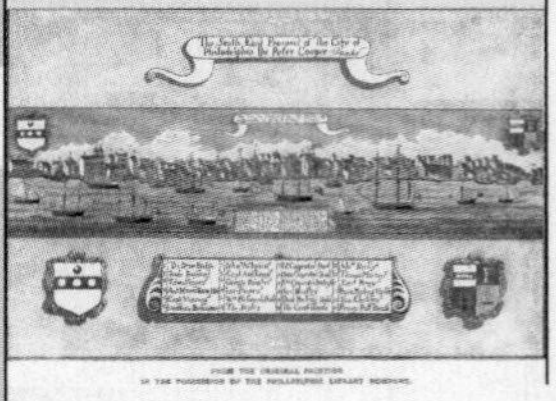

1726–1730

1729
Russian explorers Bering and Chirikov undertake their first expedition.

1731–1735

1731

Spanish missions in Texas relocate to San Antonio.

1732

Georgia is established.

1733

Molasses Act taxes molasses from the French West Indies.

Jonathan Edwards's sermons spark a religious revival in Northampton, Massachusetts, beginning the Great Awakening in the colonies.

1735

Zenger is found not guilty of libel.

1736–1739

1737

The Delaware Indians fraudulently dispossessed of their land through the Walking Purchase.

1739

Slaves rise up in the Stono Rebellion.

1740–1748

1740

King George's War/ War of the Austrian Succession breaks out.

1741

Bering and Chirikov undertake their second expedition.

1746–1769

1753

Georgia's original charter expires.

1754

Woolman publishes his first antislavery tract.

1758

Mission San Sabá is destroyed.

1769

Junípero Serra establishes Mission San Diego in Alta California.

1770–1799

1770

Spain takes possession of Alta California at Monterey.

1777

Pueblo of San José is established in Alta California.

1781

Pueblo of Los Angeles is established in Alta California.

1799

Russian-American Company is chartered.

Go to MindTap® to engage with an interactive version of the timeline. Analyze events and themes with clickable content, view related videos, and respond to critical thinking questions.

6 Imperial Conflicts and Revolution

1750–1783

Thomas Paine claimed that the American people were strong because they were unified, but people living in North America were divided by economy, culture, and imperial connections.

6-1
Seven Years' War, Years of Global Warfare

6-1a Trade and Empire
6-1b Seven Years' War
6-1c Postwar Landscape
6-1d Pontiac's Rebellion

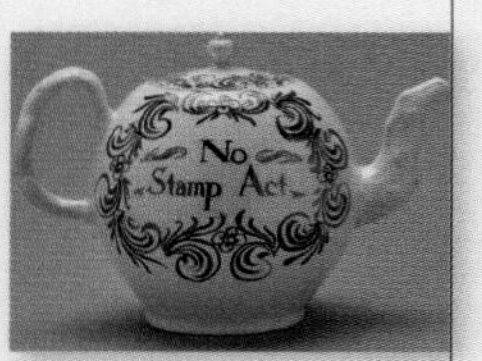

6-2
Imperial Reorganization and Colonial Resistance

6-2a Tightening Imperial Ties
6-2b Stamp Act
6-2c Rights and Liberties
6-2d Nonconsumption and Nonimportation Movements
6-2e Violent Conflict in the Interior and on the Coast

6-3
From Resistance to Revolution

6-3a Imperial Laws and Escalating Colonial Reactions
6-3b Continental Congress
6-3c Early Fighting
6-3d Declaring Independence

6-4
War for Independence

6-4a Military Strategy in the Early Stages of War
6-4b American Revolution as Imperial Conflict
6-4c American Revolution as Civil War
6-4d Surrender and Settlement

Thomas Paine grew up making foundation undergarments in a small English town but soon ran away to sea to become a privateer. Paine and the other 250 crewmen aboard the *King of Prussia* in 1757 were sanctioned by British King George II to attack enemy merchant ships and sell the spoils for personal profit. A new, global war among European powers made this kind of work lucrative and plentiful, but also dangerous. After eight months at sea, Paine returned to corset making, followed by a new career as a government tax collector. In London, Paine published a pamphlet on behalf of his fellow tax collectors, contrasting their poverty and misery with "the rich, in ease and affluence." He became acquainted with a group of men who called themselves "The Club of Honest Whigs" that gathered every two weeks in a coffee shop to talk politics and philosophy. One of its members, Benjamin Franklin—a Philadelphia printer, inventor, and politician—gave Paine the letter of introduction that set him on course to be an international revolutionary.

German artist Balthasar Friedrich Leizelt created this idealized image of Philadelphia, making it look similar to European ports engaged in Atlantic trade. ▲ Library of Congress Prints and Photographs Division

With Franklin's letter in hand, Paine crossed the Atlantic to the bustling port of Philadelphia in 1774, where new political associations were organizing North American colonists to protest what they saw as Britain's unfair treatment. Paine began publishing essays criticizing British corruption and praising American colonists' virtue. He created a sensation in January 1776, when his pamphlet *Common Sense* became the bestseller that urged colonists to reject reconciliation with Britain and support independence. He championed the revolution that erupted, boosted spirits during the war, and celebrated victory afterward.

In 1787, Paine moved to Europe, where he joined a new revolutionary movement, this one in France. In 1791 and 1792, he published his most famous work, *The Rights of Man*, praising the French Revolution and proclaiming that God had created all people equal and equally deserving of political rights. He was a champion of the poor who believed that governments in which the people ruled made better societies than monarchies did. "I see in America," he wrote, "the generality of people living in a style of plenty unknown in the monarchical countries."

Paine traveled in a world of competing imperial structures—armies, courts, trade monopolies—that had broad reach but uneven strength. The British Empire deployed him as a tax collector and privateer to keep profits away from rivals, but he also found ways to cross boundaries and seek his fortune, a strategy many adopted. Native Americans used strategic alliances with European empires to gain access to trade goods and military strength against those who would claim their land. At the

In what ways do Thomas Paine's actions within and against empires reflect the struggles of the various peoples who lived within the Atlantic World?

Go to MindTap® to watch a video on Paine and learn how his story relates to the themes of this chapter.

same time, colonial American farmers disregarded boundary lines drawn by distant empires, hoping to make their own deals locally. American colonists eagerly imported European goods along trade routes protected by powerful navies. But many colonists chafed at rules demanding that they trade only within their own empire and smuggled their way to new markets. Enslaved people were ruthlessly exploited as profitable commodities by empires that then needed them as soldiers in the ongoing warfare of the eighteenth century.

With each war over trade and territory, Europe's empires redrew borders and swapped colonial holdings. Both the Seven Years' War and the American Revolution were part of the ongoing eighteenth-century contest of Britain and its allies against France and its allies. Yet the cycle launched a new trajectory in 1763, setting in motion what would become second and third dimensions of colonial revolution: between Native Americans and colonists and between British colonists and the government in London. In all three, the desires of average people for land, personal freedom, and self-governance were prominent and often in conflict with one another.

In calling for the creation of a new country, Thomas Paine claimed that the American people's greatest strength was "in unity," but the sense of common cause needed to wage a war of independence came from different political and economic motivations. People across North America wanted personal freedom, access to land, and economic opportunity. These desires led some to join the cause for colonial independence and reject monarchies in favor of a republic. For thousands of others, especially enslaved Africans and displaced Indians, those same desires confirmed their sense in 1783 that although they lived in North American territory, they were not part of the new United States.

6-1

Seven Years' War, Years of Global Warfare

This image depicting 1764 negotiations for the return of 206 colonial captives taken from the Virginia and Pennsylvania backcountry during wartime was created by American artist Benjamin West. Around a council fire, British Colonel Henry Bouquet and his aides use paper and ink while a group of Senecas, Shawnees, and Delawares use a wampum belt to record diplomatic agreements. Both wear fabrics made in Europe.

How does this image use space, framing, posture, and props to illustrate the bargaining positions of Indians and Europeans at council fires? Why are the colonial captives not pictured? ▶

Library of Congress Prints and Photographs Division Washington, D.C.[LC-USZ62-104]

European empires competed for wealth and power by warring over territory and trade. Between 1689 and 1748, a series of wars had focused on the European continent but included armed conflict in North America. In 1754, a new cycle in these imperial contests began, and this time North America was the primary focus rather than an afterthought. Fighting among European empires and their Indian allies in this conflict, called the *French and Indian War* in North America but the *Seven Years' War* in Europe, in fact lasted for more than nine years. British victory ended French claims to North America but did not stop ongoing warfare between Native Americans and American colonists. In the Great Lakes and Ohio Valley

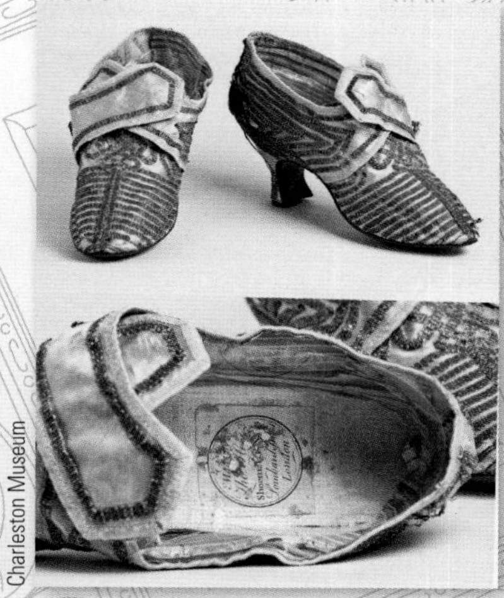

Eliza Lucas Pinckney's Silk Shoes, Ordered from London

Global Americans **Eliza Lucas Pinckney**, born Eliza Lucas on the island of Antigua in 1722, finished her education in England like many daughters of wealthy British families posted around the empire. Her family moved to become plantation owners in South Carolina when she was a teenager. With her father sent back to the Caribbean as an army officer, Lucas took over management of the family plantations, overseeing the labor of enslaved Africans and experimenting with new crops. Joining business and scientific interests, she developed a strain of indigo, a blue dye plant, and a method of producing dye cakes, which became the second most prominent and profitable export of South Carolina after rice. South Carolina indigo competed with French dyes to color the quickly expanding international commerce in new printed fabrics.

In 1744, Eliza Lucas married Charles Pinckney, a much older lawyer and politician. Raising her children "according to Mr. Lock's method" to "play [themselves] into learning," she lived to see two of her sons become revolutionary leaders. The occupation of Charles Town resulted in the loss of many of her trappings of wealth and taste. Widowed, she wrote to one creditor that her slaves had been seized for military work, her house filled with foreign soldiers, and her elegant trees cut down for army use. Like most wealthy South Carolina slave owners at the time, her identity was oriented toward the Caribbean and transatlantic commercial and intellectual networks; only during the Revolution did she remake herself as an American. At her funeral in 1793, George Washington was a pallbearer.

regions, allied Indians, inspired by religious visions and a charismatic leader named Pontiac, continued to violently oppose British and colonial American presence in the North American interior.

☞ As you read, think about how local struggles between neighbors in North America influenced imperial actions between 1754 and 1763. What types of alliances were possible? How did war change them?

6-1a Trade and Empire

Trade goods shape power politics locally and globally.

In 1757, one French diplomat observed that the "balance of commerce of the nations in America" and the "balance of power in Europe" were ultimately the same. Integrated global trade shaped settlement patterns, alliances, and the shifting fortunes of empires in the eighteenth century. Around the Atlantic, British, French, and Dutch governments sponsored companies that shipped guns and cloth to West Africa in exchange for captive humans who were transported to work on plantations in the Americas. From the Americas, slave-grown sugar, tobacco, indigo, and rice traveled back to Europe, transforming daily diets and enriching investors. The wealth generated by this trade established Dutch banks and English factories that in turn spurred global investment and local economic development. Another global circuit, connecting French and British traders with Indian fur trappers in North America, built substantial fortunes in Europe and dressed men and women on three continents.

Across the Pacific, the Spanish empire dominated global trade, shipping the silver mined by coerced laborers in Mexico and Peru to China in exchange for silks, spices, and porcelain. But the Russians were rising competitors, in the form of traders crossing from Siberia to the Aleutian Islands in search of valuable seal, fox, and sea otter pelts. Imperial taxes on the trade plumped state coffers. By the 1770s, the fur trade yielded 8 percent of Russian revenues. Spain, France, and Britain likewise depended on import taxes from their colonies to fund wars they waged to expand their territories.

Oceanic circuits for goods needed Native American labor, expertise, and trading connections. To keep relations friendly and access to animal skins open, France sent cloth, tools, cooking pots, guns, and ammunition to Indian allies as gifts. England learned to do the same with the Haudenosaunee confederacy, now known as the Six Nations. But trade-based alliances also spread disease and spurred overhunting that profoundly disrupted Indian lives. White settlers followed early traders and set up cabins as **squatters** on Indian land.

In the late 1740s, North American alliances began to break down. European wars had drained the reserves of European kings and left them with less money for diplomatic gifts. Native Americans wanted to negotiate new diplomatic and trade terms. A group of displaced Delaware and Shawnee Indians living in the Ohio River valley firmly proclaimed their neutrality and insisted on the right to deal with any trader, regardless of political ties. As they watched Scots-Irish and German migrants freely settle on their lands, claimed by both Pennsylvania and Virginia, Delawares and Shawnees rejected Haudenosaunee efforts to negotiate on their behalf and broke the old Covenant Chain that had bound allied tribes together and to the British.

squatter Person who lives on land without legal or customary claim to it, often insisting that working on land confers ownership. Squatters often claimed Indian lands.

The region between the Ohio River and the Great Lakes had long been one of the great crossroads of cultures because it linked two essential waterways of trade and travel: the route from the Atlantic along the St. Lawrence River into the Great Lakes and the Mississippi watershed that connected the interior of the continent down to the Gulf of Mexico. In 1753, French officials responded to escalating tension in the region by constructing a new line of forts between Montreal and New Orleans to secure their trading posts from British competition and American colonists in search of farmland. The crossroads of cultures became a proving ground of power.

Library of Congress Prints & Photographs Division,[LC-USZC4-5315]

Join or Die Borrowing imagery from European emblems, Benjamin Franklin published this illustration of an eight-segmented snake in the May 9, 1754, edition of the *Pennsylvania Gazette*. The image represented his belief that only centralized colonial government with power to govern North American affairs would ensure the health of the empire as a whole. The colonies, represented in this image by their initials, disagreed. Georgia and Delaware were not included in the Albany Plan or the snake image. ▲

6-1b Seven Years' War

Imperial conflicts reignite, involving people around the world.

In 1754, threatened by new French forts and Indian alliances, British authorities convened the **Albany Congress**. Delegates from seven British colonies met with representatives of the Six Nations to try to repair the Covenant Chain and secure support against the French. Extensive gifts and the naming of influential trader William Johnson to a new office, the Superintendent of Indian Affairs, convinced the Haudenosaunees to pledge limited military assistance in the form of individual warriors and scouts. Delegates also passed Pennsylvanian Benjamin Franklin's proposed Albany Plan of Union, which would have created a central government made up of representatives from British North American colonies and a crown-appointed "president general" to oversee Indian land treaties, trade, and military affairs. Preferring to retain local control, colonial assemblies rejected the idea.

As the delegates debated, fighting was breaking out. Seeking to assert authority on Virginia's borderlands, Governor Robert Dinwiddie sent a small force commanded by twenty-two-year-old George Washington to seize Fort Duquesne, a new French fort at the forks of the Ohio River, where it controlled access to the Mississippi River. Washington and Dinwiddie were shareholders in the **Ohio Company of Virginia**, a land speculation company with claims to the same valuable Ohio territory claimed by France, Britain, the Haudenosaunees, the Shawnees, and the Delawares. This gave both men personal and political reasons for expelling the French. Tanaghrisson, a Seneca chief who accompanied Washington, hoped that war between the French and British would drive both out of Indian territory, and he encouraged Washington to launch an attack. The ill-planned ambush resulted in multiple French casualties and the capture of twenty-one prisoners but left Washington's small force exposed and vulnerable at a quickly constructed Fort Necessity. More French troops soon forced Washington's ignominious retreat. Although there was no formal declaration until 1756, the **Seven Years' War** between France and its allies and Britain and its allies had begun. In the words of one British politician, "A volley fired by a young Virginian in the backwoods of America set the world on fire." People around the world were caught in the conflagration.

Albany Congress Meeting in 1754 of representatives from British colonies and Six Nations to reestablish alliances at which Franklin proposed centralized multicolony government.

Ohio Company of Virginia Land development company with powerful investors who hoped to sell land in contested Ohio River Valley.

Seven Years' War Conflict involving European empires, their colonies, and indigenous people around the globe.

militia Local defense force in every colony headed by a governor and led by local elite officers in Indian warfare and patrolling runaway slaves.

From the perspective of European power centers, the war was another clash of empires. As Britain, France, and then Spain sought to defend and expand colonial holdings in North America, they pursued similar designs in Central America, India, and the Philippines. In Europe, Britain, France, and Spain formed new strategic alliances and fought over territory in response to the rising military power of Prussia under Frederick the Great. From West Africa to the Caribbean, European empires battled to control valuable international trade routes fueling the enormous profits in enslaved people, sugar, and coffee. The British and French East India companies took advantage of political turmoil in the Mughal empire, a Muslim dynasty ruling much of India, to pursue control over textile-producing hubs. As before, European empires depended on a combination of their own troops, auxiliaries hired from other countries, and local fighting forces, many of whom had their own agendas in taking up arms (see Map 6.1).

In North America, Britain had great difficulty convincing colonists that the war was their fight. Colonial defense forces relied on **militia** units consisting of adult

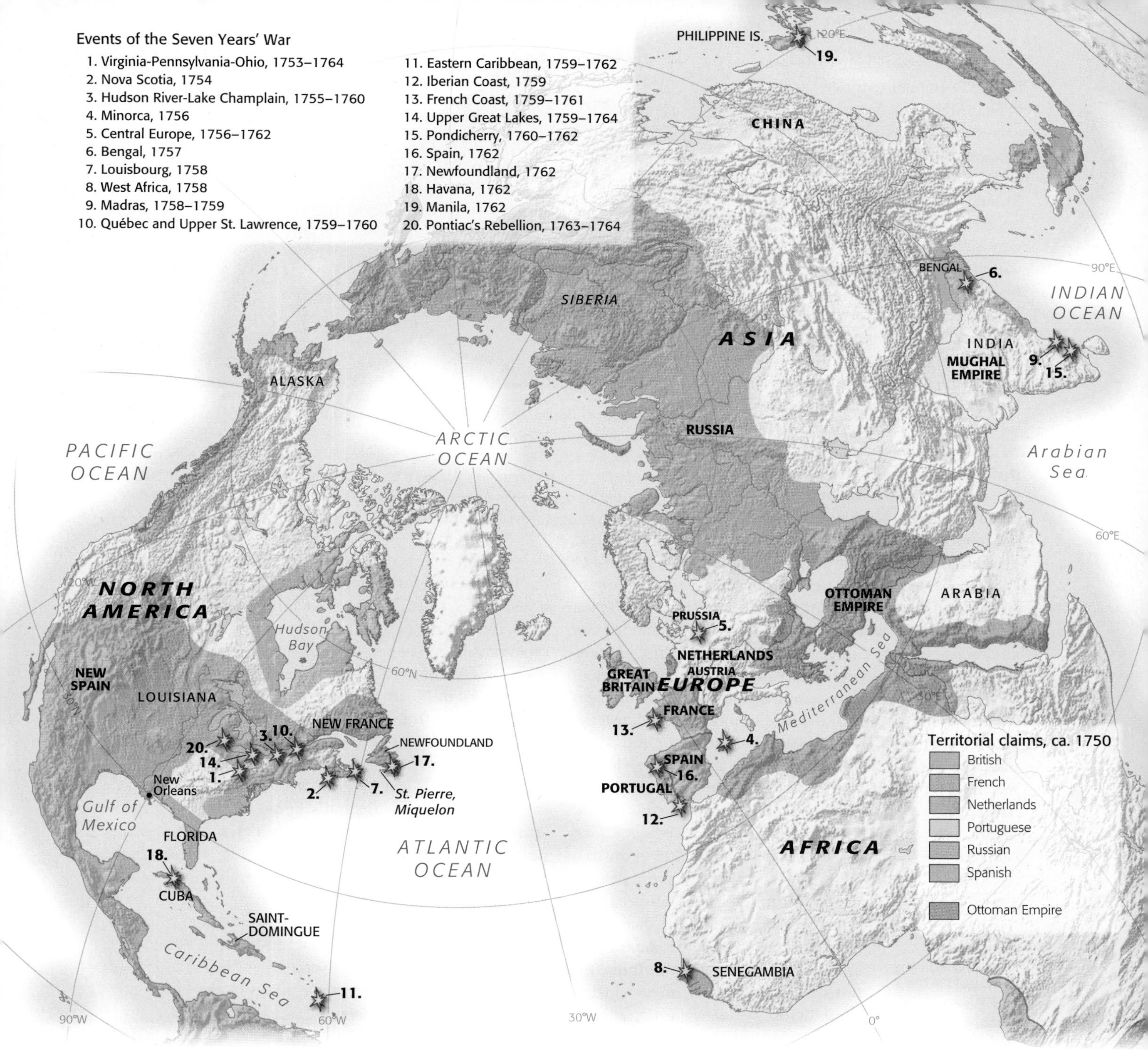

Map 6.1 Seven Years' War as a Global Conflict, 1754–1763 As with all clashes between empires in the eighteenth century, this war involved colonial settlers, indigenous people, and imperial soldiers in violent conflict around the world. In the Seven Years' War, territorial claims in North America and Native American alliances were a primary cause, but events in one theater shaped outcomes for people thousands of miles away. ▲

property-owning men. Mirroring community social structure, militias were led by local elite officers who presided over occasional public mustering exercises and organized runaway slave patrols. Militias were local in their outlook. When the war began, therefore, members of the Virginia militia refused to leave their farms unworked and their enslaved population unguarded to fight at the forks of the Ohio River. Virginia's House of Burgesses was forced to draft men to fill Britain's military quotas. Because the militia was composed of men who were also voters, elected authorities tried to conscript poor men and outsiders.

Following shocking early losses, in 1757, British cabinet secretary William Pitt took over control of the war effort and made North America his first priority. Relying on Britain's ally, Prussia, to fight the alliance of France, Austria, and Russia that had entered combat on the European continent, Pitt poured money and supplies into North America, ultimately amassing forty-five thousand troops to overwhelm France's ten thousand. Pitt also promised British Americans compensation for their participation in the war effort. Telling colonists that this was a global war of Protestants against Catholics, he drew on religious antagonisms to fuel loyalty to the British Empire.

World History Archive/Image Asset Management Ltd/Alamy Stock Photo

Death of General Wolfe The capture of Quebec was a military victory that turned Wolfe into a martyr and national hero celebrated in songs and sermons across the British Empire. Pennsylvania-born artist Benjamin West mixed classical poses with contemporary settings and costuming to create a painting that was a sensation when exhibited in London in 1771. It was quickly copied onto affordable textiles, ceramics, and engravings—materials of eighteenth-century consumer culture. ▲

The new investment in North American colonies paid off in battlefield victories that won support from Haudenosaunees in the North. The siege and capture of Quebec in 1759 was the dramatic turning point of the war. After three months of skirmishes, General James Wolfe led four thousand British troops over steep cliffs behind the city and engaged French forces on the Plains of Abraham outside city walls. Following a short engagement, in which both Wolfe and the French general Louis-Joseph de Montcalm were mortally wounded, the British took the field and the city. Within a year, after British forces had captured Montreal, the French surrendered all of Canada. The victory, which cost the British more than ten times what the French had spent, was a testament to Britain's economic power and organization, especially its large and well-funded navy. That same navy helped defeat France in other theaters of the war.

Britain's victory over France had profound consequences for native people around the globe who had used the strategy of playing one empire against the other. In India, the **British East India Company** wielded a combination of military and commercial might to exploit Indian riches in cotton textiles, silk, and tea on behalf of the British Empire. Native Bengal leaders had relied on an insistent French presence to counterbalance the company's power. When the French were defeated and driven out in 1761, Bengal Indians lost their main leverage against consolidating British control. The same happened in the Great Lakes region of North America. With the defeat and departure of the French, the Wendats (Hurons) and the Potawatomis lost negotiating leverage.

British East India Company Joint-stock company originally chartered in 1600 that by mid-eighteenth century had a trade monopoly in the East Indies and substantial military and administrative powers.

Treaty of Paris Agreement signed in 1763 ending the Seven Years' War among European powers in which France lost claims to North America and Native Americans were not represented.

Acadians Culturally mixed French and Native people who lived in British Nova Scotia; those who refused to pledge loyalty to Britain in 1755 were driven from homes, many to Louisiana.

On February 10, 1763, the **Treaty of Paris** marked the formal end of the Seven Years' War that had claimed a million lives. Confident in their power to redraw political maps moving people and land from one empire to another, diplomats in Paris upended the balance of power, granting enormous territorial claims to Great Britain. France lost all its territory in North America with the exception of two fishing islands off the coast of Newfoundland and a handful of islands in the Caribbean, including sugar-producing Saint-Domingue. Spain, a latecomer in declaring war on Britain in 1762, lost Florida but gained Louisiana in a separate agreement. Britain claimed all lands from the Atlantic coast to the Mississippi River. Native Americans, no matter on which side they had fought, were excluded from peace negotiations.

6-1c Postwar Landscape

Displacements fragment communities and force new identities.

New boundaries dictated displacements. Britain split its new colony of Florida in two, creating West Florida and East Florida. Thousands of Spanish-speaking colonists, officials, soldiers, and enslaved Africans living in the region evacuated permanently to Spanish Cuba as did a group of Catholic Yamasee Indians. Creeks who objected to the terms of the treaty had to sail to Havana to seek Spanish military support against encroaching English settlers. They were "surprised," the Creeks said, "how People can give away Land that does not belong to them."

British soldiers took a more violent approach to removing the **Acadians** from Nova Scotia. These French Americans, who often intermarried with local Micmacs, had lived under British rule since the end of the War of

Spanish Succession in 1713. In 1755, those who refused to take a loyalty oath to Britain were forced from their homes. Some fled north, some escaped to France, but many were exiled to other British colonies. British troops continued to seize territory and burn homes and fields, removing Acadians and sending them into servitude in New England or imprisoning them in ships and workhouses. Thousands died during the eviction. Eventually, several thousand Acadians moved to Louisiana, where their descendants became known as *Cajuns*.

Thousands of British American colonists died in the war, either in battle or from diseases contracted at forts and garrisons, and their deaths prompted more relocations. As families left behind struggled to support themselves, cities such as Boston filled with widows and orphans seeking financial support. Unable to raise enough money to aid them, communities in New England increased the practice of "warning out," whereby local authorities sent residents back to the town of their birth (or, in the case of free married women, their husband's town) to receive charitable assistance there. Economic losses compounded demographic ones. Lucrative military contracts for ships, weapons, clothing, and provisions dried up, and the removal of forty thousand British troops meant no more customers for food, lodging, and other services. At the very moment that they were celebrating victory in what some called the Great War for Empire, many in the colonies faced economic misery.

Less miserable, but equally uncertain, were new members of the British and Spanish empires. By claiming vast lands inhabited by mixed villages of French, Spanish, and Native American people, Britain gained an empire that was more heterogeneous than it had been in 1754. Some new subjects spoke French or Spanish; many were Catholic. But British authority was spread thin in lands once claimed by France. Kinship ties forged between French fur traders and Indian women were more influential in many places than British administrators and merchants sent to enforce the new map. Likewise, Spanish officials in Havana struggled to administer and defend the large and distant Louisiana territory. They relied on experienced French traders and a regular supply of gifts to encourage Indian allegiance. Consequently, for many living in Louisiana, the new Paris-born lieutenant governor's declaration that "we are all Spaniards" meant little. Osage traders near St. Louis took advantage of the limited colonial oversight to expand their commercial power over the Mississippi River by partnering with French, British, or Spanish traders as opportunities arose.

6-1d Pontiac's Rebellion

Allied Indians continue to fight for territory and sovereignty.

French troops withdrew from North American forts after the fall of Montreal, but warfare in the Great Lakes region continued between Indians and the British. Although it was in some ways a continuation of the Seven Years' War, the conflict was also a war for independence fought by a diverse group of Native Americans newly united by a shared desire to drive the British out of the Ohio Valley and stop further colonial settlement. This common cause drew strength from a sense of spiritual purpose. Since the 1730s, Native American prophets from various communities had called for a renewal of old rituals. By the 1750s, Delaware prophets had a new message: The Master of Life wanted them to "destroy the poison among them." Neolin, the most influential of these prophets, proclaimed that the path to heaven was blocked by European vice. He urged his followers to cease trading with the French and English and stop using their goods. His words inspired Pontiac, an Ottawa war chief, who emphasized the most militant part of Neolin's message: Indians must join together not only to resist European contact but also to force European colonists from the land. Spiritual and tactical arguments created a new sense of unity, a belief that Native Americans were a distinct people with a common identity, regardless of tribe or clan.

In the spring of 1763, a coalition of Native American people seized all but three of Britain's dozen forts and besieged Fort Niagara and Fort Pitt. During **Pontiac's Rebellion**, Indian warriors attacked settlements on the Pennsylvania and Virginia frontiers, forcing colonists to flee to refugee centers near the coast. Some turned against their Native American neighbors. In late December 1763, the Scots-Irish "Paxton Boys" murdered unarmed Christian Indian families near Lancaster and then marched to the capital city of Philadelphia, determined to kill the Indians who had fled there. Colonial officials, led by Franklin, turned them away after hearing their demands, which included military protection and increased political representation.

British Commander-in-Chief Jeffrey Amherst, who had declared a desire to "remove that Vermin" of Native Americans, was short on troops, and Pontiac's forces lacked ammunition and had to contend with devastating illness. The result was a stalemate rather than clear victory for either side. News in October 1763 of the signing of the Treaty of Paris extinguished Pontiac's hope for aid from the French, and some tribes, such as the Senecas, made their own separate peace. Pontiac and Charlot Kaské, a Shawnee war chief, continued to recruit warriors and mobilize resistance, but in 1766 they accepted a peace negotiated by William Johnson at Oswego, New York. Twelve years of warfare that had begun in 1754 ended.

Although it was incomplete and did not last, joint Indian resistance did compel the British to abandon their plan to dictate terms to them. Amherst was removed as commander, and former French forts were re-established with British soldiers and officers who restored the trading and gift exchanges that had made diplomacy possible

Pontiac's Rebellion Coordinated warfare in 1763 by Indians in Great Lakes against continuing British presence that ended in stalemate.

Royal Proclamation of 1763 Decree setting a line of settlement along the Appalachian Mountains marking the limit of legal colonial settlement.

before the war. Troops enforced the **Royal Proclamation of 1763**, a decree planned before the outbreak of Pontiac's Rebellion that forbade colonial governors from granting land patents west of the Appalachian Mountains. Those lands were to be the possession of "several Nations or Tribes of *Indians*" under the protection of the British Empire (see Map 6.2). Although a type of declaration of property rights for Native Americans, the prohibition meant little to settlers and squatters who already lived in the territory. By formally walling off Indian land, however, the Proclamation Line was a blow to those colonial elites who had formed the Ohio Company of Virginia, launched the war, and hoped to profit from land speculation once the French were gone. Indians kept copies of the Proclamation and the wampum belts that had circulated with it to hold Britain to its promises.

Map 6.2 North America in 1763 The Treaty of Paris ended French claims to vast territories on the continent. Drawing new boundaries, the British and Spanish empires forced the migrations of thousands of people living in newly claimed land. In the same year, the British established a Proclamation Line along the Appalachian Mountains, officially dividing Indians' and British colonists' lands within the empire. ▶

6-2

Imperial Reorganization and Colonial Resistance

This creamware teapot, protesting British tax policy for the American colonies, was made in Britain for export to those colonies. Potters in Cornwall, England, used local clay to develop this new form of ceramic in the 1750s in order to compete internationally with Chinese porcelain. Benjamin Franklin, testifying in Parliament in 1766, said that the goods Americans imported from Britain were "either necessaries, mere conveniences, or superfluities," all of which could be replaced.

What does this teapot suggest about the cultural and economic relationship between Britain and the British colonies? Why were goods exported from Britain the focus of British colonial policy? ▶

National Museum of American History, Smithsonian Institution, Behring Center

War brought Britain and Spain vast new territories at great cost. To reduce their war debt—and to tighten imperial control—Spain boosted trade within its empire while Britain decided to shift more costs of empire onto the colonists by taxing imports. These policy shifts signaled the recognition of colonies as markets for goods, not merely sources of raw materials. In return, American colonists soon recognized that, as consumers, they could assert power and influence policy by refusing British goods. Just as Pontiac had united diverse groups of northern Indians behind a rejection of European goods, so, too, did colonial boycotts unite disparate colonies though a sense of shared sacrifice. But new protest measures also tapped into a rumbling sense that the inequalities of colonial society—whether at the hands of local elites or British agents—were fundamentally unjust.

☞ As you read, identify the various forms of resistance that developed in North America after the Seven Years' War. What was the relationship between imperial actions and colonial reactions?

6-2a Tightening Imperial Ties

Spain and Britain re-assert political and economic power over their colonies.

The Seven Years' War left Europe's empires deeply in debt and maneuvering to re-establish themselves in the global balance of power. Spain and Britain, empires that seemed to have gained the most during the war, attempted to capitalize on their gains by raising more revenue from their American colonies, imposing closer political control, and establishing a military presence along borderlands.

In a series of actions later known as the **Bourbon Reforms**, Spain pressured its silver mines in New Spain and Peru to increase their output and send more money back to Spain. The empire opened Spanish ports to direct trade with Spanish colonies. And the crown counteracted local colonial elites by appointing loyal Spanish to the *audiencias*. In 1767, the viceroy of New Spain reminded colonial subjects of their subordinate status, declaring that they "should know once and for all that they were born to keep silent and obey, and not to discuss or express opinions on high matters of government." Residents of Spanish New Orleans, accustomed to free-flowing trade with the English under a distracted French government, refused to keep silent, and in 1768 revolted against their crown-appointed governor, Antonio de Ulloa. Spain sent a replacement, but French language and culture remained dominant.

Trade around the Pacific was also essential to refilling Spanish coffers, and Spanish King Carlos III sought to extend control over Alta California in the aftermath of war. In 1776, the year Spanish settlers and soldiers founded San Francisco, Carlos III separated the large region covering California, New Mexico, and Texas into its own province, the "Provincias Internas" (Interior Provinces) under direct control of the crown.

Britain likewise concentrated on raising revenue and tightening control. The Seven Years' War had nearly doubled Britain's national debt, and interest on it consumed half the government's annual revenues. Faced with a home population that paid ten times what a colonial American one paid in taxes, the British government concluded that Americans should pay more.

According to the outraged reports of officials, American colonists were openly ignoring trade regulations, thus evading payments rightfully due to Britain. During the Seven Years' War, New England merchants continued to import molasses from French sugar colonies to make their rum, bribing customs officers to avoid having to pay the duties intended to force them to buy British. To stop smuggling, customs officers in Boston asked the Superior Court to issue general search warrants, called **writs of assistance**, to aid them in their searches for illegal goods. In a 1761 court case, James Otis of Boston challenged the writs as an unconstitutional violation of rights. He further charged that England was crippling the American economy with measures that "destroyed all our security of property, liberty, and life." Few debated Great Britain's right to make laws regulating colonial commerce, but Otis's choice of words, equating unimpeded trade with security, liberty, and life, shortly became core principles of resistance to British authority.

In 1764, the British government took the first step in raising revenues to support its global empire with the American Revenue Act, better known as the **Sugar Act**. This law, backed by a vigorous lobby of British Caribbean sugar planters who stood to gain, actually lowered the tax on British molasses from six pence per gallon to three pence per gallon. But it sought to eliminate the illegal trade in French molasses by funding new customs officers, requiring merchants to post bonds pledging their observance of the law, and strengthening the vice admiralty courts where accused smugglers and tax evaders would be judged by crown-appointed judges, not a jury comprised of sympathetic neighbors. The Currency Act of 1764 outlawed another common practice—that of colonies printing their own paper money and using it, rather than silver or gold, to pay their debts. These acts generated local opposition but no coordinated response.

Bourbon Reforms Policies of Spanish King Carlos III influenced by European Enlightenment ideals placing state power over church power to strengthen imperial control over New Spain.

writs of assistance General search warrants that permitted customs officials to search merchant warehouses for smuggled goods.

Sugar Act British 1764 law that lowered the tax on British molasses but increased enforcement of mercantilist principles to strengthen the empire.

Stamp Act Law proposed in 1765 to raise revenue on daily colonial legal and commercial transactions that sparked protest across British colonies.

6-2b Stamp Act

A new British tax sparks widespread opposition in its colonies.

Pushing for a more direct way to raise revenue from the colonies, British prime minister George Grenville proposed that a stamp tax, long in force in England, be applied to the colonies. The **Stamp Act**, passed in February 1765, required that paper to be used for newspapers, playing cards, or legal documents carry a stamp indicating that the tax had been paid. Those who wanted the paper had to buy it from licensed distributors and pay the tax. The new tax revenue would support soldiers stationed in the North American interior, recently vacated by the Spanish and French. To British officials, the tax seemed reasonable, but to colonists, it was an outrageous new way to extract money from them.

Slated to take effect in November 1765, the Stamp Act drew unprecedented public opposition from all ranks of society because of its broad reach. Editors, lawyers, merchants, and tavern keepers objected to paying a tax on something they used every day. They formed associations called the **Sons of Liberty**, who organized protests and wrote letters that were circulated between colonial centers and printed in local newspapers. Prosperous tradesmen and common laborers employed the **politics of the streets**. They staged mocking "stamping" rituals to ridicule the regulations. On the evening of August 14, a Boston crowd hanged an effigy of stamp distributor Andrew Oliver and destroyed his home. Similar protests, including the violent tarring and feathering of stamp distributors, occurred in colonial port cities from Rhode Island to St. Kitts and Nevis in the Caribbean. Loosely coordinated crowd protests, denigrated as "mobs" by their targets, were common in the 1760s. In England, Spitalfields weavers marched in London and hanged effigies to protest unemployment and the importation of French silk.

In some protests, outrage at the provisions of the Stamp Act merged with deeply running tensions over economic inequality. Two weeks after attacking the stamp distributor's home, thousands of average Bostonians turned on the mansion of Boston-born Lieutenant Governor Thomas Hutchinson, seizing and destroying the French wines, Spanish silver, and English furniture and fabrics that marked him as a man of wealth and style.

Urged on by the Sons of Liberty, American merchants also devised a new protest measure, the **nonimportation** pledge. Merchants who signed these agreements promised to stop all trade with Britain. By refusing to import cloth, ceramics, tools, and other goods, they believed that they would hurt British manufacturers, prove their own self-sufficiency, and force a repeal of the law. A 1765 pamphlet by Pennsylvanian John Dickinson urged Americans to follow the Swiss, whose "coarse clothes and simple furniture" helped them "defend their liberty." Although the idea was innovative, commitment was uneven, and British imports continued to flow into North American colonies.

Assemblies in nine colonies elected delegates who met in October in New York at a Stamp Act Congress to draft a unified response to Parliament, objecting to the stamp tax as a dangerous break with past methods of ruling the empire. As participants in Britain's empire of trade, colonial North Americans grudgingly accepted the government's right to regulate imports and exports to strengthen the empire. The stamp tax was different because it was a direct tax on daily life intended to raise revenue that had no connection to trade policy. Without conceding its right to tax the colonists for this purpose, Parliament responded to the unprecedented opposition by repealing the Stamp Act in March 1766.

Sons of Liberty Intercolonial associations of men protesting British imperial crackdown in the 1760s and 1770s.

politics of the streets Public protest rituals that included parades, tarring and feathering, and effigies; called *mob rule* by opponents and victims.

nonimportation Protest measure consisting of written promises to stop importing British goods with the intention of using economic pressure to force a change in tax laws.

virtual representation Political theory dominant in Britain that members of Parliament represented the interests of residents in the entire empire.

actual representation Political theory emerging from colonial experience with representative assemblies maintaining that elected legislators should respond to the specific needs of constituents.

6-2c Rights and Liberties

Protesters draw on multiple ideologies of rights.

Globally, the British Empire had no single method of colonial government after the Seven Years' War. In India, the British East India Company established courts, collected revenues, raised troops, and commissioned officers to lead them, all on behalf of Britain. In Quebec, a crown-appointed governor and his council made and administered local laws. Long-standing British colonies in North America and the Caribbean had representative assemblies in which elite local men made law. In theory, all were **virtually represented** by members of Parliament, who supposedly represented the needs and interests of subjects all over the empire, not just the small group of propertied men in Great Britain who voted for them.

By the 1760s, many adult white men in British North America objected to the idea of virtual representation. Their experience of their own assemblies, in which voters had **actual representation** by individuals directly answerable to them, gave them an expectation of self-governance. The majority of people living in the colonies still had to accept virtual representation because age, sex, color, or lack of land disqualified them from the vote. Yet because the Stamp Act was imposed by Parliament rather than locally elected assemblies, the men of the Stamp Act Congress believed that Parliament had violated their rights. Their resolutions proclaimed it "inseparably essential to the freedom of a people, and the undoubted rights of Englishmen" to be taxed only by their own representatives.

Americans familiar with British political thought sensed another threat to liberty. Since the 1720s, the Radical Whigs had been convinced that the British government was being destroyed from within by corruption in Parliament and a tyrannical king. They promoted their conspiratorial outlook in essays that literate Americans such as Patrick Henry reread in light of the Stamp Act. Henry, fiery new member of Virginia's House of Burgesses, declared that any attempt to give taxation power to a nonrepresentative assembly "has a manifest Tendency to destroy British as well as American Freedom."

Individual liberty was at the core of British identity by the 1760s, bolstered by national pride in the English mixed and balanced constitution. Yet protests following the Stamp Act cracked open the broad implications of a commitment to individual rights when enslaved men and women took to street protest and transformed its politics. In fall 1765, the avenues of Charles Town, South Carolina, were filled with white protestors shouting "Liberty and no Stamp Act." In January 1766, enslaved Charlestonians followed suit, shouting "Liberty!" as they marched. Whites in power immediately understood the radical implications for the tens of thousands of recently arrived Africans. The South Carolina assembly stopped all slave importations for three years, and the city enforced a strict curfew for two weeks. Riders traversed the colony warning slave owners to restrict the freedoms of their human property as more than one hundred slaves escaped to the woods and swamps.

Fear of a slave rebellion overpowered British colonists' desire for self-government in the Caribbean, even though the Stamp Act specifically targeted them for higher taxes. The tax on wills and estate documents in the islands was double that of the mainland colonies and taxes on land grants triple. Yet with the exception of St. Kitts and Nevis, Caribbean colonies largely complied with the Stamp Act. Fearful of their enslaved population, which vastly outnumbered them, white West Indians had accepted the imperial clampdown. They even offered to pay the costs of additional troops to protect them from slave uprisings. New England traders were disgusted. Calling the West Indians "poor, mean spirited, Cowardly, Dastardly Creoles," New Englanders stopped shipping provisions to the islands, cutting off food for enslaved workers.

Yale Center for British Art, Paul Mellon Collection

Army and Church in the British Caribbean British slave owners in West Indian colonies encouraged imperial shows of force to subdue the colonies' majority enslaved population and fend off attacks from French ships. Thomas Hearne's watercolor of Antigua places the large army barracks and the spire of St. John's Anglican church at its center. No slaves are depicted working in the sugarcane fields; instead, they relax together with a mixed-race free soldier in the shadow of the hospital. ▲

6-2d Nonconsumption and Nonimportation Movements

Boycotts tie politics to daily life.

Parliament tried again to raise revenues in 1767 with a new set of taxes. The **Townshend Duties** taxed paper, lead, glass, paint, and tea imported into the colonies and created a new Board of Customs Commissioners to enforce them. New taxes sparked another round of protests, once again centered on a nonimportation movement that gained support in the southern colonies for the first time. This new round of boycotts not only specified forbidden imports but also drew average consumers into a growing **nonconsumption** movement. Although nonimportation depended on merchants to accept or refuse shipments of goods, nonconsumption could be practiced by anyone who bought muskets or wore calico.

Free women, often calling themselves the **Daughters of Liberty**, were at the forefront of the nonconsumption movement, signing public pledges not to buy imported fabric, thread, hats, ceramics, silverware, furniture, pins and nails, cheese, and dozens of other goods. They denounced merchants who violated nonimportation agreements and advocated the use of American-made goods. Championing **homespun**, a textile made by local families, women made their protest public by staging spinning contests on town greens. As one poem celebrating spinning bees proclaimed, "Britain, behold thy Trade stole from thy Hand." For some women, these movements connected their daily life's work to larger political importance and imparted a new sense of public power. Enslaved women seldom reaped power, but they did occasionally receive training in new kinds of work such as spinning and weaving when slave owners wanted to avoid purchasing imported cloth.

The renewed nonimportation and nonconsumption movements achieved the goal of disrupting British commerce. In 1769, the value of British North American exports

Townshend Duties Taxes imposed in 1767 on imported lead, glass, paper, paint, and tea, paid at colonial ports.

nonconsumption Boycott agreement engaging regular consumers—most prominent of whom were women—who agreed to stop purchasing and using British imports.

Daughters of Liberty Self-identification of women who protested British policies by boycotting imports and creating substitutes.

homespun Rough fabric spun and woven by families in colonial America and worn primarily by slaves until it became a political rallying point.

exceeded the value of imports for the first time. Parliament responded the way that many merchants had hoped by repealing nearly all of the Townshend taxes in 1770. Merchants resumed importing and consumers returned to stores.

6-2e Violent Conflict in the Interior and on the Coast

British troops become embroiled in local conflicts.

In the **backcountry**, a region of mixed colonial and Native American settlement bordering New York, Pennsylvania, and the Carolinas, colonists developed their own politics of protest, although often the flashpoint was land rather than import taxes. Residents and British officials clashed frequently over who had the right to live on, use, and profit from land on the border of settlements. Native Americans sold land through agreements arranged by chiefs, warriors, and matrons in public councils. They marked territory with slashes on trees and piles of stones. British colonists relied on mortgages signed with speculators, most of whom had received land grants from colonial governors in defiance of the Proclamation Line of 1763. These colonists were frequently in debt and faced eviction when lenders demanded payment. Under British law, debtors could be imprisoned until they or their families sold property or found some other way to pay what they owed. Because backcountry colonists were underrepresented in colonial assemblies, they seldom found institutional solutions to their problems. Petitions to colonial assemblies and letters to newspapers demanding tax relief and judicial reform got little response.

As boycotts roiled the coast, white farmers in the backcountry who felt exploited by Indians, speculators, and government officials staged a series of popular uprisings known as the **regulator movement**. North Carolina farmers turned increasingly to violent measures, forcibly closing courthouses to prevent foreclosure hearings, whipping lawyers, and breaking debtors out of jail. In 1770, they broke into the house of Assembly member Colonel Edmund Fanning and destroyed it the same way crowds in Boston had destroyed Andrew Oliver's home. Herman Husband, a leader of the North Carolina Regulators, denounced "the unequal chances the poor and weak have in contention with the rich and powerful."

While western colonists demanded the attention of colonial elites, Indians sought aid from the British army as diplomatic allies against those colonists. In 1768, in return for an enormous gift of trade goods, Haudenosaunees signed away rights to land occupied by Shawnees and Delawares on the border with Pennsylvania and Virginia. The **Treaty of Fort Stanwix** (1768) essentially moved the Proclamation Line of 1763 west to the Ohio River. From the Haudenosaunee perspective, it was a strategic move to secure British friendship and enforce a new boundary between colonists and Indians. For the Shawnees and Delawares, who had already relocated, it was one more Haudenosaunee betrayal. Militant Shawnees and Delawares organized a series of diplomatic conferences on the Scioto River to convince southern Cherokees and Creeks to join them in an anticolonist alliance independent of the Six Nations. British officials, fearing a large coordinated Indian attack, attempted to hold back Virginia speculators and settlers.

Unable to defend the Proclamation Line and facing street protests over the Stamp Act and Townshend Duties, Britain shifted troops from the interior to the coast. In 1768, the first of four regiments of British troops arrived in Boston Harbor, ultimately bringing two thousand fighting men and more than one thousand women and children as supporters and dependents with them. The **standing army** not only patrolled the streets but also lived in Bostonians' houses and yards. Soldiers shared meals, joined families through marriage and godparentage, and competed with Bostonians for scarce jobs by taking on part-time work to supplement insufficient wages.

In March 1770, tensions between British soldiers and Boston teenagers turned a taunting snowball fight into a deadly shooting; five Bostonians died, including Crispus Attucks, a forty-seven-year-old runaway slave of African and Indian ancestry who worked as a sailor. Lawyer John Adams defended the soldiers and officers in a prominent trial and won their acquittal, but his cousin, political organizer Samuel Adams, turned the event into anti-British propaganda. He arranged a funeral procession of ten thousand mourners and, by calling the incident the **Boston Massacre**, linked it to the recent St. George's Field Massacre (1768) in which British soldiers in London had killed seven people by firing into a crowd. The London crowd, too, was protesting British displays of arbitrary power. That group demanded the release from prison of radical British politician John Wilkes, a champion of freedom of speech, a critic of governmental corruption, and an opponent of the Townshend Duties who had corresponded with Boston's Sons of Liberty. In the hands of Sam Adams, Boston's conflict, rooted in labor competition, became part of transatlantic opposition to imperial might.

backcountry Region bordering Indian lands and colonial settlements in Western New York, Pennsylvania, and the Carolinas unified by intermarriage and undermined by competing land claims.

regulator movement Coordinated activities of backcountry colonists to protest their lack of political representation and vulnerability to Indian warfare and debt collectors.

Treaty of Fort Stanwix Agreement between Britain and the Six Nations signed in 1768 marking the Ohio River as the western border of British land claims. It voided the 1763 Royal Proclamation.

standing army Permanent military force in peacetime or wartime. British standing army was controlled by Parliament.

Boston Massacre Inflammatory label given to a violent clash between British soldiers and Bostonians in which five Americans died.

6-3
From Resistance to Revolution

Thomas Paine's *Common Sense* was a widely read seventy-seven-page pamphlet urging "the Inhabitants of America" to separate from Great Britain. Published after fighting had begun but before independence was declared, it combined political theory and history with polemic, as this portrait and cover page text suggest. By using common language and familiar stories, Paine declared "it is my design to make those that can scarcely read understand."

How did the timing and style of *Common Sense* influence those who read it? How would its influence on the people living in the American colonies differ from the influence of protests or boycotts? ▶

Go to MindTap® to practice history with the Chapter 6 **Primary Source Writing Activity: From Resistance to Revolution.** Read and view primary sources and respond to a writing prompt.

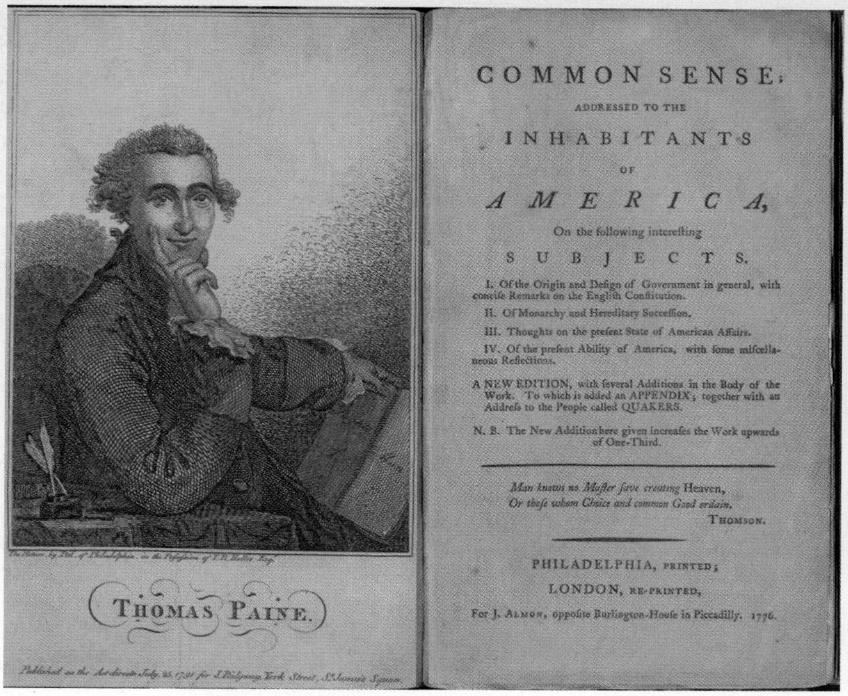

The Charles J. Tanenbaum Collection of the Eighteenth Century/British Museum

Turmoil on the East Coast and in the North American interior intensified in the early 1770s as conflicts between British colonists and London on the one hand and between Native Americans and colonists on the other, hardened into opposing camps. People across colonial North America connected their personal grievances to larger political goals. Initially, Britain attempted to treat colonial rebellion as a police matter, focused on subduing rowdy Bostonians. For some colonists, however, 1774 marked a transformation from separate colonial protests into a coordinated opposition movement. In a matter of months, debate and protest turned to armed conflict and a new political body linked thirteen of Britain's North American colonies. By 1776, one segment of the population was committed to political independence from Britain. Another—enslaved African Americans—sought liberty with Britain.

☞ As you read, think about how the events between 1754 and 1776 changed the context and meaning of colonial protests and shaped the Declaration of Independence.

6-3a Imperial Laws and Escalating Colonial Reactions

When it repealed the Townshend Duties in 1770, Parliament retained the tax on tea to affirm its right to tax colonies directly. As an Asian-grown, British-imported daily habit, tea held powerful symbolic significance for the nonconsumption movement. "The produce of the West-Indies debauches the country," declared one critic, bemoaning the fact that many continued to buy and drink that "Chinese drug," often from smuggled Dutch sources. Their inability to give up tea seemed to demonstrate colonial Americans' inability to sacrifice for the common good.

The increasing presence of tax collectors and imperial troops begins to create a sense of shared colonial struggle.

Sacrifice was a key theme of the nonconsumption movement as it turned from its original goal—to hurt Britain financially—into a broader critique of colonial society. Boycotters drew on a blend of Protestant belief and classical **republicanism** in promoting the ideal of self-sacrifice. As a philosophy of governance, republicanism rested on a moral, utopian model in which leaders sacrificed individual interests for the sake of the greater good. This selflessness, called public **virtue**, was what entitled leaders to their power. A society of people willing to sacrifice for the common good could govern itself whereas a society of weak and selfish people would fall under the rule of a tyrant. Sons and Daughters of Liberty used the ideas of republicanism to rally supporters.

The 1773 Tea Act tested American virtue by making taxed British tea cheaper than the smuggled Dutch alternative. Under its provisions, the British East India Company gained permission to ship tea directly to America rather than stopping in England first to pay a tax, as was required of all other tea merchants. The law rescued the East India Company, which faced debts it could not pay, and tempted North American customers to buy British. Rather than celebrate cheaper tea, though, Americans in New York,

republicanism Originating in antiquity, political theory arguing that a class of independent citizens, sacrificing self-interest for the common good, can best govern society.

virtue Bravery and selflessness expressed by free men acting to protect their societies from corruption within or tyranny from without.

Library of Congress Prints and Photographs Division [Robert Sayer and John Bennett/LC-DIG-ppmsca-19468]

British View of Patriotic Ladies British satirists mocked American revolutionaries as bullies or fools, using revolutionary politics for personal gain. This English cartoon ridicules the women of Edenton, North Carolina, who signed a pledge to boycott British tea. The artist depicts the women flirting and neglecting their duties as mothers. A dog chews on the child's ear while urinating on a tea canister. ▲

Philadelphia, Charles Town, and Boston organized to refuse the shipments of the British monopoly. On December 16, 1773, a group of colonists—merchants, builders, artisans, farmers—dressed in Indian styles boarded three ships carrying East India tea and dumped £10,000 worth into Boston Harbor. Shoemaker George Hewes remembered that to prevent scavenging, sailors and Bostonians rowed out to sink any floating remains by beating them with their paddles "to render its entire destruction inevitable."

Parliament responded to what became known as the *Boston Tea Party* with a series of laws designed to punish and isolate the city. Conceived as Coercive Acts (to coerce obedience), the laws closed the port of Boston to international commerce, forbade most coastal trade (see Table 6.1), and replaced Massachusetts's representative government and public meetings with appointed officials. These appointments removed the beleaguered Thomas Hutchinson, putting commander Thomas Gage in his place. They also gave British officers the right to commandeer privately owned uninhabited buildings and house troops in them, a practice called **quartering**.

Finding themselves economically isolated and under military occupation, Bostonians called the laws **Intolerable Acts**. Stories of food scarcity and the brutal behavior of imperial officials, which spread through newspapers, pamphlets, and letters circulating among the Sons of Liberty, helped to engender sympathy for Bostonians. From other regions, colonists sent sheep, rice, firewood, and other provisions to Boston's poor in the crisis. One group in Durham, New Hampshire, noted, "the methods by which the ministry sought to divide, have happily united us."

That same spring of 1774, Parliament's **Quebec Act** addressed turmoil in the backcountry with another sweeping assertion of power. The act merged the Ohio Valley region

Table 6.1 The Escalating Crisis

Between 1764 and 1774, the British government sought tighter economic and political control over its American colonies from Quebec south to the West Indies. People in the coastal mainland colonies responded with increasingly coordinated resistance. Twice, Britain had to back down, repealing the Stamp Act and most of the Townshend Duties.

Act	Provisions	Reactions
Sugar Act 1764	Reduced tax on molasses and added tax on sugar, coffee, calico, etc.; established vice-admiralty court	Individual colonies petition for repeal
Currency Act 1764	Outlawed colonial paper money	Scattered protests; circulation of pamphlets
Stamp Act 1765	Placed tax on printed materials to be purchased with specie	Street protests; nonimportation movement; formation of Sons of Liberty; Stamp Act Congress; repealed in 1766
Declaratory Act 1766	Asserted Parliament's authority to tax American colonies	Scattered protests
Townshend Acts 1767	Placed tax on imported paper, lead, glass, paint, tea; revenues to pay British administrators	Nonconsumption movement; formation of Daughters of Liberty; repealed in 1770 except for tax on tea
Tea Act 1773	Permitted East India Company to sell tea in colonies with lower tax	Protests dumping and confiscating tea
Coercive (Intolerable) Acts 1774	Closed Boston port, cut powers of Massachusetts elected officials, permitted troop quartering in private buildings	First Continental Congress, 1774
Quebec Act 1774	Acknowledged large British colony with protected Catholicism and French civil law	First Continental Congress, 1774

with former French Canada into a single colony with a centralized administration. In keeping with former French colonial practice, there was no representative government, and Catholics could continue practicing their religion freely. To the Protestant community on the North Atlantic coast, the act seemed to endorse arbitrary and tyrannical authority on the continent, a threat to all. Even more pressingly, colonists who wanted Ohio Valley land for themselves—as speculators, traders, or farmers—believed themselves to be shut out, victims of British tyranny.

6-3b Continental Congress

A new political body coordinates protest movements in individual colonies but neglects borderland conflicts.

In May and June 1774, political leaders in Boston, Providence, Philadelphia, New York, and Williamsburg called for an intercolonial congress to address Britain's escalating measures. When royal governors attempted to stop the election of delegates by dismissing colonial assemblies, organizers created independent conventions to choose representatives. In September 1774, fifty-five men from twelve North American colonies attended the **First Continental Congress** in Philadelphia. Delegates came together intending to use protest measures developed over the previous ten years in a newly coordinated style. They drafted a petition to King George III for relief from the Coercive Acts and the tea tax. They agreed to nonimportation and nonconsumption of British goods. They resolved to cut off Britain and the British West Indies from North American products. And they committed themselves to commercial independence by starting cloth manufactories.

To enforce these agreements, Congress authorized local **Committees of Observation and Inspection** to operate outside British law but within the spirit of boycott. Committee members, totaling seven thousand to eight thousand throughout the mainland colonies, were elected by the same men eligible to vote for colonial assemblies. Over time, these committees became temporary governments, aligning practical administration with the emerging rebellion. The **patriot** cause, opposed to the existing British rule, built on this shared structure of self-rule and sacrifice. Americans who still felt loyal to Britain accused the committees of mob mentality. Anglican clergyman Samuel Seabury warned New Yorkers about this quasigovernment "chosen by half a dozen fools in your neighborhood" who claimed the right to "examine your tea canisters, and molasses-jugs, and your wives' and daughters' petty-coats . . . if I must be enslaved, let it be by a king at least, and not by a parcel of upstart lawless committee-men."

The Continental Congress's *Declaration of Resolves* included a bill of rights for "the inhabitants of the English colonies in North America" that they believed to be fundamental: the right to life, liberty, and property; the right to local representative government; and the right to be free from a standing army imposed without consent. Overall, the Congress hoped to return to the situation of 1763 before the new taxes and increased presence of British imperial agents as well as the imposition of what they called "a ruinous system of colony administration . . . evidently calculated for enslaving these colonies, and with them, the British Empire."

Native Americans were not represented in the Continental Congress and most did not share its desire to roll back the presence of the British Empire. The Creeks in the Georgia backcountry valued British support against the tide of farmers and land speculators simultaneously attending the Continental Congress. Shawnees, Mingos, and Delawares in the Ohio River valley were combating a similar pattern of American land speculation and settlement and hoped British officials would intervene in the local violence. They were disappointed. In April 1774, Virginians who had crossed the Appalachians attacked and killed a group of Shawnee women and children. Retaliatory raids escalated into **Dunmore's War**, named for Lord Dunmore, royal governor of Virginia, who led the militia against the Shawnees and their allies. Typical of frontier fighting, Dunmore's War had members of the same family on both sides. John Ward, who as a child had been kidnapped and raised a Shawnee, fought for his adopted family; his father James, fighting for the Virginians, died in battle against him. When the Indians were defeated and forced to yield significant land in Kentucky territory, their ally the British government offered little real assistance. From Boston, Gage ordered the Virginians to retreat; he was ignored.

6-3c Early Fighting

Local militias take up arms while British leaders hope to put down opposition.

Although the Continental Congress had put its grievances in the form of a loyal petition to King George, he received the request as defiance and declared the colonies in rebellion: "blows must decide whether they are to be subject to this country or independent." His ministers agreed, and in April 1775, the king ordered Gage to seize military supplies in Concord, outside of Boston. British soldiers and the Massachusetts

quartering Practice of housing occupying soldiers in civilian buildings rather than in separate barracks.

Intolerable Acts Protestors' name for Coercive Acts of 1774, British police actions that closed the port of Boston and removed Massachusetts's elected government to quash rebellion.

Quebec Act Parliamentary law passed in 1774 that created a large British colony retaining Catholicism and a nonrepresentative government that had existed under French control.

First Continental Congress Philadelphia meeting of representatives from twelve British North American colonies in 1774 to coordinate protests against escalating punitive British measures.

Committees of Observation and Inspection Elected groups in each colony who enforced the agreements of the Continental Congress.

patriot Term identifying someone who openly supported the cause of independence in the American Revolution. Also called Whig or rebel.

Dunmore's War Conflict in 1774 in which the Virginia militia and a Shawnee alliance fought over violations of the 1763 Royal Proclamation.

Stock Montage/Archive Photos/Getty Images

Global Americans **Daniel Boone** was born into a large Pennsylvania family in 1734 and grew up with Indians as neighbors. After serving with British forces in the Seven Years' War, Boone, his wife, and their children settled in backcountry Virginia. Supporting his family as a hunter and trapper brought him deep into Native American hunting grounds west of the 1763 Proclamation Line. In 1773, he and a group of Virginians attempted to establish a settlement there; they were turned back by Delawares, Shawnees, and Cherokees in a clash that killed Boone's son and fueled Dunmore's War. Two years later, the families established Boonesborough on the Kentucky River. Defending his town during the fighting of the Revolutionary War required shifting alliances because neutrality was not possible. In 1778, Boone was captured and adopted into a Shawnee community and then was charged with treason by Virginians for his negotiations with Shawnee and British allies. By the end of the war, Boone had become a Virginia militia officer and elected assemblyman.

Boone's 1784 biography made him into an American folk hero who fought Indians to clear the path for the "sweets of liberty." In Europe, he was celebrated as a "natural man" uncorrupted by civilization. After the war, a disputed land title sent him in search of a new identity once more, and he moved with his family across the Mississippi to live on Spanish-claimed land as a local official of Spain. As with many in the late eighteenth century, Boone was committed to land and personal independence and was willing to seek them within empires or as part of new polities.

militia had been in a stalemate for months and when Britain forced the issue by sending 700 troops to capture ammunition, fighting broke out. Militiamen defeated British soldiers at Lexington and nearby Concord, forcing them to retreat, with 272 casualties against 93 American casualties. The following month, Ethan Allen, Benedict Arnold, and a small force seized Fort Ticonderoga in northern New York, capturing British artillery that they then transported to Boston.

Such conflicts were typical of the first year of undeclared war: Standing British troops fought local colonial militias with little oversight from the rebel side. The Continental Congress initially relied on militias for practical and political reasons. Politically, members of Congress believed that adult male citizens were the best defenders of the community. Practically, there was neither money nor time to raise an army, and so in May 1775, the Continental Congress turned the Massachusetts militia into the Continental Army, supplemented with expert riflemen from Pennsylvania, Maryland, and Virginia and under the command of George Washington, a Virginian.

Initially, the Continental Congress insisted that the conflict with Britain was a limited one. In July 1775, it prepared a speech for the Six Nations to accompany wampum belts that referred to Native Americans as "brothers." Attempting to re-establish the Covenant Chain as an American, rather than a British, alliance, agents representing Congress urged neutrality: "This is a family quarrel between us and Old England. You Indians are not concerned in it. We don't wish you to take up the hatchet against the king's troops. We desire you to remain at home, and not join on either side, but keep the hatchet buried deep." Six Nations chiefs largely agreed, at least temporarily, waiting to see how best to use the British–American conflict to their own advantage.

Although they called themselves the Continental Congress, the rebellious alliance did not include the northern territories won from France in the Seven Years' War. Early on, Congress authorized an attack on Quebec, hoping to win it from Britain as a fourteenth rebelling colony. In December 1775, two forces led by General Richard Montgomery coming from New York and Colonel Benedict Arnold traveling across Maine arrived at the walls of Quebec city. The soldiers were exhausted and weakened by smallpox. Yet knowing that

Newspapers Forge Connections Eighteenth-century newspapers circulated beyond their hometowns via packet ships and family correspondence. Papers in one city frequently reprinted material from another. This masthead of the *Massachusetts Spy*, published in the wake of fighting at Lexington and Concord, used a familiar image of Liberty and a quotation—"Liberty or Death!"—from a British play about the last Roman republican in order to appeal to "Americans" as a group. ▼

Old Paper Studios/Alamy Stock Photo

short-term militia enlistments would expire on January first, on December 31, in the midst of a blizzard, the American generals attacked. Montgomery was killed, Arnold wounded, and hundreds of Americans wounded or captured. Arnold's siege that followed was a disaster and by the summer of 1776, American forces had been permanently driven from Canada.

Faced with disloyal militias, Britain turned to potentially loyal enslaved men. As early as September 1774, a group of New England slaves had written to Gage, offering to fight for him in return for their freedom. Parliament discussed a measure to emancipate enslaved people in order to humble "the high aristocratic spirit of Virginia and the southern colonies." In November 1775, Virginia's royal governor Dunmore declared martial law in his province and offered freedom to any servants or slaves belonging to rebels who joined the king's forces. Dunmore's intent was tactical: to mobilize slaves and unnerve white rebels, not spark a general uprising. But enslaved people interpreted **Lord Dunmore's Proclamation** much more broadly. Among the first to join his "Ethiopian regiment" were eight of the twenty-seven slaves on the plantation of Peyton Randolph, a delegate to the Continental Congress. Within months, nearly one thousand slaves had joined and hundreds were captured trying. Outfitted in uniforms with "Liberty to Slaves" stitched across their chests, the men of the Ethiopian Regiment fought the patriot Virginia militia in December 1775 near Norfolk but were defeated. They retreated with the governor onto ships in the Chesapeake Bay. Only a fraction made it farther; most contracted smallpox in the close quarters of military accommodations and perished or were abandoned to die on Gwynn's Island.

In the same month that Dunmore issued his proclamation, the Continental Congress formally declared all blacks, slave or free, ineligible for military service. They gave many of the same reasons that opponents to the idea in Britain had: that merchants owed their livelihood to the slave trade, that arming enslaved people violated the honor of soldiers, and that it would provoke retaliation. Many whites also feared that enslaved people in colonies such as Jamaica would take the opportunity to launch an Atlanticwide slave insurrection. Washington, himself a slave owner, initially agreed but soon, in need of troops, changed his mind.

6-3d Declaration of Independence

Thirteen American colonies resolve to separate from Britain.

Even as Congress formed an army and engaged in combat, many were reluctant to support a full independence movement that, should it fail, would mark them as traitors. Conservative members of the Continental Congress feared wartime instability would ignite rebellions from below, and those who profited from trade with or protection from the British Empire opposed the idea of separation. Thomas Paine's *Common Sense*, published in January 1776 and broadly distributed, reminded American colonists of the blood already shed and told them it was too late for reconciliation. Instead, they could "begin the world over again." Theirs was a struggle not "of a city, a country, a province, or a kingdom, but of a continent—of at least one eighth part of the habitable globe."

Paine linked independence with republicanism, highlighting the dangers of hereditary privilege and the corruption of European politics and optimistically envisioning a society united by a common good. John Adams, long a vigorous advocate of independence, complained that *Common Sense* was "a tolerable summary of the arguments which I had been repeating again and again in Congress for nine months." Those arguments, familiar on both sides of the Atlantic, came together in a new, compelling way in Paine's writing. Paine instructed readers to see European history as leading inevitably to the independence of North American colonies. It was only common sense for them to separate. And when they did, they would be leading a world-changing movement away from monarchy and toward republican freedom.

On June 7, 1776, Richard Henry Lee of Virginia proposed to Congress: "That these united colonies are, and of right ought to be, free and independent states, that they are absolved from all allegiance to the British crown, and that all political connection between them and the state of Great Britain is, and ought to be, totally dissolved." Voting on the proposal was postponed until July; in the meantime, a five-man committee, consisting of Adams, Franklin, Thomas Jefferson of Virginia, Roger Sherman of Connecticut, and Robert Livingston of New York, set to work writing a declaration. Because it would mark the point of no return in the conflict between Britain and the colonies, the declaration had to explain the reasons for separation and establish the new nation. It also would proclaim the ideals of the "one people" it spoke for. Jefferson wrote a draft that was edited and revised by the committee and Congress as a whole. To secure the support of slaveholding South Carolina, Congress removed a paragraph in which Jefferson blamed the English king for the slave trade, which he called a "cruel war against human nature itself, violating it's most sacred rights of life & liberty."

The **Declaration of Independence** drew on the experience and rhetoric of the anti-Stamp Act protests, the nonimportation and nonconsumption movements, and the Regulators. The document pulled together the political theories that had influenced Paine. Its opening section declared that "all men are created equal" and

Lord Dunmore's Proclamation Policy announced in 1775 that slaves belonging to patriots could win freedom by joining the Virginia governor's forces.

Declaration of Independence Document establishing the United States as an independent nation, enumerating the causes for separation, and declaring the classically liberal ideas of its signers.

History without Borders

Declarations of Independence

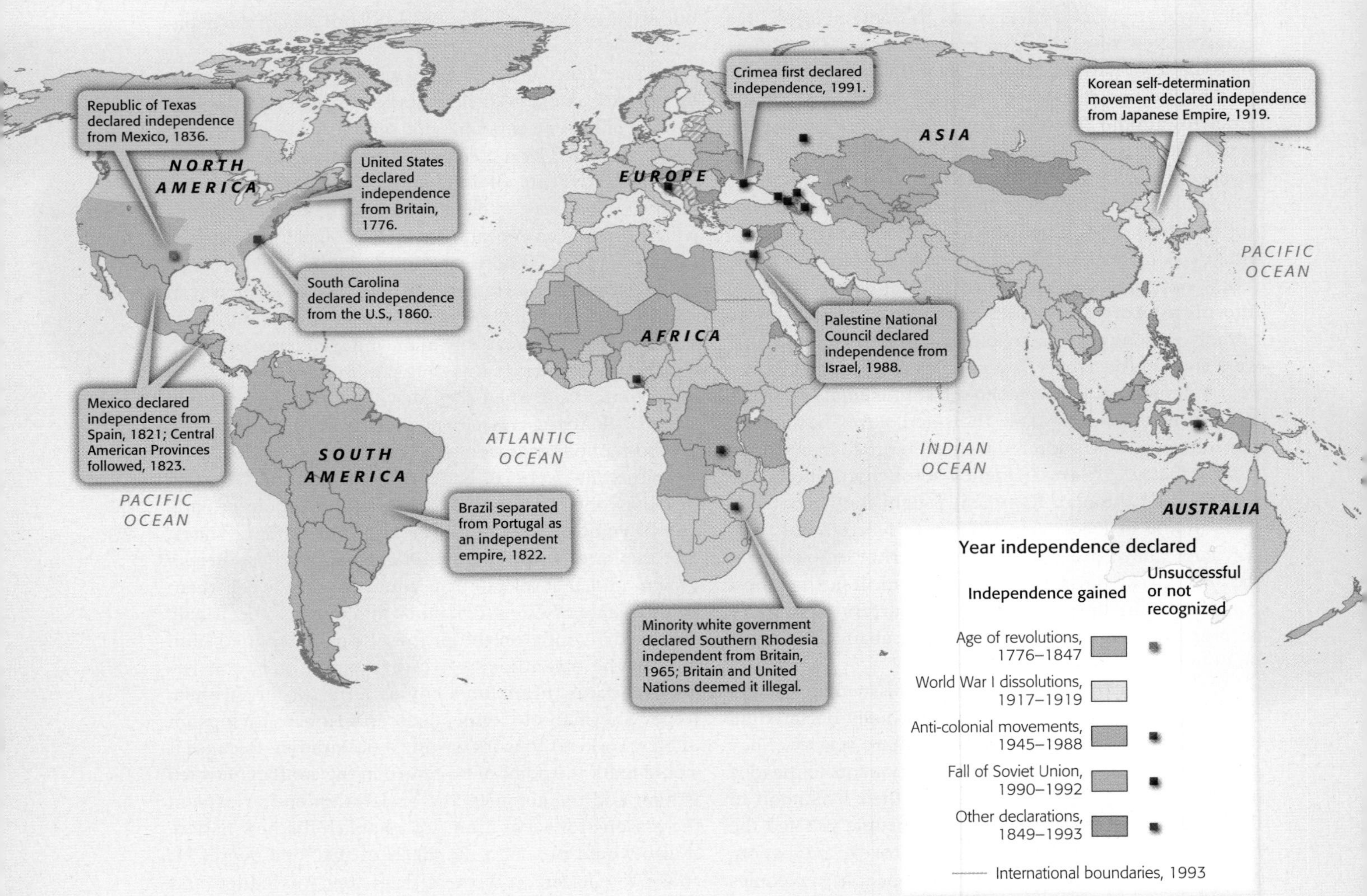

Republic of Texas declared independence from Mexico, 1836.

NORTH AMERICA

United States declared independence from Britain, 1776.

South Carolina declared independence from the U.S., 1860.

Mexico declared independence from Spain, 1821; Central American Provinces followed, 1823.

SOUTH AMERICA

ATLANTIC OCEAN

PACIFIC OCEAN

Brazil separated from Portugal as an independent empire, 1822.

Crimea first declared independence, 1991.

EUROPE

ASIA

Korean self-determination movement declared independence from Japanese Empire, 1919.

PACIFIC OCEAN

AFRICA

Palestine National Council declared independence from Israel, 1988.

INDIAN OCEAN

AUSTRALIA

Minority white government declared Southern Rhodesia independent from Britain, 1965; Britain and United Nations deemed it illegal.

Year independence declared

Independence gained	Unsuccessful or not recognized
Age of revolutions, 1776–1847	▪
World War I dissolutions, 1917–1919	
Anti-colonial movements, 1945–1988	▪
Fall of Soviet Union, 1990–1992	▪
Other declarations, 1849–1993	▪

—— International boundaries, 1993

Declarations of Independence, 1776–1993 More than 100 nations have issued declarations of independence, in four main waves. In the first "Age of Revolutions," the people of Haiti and of Spanish and Portuguese America broke away from their European rulers. After World War I, nations demanded the right to separate from the large land empires of Europe. A third round of anticolonial independence movements accompanied the end of World War II. Most recently, many states sought independence with the fall of the Soviet Union. ▲

From the beginning, the Declaration of Independence was both a distinctively American artifact and a global one. The fifty-five original signers dipped their pens into an inkstand crafted by an Irishman from silver mined in Spanish America by enslaved Africans and native South Americans. Nine signers had been born in England or Ireland; a quarter of them had been educated in Europe. Thomas Jefferson and the other men who wrote the Declaration of Independence blended global ideals, such as that of natural rights, with a specific claim to have become "one people," a new state in the international community.

The first printed copies of the Declaration began their global journey as Dutch undershirts. Papermakers in the Netherlands collected linen rags from old shirts, shredded them into a pulpy soup, dipped frames set with a fine mesh into the mixture, and smoothed and dried each sheet to

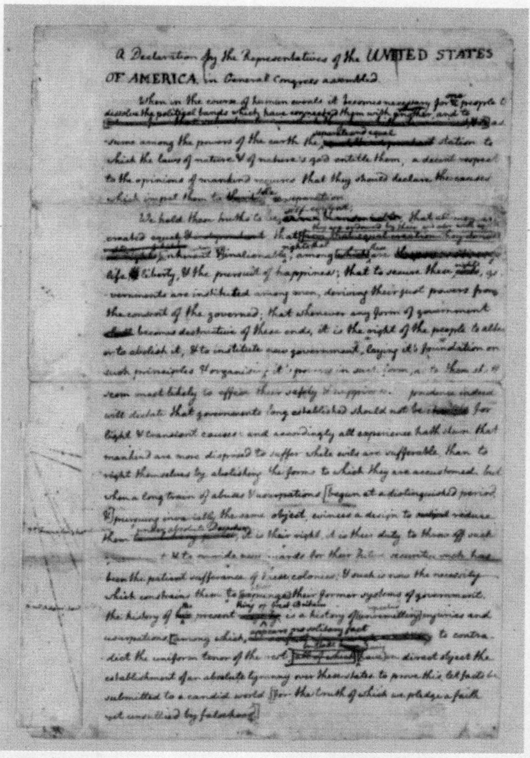

Library of Congress, Manuscript Division

Draft of the Declaration This detail of Thomas Jefferson's handwritten draft of the Declaration of Independence shows the edits added by Adams and Franklin. The final document was a product of negotiation and discussion. ▲

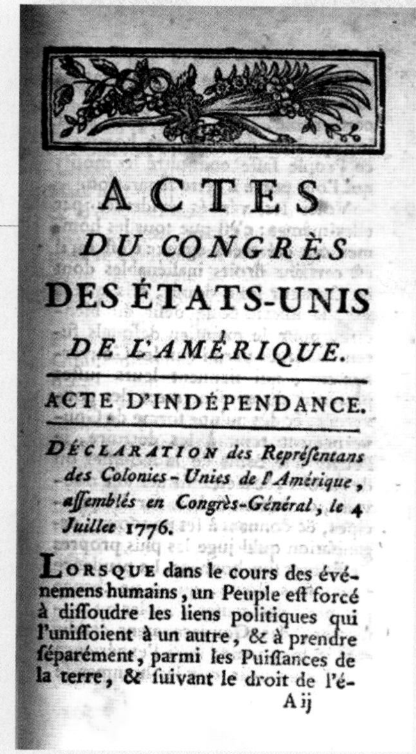
ACTES
DU CONGRÈS
DES ÉTATS-UNIS
DE L'AMÉRIQUE.

ACTE D'INDÉPENDANCE.

DÉCLARATION des Repréſentans des Colonies-Unies de l'Amérique, aſſemblés en Congrès-Général, le 4 Juillet 1776.

LORSQUE dans le cours des événemens humains, un Peuple eſt forcé à diſſoudre les liens politiques qui l'uniſſoient à un autre, & à prendre ſéparément, parmi les Puiſſances de la terre, & ſuivant le droit de l'é-

A ij

John Adams Library copy transferred from the supervisors of the Temple and School Fund. Quincy, Mass., 1894

French Translation of the Declaration of Independence, 1778 Philadelphia printers arranged for translations of the Declaration of Independence that they then sold abroad with translated copies of state constitutions and other Revolution-era political documents. In this way, a document intended for one audience was repackaged and circulated in another context. ▲

create fine-grained paper. The paper traveled to England, where it was taxed and placed on a British ship, as imperial law demanded, and next exported to Philadelphia. John Dunlap, the man who bought the paper in 1776, had emigrated from his home country of Ireland in the middle of the Seven Years' War. He used a British printing press to stamp words on Dutch-made paper to announce a new entity to the world, the United States of America.

Assembled in Philadelphia in the summer of 1776, copies of the Declaration of Independence soon traveled the oceans again. Within a month, the document was reprinted in London newspapers. The following month, people in Copenhagen and Warsaw were reading translations of the Declaration in their publications. A vast communication network of newspapers, businessmen, soldiers and spies carried copies around the world. Some foreign readers pointed out the hypocrisy of slaveholding authors claiming "life, liberty, and the pursuit of happiness" as universal rights. Others were inspired by the idea of colonized people breaking away from the imperial power that ruled them and establishing a government that had to respond to its citizens.

More than one hundred times since 1776, foreign states have broken off from their earlier affiliations, declared independence, and presented themselves as sovereign to face the international community with written proclamations. The 1918 Czechoslovak Declaration of Independence explicitly cited the "American Declaration of Independence." Ho Chi Minh proclaimed an independent Vietnam in 1945 with 150-year-old words. Internationally, declarations of independence marked the change from a world of empires in the eighteenth century to a world of independent states in the twenty-first century.

Passages from the Declaration opposing tyranny and promoting equality became the tools of international revolutionaries and reformers. French radicals published the *Declaration of the Rights of Man and Citizen* in 1789. In 1848, Elizabeth Cady Stanton launched the American women's suffrage movement with a "Declaration of Sentiments" that included the line "all men and women are created equal." Independent states formed after World War II, joined together at the United Nations, likewise embraced revolutionary claims of human equality. The UN's 1948 Universal Declaration of Human Rights recognized the equality not only of nations, but also of "all members of the human family."

Critical Thinking Questions

► Why has this eighteenth-century document, a product of a specific context, proved so versatile a tool for radically different groups?

► Which parts of the Declaration have had the widest resonance in the years since its publication?

Go to MindTap® to engage with an interactive version of **History without Borders: Declarations of Independence.** Learn from an interactive map, view related video, and respond to critical thinking questions.

asserted humanity's rights to "life, liberty, and the pursuit of happiness." It went on to accuse the king of planning to establish "an absolute tyranny over these states," and to object to Parliament's acts regarding taxation and the presence of British troops, objections that had filled the petitions of previous years.

The Declaration asserted that "these United Colonies are, and of Right, ought to be free and independent states." It did not define territorial borders but referred to a western "frontier" as a place where the king encouraged "the merciless Indian savages, whose known rule of warfare is an undistinguished destruction of all ages, sexes and conditions." Frontier warfare was vicious, but by tying the backcountry conflict to alleged indiscriminate Indian warfare, the Declaration tried to dismiss specific grievances over treaty violations that drew Native Americans into the larger conflict.

By proclaiming a distinct nation, the Declaration of Independence invited European involvement in what had been a contest within the British Empire. France and Spain both covertly gave substantial sums to the rebelling colonists through a company created to launder the money on its way across the Atlantic. This fund purchased 80 percent of the gunpowder American forces used that year. The Declaration's assertions about natural rights held by "all men" would prove to have a significant international legacy in the long run, even though their short-term relevance seemed precarious.

6-4 War for Independence

Jean Baptiste Antoine de Verger, a French officer in Rochambeau's army, painted this watercolor in the diary he kept as eyewitness to war. It depicts four soldiers of the Continental forces at Yorktown in 1781: a black soldier from the First Rhode Island Regiment, a New England militiaman, a backcountry rifleman, and a French officer.

What does this painting indicate about the makeup of pro-independence forces? What can you surmise about their different motivations? How did that makeup matter politically? ▶

Soldiers in Uniform, 1781–1784 (w/c on paper), Verger, Jean Baptiste Antoine de (1762–1851)/Brown University Library, Providence, Rhode Island, USA/The Bridgeman Art Library

As a war fought in towns and villages as well as on battlefields, the American Revolution profoundly altered the daily lives and political fortunes of all involved. Everyone contended with shortages and death as the fighting dragged on for more than six years in North America and two more around the globe. For Continental soldiers, early enlistees' confidence that the virtuous cause of independence would ennoble warfare gave way to the grinding reality of military discipline and insufficient resources. For noncombatants caught between warring forces, the fighting was a bloody civil war manifested in racial and gender violence. For European empires, the war was a chance to settle old imperial scores in the global balance of power. The resolution of the war redrew the map of the world for a second time in two decades by creating a new, large, and independent United States.

☞ As you read, seek to understand the Revolution from various perspectives. In what ways was it an imperial conflict? In what ways was it a civil war?

mercenary Professional soldier who fights for a country other than his own, many of whom were employed by the British army during the Revolutionary War.

6-4a Military Strategy in the Early Stages of War

British and U.S. leaders devise and revise their strategies.

In 1776, the government of Prime Minister Lord North planned to defeat the Continental Army the way that Britain had defeated the French army a decade earlier—by outmaneuvering it in battlefield engagements, winning, and then dominating peace negotiations. British forces concentrated on taking colonial centers such as New York City, which they occupied by fall of 1776, forcing Washington to retreat through New Jersey, which the British soon controlled as well. Britain relied on its powerful navy, standing army, and thousands of soldiers from northern Germany, whom the colonists called *Hessians*. The Hessians were **mercenaries**, men who fought on behalf of the foreign country that hired them. The British also expanded Lord Dunmore's policy of recruiting runaway slaves. Although his Proclamation had called for able-bodied warriors, one-third of those

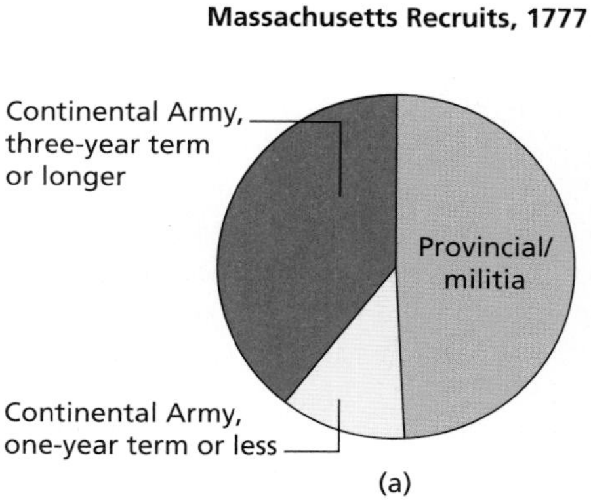

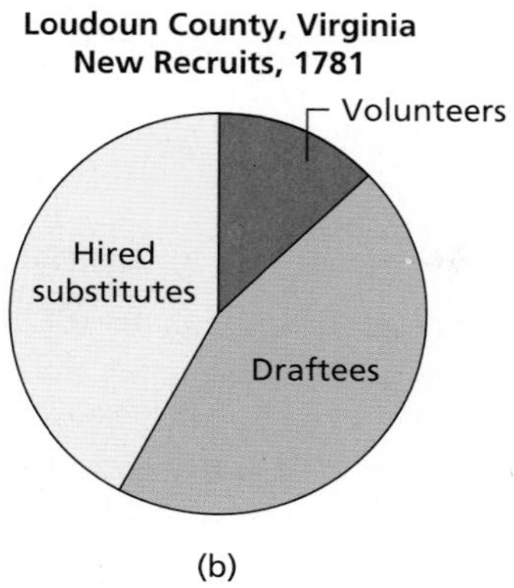

Figure 6.1(a) Massachusetts Recruits, 1777 The year 1777 marked a turning point when soldiers signed enlistments of three years or more in the Continental Army. Nonetheless, many men in Massachusetts preferred the shorter commitments of the militias, which were sent on brief expeditions of a month or two. ▲ Source: Walter Sargent, "The Massachusetts Rank and File of 1777," in *War and Society in the American Revolution*, ed. John Resch and Walter Sargent (Northern Illinois University Press, 2006).

Figure 6.1(b) Loudoun County, Virginia, New Recruits, 1781 In 1781, the Virginia Assembly set quotas for counties to supply recruits for the Continental Army. In Loudoun County, those who enlisted voluntarily were all landless laborers who were promised a bounty of cash, land, and a slave if they served for the duration of the war. Draftees and substitutes hired by draftees served eighteen months. ▲ Source: Michael A. McDonnell, "'Fit for Common Service?': Class, Race, and Recruitment in Revolutionary Virginia," in *War and Society in the American Revolution*, ed. John Resch and Walter Sargent (Northern Illinois University Press, 2006).

who reached British lines were women and children. Soon, anywhere there were British ships, there were slaves trying to get to them. Most ended up in noncombat support roles, segregated and underfed. The lucky ones traveled with the troops; the unlucky suffered disproportionately from malnutrition and smallpox.

Underfunded and underequipped, the Continental Congress ran the war in the North as one of attrition, depending on hit-and-run strikes and hoping for enough local successes to convince the British public that fighting Americans was not worth the cost. Often in retreat, the Continental Army had a few victories. Crucially, on Christmas Day in 1776, Washington, with soldiers eager for their enlistments to end in the new year, crossed the frigid Delaware River to surprise Hessians camped at Trenton, New Jersey. Capturing most of the garrison, the soldiers stayed with Washington to attack again, at Princeton, on January 3, 1777, forcing a British retreat.

As the initial enthusiasm and prospect of quick victory faded, Congress abandoned the idea of a militia-style force in favor of a standing army. In April 1777, it approved a draft and encouraged enlistment standards that changed the profile of the Continental Army (see Figures 6.1a and 6.1b). Many states permitted draftees to send substitutes, either free or enslaved, to serve in their stead. In New Jersey, as many as 40 percent of soldiers were substitutes. Pennsylvania and New Jersey also enlisted large numbers of recent German and Irish immigrants who had been working as bound servants.

To attract a fighting force for the duration, Congress offered varieties of freedom to enlistees. To recent immigrants and indentured servants, it promised land, which for most colonists was the bedrock of individual liberty. To enemy deserters, prisoners of war, and people who had failed to pay their taxes, Congress granted freedom from imprisonment or execution. For slaves, Congress changed the existing policy and offered freedom from enslavement. To free blacks, it offered the dignity of service, which had long been associated with civil rights. Although a majority of African Americans sided with the British, about five thousand served in the Continental Army and still more in racially integrated state militias. The result was that more soldiers served longer terms and were subject to stricter discipline, but the idea of a patriot–citizens' army died. Congress also sent Silas Deane to Europe to attract officers with expertise that the Americans lacked. Among his recruits was the young and idealistic Marquis de Lafayette, a French army officer who became a close friend of Washington.

These American regulars marched against British forces in New York and Philadelphia in the summer and fall of 1777 (see Map 6.3). Britain planned a pincer movement to deal a decisive defeat to American armies and cut off New England, the center of colonial resistance. Because the pincer's timing failed, separate engagements yielded opposite results. Outside Philadelphia, General William Howe defeated Washington at Brandywine Creek and Germantown with troops outnumbering the Americans three to one. The British occupied the colonial capital of Philadelphia while Continental Army units retreated to nearby Valley Forge for the winter, hungry, injured, and undersupplied. To the North, British General John Burgoyne made slow progress from Quebec. After skirmishes with American troops, he was forced to surrender his entire force to American General Horatio Gates at Saratoga in October 1777. Britain sent Sir William Howe to replace Burgoyne.

The experience at Valley Forge, where two thousand of eleven thousand soldiers spent the winter shoeless, forced

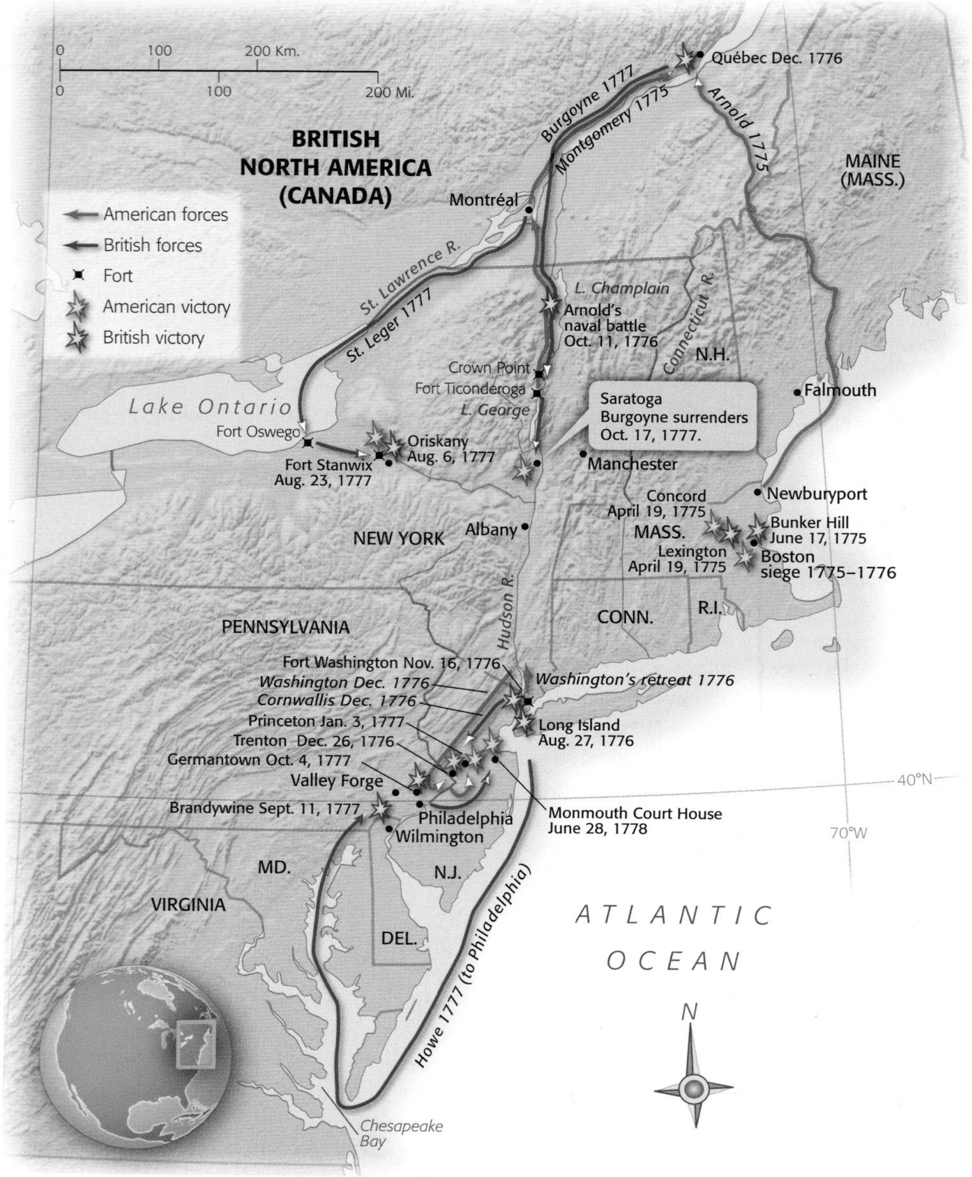

Map 6.3 Fighting in the North Revolutionary warfare began in Massachusetts. The British hoped to isolate rebellious New Englanders by occupying New York City and then Philadelphia. Troops of British general Burgoyne were successful at Quebec and in engagements along the St. Lawrence River and its connected waterways, but the American rebels defeated him at Saratoga. ▲

Americans to reconsider their scorn for British military organization, starting with support staff. While the British army maintained a standard of one woman for every ten men to do the work of cooking, cleaning, mending, and nursing, the Continental Army had only one woman for forty-four men. Washington, like other American generals, assumed that women among the troops encouraged prostitution and immorality. Consequently, two thousand five hundred soldiers died that winter and spring from disease, malnutrition, and hypothermia. Frederich Wilhelm, Baron von Steuben, a Prussian officer, arrived at Valley Forge and promptly hired more women. He also imposed a regime of drill and discipline for American soldiers that began to convert them into a more effective force. In June 1778, Washington's army fought a more evenly pitched, though inconclusive, battle against Henry Clinton's army at Monmouth, New Jersey, and the theater of war shifted to the South.

6-4b American Revolution as Imperial Conflict

People around the world experience the Revolution as an imperial conflict with local consequences.

American victory at Saratoga brought France openly into the war as an ally, decisively turning the American Revolution into one more imperial conflict. Hoping to see their longtime enemy Britain thwarted, the French court and French public had been inclined to the pro-independence side from the beginning. "There is a hundred times more enthusiasm for this Revolution in any Paris café than in all the colonies together," claimed Louis Duportail, a Frenchman who worked as chief engineer of the Continental Army. Benjamin Franklin, envoy of the Continental Congress living in Paris during the war, stoked that enthusiasm by entertaining French high society, but the French government wanted evidence that the United States could win, and Saratoga provided it. In February 1778, Franklin and French foreign minister Charles Gravier, Comte de Vergennes signed the **Treaty of Alliance** between the two countries, promising military and financial support in return for French dominion over any Caribbean islands it captured in the course of fighting. France and the United States also signed the Treaty of Amity and Commerce promoting open trade between the two. Spain declared a separate war against Britain in June 1779. Seeing an opportunity to seize valuable plantations, France and Spain spent heavily on troops in the Caribbean, India, and elsewhere. France also sent six thousand French regulars under the command of Comte de Rochambeau to Rhode Island in 1780 (see Map 6.4).

The Caribbean was the main focus of France's attempts to avenge the losses of 1763 because of its tremendous wealth and the shaky loyalties of merchants and traders there. Although West Indian colonial assemblies proclaimed loyalty to Britain—largely because they needed military protection from slave revolts and American privateers—traders from British, French, Dutch, and Spanish islands all smuggled military supplies to the American forces in small, nighttime boat deliveries. The people in ostensibly neutral Dutch St. Eustatius (with a population that included 40 percent British merchants) supplied a weekly convoy of French merchant ships to aid the war effort.

The entry of France, Spain, and finally the Netherlands into the American Revolution in 1780 turned a colonial uprising into a far-flung conflict in which multiple empires had a stake. Following the early examples of Lafayette and Von Steuben, aristocratic officers from Poland, France, and Germany journeyed to America to offer their expertise to the Continental Army. Except for some troop support from Prussia, Britain had no European allies. Its navy attacked

Treaty of Alliance Agreement signed in 1778 by the United States and France confirming French military and financial support in exchange for French territorial expansion in the Caribbean.

Map 6.4 The Revolution Worldwide, 1775–1783 Like the Seven Years' War, the American Revolution was in part an imperial conflict over trade and territory between Britain and its adversaries around the world. Many of the earlier sites of warfare reignited as Europe's empires sought to undo Britain's earlier gains. ▼

National Portrait Gallery, London

Diplomat Benjamin Franklin Scientist, printer, and politician, Franklin served as a minister to the French court during the Revolution. French people loved his "American" identity, typified by the backwoods fur hat he wears in this French portrait. His credibility, however, came from his highly respected position as a learned scientist and erudite "citizen of the world." Across the Atlantic, his son, William Franklin, was the loyalist governor of New Jersey who was arrested, imprisoned, and then exiled from the United States. ▲

The War at Sea French involvement in the American Revolution expanded the naval war. John Paul Jones of the Continental Navy commanded the *Bonhomme Richard*, a ship he received from France and renamed after Franklin's *Almanac*. In September 1779, Jones attacked the British vessel *Seraphis* off the West Coast of England, where it was protecting a merchant convoy. Jones's victory, against long odds, made him a celebrated hero; depictions of the battle were copied and republished across Europe as in this French engraving. ▼

Library of Congress Prints and Photographs Division

merchant ships from any nation suspected of transporting military supplies to the United States. In 1780, Russia, the Holy Roman Empire, the Ottoman Empire, the Scandinavian countries, and others signed a League of Armed Neutrality, insisting that any ship under the flag of a neutral country should be able to travel and trade freely.

6-4c American Revolution as Civil War

Native Americans and Loyalists discover that neutrality is impossible.

In the streets, villages, farms, and forests of North America, people experienced the American Revolution as a civil war. A significant minority—perhaps 20 percent—in the thirteen colonies openly opposed the patriot cause; others resisted passively. Called **Loyalists**, for their loyalty to Britain, or Tories, by their enemies, to link them with political enemies in Parliament, these people did not share a single ideology or motivation for remaining committed to Britain. Some living in the backcountry, as well as religious and ethnic minorities, considered the empire to be their protector against locally powerful colonial Americans. Many Native Americans, too, saw the British Empire as the only remaining counterweight to colonists' encroachments on their land. For wealthy elites with close ties to British leadership, the empire was the source of their livelihood and identity.

Neutrality proved impossible. Thomas Brown, an English-born plantation owner in Georgia believed that events in New England had "no connection or concern" to his life, but when he refused to sign a patriot association list in 1775, six of his neighbors attacked him. They broke his skull, tied him to a tree, poured tree sap on him, burned him, and scalped him. He recovered sufficiently to rally backcountry residents into a Loyalist militia renowned for its brutality.

Wherever rebel militias, loyal militias, Indian forces, and regular British and Continental troops converged, civilians suffered. Soldiers commandeered livestock and burned crops. Both European and American colonial armies used rape to terrify and conquer. The Continental Congress commissioned a report on wartime rape to document British atrocities but was unable to get fearful women to report the attacks. Indian warriors viewed terror tactics and captive-taking differently. They, too, sought revenge on enemy communities but did not rape. Starving and fearing for their safety, thousands of Native Americans,

Global Americans **Joseph Brant** (or **Thayendanega**) was born to a Mohawk Wolf clan family along the Ohio River in 1743. As a young teenager, he followed his sister Molly Brant's husband Sir William Johnson into battle during the Seven Years' War. He attended Moor's Charity School (later Dartmouth College) in Lebanon, Connecticut, where he converted to the Anglican religion and became skilled in English language and European history. He also met his first wife, Margaret, an Oneida with whom he had two children before she died. When the American Revolution broke out, Brant organized Haudenosaunee warriors to attack American settlements. His success and leadership against the American rebels earned him a captain's commission in the British army, although he continued to fight as a Haudenosaunee war chief and labored to forge a pan-Indian alliance to hold back U.S. settlement.

After the Treaty of Paris, Britain rewarded him for his loyalty to the empire with a grant of land for his family (he had married a Mohawk woman, Catharine) and his followers along the Grand River in British-held Canada. His decision to side with Britain had made him and his people exiles. Brant committed to international missionary work, traveling to England to raise money and translating selections of the Bible into the Mohawk language, before dying in 1807. His comfort both in front of the English court and at the Haudenosaunee council fires exemplified his skill in manipulating imperial structures for the benefit of Indian peoples.

colonists, and enslaved people fled, often to live as refugees in cities occupied by the British.

The Haudenosaunee alliance broke apart over whether to continue support for the British. Joseph Brant and Molly Brant, Mohawk siblings with deep ties to British institutions and officials, organized raids on American settlements and mobilized warriors to add troop strength to British campaigns in New York and Pennsylvania. In return, British outposts such as Fort Niagara sheltered and provisioned thousands of Indians from nearly twenty-two different tribes and family groups. Yet Oneidas and Tuscaroras, members of the Six Nations Confederacy, fought on the side of the rebelling Americans at the Battle of Oriskany in August 1777. In 1779, when American troops burned their towns and fields, the Onondagas, another member of the Six Nations, joined the British. Mary Jemison, kidnapped as a child to live as a Seneca in New York, recalled that the American forces destroyed her town, "burnt our houses, killed what few cattle and horses they could find, destroyed our fruit trees, and left nothing but bare soil and timber."

For Cherokees, the decision to join the fighting in the South grew from a generational power struggle that split the community into its own civil war. Like the allied Shawnees to the North, Cherokee families faced frequent border attacks from colonists eager for land. Led by matrons and older clan leaders such as Attakullakulla, who urged a limited response to frontier murder, many Cherokees attempted to maintain neutral relationships. As their economy had grown more focused on the deerskin and slave trades, they had become more dependent on the gunpowder, bullets, and trading partnerships offered by British connections. But younger warriors strongly opposed the program of neutrality and appeasement, especially as it involved selling off Cherokee land to mixed-race traders. Well aware of the ambivalent loyalties within the Cherokees, both South Carolina patriots and British Indian agents sought in 1775 and 1776 to win them over with trade goods and diplomatic missions. Delegates from Shawnee and Delaware communities who had been urging unified action since the Treaty of Fort Stanwix joined new emissaries from northern Six Nation tribes to press for a British alliance. Young Cherokee warriors were less interested in alliance than in attacking the immediate threat to their well-being. Declaring that it was "Better to die like men than to diminish away by inches," Attakullakulla's son, Dragging Canoe, launched an attack in 1776 against South Carolinians living on the Cherokee side of the 1763 Proclamation Line. The fighting lasted into the 1780s.

Britain's strategy in the South exploited the civil war dimension of the conflict. Enlisting the assistance of Loyalists, enslaved people, and pro-British Indians, the British seized territory in Georgia and South Carolina between 1778 and 1780, occupying Savannah and Charles Town (later Charleston). Soldiers commanded by Lord Charles Cornwallis crushed American forces dominated by militiamen at the Battle of Camden in August 1780. As retribution and revenge intensified the violence in the South, prisoners on both sides suffered the consequences. In North Carolina in 1781, patriot militiamen "hewed [Loyalist prisoners] to pieces with broadswords."

The British hoped to hand control of the South over to Loyalists and then sweep northward. Instead, the British army under Lord Cornwallis became dispersed and overextended as it pursued Continental forces, trying to force an engagement (see Map 6.5). In 1781, Nathanael Greene, the new commander of the American Southern Department, devised a strategy of divide and

Loyalists People who opposed the cause of independence, some of whom were motivated by personal gain, others by a desire for protection offered by the British Empire.

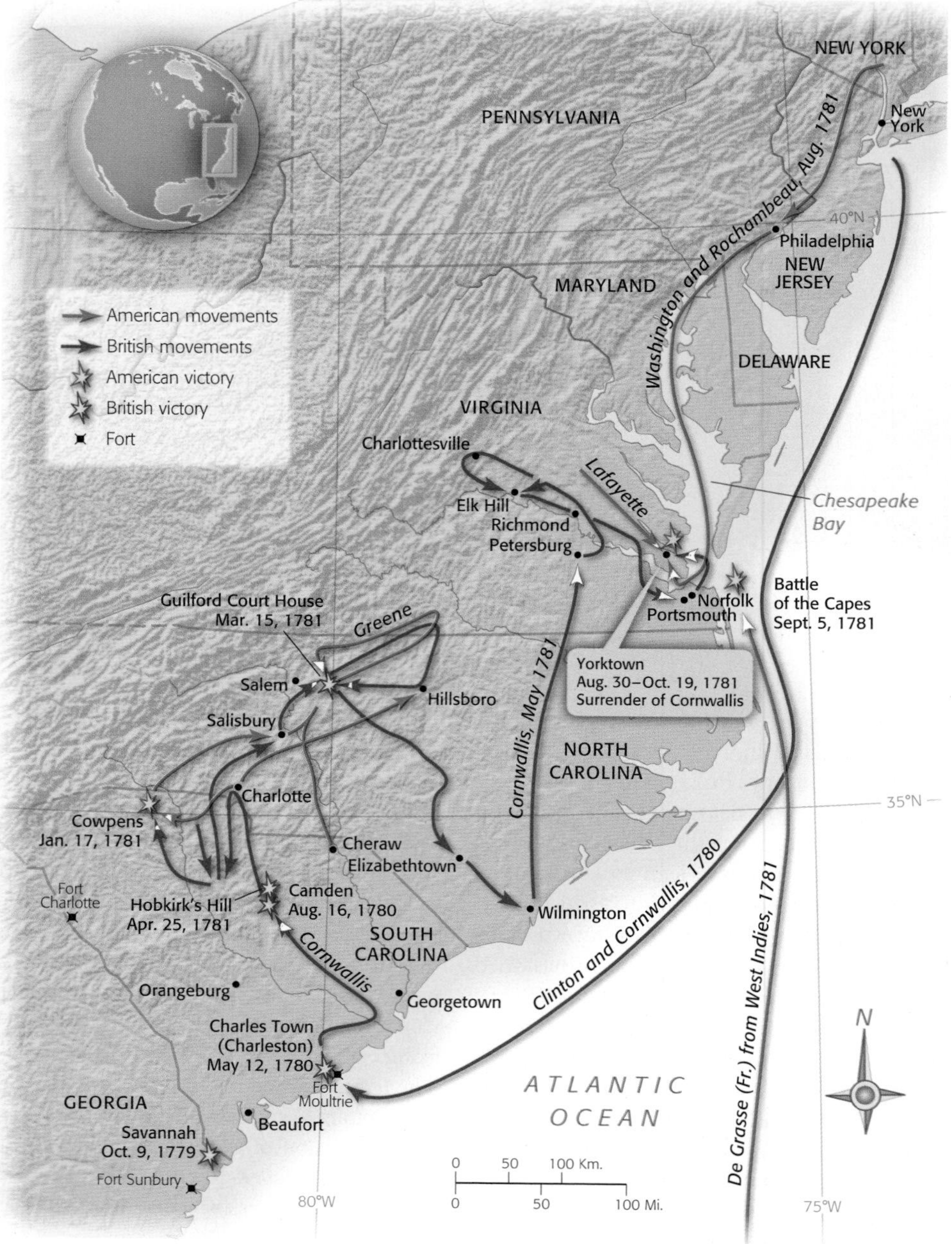

Map 6.5 Fighting in the South British strategy depended on loyal militias, enslaved runaways, and supportive Indians in the South. British troops, however, became overextended as rebellious Americans divided and evaded them. The final continental confrontation at Yorktown depended on timing and the arrival of the French. ▲

conquer that eventually outmaneuvered the British forces. Separate contingents of the American army joined with local patriot militias to engage the British army at different times and different places: Cowpens in January 1781; Guilford Court House in March; and Hobkirk's Hill in April. Cowpens was a surprising victory for Americans; the other two were losses but inflicted heavy casualties. Between battles, the American army used strategic withdrawals to force British troops to chase them beyond established supply lines. By the summer, Cornwallis moved his diminished forces north to Virginia and encamped at Yorktown on orders from General Clinton to fortify an anchoring point for the British Navy.

Treaty of Paris Agreement between Britain and the United States ending the war and redrawing the map of North America without reference to the claims of Native Americans.

6-4d Surrender and Settlement

The United States wins independence.

In August 1781, when Washington learned that a French fleet was heading north from the Caribbean, he and French commander Rochambeau abandoned plans to retake New York and rapidly marched south to meet Cornwallis's

The New York Public Library/Art Resource, NY

Reconciliation at War's End The Revolutionary War ended with another treaty in Paris that from the European perspective left the future open. This 1782 British cartoon, "The Reconciliation between Britania and Her Daughter" depicts the United States as a Native American embracing her "mother." On the left, a Frenchman tugs at America, worrying "Begar they will be friends again if you don't pull a little harder here." A Dutchman, leaning on a barrel, vows to wait before choosing sides again. ▲

troops. By September, the fleet of Comte de Grasse had defeated a British fleet and blockaded the mouth of the Chesapeake. Washington and Rochambeau arrived at Yorktown and with 7,800 Frenchmen, 5,700 Continental soldiers, and 3,200 militiamen, surrounded Cornwallis on land. The allied army dug besieging trenches and bombarded the British with artillery fire. In little over a week, Cornwallis surrendered. At the surrender ceremony, October 19, 1781, Cornwallis's representative attempted to deliver his sword to Rochambeau, who deferred to Washington, crediting the new United States with a victory that had depended upon French assistance.

Fighting in the Caribbean, however, did not stop. Although U.S. independence had been won, the imperial balance of power around the globe was still in play. France captured St. Kitts but failed to conquer St. Lucia and Jamaica. On the other side of the world, France fought in West Africa and India while Spain tried and failed to capture Gibraltar. These actions shaped each empire's standing as they went into final peace negotiations although in the end, most of what had been won was returned.

Meeting in Paris, Spanish and French representatives attempted to manipulate negotiations to support their own imperial ambitions against Britain. They hoped the new United States would become a politically and geographically limited nation dependent on its commercial connections to them. But the American commissioners, Franklin, Adams, and John Jay, moved first to establish a separate peace with Britain, hoping to use European rivalries to their own benefit. The British, who wanted American trade for themselves, offered territory belonging to Native Americans to sweeten the deal. The **Treaty of Paris**, signed in September 1783, set the boundaries of the newly independent United States to the north at the border with Canada, to the west at the Mississippi River, and to the south just above East and West Florida, which once again passed to Spain. Britain also signed peace treaties with France, Spain, and the Netherlands (see Map 6.6).

Wyandot chiefs, calling themselves "your children," had pressed to be "remembered in the Treaty," but the territorial claims of Native Americans—not present at the treaty negotiations—were ignored. They felt betrayed by their allies and asserted that Britain did not have the right to give up land it did not possess. Furthermore, they recognized that they were now left to deal with enemy Americans on their own.

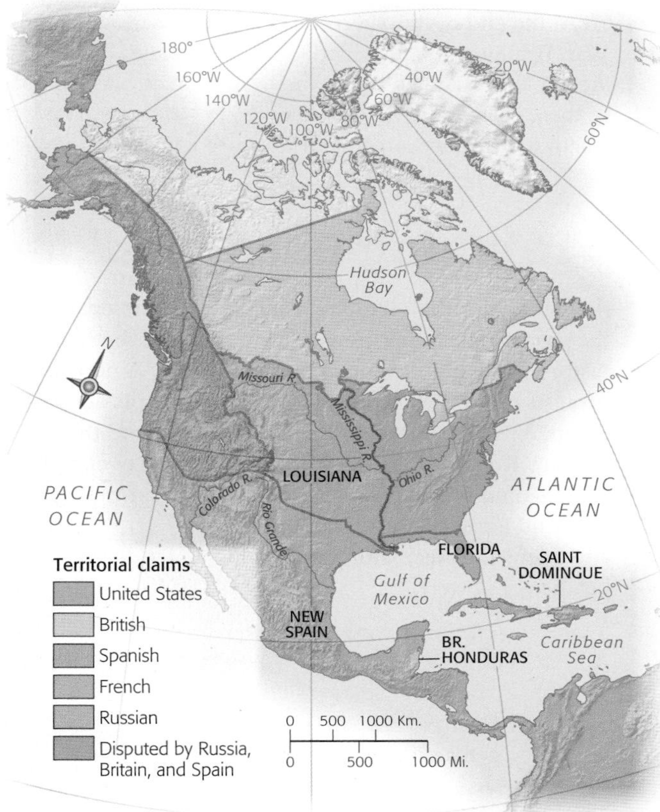

Map 6.6 North America in 1783 The 1783 Treaty of Paris redrew territorial boundaries, creating the new nation of the United States. As with the 1763 treaty meetings, Indians were not represented. The 1783 treaty disregarded Indian claims altogether. ▲

Summary

People seeking land and trade shaped North America at mid-eighteenth century. Native American and European fur trappers pursued dwindling animal populations deep into the interior. European settlers migrated north along the West Coast and west from the East Coast in search of farmland. Thousands of African people were forced ashore to live as slaves. Migrations fueled competition among European empires that saw North America as a proving ground of power. Native coalitions and colonial settlers had their own stake in global struggles over land and trade, which had yielded decades of conflict. Early in the 1750s, these conflicts erupted again in the Ohio River Valley among refugee Indian groups, land speculators, French soldiers, and European settlers. Local conflict escalated into global war.

At the end of the Seven Years' War, Britain won a lopsided victory that changed the terms of these ongoing struggles. The ejection of France left Indian diplomatic alliances and trade patterns in disarray. The assertion of unified British authority over a multicultural population seemed at odds with local ideas about identity and self-government. A wave of protests, incorporating new formats such as the boycott and forging new alliances among Great Lakes Native Americans, challenged new policies. In coalescing resistance movements, colonists, Indians, and Africans debated power and human rights. But they did not agree on an answer. Because trade and land remained core issues, people frequently turned against neighbors rather than joining with them. Over a decade of resistance, two main dimensions of conflict emerged: between Indians and colonists and between British colonists and the central government.

The Declaration of Independence asserted the existence of a "United States," but the process of deciding who was part of this new nation took decades. The long Revolutionary War was fought as a civil war that itself cemented alliances. Indians from the Mohawks in New England to the Cherokees in South Carolina formed a resistance movement in opposition to the new United States. Enslaved people who saw that rebel calls for "liberty" would not end slavery took their chances with the British army. Backcountry farmers who hoped to remain neutral were drawn into patriot or loyalist ranks in reaction to brutal home front fighting that targeted crops, homes, and families as well as soldiers.

The third dimension of the American Revolution—the global struggle of France, Spain, and the Netherlands against Britain—emerged after the Declaration as these empires all supported the rebel Americans in order to halt British imperial power. The 1783 Treaty of Paris acknowledged that the United States had won independence and emerged as a new separate nation in the world, but the people living within its boundaries did not all agree on what kind of nation it would be.

<Thinking Back, *Looking Forward*>

As you review this chapter, evaluate the role of rebellion in American history. How did the anticolonial protests of the 1760s and 1770s compare with the Pueblo Revolt or Bacon's Rebellion? How did rebel leaders bind followers together? How did local struggles over money and status intersect with the global balance of power?

In the next chapters, trace the aftermath of rebellion. How did the American Revolution disperse people across the continent and around the world? What ideas about liberty or rights did they take with them?

To make your study concrete, review the timeline and reflect on the entries there. Think about their causes, consequences, and connections. How do they connect events in North America to global trends?

Additional Resources

Books

Anderson, Fred. *The Crucible of War: The Seven Years' War and the Fate of Empire in British North America, 1754–1766*. New York: Vintage, 2001. ▶ Narrates the Seven Years' War as a global struggle over empire.

Armitage, David. *The Declaration of Independence: A Global History*. Cambridge, MA: Harvard University Press, 2007. ▶ Comparative examination of the influence of the U.S. Declaration of Independence on subsequent movements.

Calloway, Colin. *The Scratch of a Pen: 1763 and the Transformation of North America*. New York: Oxford University Press, 2004. ▶ Explores the consequences of the Seven Years' War for Native Americans, both locally and in global context.

Frey, Sylvia. *Water from the Rock: Black Resistance in a Revolutionary Age*. Princeton, NJ: Princeton University Press, 1992. ▶ Explores the Revolutionary War in the South as a three-way struggle between Britain, American rebels, and African Americans.

Gould, Eliga. *Among the Powers of the Earth: The American Revolution and the Making of a New World Empire*. Cambridge, MA: Harvard University Press, 2012. ▶ Political and economic history of the emergence of the United States as a "treaty-worthy" nation.

Gray, Edward G., and Jane Kamensky, eds. *The Oxford Handbook of the American Revolution*. New York: Oxford University Press, 2012. ▶ Wide-ranging collection of essays covering multiple dimensions of the revolutionary conflict and its aftermath.

Hartigan-O'Connor, Ellen. *The Ties That Buy: Women and Commerce in Revolutionary America*. Philadelphia: University of Pennsylvania Press, 2009. ▶ Places revolutionary boycotts in broader context of Atlantic urban economies with women at the center.

Nash, Gary B. *The Unknown American Revolution: The Unruly Birth of Democracy and the Struggle to Create America*. New York: Penguin Books, 2006. ▶ Lively account of the perspectives of native, working, and enslaved people toward the war for independence.

O'Shaughnessy, Andrew Jackson. *An Empire Divided: The American Revolution and the British Caribbean*. Philadelphia: University of Pennsylvania Press, 2000. ▶ A study of the American Revolution in the nonrebelling British Caribbean colonies.

Saunt, Claudio. *West of the Revolution: An Uncommon History of 1776*. New York: W.W. Norton, 2014. ▶ Examines native and imperial relationships in 1776 North America away from the East Coast.

Go to the MindTap® for **Global Americans** to access the full version of select books from this Additional Resources section.

Websites

American Revolutionary War Era Maps (1750–1800). http://maps.bpl.org/highlights/ar/american-revolutionary-war-era ▶ Norman B. Leventhal Map Center links to multiple libraries' digitized maps of the Revolution.

Common-Place. http://www.common-place.org/ ▶ Journal covering Revolution-era topics cosponsored by the American Antiquarian Society and the University of Connecticut.

A Guide to the American Revolution, 1763–1783. https://www.loc.gov/rr/program/bib/revolution/memory.html ▶ Organizes links to the thousands of digital sources on the Revolutionary era at the Library of Congress.

MindTap®

Continue exploring online through MindTap®, where you can:

- **Assess your knowledge with the Chapter Test**
- **Watch historical videos related to the chapter**
- **Further your understanding with interactive maps and timelines**

Imperial Conflicts and Revolution

1754–1762

May 1754

Seven Years' War breaks out in Ohio Valley.

June–July 1754

Albany Congress brings representatives of Six Nations and seven British colonies to discuss anti-French alliance.

1762

Spain declares war on Britain and is defeated at Havana.

1763

February

Treaty of Paris formally ends war, stipulating that France give up territorial claims to North America.

May

Coalition of Native people seizes British forts around the Great Lakes in Pontiac's Rebellion.

October

King George III issues Royal Proclamation marking line of settlement between colonial and Indian lands.

1764–1767

April 1764

Sugar Act lowers tax on British molasses while increasing enforcement of customs laws.

Currency Act outlaws colonial paper money.

March 1765

Stamp Act places tax on newspapers, playing cards, and legal documents; repealed in 1766.

Stamp Act Congress meets in New York with delegates from nine British colonies.

Nonimportation movement in response to Stamp Act urges merchants to boycott British imports.

January 1766

Slaves march in Charles Town streets, shouting "liberty!"

June 1767

Parliament passes new taxes on everyday goods, called Townshend Duties; most repealed in 1770.

Nonconsumption movement urges regular consumers to boycott British goods.

1768

October 1768

Treaty of Fort Stanwix cedes Shawnee and Delaware land to Pennsylvania.

Creole-dominated Superior Council in New Orleans banishes Antonio de Ulloa, first governor of Spanish Louisiana.

1769–1773

March 1770

Tensions between occupying British troops and Bostonians leads to Boston Massacre.

June 1770

Junipero Serra establishes Franciscan mission in Monterey.

May 1773

Tea Act makes British tea cheaper than smuggled Dutch tea.

December 1773

Boston protestors dump 90,000 pounds of East India Company tea into harbor.

1774

March–June

Parliament passes series of Coercive Acts that close Boston Harbor, remove colonial representative government, and allow military quartering in private buildings.

June

Quebec Act consolidates larger Canadian colony, confirming no representative government and toleration of Catholicism.

May–October

Governor of Virginia leads militia against Shawnees and allied Indians, defeating them in Dunmore's War.

September–October

First Continental Congress meets in Philadelphia with fifty-five delegates from twelve colonies.

1775

April

Boston stalemate between British forces and colonial militia breaks with fighting at Lexington and Concord.

November

Dunmore's Proclamation promises freedom to rebels' slaves who join the British cause.

1776

January

Thomas Paine publishes *Common Sense*.

June

José Joaquin Moraga, with soldiers, American-born colonists, and nearly three hundred cows, establishes military garrison and Franciscan mission in San Francisco Bay.

July

Continental Congress passes Declaration of Independence.

September

British troops occupy New York City.

1777–1779

1777

Congress approves a draft, changing the profile of the Continental Army.

February 1778

France and the United States sign Treaty of Alliance and Treaty of Amity and Commerce, pledging military support and open trade.

1779

Spain declares war on Britain.

1780–1783

Summer 1780

League of Armed Neutrality pledges European countries to free trade for ships under neutral flags.

December 1780

Britain declares war on the Netherlands.

October 1781

British troops under Cornwallis surrender the Continental Army of Washington.

September 1783

Britain and United States sign Treaty of Paris, officially ending war and redrawing boundaries of United States.

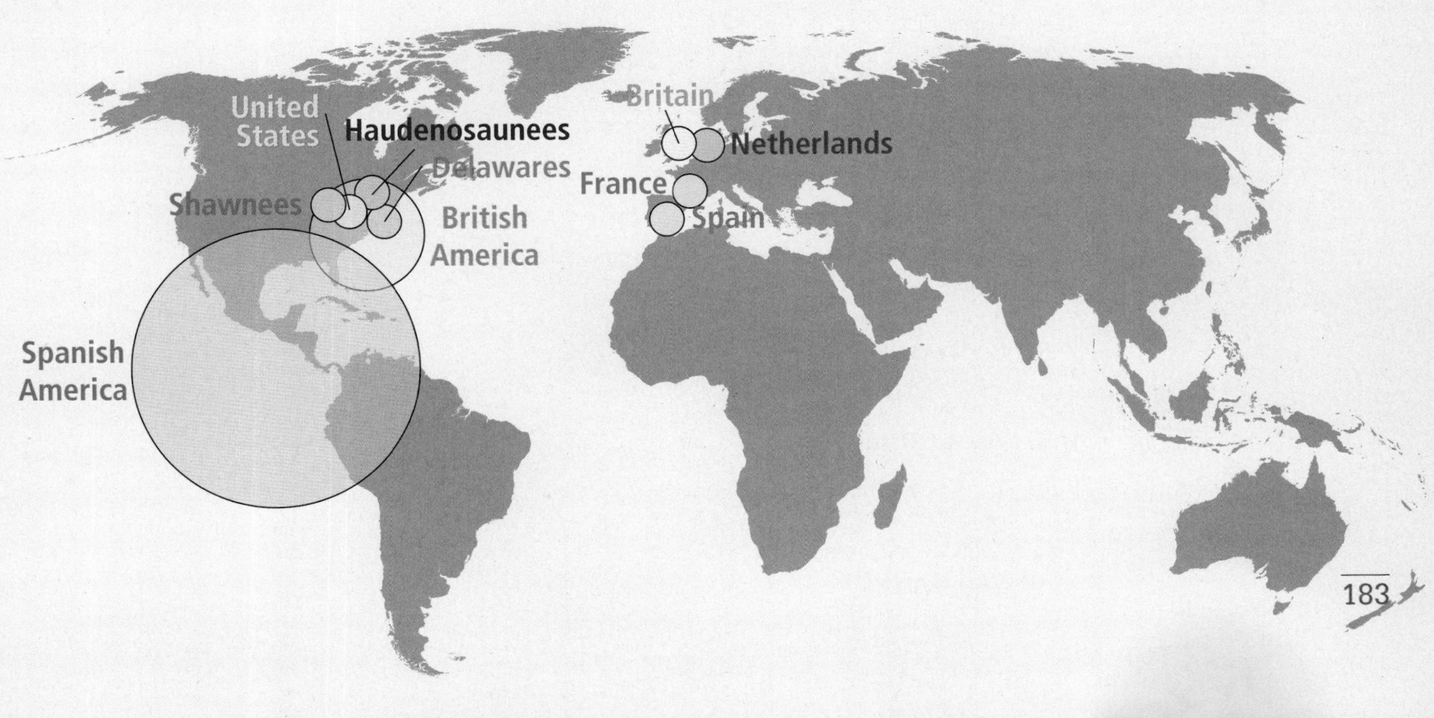

7 American Experiments

1776–1789

John White Swift, purser aboard the *Empress of China*, sailed from New York to Canton and back, 1784–1785

7-1 Institutional Experiments with Liberty

7-1a State Constitutions
7-1b Challenges to Slavery
7-1c Women and Familial Power
7-1d Emerging Religious Freedoms

7-2 Political Experiments in the Politics of Alliance

7-2a Articles of Confederation
7-2b Native American Alliances
7-2c Spanish North America after the War

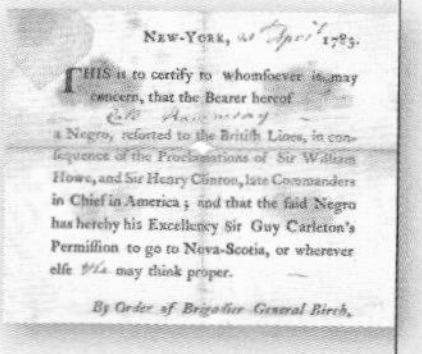

NEW-YORK, 21 April 1783.

THIS is to certify to whomsoever it may concern, that the Bearer hereof
a Negro, resorted to the British Lines, in consequence of the Proclamations of Sir William Howe, and Sir Henry Clinton, late Commanders in Chief in America; and that the said Negro has hereby his Excellency Sir Guy Carleton's Permission to go to Nova-Scotia, or wherever else she may think proper.

By Order of Brigadier General Birch,

7-3 Postwar Migrations

7-3a Loyalist Diaspora
7-3b Free Black Communities
7-3c The Trans-Appalachian West
7-3d Pacific Connections

7-4 Power in Crisis

7-4a Trade within and around Imperial Systems
7-4b American Debt Crisis
7-4c Popular Uprisings
7-4d Northwest Territory

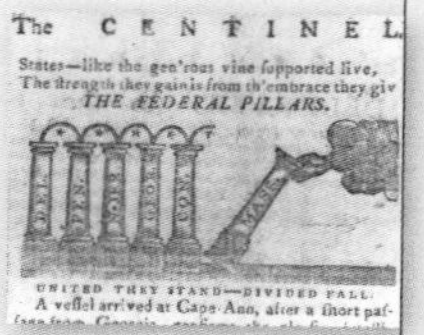

The CENTINEL.

States—like the gen'rous vine supported live,
The strength they gain is from th'embrace they giv
THE FEDERAL PILLARS.

UNITED THEY STAND—DIVIDED FALL.
A vessel arrived at Cape-Ann, after a short paf-

7-5 U.S. Constitution

7-5a The Constitutional Convention
7-5b United States Constitution of 1787
7-5c Ratification Debates
7-5d The Bill of Rights

In August 1784, when ship's purser John White Swift sailed into Canton harbor, he was optimistic about U.S. trade with China. The officers on the *Empress of China* were experienced Revolutionary War veterans. The ship had sailed out of New York harbor on George Washington's fifty-first birthday. The newly independent United States was eager to establish its own commercial relationships, especially because Britain had cut off trade between its former colonies and remaining colonies. Those aboard the *Empress* hoped that expanding commerce could help pull the new nation's economy out of its postwar slump.

Fan Depicting the *Empress of China* ▲

The *Empress of China* had set out to the east, crossing the Atlantic Ocean and sailing around the tip of Africa and then through the Indian Ocean to China—an eighteen-thousand-mile journey that took six months. In Canton, the Chinese who watched the ship arrive were cautious. It flew an unfamiliar red-and-white striped flag that looked curiously like the flag of the East India Company, but the ship was too small to be a vessel of that powerful British firm. Nor was the Chinese empire looking for more trading partners. It confined foreign sea traders to a single port and dictated all the terms of exchange, viewing it as a privilege for foreigners to associate with the Qing Dynasty.

The initial meeting with Chinese merchants was awkward, as Swift later wrote to his father: "the Chinese had never heard of us, but we introduced ourselves as a new nation." To back up that claim, the ship's captain John Green pulled out a letter of introduction stamped with the new United States seal, copies of diplomatic treaties with European powers, and the Declaration of Independence itself. Samuel Shaw, another officer, tried to impress the Chinese with a map conveying "the extent of our country, with its present and increasing population." Americans would make good customers, he asserted. But the Chinese customs officials were not impressed. Four months later they still listed U.S. ships as British.

Chinese wariness was justified. These newcomers spoke English and wanted the same goods as the English but claimed to be different. They had arrived with a French escort but insisted they were from an independent nation. Their map was continental but the United States was not. Most important, the only goods that the Americans had to offer were ginseng, a medicinal root, and furs, both trade goods provided by Native Americans. The Chinese would not have known that relationships between Native Americans and U.S. merchants were in tatters after years of brutal warfare and forced treaties.

In what ways does the fate of the *Empress of China's* trade mission to Canton reflect the problems facing the new United States?

Go to MindTap® to watch a video on the Empress of China and learn how the sailors' journey relates to the themes of this chapter.

The problems facing the *Empress of China*'s backers were the problems of the United States as a whole in the years between the Declaration of Independence (1776) and the ratification of the United States Constitution (1789). Thirteen states were independent of Britain but, although joined in a confederation, were still largely independent of each other. The conflicts that had sparked the Revolution—over land, political power, and international trade—were still urgent and unresolved. So were the imperial rivalries that could destabilize the new nation. And decades of warfare had forced tens of thousands from homes and homelands, undermining the very notion of unity.

Some liked it that way. Between 1776 and 1789, Americans engaged in a prolonged debate over whether unified or dispersed power best served an independent people. States reorganized their governments to make them more responsive to the people and then revised them when the people seemed to have gained too much control. The same process happened at the national level as new institutions dispersed and then centralized economic and political power. The United States rejected the old hierarchies of birth, but many doubted that average people deserved power and trust.

The *Empress of China* returned to New York in 1785, bearing tea, silks, nankeen trousers, and porcelain, earning backers 25 percent on their investment. The sailors re-entered a world of uncertainty and experimentation. People across the political and social spectrum, from Creeks to enslaved Africans to western farmers, knew that the end of British control meant fewer restrictions but also fewer protections. Average men and women tested the limits of revolutionary devotion to liberty and equality. Enslaved people sought freedom through courts, governments, and individual owners. Free women pressed for equal education and egalitarian marriages. Native Americans insisted that their property rights were valid. Some experiments were resolved after long debate by the principles and structures set forth in the new Constitution of the United States. But for many, like the common sailors on the *Empress of China*, the resolutions worked out in the thirteen years following 1776 felt like a revolutionary promise unfulfilled.

7-1
Institutional Experiments with Liberty

© Massachusetts Historical Society, Boston, MA, USA/Bridgeman Images

This miniature in watercolor on ivory depicts Elizabeth Freeman, painted by Susan Ridley Sedgwick in 1811. It is one of the few portraits of an African American from this period. Born into slavery, "Mumbet," as she was known, won her freedom and took her new name in a lawsuit advanced by Sedgwick's father-in-law; she became a paid servant in his home. As an old woman, Freeman was a midwife, churchgoer, property owner, and taxpayer in Massachusetts.

How does the painter use the details of costume, pose, and expression to depict her subject as a free, rather than enslaved, woman? ▶

Go to MindTap® to practice history with the Chapter 7 **Primary Source Writing Activity: Experiments with Liberty and Equality.** Read and view primary sources and respond to a writing prompt.

In 1776, rebelling Americans rejected the institutions of monarchy and aristocracy in favor of independence, self-governance, and fundamental rights. Provided that they were successful in winning the war, the implications for government seemed clear. The United States would become independent, and elected lawmakers would replace royal governors sent from Britain. Putting these principles into practice was not easy, however, because there were practical problems of who should vote and who could lead. Furthermore, the language of "liberty" and "rights" promised a broad social transformation in which traditions of deference upholding the wealth and power of the "better sort" would be replaced with fair competition among equals. How far should that transformation go? Would the institutions of slavery, family, and church also be transformed by new ideas about human liberty? Would controls over trade be abandoned? Putting liberty into practice required rethinking basic assumptions about who had the right to power over others.

☞ As you read, look for the appearance of ideas about freedom and self-governance. How did they transform institutions such as legislatures, slavery, families, and churches?

7-1a State Constitutions

State constitutions institutionalize popular control.

The Declaration of Independence asserted that governments derive "their just powers from the consent of the governed." The people, rather than God or a hereditary monarch, gave the government its power and legitimacy. One of the first proving grounds for this idea, known as **popular sovereignty**, was in the state constitutions created during and after the American Revolution. Connecticut and Rhode Island revised their old colonial charters, keeping most structures in place, but other states wrote new **constitutions** that spread power to a wider group of people. They strengthened elected legislatures, long considered the voice of free men, and weakened governors, who had previously represented imperial power. Elected legislatures, not governors, appointed judges and the governor's council, and governors lost veto power. State constitutions allocated more representation in the legislature to regular farmers living in the backcountry; in five states, representation was linked directly to population numbers. Writing new constitutions, legislators reexamined qualifications for voting.

Deciding who was eligible to vote became an exercise in defining "the people" empowered by popular sovereignty. Most states required voters to own some form of property, most commonly land, as they had throughout the eighteenth century. By holding onto this requirement, these states were following influential political theories maintaining that only free adult men who owned land and therefore had an independent stake in decisions about property could put aside selfish desires and act for the common good. Renters, wives, servants, and slaves owed their livelihoods to others, and so they were not considered able to exercise independent judgment. Many state constitutions reduced property requirements to allow more ordinary taxpaying men a voice in political decisions, but they were cautious about turning government over to what they feared was a "mob" of popular opinion. Massachusetts legislators even considered but then rejected a plan to confiscate private landholdings of more than one thousand acres and redistribtribute them to landless men in order to turn them into stakeholding farmers who could then be trusted to vote responsibly.

popular sovereignty Political theory that legitimate power resides with people who then authorize governments to act on their behalf.

constitutions Documents defining the use and limits of governmental power. State constitutions, like colonial charters, were written contracts. The British Constitution was an unwritten group of customary practice.

The most radical experiment in government was the Pennsylvania Constitution of 1776. Under its provisions, there was only a single legislative body, elected annually, whose debates were open to the public. Rather than a governor, Pennsylvania had a committee selected from among the legislators to handle executive functions. Voting was open to all free men over twenty-one years of age who had lived in the state for a year and paid any public taxes, such as the head tax levied on adult men without property, which meant that recent German immigrants and propertyless laborers could vote. Like six other early state constitutions, Pennsylvania's had a bill of rights guaranteeing citizens religious freedom, trial by jury, and freedom of speech. Pennsylvania also mandated public elementary education and forbade imprisonment for debt. The goal was both to restructure government to make it more responsive and to educate and cultivate a society of people who could become "persons most noted for wisdom and virtue," and therefore trusted with such political power.

Most states did not go as far as Pennsylvania. They retained governors and upper houses of the legislature. They required candidates for political office to own more property than average voters. But more generous voter laws and the experience of wartime self-governance led to political change. State legislatures' lower houses increasingly consisted more of artisans, backcountry farmers, and men of moderate wealth (see Figure 7.1). Governments, in the form of state capitals, moved away from the East Coast and closer to the average farmers geographically. Albany replaced New York, Harrisburg replaced Philadelphia, Richmond replaced Williamsburg, and Columbia replaced Charleston.

7-1b Challenges to Slavery

Slaves seek freedom through courts and new state governments.

Enslaved people, especially those in New England who could **petition** courts and legislatures, seized on the Revolutionary rhetoric of freedom to make the case for their release. In 1774, a group of Massachusetts slaves petitioned legislators to grant their freedom on the grounds that they had "in common with all other men a naturel right to our freedoms without Being depriv'd of them by our fellow men." The request was denied, but everywhere slaves asserted that ideas about liberty should apply to them, and they used notions

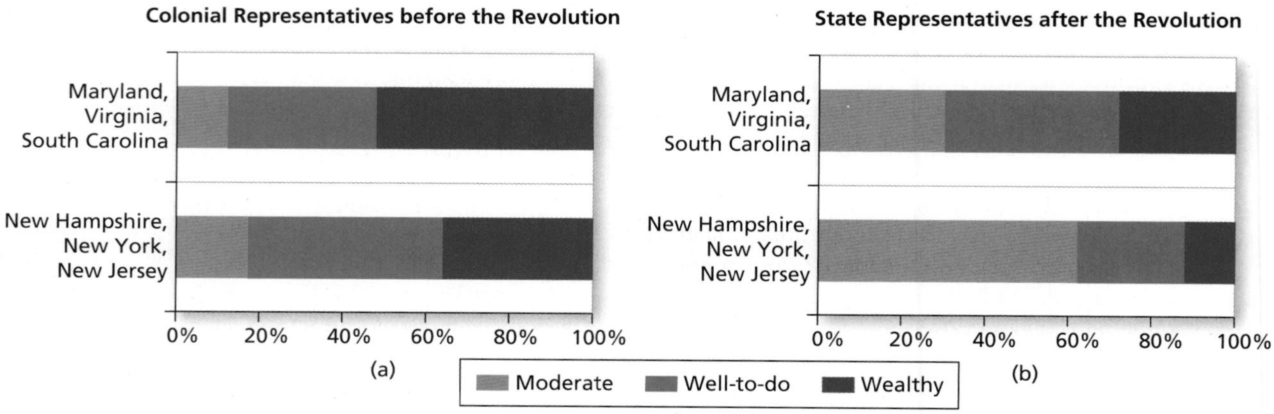

Figure 7.1a Colonial Representatives before the Revolution In the decade prior to the Revolution, men elected to serve in the colonial assemblies were prosperous, and even wealthy, as determined by the value of the property they owned: moderate (£500–£2,000), well-to-do (£2,000–£5,000), and wealthy (more than £5,000). Note that only 30 percent of the free adult male population owned property valued at more than £500; the majority owned less and were below the "moderate" level. ▲

Figure 7.1b State Representatives after the Revolution In the decade after the Revolution, legislatures were larger and more men were elected to represent western farmers to balance out the domination of men from the coast. Assemblies in the South tended to have a higher proportion of wealthy representatives, even after the war. ▲ Source: Adapted from Jackson Turner Main, "Government by the People: The American Revolution and the Democratization of the Legislatures," *William and Mary Quarterly*, 3rd ser., 23, no. 3 (July 1966)

free state State in which slavery is not permitted under law.

gradual emancipation laws State laws passed during and after the Revolutionary War that ended slavery for the future children of slaves.

about fundamental equality embedded in the language of the Declaration of Independence to try to dismantle the institution of slavery.

In Massachusetts, slaves used the first article of the new state constitution, which declared that "All men are born free and equal" and "every subject is entitled to liberty" to challenge the legality of their enslavement in court. Quok Walker, who had been promised and then denied freedom, was awarded his own freedom by the Massachusetts Supreme Court in 1781. The justices went further and declared that the words of the state constitution "effectively abolished" slavery. Elizabeth Freeman likewise won her freedom the same year. The Massachusetts legislature discussed but then failed to pass a general emancipation law that would have applied to all people held as slaves. The burden was on individual slaves to find lawyers and bring suit.

Enslaved people in other northern states had specific new laws to support their bids for freedom (see Table 7.1). In 1777, when Vermont declared independence from New York and New Hampshire, its new state constitution abolished slavery outright, and it entered the United States in 1791 as a **free state**. Connecticut, Rhode Island, and Pennsylvania followed by enacting **gradual emancipation laws**. Under these laws, people who were enslaved remained slaves for life, but their children born after the passage of the laws were freed following prolonged indentures during which they continued to work for former masters. Most gradual emancipation laws worked to protect the property rights of owners and to ensure continued access to the labor of former slaves. Once they outlawed slavery, however, free states became destinations for enslaved people seeking liberty.

In Virginia and Maryland, the doctrines of the expanding Methodist and Baptist churches that discouraged

Table 7.1 A Slow Legal End to Slavery in the North

Of the original thirteen colonies, only Vermont banned slavery outright in the Age of Revolution; other northern states relied on gradual legal processes. Because gradual emancipation laws did not apply to people born before a law was passed and because they included long periods of "apprenticeship" before freedom, thousands of people were still held in bondage in the North in the 1830s. Gradual emancipation laws were debated in Virginia and Delaware but never passed.

Year	State	Legislation
1777	Vermont	Constitution bans slavery
1780	Pennsylvania	Law frees the children of enslaved mothers at age 28
1780	Massachusetts	Constitution declares "all men are born free and equal"; courts interpret statement to refuse to uphold slavery
1783	New Hampshire	State constitution declares "all men are born equal and independent"; legal interpretation remains ambiguous
1784	Rhode Island	Law frees children of enslaved mothers at age 18 (girls) and 21 (boys)
1784	Connecticut	Law frees children of enslaved mothers at age 25
1799	New York	Law frees children of enslaved mothers at age 25 (girls) and 28 (boys)
1803	Ohio	Constitution bans slavery
1804	New Jersey	Law frees children of enslaved mothers at age 21 (girls) and 25 (boys)

Source: Joanne Pope Melish, *Disowning Slavery: Gradual Emancipation and "Race" in New England, 1780–1860* (Ithaca: Cornell University Press, 2000).

slavery, along with some pressure to remedy the hypocrisy of slave owning in a free republic, merged with a strong sense of property rights to convince legislatures to pass laws that made it easier for masters to free individual slaves. In a process called **manumission**, owners could take the initiative to free their human property; no longer did they have to seek special permission from the state assemblies to do so. In some cases, slave owners manumitted people by selling slaves to themselves, transferring title to and ownership of the human body to the person who inhabited it. In other cases, slave owners manumitted their slaves gradually. Prominent Virginian Robert Carter II manumitted five hundred slaves during his lifetime and at his death, but he was the exception. Only a minority of owners took part in manumission before laws tightened again; in fact, the number of slaves in Virginia and Maryland increased in the 1780s and 1790s.

Ellen Kelleran Gardner Fund

Republican Family Revolutionary ideals praised the free family as a place of virtuous restraint rather than abundant reproduction. In this 1788 portrait, *Samels Family* by Johann Eckstein, the mother is at the center, at the same level as her husband. An adolescent daughter is painted with a book in her hand, signifying the importance of reading and education for girls. ▲

Between the 1770s and 1790s, the number of free black people grew from a few thousand to tens of thousands, but emancipation and manumission increased racial divides and intensified hostility to blacks. Gradual emancipation laws and antislavery court decisions in New England coincided with new laws forbidding a white person to marry "any Negro, Indian, or mulatto." Even those whites who embraced the idea of natural rights rarely thought of black people as equals. The New York legislature deadlocked over a gradual emancipation bill when key supporters insisted on simultaneously denying blacks the right to vote.

7-1c Women and Familial Power

Families recalculate shared power of women and men.

Revolutionary leaders wanted to dismantle a world that put aristocrats in charge of ordinary people, but most of them preferred to keep intact a patriarchal family supported by laws that limited the rights of free women. Some women had other ideas. Writing to her husband John Adams in 1776 while he attended the Second Continental Congress, Abigail Adams asked him to "remember the ladies" in creating the new government. "Do not," she warned, put "unlimited power into the hands of the Husbands. Remember all Men would be tyrants if they could" and women "will not hold ourselves bound by any Laws in which we have no voice, or Representation." Abigail Adams ran the family farm and managed the family finances for years at a time while he was away, but John Adams belittled her request. Noting that revolutionary struggle "has loosed the bands of Government every where," that "Children and Apprentices were disobedient—that schools and Colleges were grown turbulent—that Indians slighted their Guardians and Negroes grew insolent to their Masters," he cautioned, "We know better than to repeal our Masculine systems."

The "masculine system" was not repealed. After the Revolution, as before, common law denied married women the right to make wills, control their own earnings, or move away from their husbands. But in the new nation, Annis Boudinot Stockton wrote to her daughter, "the Empire of reason is not monopolized by man," and free women prided themselves on their virtue and self-restraint. Many argued that raising generations of virtuous citizens required educated, self-disciplined mothers, and their commitment to a special kind of female republicanism made long-standing female duties newly political. Free mothers made a virtue of their legal and political limitations by proclaiming their freedom from the corruptions of money and power that came with masculine political maneuvering.

Free black and white women also began cooperating with their husbands to reduce the number of children they bore, starting their families later, spacing their children's births, and ending childbearing by their mid-30s. They used methods already available, including prolonged breastfeeding and abstinence, as well as herbal medicines to avoid or end unwanted pregnancies. Their new focus on a smaller, intensively managed family began a long decline in fertility rates that would not appear in western Europe for another century.

Enslaved black women, in contrast, bore increasing numbers of children as their owners recognized that reproduction increased their wealth. Watchful owners encouraged the birth of more children into slavery and invested more in the health of the people they owned to boost the slave population.

manumission Process by which an individual owner frees an individual slave.

disestablishment Act of ending state support for particular churches.

Act for Establishing Religious Freedom Virginia law passed in 1786 creating separation between church and state.

civil rights Personal rights, often including freedom of speech and freedom from discrimination, to which all individuals are entitled.

Motherhood lost, rather than gained, political power for women in many eastern Indian tribes. The matrilineal Cherokees, for example, had long recognized the influence of mothers as negotiators and diplomats. "We are your Mothers; you are our sons," announced Nancy Ward (Nanye'hi) to the U.S. Treaty commissioners in Tennessee in 1781. "Our cry [is] all for Peace . . . Let your Women hear our Words." But the prolonged frontier fighting and accelerated wartime diplomacy of the late eighteenth century had elevated sacrifice in battle. European commanders seeking armed support increasingly rewarded young warrior chiefs with supplies rather than entering into diplomatic relations with warrior chiefs, clan chiefs, and matrons. As young warriors distributed those goods among their allied families and clans, they increased their power relative to older male and female leaders. Trade goods and warfare upset the familiar balance of authority between men and women as well as between generations in Indian communities.

7-1d Emerging Religious Freedoms

States separate religious and political authority.

Prior to the Revolution, religious toleration was uneven, and in most colonies, a single denomination's clergy were supported by taxes and assessed fees. People who wanted the freedom to pursue their own religious beliefs without such payments used revolutionary political upheaval to challenge the idea of state-supported or established churches. New Protestant denominations such as the Baptists had flourished since the Great Awakening of the mid-eighteenth century, and their adherents chafed at being taxed to pay establishment clergy. Gradually, state after state allowed residents to direct their taxes to a wider range of religious institutions. In some cases, state governments maintained a list of acceptable churches. Other states allowed taxpayers to choose which Protestant church (or, if they were Catholic or Jewish, which school or charity) was to receive their money. Eventually, states adopted **disestablishment**, and their governments stopped collecting taxes to pay ministers or maintain congregations. Instead, religious institutions competed openly for members and financial support.

In spite of the trend toward disestablishment, most states maintained legal preferences for Protestants and required testaments of religious belief from elected officials because lawmakers believed that piety and morality were essential to virtuous leadership. Even the radical Pennsylvania Constitution of 1776 required members of the General Assembly to swear belief in the Old and New Testaments as the word of God. Evidence of Christian belief, they maintained, was evidence of moral fitness for office.

Leading Virginians, however, where the established Episcopal Church had broken its organizational ties to the Church of England, began insisting on a stronger separation of church and state. James Madison and George Mason argued that each individual should be free to follow the religion of his or her choice. As they wrote in the 1776 Virginia *Declaration of Rights*: "all men are equally entitled to the free exercise of religion, according to the dictates of conscience; and that it is the mutual duty of all to practice Christian forbearance, love, and charity, towards each other." Thomas Jefferson introduced this sentiment to the Virginia assembly in 1779 and, as the **Act for Establishing Religious Freedom**, it passed into law in 1786. The act ended compulsory taxes to support churches, mandatory church attendance, and religious oaths for those serving in political offices. Under this law, religious authority and civil authority were strictly separate. In Virginia, those who were not Protestant Christians of any denomination could profess their beliefs with no effect on their **civil rights**.

7-2 Political Experiments in the Politics of Alliance

Iberfoto/Superstock

This 1763 painting by Miguel Cabrera, *From Spanish [man] and Mestiza [woman], Castiza*, was from a popular genre known as *casta* paintings that depicted the mixed-cultural relationships common in Spanish colonialism. These paintings both categorized people by race and asserted a multiplying variety of individuals born in colonial societies.

How does this painting use clothing, pose, and background to suggest the identity of the *castiza* child born in New Spain? Is it optimistic or pessimistic about this alliance? ▶

Most people who lived in the territory claimed by the United States experienced independence and political representation as a local phenomenon. Their alliances were to family, community, or state. But after 1783, American states, European empires, and Indian tribes all experimented with ways to construct larger alliances to replace those torn apart by the war for independence. To organize on this larger level, institutions had to be calibrated to bind people together, and individuals had to accept new identities. A Virginian had to decide she was an American; a Wind Clan Creek had to decide he was an Indian. New laws were only modestly successful in pushing personal transformations, in part because all of these entities were relatively weak and could not compel adherence.

☞ As you read, think about the broad consequences of political experimentation during and immediately after the American Revolution. How important was shared identity in holding governments or military alliances together?

7-2a Articles of Confederation

A written agreement loosely unites states to conduct the war.

The **Articles of Confederation**, written in the wake of the British occupation of Philadelphia and formally adopted by the Continental Congress in 1777, codified the U.S. government as a loose confederacy joined to fight a war for independence. They institutionalized Congress as a legislative body representing the states and responsible for their common defense, whose members were selected annually by local voters, special conventions, or state legislators. Congress had the power to print money and seek loans, regulate relations with Native American tribes, and conduct foreign policy, including declarations of war and peace. Congress was to establish a post office and fix standard weights and measures to facilitate trade among the states. Calling the United States of America "a firm league of friendship," the Articles also affirmed the states' sovereignty equality: Each had one vote in Congress. The men who drafted the Articles wanted to prevent the concentration of power that they felt had led to abuse under the British colonial system. Congress had no upper legislative body reserved for aristocrats but only a single elected house. There was no prime minister and no king. The President of the Congress presided but had no separate powers.

The Articles reserved so much power for the states that Congress had trouble raising money to fight the Revolution and handling diplomacy after the war was won. Congress could not tax; it could only request revenues from the states. Because amending the Articles required the unanimous support of all thirteen states, multiple measures proposed to cope with the financial crises, such as attempts to set a national **tariff** to raise money on imports, were squashed by a single state's no vote. Most states remained committed only to their individual interests. Interstate trade, for example, was impeded by competing currencies, import taxes, and regulations that each state maintained on its own behalf.

Articles of Confederation Agreement of thirteen states passed in November 1777 to establish a confederacy for the purpose of winning independence from Britain.

tariff Tax placed on imported goods, usually to protect domestic manufacturers by making them cheaper.

western lands Areas west of the Appalachian Mountains occupied by numerous Indian groups and claimed by multiple early states under their colonial charters.

Although the Articles established a league of equals, geography and colonial history gave some states advantages that could translate into greater power. Small states and those without long-standing colonial charter claims to lands beyond the Appalachians refused to ratify the Articles for years, fearing domination by their more populous neighbors. In fact, the Articles were not ratified by all of the states until March 1781, just six months before the Siege of Yorktown ended the war. Only when Virginia, which claimed vast expanses of northwestern land under its charter, promised to give its **western lands** to the United States as a whole under Congress did its neighbor Maryland sign the confederation agreement (see Map 7.1).

With limited powers over jealous, independent, and autonomous states, Congress under the Articles of Confederation was more successful fighting the war than managing the aftermath. Under its oversight, the United States achieved victory in the American Revolution. Its agents won concessions to the United States in the 1783 Treaty of Paris that ended the war with Great Britain. But peacetime diplomacy was a series of failures in the context of shifting Indian alliances and hostile Britain and Spain that still contested North American territory. Because it lacked the ability under the Articles to enforce its own treaty agreements, Congress could do little to counteract actions of Europeans or Native Americans. Power remained firmly in the hands of the states themselves, and their interests were local.

7-2b Native American Alliances

Eastern Indians re-establish alliances as fighting continues on the borderlands.

The 1783 Treaty of Paris negotiations did not acknowledge the tens of thousands of Indians who participated in the Revolutionary conflict and for most of them, documents signed in Europe did not end the war. Fighting continued with Chickamauga Cherokees and Shawnees embroiled in border warfare with South Carolinians and Georgians. Their war became the center

History without Borders

Vermillion

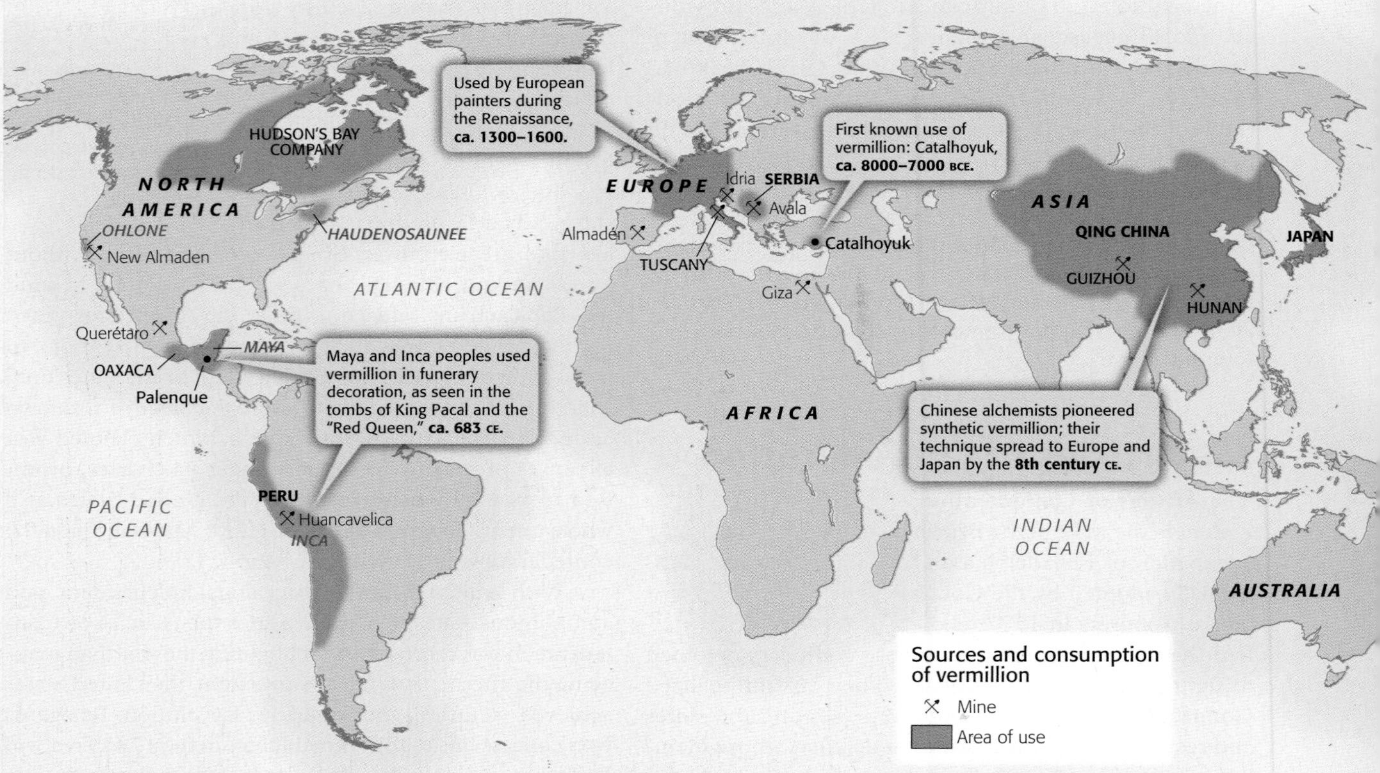

Significant Producers and Consumers of Vermillion, 8000 BCE–1800 People living near large deposits of cinnabar processed the pigment for cosmetic, decorative, and ceremonial uses. They also produced quantities for export overland and overseas, often relying on coerced labor because of the dangers of mercury poisoning. Synthetically produced vermillion also became a valuable trade good. ▲

In the eighteenth century, people around the world tapped into global trade networks because the goods they purchased improved their lives: Cooking was quicker in a bronze kettle, socializing centered on tea sweetened with sugar, and warfare was more deadly with muskets and gunpowder. Imported goods also played a role in emerging racial identities, as in the case of vermillion. Artists across the globe had long favored this orange-red pigment. Titian used it to color the gown Mary wore as she ascended to heaven in his Renaissance fresco. Qing Dynasty artists covered their carved boxes and ewers with vermillion lacquer.

A pigment of mercuric sulfide, vermillion came from two sources: powdered cinnabar, the naturally occurring ore, and an artificial process that synthesized mercury and sulfur. Mining the ore was dangerous work because of high levels of mercury, and Roman dealers sent slaves to dig it out of the rock in Almaden, Spain. Chinese chemists perfected the synthetic process in the eighth century, creating a valuable product that emperors treasured and traders sought out. Eighteenth-century records of the Hudson's Bay Company reveal that the pigment became an important part of the fur trade that connected Asia, Europe, and North America because Haudenosaunees and other Indians bought it to use for body paint, replacing the clay they had formerly used with an import that yielded more vivid hues.

Red body paint reinforced new ideas about Indian identity in the late eighteenth century. In the earliest encounters between Europeans and Native Americans, skin color garnered little attention; Indians and Europeans focused instead on differences in religion and daily life. By the end of the Revolution, however, Euro-Americans and Indians alike were dividing the world into groups of people identified as having "white," "red," or "black"

Dennis Cox/Alamy Stock Photo

Eighteenth-Century Chinese Carved Cinnabar Lacquerware To make lacquerware, Chinese artists covered wooden bowls, trays, and vases with lacquer, a tree resin colored with powdered mercury sulfide. They carved designs into the lacquer, creating objects that became desirable trade goods in Europe and North America, traveling alongside porcelain and silks. ◀

Charles Willson Peale/Independence National Historical Park

Joseph Brant In this 1797 portrait by Charles Willson Peale, Brant presents a different appearance than in the one in Chapter 6, painted by George Romney. Here his role as diplomat is prominent; he is unarmed and wearing the half-moon gorget he received earlier from the British government. Aware that the painting was intended for a collection of statesmen's portraits in Peale's Philadelphia Museum, Brant applied vermillion paint high on his cheekbones. ◀

skin. Those markers, in turn, were used to justify exclusion and separation. In the early nineteenth century, a Mikasuki chief told the governor of Florida that the Creator had initially made three men: one white, one black, and one red. He gave each a present. The white man, whom the Creator pitied, chose pens, paper, and instruments of learning. The red man, the Creator's favorite, chose weapons of war and hunting. The black man received axes, hoes, and buckets. He concluded that "the negro must work for both the red and white man, and it has been so ever since." Such explanations made racial identity seem a clear distinction of skin color, ability, and aptitude. In fact, however, as an earlier world of fluid racial identities was replaced with newer color lines, those identities were created and reinforced by global trade. North American merchants purchased redness from the Chinese to sell to the Indians.

Critical Thinking Questions

► How did globally traded goods assume different meanings for people in different locations?

► Why did people in the eighteenth century use purchased goods to communicate their sense of who they were? Did they do this differently than we do today?

Map 7.1 Western Lands Old colonial charters and competing Indian treaties created an overlapping patchwork of land claims in the western portion of the new United States. Turning that land into a reserve of potential future states owned by the United States as a whole was a significant diplomatic and economic goal of those who wanted to strengthen the confederation of united states. ▲

of a strengthened pan-Indian alliance ranging from the Creeks in the South to the Delawares in the Ohio River Valley to the Wyandots and Haudenosaunees in the North. In 1783, Indians from thirty-five native nations met at the Wyandot town of Sandusky to form an alliance. Their first goal was to roll the line of white settlement from the 1783 Treaty of Paris line back to the Ohio River border negotiated between the British and the Six Nations under the treaty of Fort Stanwix in 1768. Their larger aim was to forge a unified counterweight to American power. Among themselves, they agreed that none could sell land without the agreement of all. Looking outward, they knew that their alliance's ability to hold back the United States depended upon material support from European empires in North America.

In the North, this meant a continuing alliance with Great Britain, which still held Canada and refused to evacuate its forts on the Great Lakes. Joseph Brant, the Mohawk diplomat who had coordinated attacks with Britain during the Revolution, traveled again to London in 1785 to win British support against Euro-Americans' land claims, hoping that the British and allied Indians could make common cause against the United States. He returned with a pension, compensation for wartime losses, and a silver snuffbox but only vague promises for more. While actively seeking military support, the allied Native Americans also worked to make the United States think that they were more numerous and more strongly backed by Britain than they actually were. They spread stories of treaty meetings with the British and sent false messages by British officials still stationed in the West.

Indians in the South hoped that the Spanish, who now claimed Florida and the Louisiana territory, would provide similar leverage against the United States. Alexander McGillivray, a leader with a Creek mother and a Scottish father who had been educated in Charleston, South Carolina, dealt with the Spanish in Florida to request ammunition and support. Declaring that sovereignty over their land was one of Indians' "natural rights," McGillivray secured treaties that preserved Creek lands as a buffer between the United States and Spanish Florida. Working with the Creek National Council, which consisted of chiefs from multiple autonomous villages, he bolstered the power of Creek headmen over the traditional power of clans. McGillivray hoped that centralized power over warfare, captivity, and treaty making would strengthen Creeks as a nation and build the larger Indian alliance.

Although the British Empire had treated Haudenosaunees as spokesmen for a wide range of Indians, the United States wanted to divide and conquer individual tribes and villages by having their Indian agents meet with them separately. Piteasewa, a Shawnee speaker, countered in 1785 that "we are unanimous." The alliance was successful in forming war parties to push back white settlement in Georgia and Tennessee, but unity was always precarious. Individual Indian clans sometimes decided that a separate peace could buy them some relief from frontier warfare.

Indian alliances depended on strategic calculations, but they also increasingly drew on a sense of shared identity. Identity as Indians, unifiers argued, could combat others' efforts to seize more of their land. One group of Choctaws told the Creeks, "Brothers! . . . The same father made us all red people and desired us to live in peace . . . [I]f we continue united they can never take [our lands] from us." It was an ideology reinforced by the blood vengeance of frontier warfare during which American settlers indiscriminately raided both allied and enemy Indians.

7-2c Spanish North America after the War

Spain struggles to organize its American colonies for profit.

By the end of the American Revolution and the ensuing treaty settlements, Spain claimed vast territory in the Americas, including North America west of the Mississippi River, East and West Florida, much of Central and South America, and islands in the Caribbean including Cuba and Santo Domingo. Most valuable, and most closely governed, was the region in Mexico and to the south where large populations worked silver mines and ranches and paid taxes. In 1780, tens of thousands of Indians from multiple clans joined by *mestizos* rose up against Spanish rule and new imperial taxes in Peru and New Granada. The leader of the Peruvian revolt, Tupac Amaru, called on a shared Inca heritage to unify the insurgents and promised the return of Inca rule. The revolt turned into a house-by-house racial conflict that lasted until 1783 before pro-Spanish troops defeated it.

North of central Mexico, Spanish Texas and New Mexico consisted of presidios, towns, and missions surrounded and often dominated by Indian groups. Spanish political power was wielded by governors and Franciscan friars who competed for authority over the settlers and who often acted on their own, only later seeking approval from officials in Mexico City.

Comanches, Apaches, Caddos, and Wichitas had drawn both French traders from the north and Spanish officials into the Indian slave trade that was a key part of diplomacy and warfare in the region. These southwestern groups raided enemy communities to capture women and children, whom they then ransomed, traded as slaves, employed as slave labor, or incorporated into new families. Although enslaving and selling Indians was illegal in New Spain, trade in female captives became a key component of Spanish diplomacy. Spanish traders profited by selling Indian slaves in North America or transporting them to Havana. Retaliatory raids by Indians carried away Spanish and Indian women living in Spanish settlements. The children they bore with their captors became part of a growing *mestizo* population.

In asserting new domain over Louisiana, Spanish officials took an approach toward trade, settlement, and relationships with Native Americans that relied on negotiation as well as the exchange of goods and captives. British, French, and Indian traders along with American farmers used the interconnected Ohio, Missouri, and Mississippi Rivers to transport goods to New Orleans and from there to the Gulf of Mexico and the ocean. After the Seven Years' War, Spain had followed French practices of signing treaties with Native Americans as independent entities rather than declaring them subjects of the king. The diverse community of traders and agents made it difficult for Spain to unite its commercial and political goals for its North American colonies. The mixed loyalties of people who lived in Spanish Louisiana often thwarted Spanish efforts to retaliate against its European foes. When, at the end of the Revolution, Spain sought to deny British ships access to the central port of New Orleans, merchants in that city—many of whom were themselves British or French—violently opposed the measure.

The 1783 Treaty of Paris named the Mississippi River as the western boundary of the United States and granted the new nation right of access to trade on this major artery, worrying Spanish officials, who called people of the United States "active, industrious, and aggressive." As Spain moved to secure its borders from encroachment, it came to see the United States as more dangerous to its colonial holdings than England or France. In 1783, Britain signed East and West Florida over to Spain, rendering it a transcontinental power in North America. Yet the United States disputed the boundary of West Florida, and Georgia's government began selling land occupied by Creeks, Chocktaws, and Chickasaws to speculators (see Map 7.2).

In 1784, Spain closed the lower Mississippi River and the port of New Orleans to the United States, depriving backcountry settlers access to global markets. Instead, Spain offered land grants to lure white American settlers to migrate and become Spanish subjects. Spanish officials hoped that as these American farmers brought their African American slaves with them, the frontier trading community would develop into a profitable agricultural export economy. Spanish governors opened New Orleans to the international slave trade in order to support plantations of cotton and sugar, both of which depended on intensive slave labor, and, with tobacco and deerskins, became the most profitable crops in the lower Mississippi. These policies altered the population balance in the region as the numbers of white settlers and their slaves came to equal the number of Native Americans.

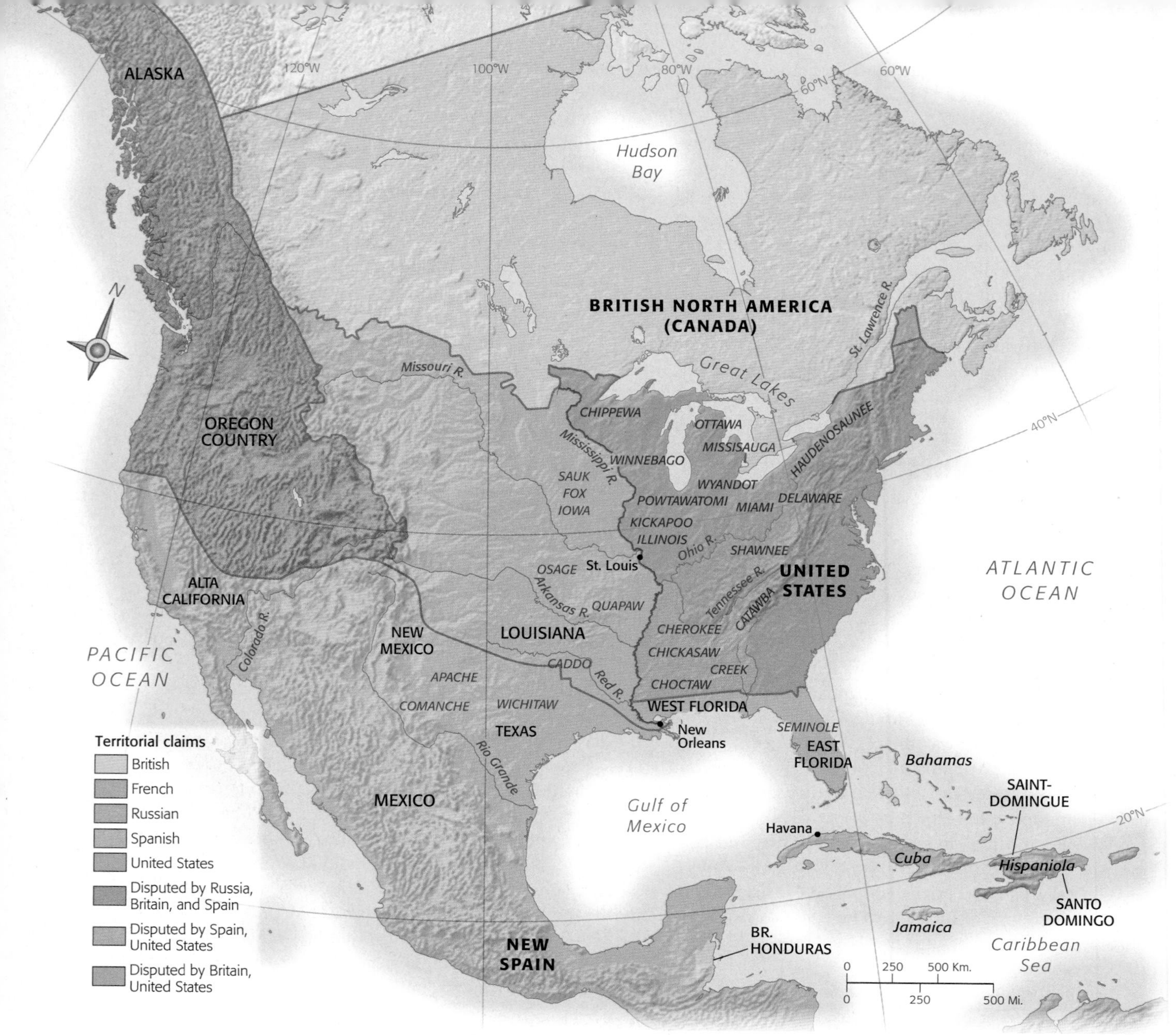

Map 7.2 Spanish America and Contested Borderlands, 1783 At the end of the American Revolution, the Spanish empire's territorial claims in the Americas were vast. Political borders drawn by overlapping treaties, as well as geographical boundaries such as the Mississippi River, created contested borderlands where Native American power and Indian alliances determined daily life, trade, and governance. ▲

New migrants were also potential allies against U.S. expansion from the east and ongoing raids by the powerful Osages and Apaches to the west. Spanish officials therefore welcomed the waves of Indian families from the Ohio River Valley and the Southeast, including Shawnees, Miamis, and Chickamauga Cherokees, who moved west of the Mississippi to live in Spanish-claimed territory. Eastern Indians likewise hoped the Spanish could provide a counterweight to U.S. expansion. In 1784, a delegation of allied Indians complained to the Spanish governor at St. Louis that the Americans were pushing into Indian lands "like a plague of locusts." The Spanish agreed.

Everett Collection Historical/Alamy Stock Photo

Global Americans **James Wilkinson** was born to an Irish family in Maryland in 1757. As a young man, he trained as a physician in Philadelphia before entering the Continental Army, where he was quickly promoted. In 1783, he moved to Kentucky as a merchant trader and property broker. Wilkinson dreamed of establishing an independent republic west of the Appalachians and in 1787 traveled to New Orleans to propose an independent Kentucky allied with Spain. Other western republics, he suggested, would break away from the United States and form a separate confederacy linked economically and politically with Spanish America along the Mississippi River. That scheme collapsed, but Wilkinson, commander of the U.S. Army, pursued other plans for an independent West. Appointed governor of the new Louisiana Territory in 1805, Wilkinson corresponded with Aaron Burr over a speculative plan to break Louisiana from the United States.

Court-martialed by President James Madison in 1811, Wilkinson was found not guilty and went on to be named U.S. envoy to Mexico where he promoted another war of independence, that of Mexico from Spain. He died in Mexico City in 1825, still hoping for a large personal land grant in Texas. His shifting identity and alliances, what his detractors called treachery and treason, were products of the mobile world of imperial rivalries and new republics in flux.

7-3 Postwar Migrations

Cato Rammsay carried this Loyalist Certificate when the British evacuated New York at the end of the American Revolution. Guy Carleton, commander-in-chief of British forces in North America in 1782, ordered the issuance of these "Birch Certificates" to secure the passage of black Americans freed by the wartime promises of the British army. Samuel Birch, who signed most of them, was the last commandant of New York City under British occupation.

What freedoms does this certificate grant Cato Rammsay and on what basis? ▶

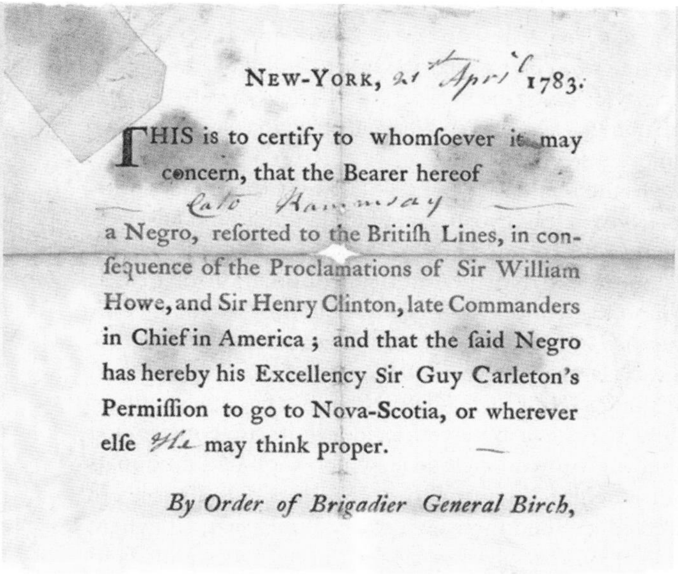

NEW-YORK, 21st April 1783.

THIS is to certify to whomſoever it may concern, that the Bearer hereof Cato Rammsay a Negro, reſorted to the Britiſh Lines, in conſequence of the Proclamations of Sir William Howe, and Sir Henry Clinton, late Commanders in Chief in America; and that the ſaid Negro has hereby his Excellency Sir Guy Carleton's Permiſſion to go to Nova-Scotia, or wherever elſe He may think proper.

By Order of Brigadier General Birch,

Black Loyalist Heritage Society

Certificate of Freedom, 1783

The American Revolution unleashed unprecedented migration in North America. Fighting in the countryside sent tens of thousands of refugees into the cities. Indians allied with the British fled to Niagara, Detroit, and St. Louis. White Loyalists and their slaves lived under protection of British garrisons in New York City, Charleston, and Savannah, but when the British were defeated, these people became refugees who were ultimately dispersed throughout the then smaller British Empire. The end of the war also ended British restrictions on settlement and trade, releasing new waves of voluntary migration west. Merchants and sailors, like those on the *Empress of China*, sought new trading partners to replace British monopolies. Blacks freed from slavery by gradual emancipation laws or individual owners migrated to U.S. cities in search of paid work and mutual support.

☞ As you read, compare the various postwar migrations of groups and individuals. How did these migrations, both forced and voluntary, reshape American societies? How did the departure of some change the communities left behind?

7-3a Loyalist Diaspora

Loyalists in exile reshape the British Empire.

Men and women who had supported the losing side in the Revolution faced tough options at the war's end. Some, uprooted and with their property seized by patriots, lived on temporary pensions funded by the British treasury while hoping to go back to their old lives. Others remained on their land and claimed that they had been neutral. Slave-owning Loyalists moved to the Caribbean to secure their property rights in exile. Slavery had been challenged as illegal in Britain since a 1772 court decision, but it remained widespread in British colonies. Between 1783 and 1785, the population of the Bahamas increased by almost seven thousand people, largely slaves taken from the rice swamps of South Carolina and Georgia to work in the sugar cane fields.

Black Loyalists, most of whom were former slaves freed during wartime, struggled to establish themselves as loyal citizens deserving refugee rights. Former owners insisted they were illegally seized property; British soldiers sometimes sold them or bestowed them as spoils of war. Many black Loyalists were ill equipped to defend their freedom in court or to recover wartime losses. When William Cooper claimed he had lost a house and land worth £500, the commission in charge of hearing claims dismissed him: "all these blacks say that they were free born and that they had property, two things that are not very probable; we did not believe one syllable of his case." But British institutions were black Loyalists' best chance to claim their freedom. The Earl of Dunmore, former Virginia governor who had issued the first promise of freedom to slaves who joined the king's forces, became governor of the Bahamas and created a "Negro Court" to rule on cases of contested freedom there.

In the final evacuation, about sixty thousand Loyalists left with the British, taking fifteen thousand enslaved people with them (see Map 7.3). Together, 2.5 percent of the British North American population dispersed around the world. One-third went to the Canadian communities of Nova Scotia, New Brunswick, and Quebec, as well as new settlements that Britain had established for them. South of Halifax, Nova Scotia, one group of white Loyalists received land grants to construct a brand-new town, Shelburne, which soon had a population of eight thousand people. Black Loyalists were directed to build their own town, Birchtown, elsewhere on Port Roseway harbor. Many did not receive the land grants promised to war veterans. Looking for a more secure footing in freedom, a third of the free black community emigrated within a decade to **Sierra Leone**, a British colony on the west coast of Africa sponsored by British antislavery activists. Located a few miles from Bunce Island, a major British slave-trading fort, the colony of Sierra Leone promised migrants land, opportunities for trade, and the chance to live in a "Province of Freedom" although still under white leaders. It was a kind of qualified freedom that would be familiar to men and women freed from slavery in North America.

Great Britain saw West Africa as a potential resettlement colony for criminals as well as for loyal free blacks. The loss of its North American colonies meant that Britain could no longer exile thousands of its convicts, most of whom had been convicted of petty property crimes, to North American ports. For a short time, the country experimented with an ill-fated venture that sent these men and women to West Africa, to operate the forts that collected and traded captured slaves. When this failed, Britain developed a prison colony in New South Wales, Australia, in 1788. First claimed for Britain by Captain James Cook in 1770, the new colony further redirected the flow of people and goods from the Atlantic empires into the Pacific.

Sierra Leone West African British colony created as a refuge for freed slaves.

7-3b Free Black Communities

Free blacks form urban communities.

Most black Americans did not leave with the British, remaining instead enslaved in the newly independent United States. But gradual emancipation and manumissions swelled the numbers of free black people, who congregated in cities. Before the Revolution, free blacks in the British North American colonies were only one-tenth of 1 percent of the U.S. population, but by 1820, they represented 2.5 percent (see Table 7.2). Many did similar kinds of work in freedom that they had done in slavery, especially hard manual labor and domestic service. In southern cities, some ran shops or negotiated their own work as carters or laundresses, and many supplemented meager wages with odd jobs and small street sales of food. Husbands and wives rented rooms in houses belonging to

Table 7.2 Free People of Color in 1790

The greatest concentrations of free people of color in the new United States were in the middle coastal states of Delaware, Maryland, New Jersey, Pennsylvania, and Virginia. Rhode Island had a high percentage of free blacks although the overall number of people was not large. Both the size of the community and their relationship to the white population shaped daily life for free people of color.

State	Free People of Color	Percentage of Total Population (%)
Connecticut	2,808	1.2
Delaware	3,899	6.6
Georgia	398	0.5
Kentucky	114	0.2
Maryland	8,043	2.5
Massachusetts	5,463	1.4
New Hampshire	630	0.4
New Jersey	2,762	1.5
New York	4,654	1.4
North Carolina	4,975	1.3
Pennsylvania	6,537	1.5
Rhode Island	3,407	5.0
South Carolina	1,801	0.7
Vermont	255	0.3
Virginia	12,866	1.7

Source: 1790 U.S. Census.

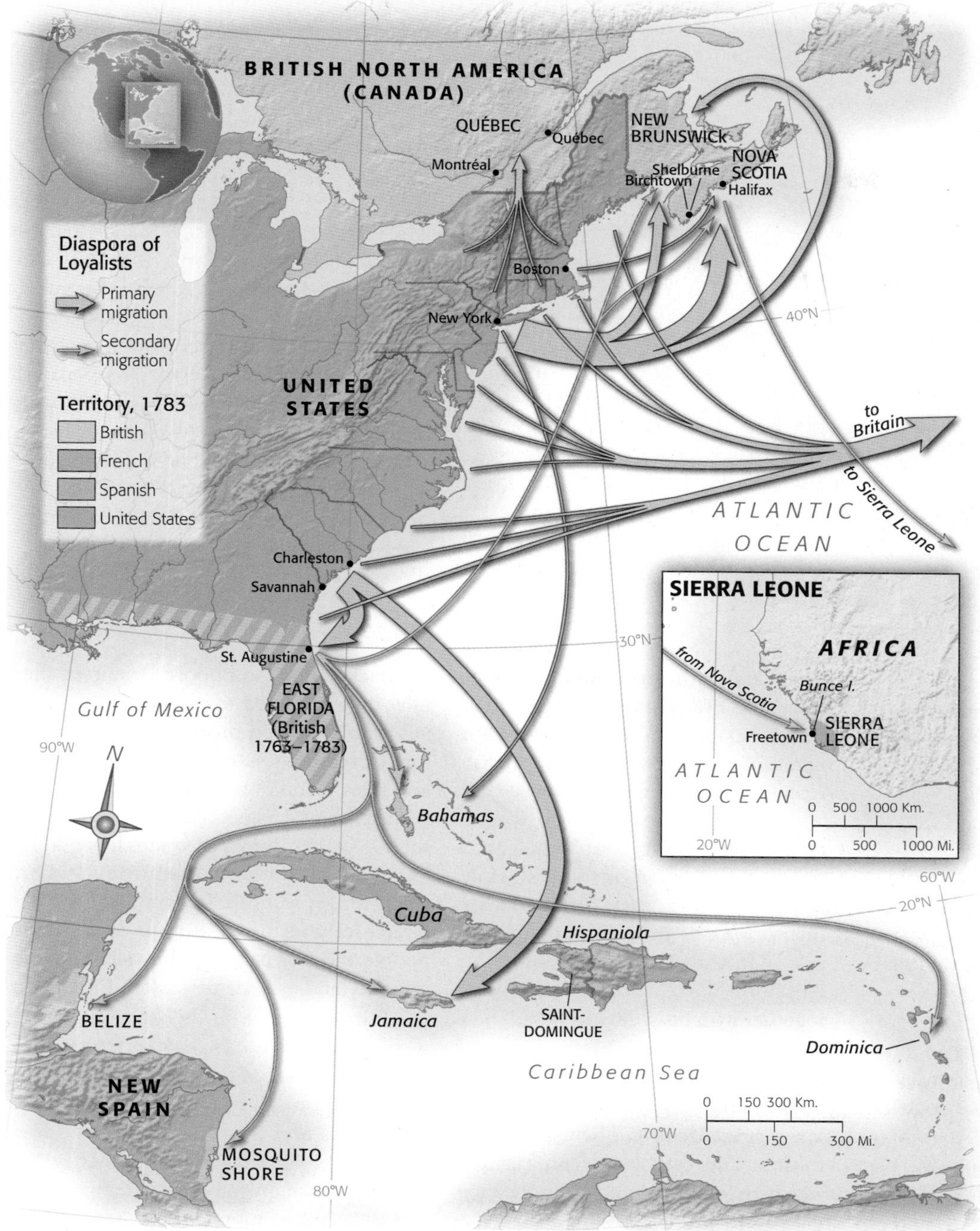

Map 7.3 The Global Loyalist Diaspora, 1783–1793 During and after the American Revolution, a total of 60,000 free Loyalists—black and white—left the United States, taking 15,000 slaves with them. Many migrated more than once. Refugees who settled in East Florida migrated a second time to the Caribbean and elsewhere when Britain returned Florida to Spanish control with the Treaty of Paris. Likewise, free blacks in Nova Scotia sought a better life in Sierra Leone. ▲

whites, scraping together income from multiple jobs. Free blacks with family members still in slavery sought to earn enough to purchase them, a process that required years of savings and, in some cases, careful petitions to state authorities.

In leaving behind slavery, free men and women created new identities, starting with new names. They shed the degrading nicknames of slavery—"Fortune," "Cesar," "Mistake"—for full, often English-sounding names such as Thomas or Sarah. They selected last names for the first

Library of Congress Prints and Photographs Division[LC-DIG-ppmsca-02947]

Global Americans The girl who grew up to be **Phillis Wheatley** was born in West Africa, "Gambia" as she remembered it, and captured into slavery around the age of seven. Massachusetts slave trader Timothy Fitch paid to transport her to North America on a voyage in which 25 percent of her fellow captives died. Purchased by the Wheatley family of Boston and named Phillis, the name of the ship she disembarked, she became a house slave. The Wheatleys oversaw her conversion to Christianity, and their daughter Mary taught her to read English and Latin and to write. In 1767, Phillis published her first poem. In 1773, when she was about 20 years old, she traveled to London to publish and promote a volume of her work; while there, she met Benjamin Franklin and secured her own manumission. Back in the United States, Wheatley became a celebrated patriot poet. Her poem "To His Excellency George Washington" depicted the Revolution as a worldwide cause against Britain's "thirst of boundless power."

In 1778 she married John Peters, a free black shopkeeper, and had several children, all of whom died young. Caught in the postwar economic depression with her husband frequently jailed for debt, she supported her remaining child by working as a servant and living in a boardinghouse. Frustrated in her attempts to publish a second volume of poetry, she died in 1784, around the age of 31 and was buried alongside her last child in an unmarked grave, her death a testament to the difficulty of free black lives after slavery.

Free African Society Organization established in multiple U.S. cities by former slaves after the Revolution to pool resources and start schools.

Treaty of Fort Stanwix of 1784 First forced treaty between Indians and the United States after the Revolution that gave up Six Nation claims to the Ohio Valley but was rejected by Indians living there.

time, and although some, such as Elizabeth Freeman, proclaimed their transformation with a descriptive last name, most selected common English names such as Smith or Brown.

Former slaves were no longer owned as property, but they lacked political and civil rights within white society. Instead, they founded new institutions to provide the support that white institutions would not. Absalom Jones, a former slave who together with his wife purchased their own freedom, and Richard Allen, a black Methodist minister, founded Philadelphia's **Free African Society** in 1787. Similar societies appeared in other northern cities, adopting "African" as a new shared identity. They sponsored schools for black children and established mutual aid funds to assist members with loans and charity in the face of illness and poverty.

7-3c The Trans-Appalachian West

U.S. and Indian migrants struggle over who should "settle" the West.

Even before the ink was dry on the 1783 Treaty of Paris, white Americans flooded across the Appalachians, especially to the Ohio country and the Tennessee River Valley, deep in the southern borderlands. As they moved, they hunted extensively, driving the bison out of Kentucky by the end of the century. They also transformed the landscape with farms and fenced pastures. Their desire for land in the West had motivated many in the backcountry to oppose Britain in the first place, and now they expected to reap the benefits of victory. Veterans who had been promised land in exchange for enlistment pressured states to open territory to development and sales. Land ownership, they insisted, would give them security as well as political and financial independence. In the 1780s, two-thirds of whites living in Kentucky did not own land but rather rented from landlords, an ominous trend for revolutionaries who believed that the lord-and-tenant relationships of Europe encouraged tyranny. Many people did not wait for the state and the surveyors but claimed land as squatters, often fighting to stay put.

Already living on the land west of the Appalachians were tens if not hundreds of thousands of Indians, including many displaced refugees from the Revolution who had moved west to escape being killed and the destruction of their fields and towns. A significant portion of Haudenosaunees followed Joseph and Molly Brant to refuge in Canada, but many moved onto land no longer under nominal British dominion and protection. As they moved and regrouped, they formed multiethnic communities along backcountry rivers.

The U.S. government insisted that Indian allies of the British were a defeated enemy with no right to live, farm, or hunt on land won by the United States. Like the white Loyalists (who were acknowledged in treaty negotiations), these Indians had forfeited their rights to property by choosing the losing side in the Revolution. To assert its claim to the spoils of war, the United States negotiated a series of Indian treaties at gunpoint. The second **Treaty of Fort Stanwix of 1784** was typical. When Haudenosaunee representatives tried to insist that the Ohio River, not the Mississippi, was the western boundary of the United States, they were told "You are a subdued people" who "stand out *alone* against our *whole* force." The fact that neither the Haudenosaunees nor the United States had the undisputed authority to negotiate over these lands, which were claimed by New York and Pennsylvania and were home to Senecas, caused more problems for the Indians who signed away lands than for the Americans who gained them. Haudenosaunee negotiators returned home to face angry Senecas who insisted that the Haudenosaunee delegates could not speak for them.

Federal commissioners exploited such divisions within Indian groups. Similar treaties took land from Delawares, Wyandots, and others at Fort McIntosh in 1785 and from Senecas at Fort Finney in 1786. Even Indians who had fought on the patriot side, such as the Pequots in Rhode Island and the Oneidas in New York, were forced to sign treaties by state and federal commissioners and burdened with neighbors who disregarded their property rights.

Treaty of Fort Stanwix, 1784 Both Haudenosaunee chiefs and U.S. agents signed and placed vermillion wax seals at the bottom of this treaty page. The treaty, which ceded the Ohio country to the United States, recognized each of the Six Nations as sovereign states and established the first Indian reservation in the United States. The United States ratified the treaty in 1785; the Six Nations never did. ▼

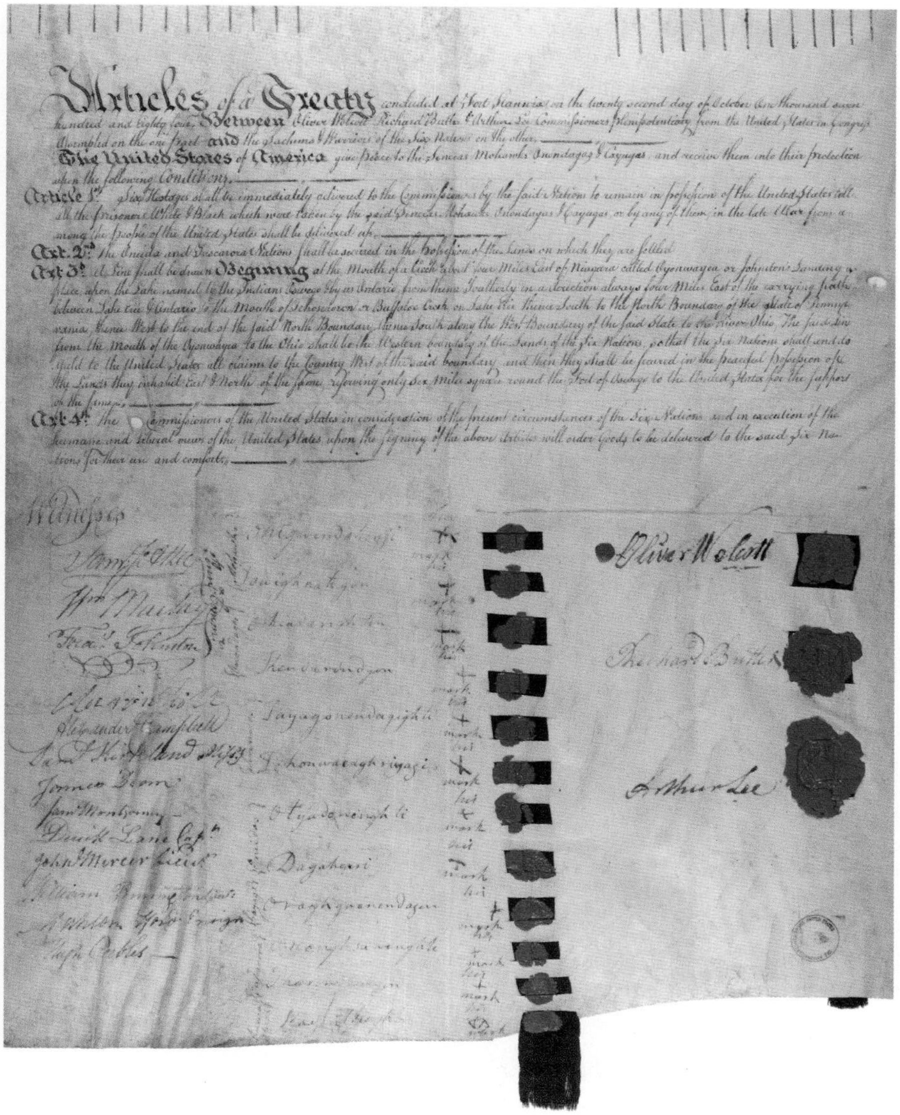
Articles of a Treaty concluded at Fort Stanwix on the twenty second day of October one thousand seven hundred and eighty four. Between ... The United States of America ...

National Archives

7-3d Pacific Connections

Traders spread commerce and disease.

Ships and crews that had fought in the American Revolution turned to ocean trade after the war, freed from British trade restrictions but also no longer protected by British monopolies or the British navy. Investors hoped that by developing independent trade relations with China, the United States could integrate itself into the Pacific Rim trading world. The Pacific Ocean had been a conduit of trading voyages for many years. In the Spanish-occupied Philippines, traders exchanged silver from Spanish mines in South America for Chinese luxury goods. In the icy waters of the North Pacific, Russian and Native American traders exchanged sea otter pelts. In 1778, British explorer Captain Cook sailed from the Pacific islands of southeast Asia toward the west coast of North America, searching for the Northwest Passage that would connect Asia, America, and Europe by an all-water route. Reports of his encounters in the Hawai'ian Islands, the territory of Alaska, and the Pacific Northwest spread interest in trade in the rest of the world.

The traders who followed Cook helped establish an expanded region of Pacific commerce linking North America, Asia, and Europe. The Spanish controlled ports in Alta California and dominated supply ships from Mexico through the early 1800s, but U.S. merchants soon came to predominate in the volume of Pacific trade, which involved traders from two dozen countries. Alta California was by the early nineteenth century a transit point where trade ships stopped to obtain sea otter pelts, timber, fish, and other commodities collected by Native Americans before heading along the Northwest coast to Alaska or to Hawai'i. Even more than in the Atlantic, entrepreneurs frequently evaded imperial boundaries and laws to create an international trading world.

Traders also brought diseases, such as tuberculosis, syphilis, and smallpox, with devastating results for Indian populations. Indigenous Pacific peoples quickly grasped the connection between disease and trading vessels. Cook islanders who fell ill developed the phrase *kua pai au*, or "I am shippy," to describe their suffering and pinpoint the obvious agent of their illnesses: the

Ledyard described the walrus hunt that was part of Cook's voyage.

SSPL/Getty Images

Global Americans Born in Connecticut in 1751, **John Ledyard** studied to be a missionary to Native Americans but instead joined a trading voyage to see the world. After stints in the British navy and army, he served as a marine officer on British Captain Cook's third exploratory voyage around the Pacific. His 1783 account of Cook's 1779 death in Hawai'i at the hands of Pacific natives was the first book to receive a copyright in the United States.

Having seen the commercial potential of Pacific trade first hand, Ledyard dreamed of leading a sea voyage across a Northwest Passage to trade in Asia. Philadelphia merchant Robert Morris eventually funded a voyage using Ledyard's scheme of trading furs for Chinese porcelain and silk and sent his ship, the *Empress of China*, to Canton. In 1785, conversations in Paris with Benjamin Franklin, Thomas Jefferson, and the Marquis de Lafayette inspired Ledyard to undertake an overland trip through Siberia that was intended to cross Alaska and end in Virginia but was cut short in Yakutsk by suspicious Russian authorities. As he met native Asian people in Siberia, he concluded that they were related to North American Indians, and historians who had "written the History of Man have begun at the wrong end."

Funded by a British antislavery activist, Ledyard took a final journey to follow the Niger River in Africa, where he died in Cairo in 1789. His global travels linked exploration, imperial influence, and commercial opportunity. Ledyard himself insisted he was "commissioned by myself to serve the World at large."

trading ships. Rates of infertility and death rose dramatically along indigenous trading routes as virgin soil epidemics spread into the interior of Indian country.

Terrible losses of life from disease forced new migrations and relationships. From the late 1770s to the 1780s, a smallpox epidemic transmitted by soldiers in the East, fur traders in Canada, and horse raiders across the plains spread across North America. When it hit previously unexposed settlements of Indians in the interior, death rates were far higher than was typical in Europe, wiping out entire villages. The epidemic of the 1780s killed as much as 80 percent of the population of the agrarian Mandans, Hidatsas, and Chipeweyans living in the Northern Plains. Sioux records referred to the 1779–1780 season as "Smallpox Used Them Up Winter." Those who survived moved west into lands emptied by dead and fleeing neighbors. The Sioux came to dominate their new territory on the northern and central plains, hunting and trading buffalo in mobile bands on horseback.

7-4
Power in Crisis

Congress printed this Continental one-third of a dollar designed by Benjamin Franklin to finance the American Revolution. It was the first American paper money to be in dollar denominations rather than pounds, shillings, and pence. After the war, the value of these dollars fell so dramatically people began to use the phrase "not worth a Continental" when talking about useless things.

What does the image of linked rings surrounding a sun suggest about the political and financial bonds of the states? ▶

CMSP Education/Newscom

Wartime dislocations contributed to an economic depression in the 1780s. During war, farms produced less for national and international markets, and plantation production sharply declined as thousands of enslaved people fled to the British. The costs of war heightened these difficulties. It was a bitter truth that to pay for a war opposing British taxation, American states had to raise their own taxes to new highs. In a republic where the people taxed themselves, the implications of popular sovereignty were felt keenly in the pocketbook, and the result was social turmoil in North America and vulnerability abroad. In another ironic twist, freedom from the British trading empire also meant isolation from the benefits of trade within the empire, and Americans struggled to establish trade connections in a world still influenced by mercantilism. Some thought the answer lay in enlarging the United States itself.

☞ As you read, consider the ways that debt, access to land, and political power were connected in the 1780s. How did people seek political solutions to their economic crises? Who succeeded and who was ignored?

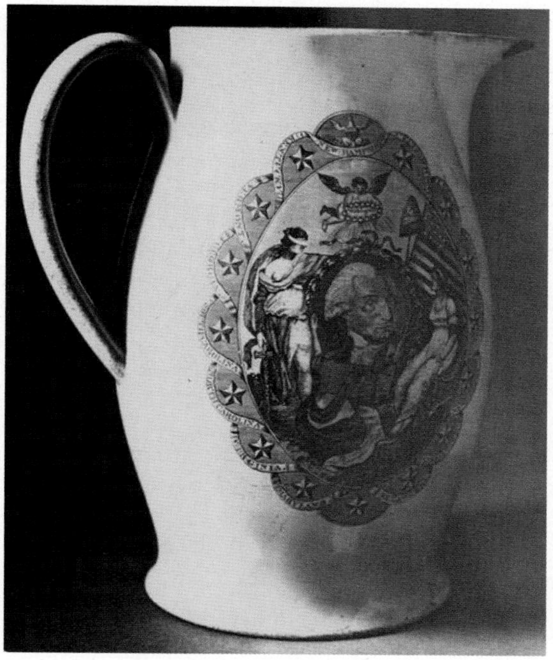

Brayton, George/The New York Public Library Digital Collections

Patriotic Dishware Produced in Britain, circa 1800 As they had before the Revolutionary War, British craftsmen made objects specifically for American markets, such as this jug featuring George Washington's portrait, surrounded by the figures of liberty and justice. Purchasing British imports such as these sunk postwar Americans deeper into debt. ▲

7-4a Trade within and around Imperial Systems

Americans struggle to establish new international trading circuits in a world plagued by war debt.

Once the war was over, British merchants flooded American markets with finished goods. The patriotic efforts of the nonimportation and nonconsumption movements fell away and were replaced with eager purchasing after years of deprivation. British ceramics manufacturers revitalized their own industry by creating patriotic dishware decorated with eagles and images of George Washington that they sold to American consumers. Personal debt grew with the new purchases, sparking a familiar call from political leaders for women to purify the nation through self-sacrifice. "Feathers and fripperies suit the Cherokees," one wrote, but they were inappropriate for "the fair daughters of independent America." Groups of free women once again took up the cause of virtuous restraint in consumption, signing agreements to dress simply as an example to all.

Planters in South Carolina and Georgia resumed the importation of Africans as slaves in 1783 after a wartime suspension of the trade. Tens of thousands of slaves had died, escaped, or been evacuated over the course of the war. In some regions, half of the slaves—representing labor and capital—were lost to owners. One Savannah merchant observed that to replace them, "the Planter will as far in his power sacrifice every thing to attain Negroes." To meet the high demand, slave traders from Great Britain, France, Denmark, the Netherlands, and the United States shipped 11,000 enslaved people into South Carolina and Georgia from Africa and the Caribbean between 1783 and 1785. In 1787, now with an oversupply, South Carolina closed the trade again.

Consumers in the United States were eager to buy British manufactured goods and cargoes of African people, but imperial trade laws made it difficult to earn the money to do so. Britain closed the British West Indies, which had remained loyal, to American ships, ending the lucrative trade of fish, grain, and livestock in exchange for sugar and molasses that had enriched colonial merchants. The French were not able to fill the gap by providing the same kind of long-term credit with which all trade was conducted. Yet there was little Congress could do to address the intertwined trade and diplomatic problems. Under the Articles of Confederation, Congress lacked power over commerce, so it could not close U.S. ports to British traders in retaliation for the British ban. Because Americans bought more than they sold internationally, they had to send scarce **specie** (gold and silver) out of the country to pay for their goods. The result was a staggering trade deficit in the millions (see Figure 7.2). An indebted nation was a weak nation. In 1783, British Lord Sheffield published a pamphlet on American commerce stating that the United States "should not be, for a long time, either to be feared or regarded as a nation."

specie Gold and silver coins preferred for payments that were believed to have a more stable, intrinsic value than other forms of money.

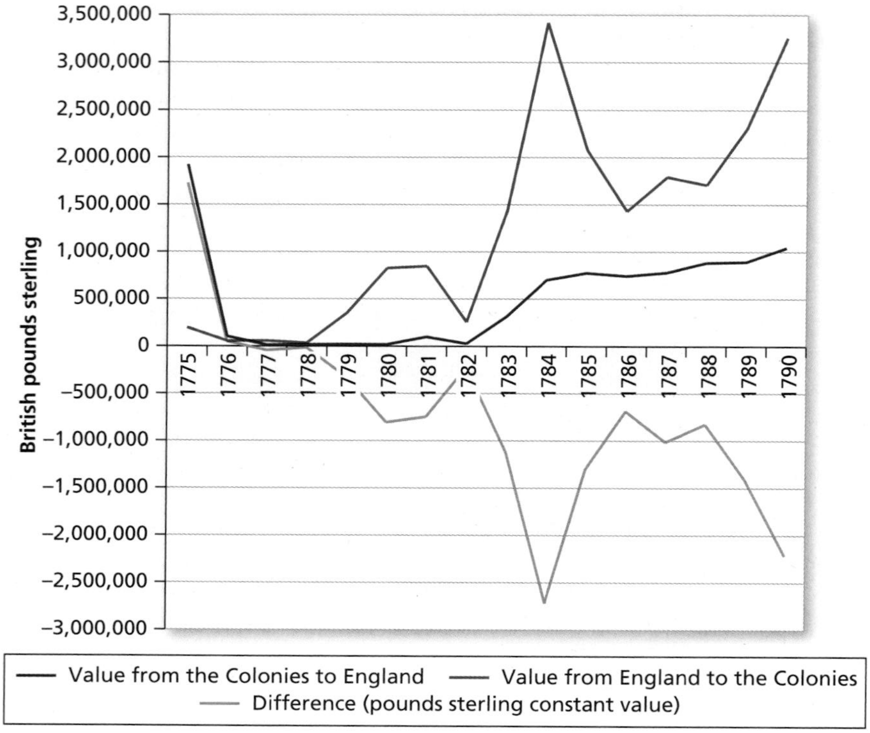

Figure 7.2 Trade Deficit with England Just as the Revolutionary War broke out, the value of goods that Britain's thirteen North American colonies exported to England was higher than the value of the goods imported from England. As the war ended, the United States resumed importing English goods, sending the new country deep into debt to its former empire. ▲ Source: *Historical Statistics of the United States*, millennial ed. Cambridge University Press, 2006.

7-4b American Debt Crisis

Government debts threaten political stability at the national level.

Congress paid for the American Revolution by borrowing money from European allies, printing paper money, and issuing promissory notes. France loaned the United States $7 million and gave several million more outright. Dutch investors loaned $2.8 million at the end of the war. Following a practice of British colonies during earlier eighteenth-century wars, Congress paid salaries and military costs with paper money, known as **bills of credit**. It declared these bills to be legal tender, meaning that people could use them, rather than specie, to pay their debts. And it planned to redeem bills of credit with specie collected from the states, which had been charged with taxing their residents to pay for the war. States, struggling to recruit and equip soldiers themselves, sent very little to Congress. Congress printed more bills, called Continentals, but they were backed by nothing more than the hope of future tax payments from the states, which were not forthcoming. Military losses undermined faith in Congress, and counterfeiting undermined faith in Continentals, whose purchasing power plummeted. By the end of the war, Congress was ordering states to accept the bills at 2.5 percent of their printed face value. Creditors rejected paper money, and the very state governments that had printed their own bills of credit refused to accept them.

bills of credit Issued by the Continental Congress and states to fund the American Revolution, paper money backed by the promise of future tax payments.

war bonds Interest-bearing notes used in exchange for money, supplies, and labor given to the revolutionary cause on which governments paid interest but could not redeem after the war.

To supplement the nearly worthless Continentals, Congress (and the states) used a variety of promissory notes to pay soldiers, farmers, and other wartime suppliers. By the end of the war, Congress had converted these notes to interest-bearing **war bonds** that it was unable to redeem. Rachel Wells of New Jersey petitioned Congress in 1786 to repay her war bond loan because "I have done as much to carry on the war as many that now sit at the helm of government." Desperate to pay their bills and rebuild their farms and businesses, bondholders sold them at a discount to speculators in exchange for usable money. Abigail Adams was a dedicated bond speculator who bought up such bonds at reduced prices. Profits were guaranteed for those who, like Adams, were wealthy enough to invest. Governments paid her interest on the face value of the bonds, not on the discounted price she had paid for them. Meanwhile, the farmers, widows, and soldiers who had originally received the war bonds lost their investment in the revolutionary effort.

At the war's end, paying interest on war bonds alone took up two-thirds of the money most states collected in taxes. Because that money was the only revenue available to run the U.S. government, state debts raised serious questions about the continued existence of the country. With no independent power to tax, Congress was unable to meet international obligations. If the United States could not pay back France, Spain, and the Netherlands for money borrowed during the Revolution, would those countries send troops to collect? Britain refused to remove its soldiers from western American forts until the United States repaid money owed to British merchants and Loyalists whose property had been seized. Furthermore, how could the United States attract foreign investors if it could not collect its own taxes?

Thomas Jefferson, serving as U.S. envoy in Paris, tried to interest French aristocrats in loaning money to Americans for land speculation, canal building, or other developments, but money was tight everywhere. Commerce had slowed for everyone during the war as British naval blockades had disrupted the business of Spanish, French, and Dutch merchants. These countries had all borrowed money from banks and private financiers to fight the war, and as much as half of their governments' income was spent on repaying that debt. European governments, like the United States, raised taxes. In France, a new finance minister proposed a stamp tax and new land taxes that would obligate nobles to pay for the debts rising out of a century of imperial wars. Nobles refused to give up their privileges, ultimately sparking another round of Atlantic revolutions that began in Paris in 1789.

7-4c Popular Uprisings

Western farmers violently protest debt, taxes, and unrepresentative government.

States responded to the debt crisis by raising taxes to three or four times higher than they had been before the war and insisting that they be paid in scarce specie. Debtors pushed back. Conflicts reminiscent of the mid-eighteenth-century Regulator movement broke out between western farmers and the merchant-dominated legislators along the coast. In 1786, the Massachusetts legislature passed one of the harshest new taxes on people and on property to pay off war bond debt. Those who could not pay had their property seized; if that was not sufficient to pay the debt, they were sent to jail, even for small sums.

Western Massachusetts farmers, mobilized in public meetings, protested the tax and its enforcement by closing the courthouses from which arrest warrants and property foreclosures were issued. The dissidents freed debtors and protestors from jail, carrying liberty poles and other emblems from the Revolutionary era. Many of the protestors were Revolutionary War veterans, still waiting for their back pay and desperate to find new markets for farm products because trade with the British Caribbean was closed. In January 1787, one veteran, Daniel Shays, led a group of more than one thousand protestors against the federal armory in Springfield to capture weapons and ammunition for their cause. A force of militiamen funded by Boston merchants engaged them, killing four and chasing the rest across New England for weeks.

Although Boston elites called the event **Shays's Rebellion**, the depth of unrest went beyond a single leader. A similar uprising in Greenbrier County, Virginia, broke out in the spring of 1787 when western farmers blocked the courthouse doors to prevent judges from issuing warrants to collect overdue taxes. The immediate goal of both uprisings was debt relief and in both cases, it was met. In Massachusetts, voters replaced the existing legislators with new men who pardoned the remaining rebels and enacted debtor relief laws. These laws reduced financial pressure on average people by letting them pay taxes in paper money, reduced the legal payments owed to bond speculators, and extended the amount of time debtors had to repay their debts. In Virginia, the legislature responded to the rebellion by repealing the tax that had sparked it.

The larger issues motivating these revolts were the responsiveness of state governments to the needs of average people and the right to determine what those needs were. Massachusetts's state constitution, like many written or rewritten in the 1780s, was conservative in apportioning power to its citizens. Although earlier constitutions, such as the Pennsylvania Constitution of 1776, had attempted to make government as responsive as possible to the people, representatives soon discovered that grassroots pressure made tax collection and tight money control difficult. By 1790, even Pennsylvania had revised its constitution to give the state government more centralized and executive power. Protestors, sensing that the government was no longer accessible through its elected representatives, took popular sovereignty into the streets.

Jefferson, U.S. minister to Paris at the time, considered these uprisings as a normal part of democratic governments. He wrote to James Madison that for the health of elected governments, "a little rebellion now and then is a good thing." But to elites in the United States, rebellion against elected government was deeply troubling. The problems of the 1780s, reported Alexander Hamilton of New York and Elbridge Gerry of Massachusetts to their fellow representatives in Congress, were due to an "excess of democracy."

7-4d Northwest Territory

Political experiment in the Northwest provides a blueprint for U.S. expansion.

To the men in Congress, selling Indian land in exchange for war bonds seemed to be a way out of the debt crisis that would simultaneously provide economic opportunities to disgruntled farmers and reward Revolutionary War veterans. The Confederation government pinned its hopes on 160 million acres of land north of the Ohio River, which had been violently contested for decades. But to achieve their goals, they had to work with the divided confederacies of the United States itself and of allied American Indians.

First, the United States had to assert national power over treaty making in the region. Massachusetts, Connecticut, and Virginia claimed parts of the territory under their old colonial charters and were reluctant to relinquish these rights and the potential profits from land sales to a shaky confederation of states. Between 1784 and 1802, states formally ceded their claims to the United States as a whole. Next, Congress had to establish a plan for surveying and selling land at auction. In the optimistic **Land Ordinance of 1785**, Congress divided the territory into a grid of six-square-mile townships, divided into 640-acre sections that could be sold individually (see Map 7.4). The hope was that by selling some smaller parcels directly, American farmers, as well as land speculators, could take ownership.

The orderly plan immediately clashed with reality on the ground.

Shays's Rebellion Insurrection by Western Massachusetts farmers (1786–1787) protesting harsh taxes, lack of adequate representation, and money policies that favored East Coast elites.

Land Ordinance of 1785 Congressional plan for land north of the Ohio River that divided the region into townships and lots to be sold to settlers and speculators.

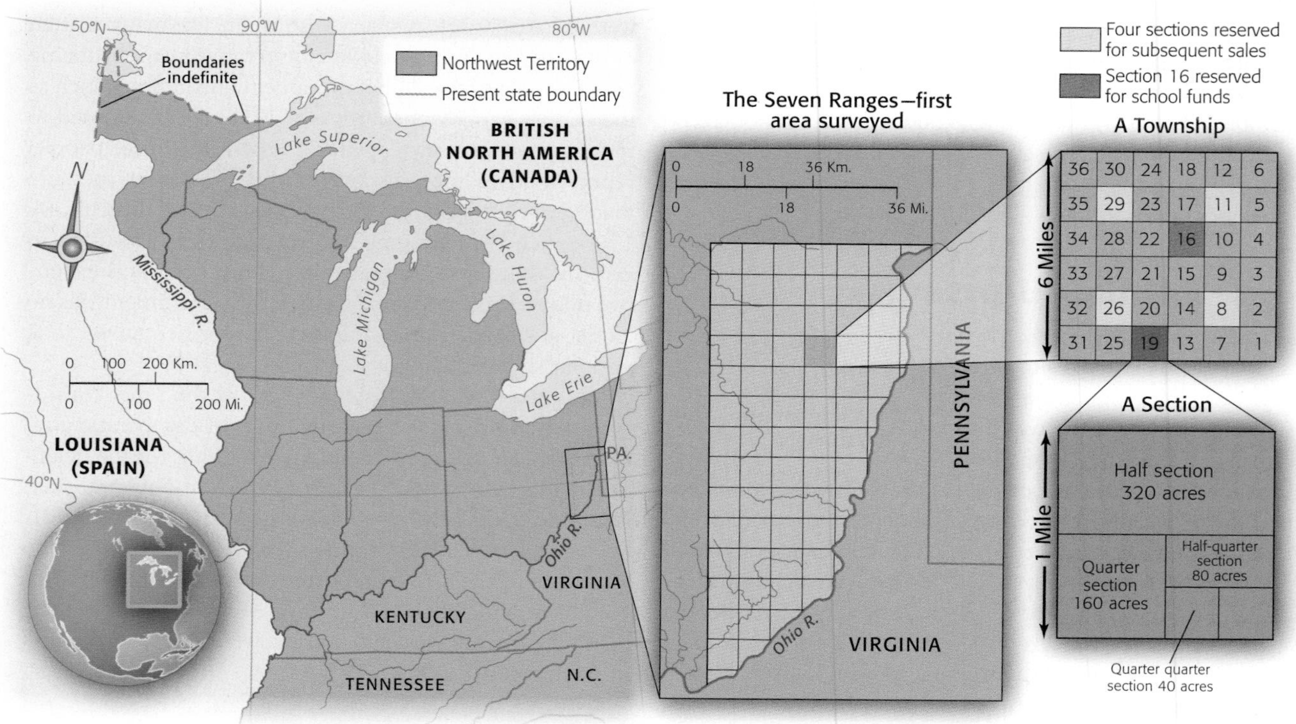

Map 7.4 The Land Ordinance of 1785 This ordinance established a plan for surveying and selling land as well as creating townships in the Northwest Territory. The experience of people in the region was at odds with the orderly plan for drawing lots along a grid. Most importantly, Indians living on the land had not ceded or sold vast portions of the Northwest Territory to the United States, and they insisted on their legal right to their homelands. ▲

With no U.S. military to protect Americans who purchased land in the Ohio River Valley, sales were slow and not profitable enough to rescue the fortunes of the new United States. Ohio River Valley Indians, rejecting the idea that the territory belonged to the United States, disrupted surveys and walked away from treaty meetings. In 1786, delegates from the Haudenosaunees, Wyandots, Delawares, Shawnees, and others sent a message to Congress repudiating earlier land treaties signed by individual tribes. For land west of the Ohio River, they reaffirmed, the United States must deal with "the united voice of the confederacy." At the same time, speculator companies formed to pressure Congress to carve land grants out of the territory.

Northwest Ordinance of 1787 Charter signed by the Second Continental Congress establishing a government, a bill of rights, and a path toward statehood for the Northwest Territory.

territories Region under the authority of the U.S. government with an appointed governor but its own elected legislature. Nineteenth-century territories gradually gained statehood.

fugitive slaves Enslaved people who escaped to states in which slavery was illegal but were subject to territorial and national laws that supported owners' rights to reclaim their human property.

The **Northwest Ordinance of 1787** attempted to solve the U.S. side of the stalemate. First, it promised that Indian lands could not be seized and sold unless in "just and lawful wars authorized by Congress." Second, it established a procedure for converting the land in the Northwest into states by inventing a new type of temporary colonial status. The provisions of the Ordinance divided the region into districts. As the land was surveyed and sold, districts became **territories**, each with its own appointed governor and elected assembly. When the population reached 60,000, a territory could ratify a state constitution and become a sovereign state of the United States. This model for expansion was a departure from that of existing empires. Rather than creating colonies to channel wealth into a metropolitan center as European empires did, the Ordinance proposed territorial status as a step toward equal statehood.

The men who devised plans for the Northwest Territory envisioned a particular social order for new states in the United States. The Northwest Ordinance outlawed slavery but provided for the capture and return of **fugitive slaves** who escaped to the territory in pursuit of freedom. Building on the Land Ordinance's provision of one lot in each township for a public school, the Northwest Ordinance stated "Religion, morality, and knowledge being necessary to good government, and the happiness of mankind, schools and the means of education shall forever be encouraged." Free white farmers—independent because of the availability of land and virtuous because of the education they had received from their mothers and their teachers—would, the designers hoped, supply the ideal citizens for an expanding republic.

7-5 U.S. Constitution

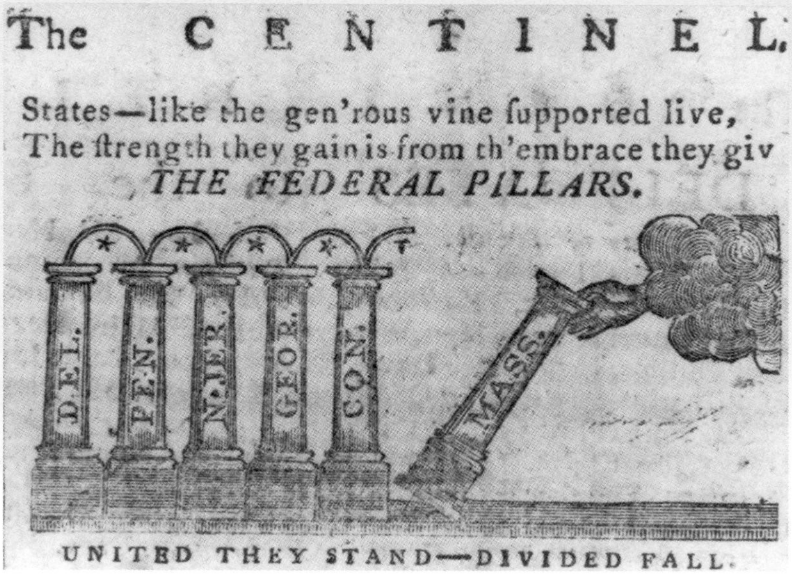

The Massachusetts Centinel/Library of Congress Serial and Government Publications Division Washington, D.C. 20540 USA

This cartoon, published in the *Massachusetts Centinel* in 1788, depicts a hand from the clouds propping up the Massachusetts pillar to the "Federal Superstructure." It was printed as the divided convention of Massachusetts debated whether to ratify the new Constitution that would replace the Articles of Confederation.

What does the cartoon suggest about the nature of the new U.S. government? How does it differ from Benjamin Franklin's 1754 image of the "join or die" snake in Chapter 6? ▶

The struggles of the period between 1776 and 1787 over unity, identity, debt, and power culminated in a Constitutional Convention. Originally convened to revise the agreement among the states, the Convention produced a new governing document for a stronger, more centralized federal government. In designing and debating this Constitution, people in the new United States faced the problems of representation and taxation that had sparked the American Revolution. They also sought political solutions to the social, military, and financial upheavals of the 1770s and 1780s. The Constitution's preamble stated that "We, the People" composed the United States, replacing the Articles of Confederation's compact of states with a collective body of citizens. But as the debates over the ratification of the new Constitution revealed, national unity and shared identity were still weak at the local level.

☞ As you read, focus on the ways in which the relationship between local and federal power was central to the framing of the Constitution and the debates over its ratification. Which side won the debate? Initially? Ultimately?

7-5a The Constitutional Convention

The Constitutional Convention rethinks the new nation's political structure.

The movement to reform the Articles of Confederation started small, when delegates from five states met in Annapolis, Maryland, in the fall of 1786 to seek a remedy for barriers to interstate trade, which was stifled by state taxes on imports across state lines. The group, calling themselves the Commissioners to Remedy Defects of the Federal Government, issued a vaguely worded report calling for a 1787 convention to discuss the Articles. In fact, their plan was more ambitious. Led by men who wanted a stronger national government, they hoped that a separate convention might be able to accomplish what the Confederation Congress could not: shift enough power away from the states to unify national and international goals. Shays's Rebellion added urgency to their desires for stronger central control. With the approval of Congress, states appointed delegations for a late spring convention in Philadelphia.

The fifty-five delegates who arrived over the course of May 1787 included Revolutionary War veterans (George Washington, Charles Cotesworth Pinckney, Alexander

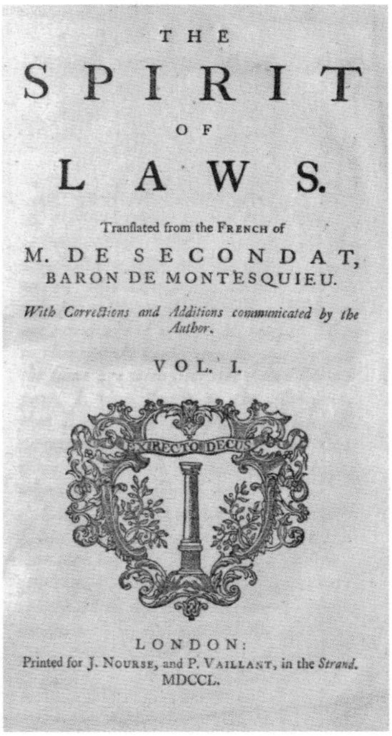
THE SPIRIT OF LAWS.
Tranſlated from the FRENCH of
M. DE SECONDAT, BARON DE MONTESQUIEU.
With Corrections and Additions communicated by the Author.
VOL. I.
LONDON:
Printed for J. NOURSE, and P. VAILLANT, in the *Strand*.
MDCCL.

Rare Books Department of Special Collections at the J. Willard Marriott Library, The University of Utah

Montesquieu's *Spirit of Laws* Among the works that James Madison consulted prior to the Constitutional Convention was Baron de Montesquieu's *Spirit of Laws*, published in France in 1748. Montesquieu theorized that history and climate shaped nations' political structures. Working from an idealized model of the English constitutional monarchy, he thought governments that granted executive, legislative, and judicial powers to separate bodies best preserved liberty. He emphasized that each of these bodies should be bound by the rule of law. ◀

Constitutional Convention Private meeting of delegates in 1787 to draft a constitution for the United States that would establish a strong centralized government.

Virginia Plan Madison's proposed structure for a new federal government that favored greater power to more populous states and limits to voters' power.

checks and balances Enlightenment political theory favoring government structures designed to curb political corruption by allowing one branch of government to overturn another's actions.

New Jersey Plan Alternative to the Virginia Plan that proposed maintaining equal representation of each state in the U.S. government.

Hamilton) and representatives to the Confederation Congress (forty-two of the fifty-five had served at some point). Most were lawyers; all were comfortably wealthy white men. Worried about public interference, they agreed to conduct business with the windows closed and with no communications to the press. Madison's detailed notes on delegates' speeches and deliberations, which give modern readers an eyewitness account, were locked away and not made public until 1840. The convention's use of secrecy, which Jefferson, from his diplomatic post in Paris, called an "abominable precedent," was not in keeping with revolutionary politics and revolutionary state constitutions, which had insisted on open debate and the publication of government proceedings. The secrecy did allow delegates to hammer out a delicate compromise.

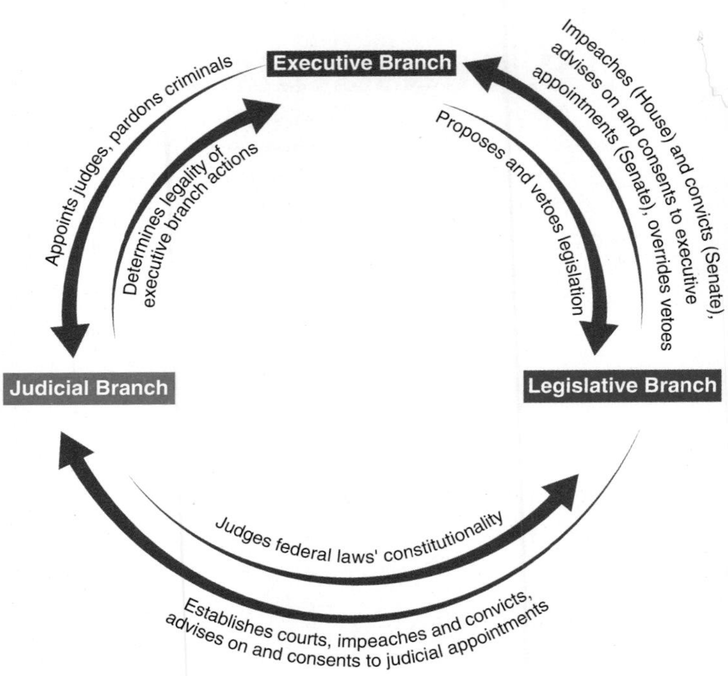

Figure 7.3 Checks and Balances in the Constitution The 1787 U.S. Constitution was designed to balance power among the branches of the federal government as well as the power between the federal government and the states. Unlike the English "mixed" government, the new U.S. government granted each branch distinct powers and gave each branch ways to check the actions of the others. ▲ Source: John G. Geer et al., *Gateways to Democracy*, 3rd edition. Boston: Cengage Learning, 2015.

Madison, part of the Virginia delegation, prepared for what would become known as the **Constitutional Convention** by immersing himself in European Enlightenment treatises on political philosophy, studies of what would later be called political science. These texts gave histories of specific kingdoms, republics, and empires since antiquity. They also proposed general theories about how governments should use and manage power. Influenced by these works, Madison believed that a proper structure of government could fix many of the problems that arose from human nature. He therefore set the terms of the delegates' discussion from the start by proposing a comprehensive plan for a new U.S. government. Called the **Virginia Plan**, it scrapped the structure of the Articles of Confederation in favor of an expanded central government. The new federal government would divide its powers among three branches with distinct roles: a congress for legislation, a president for executive authority, and a supreme court for judicial powers. The three branches would operate through a series of what came to be called **checks and balances** (see Figure 7.3). Because each branch could overturn some decisions made by another branch, none would become too powerful.

Vague on many details, Madison's plan focused on addressing what he saw as one of the main problems of the confederation: that local interests could thwart the larger common good. Under the Articles, self-interested states had equal representation in the Continental Congress; important votes required a supermajority of nine of thirteen states' support, and amending the Articles required all thirteen to agree. Under such circumstances, little legislation passed. Fixing this problem required a new approach to representation. In the proposed new structure, each state would be represented in Congress in proportion to its population. At the same time, the dangers of majority rule would be counterbalanced by making representation more indirect. Madison proposed that voters would elect only members of the House of Representatives.

Delegates from smaller states objected that the new apportionment of representation would allow states with larger populations to overrule their interests and needs. The **New Jersey Plan**, prepared as a rebuttal to Virginia's scheme, recommended a structure much more like the Articles of Confederation with a single legislature in which each state had an equal vote. This plan was appealing to small states that hoped to retain their power.

7-5b United States Constitution of 1787

The new Constitution creates a stronger central government.

The final version of the **Constitution of the United States**, signed in 1787 after months of negotiation, resolved the two approaches to representation by establishing two houses of Congress: the Senate in which each state had an equal vote and the House of Representatives in which

Birch, William Russell, 1755–1834, artist Charles Desilver (Firm)

Pennsylvania State House Yard The Constitutional Convention that met behind closed doors in the Pennsylvania State House in 1787 chose a location with deep significance for the Revolution. The Second Continental Congress had met in the same building in 1775, and revolutionaries rang its tower bell in 1776 to announce the passage of the Declaration of Independence. British soldiers turned the building into a barracks during their occupation of the city. ▲

states were represented in proportion to population. As stated in Article I, each state would have two senators in the Senate and, for every thirty thousand inhabitants, one representative in the House of Representatives. All funding bills would originate in this lower house, meaning that the majority population would control taxation. This concession to popular sovereignty was important because the Constitution granted the U.S. government extensive new powers over the economy. Congress, not the states, could coin money and regulate foreign and interstate commerce. It would have the right to tax American citizens directly rather than relying on states to raise all of the revenue.

Although slavery was not directly named in the new document, multiple clauses supported the slave system, starting with how Americans were counted. For the purposes of apportioning representatives and for the direct taxes that the federal government could demand, the government counted all free people who lived in that state as well as three-fifths of the slaves. This did not mean that a slave was three-fifths of a person or a person with three-fifths of the rights of a free citizen. Instead, the **three-fifths compromise** was a way to grant power in Congress to slave owners in exchange for acknowledging, and taxing, the slaves who produced the wealth in their states. Article I also prohibited Congress from ending the importation of slaves until 1808.

Other articles of the Constitution contained additional compromises that reflected the tension between popular sovereignty and central control. Article II outlined the executive powers of the president—an entirely new position—and put the election of the president in the hands of an **electoral college** rather than directly with voters. State legislatures chose citizen-electors in numbers equivalent to the total number of senators and representatives the state had in Congress. Those electors, in turn, chose two candidates, at least one of whom had to be from another state, and sent the names to Congress to be tallied. The person with the majority of votes became president and the one in second place became vice president. In this and other measures, the authors hoped to protect the new government from mob rule, although the final version

Constitution of the United States Document signed in 1787 establishing a new structure of U.S. government and the allocation of power within it as well as limits to that power.

three-fifths compromise Method for determining population numbers for the purposes of federal taxation and representation that counted only three-fifths of a state's enslaved people.

electoral college Institution created by the Constitution to select the U.S. president indirectly, channeling the popular vote through electors more likely to think nationally than locally.

"Federals" and "Antifederals" in Connecticut The ratification debate connected state issues to the proposed U.S. Constitution. At the top of this cartoon, Connecticut is a wagon, sinking into the mud because of its heavy load of debts and paper money. On the left, Federals urge viewers to "Comply with Congress"; on the right, Antifederals cry "the People are oprest." At the bottom, merchant vessels sailing from Connecticut to New York complain about taxes on interstate trade. State politicians feud in the middle. ▲

Doolittle, Amos, 1754–1832, engraver

Federalists Supporters of the 1787 U.S. Constitution who praised its structures of shared power between states and the national government.

federalism System of government in which a central body and regional governments share power.

Federalist Papers Eighty-five newspaper essays written by James Madison, Alexander Hamilton, and John Jay and published anonymously in New York to support constitutional ratification.

Antifederalists People who opposed the 1787 U.S. Constitution, usually on the grounds that it consolidated power at the expense of state and individual freedoms.

still allocated more power to the people than either the Virginia or New Jersey plan had. Most votes in Congress required only a simple majority to pass.

Supporters of the new Constitution called themselves **Federalists**, a term that referred to **federalism**, the sharing of power between the central government and states. Overall, however, the document was a strong statement of centralized power. Article VI stated that the Constitution and U.S. law were "the supreme law of the land," binding people in every state. Article IV declared that citizens in each state had the right to "all privileges and immunities of citizens in the several States." Finally, the Constitution itself, under Article VII, would be ratified if nine state conventions voted in favor of it. Unanimity was no longer the mark of legitimacy.

7-5c Ratification Debates

The debates over ratifying the Constitution center on federal powers and the nature of a republic.

When the delegates emerged from their closed negotiations with the final draft of the new federal Constitution in September 1787, public debate began. As was typical in British political culture, printed debate engaged public opinion that then continued in taverns, homes, workshops, and alleyways. The proposed Constitution was quickly published in every U.S. newspaper. Drafters Hamilton, Madison, and John Jay also published a series of essays, later known as the ***Federalist Papers***, making their case for the new form of government. In their essays, originally printed anonymously between October 1787 and May 1788 in New York newspapers, they elaborated on the philosophy behind the governmental structure, arguing that the new Constitution resolved problems of representation, preserved popular sovereignty, and created a state strong enough to provide defense and regulate trade in the world.

Opponents of the new Constitution likewise published numerous essays in addition to speaking to friends, family, and colleagues. **Antifederalists**, as they were labeled, were not unanimous in their reasoning but united in believing that the 1787 Constitution had betrayed the principles of the Revolution with its compromises and inventions. They were especially alarmed at the perceived restrictions on state and individual rights. Antifederalist sentiment was strong in the backcountry and in northern New England. It involved elites (including dissenting delegates to the Constitutional Convention such as George Mason) as well as middling businesspeople and struggling farmers.

Antifederalists argued that the new government was too powerful at the federal level. Instead of a union of sovereign states, the country would become a centralized state with a government that acted directly on the people. Patrick Henry, a leading patriot during the Revolution and former governor of Virginia, dismissed the celebrated checks and balances promised by the three branches of government as distracting "rope-dancing" and "chain rattling" rather than a real separation of power. Sooner or later, powers such as those to sign treaties would consolidate in the hands of a few men, he feared.

More pressing, the central government gained new powers to command a permanent army, raise taxes, and take on debts. All of these were features of European empires and all, argued the Antifederalists, threatened the liberty of U.S. citizens. While taking the power to raise troops for an army away from the states, the Constitution also granted the central government the right to control and use state militias to "suppress Insurrections and repel Invasions," a power that had been wielded against debt-burdened farmers, rebelling slaves, and Indians. In the eyes of its opponents, the Constitution was an attempt to turn the United States into a European-style empire, when, as many Antifederalists pointed out, a revolution had just been fought to separate from a European empire, its standing armies, and its corruptions.

Critics also believed that the new republic was too large to be responsive to the greater good of the community. It replaced local control by leading elected men with the distant power of those who might not know their constituents, given the large size of each congressional district. Madison, writing in *Federalist 10*, countered that the large size safeguarded the republic from special interests called **factions**, which were a great danger, Madison argued, because they favored a particular interest or passion that was at odds with the rights or needs of the community as a whole. Whereas factions representing a minority of the population would be voted out in a democracy or republic, a faction composed of the majority could easily tyrannize the country. To combat a **tyranny of the majority**, the new constitution created a large republic. In a large republic, the pool of qualified representatives was larger, and better men could be elected who could filter out the effects of faction. A larger district would also likely contain several factions that would balance each other. Madison's innovation turned around the common wisdom of republicanism by stating that its goals—a virtuous society of shared interests—were best met by increasing the size of the country rather than keeping it small.

7-5d The Bill of Rights

One of the most concrete objections to the new Constitution was that it had no bill of rights to protect individual liberties from a powerful, consolidated government. Seven state constitutions had bills of rights securing freedom of the press, trial by jury, and other individual liberties. The absence of a similar statement of rights in the proposed Constitution held up ratification for months.

The continuing importance of protecting individual rights against a powerful central government reflects the Revolution's legacy.

Table 7.3 State Ratification of the Constitution

The campaign to ratify the Constitution in state conventions began with quick success but then slowed as conventions grappled with the document's lack of a bill of rights. Votes were especially close in Massachusetts, New Hampshire, Virginia, and New York, where Antifederalist sentiment was strong. The last two states to ratify, North Carolina and Rhode Island, did so only after the First Congress sent the first twelve amendments to the states for ratification.

State	Date of Vote	State Convention Votes
Delaware	December 7, 1787	30–0
Pennsylvania	December 12, 1787	46–23
New Jersey	December 18, 1787	38–0
Georgia	January 2, 1788	26–0
Connecticut	January 9, 1788	128–40
Massachusetts	February 6, 1788	187–168
Maryland	April 28, 1788	63–11
South Carolina	May 23, 1788	149–73
New Hampshire	June 21, 1788	57–47
Virginia	June 25, 1788	89–79
New York	July 26, 1788	30–27
North Carolina	November 21, 1789	194–77
Rhode Island	May 29, 1790	34–32

Source: State-by-State Ratification Table, http://teachingamericanhistory.org/ratification/overview/, a project of the Ashbrook Center at Ashland University.

Even states that ratified the Constitution sent in a total of 124 proposed amendments focused on protecting civil liberties. Some called for a second Constitutional Convention to address these additions. The U.S. Constitution became law when New Hampshire ratified it in June 1788, but the vitally important states of Virginia and New York, which were home to significant Antifederalist feeling, followed only when their ratification was linked to an insistence that a bill of rights be added as amendments. Rhode Island held out until 1790 (see Table 7.3).

The lack of a bill of rights in the 1787 Constitution was not an oversight. Elbridge Gerry, a delegate from Massachusetts, had proposed one at the end of the Constitutional Convention and refused to sign the final draft when it failed to include a statement of rights. The majority of those assembled argued that a bill of rights was unnecessary. Because the Constitution gave the federal government only specific powers, Americans retained their liberties. Enumerating specific protected liberties would only imply that rights not listed were subject to federal intervention.

Most voters rejected this logic. As one of its first acts, therefore, the new Congress created what became the **Bill of Rights**, ten amendments

factions Group of people whose interests oppose the interests and freedoms of others. Considered by many to play a divisive and corrupting role in politics.

tyranny of the majority Concept that minority civil rights are violated in a system of majority rule addressed by *Federalist Papers* author Madison.

Bill of Rights First ten amendments to the U.S. Constitution, preserving individuals' civil rights. In several states, including it was a condition of ratification.

to the Constitution that the individual states ratified (see Table 7.4). The First Amendment protected Americans' right to speak, assemble, publish in the press, and petition the government and prohibited Congress from passing any law "respecting an establishment of religion, or prohibiting the free exercise thereof." The Second and Third Amendments countered the dangers of a standing army by protecting individuals' rights to "keep and bear arms" and form a militia as well as banning the quartering of soldiers in individuals' homes without their consent. Amendments 4 through 8 established legal rights in trials. The last two amendments covered anything left out. Amendment 9 explicitly affirmed that the rights protected in the first eight amendments were not the people's only rights. In an effort to reassert the principles of federalism, Amendment 10 confirmed that any powers not specifically given to the federal government remained powers of the individual states or of the people. The Bill of Rights therefore turned the goals of the early Revolutionaries—personal liberty, local control, freedom from tyranny—into law. Whether the Constitution could maintain these rights was an open question.

Table 7.4 The Bill of Rights

The Bill of Rights consists of the first ten amendments to the U.S. Constitution. Other amendments were sent to the states in 1789, but not ratified, including one that would have forbidden Congress to vote itself a pay raise. That amendment was eventually ratified in 1992.

Number	Subject
Amendment 1	Freedom of religion, speech, the press, assembly, petitioning
Amendment 2	Right to bear arms and form a militia
Amendment 3	No quartering of soldiers without consent
Amendment 4	No unreasonable searches and seizures
Amendment 5	Right to due process, not to testify against oneself, to compensation for property taken
Amendment 6	Right to public trial, to know charges, to confront witnesses, to legal counsel
Amendment 7	Right to a jury trial
Amendment 8	No excessive bail or fines, no cruel and unusual punishments
Amendment 9	Rights not enumerated are still maintained
Amendment 10	Powers not delegated to the federal government remain with the states

Summary

The period of experimentation between 1776 and 1789 tested the limits of the American Revolution as a true revolution as opposed to a war for independence. States, confederacies, and empires responded to wartime pressures to redistribute power among a broader group of people. Many individuals, from refugee children to freed slaves to urban mothers, wondered how the changing patterns of power might offer them new liberties. The answer they got was mixed. Wartime idealism initially motivated people to revise some old hierarchies. Slaves in northern states used petitions and new gradual emancipation laws to secure freedom; some southern masters, citing the natural law of human freedom, manumitted their slaves. Free mothers pressed for better education for girls. Many argued that freedom of religion was as important as political liberty. New state constitutions within the United States granted average men a stronger voice in their governments.

As the war dragged to its end, economic depression and bitter race warfare hardened lines between "us" and "them" that ran counter to the inspiring principles of liberty and equality that Jefferson had asserted as being self-evident. The end of the Revolution sent tens of thousands into exile around the globe, and fighting continued in borderlands, destroying long-standing sources of group identity including the Six Nations and the British Empire. Debt and its vulnerabilities ensnared everyone from western farmers to urban merchants to the governments of France, Spain, and the new United States. Disease sapped native communities across the interior of North America and down the West Coast with significant implications for U.S. efforts to secure borders and expand trade.

The United States Constitution was born in a mood of caution among political leaders who worried that the Revolution had gone too far. It also reflected a pragmatic concern for the way government could work rather than the idealistic views of the early years. As one of the *Federalist Papers* essays remarked, "If men were angels, no government would be necessary." By turning independent cooperating states into a single nation, the Constitution attempted to affirm a unity not yet cemented and to assert stronger centralized control over American citizens not yet ready to relinquish their individual rights. A hastily amended Bill of Rights addressed some of these persistent concerns. But the more radical potential of revolutionary ideals would be reignited in the decades to come, sparking first with revolution in the United States' ally, France.

Thinking Back, *Looking Forward*

As you review this chapter, think about the lasting consequences of the American Revolution. What expectations for liberty and self-government did the Revolution raise, and how were they met and unmet? In the next chapters, look for new hierarchies of race and gender that solidified in the absence of nobility and royalty. Which new rights proved permanent? Which would be denied, and to whom? Observe, too, the continuing conflict between centralized government and dispersed power.

To make your study concrete, review the timeline and reflect on the entries there. Think about their causes, consequences, and connections. How do they connect events in North America to global trends?

Additional Resources

Books

Cornell, Saul. *The Other Founders: Anti-Federalism and the Dissenting Tradition in America, 1788–1828*. Chapel Hill: University of North Carolina Press, 1999. ▶ Study of the diverse thought and influence of Antifederalism.

Duval, Kathleen. *Independence Lost: Lives on the Edge of the American Revolution*. New York: Random House, 2015. ▶ Global story of individuals on revolutionary borders and their postwar lives.

Holton, Woody. *Unruly Americans and the Origins of the Constitution*. New York: Hill and Wang, 2007. ▶ Explanation of the role of popular protest in shaping the U.S. Constitution through ratification.

Igler, David. *The Great Ocean: Pacific Worlds from Captain Cook to the Gold Rush*. New York: Oxford University Press, 2013. ▶ Intercultural history of the maritime Pacific.

Irvin, Benjamin. *Clothed in Robes of Sovereignty: The Constitutional Convention and the People Out of Doors*. New York: Oxford University Press, 2014. ▶ Social and cultural history of the Continental Congress and its public reception.

Jasanoff, Maya. *Liberty's Exiles: American Loyalists in the Revolutionary World*. New York: Alfred A. Knopf, 2001. ▶ The lives and migrations of Loyalists after the end of the Revolution.

Klepp, Susan. *Revolutionary Conceptions: Women, Fertility, and Family Limitation in America, 1760–1820*. Chapel Hill: University of North Carolina Press, 2009. ▶ Innovative examination of the Revolution's impact on families.

Nash, Gary. *Forging Freedom: Philadelphia's Black Community, 1720–1840*. Cambridge: Harvard University Press, 1991. ▶ Detailed look at the lives of African Americans before and after the Revolution in Philadelphia.

Rakove, Jack N. *Original Meanings: Politics and Ideas in the Making of the Constitution*. New York: Vintage, 1997. ▶ Political and intellectual history of the Constitutional Convention.

Wood, Gordon. *The Creation of the American Republic, 1776–1787*. Chapel Hill: University of North Carolina Press, 1998. ▶ Classic study of politics and state constitutions in the Revolutionary era.

Go to the MindTap® for **Global Americans** to access the full version of select books from this Additional Resources section.

Websites

The American Revolution, 1763–1783. http://www.gilderlehrman.org/history-by-era/american-revolution-1763-1783 ▶ Gilder Lehrman Institute of American History site with timelines, sources, and essays.

Charters of Freedom http://www.archives.gov/exhibits/charters/constitution.html ▶ National Archives site on the context and meaning of the U.S. Constitution.

Documenting the American South. http://docsouth.unc.edu/support/about/ ▶ University of North Carolina at Chapel Hill site with primary documents regarding the Revolutionary South.

Free Black Communities at the Library Company. http://www.librarycompany.org/blackfounders/#.Vden6879MiQ ▶ Exhibition including documents of free black communities after the Revolution.

Nova Scotia Museums. http://museum.novascotia.ca/our-museums ▶ Research and resources on the Loyalist diaspora, as well as other Canadian topics.

MindTap®

Continue exploring online through MindTap®, where you can:

- **Assess your knowledge with the Chapter Test**
- **Watch historical videos related to the chapter**
- **Further your understanding with interactive maps and timelines**

American Experiments

1772

June

English Justice Mansfield decides case in favor of James Somerset, a Virginia slave, challenging the legality of slavery in England.

1776

July

Continental Congress adopts Declaration of Independence, marking formal break with Britain.

September

Pennsylvania State Constitution establishes government with single legislature, broad voting rights, no governor.

1777

July

Independent Vermont's constitution outlaws slavery.

November

Continental Congress adopts Articles of Confederation as governing structure for the United States in rebellion against Britain.

1778

January

James Cook reaches Hawai'an island of Kauai on voyage seeking Northwest Passage.

1780–1781

March 1780

Massachusetts State Constitution's first article asserts all men born free and equal.

November 1780

Anticolonial Indian revolt led by Tupac Amaru in Peru
opposes Spanish taxes and imperial policy.

August 1781

Elizabeth Freeman secures freedom in Massachusetts court.

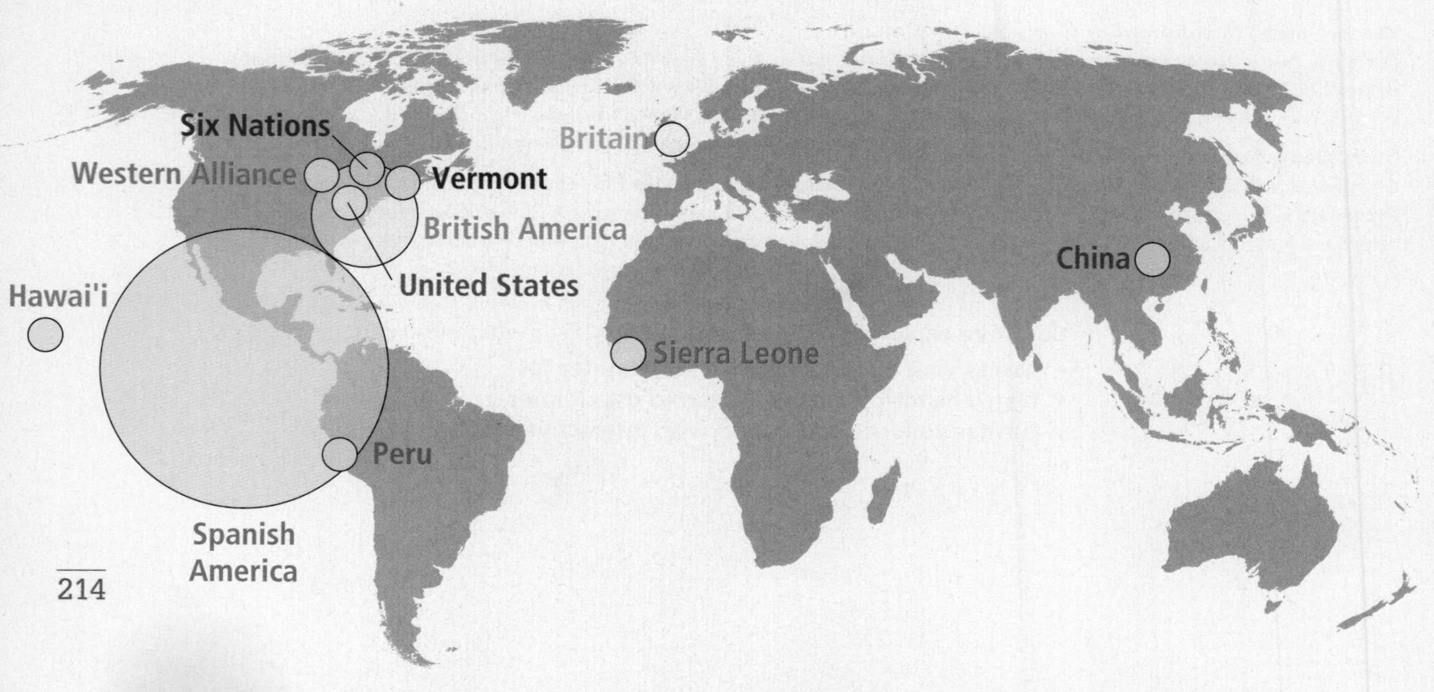

1782–1783

Twelve thousand Loyalists arrive in Spanish East Florida.

September 1783

Britain and United States sign Treaty of Paris ending Revolutionary War and redrawing national boundaries.

Fall 1783

South Carolina reopens the import of enslaved Africans and then closes it again in 1787.

Western Alliance of Native Americans meet in Sandusky to coordinate opposition to Treaty of Paris border.

November 1783

Twenty-nine thousand Loyalists evacuate New York for Nova Scotia.

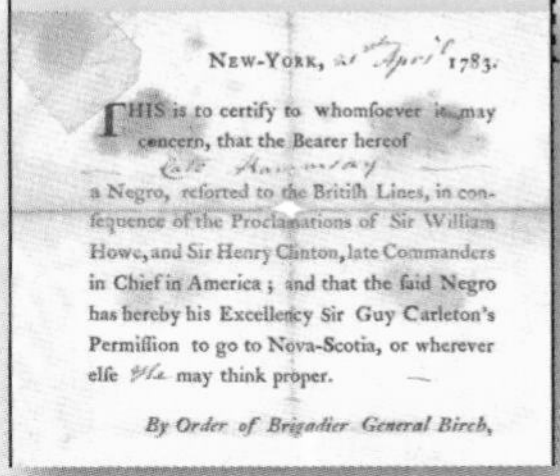

New-York, 21st April 1783.

THIS is to certify to whomsoever it may concern, that the Bearer hereof [illegible] a Negro, resorted to the British Lines, in consequence of the Proclamations of Sir William Howe, and Sir Henry Clinton, late Commanders in Chief in America; and that the said Negro has hereby his Excellency Sir Guy Carleton's Permission to go to Nova-Scotia, or wherever else he may think proper.

By Order of Brigadier General Birch,

1784

March

Spain bars U.S. trade on the Mississippi River, blocking access to New Orleans.

August

Empress of China, the first U.S. trading ship in Asia, reaches Canton.

October

Six Nations sign Treaty of Fort Stanwix with United States, relinquishing claim to Ohio territory.

1785–1786

May 1785

Land Ordinance divides Northwest Territory into townships.

November 1785

Joseph Brant travels to London to request British aid for Western Indian alliance.

January 1786

Virginia Legislature passes Act for Establishing Religious Freedom.

1787–1788

January 1787

Daniel Shays and supporters attack Springfield armory to seize weapons for the cause of western farmers but are defeated.

May 1787

British abolitionists establish West African settlement of Sierra Leone.

Delegates at Continental Congress begin debate on new national government.

July 1787

Northwest Ordinance establishes political blueprint for land north of Ohio River.

September 1787–May 1790

States debate and gradually ratify the U.S. Constitution.

October 1787–May 1788

New York newspapers publish the *Federalist Papers* arguing in favor of ratification.

1789–1791

January 1789

Ratified U.S. Constitution takes effect.

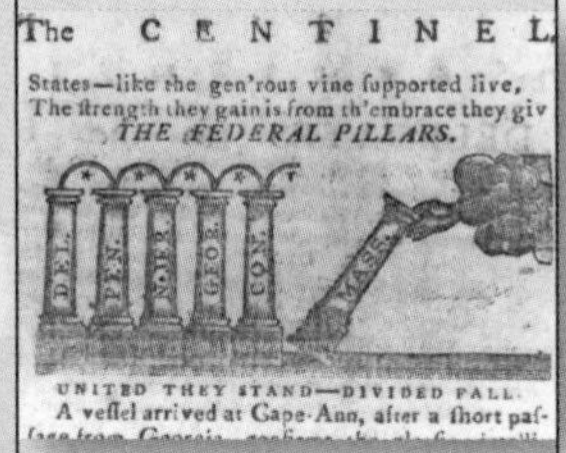

The CENTINEL
States—like the gen'rous vine supported live,
The strength they gain is from th'embrace they giv
THE FEDERAL PILLARS.
UNITED THEY STAND—DIVIDED FALL.
A vessel arrived at Cape-Ann, after a short pas-

December 1791

Bill of Rights ratified.

Go to MindTap® to engage with an interactive version of the timeline. Analyze events and themes with clickable content, view related videos, and respond to critical thinking questions.

8 Inventing Republics in the Age of Revolutions

1789–1819

From Philadelphia to Saint-Domingue, Leonora Sansay saw the spread of the revolutionary ideals of freedom and natural rights, and the violence that accompanied change.

Leonora Hassell, stepdaughter of a Philadelphia tavern keeper, spent her adolescence observing American politicians. Her family's tavern, the Sign of the Half-Moon, was located across the street from the Philadelphia statehouse, where the Continental and Confederation Congresses met. In the statehouse, at the taverns, and on the pages of newspapers, men like Leonora's friend New York senator Aaron Burr struggled—often violently—over how to interpret and implement the results of the American Revolution. In 1800, after months of intrigue and character assassination, Burr became the nation's third vice president in an election that inaugurated a new political party. That same year, Leonora married Louis Sansay, a French refugee from the revolution on the Caribbean island of Saint-Domingue. Soon after their marriage, when France moved to take the island back from black revolutionaries, Louis and Leonora Sansay sailed there too, optimistic, she said in a letter, that "order would be established" and they could reclaim the lucrative plantation.

The Library Company of Philadelphia

Incendie du Cap [Burning of Cap Francais] depicts whites fleeing the 1793 slave rebellion in Saint-Domingue. ▲

Instead, Leonora Sansay witnessed the violent birth of another new nation. Revolutionaries defeated French troops, burned the capital city of Cap Français, and in 1804, issued their own Declaration of Independence. They called the new nation Haiti, the name the island's native Taino inhabitants had given it before Europeans arrived. Sansay fled to Spanish Cuba but within a year ran again, this time from her abusive husband. She returned to Philadelphia and reconnected with Burr, who embroiled her in a plot that he and James Wilkinson had devised to colonize the Louisiana territory, which had been recently sold to the United States.

Leonora Sansay's life read like a novel and she knew it. To support herself as a woman alone in Philadelphia, she published fictionalized versions of the racial warfare and domestic violence she had witnessed in Haiti. Although novels about young women in trouble were very popular, her books, *Laura* and the *Secret History*, did not sell well. So she started over again and with the help of personal and bank loans, opened her own business making artificial flowers. A woman raised on revolution became an urban entrepreneur.

Leonora Sansay grew into adulthood in the Age of Revolution. She witnessed the spread of revolutionary ideals about freedom and natural rights that sparked uprisings in North America, France, the Caribbean, and South America as people claimed the right to govern themselves. Sansay also witnessed the violence that accompanied revolutionary change. Public protests turned to public executions on Paris streets, and the new French republic launched two decades of warfare in Europe to topple monarchies and expand French power. Millions died as French armies and the opposing forces of Britain, Austria, Prussia, and Russia sacked towns and crushed uprisings across the continent. Bound to European empires through trade

How do the events of Leonora Sansay's life reflect the uncertainties and violence of emerging nations in the Age of Revolution?
Go to MindTap® to watch a video on Sansay and learn how her story relates to the themes of this chapter.

and political alliances, the United States and Native American confederacies were drawn into global conflict; soon their towns burned and their people perished, as well. In Saint-Domingue, slaves destroyed plantations and killed the owners who had forced them to labor in the sugar fields, sending the island into thirteen years of warfare. In 1810, war spread across Latin America as colonists fought to end Spanish rule and slavery. Haiti and several Latin American republics achieved independence. Elsewhere, empires reasserted their sovereignty over colonies and territories.

The birth of revolutionary republics raised philosophical and practical questions for the United States. Should it support fellow revolutionaries or try to remain neutral in a world of constant commercial rivalry and imperial warfare? Should it follow the most radical examples, committing to citizens' rights and the end of slavery, or temper idealism with stability? Factionalism rent the political fabric of the republic as people struggled over the best direction for a country professing "Life, Liberty, and the pursuit of Happiness."

With such uncertainty, many feared, and some hoped, that the United States would collapse back into the British Empire. Instead, the United States asserted itself as a sovereign nation and extended itself as an empire. As early as 1780, Thomas Jefferson had proposed that the United States become an "empire of liberty." This new kind of empire, supported through agricultural exports, would be one that linked self-governing republics together to resist the corrupt powers of Europe. Yet implementing the vision required political and cultural choices that limited universal liberty. Commercial agriculture required land and laborers to work it, which meant driving Native Americans off their territory and expanding the institution of slavery from the coast into the interior of the continent.

8-1

The Fragile Republic

These two portraits of George Washington were both painted during his presidency. The one on the left is *General George Washington at Trenton* (1792) by John Trumbull. The one on the right is *George Washington* (1796) by Gilbert Stuart. The Charleston City Council commissioned the Trumbull painting but rejected it, preferring "a more matter-of-fact likeness." The Stuart portrait was commissioned as a gift to the Marquis of Landsdowne, British supporter of U.S. independence.

What props does each artist use to evoke the authority of Washington? How do the two portraits tell different stories about why Washington is the first president? What does each suggest about the people he leads? ▶

Trumbull, John (1756–1843)/Bridgeman Art

Painting/Alamy Stock Photo

The U.S. Constitution of 1789 created a structure for a republic with a strengthened centralized government. The future of that republic, however, seemed shaky in the next decades. The American population was culturally divided and regionally dispersed. The empires of Britain and France had deep and influential ties to the U.S. economy and government that persisted after independence. France, Spain, and Britain all formed alliances with Native Americans, who controlled the majority of North America and were pushing back against the U.S. government and individual American squatters and speculators. George Washington, the first president, was a war hero and a nationally revered figure, which helped him establish a legitimate tone of authority, and he set precedents for asserting presidential power. But powerful executives could, many feared, erode the power of the people.

☞ As you read, think about the forces pulling at the republic created by the U.S. Constitution. What held people together—culture? laws? force?

8-1a First Presidency

A new executive projects national power.

George Washington took office in New York City, temporary capital of the United States, in April 1789, having been elected unanimously by the first Electoral College. As the first president, he walked a fine line between demonstrating sufficient authority and appearing too kingly. For his inaugural suit, he sent General Henry Knox, future secretary of war, to acquire American-made cloth in the color "Congress Brown" and silver buttons stamped with eagles. He used the title "Mr. President" rather than some of the more impressive ones proposed, including the florid "His Highness, the President of the United States, and Protector of Their Liberties," favored by John Adams.

With Washington secured as president, Congress bolstered the executive by creating departments of War, State, and the Treasury, as well as Attorney General and Postmaster General. The heads of those departments appointed by the president became a **cabinet** system of advisors. Washington's two most influential advisors were Secretary of State Thomas Jefferson and Secretary of the Treasury Alexander Hamilton, men with often dramatically different ideas about the expression of federal power. Hamilton, citing the clause in the Constitution that gave Congress power "to make all laws which shall be necessary and proper" to carry out its duties, argued that the national government should be proactive. His position, later described as **loose construction** of the Constitution, was that Congress had the power to develop new offices, programs, and laws that would strengthen the economy. In his 1790 *Report on Public Credit*, Hamilton promoted the creation of a national bank, a joint venture between private investors and the federal government, that could make loans, manage government funds, and issue reliable money. Jefferson opposed the bank, insisting that only a **strict construction** of the Constitution—one that gave the government only the powers specifically mentioned in the document—could protect the people's rights to govern themselves. In the end, the Congress supported Hamilton's vision, chartering the **Bank of the United States** in 1791.

Hamilton also pushed for the United States to transform itself from a nation of farmers into a manufacturing power. As he expressed in his *Report on the Subject of Manufactures* (1791), he believed that the United States needed to nurture the "spirit of enterprise" in its citizens. First, the U.S. government had to tackle the problem of its war debts, both the money still owed to foreigners and the money that the national government and the states owed to citizens who had bought war bonds, loaned animals and tools, fed and clothed the army, and fought in the Revolutionary War. Hamilton recommended that the U.S. government pay all of these debts with money from taxes and land sales. He proposed, and Congress passed, a tariff on what he called "foreign luxuries" and an **excise tax** on distilled spirits made within the country, which damaged "the health and the morals" of the American people. The tariff, which for the next half century would provide the most reliable federal income, was relatively easy to collect at port customs houses and encouraged American manufactures by making foreign goods more expensive.

The excise tax, collected by federal revenue officers in the U.S. hinterlands, sparked a national political and military crisis that dramatized the consequences of a powerful executive. Farmers in western Pennsylvania, Kentucky, Maryland, and the Carolinas, unable to sell their grain via the Spanish-controlled Mississippi River, frequently distilled their corn and wheat into whiskey, which was cheaper and easier to transport to urban customers. Because the excise threatened their livelihoods, they resisted with violence, tarring and feathering excise officers who attempted to collect and arming themselves in preparation for a larger revolt. These protests, called the **Whiskey Rebellion**, were most violent in Pennsylvania. In September 1794, Hamilton and Washington personally led thirteen thousand federalized militia troops to put down the rebellion, which collapsed quickly. Seated on his horse, Washington was both an official elected by the voice of the people and a commander-in-chief ready to aggressively enforce federal law.

cabinet Group of presidential advisors made up of the heads of executive departments plus the vice president.

loose construction Method of interpreting the U.S. Constitution that grants the federal government powers not specifically forbidden including passing laws to accomplish its aims.

strict construction Method of interpreting the U.S. Constitution that permits the federal government only those powers specifically mentioned and reserves other powers for the states.

Bank of the United States National bank supported by private investors and federal government that held U.S. Treasury funds and controlled the money supply. It was allowed to expire in 1811.

excise tax Tax on the manufacture or sale of specific goods, such as alcohol, produced domestically that was added to the cost of the product.

Whiskey Rebellion Armed protests by backcountry farmers and distillers who opposed the excise tax on whiskey and were defeated by nationalized militia forces.

8-1b Conflicts on the Continent

Indian confederacies and European empires contest U.S. sovereignty on unstable borders.

Neither the Treaty of Paris's boundary lines or the Northwest Ordinance's blueprint for future states resolved the question of who owned and controlled the Ohio and Tennessee River valleys, and the borderlands remained a tinderbox of conflict. Initially, the U.S. Congress thought to control relations between whites and Indians with the 1790 Indian Trade and Intercourse Act, which stated that only licensed traders could work in Indian country and all land treaties and sales had to be approved by Congress. But states, squatters, and speculators regularly ignored this law. At the same time, British soldiers, stationed stubbornly at seven forts in U.S. territory, encouraged Indian warfare, hoping that an Indian state in the Northwest would act as a barrier between the United States and British Canada.

Treaty of Greenville Agreement signed between the United States and allied Indians after the Battle of Fallen Timbers, granting much of the Ohio Territory to the United States.

annuities Goods or money provided annually to Indian leaders by the government as dictated by treaties conferring Indian land to the United States.

Southwest Ordinance U.S. law outlining process for territory south of the Ohio River to become states of the United States. Unlike the Northwest Ordinance, it permitted slavery.

Most of the land included in the Northwest Ordinance was under the control of a confederacy of northwestern Indian tribes led by Miamis and Shawnees. Miami chief Little Turtle and Shawnee Blue Jacket successfully led the confederacy in battle against U.S. troops in 1790 and 1791, delivering crushing defeats with the loss of hundreds of soldiers and the near destruction of the U.S. army. The confederacy maintained a strong alliance for two years, but constant warfare requiring the coordination of numerous Indian groups proved difficult. In 1794, General Anthony Wayne led four thousand army and militia troops to defeat the unraveling confederacy at the Battle of Fallen Timbers. Retreating Indians hoped for assistance from nearby Fort Miami, still occupied by British soldiers, but the gates closed against them while Wayne's troops burned their cornfields and scalped defeated warriors. In 1795, Wayne negotiated the **Treaty of Greenville**, which both sides hoped would end the violence. The treaty handed much of Ohio and the lower Northwest Territory—lands of the Shawnees, Delawares, and Wyandots—to the United States and established **annuities** by which the federal government made annual payments to favored Indian chiefs to distribute among followers.

U.S. Diplomacy with Native Americans, 1795 The United States gave this peace medal to Wyandot chief Tarhee at the signing of the Treaty of Greenville. The United States followed European imperial protocols in distributing medals to Indian chiefs as part of treaty negotiations. At the council, General Wayne told Indians that the medals were from "your father, the Fifteen Great Fires of America," referring to the fifteen states. The treaty recognized Indian rights to all land that had not been formally ceded, a significant change from the postrevolutionary policy of conquest and forced treaties. ▲ Treaty of Greeneville Peace Medal, 1795, American School, (18th century)/© Philadelphia History Museum at the Atwater Kent,/Courtesy of Historical Society of Pennsylvania Collection,/The Bridgeman Art Library

Abandoning their Indian allies, the British tried to undermine the United States by luring citizens back as British subjects. In the Canada Constitutional Act of 1791, Britain divided its North American colony in two: Lower Canada, a French-speaking region in the East around Quebec, and Upper Canada, along the St. Lawrence River and Great Lakes, which was already populated by English-speaking Loyalists who had left the United States. A new lieutenant governor, John Graves Simcoe, offered families two hundred acres of farmland in exchange for a loyalty oath to the king of England and a small fee. Canada's Constitution further promised that subjects could not be taxed to raise revenue for the empire. Although Simcoe insisted that political loyalty to the British Empire motivated thousands of migrants and called them the "Late Loyalists," most of the migrants themselves were less political and more practical. As one said: "We fought seven years to get rid of taxation, and now we are taxed more than ever!"

Learning from its mistakes with the thirteen rebellious colonies, Great Britain designed the Canadian Constitution to limit the people's power and quash any rumblings of independence. To meet American migrants' expectations for self-government, the Constitution established an elected assembly. But the number of representatives, who shared power with a group of elites appointed for life, was kept low. A powerful lieutenant governor, appointed from London, decided when to summon or suspend the assembly. The same people regularly served in legislative, executive, or judicial positions simultaneously, so power was concentrated in a few hands.

Fights over land and trade also continued in the Southeast as one faction of Creeks and Cherokees battled U.S. settlers pressing into Kentucky, Tennessee, and Georgia. Congress passed the **Southwest Ordinance** in 1790, attempting to organize the Southwestern Territory as it had done with the land north of the Ohio River. Anticipating the spread of plantation agriculture, the Southwest Ordinance permitted slavery. As in the northern territory, however, laws could not contain struggles over power. One Cherokee headman told South Carolinians that his people were forced to move because "the Creeks and the white people . . . both love fighting." Creek Indian raids took white and black captives as prisoners who could then be ransomed back to families, sold to slave traders, or exchanged with Spanish officials for cash or livestock.

Spain, claiming jurisdiction over the continent west of the Mississippi River, hoped to lure disaffected U.S. farmers into its empire. In 1788, the Richards family of Kentucky floated down the Mississippi River to Natchez with their only possession—an ax. The Spanish colonial governor granted them—and thousands more—land for family farms in exchange for their pledged loyalty to the Spanish king and commitment to send their Protestant children to imported Irish Catholic priests for religious conversion. As individual families Americanized the border, Spain tried to use taxes on river trade and riverside forts to restrict the expansion of the U.S. nation by impeding its access to the Mississippi River. Spain also expanded its military presence in Louisiana and Florida by establishing forts on disputed territory and, in 1793, signing the Treaty of Nogales, which promised mutual assistance between the Spanish and the confederation of Cherokees, Chickasaws, Choctaws, and Creeks against U.S. expansion in the region.

Worried about the shifting loyalties on its western borders, the U.S. Congress swiftly admitted Kentucky and Tennessee as new states in 1792 and 1796. Turning disputed Indian land into national territories and national territories into states became a key strategy for the United States as it expanded its power west, adding Ohio in 1803.

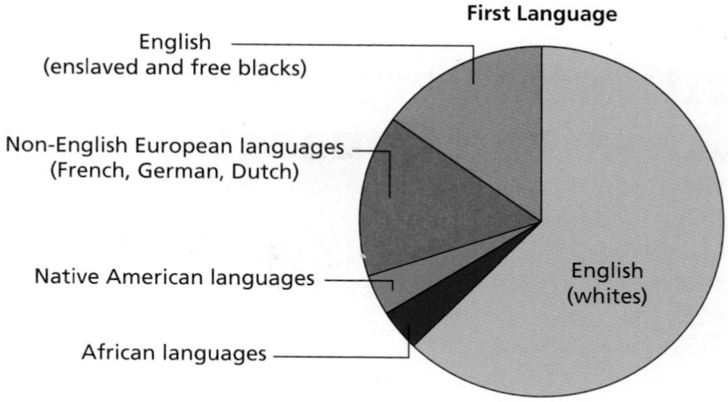

Figure 8.1 Language Diversity in the United States in 1790 The first U.S. census revealed that nearly one of four people living within the boundaries of the United States did not speak English as a first language but spoke German, French, and West African and Native American languages. English speakers had different degrees of proficiency and often used regional pronunciations and local terms. ▲ Source: Adapted from Jill Lepore, *A is for American*.

8-1c American Populations

Art and language highlight tensions within a growing population.

A year after Washington took office, the United States undertook its first census to count the residents of the United States and its organized territories. Census takers walked through communities, recording the name of the head of household, the number of free white males over and under the age of sixteen, the number of free white females, "all other free persons" (meaning people of color and Indians living in U.S. settlements), and slaves. By their count, the U.S. population was 3.9 million and growing. With birthrates higher than Native American or European settlements, the expanding U.S. population put pressure on its borders. But internal pressures divided that populace by culture, race, and language.

Jokes, essays, and plays underscored the fact that Americans regarded those living on the other side of the country as foreigners. The first play written and professionally performed in the United States, Royall Tyler's *The Contrast* (1787), featured an honest country bumpkin character, Jonathan, who lived up to all of the stereotypes of New England "Yankees" as unsophisticated and stubborn.

Noah Webster, Massachusetts teacher and lawyer, concluded that "A National language is a national tie, and what country wants it more than America?" Webster, like his mentor Benjamin Franklin, thought that a distinctive, official "American" language would unify the new country (see Figure 8.1). He started with spelling and pronunciation. In *The American Spelling Book* (1788), the most popular textbook for decades, Webster explained rules for reading and writing everyday words and simplified several common usages: *honour* became *honor*, and *musick* became *music*. Some of his later proposals to further simplify the language sparked racist satire. One newspaper mocked Webster's efforts to unify the public through language by printing fake fan mail from Irish, German, and black readers. A supposed black correspondent urged Webster as a "fello Cytzen" to add words like "hommany" and "banjoe" to the lexicon, but the satire made it clear that Native American cuisine and West African musical instruments were as unwelcome to the national culture as their words were to the national language.

Another immigrant, starring in the first U.S. bestseller, amplified the vulnerabilities of people set adrift in a mobile, polyglot country. Charlotte Temple, an English schoolgirl impregnated by a British soldier who brought her to America and abandoned her, was the heroine of *Charlotte: A Tale of Truth* (1791), written by English-born, Massachusetts-raised Susanna Haswell Rowson. Novels, a new form of literature in the eighteenth century, focused on stories of regular people rather than historical heroes or Biblical characters. People could rent copies of these books in the circulating libraries that sprung up in cities and towns.

Readers loved **seduction novels** like *Charlotte Temple* and Leonora Sansay's *Secret History* for their exciting plots and complicated moral messages. Young women, who were both the main characters and a large proportion of the audience, were free to choose their own husbands and newly independent in attaining education away from home and familiar neighborhoods. Yet with freedom came danger. In these novels, female heroines were vulnerable to tricks and betrayals from the very people who should have been reliable authorities: teachers, parents, and fiancés. The narrative of virtue under attack resonated personally and politically with Americans cast in unfamiliar surroundings. With corruption at home and betrayal abroad, many felt that the security of the young republic was at risk.

seduction novels Popular fictional stories centered around the seduction of innocent young women by male scoundrels.

8-2
Atlantic Revolutions and American Consequences

William Blake, the English poet and engraver, created this erotic image, *Europe Supported by Africa and America* (1796), to illustrate a book by J. G. Stedman, a Dutch officer sent to put down a slave rebellion in South American Suriname. The armbands on the women representing Africa and America recall the shackles of slavery. The rope, held by the white woman, binds all together.

What does the illustration suggest about the relationship among the continents in an age of emancipation? Is it to be egalitarian or hierarchical? Why are the continents represented by nude female figures? ▶

Stedman, John Gabriel/The Bridgeman Art Library

The American Revolution was part of an age of revolutions that overturned rulers and upset traditional hierarchies, military alliances, and borders. Sailors, slaves, writers, and merchants traversed the oceans, bringing with them ideas about freedom and equality, but their experiences demonstrated the social upheaval unleashed. Revolutions in France and Haiti shared dedication to liberty and natural rights and shunned the idea of privileges based on birthright. They also involved widespread participation of poor, formerly ignored people who fought for their own reasons that did not always coincide with those of the elites. Almost immediately, these revolutions became part of renewed warfare among European powers, leaving the United States clinging to neutrality abroad and politically divided at home. As war raged around the new country, political parties came to shape government decision making.

☞ As you read, think about how the American experience of revolution influenced responses to revolutions around the Atlantic. How did people understand the United States's position in global events? Did subsequent revolutions change how they thought about the American Revolution?

8-2a Revolution in France

France, like Britain and Spain, was economically devastated by the continuous warfare of the eighteenth century. Turning to a combination of new taxes and borrowing to pay its debts, the kingdom soon found itself in political and economic crisis. When the French government proposed a stamp act in 1787, protesters revived arguments from anti-Stamp Act pamphlets published 20 years earlier in North America. That same year and the next, failed harvests and harsh winters pushed peasants to riot over bread prices. To deal with the crisis in 1789, King Louis XVI convened the Estates General, a representative body that had not met for 175 years. By tradition, this assembly was divided into orders, or "estates," the first being the nobility and the second the clergy, both exempt from most taxes. The third estate—everyone else—not only paid almost all the taxes but also expected to be outvoted by the nobility and clergy because each estate had one vote. Members of the third estate wanted voting in this assembly to be by numbers of delegates. On July 14, the people of Paris seized the Bastille, an old royal prison, in a protest. Claiming a new order of "Liberty, Equality, Fraternity," they established a Constituent Assembly, overturned the traditional tax system, and voted for a constitutional monarchy. The following year, the Marquis de Lafayette, who initially supported the emerging revolution, handed the key to the Bastille to Thomas Paine, the radical writer who had rallied American patriots to the cause of independence with his *Common Sense*. Lafayette told him to deliver it to George Washington because "the principles of America opened the Bastille."

French revolutionaries express the radical potential of rights.

French Revolution Political and social revolution in France overturning the monarchy and establishing a republic.

Declaration of the Rights of Man and Citizen Document written by the French National Assembly asserting natural rights, freedom of religion and the press, and the idea of government as contract.

The **French Revolution** seemed at first to affirm the American Revolution. The Constituent Assembly's **Declaration of the Rights of Man and Citizen** of August 1789 drew on Enlightenment thought and rhetoric from the American Revolution (see Table 8.1) Expressing his admiration of the revolutionaries' goals, Paine in 1791 published the *Rights of Man*, in which he argued that human rights are inborn and governments merely human creations that can be revised and changed if they do not serve the people. French revolutionaries created a new constitution and a new elected assembly through

Table 8.1 Comparison of Revolutionary Declarations

The French *Declaration of the Rights of Man* shared ideas about human equality and inalienable rights with the 1776 U.S. Declaration of Independence. The French declaration of 1789 also proclaimed specific rights soon to be enshrined in the U.S. Bill of Rights (1791), demonstrating the transatlantic intellectual currents of the Age of Revolution.

Issue	United States (1776)	France (1789)
Motivation	"A Prince, whose Character is thus marked by every act which may define a Tyrant, is unfit to be the Ruler of a free People."	"The ignorance, neglect, or contempt of the rights of man are the sole cause of public calamities and of the corruption of governments."
Source of rights	"All men are created equal"	"Men are born and remain free and equal in rights. Social distinctions may be founded only upon the general good."
Unalienable rights	"Life, Liberty, and the Pursuit of Happiness"	"Liberty, property, security, and resistance to oppression"
Relationship of government to people	"Governments are instituted among Men, deriving their just Powers from the Consent of the Governed."	"Law is the expression of the general will. Every citizen has a right to participate personally, or through his representative."
Citizens' responsibilities	Not specified	• Submission to legal arrest • Determination and payment of taxes • No infringement on others' natural rights
Rights affirmed in law	Not specified	• Fair legal process of accusation, arrest, and imprisonment • All innocent until proven guilty • Freedom of thought, expression, religion • Property ownership

which the common people could exert power. In the new constitutional monarchy, the king—like any citizen—was subject to the rule of law. Seeing their ideals confirmed by the French revolutionaries, many in the United States celebrated with French fashions and toasts to the friendship of the United States and France. The town of Hopewell, Kentucky, renamed itself Paris. In 1793, one young Virginian vowed to cross the Atlantic to join the army of the republic and "*serve* the noblest cause in the world."

Some French revolutionaries pushed at the radical edge of universal rights. In 1791, French intellectual and playwright Olympe de Gouges published the **Declaration of the Rights of Woman and the Female Citizen**, rewriting all seventeen articles of the 1789 Declaration to explicitly include women as well as men. She insisted: "Woman, wake up . . . the tocsin of reason is being heard throughout the whole universe. . . . What advantage have you received from the Revolution?"

That was a question American women asked themselves as well. In 1790, Massachusetts author Judith Sargeant Murray published an essay entitled "On the Equality of the Sexes" challenging prevailing ideas that women were unequal in society because of their fundamental inferiority. Murray, like de Gouges and English author Mary Wollstonecraft, argued that men and women were born equal, but a limited education debased women. "Is it reasonable," Murray asked, that women "be allowed no other ideas, than those which are suggested by the mechanism of a pudding, or the sewing of the seams of a garment?" Murray and Wollstonecraft believed the solution to the problem lay in educating girls in writing, mathematics, sciences, and languages, not merely cooking and sewing. Only then could women realize their true potential. Their transatlantic influence encouraged the growth of private academies for girls who could afford them and educational books for those who could not. De Gouges's more radical proposals, including a new kind of secular egalitarian marriage and easy divorce, were not widely championed. In 1793, she was executed as the French Revolution devolved into mass executions of political rivals.

8-2b Revolution in the West Indies

Haitian Revolution overturns slavery.

People in the French Caribbean colony of Saint-Domingue largely welcomed news of the revolution in Paris, although for divergent reasons. A French colony of about six hundred thousand people located on the western third of the island of Hispaniola, Saint-Domingue generated enormous wealth for the French, producing 40 percent of the sugar and 50 percent of the coffee grown worldwide. Early on, elite white planters in the colonial assembly hoped that the Revolution would yield economic gains by transforming Saint-Domingue from a colony into a province. They wanted to be released from mercantilist restrictions and bound only by laws passed by locally elected leaders and subsequently sanctioned by the king. For the large numbers of free people of color, in contrast, the Revolution promised rights and protections that would make them equal to their free white neighbors.

Declaration of the Rights of Woman and the Female Citizen Document penned by de Gouges asserting the rights of women as being equal to those of men and claiming the Revolution for women.

Haitian Revolution Slave revolt on the French colony of Saint-Domingue that grew into a political independence movement, abolishing slavery and establishing a new nation.

Ultimately, it was the enslaved majority, who outnumbered the free population by ten to one and who seized on the notion of equality, that pushed revolution to its radical extreme. In August 1791, thousands of enslaved people marched across the island in a coordinated insurrection, killing a thousand whites, burning hundreds of sugar and coffee plantations, and plunging the island into civil war (see Table 8.2). Clearly inspired by the revolution in France, the enslaved rebels also drew on West African symbols and ideas. One rebel, when captured and killed, was carrying revolutionary pamphlets printed in Paris as well as an African amulet made of hair, herbs, and bone.

In demanding an end to slavery, the **Haitian Revolution** from 1791 to 1804 appealed to a growing international movement that proclaimed universalist messages of liberty and equality. The movement initially targeted the inhumanity of the slave trade, graphically depicted in Thomas Clarkson's 1788 engraving of the cruel crowding below decks on a slave ship. In 1789, English antislavery activists published *The Interesting Narrative of the Life of Olaudah Equiano*, which served as a template for explaining the injustice of slavery in a world speaking of liberty and equality. In 1794, France abolished slavery in the entire French Empire and declared that all were citizens with rights.

White and mixed-race slaveholders fled Saint-Domingue, taking their slaves with them to cities around the Atlantic. Between 1791 and 1805, tens of thousands of refugees arrived in

Table 8.2 The Course of the French and Haitian Revolutions

The French and Haitian Revolutions spanned more than a decade of intertwining legal, political, and military developments. Both ended with self-proclaimed emperors taking command of the nations that had emerged from the global conflict.

1789	French Estates General convenes in Versailles National Assembly organizes Paris crowd storms the Bastille National Assembly issues *Declaration of the Rights of Man*
1791	Assembly creates French constitutional monarchy
1791	Free people of color in French colonies are granted citizenship Slave insurrection begins in Saint-Domingue Thousands of slave owners flee to the United States
1792	French National Convention abolishes monarchy and declares France a republic
1793	French King Louis XVI is executed Toussaint L'Overture, leader of former slave army, allies with Spain to prevent France from reinstituting slavery in Saint-Domingue
1794	France abolishes slavery in entire empire L'Ouverture sides with French forces Napoleon stages coup, establishes Consulate
1796	L'Ouverture is declared governor of Saint-Domingue
1801	L'Ouverture proclaims new constitution, is declared governor for life
1802	Napoleon sends troops to re-establish French power in Saint-Domingue and re-instate slavery.
1803	Napoleon's troops in Saint-Domingue are defeated United States buys Louisiana territory from France L'Ouverture is imprisoned in France
1804	Declaration of independence is issued in Haiti Napoleon crowns himself emperor of France Jean-Jacques Dessalines proclaims himself emperor of Haiti
1806	United States passes Haitian Embargo Act

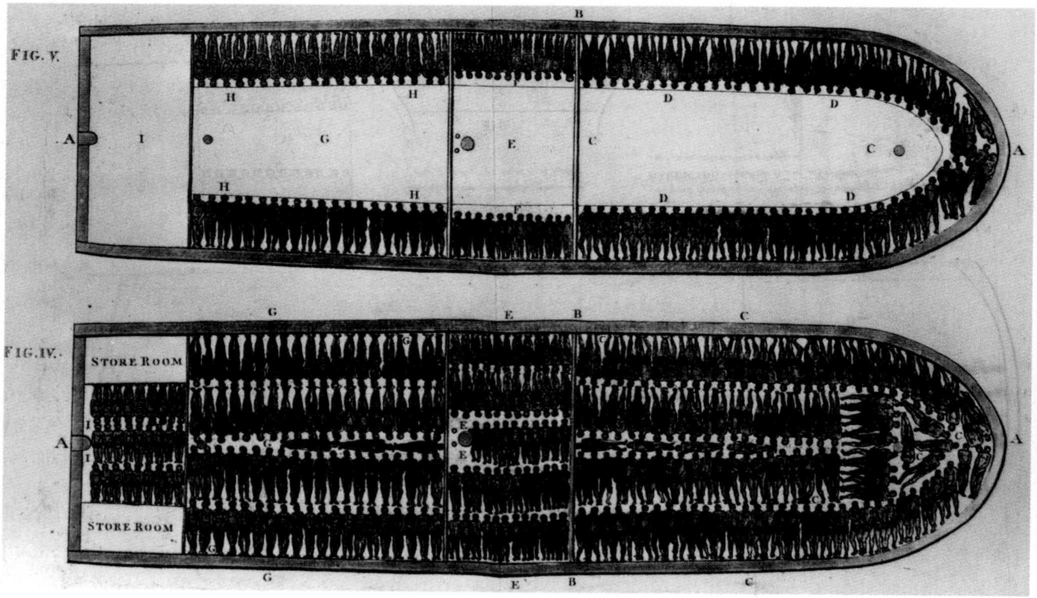

The Art Archive

Inhumanity of the Slave Trade First published in 1788 by the Plymouth Chapter of the Society for Effecting the Abolition of the Slave Trade, Thomas Clarkson's engraving *The Brookes Ship* became a widespread image of the dehumanizing Middle Passage. Reproduced on pamphlets, tokens, and other emblems of the international antislavery movement, it quickly circulated among activists. ▶

Global Americans According to his autobiography, **Olaudah Equiano** was born an Ibo in the kingdom of Benin in the middle of the eighteenth century. Kidnapped as a child and sold into the international slave trade, Equiano was shipped first to Barbados, then to Virginia, and then around the Atlantic Ocean working on merchant ships, sold and resold several times. In 1766, his Philadelphia owner allowed him to purchase his freedom, and he made his home in England. He continued to travel on trading voyages and in 1773 accompanied a polar expedition that was looking for a water passage from Europe to Asia.

In 1789, Equiano published his autobiography with the backing of British abolitionists; it had multiple editions in his lifetime and was translated into Dutch, German, and Russian. Alone and with a group called the Sons of Africa that he founded, Equiano traveled around Britain and Ireland speaking against slavery and the slave trade. He married Englishwoman Susan Cullen in 1792, and they had two daughters. He died in 1797, ten years before Britain abolished the Atlantic slave trade. Some recent scholarship suggests that Equiano was in fact born in South Carolina before beginning his journeys around the Atlantic. His autobiography, which so vividly captured the dislocation and misery of the Middle Passage, may actually be a combination of personal testimony and the collective experience of American slavery as an Atlantic phenomenon. ▲ Everett Collection Historical/Alamy Stock Photo

North American cities of New York, Philadelphia, Charleston, Savannah, and New Orleans. Initially, states such as Virginia created relief funds to provide for them, but the refugee presence was profoundly destabilizing. Many enslaved people living in the United States were inspired and encouraged. In 1793, enslaved Baptist Preacher Gowan Pamphlet was reportedly found carrying a letter stating that people of "our color" would "be in full possession of the hole country in a few weeks" aided by West Indian slaves. One Virginian claimed to have overheard his slaves discussing "how the blacks *has* kill'd the whites in the French Island." Soon white Virginians and slave owners across the United States were blaming "the example in the West Indies" for discontent in the slave population.

8-2c U.S. Diplomacy in the Age of Revolutions

The United States seeks to maintain trade relations and avoid being drawn in to Europe's wars.

Americans who had celebrated the early French revolutionaries' declarations of liberty and natural rights had different reactions as the Revolution entered a far more violent phase. In 1792, revolutionary France declared war on Austria, initiating more than two decades of warfare. By 1793, Britain and France were at war again, with Spain allied with Britain. That same year, revolutionaries executed the French king, queen, and thousands of priests and aristocrats who had been part of the old aristocratic world. Those killings were followed by months of "The Terror" as rival political factions arrested and executed each other in the tens of thousands as "enemies of the revolution."

Confronted with such violence, Americans were divided over whether to support France and Haiti as embodiments of republicanism or back their old imperial parent Britain, which still supplied nearly 90 percent of imports to the United States. Taxes charged on British imports were the main source of income for the new federal government. In addition, the more radical sentiments of revolutionaries pledging racial and gender equality worried political leaders, who had spent a decade experimenting with controls on the revolutionary impulse.

In April 1793, the recently reelected Washington proclaimed neutrality in European wars, which neither France nor Britain accepted. Edmond Genêt, representing the new French republic, arrived on American soil and promptly began using U.S. resources for French purposes, commissioning American privateers to attack and seize the cargo of British merchant ships in the Caribbean and organizing local troops to march against Spanish-controlled New Orleans. In spite of his repeated violations of U.S. sovereignty, Washington did not extradite him when a new French regime recalled him to be executed and instead, Genêt became a U.S. citizen. Britain likewise refused to accept U.S. declarations of neutrality, directing its navy to seize any American merchant ships trading with the French in the Caribbean. Washington sent Supreme Court Chief Justice John Jay to negotiate. The resulting **Jay's Treaty** (1794–1795) avoided war and gained some concessions for the United States, including a promise to remove British forces from western forts and permission to trade in the British East Indies. Opponents in Congress, outraged that the 1778 alliance with France had been violated, demanded to see the details of treaty negotiations. Washington refused, invoking **executive privilege**.

Jay's Treaty Agreement between Britain and the United States designed to ensure peace and maintain commercial ties but unpopular with some Americans.

executive privilege Concept that the president can withhold sensitive information from Congress or the courts if it concerns national security or communications within the executive branch.

Hoping to win the United States as an ally against the British on the North American continent, Spain made new trade concessions. In 1795, Spain signed the **Treaty of San Lorenzo** with the United States, opening the Mississippi River to untaxed U.S. trade and permitting American merchants to store and ship goods from the valuable port of New Orleans. The treaty betrayed Spain's promise of mutual assistance with allied southeastern Indians by establishing a U.S. border at the thirty-first parallel north of Florida, land occupied by Creeks, Choctaws, and Chickasaws. It also removed one more barrier to U.S. expansion to the west. Observing the one thousand-mile Mississippi River that now joined, as much as separated, Spanish and U.S. claims, one Spanish official concluded "You can't put doors on open country."

8-2d First Political Parties

Coalitions with competing policies and ideologies harden into two parties.

The divide between supporters and opponents of the French Revolution helped give rise to the first U.S. political parties. Factions had long been feared as promoting selfish personal interests at the expense of the public good. But in the early 1790s, those who opposed the anti-French philosophy of Jay's Treaty or Hamilton's economic plan began to express their disagreement in "democratic-republican societies." Modeled on the revolutionary Sons of Liberty, these clubs consisted of middling-rank urban artisans. Asserting that centralized power had reached too far, they supported local and state legislative caucuses. They were branded as "democrats," a term that suggested support for mob rule, by their opponents, who dug in their heels as **Federalists**. By the late 1790s, national political leaders began to draw on these coalitions, and the **first party system** took shape (see Table 8.3).

The issues that divided Federalists and **Democratic-Republicans** were not identical to those that had separated the Federalists and Anti-Federalists of the Constitutional debates. The new Federalists, many of whom were New Englanders and urban commercial people, favored a strong national government run by the rich and well born, closely tied to business and commercial elites and backed by a substantial army. They preferred a passive citizenry that deferred to its leaders. Democratic-Republicans advocated a weaker national government that preserved the revolutionary elements of the Constitution. They optimistically welcomed trade with the world and did not fear rule by the common people, either because they themselves were farmers and lower-rank men or because, as white Southerners, they lived where the common folk could not vote or were already deferential. Many believed that a radical transformation of power and social relationships around the world was still ongoing, with the United States at the forefront.

In 1796, Washington linked domestic partisanship and "foreign entanglements" as two kinds of dangerous alliances that threatened the young republic. In a letter later called his **Farewell Address** announcing that he would not seek or serve a third term as president, Washington reiterated republicanism's stress on sacrifice and unity of interest. "The common and continual mischiefs of the spirit of party" were jealousy and desire for revenge that would enflame people's passions, leading to riot or tyranny. Just like blind adherence to a party, a "passionate attachment of one nation for another" could destroy a republic by dragging it into distant wars or rendering it a "satellite" of powerful nations. Better to take advantage of the geographical distance between the United States and Europe, Washington urged, and practice a policy of **free trade** without mercantilist restrictions, as well as neutral politics toward all other nations. As republican revolutions around the Atlantic expanded into imperial wars, this idea proved difficult to realize, although it remained an enduring ideal of U.S. foreign relations.

Treaty of San Lorenzo Agreement between Spain and the United States granting Americans trading access to the Mississippi. It negated promises of military support to southeastern Indians.

Federalists Political party in power after the American Revolution that favored commercial development and ties with Britain.

first party system Emergence after 1796 of two main political parties identifying themselves as Federalists and Democratic-Republicans.

Democratic-Republicans Political party opposing the Federalists and favoring agriculture supported by recent immigrants and poor whites.

Farewell Address Letter written by Washington to "Friends and Fellow Citizens" at the end of his second term as president, cautioning against partisanship and foreign entanglements.

free trade System of international commerce with few taxes or other restrictions. It was a political ideal contrasted with mercantilism and took various forms.

Table 8.3 Comparison of the First U.S. Political Parties

Anglo-American political culture had long deplored political parties as dangerous "factions." Although a true republic could have only a single common good, competing ideas about how to deploy power abroad and at home led to the first party system in the United States.

Federalists	Democratic-Republicans
Supported protective alliance with Britain	Supported political alliance with France
Distrusted mass politics	Encouraged mass politics
Favored strong central government	Opposed strong central government
Had strongest support from merchants, property owners, city dwellers	Had strongest support from farmers and southern planters
Had Alexander Hamilton, John Adams as national figures	Had Thomas Jefferson, James Madison as national figures

8-3

Membership and Participation in the Republic

The Granger Collection, New York

In this 1796 cartoon, newspaper editor William Cobbett, who wrote under the name "Peter Porcupine," says "I hate this country and will sow the seeds of discord in it." Columbia, with the liberty cap and the American eagle, weeps over a memorial to the Declaration of Independence to the left. On the right, the Devil and the British Lion offer money to destroy liberty, trampling on the Magna Carta, U.S. flag, and 1778 Treaty of Commerce with France.

How are elements of revolutionary imagery used in this satire of politics in the 1790s? What does the presence of these elements suggest about the emerging identity of the United States? ▶

Go to MindTap® to practice history with the Chapter 8 **Primary Source Writing Activity: Political Inclusion.** Read and view primary sources and respond to a writing prompt.

In his Farewell Address, Washington asserted that "with light shades of difference," Americans had "the same religion, manners, habits, and political principles" to unify them. He attempted to minimize the very real divisions that stoked the political crisis over belonging in the new United States. As people in the United States hammered out the details of who should lead and who should follow, who could participate in governance, and whose power should be checked, they crafted new forms of citizenship. In the process of defining individual rights and to whom they would apply, a set of hierarchies rooted in race and gender hardened.

☞ As you read, reflect on the development of U.S. political culture in the decades following the ratification of the Constitution. How did people decide who deserved full participation in the republic?

8-3a Political Culture and Presidential Power

Popular political culture yields to partisanship.

Accustomed to political participation by revolutionary boycotts, spinning bees, and other politics of the streets, non-elites remained deeply involved in public demonstrations. Print culture and debating societies further encouraged voters and nonvoters to participate in political debate. This democracy of information allowed for wide participation, and disgruntled elites sarcastically complained that "Every body is wise enough to be secretary of state."

Political debate grew more sharply barbed once Washington left office. John Adams, Washington's vice president, was a leading political and intellectual figure of the Revolution and Confederation periods but personally much pricklier than the first president. When elected in 1796, Adams could not command the same loyalty as his predecessor and objections to executive power grew stronger. Jefferson, who received the second highest vote in the Electoral College, became vice president, placing partisan rivals together in the executive branch.

National leaders took a deeply personal view of political action. Like many high-ranking gentlemen, they relied on their own reputations to establish power in their communities, and their ideas about honor shaped the way they conducted business. Elected officials used the aristocratic practice of dueling, called **affairs of honor**, to appeal to the public when they felt a partisan rival had demeaned them. In an affair of honor, one man challenged another to shoot pistols at each other from an agreed-upon distance. Typically, the matter ended in negotiation before shots were fired, but the willingness to risk death to preserve one's reputation was regarded as a sign of leadership fitness. In 1804, Vice President Aaron Burr shot and killed Hamilton in a duel over reputation. For the less refined, fists could serve as well as pistols, and personal grievance coexisted with policy debates at all levels of government. In 1798, Roger Griswold, representative of Connecticut, brawled with Vermont congressman Matthew Lyon on the floor of the House of Representatives over a dispute rooted in name-calling and tobacco spit.

affairs of honor Polite name for dueling that emphasized the importance of reputation defended by face-to-face violence and was most common among southern elites and national politicians.

Global Americans **William Duane** was born in colonial New York in 1760. Widowed by colonial-Indian warfare, his mother moved the family back to Ireland, where he grew up to be a printer. He moved to Calcutta, and began *The Indian World*, a paper critical of the powerful East India Company. Deported back to England, he soon ran afoul of the government there for criticizing its crackdown on a free press and freedom of assembly. In 1795, Duane moved to the United States, where he supported himself as an assistant to Benjamin Franklin Bache's Democratic-Republican newspaper in Philadelphia. When Bache died from yellow fever, Duane took over the paper along with Bache's wife, Margaret, whom he married.

A harsh critic of Federalist policies and political repression, Duane was arrested under the Sedition Act and targeted as an alien. Together with a group of exiles from the Society of United Irishmen movement in Ireland, he helped his friend Thomas Jefferson win the presidency in 1800 and in 1802 became a naturalized U.S. citizen. He fought in the U.S. army during the War of 1812 and in 1822 traveled to Latin America to observe revolutionary developments there, publishing his experiences in *A Visit to Colombia*. Duane's influence on American politics showed the significance of international radicals who championed participatory democracy, religious freedom, and economic independence from European empires. ▲ Saint-Mémin, Charles Balthazar Julien Fevret de, 1770–1852, artist

Brawls were unusual, but nasty words were not. Revolutionary leaders who had promoted public education in the 1780s hoped that increased literacy would produce sober, moral citizens to help keep order in the new country. Instead, newly independent Americans eagerly expanded print culture to communicate ideas about society and culture that challenged the status quo. By 1790, there were more than one hundred newspapers and other periodicals in the United States, five times as many as had been available in 1760, and they accelerated partisanship in the 1790s. Colonial newspapers had mainly reprinted news from Europe, but editors in the 1790s took aggressively political stances, printing personal attacks against political opponents. The motto of *The Federalist Gazette of the United States* was "He that is not for us, is against us." Subscribing to a partisan paper signaled membership in a group of like-minded citizens.

During Adams's administration, Democratic-Republican newspapers, often edited by Irish immigrants, became the voice of political dissent over foreign policy. Following Washington's precedent, Adams attempted to remain neutral in the war between England and France, but both countries attacked U.S. merchant ships engaging in trade with the other. Finally, in 1798, Adams cut off trade with France, sparking an undeclared conflict later called a **Quasi-War** (1798–1800). He strengthened the U.S. army, supported Congress's buildup of a navy, and sent ships to the Caribbean to engage French privateers who were seizing U.S. ships. He sent ammunition, food, and other supplies to Toussaint L'Ouverture, the former slave who had become the military leader of the Haitian Revolution, thereby serving two purposes at once: opposing France and repaying a debt to the seven hundred fifty free black soldiers in L'Ouverture's army who had fought with American patriot forces during the siege of Savannah in 1779. Newspapers such as the *Aurora* lambasted Adams for betraying the American Revolution by warring against the country that had aided Americans in their fight for independence. Personal in its attacks, the *Aurora* called him "old, bald, blind, querulous, toothless."

Quasi-War Naval conflict between the United States and France conducted mainly in the Caribbean over trading rights and alliances during which the U.S. navy experienced a buildup.

Alien and Sedition Acts (1798) Targeting recent immigrants and critics of the president, four U.S. laws that many interpreted as a Federalist attack against Democratic-Republicans.

In retaliation, Federalists in Congress passed the **Alien and Sedition Acts (1798)**, a series of laws designed to silence pro-French newspaper editors. These laws made it a crime to speak, write, or print anything against the U.S. president that would bring him "into contempt or dispute" or to oppose "any measure or measures of the United States." These extremely broad laws gave the president power to deport any foreign resident whose activities he considered dangerous. More than twenty Democratic-Republican newspaper editors and politicians were arrested and several sent to prison under these laws. Similar laws in England, also passed in the 1790s, treated dissent as an unlawful attack on government. In 1794, Thomas Paine was tried and found guilty of seditious libel in English courts (although he had escaped to France) for publishing *The Rights of Man*.

Opponents of the Alien and Sedition Acts insisted that they violated the First Amendment of the Constitution, which protected freedom of speech and the press. Vice President Jefferson and Congressman Madison secretly drafted resolutions later passed by the state legislatures of Kentucky and Virginia, denouncing the acts. In these **Virginia and Kentucky Resolutions**, Democratic-Republicans articulated the idea of **nullification**, which argued that a state could refuse to enforce or obey federal laws that it deemed unconstitutional.

8-3b Citizenship and Political Rights

States expand and contract political rights.

Before the Revolution, colonists were British subjects by birth. In the new United States, people proclaimed themselves citizens, a word that implied active political participation. Because it was active, citizenship could be chosen by those born on other continents, and the first Congress had to establish the rules with naturalization laws. Under the **Naturalization Law of 1790**, any "alien" who had lived in the United States for more than two years could become a citizen as long as she or he was "a free white person" who could present proof of good character. After taking a loyalty oath, they and their children under twenty-one years of age became citizens.

Imperial powers insisted that loyalty could not be shed so easily. Desperate for sailors to fill its ranks in its ongoing struggles with French forces, the British navy practiced **impressment**, seizing sailors on U.S. merchant ships and forcing them into service, claiming that any person born a British subject remained so until death. The seizure of thousands of U.S. citizens born before the Revolution or naturalized was a direct rejection of U.S. sovereignty, and in 1796, Congress passed a law allowing any American sailor who paid 25 cents to receive a "certificate of citizenship" that he could present to British officials trying to impress sailors into the Royal Navy. Seeking something more permanent, sailors also used tattoos of eagles, liberty poles, or the date 1776 to proclaim their allegiance to the United States. Of course, actual British deserters could do the same.

Those particular inked emblems of citizenship evoked support for Democratic-Republicans and republican revolutions worldwide, demonstrating that struggles over citizenship were closely tied to partisan politics. Democratic-Republicans supported the easy inclusion of immigrants into the political body of the United States; Federalists opposed this. William Cobbett, popular Federalist editor who was himself a British migrant, sneered that "As well might we attempt to tame a Hyena, as to Americanize an Irishman." In Cobbett's Pennsylvania, tens of thousands of Irish migrants fleeing poverty and political unrest arrived in the first decades after independence. Naturalized as citizens and granted the right to vote under a 1790 state constitution that enfranchised free taxpaying men, they began voting with the newly forming Democratic-Republican party. As political control of the U.S. Congress shifted between parties, so, too, did naturalization laws. In 1798, Congress under Federalist control passed a new Naturalization Act that extended the period a person had to live in the United States before becoming a citizen to fourteen years. When Democratic-Republicans rose in power in Congress, they passed the 1802 Naturalization Act, which reduced the residency requirement to five years.

The Bill of Rights protected citizens' rights to political participation through freedom of speech, the press, and assembly. The states, however, determined who could vote. The reshuffling of voting from a privilege associated with property holding to a right associated with white adult male citizenship had begun in the Revolution-era state constitutions. In New Jersey, the state constitution granted the right to vote to "all inhabitants . . . of full age who are worth £50." Taking the gender-neutral language at its word, property-holding single women began to vote in local elections, a practice that was soon acknowledged in election laws of the 1790s, referring to voters as "he or she." In fact, when lawmakers proposed a state amendment in 1800 that would explicitly allow women to vote in congressional elections, others declared it unnecessary. One legislator said "Our Constitution gives this right to maids or widows black or white." In New Jersey, property holding, not gender or race, was what qualified a voter. It was a logic that prevailed in Canada, where unmarried women with property voted until 1834.

In New Jersey, however, Democratic-Republican claims of voter fraud during an 1807 election led to a revision of voting rights law. The new law not only banned women from voting but also took the right away from black men. Other states followed suit in the first four decades of the nineteenth century, striking down laws requiring that a voter own property and simultaneously disenfranchising white women and all blacks. Faced with a democratic population filled with rowdy and unreliable citizens, legislators decided to draw lines by color and gender rather than wealth. The Revolution had been a victory for popular sovereignty in which the people rule; the two decades that followed defined who would be included in "the people" for political purposes.

Virginia and Kentucky Resolutions Measures passed by the legislatures of Virginia and Kentucky asserting states' rights to interpret the constitutionality of laws and opposing the Alien and Sedition Acts.

nullification Legal theory that the states, as sovereign parts of the United States, retain the right to void laws passed by the federal government.

Naturalization Law of 1790 Act establishing process by which a free white person born outside the United States could become a legal citizen after two years.

impressment Practice of seizing people and forcing them into military service conducted by navies against the crews of enemy or neutral ships.

8-3c Political Exclusion and the Limits of Choice

Race and gender constrain political inclusion.

Citizenship could be chosen, but political choices, like economic choices, were often constrained. Free women, like free men, could become naturalized citizens, but only single women were obligated to pay taxes to support state and local government. Married women under the old English principle of coverture were folded within their husband's economic identity. Nor were married women held to the same standard of loyalty to the state. In the case of *Martin v. Commonwealth of Massachusetts* (1805), the Massachusetts Supreme Court ruled that a married woman Loyalist who had fled during the Revolution could not have her property confiscated. Federalist Judge Theodore Sedgwick explained, "A wife who left the country in the company of her husband did not withdraw herself—but was, if I may so express it, withdrawn by him." As Sedgwick's words suggested, free women made a single politically significant choice—the choice of a spouse—and that determined their citizenship status. In fact, American-born women who married foreigners frequently found their status as U.S. citizens challenged.

Fugitive Slave Law of 1793 U.S. law that authorized the capture and return of people who escaped from slavery and established a fine for anyone who helped a runaway.

Black Laws Acts passed in Northwestern states where slavery was illegal to exclude African Americans or limit their access to education, voting, and the legal system.

Gabriel's Rebellion of 1800 Virginia slave rebellion led by a skilled artisan slave who claimed the legacy of the American Revolution and planned to march on Richmond.

American Colonization Society Organization founded in 1816 by clergymen and politicians to raise money to send former slaves and free blacks to settle in Africa.

Liberia Colony founded by the American Colonization Society on land purchased in West Africa that was designed for the settlement of free blacks from the United States.

Free black Americans found their ability to function as citizens sharply curtailed by laws that attempted to link them with the enslaved population. The **Fugitive Slave Law of 1793** put the power of the federal government on the side of slave owners trying to recapture runaways. It established a $500 fine for interfering with the recapture of a supposed runaway and permitted slave owners to establish ownership by making a case to an individual judge. Black people kidnapped by slave catchers—whether fugitives or free people—were denied the right to jury trial and even to present evidence supporting their own case for freedom. All were presumed to be slaves unless proven otherwise, revealing the fragile protections of living in so-called free states. Even in places where slavery was prohibited, **Black Laws** reduced free black men and women to a permanent underclass. First enacted in Ohio in 1804, Black Laws in states created from the Northwest Territory forbade any "black or mulatto person" from testifying in court against a white person, joining the militia, or attending public schools. The laws required free black immigrants to carry identity certificates and to sign guardianship bonds with property holders who would be responsible for them.

Enslaved people faced violent opposition to claiming citizenship. In 1800, a skilled artisan slave named Gabriel organized a rebellion in Richmond, Virginia. He was inspired by revolutionary ideals as they recirculated during the ongoing Haitian Revolution. He also hoped to take advantage of partisan divisions within the white community. Organized among skilled urban slaves and free blacks, the rebels of **Gabriel's Rebellion of 1800** planned to march on Richmond, seize the ammunition and guns stored in the Capitol Square Building, take Governor James Monroe hostage, and demand freedom and economic justice for Virginia's poorest. Gabriel predicted that as word spread, more slaves as well as poor whites, who shared free blacks' economic and political hardships, would join the rebel army, forcing a bargain with city leaders.

When the rebellion was exposed by nervous plantation slaves and the conspirators captured and tried, several participants explicitly called upon revolutionary words. One claimed: "I have nothing more to offer than what General Washington would have had to offer, had he been taken by the British and put to trial. . . . I have adventured my life in endeavouring to obtain the liberty of my countrymen, and am willing to sacrifice in their cause." Gabriel was sentenced to death. Many of the other alleged conspirators were distributed to slave traders to sell to the Spanish in Louisiana.

The presence of free American-born blacks in Gabriel's conspiracy confirmed many white Virginians' belief that the republic could not accept them as citizens. In 1806, the state passed a new manumission law, requiring any newly freed person to leave the state within the year. Some thought moving to a new state was not enough. In 1816, a group of wealthy white ministers, lawyers, and politicians formed the **American Colonization Society** whose purpose was to raise money to deport free African Americans. Some members feared that free blacks could never find equal treatment in the United States and were better off forming their own community elsewhere. Others thought the existence of free blacks undermined the institution of slavery and to protect it, the United States needed to expel former slaves. Using private funds and money from the U.S. Congress, the Society ultimately sent thousands of African Americans to **Liberia**, a new colony they founded on the West Coast of Africa, next to Sierra Leone, the colony for freed slaves that Britain had established in 1787.

8-4

Agrarian Republic or Empire of Liberty?

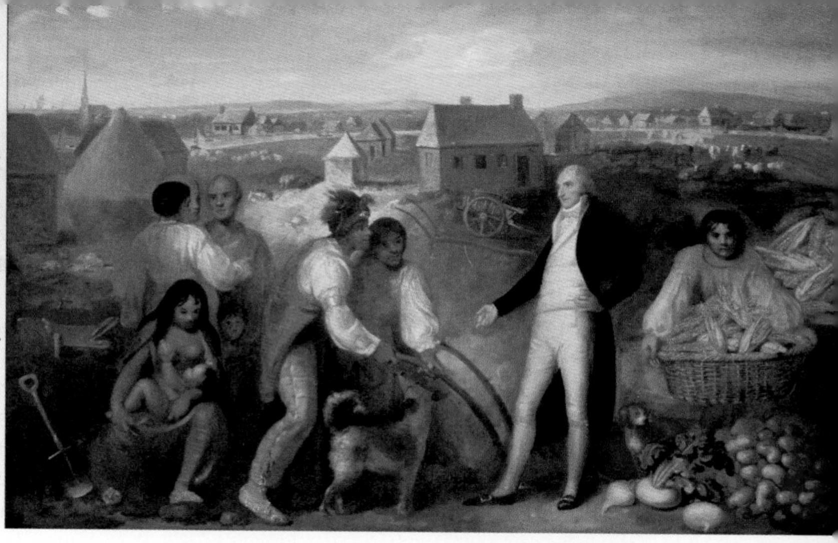

Courtesy of Greenville County Museum of Art, Greenville, S.C.

This circa 1805 painting by an unknown artist is known as "Plan of Civilization." It depicts a man like Benjamin Hawkins, superintendent of Indian Affairs for the Southeast United States from 1796–1816, who was sent to introduce European-style farming techniques to Creek Indians. In this painting, slave cabins with distinctive West African peaked roofs are visible in the background.

Compare this picture with the first seal of Massachusetts Bay Colony presented in Chapter 3. What does each image suggest about the artist's attitude toward Indians? What has changed from the colonial era to that of the early United States? ▶

Thomas Jefferson was elected president in 1800 after a bitter partisan campaign. In his first inaugural address, he attempted to draw the country back together, proclaiming "Let us, then, fellow citizens, unite with one heart and mind. . . . We are all Republicans, we are all Federalists." He spoke optimistically about the "experiment" of the United States, "Kindly separated by nature and a wide ocean from the exterminating havoc of one quarter of the globe; too high-minded to endure the degradations of the others." He praised the small farmers whose independence, he believed, would preserve the virtue of the republic. Reality did not match his rhetoric, however, because the United States could not avoid the rest of the world. As a trading nation, it depended on merchants and exchange with other countries. As a country that shared a continent with multiple groups, families, coalitions, and empires, it had to negotiate its boundaries. Although politicians articulated a fantasy of virtuous expansion, the desires and ambitions of people living on the land drew the United States into positions similar to the empires that patriots had criticized. Meanwhile, people debated whether a republic could, or should, become a new kind of empire.

☞ As you read, compare the emerging U.S. empire to other early nineteenth-century empires. How was it similar? How was it different?

8-4a Democratic-Republicans in Power

New national political leadership envisions the United States as a new type of republic.

The election of 1800 was, in the minds of Democratic-Republicans, a chance to redeem the promise of the American Revolution and to turn away from the drift toward national consolidation that had taken place under the Federalists. Campaigning against the Alien and Sedition laws, new taxes, and the undeclared war with France, Jefferson called on the voting public not to endorse the extremes of the French Revolution but to reinvigorate American republicanism. Celebrating their victory and the nonviolent transfer of power, Democratic-Republicans began to dismantle some of the Federalist program—repealing the excise on whiskey, shrinking the army, eliminating district courts, and withholding appointments for Federalist justices of the peace.

One of the justices deprived of his appointment, William Marbury, brought his case, ***Marbury v. Madison*** (1803) to the U.S. Supreme Court. Marbury did not get his job back, but in his decision, Chief Justice John Marshall established the practice of judicial review by which the Supreme Court had the power to judge whether executive actions and laws passed by Congress or the states were constitutional. Laws in conflict with the Constitution were void. It was a precedent that formally expanded the checks on congressional power by asserting the independence of the judiciary.

As his Kentucky Resolution had illustrated, Jefferson saw the United States as a compact between states as much as a centralized nation. He and the other Democratic-Republicans championed a small national government that loosely held together a country of independent farmers who sold their surplus to distant markets. Jefferson argued that the country could consist of an expanding set of politically equal states spreading freedom across the hemisphere, a concept he referred to as an "empire of liberty." Jefferson's expansionist vision initially confronted demographic and economic challenges. In 1800, 75 percent of North America was in Native American hands, including half of the supposed territory of the United States and most land claimed by Spain. The population of the United States was about 5.3 million, in contrast to the 13 to 17 million people living in neighboring Spanish America.

Marbury v. Madison U.S. Supreme court case that established the court as an equal branch of the federal government, with the power to overturn laws that violated the Constitution.

Peale, Rembrandt (1778–1860)/Collection of the New-York Historical Society, USA/
The Bridgeman Art Library

Jefferson as Natural Man Like George Washington, Jefferson was a Virginia slave owner, but he cultivated a public image different from that of the first president. Rembrandt Peale painted this portrait in 1805 at the beginning of Jefferson's second term. In it, the president wears his own hair rather than a wig, a plain, unruffled neck cloth, and a fur collar. Fur and clean linen were luxuries, but they were not aristocratic, befitting an executive who also discontinued formal presidential receptions. ▲

Jefferson's ideal of free trade on the world's oceans was undermined by the perils of merchants in the Mediterranean, where the North African states of Algiers, Morocco, Tunis, and Tripoli licensed privateers to capture ships and take hostages. In gaining independence, U.S. merchants lost the protection of the British navy, and its sailors were captured and enslaved by the **Barbary States**, which demanded millions of dollars in tribute to release them. Lurid novels and sensationalistic press accounts alarmed the American public with tales of innocent white hostages sold into slavery by dark-skinned Muslim pirates, and the government had limited tools to fight back. Treaties failed, tribute payments drained federal accounts, and U.S. shipbuilding lagged. When Tripoli declared war on the United States in 1801, Jefferson stopped the payments, sent ships to blockade Tripoli's port, and supported the building of a navy to defend U.S. sovereign rights. Conflicts, including a second war with Algiers, continued until a series of treaties was made in 1815.

Barbary States Group of North African states, some with allegiance to the Ottoman Empire, that captured merchant ships on the Mediterranean and demanded tribute payments for their return.

civilizing mission Rationalization for U.S. territorial expansion into Indian lands that involved converting natives to Protestant Christianity and spreading new family and farming patterns.

Democratic-Republicans' ideals also were tested by ongoing global crises. After a decade of warfare around the Atlantic and across Europe, some revolutionaries sought stability in strong military leaders. In France, General Napoleon Bonaparte claimed the highest political office of First Consul in 1799. In 1801, the revolutionaries of Saint-Domingue chose military commander Toussaint L'Ouverture to be governor-general of a semi-independent country. Determined to retake the island, Napoleon dispatched sixteen thousand soldiers to defeat the rebels and terrorize the population. The French captured L'Ouverture, who warned them that the "tree of liberty" would "spring up again by the roots." On January 1, 1804, new leader Jean-Jacques Dessalines announced the nation-state of Haiti with a Declaration of Independence that demanded former slaves be incorporated into society on equal terms. Haitians purged the island of white influence, first with mass killings of remaining French people and then with law. Haiti's 1805 Constitution forbade white men from owning land and declared that all Haitians would be called "black." The U.S. Congress responded by placing an embargo on trade with Haiti, and Jefferson refused to recognize the self-styled "black republic." Fearing the spread of slave rebellion, Jefferson opted for economic isolation, and other empires followed suit. The U.S. embargo and refusal of acknowledgement lasted until 1863, when President Abraham Lincoln opened diplomatic ties.

8-4b Indian Accommodation and Resistance

Eastern Native Americans confront U.S. plans for their future.

The people most pressingly facing U.S. expansion were Native American neighbors. After the Treaty of Greenville in 1795, the United States temporarily abandoned its policy of military conquest in favor of a **civilizing mission**. The federal government signed dozens of land treaties with tribal groups who ceded land to the United States. In exchange, the United States pledged to bring what leaders called "civilization" to Indians, permitting them to coexist with Americans and eventually melt into American society through intermarriage and the casting off of Indian ways. For men like Benjamin Hawkins, the U.S. Indian agent to the Creeks from 1796–1816, "civilizing" Indians meant converting them to Protestant Christianity, reorienting their economic and family lives, and pushing them toward centralized political authority. Hawkins directed Creek men to take over farming from Creek women and to employ more intensive forms of cultivation that required less land. He urged women to expand their household tasks, including spinning and weaving. He convinced the Creek National Council to take over the responsibility of punishing Creek lawbreakers rather than leave it to individual clans. The United States also supported religious schools in Indian territories that focused on training young Indians. Nancy Reece, a Cherokee girl who attended the Brainerd Mission School in Tennessee, wrote that "When school hours are over, the girls attend to domestick concerns and learn to make their own clothes and the clothes of the boys so they can do such work when they go home, to assist their parents. . . . and perhaps can learn their parents something that they do not understand."

Cherokee parents who sent their children to such schools were adopting the strategy of **accommodation**, going along with the U.S. plan in the hope of preserving their land and families. For many Southeastern Indians, including Cherokees and Creeks, the practices that white Americans called "civilized" were not distant from their own. Most were already farmers. Cherokee and Creek clans had also long been involved in the slave trade. Using slave labor to grow cotton that women could process into fabric appeared to be a good economic strategy among elite Native Americans. By accommodating to the U.S. civilization project, they hoped to confirm their sovereignty as an independent nation located next to the United States. Their accommodation, moreover, was often selective; many adopted economic practices but not gender roles. Hawkins claimed that Creek men made "slaves" of their wives by having them work in the fields, but Creek women preferred to add spinning to their farming work rather than replace one with the other. One Creek grandmother insisted to Hawkins that "she could not consent that the woman and children should be under the direction of the father" as in Euro-American families.

accommodation Indian strategy of accepting some U.S. social, cultural, and economic interventions to maintain land and political sovereignty.

Other Indians looked at the losses of land they had already suffered (see Map 8.1) and concluded that accommodation would not stop the flow of white migrants. The Senecas, who had once claimed 4 million acres in New York and Pennsylvania, were by the turn of the century confined to fewer than 200,000 acres. The formerly powerful

Map 8.1 Indian Land Cessions and Resistance The backcountry in the Age of Revolution was the site of prolonged warfare and forced treaties by which Indian groups lost their land to British American colonists and then the United States. Indians made and remade alliances between the Seven Years' War and the War of 1812 in an effort to resist the devastating loss of their lands. ▼

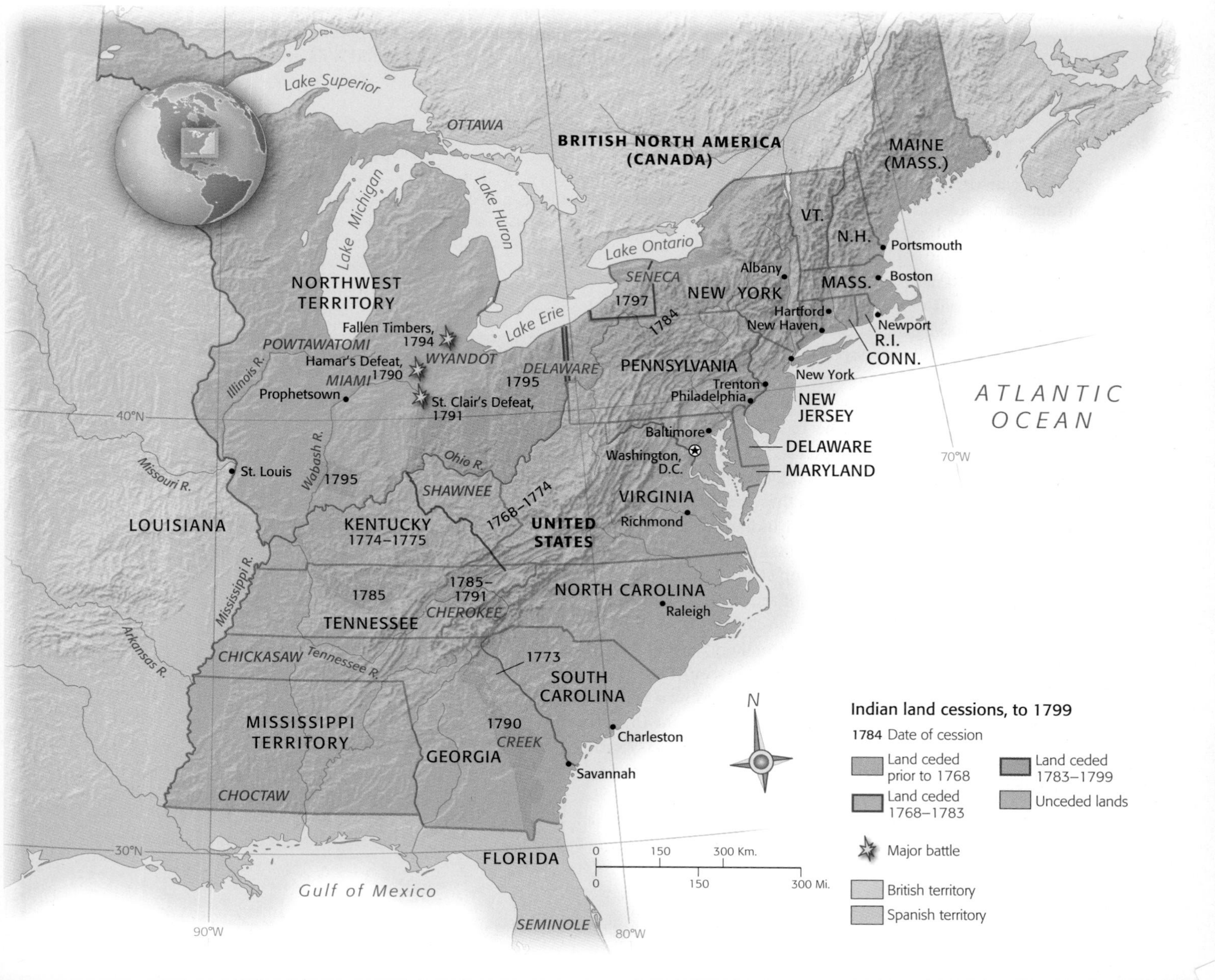

Iroquois Confederacy could no longer provide protection and diplomacy. Alcoholism, poverty, and violence plagued Indian communities torn apart by decades of war and U.S. land seizures. In 1799, Handsome Lake, a Seneca, had a religious vision that turned him away from alcohol to lead a religious revival among the Iroquois. Handsome Lake began to preach "the Good Message," a group of teachings that combined Christian and Iroquois beliefs and focused on self-renewal. He urged Indians to stop using alcohol and cease intertribal violence. Other prophets followed Handsome Lake, and the period from 1795 to 1815 became an "Age of Prophesy" for Northwestern Indians, inspiring resistance rather than accommodation.

The Shawnee Tenskwatawa (known as The Prophet) was the most influential of this group. He warned Shawnees that Americans were "children of the Evil Spirit," and Indian adoption of U.S. culture was to blame for their suffering. Denouncing Christianity, metal tools, domesticated animals, and private property, Tenskwatawa drew hundreds of Shawnees, Delawares, Ottawas, and others to the new village of **Prophetstown** on the Tippecanoe River in Indiana. Indian unity depended on turning away from white culture; prophets even argued that mixed-race children should grow up with their white relatives. Those who doubted the prophets were accused of witchcraft and some were tortured or burned at the stake.

8-4c The Louisiana Territory

Global revolutions and rivalries give the United States an opportunity to expand.

Faced with the options of resistance and accommodation, substantial numbers of Native Americans instead moved across the Mississippi River. The territory of Louisiana, stretching west from the Mississippi and including the valuable port of New Orleans, was inhabited by a diverse group of Native Americans; French, Spanish, and British traders; and U.S. farmers. In the minds of European leaders, Louisiana was also a key piece in the global balance of power. The first wave of the Haitian Revolution in 1791 had brought thousands of planters and slaves to New Orleans as refugees. Drawing on their sugar-growing and processing expertise, these refugees turned the local economy from one based on Indian fur trading and the cultivation of tobacco and indigo into one focused on slave-labor-based sugar production. New Orleans quickly became one of the main slave markets for North America.

The region's potential as a plantation-based economy attracted Napoleon, who hoped to turn Louisiana into a supply colony for the French Empire in the Caribbean. In 1800, faced with rising debt, Spain agreed to give up its Louisiana claims to France, provided that the French not sell it away again. However, recapturing the island of Saint-Domingue and re-enslaving the population proved more difficult than Napoleon had anticipated. The strength of Haitian generals L'Ouverture and Dessalines, as well as the deadly toll that tropical diseases took on French forces, caused Napoleon to abandon his vision of an integrated French Caribbean power. Without Saint-Domingue's profitable sugar plantations, Louisiana's value to France diminished. Needing money to fund imperial conquest in Europe and eager to encourage U.S. neutrality, Napoleon sold Louisiana in 1803 to the United States for $15 million, doubling the size of its territory (see Map 8.2).

The **Louisiana Purchase** of 1803 was celebrated by hunters and farmers who wanted Louisiana land and permanent trading rights on the Mississippi. What the United States lacked was the money to make the purchase. British and Dutch banks signed the loans, at 6 percent interest, which suited British political calculations because it stripped its old adversary France of a large piece of its global empire.

For Jefferson's Louisiana vision to become reality, American farmers needed water routes to the Pacific Ocean connecting the river systems of the new territory to the Missouri and Mississippi Rivers. The president commissioned the Corps of Discovery Expedition, led by Meriwether Lewis and William Clark, to cross the new

Prophetstown Indian town on the Tippecanoe River where Tecumseh and Tenskwatawa forged a pan-Indian alliance. It became the target of an attack by U.S. troops.

Louisiana Purchase Acquisition of the Louisiana Territory from France that was financed abroad and doubled the size of the United States.

Free Black Culture in New Orleans At the time of the Louisiana Purchase, the population of New Orleans was 38 percent enslaved and 20 percent free people of color. In 1786, the Spanish colonial governor had required all women of color to wrap their heads in kerchiefs, a style that women in West Africa had pioneered by using imported Indian textiles. By the nineteenth century, the practice had evolved into a fashion statement for free and enslaved women of color as depicted in François Fleischbein's *A Portrait of Betsy* (circa 1837). ▼

The Historic New Orleans Collection

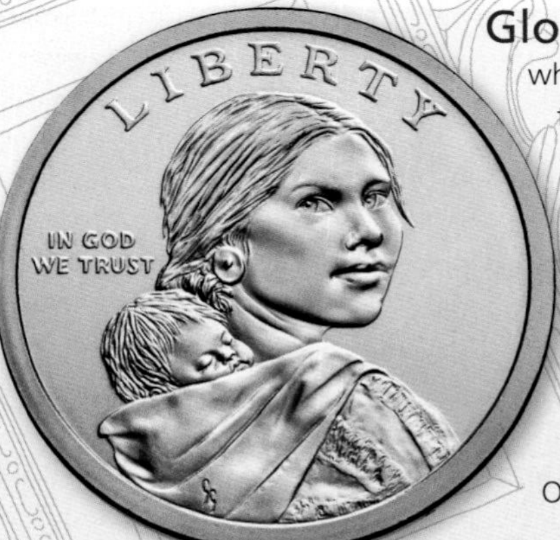

Global Americans Born around 1788, **Sacagawea** was a Shoshone Indian who as a girl was kidnapped by a raiding group of Hidatsas and taken as a slave to the northern Plains. As a teenager, she was traded to French Canadian fur trader Toussaint Charbonneau to be his wife. In the winter of 1804–1805, carrying her newborn son, Sacagawea accompanied William Clark and Meriwether Lewis in their journey across the North American continent to investigate the territory purchased from France. She provided practical skills of gathering edible plants and acting as interpreter and guide. According to Clark, her presence also "confirmed . . . our friendly intentions, as no woman ever accompanies a war party." She was unexpectedly reunited with the family of her birth, who agreed to help equip and guide the expedition over the treacherous Rocky Mountains and on to the Pacific Ocean.

After her return, Sacagawea moved with her husband and son to St. Louis, where the boy was enrolled in a boarding school that trained children in the civilization program. Sacagawea died of illness in 1812. Her short life demonstrated how much U.S. diplomacy and discovery, like that of all empires, depended on the participation of Indian women. Her experiences dramatize how people in the middle of a vast continent served as pivots of global economic flows. Yet no depictions of Sacagawea were made in her lifetime. When she was chosen in 1998 to appear on a new U.S. dollar coin, artist Glenna Goodacre used modern Shoshone college student Randy'L He-dow Teton as a model. ▲ United States Mint

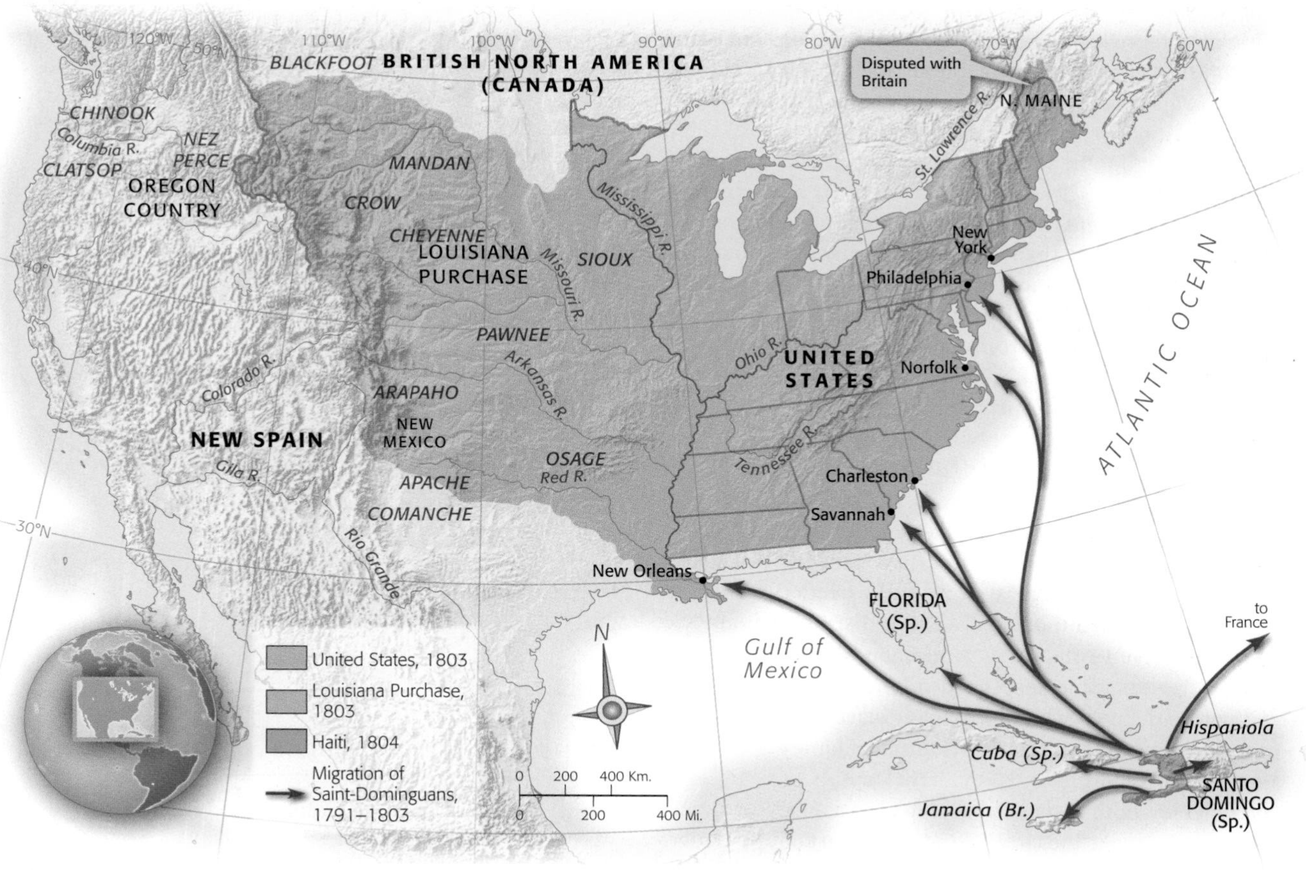

Map 8.2 Louisiana Territory and Haitian Revolution, 1803 The Louisiana Purchase connected slave rebellion with the expansion of the United States onto Indian land. Some in the United States believed that foreign ownership of Louisiana threatened U.S. security and encouraged Indian resistance to U.S. expansion. North Carolina congressman Samuel Purviance warned Congress in 1803 that if France kept Louisiana, "the tomahawk of the savage and the knife of the negro would confederate in the league, and there would be no interval of peace." ▲

territory in search of a Northwest Passage that would link his empire of liberty to Asia. In addition to staking a claim to the northwest border of the territory, the expedition was charged with gathering information on plant and animal life as well as establishing direct contacts with Native American groups. Lewis and Clark's two-year trip did not find an easy route to the Pacific; they reached its shores in an arduous journey over land. The artifacts and samples they collected were exhibited in the first American museum as unique elements of a new empire.

National Museum of American History/Kenneth E. Behring Center/Smithsonian Institution

Cotton Gin Enslaved people used Eli Whitney's cotton gin to remove seeds from cotton fibers with combs turned by a hand crank. Mills in England were ready to process cleaned and baled fibers into cotton fabric, and less than a decade after Whitney secured his patent, the United States was producing 45 percent of the raw cotton for British mills. By 1803, cotton had become the leading U.S. export; by 1820, the United States had become the world's leading producer of cotton (surpassing India); and by 1850, it produced 68 percent of total world production. ▲

8-4d Cotton Frontier

The booming market for cotton expands American slavery.

Although Democratic-Republican politics and ideas about the economy praised free and independent producers, U.S. engagement with a global marketplace ultimately boosted a dramatic expansion of slavery in the early nineteenth century. Since the 1780s, industrialists in England had been building factories to produce colorful printed cotton fabrics previously imported from India. The factories needed cotton, and the United States soon became their main source. The first cotton grown in the American colonies was sea island cotton from Barbados, which flourished in very wet areas of Georgia and South Carolina but not farther inland. Another kind of cotton, called *short-staple cotton*, could grow widely, but the seeds were hard to remove from short, fuzzy fibers. In 1794, Eli Whitney devised a machine he called the *cotton gin* that could separate the seeds from the fibers more quickly than could be done by hand. Farmers spread cotton cultivation rapidly across the lower South. The money it brought enabled the United States to buy manufactured goods from Europe, pay off foreign debt, and invest in industry.

Enslaved men, women, and children produced this wealth. Although at the time of the Revolution some politicians had predicted a gradual decline in U.S. slavery, the expansion of the cotton frontier instead encouraged a dramatic increase. In the first two decades after the ratification of the Constitution, more than one hundred thousand enslaved African people arrived on North American shores and were quickly transported inland. When Congress debated whether to allow slavery to continue in newly purchased Louisiana, James Jackson of Georgia and Jonathan Dayton of New Jersey both insisted that slavery was the only way to make the land a productive part of the U.S. republic.

In 1807, Britain banned the Atlantic slave trade, and the U.S. Congress followed suit, officially ending the importation of African captives effective January 1, 1808. To enforce these laws, both countries' navies policed the Caribbean, where the illegal slave trade continued for decades. Yet the number of U.S. slaves, increasingly laboring in cotton fields, continued to grow (see Figure 8.2).

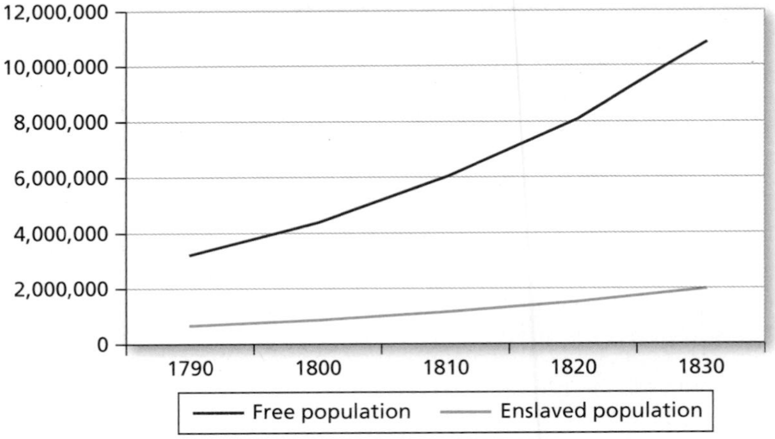

Historical Statistics of the United States, online millennial ed.

Figure 8.2 Growing U.S. Population, Free and Enslaved Although the United States banned the transatlantic slave trade in 1808, its enslaved population increased in the early nineteenth century. Under U.S. law, the children of enslaved women were deemed slaves for life. These children, in turn, gave birth to another generation of people held in slavery to increase the wealth of their owners. The free population grew through "natural increase," too, and also through immigration. ▲ Source: Historical Statistics of the United States Online Millennial edition.

Life on the cotton frontier was grueling. Enslaved people cleared the land and created the fields. Each year, men, women, and children planted, thinned, picked, ginned, baled, and shipped cotton. They also grew food crops, raised livestock, and repaired fences and buildings. Their status as valuable property made them frequent targets of Southeastern Indian raids seeking to plunder their enemies. Some captives were sold into the continental slave trade; others were enslaved by Creek and Cherokee plantation owners.

8-5 Erosion and Expansion of Empires

In John Archibald Woodside's patriotic painting *We Owe Allegiance to No Crown* (1814), revolutionary symbols such as the liberty cap are joined with new symbols, including the stars and stripes flag. The sailor representing the United States crushes a crown beneath his foot. Broken chains, evoking slavery and "enslavement" to Britain, lie on the ground. Woodside specialized in painting signs for taverns and hotels; he also decorated fire engines and painted banners for private military companies.

How would Americans have known about the symbols depicted in this painting? How would that influence the way people interpreted the painting's meaning? ▶

Erik Arnesen (c) Nicholas S. West/National Portrait Gallery, Smithsonian Institution/Art Resource.

The European wars of 1803 to 1815 marked the end of a century of conflict among European empires over land, trade, and power. Those conflicts had embroiled people around the globe, at sea and on land, and in 1812, the United States, which had vowed to stay out of foreign wars, declared war on Britain. As with the earlier conflicts, North American Indians' claims to their own territory and trade became an essential part of the global conflict, and its resolution further weakened their ability to use European antagonisms to hold back the taking of their land. For the United States, what some saw as the second war for independence cleared the way for land acquisition, cross continental expansion, and international trade.

☞ As you read about U.S. participation in the global wars of the early nineteenth century, consider the significance of the War of 1812. Was it really a second "war for independence"? Was it an entirely new conflict?

8-5a War of 1812

Americans contest independence in a second war against Britain.

Jefferson's vision of an empire of liberty was possible only if international trade allowed farmers in the West to sell their goods. In 1803, after a two-year pause, Europe plunged into another round of warfare, making U.S. trade and territory once again targets. For the next twelve years, Europe was embroiled in the Napoleonic Wars as French forces numbering in the hundreds of thousands under Napoleon invaded and conquered much of the land and people from Spain to Russia. Napoleon crowned himself emperor of France in 1804, pledging to bring stability to the French and to secure equality under the law. He pledged the same for the nations he conquered, but they allied to fight back, and battles raged across Europe, at sea, and at colonial outposts around the world.

The wars were commercial as well as military. Both Britain and France passed resolutions forbidding neutrals such as the United States from trading with the other empire or its colonies in the Caribbean. Some Americans saw these as attempts to reinstate the mercantilist trade policies, forcing the United States back into colonial status. In retaliation, Congress passed the **Embargo Act of 1807**, which cut off exports to foreign ports. Jefferson hoped that the consequences would convince France and Britain to respect the trading rights of neutrals, but the result was a crushing economic downturn for the United States. American farmers could not export their crops; American merchants could not sell their goods; and American sailors, dockworkers, and boardinghouse keepers could no longer make a living from networks of global trade. James Madison,

Embargo Act of 1807 U.S. law advocated for by Jefferson that cut off foreign trade in an attempt to assert U.S. rights against European empires.

who was elected president in 1808 at the end of Jefferson's two terms, initially sustained the embargo, but strong opposition resulted in its replacement with the Nonintercourse Act of 1809, which resumed trade with all countries except France and Britain.

Attempts to remain neutral and trade freely failed, as did U.S. efforts to coerce powerful European empires to follow its wishes. In frustration, Democratic-Republican congressmen from the South and West elected in 1810 demanded an aggressive assertion of U.S. power. Called **war hawks**, they pushed for a declaration of war, citing Britain's violations of national sovereignty: its impressment of American sailors, its alliances with enemy Indians in the West, and its encouragement of backcountry violence. In June 1812, the war hawks got it.

Canada was the first target of the U.S. offensive in the **War of 1812**. Looking at its small population of British subjects, Jefferson had declared that conquering Canada was "a mere matter of marching" up to get it and achieving, within a year, "the final expulsion of England from the American continent." Some even thought the Canadians would welcome membership in the republic of the United States. Between 1812 and 1814, U.S. forces attempted several invasions in the area around the Great Lakes, all of which failed.

U.S. soldiers ran into difficulties immediately because of their lack of experience. British soldiers, many of them recruits from Ireland, were veterans of the Napoleonic Wars, but most American soldiers were inexperienced recruits from militia units. Because soldiers were armed with smoothbore muskets that were accurate only to about one hundred yards, companies depended on disciplined, coordinated firing to disperse the enemy—just the kind of maneuver that required drill and obedience in the confusion of battle. To become an effective fighting force, as Major Thomas Melville, Jr., insisted, these men had "to forget *the Citizen* and become *the Soldier*." U.S. soldiers were also poorly paid and equipped. In 1812, Congress initially offered $5 a month to men capable of earning at least $10 per month as civilians. Even though Congress increased pay and created incentives including land in the West, the United States could not meet its targets for a fully staffed army. Nevertheless, Congress refused to accept free blacks into the army, reversing the precedent of the Continental Army of the Revolution.

war hawks Name for a group of Democratic-Republicans led by Henry Clay who favored war against Britain to resolve trade, territorial, and impressment disputes.

War of 1812 War between the United States and Britain concerning trading rights, territory, and alliances with Native Americans.

Battle of Tippecanoe Attack by U.S. troops led by William Henry Harrison against pan-Indian alliance led by Tecumseh.

Red Sticks Members of radical faction of Creek Indians who allied with the British against the United States and were defeated by Andrew Jackson and allied Indians in 1814.

The powerful British navy blockaded ports along the Atlantic and Gulf coasts, raiding eastern towns and bringing American foreign trade to a standstill. British warships, outnumbering the fledgling U.S. fleet four to one, engaged in naval battles along the coast, but the Great Lakes became the main focus of naval warfare. The United States quickly built ships to defend against British offenses and in September 1813, Commodore Oliver Hazard Perry destroyed British forces at Put-in-Bay on Lake Erie. Control of Lake Erie meant control of supply lines in the West, but neither side could gain ground, and troops at the border with Canada were in a stalemate.

8-5b Tecumseh's Confederacy

Wide-scale Indian alliance mounts its last stand.

As it had during the Revolution, the British army depended on its alliances with Indians to combat the United States, and when formal hostilities broke out, the United States was already engaged in extensive Indian warfare. In 1808, Tecumseh, brother of prophet Tenskwatawa, revived the confederacy of Blue Jacket and Little Turtle by transforming the Prophet's religious following into a pan-Indian military alliance. As a teenager, Tecumseh had fought with allied Indian forces under Joseph Brant. Perhaps, he reasoned, this new alliance of diverse Indians groups could form its own united "state" neighboring the United States. In its early stages, the alliance was vulnerable. In the fall of 1811, William Henry Harrison, governor of Indiana Territory, led troops toward Prophetstown, outnumbering and defeating the Indians there at the **Battle of Tippecanoe** and burning the community to the ground. As Prophetstown was rebuilt, Tecumseh turned to the British. Together, British and Indian soldiers captured strategic forts on the Great Lakes, took Detroit (see Map 8.3), and fought U.S. armies in Kentucky. But long supply lines through Canada and the fact that many Indian warriors returned to their families after battle weakened Tecumseh's ability to hold together his forces. Coordination with supporters in the South was difficult. In October 1813, Tecumseh was killed in a final confrontation between his warriors and the army headed by Harrison at Moraviantown, a Canadian town established by a Pennsylvania missionary for English-speaking Christian Indians. The war continued, but the Indian alliance was fatally wounded.

Fighting in the South pitted a militant confederacy of Creeks, called the **Red Sticks** because of their war clubs, allied with British troops against the U.S. forces led by General Andrew Jackson of Tennessee. Inspired by their own group of prophets preaching spiritual renewal and rejection of white ways, the Red Sticks had military backing from the Spanish. In 1813, divisions between accommodationist Creeks and the Red Sticks dissolved into a civil war that overlapped the conflict between Britain and the United States. Creeks fought on both sides over U.S. expansion into their territory. In 1814, Jackson, with Cherokee, Choctaw, and Creek allies, defeated Red Stick Creeks at the Battle of Horseshoe Bend, killing eight

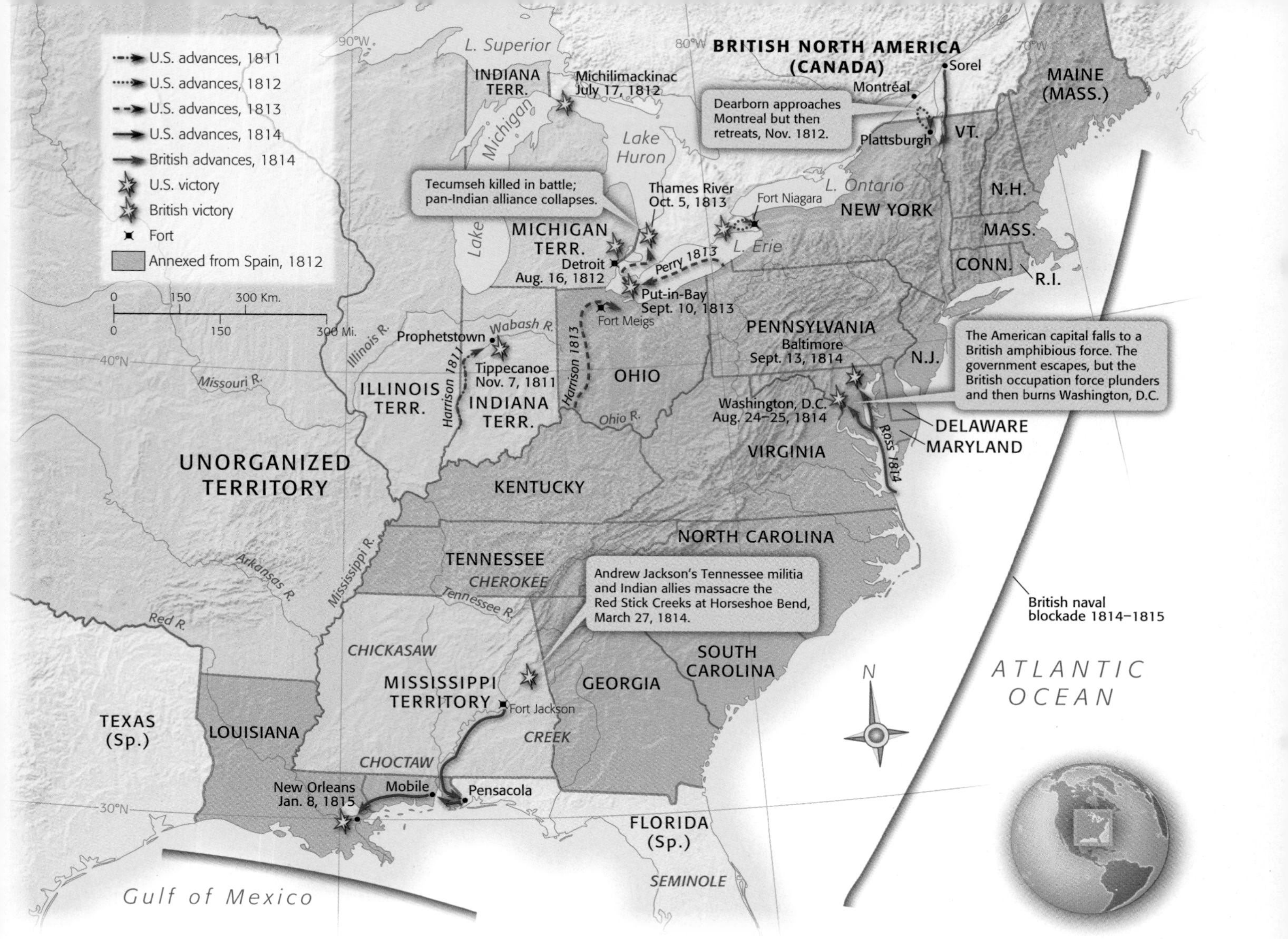

Map 8.3 Fighting the War of 1812 U.S., British, and Native American forces fought the War of 1812 in disparate locations across the eastern portion of North America. As in previous imperial conflicts, privateers and naval ships also attacked one another in the seas around Britain and the Caribbean. ▲

hundred warriors. In the **Treaty of Fort Jackson** that followed, the United States took two-thirds of Creek territory, land that belonged to both the defeated Red Sticks and the Creeks who had fought alongside Jackson. Red Stick leaders largely refused to sign the treaty; instead, they moved south to join the mixed communities of Seminole Indians and runaway slaves who lived in Spanish East Florida.

Defeats in the War of 1812 ended the pan-Indian alliance that had existed in various forms since the Seven Years' War. The many groups in the eastern woodlands—weakened by disease, outnumbered by the increasing migration of white Americans onto Indian lands, impoverished by the erosion of the animal skin trade, and divided over how much to adopt so-called civilization projects and respond to federal interference—were no longer able to sustain alliances and contain U.S. territorial claims. Pockets of militant resistance remained, particularly among the Seminoles, but the majority of Indians adjusted to new economic conditions and attempted to coexist with their neighbors.

Treaty of Fort Jackson Agreement following Jackson's 1814 defeat of Red Stick Creeks at the Battle of Horseshoe Bend that ceded the majority of Creek land to the United States.

8-5c Restoration

The end of fighting reshuffles the balance of power in Europe and returns the status quo to the United States and Britain.

In Europe, the tide turned against the French in 1812 with uprisings in France and Germany and France's failed invasion of Russia, which cost its army staggering losses. By April 1814, Paris was under foreign occupation and Napoleon was in exile. Britain then launched its most striking attack against

History without Borders

The Great Comet of 1811 and Political Prophesy

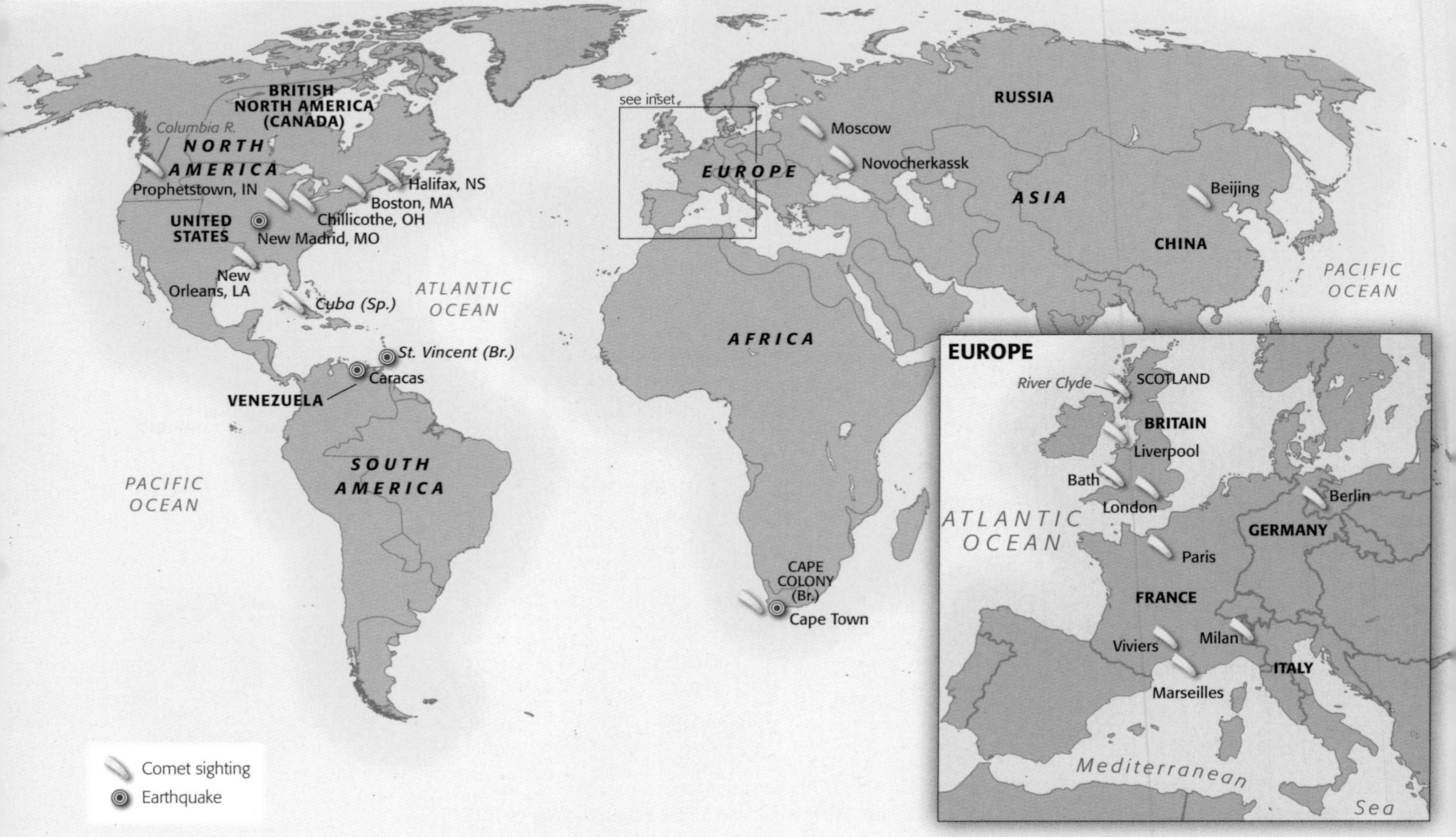

Sightings of the Great Comet, 1811–1812 People across the globe saw the Great Comet and looked for meaning in its blaze of light. In some locations, viewers wrote down their observations about the comet and its connection to earthly political events. Their accounts circulated internationally, fostering shared culture and to some degree, a shared experience. ▲

From the spring of 1811 until the summer of 1812, people around the world watched a blaze of light in the sky and wondered what it signified. Visible during the day and night, the Great Comet was first spotted with a telescope by Frenchman Honoré Flaugergues in March 1811, and could be seen by the naked eye longer than any other in history. The comet at its peak visibility in October 1811 was as bright as the third largest star in the sky and had a split tail. By the time of its last spotting by telescope in Russia in August 1812, people around the world had come to interpret this global phenomenon in the context of local circumstances, seeing in it the prophesy of dramatic changes in the balance of power among people. Others thought profit, not prophesy, would be its greatest legacy.

In America, it was called "Tecumseh's Comet" after the Creek leader whose name, chosen at birth, meant "shooting star." Drawing on a coincidence that seemed prophetic, Tecumseh and his brother The Prophet used the appearance of the comet to enhance their spiritual and political power to unify Eastern Indians against U.S. squatters. The comet coincided with a series of severe earthquakes in southeastern Missouri, northern Arkansas, and Tennessee and Kentucky between December 1811 and February 1812. These quakes, called the New Madrid Earthquakes, could be felt as far as Charleston, South Carolina, and Boston, Massachusetts. In Missouri, the land cracked and sank, and sailors on the Mississippi River reported that entire islands disappeared. The celestial object seemed a portent of earth-shattering reversals in the balance of power between native alliances and the United States.

Caricature on the 1811 Comet, c.1811 (coloured engraving), French School, (19th century)/Musee de la Ville de Paris, Musee Carnavalet, Paris, France/ Bridgeman Images

French cartoon *La Comete* (1814) This French cartoon lampoons the fashionable and foolish people who go comet viewing. Looking through telescopes, magnifying glasses, and a funnel, they are distracted from urban disorder and shady characters. The humorous image presents a stark contrast to the deadly consequences of military leaders' use of the comet. ◄

Tankard, London, 1811–12 (silver)/Emes, Rebecca & Barnard, Edward I (fl. 1808–29)/CLARK ART INSTITUTE/Sterling and Francine Clark Art Institute, Williamstown, Massachusetts, USA/Bridgeman Images

Tankard, Rebecca Emes and Edward Barnard I (London 1811/12) This tankard is engraved with the image of the Comet of 1811, three planets, and multiple stars. The comet decoration made it a souvenir of the event that would be shared as the tankard owner drank with others long after the light in the sky had faded. ◄

The comet also coincided with an earthquake in Cape Town, South Africa. William Burchell, a visiting British scientist and collector, wrote in his journal that people in town "drew from this two-fold portentous sign, the certain prognostics of the annihilation of the Cape." In fact, British and Dutch colonizers soon plunged into the Fourth War of Dispossession that pitted the Europeans against resisting Africans. In China, leaders of the Eight Trigram Sect viewed the comet as divine encouragement to plan and launch an attack on the Forbidden City to overthrow the Manchu Qing Dynasty in 1813. More than seventy thousand died as the rebellion was defeated.

In Europe, the light in the sky was called "Napoleon's Comet" and linked with another set of military prophesies and another power shake-up. Napoleon and some of his advisors saw the comet as a favorable sign to begin his assault on Russia in 1812. He was mistaken, lost most of his army in the failed invasion, and within a year was in retreat. He later wrote of this pivotal turn in the empire's fortunes that "my star was fading."

With Napoleon's army defeated and the Napoleonic Wars at last at an end, numerous enterprising Europeans turned the globally shared experience of comet watching into commercial opportunity. They sold prints of the comet, painted fans with its likeness, and etched it into beer tankards. Drawing on the belief that comets had a strong effect on the earth's atmosphere that enhanced plant and animal growth, French winemakers credited the comet with a particularly good Bordeaux crop, and "comet wine" was advertised and pursued at high prices until the 1880s. Others used a more remote connection to the comet to invoke a shared, exciting experience and encourage people to spend their money. Henry Bell, a Scottish inventor and businessman, named his new paddlewheel steamship on the River Clyde, the first commercially successful service in Europe, *The Comet*.

Critical Thinking Questions

► How did different leaders use the Great Comet of 1811 to justify military action and why?

► What role did commemoration of the Great Comet play in turning it into a type of shared culture across national boundaries? Who was included and who excluded?

the United States. British forces landed in Maryland and marched into Washington, D.C., the new capital of the United States. They burned the president's house and the capitol building as Congress and President Madison, who had been reelected in 1812, fled.

Taking advantage of southern Indian hostility and potential rebelling slaves, the British opened a southern front in Florida and Louisiana. They brought in West Indian regiments, consisting of men born in Africa and enslaved in the Caribbean, under white officers. These regiments, assigned some of the most dangerous and unhealthy work, were intended to inspire slaves to run away to the British lines as they had during the Revolution. Once again, the tactic worked. Five of Indian Agent Benjamin Hawkins's slaves escaped to join the British. But Britons were growing weary of the sprawling war.

After enforcing the punitive treaty at the end of the Creek War, Jackson took the lead in the southern fight against the British. He supported the creation of a free black battalion of soldiers drawn from the New Orleans region to defend the port from the British but also relied heavily on enslaved laborers to build fortifications and reinforce the levees. Jackson placed the city under martial law to await the final battle, which came on January 8, 1815. The **Battle of New Orleans** was a lopsided victory for the Americans, who lost only thirteen soldiers to Britain's nearly three hundred dead. Jackson was celebrated as a defender of freedom from British enslavement. Yet when the British ships retreated, several hundred enslaved Africans went with them, preferring the losing side to a life of slavery in the United States.

The **Treaty of Ghent**, which officially ended the war in December 1814, restored the territorial borders that had existed prior to the fighting. At the peace talks, the British initially proposed the creation of an Indian state in the Northwest between the United States and Canada, which the United States rejected. With no Indian representatives to speak for any of the groups in Tecumseh's alliance, the British abandoned their allies. The final treaty contained only a promise that Indian lands held before the war would be restored. They were not.

Battle of New Orleans Final military engagement of the War of 1812 that was a significant U.S. victory after the signing of the peace treaty.

Treaty of Ghent Peace treaty ending the War of 1812 that returned territorial claims to prewar status for the United States and Britain and promised the same for Indians.

Hartford Convention Meetings in the winter of 1814–1815 by New England Federalists who opposed the War of 1812 and proposed new amendments to the Constitution.

Congress of Vienna Peace convention ending the Napoleonic Wars and restoring monarchies, some with constitutions. It re-established a balance of power.

Jackson's victory took place after the treaty had been signed but before news of it had arrived in the United States. It made him the most celebrated hero of the war and a political leader on the rise. At the same moment, New England Federalists were meeting in Connecticut to pursue a new attack on Democratic-Republican power. Many opposed the war, most supported the idea of state nullification of federal laws, and some even contemplated leaving the United States to make a separate agreement with New England's strongest trading partner, Britain.

At the **Hartford Convention**, these Federalists proposed amendments to the Constitution that they hoped would protect them from the tyranny of the majority that Madison, now president, had warned about during the ratification of the U.S. Constitution. Their proposals called for limiting the representation of slaveholders, new immigrants, and backcountry farmers, all of whom tended to support Democratic-Republicans. In a piece of bad timing, they published their proposals just as the country was celebrating the end of the war. What the Federalists called dissent was attacked as treason, severely wounding the party. U.S. political culture was soon reduced to a single party, the Democratic-Republicans. In 1816, the third Virginia Democratic-Republican president in a row, James Monroe, was elected president.

In Europe, diplomats attempted to settle one hundred years of international warfare and remake the balance of power at the 1814–1815 **Congress of Vienna**. Once again, they drew lines on world maps and restored the rule of royalty. In France, the younger brother of the executed king was crowned monarch; he, like restored monarchs in Spain and Portugal, now ruled a constitutional monarchy. The defeat of Napoleon's France was interpreted as a defeat of French revolutionary ideas more broadly on the continent. One anti-French insurgent song stated, "Here's an end to equality. Here's an end to liberty. Long live God and his Majesty."

8-5d Independence in Spanish America

Spanish America enters an age of revolution while the United States strengthens national bonds.

The heavy toll of European war ultimately brought Spain's colonies into a third wave of revolutions (see Map 8.4). In 1808, the royal government in Madrid collapsed, and Napoleon placed his own brother on the throne. With the metropolitan center in turmoil, conspiracies and coups proliferated in Spanish America as American-born elites tried to take back powers eroded by the Bourbon Reforms. In 1809, the Spanish government accommodated them and declared that its American dominions were not just "colonies," but "an essential and integral part" of the kingdom, deserving of representation in the Spanish legislative body. Spain, unlike Britain in the 1770s, was willing to allow elected representation for its American entities, but it was not willing to grant equal representation. Spanish America, with a population between 15 and 16 million, was allotted nine representatives; metropolitan Spain, with 10 million people, had thirty-six. Disputes over representation and the difficulties of balancing central authority with local autonomy and popular sovereignty plagued Spanish America as it had the new United States in the 1780s.

Map 8.4 American Hemisphere in the Age of Revolution A wave of independence movements ended most of Spain's imperial claims to the Americas. Negotiations with the United States redrew boundaries that took on new meaning in the wake of Mexican independence. In spite of these changes, Spanish language, culture, and religion remained widespread. ▲

Transcontinental Treaty (Adams-Onis Treaty) Agreement between the United States and Spain acknowledging Spanish control of Texas and granting Florida and Oregon to the United States.

nationalism Identification with and feeling of loyalty to a nation, often as opposed to another group interest, such as religion.

akg-images

Simón Bolívar in Caracas The South American "Liberator" initially appealed to American politicians, who toasted him as "the George Washington of the South." The relationship later soured over political and economic power. Bolívar said of Latin American people, "We are a microcosm of the Human Race, a world apart, neither Indian nor European, but a part of each." ▲

An attempt at compromise, a new Spanish constitution of 1812 proclaimed a unified "nation" spanning the Eastern and Western Hemispheres. It granted the vote to most free adult males while taking it away from women who headed households. At the same time, the constitution formally excluded anyone with African ancestry from full rights as Spaniards and sustained legal slavery. A new, freer press spread word of the more liberal constitution. But word spread quickly, as well, when King Ferdinand VII was restored to the throne in 1814, abolished the constitution, and attempted to turn back the clock.

Revolutionaries who had spent time in the United States and Europe were already drawing on universal ideals and local cultures to lead independence movements in Spanish America. A movement in Mexico, begun in 1810, continued for a decade before ending in a new nation whose borders stretched from the Yucatan up to the Canadian border and from the Pacific to the edge of the Louisiana Territory. Simón Bolívar, leader of an independence movement in Venezuela, praised the United States as a model nation "maintained by liberty alone" in 1819. Revolutions in Latin America and South America followed, and by 1830, Cuba and Puerto Rico were all that was left of Spain's once vast Western Hemisphere empire. Many of the newly independent nations declared themselves republics but spent years in conflict over the details of how to allocate power within their multiracial communities.

The United States was slow to recognize these fellow republics and did not give official assistance to revolutionaries. It did take advantage of Spain's imperial turmoil to consolidate its own territorial claims. In 1819, the two countries signed the **Transcontinental Treaty (Adams-Onis Treaty)**, which established borders between territory claimed by Spain and territory claimed by the United States, most of it inhabited and controlled by Indians. The U.S. claimed Florida; Spain claimed land from Texas to the Pacific and down through Mexico.

In 1819, John Quincy Adams, who negotiated both the Treaty of Ghent and the Transcontinental Treaty, wrote in his diary that the "United States and North America are identical." Although far from true, his statement reflected the kind of optimistic, expansionist **nationalism** that spread in the United States after the War of 1812. This new type of patriotic loyalty and identification rested on images that had been developing since before the Revolution. The Stars and Stripes, approved by the Continental Congress in 1777 as the flag of the United States, became a prominent symbol of the nation. One flag, which had flown over Fort McHenry during its attack by British forces in 1814 inspired Francis Scott Key's poem and song "The Star-Spangled Banner." The Flag Act of 1818 formally linked the familiar symbol with the nation's expansion. Under its provisions, each time a new state joined the United States, the official flag was to gain another star. There were stars for Louisiana (a state since 1812), Indiana (1816), Mississippi (1817), Illinois (1818), and soon Alabama in 1819 as borderlands became cotton frontier states where free white men held political power through their citizenship and votes.

Summary

The War of 1812 was in one sense a second war for independence of the United States. It was part of the final confrontation of a century of warfare between Britain and its allies on one side and France and its allies on the other. Although the war itself did not change British policies toward the United States or the border with Canada, its conclusion established that the fate of the U.S. republic diverged from those of other revolutionary republics, including France, Haiti, and the new nations in Latin America. After twenty years of turmoil, the United States had not collapsed from external pressure or turned to self-proclaimed emperors to restore political order. Its political system had endured the wrenching divisions of partisan politics and dissent without dissolving into anarchy or giving way to a dictator.

Many of the American revolutionary experiments in governance and economy survived the test of the Age of Revolution, and a new form of participatory citizenship was taking hold.

There were ironies in the emerging continental empire that had come into focus by 1819. The War of 1812 solidified U.S. conquest of Indian land to the Mississippi River and beyond. With the vast territory of the Louisiana Purchase, Jefferson's vision of a continental empire seemed closer to reality. The United States had used familiar tools of empire: war, diplomatic negotiation, purchase, and national economic policy. Although the United States had joined Britain in abolishing the international slave trade in 1808, it relied heavily on a thriving interstate trade that expanded slavery to economically and politically support the nation that Jefferson had branded the empire of liberty. Finally, the egalitarian concept of citizen had replaced the old hierarchies of political subjects to a monarch, but the evolving meaning of citizenship on the ground remained contested.

<Thinking Back, *Looking Forward*>

As you review this chapter, critically evaluate Jefferson's idea that an "empire of liberty" could exist. Think about the laws, trading relationships, and military agents of empires in the colonial period. When did they restrict liberty, and when did they promote it? How did the United States in the early nineteenth century differ from the empires that had come before it?

Consider the new United States in its global context: Which political and economic relationships survived the Age of Revolution and the subsequent restoration of European monarchies, and which were transformed?

In the coming chapters, evaluate the consequences of the Age of Revolution for different groups.

How did the rights and obligations of citizenship change over the nineteenth century?

To make your study concrete, review the timeline and reflect on the entries there. Think about their causes, consequences, and connections. How do they fit with global trends?

Additional Resources

Books

Dowd, Gregory. *A Spirited Resistance: The North American Indian Struggle for Unity, 1745–1815*. Baltimore, MD: Johns Hopkins University Press, 1993. ▶ Decades-spanning exploration of eastern Indian alliances.

Egerton, Douglas R. *Gabriel's Rebellion: The Virginia Slave Conspiracies of 1800 & 1802*. Chapel Hill: University of North Carolina Press, 1993. ▶ Exploration of the political and social context of slave revolt.

Freeman, Joanne. *Affairs of Honor: National Politics in the New Republic*. New Haven, CT: Yale University Press, 2002. ▶ Lively depiction of the uses and abuses of honor in national politics.

Klooster, Wim. *Revolutions in the Atlantic World: A Comparative History*. New York: New York University Press, 2009. ▶ Engaging comparisons of the motivations and trajectories of Atlantic revolutions.

Taylor, Alan. *The Civil War of 1812: American Citizens, British Subjects, Irish Rebels and Indian Allies*. New York: Vintage, 2011. ▶ Portrayal of the northern front of the War of 1812.

Zagarri, Rosemarie. *Revolutionary Backlash: Women and Politics in the Early American Republic*. Philadelphia: University of Pennsylvania Press, 2007. ▶ Study of the mixed political legacy of the Revolution for American women.

Go to the MindTap® for **Global Americans** to access the full version of select books from this Additional Resources section.

Websites

European Explorations and the Louisiana Purchase. (http://www.loc.gov/collections/louisiana-european-explorations-and-the-louisiana-purchase/) ▶ Library of Congress collection of maps and other sources about Louisiana.

War of 1812. (http://www.nps.gov/subjects/warof1812/index.htm) ▶ National Park Service site providing maps, primary sources, and personal stories.

MindTap®

Continue exploring online through MindTap®, where you can:

- **Assess your knowledge with the Chapter Test**
- **Watch historical videos related to the chapter**
- **Further your understanding with interactive maps and timelines**

Inventing Republics in the Age of Revolutions

1789–1790

February 1789

George Washington is elected the first U.S. president.

July 1789

Parisians storm the Bastille, beginning the French Revolution.

March 1790

First U.S. Naturalization Law offers a pathway to free white immigrants to become citizens.

May 1790

Southwest Ordinance establishes plan for territory south of the Ohio River to become states.

August 1790

First U.S. census counts a population of 3.9 million people, free and enslaved.

1791–1793

August 1791

A slave revolt on Saint-Domingue launches the Haitian Revolution.

1791

Tens of thousands of refugees begin to flee Saint-Domingue for the United States, Cuba, and French Louisiana.

February 1793

Washington is reelected president.

Fugitive Slave Law commits federal government to help slave owners recover runaways.

1794

March 1794

Eli Whitney patents a cotton gin, making the hand processing of cotton fiber faster and easier than without it.

August 1794

Battle of Fallen Timbers ends in Indian defeat but begins more moderate relations with the United States.

September–November 1794

Hamilton, Washington, and federalized militia troops put down the Whiskey Rebellion tax revolts in Pennsylvania.

1795–1799

October 1795

Treaty of San Lorenzo between the United States and Spain opens the Mississippi to trade.

February 1797

Congress certifies that Adams, Washington's vice president, is elected president.

June–July 1798

Congress passes the Alien and Sedition Acts, targeting a press critical of the Adams administration.

1798–1800

France and the United States engage in an undeclared war over neutral trading rights.

1800–1802

February 1800

Jefferson is elected president in the House of Representatives, transferring executive power from one political party to another.

September 1800

Skilled slave Gabriel plans a large-scale revolt in Virginia that is uncovered and brutally put down.

1801

Barbary States begin to wage war on the United States over demands to pay tribute for captured merchant ships on the Mediterranean.

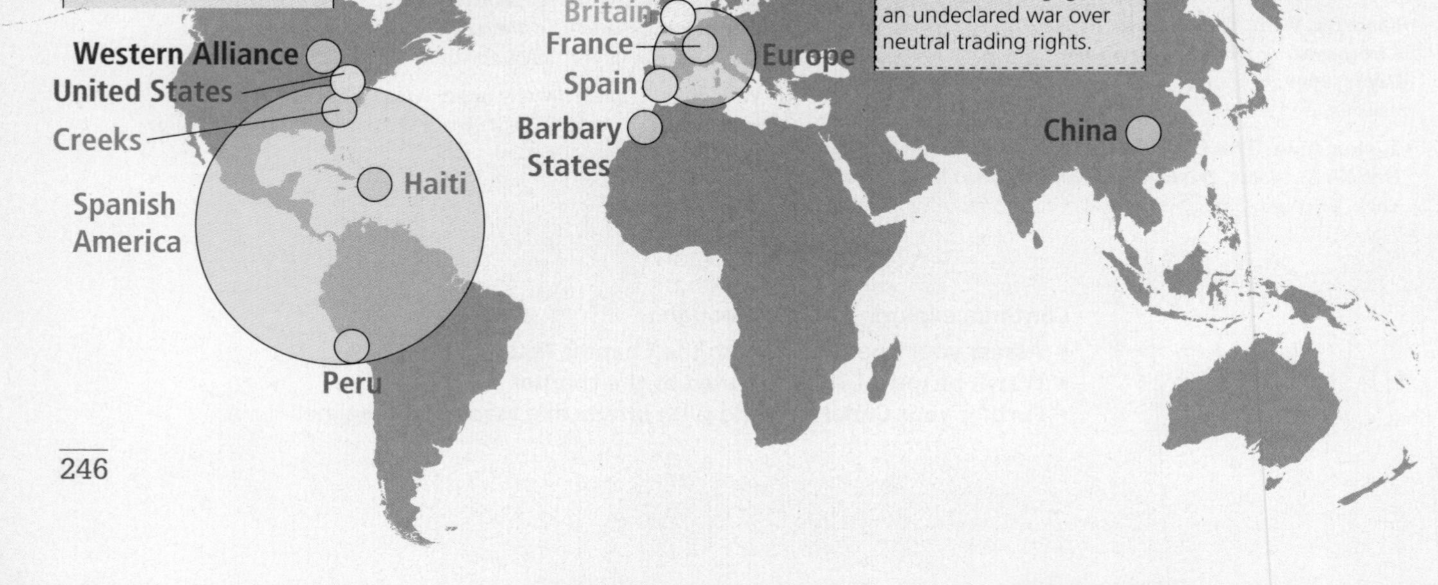

1803

February 1803

Supreme Court case *Marbury v. Madison* establishes the principle of judicial review and the independent judiciary.

October 1803

Louisiana Purchase from France adds 530 million acres of territory to the United States.

1804–1806

November 1804

Jefferson is reelected president.

January 1804

New republic of Haiti declared, ending the revolution on Saint-Domingue.

December 1804

Napoleon crowns himself emperor of France in the midst of war with European powers.

1804–1806

Lewis and Clark expedition crosses the Louisiana Territory to the Pacific Ocean and returns.

1805

Shawnee Tenskwatawa begins preaching a message of unity for Eastern Indians to shun American culture.

1807–1809

February 1807

New Jersey disfranchises unmarried women and free black men who had previously voted legally.

1807–1809

Embargo Act cuts off foreign exports, plunging the United States into an economic downturn.

1808

Leonora Sansay publishes *Secret History; or the Horrors of St. Domingo.*

January 1808

U.S. law banning the import of enslaved Africans from overseas goes into effect.

February 1809

Congress certifies that Madison, major author of the U.S. Constitution, is elected president.

1810–1815

1810

Independence movement breaks out in Mexico against imperial Spain.

November 1811

Harrison defeats Tecumseh's forces at the Battle of Tippecanoe, weakening the Indian alliance.

1812–1814

War of 1812 pits the United States against Britain and its Indian allies.

February 1813

Congress reports that Madison is reelected president.

August 1814

Treaty of Fort Jackson claims two-thirds of Creek territory for the United States.

1814–1815

Congress of Vienna ends Napoleonic Wars and restores monarchies in Europe.

December 1814–January 1815

Jackson turns Battle of New Orleans into a major victory for the United States over Britain.

1816–1819

November 1818

Monroe is elected president.

February 1819

Transcontinental Treaty establishes a new border between the United States and Spanish America, granting Florida to the United States.

Go to MindTap® to engage with an interactive version of the timeline. Analyze events and themes with clickable content, view related videos, and respond to critical thinking questions.

9 Markets and Democracy

1790–1840

C&O agents recruited men in Ireland to work on the Chesapeake and Ohio Canal, where they earned 50 cents per day, plus whiskey, for each day they worked.

9-1
Industry and Labor

9-1a Growth of Manufacturing Systems
9-1b Spread of Wage Labor
9-1c Workers and Labor Organization
9-1d The Pacific Coast in the Global Marketplace
9-1e Expansion of Slavery

9-2
Time, Space, and Money

9-2a Transportation Revolution
9-2b Corporations
9-2c National Institutional Supports
9.2d State Banking and Western Lands
9.2e Panic of 1819

9-3
Global Markets and Regional Alliances

9-3a Export Economy
9-3b Global Fur Trade
9-3c Political Compromise over Slavery
9-3d A Hemispheric Vision

9-4
Democracy in Practice

9-4a Revival of Partisan Politics
9-4b Andrew Jackson as National Executive
9-4c Global Democratic Experiments
9-4s Participatory Politics

9-5
Limits of Majority Rule

9-5a States' Rights
9-5b New Political Parties
9-5c Credit Crash and Its Consequences

In their shanty on the bank of the Potomac River in 1834, Irish immigrants Patrick and Mary Ryan bet their futures on a construction project. Patrick was a contractor hired to build a section of the Chesapeake and Ohio Canal. Funded by private investments and generous state loans, the canal joined two great waterways of North American trade—the Atlantic Ocean and the Mississippi River—to transport crops to market cheaper and faster. Patrick had to advance the capital to complete his section of the canal, so while they waited for his speculative venture to yield profits, Mary, Patrick's wife, ran a boardinghouse for the laborers, cooking, washing, and bringing in vital additional income.

The Granger Collection, New York

Barges at the Entrance to the Erie Canal, 1825 ▲

Canal work was physical and grueling. Men spent twelve to fifteen hours each day blasting through rock with gunpowder, clearing the rubble using horses and handcarts, digging deep into the dirt, and draining the passes through which barges and later steamships could travel. In return, they made fifty cents per day plus whiskey, but only for the days they worked. It was a bargain that could appeal only to men with few options, such as the men recruited in Ireland by C&O agents and transported to the Ryans' camp.

On the evening of November 8, 1834, long-simmering tensions in the camp exploded into violence. As the men gathered with their boss, drinking and gambling, John Brady, too ill at the time for canal work, got up from the table and stumbled into Mary's kitchen, where he had been helping with the cooking to pay his room and board. An argument broke out, and Brady hit his landlady, who brandished a candlestick in retaliation, shouting that she would "hammer the life out of him." Patrick ran into the kitchen. Brady, battered and bloody, staggered out into the cold alleys of the workers' camp. After Brady died the next morning, Mary and Patrick Ryan were charged with murder.

Testimony at the trial suggested that the community held Brady's life cheaply. One witness commented that "such disturbances are common in the shantees." The Ryans themselves, dismissing Brady as a despised "County Clare man," attributed the conflict to ethnic tensions brought from Ireland. The jury, considering Patrick "an excellent contractor," acquitted the Ryans. But the struggles of poor immigrant laborers were increasingly hard to ignore. Canal workers on the C & O led at least ten strikes protesting working conditions and pay. Federal troops intervened repeatedly to put down labor unrest.

Relationships between workers and employers underwent dramatic changes in the first half of the nineteenth century. American sons and daughters left their farms, and immigrants fled their homelands for work in U.S. factories where new machines set the pace of a workday measured by the clock, not the task. Canals such as the C&O, as well as turnpikes, steamboats, and railroads, moved people, products, and information faster, making goods widely available through an internal

How did the treatment of the workers who were recruited from Ireland to build the Chesapeake and Ohio Canal reflect the United States's early-nineteenth-century political and labor landscape?

Go to MindTap® to watch a video on the workers and learn how their experiences relate to the themes of this chapter.

trade. Americans' daily lives were shaped by economic forces they could not control and struggled to comprehend. New ways of organizing the production of goods devalued craft skills, altered household production, and challenged ideas about who should lead and who should follow.

Transformations in the United States were linked to global markets and industrialization. Industrial innovation, advances in transportation, and complex financial instruments created an integrated global marketplace that turned raw materials grown in one region into finished goods produced in another. Around the world, powerful empires, including the British in China, the Spanish in South America, and the Russians on the Pacific Northwest coast, competed economically with the United States, revealing the new nation's political and financial vulnerability. Global events—demand for cotton, displacement by landlords, regional famines, and political revolutions—set in motion two streams of migrating laborers: enslaved African Americans across the South and free European immigrants to the United States. The government forcibly relocated a third migrant group—Eastern Native Americans—to use their land to supply the global cotton boom.

The new market landscape raised cultural and political questions about competition. Some Americans placed their faith in its creative power, insisting that lively competition—of businesses, goods, ideas, and individuals—produced the best society. Others thought that fair competition must include protections to shelter minority viewpoints, promote valuable regional interests, and incubate emerging industries. A new national political system arose in response to this debate but excluded most individuals from formal participation because of their sex, race, or immigrant status. They expressed political will though labor organization, petitions, and protest.

9-1

Industry and Labor

This two-dollar bank note from the Sanford Bank in Maine (1861) depicts three women making textiles: the one on the left is spinning thread; those in the center are operating power looms. Artwork on bank notes was designed to foil counterfeiters but also became a cultural vehicle. Engravers produced dies with pastoral scenes or historical vignettes, and printers could select a combination of images to make an appealing or inspiring note.

The Granger Collection, New York

Why does this bank note contain multiple images of women at work? What does it suggest about the place of women in the nineteenth-century economy? ▶

Go to MindTap® to practice history with the Chapter 9 **Primary Source Writing Activity: Labor and the Global Marketplace.** Read and view primary sources and respond to a writing prompt.

In the first half of the nineteenth century, new technologies used water, steam, and human muscle power to increase the speed and profitability of U.S. manufacturing. A global flow of free workers poured into cities, where they toiled for wages in sugar refineries, distilleries, breweries, and in new factories that produced cotton cloth. New production processes reinforced dependent relationships between workers and their supervisors as the economic system increasingly treated workers as interchangeable commodities to be hired at the lowest wages possible and fired in hard times. Industrial development commandeered the labor of Indians on the Pacific coast and slaves in the South who produced the raw materials that became manufactured goods.

☞ As you read, think about how technology transformed labor patterns and the meaning of work in the United States. How did businessmen respond? How did workers respond?

9-1a Growth of Manufacturing Systems

European technology and new labor arrangements change the scale of production.

The **Industrial Revolution**, which transformed the production and distribution of goods worldwide, was built on the trade networks, political power, and wealth that European empires had developed through centuries of colonialism. In Britain, money from colonial trade allowed entrepreneurs to experiment with water-powered spinning machines and mechanized looms that could produce cotton textiles to compete in global markets with cloth made in India. Cotton textile production led the way to more innovations, including steam- and coal-powered machinery and centralized factories where workers used complex machines to mass-produce finished goods of uniform quality.

What began in Britain spread across Europe and North America. In 1789, English farm boy-turned-factory-worker Samuel Slater arrived in the United States armed with a good memory and a plan for adapting British technology to American social conditions. Flouting the British law that forbade workers in its renowned factories from sharing industrial secrets, Slater built his own mill in Pawtucket, Rhode Island. That mill, powered by a wheel turned by falling water, carded and spun cotton into thread. He employed entire households, advertising for "men with growing families" and constructing apartment buildings to house them and company stores to take their credit. Fathers managed the work of their dependents, just as they did on farms.

Once the thread was spun, Slater's mill "put out" the product to local farm families to finish. This **putting-out system** enabled manufacturers to tap into local labor markets and pay only for work completed; there was no responsibility to house or feed workers. Children and unmarried women wove thread into cloth and in some cases, sewed fabric into clothing. Returning the finished goods earned the family store credit to purchase tools and imported goods, including finer printed cloth. Manufacturers could not, however, control quality or flow of product and profit.

The Embargo of 1808 and the trade disruptions of the War of 1812 shut consumers off from English imports and opened the door for local entrepreneurs like Slater. Francis Cabot Lowell, who spent two years touring the mills of Manchester, England, returned to the United States to cofound the Boston Manufacturing Company in 1813. After building early mills in Waltham, near Boston, the company expanded in 1821 with a fully integrated cotton manufactory at Lowell, Massachusetts. The **Waltham-Lowell System** brought all of the processes of fabric production (carding, spinning, weaving, and fulling) under one management. Company salesmen promoted its cloth to urban merchants and dealers, who in turn distributed it to markets across the United States and around the world (see Map 9.1). Some cloth was shipped as far as China, where it rivaled cloth made in India by the British East India Company.

Unlike the earlier Slater-style mills, Lowell mills employed single women. The mills recruited from the same group of young farm women who had performed putting-out work for decades; in some ways, the new system reassured people anxious that industrialization destroyed families by dismantling household economic unity. In other ways, the Waltham-Lowell system marked a sharp break with the past. The "mill girls," as they called themselves, worked long hours set by the clock and enforced by a system of bells. Workers were supervised during the day by men who were not family members and at night by landladies who ran the company-approved boarding houses where they were required to live. The women could choose how to spend their wages of $12 to $14 each month—on imported fabrics, novels, or lessons. They sent some money home to help relatives. In the evenings, they organized prayer groups and published a literary

Canned Food to Feed an Army During the Napoleonic wars, Frenchman Nicolas Appert discovered a method for preserving food by cooking it in a sealed jar. British inventors improved on the technology with mass-produced tins filled with food for long military campaigns like this tin of roast veal prepared by the British firm of Donkin, Hall, and Gamble in 1823. The Industrial Revolution linked technology, mass production, and military power. ▲ Science & Society Picture Library/Getty Images

Industrial Revolution Eighteenth- and nineteenth-century transformation of economies and societies as the result of new machinery, energy sources, and labor organization.

putting-out system Early manufacturing method of distributing raw or partially processed materials to people who completed them at home using their own tools.

Waltham-Lowell System Fully integrated textile manufactory system originating in Massachusetts that centralized production and distribution and housed workers in company-managed boardinghouses.

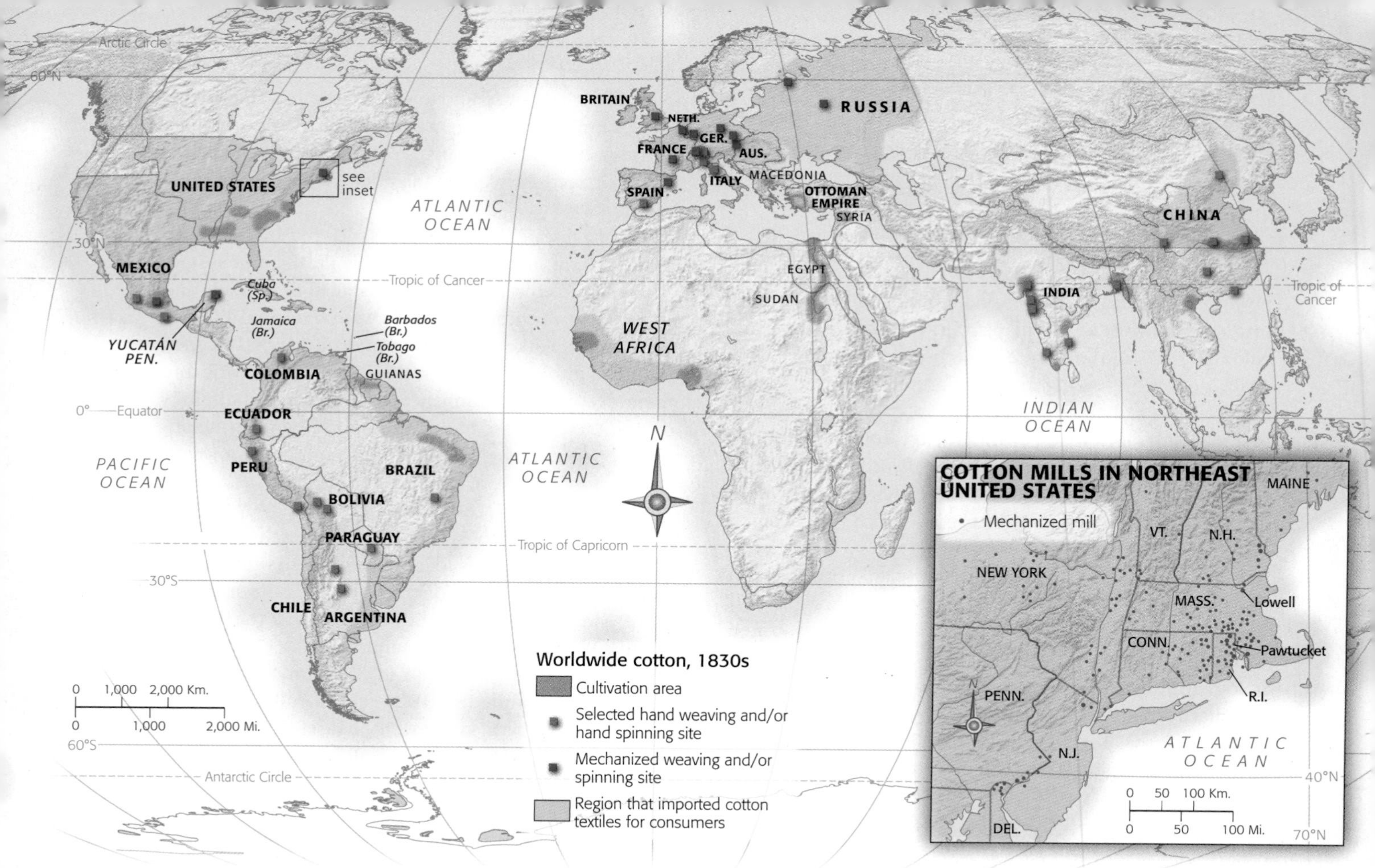

Map 9.1 Global Webs of Cotton For thousands of years, people picked, spun, and wove cotton and wore cotton clothing in warm regions of the Americas, Africa, and Asia. From local roots, this labor-intensive product became an important trade good. In China and India, manufacturers drew on nearby sources, but European and U.S. manufacturers used imperial conquest and transatlantic financing to acquire raw materials from one region and turn them to profit in another, aided by new technologies of water and steam power. ▲

surplus labor Working members of a family whose labor was not needed on the farm for household subsistence. Some found wage work that contributed to family security or comfort.

magazine, called the *Lowell Offering*. As the Waltham-Lowell System spread to other New England towns, so did paid female employment. By the 1830s, women made up 30 percent of workers in manufacturing and 80 percent of textile workers.

9-1b Spread of Wage Labor

Migrants and immigrants create a dynamic supply of waged workers, changing manufacturing systems.

The women employed in the Lowell Mills were part of a larger movement of migrants pushed out of farms along the East Coast and the villages of Europe and pulled into the developing cities and industries of the United States. As American farms became more productive, families faced a new phenomenon of **surplus labor**—young men and women who were not needed to work year-round on farms. Alternatives in manufacturing, land speculation, and urban service work drew men and women from country to city and from east to west. In the 1810s, the U.S. population in the Great Lakes region and the southern Mississippi Valley region tripled.

These same opportunities appealed to men and women thousands of miles away. Hundreds of thousands of British, Irish, and German migrants arrived in the United States in the first four decades of the nineteenth century. English textile workers brought expertise in weaving to New England's mills. Coal miners from Scotland and Wales moved to Pennsylvania where their knowledge earned them far higher wages than they had at home. Poor German immigrants labored in cities and along the canals of the expanding transportation systems of the United States while wealthier German families established trades or became Midwestern farmers. Some later became land speculators in central Texas.

The greatest proportion of immigrants came from Catholic Ireland. Largely single women and men, they were seeking relief from poverty and English repression. A few

Henry H. and Zoe Oliver Sherman Fund

Global Americans When he commissioned his portrait in 1825, wealthy Philadelphian **Patrick Lyon** insisted that he be depicted as the working blacksmith he had been at the beginning of his career. Lyon was born in 1779 in London and trained in Scotland to become a master blacksmith. Migrating to Philadelphia in 1793 to establish his own business, Lyon suffered the tragedies of early urban living when his wife and child died in a yellow fever epidemic. In 1798, he was hired to forge the locks for the vault of the Bank of Philadelphia. When the vault was breached and more than $160,000 stolen, Lyon was jailed for three months in spite of his strong alibi. After the real criminal confessed, Lyon was finally released and sued the bank directors for false imprisonment and loss of reputation. He was awarded a large settlement, equal to several years' wages, but until his death in 1829, he was resentful of the moneymen who had imprisoned an honest artisan. His portrait, depicting the nobility of work, was a response to the internationally connected bankers who had orchestrated his imprisonment and the industrialization that was undermining his craft specialization. Having immigrated for economic opportunity, he became a symbol of American egalitarianism. The judge at his trial proclaimed that "in our country . . . neither wealth nor office create an unequal standing."

with money speculated on western land, but most men worked in mills, on wharves, or they supplied the labor to build canals and roads. Irish women labored as laundresses and maids and hoped for employment in the mills. Their presence in urban enclaves and along transportation routes peaked between 1846 and 1851 when a potato blight and famine Ireland called the "Great Hunger" drove more than a million Irish to cross the ocean in desperation.

Artisan trades were transformed by the spread of cheap, flexible waged labor. In a traditional artisan's workshop, a master who was both a skilled worker and a business owner signed long-term contracts with two groups: young apprentices, who worked in return for training and board, and fully trained journeymen, who were saving money until they could open their own workshops. Living and working together in the same business, these men and women developed a sense of occupational identity that was nourished by the fact that workers could not be fired for sickness or business downturns. In contrast, immigrants, runaway servants, and teenagers on the move could be hired for a wage and fired with no lasting obligations to train and support them, making them an appealing alternative to nineteenth-century business owners.

If they were not going to invest in training workers in all aspects of a craft, business owners had to simplify the work. Artisan masters increasingly subdivided projects into smaller tasks that could be successfully completed by an untrained labor force, implementing a **division of labor** in the manufacturing process that was efficient but monotonous for workers. Merchants who wanted to compete with established workshops bypassed the old system completely, hiring a mixture of skilled and unskilled laborers to produce goods.

Standardization helped unlock the profitable potential of divided labor. In 1790, French gunsmith Honoré Blanc called politicians, intellectuals, and military officers to Paris to demonstrate how his workshop produced muskets made of **interchangeable parts**. Taking pieces of gunlock from a line of bins, he constructed a working whole. His system, developed in the workshops of Swedish watchmakers and from sketches of French military engineers, depended on precision tools and gauges as well as uniform measurements. In the United States, Eli Whitney sought to copy Blanc's success directly but struggled with musket production. Yet the idea of standardization soon permeated the manufacture of products such as clothing. While an eighteenth-century gentleman paid a master tailor for a custom-crafted suit, a businessman in the nineteenth century bought a ready-made suit. A skilled cutter used a standardized pattern to create the fabric pieces, which he then sent to a woman to sew together in her home. Because each garment earned her only a few cents, she took on as much piecework as possible to scrape out a living.

division of labor Production process in which different workers specialize in different parts of a larger task.

interchangeable parts Nearly identical components made from standardized instructions, allowing them to be exchanged for one another when assembled.

9-1c Workers and Labor Organization

Industrialization challenges the meaning of work and independence.

The expansion of a market economy, in which prices of goods and labor fluctuated rather than adhered to custom or law, had profound social and political implications. For native-born women in the textile mills, earning money of one's own meant freedom from the family-based credit that dominated the countryside. But for native-born white men, working for a wage seemed a threat, not a boon, to autonomy. Journeymen found their upward mobility severely limited by masters' efforts to pay the least and profit the most from their work. By 1815, half of the journeymen in New York were over thirty years old, typically married with several children and yet unable to afford a shop or home of their own. Since the eighteenth century, land ownership had served as the basis for independent male adulthood and civic participation. Artisans argued that their ownership of tools and craft knowledge offered them similar independence. But waged workers depended on others for basic subsistence, a status that meant they did not fit the model of republican citizenship.

Organizing to resist the changes that stripped them of their independence, journeymen wanted to maintain set fees for completing finished products and used a combination of joint demands and limited strikes, called **turn outs**, to press their case with employers. Initially, U.S. judges, relying on common law, deemed such labor actions to be illegal conspiracies, but later they began to accept limited worker's rights, opening the door to increased labor organization. In 1833, New York house carpenters, leather-dressers, cabinetmakers, and type foundry workers, among others, formed the **General Trades Union** to organize strikes and push for higher wages.

The crowded conditions in mills and factory boardinghouses also fostered collective action. In 1834, female workers at the Lowell Mills turned out for several days and paraded in the streets of Lowell to protest a wage cut—unsuccessfully. When the company in 1836 proposed to raise rents in the boardinghouses, resulting effectively in another pay cut, between fifteen hundred and two thousand women walked off the job for several months. Faced with the loss of one quarter of the work force, the company conceded and kept rents low.

Working men and women justified labor action by talking about their families. Sarah Bagley, an organizer in Lowell, explained to a skeptical public, "The whip which brings us to Lowell is NECESSITY. We must have money; a father's debts are to be paid, an aged mother is to be supported, a brother's ambition to be aided, and so the factories are supplied." Men in trade unions typically paired demands for fair wages with an insistence on their rights as householders. Like their counterparts in Europe, many agitated for a **family wage** that would supposedly allow a man to earn enough that his wife and children would not have to look for paid employment. Acutely aware of the oppressive conditions of factory workers in England, organizing workers in Philadelphia insisted that while in Europe, "slavery, labor [and] degradation" had descended since medieval times, the American "community of freemen" should award dignity to labor. Although they cast themselves as breadwinners to employers, such men depended on their wives and children to scrimp, save, salvage, and barter to make ends meet.

turn out Collective labor action, also called *strike*, in which workers leave the workplace for days or weeks to protest working conditions by revealing company dependence on them.

General Trades Union Umbrella organization of multiple separate trade unions created in 1834 New York City to coordinate labor protests across the economy and with other cities.

family wage Earnings that were theoretically sufficient to allow a man to support a wife and children who did not work for wages but were never a reality.

Expanding commercial businesses demanded a robust service industry to keep the books, sell the goods, and house and feed the workers who had left their homes. Clerks and boardinghouse keepers, two rapidly expanding ranks of service workers, embodied the challenges to ideas about independent work and household unity. Nineteenth-century clerks ran errands, moved goods, served customers, and spent days making deliveries. By the middle of the nineteenth century, New York City had fourteen thousand clerks, just over 40 percent of whom had immigrated from western Europe. Clerking appeared to be an opportunity to European immigrants and farm boys, but in their daily lives, clerks got no respect. Some critics complained that service work was too soft for a man; others scorned the physical tasks that clerks did as meaningless unskilled labor. Women expanded the service economy by taking in borders; by one estimate, 30 percent of all nineteenth-century households housed and fed nonrelatives for money. Companies such as the Lowell mills hired women to run boardinghouses that enforced church attendance, curfews, and limited mixed-sex socialization. Mary Ryan on the C & O Canal worked as part of a husband-wife team that had looser standards. All boardinghouses were suspect for selling the services that Americans expected female relatives to provide for free. Even if the food was tasty, it was tainted because the landlady had to be paid to make it. One critic claimed, "In the cold heartless atmosphere" of the boardinghouse "interest takes the management instead of affection."

9-1d The Pacific Coast in the Global Marketplace

Eastern manufacturing demands transform Pacific workplaces.

Eastern industries needed more than a boardinghouse full of workers to keep profits flowing; they needed the labor of workers thousands of miles away. Slaves on the Gulf Coast picked cotton that was spun in New England mills. Mid-Atlantic miners dug coal to fuel steam engines.

A vast network of European, Indian, and multiracial laborers turned the plants and animals of the Pacific into usable raw materials to keep the new machines running. In California, the emerging independence movement disrupted annual Spanish supply ships that had brought finished goods to California's missions, pueblos, and presidios. Into the breach came European, South American, and Euro-American traders who plied the coast. Missionaries reoriented production in the missions in response to what these foreign traders wanted, directing Indians to raise and slaughter tens of thousands of cattle annually for their hides and fat. Stripped of their hides, cattle carcasses littered California's countryside, leading to an explosion in the population of grizzly bears and other predators. Once Mexican independence officially opened California ports to global commerce (see Chapter 11), New England merchant houses sought to dominate the hide-and-tallow trade. Packaged on ships that sailed around the Cape of South America to the eastern United States, California hides became leather for shoes and machine belts. Tallow, crafted into soap and candles, brightened homes and workplaces not only along the East Coast of the United States but also in Peru, where silver miners deep underground depended on the light from tallow candles.

Factories that needed leather belts to run their machinery also required oil to keep gears turning, and the favored source of that oil was the fat of whales swimming in the waters of the Pacific Ocean. The eighteenth-century U.S. whaling industry had concentrated on short-term voyages from Massachusetts's Nantucket Island. After the War of 1812, American whalers turned in earnest to the vast number of whales in the Pacific for bones, blubber, and spermaceti, the oily liquid filling the head cavity of sperm whales that made superior, clean-burning candles. Deep-sea voyages took sailors from their homes for years as they worked on international crews.

Work on a deep-sea whaling ship followed a grueling schedule that some thought resembled factory work. Because they were away from port for such long periods of time, whaling vessels had to process and store the products of their hunt while at sea. Risking injury from sharp knives, heavy kettles, and boiling oil, sailors earned wages similar to those of factory workers, but the idea of a family wage meant little. While officers' wives back home received some company wages, the families of common sailors had to find other paying work during their long absences.

The Business of Whaling The log of the Nantucket-based *Washington* records capturing, killing, and processing whales. Each day, Captain Coffin noted the ship's location and drew blood-spouting whales to tally the daily kill. After chasing and killing their quarry, sailors sliced blubber from the animal's side and hoisted strips up to the deck for boiling. One observer commented that the work "somewhat resembled the unwinding of a lot of tape from a long bobbin." ▼

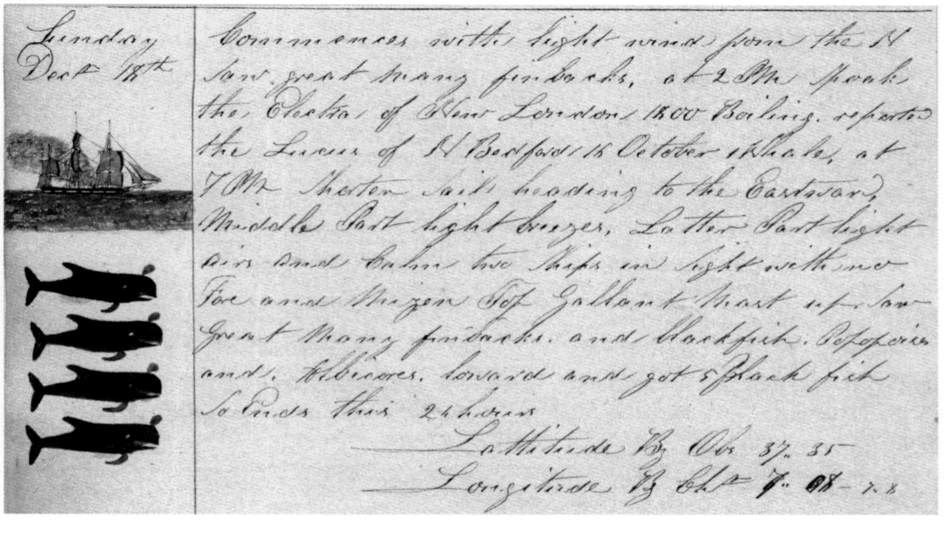
Sunday Dec 18th
Commences with light wind from the N saw great many finbacks, at 2 PM spoke the Electra of New London 1800 Boiling. reported the Lucas of N Bedford 15 October whale, at 7 PM Shorten sail heading to the Eastward Middle Part light breezes, Latter Part light airs and calm two Ships in sight with no Fore and Mizen Top Gallant Mast up saw Great many finbacks. and blackfish. Porpoises and Albicores. lowered and got 5 black fish So Ends this 24 hours
Lattitude By Obs 37. 35
Longitude By Chr 7. 08 - 7.8

Courtesy of the Nantucket Historical Association

9-1e Expansion of Slavery

interstate slave trade Forced migration of hundreds of thousands of slaves from the coastal Atlantic states to the cotton-growing Gulf states in the first half of the nineteenth century.

coffles From the Arabic word *cafila*, a chained caravan designed to prevent humans or animals from escaping.

Legal and illegal slave trade accelerates the movement of labor.

The Waltham-Lowell system produced a coarse grade of cotton fabric used to clothe the enslaved people who had picked the fibers to begin with. In the early nineteenth century, a thriving **interstate slave trade** transported people from the farms of the Chesapeake, where depleted soil made slave labor less valuable, to the cotton plantations of the Deep South and the West (see Map 9.2). As British and then New England mills demanded increasing inputs of raw cotton, the profitability of the global cotton trade drove up the prices people were willing to pay for human beings to grow, pick, and process the cotton.

The interstate slave trade began as individual speculative ventures. A trader traveled from plantation to plantation in the upper South, purchasing groups of about ten people whom he chained together in **coffles** and marched south, selling them as they walked. A slave purchased for $300 in Maryland could sell for $600 in Georgia. Soon, slave-trading firms centered in cities such as Baltimore and Alexandria took over the business from individual entrepreneurs. Crowding people into "pens" in urban centers, including the capital, Washington, D.C., slave traders shipped human beings by steamship, canal, and improved roads to auctions in New Orleans and Natchez. Between 1800 and 1840, the state of Virginia exported more than 300,000 enslaved people; Mississippi alone gained more than 130,000. One-third of slaves in this migration moved with owners as part of a familiar group; two-thirds were separated from family and sold in distant marketplaces.

Slaves caught up in forced separation experienced firsthand what it meant to be both a person and a commodity. Owners told them, "[I'll] put you in my pocket," vowing to sell a boy for a pocketful of bills to be used to purchase new goods, slaves, or land. Jacques, one slave boy in Louisiana, was mortgaged three times and sold twice between his eighth and twelfth birthdays. Slaves did anything they

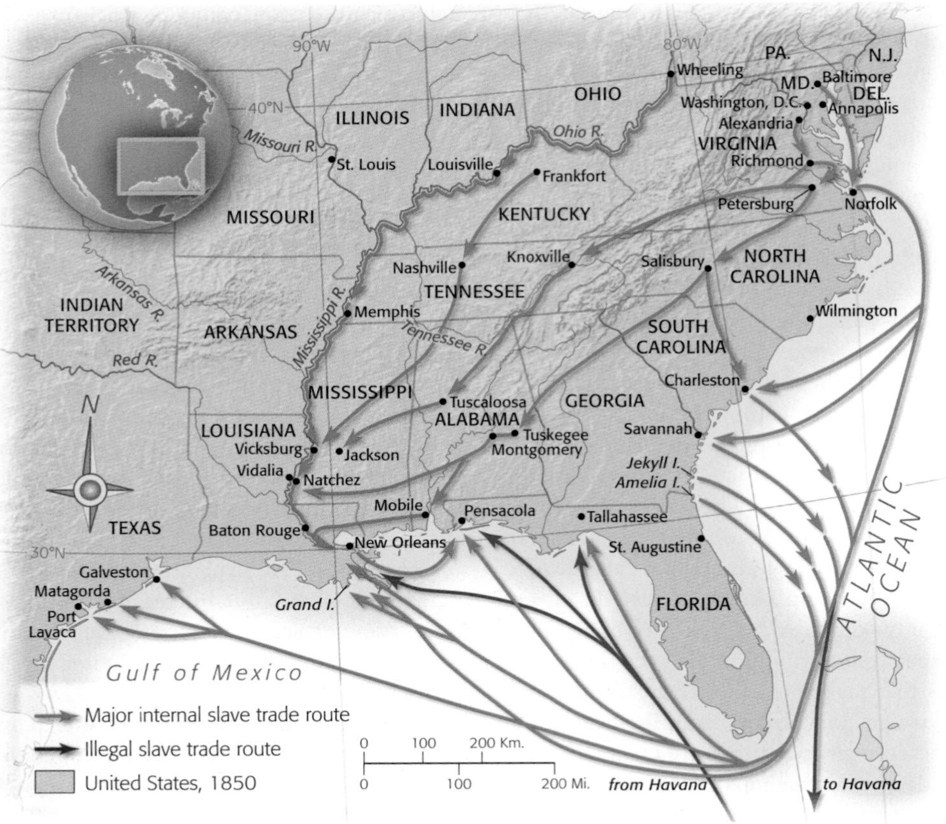

Map 9.2 The Interstate Slave Trade More than 875,000 enslaved people were dragged to the Lower South between 1820 and 1860. In addition to being a forced migration, the trade generated millions in profits for the sellers and transporters as well as income for the lawyers, doctors, blacksmiths, clothing providers, provisioners, and insurers who made the trade possible. An illegal slave trade centered on Spanish Cuba intersected with the legal slave trade across the Gulf of Mexico. ▲

Sale of Human Beings This 1812 advertising flyer categorized people as if they were exchangeable parts rather than individuals, highlighting their sex and relative age or their work experience. The advertisement did not note the names, individual preferences, or unique relationships of the people who were treated as a mobile source of cash for owners. ▶

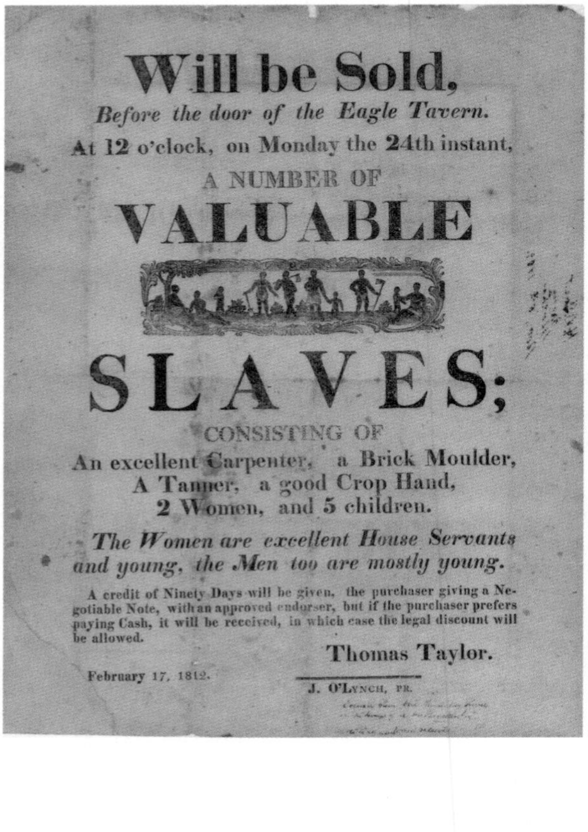
Will be Sold,
Before the door of the Eagle Tavern.
At 12 o'clock, on Monday the 24th instant,
A NUMBER OF
VALUABLE
SLAVES;
CONSISTING OF
An excellent Carpenter, a Brick Moulder,
A Tanner, a good Crop Hand,
2 Women, and 5 children.
The Women are excellent House Servants and young, the Men too are mostly young.
A credit of Ninety Days will be given, the purchaser giving a Negotiable Note, with an approved endorser, but if the purchaser prefers paying Cash, it will be received, in which case the legal discount will be allowed.
Thomas Taylor.
February 17, 1812.
J. O'LYNCH, PR.

Library of Virginia

could to hold on to some part of their lives. Mothers bargained with owners to stay with their children; husbands threatened to run away if they were not sold to a plantation where a beloved wife lived.

Although the United States had outlawed the importation of Africans in 1808, demand for slave labor boosted a thriving illegal Atlantic trade into the mid-nineteenth century, bringing Africans into Texas, Louisiana, and Florida from Spanish Cuba. U.S. shipbuilders constructed new vessels to transport captive African men and women across the Gulf of Mexico. Traders in the illegal business depended on smugglers or bribable U.S. customs agents in New Orleans and elsewhere to classify their cargo as products of the legal interstate trade, not the illegal international trade. In the slave pens of New Orleans, legally and illegally enslaved people suffered together in the interest of global profits.

9-2 Time, Space, and Money

Process of Excavation, Lockport, George Catlin (1826). This image depicts the work of Irish laborers digging a channel for the Erie Canal at Lockport, New York, where a system of locks on the canal raised the level of the water.

New York Public Library

What does the scale of this image—the canal, the workers, and the wooden cranes—suggest about the relationship of workers to their work in an expanding industrial and commercial economy? ▶

U.S. commerce depended on a political system that encouraged businessmen and investors. Federal and state governments organized and sold public land, subsidized transportation, and passed protective laws making American-produced goods cheaper than imports. Nationally minded congressmen advocated a future United States that combined commercial agriculture with manufacturing in order to make the country more independent. However, connections among markets for labor, credit, and goods meant that individuals were already dependent on global economic forces that they could not control or fully comprehend.

☞ As you read, consider the various ways that Americans promoted and paid for national economic development. Who benefited from this intersection of politics and the economy?

9-2a Transportation Revolution

New modes of transportation and communication shorten the experience of distance.

A spreading web of turnpikes, canals, steamship lines, stagecoach routes, and railroads covered the United States in the first half of the nineteenth century (see Map 9.3). Backers called these projects **internal improvements** to stress that improved transportation strengthened the national economy. These large-scale, risky undertakings depended on unprecedented levels of government sponsorship. Early turnpikes were funded by private companies that raised capital by selling shares to individual investors and earned profits from the tolls collected periodically along their course. Canals needed state support. The **Erie Canal**, running 364 miles from the Hudson River near Albany to Lake Erie at Buffalo, completed a long-desired all-water route between the Atlantic Ocean and the Great Lakes. When it was finished in 1825, New Yorkers celebrated with bonfires, songs, cannon salutes, and speeches praising national unity through better transportation. Such patriotic displays slighted the international effort involved. The state of New York raised funds for its construction through a lottery and a tax on the auction sales of goods; English investors loaned the balance of the money. Irish immigrant laborers and pardoned convicts dug the channel, modifying the specifications of Dutch and English engineers for North American landscapes.

Like canals and turnpikes, steamboats on the Mississippi River brought the global economy to the U.S. interior by making communication faster and freight fees cheaper. Robert Fulton, who developed the American steamboat in 1807, envisioned it bringing "a little Paris, a section of Broadway, or a slice of Philadelphia" to "the very doors of our cabins." By harnessing the potent power of steam, boats could travel upriver as well as down. In 1817, seventeen steamboats opened for business on the Mississippi; within thirty years, there were more than seven hundred, each larger and carrying more cargo and passengers. In 1814, it took six days and six hours for the *Orleans* to make the 268-mile trip from New Orleans to Natchez. By 1844, the *Sultana* made it in just under twenty hours. Whereas an old-style boat with a keel transported goods from New Orleans to Louisville at the rate of 5 cents per pound, the flat-bottomed steamboat took them for a half-cent a pound. Furs from animals trapped near the Great Lakes and grain and livestock from the western plains all traveled south. Cotton and sugar went north.

Railroads, first constructed on a major scale in the 1830s, were even faster and more direct. Steamships transported goods north and south on the Mississippi River, but the early railroad companies such as the Baltimore and Ohio and the Reading Railroad connected east and west, altering the axis of major

internal improvements Infrastructure and transportation projects with the goal of improving commerce that were funded in part with public money.

Erie Canal New York water route between Albany and Buffalo completed in 1825 to speed transportation of goods and people from East Coast to Great Lakes networks.

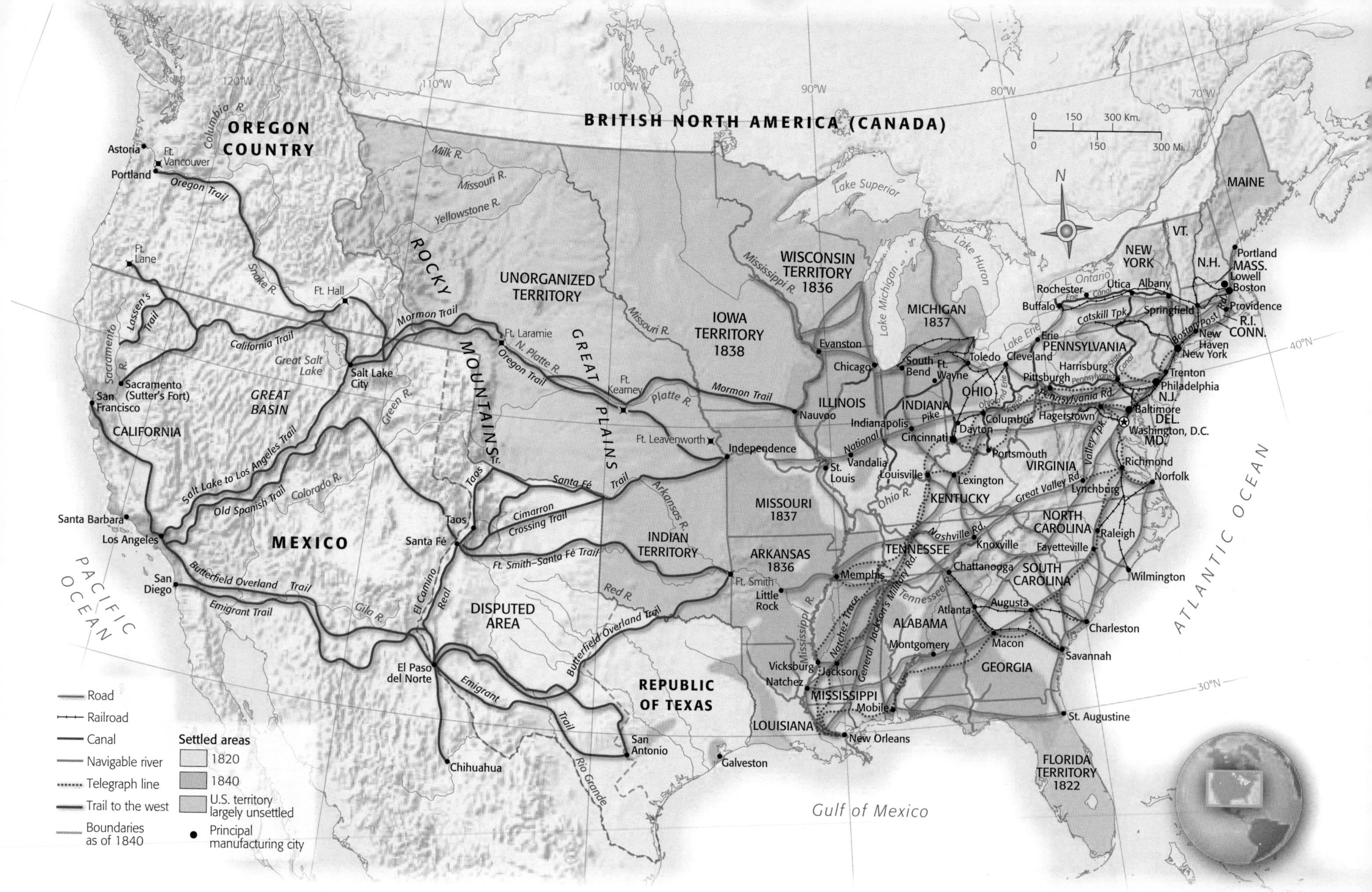

Map 9.3 Transcontinental Travel and Commerce by 1840 Canals and roads funded by states and private investors, followed by railroads and telegraph lines, formed a network with navigable rivers to connect port cities to communities in the continent's interior. New communication and transportation lines also linked up with overland trade routes in the West. The migration of people and goods became easier and cheaper, boosting commercial agriculture because farmers could transport goods to distant markets. The result was increased U.S. settlement onto lands previously or simultaneously occupied by Indian groups. ▲

commercial traffic. When construction began on the Baltimore and Ohio Railroad in 1828, Charles Carroll, the last living signer of the Declaration of Independence, told the gathered crowd that launching the new railroad was "among the most important acts of my life, second only to my signing the Declaration of Independence, if even it be second to that."

9-2b Corporations

State governments join public and private ventures.

New businesses from cotton mills to steamboat lines were organized as corporations, entities legally able to buy and sell poperty. Shareholders pooled their money and obtained **corporate charters** issued by state legislatures. In 1808, John Jacob Astor, a German immigrant who had spent decades building a beaver fur-trading business with Indians in New York and the Great Lakes, received a charter from the state of New York to found the American Fur Company. He hoped that a state charter would help him drive his British rival, Hudson's Bay Company, from U.S. borders and trade routes. Inspired by reports from the Lewis and Clark expedition, Astor chartered a subsidiary, the Pacific Fur Company, in 1810 to establish a base called Astoria at the mouth of the Columbia River on the Pacific coast and issued one hundred shares of stock in the company.

Although the pooling of investors had existed since the joint-stock companies that funded much of European colonialism, state governments in the nineteenth century created new incentives for private investment in transportation projects. Corporate charters typically granted the protection of limited liability, which reduced investor risk by preventing creditors from seizing shareholders' personal assets to satisfy business debts. Most transportation charters also included the power of **eminent domain**, a corporation's legal right to force landowners to sell property along the route of a turnpike, canal, or railroad, whether they wanted to or not. Eminent domain had previously been a power only governments could invoke to serve a common good. Because states in the nineteenth century were trying to tap into private resources to undertake major projects, state governments transferred some of their powers to corporations serving a quasi-public function.

Courts supported the sanctity of corporate charters, bolstering the power of businesses. In the 1819 Supreme Court decision ***Trustees of Dartmouth College v. Woodward***, Chief Justice Marshall declared that a private corporation had the same protected rights as a U.S. citizen. In this case, the state of New Hampshire was prevented from turning Dartmouth College into a public college. Such an alteration in the school's charter, Marshall contended, would amount to an illegal seizure of private property, and protecting private property was a cornerstone of U.S. law and politics.

9-2c National Institutional Supports

Nationalists mobilize the federal government.

Nationally minded politicians believed that the federal government should directly support economic development by backing internal improvements. With the end of the War of 1812, they insisted that the United States should cultivate markets within its own borders, free from Europe's problems and dependencies. "The crops of our plains would no longer sustain European armies," declared Daniel Webster. Instead, interstate commerce could promote the integration and independence of the United States. Tench Coxe, who before the Revolution had been a merchant with strong ties to English businesses, envisioned a new system by which farmers would feed manufacturers, who would in turn provide farmers' tools. Merchants would supplement this domestic interdependency with additional products from "foreign climates." Coxe's vision drew on decades of experience with manufacturing societies that invested in new factories and lobbied for laws to shield their products from foreign competition while permitting trade.

The federal government called the first **Patent Act** (1790) an Act to Promote the Progress of Useful Arts. It gave inventors a fourteen-year monopoly on machinery and processes that they had created, described, and licensed. As Coxe had envisioned, patents encouraged innovation in manufacturing, agriculture, and trade. Charles Newbold, David Peacock, and Jethro Wood patented cast iron plows between 1797 and 1819 that immediately outpaced damage-prone wooden plows clad in iron plates. Cyrus McCormick patented a horse-drawn reaper in 1834 that could harvest as much as fourteen individuals could with scythes. Inventions patented outside the United States were excluded from protection; the federal government sanctioned and even encouraged the industrial espionage at the heart of New England's new power looms.

Recognizing that entrepreneurs needed to take big risks, lawmakers also experimented with laws to cushion their losses. Under the short-lived national Bankruptcy Act of 1800, merchants, bankers, brokers, and insurance underwriters who could not repay their creditors could be compelled to declare **bankruptcy**, have a commission divide their assets, and start fresh.

corporate charters Written license granted by a government detailing the structure and plans of a business that often included limits on the duration and privileges of the business.

eminent domain Legal power of a government or its agent to take private property to serve a public good with compensation.

Trustees of Dartmouth College v. Woodward U.S. Supreme Court decision protecting the sanctity of private corporate charters, deeming corporations to have constitutionally protected rights.

Patent Act First federal patent law passed in (1790) that protected registered inventions from competition for fourteen years, following English practice.

bankruptcy Legal process that distributes assets among creditors and cancels the remaining debt status of a person deemed unable to pay his or her debts.

Joseph Kriehuber/The Granger Collection, New York

Global Americans Born in Germany in 1789 and largely self-educated, economist **Frederich List** fled Austria for the United States in 1825 on the advice of Revolutionary War hero General Lafayette. List worked as a newspaper editor, coal prospector, and railroad builder, all the while advocating strongly for the American System. Opposing the free-trade policies of Adam Smith, List argued in favor of the protective tariff, claiming that such a measure was well in the spirit of the U.S. Founding Fathers. At the same time, he used examples from Europe to argue that other governments were far ahead of the United States in cultivating knowledge about commerce and economy. Pointing to the polytechnic schools of France, Austria, Switzerland, and Germany, he argued that such institutions yielded not only productivity gains but also "moral riches." A fully engaged participant in the American System, List articulated the moral and ideological dimensions of taxes, banks, and internal improvements. He became a U.S. citizen and traveled back to Germany as a diplomat and railroad promoter, but financial failures contributed to the despair that drove him to suicide in 1846.

Once through bankruptcy, a commercial debtor had no enduring legal or moral obligations to make all of his or her old promises good; instead, the individual was released to make new ones. Fears of collusion between debtors and creditors forced the act's repeal in 1803.

Robust commerce also depended on good communication, and the United States Post Office, formally organized in 1792, soon employed more people than the rest of the civilian bureaucracy put together. Thousands of post offices opened in the third decade of the nineteenth century as settlers in distant parts of the country petitioned for service. Postal policies and direct investment were a boon to local economies and transportation between communities. The office subsidized stagecoaches because the mail traveled along with passengers. The mandate that post offices be open every day meant that local postmasters, commonly tavern keepers and shopkeepers, could keep their businesses open and even sell liquor on Sundays because they were exempt from laws forbidding the practice. Because printed material, such as newspapers and political pamphlets, traveled at a much cheaper rate than personal letters, the Post Office fostered a closely networked business and political world.

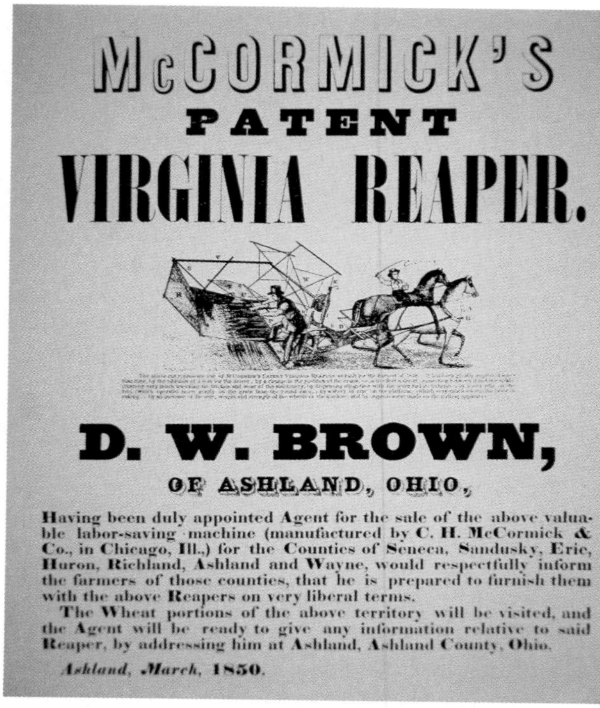

McCormick's Patent Virginia Reaper Advert, 1850 (litho), American School (19th century)/Private Collection/Peter Newark American Pictures/Bridgeman Images

Advertisement for Mechanical Reaper Cyrus McCormick invented and manufactured the Virginia Reaper, but a patent did not guarantee profits. In its first decade, his company made little money. Moving to the emerging grain belt of the Midwest, developing an extensive advertising campaign, and introducing regular improvements were essential steps to success. ▲

Building on these targeted laws and private initiatives, Kentucky congressman Henry Clay suggested a comprehensive, centralized plan for national development. His proposed **American System** consisted of a protective tariff on imports, a national bank, increased federal land sales, and federal money for internal improvements. By uniting the interests of agriculture, commerce, and industry, Clay hoped to promote success for individual Americans and make U.S. exports stronger. The American System had unifying potential across regions. John C. Calhoun, congressman from South Carolina, supported using federal funds to "bind the republic together with a perfect system of roads and canals. Let us conquer space."

American System Program of political assistance proposed for the economic development of the United States in the 1810s and 1820s. Some elements were adopted; others were contested and rejected.

But should the federal government take such an active role in commercial development? U.S. officials had debated this since Hamilton and Jefferson took opposing sides on the question of strict versus loose construction of the Constitution. One faction of Democratic-Republicans, in the tradition of Hamilton, favored expanding the powers of the federal government to serve what its proponents saw as the interests of the United States as a nation. Other lawmakers were more cautious about pushing beyond measures such as post and patent offices, which were clearly authorized by the Constitution. In 1817, President James Madison, although a supporter of economic development, vetoed a bill that would have earmarked U.S. Bank dividends to pay for transportation projects.

9-2d State Banking and Western Lands

> The spread of farming in the Midwest sends produce east and speculators west.

Clerks, landladies, canal diggers, and spinning machine operatives who were no longer directly involved in farming created new markets for foodstuffs across state lines. To capture this market, farmers wanted more land and were willing to speculate on future profits to get it. Governments and entrepreneurs eased their way, connecting the East and Midwest through land sales.

Acquired through treaty, sale, or warfare with the Indian people who lived on it, the land these farmers desired was transformed into federal territories. Following practices established by the 1785 Land Ordinance, the U.S. government hired surveyors to assess difficult terrain, marking an orderly grid over swamps, fields, forests, mountains, and rivers. As they had in the Northwest and Southwest Territories, Americans moved onto land in the Mississippi Valley long before the surveyors arrived. Congress frequently permitted squatters who had "improved" their land by building barns, houses, and fields the chance to purchase it at a minimum price of $1.25 an acre. But many white migrants who arrived after the squatters had to buy their farms from speculators, who had bought them at Land Office auctions and then resold them on credit with interest rates as high as 40 percent. The fastest way to pay back such loans was with earnings from cash crops exported east and on to Europe.

Speculators and farmers depended on **state banks** created by investors who deposited assets—usually bonds—with a state government and then began issuing money. Banks supported land booms and dramatically expanded the supply of circulating money. Under the U.S. Constitution, only the federal government could coin money; paper money, in contrast, could be issued by a wide range of institutions. State banks hired engravers to design and print **bank notes**, slips of paper promising to pay an equivalent amount of gold or silver coin when the note was presented for redemption at the bank. Other businesses, including insurance companies, railroads, and private banks printed their own paper notes. By the 1850s, more than ten thousand different kinds of paper were in circulation. These paper dollars, easily portable across distances, were a much-needed circulating medium that enabled people to undertake varied transactions.

A bank note's value rested on what the people who used it agreed it to be. As long as all users had faith that two different $5 bills could be exchanged for equivalent amounts of gold and silver, the system worked. But banks and other corporations issued far more paper money than they could redeem in gold and silver, hoping to raise more money in interest payments from the people to whom they extended loans. While the notes circulated through the hands of farmers and land agents, the system worked. But if all the holders of a bank's notes came at once for their gold and silver, the speculative bubble would burst.

9-2e Panic of 1819

> A financial crisis reveals the vulnerabilities of the new political and economic systems.

The bubble did burst, first in 1819, followed by a series of panics throughout the nineteenth century. The trouble began in Europe. During the Napoleonic wars, many western Europeans were desperate for food, and the price of U.S. corn and wheat surged, prompting midwestern farmers to expand their fields to grow crops to export. British factories' demands for cotton ensured that prices for U.S. cotton increased as well. By 1818, however, European farmers had recovered from wars and crop failures and were growing their own foodstuffs. Britain turned back to India to supply its mills, and the price paid for a pound of cotton fell 50 percent. Land purchased on the promise of high prices was not worth the money that had been borrowed to buy it.

The **Second Bank of the United States** compounded American credit woes. Chartered in 1816 for a twenty-year period, it was the most powerful of all of the new banks. In addition to having branches in multiple states, 20 percent of its stock was held by the federal government. The bank loaned money to the federal government, state banks, and individuals. It also acted as the federal government's banker, making transactions and holding its revenues. Because its paper notes alone could be used to pay federal taxes, customers daily visited its branches to exchange their various notes for Bank of the United States paper. By taking those state bank notes back to their origins for immediate redemption into specie, the Bank could exert some control over the money supply in the United States.

In late 1818, faced with worrisome evidence of a speculative bubble, its directors called in loans and contracted credit. To make their redemptions, state banks had to call in their loans and send their gold and silver to the Second Bank. Indebted farmers could not pay, nor could land speculators, who in turn owed far more to

state banks Corporation licensed by a state to print money, accept deposits, and make loans. Predominated in the nineteenth century.

bank notes Paper certificate issued by banks that circulated as currency with the promise to repay the holder the face value on demand.

Second Bank of the United States National bank chartered by Congress in 1816 to conduct business for the federal government and issue notes that could be used to pay federal taxes.

History without Borders

Paper Money

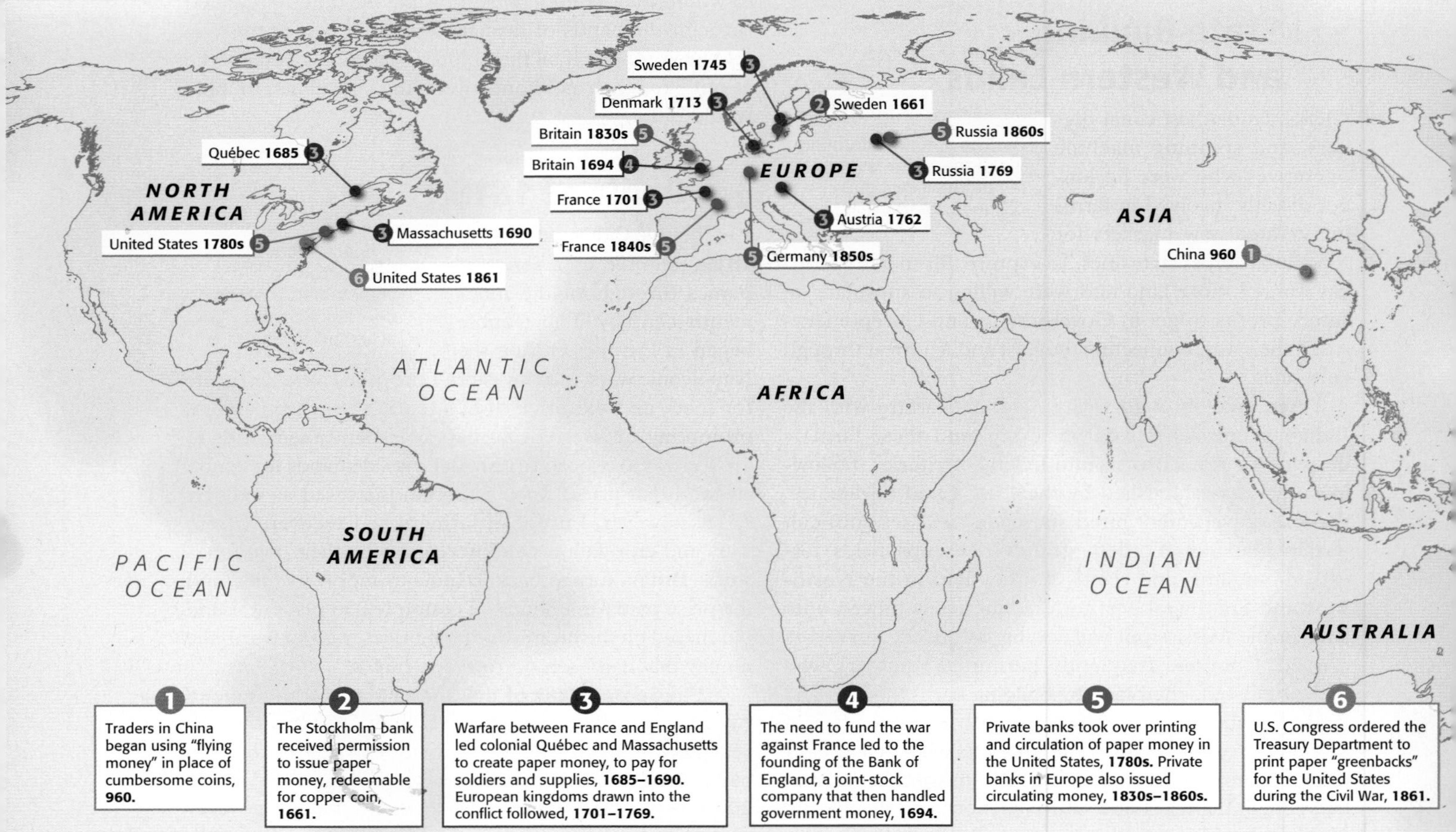
Sweden 1745 3
Denmark 1713 3
2 Sweden 1661
Britain 1830s 5
5 Russia 1860s
Britain 1694 4
EUROPE
3 Russia 1769
Québec 1685 3
NORTH AMERICA
France 1701 3
3 Austria 1762
ASIA
3 Massachusetts 1690
United States 1780s 5
France 1840s 5
5 Germany 1850s
China 960 1
6 United States 1861
ATLANTIC OCEAN
AFRICA
SOUTH AMERICA
PACIFIC OCEAN
INDIAN OCEAN
AUSTRALIA
1
Traders in China began using "flying money" in place of cumbersome coins, **960.**
2
The Stockholm bank received permission to issue paper money, redeemable for copper coin, **1661.**
3
Warfare between France and England led colonial Québec and Massachusetts to create paper money, to pay for soldiers and supplies, **1685–1690.** European kingdoms drawn into the conflict followed, **1701–1769.**
4
The need to fund the war against France led to the founding of the Bank of England, a joint-stock company that then handled government money, **1694.**
5
Private banks took over printing and circulation of paper money in the United States, **1780s.** Private banks in Europe also issued circulating money, **1830s–1860s.**
6
U.S. Congress ordered the Treasury Department to print paper "greenbacks" for the United States during the Civil War, **1861.**

Paper Money, 960–1861 As paper money systems developed around the world, their legal status and who had the right to issue bills created tensions among traders, investors, and governments. This map shows some key turning points, as paper money came to be tightly linked to the power and credibility of nations. ▲

Barter—the immediate, face-to-face exchange of one good for another—is one of the simplest methods of exchange, but every trading society has had to cope with how to transmit exchanges across distances and over time. Global trading regions developed unique markers to denote value and smooth transactions. In Africa, India, China, and other regions connected by the Indian Ocean, cowrie shells served as small-denomination money of exchange. Merchants and traders in the East Indies used small, low-value bronze coins with a hole in the center, which Europeans called *cash*. Fur traders in North America used wampum, beads that Native Americans on Long Island Sound made out of whelk and clamshells. Spanish invaders minted large deposits of gold and silver in South America into coins as part of colonial conquest. These "pieces of eight" circulated around the world as familiar global currency by the seventeenth century. Each of these forms of money had benefits, but all were bulky to transport and vulnerable to theft.

The appeal of paper money—lightweight, foldable, and easily printed with financial and political information—was clear, but its spread depended on political and financial developments. Chinese merchants in the Song Dynasty (960–1279 CE) were the first to use paper IOUs called *flying money* to transmit exchanges over long distances. By the Middle Ages, traders around the Mediterranean also used paper IOUs called *bills of exchange* that functioned as checks do today except that the bills could then circulate as money in transactions that had nothing to do with the original agreement. Florentine bankers, traders, and growers of commodities all welcomed the bill of exchange as a method of importing in one place, exporting from another, and settling up accounts in a third.

Banknote of China, Ming Dynasty, 1368–1644 (paper), Chinese School/ Ashmolean Museum, University of Oxford, UK/Bridgeman Images

Great Ming Circulating Treasury Note, 1375 This is the earliest surviving example of government-issued paper money. Paper money began in China as a convenient private tool used by traders, but Chinese emperors took over and used paper money to control international trade and centralize holdings of gold and silver. By the 1450s, however, overprinting money had made the notes lose value, and China abandoned a paper money system for silver coins. ◀

Bank of Henderson Five Dollar Bill, 1818 This bill is signed in ink by bank directors, linking these five dollars with earlier bills of exchange, signed by merchants. The Bank of Henderson was one of the unregulated banks of the nineteenth-century United States. Located in Kentucky, its notes were not backed by the reserves suggested by its issuing practices. ◀ Library of Congress/ University of Chicago. Library. American Currency Collection

Governments also began to use paper IOUs to fund their largest projects: wars. In British North America, Massachusetts authorities first issued paper money in 1690 to pay for troops and supplies in battles against the French in New France. These Massachusetts shillings promised holders gold or silver equivalents at the end of the conflict, but instead, paper money typically circulated and was used to purchase goods and pay taxes. For paper money to succeed, users had to believe that it could be exchanged for something of value, such as gold or silver. Too much paper money in circulation led to inflation, causing bills to be worth far less than the values printed on them. The disastrous experience of paper bills in the American Revolution led the framers of the Constitution to forbid states from printing money.

Between the Revolution and the Civil War, most paper money in the United States was printed and circulated by private commercial sources with state charters: banks, insurance companies, railroad and canal companies, and companies without charters. These notes, frequently counterfeited or backed with little or no security, circulated alongside thousands of different gold, silver, and copper coins minted by governments from around the world. A profusion of forms of money, intersecting with global financial flows, fed the economic growth and boom-bust cycles of the nineteenth century.

Critical Thinking Questions

▶ How does the form that money takes influence who can use it? How does it influence who can issue it?

▶ Why is the history of paper money directly linked to both trade and warfare?

Go to MindTap® to engage with an interactive version of **History without Borders: Paper Money.** Learn from an interactive map, view related video, and respond to critical thinking questions.

state banks than the land was then worth. Banks failed, the western land bubble popped, and people around the country suffered. For the next four years, Americans lost their homes and jobs as foreclosures rose and businesses collapsed. Unemployment reached 75 percent in Philadelphia. Tens of thousands were jailed for debt, and the *National Gazette* reported that debtors in New York prisons had no bedding and no food other than a quart of soup every twenty-four hours.

Who was to blame? Individuals referred to the Panic of 1819 as "hard times." Few had the idea that something as abstract as "the economy" or as difficult to grasp as the speculative value of paper money could cause such real anguish. Many assumed that moral failures were the root of the trouble. One newspaper quipped, "To dress, to visit, and to play, / To get in debt, and run away, /Are common vices of the day." Victims countered that fraud was to blame and talked of shady dealers who "laughed in their sleeves" at others' misfortune. A growing number pointed to the Second Bank, charging that insiders ran banks as monopolies. Although times improved after 1822, debt and poverty remained and suspicions about the banking system simmered. The **boom-bust cycle** of the U.S. economy persisted.

9-3 Global Markets and Regional Alliances

What does the placement and relative size of humans, wheels, and baskets of picked cotton suggest about the way cotton cultivation shaped human lives? How are the slaves' work lives depicted in comparison with the men digging the Erie Canal? ▼

Hauling the Whole Week's Picking (1842), William Henry Brown. This collage, depicting a surprisingly well-dressed family of slaves, is part of a series created to decorate the rooms of the masters' children on the Nitta Yuma plantation in Vicksburg, Mississippi. Brown specialized in the art of silhouette, which involved using scissors to cut portraits of people from black paper.

Hauling The Whole Week's Picking, c.1842 (w/c on paper), Brown, William Henry (1808–83)/The Historic New Orleans Collection/Bridgeman Images

Americans viewed their place in the global economy in starkly different ways. Farmers favored policies that sent products across borders easily to generate profit. Manufacturers opposed the idea of open competition with European products, arguing that the United States needed to favor its own industries over those of foreigners. Merchants looked for new regions to exploit, forging uneasy partnerships across racial and ethnic lines. Cotton growers, dependent on global markets, invested deeply in expanding racialized slavery. Looking inward, these competing regional economic interests threatened national political unity. The credit system concentrated profits in developed parts of the country, leaving the South and the West dependent on the East and on Britain—a relationship more fitting for a colony than a republic. Looking outward, the United States tried to project strength as part of a larger hemispheric region of linked former colonies.

boom-bust cycle Economic course typified by expansion and then contraction of business activity that came to exemplify the U.S. economy in the nineteenth century.

composite farming Farming system that grows crops for household use and also for market exchange.

☞ As you read, consider the ways that economic interests reconfigured regional politics and identities in the first half of the nineteenth century. Which new interests emerged on the national scene?

9-3a Export Economy

Agriculture unites and divides Americans.

In spite of the development of manufacturing in the United States, the vast majority of Americans lived on farms practicing **composite farming**, which included some production for the family's own use and some for sale in local and more distant markets. Husbands and wives worked all day to raise crops and livestock, maintain vegetable gardens, and process dairy products. Children performed essential labor and ran errands. To purchase goods they could not produce, families ran long credit accounts with local storekeepers that they paid off in extra eggs or homespun thread. Large families meant that new generations often had to move away to establish farms of their own, but they took the familiar forms of work and exchange with them.

Like their urban counterparts, farm families also responded to the opportunities of market development, labor migration, and improved transportation. Women in Delaware increased their dairy businesses to earn surplus profits that could be reinvested in land, opening more fields to wheat cultivation. Midwestern farmers used improved plows and mechanical reapers to specialize in corn and wheat as cash crops. Farmers, like merchants, replaced long-term worker contracts with seasonal waged work, which meant that the people who helped with the harvest did not have to be supported over the winter. Transportation opened new markets across regional lines and internationally (see Figure 9.1).

International markets meant international competition, and Americans disagreed about which industries needed protection. In 1816, Congress established a federal tariff on imports into the United States, hoping to protect the emerging textile, ironwork, and tannery industries by making their imported competitors more expensive. American businesses could be protected as they experimented with the technology, labor, and distribution systems necessary to compete with imports on their own. With subsequent revisions, by 1830, most imported goods that competed with U.S.-made goods were taxed one-third to one-half of their value.

Opponents of the tariff asked why U.S. manufacturing should be protected but not commercial agriculture. Southern planters of rice, cotton, and tobacco exported most of their crops, where they competed in markets not under U.S. tariff protection. Because their customers were abroad, southern planters earned their money in the form of credit abroad. The protective tariff that made English imports expensive meant that the credit Southerners received from English buyers was worth less than the credit U.S. manufacturers earned within the United States. Many feared that the British, who already protected their own farmers with Corn Laws, would retaliate with additional tariffs and price American export-based farmers out of their livelihood.

9-3b Global Fur Trade

Indian workers supply global markets with western plants and animals.

While farmers kept their eyes focused on the trade routes of rivers emptying into the Atlantic Ocean and Gulf of Mexico, fur trappers and traders fixed their attention on the Pacific. Following the first voyage of the *Empress of China* in 1784, U.S.–China trade had grown dramatically. By 1840, it was a $6.6 million business, making China the third largest exporter to the United States behind England and France. U.S. traders scoured the natural resources of the globe to find goods they could exchange for Chinese silks, tea, and porcelain. They soon added Hawaiian sandalwood, Rocky Mountain furs, Pacific otter skins, and Turkish opium to their shipments to Canton.

Tapping into the natural resources of North America for the China trade meant collaborating with Native Americans. In the Rocky Mountains, fur traders from the United States relied on the connections and expertise of Indians and French-speaking traders to obtain beaver fur and bison hides. Men employed by the Rocky Mountain Fur Company traveled up the Missouri River and along

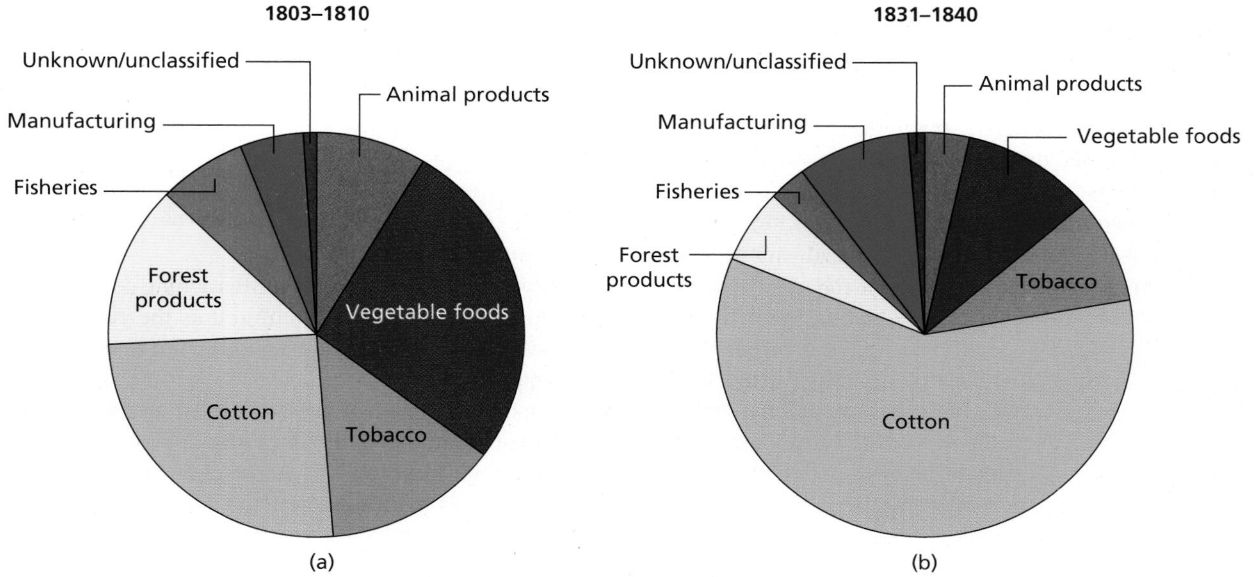

Figure 9.1 Changing Profile of U.S. Exports In the first decades of the nineteenth century, cotton increasingly dominated U.S. exports, pushing aside earlier important commodities such as tobacco. Grains and other vegetable foods also declined as exports because more U.S. grain was traded between states across new transportation lines. ▲ Source: *The Cambridge Economic History of the United States, Volume 2.*

Global Americans Born in 1825 to an influential Blackfeet family, **Medicine Snake Woman** (Natawista) married Alexander Culbertson, a trader with the American Fur Company twice her age, when she was 15. Their marriage bolstered the fur company's ambitions to replace the mobile rendezvous system with a chain of settled trading forts on the Upper Missouri River. Medicine Snake Woman's married life looked in two directions: toward the United States, where she sent five of her children to be educated in Catholic schools in St. Louis, and toward the contested West, where she worked with Culbertson to negotiate land treaties between the United States government and Blackfeet and Gros Venture Indian groups. From her home at Fort Union on the Upper Missouri River, she hosted Assiniboine, Crow, Sioux, and Blackfeet hunters; U.S. railroad surveyors; and European artists who all came to trade beaver and buffalo furs for English rifles and Chinese glass beads. Retiring in wealth to Peoria, Illinois, in 1858, Medicine Snake Woman left Culbertson ten years later to live with her Native American relatives. She died in 1893 on a Canadian Indian reservation. Through her economic, diplomatic, and family life, she negotiated the intersection of global business and Native American kinship practices, which defined life in western North America.

Native American roads to live year-round with Indian families. Indian women agreed to partner with trappers, teaching them how to treat, process, and pack furs. Traders, trappers, and Indians from multiple tribes met together at annual **rendezvous** points that were marked by peeling the bark off a set of trees near a river junction or constructing a five-foot tall mound of earth marked red with vermillion. When the parties met at these trade fairs, they exchanged goods for furs, which then traveled through St. Louis and down the Mississippi River to New Orleans, a hub of the global economy.

Native American labor, Chinese consumers, and Russian, U.S., and English ships all came together in the "great hunt" of the Eastern Pacific sea otters. Traders on the border between Russia and China had treasured and exploited the velvety fur of these small animals since the mid-eighteenth century. By kidnapping the indigenous hunters of the Aleutian and Kodiak Islands and putting them to work, the traders emptied the northern Pacific of otters, pushing the hunt down the coast toward Baja California, where British, U.S., French, and Spanish traders competed for the profitable business. In the years between 1803 and 1812, Americans and Russians joined forces in otter-hunting ventures that used U.S. ships to transport Indian men and women specializing in canoe-based hunting and pelt preparation, together with Russian overseers, to the shores and bays of California, paying bribes to the Spanish to look away. In the 1830s, sharpshooters targeted the remaining otters from the shore and within a decade, all of the "soft gold" of sea otter pelts had been hunted to near extinction.

rendezvous Annual gathering in which white and Indian trappers exchanged furs for manufactured goods as part of the Rocky Mountain fur trade industry.

Treaty of Wanghia Agreement that granted the United States the same access to Chinese ports and to trading as Britain had and that guaranteed that trading Americans remained under U.S. law.

American fortunes in the Pacific, however, continued to grow. In 1839, the Chinese government decided to halt the illegal flow of Indian and Turkish opium brought by competing U.S. and British ships. Confiscation of the contraband drug sparked the Opium War between the British and Chinese, which ended in an 1842 treaty that expanded British trading power. Not to be excluded, in 1844, the United States and China signed the **Treaty of Wanghia**, which granted the United States similar most-favored nation trading status, meaning that U.S. businessmen paid the same tariffs and received the same benefits as those from Britain, France, or any other nation. American merchants gained access to the five Chinese ports established at the end of the Opium War. In those ports, Americans could buy land, establish churches and hospitals, learn the Chinese language, and be subject to U.S. rather than Chinese law, an arrangement that put China in a subordinate position.

9-3c Political Compromise over Slavery

Internal developments reshape political regions.

By 1820, the most important regional split in the United States was no longer the East Coast versus the borderland West but rather states with slavery versus those without. This hardening sectionalism was economic, political, and cultural as the congressional crisis provoked by Missouri's admission to the United States highlighted.

Since the passage of the Northwest and Southwest Ordinances, national politics had sought compromise on the question of slavery in the republic, although free-state lawmakers grumbled that the Three-Fifths Compromise permanently granted states with slavery the edge in representation. In 1818, Missouri, where slavery existed, applied to be admitted as the second new state of the Louisiana Purchase, forcing Congress to confront the expansion of legal slavery in the United States. At the time, the country had eleven free states and eleven slave states.

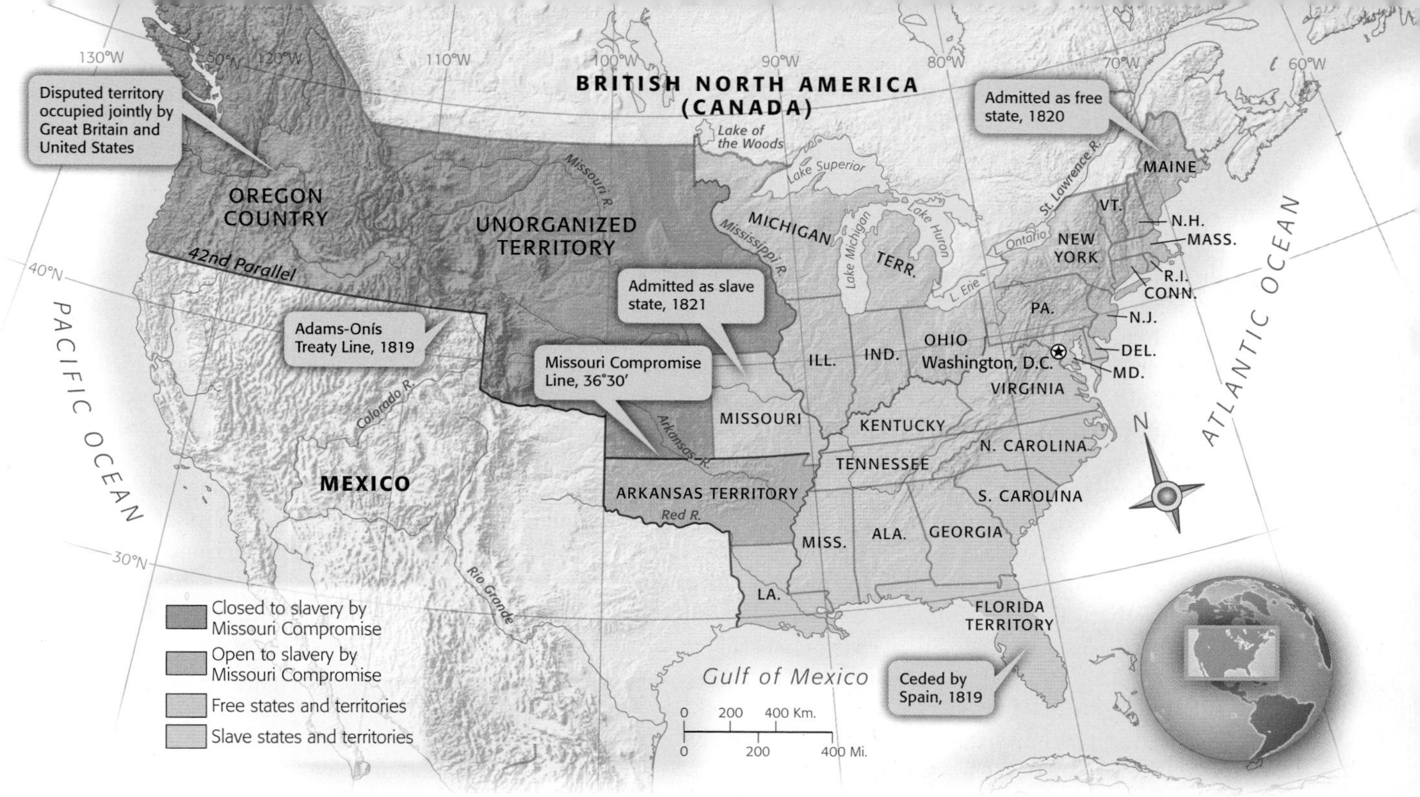

Map 9.4 Missouri Compromise, 1820 The law passed by the U.S. Congress maintained a balance of free and slave states. Nationalists were gratified that the Union could be strengthened through internal compromise and independence from European political maneuvering. But seventy-seven-year-old Jefferson lamented that the compromise was "a reprieve only, not a final sentence" on the question of extending slavery. ▲

Admitting Missouri would upset the balance between the two sides in the Senate. In addition, Missouri was geographically northern—its profile reached up over the Ohio River, which had been the dividing line between interior states that permitted slavery and those that outlawed it. Free-state congressmen moved to place conditions on Missouri's admission, including a gradual emancipation amendment, and slave-state congressmen protested that the federal government lacked the power to compel what was properly state law.

After long debate, Congress passed the **Missouri Compromise** in 1820, which allowed Missouri to enter the United States as a slave state balanced by Maine (formerly part of Massachusetts) as a free state (see Map 9.4). Seeking to pre-empt future debates, the bill also prohibited the extension of slavery in the territory of the Louisiana Purchase north of the 36–degree parallel but permitted it south of that line. Like other dividing lines in the history of imperial expansion in North America, the Missouri Compromise line helped to turn complicated political and familial identities on the ground into a starker sense of "us" versus "them." Missouri's new constitution, which prohibited free blacks from settling in the state, indicated that individual citizenship rights would continue to resist compromise.

9-3d A Hemispheric Vision

External dangers reshape political regions.

Statesmen hoping to promote U.S. economic development faced other contradictions that had always accompanied Jefferson's "empire of liberty." Lacking a strong navy and still relying on British banks for loans and seed money, the United States was vulnerable on both coasts. On the Atlantic, a Holy Alliance of European monarchies declared its commitment to put down revolutionary movements and help Spain retake its former American colonies. On the Pacific, Russian Czar Alexander I declared in 1821 that no foreign ships could come within one hundred miles of the coast of Alaska, claiming his empire's intention to maintain and extend its fur-trading operations in the Pacific Northwest. To protect itself from these perceived imperial threats, the United States needed a standing army, navy, higher taxes, and more centralized power. Yet these measures all undermined the ideals of a republic and long-standing opposition to a permanent military.

Missouri Compromise Law that admitted Missouri as a state permitting slavery and Maine as a state outlawing slavery, an attempt to maintain sectional political balance.

South America presented a political and economic solution. There, new republics and gold and silver mines offered the indebted United States a way to repay European investors and curb paper money speculation. Congressman Clay urged the United States to recognize South American independence movements and establish lucrative hemispherical trading ties that would create a region of "National Independence and Liberty" in contrast to the Old World monarchies. Others were skeptical of tying U.S. diplomatic fortunes to fledgling republics and urged a political alliance with Britain, which wanted to keep U.S. markets open and the Spanish and Russians out as colonial powers.

Monroe and his secretary of state John Quincy Adams crafted a message to Congress in 1823 that came to be called the **Monroe Doctrine**. Its central ideas were that North and South America were joined in republicanism, anticolonialism, and economic independence. Asserting that the Americas were "not to be considered as subjects for future colonization by any European power," the message warned that the United States would look on any "interposition" in the Western Hemisphere by European empires as a threat to American safety. The president's message further promised "not to interfere in the internal concerns" of Europe.

Such bold words presented a vision of regional influence that served the political interests of the United States. They did not specify what the United States would do in the event of European intervention. In fact, U.S. statesmen counted on the British Royal Navy to deter other European empires. And the Doctrine's words failed to acknowledge that in terms of trade, Britain, not the United States, was the major source of loans, trading relationships, and banking expertise to the new republics of Latin America. British traders, European diplomats, and Latin American revolutionaries all understood it as a statement of ambition rather than strength.

9-4 Democracy in Practice

The County Election (1852), by George Caleb Bingham, depicts election day in Missouri at mid-century as a social event. On the right side of the image, voters debate their options. On the left side of the image, the lone African American serves alcohol. Voting in this period was done either by voice vote or with tickets printed and handed out by political parties, decorated to make the voter's choice clear to the crowd.

How does this painting use the details of a local election day to portray the atmosphere of mid-nineteenth-century democratic participation? Who would feel welcome casting votes? ▶

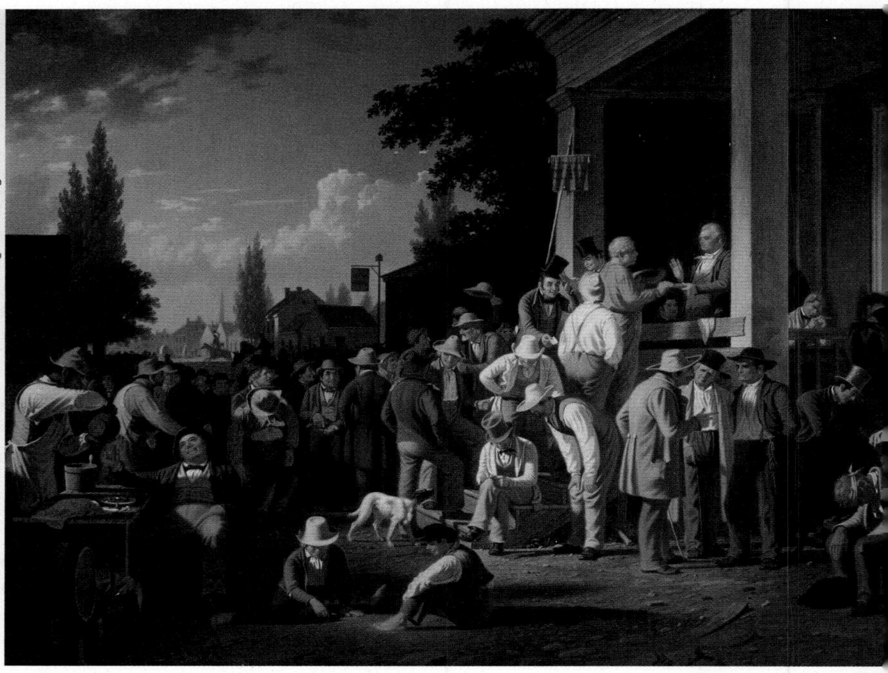

The County Election, 1852 (oil on canvas), Bingham, George Caleb (1811–1879)/Saint Louis Art Museum, Missouri, USA/Gift of Bank of America/Bridgeman Images

Americans buffeted by the forces of migration and industrialization pressed for a political system that could represent new regional and class divisions. States replaced an older conception that voting was a privilege of stable landowners who had a clear stake in society with an emerging one that the vote was connected with citizenship for adult white men. To reach this new constituency, politicians innovated an open, competitive, masculine culture focused around elections. Embracing private interests, a new party system revived partisanship. As global political movements in favor of democracy offered inclusion to some but excluded others, disenfranchised Americans experimented with alternative forms of political action.

Monroe Doctrine Foreign policy statement by Monroe asserting U.S. opposition to European efforts to colonize in North or South America.

☞ As you read, think about the social and political consequences of new laws granting most adult white men the right to vote. Did political developments extend or reverse the achievements of the American Revolution?

9-4a Revival of Partisan Politics

A new electorate requires new electioneering.

In the first decades of the nineteenth century, states removed religious tests and property requirements for voters, replacing them with the requirement that voters be male and white. In 1821, New York widened the right to vote to all white men with no property requirements and declared that only free black men who owned

$250 worth of property could vote. Of the 30,000 African Americans in New York, only 298 were eligible to vote. Similar patterns emerged in the new states created by territorial expansion. All of the states admitted to the Union after the War of 1812 permitted white men to vote without any requirement for property holding. At the same time, all of the states admitted after 1819, except Maine, prohibited black men from voting.

The consequences of enfranchising almost all white men transformed political life. In 1820, James Monroe was elected president without significant challenge. But opponents of the American System that he supported awakened from the lull in political partisanship and began to coalesce around Andrew Jackson. In 1824, Jackson was a war hero famous for his victory at the Battle of New Orleans and a wealthy lawyer and slaveholder. His origins, however, allowed him to portray himself as a striking alternative to the East Coast elites who had dominated the U.S. presidency. Son of Irish immigrants, Jackson grew up in the borderlands of the Carolinas and Tennessee, was orphaned at age fourteen, and had only sporadic education. In the 1824 presidential election, Jackson received more popular and electoral votes than any of the other four candidates for the presidency but no overall majority. Under the provisions of the Constitution, the outcome was therefore decided in the House of Representatives. Clay, who came in fourth in the Electoral College, threw his support to John Quincy Adams, a fellow **National Republican**, as their faction of the party was known. Jackson was defeated, and Clay became secretary of state. Jackson's supporters charged that a "corrupt bargain" had vanquished the will of the people. A new **Democratic Party** unified around opposition to Adams and what its members called *elitist minorities*.

The Democratic Party mobilized and secured the loyalty of new voters, embracing the idea that voters should choose party leaders who would promote their interests rather than espousing old ideas that elections should select independent men to act for the common good. The 1828 campaign used mass-produced newspapers and printed handbills with slogans such as "Who do you want—John Quincy Adams, who quotes the law, or Andy Jackson, who makes the law?" Parades, rallies, and barbecues emphasized white men's camaraderie as enfranchised citizens. Beating Adams, who ran again, Jackson won the presidency in 1828 with the overwhelming support of new voters. In the next years, political parties, following the tactics developed in evangelical reform movements (see Chapter 10), began to hold national conventions to craft platforms and select nominees. Rather than choose candidates in Congress, parties relied on popular participation to shape the careers of national politicians. The new tactics worked. In 1824, fewer than 30 percent of eligible voters cast ballots, but in 1840, 80 percent voted.

9-4b Andrew Jackson as National Executive

Jackson champions the majority by strengthening the power of the presidency.

Proclaiming that "parasitic minorities" should not rule over the majority, Jackson mobilized a diverse group who felt victimized by the economic changes of the nineteenth century. Artisans feared the loss of independence foisted by a small owner-manager class. Southern and western white farmers thought Indians should be expelled from valuable farmland. Indebted farmers worried that a cabal of moneymen were exploiting the legal and banking system for selfish gain.

The Second Bank of the United States became a prime target for Jackson's attacks that the privileges of the few should not prevail over the rights of the many. Since the Panic of 1819, opponents had argued that the Second Bank was so big and powerful that it threatened to put state banks out of business, and if it became the only source of money in the United States, the bank could do whatever it wanted. Jackson agreed. He wanted to destroy the bank and replace its paper money with a national currency of gold and silver coins. When bank president Nicholas Biddle requested a recharter for the Second Bank in 1832, Jackson vetoed the bill and then withdrew all federal deposits and put them in selected state banks. In doing so, he acted against the wishes of Congress and his secretary of the treasury, who pointed out that by law the deposits were supposed to go to the Bank of the United States.

Jackson's 1832 veto statement attacking the "Monster bank" demonstrated that his hatred for the bank was political as much as economic. He told people to blame the bank and outside corruption for the uncertainties of the market economy and played up a class warfare argument. He argued that the bank was an example of "the rich and powerful" bending "the acts of government to their selfish purposes." He pointed out that many of its stockholders were wealthy foreigners. And he argued that he, as elected president of the people, had a duty to participate directly in lawmaking because he represented the majority of Americans while congressmen, elected from state districts, represented only minorities within the whole.

The largest group to become the target of Democratic attacks on "minority" privileges was made up of southeastern Indians. Although many Creeks, Cherokees, and Choctaws had responded to the civilizing mission of the early nineteenth century, the federal government targeted them for removal to western lands. Echoing earlier ideas about the spread of U.S. civilization but with a new hardened racial edge, Jackson mischaracterized Indian-controlled lands as "covered with forests and ranged by a few thousand savages." In contrast, he declared, "our extensive republic" was "studded with

National Republican Faction within the Democratic-Republican party that supported the American System.

Democratic Party Political party formed around Andrew Jackson that opposed entrenched elitism, favored white male franchise, and pioneered boisterous mass politics.

Indian Removal Act U.S. law authorizing the president to offer Native Americans lands west of the Mississippi in exchange for their eastern homelands.

Cherokee Indian Cases U.S. Supreme Court legal decisions in 1831 and 1832 that affirmed Native American Indian tribes as sovereign entities but that Jackson refused to enforce.

cities, towns, and prosperous farms, embellished with all the improvements that art can devise or industry execute, occupied by more than 12 million happy people." The needs of the "12 million" in his eyes, trumped those of the "few thousand." In 1830, Congress passed the **Indian Removal Act**, which called for almost 100,000 Indians to relocate voluntarily from areas up and down the western borderlands of the United States across the Mississippi River to Indian Territory.

The American millions pushing Congress and the states to buy Indian land gained a new motive in 1829 when a north Georgia farmer and prospector discovered gold on a tributary of the Chattahoochee River, setting off a rush of migrants in search of quick wealth. The Cherokee Nation, a republic-style government established in 1820, owned most of the gold-producing land. The state of Georgia quickly passed laws designed to strip Cherokees of this land and their rights. As Native Americans had long done, Cherokees brought their grievance against Georgia to U.S. courts. In his *Cherokee Nation v. Georgia* (1831) decision, Chief Justice John Marshall ruled that the U.S. Supreme Court had no jurisdiction under the Constitution to hear Indian cases, but he did define the Cherokee Nation as a "domestic dependent nation," a ward rather than an independent country, that nevertheless had rights to its lands until it decided to cede control. In 1832, the Cherokee Nation brought a new test case with a U.S. citizen: Samuel Worcester, a Vermont missionary who had refused to obey Georgia's new law that non-Indians in Cherokee country pledge allegiance to the state of Georgia. In this decision, *Worcester v. Georgia* (1832), Marshall declared that the Cherokee Nation was "a distinct community" and Georgia laws had no force within its borders. Taken together, the **Cherokee Indian Cases** defined the legal status of Native American tribes as entities under the protection of the U.S. government that maintained sovereignty within their own borders.

Jackson, acting as executive, refused to enforce the decisions and supported the forcible removal of Indians in the Southeast. Seminoles in East Florida held out the longest, fighting a guerrilla war against U.S. Army and militia troops from 1835 to 1842. Some stayed in the Everglades, but ultimately most were expelled to follow the Choctaws, Creeks, Chickasaws, and Cherokees.

Smithsonian American Art Museum, Washington, DC/Art Resource, NY

Seminole Leader Osceola Born William Smith, Osceola rose to become a leader in the Seminoles' armed resistance to removal in the late 1830s. George Catlin painted this portrait in 1837, during the final months of Osceola's life in a South Carolina prison, after he was captured under a flag of truce. Catlin's gallery of hundreds of portraits of American Indians, called "Nature's dignitaries," toured the United States and Europe. ▲

9-4c Global Democratic Experiments

People around the world experiment with democratic reforms through law and independence movements.

The Cherokee Nation was one of many entities expanding men's access to their governments. In 1827, it ratified a written constitution that established a bicameral elected legislature as well as executive and legislative branches. The document extended the right to vote and to serve in office to all free adult Cherokee men. It excluded Cherokee women and all people of "negro or mulatto parentage."

In Britain, after a decades-long campaign, Parliament passed a Catholic Emancipation Act in 1829 that permitted Catholics to serve in Parliament. Three years later, the English Reform Act of 1832 further reconfigured representation. Rural districts long emptied of residents lost their members of Parliament, and urban and industrial centers such as London and Manchester gained more proportional representation. The old idea that each representative spoke for the entire empire was replaced with a more democratic model of representatives closely linked to their constituents' needs. Poor working men had protested for the right to vote, but the Reform Act took only gradual steps, granting adult men whose homes were worth £10 in annual rents the vote. The expansion increased the number of voters from about 14 percent of men to nearly 20 percent, a far more modest change than in the United States.

Inadequate representation spurred other European states to overthrow autocratic kings in favor of constitutional monarchies who would sanction freedom of the press and assembly as well as economic policies associated with free trade. In 1830, wealthy urban Frenchmen forced autocratic King Charles X to abdicate and replaced him with Louis-Philippe. A member of the royal family who had spent time in the United States in the 1790s, he was hailed as the "citizen king." Belgians, who had been united with the Netherlands at the end of the Napoleonic Wars, objected to a union in which they outnumbered the Dutch but did not enjoy greater representation in government. When petitions to William I failed, Belgians declared independence in 1830. Other peoples demanded recognition as independent nations with less success. Poles were defeated in their revolt against the Russian czar in 1831.

The wave of independence movements in Latin America produced constitutions establishing representative governments. Uruguay's first constitution of 1830 drew on U.S. and French models in creating separate branches of government to oversee lawmaking, enforcement, and judicial decision making. Chile's 1833 constitution created a republic whose government was declared to be "popular and representative," granting the right to vote to those free men over twenty-one who could read and write.

9-4d Participatory Politics

Petitions seek democracy for nonvoters.

Americans who could not vote did have the right to petition, and beginning in the late 1820s, this traditional form of gaining access to political leaders became a tool of the masses. By collecting signatures and making political demands, Americans with vulnerable political rights tried to amplify their voice as citizens. The right to petition was so closely tied to U.S. citizenship that in 1837, the U.S. House of Representatives passed a resolution forbidding slaves from submitting petitions on the grounds that they were not citizens.

Shut out from voting, white women petitioners tried to make their exclusion from partisan politics a point in their favor. Catharine Beecher, part of an influential family of educators, preachers, and writers, organized the first national women's petition drive to flood Congress with petitions opposing Cherokee removal. Claiming that "women are protected from the blinding influence of party spirit," these petitions made a nonpartisan moral case against the forcible removal of Indian men, women, and children. They highlighted feelings of distress for the Christianized Cherokees, forced out of their homes and the mission schools that many of the petitions' signers had supported for decades.

Lowell Female Reform Association Organization of female factory operatives in Massachusetts in 1845 that grew out of the earlier Lowell Factory Girls' Association.

Ten-Hour Movement International labor movement that pushed governments to legislate maximum ten-hour workdays.

Working people hoped that petitions would form a bridge between labor actions and political change. In the 1840s, the **Lowell Female Reform Association**, together with blacksmiths and carpenters in Philadelphia, joined forces with an international **Ten-Hour Movement** to petition lawmakers to limit the workday to no more than ten hours. Factory workers in the United States and Britain regularly toiled over 12 hours a day, six days a week. Pressure in Britain to regulate work, especially child labor, was gaining strength, and activists hoped to achieve results in the United States as well. In 1845, three-fourths of those who signed ten-hour petitions addressed to the Massachusetts legislature were women. The movement was a moderate success, and in 1840, the federal government mandated a ten-hour workday on federal projects. By the end of the decade, New Hampshire and Pennsylvania had adopted ten-hour days. But in many states, including Massachusetts, the Ten-Hour Movement was decried as "un-American."

9-5 Limits of Majority Rule

"Specie Claws" (1837), by H.R. Robinson, links the hard times of 1837 to national policies. In this image, rent collectors appear at the door while an out-of-work carpenter, with his tools strewn on the bare floor, tells his hungry wife and children "I have not the means, and cannot get any work." Faint portraits of Democratic presidents Jackson and Van Buren are hanging on the walls.

According to this cartoon, who is to blame for the financial crises of 1837? Who suffers? ►

The boom-bust economy of the 1830s and 1840s brought the flaws in majority rule into sharp focus as some regions rose and others suffered. In response, some states tried to renegotiate the terms of their participation in the Union. New coalitions formed political parties more responsive to the needs and interests of those states. When global markets entangled the United States in another crushing economic depression, elected representatives redesigned laws and institutions to cope with seemingly anonymous global forces. In doing so, they debated the proper balance between open competition and necessary shelter.

☞ **As you read, reflect on the ways Americans used democratic politics to rethink the meaning of individual rights. How did lawmaking reflect changing ideas about rights?**

9-5a States' Rights

A revived focus on state political power emerges as a counterweight to majority rule.

Alexis de Tocqueville, a French aristocrat and political thinker who toured the United States in the 1830s, wrote critically about the social dimensions of American democracy. The much-celebrated majority rule, he claimed, restricted true liberty: "I know of no country in which there is so little independence of mind and real freedom of discussion as in America." Madison had warned against the political consequences of this "tyranny of the majority" during the constitutional debates of the 1780s, cautioning that because the essence of democracy is the rule of the majority, government must be carefully designed to protect the rights of the minority. Tocqueville focused on social costs, arguing that democratic despotism oppressed people who did not even realize it. While the aristocratic rulers of Europe controlled people's bodies with decrees about forbidden behaviors, democracy in the United States coerced conformity by insisting that the majority was correct and opponents should be ostracized.

The political realities of majority rule combined with a rising sense of **sectionalism** dividing the country reinvigorated debate over the proper balance between the rights of states and the interests of the country as a whole. When Congress passed the **Tariff of 1828**, white South Carolinians believed that it blatantly favored northern industry at the expense of southern commercial agriculture. But how could they stop the measure, given that a majority vote had passed it? In an anonymous essay, Vice President Calhoun proposed a method for states to nullify federal laws they deemed unconstitutional. His *doctrine of nullification* stated that the federal Constitution was a compact between individual states that retained their own sovereignty. When there was a disagreement about that compact, states kept the right to interpret it as they saw fit. In other words, the states, not the federal courts, had the final say on whether a federal law was constitutional. Calhoun suggested that South Carolina hold a state convention and vote the tariff null and void and then take its cause to the other states in a specially called convention. If three-quarters of the other states disagreed, the nullifying state had two choices: either live with the law or withdraw from the United States.

sectionalism Political loyalty to one's own region of the country in opposition to other regions that in the nineteenth century was increasingly between North and South.

Tariff of 1828 Federal tax on imported manufactured goods that prompted a political crisis dividing the cotton-producing South from the North and Midwest.

Whigs Political party created to oppose the Democrats and to champion a strong federal government and, in some cases, moral reform.

The doctrine of nullification was a way to protect minority rights. In this case, southern planters were the minority. Supporters claimed to be following in the patriotic tradition of the Kentucky and Virginia Resolutions, which had suggested that sovereign states were the best check on tyrannical power. Opponents disagreed, declaring the U.S. Constitution an agreement among "we the people" of the United States, not merely a compact between independent states. That same Constitution, they argued, gave the power to regulate commerce to the federal government.

Andrew Jackson was known as a strong states' rights supporter. He was a cotton planter and a slave owner, but he opposed nullification, insisting "Our Federal Union. It must be preserved." He thought that the tariff would temporarily help the United States raise money to pay its debts and increase its military defense. He therefore signed a tariff act in 1832 that reduced the rates but insisted on the principle of protectionism. South Carolina held a convention and declared federal tariffs null and void in the state. Jackson asked Congress to pass what was called a *Force Bill,* giving him the power to use the military to collect tariff revenues. Even those representatives who opposed nullification thought that this was going too far. Pushed to the brink, Senator Clay devised a compromise to gradually lower the tariff and eventually end protectionist measures. South Carolina promptly nullified the Force Bill, an action that the federal government ignored. The crisis died down, but the issue of states' rights, particularly a state's right to protect legal slavery, would not go away.

9-5b New Political Parties

Opposition parties challenge Democrats and push for a more active government.

Native-born businessmen, defenders of displaced Indians, and antitariff Southerners saw Jackson as a tyrant. "King Andrew," they claimed, manipulated gullible supporters by using the "tyranny of the majority" to crush opposition to his power. Gathering together in a new political party that first ran candidates in the 1836 election, they named themselves the **Whigs** to honor revolutionary patriots and eighteenth-century British opponents of kingly tyranny (see Table 9.1). Whigs saw the expansion of the right to vote and the boisterous political culture of rallies, party platforms, and parades as the collapse of the Founding Fathers' vision, not its logical next step, as Democrats did. "*The Republic has degenerated*

Table 9.1 Comparison of U.S. Political Parties

Both the Democratic and Whig parties of the second party system were coalitions, made up of voters with diverse views on religion, slavery, and regional economic power. In terms of style, both parties adopted imagery that presented politics as a battle of rugged masculinity.

Democrats	Whigs
Favored weaker federal government	Favored stronger federal government
Supported state control of internal improvements	Supported federal investment in internal improvements
Encouraged immigration	Distrusted immigration
Were motivated by local rights and the "common man" against monopolies	Were motivated by social reform issues
Had strongest support from laborers, Catholic immigrants, Southerners	Had strongest support from businessmen, native-born Protestants, New Englanders, free blacks
Had Andrew Jackson, Martin Van Buren as national figures	Had Henry Clay, William Henry Harrison as national figures

into a Democracy" one Virginia newspaper lamented, using the term *democracy* in its negative eighteenth-century sense of mob rule. Whigs preferred a system in which the passions of the majority were filtered through the judgment of elites. Influenced by evangelical Christianity, they praised self-control and domesticity for men.

Whigs advocated an active central government. They championed many of the elements of the American System, including a national tariff, a new national bank, and renewed support for internal improvements. Mostly native-born Protestants, Whigs tended to concentrate in the Upper South, the North, and parts of the West focused on commercial development.

Working people's struggles to improve their conditions highlighted the importance of the ballot box. Laws forbidding unionization, imprisoning debtors, and seizing the property of bankrupts could change only by the action of elected officials, and the major parties seemed unconcerned with the suffering of workers and debtors. Inspired by similar organizations in England, Philadelphia workers formed the first Working Men's Party in 1828 to represent "the interests and enlightenment of the working classes." In 1837, workers and farmers in Utica, New York, established the Equal Rights Party to demand a legal system that would protect average people, not just propertied investors. Working Men's political parties championed several causes, including free public schools, an end to imprisonment for debt, the payment of all wages in hard currency, and a ten-hour workday. Dissatisfied with the candidates of the Democrats and then the Whigs, these **third parties** defined and spoke for a specific constituency. Most were short lived. Their success, typically, came when one of the two major parties took up their issue as its own.

9-5c Credit Crash and Its Consequences

Americans face the consequences of speculation.

The year 1836 began on a bubble of enthusiasm for speculation in the U.S. economy. The transatlantic cotton business was booming again as British firms purchased U.S. cotton at ever-higher prices and sent desirable manufactured goods to American ports. Gold and silver flowed in as well. Imported from Mexico where it was mined, silver had long been funneled to China in exchange for imports. In the 1830s, Chinese merchants preferred paper bills on British banks, which were more easily integrated into the opium trade with India. Flush with borrowed British paper that they passed on to the Chinese, U.S. state banks began to accumulate Mexican silver. To many of these banks, more silver in the vault justified the printing of more paper money. Individuals eagerly borrowed that new money, in turn, to purchase western land sold by the federal government. Borrowers speculated that the value of land would rise quickly enough to enable them to pay off their debts. But just as in 1818, such practices were vulnerable to sudden credit contractions.

Contraction came first from England, where a bad grain harvest forced the Bank of England to restrict its credit, leading to a domino effect of firms calling in their transatlantic debts. The panic spread and deepened as the consequences of new U.S. financial policies took over. Jackson, at the end of his presidency, had tried to curb speculation in 1836 by adopting the **Specie Circular**, which prohibited the federal government from accepting anything but gold and silver coin as payment for government land. Martin Van Buren, Jackson's vice-president who was elected president in 1836, left the policy in place even as the panic took hold. The effect was to reduce the value of the notes that farmers held. People rushed to the banks to obtain specie with which to repay their debts, but the banks lacked sufficient reserves to pay depositors. More than half of the nation's banks failed. As banks desperately called in their business loans to obtain specie, businesses failed in turn. Unemployment soared, and wages fell by as much as 50 percent. Following the philosophy of the Democratic Party, which called for limits on federal power, Van Buren refused to involve the federal government in stopping the panic or depression that followed.

The **Panic of 1837** had international causes, but many read the hard times that followed as an indictment of U.S. democracy. With more than 30 percent of workers in New York City unemployed, many wondered whether the U.S. government could still respond to the needs of the people or if it had become completely captive to the interests of bankers and bosses.

third parties Political parties other than the main two that have often coalesced around a specific cause.

Specie Circular Jackson's executive order requiring payments for public land in specie rather than credit or bank notes that was repealed in 1838.

Panic of 1837 Financial crisis of international origins that led to bankruptcies, bank failures, and unemployment.

Robinson, Henry R., –1850/Library of Congress

Andrew Jackson Rides the Democratic Donkey This 1837 political cartoon references a Biblical story to criticize Jackson for being a false prophet indifferent to the suffering he has caused as president. With a "Farewell Address" trailing out of his pocket, Jackson beats his donkey with a cane marked "veto." Newly elected Van Buren follows in the footsteps of his predecessor, oblivious to the specter brandishing a flaming sword to protest their actions. ▲

Increasing suspicion about the legality and utility of state charters combined with a rash of states defaulting on their loans led to the sharp curtailment of such charters in the years after the panic. Whereas 70 percent of canal construction had been financed by state and local sources, 70 percent of railroad construction came from private investment. The U.S. Supreme Court, in *Charles River Bridge vs. Warren Bridge* (1837), ruled against the types of state monopolies that had been at the heart of early nineteenth-century commercial development, preferring to bolster the rights of individual entrepreneurs to compete. The case revolved around a state-chartered toll bridge linking Charlestown and Boston that had been extremely profitable for its owners. When Warren Bridge, a rival, constructed in 1828 less than a hundred yards from the first cut into those profits, the Charles River owners sued for protection of their corporate rights. The court's decision supported the new bridge and private competition.

To cope with the fallout of so many Americans "going smash," Congress tried again to fashion a bankruptcy law that would satisfy creditors without destroying debtors. The Bankruptcy Act of 1841 offered a fresh start to anyone who obeyed court orders and gave over assets to a bankruptcy assignee. For the next two years, forty-one thousand Americans were designated bankrupts. They were not imprisoned or branded for life as cheats; most went on to waged work that offered steadier, although less potentially lucrative returns, than entrepreneurship. For some creditors, the idea of such a safety net was galling—should gamblers be allowed to cheat the people who had trusted them with no consequences? Under political pressure, Congress revoked the Bankruptcy Act in 1843.

Most free Americans continued to believe that financial failure was the fault of the individual in spite of the fact that the expanding economy had exposed average people to international and transcontinental forces they could not control. Disappointed European investors, who held the bonds that U.S. states refused to repay in the crisis, blamed governments unwilling to tax voters.

Summary

In the early decades of the nineteenth century, political revolutions and industrialization eroded imperial trade monopolies as nations competed for position in global markets. Market transformations changed labor and family patterns. Although many farm families continued to operate under an integrated household economy, urban and immigrant families increasingly consisted of a collection of waged workers who pooled their disparate resources to survive. Global labor flows further broke up and reassembled families as free sons and daughters migrated within the United States and immigration brought in new workers and communities. Enslaved families long established in the tobacco-producing coastal regions were torn apart by an interstate slave trade serving the demands of continent-spanning cotton and textile businesses.

Projects such as the C & O canal helped promote a unified United States, bridging old regional divides between the coast and the western borderlands by constructing vital links between them. But new divisions threatened to destabilize the American union. The relationship between the developing economic system and the U.S. political system underwent profound flux in the opening decades of the century as the East–West political divide of the Revolutionary era was replaced by a North–South divide over slavery. Working against these sectional trends, a new party system tried to knit together coalitions that reached across regional divides. Slave-owning Southerners and poor Irish immigrants in northern cities became Jacksonian democrats.

Faced with an economy they could not control, Americans struggled to use their political system to speak for their interests. Old debates over the contest between majority rule and minority rights in a republic took new sectional shape in the democratic system that had emerged by 1840.

Thinking Back, *Looking Forward*

As you review this chapter, compare the global forces behind early colonial migrations, both free and forced, with the global forces that were behind migrations, again both free and forced, in the first decades of the nineteenth century. How did the changing nature of labor itself affect families? How did work lives and family ties change from the mid-eighteenth century to the mid-nineteenth century?

In coming chapters, be alert to how families, religious practices, new institutions, and cultural forms responded to the disruptions caused by nineteenth-century economic transformations.

To make your study concrete, review the timeline and reflect on the entries there. Think about their causes, consequences, and connections. How do they connect events in North America to global trends?

Additional Resources

Books

Beckert, Sven. *Empire of Cotton: A Global History*. New York: Knopf, 2014. ▶ Sweeping study of capitalism and the global cotton trade.

Igler, David. *The Great Ocean: Pacific Worlds from Captain Cook to the Gold Rush*. New York: Oxford University Press, 2013. ▶ Portrayal of the international Pacific World of the nineteenth century.

Johnson, Paul. *Sam Patch, the Famous Jumper*. New York: Hill and Wang, 2004. ▶ Story of a competitive waterfall jumper and the Industrial Revolution.

Johnson, Walter. *Soul by Soul: Life inside the Antebellum Slave Market*. Cambridge, MA: Harvard University Press, 1999. ▶ Illumination of the dynamics of human commodification in the domestic slave trade.

Larson, John. *Internal Improvement: National Public Works and the Promise of Popular Government in the Early United States*. Chapel Hill: University of North Carolina Press, 2001. ▶ History of the connections between transportation projects and the shift from republic to democracy.

Mihm, Steven. *A Nation of Counterfeiters: Capitalists, Con Men, and the Making of the United States*. Cambridge, MA: Harvard University Press, 2009. ▶ Exploration of the making and distribution of counterfeit bills.

Rockman, Seth. *Scraping By: Wage Labor, Slavery, and Survival in Early Baltimore*. Baltimore, MD: Johns Hopkins University Press, 2009. ▶ Detailed study of enslaved and free workers in nineteenth-century Baltimore.

Watson, Harry L. *Liberty and Power: The Politics of Jacksonian America*. New York: Hill and Wang, 2006. ▶ Classic, engaging survey of culture and politics in the early nineteenth century.

Wilentz, Sean. *The Rise of U.S. Democracy: Jefferson to Lincoln*. New York: W.W. Norton, 2005. ▶ Interpretive synthesis of the political and cultural ramifications of nineteenth-century democracy.

Zaeske, Susan. *Signatures of Citizenship: Petitioning, Antislavery, and Women's Political Identity*. Chapel Hill: University of North Carolina Press, 2003. ▶ Study of the form and use of petitions as political tools by women.

Go to the MindTap® for **Global Americans** to access the full version of select books from this Additional Resources section.

Websites

Capitalism by Gaslight at the Library Company. (http://www.librarycompany.org/shadoweconomy/index.htm) ▶ Exhibition with documents featuring the illicit economies of the nineteenth century.

Cotton Town. (http://www.cottontown.org/Pages/default.aspx). ▶ Extensive collection of documents and analysis of the English cotton industry.

Railroad Maps at the Library of Congress. (http://www.loc.gov/collection/railroad-maps-1828-to-1900/about-this-collection/). ▶ Collection of 623 railroad maps and associated documents.

Transatlantic Slave Trade Database. (http://www.slavevoyages.org). ▶ Detailed numbers and maps of the slave trade into the nineteenth century.

Women Working, 1800–1930. (http://ocp.hul.harvard.edu/ww/index.html). ▶ Valuable collection of primary sources and essays on women at work.

MindTap®

Continue exploring online through MindTap®, where you can:

- **Assess your knowledge with the Chapter Test**
- **Watch historical videos related to the chapter**
- **Further your understanding with interactive maps and timelines**

Markets and Democracy

1790–1792

April 1790
Congress passes the first patent act, granting fourteen-year monopoly on registered inventions.

November 1790
Blanc demonstrates the principle of interchangeable parts on gunlocks in Paris.

February 1792
Congress formally organizes the United States Post Office.

1807–1810

March 1807
Congress abolishes the international slave trade, effective 1808.

November 1808
Madison wins election as president.

June 1810
Astor charters the Pacific Fur Company to establish a fur trading post on the Pacific Coast.

1812–1816

November 1812
Madison wins reelection as president.

1812–1814
War of 1812 pits the United States against Britain and its allies.

April 1816
Second Bank of the United States created.

Congress passes a protective tariff on imported cotton and wool textiles.

November 1816
Monroe wins election as president.

1819–1820

1819
Panic of 1819, sparked by European postwar recovery, sends U.S. economy into downturn.

March 1820
Missouri Compromise admits Missouri to the United States as a slave state and Maine as a free state.

November 1820
Monroe wins reelection as president.

1821–1825

1821
Boston Manufacturing Company creates cotton textile manufactory in Lowell, Massachusetts.

September 1821
Russian Czar Alexander I declares the Alaskan coast forbidden to non-Russian ships.

December 1823
Monroe Doctrine states that the American Hemisphere must remain free from European interference.

February 1825
John Quincy Adams wins election as president in a decision made in the House of Representatives.

October 1825
Erie Canal connecting Albany to Buffalo is completed.

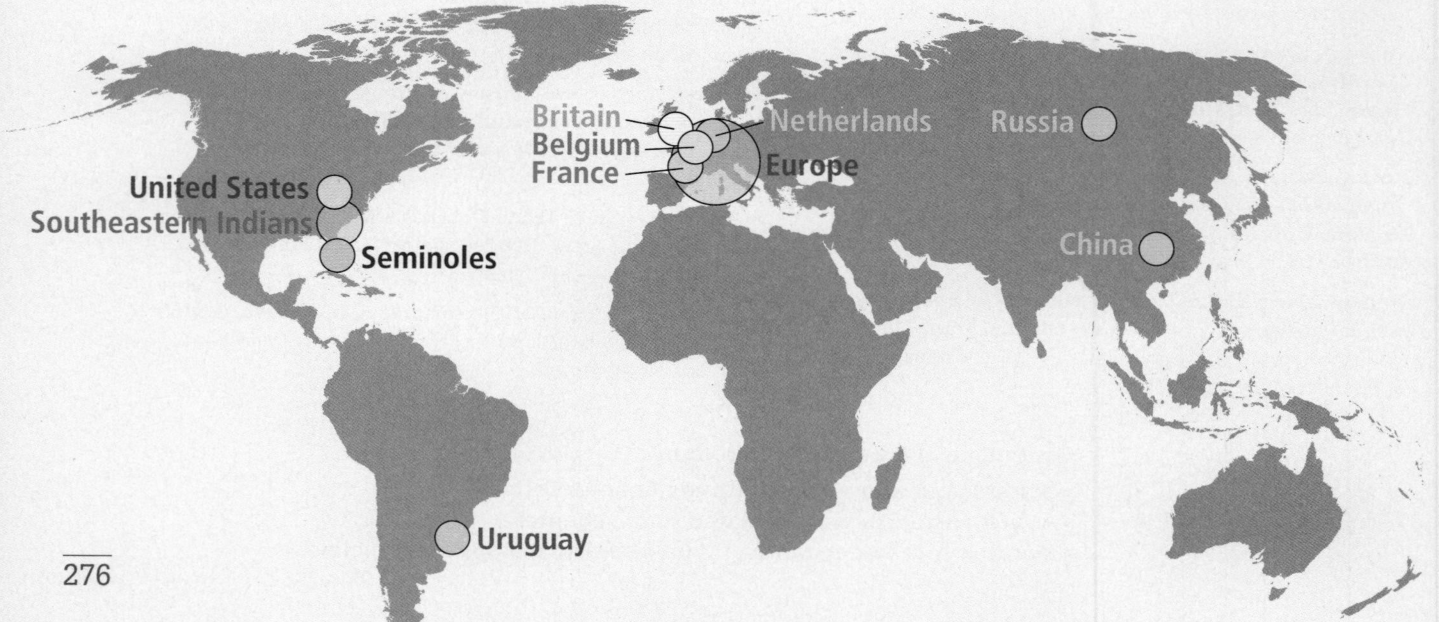

1828–1829

May 1828

Congress passes Tariff of 1828 over South Carolina's objections.

July 1828

Construction begins on the Baltimore and Ohio Railroad, connecting the Potomac and Ohio Rivers.

November 1828

Jackson wins election as the first president from the new Democratic Party.

April 1829

British Parliament passes Catholic Emancipation Act, permitting Catholics to serve in government.

1830

May

Jackson signs the Indian Removal Act, authorizing land grants for Indians west of the Mississippi.

July

Independent Uruguay models first constitution on U.S. and French examples.

August

French King Charles X abdicates in favor of Louis Philippe, the "citizen king."

November

Belgians declare independence from the Netherlands.

1832

July

Jackson vetoes the recharter of the Second Bank of the United States.

November

Jackson wins reelection as president.

1833–1836

August 1833

Workers from diverse trades form the General Trades Union in New York.

1835

Seminoles fight guerilla war against the United States to oppose removal (to 1842).

1836

Female mill workers in Lowell organize a turn-out that lasts months.

November 1836

Van Buren wins election as president, defeating candidates from the new Whig Party.

1837–1844

1837

Bank failures and unemployment soar in the Panic of 1837.

February 1837

House of Representatives resolves that slaves lack the right to petition because they are not citizens.

August 1841

Congress passes Bankruptcy Act that applies to average Americans, not just elite businessmen.

July 1844

Treaty of Wanghia with China grants the United States trading privileges equal to those of Britain and France.

10 Personal Transformations and Public Reforms

1800–1848

Lucretia Mott and Elizabeth Cady Stanton met when both traveled to London for the World's Anti-Slavery Convention, where the younger Stanton in particular was awakened to a larger world.

10-1
American Communities

10-1a U.S. Cities
10-1b The Middle Class
10-1c Families in the West and Midwest
10-1d Plantations and Slavery
10-1e Farming Communities

10-2
Religious Awakenings and Social Experiments

10-2a Evangelical Christianity
10-2b American Missions
10-2c Christianity's Multiple Messages
10-2d Experimental Communities

10-3
American Cultures

10-3a Feelings and Behavior
10-3b Nature and Self-Improvement
10-3c Print and Public Performance

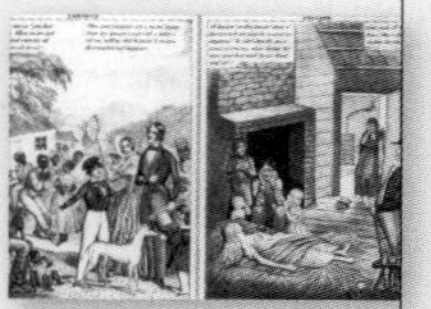

10-4
Ideologies of Race and Slavery

10-4a Legal Contexts for Slavery
10-4b Proslavery Arguments
10-4c Scientific Racism
10-4d Resistance to Slavery

10-5
Individual Rights and Social Good

10-5a Temperance Movement
10-5b Institutions of Rescue and Reform
10-5c Expansion of Antislavery
10-5d Women's Rights

When they met in 1840, Elizabeth Cady Stanton was a 25-year-old bride on her honeymoon and Lucretia Mott was a 47-year-old international activist. Both had traveled to London for the World's Anti-Slavery Convention, Stanton as a supportive observer and Mott as a delegate from the Philadelphia Female Anti-Slavery Society. The British and Foreign Anti-Slavery Society, organizer of the convention, had invited "the friends of the slave of every nation and every clime" to come to coordinate international efforts. Britain had legally emancipated slaves in its colonies in 1833, and British abolitionists wanted to end slavery everywhere. Responding to the call, nearly five hundred activists from across England and Ireland, the Caribbean (Jamaica, Antigua, Barbados, Haiti, and Mauritius), Africa (Sierra Leone), France, Spain, Canada, and the United States met in London.

The Library of Congress

Elizabeth Cady Stanton with Her Daughter, Harriot, 1856

The U.S. delegation included seven women, many of them Quakers like Mott, who were leaders in American antislavery societies. But when the women tried to present their credentials and take their places, the conference organizers refused, stating that it was against "English custom and usage" to permit women equal participation in men's antislavery work.

The first day of the conference was devoted to debating this issue with opponents stating that they would be "embarrassed" to talk about the horrors of slavery in front of ladies. One black male delegate from Jamaica thought that including women would "lower the dignity" of the proceedings and make it a subject of ridicule. London attorney William Ashurst called these delegates out for their hypocrisy. How could it be, he asked, that a convention in favor of universal humanity was opening by "disfranchising one-half of creation"? The delegates were unconvinced and voted overwhelmingly to make the women sit silently behind a divider. Some American men, including leading abolitionist William Lloyd Garrison, joined them in solidarity.

To Mott and the other longtime activists, the debate highlighted a familiar dilemma. Efforts to reform social ills—from drunkenness to prostitution to poverty to slavery—depended on women as speakers, writers, fund-raisers, and organizers. Yet women could not vote, and powerful cultural ideals demanded they remain in the background. Undaunted, Mott continued with her European tour, lecturing and meeting allies interested in ending these limitations to women's rights. Stanton was electrified by her new transatlantic acquaintances: "It was intensely gratifying to hear all that . . . I had dimly thought, so freely discussed by other women."

Many in the nineteenth century experienced a newfound sense of living in a larger world. Some, like Stanton, were energized and inspired. Garrison's antislavery newspaper bore the motto "Our country is the world—our countrymen are mankind." Cheaper travel, faster printing presses, and more widespread literacy made it possible to spread culture and ideas quickly through neighborhoods and across international political boundaries. New ideas about human nature and human capacities made forging these connections imperative.

At the same time, industrialization, displacement, and urbanization created social problems that divided people in new ways. Manufacturing

What do Lucretia Mott and Elizabeth Cady Stanton's experiences at the World's Anti-Slavery Convention reveal about the relationship between democracy and reform in the nineteenth century?

Go to MindTap® to watch a video on Mott and Stanton and learn how their stories relate to the themes of this chapter.

boomtowns and cities were crowded with poor and transient people competing for low-wage work. The territorial expansion of the United States forced Native, French, and Spanish communities to adapt their own legal systems and family patterns. Regimented labor brutalized slaves on cotton fields and demoralized workers in factories. The boom-bust economy left farmers and clerks scrambling to plan for the future. An economy and political culture built on competition was ruthless to losers.

Remedies took one of two main approaches: strengthening communities or asserting individual rights. In city neighborhoods, free black people created mutual aid societies. In rural areas, men and women experimented with new forms of communal living. Everywhere, churches hoped to change behavior and reform society by reinforcing the bonds between believers. At the same time, and often in the same regions, men and women stressed autonomy as much as community. Thinkers sought wisdom in self-reliance. Slaves escaped to free themselves. Women, white and black, continued to expand the claims of equality.

10-1 American Communities

George Catlin's *Five Points* (1827) depicts black and white New Yorkers working, fighting, and socializing in the streets. The painting details nineteenth-century urban life, including people pumping and carrying water, a prostitute soliciting customers from an upper-story window, and the proliferation of grocery shops, most of which sold alcohol. Catlin's picture also highlights contrasts: A pig is foraging in the garbage at the feet of a man in a top hat.

How does the artist portray relationships among these neighbors? Is he depicting one community? ▶

The Five Points, Junction of Baxter, Worth and Park Streets, New York (hand-coloured engraving), Catlin, George (1796–1872) (after)/© Museum of the City of New York, USA/Bridgeman Images

Migration, industrialization, and global trade restructured nineteenth-century U.S. communities, gradually in some regions and dramatically in others. From the countryside and from Europe, people flocked to cities to work in factories, offices, and service industries. In search of productive land, farmers pushed west onto former Indian territory. Across the South, export-minded cotton growers dragged enslaved African Americans away from families and work lives. Up streams and over mountains, Native Americans and fur traders joined distant markets. All confronted new lives among strangers who differed in wealth, religion, and culture. In most cases, families bore the brunt of economic change.

☞ As you read, think about how the economic forces of the early nineteenth century, including migration, industrialization, and global trade, reshaped communities in the United States. Were people aware of larger patterns, or was their context mainly local?

10-1a U.S. Cities

Urban communities fracture along lines of class, race, and religion.

The majority of Americans lived rural lives in the nineteenth century, but between 1820 and 1850, a significant proportion of the population was caught up in a quick urbanization (see Table 10.1). Old ports grew as industries in them expanded, and transportation networks created new boomtowns along canals and railroads. In 1820, only 7 percent of Americans lived in cities of more than twenty-five hundred people, but thirty years later, 18 percent did. Three groups—migrants from rural surroundings, free black people, and immigrants from abroad—accounted for the bulk of this increase.

They found, especially in the larger cities, the same problems of poverty, crowding, and illness that American

Table 10.1 Urban Population and Growth around the World (in thousands)

In the first half of the nineteenth century, city populations in the United States increased dramatically. By mid-century, some equaled the size of European urban centers, although most were dwarfed by the major cities of Asia and Europe. Slave labor and transatlantic trade led to large population increases in Brazil's Rio de Janeiro, where slave-grown coffee became a significant export, and in England's Manchester, home to industrial cotton manufacturing.

City	Population in 1800	Population 1850–1851	Percent Increase (%)
New Orleans	8	116	1,350
Boston	25	137	448
Baltimore	26	169	550
New York City	60	696	1,060
Philadelphia	69	340	393
Rio de Janeiro	43	166	286
Mexico City	137	170	24
Manchester	90	303	237
Berlin	172	419	144
Amsterdam	217	224	3
Vienna	247	444	80
St. Petersburg	336	485	44
Paris	581	1,053	81
London	1,117	2,685	140
Edo (Tokyo)		1,150	
Osaka		330	
Beijing		850	
Suzhou		700	

Sources: International Historical Statistics; Saito Seji, "Edo jidai no toshi jinko [Urban Population of the Edo Period]," Chiiki kaihatsu [Local Development], September 1984, pp. 48-63, Sekiyama Naotaro, Kinsei nihon no jinko kozo [The Population Structure of Early Modern Japan], Tokyo: Yoshikawa Kobunkan, 1958: Chinese statistics are for the 1840s, from G. William Skinner, The City in Late Imperial China.

statesmen and wealthy travelers had always condemned in European cities. In poor neighborhoods, men worked for low wages as manual laborers, women took in sewing and did cleaning work, and children scavenged in the streets for trash that could be resold. They lived in crowded wooden buildings with nowhere to dump garbage but out the window. The infamous **Five Points** neighborhood of Lower Manhattan sat at an intersection of streets and had once been a skating pond. Decades of garbage and run-off from urban tanneries and landfill turned it into a place where disease passed quickly through the water supply.

Filthy conditions and international trade exposed Americans to global epidemics. Cholera, a disease originating in South Asia, had begun traveling with sailors by 1817 (see Map 10.1). An 1831 outbreak in London spread to Canada and then to New York in 1832, hitting the poor of the Five Points especially hard. Children who seemed well in the morning died by evening, their bodies shaking with cramps. Of the city's 250,000 residents, 3,515 died before the epidemic subsided. As they fled, traveling on mail coaches and canal boats, people carried the disease as far north as Maine, deep into the Midwest, and down the Mississippi to New Orleans, where it claimed thousands more lives. No one at the time knew that water contaminated by human and animal waste was to blame. Instead, cholera was called the "poor man's plague," both because the poor were disproportionately victims and, some wealthy New Yorkers believed, they were the perpetrators. "They have brought the cholera this year," wrote former mayor Philip Hone, "and they will always bring wretchedness and want." Charles Dickens, the popular British author, likened the Five Points to London slums on his visit in 1842: "All that is loathsome, drooping, and decayed is here."

Competition for work among free blacks, native-born poor whites, and recent European immigrants was intense. Male laborers could earn $1 a day for construction or dock work, but work was not available every day. A woman in Baltimore might earn six cents for every pair of pants she sewed, but in the next building would be another woman, sewing faster and enlisting her children to help. Discriminatory laws barred African Americans from many jobs and membership in institutions.

Sometimes hostility among neighbors erupted into violence. On the evening of July 7, 1834, a group of musicians from the New York Sacred Music Society arrived at the Chatham Street Chapel and discovered an African American choir had

Five Points Neighborhood in New York City named for the "points" created where three streets intersected that was internationally known for poverty, crowding, and violence.

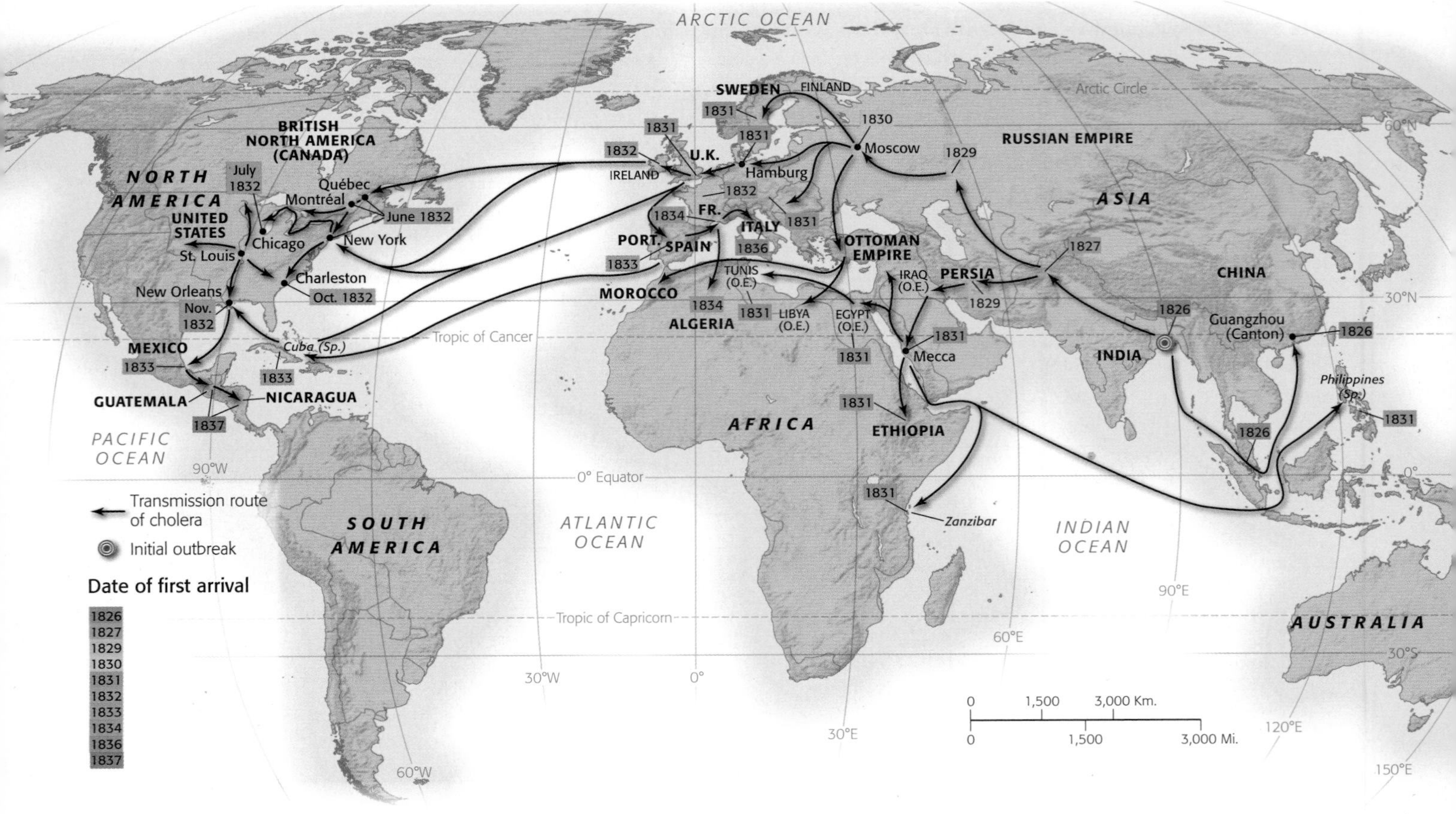

Map 10.1 The Global Cholera Epidemic of 1829–1836 The cholera epidemic spread along the same routes as imperial armies, religious pilgrims, and traders. Death tolls were highest in urban areas, leading many observers to conclude that it was a disease of the urban poor. But improved transportation, including canals, turnpikes, trails, and steamships also spread the disease to rural parts of Europe and Asia, and deep into the North American interior. ▲

received permission to use the large hall to celebrate the seventh anniversary of New York's final, full emancipation of slaves. A brawl between musicians escalated into days of violent rioting as thousands of white New Yorkers pulled down the houses of African Americans, desecrated black churches, and assaulted blacks in the city.

In response to this environment of violence and discrimination, African Americans formed tight-knit subcommunities around racial solidarity that often transcended class or family background. They organized mutual aid societies and established their own churches. They protected runaways from slave catchers and protested attempts to enslave free people. Even blacks who had been born to free parents participated in annual public commemorations of the end of the Atlantic slave trade in 1808.

nativism Ideology opposing immigrants in favor of preserving the privileges of existing citizens.

Using the Catholic church as a foundation, Irish immigrants built their own subcommunities supported by a network of aid associations, schools, militia companies, and political organizations. In Philadelphia, the Hibernian Society for the Relief of Immigrants met incoming ships at the docks with clothing, cash, and offers of assistance to help immigrants find work and housing. Skilled Irish workers joined together in businesses and craft associations to form contracts that competed with U.S.-born workers, often by working for less money.

Cultural and religious clashes between immigrant Irish Catholics and native-born Protestants layered on top of labor competition. Nineteenth-century American Protestants inherited anti-Catholic biases that had taken root during centuries of Europe's wars of religion. Sensational Protestant publications, such as the 1836 *Awful Disclosures of Maria Monk*, accused Catholic priests and nuns of secret immorality and asserted that Catholic institutions in the United States were populated by conspiracists hoping to undermine American institutions. Popular publications fed the political **nativism** that opposed immigrant rights.

10-1b The Middle Class

New ideologies of the home structure middle-class life.

On the outskirts of crowded cities lived a group of U.S.-born white Americans who worked with their brains rather than their muscles and lived not on the streets but in homes as part of the **middle class**. This class, created by the developing system of capitalism, was in one sense an economic standing between poverty and aristocratic wealth. It was also a culture practiced initially in the urban Northeast but expanding into the South and West. Middle-class Americans were self-conscious about their economic standing and anxious that the boom-bust economy could take it away. They placed their faith in a culture of sober respectability involving Protestant churchgoing, thriftiness, and moderation to keep them secure.

The most significant social hallmark of the middle class was the separation of home and work. Factories, banks, loan offices, canal companies, and other expanding industries created new occupations for men as lawyers, engineers, bankers, and managers. Rather than toil side-by-side with their wives and children in shops or on farms, these men went out to work. Farm life had always involved a gendered division of labor in which men plowed and harvested, repaired tools, and built fences while women made and preserved food, washed and repaired clothing, and cared for children. But as adult men moved into paid work away from home, the gendered division of labor became a profound separation in the daily lives of middle-class men and women. Middle-class wives still engaged in housework and child care, alone and with the help of servants, but out of the sight of men and for no compensation.

As unpaid domestic work lost its status as an overtly economic contribution, many came to see it as a labor of love. Across industrializing Europe, women's skills in cooking, cleaning, and nurturing were loudly praised as evidence of their natural destiny, and the U.S. middle class took up the message. For centuries, philosophers and ministers had insisted that men needed to be in charge of children and household because they were more rational and God had granted them more power. But new times demanded new explanations for family life. Magazines like *Godey's Lady's Book* founded in 1830 promoted a new culture of the home, led by women, called **domesticity**. Through pictures and text, the magazine insisted that men and women lived in different "spheres" of life, each one appropriate to inborn differences in the sexes. Men dominated business and politics because they were fundamentally rational, aggressive, and competitive. Women presided over homes because these spaces required people who were emotional, nurturing, and self-effacing. In the evenings, men and women reunited.

Domesticity contained many contradictions at the heart of middle-class life. Superior mothering depended on having fewer children. Over the course of the nineteenth century, the white birthrate fell from seven to five children per woman as husbands and wives cooperated to use periods of abstinence, herbs such as savin and pennyroyal, and, after mid-century advances in rubber technology, condoms and other devices. On farms, additional children meant additional laborers, but in a middle-class urban setting, more children required more resources to educate, place in careers, and establish in marriages. Domesticity also praised the home but required regular trips out to obtain the appropriate clothing, toys, and home decoration from an expanding consumer culture. Finally, although domesticity celebrated women as natural caregivers, a growing industry offered expert instruction. In her 1841 *Treatise on Domestic Economy*, educator Catharine Beecher outlined a chore for middle-class women to do every hour of the day.

Domesticity also highlighted the distance between middle-class lives and those of poorer neighbors. Black, white, immigrant, and U.S.-born poor people lived in crowded, chaotic spaces that doubled as workplaces; they had no hope of practicing the ideals of domesticity.

10-1c Families in the West and Midwest

Mixed-race communities bind western settlements.

From St. Louis to Santa Fe and north along the Pacific Coast, men from the United States claimed a place in the fur trade. Just as the French and Spanish had, they forged trading networks centered on families formed through marriage, adoption, and guardianship. In 1800, in the fur-trading hub of St. Louis, 80 percent of people born were *métis*, meaning that they had Indian as well as European ancestors. New cross-cultural families formed when Euro-American men sought Indian wives who possessed the skills and connections to help them succeed in the trade. A. P. Chouteau, West Point graduate and oldest son of a powerful fur-trading family, left his wife, Sophie, and children in St. Louis in 1822 when he obtained a U.S. license to trade with Osages and Kickapoos along the Arkansas River. The new venture depended on strong Indian allies, and for Chouteau, that meant Osage wives. Just as powerful Osage men did, Chouteau married several women over the course of his time on the Arkansas and Missouri Rivers, creating a broad network of allies whom he depended on for the business and eventually for diplomatic missions between the United States and Indian tribes on the Plains. His Osage household raised the next

middle class Part of society that had to engage in work to survive but had enough income to enjoy leisure and self-improvement with the aid of consumer goods.

domesticity Ideology praising home life as a peaceful oasis sheltered from the public in which middle-class women oversaw the emotional comfort of the family.

History without Borders

The Middle Class

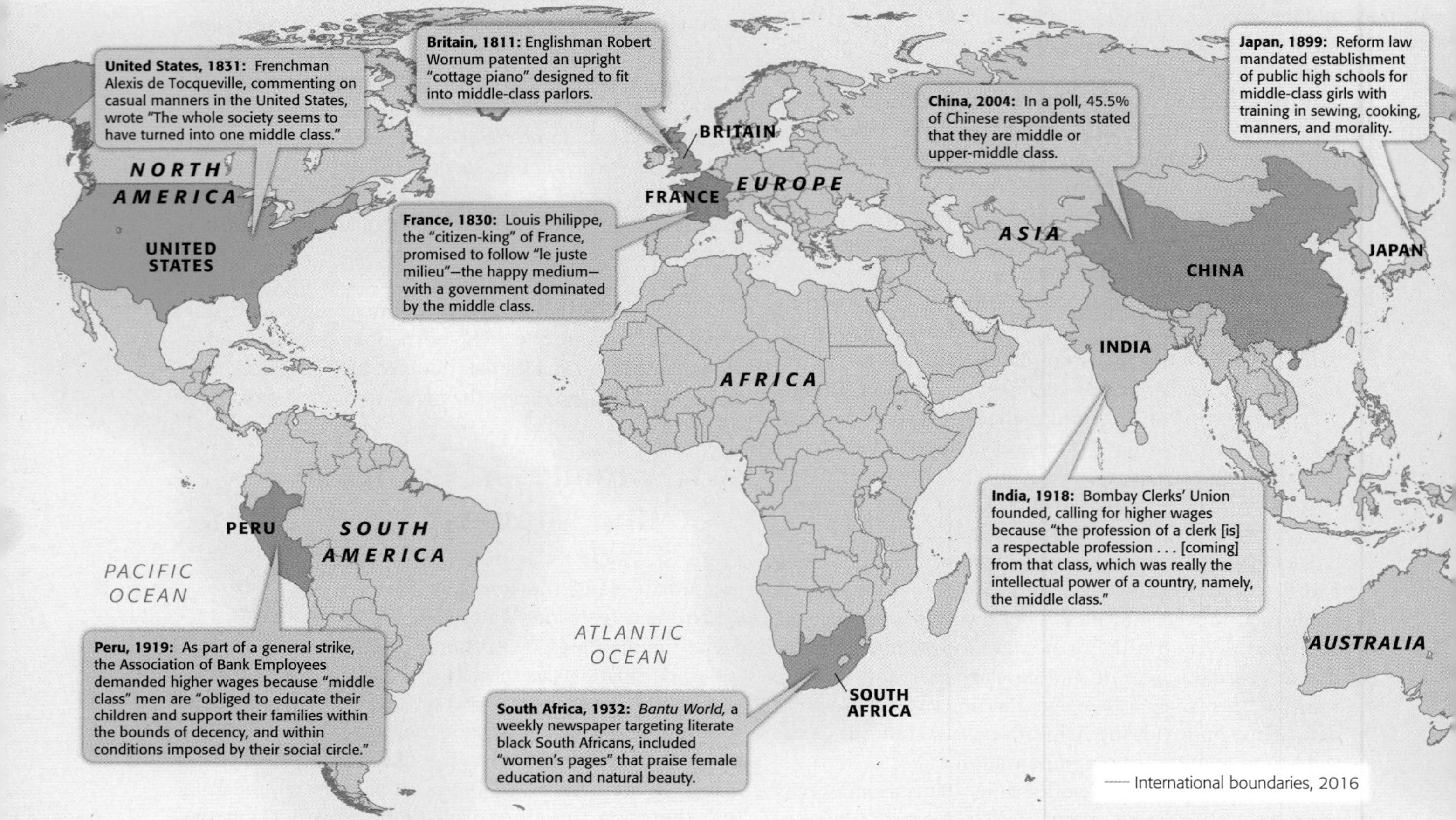

United States, 1831: Frenchman Alexis de Tocqueville, commenting on casual manners in the United States, wrote "The whole society seems to have turned into one middle class."
Britain, 1811: Englishman Robert Wornum patented an upright "cottage piano" designed to fit into middle-class parlors.
China, 2004: In a poll, 45.5% of Chinese respondents stated that they are middle or upper-middle class.
Japan, 1899: Reform law mandated establishment of public high schools for middle-class girls with training in sewing, cooking, manners, and morality.
France, 1830: Louis Philippe, the "citizen-king" of France, promised to follow "le juste milieu"—the happy medium—with a government dominated by the middle class.
India, 1918: Bombay Clerks' Union founded, calling for higher wages because "the profession of a clerk [is] a respectable profession . . . [coming] from that class, which was really the intellectual power of a country, namely, the middle class."
Peru, 1919: As part of a general strike, the Association of Bank Employees demanded higher wages because "middle class" men are "obliged to educate their children and support their families within the bounds of decency, and within conditions imposed by their social circle."
South Africa, 1932: Bantu World, a weekly newspaper targeting literate black South Africans, included "women's pages" that praise female education and natural beauty.
NORTH AMERICA
UNITED STATES
BRITAIN
FRANCE
EUROPE
ASIA
CHINA
JAPAN
INDIA
AFRICA
PERU
SOUTH AMERICA
PACIFIC OCEAN
ATLANTIC OCEAN
SOUTH AFRICA
AUSTRALIA
International boundaries, 2016

The Middle Class Around the World Arising along with industrialization at different periods, middle classes around the world often announced their existence in order to claim political rights. The term "middle" was not usually a measure of wealth; instead, it was meant to imply the group's separation from corrupt aristocracy on the one hand and ignorant poor on the other. ▲

Emerging in different locations at different points in the late eighteenth, nineteenth, and twentieth centuries, middle-class status was made in manufacturing enterprises, private homes, and elected governments. Industrialization created more opportunities for men to work as professionals, bureaucrats, and business owners who earned incomes in the form of profits and wages. The consequences were financial: economic comfort and access to consumer goods unknown to most people. The results were also political because income and financial independence, not family background, increasingly qualified men to participate in political leadership. As the middle class expanded, nations adopted new laws abolishing privileges associated with birth. The British Reform Bill of 1832 extended the vote to industrialists and shopkeepers. The Meiji Reforms in late nineteenth-century Japan abolished feudal ranks and created railroad and mining industries that they sold to newly made businessmen. Those businessmen held political offices formerly reserved for elite samurai families.

Middle-class women's work in their own homes was the stabilizing counterpart to marketplace activity. Just as *Godey's Lady's Book* trained middle-class American women to preside over families in the 1840s, a half century later *Jogaku zasshi* (*Women's Educational Journal*) used articles about child rearing, temperance meetings, and inspiring literature to turn young urban women in Japan into "good wives and wise mothers." Domesticity ensured morality, whether joined to formal religious observance or not.

Middle-class people proudly identified themselves as moderate in their behavior and material lives: neither too showy nor too coarse, neither too passionate nor too lazy, and neither

THE SPHERE OF WOMAN.
TRANSLATED FROM THE GERMAN OF GOETHE.

Godey's Lady's Book, March 1850

Mother-Centered Domesticity After 1836, Sarah Josepha Hale, a young widow supporting five children, edited the women's magazine *Godey's Lady's Book*. Because it cost only $3 per year, mill workers as well as middle-class wives could afford it, and circulation reached one hundred fifty thousand by mid-century. The magazine introduced readers to new images of family, centered around a fashionable mother dedicated to the emotional comfort of her children. The domesticity industry also offered literate women new opportunities to support themselves. ▲

高木商店樂器着荷廣告

○弊店義兼テ歐米ヘ注文致置キ候ピヤノ。オルガン。ヴァイオリン。並ニ歐米諸大家ノ音樂書籍數百種今回着荷致候ニ付キ非常廉價ニテ販賣可致候間御一覽ノ上御購求被下度伏テ是祓ル。

○和製オルガン儀モ近頃諸機械ヲ設置キ凡テ歐米製ト異ナル無キ品ヲ製スルニ至レリ貳拾圓以上百貳拾圓迄數種

○ピヤノ。オルガン等深切ニ調律修繕可致候

東京市神田區通鍋町拾番地

但雛形代價附御入用ノ節ハ御申越次第直ニ郵送ス

高木商店

東京經濟雜誌

社說

論說

寄書

銀行及商業之景況

官令（數件）

定價一冊金七錢（市外郵税五厘増）

東京市京橋區彌左衛門町

經濟雜誌社

帝國議會の怪問題女人禁制の案に關したる坂垣伯の意見、並に清水豊子が同件に付き「泣て姉妹に訴ふ」の沈痛なる論辨。並に、之に對する巖本善治氏が意見は、載せて女學雜誌第二百三十四號の附錄にあり。同號は附錄あるに關はらず、定價依然六錢なり。殘冊少々あり郵券代用の注文に應ず。

Jogaku zasshi

***Jogaku Zasshi*, December 1890.** This page from the popular Japanese ladies' magazine features a parlor pump organ, an instrument for entertaining in the home. Middle-class domesticity required consumer purchases and leisure time to cultivate artistic skills and emotional expression. Music lessons for children or adults were part of cultivating social development. As with the pump organ, middle-class purchases were also for performance, allowing the user to demonstrate status to guests. ▲

aristocrat nor peasant. The concept that most middle-class people used, whether they lived in London in 1780, in Baltimore in 1830, or Johannesburg in the 1930s, was "respectability," which described self-controlled, law-abiding, educated, moral, thrifty families. Respectability, they claimed, was what kept them secure in a modern market susceptible to dramatic swings in fortune. Middle-class status knit together a comfortable level of wealth and a culture demonstrating that the possessor of that wealth deserved it.

These ideals became a central plank of colonialism and conquest in the nineteenth and early twentieth centuries. Whereas early fortune seekers and traders in the American Northwest lived in racially mixed outposts, conquest by the United States in the second half of the nineteenth century brought the shuttering of multiracial dance halls and the creation of reform societies, a pattern that repeated in other regions. Colonial guides for Frenchwomen traveling to Indochina in the early twentieth century told them they were "auxiliary forces" for the French empire by making sure their homes were "happy and gay and that all take pleasure in clustering there." Native people who did not live by middle-class codes were barred from political privileges.

In some times and places, middle-class respectability became a tool that racially marginalized people used to secure better treatment. Black women in 1896 formed the National Association of Colored Women, whose motto, "Lifting as We Climb," stressed the significance of middle-class charity work among poor blacks for improving the image and status of all African Americans. Black men and women in Sophiatown, South Africa, in the 1940s united around an identity as respectable property owners to establish better schools and demand that the police respond to urban crime in their neighborhoods.

Critical Thinking Questions

► Why did groups of people identify themselves as being part of a shared "middle class"? From whom were they separating themselves?

► What did "middle-class values" offer people engaged in power struggles over land, resources, and political access?

Go to MindTap® to engage with an interactive version of **History without Borders: The Middle Class.** Learn from an interactive map, view related video, and respond to critical thinking questions.

Bent's Fort Trading outpost built in 1833 by William and Charles Bent for their business in furs and buffalo hides, connecting Indian hunters to global markets.

generation of bicultural children to own land and conduct trade in the Midwest by educating them in mission schools (see Table 10.2) and sending them to St. Louis to spend time with French-American relatives.

The Granger Collection, New York

A Fur-Trapping Family American men in the fur trade married into Indian families, such as those depicted in *The Trapper and His Family* (1840–1841), by Charles Deas. Deas had a studio in St. Louis, which was a trading hub populated by generations of families with Indian and Euro-American members. In the painting, the trader and his wife have a canoe filled with children, a dog, and a covered pile of animal skins. ▲

Mixed-culture families also anchored the trading posts and forts in the contested West. **Bent's Fort**, located at the foot of the Rocky Mountains in 1833, was a center for trade in buffalo robes, tools, and horses. William Bent gained diplomatic and economic power from his Cheyenne wife, Owl Woman, daughter of a chief who acted as an intermediary between U.S. traders and warring Indian groups. Their children went to schools in St. Louis but spent much of their time with their Cheyenne communities; one observer talked of them "chattering now Indian, and now Spanish or English." Life in and around the adobe fort involved frequent moves among cultures, and Bent's employees typically had families that included European and Indian members. Seasonal trading patterns brought camps of Arapaho, Sioux, Kiowa, and Comanche hunters and their families.

Table 10.2 Harmony School Population, 1824–1825

Missionary records from the Harmony School in Missouri document the multicultural backgrounds of children of the fur trade in the early years of Missouri statehood. They also hint at the personal toll of the civilizing mission. Mary E. Sibley was the daughter of Osage chief Sans Oreille and one of his three wives. She was briefly adopted by the Sibleys and renamed before her own mother came to Harmony to bring her home.

Name	Parentage
Catherine Strange	U.S. and Osage
Susan Larivive	Sioux, French, Osage
Rebecca Williams	Pawnee, French, Osage
Mary Ludlow	Pawnee, French, Osage
Louisa Anna Bean	Pawnee, French, Osage
Maria Seward	Osage
Mary Williams	Osage and U.S.
John B. Mitchell	Osage and French
James Chouteau	Osage and French
Julia Michael	Osage and French
Lewis Michael	Osage and French
Gabriel Marlow	French and Pawnee
Augustus Chouteau	French and Osage
William C. Brownlee	Delaware
William Rogers	Pawnee
John B. Packett	Sauk
John McDowell	Osage
Mary E. Sibley	Osage
Jane Renick	Osage and French

Sources: Louis F. Burns, *A History of the Osage People* Anne Hyde, *Empires, Nations, Families*.

As they moved in and out of the orbit of trading posts, mixed-culture families helped negotiate the strain of migration and overhunting west of the Mississippi River in the 1830s and 1840s, when the political power of the United States and Mexico was distant and often weak. Mixed families on the Southwestern Plains brokered deals between Comanches and Cheyennes who warred over who would control the lucrative hide trade. As refugee Indians moved or were forced west from their origins east of the Mississippi River, they sometimes intermarried with existing Indian and mixed-culture families as an alternative to warring over land.

Intercultural marriages between wealthy California women and ambitious traders settling in Alta California formed the core of an elite group of landholders who rose to power after the province became part of independent Mexico in 1821. Beginning in 1833, successive Mexican governors won approval from their country's central government to break apart the mission system in a process known as *secularization.* They exiled Franciscans, converted missions into parish churches, emancipated Indians from the missions, and granted enormous tracts of land to their friends, subordinates, and relatives. Some native people formed refugee communities with Indian groups nearly depleted by disease. Others became servants or laborers on the reconfigured farms, ranches, and manufactories. Intercultural marriages, representing 15 percent of marriages recorded in California, helped cement "respectable society" that controlled the area's wealth.

10-1d Plantations and Slavery

An expanding institution shapes all southern lives.

The global cotton economy enmeshed southern communities along with the rest of the country in industrialization and territorial expansion, and the South's distinctive plantation slavery systems adapted. Slave owning itself was concentrated in a minority of the population: In 1830, only 36 percent of southern whites owned slaves (see Figure 10.1). The average slave owner was a farmer who bet that an investment in owning another human being would allow him to build something bigger. Such slave owners worked in the fields with their slaves—male or female—and hoped to earn enough to purchase additional human property, which would lift them into the upper levels of southern society.

If the average white Southerner lived with one or no slaves, the average enslaved Southerner lived with both whites and blacks. Half of the slaves in the South lived on plantations with between ten and fifty other slaves. The overwhelming majority were U.S. born, which set the South apart from other major slave populations of the nineteenth century. Brazil and Cuba, where slaves numbered more than 40 percent of the population in the 1840s, relied on a constant supply of captured Africans to work—and die—on sugar plantations and in towns and industries. The enslaved majorities in South Carolina and Mississippi who emerged by mid-century, in contrast, shared language, culture, and history with the free population.

Close contact between slaves and owners meant close supervision, which intensified on the expanding cotton plantations of the lower South. On Lowcountry rice and indigo plantations, slaves worked a set task and then turned to different crops—corn, squash, potatoes—that they grew in their own gardens to supplement inadequate food supplies. But most enslaved people sold to the cotton growers were from Chesapeake tobacco farms or Caribbean sugar plantations, where they labored from dawn to dusk as part of a gang. On cotton plantations, they found gang labor intensified by a "pushing system" driven by a white overseer hired to whip more work out of them. Cotton planters kept detailed records of each slave's daily work and devised quotas to demand increased productivity. When in the 1830s Israel Campbell picked only ninety pounds in one day rather than one hundred, his owner declared he would suffer "as many lashes as there were pounds short."

Slaves who labored in workshops, stables, or homes avoided some of the physical strain of the fields but suffered even closer attention from slave owners. A plantation was both home and workplace; there could be no isolated domesticity. Cooking, cleaning, sewing, and caring for large families required the work of mistresses and slaves. Slave masters prided themselves on offering hospitality to travelers and visiting family members because the gifts of food, lodging, and conversation expressed a man's honor as well as his wealth. More visitors meant more laundry, however, and failure to perform daily household drudgery sparked violence against slaves just as unmet cotton quotas did.

Slave families tried to mitigate the personal costs of violence and exhaustion by creating networks of love and support. Even though marriages between slaves were not legally recognized, many owners encouraged them, either with people on the same plantation or on neighboring ones, in what were called **abroad marriages**. Slave owners hoped that giving people a stake in family life would keep them docile and prevent runaways. They used the threat of separation to bind mothers, who were more likely to live together with their children, to their owners. Harriet Jacobs, a slave in North Carolina, remembered that her owner threatened to send her children away to a distant plantation unless she did as he commanded. When she resisted, he said, "Your boy shall be put to work, and he shall soon be sold; and your girl shall be raised for the purpose of selling well." In fact, one-third of slave marriages in the nineteenth century ended in forced separation, and parents could expect owners to sell their children away.

The majority of white Southerners supported slaveholding even though they did not themselves own slaves. All free white men were required to donate time to serve on slave patrols, which rode through the countryside on horseback, looking for and capturing runaways. White men elected elite planters with multiple plantations to serve the highest

abroad marriages Marriages between enslaved people who lived on separate farms or plantations in which the husband's visit to his wife and children required permission or secrecy.

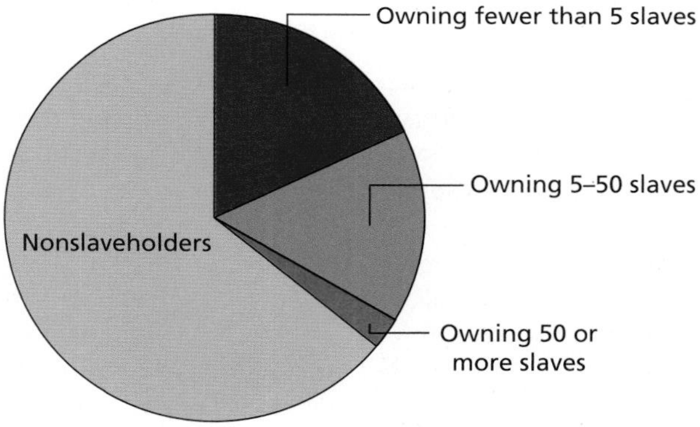

Figure 10.1 Slaveholding in the South, 1830 (in percentages)
Slave owners in the South wielded economic, political, and cultural power, but this wealthy group was greatly outnumbered by those who owned no slaves. Over the course of the middle of the century, the number of slaves increased, but the proportion of slaveholders decreased. By 1860, just 25 percent of white Southerners owned slaves. Yet most white Southerners supported slavery, practically and ideologically. ▲ Source: U.S. Bureau of the Census.

brawling Style of bare-knuckle fighting used by white men in the backcountry South to defend their honor.

political offices rather than insisting on representatives closer to their own rank. In part, white men and women supported the power of slave owners because they hoped one day to own slaves themselves. Even without the direct use of slave labor, small white farmers operated within an economy organized around plantation agriculture and planter dominance. Big plantation stores bought these farmers' surplus produce to feed their slaves, and skilled artisan slaves provided services for the community.

10-1e Farming Communities

Farm families develop distinct rural cultures.

Whites who lived in the borderland South, far from cotton fields or growing markets, developed a more insular culture. They farmed for their own use and hunted and pastured animals in woodlands shared with neighbors. They lived in a local, kin-based society of rural villages. Impassible roads isolated people from the types of internal improvements and international commerce that fed the cotton trade. In contrast to the cities of the North or the plantations of the deep South, work was not specialized or rationalized. Family life, too, was strikingly different from the middle-class ideals of the industrializing areas because men and women toiled all day to meet basic needs.

Masculinity for these families was grounded in toughness and ferocity, not reliable breadwinning or gentlemanly hospitality. Told they were political equals, poor white men held little economic or social power as compared to that of the slave owners who dominated southern public life. Instead, these men often fought over small insults to assert their own honor in a **brawling** style of fighting that involved kicking, pulling hair, biting ears, and especially gouging out an opponent's eyes. Mike Fink, a celebrated gouger and hunter, boasted: "I can outrun, out-jump, out-shoot, out-brag, out-drink, an' outfight, rough-an'-tumble, no holts barred, ary man on both sides of the river from Pittsburgh to New Orleans an' back ag'in to St. Louiee."

Some upland farmers left the South and joined the migrating New Englanders and New Yorkers who settled in the Northwest. Treaties signed at the end of the War of 1812 pushed the Kickapoos, Potawatomis, and Chippewas from their land in the Ohio River Valley. U.S. agents and private speculators sold that land, in turn, to farmers from New England, New York, Pennsylvania, and Kentucky. Some were in search of profits from land booms, but many desired the independence and stability that land brought. Initially, these families practiced mixed farming. They bartered small surpluses of corn, hogs, and homespun cloth for salt, coffee, and tools sold by traveling peddlers. They raised larger families than Americans in the East or their remaining Indian neighbors. Women married in their late teens or early twenties and gave birth to children

AKG Images

German Immigrants' Dream versus Reality German migrants, like those from the East coast, hoped for the good life on farms in the Midwest. Some were disappointed, as this 1845 German cartoon, "The German Emigrant," depicts. This man dreams of the life of a southern planter but finds "I perish here a poor wretch behind the plow/Whilst lion and vulture devour my wife and child." ▲

every two years until their forties. Visiting from New York, Washington Irving joked that he was "in [a] house with nineteen children and thirty-seven dogs."

Over time, developments of the transportation and industrial revolutions transformed these communities. Settled families accumulated land and better tools, including mechanical harvesters that allowed them to increase the size of their surpluses. Ohio canals, stagecoaches, and railway lines meant cheaper access to markets in New York and New Orleans. Soon, Midwestern grain fed New York seamstresses and Mississippi slaves. Transportation lines also carried new immigrants to the Midwest. In the 1840s, German-speaking migrants joined native-born Americans and descendants of French and Indian traders in the Midwest. Many of the newcomers were unable to purchase independent farms and instead became tenants of landowners, locked into rental agreements that earmarked a portion of their proceeds to landlords.

10-2 Religious Awakenings and Social Experiments

Bettmann/Corbis

Certificate of the Missionary Society of the Methodist Episcopal Church (engraved circa 1838), registers a $20 contribution by Philip Harper. The certificate is both a receipt and a decorative object to be displayed at home. Nathaniel Currier, later part of Currier and Ives, was the most successful commercial lithographer of the nineteenth century, using new printmaking techniques to offer inexpensive popular art to wide swathes of the U.S. and, eventually, European public.

Look at the circle of seated Indians wrapped in blankets and the dark-skinned family on their knees, surrounded by palm trees. What do these images suggest about the relationships among missionaries and the people they served? Why would Philip Harper have wanted to join this society? ▶

By accelerating impersonal labor, low wages, and disruptive migrations, industrialization led many individuals to rethink their religious lives. Uprooted from settled places of worship and religious leaders who had guided communities for decades, they searched to understand the individual's relationship to God. Originating in the borderlands, religious revivals swept the Midwest, the South, New York, and New England. Expanding Protestant denominations espoused a mixed message of both individual freedom and community responsibility. Enslaved people adopted Christianity's emphasis on liberation whereas slave owners and other elites chose messages that stressed social control. Missionaries sought converts and established schools and churches that linked salvation and U.S. power from the Middle East to the far West.

☞ As you read, consider the ways that evangelical Christianity spread new ideas about an individual's connection to God. What were the implications for how the people of the world should live together?

10-2a Evangelical Christianity

Expanding Protestant denominations reinvigorate religious practices.

In 1801, twenty-five thousand people gathered in Cane Ridge, Kentucky, to pray, sing, and listen to sermons as part of a life-changing religious revival. As they tied up their wagons, pitched their tents in the woods, and gathered in front of the stages that organizers had built for the visiting ministers, the crowd became part of an outpouring of religious feeling and enthusiasm known as the **Second Great Awakening**. This Protestant movement of the early nineteenth century greatly increased church attendance and made evangelical Christianity a powerful cultural force in the United States.

Second Great Awakening Name of a series of religious revivals and expanded church attendance that made evangelical Christianity the main religious force in the United States.

Library of Congress Prints and Photographs Division [LC-DIG-ds-030915]

Camp Meeting Part of the appeal of outdoor revivals was that dancing, singing, and extreme emotions were welcomed as part of the religious experience. Benjamin Latrobe, who sketched the layout of an 1809 camp meeting in Fairfax, Virginia, noted that right in front of the stage there was "a boarded enclosure filled with straw, into which the converted were thrown that they might kick about without injuring themselves." In this picture, observers are fascinated, but skeptical. ▲

In the early years of the republic, few Americans attended church regularly; some estimate that perhaps only one in twenty were frequent churchgoers. By 1830, that number had swelled to one in seven. New members joined congregations of Methodist, Baptist, and African Methodist Episcopal churches that were experimenting with ways to reach potential believers. Following disestablishment, states no longer compelled citizens to support a particular church; instead, Americans attended and paid to support those churches that appealed to them in message and method.

Evangelical Christians believed that all humans had the potential for salvation but it was up to the individual to accept God's grace in an act of free will. Once she did, she could conquer sin in herself, a doctrine of self-transformation known as **perfectionism**. Offering believers a vision of individual self-respect and collective self-confidence, the evangelical movement asserted that people had the obligation and the right to read the Bible, pray, and decide for themselves on spiritual matters rather than relying on an educated elite to instruct and test them. Lay speakers as well as ordained ministers strove to reach individual souls. One of the most famous Awakening preachers, Charles Grandison Finney, asserted that "we must have exciting, powerful preaching, or the devil will have the people." At **camp meetings** such as the one at Cane Ridge, the result was a full-body experience. In 1832, British observer Fanny Trollope described "Hysterical sobbings, convulsive groans, shrieks and screams" as participants "threw about their limbs." Although Trollope claimed to feel "sick with horror" at the spectacle, the outdoor meetings increased evangelical denominations' influence.

perfectionism Protestant tenet holding that humans can work to free themselves from sin during their lives.

camp meetings Outdoor religious revivals held in the United States and Britain at which people stayed for several days to pray, sing, and listen to a variety of ministers and lay preachers.

Evangelical culture spread through travel and publications. Ministers themselves traveled to audiences, either at revivals or as part of a regular circuit, visiting communities with no established churches. Evangelical publishers supported ministers' work by selling pamphlets to help organizers plan their own revivals. In a constant transatlantic exchange, U.S. and British Methodist magazines reprinted affecting stories of sinners converted by the power of God. The American Bible Society, founded in 1816, raised money to print and distribute Bibles in English and by 1823 had arranged for a Spanish translation to spread Protestant Christianity throughout the hemisphere.

Perfectionism was an individual undertaking whose results could be multiplied across societies. Business owners tapped into the personal responsibility vein of evangelical theology and linked a strong work ethic to salvation. In the winter of 1830–1831, Finney accepted an invitation to bring revival to the Erie Canal boomtown of Rochester, New York. Drawn by exciting preaching and often led by the women in their families, hundreds converted and established Bible study groups in their homes. Inspired by their own conversions, Rochester residents founded churches for workers and set up savings banks

Oberlin College Archives

Global Americans

Connecticut-born, New-York raised **Charles Grandison Finney** (1792–1875) studied to be a lawyer, but a conversion experience in 1821 led him to abandon the law and become a Presbyterian minister. In the 1820s and 1830s, his preaching tours, with their message of universal salvation delivered to women and men in exciting, relatable language, sparked revivals across the northeastern United States and Britain. In 1835, he became a professor at Oberlin College, where he later (1851) was president. Oberlin, the first U.S. college to regularly admit white women and African Americans, was part of abolitionists' efforts to help runaway slaves escape to freedom in Canada.

Finney's tours and publications ensured that the Second Great Awakening was a transatlantic religious movement. In 1835, he published *Lectures on Revivals of Religion*, in which he explained that enthusiastic preaching worked only on a soul that was prepared. He urged readers, "You must begin by looking at your hearts" and write down an inventory of specific sins committed (pride, envy, lying) as well as sins of omission (ingratitude, neglect of the Bible, failure to pray with family). The book was soon translated into French and Welsh. He and his second wife, Elizabeth, traveled to Britain in the 1850s where he preached and she held religious meetings for women, spreading the "new measures" of revival.

to encourage thrift in others. Women started the Female Charitable Society to collect and distribute relief funds for families and the unemployed. Poverty, drunkenness, and laziness, they concluded, were not regrettable consequences of hard lives but sins to be redeemed.

10-2b American Missions

Missionaries forge international networks.

Catholic missionaries had worked in the Americas for centuries, and their efforts continued in the nineteenth century. Religious orders ran convent schools in cities such as St. Louis, where they educated Indian and métis children. Privately funded organizations expanded in Catholic countries in the early nineteenth century, backing missions to Africa and Asia as well as to the Pacific islands of Hawai'i. Increasingly, those priests and nuns competed with Protestant missionaries from New England for converts.

Protestant evangelical missionaries believed that salvation in an individual life was part of a larger, thousand-year cycle of sin and redemption set by God's time. A belief called **millennialism** held that mass conversion would bring about the final thousand-year reign of Jesus Christ on earth. The belief inspired particular attention to the Middle East because some evangelicals were convinced that the conversion of Jews in the old city of Jerusalem was essential to securing Jesus's return. In 1810, a group of ministers, businessmen, doctors, and lawyers in New England founded the **American Board of Commissioners of Foreign Missions (ABCFM)** as the first U.S. missionary organization. Through its fund-raising and organization, it sent missionaries—often a husband and wife—to China, Ceylon, and the Ottoman-controlled territory of the Middle East. Missionary couples inspired by religion and nationalism established schools and churches teaching spiritual salvation through the adoption of English language and middle-class culture. Missionary Elizabeth Dwight wrote in a letter from Constantinople to *Mother's Magazine*, an American publication, "The heathen want not only ministers of the word, but *pious, well-educated families* . . . to be the living, bright examples of the doctrines of Christianity."

Evangelical missionaries also targeted American Indian settlements, where they became embroiled in the power politics of U.S. expansion. In 1819, African American lay minister John Stewart began a mission to the Wyandot Indians in Ohio. Working with a former slave who had been captured by the Wyandots and knew their language, Stewart converted several high-ranking members. His efforts soon inspired the Methodist Episcopal Church to open its own missionary society in the region. Converted Wyandot Indians, in turn, convinced missionaries to intervene in border disputes with the United States and used evangelical fund-raising channels to purchase clothing and food.

millennialism Belief held by some Christian denominations that there will be a one thousand-year period of Christ's reign on earth before the final judgment.

American Board of Commissioners of Foreign Missions (ABCFM) Organization established in 1810 as the first U.S. society dedicated to sending Protestant missionaries to convert people in Asia, Africa, and the Middle East.

Native Americans in more distant settlements found missionaries' messages less compelling. In 1835, ABCFM sponsored newlywed Marcus and Narcissa Whitman's journey from New York to Oregon Country. There, they built a mission for the Cayuse Indians in the Walla Walla Valley, urging the seasonally migratory people to take up permanent farming and Protestant Christianity together. Unsuccessful in its conversion efforts, their mission became a way station and first-aid center for settlers traveling into the Oregon territory in the 1840s. Those migrants soon brought a devastating measles epidemic to the Cayuses, who saw in their misery the fulfillment of their own prophesy, that strangers would bring destruction followed by community rebirth into a new world. When Marcus Whitman, a doctor, was unable to cure the suffering people, a group of Cayuses killed both Whitmans and twelve others at the mission in 1847. Subsequent retaliatory violence escalated into a decade of warfare.

10-2c Christianity's Multiple Messages

Christianity fills divergent purposes in a pluralistic society.

Evangelical Protestantism became a major religious and cultural force in the nineteenth-century United States in part because it carried messages of both liberation and conservative control. In the slaveholding South, Baptists and Methodists gained converts among whites by abandoning their earlier insistence on the equality of souls and preaching instead the duty of fathers to lead the members of their households to Christian conversion. Sermons and print culture stressed the responsibility of masters and the necessary obedience of inferiors, including children and slaves. Baptist congregations in the South encouraged women's prayers but revoked their power to speak on church business.

At the same time, the Bible offered profoundly moving stories for enslaved people. Some found inspiration in the story of Exodus, in which Moses led Israelites out of slavery, and in the nobility of Jesus Christ's suffering. One song sung by slaves in the nineteenth century drew direct parallels between Bible stories and their own lives: "He delivered Daniel from the lion's den, / Jonah from the belly of the whale, / And the Hebrew children from the fiery furnace, / And why not every man?" Regular, enthusiastic group worship gave enslaved people chances to meet and form relationships. All of these practices, essential to Christianity's message about a deep, personal religious experience, at the same time nurtured independence, knowledge, and the networks that enabled resistance to slavery.

African Methodist Episcopal First independent black denomination in the United States, recognized in 1816.

utopian communities Settlement that experimented with communal living arrangements organized around religious or philosophical principles designed to perfect society.

Shakers Utopian community founded by Briton Ann Lee that believed in celibacy; men and women lived and worked apart.

Mixed messages of inclusion and exclusion sparked the creation of new Protestant denominations. Evangelical churches initially encouraged black participation and nurtured free black preachers, encouraging them to speak to mixed-race groups. Blacks and whites both attended the Cane Ridge camp meeting and because revivals welcomed new authorities, the number of black ministers and lay speakers increased. But many congregations retained discriminatory practices. Some did not allow black members to be buried in the same church cemeteries, and others required African American participants to sit upstairs in special galleries around the sanctuary rather than joining white congregants. The **African Methodist Episcopal** (AME) church, which had begun as an all-black affiliate of a Philadelphia congregation created by the Free African Society, sought and won legal recognition as an independent church in 1816. It was the first fully independent black denomination in the United States with its own bishops and national structure. Like other evangelical churches, it encouraged black women to speak as lay ministers although it did not make them full ministers.

Slavery itself divided denominations as they debated whether slavery was a sin or was part of the God-ordained order of the world. The American Presbyterian (1837), Methodist Episcopal (1844), and Baptist (1845) churches each divided into separate conferences that either accepted slavery or rejected it.

10-2d Experimental Communities

Social experiments counter the culture of individualism.

Significant numbers of Americans despaired at the divisions between rich and poor created by industrialization as well as the social isolation of both middle-class parlors and urban construction sites. They decided to withdraw into communities that would pursue cooperation rather than competition. Some of these **utopian communities** were based on a religious vision. Others were living expressions of carefully designed blueprints informed by scientific principles. All shared a conviction that a good society required reformed relationships between men and women.

One of the oldest utopian communities, the **Shakers**, decided that separation of the sexes was the only way to preserve the dignity of both. Founded in late eighteenth-century Britain by Ann Lee, the community was officially called the United Society of Believers in Christ's Second Appearing. Lee preached that God was both male and female and that each individual communicated personally with the divine in the form of artistic expression and work. The Shakers, whose name came from the religious ecstasy of their dancing, believed in total celibacy. Men

Buttre, John Chester, 1821–1893, engraver; Gorbitz, J., artist

Global Americans Born in Scotland in 1795, orphaned as a toddler, and raised in London, **Frances ("Fanny") Wright** became an international traveler and writer in her early twenties, befriending the marquis de Lafayette and touring with him across the United States in 1824. The following year, she became a U.S. citizen, purchased land in western Tennessee, and published *A Plan for the Gradual Abolition of Slavery in the Western United States without Danger of Loss to the Citizens of the South*, outlining a plan to establish a colony for freed slaves. Her own colony, Nashoba, was a failure, and in 1828 she joined Robert Dale Owen's New Harmony utopian society in Indiana.

Wright became a popular public speaker not as a moral reformer but as a freethinker dedicated to equality. Labeled a "female Tome Paine" by one of her critics in 1829, Wright was sharply critical of evangelical preachers who, she charged, preyed upon "the minds of weak and deluded women" who were easy, poorly educated victims. She championed women's education as well as sexual and economic rights within marriage. She traveled frequently between France and the United States and stumped for the Democratic Party in 1836 and 1838. She died in 1852 in the midst of a legal battle with her ex-husband over her own earnings, a symbol of both international radicalism and its limits for women.

and women lived and worked apart, each group contributing to the success of the whole. They relied on converts, including orphans, widows, and poor families who asked to join. Because they did not recognize blood ties as more significant than other connections, a mother and daughter who joined together became "sisters."

Other British transplants created societies that were not religiously inspired but equally radical in re-envisioning the ties binding humans into a society. Robert Owen, a Scottish factory owner, traveled to the United States in 1824 to invest his industrial fortune in an experimental community, New Harmony, in Indiana. Having witnessed the misery of British mill towns, Owen declared that human beings needed to be liberated from "the trinity of evils responsible for all the world's misery and vice: traditional religion, conventional marriage . . . and private property." In spite of his business experience, Owen was unable to secure a solid financial footing for the community, and he returned to Europe to promote what he had come to call *utopian socialism*.

Frances Wright, another Scot, purchased former Chickasaw land in Tennessee to found the society of Nashoba, where she believed that she could help end slavery and thus bolster American liberty. She planned to fill the model farm at Nashoba with enslaved African Americans who, working under a cooperative labor system, would earn enough to buy their own freedom within five years and pay for their own relocation to Haiti or Liberia. She predicted that as the idea spread, slavery would become unprofitable and ultimately extinct. Unable to acquire enough investment or slave labor, Wright re-tooled Nashoba as a utopian community of whites, but ultimately that vision collapsed in scandal.

The miseries of industrialization in France inspired the most successful imported utopian movement. Frenchman Charles Fourier believed that the progress of civilization depended on a very specific form of community living: 1,620 people living in a large building complex set on six thousand acres of well-tended land. Leisure, not work, would fill their days. A dazzled American visitor, Albert Brisbane, brought the Fourierist movement to the United States in the 1840s, eventually involving fifteen thousand Americans in communal living experiments, clubs, mutual insurance associations, and cooperative stores.

American Joseph Smith's vision of new religious and social bonds proved far more enduring and influential in the United States than any of the transatlantic experiments. Smith grew up poor in a farming family in western New York who had lost everything in a speculative ginseng shipment to China. As a boy, he witnessed multiple revivals sweeping through the region and concluded that none of these competing factions represented the true church. In his 20s, Smith experienced visions in which God called him to be a prophet, redeeming society from its excess of individualism. In 1830, he published his revelations in the *Book of Mormon* and established the Church of Jesus Christ of Latter-day Saints, or **Mormons** in New York. They resolved the conflicts between the claims of the individual and the need for social order by establishing a highly controlled, patriarchal society.

Mormons Church founded by Joseph Smith in 1830. Organized in New York, the group moved west after being the focus of attacks.

10-3

American Cultures

A.W. Graham, Laurel Hill (1844). This engraving, depicting a new "rural cemetery" outside of Philadelphia, appeared in *Godey's Lady's Book* and was later reprinted in a cemetery guidebook. Carefully landscaped rural cemeteries offered urban Americans a respite where they could picnic in nature. Nearby, merchants sold industrially produced monuments, iron fences, and outdoor furniture to decorate these "cities of the dead."

How does the artist use costume and scale to suggest human beings' relationship to nature? What does the image imply about the relationship between the living and the dead? ▶

The Library Company of Philadelphia

The boom-bust economy of the first half of the nineteenth century generated new wealth but also great insecurity. Surrounded by strangers and stalked by financial failure, Americans developed cultural responses to the difficulty of judging truth from fiction in an expanding world. Some sought authenticity, in manners that conveyed genuine emotions or in time spent in nature. Others turned harmless frauds into public amusements. The technologies of the early nineteenth century, including expanding transportation systems, cheaper printing processes, and robust communication networks, allowed performers and publications to transmit culture around the world as never before.

☞ As you read, identify the ways that culture helped people interpret new social and economic conditions. How did books, newspapers, lectures, and songs shape behavior?

10-3a Feelings and Behavior

Middle-class culture cultivates sincere feeling as a sign of respectability.

Middle-class Americans believed that they had earned their wealth, but because it was held in paper mortgages, bank notes, and insurance certificates, they knew it could quickly be lost. So they struggled to act as if their status was secure. They bought etiquette books that explained in minute detail how a middle-class person should dress and behave with rules that stressed restrained and predictable movements: "The general positions for the arms are about the level of the waist, never hanging down or being quite stiff, but being gently bent, the elbow a little raised, the fingers not stretched out stiffly, but also a little bent, and partially separated." Proper behavior would demonstrate true worth. "The manners of a gentleman are the index of his soul," one book pronounced. Yet people in a city of strangers feared that fakers surrounded them. How could one know whether a well-mannered new clerk was an honest associate or an ambitious fraud? What kind of society would there be if each member were only pretending to belong? Middle-class Americans looked for sincerity in others and worked to foster it in themselves.

Sincere feeling, they hoped, was the true glue of society. **Sentimentalism**, the idea that human beings could connect emotionally by understanding each other's feelings, pervaded nineteenth-century middle-class life. Men and women believed that sensitivity to the feelings of others was the most refined character trait a person could possess. It was a mark of superiority and the only true motivator of benevolent behavior. To cultivate those feelings, middle-class Americans developed new forms of leisure focused on the home. In the evenings, families gathered in their parlors, special rooms that were devoted to reading out loud, sincere conversation, and music. **Parlor music** sung to the accompaniment of a wife or daughter playing the piano offered short, melodic songs that evoked powerful emotions of love and loss, such as the wildly popular "Home! Sweet Home!" Originally written in 1823 by American actor John Howard Payne for an English opera, it proclaimed "Be it ever so humble / There's no place like home."

Mourning culture was another way to experience and demonstrate sentimentalism. Middle-class women wove connections between the living and the dead by making jewelry out of the hair of deceased loved ones. They embroidered "mourning pictures" with weeping willows and the names of the deceased. Men and women visited vast new cemeteries. Mourners believed that their experience of deep grief helped awaken them to Christian sympathy and realize the emptiness of worldly happiness.

sentimentalism Theory that humans can understand each other through sympathy for others' feelings and that those feelings allow people to bond in societies.

parlor music Popular songs with subjects such as family, love, patriotism, and history sold as sheet music for families to sing in their parlors.

10-3b Nature and Self-Improvement

Urbanizing, competitive Americans seek truth in nature.

"Nature," wrote Ralph Waldo Emerson in 1836, is "essences unchanged by man; space, the air, the river, the leaf." In these essences, he believed, was a truth obscured by nineteenth-century society. With like-minded thinkers, he founded **transcendentalism**, an intellectual movement in New England during the 1830s and 1840s that came to have a major influence on U.S. culture. Transcendentalists were inspired by European romanticism, a movement in art and thought that challenged Enlightenment rationalism. They also read translations of Chinese Confucian and Indian Hindu texts brought home by missionaries. Transcendentalists argued that human reason was not the best tool for understanding; instead, humans should seek to transcend their senses and come to understand truth.

The term *transcendentalism* originated with the German philosopher Immanuel Kant, who argued that there was a kind of "transcendental" knowledge in intuition. Emerson, a former Unitarian minister who ultimately deemed the denomination a "corpse cold" form of Christianity, championed "Self-Reliance," the title of an essay he published in 1841. Calling on readers to defy conventions and "trust thyself," Emerson's celebration of individualism suited U.S. democratic politics and the middle-class ideal of the self-made man. His friend Henry David Thoreau experimented with solitary existence, moving to a cabin on Massachusetts's Walden Pond in 1845, but it was intellectual rather than physical independence that the transcendentalists sought. In his cabin, Thoreau entertained like-minded reformers and had regular visits from his mother and sisters.

Transcendentalists benefited from the **lyceum movement**, which also emerged in the 1830s in New England. Local associations, called *lyceums* after the school in Athens where Aristotle taught, promoted adult education in the form of public lectures and debates that by the middle of the century reached four hundred thousand people weekly. Each local lyceum collected subscriptions to pay for speakers, who traveled along regular circuits. Arriving in town by stagecoach or rail car, lyceum speakers gave talks on reform, women's rights, science, art, medicine, and politics. In 1838, a young Abraham Lincoln spoke about "The Perpetuation of our Political Institutions" to the Young Men's Lyceum in Springfield, Illinois. Middle-class self-improvers believed that adult education could reform society by training citizens in the arts of public speaking and persuasion.

Tomas Abad/Alamy Stock Photo

Romanticism and the Natural Landscape European romanticism inspired American painters to portray the beauty and power of nature in harmony with or in contrast to settled farmland as in this painting, Thomas Cole's 1836 *The Oxbow*, which measures six feet wide. Cole, who emigrated from England to Ohio with his family as a child, founded the Hudson River School, a group of landscape painters greatly admired by transcendentalists. ▲

10-3c Print and Public Performance

Truth and fraud compete in new cultural media.

The industrial revolution made printing faster and cheaper, allowing publishers to reach a new public. In 1825, the cylinder printing press, combining German technology and English steam machinery, reached the United States. It was self-inking and had a continuous process, which meant that fewer operators could produce thousands of copies an hour rather than hundreds. In 1833, Benjamin Day brought the benefits of mass printing to crowds of urban workers with his *New York Sun*, four pages of opinionated essays, crime reporting, and sensational stories of life on the moon and in the Five Points neighborhood. Costing only a penny a paper, the *Sun* and others of the **penny press** pioneered a new kind of news. Before the *Sun*, newspapers were called "blanket sheets"—large papers that were four feet by three feet when opened. Businessmen subscribed to them, paying six cents an issue for political and international economic information. The penny press, in contrast, was supported by advertising and sold on street corners.

The new audience demanded a new kind of reporting. Penny press reporters did not wait for information to be submitted but instead interviewed crime victims and gathered evidence to wrap in sensationalist language for an eager public. Coverage of the 1836 trial of New York clerk Richard Robinson, accused of murdering the prostitute Helen Jewett, typified the new relationship between the people and

transcendentalism Literary and philosophical movement organized around the belief that people have an intuitive knowledge of themselves and the world that does not depend on rational belief.

lyceum movement Network of organizations that sponsored adult education through public lectures on political and literary subjects.

penny press Daily and weekly urban newspapers, sold on street corners for a penny, that covered local crime and sensational stories and pioneered investigative journalism.

minstrel show Popular musical theatrical performance by white Americans dressed to look like stereotypical African Americans presented on national and international tours.

the press. Highly emotional reporting from the scene of the crime combined with investigations into the family backgrounds of Robinson and Jewett turned the trial and Robinson's hasty acquittal into lucrative entertainment. Most readers believed in Robinson's guilt and thought the whole event a cautionary tale about young people in the anonymous city and the dangers of prostitution.

Printed sensations took advantage of improved roads and faster steamships to advertise public amusements to an extended crowd. One of the most popular show promoters of the nineteenth century, P.T. Barnum, won national attention and a personal fortune by inviting audiences to test the truth of his outrageous claims. He exhibited a "feejee mermaid," a sewn-together taxidermy creature combining animal parts that he insisted was an actual mermaid. Thousands lined up to pay to be tricked in this new form of mass entertainment. In 1843, Barnum enlisted his five-year-old distant cousin, Charles Stratton, who had a form of dwarfism, to tour Europe and then Cuba under the name of "General Tom Thumb," singing, dancing, and impersonating Napoleon.

Another type of dress-up and trickery was the basis for a new American form of popular culture, the **minstrel show**. These productions featured white performers who blackened their faces with burnt cork and sang and acted out stereotyped African American characters. Stock types, such as "Zip Coon," a free black man who boasted of his independence yet misused complicated words, populated minstrel shows, which also included songs about southern slave plantations (such as "Dixie" and "Old Folks at Home"). The most eager audiences for minstrel shows were urban white working men, who felt themselves threatened on one side from free black laborers and on the other by religiously minded reformers who scolded them and spoke of their need to adopt sobriety and self-discipline. Minstrel shows also toured Europe, and Stephen Foster's "Oh! Susanna!" was performed by buskers on the streets of London and sung by Juan Bega, an African American boatman working on the Isthmus of Panama, within months of its publication.

Image courtesy of Images Musicales

Music for Stephen Foster's "Oh! Susannah!" The cover of this sheet music notes that the song was popularized by the Ethiopian Serenaders, a blackface minstrel group that performed in various places in the United States, including at the White House, and in Europe. This copy of the music was printed in London, meaning that the emerging middle class there could sing songs about the U.S. South in their parlors. ▲

10-4 Ideologies of Race and Slavery

These lithographs of "Black and White Slaves" by Edward Williams Clay (New York, 1841) contrast the supposed paternalism of the U.S. South with the cruelty of English factory owners. The slave owner on the left says "These poor creatures are a sacred legacy from my ancestors"; the industrialist on the right tells the starving family to "pack off to the work house." Clay was a Philadelphia artist and cartoonist whose stereotyped images helped develop a visual culture of race and racism.

How does the artist, a Northerner, depict the lives of "slaves" in the United States and England? What does he suggest about their relationship to those who own them? ▶

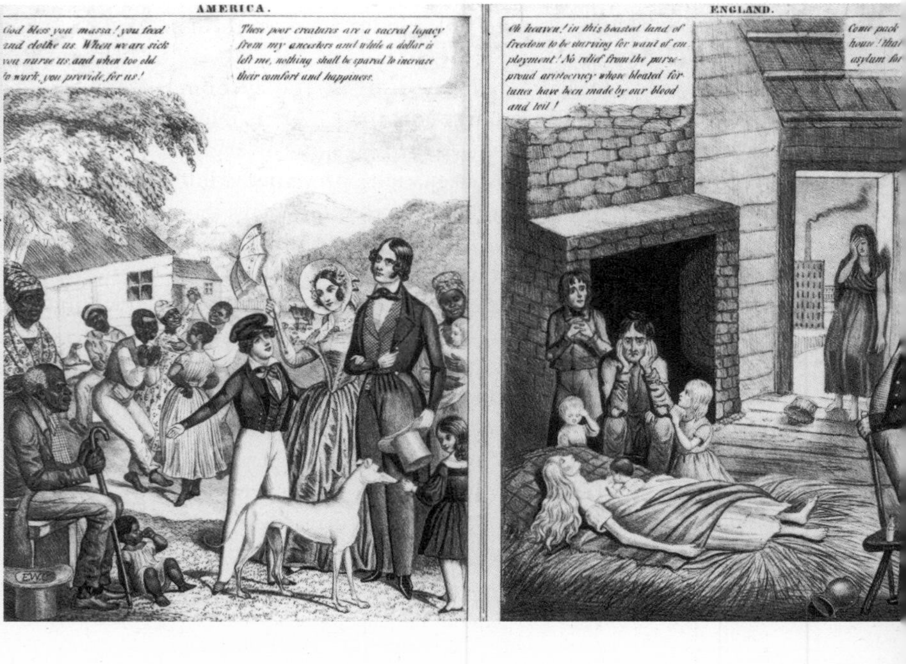

Smithsonian Institution National Museum of American History, Behring Center

Slavery expanded in the nineteenth century to fill the labor demands of global trade and industrial production. Scientists, ministers, politicians, and slaveholders devised racial and religious ideas that argued with new strength and conviction for the cruel system of racial hierarchy that supported slavery. At the same time, the Age of Revolution and the agreement of European nations and the United States to abolish the international slave trade increased debate about the morality of holding humans in permanent bondage. People trapped in slavery drew on their intimate knowledge of law, faith, and the personal lives of their enslavers to carve out moments of independence in an exploitative world that occasionally widened into rebellion.

☞ As you read, note the ways that slavery adapted to changing global politics and economies in the nineteenth century. How had discussions linking race, slavery, and politics changed?

10-4a Legal Contexts for Slavery

Slave laws respond to evolving national and international contexts.

The laws governing American slavery developed over centuries of experimentation within European empires, and they continued to adapt in the nineteenth century. The abolition of the Atlantic slave trade in 1808 was followed by treaties designed to enforce it, which altered the landscape of slavery along the U.S. coast. The **Anglo-Spanish Treaty of 1817** pledged Spain to end the slave trade north of the equator immediately and to the south by 1820. It also gave the British navy the right to board suspected slave ships, seize human cargo, and fine the captain. Yet slavery thrived on the plantations of Brazil and on Spanish Cuba, where ships from West African kingdoms such as the expanding Dahomey still delivered hundreds of thousands of captive humans.

In 1839, this international framework was put to the test in U.S. courts when U.S. forces seized forty-three Africans aboard the ship ***Amistad*** in Long Island Sound. Captives on the Cuban-bound voyage had waged a shipboard revolt, killing the captain and cook and demanding that the remaining crew divert the ship to Africa. When they ended up in the United States instead, the question for the courts was: Were they murderous pirates or freedom fighters? The verdict hinged on uncovering the captives' origins. If they were slaves in Cuba, they should be returned as property; if they were newly enslaved victims of the outlawed international slave trade, they deserved freedom. They were ultimately declared free, acquitted of murder, and allowed to return to West Africa.

Within the United States, legislators in Alabama, Georgia, and Louisiana responded to charges that slavery destroyed families by passing laws in the 1820s and 1830s that prevented owners from selling children under ten away from their mothers. To get around such laws, however, owners often rented out their slaves, including very young children they sent to farms needing "little negroes" who could be trained to babysit white children or help in the fields. Slave owners viewed small black children, just like adults, as flexible laborers who could produce income for them during plantation slack times.

Industries in the South took advantage of the practice of slave rentals to fill out their labor force. The **Tredegar Iron Works** in Richmond, Virginia, which provided material for the expanding railroad system in the United States, had a 50 percent enslaved workforce. The company, chartered in 1837, bought some of its slaves but rented the rest through contracts signed with Virginia slave owners. Through such contracts, slave owners held on to their human property but handed the management and maintenance of these workers to company supervisors.

10-4b Proslavery Arguments

Defenders reimagine slavery from a necessary evil to a positive good.

Whites who justified slavery in the eighteenth century typically cited the economic benefits of an enslaved labor force. By 1820, a new **proslavery doctrine** had emerged in the United States. Building on the concepts of paternalism forged on eighteenth-century tobacco plantations, this notion held that slaves by their natures were unable to take care of themselves, and whites had been appointed by God to watch over their bodies and souls. Southern slave owners said that they were providing what blacks required, oversight and protection: "The Southerner is the negro's friend, his only friend."

Proslavery speakers embraced the paternalistic view of U.S. slavery in part because it was economically self-serving. With the international slave trade abolished, slave owners had to rely on "home-grown" slaves. Breeding human beings, like breeding animals, was a concept they embraced eagerly. One planter wrote from Texas in 1849 to his nephew: "Get as many young negro women as you can. Get as many cows as you can. . . . It is the greatest country for an increase that I have ever saw in my life." Slavery increased dramatically. By 1860, the United States had 4 million slaves in a population of 31 million people. Evangelical religion also bolstered proslavery paternalism. White Southerners converted in large numbers during the Second

Anglo-Spanish Treaty of 1817 Agreement signed between England and Spain in which Spain pledged to end the slave trade and to permit the British navy to inspect Spanish ships suspected of carrying slaves.

Amistad Spanish schooner carrying rebellious illegal slaves that landed in the United States, leading to a series of trials to determine the status of the people aboard.

Tredegar Iron Works Virginia plant manufacturing iron hardware and locomotives established in 1836 by Francis B. Deane that employed slave laborers alongside free blacks, immigrants, and United States-born workers.

proslavery doctrine Ideology drawing on law, religion, history, and racist science in defense of slavery as a positive institution for whites and blacks.

William H. Townsend, Sketches of the Amistad Captives. General Collection, Beinecke Rare Book and Manuscript Library, Yale University

Global Americans The woman who became **Sarah Mar'gru Kinson** was born Mar'gru to a large family around 1832 in Bendembu, West Africa. After her father pawned her for a debt, she marched with a group of captives to the coast of Galinhas and was sold into the Spanish-Cuban slave trade. Mar'gru was confined in slave pens on Lomboko Island and then transported to Cuba, where she was sold at auction as a slave. On route to her new plantation aboard the ship *Amistad*, Mar'gru was caught up in a mutiny led by Cinque, one of the adult slaves on the ship. After three grueling months at sea, the ship ended up near Long Island Sound, where it was seized by U.S. maritime forces. Its occupants became the focus of a famous trial. Abolitionists demanded their freedom; Cuba insisted that they were legal slaves.

Along with the other *Amistad* survivors, Mar'gru traveled to Sierra Leone in 1841, sponsored by the Amistad Committee and Union Missionary Society. Then going by the name Sarah Kinson, she was unable to integrate into Mende culture. Instead, she returned to the United States in 1846 and studied at Oberlin, the first college in the United States to accept black and white students together. She returned to West Africa to teach at a mission school and married Edward Green in 1852. Soon after, she disappeared from written records. Sarah Mar'gru's life was extraordinary, but its Atlantic dimensions demonstrate that the expansion of slavery and the emergence of abolition in the nineteenth century were fundamentally international developments.

Great Awakening and began to use Biblical rather than economic language to talk to and about their slaves. They quoted Paul's letter to the Ephesians in the Bible: "Servants, be obedient to them that are your masters according to the flesh with fear and trembling, in singleness of your heart, as unto Christ."

Forged in paternalism, proslavery language became a sectional strategy for the South. Southerners claimed that they were maintaining the true bonds of caring dependence that had been disrupted by industrial growth elsewhere. They accused northern industrialists of merely exploiting those who labored, giving them no guidance, training, compassion, or security in return. Slave owners, they countered, had a duty to support their slaves even when they were sick or old. Northerners were vulnerable to these claims, because they heard the same arguments from a growing labor movement. Proslavery barbs targeted Britain as well. In 1833, South Carolina planter James Henry Hammond condemned the British as hypocrites who forced the Irish into "absolute & unmitigated slavery."

Proslavery ideology ignored the basic truths of American slavery. Slaveholders declared themselves committed to supporting enslaved people throughout their lives, but the thriving interstate slave trade demonstrated that they were quick to sell human property to pay debts. The myth of the large benevolent family was especially cruel. Slave masters were legally free to rape their slaves, father children with enslaved women, and continue to hold those children as property rather than family members. White women reacted to this open secret with rage, beating and punishing the enslaved women, or with bitter resignation.

scientific racism Body of knowledge created by so-called scientific studies of human traits that declared permanent hierarchical differences among distinct racial groups.

10-4c Scientific Racism

The "science" of difference links race, slavery, and conquest.

New ideas about human origins bolstered proslavery arguments and spread racism in free states and territories. Earlier race prejudice had various explanations for physical differences between groups of human beings, but most Euro-Americans had believed in the Biblical story that all humans came from a single origin. In the nineteenth century, this idea, called *monogenesis*, was challenged by *polygenesis*, the idea that human beings had fundamentally different origins. Polygenecists believed that from these different origins had grown separate races that were fundamentally and permanently different. In fact, proponents argued that a hierarchical chain of races separated the people of so-called superior appearance, intelligence, culture, and temperament from those with "inferior" qualities.

Scientific racism linked physical appearance to character, a connection that had broad support in the nineteenth century. Phrenologists, who believed that bumps on one's skull corresponded with over- or underdeveloped parts of the brain, applied their analysis to individuals. A person with a bump near the part of the brain that controlled envy had an envious temperament. Scientific racism insisted that entire groups of human beings, or races, shared physical traits linked to intellectual and moral capacity. Philadelphia physician Samuel George Morton measured the size and capacity of thousands of skulls and, in his 1839 *Crania Americana*, published his conclusions about the link between skull capacity, intellect, and moral character. He divided humanity into four groups: Caucasians, Mongolians, [Native] Americans, and Negroes. According to his reported measurements, Caucasians had the largest brains and were the most intellectual and cultured whereas Negroes had the smallest brain capacity although they were talented in music. The idea that human beings fell into unchangeable categories that could be easily perceived gained popular appeal among scientists and the public. Even the *Amistad* captives were subjected to a phrenologist's scrutiny while they awaited their legal fate.

Scientific racism blurred categories of culture and appearance, forging a tool for expansionist political rhetoric. In 1844, Mississippi senator Robert J. Walker argued that Mexico did not deserve independent status because Mexicans were an "ignorant and fanatical race" due to their Catholicism and the prevalence of multicultural families. In fact, race was neither obvious nor fixed, and nineteenth-century migrations allowed people to shift from one race to another, passing with a new identity. Joshua Peavy was born a free black farmer in North Carolina in the early nineteenth century. Converting to Methodism in the Second Great Awakening, he moved to Alabama to become an ordained minister. Neighbors described him as a "Frenchman" with a "very dark complexion."

Public Domain

Frederick Douglass Born into slavery in Maryland, Douglass learned to read and write in Baltimore in spite of bans on slave literacy. He escaped to freedom in New York in 1838 and became active in the American Anti-Slavery Society. His 1845 autobiography, *Narrative of the Life of Frederick Douglass*, countering proslavery claims, was a best seller in the United States. Within a decade, it had been translated into Dutch, French, and German. ▲

10-4d Resistance to Slavery

Enslaved people use a range of methods to resist slavery in their daily lives.

White Southerners deepened their commitment to slavery; enslaved people continued to resist it daily. To disrupt the punishing workday, some broke tools or pretended to be sick. They ran away for short periods of time to visit family members on nearby plantations. Some retaliated against vicious treatment by poisoning masters and mistresses. The multiple forms of resistance to slavery depended on an individual's calculation of the personal risks of each action, and many relied on slave owners' misunderstanding of the people they claimed to know. Frederick Douglass, a former slave who became one of the most prominent U.S. antislavery crusaders, wrote in his autobiography that whites often thought slaves' singing was evidence of their contentment, but they were profoundly mistaken: "The songs of the slave represent the sorrows of his heart; and he is relieved by them, only as an aching heart is relieved by tears."

Although large-scale rebellions coordinated by multiple slaves were rare in the United States, one of the largest occurred in 1831 when enslaved Virginian Nat Turner, inspired by a religious vision, led dozens of slaves in an uprising known as **Turner's Rebellion**. Armed with axes, knives, and guns, the group killed sixty people, starting with Turner's owners. Terrified whites called in militias and vigilantes from Virginia and North Carolina. Thousands went on a rampage of retaliation, killing two hundred slaves at random in Virginia and neighboring states. Turner was caught. While he was in prison, awaiting conviction and then execution, he was interviewed by a slave-owning lawyer named Thomas Gray, who published *The Confessions of Nat Turner*. In this account, Turner did not claim that he was mistreated by specific owners. Rather, he saw in the Bible and in heavenly visions the truth that slavery was a sin committed by whites against blacks. When the lawyer asked if he had any regrets, Turner reportedly said, "Was not Christ crucified?"

White Southerners took two lessons from Turner's Rebellion. First, the killings graphically reminded those clinging to paternalism that slavery was in fact violent and dangerous. The following year, the Virginia legislature debated a measure that would have gradually ended slavery and sent all free blacks out of the state. Those in favor of the measure argued that the safety of whites depended on eliminating black people from their communities; those opposed insisted that they could not afford to end slavery in the state. Virginia legislators ultimately defeated the measure seventy-three to fifty-eight. The second effect of Turner's Rebellion was to convince white Americans in the South that Christianity and literacy could be dangerous because they encouraged enslaved people to think about and act on their desire for freedom. In the early 1830s, both before and after the Turner rebellion, southern states passed or tightened laws against teaching enslaved people to

Turner's Rebellion Slave uprising led by Nat Turner in Southampton County, Virginia, that had the most casualties of any U.S. revolt.

read, hoping to close off access to the Bible and antislavery works. After the rebellion, Virginia and Alabama forbade teaching enslaved or free black people to read or write.

A violent uprising in Jamaica also in 1831 had a starkly different effect on the British Atlantic. Led by Samuel Sharpe, an enslaved Baptist deacon and speaker, the protest began as a labor strike after Christmas. Peaceful protest soon turned to armed conflict between fifty thousand slaves and British colonial authorities. Fourteen whites and one hundred eighty-six slaves died in the **Christmas Rising**; more than five hundred more slaves were captured, tried, and hundreds executed in the aftermath. British public opinion, shocked by the uprising and its brutal suppression and at the same time comfortably separated from the realities of living among freed and enslaved people, finally supported the British abolitionists' cause. They pushed Parliament to vote for emancipation, which passed in 1833. The **Slavery Abolition Act**, which took effect on August 1, 1834, declared most enslaved people in the British Empire free from slavery and instead put to work as apprentices for several more years. The British government compensated former slave owners for the loss of their property with money.

10-5 Individual Rights and Social Good

The image on the left was originally created for the Society for the Abolition of Slavery in England in the 1780s and became widely used on both sides of the Atlantic. In the United States, Maria M. Stewart, a free black abolitionist, used the image on the right in the 1830s to accompany her publications.

Compare the bodies, clothing, and poses of the people in the two images. What are the key differences between the earlier image and the later one, and how do they influence the universalism of the message? Do they present different rationales for emancipation? ▶ Everett Collection, The Granger Collection, New York.

Go to MindTap® to practice history with the Chapter 10 **Primary Source Writing Activity: Social Ills and Social Good.** Read and view primary sources and respond to a writing prompt.

The problems of nineteenth-century American societies, including poverty, prostitution, alcoholism, crime, slavery, and inequality struck many Americans as incompatible with democracy and the evangelical mission. Some reasoned that a self-governing society needed healthy, informed, equal citizens. Others believed that achieving God's kingdom on earth required the eradication of sins. But how could they best achieve reforms when many reformers and their targets lacked the vote? The answer came from private organizations that drew on networks of churches and intellectuals to spread ideas. They used technologies of print, publicity, and transportation to gain supporters. Public opinion, they hoped, could be a political tool.

Christmas Rising Slave rebellion on the British colony of Jamaica led by Samuel Sharpe, an enslaved Baptist lay preacher that helped push Britain toward abolition.

Slavery Abolition Act Legislation (1833) that abolished slavery in most British colonies although former slaves had to serve a period of apprenticeship. Slave owners received financial compensation for their lost property.

American Temperance Society Organization founded in 1826 to promote reducing the use of alcohol that sparked a national cause and eventually had numerous local branches.

☞ As you read, think about how connections of people, ideas, and publications shaped the development of reform movements in the first five decades of the nineteenth century. How did Americans use international movements to address local issues?

10-5a Temperance Movement

Efforts to get Americans to curb alcohol consumption gain diverse supporters.

For centuries, Americans drank ale, cider, and beer with meals, at public celebrations, and as medicine. In the early nineteenth century, people began to drink more, replacing ale with increasingly high alcohol beverages. Employers such as Patrick Ryan served whiskey rations to the men performing difficult and dangerous work on canals. Binge drinking and drinking alone were also on the rise as people moved far from their families and familiar communities. By 1830, per capita alcohol consumption by U.S. adults peaked; across Europe, only the Swedish and French drank more (see Figure 10.2).

American religious leaders viewed these developments with alarm. Minister Lyman Beecher condemned excessive drinking for "the moral ruin which it works in the soul," with consequences for Americans and "the hopes of the world, which hang upon our experiment of civil liberty." In 1826, he and other Boston ministers founded the **American Temperance Society**, which soon inspired the opening of thousands of local chapters. Their goal was to encourage people to moderate their

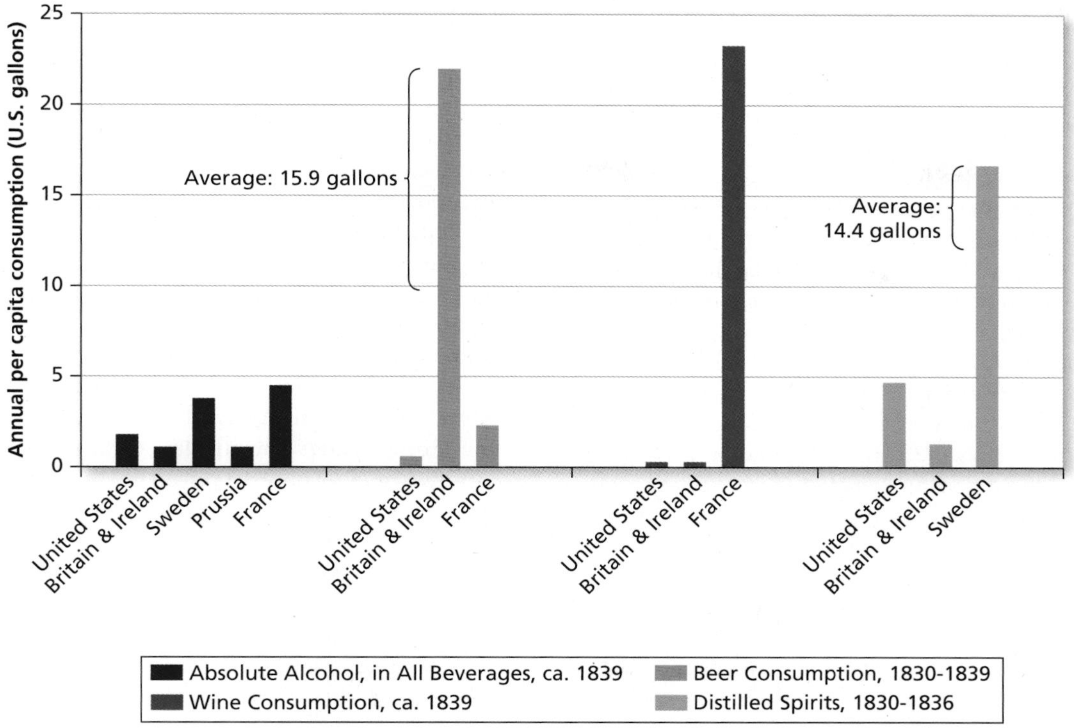

Figure 10.2 Alcohol Consumption in the 1830s Improved transportation, urbanization, and international trade increased the amount of alcohol that people drank in the early nineteenth century and influenced what they drank. Western U.S. farmers distilled surplus grain into whiskey, which was less bulky and expensive to transport. For American drinkers, this meant that whiskey was more widely available than in previous generations. In France, rural farmers moved to cities and became wine drinkers, in part to avoid the contaminated water common to urban centers around the world. ▲
Source: W. J. Rorabaugh, *The Alcoholic Republic*.

drinking by limiting consumption and switching to beer and wine rather than the "ardent spirits" of whiskey or rum.

The expanding movement had wide appeal, as well as support from churches and business leaders. The Georgia State Temperance Society, founded in 1828, initially held its annual meetings with the state Baptist convention. Baptists charged that drinking violated the Sabbath because workers who had only a single day off in the workweek spent it in the bar rather than in church. Others focused on the social costs of excessive drinking. Men and women argued that alcoholic fathers failed in their duties as head of household by drinking up the family's earnings and physically abusing their wives and children. By the mid-1830s, the American Temperance Society claimed that 1 million people had signed pledges to give up drinking, and temperance stories, songs, and poems rolled off printing presses.

Increasingly, temperance movements pushed for total abstinence from alcohol. Thomas P. Hunt, a Presbyterian minister, founded the Cold Water Army to recruit children to the cause, getting them to sign pledges that they would drink cold water, not alcohol. In 1840, working-class people formed the **Washingtonian movement** whose members drew on their pasts as hard drinkers and shared stories of lives destroyed by drink. By focusing on the links between drinking, poverty, and family violence, Washingtonians encouraged a type of grass-roots reform. As they lectured, they offered one another practical assistance in the form of food and clothing to restore families torn apart by alcohol abuse.

Temperance leadership was male but depended on female members to work for the cause. Maria Stewart, a widowed free black woman speaking in Boston in 1832, linked temperance with better living conditions for free blacks, proclaiming that were "the American free people of color to turn their attention more assiduously to moral worth and intellectual improvement, this would be the result: prejudice would gradually diminish, and the whites would be compelled to say, unloose those fetters!" But by saying these words in a public hall rather than in her home, Stewart and other female speakers were challenging expectations about proper female behavior. Stewart's audiences pelted her with tomatoes and jeered at her presumption.

Washingtonian movement Group of working-class societies in the 1840s that advocated total abstinence from alcohol by using the stories of former alcoholics as cautionary tales.

10-5b Institutions of Rescue and Reform

Expanding institutions combat social ills.

Temperance was the first and most widely supported reform movement, but it encouraged and trained generations of reformers who tackled other social problems. As the case of Helen Jewett demonstrated, rootless men and women moving into cities contributed to a significant expansion in the commercial sex trade. The number of established brothels in New York City tripled between 1820 and 1860, where as many as 10 percent of women engaged in prostitution at some point to make ends meet. In 1834, middle-class women established the **American Female Reform Society** in New York, targeting both the men and women caught up in the sex trade. Decrying the sexual double standard that permitted middle-class men to visit prostitutes discreetly, female reformers published the names of men seen exiting brothels in newspapers and organized raids to drive them onto public streets. Challenging the idea that poor prostitutes deserved ostracism, they tried to rescue them with training to be domestic servants in Magdalen charities, modeled on English institutions that took prostitutes away from their former neighborhoods.

American Female Reform Society Organization founded in New York in 1834 by women dedicated to ending prostitution and helping former prostitutes.

asylum movement International campaign led in the United States by Dorothea Dix to establish institutions in which the mentally ill could receive care and treatment.

Philadelphia Quakers were at the forefront of another transatlantic development in reforming institutions: the penitentiary. Most existing jails held a mix of offenders, including debtors, people awaiting trial, and convicted criminals held for whipping or branding. Rather than punish the body, reformers insisted that time in a penitentiary, properly supervised, could reform a criminal's character. Philadelphia's penitentiaries used a combination of clean conditions, strict routine, religious self-reflection, solitary confinement, and training in a marketable skill to transform prisoners. In 1816, New York State modified these methods in its new state penitentiary where inmates toiled in gang labor during the day but were confined to solitary cells at night. Alexis de Tocqueville journeyed to the United States specifically so that he could pay twenty-five cents to observe prisoners.

When Dorothea Dix, daughter of an alcoholic Methodist itinerant father and mentally ill mother, entered a Boston-area jail in 1841 to teach religious classes, she discovered that numerous inmates were not criminals but mentally ill. Chained to walls, inadequately clothed, and generally ignored, these women and men were confined with convicted criminals because their families were unable to care for them. Drawing from the ideas of French and British doctors, Dix plunged into research and writing, presenting her findings to the state legislatures of Massachusetts, New York, New Jersey, and Pennsylvania. She became a leader of the **asylum movement**, which pushed states to establish public institutions for the treatment of the mentally ill.

Prisoners at the State Prison at Auburn.

Penitentiary Prisoners New York's Auburn System combined a form of slave labor with progressive belief in human self-improvement. Prisoners wore uniforms, marched in formation, and kept silent. The state of New York sold the shoes and furniture made by prisoners behind bars for a profit. Initially, neighboring industries objected to having to compete with prison laborers; soon, prison officials began to contract out inmates' labor. ▲ The Granger Collection, New York

Concentrating the "insane" within institutional walls created a laboratory for reformers and physicians. Doctors and directors of asylums in the United States, Europe, and Asia published studies and shared correspondence concerning the proper definition and treatment of people with this baffling illness.

Other reformers targeted schools. Physician Samuel Gridley Howe was a veteran of the Greek War of Independence (1821–1832) when he retuned to head the New-England Institution for the Education of the Blind in 1832. He joined with educator Horace Mann to promote a new kind of teacher training emphasizing patient guidance, rather than threats of physical punishment, to instruct students. Mann, like Howe and Dix, urged state legislators to fund institutions that would develop Americans' capacities. Mann argued in 1832 that a system of **common schools** offering basic education to all children was essential in a democracy: "For what value is it, that we have the most wisely-framed government on earth," he asked, "if this people has not the intelligence to understand" or uphold it?

10-5c Expansion of Antislavery

Local contexts shape the international movement to end slavery.

By the 1830s, the United States stood as a contradiction to its neighbors. It permitted the broadest range of citizens to vote, yet those citizens supported an expanding population of people held in permanent slavery. Independent Mexico abolished slavery in 1829. Britain had ended slavery in its North American colonies in 1833. Charles Follen, a German immigrant, asked in 1833, "Shall the United States, the Free United States, which could not bear the bonds of a King, cradle the bondage which a King is abolishing?"

Follen was part of a transatlantic network of antislavery activists whose message had grown increasingly radical. Antislavery organizations first emerged in England, where Quakers, who had previously prospered in the slave trade, rejected the institution as a violation of their faith in the equality of human souls. In their commitment to egalitarianism, Quakers opposed hierarchical titles, refused to practice rituals of deference to elites, and welcomed both men and women as public speakers of the faith. From those origins in the 1750s, a network of antislavery activists grew, championing the abolition of the international slave trade, gradual emancipation, and the resettlement of former slaves in African colonies such as Sierra Leone and Liberia.

Originating in the free black community, **abolitionism** demanded the immediate and universal end to slavery. Abolitionists identified slavery as an entrenched social system of violence and immorality that had to be actively defeated. In 1829, David Walker, a free black man born to a white mother and an enslaved father, published his ***Appeal to the Coloured Citizens of the World***, tracing the global history of slavery and its spread throughout the United States. He called out the hypocrisy of the Founding Fathers and all Americans celebrating the Fourth of July for espousing equality while upholding both slavery and racism. "America is more our country, than it is the whites—we have enriched it with our blood and tears," he wrote, appealing to free blacks and those in slavery. He directed Americans to look to Spain and Portugal, where repression and revolution had men "cutting each other's throats" and see the judgment of God on countries that had been "oppressing the Lord's people" in their former American colonies. Walker argued that the violence of slavery could be met with violent antislavery: "kill or be killed."

Whites and blacks formed the **American Anti-Slavery Society** in 1833, committed to the immediate and full abolition of slavery. Eschewing the violence of Walker, their early tactics drew on the experience of reformers in the temperance and evangelical movements at home and in Europe. Hoping to create an intense antislavery moral climate by evoking sympathy for slaves, they published a flood of antislavery literature, totaling more than 1 million pamphlets in 1835. They produced children's picture books and parlor music. Their message stressed the sins of slavery, including the sexual abuse of slave women, the separation of families, and the murderous violence that was part of slave discipline. Southern states passed laws forbidding the post offices from carrying or delivering such literature, cutting abolitionists off from moderate whites in the South.

Abolitionists turned to spreading their message among Northerners, many of whom cared little about what they saw as someone else's problem. Angelina and Sarah Grimké, two sisters who had grown up in a slave-owning family but became Quakers and leading abolitionists published *American Slavery As It Is: Testimony of a Thousand Witnesses* with activist Theodore Dwight Weld in 1839. The book brought the voices of former and escaped slaves to northern readers. Former slaves Sojourner Truth and Frederick Douglass spoke to audiences of the horrors of slavery, describing their experiences in vivid detail. Revival-style abolitionist meetings won converts but also stoked violent opposition from mobs.

Simultaneously, the Anti-Slavery Society bombarded Congress and other legislative bodies with more than seven hundred thousand petitions designed to chip away at the more vulnerable parts of the laws supporting slavery. These petitions called for the abolition of slavery in Washington, D.C.; the abolition of the interstate slave trade; the removal of the Three-Fifths Compromise from

common schools Tax-supported public elementary and secondary schools designed to educate all children equally.

abolitionism Political movement demanding the immediate end to slavery and the emancipation of all slaves without compensation for slave owners.

Appeal to the Coloured Citizens of the World Radical abolitionist essay written by David Walker calling for the violent overthrow of slavery.

American Anti-Slavery Society Abolitionist organization founded in 1833 led by William Lloyd Garrison dedicated to nonviolent moral opposition slavery by women and men.

the Constitution; and the denial of admission of new slave states to the United States. In response, Congress in 1836 passed a **gag rule** that forbid the national legislative body from even discussing antislavery petitions.

10-5d Women's Rights

Wide-ranging women's rights movements emerge from religious and reform activism.

The accumulated experiences of nineteenth-century reform produced another transformative movement for social justice: women's rights. From the start, critiques of women's degraded status depended on international comparisons and connections. American women who traveled as missionaries used their experiences in Asia to highlight the inferior condition of women outside the United States. Anne Hasseltine Judson, a missionary who worked in India, Thailand, and Burma in the 1810s and 1820s, returned to the United States in 1822 and told U.S. women that supporting missionary work would elevate the position of women around the world. Shocking her audience, she claimed that Hindu women were kept ignorant and debased, that "mothers consider female existence a curse." Christian education and conversion, she declared, would elevate these women to the privileged status of their white sisters in the United States because Protestant Christianity proclaimed the spiritual equality of men and women.

Missionaries were not the only ones debating women's status worldwide. In France, female socialists demanding wage equity for working people concluded that the fruit of women's labors should belong to them, not to the men of their families. They moved beyond most male activists in promoting financial autonomy for women. In England, a Chartist movement of working people had formed following the limited gains of the 1832 Reform Act. But when movement leaders demanded "universal suffrage," and yet intendeded to extend the vote only to men of the working class, female activists began to advocate on behalf of women. In German states, women in "free congregations" that rejected Christian establishments and emphasized free thought objected when these churches limited female opportunities for leadership.

The contradictions that women faced in reform movements forced them to confront the larger question of equality and human capability. When Angelina Grimké was called "unnatural" and unfeminine for speaking publically against slavery, she asked: "What then can *woman* do for the slave when she is herself under the feet of men and shamed into *silence*?" At the same time, connections forged through one type of reform strengthened work for women's rights. English activist Anne Knight wrote to American abolitionist Maria Weston Chapman, recommending that she read Scottish author Marion Reid's *A Plea for Woman* because "These things ought to be sent darting off like lightning to all the world if possible." Women's rights activists built international networks through personal correspondence and printed pamphlets that connected efforts across the oceans.

Women and men deepened these networks by holding conventions, which enabled them to meet and develop policy programs. In 1848, Lucretia Mott and Elizabeth Cady Stanton organized a Women's Rights Convention at Seneca Falls, New York, where Stanton lived. Mott knew the town from her missionary work there with a community of Seneca Indians. At this convention, three hundred people, including prominent abolitionist Frederick Douglass, met to listen to speeches about the social, political, and economic condition of women. They also presented the **Seneca Falls *Declaration of Sentiments***, written largely by Stanton. Signed by sixty-eight women and thirty-two men, the document was modeled on the Declaration of Independence and presented the demands of a wide-ranging "woman movement" that claimed both rights and a central place in public life for women. The declaration objected to laws that gave husbands the right to their wives' earnings and awarded child custody in divorce cases to fathers, never mothers. It protested practices that denied women access to higher education and higher wages for their work. And it insisted that women should have the right to vote. This last, most radical demand became the main goal of the women's suffrage movement that spanned the next seventy-two years. Of the one hundred people who signed the Declaration, only two were still alive when the U.S. Constitution was amended to allow women to vote.

State legislatures, responding to political pressure, began to pass laws modifying the status of married women who lived under coverture. Under these acts, which began in Arkansas territory (1835) and Mississippi (1839), married women were permitted new rights to own and eventually control property in their own names. In 1848, New York passed a comprehensive **Married Women's Property Act** that became a model for other states in the 1850s (see Table 10.3). This act determined that the property a woman owned at the time of her marriage, whether it was the clothes on her back or the land her parents had given her, belonged to her, not her husband. His creditors could not seize her property. She controlled the profits that her property yielded. These early laws focused on wealthier women; only later in the century did married women who worked for wages gain legal rights to those wages.

gag rule (1836) Resolution passed in the U.S. House of Representatives forbidding the consideration of antislavery petitions. It was rescinded in 1844.

Seneca Falls *Declaration of Sentiments* (1848) Document by Elizabeth Cady Stanton signed at the Seneca Falls Convention that was modeled on the Declaration of Independence and demanded rights for women.

Married Women's Property Act Name for diverse state laws in the nineteenth and twentieth centuries that granted married women relief from coverture and gave married women rights to their own inheritances and wages.

Table 10.3 Married Women's Property Acts, 1808–1860

Laws expanding the property rights of free women fell into broad categories concerning wills, property holding, and earnings. Individual states attached specific limitations. For example, a state that permitted married women to write their own wills might require the husband's permission. Years later, that provision could be eliminated in another law. The result was a complex patchwork of legal rights that changed in response to husbands' and fathers' demands as well as those of women themselves.

	Married Women Permitted to Write Their Own Wills	Married Women Permitted to Own Poperty Free from Husband's Debts	Married Women Permitted to Control Their Own Earnings
1800–1820	1808 Ohio		
	1809 Connecticut		
	1810 Ohio		
	1818 Massachusetts		
1820–1840	1823 Florida		
	1825 Florida		
	1833 Pennsylvania		
		1835 Arkansas Territory	
		1839 Mississippi	
1840–1845	1840 Ohio		
	1841 New Hampshire		
	1842 Massachusetts		
	1843 Maryland	1843 Maryland	
		1844 Maine, Michigan	
		1845 Florida, Connecticut, Vermont, Texas, Massachussetts	
1845–1850	1846 Alabama	1846 Alabama, Arkansas, Iowa, Kentucky, New Hampshire, Ohio	
	1847 Indiana		
	1848 Pennsylvania	1848 Alabama, Arkansas, New York, Pennsylvania, Rhode Island	
	1849 New York	1849 Connecticut, Missouri	
	1850 Michigan	1850 Oregon, Tennessee, Wisconsin	
1850–1855	1852 Tennessee, Ohio	1852 New Jersey	
	1853 Oregon		
	1854 New Hampshire		
	1855 Massachusetts	1855 Florida, Michigan	1855 Massachusetts, Pennsylvania
1855–1860	1856 Rhode Island		
			1858 Kansas
			1860 Maine, Maryland, New York

Source: Joan Hoff, *Law, Gender, and Injustice: A Legal History of U.S. Women* (New York: New York University Press).

Summary

Economic and political developments in the first half of the nineteenth century transformed religious practice, personal life, and culture. Migration for jobs created new multiethnic urban communities that divided along racial and religious alliances. Boom-bust cycles of economic instability drove some to drink and others, as part of a new middle class, into a sober celebration of private home life. Global markets in cotton and animal skins rewarded families that could take on new members and abandon others, leaving Indian wives, enslaved husbands, and mixed-race children behind. In every region of the United States, individuals and communities adapted their personal beliefs and private lives to cope with the opportunities and uncertainties of national and global forces.

Evangelical Christianity, with its emphasis on both personal perfectionism and community obligation, became a powerful force in the United States and was soon exported by missionaries around the globe. Reformers insisted that sin was the poison causing most social problems and personal effort was the antidote. At times, reformers' message seemed to punish those suffering. In other cases, they demanded that the powerful invest time and money to help weaker members of the community. Both enslaved people and enslavers found support in Biblical messages, but as Native Americans had discovered, religious goals intersected with political ones in ways that could be difficult to control.

Improved transportation and printing technologies encouraged cultural forms created locally to be exported globally. Songs written in the North about slavery in the South entered popular culture across the Atlantic. American artists, inspired by European celebrations of untamed nature, painted wild North American landscapes. Escaped slaves shared their testimony with Midwesterners through public speaking and with Europeans in the pages of their autobiographies.

New cultures and new ideas, in turn, shaped the politics and economy of nineteenth-century America. Notions about middle-class domesticity bolstered the practice of paying women workers less. Scientific racism, nurtured in transatlantic intellectual circuits, offered an explanation for why slavery was expanding in a democracy and ensured cotton planters' reliance on an enslaved labor force. The conviction that humans had an obligation to choose their own church and actively seek salvation fueled a profitable international marketplace in religious publications and speakers. The national political system, oriented around individualism and competition among free men, could not remain aloof to the interests of non-voters.

<Thinking Back, *Looking Forward*>

As you review this chapter, think about the history of culture and how seemingly essential concepts, such as sex, religion, and human nature, were transformed by local circumstances and global trends. How did circulating scientific knowledge or new ideas about natural rights alter the ways people worshipped God? Why were ideas about women's "nature" in the nineteenth century different from those in the seventeenth century? In the chapters to come, look for the consequences of cultural change. How did new ideas about race determine foreign policy and the growth of new empires? Did nineteenth- and twentieth-century conquests in the West and the Pacific draw on different cultural ideas than sixteenth- and seventeenth-century European conquests?

To make your study concrete, review the timeline and reflect on the entries there. Think about their causes, consequences, and connections. How do they connect events in North America to global trends?

Additional Resources

Books

Anderson, Bonnie. *Joyous Greetings: The First International Women's Movement*, 1830–1860. New York: Oxford University Press, 2001. ▶ Intellectual history of transatlantic women's rights movements.

Boydston, Jeanne. *Home and Work: Housework, Wages, and the Ideology of Labor in the Early Republic*. New York: Oxford University Press, 1994. ▶ Pioneering study of women's household labor in the nineteenth century.

Camp, Stephanie. *Closer to Freedom: Enslaved Women and Everyday Resistance in the Plantation South*. Chapel Hill: University of North Carolina Press, 2004. ▶ Provocative interpretation of how gender shaped slave resistance.

Cook, James. *The Arts of Deception: Playing with Fraud in the Age of Barnum*. Cambridge, MA: Harvard University Press, 2001. ▶ Study of nineteenth-century popular entertainments.

Davis, David Brion. *Inhuman Bondage: The Rise and Fall of Slavery in the New World*. New York: Oxford University Press, 2008. ▶ Sweeping portrayal of American slavery in global context.

Dunn, Richard S. *A Tale of Two Plantations: Slave Life and Labor in Jamaica and Virginia*. Cambridge, MA: Harvard University Press, 2014. ▶ Comparative study of slave experiences in Jamaica and Virginia in the nineteenth century.

Hatch, Nathan. *The Democratization of American Christianity*. New Haven, CT: Yale University Press, 1999. ▶ Historical study that links the Second Great Awakening with democratic impulses.

Howe, Daniel Walker. *What Hath God Wrought: The Transformation of America, 1815–1848*. New York: Oxford University Press, 2007. ▶ Synthetic history of nineteenth-century politics, economy, and culture.

McDaniel, Caleb. *The Problem of Democracy in the Age of Slavery: Garrisonian Abolitionists and Transatlantic Reform*. Baton Rouge: Louisiana State University Press, 2015. ▶ An interpretation of American abolitionism that highlights its transatlantic contexts.

Go to the MindTap® for ***Global Americans*** to access the full version of select books from this Additional Resources section.

Websites

Ardent Spirits at the Library Company. (http://www.librarycompany.org/ArdentSpirits/index.htm) ▶ Exhibition exploring the many dimensions of the temperance movement.

Home, Sweet Home: Life in Nineteenth-Century Ohio. (http://lcweb2.loc.gov/diglib/ihas/html/ohio/ohio-home.html) ▶ Library of Congress collection of parlor music with explanatory essays.

Immigration to the United States, 1789–1930. (http://ocp.hul.harvard.edu/immigration/) ▶ Harvard University Library collection of sources on nineteenth-century immigration.

Inland Waterways. (http://americanhistory.si.edu/onthewater/exhibition/4_1.html) ▶ Smithsonian National Museum of American History exhibit on life along inland waterways.

MindTap®

Continue exploring online through MindTap®, where you can:

- **Assess your knowledge with the Chapter Test**
- **Watch historical videos related to the chapter**
- **Further your understanding with interactive maps and timelines**

Personal Transformations and Public Reforms

1801–1810

August 1801

Camp meeting in Cane Ridge, Kentucky, draws tens of thousands.

1808

Charles Fourier publishes his first major work, influencing utopian communities.

June 1810

New England ministers and businessmen found the American Board of Commissioners of Foreign Missions (ABCFM).

1816–1817

1816

New York builds a state penitentiary following the Auburn System of prisoner control.

April 1816

African Methodist Episcopal Church becomes an independent denomination.

May 1816

American Bible Society dedicated to printing and distributing Bibles is founded.

September 1817

Anglo-Spanish Treaty commits Spain to ending the international slave trade to be enforced by Britain.

1821–1826

September 1821

Mexico achieves independence from Spain.

May 1823

American John Howard Payne premiers "Home! Sweet Home!" in London.

1825

Robert Owen founds New Harmony, an experimental community, in Indiana.

February 1826

Boston ministers found the American Society for the Promotion of Temperance to encourage moderation in alcohol consumption.

1828–1830

November 1828

Andrew Jackson elected president of the United States.

1829

David Walker publishes *Appeal to the Coloured Citizens of the World*, decrying slavery and racism.

September 1829

Independent Mexico abolishes slavery.

1830

Joseph Smith publicizes the *Book of Mormon*, the founding text of the Church of Jesus Christ of Latter-day Saints, also known as the Mormon Church.

June 1830

Godey's Lady's Book begins publication.

1831–1832

1830–1831

Finney leads religious revival in Rochester, New York, during high point of Second Great Awakening.

August 1831

Turner leads largest U.S. slave rebellion of the nineteenth century.

December 1831

Sharpe leads Christmas Rising slave revolt in Jamaica, resulting in two hundred deaths.

1832

Cholera outbreak in New York City kills thousands of mainly poor residents.

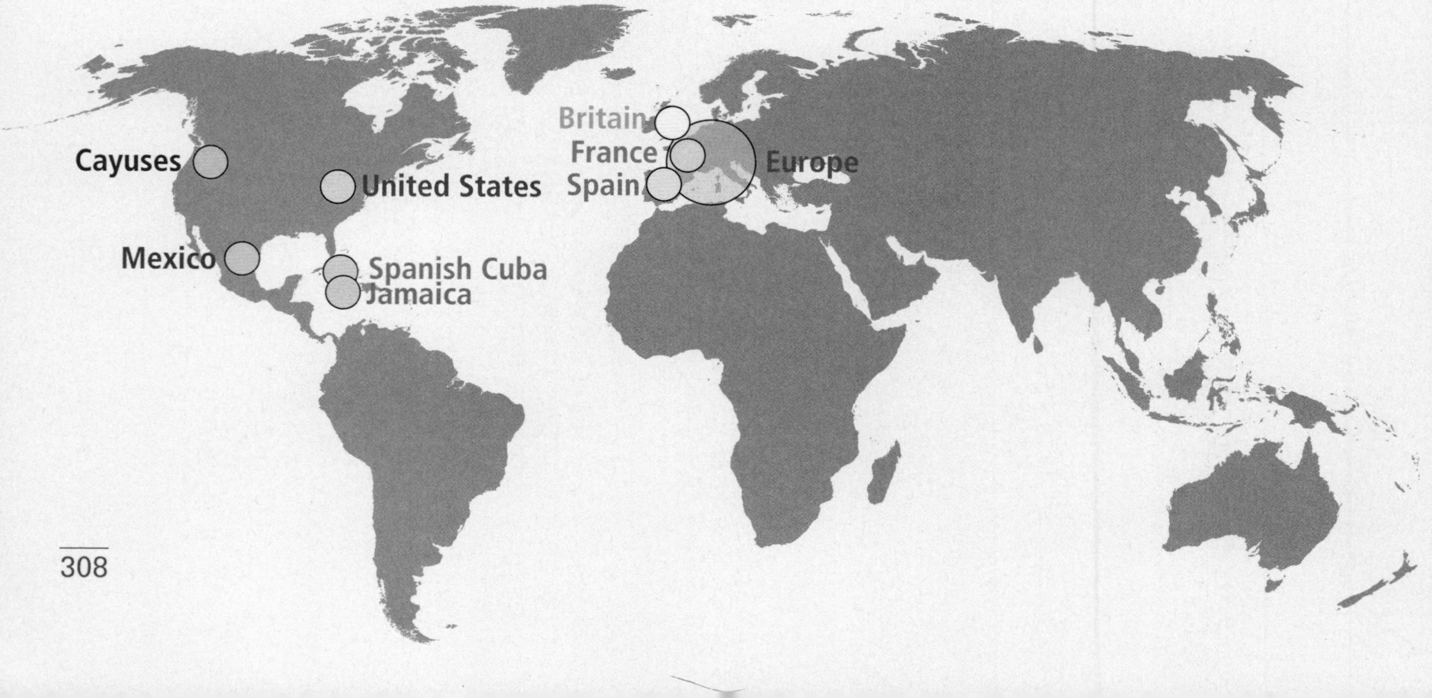

1833

August 1833
British Parliament passes the Slavery Abolition Act, ending slavery in most of the British colonies.

September 1833
Day publishes the *New York Sun*, first of the penny press papers.

December 1833
Garrison and others found the American Anti-Slavery Society.

1834–1836

May 1834
New York women found the American Female Reform Society to combat prostitution.

July 1834
Antiblack riots in New York City are sparked by anniversary celebrations for state emancipation.

1834–1836
Mexican officials break up the Franciscan missions in Alta California.

1835
ABCFM sends missionaries Marcus and Narcissa Whitman to Cayuse Indians.

May 1836
Congress passes a gag rule, forbidding the further consideration of antislavery petitions.

1837–1839

February 1837
Richmond, Virginia, businessmen receive charter for the Tredegar Iron Works.

June 1839
Chartists' Petition demanding universal male suffrage presented to Parliament.

August 1839
U.S. navy seizes the *Amistad*, launching a series of trials concerning the passengers' free status.

1839
Physician Samuel George Morton publishes *Crania Americana*, fueling scientific racist thought.

1840–1844

June 1840
World's Anti-Slavery Convention meets in London with nearly five hundred delegates.

1841
Ralph Waldo Emerson publishes "Self Reliance."

1843
U.S. promoter P. T. Barnum tours Europe and Cuba with his distant cousin posing as "Tom Thumb."

1845–1848

May 1845
Baptist Church splits over whether to accept slavery, forming two conferences.

July 1848
One hundred women and men sign the Seneca Falls Declaration of Sentiments for women's rights.

Go to MindTap® to engage with an interactive version of the timeline. Analyze events and themes with clickable content, view related videos, and respond to critical thinking questions.

11 A Continental Nation

1815–1853

Texas in the 1830s and 1840s was a difficult place for *Tejanos*. By the time he died in 1890, Juan Seguín had exiled himself to Mexico. People on both sides of the border questioned his loyalty because he had fought for both Mexico and the United States during his lifetime.

On the night of February 25, 1836, Juan Seguín slipped out the back of Mission San Antonio de Valero in Texas. Mexican forces had surrounded him and his comrades in the Spanish mission, better known today as the Alamo. The situation appeared hopeless for the Texas rebels who were fighting for their independence from Mexico. Their commander sent Seguín to ride north and bring back reinforcements to help save the men from certain attack, capture, and perhaps death. Although Seguín carried his message to Sam Houston, president of the newly formed Texas Republic, he was too late. The Mexican army attacked before he returned, killing virtually every man who stayed to defend the Alamo. Seguín later helped defeat Mexican forces at the Battle of San Jacinto. He was among the victors who accepted General Antonio Lopez de Santa Anna's surrender when he laid down his arms and recognized Texas independence.

Juan N. Seguín, Jefferson Wright (1838)/The State Preservation Board, Austin, Texas

Seguín, a wealthy and prominent man, was elected as a state senator, the only *Tejano* (Texan) in that body, and later mayor of his hometown, San Antonio. As he returned to domestic life, he envisioned a world where former Mexican citizens would live side-by-side with their Anglo neighbors who had emigrated from the United States over the past two decades. Together they would all be *Tejanos*, a people united by the shaping of a new democratic nation.

But Texas in the mid nineteenth century was a difficult place for Mexican Americans, even those as wealthy as Seguín, to maintain their status in the Lone Star Republic's evolving society. By the time Seguín died in 1890, he had held many offices, been exiled to Mexico because people questioned his loyalty to Texas, lived on both sides of the U.S./Mexican border, and fought for both the Lone Star Republic against Mexico and for the Mexican government against the United States. He eventually lost all of his property and died a destitute man who wondered in his memoir how he had become a "foreigner in my native land." The world was changing around Seguín. He and others born in Mexico's northern provinces were remade as Americans as the United States expanded its border to the Pacific.

The story of Juan Seguín reveals the complexities of living in the territories between the Mississippi River and the Pacific Ocean, which in 1815 were either colonies of Spain and Britain or the unorganized Louisiana Territory, which had been a colony of both Spain and France. By 1850, the American West would be organized into U.S. territories. The process of incorporation was marked by experimentation, violence, political turmoil, and accommodation. Across these vast spaces, imperial nations and Indian empires competed for trade monopolies and power even as individuals—Native Americans, Mexicans, and Euro-Americans—competed for land and wealth.

How does Juan Seguín's experience as a *Tejano* in Texas illustrate the complexities of living in the territories between the Mississippi River and the Pacific Ocean?

Go to MindTap® to watch a video on Seguín and learn how his story relates to the themes of this chapter.

On the northern Great Plains, the Sioux sought to dominate their neighbors. In Indian Territory, tribes from the southeast United States re-established themselves. In Texas, white U.S. settlers and their slaves crossed international boundaries to establish cotton plantations. In Oregon, fur trappers from around the world created monopolies for their enterprises even as families from the eastern United States worked to build farming communities. In California, the discovery of gold drew men and women from all over the world. As these peoples and cultures clashed, the U.S. government asserted its control by sponsoring expeditions, relocating Native Americans, improving transportation and communication to promote commerce, negotiating treaty settlements, and making war that forced territorial transfers. Between 1815 and 1850, the nation expanded by more than 50 percent.

The repercussions were not limited to the United States. As Spain's empire contracted in the face of independence movements throughout the Americas, France and Britain threatened to seize new territories. The British took a renewed interest in Pacific Coast enterprises. France intervened in Mexico. The Texas province of Coahuila y Tejas broke away to form an independent nation (the turmoil in which Seguín was caught). Aggressive overtures by Britain in what would become the Pacific Northwest accelerated annexation by the United States.

11-1 Pulled and Pushed West

Winter Counts, or as Lakotas call them *waniyetu wowapi*, are calendars that tell history. They were drawn on bison hides, and each year people added information. They were called Winter Counts because they were created during the cold months when people were inside and not engaged in hunting, planting, or harvesting. ► Fine Art Premium/Corbis

As you study the image, describe the narrative being told. How could it help historians tell a more comprehensive account of migrations on the Great Plains?

Continuing the migrations of the early nineteenth century, Americans pushed beyond the former frontier lands of Ohio, Kentucky, and Tennessee, across the Mississippi River. Establishing plantations that used slave labor as in the South and small farms with commercial connections as in the North, these pioneers came into direct contact and conflict with Indians up and down the western frontier. The settlers' presence dispossessed Sac, Fox, and Sioux in the North and Cherokees, Seminoles and others in the South. The importance of Mississippi River towns, including New Orleans and St. Louis, increased as hubs for trade in cotton, wheat, and slaves. Pushing farther west, fur trappers and traders from the United States, France, Britain, and Mexico competed for the region's rich resources of beaver pelts and bison hides. In an attempt to bring order and control over this mix of people, the U.S. government sent mapping and scientific expeditions to bolster knowledge about the region and to help formulate plans for increased influence.

Indians were not the only people pushed unwillingly west. Black slaves were chained and marched from the failing tobacco fields of the Chesapeake to the southwestern frontiers. Mormons, adherents to a new American religion, fled to Utah beyond the reach of their persecutors and the U.S. government. Like the traders and planters, many migrants in the trans-Mississippi West paid little regard to national boundaries or Indian lands, eager to get what they wanted and willing to move farther west. In the vast places not yet mapped or even marched over by Euro-Americans, control by the United States, Mexico, or Britain was not much in evidence but that of the Indians was clear.

☞ As you read, consider why people were pushing —or being pushed—across the Mississippi River. How did they interact with those they encountered?

11-1a Sioux Destiny on the Great Plains

Sioux dominate the trade of the region's natural resources.

Sioux, who referred to themselves as *Oceti Sakowin*—Seven Council Fires—did not always live on the Great Plains or hunt bison. By studying

Winter Counts, historians know that although the Sioux originally lived in the Great Lakes region, white and other Indian migrations earlier in the nineteenth century had pushed them out of the Upper Missouri Valley and westward. The move disrupted not only their day-to-day lives but also their sense of themselves as a people. To combat that disruption, the Sioux told a story of their origin to explain their migration onto the Great Plains.

In their explanation, **White Buffalo Calf Woman** came to the Sioux and prophesized their success if they moved onto the Great Plains. The Sioux then reimagined themselves as a nation destined to live on the Great Plains and control the magnificent bison herds that roamed that portion of North America. This narrative provided them a religiously ordained justification for the conquest of their neighbors and their dominance of the bison hide trade, which were in high demand globally. The first population pressure on other Indians living on the Great Plains came not from Euro-Americans looking for "free" land but from the Sioux, who were pushing westward to fulfill their own prophesized destiny.

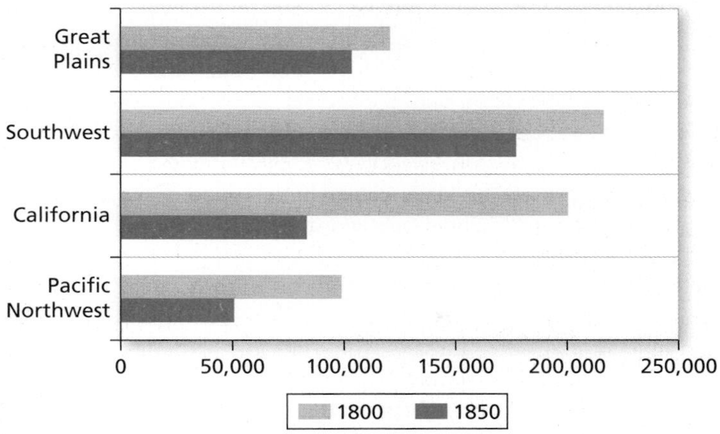

Figure 11.1 Decline in Native Populations in the U.S. West by Region, 1800–1850 Inaccuracies of census data make determining the population of Native Americans during this period difficult. For instance, the Great Plains census shows a slight decline, but historians know that the population of the Mandan decreased more than 75 percent whereas that of the Lakotas increased. These relative numbers, however, reflect the population decline that would continue through the mid-twentieth century, when they finally began to increase. ▲ Source: D. H Ubelaker. "North American Population Size, A.D. 1500 to 1985." *American Journal of Physical Anthropology* 77 (1988): 292.

The Sioux created alliances in order to move freely along the plains and control the regions' resources. The Sioux could not do all the hunting and preparing bison hides themselves, so they acted as intermediaries between other Indians and European and U.S. traders. The Sioux were spared the most dramatic impact of a smallpox epidemic when it swept through the Missouri River Valley in 1837 because their mobility allowed them to disperse themselves, fleeing the settled villages where disease spread easily. In contrast, almost half of the Indian population, forced to stay in their circumscribed territory because they feared Sioux depredations, perished in the epidemic (see Figure 11.1). The Sioux took advantage of rivals' population loss and pushed farther west and south, displacing Mandans, Hidatsas, Pawnees, Crows, and others from their hunting lands and agricultural plots. Moreover, Sioux population increased from five thousand in 1804 to more than twenty-five thousand in 1850.

Sioux expansion and ties to global markets began to decimate the vast bison herds. They moved away from hunting for subsistence and the demands of a regional economy toward fulfilling the greater demands of a market economy in bison hides, which were increasingly used for making industrial grade leather as well as fur coats. In partnership with the increasing number of Euro-American traders, the Sioux began to overhunt to meet the market demands from competing fur trade companies. To dominate this trade, the Sioux relentlessly attacked their neighbors. Although U.S. citizens, who by the early 1840s were moving across the Plains on their way to Oregon, were rarely the target of Indian attacks, they were often caught in the cross fire and competition over territory.

To settle Great Plains warfare among Indians and to open a path across the continent for those heading west, the U.S. government negotiated the **Fort Laramie Treaty** in a 1851 conference to secure safe passage so that the migrants could move west unimpeded. In addition to securing safe travel for Americans, the treaty established set boundaries (the beginnings of reservations) for many of the weaker Plains groups and defined all political relationships on the Great Plains until the 1890s. The Sioux, in alliance with Cheyennes and Arapahoes, kept other groups away from the proceedings and dominated the conference. They made a treaty that solidified their alliance with the Americans. Although the signed treaty proclaimed U.S. military presence on the Plains, it was also the U.S. government's recognition of the power of the Sioux.

11-1b Indian Removal

The U.S. government pushes Indians west.

During the same period, Choctaws, Chickasaws, Cherokees, Creeks, and Seminoles continued their ongoing warfare with the state and federal governments in the Southeast (particularly in Georgia) and the U.S. government. In the North, tribes constantly resisted their forced movement imposed on them by the Indian Removal Act of 1830.

In 1828, the "British Band" of the Sauk led by Black Hawk resisted U.S. expansion and dismissed the treaty of 1804, which they had signed, as corrupt and unjust. Black Hawk said, "Whites were in the habit of saying

White Buffalo Calf Woman Protagonist in the Sioux origin narrative that justified tribal migrations onto the Great Plains and domination over their neighbors.

Fort Laramie Treaty Agreement between the U.S. government and Plains peoples to establish boundaries and to allow white immigrants to pass safely through Indian country.

one thing to the Indians and putting another thing down on paper." The **Black Hawk War** in 1832, however, was not just a military engagement between the United States and the Sauks; it also involved a complicated set of previous alliances and enmities between France, Great Britain, the United States, Sauks, Meskwakis, and Potawatamies.

Black Hawk and his allies won an initial round of skirmishes that left the Illinois militia stunned. In response, President Andrew Jackson ordered General Winfield Scott to take over the operations and promise no treaty negotiations. Jackson wanted Black Hawk to be made an example so that other Indians would not resist the U.S. government and their removal. Black Hawk surrendered and was taken to prison in Virginia. Before being released a few months later, he toured Baltimore, Philadelphia, and New York City. He was to report back to his people about the power and size of the United States and to counsel against any future resistance to U.S. removal policy. The conclusion of the Black Hawk War opened Iowa to white settlement.

Black Hawk War Battle between the United States and the "British Band" of Indians led by Black Hawk, who crossed into U.S. territory trying to avoid conflict in their homelands.

Indian removal had long been U.S. government policy, which had been engaged in convincing Indians to move west across the Mississippi River (see Map 11.1). Along the western frontier from Michigan to Georgia, the U.S. government pushed Indians west to the Great Plains, which were already under pressure from the Sioux. The Plains were also being populated by Indians such as Kiowas and Apaches, who were fleeing the expansion of the Comanche in the southern Plains.

John Ross, the principal chief of the Cherokee nation, condemned the Indian Removal Act. In two Supreme Court case decisions, the Cherokees prevailed (see Chapter 9). The court victories, however, proved to be merely symbolic. Rather than enforce the Court's rulings granting Cherokee sovereignty, Jackson worked with officials in Georgia and the U.S. Congress to forcibly remove the Indians. He also called on a Cherokee ally, Major Ridge, who led the opposition to Ross. Ridge and Jackson had fought together during the War of 1812. Ironically, Ridge had risen to a position of power partly because in 1807 he had killed Doublehead, a Cherokee leader in the pay of the United States who had been bribed to violate a blood oath against

Map 11.1 U.S. Removal of Indians, 1830–1845 After the passage of the 1830 Indian Removal Act, the federal government legally pushed Indians from their homelands in the regions noted in the map to the far West. Tens of thousands lost their property and family networks and had to start over in Indian Territory, part of which was later organized as the state of Oklahoma. By 1837, the Jackson administration had relocated more than fifty thousand people and opened 25 million acres of land for white settlement. ▼

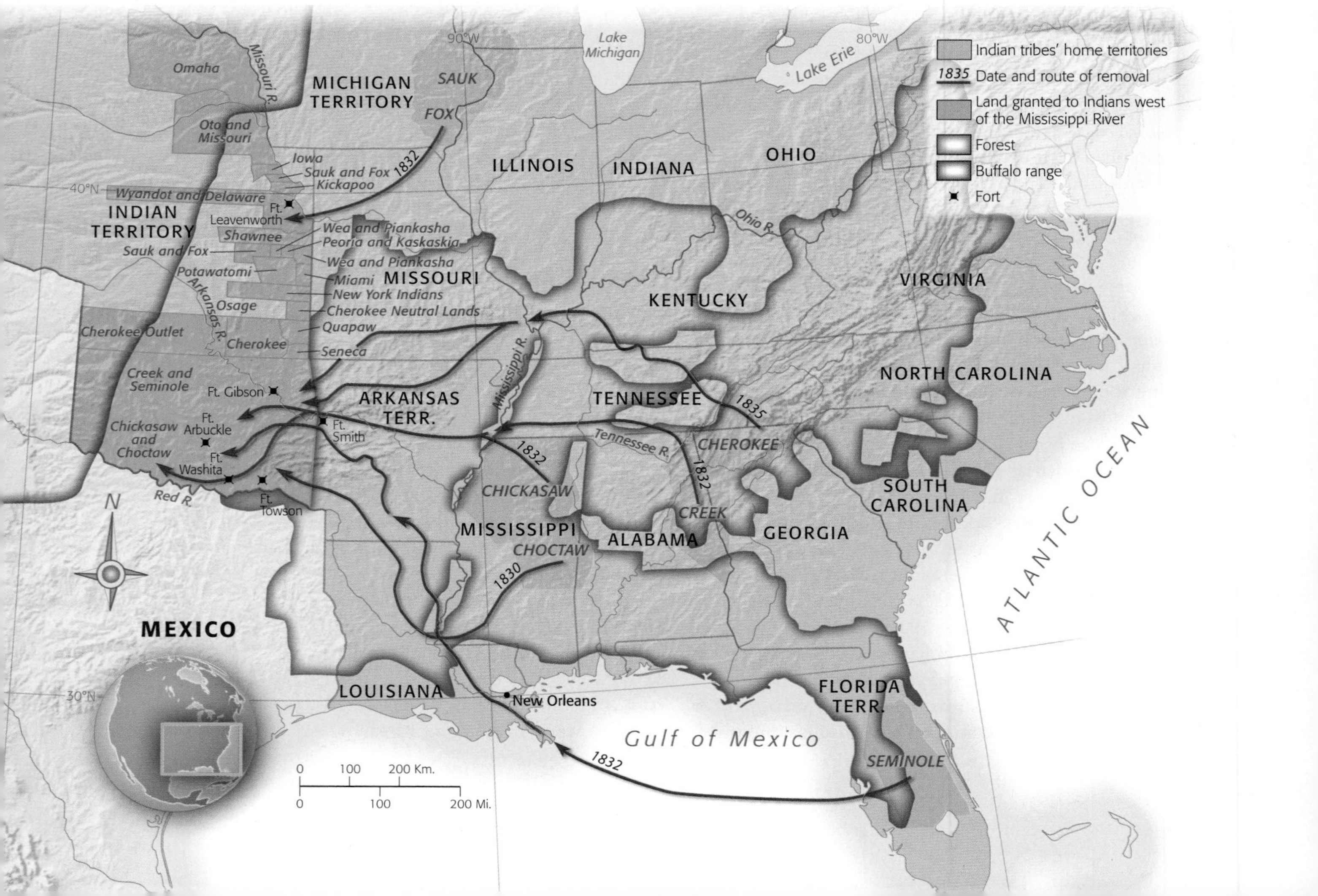

signing treaties that ceded Cherokee lands. But twenty-eight years later, Ridge led the Cherokees, who believed that it was pointless to oppose removal and instead sought the land in the West as compensation.

In 1836, the U.S. government negotiated the **Treaty of New Echota** with the Treaty Party, a small group of Cherokees led by Major Ridge and his son John Ridge; they did not represent the majority and were not the elected government. The Treaty promised to pay $5 million to Cherokees to be paid in per capita payments, promised to cover the traveling costs of those who moved, and gave Cherokees an amount of land, equivalent in acreage to that lost in Georgia, in **Indian Territory** (present day Oklahoma). Many Americans who opposed the treaty saw the inherent unfairness to the Cherokees. Others questioned the wisdom of siding with President Jackson against the Supreme Court. Some who opposed the treaty would eventually become antislavery advocates in Congress—most famously, the former president, John Quincy Adams. Despite heated opposition, the U.S. Senate ratified the treaty by a margin of one vote. It gave the Cherokees two years to remove themselves to Indian Territory.

Those who followed Ridge left almost immediately. Many in the Ross party, however, continued to hope that they could negotiate to stay in their homes. But the state of Georgia ignored their petitions and held a lottery in which whites received Cherokee lands, houses, and improved fields. As the 1838 deadline approached, General Scott arrived to round up Cherokees from their homes, put them into holding pens, and then lead them overland in the winter to Oklahoma in what has become known as the **Trail of Tears**. The conditions on the trail were brutal as families struggled to stay together and survive in the face of inadequate provisions, drought, harsh weather conditions, and disease. In the winter of 1838–1839 as they moved to their lands across the Mississippi, leaving behind their property and most of their possessions, more than 25 percent of those who had set out on the trail died. Estimates range from 4,000 to 8,000 lives lost during the entire removal process. Quatie, the white wife of John Ross, died of exposure after giving her only blanket to a small child who had none. No Cherokee family was left unscathed by the process of removal.

In Oklahoma, Cherokees came into conflict with U.S. settlers who were pushing into Mexican-controlled Texas to the south and other Indians who were fleeing from Sioux and Comanche dominance. Despite a harsher and drier climate than the one they had left in Georgia, Cherokees built homes and businesses and created a new government while the Ross and Ridge factions vied for political power. The bitter division between the factions escalated as the majority of Cherokees blamed the Ridge family for their hardships in Oklahoma. On June 22, 1839, Major Ridge, his nephew, and his son were murdered for what many Cherokees considered their treason in selling land in Georgia. Revenge killings continued until 1845 when U.S. federal troops were called in to prevent a civil war among the Cherokees.

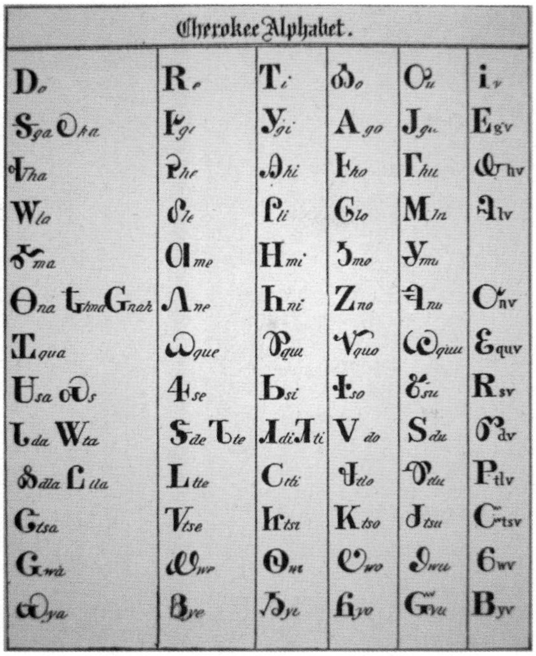

Sequoyah and the Syllabary In the late 1810s, Sequoyah developed a syllabary (a series or set of written characters) so that Cherokees could communicate with one another in writing. Sequoyah did not know how to read or write in any other language. Each of the eighty-five characters in his syllabary represents a syllable. Within a decade, Cherokees had achieved almost 90 percent literacy (much higher than anywhere else in North America). The Cherokee community had a printing press that published a newspaper, books, fliers, and hymnals. ▲

11-1c Maps, Trails, and Trade

Global and local economies become increasingly intertwined.

After the success of the Lewis and Clark Expedition and the acquisition of territory from the Transcontinental (Adams-Onis) Treaty, the U.S. government wanted to explore and map these new acquisitions (see Map 11.2). Its curiosity extended far beyond the North American continent. In 1836, President Jackson authorized the U.S. Exploration Expedition to survey and collect data from the South Pacific and Antarctic regions. The military venture included civilian scientists who collected plant samples, drew images, and wrote scientific entries about all they encountered. Between 1838 and 1842, the expedition of six ships commanded by Navy Lieutenant Charles Wilkes encountered many indigenous peoples, often using violence. Wilkes

Treaty of New Echota Agreement signed by the U.S. government and the Treaty Party of the Cherokees, who agreed to remove themselves to present-day Oklahoma.

Indian Territory Area of federal lands in the western United States that was set aside for Indians who were removed from their ancestral homelands.

Trail of Tears Name of a series of forced migrations of Native Americans from their homelands in the southeast United States to federal territories in the U.S. West.

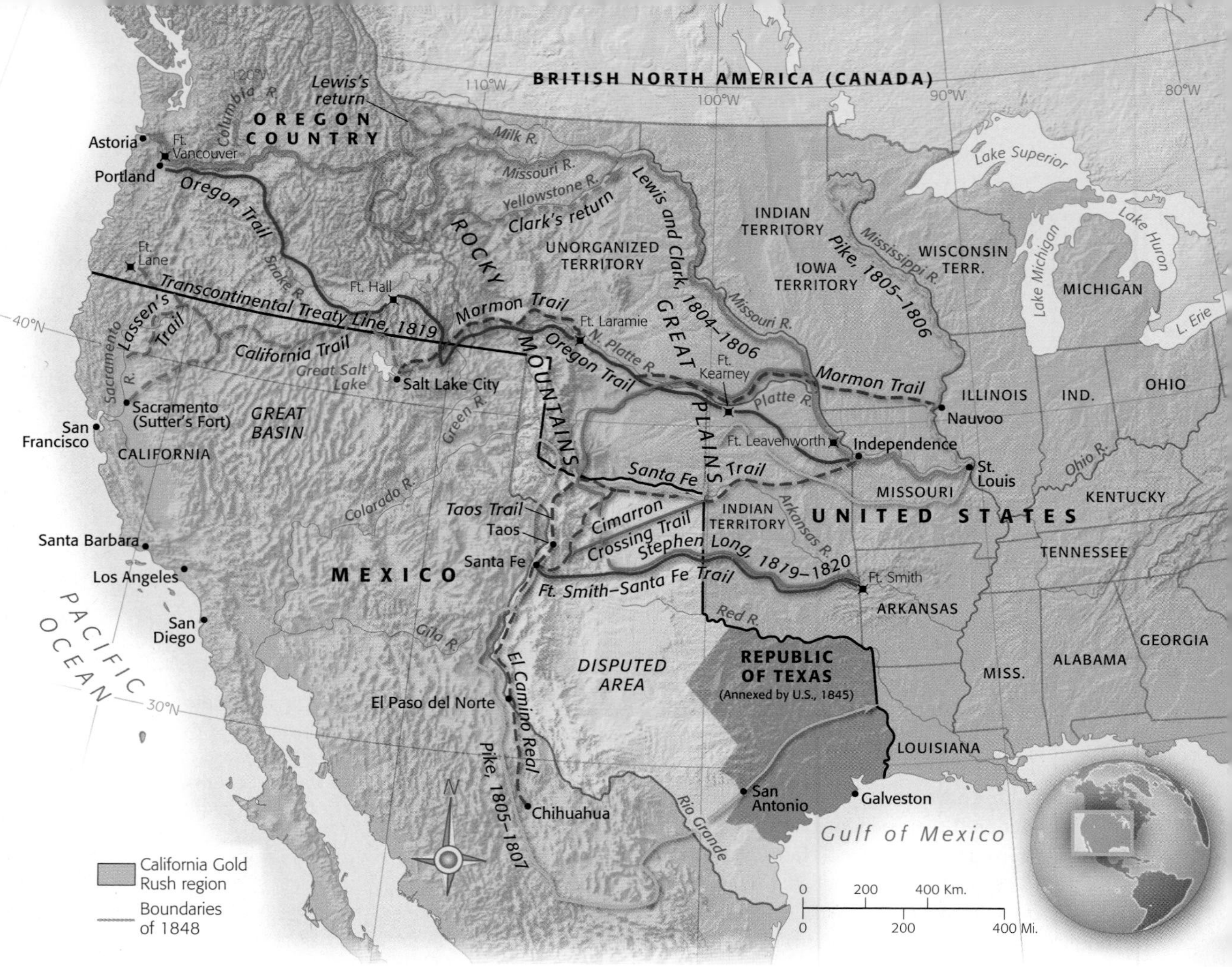

Map 11.2 Trails to the West, 1804–1850 Far from being an empty space when white settlers began their migration, what would become known as the U.S. West was already filled with thousands of Native Americans who had complex economies and thriving communities. These routes into the interior of the West show how white settlers followed rivers and Indian trading trails to make their incursions. These were well-known paths that had served indigenous communities for generations but became the highways that brought settlers into Indian country. ▲

found it difficult to balance the military and scientific missions. Upon the expedition's return, its collections became the basis for both the National Botanical Garden and the newly created **Smithsonian Institution**.

Exacerbating the contest over lands and trading routes in the middle part of the North American continent, thousands of Americans and Europeans came in search of economic opportunities. Throughout the first part of the nineteenth century, the Mississippi and Missouri Rivers had been the highways on which trade was conducted through the continent's interior. The U.S. government sent out expeditions and created bureaucracies to control and map these lands in preparation for settlement. In addition to these government-sponsored explorers and some early settlers trekking along the trails, U.S. and European fur trade companies led by John Jacob Astor, Manuel Lisa, and the Choteau family dominated the region economically.

Smithsonian Institution U.S. national museum with headquarters in Washington, D.C., funded by a bequest from the British scientist, James Smithsonian.

The Lewis and Clark expedition was only the first of many government-sponsored forays into the West to map and explore the region from the Mississippi to the Pacific Ocean and, when possible, from the northern reaches of Mexico's territories north to British territory. In 1806, Zebulon Pike headed west to map the Louisiana Purchase and to find the headwaters of the Arkansas and Red Rivers. He entered Spanish territory in present-day southern Colorado and built a fort for the winter. The Spanish government arrested Pike for trespassing and took him to Mexico City where he was able to observe and then report back on the landscape, resources, and peoples of the region.

Global Americans **William** and **Charles Bent**

made their lives on the edge of three cultures: the United States, Mexico, and Indian country. The brothers came from a large prosperous family in St. Louis, Missouri. They headed west to find their fortunes in the emerging fur markets. In 1833, along with their friend Ceran St. Vrain, they established Bent's Fort, which sat on the Santa Fe Trail and in Mexican territory.

Bent's Fort was the only outpost between St. Louis and Santa Fe and functioned as a free trade zone. It was not under the control of the United States, Mexico, or any particular Indian tribe, although the Bents worked closely with the local Indians to establish the post. This freedom extended beyond the economic and into the social realm. It was a place where people from many nations intermingled with Americans and Indians from a wide range of plains groups. The Bents also brought three slaves, the Green family, to the Fort.

The Bents made strategic marital alliances. William married Owl Woman, the daughter of White Thunder, a Cheyenne elder of considerable stature. They had four children. Charles wed Maria Ignacia Jaramillo, who was from a prominent *Hispano* family. He used this connection to promote the trading posts and to acquire thousands of acres of land. The Bents' network across this borderland between nations represented a world where exchanges flowed freely with little constraint from government or society.

▲ (Left) The Granger Collection, New York. (Right) Center for Southwest Research, University Libraries, University of New Mexico

The **U.S. Army Corps of Engineers** had been established in 1779 to coordinate military efforts, propose infrastructure improvements, and to map the West. In 1824, Congress passed the **General Survey Act**, which provided the authorization for the Corps to survey road and canal routes into the interior of North America. One of the most effective surveyors during this period was Stephen H. Long. He completed five surveys, covered 26,000 miles, and was the first to label the Great Plains as the Great American Desert.

Official government expeditions acquired much knowledge and shared it through informal trade networks. For example, William Clark kept a map in his St. Louis office where fur traders, explorers, and travelers to the West would come and add to the map what they had seen or just study it to understand what type of terrain they were heading into. The **Clark Map**, as it came to be known, was the physical embodiment of knowledge about the American West as it changed over time.

Enterprise and trade often preceded the government into the West. The development of the **Santa Fe Trail** from St. Louis to Santa Fe, where it met the Chihuahua Trail, began in earnest after Mexico had gained independence from Spain in 1821. The trails, which were based on known Indian trade routes, created a highway of multinational people who traded everything from furniture and cloth to foodstuffs and raw goods in a trading system that linked the West to New York, Mexico City, London, and China. By the 1830s, fur trapping had also become an important part of this developing economy along the Santa Fe Trail. In 1833, William and Charles Bent and their partner Ceran St. Vrain established Bent's Fort. Long

Clark's Map, 1810 Upon his return from the Lewis and Clark expedition, William Clark drew a map of the trans-Mississippi West. During his time as territorial governor of Missouri, he kept the map in his office where returning travelers would stop by to talk about their travels and make additions and edits to the map. ▼

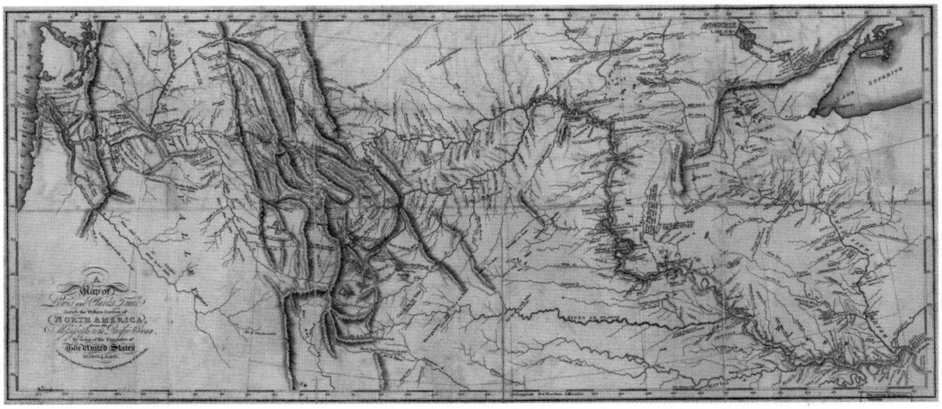

American Memory, Geography and Map Division, Library of Congress

U.S. Army Corps of Engineers Military division created to provide domestic and military engineering services including the building of canals, roads, and dams.

General Survey Act Legislation passed after *Gibbons v. Ogden* decision that gave the federal government authority over interstate commerce to fund the building of roads and canals.

Clark Map Master map created by Clark in 1810 when he returned to St. Louis after his expedition with Lewis, providing essential cartographic information for the next twenty-five years.

THE MORMON HAND-CART COMPANY CROSSING THE PLAINS.
North Wind Picture Archives/Alamy Stock Photo

Mormon Migration Mormon migrations differed significantly from other white migrations into the U.S. West. Whereas most families who migrated brought as many possessions and provisions as they could carry, Mormon families traveled light because they wanted to get to Utah as quickly as possible. As a result, families used these pushcarts, taking only what would fit and what one man could pull over more than 900 miles from Winter Quarters to Salt Lake City. ◄

before the U.S. government could dominate the region, these traders and their Indian allies had created a thriving economy and multinational community.

The West was crisscrossed with various trade routes that would eventually become overland trails for settlers moving from the East into California and Oregon. By the early 1840s, settlers moved across the Oregon Trail, the Santa Fe Trail, the Platte Road, and what became known as the **Mormon Trail**. Migration to the West depended on the U.S. government's ability to control Indian violence by creating a system of forts that could aid settlers.

Unlike the market-driven movement of fur traders and trappers, the Mormon migration by members of the Church of Jesus Christ of Latter-day Saints (see Chapter 10) was one of the most organized and hierarchical migrations into the U.S. West. Because they were persecuted for their religious beliefs, their forced westward trek from 1831 to 1838 took them through western New York, Ohio, Illinois, and Missouri. They created thriving communities that grew rapidly but were always harassed by suspicious locals. In 1843, their prophet Joseph Smith claimed to have received a revelation regarding **polygamy**.

Santa Fe Trail Overland trade route from Franklin, Missouri, to Santa Fe, New Mexico where it connected with the *Camino Real*, linking the region directly to Mexico City.

Mormon Trail Overland route used by Mormons fleeing persecution, linking Nauvoo, Illinois, with Salt Lake City, Utah.

polygamy The practice of one man marrying multiple women that Joseph Smith declared in 1831 to be a tenet of the Mormon Church.

The revelation was immediately controversial. Smith constantly defended himself against outsiders, and many Mormons doubted the revelation and the place of polygamy in their religious practice. After a series of confrontations between Smith and the Illinois government, Smith turned himself in to the local sheriff at Carthage. While he was in jail, a mob attacked, killing him and his brother Hiram. To avoid more attacks, the Mormons, under the leadership of their new prophet, Brigham Young, pushed westward to find a new home.

Fearing interference from the U.S. government, Young wanted to move the immigrants westward into Mexican territory in February 1846. He then struck a bargain with President James K. Polk, who had just declared that a state of war existed with Mexico. The Mormons were allowed to make their encampment on U.S. government land in Nebraska and agreed to send 543 men, the Mormon Battalion, to fight Mexico. The government wages provided much needed cash to aid Mormon families who were slowly moving westward. They, like the Sioux in the Treaty of Fort Laramie, exchanged their military cooperation for access to land.

In the spring of 1847, after making his way across the Great Plains, Young stood atop the Wasatch Range and looked into the Utah Valley and proclaimed, "This is the place." But "this" turned out to be territory held by Utes, who were not interested in sharing the fertile valley with the Mormon immigrants. Sensing that they could not challenge the powerful Utes, Young moved south and settled in the arid and desolate Salt Lake Valley. The advance group began planting crops, building shelter and fences, and preparing for an onslaught of immigrants while Young returned to Nebraska to lead his flock to the Salt Lake Valley. Sixteen thousand men, women, and children with their household goods and animals walked to Utah. The poorer immigrants took only what they could carry in handheld pushcarts or on their backs. In 1849, to ensure their success, Young, under the guidelines of the Northwest Ordinance, established a territorial government and the state of Deseret (meaning honeybee) of which he was the governor.

11-2 National Destiny

MPI/Archive Photos/Getty Images

The Fall of the Alamo by Robert Jenkins Onderdonk (1903) depicts the way that many Americans, Texans in particular, choose to remember the battle at the Alamo. It depicts Davy Crockett, out of ammunition, beating off Mexican soldiers before he dies a valiant martyr's death. Although contemporary witnesses and historians later disputed the events as shown here, some suggesting that Crockett had been captured and executed, most chose to believe the myth that had been created about the defenders of the Alamo.

How does Onderdonk portray Davy Crockett in the painting? How does he depict the Mexican army's attack on the Alamo? ►

In the 1830s and 1840s as Indian treaties and removals opened land across the Mississippi to settlement, many Americans began thinking of themselves as part of a continental nation. What would it take to realize a nation that would stretch from the Atlantic to the Pacific? Already, American settlers were ignoring national boundaries to take up residence in the Mexican province of Coahuila y Tejas, as well as in Oregon where a joint occupation with Britain had followed treaties negotiating the withdrawal of both Russian and Spanish claims. By the 1830s, the presence of Americans in Texas and Oregon accelerated interest in making these regions part of the United States. But with that land came the people who had inhabited it for centuries, and Americans reacted in different ways to the prospect of incorporating them into the United States.

☞ As you read, consider how U.S. settlers regarded national boundaries. Why did Americans continue to look beyond their established borders to expand U.S. influence?

11-2a Conflict in the Texas Borderland

A new republic breaks away from Mexico.

After the Louisiana Purchase in 1803, the boundary with Mexico was uncertain. The United States sponsored explorers such as Pike and John C. Fremont to mark the boundaries of the nation and spy on their Mexican neighbors. Illegal explorations, **filibusters**, also crossed these unmarked borders. For example, Augustus Magee, a former lieutenant in the U.S. army, raised a force of three hundred men to cross into Texas to help free the province from the Spanish in 1812. While the expedition was unsuccessful, it revealed a pattern of U.S. citizens crossing borders to further U.S. interests, even if unsanctioned by the government. Although the Treaty of 1819 specified the U.S.-Mexico border and renounced all U.S. claims to Texas, the border still remained a porous and largely symbolic line that few recognized. Southerners in particular resented that Texas, along with Florida, had not been ceded by the Spanish as they wanted to push slavery farther west into Texas's cotton-growing areas.

Tejas y Coahuila was sparsely populated by Spanish, and later Mexican citizens. Because of its distance from Mexico City, the province was poorly served by the government. The outposts continually confronted Comanches who raided their communities for horses, cattle, and captives. Nevertheless, the province's struggling missions, along with the settled population of farmers, maintained cattle ranches and strong communities that drew the attention of slaveholders in the U.S. South.

Once Mexico gained independence from Spain in 1821, the Mexican government worked to secure its northern border against the United States. The government worried that foreigners—Americans, Russians, and the British—would overrun New Mexico, Alta and Baja California, and Tejas y Coahuila. Because Texas seemed the most susceptible of these to foreign and Indian incursions, the Mexican government encouraged foreigners, particularly Americans, to emigrate under the Mexican government's terms. These immigrants would gain property rights to millions of acres if they agreed to become Mexican citizens and convert to Catholicism. Thousands of U.S. citizens, particularly those moving from Tennessee and Kentucky, accepted the offer and started new lives as Mexican citizens. Many of them married into elite, property-owning *Tejano* families, like the Seguíns (see Table 11.1).

In 1821, Moses Austin, a New Englander who had sought his fortune in lead mining in upper Louisiana, was drawn by Mexico's offer and negotiated an ***empresario*** contract whereby he would settle 300 families on 100,000 acres of Texas land. Austin died before he could fulfill his contract, and in 1821 the colonial government was overthrown and the Republic of

filibusters A person who enters a foreign territory with the intention of starting a rebellion or uprising, which was associated with U.S. presence in Latin America.

empresario A person to whom the Spanish and later Mexican governments granted large areas, sometimes millions of acres, of land.

Table 11.1 Racial Terminology Used in North America circa 1820–1850

The historical terms listed here describe ethnic groups mentioned in this chapter who populated the North American continent. In addition to these terms, groups would have also had derogatory terms to describe one another.

Term	Definition
Tejana/o	People of Mexican descent residing in Texas and who became U.S. citizens after 1845
Hispana/o	People of Mexican descent residing in New Mexico and who became U.S. citizens after 1912
California/o	People of Mexican descent residing in California and who became U.S. citizens after 1848
Mestiza/o	People of mixed racial or ethnic backgrounds
Mexicana/o	U.S. citizens of Mexican descent
Mexican	Citizen of Mexico
Mexican–American	U.S. inhabitants of Mexican descent
Anglo	People of European descent
Gentile	Term used by Mormons to describe non-Mormons; could apply equally to Catholics, Protestants, and Jews
Indian	General term used to describe indigenous peoples of North America
Métis	People of mixed heritage from European and Indian parents; used mostly by the French
Pueblos	Native Americans who lived along the Rio Grande Valley in New Mexico

Mexico soon established. Moses Austin's son, Stephen, renegotiated the arrangement with the newly independent Mexico, fulfilling the requirement that he convert to Catholicism, and eventually settled more than nine hundred people in Texas. Ninety percent of them were southerners who intended to grow cotton using slave labor. Although Mexico abolished slavery in 1829, Tejanos ignored the law and blacks remained enslaved.

Texas, like New Mexico and California, was far from the seat of political power in Mexico City. Like the Regulators in backcountry North and South Carolina, these *Tejanos* on the nation's northern frontier often felt neglected in receiving adequate government financial aid and military protection against Indians. Most of the immigrants to Texas had strong ties to the United States, looked eastward for cotton markets, and hoped for eventual union with the United States. In 1826, Haden and Benjamin Edwards rebelled against the Mexican government and formed an alliance with Indians and *métis*. The group seized Nagadoches, Texas, in an effort to wrest independence from Mexico. Stephen Austin, who supported the emerging Mexican republic, and his men subdued the rebellion. Perceiving the revolt to be a result of southern U.S. influence, the Mexican government banned the further importation of slaves and prohibited any further immigration from the United States. Austin and other Texas leaders accepted these limitations reluctantly.

Alamo A Texas mission in which the Mexican government laid siege to Texas rebels for 13 days in the spring of 1836 before defeating them.

The Treaty of Velasco The 1836 treaty that ended hostilities between the Mexican government and the Texas rebels after the defeat of Santa Anna at San Jacinto.

Eight years later, however, General Antonio Lopez de Santa Anna renounced the republican, federal form of government and declared himself dictator, preferring a more centralized form of government. Santa Anna dissolved the Constitution of 1824, angering the Texans who expected to live under a democracy. Austin and other leaders, including Juan Seguín, pushed for Texas independence. In rhetoric recalling the American Revolution, leaders stated that they were preserving the Mexican Republic and were rebelling only against Santa Anna's tyranny.

While many immediately hoped for Texas to be granted U.S. statehood, their public rhetoric merely called for a return to Mexico's own republican ideals. On March 2, 1836, Texas leaders declared independence from Mexico and wrote a constitution that borrowed heavily from the U.S. Constitution but prohibited the Texas legislature from interfering with slavery and free blacks from residing in the territory. A number of prominent *Tejanos* signed their names to the document, including Lorenzo de Zavala who became vice president of the new republic.

General Santa Anna amassed a force of seven thousand troops to squash the rebellion outside the **Alamo** in San Antonio. William Travis, the commander at the fort, sent Juan Seguín to tell the newly elected president, Sam Houston, of the Alamo's siege and to bring back reinforcements. After a two-week siege, he attacked the garrison, killing almost all of the 187 men, 10 percent of whom were *Tejanos*. Santa Anna sustained a serious loss of 1,500 men, but he continued his march north wiping out the Texas forces at Goliad, including summary executions of 300 *Tejanos*.

Following a month of preparation and recruiting volunteers from the United States, President Sam Houston, the commander of the Texas forces, led a surprise charge on Santa Anna's forces at San Jacinto. In just over fifteen minutes, Houston's troops defeated the Mexican forces and captured Santa Anna. After such a humiliating defeat, Santa Anna could do little but accept Texas independence under the terms of the **Treaty of Velasco**. The Mexican Congress, however, repudiated the treaty, refused to recognize Texas independence, and stripped Santa Anna of his power, banishing him to Cuba. The United States recognized Texas as a sovereign nation but did not consider it for statehood because doing so would shift the balance of free and slave states. From 1836 to 1845, Texas was known as the *Lone Star Republic*.

AP Images/Harry Cabluck

***The Surrender of Santa Anna*, 1896** This painting by William H. Huddle depicts Santa Anna surrendering to Houston, who is shown injured, lying under an oak tree with a bandaged leg. The defeated Santa Anna is depicted wearing the white pants of a private. ◄

11-2b The West as the Future

Politicians discuss the West and the expansion of slavery.

In 1839, John L. O'Sullivan, a prominent political commentator and editor of *The Democratic Review*, published "The Great Nation of Futurity." He argued that Americans were uniquely free from the brutality of European history. He wrote, "The expansive future is our arena, and for our history. . . . We are the nation of human progress." O'Sullivan often spoke for the expansionist wing of the Democratic Party, extolling the need to push west for the sake of expanding the nation's democratic principles to those in the Mexican and British provinces, which he claimed would not otherwise enjoy those freedoms.

National politics between 1835 and 1845 increasingly focused on the West. The slavery issue came into play with each new territory that petitioned for statehood (see Table 11.2). Politicians strove to maintain the precarious balance between free and slave states in the Senate that had been achieved with the Missouri Compromise in 1820.

Presidential elections began to reflect the increasing political importance of the West. In 1828, Andrew Jackson became the first president elected from a state west of the Appalachian Mountains. In 1840, the Whigs ran William Henry Harrison of Indiana, another famed Indian fighter and the military hero of the Battle of Tippecanoe. Although born wealthy on a Virginia plantation, he was recast as a hard-drinking westerner, a man of the people born in a log cabin. John Tyler, a former Democrat, was his running mate. The Whigs rallied their supporters with parades featuring barrels of hard cider, miniature log cabins, and the slogan "Tippecanoe and Tyler Too!"

The Democratic nominee, President Martin Van Buren of New York, had faced the Panic of 1837 and the ensuing depression. Whigs blamed the economic downturn on the inactivity of the federal government and lampooned the president as "Martin Van Ruin." In contrast to Harrison's tough warrior image, they derided the president's masculinity, declaring "Van, Van is a used-up man." James G. Birney, a former slaveholder, ran on the **Liberty Party** ticket, a single-issue, electorally weak party that aimed to bring opposition to slavery to the forefront of national

Liberty Party Third-party that broke away from the U.S. Anti-Slavery Society to advocate the use of the Constitution to abolish slavery.

Table 11.2 Free and Slave States Admitted between 1800–1850

During the first half of the nineteenth century, the balance of power between free and slave states was precarious. The eight states admitted as slave states allowed settlers to import their human property without fear of confiscation. National confrontations over the place of slavery played out in the western territories to which immigrants moved. To make way in these regions for the settlers and their new labor systems, whether free or slave, Indians were removed from their homelands.

Year	State	Status
1803	Ohio	Free
1812	Louisiana	Slave
1816	Indiana	Free
1817	Mississippi	Slave
1818	Illinois	Free
1819	Alabama	Slave
1820	Maine	Free
1821	Missouri	Slave
1836	Arkansas	Slave
1837	Michigan	Free
1845	Florida	Slave
1845	Texas	Slave
1846	Iowa	Free
1848	Wisconsin	Free
1850	California	Free

politics. For the next twenty years, every national politician would need to address the issue directly.

Harrison won the election of 1840 by a landslide, taking 234 electoral votes to Van Buren's 60. Refusing to wear a hat or overcoat on a cold, wet day, Harrison gave a nearly two-hour inaugural address, the longest in U.S. history. He developed pneumonia and died only a month after taking office, leaving the presidency to John Tyler. A lifelong Democrat, Tyler had joined the Whig Party only because he opposed Jackson's promise to use force against South Carolina during the nullification crisis. As president, Tyler opposed all efforts by the Whigs to pass their program of federally financed improvements, vetoing their efforts to raise the tariff and create a bank. Furious over his vetoes, which Whigs compared to Jackson's veto of the Bank Bill, they expelled Tyler from the party. For the next four years, the federal government was gridlocked.

Preemption Act Legislation that permitted settlers, also known as squatters, to purchase the land they occupied on federal claimed lands for $1.25 an acre.

The only policy the parties could agree on was westward expansion and allocation of public lands (see Map 11.3). Congress enacted the **Preemption Act** in 1841, which allowed squatters on public land to purchase 160 acres at the minimum price of $1.25 an acre. Much of this land was in newly acquired territories in the old northwest and southeast, sites of intense efforts to remove Indians and promote white settlement. Western expansion was one of the few areas of bipartisan consensus at a time when the parties were deadlocked over the proper role of the federal government. Ever since Jefferson had bought the Louisiana Purchase, Democrats had understood that western expansion was an exception to their philosophy of limited federal government. Southern Democrats rallied to the idea of more slave states and called for the annexation of Texas, and nationalists denounced the British and called for the annexation of Oregon Territory. Even President Tyler, a "states' rights" politician who was otherwise suspicious of vigorous federal power, could see the political benefits of western expansion.

The issues of westward expansion, particularly the issue of Texas **annexation**, and slavery dominated the election of 1844. The Democratic Party was divided on the issue of slavery. Antislavery Democrats, such as Van Buren, opposed

Map 11.3 U.S. Geographic Expansion, 1800–1860 During the first half of the nineteenth century, the United States more than doubled its territory and became a continental nation. In the process of expansion it overtook Native American communities as well as pushed out foreign nations such as Great Britain, France, Spain, Russia, and Mexico. The U.S. military and settlers used well-established trails to make their incursions, and by 1850 most of the continent was occupied and controlled by the United States. ▼

annexation, but proexpansion Democrats engineered the presidential nomination of James Polk, a Tennessee congressman who pushed for the annexation of both Oregon and Texas. On the other side, most Whigs were hostile to the idea of adding a slave state to the Union. Their nominee, Henry Clay, took an ambiguous position on the annexation of Texas. In a close race, Polk won on a platform of expansion.

Tyler, a lame-duck president, denied Polk the chance to annex Texas by pressing Congress to pass a joint resolution inviting Texas to join the Union. Unlike a treaty, the resolution did not require a two-thirds vote in the Senate and, therefore, could not be blocked by antislavery Democrats and Whigs. Proslavery Americans had been migrating in large numbers to Texas for a decade, and they outnumbered *Tejanos* by a margin of eight to one. Even influential *Tejanos* such as Juan Seguín were marginalized. Not surprisingly, the Texas legislature ratified the annexation resolution treaty, and Texas joined the Union as a slave state on December 29, 1845. Once Texas was open to U.S. settlement, southerners pushed westward into the area around its eastern rivers where cotton plantations worked by slaves had sprung up and was ripe for the expansion of slavery. The annexation also created a diplomatic crisis with Mexico.

Two earlier events contributed to the crisis. In March 1845, Florida, a former colony of both Spain and Britain, had joined the Union as a slave state. Then, in the summer of 1845, in the midst of the debate over Texas, O'Sullivan suggested in the *Democratic Review* that it was the "manifest destiny" of the United States "to overspread the continent allotted by Providence for the free development of our yearly multiplying millions." He articulated the ideology underlying the U.S. expansion, which had been in place since President Jefferson had sent Lewis and Clark west to explore the northwest. The term **manifest destiny** resonated in public and political discourse. O'Sullivan warned that "other nations" had "intruded" themselves in Texas, a violation of the Monroe Doctrine. He also asserted the superiority of U.S. political institutions over those of Mexico and predicted that California would naturally "next fall away" from Mexico's tenuous ("imbecile and distracted") hold. "The Anglo-Saxon foot is already on its borders." O'Sullivan's words spoke to Americans who wanted to secure territory for the expansion of the U.S. economy in general and slavery specifically. Just as the Sioux used the White Buffalo Calf Woman narrative to justify their claims, so the U.S. found in the ideology of Manifest Destiny a religious justification for expansion.

The U.S. annexation of Texas portended war against a neighboring republic. Since 1824, Mexico had been an independent republic with a constitution that had established a federal republic of nineteen states and four territories. Unlike the U.S. Constitution, the Mexican Constitution included Indians as citizens, outlawed slavery, and had fewer racial or property restrictions regarding suffrage or holding public office. But the Mexican Constitution proved incapable of constraining the power of the central government. As the rhetoric of Manifest Destiny became heated, most Americans willingly set aside Mexico's sovereignty to take advantage of its weaknesses.

11-2c U.S.–Canada Border and the Oregon Question

The U.S. government finally resolves its border issues with Great Britain.

With the nation's political focus on the West and the escalation of hostilities with Mexico over Texas, pressure built to settle the question of the Oregon border peacefully. Since the Revolutionary era, Britain and the United States had been in constant dispute about their shared border at various locations from Maine to Oregon. In an effort to avoid hostilities, the two nations had jointly occupied Oregon since 1818. In 1842, after clashes over the boundary between New Brunswick and Maine, the two countries signed the **Webster-Ashburton Treaty** to clarify the northeastern border between the two nations.

In the far west, Great Britain had discouraged settlement in order to protect its fur trade, but the U.S. government promoted the settlement of family farms. What began in the late 1830s as a trickle of missionaries, such as the Whitmans (Chapter 10), and fur traders trekking westward picked up momentum, and by 1843, almost one thousand immigrants were making their home in the jointly occupied territory. By 1845, two thousand five hundred people had crossed the Great Plains through Indian lands to get to Oregon. As John C. Calhoun noted, it was "wise and masterly inactivity" that had allowed what was called the **Great Migration** and would also allow the Oregon Question to be decided by the settlers in the territory.

Tensions with Mexico made the settlement even more imperative. The settlers and their expansionist allies pressured the newly elected President Polk to resolve the dispute as he had promised in his 1844 campaign slogan of "Fifty-four forty or fight!" that is, setting the northern border of Oregon at the latitude line of fifty-four degrees, forty minutes. In the Oregon Treaty of 1846, however, Polk compromised and retained only half of the U.S. claim, making the **forty-ninth parallel** the border with Canada. Great Britain kept the Vancouver Islands. As tensions with Mexico rose, Polk wanted to avoid a simultaneous war with a much stronger British foe. Because Oregon Territory was not conducive to slavery, Polk's settlement also provided a way to balance the recent annexation of Texas, a slave territory. It was a precarious balancing act for Polk.

annexation The addition of territory, sometimes by force, to another nation, state, or city.

manifest destiny Popular belief in the United States in the early nineteenth century that the nation was destined to rule over North America.

Webster-Ashburton Treaty Agreement between the United States and Great Britain that established the border between the two countries in the eastern half of North America.

Great Migration (1843) Movement of almost one thousand U.S. settlers to Oregon Territory, overwhelming their British counterparts.

forty-ninth parallel Latitude used by the Oregon Treaty of 1846 to mark the international boundary between Canada and the United States.

History without Borders

Violence on Settler Frontiers

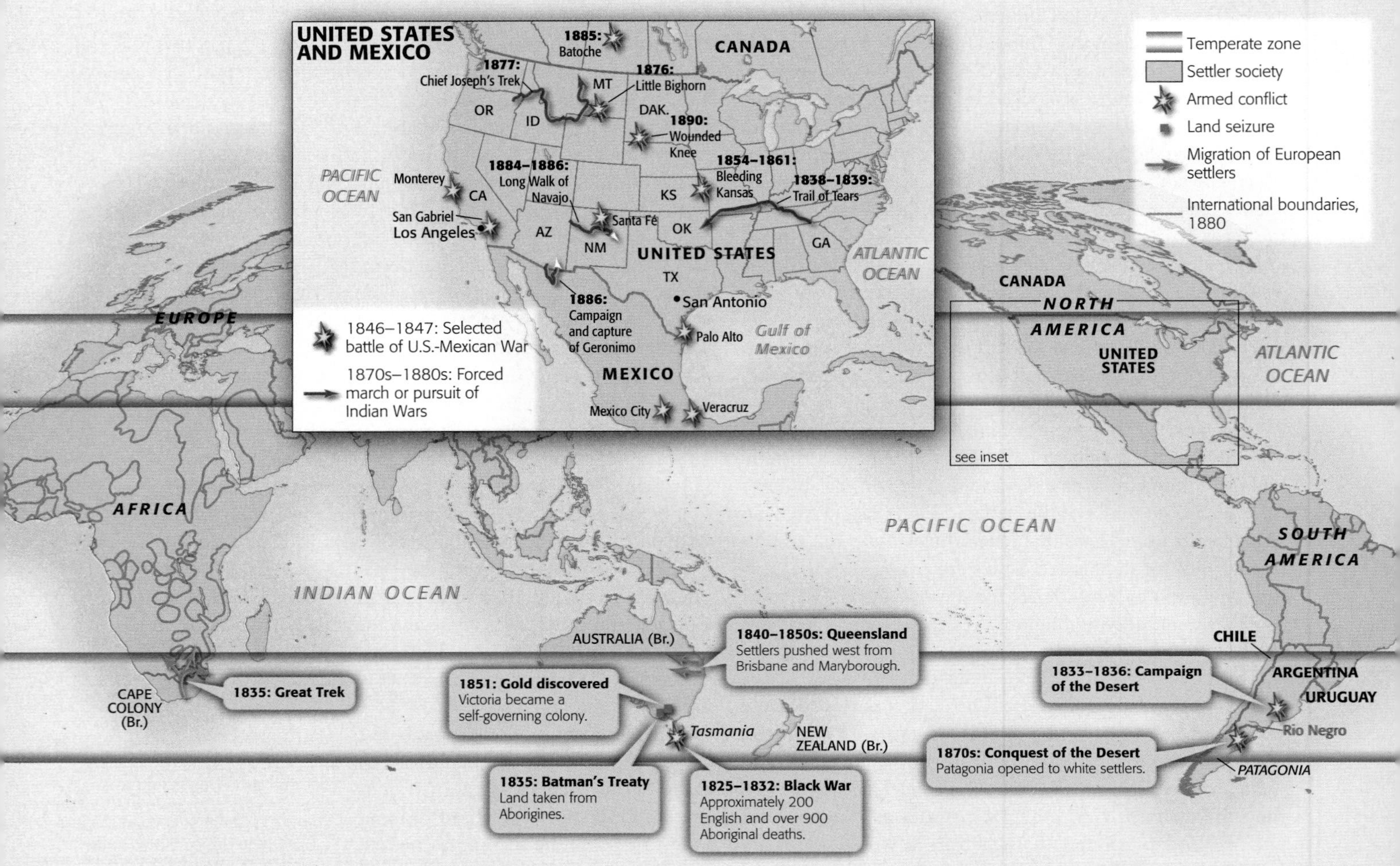

Migrations and Frontier Conflicts, 1825–1890 During the nineteenth century, other nations, as well as the United States, were expanding their global reach through warfare, trade, and colonialism. These countries tended to migrate towards the temperate zones where they found comfortable climates and abundant natural resources. These colonizing enterprises also found resistant native peoples who did not want to share their resources with the interlopers. The nineteenth century, as depicted on this map, is marked by violence as settler societies imposed themselves on native communities. ▲

Once we discard the myth that the American interior was unoccupied land, it becomes another example of borderland conflict that spread globally as Europe's descendants pushed inland onto continents they claimed. Territorial expansion, settler migration, and dispossession of native peoples in the young United States paralleled events taking place simultaneously on other nineteenth-century frontiers. In the temperate-zone, new nations of the Americas, and the British colonies of Australia and South Africa, white-dominated "settler societies," embarked from coastal settlements to pursue wealth and opportunity in the continents' interior.

Such frontiers were often violent places. Because pioneer settlers preceded lawful government, vigilante justice prevailed. Miners fought over conflicting claims during gold rushes. Ranchers and farmers who had rival agendas for land use competed for government support. In the United States, the expansion of slavery caused a frontier war with Mexico and western settlers. The most common source of violence, however, was settlers' determination to push aside native inhabitants of the land.

In Argentina, General Juan Manuel Rosas, a frontier rancher and military strongman whom historians have compared to Andrew Jackson, initially negotiated peace agreements with the Indians of the Pampas but then turned to conquest and removal. During the Campaign of the Desert (1833–1836), Rosas led a

MPI/Getty Images

Geronimo with Apache Warriors, 1886 Geronimo (far right), Apache leader, fought against the encroachment of Mexican settlers. In 1885, Geronimo and his band fled the San Carlos Reservation in Arizona, fighting against and eluding U.S. troops before finally surrendering in September 1886. Geronimo later claimed that the surrender had been conditional, a fact disputed by the U.S. government. ◄

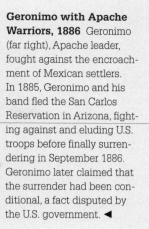

The Granger Collection, New York

Voortrekkers Make the Great Trek in South Africa, 1835–1843 Beginning in 1835, wagon trains like this one made the Great Trek from the Cape Colony to Natal as the Boers sought frontier in the eastern interior outside of British rule. ◄

military drive to force Indians south of the Rio Negro, which divided the nation into north and south. He allowed tribes that agreed to stay south of the line to be provided rations and horses and attacked those who refused. A similar situation occurred in Australia where white settlers, many of whom were convicts transported from Britain, collided with aboriginal people on several frontiers and perpetrated notorious massacres despite the efforts of missionaries and humanitarians.

In the British Cape Colony of South Africa, the Boers, descendants of the original Dutch colonizers, stretched the frontier as they sought land for cattle ranching and resisted British edicts that had ended the enslavement of African natives. In 1835, twelve thousand Boers embarked on a Great Trek into the eastern interior, where they set up three republics in defiance of British rule. The Great Trek and the U.S. "Trail of Tears" happened simultaneously and made a striking contrast. In South Africa white ranchers pushed past native peoples toward the far frontier, protesting Britain's refusal to seize native lands.

In the United States, the full force of state and federal governments bore down on Native Americans in order to remove them farther westward and open lands for white settlers. Even so, in the 1870s, when gold was discovered in the Boer regions of South Africa, the British quickly seized the land and exploited the natives brutally as mine workers. In the United States, Argentina, Australia, and South Africa during the 1870s, campaigns against native peoples resumed with greater force on the next frontiers, transported by railroads and with powerful new weapons to confine natives to out-of-the-way colonies, "homelands," or reservations.

Violence was only part of the settler frontier story, which also included transnational immigration, family homesteading, and boom-and-bust economies. Expansion was tied to economic development as frontier farm products were shipped internationally. The United States promoted the growth of banks and factories in eastern cities. Almost everywhere, however, indigenous peoples were targeted for removal and faced painful choices about whether to adopt white ways, accept forced relocation, or organize resistance.

Critical Thinking Questions

► How did European and U.S. expansion into the interior of North America compare with similar migrations in other parts of the world?

► How did Native peoples, both in North America and elsewhere, respond to these violent encroachments?

11-3

Transcontinental Nation

This lithograph depicts the U.S. army's victory over Mexican forces in the heart of Mexico City. The battle, in which the United States captured the San Patricio Brigade, was brutal and included hand-to-hand combat. It marked the first time that the United States had occupied the capital of a foreign nation.

This painting appeared just one year after the end of the war. How do you think Americans reacted to images such as this one, which depicts U.S. armed forces taking the capital of Mexico? ▶

UniversalImagesGroup/Getty Images

Between President Polk's election in 1844 and the Treaty of the Guadalupe-Hidalgo in 1848, which ended the hostilities between the United States and Mexico, the two countries fought a fierce military and ideological battle over who would control what later became known as the U.S. Southwest. The United States pushed across national boundaries and directly attacked Mexico's capital. When the war ended and U.S. troops occupied Mexico City, both U.S. citizens and politicians wondered what to do with this conquered nation. Now that the territory had been won, what were the consequences of bringing thousands of Mexicans and Indians into the Union? The debate that ensued publicly exposed U.S. nativist prejudices against Mexicans and Indians. For some Americans, the potential acquisition of so much territory also fueled the national debate about the spread of slavery to the territories. But with the ratification of the treaty, some U.S. politicians realized the promise of Manifest Destiny—a country that spread from the Atlantic to the Pacific coasts.

☞ As you read, consider the results of U.S. expansion. As the country became a nation that stretched from coast to coast, how did it deal with the issues raised by the incorporation of nonwhite citizens from Mexico and the potential spread of slavery?

11-3a Start of and Opposition to the U.S.–Mexican War

Americans debate the merits of the war.

Tension between Mexico and the United States had been rising since the founding of the Republic of Texas in 1836. Mexico never recognized Texas as an independent republic and warned the United States that its annexation of Texas would be considered an act of war. Complicating the diplomatic situation between the two nations was the political instability in Mexico and the covetous gaze of the United States on Mexico's north. Between 1821 and 1876, the presidency of Mexico changed fifty-five times, most often through coup and violent overthrow. Santa Anna served eleven times as president during crucial moments of U.S.–Mexican diplomacy and hostilities. The constant change in governments made diplomatic negotiation difficult.

Nueces Strip The territory between the Nueces River and the Rio Grande, which was the source of territorial dispute between the United States and Mexico prior to their war.

President Polk sent John Slidell, Louisiana congressman and diplomat, as his envoy to negotiate with the Mexican government about acquiring territory and settling U.S. citizens' claims against the Mexican government. Slidell offered Mexico $30 million to purchase California and New Mexico territories. The Mexican government never officially recognized his diplomatic mission, and the public was angered by the audacity of the "yankees" who thought they could purchase their way out of the dispute. Slidell left Mexico disgusted by the government's unwillingness to negotiate and suggested to Polk that he station troops at the border to pressure Mexico to negotiate.

The most sensitive issue was their shared border. Mexico believed that the border between Mexico and the renegade Texas was the Nueces River. Texas, however, and consequently the United States, insisted it was farther south, along the Rio Grande. Even before Slidell had left Mexico, President Polk ordered General Zachary Taylor to move his troops across the Nueces River and into the disputed territory, the **Nueces Strip**. On April 12, 1846, Mexican forces ordered Taylor to retreat across the river. He refused and directed the U.S. navy to blockade the mouth of the Rio Grande, thus cutting off supplies to the Mexican troops. On April 25, the Mexican army attacked the U.S. military in the strip, killing eleven, wounding five, and taking forty-seven prisoners. This was the provocation that Polk needed. When he received the news on May 9, 1846, he announced to Congress that "by the act of Mexico" a state of war existed. Mexico, he said, "has invaded our territory and shed American blood upon the American soil." Despite opposition from both Whigs and Democrats, many of whom recognized the duplicity of Polk's claims, the war resolution passed Congress on May 13, 1846.

The war garnered significant initial public support, including a massive rally in New York City in May. The rally included speeches that vilified Mexicans as Catholic, half-breed mongrels and called for the United States to invade their land. Newspapers such as the *New York Herald* supported the war. Walt Whitman, the editor of the *Brooklyn Daily Eagle*, wrote that "Mexico must be thoroughly chastised" for its aggression.

Others viewed the war as a southern Democratic ploy to acquire territory for the extension of slavery. In August 1846, David Wilmot, an antislavery congressman from Pennsylvania, tried to add a proviso to an appropriation bill to outlaw slavery in any territory that might be gained from war with Mexico. Denouncing both the war and slavery, Henry David Thoreau penned "On Civil Disobedience." He refused to pay taxes to support the war, spent a night in jail, and argued that if government "is of such a nature that it requires you to be the agent of injustice to another, then, I say, break the law." His call for **civil disobedience** has reverberated to the present. Some northern women, who were antislavery as well, opposed the war on moral grounds. Women's rights advocate Lucretia Mott read a public antiwar statement to a large crowd in Philadelphia in June in response to a petition from the women of Exeter, England. The women of these two cities did not want war. More than three thousand women signed Mott's antiwar speech, and the British Consul forwarded their antiwar response to their counterparts in Exeter.

civil disobedience Refusal, often in the form of nonviolent resistance, to obey laws considered to be immoral or unjust.

11-3b Waging of the War

Once Congress acknowledged the state of war with Mexico in 1846, the military struggle was fought on three fronts across the present-day U.S. Southwest, northern Mexico, and Mexico City (see Map 11.4). President Polk ordered General Taylor to move his troops farther south into Mexico's territory in

The United States invades Mexico and meets resistance on multiple fronts.

Map 11.4 Major Campaigns of the U.S.–Mexican War The war that the United States waged against Mexico covered much territory and was fought on at least three fronts at any given point in the war. While U.S. troops fought on foreign territory, Mexicans fought on their home territory. Involving civilians made the war more difficult to wage, making the progress of U.S. troops slow but steady through Mexico's interior. ▼

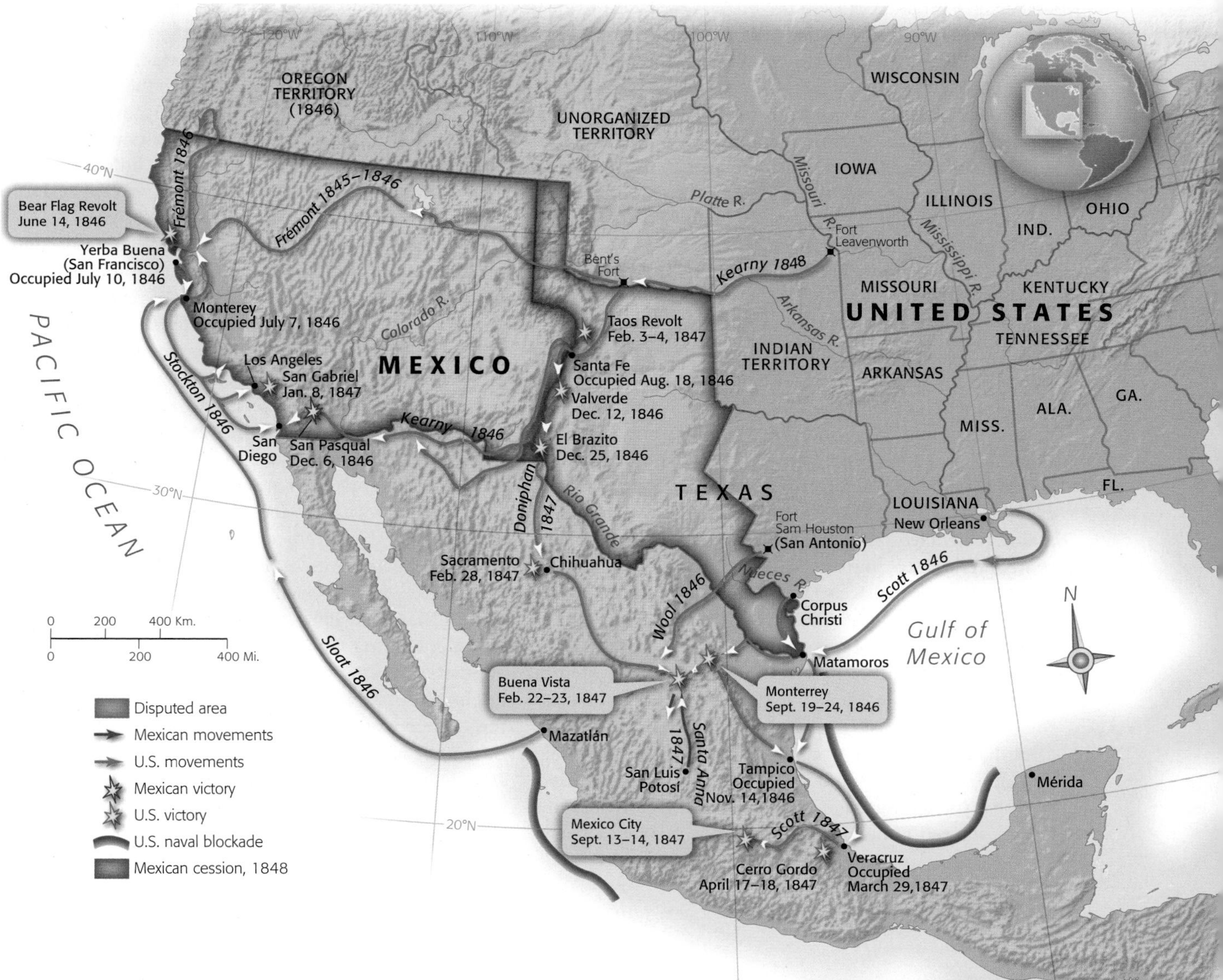

Riley was taken prisoner at the Battle of Churubusco, about a year after the capture of Monterrey, shown here.

Global Americans

John Patrick Riley, born in County Galway Ireland around 1818, was a British soldier before migrating to Canada during the Great Famine. He quickly crossed into Michigan and joined the U.S. army. Immigrants often joined the military because of the wages it paid, the stability it provided, and the path to citizenship it offered. These immigrants, however, often faced anti-immigrant and anti-Catholic prejudice from enlistees and officers, at which Riley bristled. With the outbreak of the U.S.–Mexican War, he was sent south to fight against Mexico.

After six months, Riley and Patrick Dalton deserted the U.S. army and formed the Saint Patrick's Battalion to fight for the Mexican army. The battalion, made up of hundreds of deserters of mostly Irish and German descent, also included former slaves who had crossed into Mexico for their freedom. The men who joined the battalion did so for a number of reasons: prejudice they faced in the United States made them eager to leave, sympathy for Catholic Mexico for what they perceived as U.S. aggression, and the promise of free land for their service to the Mexican cause.

Captured by U.S. troops at the Battle of Churubusco, battalion members were tried for treason and desertion. Although Riley escaped execution, he was convicted of desertion and branded with a "D" on his cheek. He never returned to the United States but remained in Mexico where he and his battalion members were revered as heroes in Ireland, Mexico, and among Irish immigrants in the United States.

the summer of 1846. On September 25, Taylor's troops captured Monterrey, Mexico. Taylor's men captured Saltillo in November and by the end of the year controlled all of northeastern Mexico. In early 1847, Taylor's troops continued to take territory, culminating in the battle of Buena Vista in February, the bloodiest confrontation of the war. It cost the lives of 665 Americans and more than 3,500 Mexicans.

While Taylor fought on the southern side of the Rio Grande, Brigadier General Stephen Watts Kearny pushed west along the Santa Fe Trail from Kansas toward New Mexico and California. Although his main mission was to secure Mexico's northern territories, he was also under orders to intimidate the Plains Indians, particularly the Comanches. Kearny told them that "the road opened by the dragoons [horse-mounted infantry] must not be closed . . . and that the white people traveling upon it must not be disturbed, either in their persons or property." His expedition highlighted U.S. military presence on the Great Plains. It signaled that the U.S. government was willing to protect its citizens during violent encounters with Indians. Polk also asked Kearny to incorporate the 543 men of the Mormon Battalion that Brigham Young had sent to re-enforce Kearny's march west.

Kearny and his troops met relatively little resistance as they entered New Mexico in the summer of 1846. New Mexico Governor Manuel Armijo mustered a defensive force that met Kearny's troops east of Santa Fe. But Armijo abandoned his troops and fled more deeply into Mexico, leaving a small, overmatched force. When Kearny and his troops entered Santa Fe, they met no resistance. Many New Mexico residents welcomed the Americans, whom they regarded as potentially wealthy trading partners who would boost the economy and develop the region. Kearny and his men set up a U.S. territorial government with Charles Bent as governor. The occupation happened so quickly that Kearny left Santa Fe after little more than a month and took most of his men west toward California to aid the uprising there.

A year earlier, the U.S. government had sent John C. Frémont and a small group of men to find the headwaters of the Arkansas. Without explanation, Frémont headed to the far west. While in California, Frémont met with Thomas O. Larkin, the American consul to Mexico, and they discussed California's revolting from Mexico in the same way that Texas had done nine years earlier. The Mexican government, suspicious of Frémont's exhortations to American citizens, encouraged him to leave. But, after crossing into Oregon, Frémont retraced his steps and headed back into the heart of California. Frémont spent June and July inciting military unrest. On July 4, 1846, the Bear Flag Republic declared its independence from Mexico. Once the new republic received word that the U.S. had declared war on Mexico, it allied itself formally to the United States.

Conquering California was an involved and bloody conflict for the United States. Frémont, placed under the command of naval Commodore Robert F. Stockton, led the California Battalion south toward San Diego and the onslaught of Mexican troops. Taking San Diego and Los Angeles proved difficult because the *Californios* and the Mexican army protected the two cities from U.S. capture. By January 1847, Kearny, Stockton, and Frémont had taken control of California, but at a significant cost to U.S. troops. Kearny was wounded and lost one-third of his men. In that month, however, General Andres Pico signed the **Treaty of Cahuenga**, which turned California over to the United States but guaranteed *Californios* the same rights as U.S. citizens.

New Mexico also did not submit easily to U.S. rule. Despite the appearance of calm when Kearney had left, tensions ran high. A rebellion against U.S. rule erupted in December 1846 in the northern town of Taos. A coalition of *Hispanos* and Pueblo Indians intended to assassinate Governor Charles Bent and attack the U.S. troops. Bent had the plotters arrested and went to Taos in January 1847, believing his trading and family connections would calm any lingering hostile feelings. During his visit, rebels attacked his entourage and murdered Bent and a number of the group. Over the next few weeks, more than three thousand rebels mounted a counterinsurgency, and U.S. troops had to be sent north from Santa Fe. They crushed the rebellion after three months of skirmishes. Eventually, twenty-eight *Hispano* and Pueblo men were convicted and executed for treason and murder.

With the U.S. troops' steady success in taking the northern provinces of Mexico, President Polk decided to send troops under the leadership of Major General Scott into central Mexico. His troops landed in Veracruz on the eastern coast of Mexico and marched toward Mexico City. Between November 1846 and September 1847, U.S. troops made steady progress across the interior of Mexico. Their invasion provoked resistance and bloody battles at Cerro Gordo, Puebla, Contreras, Churubusco, and the climactic battle in Mexico City at Chapultepec Castle, which housed a military academy. On the morning of September 13, 1847, U.S. forces began attacking the castle. Shelling continued throughout the day. The next morning, infantrymen attacked and pushed into the castle and through the city, where they met troops and citizens led by their president and military commander, General Santa Anna. By September 16, the U.S. flag flew over the capital city of Mexico—the first time that the U.S. flag had flown over a foreign country. The war that President Polk had proclaimed a defensive measure against Mexican encroachments across the Rio Grande had become a war of conquest and domination. For Mexicans, the war brought political turmoil and humiliation with the presence of an invading force in their capital.

11-3c Politics of Victory

The United States comes to terms with massive land acquisition and new citizens.

The U.S. military success created a host of problems in dealing with a conquered Mexico and its people. The United States could now lay claim to more than half of Mexico's territory from the capital of Mexico City north to California's boundary with Oregon. Those who pushed for keeping all of this land were part of the **All Mexico** movement. These supporters tended to be Democrats who either wanted to expand slavery or who saw it as the U.S. mission to bring "progress" to Mexico and its peoples. In the All Mexico movement, supporters of Manifest Destiny had to confront its logic. If it was the Manifest Destiny of the United States to acquire all the lands between the Atlantic and Pacific Oceans was it also its destiny to incorporate all of the land's inhabitants, including Mexicans and Indians? What was the meaning of citizenship for those who had been conquered by U.S. aggression? The U.S. public and politicians had to contemplate what the results of this war meant within the context of a democratic and republican society.

Most Americans opposed the naked aggression reflected in the All Mexico movement. Conscience Whigs had opposed the U.S.–Mexican War on ideological grounds. Abraham Lincoln, a young congressman from Illinois, voiced the position that true democracies should not be in the business of conquering foreign nations, their people, and their land. These actions stood in opposition to the principles on which the United States was founded. In addition, those who opposed slavery also were against the acquisition of Mexican territory because they feared the spread of slavery farther west. Because of their history, isolation, and arid geography, neither California nor New Mexico seemed likely candidates for the extension of slavery, but Texas encouraged slaveholders to bring their human property to the state and extend cotton culture. Finally, racist and anti-Catholic arguments surfaced as Americans confronted the prospect of thousands of Catholic Mexicans becoming U.S. citizens. John Calhoun, one of the most outspoken critics of the All Mexico movement said, "Ours, sir, is the Government of a white race. The greatest misfortunes of Spanish America are to be traced to the fatal error of placing these colored races on an equality with the white race."

In 1848, the **Treaty of Guadalupe Hidalgo**, which required Mexico to give up all claims to Texas and recognize the Rio Grande as the international boundary, was negotiated in this political context and after a difficult series of diplomatic exchanges. When negotiations broke down over the extent of U.S. territorial ambitions, President Polk recalled his envoy, Nicholas P. Trist, believing there was no room for negotiation. The war and occupation would simply continue. The Mexican government, sensing that Trist was their best option in obtaining a somewhat favorable treaty, hurriedly finished negotiations, which clearly favored the U.S. position. Although some Mexicans wanted to continue the fight, the defeat at Chapultepec combined with political upheaval in the Mexican capital made it difficult to launch a united front.

The treaty established the U.S.–Mexican border along the Rio Grande and then due west along a surveyed and marked border through the desert. The United States agreed to

Treaty of Cahuenga Agreement that ended the California front of the U.S.–Mexican War and gave *Californios* the same rights as U.S. citizens.

All Mexico Political movement at the close of the U.S.–Mexican War that pushed to acquire and take over all of Mexico as opposed to annexing only the northern provinces.

Treaty of Guadalupe Hidalgo Agreement ending the U.S.–Mexican War that required the United States to pay $30 million and Mexico to give up the present-day U.S. Southwest.

pay Mexico $15 million for the territory it would acquire. It also assumed claims that U.S. citizens had against the Mexican government for any losses they suffered during the war or from hostile encounters with Indians along the border. The two governments also committed themselves to arbitrating their future differences. Two points, however, were not amicably negotiated: citizenship and property rights of former Mexican citizens (see Table 11.3).

Table 11.3 Treaty of Guadalupe Hidalgo

Two important clauses of this treaty affected former Mexican citizens who came under U.S. jurisdiction. Article IX provided that they would become full U.S. citizens "as soon as possible." However, the Senate changed this to "be admitted at the proper time (to be judged of by the Congress of the United States)," causing many to wait more than sixty years for citizenship. Article X promised to recognize property rights existing under Mexican law. However, the Senate forced these Mexicans to go through an arduous legal process to document their land titles.

As Written during Negotiations	As Ratified by U.S. Senate
Article IX	**Article IX**
The Mexicans who, in the territories aforesaid, shall not preserve the character of citizens of the Mexican Republic, conformably with what is stipulated in the preceding Article, shall be incorporated into the Union of the United States, and admitted as soon as possible, according to the principles of the Federal Constitution, to the enjoyment of all the rights of citizens of the United States. In the mean time, they shall be maintained and protected in the enjoyment of their liberty, their property, and the civil rights now vested in them according to the Mexican laws. With respect to political rights, their condition shall be on an equality with that of the inhabitants of the other territories of the United States; and at least equally good as that of the inhabitants of Louisiana and the Floridas, when these provinces, by transfer from the French Republic and the Crown of Spain, became territories of the United States. The same most ample guaranty shall be enjoyed by all ecclesiastics and religious corporations or communities, as well in the discharge of the offices of their ministry, as in the enjoyment of their property of every kind, whether individual or corporate. This guaranty shall embrace all temples, houses and edifices dedicated to the Roman Catholic worship; as well as all property destined to its support, or to that of schools, hospitals and other foundations for charitable or beneficent purposes. No property of this nature shall be considered as having become the property of the American Government, or as subject to be, by it, disposed of or diverted to other uses. Finally, the relations and communication between the Catholics living in the territories aforesaid, and their respective ecclesiastical authorities, shall be open, free and exempt from all hindrance whatever, even although such authorities should reside within the limits of the Mexican Republic, as defined by this treaty; and this freedom shall continue, so long as a new demarcation of ecclesiastical districts shall not have been made, conformably with the laws of the Roman Catholic Church.	The Mexicans who, in the territories aforesaid, shall not preserve the character of citizens of the Mexican Republic, conformably with what is stipulated in the preceding article, shall be incorporated into the Union of the United States and be admitted at the proper time (to be judged of by the Congress of the United States) to the enjoyment of all the rights of citizens of the United States, according to the principles of the Constitution; and in the mean time, shall be maintained and protected in the free enjoyment of their liberty and property, and secured in the free exercise of their religion without; restriction.
Article X	**Article X**
All grants of land made by the Mexican Government or by the component authorities, in territories previously appertaining to Mexico, and remaining for the future within the limits of the United States, shall be respected as valid, to the same extent that the same grants would be valid, if the said territories had remained within the limits of Mexico. But the grantees of lands in Texas, put in possession thereof, who, by reason of the circumstances of the country since the beginning of the troubles between Texas and the Mexican Government, may have been prevented from fulfilling all the conditions of their grants, shall be under the obligation to fulfill said conditions within the periods limited in the same respectively; such periods to be now counted from the date of exchange of ratifications of this treaty: in default of which the said grants shall not be obligatory upon the State of Texas, in virtue of the stipulations contained in this Article. The foregoing stipulation in regard to grantees of land in Texas, is extended to all grantees of land in the territories aforesaid, elsewhere than Texas, put in possession under such grants; and, in default of the fulfillment of the conditions of any such grant, within the new period, which, as is above stipulated, begins with the day of the exchange of ratifications of this treaty, the same shall be null and void.	*Stricken*

Source: http://www.ourdocuments.gov/doc.php?flash=true&doc=26.

The U.S. Senate ratified the Treaty of Guadalupe Hidalgo on March 10, 1848. Finally, in 1853, the last piece of what is known today as the continental United States was acquired when President Franklin Pierce directed James Gadsden, the minister to Mexico, to purchase a parcel of land in present-day southern Arizona. Manifest Destiny, as envisioned by many U.S. citizens, had finally been realized. Americans were then free to push westward in search of new lives and lands.

11-4 The World Rushed In

As "gold fever" caught in 1849, people from the East Coast, the Midwest, and outside the U.S.—Britain, France, Central America, Chile, Hawai'i, and China—flocked to try their hand at panning for gold and getting rich quick. Many advertisements induced forty-niners to take the stemship route rather than the overland route to the goldfields of California. This Nathaniel Currier cartoon titled "The Way They Go to California" offers a fantastical satire on the desperation of miners looking to make a fast journey by any means—even rocket.

How did new modes of transportation and communication promote passage to California? ▶

THE WAY THEY GO TO CALIFORNIA.

The Granger Collection, New York

Go to MindTap® to practice history with the Chapter 11 **Primary Source Writing Activity: Promise of the West.** Read and view primary sources and respond to a writing prompt.

People in San Francisco learned about the end of the U.S.–Mexican War just as news of the discovery of gold at Sutter's Mill, outside of Sacramento, spread through the city. The irony of discovering gold just as Mexico had turned California over to the United States was not lost on *Californios*. Now that this *El Dorado* had been discovered, it belonged, from the perspective of *Californios*, to Americans who poured across the Great Plains on their way to California.

Farther north in Oregon, immigrants were drawn by the promise of fertile and plentiful land rather than gold. Eastern families sold their land, homes, and belongings and packed up wagons for the move west. This decision was often an agonizing one that meant leaving behind all community ties and comforts. Life on the trail was difficult and often treacherous. Families had to redefine how work was divided and accomplished to survive. Thousands of migrants took a toll on the environment along the trail, which could barely sustain such a vast movement. This massive migration also forced new relationships between Euro-Americans, indigenous peoples, and Mexican-Americans. Both violence and accommodation marked these new relationships.

☞ As you read, consider the consequences of this migration. How did it affect the Indians, *Californios*, and the landscape? How did the end of the war and the Gold Rush shape Americans' perceptions of themselves?

11-4a The Move to the West

Families remake themselves in the new territory.

California's Indian and *mestizo* population had been under Spanish control until 1820 followed by Mexican rule until 1848. The Spanish military, Catholic missionaries, and Spanish settlers had colonized California Indians. The Spanish encouraged the Indians to move to missions and worked them as unfree labor to bring intensive agriculture to the region. The *Californio* population thrived during the Mexican period by engaging in extended trade with merchants from all over the world who came into the ports of San Francisco, Monterey, and Los Angeles to buy cowhides and tallow. The California Indian population continued to decline, however, particularly after smallpox spread through the region in 1836 and 1844. Forced labor, disease, and land loss through privatization of property for eight hundred *ranchos* were responsible for the Indians' rapid population decline. In California, Americans remade the economy and society based on gold, commerce, and immigration.

On January 24, 1848, two weeks before the Treaty of Guadalupe Hidalgo was signed, James W. Marshall, a foreman working for Sacramento businessman John Sutter, found pieces of shiny metal near a lumber mill along the American River in what is now Coloma, California.

The two men privately tested the findings and confirmed that indeed it was gold. Sutter wanted to keep the news quiet because he feared the onslaught of settlers into his valley in a frenzied search for gold. However, rumors soon started to spread and were confirmed in March 1848 by a San Francisco newspaper publisher who strode through the streets of San Francisco, holding aloft a vial of gold, shouting "Gold! Gold! Gold from the American River!"

News of the gold discovery met with skepticism. On August 19, 1848, the *New York Herald* was the first major newspaper on the East Coast to report the news. But not until December 5, when President Polk confirmed in an address to Congress the discovery of gold did the vast majority of Americans take the news seriously. That winter, families discussed whether to allow their husbands, fathers, and sons to head off to the goldfields. The migration of 1849 primarily included young white men from the East Coast and Midwest who used any means necessary to get to California. Some boarded ships in Boston and sailed around Cape Horn or through the Straits of Magellan in South America. Some traveled on ships down the East Coast to Panama where they disembarked, walked across the Isthmus of Panama, and then boarded another ship on the Pacific side and sailed north into the port of San Francisco. Most packed their wagons with supplies of food staples, tools, and animals and headed west across the open prairie to make it to California before all the gold was gone. As word spread about a gold rush, people caught what the Sioux leader, Black Elk, described as "gold fever." They impulsively abandoned their homes and families and went west in search of easy riches.

The Gold Rush and ensuing migration of hundreds of thousands of people, mostly men, as well as the wealth that the gold rush created transformed the way Americans thought about money and the definition of success. In the first year after news of the gold rush hit the eastern United States, eighty thousand people headed west, four times as many as had gone in the past. By the end of the Gold Rush in 1854, more than three hundred thousand people, mostly men, from around the world had gone to California to try to make a quick fortune. About one-third of these migrants came from abroad. Mexican and Chilean miners came to try their expertise in the goldfields. Chinese immigrants came in search of *Gum Sham* (Gold Mountain). And Europeans, mostly German and French, fled the revolution of 1848 to find prosperity and a new home. These adventurers (later called **forty-niners**) and settlers were not entering empty territory but a region that had a long and rich history of Indian and Mexican expansion, conquest, and settlement.

forty-niners Adventurers from around the world who came to the California goldfields in 1849.

placer mining Process of removing mineral deposits from river beds by placing dirt in a pan, swishing it with water, and letting the heavy metals sink to the bottom of the pan.

Between 1849 and 1855, $300 million worth of gold was pulled out of the Sierra Nevada Mountains and its foothills and rivers. The California Gold Rush combined with the discovery of gold in Australia in 1852 influenced families' behaviors around the globe. Friedrich Engels noted to Karl Marx in 1852, "California and Australia are two cases not provided for in the [*Communist*] *Manifesto*: the creation of large new markets out of nothing. We shall have to allow for this." The Gold Rush caused Americans to question how democracy would work in a frontier society and what it meant to have potential access to so much money in such a short time. For example, Eddin Lewis, a farmer in Sangamon County, Illinois, who exported livestock and corn, recorded that he had earned $350 in 1847. Meanwhile, C.C. Mobley, one of the first to reach the California goldfields recorded that he and his companions had made $205 each that week and the week before had made $150 each. Mobley and his friends, with just a pick and shovel, had made as much in two weeks as Lewis, one of the most prosperous farmers in Sangamon County, had made in a year from a farm he had built over a lifetime.

11-4b Life in the Goldfields

Gender imbalance and racial diversity characterize the Gold Rush.

Those who left their homes in 1848 to search for the precious substance did not arrive in California until 1849. Travelers arriving in San Francisco described the city as a ghost town because all able-bodied people had left the city to head into the Sierras to try their luck at getting rich quick. That first season of panning for gold in 1848 was a family venture with *Californio* and Indian families working the rivers for their own benefit or for the benefit of California *rancheros*. Panning for gold required little investment or infrastructure. People just put a pan in the water, dropped in the gravel, and swished it around looking for pieces of gold. Prospectors competed for places along the river to use **placer mining**, which used the technology of panning but could require more intensive labor.

In many ways, class divisions softened. One American noted of the changes brought by the discovery of gold, "The millionaire is obliged to groom his own horse, and roll his own wheelbarrow; and the *hidalgo*—in whose veins flows the blood of Cortes—to clean his own boots." Economic competition, however, seemed to fuel racial tensions. After the spring of 1849, thousands of foreigners poured into California and upended what had emerged as a precarious balance among Californians. This mix of Americans, Europeans, Chinese, Chileans, and Mexicans led to violence and legal restrictions.

In particular, the Chileans faced the most overt hostility because of their long history of mining and their immediate success. They attracted the animosity of the less capable Americans, who asserted that because California was a U.S. territory, the mines should be reserved for U.S. citizens. Physical violence and racial harassment plagued the miners from Chile, Peru, Mexico, and China. This prejudice peaked with the passage of the

Chinese during the Gold Rush, 1852 Chinese, like other sojourners, were looking to get rich quickly, send money back to their families, and then return home. Unlike white migrants, however, Chinese men faced nativist hostilities from men who resented their mining skills and were suspicious of their different appearance and religion. The Chinese were quickly barred from the goldfields and found a niche providing domestic services such as laundry and cooking to other miners. They were also segregated into separate camps and Chinatown neighborhoods in cities such as Sacramento and San Francisco. ◄

Foreign Miner's Tax of 1850, which charged non-U.S. citizens a $20 fee to mine, essentially barred all foreigners from working the goldfields. Some groups, particularly the French, complained, but the law remained in place, although the tax was eventually lowered to $3 a month—still a hefty sum given that the mines were not as lucrative as more people mined.

The majority of Chinese did not arrive until 1852, after the height of the rush was over. More than twenty-five thousand disembarked in San Francisco, and like the other immigrants, they were drawn by stories of quick wealth. Most of them came from the Pearl Delta Region, an area with a long history of trade with the Pacific Coast of North America. Because many American Christian missionaries had come to that region, the Chinese were familiar with the United States and English and had connections that brought them news of the Gold Rush. Most of the Chinese who went to California were men with some means who were capitalizing on their knowledge of gold mining, trade routes, and sense of adventure. Like all other immigrants to the goldfields, the Chinese, too, had dreams of getting rich quickly and returning to their families in China.

These dreams were quickly shattered. Upon their arrival, the middle-class Chinese immigrants became the primary target of amplified American nativism because the boom days of the gold rush had passed. The miners who were still working their claims worked long and difficult hours with little profit. The Chinese were not only worthy competitors but also had a culture and appearance that seemed frightening to many Americans. Some people found Chinese clothes, food, and worship of Buddha curious and intriguing, but most found the Chinese threatening and wanted them to go away. Americans quickly pushed them out of the goldfields through violence and intimidation. But the Chinese adapted and found a niche open to them because there were few women in the goldfields. They did work that American men did not want to do for themselves and for which they were willing to pay: cooking and laundry.

Panning for gold was anything but easy and very few people made themselves rich by it. The money made was quickly spent on the few consumer items and services available, which came with a steep price tag. The people who did make fortunes were those like Levi Strauss (the inventor of jeans) and Henry Wells and William G. Fargo (creators of California's early bank) whose businesses supplied the hungry and desperate miners. Those who did work the placer mines struggled to find lucrative spots and to maintain their claims. Many of the Americans banded together in groups that adopted constitutions and rules for how they would work communally once they reached California. Others chose to work as individuals or in pairs, preferring more informal arrangements for balancing work on the actual claim with the "support" work of cooking, purchasing supplies, cleaning, and accounting.

Because this was primarily a migration of men, the lack of women to provide "support" work created an opportunity for arrangements that defied conventional gender norms. Plentiful gold dust circulating through the economy created a situation in which men were willing to pay for domestic work. Chinese immigrants filled part of the void. Some enterprising white women who came out with their

Foreign Miners Tax of 1850 A $20-per month tax placed on foreigners who wanted to prospect in California during the Gold Rush.

Global Americans Few people who came to the Gold Rush got rich. Those who did made their money from servicing the forty-niners rather than mining. Such was the case with the Ghirardellis. **Carmen Alvarado Domingo Ghirardelli** was born in Lima, Peru, in 1829. She married a French physician, and had one daughter, Carmen. Her husband's ship, however, was lost at sea and Carmen was widowed in 1845. In 1847, she met and married Domingo Ghirardelli, who was also recently widowed. He had been born near Genoa, Italy, and apprenticed with a confectioner. He left Italy in the 1830s during the violent reunification process. He first went to Uruguay, and then to Lima where he set up a sweet shop. He caught gold fever and headed to California, leaving Carmen behind with three young children. Like thousands of women worldwide, she stayed behind, kept the house and children, and ran the business in Lima, while Domingo pursued his dream in California.

In California, Domingo started prospecting but soon found that he made more money selling provisions to the miners than by mining himself. He and his friend had brought six hundred pounds of chocolate with them. He opened stores in both Stockton and San Francisco before founding the Ghirardelli Chocolate Factory in San Francisco in 1852. In 1853, Carmen sold the business in Lima and moved to San Francisco to join her husband. Their growing family lived above the factory and by the 1860s, they were importing thousands of pounds of chocolate and gaining a reputation for their exquisite confections. ▲ National Portrait Gallery

menfolk or by themselves ran successful bakeries, restaurants, and boarding homes that appealed to men who missed domestic comforts. The balance between the sexes was so skewed (in 1850 there were twelve men for every woman) that women had their choice of husbands. Many men complained about the lack of marriage prospects, and a few feared that their wives would find someone more to their liking.

Others viewed the imbalance as an opportunity to make money by exploiting the sexual desires of men. William Stewart told the story of a man who created quite a scene when he brought his young wife into a camp and allowed the men to look at her as she peeked out from the wagon's curtains. "She repeated this performance several times, and I kept slowly moving back so the boys could have a good view of her." Other women sold their time and company to men who were eager for their attention. In many situations, sex was exchanged without fear of reprisal because there were no laws to prevent prostitution. Some encounters did not involve sex. An attractive woman could earn up to $20 for the evening just to sit at a poker table and entertain the men.

11-4c Families in the West

Diverse peoples form new communities.

The Gold Rush disrupted the lives of most families who were pulled into the vortex of its power. The influx of prospectors from around the world upended the delicate balance that the families already living in the region had created for themselves. Western families were a diverse group, who, prior to the gold rush, had come together to create stable economic and social groups that provided nurturing homes. These families tended to congregate around the emerging institution such as the town, mission, military garrison, or trading post. At Fort Vancouver on the banks of the Columbia, mixed families made up of British, American, and Indian peoples came together to trade and develop one of the strongholds of the Pacific Northwest. Bent's Fort on the banks of the Arkansas was such an enterprise that provided a safe haven for families from the depredations of the Comanches.

By the early 1840s, however, fur-trading families began to realize that the world was shifting, and their place as successful intermediaries between Indians in the Far West and the trading houses in the East was being eroded. These traders worked hard to find a place for their mixed families in this rapidly changing world that would come to see mixed-race children as a problem. Kawsmouth (Kansas City), on the banks of the Missouri River, had been founded by the Chouteau family in 1821 as a trading post. By the 1840s, it was almost a mixed race community where fur-trading families could purchase property and raise their children in relatively stable conditions with access to schools provided by both Protestant and Catholic churches. Prominent fur traders, such as the Bents, Bridgers, and McKenzies, ensconced their families there. The families worked as guides, farmers, and traders for the growing number of people who passed through. Places such as Saint Louis helped these families make the transition from frontier fur-trade economies to the more settled world of commerce and trade that was taking over the Great Plains and Mountain West with the increased traffic of immigrants from Europe and the eastern United States.

The Granger Collection, New York

Fort Vancouver, WA, 1824 Encampments such as the one shown here became gathering points for the emerging mixed families in early nineteenth century North America. Places such as this one, Bent's Fort, and at Kansas City were fortified against outside incursion and provided a space for families to grow crops or hold livestock (notice the fences). These places also fostered the trade of goods, ideas, and cultures. ◀

The Gold Rush unraveled the alliances that fur traders and their families had been nurturing. As word filtered back east from early migrants, many Americans began to look to the far west as a new place to take their families and make a living. From 1843 through the end of the 1850s, thousands of families made their way every year across the Great Plains or took ships to Oregon and California. This migration was a movement of whole families who came to a collective decision about their permanent move to a new place. Families began preparing in the early spring and sold all but the most essential items that they could load into their wagons. They took the cash they had raised from selling their homes, farms, businesses, and household goods and set out on the trail, not knowing whether they would have enough money or supplies to make it to California or Oregon by the time snow fell in late autumn.

Despite the hardships of such an arduous trip, thousands of families made the trek to their new homes. When they arrived, they encountered Mexican, Indian, and mixed-race families who had been living for generations in the region where they had established communities, churches, schools, and governments. At first, the settlers engaged peacefully with the local populations, but as the population pressure increased, these encounters became more violent.

11-4d Legacy of Colonialism

> The process of incorporating territories was uneven and arduous.

Between 1815 and 1850, the United States became a continental nation. Much of the land between the Mississippi River and the Pacific Ocean had been taken from Indians and came under U.S. control. It was mapped and organized into states and territories. Oregon, Colorado, New Mexico, Arizona, Nevada, and Utah became territories in 1848 with the transfer of Mexican territory, which had been owned at various times by Britain, France, Spain, and Mexico. The transfer of this territory to U.S. control had a lasting impact on those arriving in the West. They felt as if they were bringing their nation with them to this new territory. But the transition placed a deep mark on those who were already settled there, mostly Mexicans and Indians. They suffered land loss and death at the hands of encroaching settlers and then had to remake themselves to fit their property, customs, and families into the legal, social, and economic regime that the United States imposed.

Through the process established by the Northwest Ordinance in 1787, these newly acquired western territories were to be incorporated into the United States as equal states with citizens. This was the promise also made in the Webster-Ashburton Treaty and the Treaty of Guadalupe Hidalgo. The reality of the process, however, differed from the ideal and the earlier incorporation of lands acquired by earlier treaties and the Louisiana Purchase. Some areas—Utah, because of the presence of Mormons, and New Mexico, Arizona, and Oklahoma, because of their mixed race populations—had exceptionally long territorial periods before they were granted statehood. Mixed-race fur-trading families as well as Mexican and Indian families experienced first-hand the hardening racial structures in the United States. As tensions over the place of slavery in the western territories mounted and conversations concerning race, citizenship, and rights became more fraught, violence often erupted.

By 1850, the United States had managed to become a continental nation and strove to be the "empire of liberty" that Thomas Jefferson had envisioned. That expansion came, however, with difficult growing pains as some of the multiracial population was not convinced that it wanted to be incorporated into the new nation.

Summary

Following Lewis and Clark's trek across the West, Americans thought about how to incorporate the western territory into the nation. Some used diplomacy and war, and others, such as the fur traders, used their economic power to subdue Indians and conquer territories. Some Americans had conflicting ideas about their place within the encroaching United States. In the case of the Sioux, accommodation in the form of the Fort Laramie Treaty of 1851 secured safe travel across the Great Plains for immigrants going to California. In the case of Cherokees and Sauks, the conflict with whites ended in forced removal to Indian Territory. The Mormons were also pushed west, not out of a desire to take land but because their neighbors persecuted them for their religion. The tensions over ideologies, power, land, and resources marked this period as contested and violent.

Many Americans embraced Manifest Destiny, which justified taking territory and displacing its inhabitants, primarily Mexicans and Indians, from their homes. Many believed that their actions were justified because they were improving the land they conquered and the peoples they encountered. Throughout this period, the national political parties vied with one another to determine how to incorporate the West into the new nation. This conflict defined political parties and set the stage for the sectional conflicts of the 1850s.

The first test of Manifest Destiny was the U.S.–Mexican War. The U.S. military attacked Mexico, which ended with the acquisition of Texas, New Mexico, Arizona, and portions of Colorado and Utah. In the last days of the war, the United States occupied Mexico City. The Treaty of Guadalupe Hidalgo established a new boundary between the two nations and then specified how former Mexican citizens and their property would be incorporated into the U.S. system.

As continental dreams became a reality, Americans migrated west. The lure of the Gold Rush drew people, mostly men, from around the world. They hoped to strike it rich and then return home to their families. Although the majority never earned vast riches, many decided to stay and make their homes in California. The rush to the West also fueled a later wave of immigrants who moved with their families to start new lives. With all of these people moving through the Great Plains and creating new communities in the West, conflict and accommodation emerged as these new immigrants came into constant contact with Indians and Mexican Americans who had been making their homes there for generations.

Thinking Back, *Looking Forward*

As you review this chapter, think about the role that westward expansion played in the development of the United States as a diverse nation. How were these various groups incorporated into the expanding nation? In what ways was their participation limited? What was the role of violence in westward expansion and incorporation? In the next chapters, think about how violence continues to play a role in U.S. conquest. Also consider how the lessons learned from the U.S.–Mexican War and U.S. westward expansion play a role in U.S. conquest after the Civil War.

To make your study concrete, review the timeline and reflect on the entries there. Think about causes, consequences, and connections. How do they fit with global trends?

Additional Resources

Books

Chavez, Ernesto. ***The U.S. War with Mexico: A Brief History with Documents***. **New York: Bedford/St. Martins Press, 2007.** ▶ Comprehensive history and analysis of the war from the perspective of people on both sides of the border.

Faragher, John Mack. ***Frontiers: A Short History of the American West***. **New Haven, CT: Yale University Press, 2007.** ▶ Comprehensive work on this period and the U.S. West.

Greenberg, Amy S. ***A Wicked War: Polk, Clay, Lincoln and the 1846 Invasion of Mexico***. **New York: Knopf, 2012.** ▶ Description of the political landscape and antiwar sentiment prior to the U.S.–Mexican War.

Hämäläinen, Pekka. ***The Comanche Empire***. **New Haven, CT: Yale University Press, 2008.** ▶ The rise of the Comanches as they came to dominate the southern Great Plains against other Indian and Euro-American groups.

Holliday, J.S. ***The World Rushed In: The Gold Rush Experience***. **Norman: University of Oklahoma Press, 2002.** ▶ Widely considered the most comprehensive study of the Gold Rush.

Hyde, Ann. ***Empires, Nations, and Families: A History of the North American West, 1800–1860***. **Lincoln: University of Nebraska Press, 2011.** ▶ Award-winning narrative that looks at the relationships between families and how empires developed in the U.S. West.

Johnson, Susan. ***Roaring Camp: The Social World of the California Gold Rush***. **New York: Norton, 2000.** ▶ Award-winning account of the multifaceted nature of the Gold Rush and the ways the event upended social mores.

Montejano, David. ***Anglos and Mexicans in the Making of Texas, 1836–1986***. **Austin: University of Texas Press, 1987.** ▶ Analysis and explanation of the complex racial relations during the economic development of Texas.

Purdue, Theda, and Michael Green. ***Cherokee Nation and the Trail of Tears***. **New York: Penguin, 2008.** ▶ Comprehensive examination of the federal policies that led to the Cherokee tragedy and the response to it.

Weber, David. ***The Mexican Frontier: The American Southwest Under Mexico***. **Albuquerque: University of New Mexico Press, 1982.** ▶ Study of the region's history prior to its conquest and occupation by the U.S. government.

Go to the MindTap® for **Global Americans** to access the full version of select books from this Additional Resources section.

Websites

100 Milestone Documents. www.ourdocuments.gov ▶ Primary source site from the U.S. government with full text of important U.S. government documents.

Smithsonian Winter Count Project. www.wintercounts.si.edu ▶ Comprehensive digital collection of numerous Winter Counts with explanations.

MindTap®

Continue exploring online through MindTap®, where you can:

- **Assess your knowledge with the Chapter Test**
- **Watch historical videos related to the chapter**
- **Further your understanding with interactive maps and timelines**

A Continental Nation

1815–1821

October 1818

The U.S. Senate ratifies the Treaty of 1818, establishing the joint occupation of Oregon Territory with Great Britain.

February 1819

The U.S. Senate ratifies the Transcontinental Treaty, establishing the boundary with Spain in North America.

November 1820

James Monroe is elected president.

August 1821

Mexico and Spain sign the Treaty of Cordoba, which grants independence to Mexico.

1822–1829

April 1824

General Survey Act passes and allows the president to commission surveys for roads and canals.

August 1824

Republic of Mexico is established.

October 1824

Mexican Constitution abolishes slavery and frees all current slaves.

November 1824

John Quincy Adams is elected president.

November 1828

Andrew Jackson is elected president.

1830–1833

May 1830

Indian Removal Act authorizes the president to negotiate with tribes for their removal to western federal territories.

July 1831

Joseph Smith, leader of the Church of Latter Day Saints, reveals the practice of polygamy to his followers.

November 1831

Chocktaws begin their forced migration to Indian Territory in a process known as the *Trail of Tears*.

April 1832

Black Hawk War between the United States and Sauks begins.

November 1832

Andrew Jackson is reelected president.

May 1833

Bent's Fort is established as a major trading post for fur trappers.

1834–1836

December 1835

United States and Cherokees sign the Treaty of New Echota.

March 1836

Texas convention declares independence from Mexico, forms a government, and adopts a constitution.

April 1836

Sam Houston defeats General Santa Anna at the Battle of San Jacinto.

November 1836

Martin Van Buren is elected president.

1837–1841

Spring 1837

Smallpox epidemic in the Missouri River Valley kills thousands of Indians on the Great Plains.

August 1838

U.S. Exploration Expedition, led by Charles Wilkes, leaves Virginia.

December 1838

Cherokees begin their one-thousand-mile forced migration along the Trail of Tears.

November 1840

William Henry Harrison is elected president.

April 1841

John Tyler becomes president after the death of President Harrison.

September 1841

Preemption Act passes, allowing squatters living on federal lands to purchase up to 160 acres for $1.25 an acre.

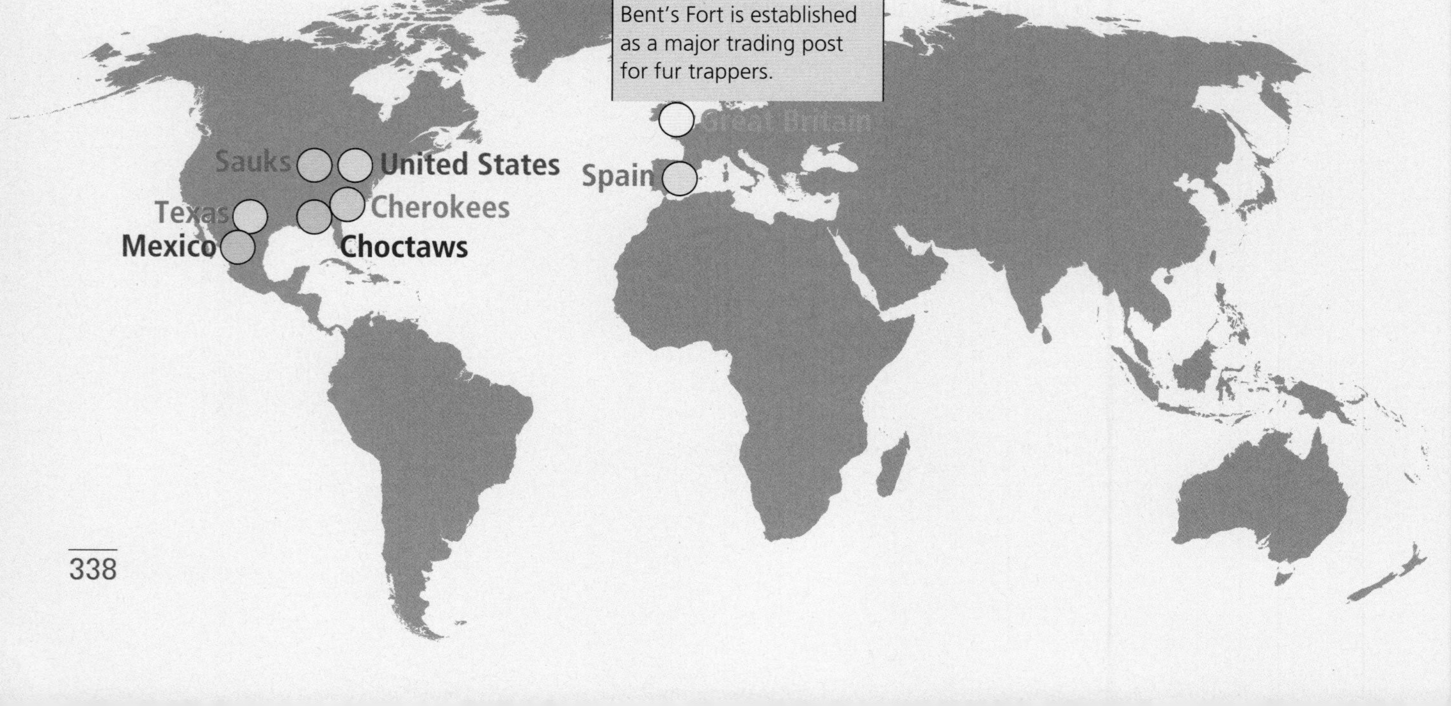

1842–1845

August 1842

U.S. Senate ratifies the Webster-Ashburton Treaty, resolving the territorial disputes between the United States and Great Britain.

October 1843

Almost a thousand immigrants, in what became known as the *Great Migration* to Oregon, arrive in the Willamette Valley.

November 1844

James K. Polk is elected president.

March 1845

Tyler annexes Texas to the United States. Florida joins the Union as a slave state.

December 1845

John Slidell arrives in Mexico and offers $30 million for California and much of the U.S. Southwest.

1846

February

Brigham Young leads his followers onto the Mormon Trail westward.

May

U.S. Congress approves a declaration of war against Mexico.

June

California declares its independence from Mexico and name it the Bear Flag Republic.

July

Mexico declares war on the United States.

1847

January

Taos Revolt against the United States occurs, killing Governor Charles Bent.

Treaty of Cahuenga is signed, and Mexico releases all claims to California.

June

Mormons under the leadership of Brigham Young arrive in present-day Utah.

August

At the Battles of Contreras and Churubusco, most of St. Patrick's Battalion are killed or captured.

September

After the Battle of Chapultepec, General Winfield Scott occupies Mexico City.

Polk recalls Trist from Mexico, but he remains.

1848–1850

January 1848

Gold is discovered at Sutter's Fort in California Territory.

February 1848

United States and Mexico agree to the terms of the Treaty of Guadalupe Hidalgo.

July 1848

Last U.S. troops depart from Mexican territory.

August 1848

New York Herald reports that gold has been discovered in California Territory.

December 1848

Polk confirms report of gold in California Territory.

Spring 1849

Thousands from around the world migrate to the California goldfields.

September 1850

U.S. Congress grants California statehood as part of the Compromise of 1850.

1851–1853

September 1851

The Fort Laramie Treaty between the United States and representatives from the Cheyennes, Arapahoes, Crows, Assiniboines, Mandans, Hidatsas, and Arikaras is signed.

December 1853

Gadsden Purchase adds territory from Mexico for a transcontinental railroad

Go to MindTap® to engage with an interactive version of the timeline. Analyze events and themes with clickable content, view related videos, and respond to critical thinking questions.

12 Expansion, Slavery, and the Coming of the Civil War

1848–1861

John Brown left rural New York for the Kansas territory, where he and his sons engaged in guerrilla warfare between his antislavery bands and proslavery militias. Brown would later launch the unsuccessful raid on Harpers Ferry and be executed for his efforts.

William Walker sailed from San Francisco to Nicaragua, eventually declaring himself president, legalizing slavery, and offering land grants to American plantation owners. Walker was eventually killed by a Honduran firing squad.

12-1

Continental Expansion, Conflict, and Compromise

12-1a Debate over Slavery in the Territories
12-1b Election of 1848
12-1c The Compromise of 1850

12-2

The United States Overseas

12-2a Americans and the Revolutions of 1848
12-2b American Commerce and Markets in Asia
12-2c U.S. Expansionism in Latin America

12-3

Reemergence of the Slavery Controversy

12-3a Abolitionists and Fugitive Slaves
12-3b *Uncle Tom's Cabin*
12-3c The Kansas-Nebraska Act

12-4

The Politics of Sectionalism

12-4a Anti-immigrant Sentiment and the Know-Nothings
12-4b Republicans and the Sectional Debate
12-4c Violence in Kansas, Congress, and California
12-4d *The Dred Scott* Case and Lincoln-Douglas Debates

12-5

Road to Disunion

12-5a John Brown's Raid
12-5b Election of 1860
12-5c The Secession Crisis
12-5d "And the War Came"
12-5e Slavery, Nationalism, and Civil War in Global Perspective

In the spring of 1855, William Walker and John Brown, two Americans of opposing sectional backgrounds and views, set out to resolve the status of slavery in new lands open to settlers. Walker sailed to Central America, whose tropical climate and fragile governments tempted U.S. adventurers, especially Southerners eager to extend U.S. rule and slave-labor plantations. Brown headed to the Kansas territory, where Congress had recently set off a small-scale civil war by declaring that the settlers themselves should decide whether to allow or ban slavery. Consumed by visions of fame and righteousness, both men believed themselves agents of destiny.

Boston Athenaeum
John Brown

Library of Congress Prints and Photographs Division[LC-USZC4-10802]
William Walker

A mildly successful lawyer from Tennessee, Walker had caught the fever for U.S. expansionism in Latin America. In May 1855, he sailed from San Francisco to Nicaragua with a small volunteer army that gained local allies in Central America, defeated the Nicaraguan army, and installed a puppet regime there. Following a sham election, Walker declared himself president of Nicaragua and legalized slavery. Describing Nicaragua as better suited to plantation agriculture than Kansas, he offered land grants to Southerners who would bring their slaves to grow cotton, sugar, and coffee.

John Brown was a restless tanner, sheep farmer, and land speculator who moved among several northern states seeking to support his large family. Although he was white, Brown settled for a few years in a rural New York black community on land donated by the wealthy abolitionist Gerrit Smith. Before long, Brown became convinced that he was divinely appointed to destroy slavery. In 1855, he followed his sons to Kansas territory to spearhead the fight against slaveholding settlers. There Brown led a raid on a proslavery settlement that killed five residents. For months afterward, guerrilla warfare raged in Kansas between Brown's antislavery bands and armed proslavery militias, some sent from neighboring Missouri.

Walker and Brown failed in their missions. A Central American army led by Costa Rica forced Walker out of Nicaragua, while Brown, his men badly outnumbered by proslavery guerrillas, fled Kansas to safety in New England. Yet these self-styled freedom fighters remained undeterred. Walker launched several more expeditions to Nicaragua, the last an attempt in 1860 to penetrate the country through neighboring Honduras. Meanwhile, in October 1859, Brown electrified Americans by leading an unsuccessful raid on the federal arsenal at Harpers Ferry, Virginia, in hope of stirring a rebellion among local slaves. Captured by U.S. marines, he was convicted of treason and executed by hanging. Less than a year later, Walker was taken into custody and killed by a Honduran firing squad.

How do the fanatical actions of John Brown and William Walker in the name of their causes reflect America's intensifying divisions in the mid-nineteenth century?

Go to MindTap® to watch a video on Brown and Walker and learn how their stories relate to the themes of this chapter.

Not all proslavery and antislavery enthusiasts were as fanatical or as prepared as Walker and Brown to die for their cause. During the 1850s, however, Americans became increasingly divided into opposing camps. As the nation's borders expanded in the Southwest and settlers filled in the Great Plains, the contest between proslavery and antislavery advocates intensified. Each expansionist move—the purchase of California and New Mexico as prizes of the U.S.–Mexican War, the opening of Kansas and other western prairie lands, and the prospect of annexing Cuba and other Caribbean territories—led to a showdown between impassioned citizens of the northern and southern states over the issue of extending the South's slave society into the nation's territories. Despite a temporary congressional compromise in 1850, sectional tensions mounted in the following years during a series of crises based in one way or another on differences over slavery. The confrontation culminated when the majority of slave states seceded from the Union and war broke out between the United States and the rebellious Confederacy.

Viewed in global context, the American sectional struggle over slavery in the territories was part of a transatlantic upsurge in nationalist feeling in the 1840s and 1850s. Nationalist and republican revolutions swept through Europe in 1848 while wars of national unification or expansion raged in Mexico and South America. Almost everywhere, competing visions of national futures led to conflicts over territorial boundaries, forms of representative government, central versus local control, and degrees of personal freedom. Many Americans sympathized with overseas struggles against kings and tyrants, but when their own nation's expansion became intertwined with fierce sectional divisions over slavery versus freedom, its political leaders inched step-by-step toward a homegrown nationalist war.

12-1 Continental Expansion, Conflict, and Compromise

Library of Congress Prints and Photographs Division[LC-DIG-pga-02601]

This 1852 engraving by Henry S. Sadd after a painting by Tomkins Harrison Matteson, entitled *Union*, commemorates the Compromise of 1850, an agreement forged in Congress to resolve the dispute over the status of slavery in territories acquired after the U.S.–Mexican War. Most of the key individuals who debated the compromise are posed formally, including General Winfield Scott, Lewis Cass, Henry Clay, John C. Calhoun, and Daniel Webster.

Analyze the symbolism of the print. Why are Webster, who approved the compromise, and Calhoun, who opposed it, both depicted next to a bust of George Washington? Why do they rest their hands on the U.S. Constitution? Why is Clay seated at the center? Why does an eagle help to part the curtain in the background, revealing a gleaming classical temple? What is meant by the engraving's title? ▶

Many Americans took pride in their nation's expansion across the continent, but some wondered whether the growing "empire of liberty" should extend the institution of slavery. Victory in the U.S.–Mexican War aroused northern fears that southern politicians would turn the new territories thus gained into slave states. Some claimed to detect a conspiracy to expand the South's "peculiar institution" and use slave-state votes to control national politics. At stake in the struggle over the West were the competing political fortunes of the North and South and the future of the nation. Out of this volatile mix of ambitions and fears emerged a proposal to outlaw slavery in the new territories that opened a fierce debate in Congress and sparked talk of southern states' quitting the Union. Tensions were neutralized only when Congress approved a shaky sectional compromise.

☞ As you read, consider the opposing positions Americans took on the issue of slavery in the territories. How did the Compromise of 1850 attempt to reconcile them?

12-1a Debate over Slavery in the Territories

Partisans of free soil, states' rights, and popular sovereignty vie for control over western lands.

A few months into the U.S.–Mexican War, David Wilmot, a Pennsylvania Democrat, offered an amendment to a funding bill pledging that "neither slavery nor involuntary servitude" would be permitted in any lands acquired from Mexico. The **Wilmot Proviso** echoed the wording of the Northwest Ordinance to emphasize that Congress was empowered by the framers of the Constitution to prohibit slavery in federal territories. Although it never passed both houses, for the next few years, the proviso focused and escalated the national controversy over the expansion of slavery.

In the debates of 1846–1848, three main positions emerged, two aggressively sectional and one aimed at compromise. Wilmot's idea that the federal government could and should prohibit slavery in the territories was labeled **"free soil."** A diverse coalition of Northerners rallied under its banner. Political abolitionists supported the free-soil position as a key step toward ending slavery. Yet one could oppose slavery's extension without being an abolitionist. Wilmot, for example, declared that "the negro race already occupy enough of this fair continent." He and many white Northerners believed that slave plantations in the West would shut out the North's aspiring white farmers. Promotion of white economic opportunity in the West was often tinged with prejudice against blacks, free as well as slave. In 1848, Illinois voters approved a law forbidding free blacks from entering the state, and Indiana soon followed suit.

Alarmed by Northerners' support for free soil, prominent Southerners sought a secure future for their slave society. John C. Calhoun argued that the Constitution and the Fugitive Slave Law of 1793 defined slaves as property and that protection of owners' rights meant that they could take their slaves into territories. This position extended Calhoun's states' rights doctrine beyond state borders. It reflected not only slave owners' ambitions to expand their realm but also the hopes of nonslave-owning Southerners who looked to western territories for the chance to raise their social and economic standing.

A potentially attractive compromise beckoned in the idea of **"popular sovereignty,"** which was formulated by Lewis Cass of Michigan and later championed by his fellow Democrat, Stephen Douglas of Illinois. Why not let the territorial settlers decide for themselves the status of slavery? This formula took the controversy out of Congress and invoked U.S. traditions of self-government and local control. It fudged crucial questions with ambiguous language by not specifying how and at what stage slavery could be banned. Both proslavery and free-soil settlers warmed to "popular sovereignty" because each saw how it might bring victory.

12-1b Election of 1848

Party divisions over slavery give the presidency to the Whigs' Zachary Taylor.

The question of slavery in the territories remained unresolved during the election of 1848. Polk declined a second term, so the Democrats turned to Cass, a party veteran who ran on the platform of popular sovereignty. The Whigs again sought victory by running a war hero; this time it was General Zachary Taylor of U.S.–Mexican War fame. Because Taylor was a southern slaveholder and the Whigs refused to endorse the free-soil position, many southern Democrats crossed party lines to vote for the general. Meanwhile, Northerners opposed to extending slavery, who were snubbed by the two parties, formed a new organization. The **Free-Soil Party** appealed to Democrats who favored the Wilmot Proviso, antislavery Whigs, and former Liberty Party men. It nominated former president Martin Van Buren.

Van Buren attracted one in seven northern voters, not enough to win any northern state but sufficient to play "spoiler" by dividing these states along East-West lines between Taylor and Cass. As a result, the soldier-planter Taylor, who was stronger than Cass in the South, won a narrow victory. The Free-Soil Party won ten seats in Congress, another sign that the major parties were beginning to crack under the strain of the slavery question. It was left to the aged General Taylor, who had no political experience and had never even voted, to resolve the conflicted legacy of the war he had helped the United States to win.

12-1c The Compromise of 1850

After much maneuvering, Congress adopts measures to settle the sectional dispute over slavery.

By the time Taylor took office in March 1849, the slavery issue had become pressing because the Gold Rush had populated California so quickly with new settlers that it skipped territorial status and qualified for statehood. A strong proponent of Manifest Destiny, Taylor believed that the slavery controversy should not block the path to continental empire. Encouraged by the new president, California voters drew up a state constitution that prohibited slavery. Southerners closed ranks to oppose the state's admission. Because the ratio of free to slave states was fifteen to fifteen, admitting California would give the North a critical edge in the Senate and add to its majority in the House.

With Congress deadlocked, Henry Clay, the venerable Whig leader who had helped forge compromises over Missouri in 1820 and

Wilmot Proviso Proposal in 1846 for Congress to ban slavery from all territory gained from the U.S.–Mexican War that touched off heated sectional debate.

free soil Political platform declaring that Congress should exercise its constitutional power to prohibit slavery in the western territories.

popular sovereignty Position taken by many Democrats in the debate over slavery in the territories that asserted local, not congressional, control over the issue.

Free-Soil Party Third political party organized in 1848 by Democratic and Whig dissidents who opposed the expansion of slavery into western territories.

the tariff in 1833, constructed a compromise "omnibus bill" that addressed several contentious issues, including California statehood and the status of slavery in other lands acquired from Mexico. Clay's bill touched off a six-month debate in which the Senate's aging giants, John C. Calhoun and Daniel Webster, mustered their best arguments and oratory. Calhoun warned that the Union was doomed unless Northerners ceased attacking slavery and Southerners were given a permanent veto over laws related to it. Webster rose, speaking "not as a Massachusetts man, nor as a Northern man, but as an American," to support sectional compromise.

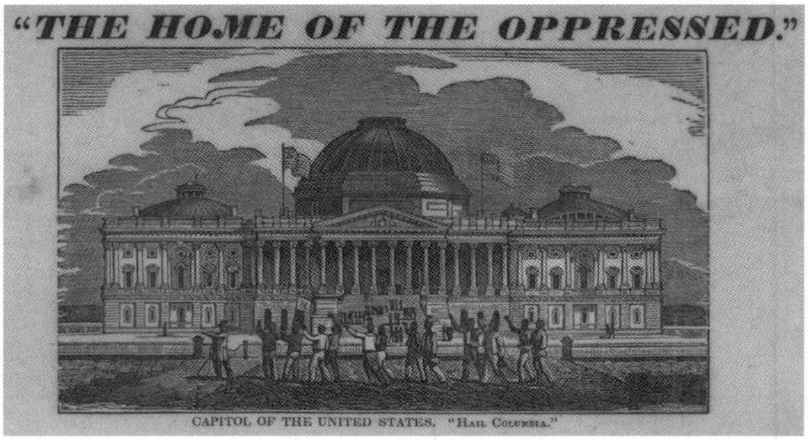

"THE HOME OF THE OPPRESSED."
CAPITOL OF THE UNITED STATES. "HAIL COLUMBIA."

A Capital under Slavery's Shadow This abolitionist engraving dramatizes a national embarrassment: a line of shackled African Americans being marched past the U.S. Capitol on their way to slave markets. This blatant juxtaposition of white liberty and black slavery stunned many foreign visitors and appalled Illinois congressman Abraham Lincoln, who introduced a bill in 1849 to abolish slavery in the District of Columbia. The Compromise of 1850 outlawed slave trading, but not slaveholding, in the nation's capital. ▲

In July, hopes for compromise were shattered when Congress defeated Clay's proposal. Calhoun was dead, the exhausted Clay left Washington, and Webster, bitterly attacked in Massachusetts for his concessions, resigned to become secretary of state. Just when all appeared lost, two events allowed a deal to be struck. First, President Taylor, who had opposed Clay's bill, died suddenly of an intestinal ailment. His successor, Millard Fillmore of New York, was a milder man and a political veteran who persuaded other Whigs to join the compromise. Second, Clay's younger ally, Stephen Douglas of Illinois, took charge of the bill, and the "Little Giant," a five-feet, four-inch dynamo, brought new energy to the fight. Douglas shrewdly broke up Clay's package and introduced the measures separately, building a different coalition to pass bills that admitted California as a free state, placed the New Mexico and Utah Territories under popular sovereignty, adjusted the Texas state boundary, strengthened federal sanctions against fugitive slaves, and banned slave trading in the nation's capital. Few senators voted for all these measures, but taken together, they became known as the **Compromise of 1850** (see Table 12.1).

President Fillmore hailed the deal as the "final and irrevocable" settlement of the sectional dispute over slavery. For all its shortcomings, the Compromise of 1850 had two big advantages. First, massive victory rallies in Washington and other cities seemed to indicate that the majority of voters was relieved to end the crisis. Second, the status of slavery in all U.S. territories was now confirmed. Although there was still the potential for overseas expansion, within the nation's boundaries there were no new lands to fight over.

Compromise of 1850 Cluster of five bills passed by Congress to resolve the dispute over the status of slavery in lands acquired after the U.S.–Mexican War.

In the presidential campaign of 1852, both major parties endorsed the sectional compromise, but the Democrats were the more united party. Torn between "Conscience" Whigs who opposed Fillmore and "Cotton" Whigs who appeased the South, the Whigs nominated another U.S.–Mexican War hero, the Virginian Winfield Scott. Some antislavery northern Whigs bolted to support John P. Hale of the Free-Soil Party. The Democrats chose Franklin Pierce, a New Hampshire politician whose enthusiasm for expansion and silence on slavery satisfied the party's southern wing. Pierce won easily with 254 electoral votes to Scott's 42.

Pierce interpreted the results as popular approval of the 1850 congressional deal. His inaugural address contrasted Europe convulsed by revolutions and the United States, which was blessed with prosperity and calmed by sectional compromise. Proclaiming the United States exempt from "their wars, their tumults, and anxieties," Pierce called "unfounded" the fear that "extended territory [and] multiplied States" posed dangers to the republic. Events at home and abroad soon challenged such confidence.

Table 12.1 The Compromise of 1850

Because only a handful of senators voted for all of its measures, the Compromise of 1850 did not represent an agreement forged by concessions on both sides. In hindsight, it may be more accurate to label it an uneasy truce than a genuine compromise.

Pro-North Provisions	Pro-South Provisions
California admitted as a free state	Slavery permitted in New Mexico and Utah territories under "popular sovereignty"
Texas boundary dispute settled by granting lands east of Rio Grande to New Mexico Territory	Texas given $10 million by U.S. government to pay state debts and drop its claim to New Mexico lands
Slave trade prohibited in Washington, D.C.	Tough new Fugitive Slave Law adopted

12-2

The United States Overseas

Glenn Asakawa/The Denver Post/Getty Images

On July 8, 1853, U.S. naval commodore Matthew Perry led a flotilla of steamships under a cloud of black smoke into Tokyo Bay to force the long-secluded country to open its doors. Ocean-going steamships were unfamiliar to Japanese artists, and this colorful woodblock print dramatically portrays Perry's vessel.

What kind of human features did the Japanese artist give Perry's ship, and why? Does the image convey fear of Western technology, fascination with it, or both? ▶

Once the United States spanned the continent, the nation's leaders looked beyond its borders to project American power. President Pierce held visions of U.S. global influence that reflected agreement among business and political elites from both parties that American ideals, trade, and territory should spread wherever possible. Many hoped that European nations would adopt the U.S. republican model, especially after nationalist and democratic revolutions broke out in 1848. Some sought new U.S. territories in Mexico and Central America. Others, eager to follow up on overland expansion to California, pushed American commerce to the Pacific and predicted fabulous profits from the China trade. As an added benefit, Pierce hoped that initiatives abroad would divert Americans' energies from festering domestic divisions. Yet Europe's revolutions and U.S. initiatives in Latin America quickly became entangled in controversies at home over the slavery question.

☞ As you read, consider the various locales, goals, and methods of U.S. expansionism after 1848. Where did U.S. expansionists look to project the nation's power, and how? How successful were they? How did the slavery issue intrude?

12-2a Americans and the Revolutions of 1848

Support for European revolutions reflects Americans' international ambitions and their internal divisions.

President Pierce was part of **Young America**, a cohort of emerging journalists and politicians who rose to prominence as Clay, Webster, and Calhoun faded with age. The group's label replaced *United States* with *America*, a term that absorbed the entire hemisphere and referred to national ideals as well as a particular place. The label also reflected transatlantic crosscurrents. "Young Italy" and "Young Germany" were nationalist movements of the 1840s whose members, inspired by the U.S. example, sought to unify their nations under republican governments. The Young Americans were energized by this European ferment and by pride in their nation's prosperity and territorial gains. They became a vocal faction in the Democratic Party, promoting an aggressive, male-dominated literary and political nationalism. Their leading magazine, the *Democratic Review*, championed a unique national identity for American literature, publishing works by Ralph Waldo Emerson, Henry David Thoreau, Nathaniel Hawthorne, and Walt Whitman. In politics, Young Americans updated the Democrats' agrarian stance by accommodating banks and promoting railroads. They advocated aggressive expansion into western territories and support for republican movements abroad.

Young America's hopes for the spread of democratic institutions seemed to be confirmed by the **Revolutions of 1848** that swept through Europe. Popular demands for reform first erupted into revolution in Paris, where a crowd invaded the royal palace and proclaimed the Second French Republic. This was followed by nationalist uprisings in the German states, Italy, and the Austrian empire. In Germany and Italy, revolutionary leaders aimed to unify a patchwork of small states under a national republic. In the Austrian empire, the Hungarians and other ethnic groups sought independence. Whether they promoted breakaway or consolidating nationalism, most European revolutionaries fought to create republican governments.

Americans welcomed news of the uprisings against kings with massive rallies in several American cities. The United States was the first nation to recognize the new French republic. Beyond this, what form American assistance to European revolutionaries should take proved controversial. To aid an insurrection against Britain planned by the "Young Ireland" movement, a band of Irish Americans sailed across the Atlantic, but they were arrested and detained until U.S. diplomats apologized to the British

Young America Circle of writers and Democratic politicians promoting expansion of U.S. influence and institutions through North America and overseas.

Revolutions of 1848 Wave of nationalist and republican uprisings that swept Europe in 1848, most of which failed or were suppressed.

Library of Congress

Global Americans The Young America movement not only inspired writers and politicians; it also spawned ambitious entrepreneurs who promoted U.S. business ventures abroad and coupled them with republican values. William Wheelwright built railroads in Chile; Freeman Cobb set up stagecoach lines in Australia; and Perry Collins proposed constructing a telegraph line across Russia. None of these men was more colorful than **George Francis Train**, a publicity-seeking Massachusetts merchant who became a shipping magnate, railroad organizer, travel writer, and confidant of European revolutionaries. In 1853, Train sailed to Melbourne, Australia, to set up a shipping business connected to England and California. He described his return journey in *Young America Abroad* and *An American Merchant in Europe, Asia and Australia*, books published in 1857. A zealous believer in the United States as a model for the world, Train urged the Australians and Irish to declare independence from Britain, rejoiced to find Crimean War soldiers swigging New England rum, and promoted democratic ideas wherever he went. "He would have every place Americanized, including Jerusalem and Athens," an English critic complained. In the 1850s, Train built London's first horse-drawn street railway and then returned to promote a U.S. transcontinental railroad. Two decades later, he circled the globe in record time, a feat that inspired Frenchman Jules Verne's adventure novel, *Around the World in Eighty Days* (1873). Increasingly eccentric, Train died a forgotten man in 1904. Fifty years earlier, however, his colorful promotion of American technology and ideals abroad made him a famous "Young American" on three foreign continents.

government. Despite public pressures, Polk and later U.S. presidents adhered to the policy of noninterference in European affairs, and Congress sent no military aid to Europe's freedom fighters.

After 1848, the forces of European reaction regrouped to suppress the nationalist revolts. French conservatives rallied around Louis Napoleon, nephew of the former emperor, who declared himself Emperor Napoleon III in 1852. In Austria, the Hapsburg monarchy accepted the revolutionaries' decree ending serfdom but ruthlessly put down uprisings in Vienna, Prague, and Budapest, the last with aid from Russia.

Americans' reactions to the failures of 1848 reflected their stance toward growing sectional divisions at home. Some Northerners blamed Europe's aristocratic classes for squelching reforms and vowed to fight against undemocratic "despots" at home and abroad. To anxious onlookers in the South, the revolutions showed that popular agitation could easily slide toward radicalism. In 1848, France's revolutionary government abolished slavery in overseas colonies, and legislators influenced by socialist ideas set up National Workshops that guaranteed workers employment. That same year, a pair of exiled German revolutionaries, Karl Marx and Friedrich Engels, published the *Communist Manifesto*, which predicted that class struggles would soon topple capitalism and inaugurate rule by the working class ("proletariat") for the equal benefit of all.

In practical terms, the suppression of European revolutions strengthened the free-soil movement by sending a vocal group of German "Forty-Eighters" into exile. Deeply influenced by democratic ideas, these immigrants settled chiefly in free midwestern states and often voted against proslavery interests. In the 1850s,

Kossuth in America In 1851, exiled Hungarian patriot Louis Kossuth arrived for a U.S. fund-raising tour. A Kossuth mania overtook Americans as they renamed towns for him and beards like his became fashionable, replacing the clean-shaven look of the Founders. But Kossuth alienated many Americans with his noncommittal stance on slavery. This Hungarian Fund certificate shows Kossuth in the center and promises the donor repayment one year after Hungary wins independence. Kossuth departed with meager donations and no pledge of U.S. government aid. ▼

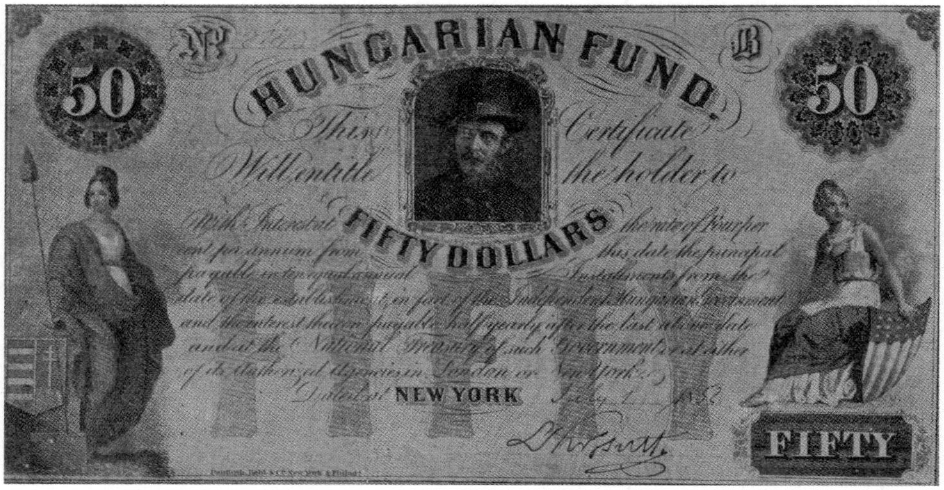

Facsimile of a fifty dollar note of the Hungarian Fund, signed by Kossuth (engraving), English School, (19th century)/Private Collection/© Look and Learn/Illustrated Papers Collection/Bridgeman Images

leading Forty-Eighters such as Carl Schurz of Missouri and Friedrich Hecker of Illinois rallied support among German Americans for the newly formed Republican Party and its free-soil platform.

Despite their failure, the European revolutions heightened popular zeal to have the U.S. republican experiment succeed and its institutions imitated elsewhere. Whether such institutions should include slavery and whether American influence should be spread by example or intervention remained divisive questions.

12-2b American Commerce and Markets in Asia

U.S. commercial influence extends with pressure on China, Japan, and Hawai'i.

In the 1850s, Asia was another focal point for Americans' overseas ambitions, with trade the primary objective. Since Jefferson, U.S. presidents and diplomats had pursued a strategy of finding markets abroad for the nation's goods and of keeping sea-lanes open for commerce. As the nation reached the Pacific, this strategy stretched to Asia. Senator William H. Seward, later secretary of state, urged U.S. businessmen to "multiply your ships, and send them forth to the East," declaring that the nation that dominated Pacific trade would become "the great power on earth." Like Seward, many Americans viewed the plunge into the Pacific as the culminating phase of frontier expansion. Protestant missionaries eyed the West Coast as a staging ground for evangelizing in Asia. Congressional orators predicted that the United States would carry Western science and republican institutions to China and Japan while American farms became Asia's granary.

The reality fell short of the rhetoric. Americans' desire to trade with Asia ran up against the desire of China and Japan to fend off Western pressures. U.S. shippers traded ginseng, furs, and (in some cases) opium to obtain tea, textiles, and porcelains from Chinese merchants, but Western rivals outpaced them. The British, French, and Russian empires vied for colonies as well as **spheres of influence**, concessions that included control over certain territories, ports open to foreign ships, access for missionaries, and even "extraterritoriality," the right to enforce European rather than indigenous laws. In the 1850s, U.S. policy makers' most realistic goals in Asia were treaties that granted the same trade privileges given to other Western nations.

In China's second opium war, called the *Arrow War* (1856–1860), the United States offered modest naval support when the British and French invaded Beijing. At the war's end, the United States obtained access to treaty ports that Europeans forced China to open. This conflict occurred in the middle of the **Taiping Rebellion** (1850–1864), the century's bloodiest civil war, in which more than 20 million Chinese people perished, mainly from starvation and disease. Britain, France, and Russia took advantage of the crisis to grab territory on China's coast and borders, and some Americans proposed seizing Formosa (now Taiwan). But U.S. leaders' vision of empire did not yet include annexing land in Asia. The China trade failed to meet Westerners' inflated expectations, and the United States lagged behind Britain in gaining a share.

American relations with Japan were a different story because the United States took the lead in prying open the Japanese market. The Shogun, Japan's military ruler, had prohibited all but a few contacts with Westerners after European missionaries and traders were expelled in the 1630s. That isolation ended suddenly. Ordered by President Fillmore to survey the Asian coast and to negotiate a trade treaty with Japan, U.S. naval commodore Matthew C. Perry cruised up Tokyo Bay in July 1853 with a squadron of steam-powered warships. The Americans believed that a show of strength would win concessions that the British and Russians had failed to get. After much hesitation, Japanese officials, aware of China's recent military defeats against Western powers, relented. By agreeing to the **Treaty of Kanagawa** (1854), modeled on the **unequal treaties** that China had signed, Japan opened two ports to American ships, offered protection for shipwrecked crews, and allowed American vessels to buy provisions. A second treaty in 1858 opened full diplomatic relations between the United States and Japan and placed a low tariff on imported American goods. Such treaties set the unequal, and to the Japanese, humiliating, terms of Japan's commercial relations with Western powers for the rest of the century.

Increasing trade with Japan amplified Hawai'i's importance as a stopover where steamships could refuel. Already significant as a whaling port and the site of sugar plantations owned by Americans, Hawai'i allowed U.S. businessmen and missionaries to exercise growing influence on its government. In the 1840s, rival U.S., French, and British officials pledged to respect Hawai'i's independence under King Kamehameha III, but their truce was uneasy. Americans who held key ministerial posts in the Hawaiian government pushed for closer ties. In 1854, an envoy of President Pierce negotiated a treaty of annexation, but it was never signed because of foreign protests and disputes over whether slavery would be permitted. U.S. policy makers remained determined to dominate the Hawaiian economy and to prevent other nations from taking over the islands.

spheres of influence Areas outside a nation's territory but still under its sway; in the case of empires, lands that conceded trading and other rights to imperial powers.

Taiping Rebellion Long and bloody Chinese civil war that allowed Western powers to increase their local influence.

Treaty of Kanagawa Agreement between the United States and Japan that opened Japanese trade to American merchants.

unequal treaties Nineteenth-century treaties signed by China and Japan under duress ceding trading privileges, missionary access, or territorial concessions to Western powers.

12-2c U.S. Expansionism in Latin America

American moves to purchase or seize Caribbean lands heighten the domestic dispute over slavery.

When Hawaiian annexation failed, southern politicians' hopes for slave plantations in the Pacific turned to the Caribbean, whose nearby location, tropical climate, and colonial history appeared hospitable to slavery. Sugar plantations worked by half a million slaves still thrived in Spanish Cuba and Puerto Rico, and unstable governments in Spain's former Central American lands seemed to invite intervention. Potential U.S. possessions in the Caribbean and Latin America might become slave states that could, one proslavery politician claimed, give the South "more power & influence than . . . a dozen wild deserts" of the Southwest. Such lands (see Map 12.1) might be purchased or seized by filibusterers. Southern expansionists had found important allies in Presidents Polk, Pierce, and Buchanan, who were strong supporters of slavery, Manifest Destiny, and expanded overseas trade.

The defensive part of Southerners' strategy involved quarantining Haiti. For decades after Haiti's blacks had abolished slavery and won independence from France, the United States withheld diplomatic recognition of the country. Trade in sugar and grains flourished between the two nations, and many U.S. merchants and abolitionists supported formal relations, but southern politicians stood in the way. A free black republic was too dangerous to befriend for American slaveholders, who feared the influence of Haiti's example and its refugees among their slaves.

In contrast, Cuba, just ninety miles off the Florida coast, struck white Southerners as a candidate for annexation. Before the 1840s, U.S. officials backed Spanish rule in Cuba to preserve regional stability and to avoid a "second Haiti." When wealthy Cuban exiles began agitating for Americans to assist Cuban independence, southern politicians saw a chance for the Democrats to acquire it "for the planting and spreading of slavery," as a Mississippi senator admitted. In 1848, President Polk authorized $100 million to purchase Cuba, but Spain's foreign minister ruled out selling the island, which he considered a jewel in the Spanish empire's crown.

One response to Spain's refusal came from Narciso López, a Venezuela-born Cuban who recruited a private invading force in the U.S. South. In 1850 and 1851, he sailed from New Orleans to Cuba with a small army. The first time, López failed to win local support in Cuba and retreated in defeat to Florida. The second time, Spanish soldiers killed two hundred of his men and executed fifty, including López himself. Another response to Spain's defense of Cuba was to escalate U.S. pressure to purchase the island. The U.S. minister to Spain, Pierre Soulé of Louisiana, tried to use an incident involving the illegal seizure of an American ship to threaten Spain with war. In October 1854, Soulé and the U.S. ministers to England and France met in Belgium and drafted a memorandum to Pierce declaring that the United States should seize Cuba if Spain refused to sell it. But this **Ostend Manifesto** was leaked to the public, and an outcry among Northerners forced the Pierce administration to disavow it. The dream of a Cuban slave state died hard, however, and purchasing Cuba remained on the Democratic Party's platform until the Civil War.

Ostend Manifesto Letter from U.S. ministers in Europe to President Pierce in 1854 recommending purchase or seizure of Cuba from Spain.

Clayton-Bulwer Treaty Accord in which the United States and Britain disavowed plans to colonize Central America and agreed to permit mutual access to any canals constructed there.

Another target for expansion southward was Mexico. The All-Mexico movement had faltered after the U.S.–Mexican War (see Chapter 11), but the cession of California and New Mexico whetted some expansionists' appetite for additional chunks of Mexican land. Southern-born filibusterers launched unsuccessful private invasions of Mexican border provinces from California in the 1850s. In 1853, President Pierce sent an envoy to offer Mexican ruler Santa Anna up to $50 million for several areas, including Baja California. In the Gadsden Purchase, Pierce settled for a much smaller addition to southern New Mexico to ease construction of a transcontinental railroad (see page 352).

As it turned out, Americans built the first transcontinental railroad outside, not within, their nation's borders. U.S. interest in Central America intensified after the Gold Rush showed the importance of a shorter passage between the Atlantic and Pacific Oceans than sailing around Cape Horn. In 1855, after New Granada (present-day Colombia) ceded the right of transit across Panama, a U.S. company completed the forty-eight-mile Panama Railway connecting Colón on the Atlantic coast to Panama City on the Pacific. Westward expansion across the continent came to depend heavily on the steamship route to and from the isthmus and the railroad route across it, which transported more gold seekers than the Overland Trail. In the next decade, the Panama route carried the bulk of U.S. mail as well as gold and silver shipments from California to eastern banks.

In Nicaragua, where a large interior lake aided the crossing between oceans, the United States confronted Great Britain's prior claim to coastal lands. The two nations agreed in the **Clayton-Bulwer Treaty** of 1850 not to exclude others from any waterway they built. Although high costs and engineering difficulties prevented construction of a canal, U.S. business tycoon Cornelius Vanderbilt established a road and steamship route through Nicaragua that carried two thousand Americans between the oceans each month.

Into this strategic and contested terrain came William Walker, seeking fame, fortune, and territory for slavery. In May 1855, he sailed from San Francisco to Nicaragua with a band of fifty-six men that was later reinforced by local opponents of the Nicaraguan government. Aided by repeating rifles, Walker's men defeated the Nicaraguan army and installed a puppet government. In 1856, Walker declared himself president of Nicaragua, legalized slavery, and announced plans to reopen the African slave trade.

Despite bitter opposition from antislavery politicians, the Pierce administration immediately recognized Walker's government. Nicaragua's tropical farms could "never be developed without slave labor," the U.S. minister to Nicaragua explained. But Walker's triumph was short lived. Troops from Costa Rica, inspired by nationalist hero Juan Santamaria and subsidized by Walker's rival Vanderbilt as well as Great Britain, invaded and helped the Nicaraguans defeat Walker's army. Southerners' dream of a proslavery empire in the Caribbean did not become reality, but it scarred U.S. politics throughout the 1850s. Pierce and other Young America supporters had hoped that overseas expansion might quell the domestic debate over slavery, but filibustering and overtures to buy territory only sharpened the sectional conflict.

Map 12.1 Filibustering Expeditions in Latin America, 1850–1860 Throughout the 1850s, U.S. adventurers mounted illegal private expeditions to grab land from northern Mexico, independent Central American republics, and the Spanish colony of Cuba. Filibusterers sought fame and fortune as well as expanding U.S. territory, including areas where slavery could take root. ▲

12-3

Reemergence of the Slavery Controversy

In the climax to Harriet Beecher Stowe's bestselling novel, *Uncle Tom's Cabin* (1852), the runaway slave Eliza crosses the half-frozen Ohio River to freedom with her child. This poster for a British-American theatrical coproduction shows Eliza making the treacherous nighttime crossing while fending off hounds sent by slave catchers visible on the far shore.

How would this scene, taken from Stowe's novel, evoke the northern public's sympathies for slaves and suggest slavery's relevance to their lives? ▶

Library of Congress Prints and Photographs Division[LC-USZC4-1298]

Plans for expansion beyond existing U.S. borders escalated sectional divisions over slavery. Closer to home, the controversy over fugitive slaves showed how the Compromise of 1850 had heightened Northerners' awareness of their entanglement with slavery and its impact on their daily lives. African American and white abolitionists' challenges to the strengthened Fugitive Slave Law combined with a best-selling novel dramatizing the plight of the South's slaves captured the public's attention. Tensions reached the boiling point, but only after the question of slavery in the territories reemerged unexpectedly in 1854. That year, a law that opened the Kansas territory to slave owners shattered the sectional truce.

☞ As you read, consider the events that reignited controversy over slavery in the United States in the early 1850s. How did black and white abolitionists revive the debate over slavery after the Compromise of 1850? How did the question of slavery in the territories resurface?

Library of Congress Prints and Photographs Division

Global Americans The most famous of the Underground Railroad's "conductors," **Harriet Tubman** exemplifies the transnational dimension of U.S. slaves' journey to freedom. Born into slavery on a Maryland plantation, Araminta "Minty" Ross became a muscular laborer and a habitual rebel who married freeman John Tubman in 1844. Emboldened by stories of successful runaways he told and by fears that her family would soon be sold, she fled to Philadelphia in 1849, where she adopted her mother's name, Harriet. Determined to lead others to freedom, Tubman returned to Maryland and, after the Fugitive Slave Act of 1850 raised the risk of capture, began to guide escaped slaves on a long and dangerous route through Pennsylvania and western New York to Canada, where Britain had outlawed slavery in 1833. Carrying a revolver and using the North Star as a guide, Tubman traveled with her "passengers" at night and relied on local free blacks and white abolitionists for assistance. Slaveholders posted rewards for her capture, but she was never apprehended. After Tubman established her home in St. Catharines, Canada West (present-day Ontario), she made it a haven for fugitive slaves, including many friends and family members. In the 1850s, she returned to the South more than a dozen times to conduct runaways to Canada. Abolitionist William Lloyd Garrison called her "Moses" for leading hundreds of escapees to the "Promised Land"—which before the Civil War meant Canada for those seeking legal protection from recapture.

12-3a Abolitionists and Fugitive Slaves

> Abolitionist agitation and the new fugitive slave law bring slavery home to Northerners.

Abolitionists played a major role in keeping the moral issue of slavery in public view after the Compromise of 1850. Fearing recapture after his escape from slavery, Frederick Douglass left the United States in 1845 to lecture in England and Ireland, where abolitionist sympathizers purchased his freedom. When he returned, Douglass resolved to take an independent stand against all forms of white racism. Breaking with his antipolitical mentor, William Lloyd Garrison, Douglass supported the Free Soil Party's campaign against slavery in the territories. His newspaper, the *North Star*, supplemented news of the antislavery movement with exposés of segregationist practices in northern schools, streetcars, and railroads. In an 1852 Independence Day speech, Douglass asked pointedly "What to the slave is the Fourth of July?" His answer: "A day that reveals to him, more than all other days in the year, the gross injustice and cruelty to which he is the constant victim."

Douglass hoped to change attitudes and practices—North and South—with appeals to conscience, but not all black leaders were as optimistic as he was. In the wake of the Compromise of 1850, Martin Delany promoted plans to leave the United States. Delany, who had been dismissed from Harvard Medical School after white students objected to a black man's presence, suggested in *The Condition, Elevation, Emigration, and Destiny of the Colored People of the United States* (1852) that free blacks and slave runaways build a black homeland in Central America or West Africa. In 1859, he negotiated a treaty with Yoruba leaders to settle free African Americans on land that is now part of Nigeria. However, the vast majority of northern blacks remained in the free states, determined to fight for civil rights and an end to slavery. Even male and female delegates to the 1854 National Emigration Convention in Cleveland approved a resolution demanding "every political right, privilege and position to which the whites are eligible in the United States."

Some northern blacks organized campaigns to end discrimination in employment and education. After five-year-old Sarah Roberts was refused admission to a nearby white school and assigned to a distant and poorly funded all-black school in Boston, her father took the case to court. Robert Morris, the first black lawyer to argue a jury case in the United States, cocounseled with Charles Sumner to challenge Boston's segregated school system. They lost their case in an 1850 state court decision that was later cited to justify segregation laws. But through protests, boycotts, and alliances with white abolitionists, Boston's free blacks eventually won over the state's lawmakers. In 1855, Massachusetts became the first state to legally desegregate its public schools.

African American abolitionists and white allies also formed associations to protect runaway slaves against capture and re-enslavement. More than a thousand southern slaves managed to escape north to freedom each year, often with assistance. The loose network of abolitionist agents and safe houses that became known as the **Underground Railroad** helped many escaped slaves reach the relative safety of the North's cities or a more certain refuge in Canada (see Map 12.2).

The new **Fugitive Slave Law**, part of the Compromise of 1850, was intended to stem this northern flow, but its effects were broader. It tightened enforcement of the federal law of 1793 by adding restrictions on runaways and their sympathizers. Captured suspects were denied a trial by jury or the right to present evidence to federal commissioners who heard their case, and local governments were prevented from intervening. The law

Underground Railroad Secret network of abolitionist safe houses and conductors that helped southern slaves escape to northern free states or Canada.

Fugitive Slave Law Legislation passed as part of Compromise of 1850 that strengthened federal government control over the capture and prosecution of runaway slaves.

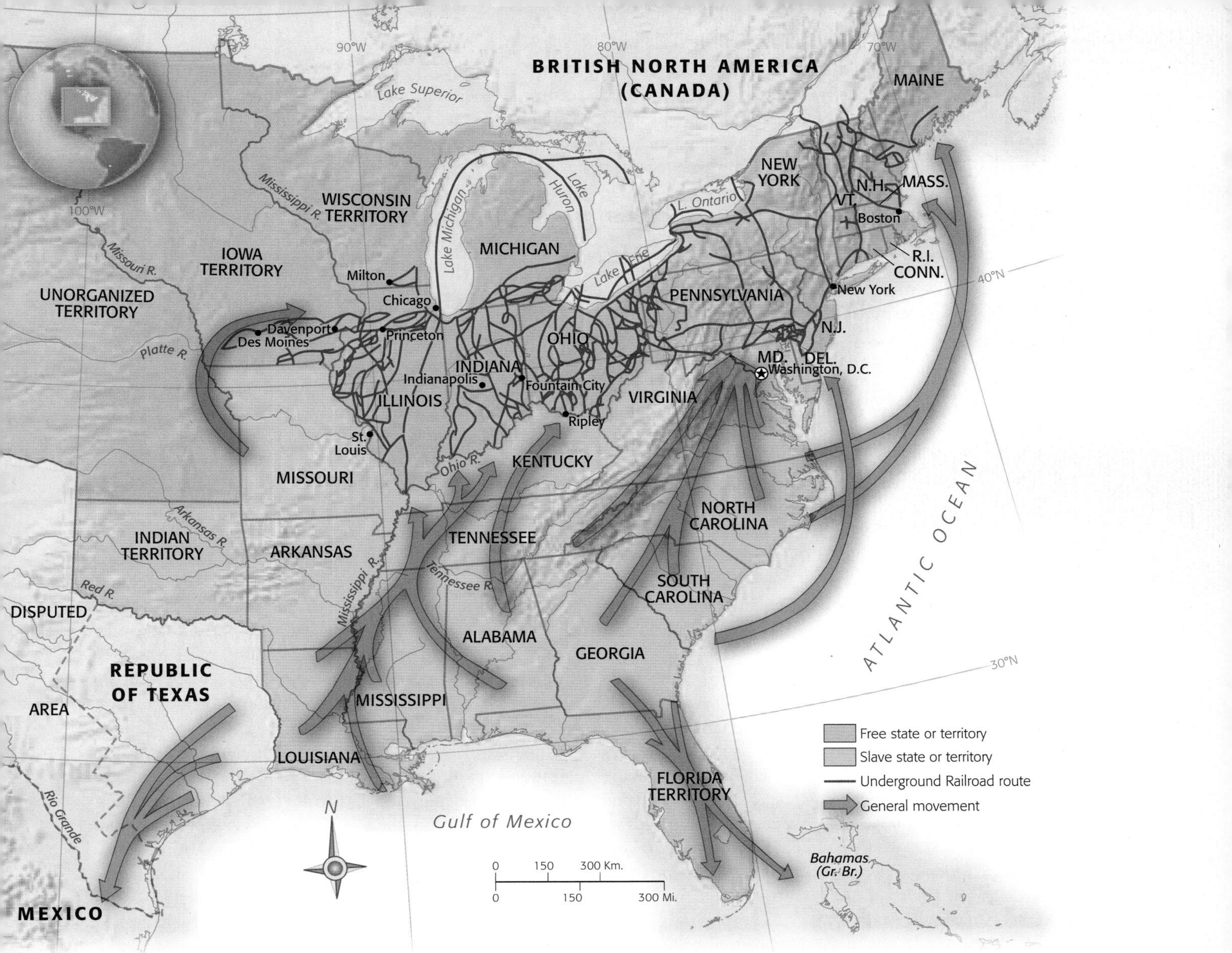

Map 12.2 Escape from Slavery A few thousand slaves successfully escaped each year from slavery in the South. Although some fled south to Mexico and the Caribbean, most headed north by roads, trains, or boats and were often assisted by Vigilance Committees on the Underground Railroad. Many runaways followed routes to Great Lakes ports or other border crossings to seek a safe haven from slave catchers in British Canada. ▲

threatened free blacks with potential enslavement, decreed that citizens could be compelled to join the hunt for fugitives, and made it a felony for anyone to harbor them.

A string of dramatic rescues and court cases intensified opposition to the new law. In 1851, a group of black resistance fighters in Christiana, Pennsylvania, led by escaped slave William Parker killed a Maryland slave owner who was attempting to recapture fugitives. Parker fled to Canada, assisted by Frederick Douglass. Three years later, an interracial crowd of abolitionists stormed a Boston courthouse to free the captured runaway Anthony Burns, and a prison guard was killed in the failed attempt. President Pierce sent federal troops to Boston to escort Burns south. Each episode attracted new sympathizers. Enraged by the Burns case, Massachusetts businessman Amos Lawrence declared that he and his friends "went to bed one night old fashioned, conservative, Compromise Union Whigs & waked up stark mad Abolitionists."

12-3b *Uncle Tom's Cabin*

An influential antislavery novel dramatizes the evils of slavery.

The plight of fugitives and the horrific fate of relatives they left behind were the subject of a best-selling novel published in 1852, Harriet Beecher Stowe's ***Uncle Tom's Cabin***. A white abolitionist, Stowe had never seen a slave plantation, but her family had harbored runaways at their home in Cincinnati. Her book

Uncle Tom's Cabin Stowe's best-selling novel that dramatized the evils of slavery and plight of fugitive slaves.

settler societies New World nations or British colonies where European settlers dispossessed native peoples and African slaves, pushed inland, and transplanted their way of life.

Gadsden Purchase Agreement with Mexico by which the United States paid $10 million for southwestern lands to ease construction of a transcontinental railroad.

Kansas-Nebraska Act Law pushed by Democrat Douglas that repealed the Missouri Compromise and opened Kansas Territory to slavery under popular sovereignty.

absorbed their stories into a fictional saga that brought the cruel realities of the slave quarters and the whipping post into tranquil northern parlors.

Unabashedly sentimental, Stowe's novel traced the fate of several slaves, including Eliza, who flees northward carrying her child across ice floes on the Ohio River; Lucy, who commits suicide when her infant is sold away; and the saintly Uncle Tom, who forgives a cruel master even as he is beaten to death. All suffer the evil effects of the slave system. Stowe drew on ideas of womanhood that transcended racial and class differences by highlighting the agony of enslaved mothers. Convinced that slavery also corrupted the master class, she avoided blaming southern slaveholders, portraying most as good Christians trapped in their roles and making the cruelest master a New England-born overseer. Her intent was to stir readers' consciences and awaken them to their complicity with slavery.

Uncle Tom's Cabin tugged at the heartstrings of the quarter of a million Americans who read it in its first year as well as those who attended theatrical adaptations. Many Northerners accepted Stowe's portrait of slavery as accurate whereas white Southerners condemned it as misleading propaganda. Translated into many languages, *Uncle Tom's Cabin* became the world's best-selling novel in the nineteenth century. It was a huge hit in Europe, where Romantic literature prevailed, the South provided an exotic setting, and the recent abolition of slavery in British and French colonies allowed readers to pity Americans. At the end of the novel, Stowe linked the antislavery movement to the European revolutions of 1848. Both gave voice to the hunger for freedom among the oppressed, she declared, and every nation that failed to heed this call would face God's wrath on the Day of Judgment.

12-3c The Kansas-Nebraska Act

Stephen Douglas reopens the political fight over slavery in western territories.

Despite controversies over *Uncle Tom's Cabin*, fugitive slaves, and Central American filibusterers, the most explosive issue in the struggle over slavery in the 1850s remained the question that the U.S.–Mexican War had raised: the status of slavery in the western territories. The man who shattered the sectional truce of 1850 was the same one who had steered it through Congress. When Stephen Douglas proposed in 1854 to organize the remaining Louisiana Purchase lands west of the Missouri River into territories where slavery might take hold, he created a furor that convulsed American politics.

The dispute grew out of two manias that nineteenth-century Americans shared with **settler societies** such as Canada and Argentina: land hunger and railroads. Midwestern farmers had long coveted fertile lands in the vast prairies between the Mississippi River and the Rockies. Attempts to open them for sale and settlement were held back because the federal government had set aside some tracts in 1830 as a permanent Indian reserve. Meanwhile, plans for a transcontinental railroad anchored the dreams of many U.S. expansionists. Enormous profits could be made by linking existing lines east of the Mississippi with the Pacific. For the eastern terminus, Northerners' hopes focused on Chicago, the booming Great Lakes port and commercial hub. Southerners pushed for New Orleans, Memphis, or St. Louis, all located in slave states. As sectional rivalry for the transcontinental railroad heated up, it inevitably became entangled with slavery.

Prodded by expansionists, federal officials opened new western lands to settlers and railroads. In 1853, the Pierce administration purchased from Mexico thirty thousand square miles of desert land south of the Gila River in present-day Arizona and New Mexico. Costing $10 million, the **Gadsden Purchase** skirted the southern end of the Rocky Mountains to create a level railroad route from the South to the West Coast. The path was less smooth than expected. This borderland had long been contested between the Apache people and Mexican frontiersmen, and the U.S. government joined the violent struggle as a third party. Farther north, the Pierce administration pressured tribal leaders in Nebraska to give up their lands for railroads and white settlement. In treaties signed early in 1854, the Delawares, Shawnees, Iowas, and Kickapoos ceded all but a few small reservations. Most Indians were eventually forced to move to Oklahoma territory, where they were squeezed onto small grants bordering the Native Americans who had been sent there earlier by the Indian Removal Act in the 1830s.

Early in 1854, Douglas, eager to promote a transcontinental railroad that would benefit his state of Illinois, introduced a bill to organize the remaining Louisiana Purchase lands into two territories, Kansas and Nebraska. To attract Southerners' support, Douglas's bill raised the possibility that slavery could be established in these territories by leaving the issue to local voters, his trademark formula of popular sovereignty.

This time the Little Giant had miscalculated. Douglas was indifferent to slavery and believed it had little chance to take root on the Great Plains. By 1854, however, many Northerners and Southerners were ready to argue vehemently over that possibility. Free-soil advocates saw popular sovereignty as a proslavery formula, especially after the Utah Territory had used it to legalize slavery in 1852. Besides that, the Kansas and Nebraska Territories lay above the line where slavery had been forbidden in the Louisiana Purchase lands by Congress in 1820. After a heated debate, the **Kansas-Nebraska Act** was passed by Congress in May 1854 (see Map 12.3).

Map 12.3 The Kansas-Nebraska Act and Slavery in the Territories, 1854 Stephen Douglas's Kansas-Nebraska Act reopened the slavery controversy by applying the formula of popular sovereignty from the Compromise of 1850 to new territories in remaining lands from the Louisiana Purchase. The Missouri Compromise of 1820 had banned slavery from those lands, but the new law repealed it, causing a political firestorm. ▲

Douglas's victory reopened sectional divides and strained existing political parties to the breaking point. Southern Democrats strongly backed the Kansas-Nebraska Act while Democrats in the North, wary of a popular backlash, split their votes. Their fears proved well founded in the 1854 elections, when northern Democrats lost most of their seats in Congress and were left in control of only two free-state legislatures. As the Democratic Party became more southern dominated, dissatisfied northern members began to seek alternatives. Meanwhile, the Whig coalition shattered entirely. Northern Whigs voted unanimously against the Kansas-Nebraska Act, southern Whigs decisively for it. The national Whig Party, already weakened by divisions over the Compromise of 1850, simply dissolved. The stage was set for a dramatic realignment of the American political system.

12-4

The Politics of Sectionalism

After the Kansas-Nebraska Act became law, settlers rushed into the new territories and formed free-soil and proslavery factions who vied for control, sometimes violently. This northern cartoon blames Democratic Party leaders such as Franklin Pierce and Stephen Douglas for forcing a "freesoiler" to swallow slavery.

Why did the struggle over popular sovereignty devolve into armed conflict? How does the cartoon link slavery's spread to western territories with U.S. expansionism in Latin America? ▶

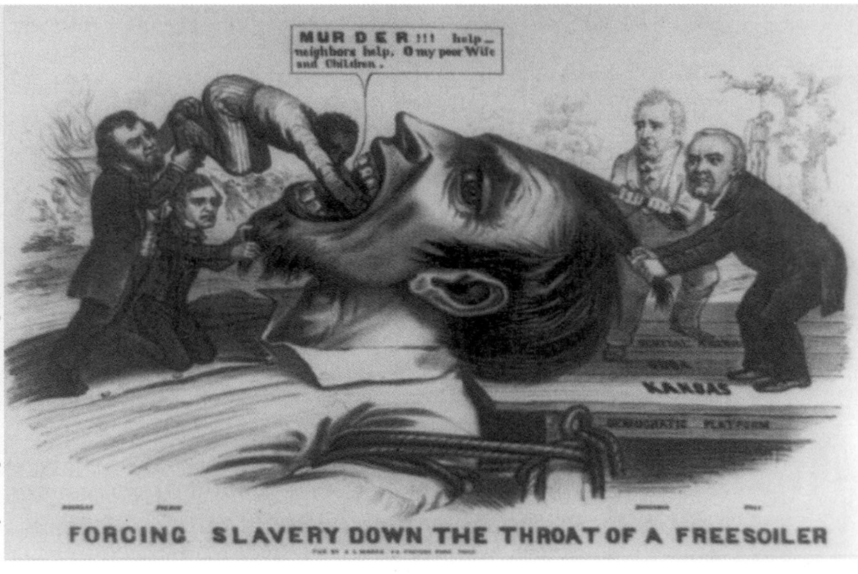

political machines Urban political organizations, often headed by a boss, that rely on party discipline and distribution of rewards to gain power and retain voters' loyalty.

Know-Nothings Secret society founded in the 1850s to prevent Catholics from voting and holding office that elected members to Congress through the American Party.

In the wake of the Kansas-Nebraska Act, old political parties splintered and new ones emerged, one of them a short-lived anti-immigrant coalition, the other a rapidly growing northern party dedicated to preventing slavery's spread. The shake-up signaled a move toward political parties that starkly reflected sectional ideas and interests. As each of the major parties, the older Democrats and the new Republicans, consolidated their control over voters in the South and North, respectively, the venerable tradition of sectional compromises engineered by cross-sectional parties, long the glue of the U.S. political system, was rapidly melting away.

One symptom of the intensifying sectional rift was the outbreak of guerrilla warfare between proslavery and antislavery settlers in the territories. Another was the failure of an ambitious Supreme Court decision to settle the question of slavery's expansion into those territories. If political parties, the courts, and the people themselves could not resolve their differences peacefully, what alternatives were left?

☞ As you read, consider the impact of the Kansas-Nebraska Act, the formation of new political parties, and the Dred Scott decision. How did these developments escalate sectional tensions over slavery?

12-4a Anti-immigrant Sentiment and the Know-Nothings

A short-lived nativist coalition bids to disrupt the political party system.

When northern voters sought new political moorings after the Whig Party dissolved, substantial numbers rallied around nativism. Almost 3.5 million immigrants landed in the United States between 1848 and 1860, the largest influx in U.S. history in proportion to the resident population (see Figure 12.1). Native-born American Protestants generally welcomed the German Forty-Eighters and middle-class German Protestants, who scattered on farms in the Midwest, established prosperous businesses in river ports, and shared northern Protestants' free-soil beliefs. But Catholic immigrants, especially 1 million poor Irish Catholics escaping the "Great Hunger," a potato blight and famine that lasted from 1846 to 1851, aroused opposition. Nativist fears focused on poverty, crime, and cultural differences between Catholics and Protestants over temperance laws and separate schools. After a republican revolt in Rome was suppressed and the Papal States restored, Protestant propagandists portrayed Catholic immigrants as the advance troops of a papal plot to take over the United States and destroy free institutions.

Political opposition to immigrants crystallized when the newcomers began voting. Irish immigrants and German Catholics preferred the Democratic Party, which organized their votes into urban **political machines**, which distributed jobs and favors in return for party loyalty and promised protection from religious persecution. In response, secret anti-Catholic organizations such as New York's Order of the Star-Spangled Banner (1850) were formed in northern states. Going public, these secret societies nominated local candidates who attacked crime and corruption and stirred voters' Protestant loyalties and patriotic sentiments. By 1851, nativist parties succeeded in electing prominent city officials in Boston, Philadelphia, New Orleans, and San Francisco.

In 1854, the anti-immigrant crusade went national, in part to fill the void left by the Whigs' demise. Nativist organizations coalesced into the American Party, also called the **Know-Nothings**, after a secret organization whose members were supposed to reply "I know nothing" to inquirers.

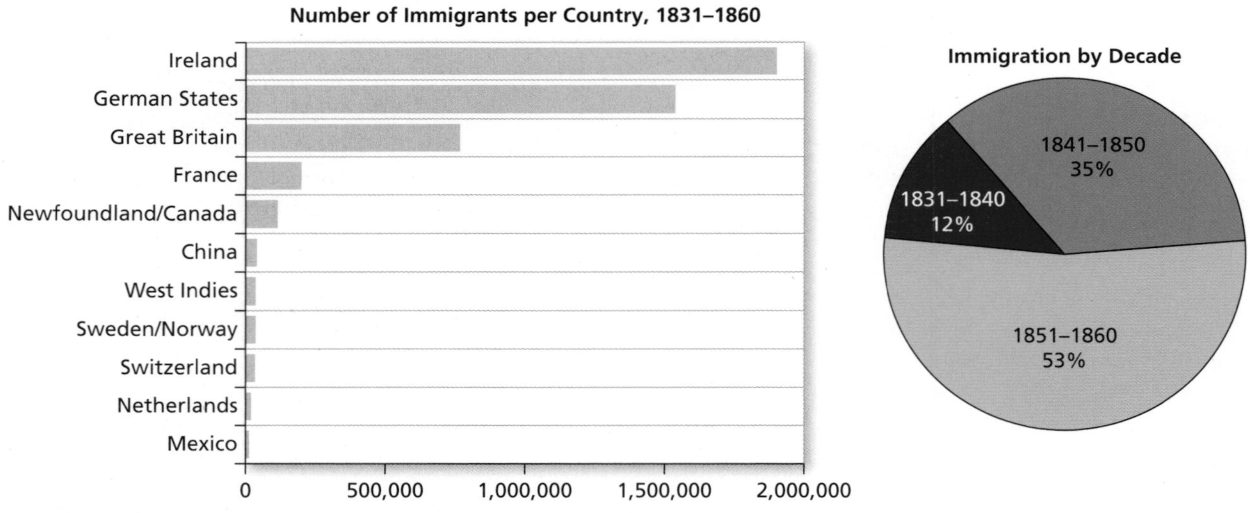

Figure 12.1 Major Sources of Immigration to the United States, 1831–1860 The majority of immigrants into the United States came from Ireland and the German states with Great Britain a distant third. More than half arrived during the sectional struggle over slavery in the 1850s. By 1860, 15 percent of the white population was of foreign birth, and 90 percent of immigrants lived in northern states.

▲ Source: Data from Stephan Thernstrom, ed., Harvard Encyclopedia of American Ethnic Groups (Cambridge, Mass., and London: Harvard University Press, 1980), 1047.

Know-Nothings pledged to extend the time to citizenship for immigrants (naturalization) from five to twenty-one years, to restrict voting rights to native-born Americans, and to bar Catholics from holding office. The new party achieved a stunning success in the 1854 elections by running its own candidates or forming alliances with local parties, usually Whigs. Know-Nothings captured most state offices in Massachusetts, Delaware, and Pennsylvania, gained ground in Upper South cities such as Baltimore and Louisville, and elected seventy-five congressmen pledged to their program.

Fearing that the question of slavery could destroy the Union, the Know-Nothings tried to ignore it by appealing to constitutional agreements and patriotic sentiments. But the issue was impossible to avoid, and playing on religious and ethnic prejudice proved an unsuccessful diversion. In short order, the Know-Nothings, like the Whigs before them, split along North-South lines over slavery. When Know-Nothing leaders introduced a platform in 1856 that endorsed the Kansas-Nebraska Act, most Northerners walked away from the new party.

12-4b Republicans and the Sectional Debate

A new northern party polarizes the political dispute over slavery.

Another new coalition, the **Republican Party**, got off to a later start than the Know-Nothings but proved more durable. The party sprang up in 1854 in midwestern states out of spontaneous protests over the Kansas-Nebraska Act and then spread eastward. Its coalition of antislavery Whigs, dissenting northern Democrats, and Free Soilers began with divergent views on such issues as immigration and tariffs, but they agreed on one powerful cause: opposition to slavery's extension westward. Its clout was demonstrated in the 1854 elections when the fledgling party won a surprising victory, capturing a majority of northern states' seats in the House of Representatives.

The Republicans' motto, "Free Soil, Free Labor, Free Men," summarized their appeal. Free-soil antagonism to slavery in the territories reflected varied concerns, ranging from prejudice against blacks in the North to the search for economic opportunity in the West unhindered by competition with slave labor. Only a small minority of prominent Republicans held abolitionist views; others, like northern bankers and manufacturers of clothing, profited directly from the trade in slave goods. Most were willing to leave southern slavery alone and did little to improve the condition of the North's free blacks.

The ideology of **free labor** highlighted Northerners' confidence in their prosperous system of competitive capitalism. Northern farms and factories had created a high standard of living compared to that of the "backward" South. A free-labor society, Republicans believed, dignified work and rewarded initiative. Prominent Illinois lawyer Abraham Lincoln and other Republicans tied free labor to U.S. nationalism, asserting that the North's thriving economy and open frontier exempted the United States from class antagonisms that divided Europeans. Preserving western lands as a **safety valve** that offered an escape for discontented eastern wage workers would guarantee America's fortunate difference into the future.

For the great majority of Republicans, free men meant free white men unpressured by the "Slave Power," a conspiracy of influential planters that threatened majority rule and compromised the nation's global posture. The South's promotion of slavery, Lincoln and other Republicans believed, tarnished the image of the United States abroad and prevented foreign liberals from adopting its republican institutions. Despite the emphasis on free men, Republicans celebrated middle-class women's moral influence and encouraged their participation in political events in contrast to the Democratic Party's emphasis on male mastery of households and plantations.

The Republican Party was the first major sectional party in U.S. politics. In their heyday, the Whigs and Democrats, with substantial membership in the North and South, often put aside sectional views to promote compromise. Without southern members to appease, Republicans appended a northern-flavored economic program to their platform. They updated the old Whig American system of federal support for internal improvements with calls for federal subsidies for a Pacific railroad and free homesteads of one hundred sixty acres for western settlers. This economic package and, after party leaders denounced nativist views, a friendlier attitude toward immigrants attracted additional northern voters.

The Democratic Party remained a cross-sectional coalition but became increasingly dominated by southern leaders. Franklin Pierce and other "northern men of southern principles," called "doughfaces" for their pliable views, rose in the party at the expense of neutral nationalists such as Stephen Douglas. The core strategy of the Democrats' vocal Deep South **"fire eaters"** was an aggressive defense of slaveholders' rights. Their growing influence among Democrats pushed aside the Upper South tradition of sectional compromise. Without a viable opposition party to replace the Whigs, Southern politics became a one-party system dedicated to sectional loyalty and defense.

Southern Democrats' growing militancy derived from other sources besides party reshuffling. The cotton boom required expansion, and access to western lands promised social mobility for poor whites who aspired

Republican Party Political coalition created to oppose extension of slavery to western territories that adopted the economic program formerly advocated by Whigs.

free labor Ideology that celebrated the virtues of property ownership, waged work, self-discipline, and upward mobility under competitive capitalism.

safety valve Idea that access to western lands offered relief for poor or discontented eastern workers and farmers, and a chance for upward mobility.

fire eaters Outspoken defenders of white Southerners' rights to own and dispose of slaves under government protection; the first advocates of the South's secession.

Architect of the Capitol

Global Americans Born in Germany, **Emanuel Leutze** was brought to the United States as a child by his immigrant parents. He took painting lessons in Philadelphia and returned to Germany for advanced training. At first practicing his craft abroad, Leutze specialized in historical subjects painted dramatically and in painstaking detail, many of them illustrating the virtues of America. A strong supporter of the Revolutions of 1848, Leutze painted his iconic *Washington Crossing the Delaware* (1850) to inspire European liberals with the example of the American Revolution. In 1859, he returned permanently to the United States. As the sectional struggle over slavery in the territories heated up, Congress commissioned Leutze to produce a stairway mural for the U.S. Capitol Building. *Westward the Course of Empire Takes Its Way* portrayed Manifest Destiny on an epic scale. It features a procession of pioneer men and women, including recent Irish and German immigrants, who pilgrimaged from the Valley of Darkness toward the golden light of San Francisco Bay. Like many German immigrants, Leutze warmed to the Republicans' free-labor ideology. For the mural's final version, Leutze linked westward expansion with antislavery sentiment by inserting a freed black boy guiding a mule near its center.

to own slaves—a southern white version of the free-labor safety valve. In the eyes of southern Democrats, Republicans looked no different from abolitionists, for both threatened to strangle the slave system. Also at stake was the shifting balance of sectional power in Congress. Additional free states remained to be carved out of the Oregon, Louisiana Purchase, and Northwest Ordinance territories whereas slaveholders could count only on dry and distant New Mexico. Unless slavery could be extended, the Democrats' control of Congress and the presidency appeared doomed. Finally, Deep South politicians worried about the loyalty of Upper South farmers, who were less tied to the cotton boom and might compromise slaveholders' interests. The fire eaters believed that confrontations over slavery would ensure a united southern front.

During the intensified sectional debate of the 1850s, proslavery advocates extended the religious, racial, historical, and economic arguments they had developed earlier to defend their views and attack opponents (see Chapter 10). Josiah Nott, an Alabama physician, claimed in *Types of Mankind* (1854) that black Africans and their descendants constituted a separate, unchanging racial type unable to rise from "barbarism." International perspectives also informed the controversy. South Carolina senator James Henry Hammond, in his famous "mud-sill" speech, used Roman history to argue that a servile laboring class was necessary to support "civilized" free men. To discredit the North's free-labor system, proslavery spokesmen borrowed heavily from British and French critics of industrialism. Northern workers toiling in factories and living in squalid new industrial slums were "wage slaves" whose plight was far worse than that of southern blacks, the Virginia proslavery apologist George Fitzhugh charged in *Sociology for the South; or The Failure of Free Society* (1854). At the same time, proslavery politicians' aggressive stance fed on their discomfort that slavery and other forms of bound labor were in obvious decline throughout the western world. The revolutionary upheavals of 1848 outlawed slavery in French colonies and ended serfdom in the Austrian empire and German states. To antislavery Northerners, these developments showed that the tide of history was rising with them. Both sides were determined to make a stand in Kansas.

12-4c Violence in Kansas, Congress, and California

Conflict over territorial slavery produces bloodshed in western lands and the U.S. Senate.

Far from resolving growing tensions over slavery, the Kansas-Nebraska Act simply shifted animosities from Congress to Kansas. Goaded by the popular sovereignty provision, a race began between proslavery and antislavery forces to recruit settlers and build a majority among Kansas voters, and their animosity degenerated into a mini-civil war. Southerners initially gained the upper hand because Kansas lay west of slave-state Missouri. In 1855, thousands of Missouri "border ruffians" crossed over and voted fraudulently to give proslavery candidates a large majority in the territorial legislature, which established Lecompton as its capital. Northern abolitionists and religious societies responded by sponsoring free-soil settlers, in some cases providing them with guns. Abolitionists such as Angelina Grimké and Lydia Maria Child who had previously embraced pacifism now declared that violence was necessary to defend Kansas free soilers. Republican politicians declared that Americans in Kansas faced a homegrown Revolution of 1848 between the forces of freedom and despotism. When the Lecompton legislature legalized slavery, the free soilers convened in Topeka and established their own territorial government and constitution.

By early 1856, guerrilla warfare had erupted between partisans of the two Kansas governments, and President Pierce pledged armed federal support for the proslavery regime. In May, a posse organized by a federal marshal sacked the free-state town of Lawrence. In retaliation, abolitionist agitator John Brown led four of his sons and a few followers in a raid on a proslavery settlement on Pottawatomie Creek. Wielding broadswords, they hacked five men to death. After that, armed bands of guerrillas roamed through eastern Kansas, clashing over slavery and rival claims to turf. What the eastern press called **"Bleeding Kansas"** became a living symbol of sectional polarities.

Meanwhile, violence reached the floor of Congress when Massachusetts Republican Senator Charles Sumner gave a stinging speech condemning "The Crime Against Kansas." An abolitionist and florid orator, Sumner portrayed proslavery voter fraud as "the rape of a virgin territory" and singled out Senator Andrew Butler of South Carolina as one who had taken "the harlot, slavery" as his mistress. Sumner's abusive personal references provoked an attack by South Carolina representative Preston Brooks, a relative of Butler, who beat Sumner unconscious with his cane. The injured Sumner became a hero to Republicans, his vacant senate chair a symbol of slaveholder violence. Brooks was censured by Congress but reelected by South Carolina voters and received dozens of congratulatory canes as replacements for the one he broke in the attack.

The presidential contest of 1856 provided a snapshot of the political divisions and realignments that followed the Kansas-Nebraska Act. Passing over Pierce and Stephen Douglas as too controversial, the Democrats turned to Pennsylvania's James Buchanan, a reliable doughface who had been an overseas diplomat during the sectional debate. For their first national election, the Republicans chose John C. Frémont, a military hero and western adventurer who relied on his youthful good looks—and his politically savvy wife, Jessie Benton, the daughter of a powerful Missouri senator—to unify the new party's ranks. The Know-Nothings, now split by slavery into northern and southern wings, fretted as the first organization endorsed Frémont while the second nominated former president Millard Fillmore.

With the support of southern voters, who preferred Buchanan to Fillmore in every slave state but Maryland, the Democratic candidate won the three-way election. Frémont, however, ran remarkably well, carrying eleven of the sixteen free states. If the Republicans had taken Pennsylvania and one other heavily populated free state, Frémont would have entered the White House; by this time, a northern sectional party could win the presidency without even campaigning in the South.

That lesson was not lost on James Buchanan. Perhaps seeking to appease Republicans, who had campaigned against the "twin relics of barbarism," polygamy and slavery in the West, the new president sent U.S. forces to the Utah territory to replace Mormon leader Brigham Young as governor. The expedition led to a prolonged standoff known as the *Utah War* (1857–1858) whose worst casualties were not armed men from either side but a band of one hundred twenty California-bound emigrants ambushed in a remote area by local Mormon militiamen. Eventually, the two sides negotiated an agreement whereby Young stepped down, federal troops remained as peacekeepers, and those who took part in the "Mormon Rebellion" were pardoned.

Buchanan also took steps to resolve the Kansas question but only made things worse. The new president announced that he supported Kansas's admission to the Union as a slave state. A proslavery constitution was drafted at Lecompton in 1857 and eventually submitted to Kansas voters, who rejected it. Nevertheless, Buchanan insisted that the **Lecompton constitution** was legitimate and pressured northern Democrats in Congress to join southern colleagues and admit Kansas to statehood under it.

Stephen Douglas broke with the administration. Angered by Buchanan's violation of popular sovereignty, Douglas believed that midwestern Democrats like him could not cave in to proslavery politicians without endangering their own reelection. Douglas's independent stand infuriated southern Democrats and ended his dream of winning the South's support for his presidential ambitions. The Lecompton controversy revealed a growing sectional fissure in the Democratic ranks.

In California, where the Democrats were divided between migrants from the free and slave states, the Lecompton rift sparked intraparty violence. Newly elected U.S. Senator David Broderick was a second-generation Irish American and a Democratic political boss who sided with Douglas. His bitter rival, Kentucky-born David Terry, had been chief justice of the California Supreme Court and led the state's proslavery Democratic faction. The two men exchanged insults and then fought a duel south of San Francisco, where Terry shot Broderick in the chest. "I die because I was opposed to a corrupt administration and the extension of slavery," the senator reportedly proclaimed on his deathbed. In 1854, the Whig Party had shattered over slavery; a few years later, the nation's Democrats headed toward their own breakup.

"Bleeding Kansas" Label given by northern newspapers to guerrilla war in Kansas Territory after 1854 as armed conflict raged between antislavery and proslavery supporters.

Lecompton constitution Proslavery constitution that was drafted for Kansas Territory but not approved by Congress when Democrats split into sectional factions.

Library of Congress Prints and Photographs Division (LC-USZ62-107588)

Missouri History Museum, St. Louis

Roger Taney and Dred Scott These photographs suggest the gravity of the *Dred Scott* case and the dignity of both principals. Roger Taney was a Maryland attorney and Jackson appointee who had freed his own slaves but who championed white man's democracy and condemned antislavery agitation as "northern aggression." Dred Scott's master had allowed him to marry and promised that he could earn his freedom, but when the master died, his widow reneged, prompting Scott's suit against her and her brother, John Sandford. Shortly after the Supreme Court's decision, the sons of Scott's first owner purchased him and his family and freed them. ▲

12-4d *The Dred Scott* Case and Lincoln-Douglas Debates

A Supreme Court decision opens the territories to slavery and deepens sectional divisions.

In his inaugural address, President Buchanan referred to a pending Supreme Court decision that he hoped would settle the slavery controversy once and for all. Dred Scott, a Missouri slave, had been taken by his owner, an army surgeon, to various posts in Illinois and Wisconsin, the latter a territory where slavery had been banned by the Missouri Compromise. In Wisconsin, Scott met and married another slave, Harriet Robinson. When their owner took them back to St. Louis, Harriet Scott, who attended an abolitionist church, convinced her husband to sue for freedom. Arguing that residence in a free territory had made him and his family free, Scott's lawyers pursued his appeal to the Supreme Court.

At stake were two key issues. First, did Scott have the right of U.S. citizens to sue in federal court? Second, did Congress, or a federally sanctioned territorial legislature, have the power to prohibit slavery in a territory? In March 1857, Chief Justice Roger Taney delivered the majority opinion of a court that tilted toward the South. Scott, Taney declared, could not be a citizen. Ignoring African Americans' citizenship in several northern states since the 1780s, Taney asserted that the founding generation had agreed that blacks were "beings of an inferior order" with "no rights which the white man was bound to respect." Moving on to the question of slavery in the territories, Taney declared that the Missouri Compromise was unconstitutional. The Constitution did not give Congress authority over territory acquired after 1787. More important, said Taney, the Fifth Amendment to the U.S. Constitution forbade taking a person's property, including slaves, without their consent or "due process of law."

***Dred Scott* decision** Supreme Court case (*Dred Scott v. Sandford*) that declared blacks ineligible for U.S. citizenship and overturned federal laws prohibiting slavery in territories.

Instead of settling the controversy over slavery, the ***Dred Scott* decision** of 1857 deepened it. Southern whites, whose constitutional arguments had won crucial support, rejoiced whereas Republicans, whose free-soil views the Court dismissed, were outraged. African American conventions held in northern cities denounced the decision. For northern Democrats such as Stephen Douglas, the Court's decision posed a fatal obstacle. Because territorial legislatures were then prohibited from interfering with slave owners' property rights, Douglas's formula of popular sovereignty became meaningless: Kansas could not prohibit slavery even if its citizens wished. Polarized reactions to the decision indicated that by 1857, the Supreme Court could not keep together a union of states that slavery was pulling apart.

The biblical adage that "A house divided against itself cannot stand" struck Abraham Lincoln as an apt metaphor for the situation in the United States. Either the opponents of slavery would blockade it into extinction, as Republicans proposed, or its advocates would press until the nation legalized slavery everywhere inside its borders. During the Illinois senatorial campaign of 1858, Lincoln, the Republican challenger, engaged the incumbent Douglas in a series of debates. Lincoln charged that the *Dred Scott* decision prefigured the spread of slavery to free states. Declaring slavery a "vast moral evil," Lincoln asked Douglas whether popular sovereignty remained a viable way to curb it.

In reply, Douglas asserted that despite the *Dred Scott* decision, citizens in territories could exclude slavery by denying it legal protection—a response that appeased Illinois voters but further damaged the Little Giant's standing in the South. When Douglas labeled Lincoln a "Black Republican" who favored racial equality, Lincoln responded that he was not in favor of "bringing about the social and political equality of the white and black race." Lincoln's racial views stood at the moderate Republican center, positioned between the abolitionists and antiblack free soilers, and his debate performance enhanced his reputation among Republicans nationally. Douglas hung onto his seat, but other northern Democrats felt the backlash from the *Dred Scott* decision in the 1858 elections. Propped up by the solid South, the party kept control of the Senate but it lost its majority in the House, which only tightened the political deadlock in Washington.

12-5
Road to Disunion

This political cartoon produced by New York printmakers Currier & Ives depicts the movement among southern states to leave the Union in the winter of 1860–1861. It shows Florida, Alabama, Mississippi, and Louisiana as men riding donkeys, following South Carolina's man riding a pig toward a dangerous cliff. South Carolina's rider shouts that "Old Hickory [Andrew Jackson] is dead, and now we'll have it," while Alabama declares that "Cotton is King!" The Georgia rider detours down a hill, expressing "doubts about 'the end' of that road."

What does this northern cartoon suggest about the motives of the seceding southern states? How does the cartoonist view their prospects? ▶

Go to MindTap® to practice history with the Chapter 12 **Primary Source Writing Activity: Domestic Divisions.** Read and view primary sources and respond to a writing prompt.

Library of Congress Prints and Photographs Division (LC-USZ62-32995)

With the status of Kansas unresolved, an unpopular Supreme Court decision under debate, and Congress locked in stalemate, the issue of slavery in the territories seemed to paralyze the U.S. political system. Some white Southerners, surveying the gains that opponents of slavery had made at home and abroad, preached disunion as the only solution. By withdrawing from the Union, southern whites could transform themselves instantly from a minority to a majority and build a new nation founded on slavery and states' rights. Disunion remained a distinctly minority view among white Southerners, however, until an attempted slave insurrection in 1859 and the Republicans' presidential victory the following year seemed to confirm the fire eaters' dire prophecies. When South Carolina renounced the federal union after Lincoln was elected president, it set off a chain reaction that led to civil war. As it turned out, Americans disagreed just as fiercely over the meaning and permanence of the Union as they had over the extension of slavery within it.

☞ As you read, examine key events along the road to the Civil War. What did the response to John Brown's raid reveal? Why did several slave states secede from the Union following Lincoln's election? Why did Republicans reject political compromise and Northerners refuse to let the secessionists depart? How did the Civil War break out?

12-5a John Brown's Raid

An abolitionist attempt to provoke a slave insurrection electrifies the nation.

As political positions on slavery polarized, John Brown again pushed the conflict over the line into violence, as he had in Kansas. On October 16, 1859, Brown led an interracial band of eighteen followers in a raid on the federal arsenal at Harpers Ferry, Virginia. His intent was to steal firearms and establish a fortress in a mountain hideaway in Virginia, inspiring slaves to rebel and take refuge there. Brown knew about successful Latin American maroons—colonies of runaway slaves—and he absorbed tactics of guerrilla warfare from writings of the Italian revolutionary of 1848, Giuseppe Mazzini. But his raid failed badly, and his men were besieged in the arsenal's engine

John Brown Confers with Frederick Douglass Brown sought the support of abolitionist Douglass shortly before leading the raid at Harpers Ferry. Douglass disapproved, warning that attacking federal property was suicidal and would provoke a violent backlash. After the raid, Douglass fled for a time to Canada, fearing arrest as a coconspirator. To the South's whites, the web of guilt by association spread beyond abolitionists like Douglass to include mainstream Republicans. In this 1941 painting by black artist Jacob Lawrence, Brown makes his appeal and Douglass resists. A cross on the wall suggests their shared religious inspiration. ▶

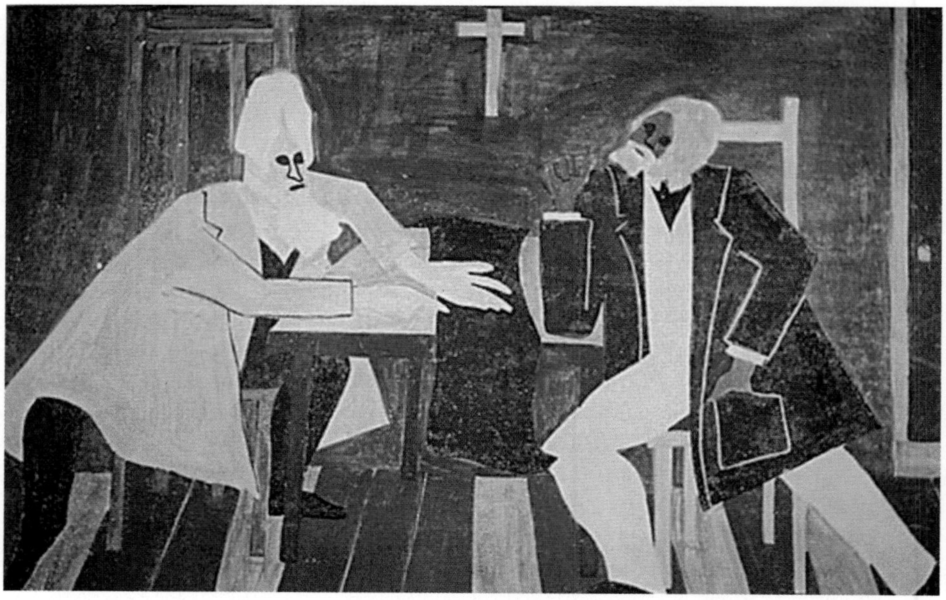

U.S. National Archives and Records Administration

John Brown's Raid Failed 1859 attack by militant abolitionists on the federal arsenal at Harpers Ferry, Virginia, intended to spark a slave insurrection.

house by the local militia and then U.S. troops commanded by Colonel Robert E. Lee. After surrendering, Brown and six of his followers were convicted of treason against Virginia and executed.

John Brown's Raid electrified the nation, and his death stirred strong emotions at home and abroad. Impressed by Brown's courage, transcendentalist Henry David Thoreau praised him as a martyr who "would make the gallows as glorious as the cross." In an impassioned plea to stay Brown's execution, the French romantic novelist Victor Hugo published a letter calling Brown a "liberator" and "the champion of Christ." Southern planters' reactions formed a stark contrast, for the raid revived their worst nightmare: a violent insurrection by their own supposedly loyal slaves. Once it became known that Brown had received financial support from a circle of New England abolitionists, Southerners saw proof that northern abolitionists aimed to incite a slave rebellion. Proslavery leaders had threatened to desert the Union for a decade, but Brown's raid convinced many rank-and-file white Southerners that they were no longer secure in confederation with free states.

12-5b Election of 1860

A four-party contest gives the presidency to Republican candidate Lincoln, elected by a sharply sectional vote.

When Congress reconvened after John Brown's raid, tensions ran so high that according to one senator, many members carried concealed revolvers and knives on the floor of Congress. In February 1860, Democratic Senator Jefferson Davis of Mississippi demanded congressional action against states harboring fugitive slaves and federal guarantees that slavery would be protected in the western territories. For the South's fire eaters, the Davis resolutions were the minimum price the North had to pay to keep southern states in the Union.

That price was too high even for northern Democrats. Fearing rejection by voters in their own states, Stephen Douglas and other free-state champions of popular sovereignty refused to switch to Davis's position. In April 1860, the Democrats met to nominate a presidential candidate, and when Douglas secured the majority, the Deep South delegates walked out. The same drama was repeated at a later convention. Hopelessly divided, the Democrats offered two candidates to the public: Douglas for the northern wing of the Party, and Vice President John C. Breckinridge of Kentucky for the southern.

Republicans, sensing victory, sought a moderate candidate and a broad platform. Lincoln appealed as a Midwesterner who could win interior states. He was untainted by Know-Nothing views and less militant on slavery than the early favorite, Senator William Seward of New York. The Republican platform condemned John Brown's raid and pledged noninterference with southern slavery but held the line against its extension. Republicans also widened their appeal by advocating immigration, homestead laws, and a transcontinental railroad.

None of these candidates pleased political veterans in the Upper South. Desperate to preserve the Union, they hastily formed the Constitutional Union Party. Their nominee, John Bell of Tennessee, conjured the spirit of Henry Clay but had no specific compromise to offer.

The election of 1860 became a four-way race that was sharply sectional in character. Lincoln took every northern state except New Jersey, which he split with Douglas. Breckinridge carried nine states in the Deep South. The Upper South was divided among Bell, Breckinridge, and Douglas, who won only Missouri. Lincoln won just under 40 percent of the popular vote, but his margin in the Electoral College was decisive. The Republicans had learned the lesson of 1856: A presidential candidate no longer needed Southerners' votes to win. South Carolina's proslavery leaders understood this, too.

12-5c The Secession Crisis

Deep South states bolt from the Union, and the Republican Party rejects compromise.

In December 1860, not long after the election results were official, South Carolina passed an ordinance of **secession**, withdrawing the state from the Union. Proslavery politicians in that state were emboldened by lame-duck president Buchanan, who denied the right of secession but said the federal government could do nothing to stop it. South Carolina leaders argued that the incoming "Black Republican" Lincoln would do all he could to abolish slavery. The Republicans' victory signaled that the Democrats' control over the presidency and Congress was ending, and their dominance of the Supreme Court would soon follow. Because the Union was no more than a compact among sovereign states, proslavery leaders contended, state conventions or legislatures could vote to withdraw from it. Secessionists portrayed their cause as the true heir to the American Revolution's revolt against tyranny and the proper response to Republicans' abandonment of the Framers' constitutional guarantees to slave owners. The only course left was to form a new nation dedicated to slavery and states' rights.

South Carolina's secessionists hoped to force other southern states to declare their slave-state loyalties and forswear sectional reconciliation. The response was mixed. State conventions in the Deep South passed secession ordinances, and by February 1861, six states—Georgia, Florida, Alabama, Mississippi, Louisiana, and Texas—had joined South Carolina to form the Confederate States of America (see Map 12.4). Convened in Montgomery, Alabama, the delegates drafted a constitution little different from that of the United States with a few telling exceptions: It declared the Confederacy a union of sovereign states (not of "the people"), prohibited tariffs, and protected slavery in Confederate states and territories. The delegates chose Jefferson Davis as their president, organized the Confederate legislative and executive branches to function as an independent government, and began seizing federal forts and installations in the South.

This show of southern unity was deceptive. Four states of the Upper South—Virginia, North Carolina, Tennessee, and Arkansas—rejected secession, at least for the time being. Slaves constituted less than one-third of these states' population. Many Upper South voters were "conditional Unionists" who advocated waiting to assess the new Republican administration's policies on slavery and secession. Others were nonslaveholders who had always been wary of planter domination. As the South's poor whites weighed their class interests against their sectional loyalties,

secession Formal withdrawal from the United States declared by the southern states that formed the Confederacy in 1861 but was not recognized by Unionists.

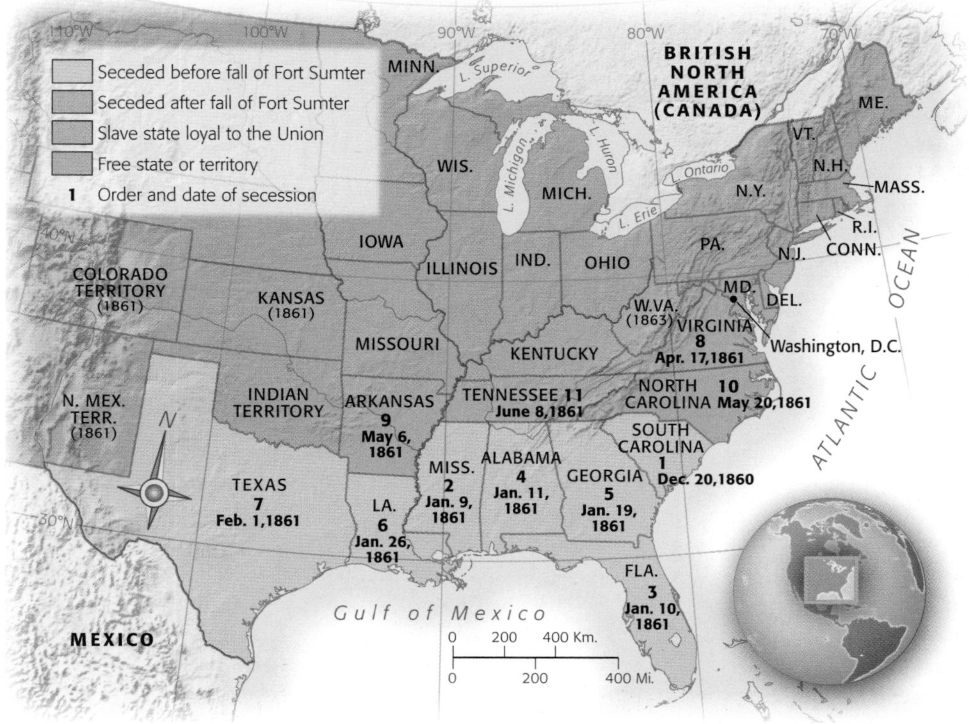

Map 12.4 The Course of Secession, 1860–1863 Secession from the Union occurred in two waves that reflected white Southerners' response to events and the regional importance of slavery to states' economies. After Lincoln's election, South Carolina passed an ordinance of secession and was soon joined by six Deep South states. Four Upper South slave states waited and seceded only after fighting began in April 1861. Four border slave states remained loyal to the Union. ▲

History without Borders

Secession

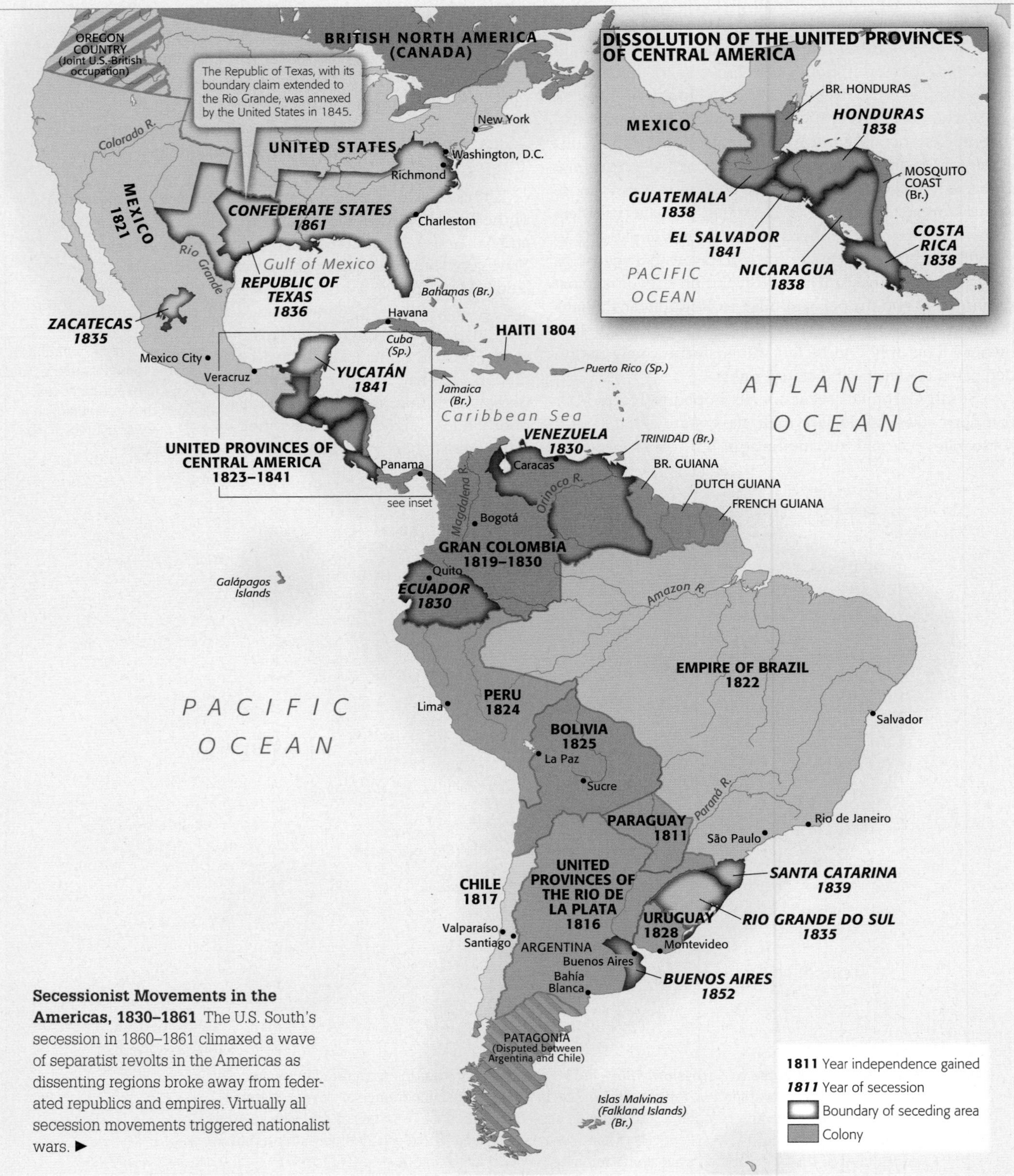

Secessionist Movements in the Americas, 1830–1861 The U.S. South's secession in 1860–1861 climaxed a wave of separatist revolts in the Americas as dissenting regions broke away from federated republics and empires. Virtually all secession movements triggered nationalist wars. ▶

Alfredo Dagli Orti/The Art Archive at Art Resource, NY

Garibaldi in Two Worlds Italian nationalist hero Giuseppe Garibaldi fought for republican self-government on both sides of the Atlantic. Committed to national self-determination, Garibaldi veered between supporting secession movements in Brazil (1835) and the Papal States (1848) and fighting wars of national consolidation in Uruguay (1842) and, most famously, Italy. By conquering Sicily in 1860, Garibaldi and his Redshirt army helped create a consolidated Kingdom of Italy free from foreign control. When the U.S. Civil War broke out, President Lincoln unsuccessfully offered Garibaldi a generalship in the Union army. ▲

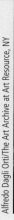

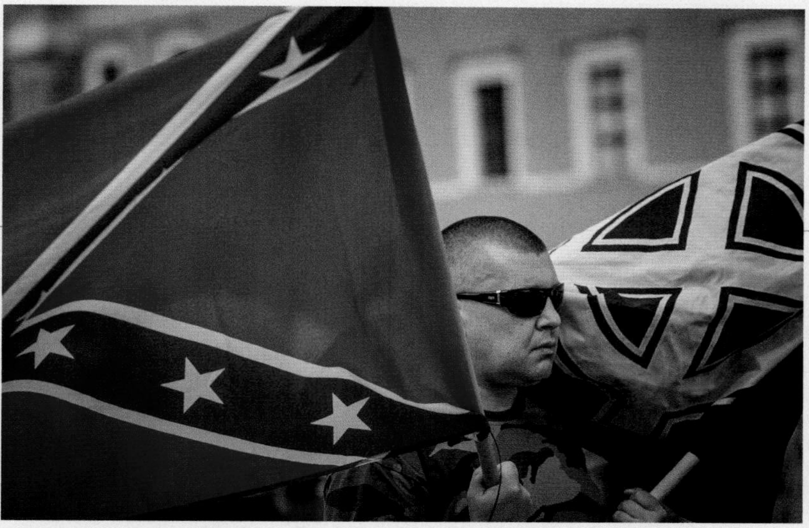

WOJTEK RADWANSKI/AFP/Getty Images

The Confederate Flag Abroad Despite its removal from South Carolina's capitol building in 2015, the Confederate battle flag remains embroiled in controversy at home and abroad. It flies around the world, sometimes expressing white supremacist ideology (as with neo-Nazi groups in Germany) and other times symbolizing defiance by ethnic or regional minorities. In this photo, a Polish far-right activist holds a Confederate flag and a "White Pride" banner during a July 2015 demonstration against accepting over two thousand Middle Eastern immigrants to Poland. In recent years, Confederate flags have also been displayed by pro-Russian separatists in Ukraine. ▲

The slaveholding South's strategy of secession was not unique. The mid-nineteenth century was a global age of nationalism in which popular fervor was mobilized not only to incite democratic revolutions or unify small states into national governments but also to carve new nations out of centralized republics or monarchies through acts of secession. In the latter category, the European revolutions of 1848 featured revolts intended to establish Hungary and Poland as independent nations throwing off Austrian and Russian imperial rule. But the closest parallels to the U.S. secession crisis were the separatist movements that threatened new nations in Latin America.

After winning their independence from Spain and Portugal by the 1820s, many Latin American nations adopted federal-style governments, often modeled on the United States, to forge national unity out of local differences. Like the young United States of America, these countries were "unions" that had not yet become tightly knit nations. Some, like the United Mexican States and the United States of Colombia, copied the name of their northern neighbor, and they experienced many of the same sectional tensions. Disputes over tariffs, political representation at the capital, church-state relations, and powers of national versus local government provoked regional secession movements and wars to suppress such revolts in Brazil, Argentina, Colombia, and other new Latin American republics.

Next door to the United States, the republic of Mexico faced a series of regional revolts in the antebellum decades. The struggle for Texan independence was, from the viewpoint of the Mexican government, one of several linked secession movements. In the mid-1830s, after President Santa Anna suspended the federal constitution, enlarged his powers, and decreed new local taxes, the Mexican states of Yucatan, Zacatecas, and the section of the state of Coahuila known as Tejas declared themselves in revolt. The Texans' secession movement, which was led by transplanted white Southerners, set a precedent that South Carolinians followed twenty-five years later.

The Yucatan Republic maintained its fragile independence for more than a decade before internal divisions and lack of foreign support caused its demise. To suppress a revolt by native Mayan peoples, Yucatan's leaders sought an alliance with the United States during the U.S.–Mexican War, but Congress declined to take on another war. In desperation, Yucatan secessionists agreed in 1848 to rejoin Mexico in exchange for military assistance against the Mayans.

Mexico's violent divisions persisted to the late 1850s, when a revolt by conservatives who were outraged by a new republican constitution of 1857 that separated church and state ousted Mexico's reform administration and forced its leader, Benito Juárez, into internal exile. The resulting civil war (the Reform War of 1857–1861) overlapped the U.S. secession struggle. North of the border, president-elect Lincoln supported Juárez and likened seceding Southern slaveholders to the Mexican usurpers. Both groups, he declared, were attempting to destroy legitimate republican constitutions through illegal means, substituting bullets for ballots.

Critical Thinking Questions

► How was the secession of the U.S. South in 1860–1861 similar or different from other secessionist movements in the age of nationalism?

► Why did nineteenth-century secession movements nearly always result in civil wars?

Go to MindTap® to engage with an interactive version of **History without Borders: Secession.** Learn from an interactive map, view related video, and respond to critical thinking questions.

Crittenden Compromise Eleventh-hour proposal to stop secession and prevent sectional war that Republicans rejected because it allowed slavery in future territories.

Fort Sumter Federal fort in harbor of Charleston, South Carolina, whose bombardment by Confederates began the Civil War in April 1861.

border states Four slave states in the Upper South—Maryland, Delaware, Kentucky, and Missouri—that remained in the Union after secession.

many hesitated or even opposed secession. Whites in Kentucky and Missouri had additional reasons to waver, for if a sectional war followed secession, it would divide their families and almost surely be fought on their soil. Before Lincoln took office in March 1861, secession was a half-successful revolution but a determined one.

At first, Lincoln considered secession a bluff staged by the South's proslavery minority to gain concessions from the national government. As the breakaway movement gathered momentum, Lincoln marshaled arguments against it. The Union, he asserted, was not a revocable agreement among the states but a perpetual trust inherited from the Founders' generation. Secession violated the nation's fundamental right to ensure its survival, a task that was especially critical, Lincoln believed, because the failure of the U.S. experiment in self-government would set back the global spread of democracy for a century.

In the midst of the secession crisis, Senator John J. Crittenden of Kentucky proposed a compromise intended to prevent further defections and perhaps lure back the seceded states. Its main provision extended the old Missouri Compromise line to the Pacific and declared all present or future territories above the line free and those below it open to slavery. Lincoln, not yet sworn in as president, urged Republicans to oppose the **Crittenden Compromise** of 1861. To accept it would be to renounce the antiextension platform on which he had just been elected. Lincoln was willing to concede defeat in New Mexico, whose territorial legislature had approved black and Indian bondage, but he stood adamantly against proslavery expansionism in the Caribbean. Recalling William Walker, he warned that Crittenden's proposal would encourage "filibustering for all South of us," including Nicaragua and Cuba, and "making slave states of it." The prospect of slavery expanding outside U.S. borders, not its extension within, became the final obstacle to negotiating a halt to secession. Lacking the Republicans' support, Crittenden's proposal died in Congress. Whether proslavery extremists would have accepted it is debatable, but its failure guaranteed that the nation would be divided into contending governments when Lincoln assumed office.

12-5d "And the War Came"

Confederates fire the first shot when the Union tries to provision Fort Sumter.

After the lower-South states seceded, two questions remained: Would the remaining slave states leave the Union? Would secession lead to war? The second was answered first.

In his inaugural address of March 1861, Lincoln appealed to Southerners' unionist sentiments and pledged not to touch slavery in states where it existed. While committed to maintaining federal authority over the South, Lincoln sought to avoid war by adopting a cautious strategy. No federal troops were sent to punish secessionists or to collect tariffs. Instead, Lincoln resolved to hold onto key forts off the coast of the rebellious states.

At **Fort Sumter** in Charleston harbor, the decisive collision occurred. When federal soldiers stationed there ran low on supplies, Lincoln notified South Carolina authorities that he would dispatch a relief ship to off-load food but no guns or ammunition. Faced with the choice of accepting this show of federal authority or attacking the fort, the Confederates chose war. On April 12, the Confederate government ordered local commanders to compel the surrender of Fort Sumter. Lincoln had maneuvered Confederates into firing the first shot, which signaled to Unionists that the South's action was a rebellion against legitimate national authority. "Both parties deprecated war," he later wrote, "but one of them would *make* war rather than let the nation survive, and the other would *accept* war rather than let it perish, and the war came." After two days of relentless bombardment, the federal garrison surrendered Fort Sumter. Miraculously, no soldiers were killed in the battle that began the bloodiest war in American history.

In response to the attack on Fort Sumter, Lincoln called for seventy-five thousand Union militiamen and began mobilizing the North for war. Political leaders in the Upper South, who had been waiting to see whether Lincoln would force secessionists to return, now cast their lots. During the next two months, four more slave states seceded to join the Confederacy: Virginia, Arkansas, Tennessee, and North Carolina. In recognition of Virginia's importance, the Confederate capital was moved to Richmond. Four **border states**—Maryland, Delaware, Kentucky, and Missouri—remained in the Union, held there by intense political pressure and, in the case of Missouri and Maryland, the firm presence of federal troops. By the summer of 1861, the two sides were formed to settle the issues of slavery and secession on the battlefield.

12-5e Slavery, Nationalism, and Civil War in Global Perspective

The South's commitment to slavery prevents peaceful emancipation, and the cotton boom feeds Southern nationalism.

Focusing on the raging domestic conflict over slavery in the territories helps explain the nation's descent into civil war, but seen from a global perspective, this outcome was highly unusual. Popular opposition to slavery mounted throughout the nineteenth-century Western world, but it led to civil war almost uniquely in the United States. Besides Haiti, where the abolition of slavery had merged into a war for colonial independence, all other slave societies in the Americas abolished slavery peaceably through national laws or imperial decrees in the 1800s.

In an age of intense nationalist feeling, slavery's entanglement with rival definitions of nationhood dramatically raised the stakes of the U.S. conflict. Lincoln's insistence that the Union could not endure half-slave and half-free represented an ambitious program to enact the Founders' ideals and make freedom national. Meanwhile, Southern states opted to form an independent nation in 1860–1861 to protest Republicans' "betrayal" of a tradition of compromise going back to the 1787 Constitution. Both the North's consolidating version of nationalism and the South's breakaway version followed transatlantic precedents. The Republicans' push for uniformity under the central government echoed contemporary national unification movements in Italy and Germany. In contrast, Southern proslavery spokesmen resorted to a familiar contemporary strategy by seceding from the federal union. On both sides of the Atlantic, secession movements led to wars between competing national claimants.

Only in the United States, however, was slavery at the root of the nation's splintering. In the face of growing antislavery sentiment, Southern leaders were fiercely determined to preserve their slave system. Unlike European colonists in the West Indies and slave owners in South American nations, the South's planters rejected plans for gradual or **compensated emancipation** and looked toward the nation's expanding frontier to extend the plantation system. Because slavery was highly concentrated in one U.S. region (unlike in Brazil, for example), Southern politicians formed a powerful sectional bloc against Republicans' efforts to contain the slave system. Also, because of the booming global demand for cotton, Southern elites wielded enough economic clout on the world market to envision the Confederacy as a successful independent nation. When Northerners disputed the South's right to quit the Union, the sectional conflict rooted in slavery exploded into civil war.

compensated emancipation Process to end slavery by reimbursing owners after slaves were freed by manumission or legal decree.

Summary

In the 1850s, the expansion of slavery westward and its potential extension south of U.S. borders triggered a national crisis. Inflamed by national pride, most Americans favored spreading their nation's territory across the continent and its influence around the globe. Yet national expansion added fuel to the sectional rivalry over slavery. The nation's rapid westward push set off a prolonged debate over extension of the South's slave system into newly acquired territories. Involvements abroad provided no respite. American reactions to the European revolutions of 1848 reflected domestic divisions over slavery, and the nation's threatened movement south into Cuba and Central America injected the slavery question directly into foreign affairs.

The U.S. acquisition of California and New Mexico following the war with Mexico brought the slavery issue to center stage. Most white Northerners were not abolitionists; they refused to attack slavery in the South or support African Americans' push for racial equality in the North. But northern free soilers clashed with militant slaveholders over western lands, which both sides saw as the key to economic opportunity and the nation's future. Political divisions heightened sectional tensions as new northern-dominated coalitions such as the Republicans and the Know-Nothings appeared in the wake of the Whig Party's collapse. The Compromise of 1850, the Kansas-Nebraska Act (1854), and the Supreme Court's Dred Scott Decision (1857) failed to resolve the territorial dispute. In Kansas, guerrilla fighting between free-soil and proslavery partisans presaged a national civil war. John Brown's raid at Harpers Ferry raised the specter of abolitionist-inspired slave insurrections in the South itself.

In 1860, slaveholders' demand for federal guarantees of slavery in the territories split the Democratic Party, giving the presidency to the Republicans' Abraham Lincoln. Seeing that the control over the national government they had exerted since Presidents Jefferson and Jackson was now over, proslavery leaders resorted to a common practice in federative nations of the Americas: They seceded. As happened elsewhere, secession led to armed conflict, but only in the United States did the struggle over slavery provide the spark for secession and civil war. Whose vision of nationalism prevailed—the Union's or the Confederacy's—and the fate of the root cause of division, slavery itself, would be decided on the battlefield.

<Thinking Back, *Looking Forward*>

As you review, consider how the contest over slavery in the territories culminated two nineteenth-century topics discussed earlier: continental expansion and the growing debate over slavery and race. How did westward expansion heighten tensions between free and slave labor in America's "empire of liberty"?

How was U.S. abolitionism connected to freedom struggles in other nations? Why was antislavery such an explosive cause in the United States? Did the outbreak of Civil War mean that the U.S. republican experiment had failed? In the next chapters, look for the consequences of a nationalist war rooted in slavery.

How did the Civil War play out as a war of competing nationalisms? As a struggle over freedom and equality?

To make your study concrete, review the timeline and reflect on the entries there. Think about their causes, consequences, and connections. How do they fit with global trends?

Additional Resources

Books

Anbinder, Tyler. *Nativism and Slavery: The Northern Know-Nothings and the Politics of the 1850s*. New York and Oxford: Oxford University Press, 1992. ▶ Explanation of the rapid rise and fall of the influential anti-immigrant political party.

Fleche, Andre M. *The Revolution of 1861: The American Civil War in the Age of Nationalist Conflict*. Chapel Hill: University of North Carolina Press, 2012. ▶ Placement of the divergence of northern and southern nationalism in a transatlantic context, including the revolutions of 1848 in Europe.

Foner, Eric. *Gateway to Freedom: The Hidden History of the Underground Railroad*. New York: W.W. Norton, 2015. ▶ Presentation of fresh evidence to reconstruct the network of black and white abolitionists who assisted fugitive slaves.

Freehling, William W. *The Road to Disunion: Secessionists Triumphant, 1854–1861*. New York and Oxford: Oxford University Press, 2007. ▶ A powerful analysis of how secessionist fire eaters overcame Upper South-Lower South divisions.

Gienapp, William. *The Origins of the Republican Party, 1852–1856*. New York and Oxford: Oxford University Press, 1987. ▶ A comprehensive history of the party's rapid rise.

Horwitz, Tony. *Midnight Rising: John Brown and the Raid That Sparked the Civil War*. New York: Henry Holt, 2011. ▶ A riveting account of the raid and its background, including a complex portrait of Brown.

May, Robert E. *Manifest Destiny's Underworld: Filibustering in Antebellum America*. Chapel Hill and London: University of North Carolina Press, 2002. ▶ An eye-opening history of nearly forgotten expansionist adventures.

Potter, David M. *The Impending Crisis, 1848–1861*. New York: Harper & Row, 1976. ▶ The best single-volume overview of the coming of the Civil War.

Stampp, Kenneth M., ed. *The Causes of the Civil War*. New York: Simon and Schuster, 1991. ▶ Indispensable collection of documents, essays, and interpretations.

Wiley, Peter Booth. *Yankees in the Land of the Gods: Commodore Perry and the Opening of Japan*. New York: Viking, 1990. ▶ A colorful account of the historic encounter of East and West.

Go to the MindTap® for **Global Americans** to access the full version of select books from this Additional Resources section.

Websites

Brady-Handy Collection of Photographs, Library of Congress. (http://www.loc.gov/pictures/collection/brhc/) ▶ Archive of ten thousand photographs of political and social leaders of the 1850s and the Civil War era.

Civil War Primary Sources. (http://www.civilwar.org/education/history/primarysources/#photos) ▶ Source of political speeches, acts of Congress, and party platforms of the 1850s as well as secession ordinances of the thirteen Confederate states.

Harpers Ferry National Historic Site. (http://www.nps.gov/hafe/index.htm) ▶ Gateway website for the well-preserved West Virginia town with exhibits on John Brown, munitions technology, and antebellum African American life.

Library of Congress Primary Documents in American History: *Dred Scott v. Sandford*. (http://www.loc.gov/rr/program/bib/ourdocs/DredScott.html) ▶ The text of the 1857 Supreme Court decision and dozens of related primary sources.

Lincoln-Douglas Debates of 1858. (http://lincoln.lib.niu.edu/lincolndouglas) ▶ Complete text of the seven debates of the Illinois senatorial campaign plus newspaper commentary.

MindTap®

Continue exploring online through MindTap®, where you can:

- **Assess your knowledge with the Chapter Test**
- **Watch historical videos related to the chapter**
- **Further your understanding with interactive maps and timelines**

Expansion, Slavery, and the Coming of the Civil War

1846

August

Wilmot Proviso opens congressional debate over slavery in territories acquired through U.S.–Mexican War.

1848

February

Republican revolution erupts in France and spreads antimonarchy uprisings across Europe.

April

Revolutionary government in France abolishes slavery in French colonies.

August

Free-Soil Party is formed to ban slavery from U.S. territories.

September

First wave of German "Forty-Eighters" arrives in United States as German revolutions are suppressed.

November

Whig candidate Zachary Taylor is elected president.

1849

December

California applies for admission to statehood.

1850

September

Congressional compromise admits California as free state and enacts new Fugitive Slave Law.

1851

September

Filibusterer Narciso López is captured in Cuba and executed.

December

Defeated Hungarian nationalist Louis Kossuth lands in the U.S. to seek official support.

1852

March

Uncle Tom's Cabin is published and becomes a best-selling antislavery novel in the United States and Europe.

November

Democrat Franklin Pierce is elected president.

December

Louis Napoleon declares himself Emperor Napoleon III of France, signaling end of 1848 Revolutions in Europe.

1853

July

U.S. Commodore Matthew Perry sails into Tokyo Bay to force open trade with Japan.

December

Gadsden Purchase adds territory from Mexico for a transcontinental railroad.

1854

March

In Treaty of Kanagawa, Japan agrees to open specified ports to the United States and other Western nations.

May

Kansas-Nebraska Act rekindles political controversy over slavery in the territories.

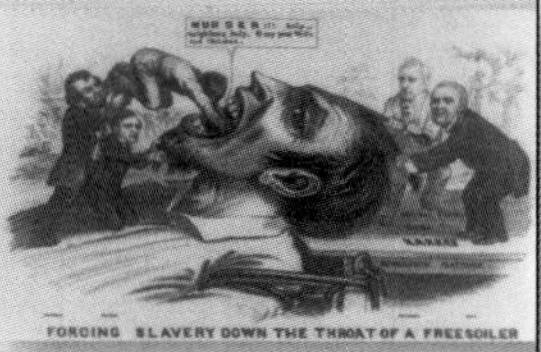

July

Republican Party forms political coalition in opposition to Kansas-Nebraska Act.

August

U.S. negotiates annexation treaty with King Kamehameha III of Hawai'i, but it goes unsigned.

October

U.S. foreign ministers draw up Ostend Manifesto urging purchase or forced cession of Cuba from Spain.

November

Know-Nothing movement organizes nationally as the American Party after winning local elections.

1855

January

New York company completes Panama Railroad crossing the isthmus between the Atlantic and Pacific Oceans.

October

William Walker's filibustering expedition overthrows Nicaragua's government.

1856

May

Massachusetts Senator Charles Sumner attacked in Congress after speech against extending slavery to Kansas.

Guerrilla war rages in Kansas territory between free-state and proslavery partisans.

October

Arrow War (Second Opium War) opens as England and France attack China, resulting in U.S. access to additional Chinese ports.

November

Democrat James Buchanan is elected president.

1857

March

Supreme Court issues *Dred Scott* decision permitting slavery in territories and denying blacks U.S. citizenship.

December

Mexican civil war (Reform War) begins over new republican constitution and laws separating church and state.

1858

August–October

Abraham Lincoln and Stephen Douglas debate free soil versus popular sovereignty in the Illinois race for U.S. Senate.

1859

October

John Brown attacks arsenal at Harpers Ferry, Virginia, in an attempt to spark a slave insurrection.

1860

April

Deep South's demand to guarantee slavery in the territories splits the Democratic Party.

September

Filibusterer William Walker is executed in Honduras.

November

Republican candidate Lincoln is elected president in sectional four-party election.

December

South Carolina convention approves ordinance of secession from the Union.

1861

January

Last-minute Crittenden Compromise fails to pass Congress.

February

Six Deep South slave states join South Carolina in seceding from the Union, forming the Confederate States of America.

April

Civil War erupts when Confederates bombard Fort Sumter off South Carolina coast.

April–June

Four additional slave states join the Confederacy.

13 The American Civil War

1861–1865

In 1863, William Andrew Jackson toured England, Scotland, and Wales, giving vivid testimony about slave life in the Confederacy to help rally British public opinion behind the Union.

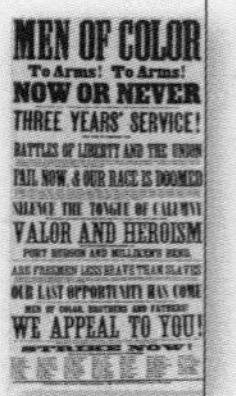

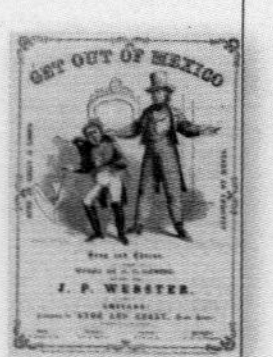

Like many Americans, William Andrew Jackson, a twenty-nine-year-old slave from Virginia, was transformed by the Civil War. Born in the countryside, he was taken to Richmond and hired out by his master, eventually as coachman for Confederate President Jefferson Davis. Davis's slaves constantly talked about fleeing bondage, Jackson recalled, making sure that "when the time came they would be found ready." Jackson seized his chance in April 1862. When Davis left Richmond to confer with his generals, Jackson escaped to nearby Union camps, where he provided details of Richmond's fortifications and Confederate troop movements.

New York : Harper & Brothers, June 7, 1862.

As Jackson made his way north, he became a celebrity. "Jefferson Davis's Coachman" was profiled in *Harper's Weekly* and the New York press. Literate and an eloquent speaker, he was, said the *New York Tribune,* as "black as a Congo negro" yet "much more intelligent than a good many white folks." Pressed for details about the Davis family, Jackson revealed that Varina Davis, the Confederate first lady, lacked faith in the Confederacy, which she privately declared was "about played out."

Varina Davis "used to talk a great deal about England and France helping them [the Confederates]," Jackson recalled, and in the fall of 1862 he sailed to England to prevent such an outcome. With letters of introduction from abolitionist William Lloyd Garrison, Jackson spoke at public meetings in Britain, giving vivid testimony about slave life and stressing that the Confederates were fighting to preserve slavery, not simply to win independence. In 1863, he toured England, Scotland, and Wales as an agent of the Union and Emancipation Society, which had organized to support President Lincoln's Emancipation Proclamation. Jackson's campaigning and that of other former slaves on tour helped rally British public opinion behind the Union.

Jackson's transatlantic journey from the stables of the Confederate White House to speakers' platforms in British lecture halls was unique. Yet his experience illustrates two of the Civil War's most far-reaching developments: the way that the South's slaves and their northern allies seized wartime opportunities to achieve emancipation and the way that the war threatened to escalate from a domestic dispute into an international conflict. Union leaders announced that their objective was to restore the Union, but a year and a half into the war, President Lincoln declared his intention to free secessionists' slaves. Emancipation had enormous implications for the war's outcome overseas as well as at home because the political leaders of Britain and France, although eager to support the South's independence, were reluctant to defend slavery, having abolished it in their own colonies decades earlier.

How do William Andrew Jackson's experiences as coachman to Jefferson Davis and later rallying Union support in the United Kingdom illustrate the role of emancipation in the war's outcome both domestically and overseas?

Go to MindTap® to watch a video on Jackson and learn how his story relates to the themes of this chapter.

The end of slavery in the United States and the struggle over foreign intervention were only two of the wartime developments that wrought huge changes in American life. In the North, the demands of war production boosted industrial capitalism, and in both sections of the divided nation, the reach of central governments expanded. The war itself, begun as a gentlemanly affair between West Point generals, devolved into fierce campaigns in which powerful new cannons crumbled masonry forts and marching armies destroyed farms and homes. When the Union finally prevailed in 1865, all Americans faced adjusting to personal traumas and the social and economic transformations brought by war.

The American Civil War was not the only mid-nineteenth century nationalist conflict between centralizers and secessionists, republicans and aristocrats. The North's aim to unify the states under the national government and the southern states' resistance aligned with similar struggles in Latin America and Europe. In Germany and Italy, centralized nation-states replaced weak federations and alliances between dukes or kings. In Mexico and South America, national governments triumphed by tightening constitutional controls. The creation of new national governments often coincided with movements to end forced labor and extend political participation to common people. Almost everywhere, entrenched elites opposed democratic changes, and clashes over the meaning of freedom and nationhood were settled on the battlefield.

13-1 Beginning of the War, 1861

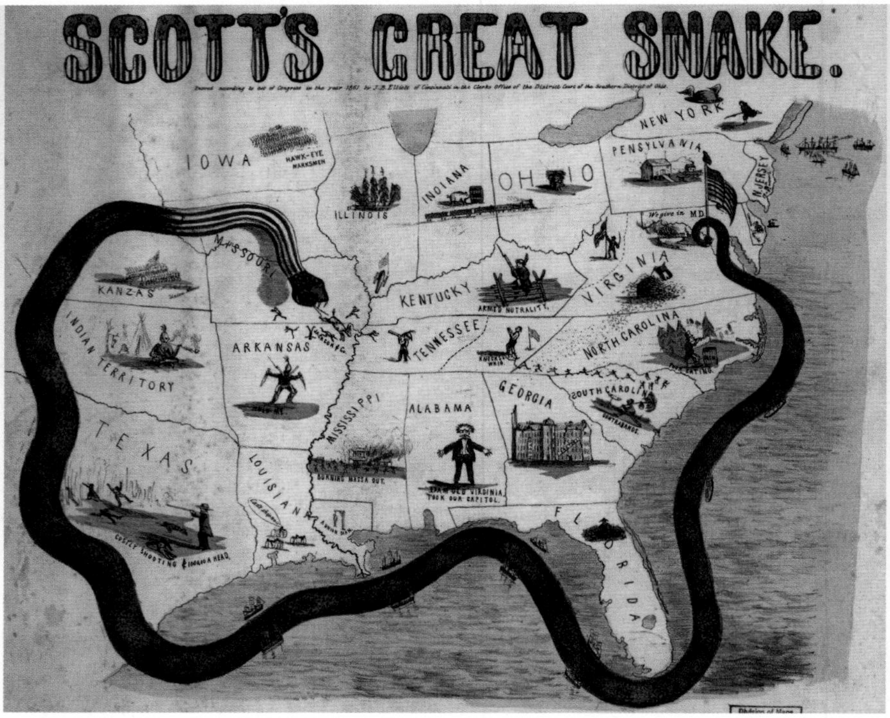

This Union propaganda map, published in 1861, shows General Winfield Scott's Anaconda Plan to surround the Confederacy by land and sea and squeeze it into submission. Notice how Georgia's cotton factories close down and Mississippi slaves rise up, "burning massa out." Northern farms prosper while North Carolinians are reduced to eating rosin (cakes of pine resin).

How does the map envision the Anaconda Plan's operations and its success? How are states in the Upper South portrayed? ▶

Elliott, J. B.

Each side in the Civil War predicted a quick and easy victory, the Union by penetrating and blockading the South, the Confederacy by repulsing the invaders. The Union's superior industrial and labor force resources promised an important material edge. Confederates, however, counted on their fighting spirit and the advantages of defending their homeland. Linked to Europe by ties of trade and national self-interest, the South also hoped to secure an alliance with Britain and France that would tip the war scales in its favor. Neither side was prepared for combat. The Confederacy lacked an army and navy, and the regular Union army totaled only seventeen thousand men, most of whom were deployed on the western frontier. It took time and effort to mobilize for the war. In the meantime, the first major battle at Bull Run and the struggle over the allegiance of border states such as Missouri demonstrated that the war would be neither brief nor painless.

☞ As you read, consider the resources, war aims, and strategies of the Union and the Confederacy. What were each side's strengths and weaknesses?

13-1a Mobilization and Strategy

Planning a war to restore the Union, the North invades while the South defends.

President Lincoln's call for seventy-five thousand volunteers after the attack on Fort Sumter spurred both sides to action. Northern politicians closed ranks behind the Union. Stephen Douglas, Lincoln's northern opponent in the 1860 presidential election, pledged his support, as did many prowar Democrats. A quarter of a million New Yorkers attended a patriotic rally in Union Square, the largest public gathering in North America up to that time. In the South, conditional Unionists in Virginia, North Carolina, Tennessee, and Arkansas responded to Lincoln's call for troops by siding with the Confederacy. They joined earlier secessionists at enlistment rallies and elaborate balls held to celebrate departing troops.

Both sides invoked the nation's history and principles to justify their cause. Northerners declared that Union victory would preserve the Founders' legacy and promote democracy around the world. "If we should fail," one Ohio soldier wrote, "the onward march of Liberty in the Old World will be retarded at least a century, and Monarchs, Kings and Aristocrats will be more powerful against their subjects than ever." In contrast, Confederates likened their cause to the patriots of 1776 who had declared their independence against a tyrannical king. A young Virginia officer wrote his mother that the North's "war of subjugation against the South" was just like "England's war upon the colonies."

At the war's outset, Lincoln and Congress emphasized that their goal was to restore the Union. They viewed the Confederacy not as a sovereign nation but as a conspiracy of states in rebellion against the national government. Taking a global view, Lincoln felt a kinship with advocates of national unification in Mexico, where President Benito Juárez had just defeated a conservative revolt, and in Italy, where a patchwork of kingdoms and states was coalescing through diplomacy and war into a unified constitutional monarchy. Impressed by the Italian nationalist hero Giuseppe Garibaldi, Lincoln offered him a generalship, but Garibaldi refused because the Union was not committed to abolishing slavery.

For Lincoln, preserving the Union required leaving slavery untouched. On the day before Lincoln's inauguration, Czar Alexander II, intent on modernizing Russia after its humiliating defeat by the French, British, and Ottoman Turks in the Crimean War (1853–1856, see also figure 13.2 on page 396), freed Russia's 23 million serfs by edict. Lincoln applauded the Czar's action but rejected similar steps against U.S. slavery. Most Northerners were not abolitionists, and many were Democrats who might withhold their support if the war targeted slavery. Pressing the issue might also drive slave owners in the border states to the Confederacy. In his July 4, 1861, message to Congress, Lincoln reaffirmed that he had "no purpose, directly or indirectly, to interfere with slavery in the states where it exists." Congress agreed.

Lincoln's assurances meant little to Confederates, who sought independence without interference. To fend off invasion and blockade, Confederate leaders planned a defensive war. This strategy had several advantages. Confederate forces could rely on local knowledge and assistance to outmaneuver invaders. Defense required fewer soldiers than occupation, and Southerners had only to hold on while their troops won enough military victories or Northerners grew weary enough to call the war off. Prolonging the war, however, risked stretching Confederate resources to the breaking point (see Figure 13.1).

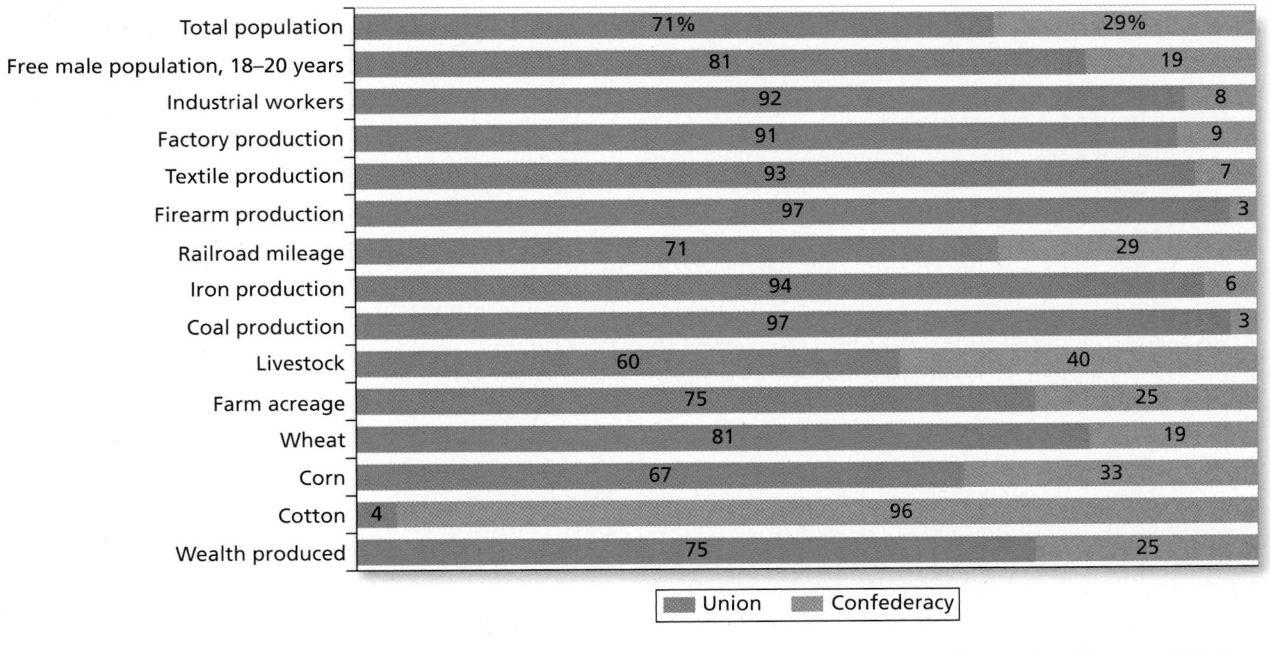

Figure 13.1 Comparison of Union and Confederate Resources, 1861 At the start of the war, the Union enjoyed huge quantitative advantages in population, industry, railroad mileage, and wealth. Confederates had the advantage of fighting a defensive war and relying on slave labor to sustain domestic production while white men fought. The South's strategists believed that a short war might give the Union insufficient time to mobilize its resources and that a prolonged one would allow Confederates to rely on the global demand for cotton to attract funds and foreign support. ▲

Battle of Bull Run First major battle of the Civil War, fought in northern Virginia in July 1861, in which Union troops' panicked retreat gave Confederates a decisive victory.

King Cotton Diplomacy Confederate strategy of withholding cotton from Britain and France as pressure to recognize the South's independence and provide armed support.

***Trent* Affair** Anglo-American diplomatic crisis in 1861 that was resolved peacefully after Union officials apologized for seizing Confederate envoys on a British ship in the Caribbean.

To counteract the Union's material advantages, the Confederacy hoped for European allies.

Both sides' ideas about a quick and decisive victory were tested in July 1861 when Union general Irvin McDowell marched thirty-five thousand raw recruits into Virginia. Awaiting them across a stream called Bull Run at Manassas, a railroad junction thirty miles southwest of Washington, were twenty thousand Confederates. With little expectation of bloodshed, some Washington dignitaries picnicked on a nearby hill to watch the action. The Union soldiers initially pushed back the enemy, but the Confederates, rallied by General Thomas ("Stonewall") Jackson, held firm. When Rebel reinforcements arrived by train in the middle of the battle—a first in the history of warfare—the Confederates counterattacked, and Union soldiers fled in disorganized panic, some all the way to Washington. The **Battle of Bull Run** boosted Confederates' confidence and revealed to Northerners that the war would be no afternoon picnic.

13-1b Potential European Involvement

> Britain and France tilt toward the Confederacy, and the Union escapes a diplomatic crisis.

Most nineteenth-century civil wars became international wars, and the U.S. war threatened to join the list. The nation's growing economic stature made it a rival that European powers would have been pleased to see splintered. Especially because the South's cotton exports were important to their economies, Britain and France leaned toward intervening on the Confederacy's behalf. France also sought to regain a New World empire in Mexico. In December 1861, Britain, France, and Spain sent troops to collect debts owed by Mexico's beleaguered liberal government under President Juárez. Britain and Spain soon withdrew their forces, but Napoleon III, who aimed to install a Catholic monarch beholden to France, sent additional soldiers.

Europeans held conflicting attitudes toward the Civil War. Although British mill owners depended on cotton, factory workers and abolitionists sympathized with the Union and the idea of free labor. Writing in exile from London, Karl Marx predicted that the defeat of slave owners would help liberate workers everywhere. Meanwhile, Britain's landed elites, like Europe's ruling classes generally, identified with wealthy southern planters and opposed democratic reforms. National self-interest influenced European policies more than public opinion. But before allying with the Confederacy, European rulers wanted assurance that it was a viable nation. They also eyed each other with suspicion, worrying that intervention might drag them into a distant war to the benefit of rivals. Napoleon III resolved not to recognize the secessionists unless Britain did.

Thus, the Confederates' diplomatic objective became securing Britain's recognition, which Union leaders aimed to prevent. If Britain allied with the South, it could destroy the Union navy, supply the Confederacy with war materiel, and open a second fighting front on the Canadian border. Cotton was the Confederacy's primary lure. In the war's first year, Southerners imposed a voluntary embargo, gambling that withholding cotton would increase pressure in Britain on their behalf—a strategy that became known as "**King Cotton Diplomacy**."

Union leaders sought to stop Confederate overseas trade entirely. A few days after Fort Sumter fell, Lincoln proclaimed a naval blockade of Confederate ports, opening a prolonged diplomatic controversy with Britain. Under international law, the blockade implied that the Confederacy was a sovereign state free to trade with neutral nations like Britain and France—exactly what the Union was trying to prevent. Union leaders were fortunate that Britain did not challenge the blockade directly but relied on Confederate ships to carry goods. Initially, most Confederate merchant ships passed through unscathed, but by 1863, the blockade tightened enough to deter Rebel runners.

Long before that, the South's cotton strategy faltered. British merchants warehoused a surplus of cotton when the war began, and a year later, when the cotton famine loomed, they developed alternative supply sources. The South reversed its embargo policy in 1863, but it was too late. Meanwhile, European trade with the North increased, and poor grain harvests in England meant that Britain needed the North's wheat even more than the South's cotton.

Despite the blockade and the cotton embargo's failure, a brisk trade flourished in arms and ships between the British and the Confederates. British shipyards supplied powerful commerce raiders such as the *Alabama* to the Rebel navy, which used them to sink Yankee merchant ships on the high seas. In November 1861, a confrontation in international waters came close to sparking an Anglo-U.S. war. A federal warship stopped the British mail packet *Trent* as it left Havana carrying Confederate envoys James Mason and John Slidell, who were bound for London and Paris. The two diplomats were removed and imprisoned in Boston, outraging British officials, who began preparing for war. Cooler heads prevailed when U.S. secretary of state Seward acknowledged that the Union captain had acted without authorization, and President Lincoln ordered the diplomats' release. The ***Trent* Affair,** the first of several war scares with Britain, blew over, and the Rebels resumed their mission to secure British and French support.

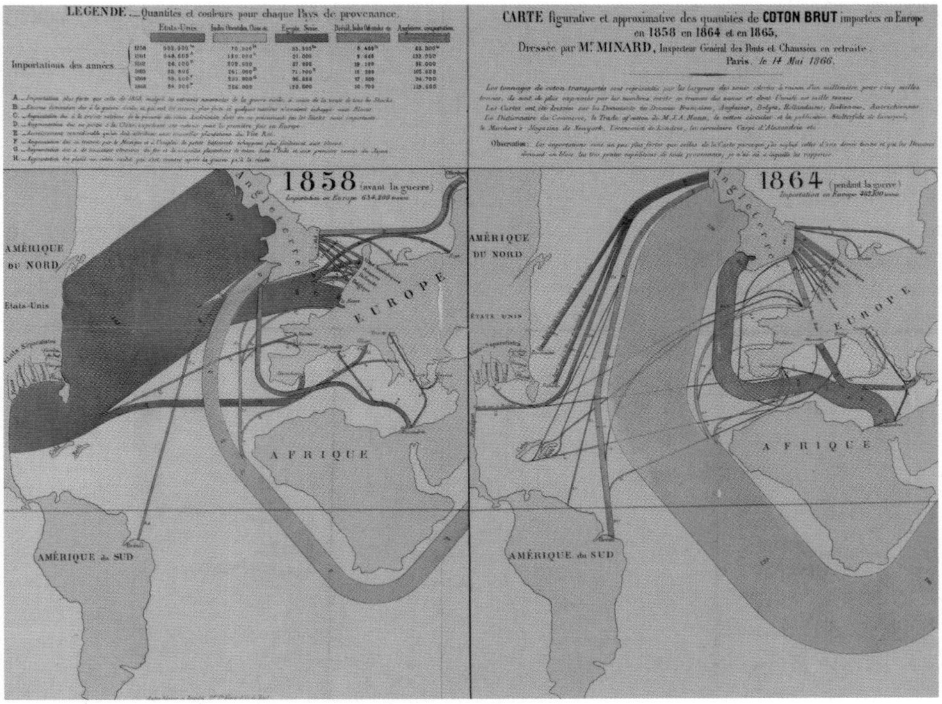

Minard, Charles Joseph, 1781–1870.

King Cotton Diplomacy Fails These maps created by French cartographer Charles Joseph Minard in 1866 show the dramatic shift in cotton imports to Europe before (1858) and during (1864) the Civil War. The South's voluntary embargo and the North's coastal blockade brought the huge flow of cotton from the United States (blue band) to a virtual halt. To compensate, England and France developed new sources of supply in India and China (orange band), Egypt and Syria (brown band), and Brazil and the West Indies (lavender band). ◄

13-1c Struggle for the Border States

The Union retains four border slave states by various strategies.

After Fort Sumter and the secession of four upper-South slave states, the fate of four remaining slave states—Maryland, Delaware, Kentucky, and Missouri—remained undecided. Gaining these states would shift badly needed resources to the Confederacy and give it strategic advantages. Lincoln viewed holding the border states, especially Kentucky, as key to Union victory. "I think to lose Kentucky is nearly to lose the whole game," he fretted.

The centerpiece of Lincoln's border-state strategy was his emphasis on restoring the Union, not attacking slavery. Otherwise, the president varied his tactics according to local conditions. Tiny Delaware, with few slaveholders, was safe for the Union, but in neighboring Maryland, slaveholders and pro-Confederate sympathizers were a serious threat. In mid-April 1861, a Baltimore mob attacked a Massachusetts regiment en route to Washington, killing four soldiers. Acting swiftly, Lincoln placed the state legislature under military watch, suspended the writ of **habeas corpus** (which prevented arbitrary arrest and detention), and put pro-Confederate officials behind bars. One case was appealed to the Supreme Court's chief justice, Roger Taney, who in *ex parte Merryman* (1861) declared that only Congress could suspend habeas corpus. Lincoln ignored the ruling, outraging but neutralizing dissenters in the North.

Whereas Maryland was saved for the Union by force, Kentucky was won by restraint. In the native state of both Lincoln and Jefferson Davis, the conflict became a "brothers' war" that divided family members. Kentucky's officials attempted to remain neutral, threatening to turn against whichever side sent an army across its borders. The federal army shrewdly outwaited its foe. In September 1861, a Confederate army seized the heights commanding the Mississippi River at Columbus, Kentucky. The state legislature denounced the "invaders" and invited Union troops to drive them out. Kentucky officially became a Union state, although the Confederates also claimed it and recruited soldiers there.

A more complex and drawn-out series of events took place in Missouri, where the pro-Confederate state militia and German-American Unionists from St. Louis squared off and regular Union and Confederate armies massed for a showdown. In August 1861, the Confederates under General Sterling Price pushed northward, claiming half the state. John C. Frémont, the Union's local commander, drove Price back but could not control the feuding population. For much of the war, bands of **guerrillas** roamed Missouri, "bushwhacking" (ambushing) enemy patrols, terrorizing neighborhoods, and carrying on local feuds. In the pro-Confederate gang of William Quantrill, from whom postwar outlaws Frank and Jesse James learned their trade, guerrilla tactics descended into robbery and wanton killing.

habeas corpus The right of an arrested person to be brought before a judge or into court.

guerrillas Armed bands of civilians or irregular combatants rampant in Civil War border states and Appalachia who attacked soldiers and civilians.

West Virginia New Union state created when pro-Union counties of western Virginia separated from Confederate Virginia under protection of occupying federal troops.

Some states that were firmly committed to the Union or Confederacy divided geographically. In the backcountry of eastern Tennessee and western Virginia, nonslaveholding whites sabotaged Confederate operations and fought Rebel guerrillas. In the summer of 1861, the Union army cleared Confederate forces from western Virginia. Protected by a strong federal presence, local officials seceded from Virginia and entered the Union as the state of **West Virginia** in 1863. In contrast, the southern counties of Ohio, Indiana, and Illinois, where many migrants from Tennessee and Kentucky resided, became hotbeds of resistance to Union war measures. In distant California, many transplanted Southerners sided with the Confederacy. Around San Francisco Bay, Union officials foiled plots to divert shipments of California gold to Confederate coffers.

13-2 The Seesaw War, 1862

Library of Congress Prints and Photographs Division Washington, D.C.[LC-DIG-cwpbh-03384]

The Civil War was the first to be extensively captured by camera. Photographers accompanied the armies, and in October 1862, Mathew Brady displayed photographs of *The Dead of Antietam* at his New York City studio, including this view of slain Confederate artillerymen at Dunker Church. One reporter wrote, "Mr. Brady has done something to bring home to us the terrible reality and earnestness of war. If he has not brought bodies and laid them in our door-yards and along the streets, he has done something very like it."

What emotions did photographs of the battlefield dead evoke in viewers? How did such pictures contrast with participants' expectations of the war's fighting and outcome? ▶

The war's second year demonstrated that it would not be over soon. Momentum on the battlefront tilted in opposite ways in different regions. In the West, Union forces secured key areas and penetrated southward along the Mississippi River. In the East, where fighting concentrated in Virginia, Confederate generals turned back offensives by larger Union forces aiming to capture Richmond. Both sides struggled to care for the unprecedented number of sick and wounded soldiers. Only after a Confederate move northward into Maryland was thwarted did Lincoln's administration seize the initiative by shifting its strategy on slavery.

☞ As you read, look for reasons the Civil War proved to be so long and deadly. What geographic, military, and medical factors contributed to the toll?

13-2a Union Gains in the West, Confederate Victories in the East

Lincoln and Davis split victories, but both find fighting generals.

After Bull Run, Lincoln turned to General George B. McClellan, fresh from success in western Virginia, to command of the Army of the Potomac. He had been an official U.S. military observer at the Crimean War, where he watched British and French forces practice maneuver and siege against Russia. As a northern Democrat, McClellan wanted to avoid an all-out war that might loosen the South's control over slavery. Hailed as the "Young Napoleon" by the press, McClellan

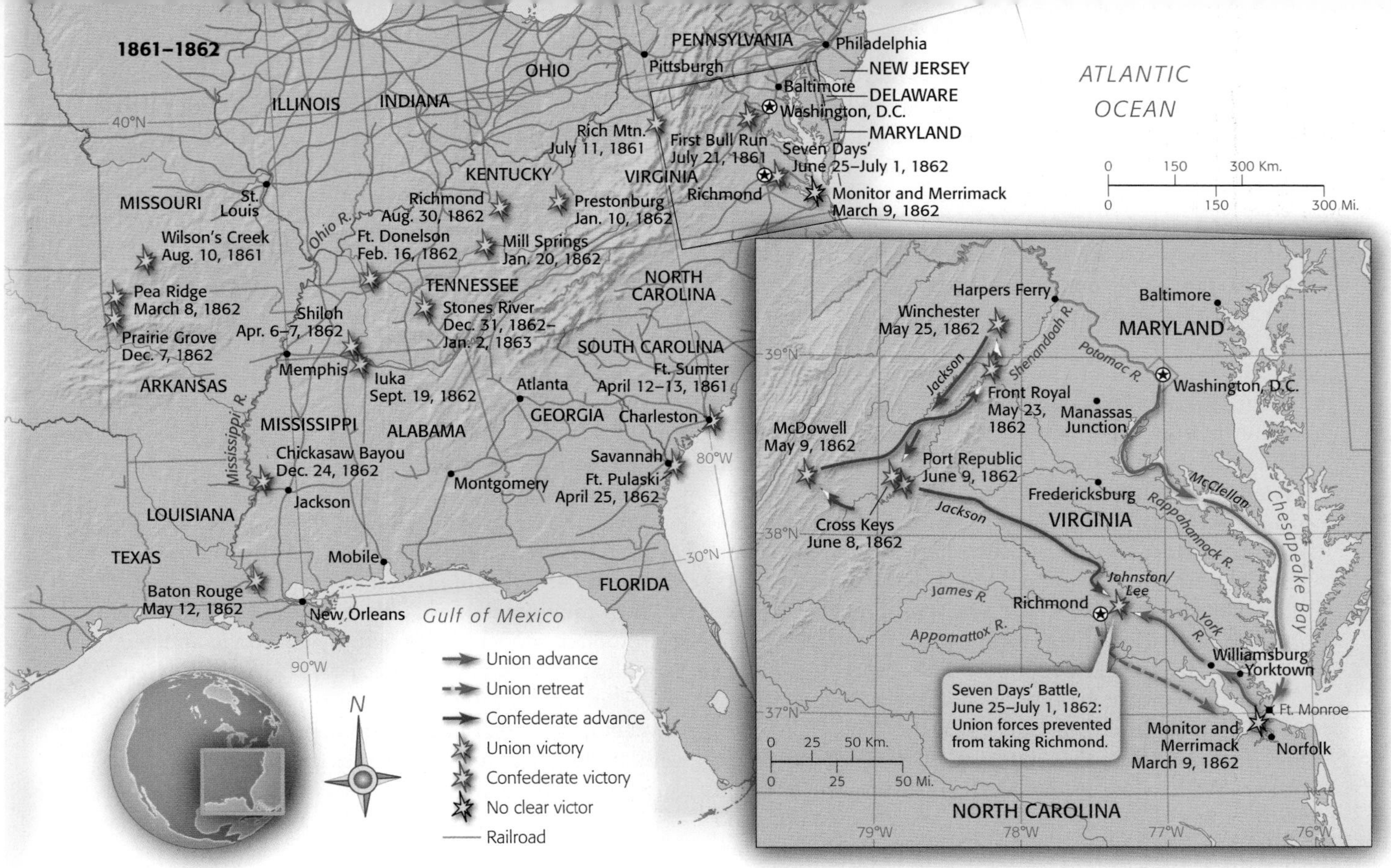

Map 13.1 The Civil War, 1861–1862 Victories in Kentucky, Tennessee, and Missouri swung momentum in the West to the Union in 1862. Two Tennessee forts surrendered to forces led by Grant, who continued south. In the East, Confederates dominated on battlefields between Washington and Richmond. "Stonewall" Jackson outmaneuvered the federals in western Virginia and then joined Lee in the Seven Days' Battle to turn back Union forces near Richmond during McClellan's Peninsular Campaign. ▲

had all of his namesake's vanity but none of his daring. An excellent organizer, he trained the Union's new recruits into a disciplined army but hesitated to deploy it. He stalled for several months despite public clamor to march his huge army toward Richmond.

Across the Appalachians, the Union army fared better (see Map 13.1). The Mississippi River and its tributaries allowed federal troops and gunboats to penetrate the Confederacy. Lincoln also found an aggressive commander in Ulysses S. Grant. A quiet, unpretentious man, Grant was a Mexican War veteran who entered civilian life in the 1850s and struggled to earn a living. Rejoining the army when the war broke out, Grant displayed determination, calmness in battle, and grasp of military strategy. In February 1862, he coordinated a land and river campaign against Fort Henry on the Tennessee River and nearby Fort Donelson on the Cumberland River that forced the surrender of thirteen thousand Rebel soldiers. These first major Union victories boosted morale in the North and pushed the Confederates out of Kentucky and half of Tennessee.

As Grant advanced south toward Corinth, Mississippi, the Confederates launched a surprise attack in the two-day **Battle of Shiloh**, April 6 and 7, 1862. Initially driven back, the federals were reinforced by troops arriving by steamboat and recovered their ground. Shiloh introduced Americans to the bloodbath of the Civil War: More than 23,000 of the 77,000 soldiers engaged were killed or wounded. Grant's career suffered a temporary setback, but Union forces soon occupied Corinth. These victories on the Mississippi River were complemented by an attack farther south in which Union Admiral David Farragut forced the surrender of New Orleans. By the summer of 1862, only two hundred miles of the Mississippi remained in Confederate hands.

West of the Mississippi, Union forces also made gains. They chased Confederate Missourians into Arkansas, where at Pea Ridge in March 1862, they repelled a Rebel attack. Eight hundred miles farther west,

Battle of Shiloh Bloody Union victory fought in southwestern Tennessee between forces under Union general Grant and Confederate generals Johnston and Beauregard.

Confederates from Texas drove up the Rio Grande to occupy Albuquerque and Santa Fe. A band of Colorado miners who enrolled in Union regiments marched over the Rockies to confront the Texans at **Glorieta Pass** on March 26–28 and sent them homeward in retreat. This battle, combined with the advance of California volunteers eastward along the Gila River, secured Arizona and New Mexico for the Union and thwarted Confederates' hopes for an overland connection to gold and sympathizers in California.

In the compact Washington-Richmond corridor, Confederates could concentrate their forces more effectively than in the sprawling West. Against the Atlantic blockade, they unveiled a new weapon, the ironclad ram *Virginia*, rebuilt from the captured Union frigate *Merrimack*. The *Virginia* destroyed several U.S. Navy ships off Hampton Roads, Virginia, before it encountered a Union counterpart, the *Monitor* on March 8, 1862, in history's first battle between **ironclads**. The ships fought to a draw, but the *Virginia*, unable to escape to open water, was soon scuttled by the Confederates. The superior *Monitor* became the model for dozens of shallow-draft ironclads the Union used to tighten the blockade.

In April 1862, General McClellan finally advanced toward Richmond (see Map 13.1). His **Peninsular Campaign** was an elaborate offensive in which one hundred thousand federal troops were transported by ship to the peninsula between the James and York Rivers from which to fight their way to Richmond, seventy miles northwest. It took six weeks for them to reach the outskirts of Richmond, where Confederate general Joseph Johnston's men attacked, and the two armies fought to a draw in the Battle of Seven Pines (May 31–June 1). When Johnston was wounded, President Davis replaced him with General Robert E. Lee.

Born into a prominent Virginia family, Lee had served in the U.S-Mexican War and later commanded the federal troops that forced John Brown's surrender at Harpers Ferry. Although personally reserved, Lee preferred an aggressive strategy of mounting swift counterattacks wherever Union forces appeared vulnerable. Sensing McClellan's hesitation, Lee attacked the separated Union lines. For the next week, the armies fought almost daily as the unnerved McClellan retreated down the James River. The Seven Days' Battles left thirty thousand men dead or wounded. Although the Union army fought well, McClellan gave up the Peninsular Campaign and returned to Washington. Emboldened by his success, Lee moved north to attack McClellan's replacement, General John Pope. In the Second Battle of Bull Run (August 29 and 30), Lee's nimble army isolated elements of Pope's forces and routed them. An exasperated President Lincoln removed Pope from command and, lacking alternatives, reappointed McClellan to restore the discipline and morale of the Army of the Potomac.

Glorieta Pass (1862) Westernmost major battle of the Civil War, in which Union soldiers drove an invading Confederate army from New Mexico Territory.

ironclads Iron-protected gunships, a key Civil War technological innovation, developed by both sides in 1862 to contest the Union's river and coastal blockade.

Peninsular Campaign (1862) Massive offensive planned by McClellan to attack Richmond via the Yorktown Peninsula but defeated by indecision and Lee.

United States Sanitary Commission Private agency chartered by the federal government to assist sick and wounded Union soldiers, a key outlet for women's volunteer work.

13-2b Death, Medical Care, and the Soldiers' Life

The war compels advances in medicine and nursing.

As Shiloh and the Seven Days' Battles showed, most Civil War engagements were deadly contests whose victor was determined only by which side retreated afterward. One reason for high death tolls was new weaponry to which generals were slow to adjust. Taught at West Point to concentrate foot soldiers for frontal attacks, they continued the practice even though modern rifles had greater range and accuracy than older smooth-bore muskets. Armed defenders behind earthworks or in trenches decimated lines of advancing soldiers, and their fire was often supplemented with artillery that spewed canister or grapeshot (clusters of small metal balls).

Civil War doctors refined amputation and other surgical techniques, but they could not stop infections. Disease killed twice as many soldiers as bullets. Overcrowded and unsanitary conditions in soldiers' quarters bred smallpox, dysentery, typhoid ("camp fever"), pneumonia, and malaria. The Peninsular Campaign revealed that neither side could effectively care for the wounded. Building on a report by Crimean War observers, the Union army organized an ambulance corps that became a model for all armies into the twentieth century. Away from the front, federal authorities constructed more than three hundred fifty hospitals, many in an airy pavilion style that retarded the spread of disease.

Many women seized the chance to aid the war effort by assisting sick and wounded soldiers. Northern women, already schooled in activism through temperance, abolitionist, and other reform movements, were especially well organized. They formed the rank and file of the **United States Sanitary Commission**, founded in the spring of 1861. Patterned on the British Sanitary Commission, which had improved hospital care during the Crimean War, the Commission donated blankets and medical supplies procured with funds raised by volunteers. Northern women also learned from British nurse Florence Nightingale's success in mobilizing care for the Crimean War's wounded. Over the objection of most army doctors, a corps of female nurses was added to the service. Dorothea Dix, a veteran of mental health reform, became superintendent of nurses in Washington. More than three thousand Union women worked as paid army nurses and many more, including Susie King Taylor, an escaped slave from Georgia attached

JT Vintage/Glasshouse Images/Alamy Stock Photo

Global Americans Before her career as a pioneer nurse and humanitarian, Massachusetts-born **Clara Barton** worked as a teacher and then as a clerk in the Washington, D.C., Patent Office, to which she returned at the start of the Civil War. Seeking a more active wartime role, Barton joined other women volunteers to gather food, clothing, and bandages for Union soldiers. In 1862, after the battles of Second Bull Run, Antietam, and Fredericksburg, she gained permission to work at field hospitals tending wounded men. Later in the war, she distributed supplies and oversaw hospitals for Union armies in South Carolina and Virginia. The Civil War served as a springboard for Barton's career as a global humanitarian. At first, she ran the government's Office of Missing Soldiers, established to find and identify individuals imprisoned, killed, or missing in action. On vacation in Geneva, Switzerland, she learned about the International Committee of the Red Cross, a neutral relief society founded by Swiss activist Henry Dunant in 1863. During the Franco-Prussian War (1870–1871), Barton helped to run German hospitals and distributed supplies to civilians in Paris. After returning to America, she campaigned for the U.S. government to recognize the Red Cross and the Geneva Convention that enabled its operations. In 1881, she organized the American branch of the Red Cross and for two decades directed relief efforts during wars and emergencies in the United States and overseas, including Cuba and Ottoman Turkey. Honored for her humanitarian work in Europe as well as at home, Clara Barton believed that charity recognized no national borders.

to a black Union regiment, served as volunteers. This collective effort turned nursing into a female occupation and helped professionalize it after the war. Although the Confederacy lagged behind the Union in providing adequate hospitals and medical care, Confederate women organized locally to furnish clothing and bandages to Rebel soldiers, and many served selflessly as nurses. Sally Louisa Tompkins, who ran a model hospital for wounded Confederates in Richmond, was commissioned a captain by Jefferson Davis so that she could remain in charge after the military took it over.

Some women accompanied troops in camp as cooks or laundresses, and others sold sexual services. Still, for soldiers who escaped death, wounds, or disease, camp life was monotonous. "The first thing in the morning is drill," one Pennsylvania soldier explained, "then drill, then drill again. . . . Between drills, we drill and sometimes stop to eat a little and have roll call." Soldiers relieved boredom with gambling, sports, drinking, and letter writing. As the war dragged on, many soldiers became hardened and fatalistic, but patriotism, duty, and comradeship kept them at their posts.

13-2c Debate over Emancipation

"Contrabands" and Congress open the path to emancipation.

Wherever the North's army penetrated, African American slaves escaped to seek freedom behind Union lines. These fugitives forced the issue that Lincoln's administration had tried to avoid. In response, Union generals improvised. Some returned the runaways under the Fugitive Slave Law, but others crowded them into makeshift camps. When two Union generals proclaimed them free, Lincoln countermanded their orders. Union general Benjamin Butler found a halfway solution: declaring the fugitives "**contraband**," or captured enemy property, he refused to return them and put them to work.

Butler's policy was aligned with the first Confiscation Act passed by Congress in August 1861, which permitted the seizure of property employed by the Rebel army, including slaves, but did not give them freedom. Lincoln remained committed to a hands-off policy, but mounting pressures and the logic of the war pushed him toward bolder measures. Emancipation, Lincoln admitted in August 1862, would "help us abroad." Britain and France had previously abolished colonial slavery and both would hesitate to oppose a U.S. antislavery war. Republican abolitionists argued that slavery was the root cause of rebellion and should be eradicated. Frederick Douglass tied emancipation to the advantage that black soldiers, initially rejected by recruiters, could give the Union. Others pointed out that encouraging slaves to escape would cripple the Confederate economy. In July 1862, a second Confiscation Act allowed the seizure of land from rebellious Southerners, freed runaway slaves, and authorized the president to use blacks as soldiers.

Lincoln still preferred gradual, compensated emancipation and offered such a proposal to the loyal border states coupled with a plan to resettle willing former slaves in the West Indies or Central America. He pleaded with Delaware and Kentucky to take the deal. When they refused and northern blacks angrily rejected resettlement, Lincoln changed course.

In mid-1862, Lincoln decided to proclaim slaves in Rebel states free, striking a moral and a practical blow against the Confederacy. He prepared

contraband Term that fixed the legal status of slaves who fled to Union lines prior to the Emancipation Proclamation as captured, unreturnable enemy property.

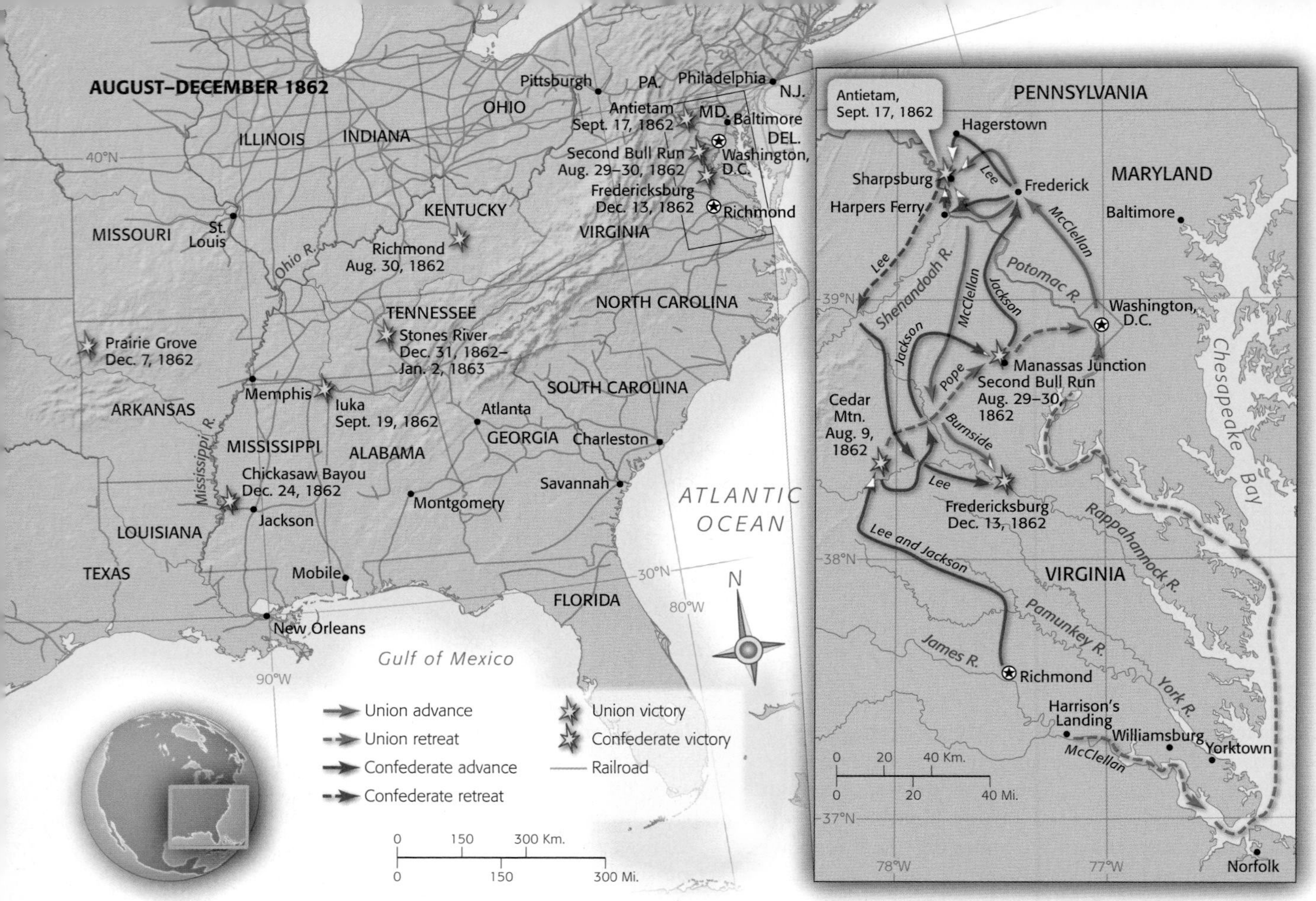

Map 13.2 The Civil War, Late 1862 In 1862, Union armies made steady progress penetrating Tennessee and clearing Confederate regulars from Missouri. In the East, Lee, after success at the Second Battle of Bull Run, invaded Union territory. McClellan's defenders repulsed Lee's advance at Antietam Creek in Maryland. Although a limited victory, Antietam allowed Lincoln to announce his pending Emancipation Proclamation. Union fortunes in Virginia were again set back at Fredericksburg, where Lee's men inflicted a lopsided defeat. ▲

northern public opinion by linking emancipation to Union victory. "My paramount object in this struggle is to save the Union," he wrote antislavery editor Horace Greeley. "If I could save the Union without freeing *any* slave, I would do it; and if I could save it by freeing *all* the slaves, I would do it; and if I could do it by freeing some and leaving others alone, I would also do that." Lincoln had already decided on the third option. After informing his cabinet, he agreed to wait for a decisive Union military victory so his announcement would not look like an act of desperation.

Battle of Antietam Standoff in which McClellan stopped Lee's advance into Maryland, the Union victory that allowed Lincoln to announce plans for emancipation.

That victory came in September 1862 at the **Battle of Antietam** (see Map 13.2). Lee had invaded Maryland, hoping to secure that state for the Confederacy, impress European powers, and scare Northerners into voting for peace. He collided with McClellan's army near Sharpsburg, on Antietam Creek, on September 17. With twenty-three thousand men killed or wounded, it was the bloodiest one-day battle of the war. Technically, Antietam was a Union victory because Lee's offensive was stopped, but McClellan failed to break Lee's lines or to cut off his retreat to Virginia. Frustrated by the missed opportunity, Lincoln again removed McClellan from command, this time for good.

Although Antietam was not the crushing blow Lincoln sought, it served his purpose. Five days later, he issued a Preliminary Emancipation Proclamation announcing that all slaves in rebellious states would be freed on January 1, 1863, unless those states declared loyalty to the Union before the deadline. No Rebel states accepted the offer.

13-3

Turning Points, 1863

After the Emancipation Proclamation, Frederick Douglass, William Forten, and other African American abolitionists issued a national call for black recruits. This poster from 1863 appealed to free and newly freed blacks to "join the Battles of Liberty and the Union." Invoking the revolutionary heroes of 1848 in Europe and black Union soldiers who had already fallen, the signees declared, "Let us rather die freemen than live to be slaves."

How did these abolitionists give global significance to black enlistment? What did they mean by "fail now & our race is doomed"? Why did they ask, "Are freemen less brave than slaves"? ▶

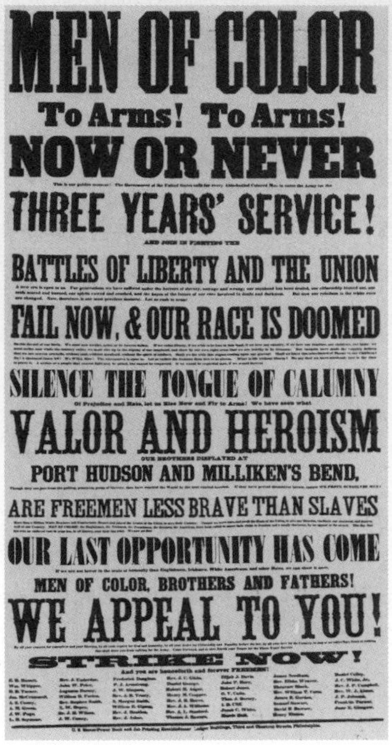

Archive Photos/Getty Images

Go to MindTap® to practice history with the Chapter 13 **Primary Source Writing Activity: A War for the Union, A War against Slavery**. Read and view primary sources and respond to a writing prompt.

By officially aligning the United States with the global movement to end slavery, Lincoln's decision for emancipation deterred foreign support for Confederates. Closer to home, it helped tip the war's balance by weakening the South's economy and enlisting thousands of black Union soldiers. Later in 1863, Union military forces won strategic victories in Pennsylvania and Tennessee and on the Mississippi River. Much bloodletting remained, including continued conflict in Indian country. But after the summer of 1863, the Confederate army was permanently on the defensive, and the path to Union victory became visible.

☞ As you read, look for several key turning points in the Civil War during 1863. How did each help to turn the tide in the Union's favor, and how did each reinforce the others?

13-3a The Emancipation Proclamation and African American Soldiers

Emancipation transforms the Union's war aims and armies.

Issued on New Year's Day 1863, Lincoln's **Emancipation Proclamation** fell short of complete abolition. It freed slaves in states still in rebellion, but specifically excluded slaves in the loyal border states and in areas under federal occupation, just as the president had hinted to Greeley. Lincoln's approach was both conservative and radical. Declaring emancipation a "military necessity," he pacified the North's conservatives by stressing its damage to the Confederacy. By casting it as an "act of justice," he pleased abolitionists and turned Union soldiers into liberators. Most important, the proclamation grafted a war against slavery onto the war for the Union.

Reactions to the Proclamation underscored this change. Confederate spokesmen deplored it as a revolutionary measure intended to provoke a race war in the South. Some northern Democrats stoked fears about white intermarriage with free blacks. Most Northerners, however, supported Lincoln's decree, seizing on either its military or moral justifications as they saw fit. African Americans in the North celebrated the news at impromptu rallies, and as word spread to southern plantations, slaves voted for freedom with their feet. More than one-fifth of the South's blacks ran away. This massive exodus reduced the South's plantation output and boosted the Union's potential resources.

The Proclamation cleared the way for the Union to enlist African American soldiers. Frederick Douglass, Martin Delany, and Sojourner Truth joined recruiting tours through the North, and freedmen were signed up in refugee camps near the front. By the war's end, 186,000 African Americans served in the Union army and another 20,000 in the navy. More than half were former slaves and free blacks from Confederate states. Douglass claimed that military service would cement black claims to legal equality: "Once let the black man get . . . a musket on his shoulder and bullets in his pocket, and there is no power on earth which can deny that he has earned the right to citizenship." His optimism was premature. Black soldiers served in

Emancipation Proclamation Lincoln's edict of January 1, 1863, freeing slaves in rebellious states and encouraging their recruitment as Union soldiers.

History without Borders

Slave Emancipation in the Americas

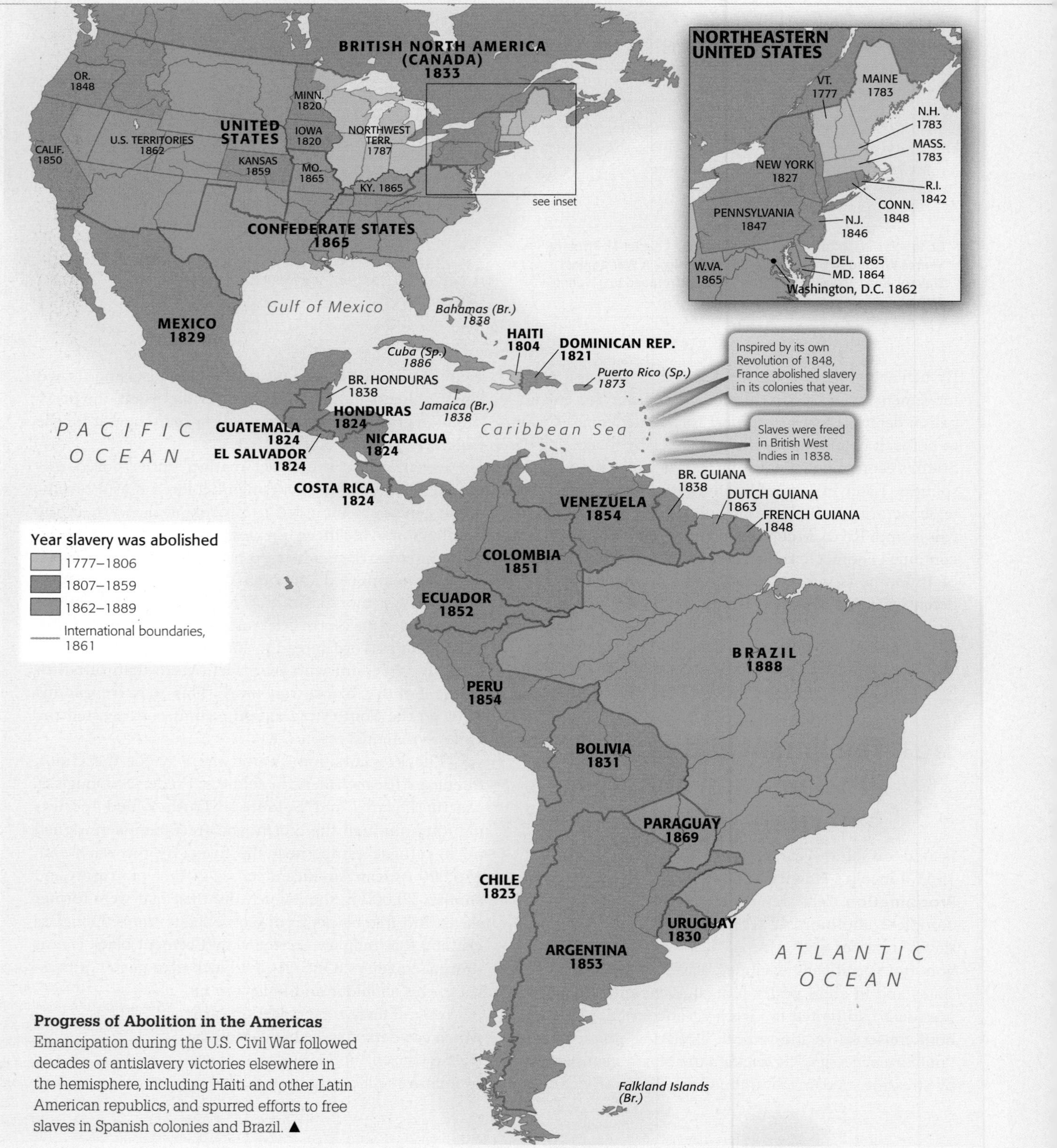

Progress of Abolition in the Americas
Emancipation during the U.S. Civil War followed decades of antislavery victories elsewhere in the hemisphere, including Haiti and other Latin American republics, and spurred efforts to free slaves in Spanish colonies and Brazil. ▲

Liberation of Slaves by Simon Bolívar (1783–1830) (w/c on paper), Cancino, Fernandez Luis (19th century)/Casa-Museo 20 de Julio de 1810, Bogota, Colombia/Bridgeman Images

Liberation of Slaves by Simón Bolívar This watercolor by F.L. Cancino presents a top-down view of Bolívar's declaration ending slavery during the independence war in Gran Colombia (present-day Venezuela). Although he personally opposed slavery, Bolívar also acted to ensure the support of Haiti's president and Gran Colombia's blacks in the war against Spain. ▲

mauritius images GmbH/Alamy Stock Photo

Samuel Sharpe Monument in Jamaica These statues in Montego Bay memorialize the Jamaican slave uprising of 1831–1832. Sharpe, a Baptist convert, preached nonviolence and led a general strike against slavery that evolved into the Christmas Rebellion of 1831, during which Sharpe and hundreds of slaves were captured and murdered. The statues show Sharpe preaching to a group of Jamaican slaves, dramatizing their active struggle for freedom. ▲

By the time the Civil War began in the United States, slavery in the Americas had been under attack for nearly a century. Despite resistance from planters and their political allies in imperial centers and national governments, the abolition of slavery progressed in three overlapping waves. The first coincided with wars for colonial independence and the second followed efforts to outlaw the African slave trade after 1807. In the third, which was spurred by the American Civil War, emancipation spread to the United States, Brazil, and the Spanish Caribbean, plantation societies where global trade in cotton, sugar, and tobacco had kept the institution profitable.

The Age of Revolution (1776–1830) spread ideals of freedom and equality through the Atlantic world. All the northern U.S. states took measures to extinguish slavery after independence, and the Haitian Revolution (1791–1804), which evolved from a slave rebellion, provided inspiration for slaves elsewhere. Several new republics in Latin America adopted gradual emancipation measures between 1814 and 1830 during their struggle for independence from Spain.

Great Britain, whose Parliament banned the slave trade in 1807, exerted strong pressure on remaining slaveholding nations. The moral agitation of evangelical reformers blended with economic incentives as England transitioned to contract labor in colonial lands and sought to deny cheap slave labor to its rivals. In 1808, the United States outlawed the slave trade, and the Netherlands and France soon followed. By the 1850s, Britain's powerful navy had effectively ended the transit of slaves to the Americas except for Spanish Cuba and Puerto Rico. With their enslaved populations dwindling, Colombia, Argentina, Venezuela, and Peru abolished the institution.

Britain also took the lead in ending colonial slavery. Frightened by a massive slave rebellion in Jamaica in 1831–1832, Parliament emancipated seven hundred fifty thousand slaves in the West Indies, effective in 1838. The French Revolution of 1848 freed three hundred thousand slaves in France's overseas colonies. These actions bolstered antislavery efforts by U.S. reformers and transatlantic ties between Anglo-American abolitionists.

Despite antislavery activism, slavery was still thriving in 1860 in Dutch Surinam, the Spanish Caribbean, and the two largest slave societies of the Americas, the United States and Brazil. Union victory in the Civil War dealt the death blow to slavery in the U.S. South and sealed its fate in the hemisphere. The remaining slave strongholds in the Americas were pressured by Britain and the United States, which joined Britain in 1862 in suppressing the African trade. The Dutch Empire ended colonial slavery in 1863. Spain abolished slavery in Puerto Rico in 1873 and Cuba in 1886. Brazil began gradual abolition in 1871, which culminated in 1888.

Throughout the Americas—with the exceptions of Haiti and the United States—emancipation occurred by legislation or decree without causing a war of its own. Many governments adopted compensation schemes that appeased masters and gradually freed their slaves. In the British West Indies, slaves had to endure a six-year "apprenticeship" to their owners prior to freedom. Because emancipation in the U.S. South began as a wartime measure, it was more abrupt and radical. As announced by Lincoln's Proclamation, emancipation was immediate and uncompensated. By aiding the Union cause, African American men and women, many of them former slaves, laid the basis for claims to full citizenship and voting rights.

Just as moral and military motives mingled in Lincoln's Emancipation Proclamation, historians have argued over the main drivers of abolition in the wider Atlantic world. Growing moral and religious revulsion over slavery, preference for wage-labor capitalism, crises prompted by wars for independence and slave revolts, national self-interest, and the courageous struggles of slaves and abolitionists all played roles in ending this long-standing injustice.

Critical Thinking Questions

▶ What shared or unique factors spurred the emancipation of slaves in the Americas? What considerations slowed the abolition movement?

▶ What role did Great Britain play in ending transatlantic slavery? How and why did the United States follow its lead?

Go to MindTap® to engage with an interactive version of **History without Borders: Slave Emancipation in the Americas**. Learn from an interactive map, view related video, and respond to critical thinking questions.

Fort Pillow Union fort in Tennessee where Confederates murdered African American soldiers after they had surrendered.

Battle of Chancellorsville Daring Confederate victory by Lee's outnumbered forces over Hooker in Virginia.

Second Mexican Empire Short-lived (1864–1867) reign of Maximilian I, who assumed the throne after French military intervention.

segregated units and faced opposition from white officers, some of whom resigned their commissions. Others only grudgingly accepted "anything that will kill a rebel."

Initially, black soldiers were paid less than white soldiers. They were given lackluster training and inferior equipment and assigned to labor detachments or garrison duty. African American soldiers protested these inequities, and one black South Carolina sergeant was executed for leading his men in a camp walkout. Attitudes began to change when black soldiers fought heroically at Milliken's Bend in Louisiana and in a futile assault on Fort Wagner, near Charleston, by the 54th Massachusetts regiment. Finally, in June 1864, Congress equalized the pay of black and white soldiers. That same month, black soldiers in the Army of the Potomac won the personal thanks of President Lincoln when he visited the Virginia front.

Confederate policy classified captured black soldiers as insurrectionists who could be enslaved and even executed. The Lincoln administration responded by suspending prisoner exchanges until the Confederates treated black prisoners equally with whites. The standoff meant that after 1863, Confederate and Union prisons became overcrowded, deadly pens. More than fifty thousand soldiers of both sides died in captivity, a quarter of them Union soldiers at the infamous Confederate prison at Andersonville, Georgia.

In April 1864, two Confederate armies committed mass murder against black soldiers. Led by General Nathan Bedford Forrest, a founder of the Ku Klux Klan after the war, Confederate soldiers massacred more than two hundred black soldiers who had surrendered at **Fort Pillow**. Farther west, a Confederate regiment of Choctaw Indians scalped and mutilated a similar number of captured black soldiers at Poison Spring, Arkansas.

Despite such atrocities and prejudice in their own army, African Americans who joined Union forces took pride in their service. Putting on the federal blue uniform, one remembered, was "the biggest thing that ever happened in my life." Like slave runaways of both sexes, African American soldiers and those who toiled in Union camps seized their freedom, rather than being given it.

13-3b The Contest over European Intervention

Britain and France back away from supporting the Confederacy.

By announcing the end of slavery in the South, Lincoln reduced the probability that Britain would support the Confederates. A few weeks after the Proclamation, Henry Adams, son of Charles Francis Adams, the U.S. minister to London, wrote his brother in the Union army that Lincoln's action meant more than "all our former victories and all our diplomacy. . . . If only you at home don't have disasters," Adams continued, "we will give . . . a checkmate to the foreign hopes of the rebels."

Yet more Union disasters awaited. In May 1863, General Joseph Hooker's army was outmaneuvered by General Lee's bold splitting of his smaller force into separate wings at the **Battle of Chancellorsville**. Although Lee lost Stonewall Jackson, who was mistakenly shot by his own men, Chancellorsville sealed Lee's reputation for daring generalship and lent his army an air of invincibility.

Lee's victories impressed British and French authorities. French bankers awarded the Confederacy a $15 million loan and their government resumed backroom scheming for Anglo-French mediation of the conflict. British shipyards secretly contracted with Confederates to build ocean-going ironclad rams that could destroy the Union blockade's wooden ships. Only when U.S. Minister Adams threatened war did the British government seize two warships known as "Laird Rams" that were under construction. At the same time, the Union victories at Gettysburg and Vicksburg (see page 386) demonstrated that the tide of battle had turned decisively in the Union's favor. These events put an end to the Confederates' hopes for British support.

Yet British-built commerce raiders continued to stoke Anglo-American tensions. The *Alabama* destroyed more than sixty merchant vessels before the *U.S.S. Kearsage* sank it off Cherbourg, France, in June 1864. Later that year, Confederate agents crossed the border from British Canada to rob banks in St. Albans, Vermont, and set fires in New York City. Union leaders protested to British officials, but none of these incidents led to war.

Once Britain backed off, Confederate hopes for foreign intervention rested on Napoleon III and his intrigue in Mexico. After the Mexicans defeated French forces in the Battle of Puebla on May 5, 1862 (commemorated as *Cinco de Mayo*), Napoleon sent reinforcements, seized Mexico City, and overthrew President Juárez in June 1863. Allying with Mexican royalists, Napoleon installed Archduke Maximilian of Austria as emperor of Mexico. Confederates hoped the Lincoln administration would condemn this takeover and declare war on France or that Napoleon III would recognize the Confederacy if Confederates recognized Maximilian's **Second Mexican Empire**. Neither happened. Napoleon shied away from provoking the Union, and although secretary of state Seward condemned France's invasion as a violation of the Monroe Doctrine, President Lincoln understood that Union forces already had their hands full. "One war at a time," he advised his cabinet.

New York: Harper & Brothers

Russian Fleet Visits New York City, 1863 In October 1863, Russia's Czar Alexander II dispatched squadrons of warships to New York and San Francisco harbors. The move was intended to protect Russia's navy from winter freezing and British threats in Europe, but the North's public interpreted it as a promise of Russian assistance should Britain and France intervene in the Civil War. Union officials gave the Russians a hero's welcome. ◄

13-3c The War in Indian Country

The war divides Indian peoples and inflames frontier disputes.

The peculiar legal status of Native American peoples in the United States as "domestic dependent nations" shaped their Civil War experience. As "nations," they negotiated treaties of alliance with the Union or Confederacy; as "dependents," they remained subject to white domination no matter which side they chose. Approximately 20,000 Native Americans served in Civil War armies, the majority with the Confederacy. Either way, most tribes emerged worse off than before the war.

In Indian Territory—present-day Oklahoma—the southeastern tribes forced there by Indian Removal were bitterly divided during the Civil War. Full-blooded Cherokees who had opposed removal generally favored neutrality, while mixed bloods who had married southern whites and sometimes owned slaves favored the Confederacy. Initially, Confederate sympathizers held the upper hand. Leaders of the Cherokees, Creeks, Chickasaws, Choctaws, and Seminoles signed treaties of alliance with the Confederacy, held seats (but could not vote) in the Confederate Congress, and organized Confederate units. Meanwhile, pro-Union Cherokees rallied around John Ross, principal chief of the Cherokee Nation, who enrolled three of his sons in the Union army. Cherokee factions staged raids against each other, vandalizing homes and burning crops.

In the summer of 1863, the momentum shifted toward the Union. Federal troops invaded Indian Territory, forcing pro-Confederate Cherokees to flee southward. Confederate authorities failed to aid their Indian allies, and more than 10,000 huddled in refugee camps, their tribal governments and economies devastated. After Cherokee chief Stand Watie became the last Confederate general to surrender in June 1865, the U.S. government treated the Cherokees as if all had supported the Confederacy, compelling new cessions of land as punishment for alleged wartime disloyalty.

Some Indians on the northern Plains seized on the absence of federal soldiers to oppose oppressive treaties and corrupt white agents. In August 1862, the eastern (Santee) Sioux of Minnesota, led by Little Crow, killed more than 400 whites. President Lincoln dispatched a Union force commanded by General Pope, who suppressed the revolt. Thirty-eight Sioux leaders were executed, and the tribe fled west to the Dakotas.

Farther west, Union volunteers who had organized to fight Confederates turned on local Indians. In New Mexico, Army colonel Christopher ("Kit") Carson, who had helped stop Confederate advances in the Southwest, led his troops into Navaho country in retaliation for Indian raids on Anglo settlers. After Carson destroyed cornfields and villages, 8,000 Navajos were marched four hundred miles south to a reservation at Bosque Redondo. Several hundred died along the way, and the rest were held captive until released by a treaty in 1868.

A similar hatred of Indians festered among the Colorado volunteers returned from the Battle of Glorieta Pass. Under the command of Col. J. M. Chivington, they indiscriminately attacked Native American groups who resented tribal cessions of vast lands during the Pike's Peak gold rush. In November 1864, Chivington's army attacked a village of friendly Cheyennes and Arapahos encamped near Fort Lyon, killing and mutilating more than one hundred fifty Indians, mostly women and children. A congressional committee condemned the **Sand Creek Massacre**, but no charges were brought. The massacre enraged young Indian warriors who opposed treaty concessions, and the cycle of retaliatory raids continued after the war.

Sand Creek Massacre Brutal attack on a peaceful village of Cheyenne and Arapaho Indians by a Colorado militia under Union officer Chivington in November 1864.

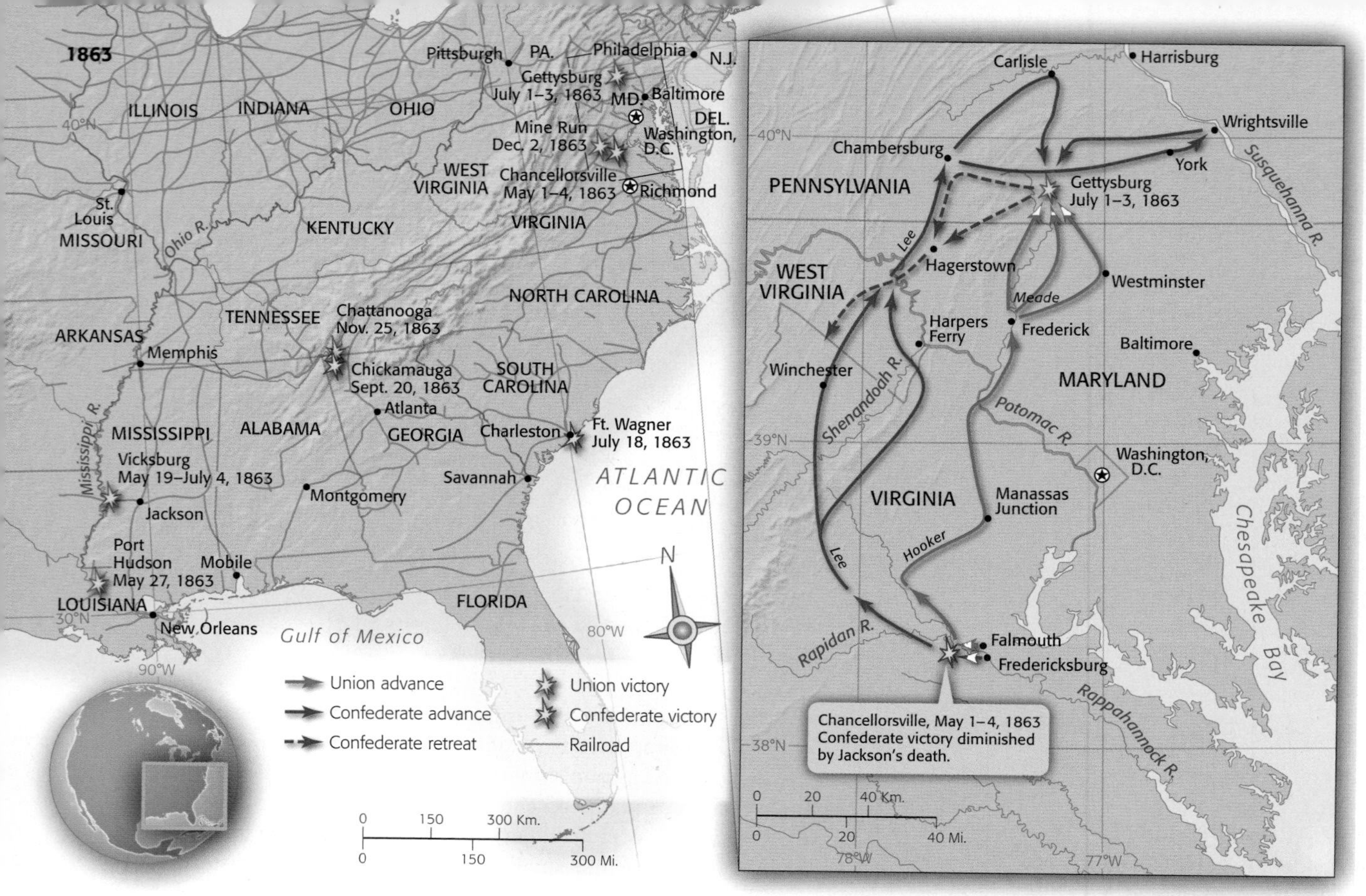

Map 13.3 The Civil War in 1863 Three Union victories turned the military tide in 1863. Vicksburg's surrender to Grant gave the federals control of the Mississippi River and isolated western Confederates. Meade's forces stopped Lee's second invasion of the North after his success at Chancellorsville during a massive three-day struggle at Gettysburg, and Lee retreated to Virginia. At Chattanooga, Grant avenged an earlier Union defeat at Chickamauga, solidified Union control of Tennessee, and opened the route to Atlanta. ▲

13-3d Gettysburg, Vicksburg, and Chattanooga

The Union wins three crucial battles.

In the summer of 1863, Union forces turned the tide of the war in three key battles (see Map 13.3). Lee again invaded the North, believing that a victory there would demoralize the Northerners and win European recognition of the Confederacy. In mid-June, his army of 75,000 men crossed the Potomac, where they foraged for food and demanded payments from frightened townspeople. When Hooker followed Lee too cautiously, Lincoln replaced him with the steadier George G. Meade. In the **Battle of Gettysburg**, an epic three-day struggle, Meade's Union troops repulsed repeated attacks by Lee's army. Total casualties of nearly 50,000 men made it the largest battle ever on North American soil. Lee lost one-third of his soldiers and retreated south. Although Meade failed to cut off Lee's escape, the Union victory at Gettysburg was decisive. President Lincoln, dedicating the battleground cemetery the following November, honored the Union dead for sacrificing their lives so that "government of the people, by the people, for the people, shall not perish from the earth."

Battle of Gettysburg Crucial three-day Civil War battle of July 1863 in which Meade's Union forces defeated Lee's Confederates in Pennsylvania, forcing a retreat to Virginia.

Vicksburg Fortress town in Mississippi surrendered by Confederate defenders to Grant on July 4, 1863, after a prolonged siege, ensuring Union control over the Mississippi River.

The day after the Gettysburg victory, General Grant occupied **Vicksburg**, climaxing a prolonged struggle for that Confederate stronghold on the Mississippi River. After a six-week siege in which Vicksburg's soldiers and civilians were reduced to eating rats, Confederate John C. Pemberton surrendered 30,000 men to Grant on July 4. When the Confederate garrison at Port Hudson, Louisiana, surrendered a few days later, Union forces controlled the entire Mississippi River, cutting the Confederacy in half.

Bettmann/Corbis

Global Americans

Carl Schurz, a military officer in the failed Frankfort revolution against the German monarchy, sought exile in France and England and then migrated to the United States. Like most of the four thousand German "Forty-Eighters," Schurz had strong antislavery convictions. Settling in Wisconsin, he helped to organize the state's Republican Party, attacked the Fugitive Slave Law, and gave rousing speeches—often in German—at pro-Lincoln rallies. Once elected, Lincoln sent him to Spain as an ambassador to help dissuade it from supporting the Confederacy. In 1862, Schurz was commissioned a Union general; he later fought at Second Bull Run, Chancellorsville, Gettysburg, and Chattanooga, and became the best known of the German-American Union officers, a group that included Franz Sigel, Friedrich Hecker, and Alexander von Schimmelfennig. News of their military exploits and antislavery efforts heightened the interest of European liberals and revolutionaries, including their fellow German exile, Karl Marx, in the Union cause.

At the war's end, Schurz turned to politics. A prominent advocate of clean government and aid to former slaves, he was elected to the U.S. Senate from Missouri in 1868, becoming its first German-American member. He later served as secretary of the interior under President Rutherford Hayes. Schurz fervently hoped that U.S. institutions would spread worldwide, but his belief in self-government made him an outspoken critic of U.S. imperialism. Throughout his career, Schurz was an authoritative and influential transatlantic voice for freedom.

Lincoln next sent Grant to Chattanooga, Tennessee, where Union General William Rosecrans was in danger of surrendering to a siege by Confederate Braxton Bragg. In the **Battle of Chattanooga**, November 23–25, Grant's troops stormed the heights east of the city and drove Bragg's disorganized Confederates back into Georgia. Although less celebrated than the Union victories at Gettysburg and Vicksburg, the capture of Chattanooga was equally important. It secured all of Tennessee for the Union and cleared the path to Atlanta, the gateway to the southern Confederacy.

Battle of Chattanooga Victory by Grant over Confederates under Bragg that secured Tennessee for the Union and opened the route to Atlanta.

13-4
War on Two Home Fronts

These two engravings by American artist Winslow Homer featuring women's wartime activities appeared in *Harper's Weekly,* the North's most popular illustrated magazine. The first is titled *Filling Cartridges at the U.S. Arsenal, Watertown, Massachusetts.* The second, *The Influence of Woman: The Sister of Charity, Sewing Shirts, Washing, Home Tidings,* appeared in a series "Our Women and the War."

Compare and contrast the two illustrations. How do the activities they portray suggest both continuities and changes in gender roles during the war? ▶

Library of Congress Prints and Photographs Division[LC-USZ62-96445]

Homer, Winslow (1836–1910) (after)

"An army marches on its stomach," Napoleon once declared, and his campaigns demonstrated the success of massive wartime mobilization overseen by a powerful government. Union and Confederate political leaders took this lesson to heart. Both sides raised revenue, drafted soldiers, and stimulated factory and farm production to sustain their armies. In the process, they enlarged the powers of the national government in ways that alarmed dissenters. The war's outcome hinged on how well each side handled home front political and economic problems, not simply on how their armies fought.

☞ As you read, consider the political, social, and economic transformations that took place on the Union and Confederate home fronts. How did they help or hinder each side's war effort?

13-4a Centralization and Resistance

Drafts, taxes, and martial law arouse dissent in the Union and Confederacy.

Among the war's changes, none was more startling to Southerners than the growing power of their new national government. Waging the best possible fight required subordinating states' rights and local prerogatives to war needs. Understanding this, Confederate President Jefferson Davis asserted government control over arms, supplies, and troops. The Confederate Congress established a draft in April 1862, passed a 10 percent tax to be paid in farm products, and gave the executive control over railroads. The army impressed slaves to build fortifications and confiscated crops and animals to feed troops. Overnight, a bureaucracy sprang up in Richmond that rivaled the Union's in proportion to the overall population.

As the Rebel government's claim on men and resources escalated, opposition to its centralized power grew. Vocal states' rights zealots, led by Vice President Alexander Stephens and the governors of Georgia and North Carolina, denounced the Davis administration as despotic. More damaging dissent arose among ordinary Southerners. Nonslaveholders in the backcountry refused to cooperate with tax collectors and impressment officers. The Confederate draft law, which allowed men to hire substitutes and exempted one white man on a plantation with twenty or more slaves, spurred charges that the conflict was "a rich man's war but a poor man's fight." Many poor whites who resented planters refused to "go fight for their infurnal negroes." Conscription bolstered the desperate Confederate army—more than 25 percent of Confederate soldiers were draftees and substitutes, compared to 8 percent for the Union (see Table 13.1). But the Confederacy paid a price in home front morale and unity.

The Confederate Congress prevented Davis, who had invoked martial law in embattled Confederate districts early in the war, from detaining draft and tax evaders.

Table 13.1 Social Profile of Civil War Soldiers

Despite complaints over "a rich man's war and a poor man's fight," both sides in the Civil War organized an army of soldiers that roughly reflected their population's social origins. The major exception was the Union's recruitment of African American men after 1862 and the Confederacy's refusal to do so. Union recruiters also benefited from a sizeable pool of white men, including many immigrants, whereas the Confederacy faced shortages and relied heavily on the draft to supply soldiers.

	Union	Confederate
Total number who served in the military	2.1 million	0.9 million (est.)
Percentage of total who were drafted	2	20
Percentage of total who paid for substitutes	6	8
Percentage of living West Point graduates who joined	66	23
Social Origins (approximate percentage of total)		
Native-born whites	67	89
Foreign born	24	9
African American	9[a]	0[b]
Native American	<1	2
Farmers and farm laborers	48	62
Unskilled laborers	16	9
Skilled laborers	25	14
White collar and professional	8	12

[a] Approximately half of this number were runaways or recently freed slaves from Confederate states.

[b] Southern slaves were often impressed into assisting the Confederate army in camps, hospitals, and defensive lines, but the government did not officially enroll any as soldiers until the war was virtually over.

Sources: Steven Woodworth and Kenneth J. Winkle, *Atlas of the Civil War* (New York: Oxford University Press, 2004), 364; James McPherson, *Ordeal By Fire*, 4th ed. (New York: McGraw-Hill, 2009), 387–388; E.B. Long, *The Civil War Day by Day* (Garden City, NY: Doubleday, 1971), 705–708.

Stephens declared that losing the war would be preferable to curbing Southerners' liberties. Such sentiments underscored the dilemma of white Southerners' fixation on individual and states' rights during wartime, signaling the failure of Confederate nationalism.

On the Union home front, the Lincoln administration pursued similar policies of centralization and also met with opposition. Yet discontent in the North was muted by several factors, including a strong political and military response, the increasingly positive momentum of the war, and general wartime prosperity.

In 1861, Congress created the nation's first income tax. In the following year, the **Internal Revenue Service** began collecting it and a new series of excise taxes on tobacco, liquor, and other items, which had been eliminated by President Jackson. These measures met little opposition, partly because the income tax was progressive, with rates rising according to income. Congress raised the tariff to produce additional revenue. In the end, the Union covered 21 percent of its war costs through taxation, compared with the Confederacy's less than 10 percent.

The Union's draft lottery, enacted in 1863, aroused heated opposition. Like the Confederate measure, it allowed draftees to hire substitutes or pay a fee to avoid serving. Workers and immigrants in the North's cities condemned the system as discriminatory, although statistics showed that they were not selected disproportionately (see Table 13.1). Among working-class Northerners, the war was increasingly unpopular for its enrichment of bosses and the threat of competition for jobs posed by newly emancipated slaves. Anger erupted into violence in New York City in July 1863 when the first draft lists were posted. A predominantly Irish mob destroyed local draft headquarters, looted homes of the rich, and turned on African Americans, burning the city's Colored Orphan Asylum and murdering black bystanders. Class resentments and racism fueled three days of street warfare that claimed more than one hundred lives. Army units rushed from Gettysburg and gunboats borrowed from the Union blockade finally suppressed the **New York City Draft Riot**.

The Lincoln administration asserted military control over civilian dissenters more forcefully than its Confederate counterpart. After September 1862, when Congress gave the administration permission to suspend habeas corpus at will, Lincoln authorized the arrest of those suspected of evading the draft, trading with the enemy, or "any disloyal practice." All told, military authorities detained more than thirteen thousand civilians during the war, and federal courts refrained from interfering. After the war, in ***ex parte Milligan*** (1866), the Supreme Court ruled that federal authorities had overstepped their bounds and that citizens could not be tried by military tribunals in areas where loyal civilian courts were functioning. The decision came too late to assist wartime detainees, however. The Union's practice of aggressively using courts and prisons to deter disloyalty created abuses but was undeniably effective.

13-4b Comparative Politics and Leadership

The Union's political institutions and leadership help ensure its success.

Contrasts between political systems and leadership added to the Union's comparative advantage over the Confederacy. In a display of unity, members of the Confederate Congress renounced party affiliations, yet this strategy backfired. Lacking a disciplined party organization, President Davis could not assemble votes to pass legislation or build loyalty through patronage. As a result, Confederate politics splintered into multiple warring factions divided along personal or ideological lines. Congressmen engaged in fistfights and brandished weapons. The Confederate Cabinet was similarly unstable. Most of the South's ablest leaders chose to join the army, and Davis relied on a dwindling cadre of efficient advisers. Resignations and cabinet reshuffling produced five Confederate secretaries of war in four years.

Davis was too icy and inflexible to guide the Confederacy through its embattled infancy. An honorable but proud aristocrat, he combined the self-assurance of a wealthy planter with an engineer's penchant for micromanaging the war. He quarreled with key generals, took political criticism personally, and lacked the common touch to inspire affection among ordinary Southerners.

Internal Revenue Service Federal agency established in 1861 to collect income and excise taxes during the Civil War.

New York City Draft Riot Violent protest against Union conscription, targeting wealthy residents, antislavery journalists, and especially African Americans.

ex parte Milligan Supreme Court ruling against military tribunals in the case of pro-Confederate civilians in Indiana who plotted to take over the state's government.

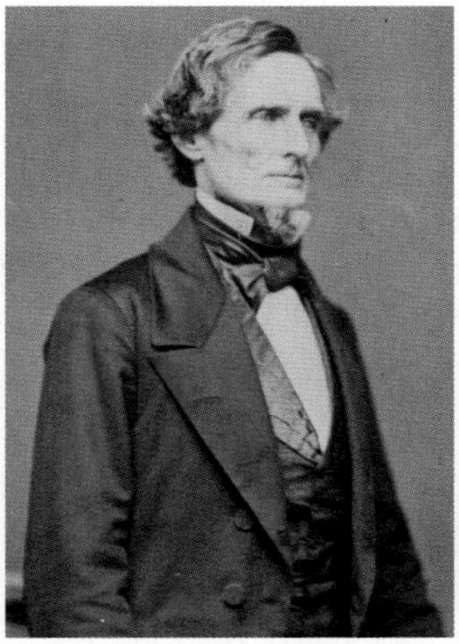
Library of Congress

Brady National Photographic Portrait Galleries, photographer

Two Civil War Presidents Photographs of Jefferson Davis (left) and Abraham Lincoln (right), both taken by Mathew Brady, show similarities in appearance and bearing between the two. Beneath surface appearances, however, Davis and Lincoln had important differences in temperament and political skill that gave an edge to the Union war effort. ▲

In the 1863 elections, openly antiadministration candidates came close to winning majorities in the Confederate Congress. Meanwhile, as the Union army occupied more and more Confederate territory, Davis's government lost control over local conditions. Dissenters took possession of several mountain districts. A group of nonslaveholding whites in isolated Jones County, Mississippi, declared the Free State of Jones and defied Confederate authorities.

The North's political institutions and leadership proved more resilient than the South's. Like Davis, Lincoln faced opposition to his policies, but he used his personal skills, the North's reservoir of talent, and the tools of party politics to neutralize foes and further the war effort.

Although reduced to a minority, the Democratic Party remained a powerful force in Union politics and a conduit for wartime dissent. The Democrats contained war and peace factions, both of which promised a return to "the Union as it was," the former by force and the latter by negotiation. Democrats closed ranks by blaming the Lincoln administration for the war's high death toll, its economic upheavals, and especially the emancipation of slaves. Many Democratic leaders also condemned the draft and martial law. These positions, along with warnings that freed slaves would inundate the North, appealed to many Midwesterners with southern roots and to workers and immigrants in northern cities.

Lincoln both accommodated and countered the Democrats. He lured War Democrats by offering appointments to federal offices and commissions as Union generals. He played tough politics, too, secretly subsidizing Indiana's budget so the state's Republican governor could dismiss its Democratic-controlled legislature. Outspoken **Peace Democrats** were accused of disloyalty. When Ohio congressman Clement L. Vallandigham denounced emancipation and the draft and labeled Lincoln a "dictator," military authorities imprisoned him for treason. Lincoln commuted Vallandigham's sentence, avoiding a judicial confrontation, and shrewdly exiled him to the Confederacy. A small cadre of Peace Democrats formed shadowy secret societies and hatched plots to sabotage Union communications or free Rebel prisoners in the North. Such activities gave Republicans the chance to label all Peace Democrats "**Copperheads**" (after the poisonous snake) and associate them with treason.

Within his own party, Lincoln faced near-constant challenges from radicals who decried his caution on emancipation or his management of the war. But the president maneuvered deftly to balance Republican factions and preserve party unity. He appointed factional leaders to his Cabinet, a talented group that included Seward and Treasury secretary Salmon Chase, and he managed this "team of rivals" with skill. As a result, his administration was efficient with little of the turnover that plagued Davis's cabinet.

"This is essentially a people's contest," Lincoln had told Congress on Independence Day, 1861. He identified the Union with the goal of "afford[ing] all an unfettered start and a fair chance in the race of life." In such speeches, Lincoln voiced the egalitarian aspirations of American nationalism. In contrast to Davis's aristocratic demeanor, "Old Abe" offered plain speech and folksy humor that captured the Union public's imagination and held their allegiance through the war. Lincoln's leadership, together with his able cabinet and the Republicans' domination of politics, sustained the Union in wartime.

Peace Democrats Faction of the North's Democratic Party that opposed wartime legislation and emancipation, calling for negotiations to restore "the Union as it was" peacefully.

Copperheads Republican label for Northerners who sympathized with the Confederacy, smearing them as traitors by likening them to poisonous snakes.

Pacific Railroad Act Federal law that subsidized construction of a transcontinental railroad from Omaha, Nebraska, to Sacramento, California.

greenbacks Paper money, printed in green ink on one side, issued by the U.S. government during the Civil War and not backed by gold or silver.

13-4c Economic and Social Transformations

The Union booms while the Confederacy busts.

The war's economic impact dramatically highlighted contrasts between the Union and Confederate home fronts. By 1861, the North had a large network of factories and railroads, and its farms were increasingly mechanized. Wartime government spending pumped enormous sums into the economy, including nearly $2 billion on weapons, supplies, food, horses, and wagons. To oversee such expenditures, the War Department built a bureaucracy of one hundred thousand employees and established procedures for issuing contracts and inspecting goods. Nevertheless, fraud occurred. Corrupt contractors sold the government blankets and uniforms made from "shoddy," compressed wool that quickly disintegrated. Some government agents accepted bribes or handed contracts to relatives and cronies. In the short term, the War Department's close relations with business filled the massive needs of military mobilization; in the long term, the relationship prefigured the fraud and scandals of the postwar "Gilded Age."

Republican legislation also fostered the partnership between capitalism and government. With their congressional majority bolstered by the exit of southern members, Republicans passed probusiness measures from their prewar agenda. They raised the tariff to protect the North's industries. They approved the **Pacific Railroad Act** (1862), which gave railroads land grants and loans to build a line to California. In 1863, Congress created a national banking system that issued a paper currency of **greenbacks**, which were not backed by gold or silver but nevertheless held their value during the war. These and similar measures expanded the reach of the federal government into Northerners' daily lives.

Such laws benefited affluent groups at the expense of average Northerners. Central banking created a more stable currency but also tighter credit that squeezed western farmers. Republicans, however, specifically added two laws to promote Lincoln's goal of opportunity for all. The **Homestead Act** granted one hundred sixty acres of public land to settlers who remained for five years. The **Morrill Act** used sales of other public land to establish state universities specializing in agriculture and engineering. Before the war ended, twenty thousand homesteaders had taken up new western farms, and eleven campuses in the Northeast and Midwest had been designated state land-grant colleges.

Despite the wartime boom, many ordinary Northerners experienced hardship. Taxes and inflation raised the price of consumer goods while wages lagged. Faced with replacement by labor-saving machines or competition from young rural migrants, workers organized protests. Some, including tailors, cigar makers, and railway engineers, formed national unions and threatened strikes. Employers denounced worker activism as unpatriotic and recruited women, blacks, and immigrants as strikebreakers. One spark that lit the New York City Draft Riots, for example, was the hiring of African Americans to break a longshoremen's strike. In other cases, federal troops were called in to suppress labor protests at arsenals and munitions factories. Overall, the North benefited from an economy balanced between farms and industry, but its wartime prosperity was far from evenly shared.

The South's economy, ill prepared for the agricultural and industrial demands of war, simply collapsed under the combined weight of declining production and escalating destruction. Understanding their comparative disadvantages, Confederate officials asserted control over the economy, hastily building new railroad lines, factories, and foundries. Through trade and domestic production, Confederate soldiers received enough rifles and ammunition to persevere. But the South's food production could not meet basic civilian and military needs. As young men enlisted, farms declined, and slaves who escaped to Union lines left plantations shorthanded. The shrinking grid of working railroad lines could not distribute corn and hogs. And as Union troops occupied the South, they consumed or destroyed most livestock and crops.

By 1863, shortages of food and clothing were severe. Food riots broke out in Richmond and Atlanta to protest high prices and the scarcity of bread and salt. Marching under banners that read "Bread and Peace," the women of Mobile, Alabama, looted stores for sustenance. Some families on the home front lined their threadbare clothes with newspapers to keep warm; others stripped furniture for fabric.

Unable to finance the war, the Confederates printed paper money. For the Union, "greenbacks" solved a shortage of cash, not goods; for Confederates, the shortage was goods, and inflation surged. By mid-1864, Confederate dollars were practically worthless. It was said that Southerners had earlier gone to market with money in their pockets and returned with potatoes in carts, but this time, they brought carts of money to return with a single potato in their pocket. Despite hardships, people managed by bartering, improvising, and sacrificing. The South's unbalanced agricultural economy, overly dependent on cotton and tobacco exports, never adjusted to the demands of war.

13-4d Women and the War

Wartime needs bring welcome opportunities and unwelcome hardships for women.

Wartime requirements opened new opportunities for women. In the North, prosperity widened women's sphere, and many drew on prewar experiences in reform movements or factory work to take advantage. More than one hundred thousand women toiled in northern factories, stitching boots, manufacturing ammunition, and canning foods for soldiers at the front. Less than a decade after Americans Elias Howe and Isaac Singer had introduced the first commercially viable sewing machines, women in the North used them to mass-produce Union uniforms, tents, and flags. The federal government hired thousands of women as clerks and copyists. In private businesses, unlike government, women were often paid less than men for the same work, yet in both cases, war work for wages gave women a measure of independence and a way to contribute publicly to the Union cause.

How far the war permanently changed women's roles in the North is unclear. Clerical work, nursing, and teaching (where women replaced men who had gone to fight) continued to be "women's work" after the war, but opportunities in factories declined when soldiers came back. After the war, several state universities permitted women to enroll and more private colleges went coeducational. Women's rights advocates used women's war work to call for social and political rights, especially the vote. Nevertheless, conservative ideas about women's domestic role remained popular, and many middle-class women—and their soldier husbands—longed to return to home and hearth. The war chipped away at rigid restrictions on women's lives but brought no large-scale changes.

On both the Union and Confederate sides, a few hundred women disguised themselves as men to fight in the armies. Some had identified as men before the war; others joined from a sense of patriotism, adventure, or loyalty to the brothers and husbands they accompanied. Both sides benefited from well-placed female spies. Rose Greenhow picked up gossip in Washington for the Confederacy, and actress Pauline Cushman toured Confederate camps for the Union. Locally, civilians often provided valuable intelligence to Union and Confederate army officers.

In comparison with northern women, white women's lives in the South were more rigidly shaped by traditional gender

Homestead Act Federal law that granted one hundred sixty acres for a small fee to settlers on public lands in the West.

Morrill Act Federal law allotting land grants whose sales funded state colleges for agriculture and the mechanical arts.

roles. In the war's early days, newspapers and magazines urged women to remain exemplars of purity and self-sacrifice. Staying within the domestic context, Confederate women joined together to sew flags, roll bandages, and collect jewelry and silverware to donate. As war needs escalated, many took on traditionally male tasks. Like their Union counterparts, they managed farms in their husbands' absence and made tents and munitions at nearby factories. Young women migrated to capitals to take government jobs as clerks and secretaries or to serve as nurses. Schooled by traditional ideals, many regarded these tasks as temporary and often distasteful necessities, recording in their diaries their longing to return to the ordered and peaceful prewar world.

Unlike Northerners, southern women faced the ordeal of invasion, dislocation, and economic collapse. As the war turned against the South, battlefield deaths and everyday hardships chipped at their loyalties and undermined any enthusiasm for expanded roles. By 1864, many women focused on nothing but survival. For northern reform women, the Civil War was building the ground for progress and equality; for southern white women, the war was destroying the ground under their feet.

13-5 Union Success, 1864–1865

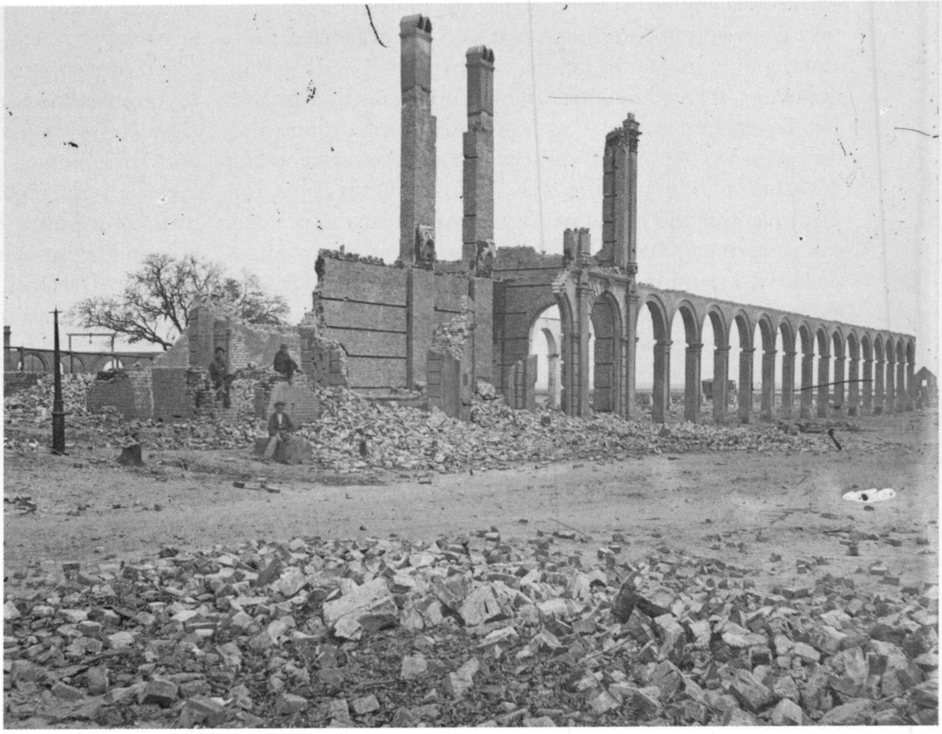

This photograph by George Barnard depicts the ruins of Charleston's railroad station after its destruction by Union general William T. Sherman's troops in early 1865.

What effects did the wholesale destruction of railroads, factories, and public buildings have on the South's resources and morale? Why did Union armies target civilian property? ▶

Library of Congress

By the spring of 1864, the stage was set for coordinated offensives that, Union leaders hoped, would bring victory. Lincoln appointed the tenacious Grant commander of all the Union armies, leaving tough-minded General William T. Sherman in charge of the western army at Chattanooga. Grant advanced toward Richmond to force Lee's army into a decisive battle while Sherman pushed southeast to take Atlanta. Both offensives took longer than expected, complicating Lincoln's bid for reelection in the fall. Not until April 1865 did the two major Confederate armies surrender. Northerners at last won the Civil War, but their celebration was cut short when an assassin's bullet felled the president who had led them to victory.

☞ As you read, think about what forced the Confederate armies to surrender. Why did the North win and the South lose?

13-5a Grant and Sherman on the Move

The Union begins its final offensives in Virginia and Georgia.

In May 1864, Lee's 75,000 soldiers repulsed Grant's massive 115,000-man army in the thick underbrush of the Wilderness, near Fredericksburg, Virginia. Undeterred, Grant resumed his southward march, hoping to outflank Lee and draw him into open battle. Lee, on the defensive, fought behind earthworks. Fighting broke out with brutal regularity during the **Overland Campaign**, and the blood flowed apace (see Map 13.4). In four weeks, the two armies fought five pitched battles. At Cold Harbor, Grant lost seven thousand men before calling off the morning assault. Some Union

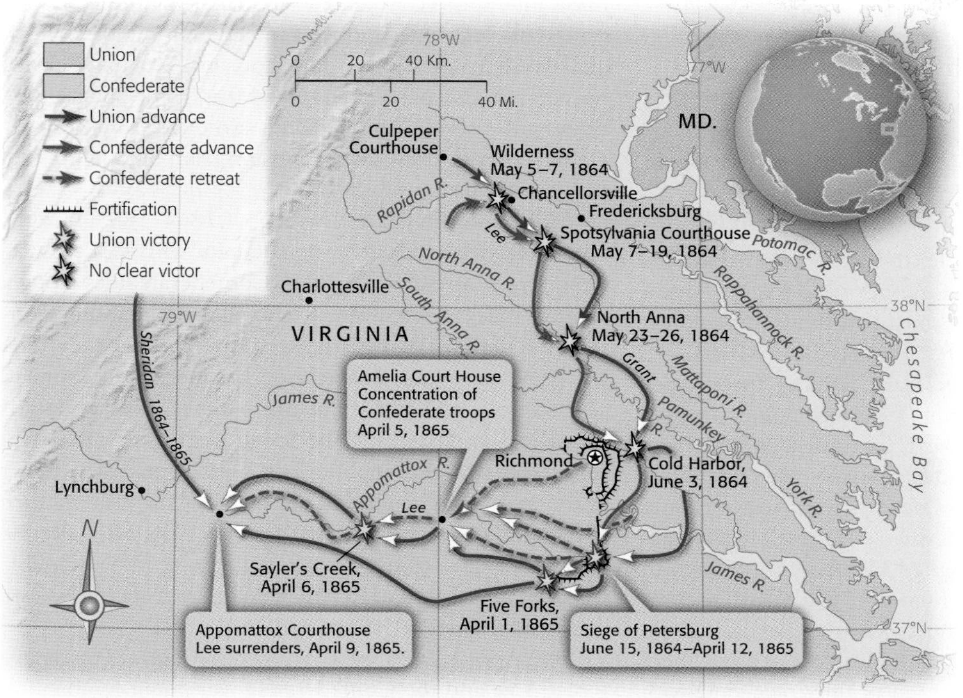

Map 13.4 Grant and Lee in Virginia, 1864–1865 Grant's relentless attacks during the Overland Campaign eventually wore down Lee's smaller army and stretched its lines to the breaking point. From the Wilderness to Petersburg in spring 1864, the Confederates withstood almost daily Union assaults and inflicted horrendous casualties. The next year, Grant's forces slowly encircled Petersburg, and Lee's dwindling army fled westward before he surrendered to Grant at Appomattox Court House. ◀

soldiers, sure they would die, pinned their names to their uniforms so their bodies could be identified.

Checked in front of Richmond, Grant bypassed the capital to seize the railroad center at Petersburg twenty miles south. There his army settled into a prolonged siege. The Overland Campaign had cost Grant 65,000 casualties to Lee's 35,000, but the Union army could replace lost soldiers while the Confederate force could not.

In Georgia, Sherman's flanking moves pushed Joseph Johnston's Confederates back ninety miles into Atlanta's stout defenses. But in mid-July, when Davis replaced Johnston with the combative John B. Hood, the Confederates counterattacked, slowing Sherman's progress. After a month of frustration, the Union army circled south to cut off Atlanta's supply lines, forcing Hood to evacuate the city. "Atlanta is ours, and fairly won," Sherman telegraphed Lincoln triumphantly on September 2.

13-5b Election of 1864

Lincoln wins reelection thanks to timely Union victories.

Sherman's victory at Atlanta came just in time for the president, who was fighting a battle of his own to be reelected. The Republicans renominated Lincoln in July but with little support from the party's radicals, who decried his lenient plans for readmitting conquered southern states. At the Republican convention, Lincoln's managers engineered a bipartisan National Union ticket by nominating Andrew Johnson of Tennessee, a strongly prowar Democrat, as vice president. His place on the ticket was meant to expand Lincoln's base of support and exploit division among Democrats.

Overland Campaign A six-week series of bloody battles between Grant's Union army and Lee's troops defending Richmond.

The Democrats nominated Lincoln's former commander, George B. McClellan, who favored continuing the war until the Union was restored. When vocal Peace Democrats passed a platform calling for an immediate armistice and negotiations, Republicans charged treason, and McClellan was forced to repudiate the platform. Despite the Democrats' divisions, there was concern that Lincoln could lose an election that was widely seen as a referendum on the war. In August, Grant's army was bogged down at Petersburg and Sherman's was stalled before Atlanta, and the North's public was stunned by the war's death toll.

Quite suddenly, the military situation improved. The Union navy closed the port of Mobile, Alabama, on August 23. Ten days later, Sherman occupied Atlanta, and by October, General Philip Sheridan had secured Virginia's Shenandoah Valley. This string of victories lifted Unionist morale and ensured Lincoln's reelection. In November, he won 55 percent of the popular vote and 212 of 233 electoral votes. Despite their grief and fatigue, the northern public voted to see the war through. Lincoln's reelection—the first of a sitting American president during wartime—was the war's most important political turning point.

13-5c Surrender and Assassination

The war ends with triumph and tragedy for the Union.

While Grant pinned down Lee's army in Virginia, Sherman cut loose in Georgia. Exemplifying the Union's new hard war strategy, Sherman aimed to "make war so terrible" to Southerners "that generations would pass away before they would again appeal to it." From Atlanta, he led sixty-two thousand soldiers on a **March to the Sea** toward Savannah (see Map 13.5). Abandoning their supply lines, the federals foraged for food and destroyed everything else that could support the South's war effort: railroads, foundries, barns, crops, courthouses, and livestock. Advancing ten miles a day, they left a sixty-mile wide wake of devastation. Nearly twenty thousand slaves followed Sherman's troops. Their defection and Sherman's pillaging led Confederate women to plead with soldiers to return home. "If you put off a-coming," one wife wrote to her husband at the front, "'twont be no use to come, for we'll all hands of us be out there in the garden in the grave yard with your ma and mine." In response to such desperate appeals, Confederate desertions soared.

March to the Sea Sherman's destructive path from Atlanta to Savannah, intended to crush the Confederacy's resources and morale.

Sherman entered Savannah by Christmas and in February turned north into South Carolina, where his men gutted the state capital of Columbia, and then marched into North Carolina. Confederate General Johnston, with a ragtag army of twenty-two thousand men, faced the Union juggernaut. Sherman's objective immediately switched from destroying property to preventing Johnston from linking up with Lee in Virginia.

Through the fall and winter of 1864–1865, Grant's army had been locked in a stalemate with Lee's dwindling forces, stretching the thin Confederate lines along a seventy-mile front and slowly encircling Petersburg. Confederate authorities became so desperate that they took the previously unthinkable step of offering freedom to slaves who would enlist. The irony was not lost on southern whites and blacks. "The South went to war to defeat the designs of the abolitionists," a Virginia newspaper thundered, "and behold! in the midst of the war, we turn abolitionists ourselves!" Few slaves took the offer. As one prominent slave owner recognized, why fight for possible freedom in a slave society when all blacks "are pretty sure of having it anyway" after a Union victory.

On April 1, 1865, a Union breakthrough at Petersburg forced Lee and the Confederate government to abandon Richmond (see Map 13.4). Grant's army pursued Lee's haggard remnants and cornered them at Appomattox Court House. On April 9, Lee accepted Grant's respectful terms and surrendered. Two weeks later, Johnston surrendered to Sherman in North Carolina. In May, the

Map 13.5 Sherman's Campaign in the South, 1864–1865 While Grant tied Lee down in Virginia, Sherman pushed south to Atlanta. He maneuvered Confederates under Hood into abandoning the city and then led a rapid March to the Sea, destroying Confederate resources and morale. Hood invaded Tennessee trying to divert Sherman but was badly defeated at Franklin and Nashville. From Savannah, Sherman turned north to ravage South Carolina and prevent Johnston from joining Lee's retreating forces. News of Johnston's surrender reached Washington during mourning over Lincoln's assassination. ▼

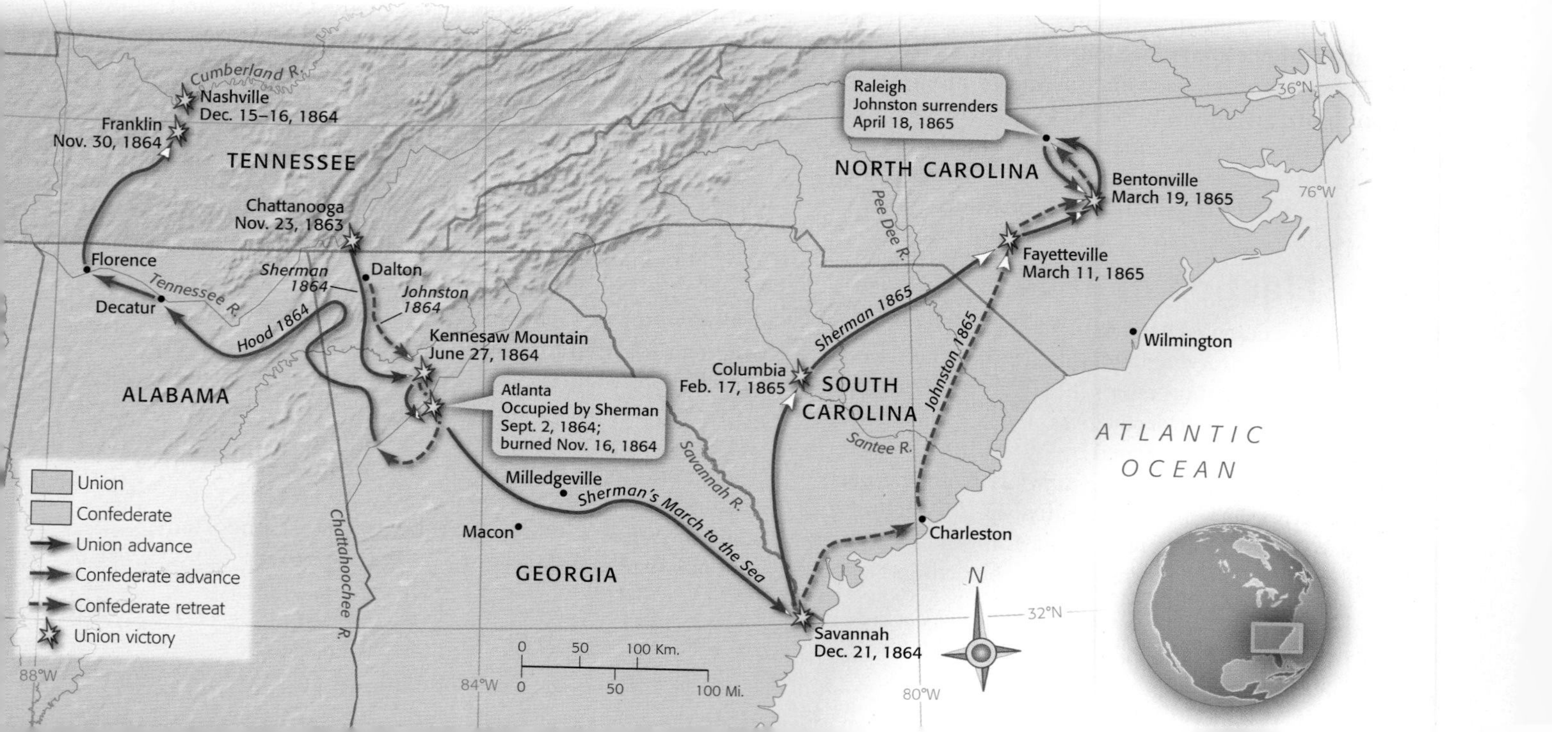

Confederates' trans-Mississippi army under General Kirby Smith gave up its arms. The Civil War had finally ended.

Northerners had barely begun celebrating when unprecedented tragedy struck. Five days after Lee's surrender, John Wilkes Booth, a rabid Confederate sympathizer and the brother of a well-known stage actor, assassinated Lincoln. Booth had stalked the Union president for months, initially with a kidnapping plan in mind, but he turned to murder after Lincoln began supporting voting rights for blacks. On the night of April 14, he shot the president at Ford's Theatre in Washington. Fleeing across the Potomac, Booth was tracked down by Union soldiers and killed. Eight of his accomplices, one of whom stabbed Secretary of State Seward (who recovered) and another who was assigned to kill Vice President Johnson but balked, were arrested. Four were convicted in the murder conspiracy and hanged. On April 15, the day Lincoln died, Andrew Johnson was sworn in as president.

A month earlier, in his Second Inaugural Address, Lincoln had noted the "fundamental and astounding" changes the war had brought. "Neither party expected for the war the magnitude or the duration which it has already attained," he said. "Neither anticipated that the cause of the conflict [slavery] might cease with or even before the conflict itself should cease." Lincoln had skillfully guided the Union through these transformations. As he considered the coming peace, the president reaffirmed his commitment both to end slavery forever and to "bind up the nation's wounds." Now this daunting dual agenda was left to his successors.

13-6 National and Global Impacts of the War

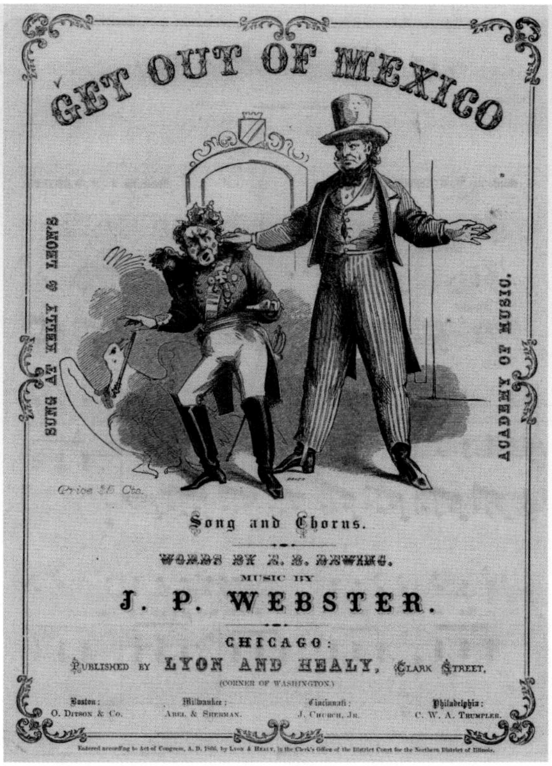

Lyon and Healy, Chicago, 1866

After Appomattox, Union veterans were sent to the Southwest to pressure France's puppet regime in Mexico. This sheet music conveyed their message in song. The lyrics explain that Napoleon III had sneaked in a Hapsburg prince "while Old Uncle Sam was busy . . . with his dear rebellious children." But "now our cruel war is over, we're united all once more. . . . Poor Max, there's no use talking, so pack up your kit and go, for the Universal Nation says 'Get Out of Mexico!'"

How does the illustrator portray the victorious Union's strong international posture? Why do the lyrics refer to the Civil War and call the United States "the Universal Nation"? ▶

The Civil War was the most traumatic event to date in the nation's history. As many as 700,000 soldiers died in the conflict, fourteen times the number killed in the Revolutionary War. Confronted with death on a monumental scale, Americans struggled to ennoble it. Northerners took pride in the Union's preservation and prosperity while white Southerners bewailed their lost pride and privilege. Emancipation, the war's most radical change, aligned the nation's laws with its ideals but also opened a hotly contested social revolution in the South. Outside the nation's borders, the conflict industrialized warfare and escalated its destructiveness. Its outcome solidified republican government in Mexico and inspired European reformers to press for democratic changes. Cleared of slavery's taint, many Americans hoped that their reunited states might be a beacon of freedom to the world's peoples.

☞ As you read, consider the many ways the Civil War changed Americans and others. How did the political, social, economic, and technological effects of the war reverberate inside the nation and beyond it?

13-6a Legacies of the War for the Nation

The war strengthens the national government, hardens sectional loyalties, and ends slavery.

The war had devastated the South, where most battles were fought, destroying railroads, industries, and farms and defacing the landscape. Defeat

Lost Cause Nostalgic postwar defense of the Confederacy by southern whites.

also scarred white Southerners' consciousness, ending a way of life based on slavery and instilling harsh memories of invasion and occupation. The experience fed their regional pride and defiance, cementing their devotion to the **Lost Cause**. Talk of secession ended, but states' rights remained a potent dissenting ideology. In this sense, the Civil War did not close the book on sectionalism but added a new chapter to its history.

Economically, the war had brought prosperity to the North and set the foundation for future growth. Whereas the South's share of the nation's wealth fell by more than 60 percent, the aggregate wealth of the North increased significantly. This bonanza was not distributed equally, however. Industrialists and entrepreneurs benefited but business and government did little to moderate class and gender inequalities.

Battlefield victories enforced Lincoln's claim that the Union was perpetual and achieved its preservation. In fact, the national government emerged from the war more powerful than before, having exercised authority over banking, taxation, railroads, and the disposition of western lands. For African Americans and their abolitionist allies, emancipation was the war's most far-reaching achievement. At the war's outset, most Northerners were not abolitionists, and few observers foresaw that Lincoln would align the goal of "assur[ing] freedom to the free" with "giving freedom to the slave." Yet white racial attitudes shifted only gradually. Many Northerners still balked at extending voting rights to blacks and considered them racially inferior. White Southerners stiffened their defense of white supremacy.

The Civil War ended slavery and secession but left other questions unresolved. Disputes over the balance of federal and state authority persisted, and issues that cut across sectional lines, such as the tariff, currency, and immigration, remained controversial. Most immediately, the war's outcome left two pressing and fundamental questions: On what terms would northern and southern states be reunited, and what place would the freed slaves take in American society? Answering them became the central challenge of the postwar years.

13-6b The Transnational Technology of War

The Civil War revolutionizes weaponry, making future wars deadlier.

Because it was the first great conflict fought with the weapons of the Industrial Revolution, the Civil War changed the nature of warfare. Some new weapons, such as British sharpshooter rifles and French conical bullets (minié balls), had not been previously used on a massive scale. Others, such as repeating rifles, submarines, and land mines, were U.S. innovations. These new weapons helped to make the Civil War the deadliest of the era's nationalist conflicts outside of Asia (see Figure 13.2). The war conclusively demonstrated the importance of railroads and telegraph lines in conducting large-scale combat and the superiority of ironclad warships over wooden fleets. Taken together, the Civil War's technological changes marked it as the first "modern war." Its new weaponry made subsequent wars even deadlier.

European military observers criticized America's volunteer soldiers as "armed mobs from which nothing could be learned," as one Prussian general concluded. Few realized how the Civil War's repeating guns, trench warfare, and indecisive battles foreshadowed the devastation of World War I. Yet the U.S. experience did influence European practice. Successful bombardments demonstrated that new rifled cannons made masonry forts obsolete. After observing Union monitors and Confederate rams, European navies rushed to build fleets of ironclad warships. The world's first ocean battle between ironclads occurred between Austria and Italy just one year after the Civil War ended.

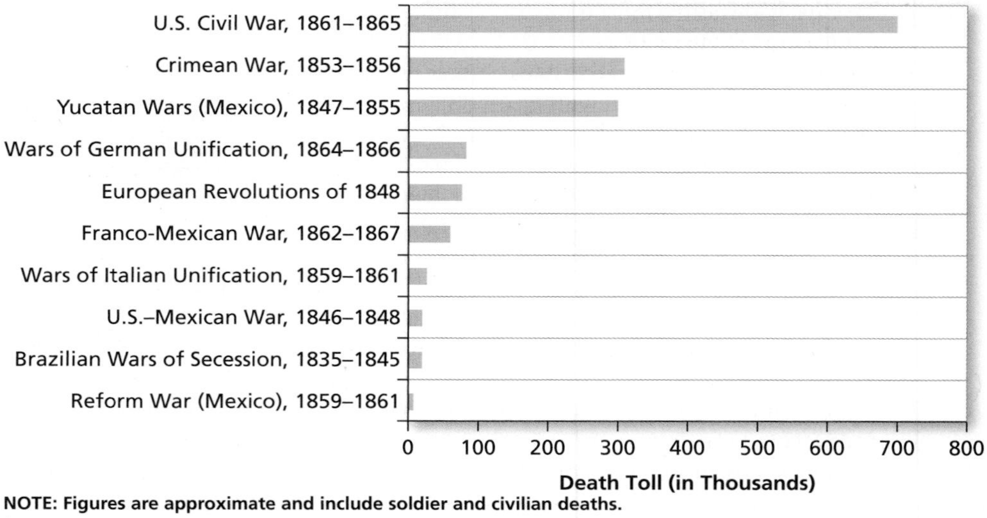

Figure 13.2 Death Toll of Mid-Nineteenth-Century Nationalist and Civil Wars Although it was dwarfed by China's Taiping Rebellion (1850–1864), in which 20 million people lost their lives, the U.S. Civil War was the deadliest Western conflict in an age of many nationalist and civil wars. Disease continued to cause most war deaths, but conscription and massive armies, more powerful and accurate weapons, and civilian targets increased casualties in the mid-1800 conflicts and later wars. ▶ Source: Estimates derived from annotated lists in *Statistics of Wars, Oppressions and Atrocities of the Nineteenth Century* (http://necrometrics.com/wars19c.htm)

Harper's Weekly

Global Americans Born in Massachusetts in 1831, **Frederick Townsend Ward** was an international adventurer who sought military glory and was willing to shift allegiances to achieve it. He sailed on clipper ships to China, joined a U.S. filibuster expedition to Mexico, and fought for the French in the Crimean War. On a trading voyage, Ward arrived in Shanghai in 1860 at the height of the Taiping Rebellion (1850–1864), a massive religious and political uprising against the Qing emperor. At first, he planned to join the rebels but switched sides when Shanghai bankers and merchants offered him financing. To defend the emperor, Ward organized the Ever Victorious Army, an elite body of five thousand Chinese troops led by Western officers and trained in modern weaponry and tactics. When news of the American Civil War reached China, Ward wavered but eventually sided with the Union. His army protected Shanghai's small American expatriate community from attacks by the British navy, and he pledged much of its booty to the Union cause. In 1862, Ward led the Ever Victorious Army to several victories over rebel Taiping forces that greatly outnumbered his men. His spectacular success ended when he was mortally wounded in the Battle of Cixi in September 1862. In the United States, the events of the Civil War overshadowed Ward's exploits during his lifetime and afterward, but he is better known in China. Some historians credit him with saving Shanghai for the Qing dynasty, but most believe that exporting Western arms and military training to China was his major legacy.

One U.S. military innovation aimed at humane effects. In 1863 at Lincoln's request, the German-American legal philosopher Francis Lieber drew up a code of conduct for Union soldiers. Known as General Orders No. 100, or simply the **Lieber Code**, it was prompted by Confederate brutality toward captured black soldiers. The code prescribed treatment of prisoners of war, civilians, and spies. It became the basis for later international agreements, including the Hague Regulations of 1907, which absorbed it into international treaty law. As modified by subsequent Geneva Conventions, it remains in effect today.

13-6c Political and Economic Reverberations Abroad

The war encourages nation building in North America and liberal nationalism in Europe.

The North's victory not only reunited the Union but also helped to consolidate neighboring nations. Following the Confederates' surrender, fifty thousand federal soldiers under General Sheridan marched to the Texas-Mexican border. U.S. officials pressured France to withdraw from Mexico and established a naval blockade to prevent Austrian reinforcements. After Napoleon III withdrew French forces in 1866, Maximilian's monarchy collapsed, President Juárez was restored to office, and the Mexican republic was saved. The Civil War also spurred, more indirectly, the creation of modern Canada through the British North America Act of 1867 (see Chapter 14).

Trade disruptions spread the Civil War's effects around the globe. Cotton growers in India, Egypt, West Africa, Turkey, and Brazil expanded farms to replace exports from the South. After emancipation, production shifted from slave economies to sharecroppers, tenant farmers, and peasants. The South's cotton exports recovered but no longer monopolized the global market. Meanwhile, wartime Confederate raiding and the Union demand for ships devastated the American whaling industry in the Pacific. Merchants in Hawai'i lost their lucrative restocking business and turned to growing sugar, making it the island kingdom's chief industry by the war's end.

In rallying the public behind the war, Lincoln had described the United States as the world's "last best hope" for democracy. The European Revolutions of 1848 had failed to replace monarchies with lasting republics and constitutions. In some cases, such as Germany under Chancellor Otto von Bismarck, nationalist movements had embraced authoritarian politics. Lincoln, in contrast, had aligned U.S. national unification with political equality. The Union's victory reinvigorated the idea of democratic self-government and encouraged European liberals to promote reforms. Britain extended voting rights to workers and small landholders. French jurist Edouard Laboulaye, a strong supporter of the Union and emancipation, proposed constructing the Statue of Liberty as a congratulatory gift to the United States. In India, Australia, and elsewhere, emerging colonial nationalists took heart from the U.S. example. Confident American victors anticipated that the "new birth of freedom" forecast by Lincoln in his Gettysburg Address would spread worldwide. The most perceptive observers realized, however, that its promise first had to be kept at home.

Lieber Code Rules of warfare codified at President Lincoln's request by legal scholar Francis Lieber, which influenced later international agreements covering combat and prisoners.

Summary

The American Civil War took place among parallel struggles over national unity and the extension of freedom that had begun with the European Revolutions of 1848, continued with Latin American civil wars, and concluded with Italian and German unification in 1871. Although both the Union and the Confederacy anticipated a quick victory, the war became a long and deadly struggle as the Union's mobile troops and gunboats won victories in the Mississippi Valley that were countered by Confederate triumphs on the battlefields of Virginia. Mass mobilization of soldiers and civilians provided men and supplies, railroads and steamboats took them to battle zones, and the new technology of rifled muskets and cannons littered battlefields with the dead and wounded.

As the war dragged on, it took on larger dimensions, some of them unanticipated. Native Americans became involved as participants or as rebels against treaties imposed by white governments. Britain and France threatened to intervene, potentially tipping the scales in the Confederates' favor or embroiling Europe's powers in a global war. The Confederate and Union central governments expanded their powers, the latter in permanent ways. Above all, the war's erosion of social institutions, accelerated by occupying armies and runaway slaves, led to Lincoln's momentous decision to emancipate the South's slaves.

By 1864, the Union's superior leadership and resources began to take effect. After the Union's campaign of destruction in the lower South and gradual encirclement in Virginia, the Confederates were forced to surrender. The South's landscape lay devastated and its racial order overturned. Victorious Northerners cheered the Union's preservation and its example of republican self-government to the world. Looking ahead, Americans of all regions and races faced the formidable task of healing sectional wounds, deciding the proper role of government, and enacting the pledge of freedom given to former slaves.

<Thinking Back, *Looking Forward*>

As you review this chapter, think about how the Civil War continued a centralizing trend for the nation and the federal government. What other nations experienced similar nationalizing struggles, even civil wars, at this time? In the next chapters, look for the consequences of a strong central government and for continuing conflict over its powers. Compare slave emancipation in the United States with emancipation of unfree people elsewhere. Did governments translate freedom into equality?

To make your review concrete, review the timeline and reflect on the entries there. Think about their causes, consequences, and connections. How do they fit with global trends?

Additional Resources

Books

Berlin, Ira, et al. ***Free at Last: A Documentary History of Slavery, Freedom, and the Civil War*****. New York: New Press, 2007.** ▶ A revealing collection of documents from enslaved and free African Americans.

Blight, David. ***Race and Reunion: The Civil War in American Memory*****. Cambridge, MA: Harvard University Press, 2002.** ▶ Pioneering exploration of how the war was remembered and commemorated.

Clinton, Catherine, and Nina Silber, eds. ***Divided Houses: Gender and the Civil War*****. New York: Oxford University Press, 1992.** ▶ Essays on the varied wartime roles of men and women.

Doyle, Don H. ***The Cause of All Nations: An International History of the Civil War*****. New York: Basic Books, 2015.** ▶ An engaging history of wartime diplomacy and public opinion abroad.

Gallagher, Gary. ***The Confederate War*****. Cambridge, MA: Harvard University Press, 1999.** ▶ An expert contribution to the debate over why the Confederacy lost.

Goodwin, Doris Kearns. ***Team of Rivals: The Political Genius of Abraham Lincoln*****. New York: Simon and Schuster, 2006.** ▶ Colorful narrative of how Lincoln led his administration and the Union to emancipation and victory.

Guelzo, Alan. ***Gettysburg: The Last Invasion*****. New York: Knopf, 2013.** ▶ Detailed, dramatic study of an epic battle and key military turning point.

Hauptman, Laurence M. *Between Two Fires: American Indians in the Civil War*. New York: Free Press, 1995. ▶ An informative survey of wartime activities and divisions among Native Americans.

McPherson, James. *Battle Cry of Freedom: The Civil War Era*. New York: Oxford University Press, 1988. ▶ The best single-volume overview of the period.

Sutherland, Daniel E. *A Savage Conflict: The Decisive Role of Guerrillas in the American Civil War*. Chapel Hill: University of North Carolina Press, 2013. ▶ Excellent overview of an often-neglected and sometimes romanticized aspect of the war.

Go to the MindTap® for **Global Americans** to access the full version of select books from this Additional Resources section.

Websites

Abraham Lincoln Papers at the Library of Congress. (http://memory.loc.gov/ammem/alhtml/malhome.html). ▶ A collection of twenty thousand documents by or relating to President Lincoln.

The Civil War Home Page. (http://www.civil-war.net). ▶ Excellent gateway to Civil War documents on the Internet from printed and archival sources.

The Civil War in *Harper's Weekly*. (http://sonofthesouth.net/). ▶ A complete file of the popular northern illustrated magazine during the war.

Civil War Photographs from the Library of Congress Collections. (http://www.loc.gov/pictures/collection/civwar/). ▶ More than seven thousand photographs on varied aspects of the war.

Making of America: The War of the Rebellion. (http://ebooks.library.cornell.edu/m/moawar/waro.html). ▶ Searchable copy of the one hundred twenty-eight-volume Official Records of the Union and Confederate Armies, originally published in 1880–1901.

National Park Service. (http://www.nps.gov). ▶ Gateway site to Civil War National Military Parks and Soldiers and Sailors database.

The Valley of the Shadow. (http://jefferson.village.virginia.edu/vshadow2/). ▶ A rich collection of sources on how the Civil War affected two counties, one in Pennsylvania, the other in Virginia.

MindTap®

Continue exploring online through MindTap®, where you can:

- **Assess your knowledge with the Chapter Test**
- **Watch historical videos related to the chapter**
- **Further your understanding with interactive maps and timelines**

The American Civil War

1861

March

Czar Alexander II issues edict freeing Russia's serfs.

Benito Juárez is elected president of the Mexican Republic after Reform War ends.

Lincoln is inaugurated as U.S. president.

April

South Carolina bombards Fort Sumter, opening the Civil War.

June

Northern women form U.S. Sanitary Commission, modeled on British organization from Crimean War.

1861

July

Confederate army is victorious at First Battle of Bull Run in Virginia.

November

Trent Affair sparks Anglo-American diplomatic crisis and war scare.

1862

February

Grant's victories at Forts Henry and Donelson spearhead Union advances down the Mississippi Valley.

March

Standoff between *Monitor* and *Virginia* opens global era of ironclad warships.
Union victory at Glorieta Pass, New Mexico, thwarts Confederate designs on California.

May

Federal Homestead Act offers free farms to loyal Northerners and immigrants.

1862

July

Peninsular Campaign ends in Union retreat from outskirts of Richmond.

U.S. Congress passes Pacific Railroad Acts, strengthening economic ties to West.

September

Battle of Antietam halts Lee's invasion of Maryland.

Lincoln announces Preliminary Emancipation Proclamation.

1863

January

Emancipation Proclamation frees slaves in rebel areas, welcomes black Union recruits, gains support for the U.S. abroad.

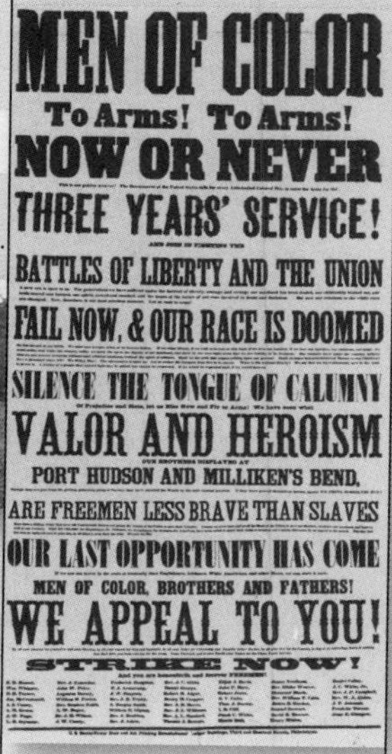

April

Lieber Code, written to counter Confederate mistreatment of black Union soldiers, prescribes globally influential rules of military conduct.

May

Battle of Chancellorsville caps Lee's successes, Union failures in Virginia.

June

West Virginia separates from Virginia and joins the Union, highlighting border-state divisions.

Napoleon III's French army seizes Mexico and installs Maximilian, Archduke of Austria, as emperor.

1863

July

Union victories at Gettysburg and Vicksburg turn military tide in the Union's favor.

New York City Draft Riot dramatizes dissent on Union and Confederate home fronts.

September

Russian fleet makes friendly visits to New York and San Francisco.

British government seizes ironclad *Laird Rams* intended for Confederacy.

1864

April

Confederates massacre surrendering black Union soldiers at Fort Pillow, Tennessee.

May–June

Overland Campaign in Virginia produces bloody stalemate between Grant's and Lee's armies.

1864

September

Sherman captures Atlanta, boosting Republican fortunes in election year.

October–November

Confederate agents enter U.S. from Canada to raid Vermont and New York City.

November

Lincoln is reelected over Democrat George McClellan, the war's pivotal political event.

Union soldiers annihilate Cheyenne and Arapaho Indians in the Sand Creek Massacre in Colorado.

November–December

Sherman's March to the Sea destroys Confederates' resources and resolve.

1865

April

After breakthrough at Petersburg, Virginia, major Confederate armies surrender, ending the Civil War.

Lincoln is assassinated, succeeded by Vice President Andrew Johnson.

June

Stand Watie, Cherokee chief, is last Confederate general to surrender.

1866

January

Under U.S. pressure, Napoleon III announces withdrawal of French troops from Mexico, hastening fall of Emperor Maximilian.

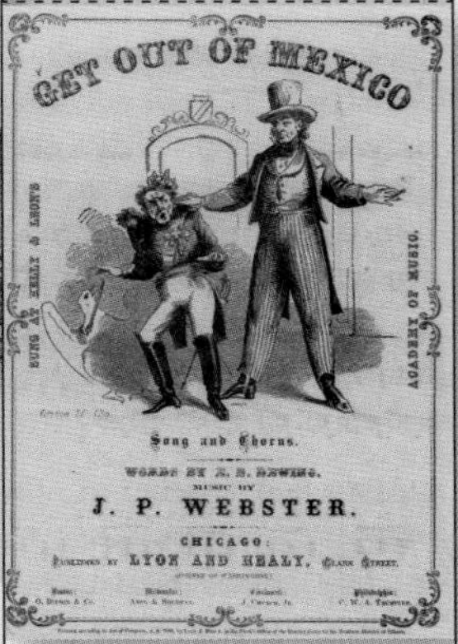

April

Supreme Court rules in *ex parte Milligan* against trying civilians in military tribunals when civil courts are functioning.

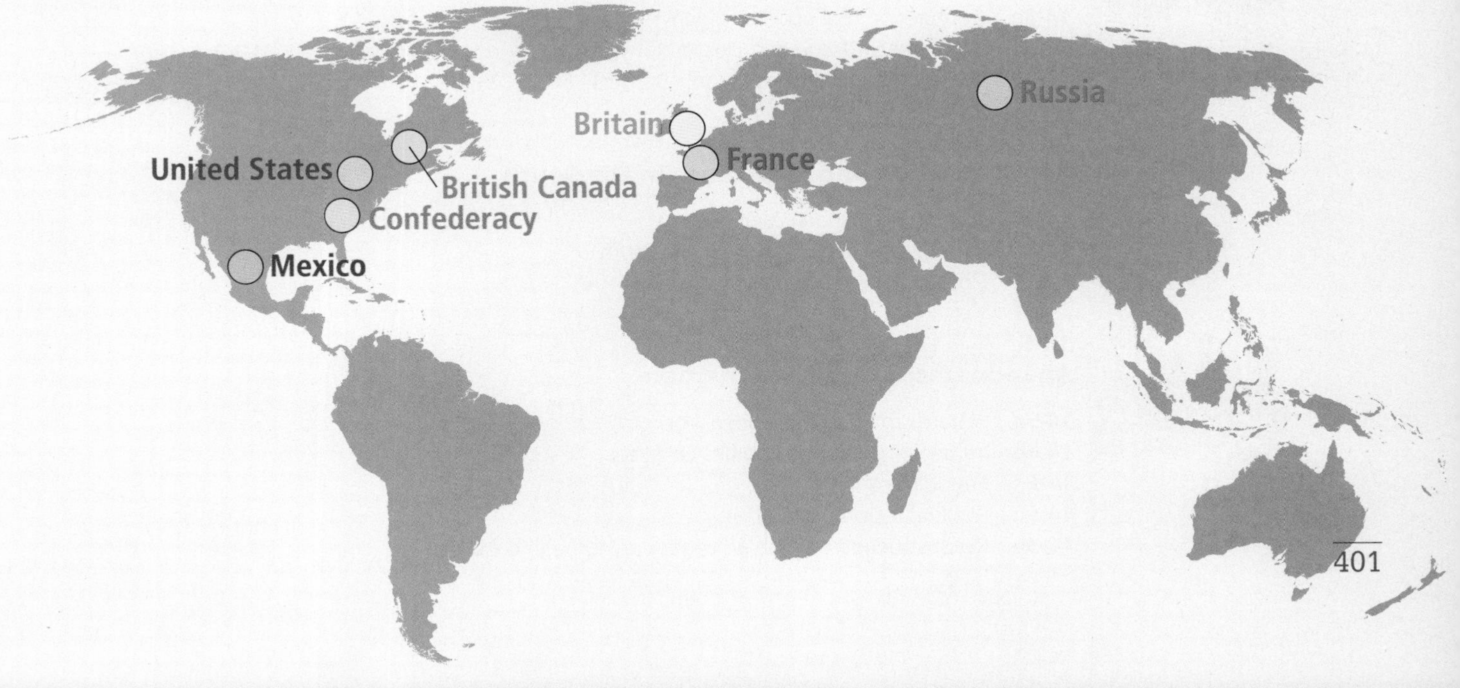

14 Reunion and Retreat: Reconstruction

1865–1877

The son of immigrants from Haiti and Cuba, Rodolphe Desdunes worked throughout his life for equal rights for people of color in Louisiana. This included organizing support for Homère Plessy, the plaintiff in the landmark *Plessy v. Ferguson* case, which ultimately upheld segregation and proved a deep disappointment to Desdunes.

For Louisiana people of color like Rodolphe Desdunes, emancipation was a transnational movement and a multigenerational commitment. Carried by slaves and other migrants, the ideal of racial equality coursed across the Atlantic and stretched in time from the French and Haitian Revolutions of the 1790s to the American antisegregation campaigns a century later. Desdunes's parents were from Haiti and Cuba; he grew up in the New Orleans community of Creoles or "free coloreds" whose French language associations protested racial restrictions and advocated abolition. When federal troops occupied New Orleans during the Civil War, many Creole men joined the Union army, cementing their claim to full citizenship. After the war, Louisiana's new Constitution of 1868 guaranteed "equal civil, political and public rights" to all citizens. Six years of Republican rule built freed people's schools, enlisted blacks in the state militia, and elected dozens of American-born and Caribbean-origin blacks to office.

Louisiana Division/City Archives

Desdunes was too young to vote for the 1868 Constitution, but he defended it when black civil rights came under attack by violent white-supremacist groups. Serving on the New Orleans Metropolitan Police, Desdunes was wounded in 1874 when more than three thousand armed White Leaguers, mostly Confederate veterans, stormed city hall and the statehouse. They withdrew only after President Grant rushed federal troops to the city.

As the rights of people of color were assailed, Desdunes began studying law to take their grievances to the federal courts, where postwar constitutional amendments could be used to challenge state laws. When Louisiana mandated racial segregation on railroads, Desdunes enlisted his son to test the statute and won a verdict that integrated interstate trains. Because railroad travel *within* Louisiana remained segregated, Desdunes organized support for Homer (born Homère) Plessy, another Creole of Haitian descent, to mount a legal challenge that climbed to the U.S. Supreme Court. *Plessy v. Ferguson* (1896), which upheld Louisiana's segregationist practices, broke the promise of Louisiana's 1868 constitution and signaled the final unwinding of Reconstruction. Heartbroken, Desdunes withdrew from public life to write a history of black Creole activism in New Orleans meant to inspire future generations to renew the struggle.

Desdunes's post-Civil War experience had unique features that stemmed from Louisiana's Afro-French community and its cosmopolitan outlook. Still, Louisiana blacks played an important role outside the state as prominent advocates for civil equality. Moreover, the struggle in Louisiana broadly resembled the course of postwar debates elsewhere in the nation. What political and social rights would be guaranteed to emancipated African Americans? How far would the northern victors and newly empowered freed people restructure southern society and politics to embody those rights? How would the former Confederate states be restored to the Union, and who would control that process? How much authority should the federal government exert over the states?

How do the experiences of Rodolphe Desdunes reflect the struggle of Louisiana blacks and the role that they played as prominent advocates for civil equality?

Go to MindTap® to watch a video on Desdunes and learn how his story relates to the themes of this chapter.

The answers to such questions were hotly debated among different political, economic, and racial groups. Control over events veered between the president and Congress, the states and the federal government. All knew that the outcome was as important as the Civil War's battles, for it was possible to win the war and lose the peace. The questions themselves implied a dilemma: Rapid and lenient restoration of Rebel states to the Union would mean letting go of transforming the South and enforcing racial equality, whereas determination to revolutionize the South's economic and racial order would mean a long, costly, and potentially bloody struggle.

Of the two main postwar tasks Americans faced—restoring political relations with former rebels and reshaping southern life after slavery—the first was the residue of civil war, and the second was the aftermath of emancipation. Viewed in a global context, the postwar political settlement resembled national unification in countries such as Italy and Germany, where the northern victors dominated the national government but North-South differences remained and regional resentments festered. The struggle over emancipation was also a familiar global theme. Around the world, other slaveholding nations, including Spain (in Cuba), Britain (in Jamaica), and Brazil, faced similar conflicts over emancipating slaves and defining justice once they were liberated. Emancipation during the Civil War gradually undermined the existence of slavery elsewhere, including Cuba and Brazil. Yet the abandonment of the North's Reconstruction program indicated that for the time being, the United States would follow a conservative path similar to that of other postemancipation societies in the Americas, which retreated from equality, limited the rights won by freed people, and appeased their former masters.

14-1 Wartime Origins of Reconstruction

As the Civil War ended, the Freedmen's Bureau, northern charities, and former slaves collaborated to construct local schools in the South. This photograph shows the Freedmen's School and its students on James Plantation in North Carolina.

Examine the photograph and the placement of its subjects. Who is the woman on the left? What can we learn from the varied heights and two sexes of the pupils? What can this photograph tell you about freedmen's schools and black Southerners' attitudes toward education? ▶

The Granger Collection, New York

Reconstruction began long before the Civil War ended. When the federal army occupied areas in Louisiana, Tennessee, and Virginia, local Unionists made preparations to rejoin the federal government. Before and after President Lincoln's Emancipation Proclamation, hundreds of thousands of runaway slaves migrated behind Union lines, seeking freedom and enlisting as federal soldiers or hospital workers. Wartime debates in Congress over readmitting rebellious states, addressing freed people's aspirations for land and labor, and adopting Union policies to meet the needs of the refugee influx provided a rehearsal for the postwar struggle over Reconstruction.

☞ As you read, consider how the Union's actions during wartime helped to set up conflicting expectations for postwar reconstruction. Were Union policies meant to raise former slaves' economic status or to keep them as farm laborers?

14-1a Lincoln versus Congress

The president and congressional Republicans quarrel over Reconstruction.

In his Proclamation of Amnesty and Reconstruction of December 1863, President Lincoln set lenient terms to entice Confederates back to the Union. While holding firm on emancipation, the president offered pardons and restoration of property to Confederates (except to high military and civil officials) who would swear an oath of allegiance to the United States. According to Lincoln's **Ten-Percent Plan**, as soon as 10 percent of those who had voted in 1860 took the oath, new state governments could be formed. He imposed no requirements for freed people's civil and political rights.

Most congressional Republicans criticized Lincoln's plan of "restoration" and favored a more thorough "reconstruction" of the South. Republican radicals, about one-third of the party's congressmen, wanted to "revolutionize Southern institutions, habits, and manners," according to spokesman Thaddeus Stevens. Moderates favored less drastic changes but agreed that Congress, not the president, should control reconstruction. The gap between Lincoln and **Radical Republicans** was exposed in the struggle over reconstruction in Louisiana, where the new state constitution of 1864, ratified by only 10 percent of Louisiana's adult white males, rejected black suffrage. In response, Congress denied admission to Louisiana's representatives.

In July, Republicans in Congress countered Lincoln's plan with the **Wade-Davis Bill**. It required 50 percent of voters to take an oath of allegiance to the Union and mandated that new state constitutions be drawn up by delegates elected by those who had never supported the rebellion. Lincoln, fearing that this bill would halt the process underway in Louisiana and Arkansas, killed the legislation by using a pocket veto, refusing to sign it before Congress's session ended.

Lincoln's reelection in 1864 paved the way for passage of a measure that the president and Republican radicals agreed on: the **Thirteenth Amendment**, abolishing slavery nationwide. Republicans feared that Lincoln's Emancipation Proclamation would be overturned by the courts in peacetime or reversed by new state governments in the South. The solution was to amend the federal constitution. Fall elections in 1864 gave the Republicans a strong congressional majority, and in January 1865, the House of Representatives passed the Thirteenth Amendment after several wavering Democrats were wooed by Republican lobbyists to their side. When the amendment was ratified by three-quarters of the states, emancipation became the law of the land in December 1865.

14-1b Emancipation on the Ground

Northern volunteers and the Union government assist the freed people.

In regions far from the invading Union armies, most black Southerners did not learn about emancipation until the spring of 1865. *Juneteenth*, the official announcement of emancipation in the holdout state of Texas on June 19, 1865, became a special day of celebration for African Americans. Long before that, slaves in coastal regions and the upper South had taken steps to free themselves. More than a million fled the South's plantations during the war, and half ended up in Union-occupied areas.

Union army officers' response to the influx of freed people was shaped by the desire to maintain order and agricultural production more than humanitarian motives. Herded into makeshift camps, some freed people were supplied rations and hired by the army and navy for meager wages as laborers, cooks, or hospital workers. Others were contracted to work on plantations seized by Union armies and leased to loyal southern whites or Yankee entrepreneurs.

For freedmen intent on staying in the agricultural South, leasing or buying confiscated lands was the preferred alternative. By the end of the war, nearly one-fifth of the farmland in areas under Union occupation was being worked by independent black families. When General Sherman passed through coastal Georgia and South Carolina in January 1865, local black leaders persuaded him to draft **Field Order No. 15** to give each freed family provisional title to forty acres of land confiscated from slaveholders. Union officials settled more than forty thousand freed people there. Elsewhere in the South, small pockets of freed people had been able to purchase land during the war.

Freed people's thirst for education was quenched more readily than their hunger for land. Freedmen's aid societies formed in the North sent more than one thousand teachers to the South during the war, and the influx increased after Appomattox. Three-quarters were women and perhaps one-fifth were black. Charlotte Forten, a young African American woman who journeyed from Philadelphia to teach in South Carolina's Lowcountry, told her

Ten-Percent Plan Lincoln's lenient wartime program to restore pacified Confederate states to the Union.

Radical Republicans Party faction intent on ensuring civil rights for former slaves and transforming the South's society and economy during Reconstruction.

Wade-Davis Bill Congressional measure that required stiff loyalty tests for readmitting former Confederate states but that Lincoln pocket vetoed.

Thirteenth Amendment Constitutional addition outlawing slavery in the United States that was ratified eight months after the Civil War ended.

Field Order No. 15 Sherman's 1865 decree setting aside land confiscated from slaveholders in coastal South Carolina, Georgia, and Florida for settlement by freed people.

Freedmen's Bureau Federal agency created under the War Department to oversee education, labor contracts, and welfare of former slaves.

students about "the noble Toussaint [L'Ouverture]," the black liberator of Haiti, so that they "should know what one of their own color could do for his race." Teachers like Forten promoted basic literacy and numeracy but also strove to help freed people "unlearn the teachings of slavery" by promoting pride, self-discipline, and the dignity of work.

Higher education for freed people was offered in seminaries, colleges, and "normal schools" (teacher training institutions) that were founded by northern charitable organizations and biracial missionary societies. Howard University in Washington, D.C., Fisk University in Tennessee, and Hampton Institute in Virginia trace their origins to Reconstruction; all were named after or led by prominent Civil War generals.

Congress assisted these philanthropic ventures and independent schools through the **Freedmen's Bureau**, established in March 1865. Run by the War Department, the bureau allocated one-third of its budget to schools from primary education to colleges such as Howard and Fisk. It took over the Union army's wartime mandate to provide relief to refugees and to enforce labor contracts between planters and former slaves.

Prevailing stereotypes and ideologies compromised most types of help available to the freed people, whether it was provided by the federal government or private volunteers. Many army supervisors and Unionist whites envisioned southern blacks as permanent farm workers, not owners. Free-market practices meant that whites often outbid former slaves who had scraped together money to buy land. And the free-labor ideology decreed that blacks should be left to fend for themselves after a short period of aid and tutelage. These assumptions persisted and undermined Northerners' plans to reconstruct the South.

14-2

Postwar Conditions and Conflicting Agendas

Library of Congress Prints and Photographs Division

Thomas Nast's widely distributed cartoons in *Harper's Weekly* magazine both shaped and reflected northern views of Reconstruction. This cartoon of August 5, 1865, features contrasting episodes. On the left panel titled *Pardon,* Columbia, a symbol of the United States, wonders "Shall I trust these men?" referring to the prostrate figures of Robert E. Lee, Jefferson Davis, and other former Confederate leaders. On the right panel called *Franchise,* Columbia clasps the shoulder of a disabled black Union veteran and asks, "And not these men?" The globe-shaped object on the pedestal is a ballot box.

How does the cartoonist contrast President Johnson's plan to pardon former Confederate leaders with mainstream Republicans' program to give voting rights to male African Americans? Which position does the cartoonist favor, and how does his portrayal indicate it? ▶

Go to MindTap® to practice history with the Chapter 14 **Primary Source Writing Activity: Responses to Reconstruction.** Read and view primary sources and respond to a writing prompt.

At the end of the Civil War, white Southerners were demoralized and resentful while the region's blacks looked forward to free and independent lives. All realized that postwar life would require changes, and each group developed its own agenda. Dramatic divisions formed among white and black Southerners, political parties, the president, and Congress over restoring the Union and defining the role of former slaves. The debate over Reconstruction paralleled struggles that followed the emancipation of slaves and other unfree laborers in overseas lands, but control by congressional Republicans seemed to promise a more equitable outcome than elsewhere.

☞ As you read, consider the agendas of different political groups in the North and South for postwar Reconstruction. How did the varied positions of former slaves, southern whites, President Johnson, and the Republican-dominated Congress lead to conflict, and over which issues?

14-2a Freedom in Action

At the war's end, slavery was gone and the Confederacy dissolved, but no new social or political system emerged to take their place. Despite the initial confusion, the lines were quickly drawn between southern blacks and whites over the fundamental issues of land, labor, and political power.

African American families reunite and organize to secure equal rights.

Former slaves had firm ideas about what they expected from freedom. For many, the first task was to reunite families who had been separated by slavery or the war. Freed people used their communal grapevine to locate relatives and took to the roads to find them. They enlisted help from the Freedmen's Bureau or paid for newspaper advertisements. Some relatives were never found, but most families broken by slavery were mended in the postwar years, and by 1870, the two-parent household became the norm.

Reconstituted African American families had to decide where to live. Some returned to the familiar surroundings of their old plantation, but many others fled the places where they had labored. As one slave told her former owner, "If I stay here I'll never know I'm free." Thousands moved to cities, believing that life would be freer there and Union troops would provide protection. The black population of major southern cities doubled in the five years after the war. Urban black enclaves were segregated "across the tracks" from whites, and occupational choices were restricted by prejudice. The majority of males became unskilled manual laborers and women were hired as maids, washerwomen, or seamstresses. Still, their neighborhoods provided precious space where African Americans established schools, clubs, benevolent societies, and other community institutions.

Whether in towns or the countryside, African Americans organized and built separate Protestant churches. Predominantly Baptist and Methodist, they became focal points for religious life and other community activities from educational classes and festivals to political meetings. Black women played prominent roles in these events, and male ministers emerged as respected community leaders who dispensed political as well as spiritual guidance.

In an agricultural society, economic independence entailed access to land. Stimulated by the Freedman's Bureau, "forty acres and a mule" became the rallying cry for freed people who demanded a portion of the lands they had worked for generations. They were deeply disappointed when "Sherman's lands" were restored to white owners and various proposals to confiscate and redistribute Rebel plantations failed to win passage in Congress.

The majority of newly emancipated blacks had little choice but to work on plantations for wages. Determined to get their full worth, blacks bargained hard over wages and hours and turned to the Freedmen's Bureau for help in enforcing annual contracts with white employers. Many African American women refused to return to full-time fieldwork, eager to raise their children and tend their own households. Labor shortages gave freedmen bargaining power, but they hated working in gangs, which reminded them of slavery, and distrusted their former masters as employers.

Freedmen realized that political organizing was necessary to demand equal rights. Even before the war ended, freedmen had joined Union Leagues, Republican clubs that had been organized in occupied districts, and used them to call for the rights of "all loyal men, without distinction of color." In the summer and fall of 1865, freedmen's conventions assembled in most former Confederate states,

Dressing for the Carnival In the 1870s, northern artist Winslow Homer captured this image of a freed Virginia family preparing for the Afro-Caribbean festival of Jonkonnu, a celebration that former slaves merged with the Fourth of July. In the painting, two women sew colorful shards on a man dressing like a harlequin, while children look on, one holding a lowered American flag. Homer celebrated the freed people's creative mix of cultures while subtly contrasting hopes for Reconstruction with its harsh realities. ◄

several in black churches. Delegates addressed petitions to white-dominated constitutional conventions, demanding equal participation and the right to vote. The new white governments ignored these demands, indicating how far apart former masters and former slaves stood at the dawn of the new era.

14-2b White Resistance

In defeat, white Southerners are devastated but defiant.

The war's physical and economic devastation demoralized white Southerners, who had controlled the region's resources. Much of Atlanta, Charleston, and Richmond lay in ruins. Slave emancipation and farms destroyed by marching armies diminished planters' wealth, and the wartime deaths of one in five white southern men deprived households of traditional heads. With no new legal system in place, crime rates rose sharply.

Many former Confederates feared being subject to occupying troops who had recently killed the South's soldiers. White Southerners especially dreaded reprisals from their former slaves, who might claim former masters' possessions or even murder them. In late 1865, rumors of a pending Christmas insurrection of violent freedmen, stirred by recollections of a similar revolt in Jamaica, sent chills through the South's white communities. A South Carolina planter's wife foresaw "the foulest demonic passions of the negro, hitherto so peaceful & happy, roused into being & fierce activity by the devilish Yankees."

Paranoia about potential black violence prompted immediate attacks by whites. The Civil War left a legacy of guerrilla warfare, racial hatred, and gun carrying in the South that continued to fuel violence after Appomattox. On Christmas Eve 1865, a group of Confederate veterans gathered in Pulaski, Tennessee, to organize the **Ku Klux Klan**. This secret vigilante group pledged to suppress all freedmen's assertions of equality and restore white supremacy by intimidation and violence. Its membership grew rapidly in the following year as it allied with opposition to black voting. Even white Southerners who renounced the Klan's tactics could not imagine peaceful coexistence of the two races under legal equality.

Southern whites especially worried about losing the cheap and disciplined labor of African American slaves on their farms. In the summer of 1865, white-dominated state legislatures passed restrictive **Black Codes** designed to return freed people to conditions as close to slavery as possible. They forbade blacks from owning guns, consuming alcohol, and marrying whites. Vagrancy laws forced black men and women to carry permits and mandated fines or imprisonment for the unemployed. The Black Code in South Carolina required freedmen to pay hefty fees to set up businesses, and Mississippi's made it illegal for blacks to own or lease farmland. These codes announced that southern whites' immediate postwar agenda was to reestablish social and economic dominance over African Americans.

Ku Klux Klan White supremacist secret society organized by former Confederates that terrorized southern blacks and their supporters during Reconstruction.

Black Codes Restrictive laws passed by Democratic-controlled southern states that denied civil rights and economic advancement to former slaves.

14-2c Johnson's Reconstruction Plan

President Johnson seizes the initiative and conciliates former Confederates.

Ex-Confederates' aspirations were bolstered by the new president, Andrew Johnson, who developed a surprisingly lenient Reconstruction plan.

In some ways, Johnson was a worthy successor to the slain president. Like Lincoln, he was born in humble circumstances in the upper South's backcountry, had little formal education, and rose through hard work. Johnson was also an ardent Unionist. A Democrat and the only senator from the South to remain in Congress after secession, he had been appointed military governor of occupied Tennessee and inserted as Lincoln's running mate in 1864 on a bipartisan Union ticket. Johnson once owned slaves but during the war supported emancipation, mainly as way to punish the South's aristocrats, whom he resented. At the war's end, he declared repeatedly that "treason is a crime and must be made odious." Some Radical Republicans who had criticized Lincoln's generous reconstruction terms saw Johnson as a potential ally.

Yet as a former southern Democrat with states' rights leanings and unreconstructed racial views, Johnson had as much in common with the war's vanquished as its victors. His plan, introduced in May 1865, called for swift restoration of the Rebel states, which he claimed had never legally left the Union. Nearly all Southerners who swore an oath of allegiance to the Union would regain their political and property rights. Confederate civilian and military officers and those owning more than $20,000 in property had to obtain a presidential pardon. Except for having southern states ratify the Thirteenth Amendment, the plan was silent on civil or voting rights for the freed people.

Over the summer of 1865, Johnson dropped his call to punish Confederate leaders and granted more than thirteen thousand pardons to wealthy former Confederates. Meanwhile, southern states largely accepted Johnson's mild conditions and created new governments little different from prewar regimes. Some refused to ratify the Thirteenth Amendment or repudiate their Confederate debts. No reorganized southern state allowed black votes, and the former Confederates who led those states adopted harsh Black Codes. To underscore their defiance, white Southerners sent Alexander Stephens, the former Confederate vice president, to the U.S. Congress along with ten Confederate generals and fifty-eight former Confederate congressmen. Eight months after the war's end, Republican leaders wondered aloud who had actually won it.

14-2d Congressional Response

When Congress reconvened in December 1865, angry Republicans refused to seat representatives from the former Confederate states. Moderates agreed that the former slaves' civil rights should be protected, and most Republicans believed that southern states should not be readmitted until they renounced secession and repudiated Confederate debts. Many worried that unrepentant southern Democrats might undo Republican wartime legislation. Emancipation had nullified the constitution's clause that African Americans represented three-fifths of a person or citizen. Because freedmen were then counted as one whole person, southern states stood to gain as many as two dozen representatives in Congress. These concerns moved congressional Republicans toward extending voting rights to the former slaves on political as well as moral grounds.

Congress opposes Johnson and forges an alternative Reconstruction program.

Taking aim at the Black Codes, Congress in early 1866 reauthorized the Freedman's Bureau, directing it to prosecute state officials who violated blacks' civil rights. President Johnson vetoed the bill. Clinging to old racial fears, he was convinced that efforts to empower freedmen would come at poor whites' expense. Congress next sought to broaden its protection of freed people by passing the **Civil Rights Act of 1866**, a landmark bill that specified that blacks enjoyed the same rights guaranteed to other U.S. citizens. It directly aimed to overturn the Supreme Court's *Dred Scott* decision of 1857. Again, Johnson vetoed the measure, denouncing its expansion of federal power as well as its assertion of equal rights. In both cases, the president's refusal to compromise helped to unite his Republican opponents, who mustered the two-thirds majority necessary to override his veto.

To counter white Southerners' opposition, Republican leaders sought constitutional protection for equal rights. In June 1866, Congress passed the **Fourteenth Amendment**, which absorbed the new Civil Rights Act into the federal charter. It declared that all persons born or naturalized in the United States (except Native Americans) were citizens entitled to due process and equal protection of the law. When ratified by the states in 1868, this sweeping provision established a policy of **birthright citizenship**, automatic granting of citizenship to those born within the nation's borders. This policy was later adopted by nearly all Western Hemisphere republics—most immediately, Argentina in 1869—but was resisted by European nations that relied on ties of language or blood lineage to bind their nationality.

Other sections of the Fourteenth Amendment repudiated the Confederate debt and disqualified Confederate officeholders from state and national positions. Rather than give black people the vote outright, the amendment specified that states denying suffrage to black men would have their representation in Congress reduced proportionally. Many Republicans represented northern states that denied blacks the vote and balked at mandating universal male suffrage. Some hoped that Johnson would accept the amendment as a compromise and a minimum condition for Reconstruction.

Johnson flatly opposed the Fourteenth Amendment and encouraged white Southerners and northern conservatives to remain defiant. In the summer of 1866, he launched an unprecedented speaking tour across the

Civil Rights Act of 1866 Law that recognized citizenship rights of former slaves and gave the federal government power to enforce them.

Fourteenth Amendment Constitutional addition ratified by the states in 1868 that gave citizenship to nearly all persons born or naturalized in the United States, including former slaves, and penalized states that restricted male suffrage.

birthright citizenship Automatic provision of citizenship to children born within a nation's borders or territories, which became common practice in the Americas after U.S. adoption.

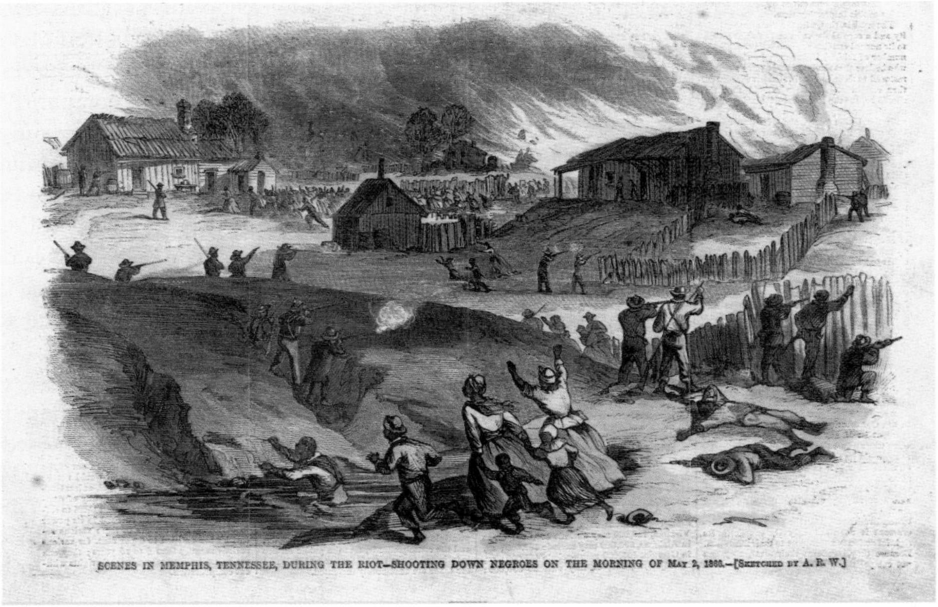

SCENES IN MEMPHIS, TENNESSEE, DURING THE RIOT—SHOOTING DOWN NEGROES ON THE MORNING OF MAY 2, 1866.—[SKETCHED BY A. R. W.]

Memphis Riots, May 1866 Three days of violence erupted after a white policeman tried to arrest a black Union veteran. Memphis's whites, who resented policing by black Union soldiers and competition with former slaves for jobs, attacked a black shantytown, shooting at will and setting buildings ablaze. Forty-six blacks and two whites died and one hundred buildings were burned, but no arrests were made. Accounts of the riot influenced passage of the Congressional Reconstruction Act. ▶

Tennessee State Library and Archives

Print Collector/Hulton Archive/Getty Images

Global Americans The son of a Cuban schoolmaster, **Ambrosio Gonzales** was educated in New York and returned to Havana to earn a law degree and teach languages. There he joined a secret organization that advocated U.S. annexation of Cuba without ending slavery. In 1849 and 1850, Gonzales helped organize two failed filibusters to invade Cuba from the United States. Through these activities he became associated with prominent southern planters, and in 1856, he married into a wealthy South Carolina slaveholding family. During the Civil War, Gonzales served as a Confederate artillery chief under General P.G.T. Beauregard, his former schoolmate in New York. Reconstruction turned Gonzales's privileged plantation life upside down. The family estate languished when black workers departed and cotton prices fell, and Gonzales's Caribbean import business in Charleston was destroyed in a race riot. An experiment in hiring Chinese and European contract laborers for his sawmill ended in bankruptcy. In 1869, the family sailed to Havana, counting on wealthy relatives and the legality of Cuban slavery to escape the reversals of Reconstruction. Less than a year later, Gonzales's wife died of yellow fever. Returning to the United States in the 1870s, he scraped together a living by teaching in various cities and repeatedly urged Grant and others to annex Cuba. Although his Cuban background was unusual for the South's planter elite, Gonzales's career embodied their Caribbean connections, expansionist dreams, and resistance to emancipation and Reconstruction.

northern states to rally public support for his resistance to equal rights legislation. Scheming to bypass Republicans and forge a new centrist coalition, Johnson labeled his congressional opponents traitors who should be hung.

These crude attacks alienated the North's public. Meanwhile, two bloody race riots that broke out in southern cities suggested the violence Johnson's stand appeared to encourage. In May 1866, a mob of whites stormed a freed people's neighborhood in Memphis, killing nearly fifty and burning schools and churches. Three months later, armed whites in New Orleans attacked a black parade for voting rights; nearly eighty citizens were killed or wounded, most of them African Americans. These outrages prompted a backlash against Johnson and his policies. The 1866 congressional elections returned a veto-proof Republican majority to Congress. Republicans were poised to replace the president's discredited program of "restoration" with a more sweeping "reconstruction" agenda.

14-2e Reconstruction in a Global Perspective

> The United States stands out among postemancipation societies in granting freed slaves the right to political equality.

During the Reconstruction years, Americans battled over the aftermath of civil war and the meaning of emancipation. Viewed in global perspective, neither struggle was unique. In the mid-nineteenth century, many countries faced continued turmoil after civil wars and emancipations. Their histories served as important points of influence and comparison for U.S. developments.

Former Confederates complained that Reconstruction was unduly harsh on the South, but most groups defeated in nineteenth-century civil wars were treated more brutally. The victorious Chinese imperial forces who suppressed the Taiping Rebellion (1850–1864) executed more than 1 million captives. Defeated spokesmen for the 1848 revolutions in Europe, when not imprisoned, were forced into exile. After the failed Hungarian revolt, Louis Kossuth never returned to his native land, and thousands of his fellow secessionists languished in Austrian prisons.

Some Confederate partisans who refused to accept defeat went into voluntary exile. Confederate cabinet member Judah Benjamin fled to England, where he began a successful second career as a barrister. Colonies of Confederate expatriates were formed in Mexico, Cuba, and British Honduras (now Belize). About twenty thousand whites from the Deep South migrated to Brazil, whose emperor offered subsidized transport and cheap land and where slavery was still legal. These *Confederados* established cotton plantations and introduced Baptist Christianity to the region north of Sao Paolo.

In comparison to conquerors in civil wars elsewhere, victorious Unionists were remarkably lenient. A few Radical Republicans declared that "the leaders of this rebellion must be executed or banished," yet neither Jefferson Davis nor Robert E. Lee was tried for treason and the victors imposed no exile or mass imprisonments. Federal laws disfranchised a small number of high-ranking Confederates, but pardons and amnesty acts restored their property and political rights.

In contrast to this relatively mild political punishment, many Republicans favored wholesale social changes in the conquered South. Compared to emancipation elsewhere in the Western world, postwar Reconstruction made possible a more abrupt break with the past. In Russia, where Czar Alexander II emancipated the serfs, and in the British Caribbean and Brazil, where plantation slavery was abolished gradually, masters were compensated for losing their human property and strongly influenced the terms of emancipation. When Confederates rejected President Lincoln's offer of compensated emancipation, they triggered his Emancipation Proclamation—the largest confiscation of property in the nation's history. The Union's military victory meant that in the postwar period Congress excluded former masters from setting the terms of the new order.

In most plantation societies in the Americas, landed white elites retained the upper hand after emancipation and used it to keep political power and force former slaves back to work. In Jamaica, for example, freed people had to accept a four- to six-year apprenticeship working for their former masters without wages. Although full civil rights were supposed to follow, freed slaves were prevented from voting by prohibitive property requirements and eventually outright exclusion. Reconstruction in the United States got off to a more promising start. When the Republican-dominated Congress passed laws guaranteeing civil and political rights regardless of race, the United States became unique among postemancipation societies in granting freed slaves the right to political equality.

As Americans debated Reconstruction, they looked for lessons as emancipation unfolded in the Caribbean. In October 1865, freed black farm workers in Jamaica rose up to protest lack of access to land. The **Morant Bay Rebellion** was brutally suppressed, and Jamaican whites returned control of the colony to Britain. When news of the rebellion reached North America, the South's newspapers warned that demands for land and similar "incendiary teachings" would produce violent uprisings among former slaves. Meanwhile, northern abolitionists such as Lydia Maria Child compared the Jamaican freed peoples' restrictions to the South's Black Codes, declaring that such schemes for "legislating the blacks back into slavery" must be stopped.

Morant Bay Rebellion
Uprising in Jamaica by freedmen asserting their right to land to which whites retaliated by killing more than four hundred blacks and revoking colonial self-rule.

14-3 Congressional Reconstruction

This political cartoon was published during the impeachment trial of President Andrew Johnson in 1868 when Republicans in Congress charged him with obstructing enforcement of the Constitution and recent Reconstruction laws. "This little boy would persist in handling books above his capacity," the caption reads. "And this was the disastrous result." The cartoon reflects Republicans' confidence that Johnson would be convicted.

Why would political opponents portray Johnson as a "little boy" involved in matters "over his head"? Why is it significant that Johnson is shown crushed by "Vol. 14" of the Constitution? ▶

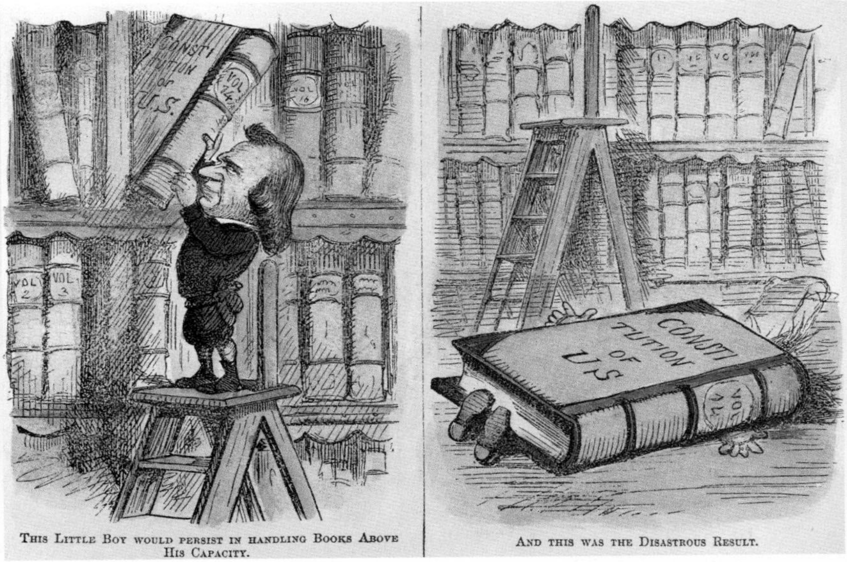

THIS LITTLE BOY WOULD PERSIST IN HANDLING BOOKS ABOVE HIS CAPACITY.

AND THIS WAS THE DISASTROUS RESULT.

The Granger Collection, New York

Under "radical" Reconstruction, congressional Republicans used their strong majority to impose plans to restore the Union and reconstruct the South politically. Their program did not distribute land to freed people; it did not enfranchise women or prevent indirect disfranchisement of African Americans. But it amended the constitution to make voting rights colorblind and federally protected. And it installed loyal Republican governments in the former Confederate states. This expansion of federal power paralleled the growth of national influence abroad following the Union's victory in the Civil War.

☞ As you read, think about how the Union victory in the Civil War and growing federal powers reconfigured sectional relations in the United States as well as foreign relations in North America. How did Congressional Reconstruction attempt to make over the South politically and socially? How did expanding U.S. power redraw the map of North America?

14-3a Military Occupation and Impeachment

After debating several proposals, Congress drew up a comprehensive blueprint for overhauling the South's political framework. The

Congress takes charge of Reconstruction during a constitutional crisis.

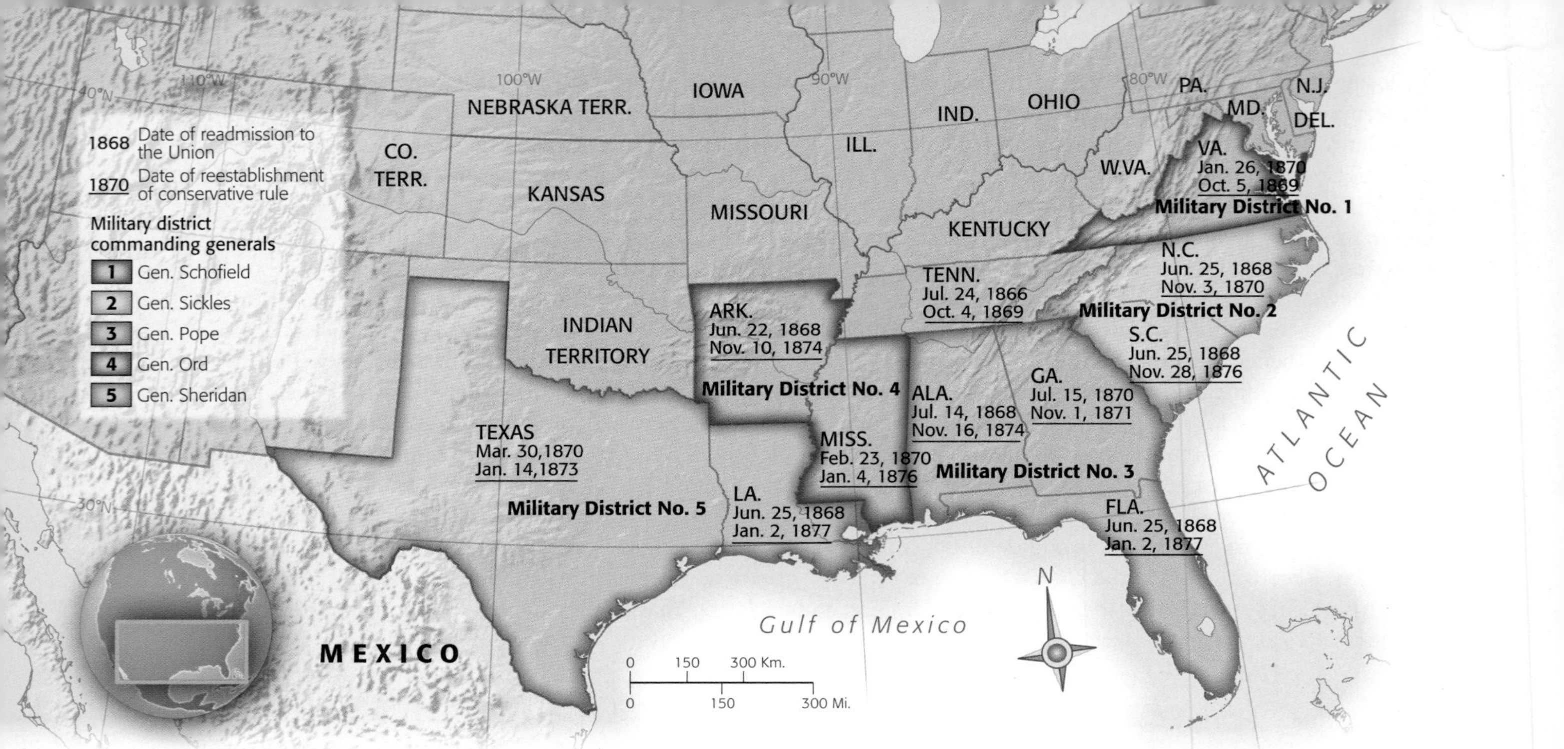

Map 14.1 Course of Reconstruction This map shows the five military districts established when Congress passed the Reconstruction Act of 1867. As the dates within each state indicate, by 1870 all southern states had been readmitted to the Union. Almost immediately, however, conservative Democratic forces began regaining control of state governments, and so-called radical Reconstruction was in retreat. ▲

Reconstruction Act of 1867 rolled back the restoration process begun under Johnson. It divided ten former Confederate states—excluding Tennessee, which ratified the Fourteenth Amendment—into five military districts overseen temporarily by the Union army (see Map 14.1). These states were required to call constitutional conventions with delegates elected by blacks and whites. For states to win readmission to the Union, their new constitutions had to guarantee black men's voting rights, Congress had to approve the new charters, and the states had to ratify the Fourteenth Amendment. Congressional Reconstruction met Republicans' call for freedmen's rights, loyal southern governments, and federal control of the process.

Reconstruction Act of 1867 Legislation that returned former Confederate states to military rule and set conditions for readmission, including new constitutions and ratification of the Fourteenth Amendment.

Tenure of Office Act Law passed in 1867 to prevent Johnson from firing cabinet members without Senate approval.

impeachment Constitutional process of bringing federal officials to trial in the Senate for "high crimes and misdemeanors" that requires a two-thirds vote to remove them from office.

Expecting Johnson to oppose their plans, Republicans passed laws to limit his power. The **Tenure of Office Act**, which prohibited the president from removing cabinet members and other high officials without the Senate's consent, became the focus of conflict. It was designed to protect Secretary of War Edwin Stanton, a Radical Republican who supervised military occupation in the South. Johnson, believing the law unconstitutional, fired Stanton in February 1868. Congress responded immediately by initiating the first **impeachment** of a U.S. president. By a vote of 126 to 47, the House approved eleven articles of impeachment. Nine centered on the Tenure of Office Act; the others accused Johnson of insulting Congress and—the crux of the matter—holding up enforcement of its Reconstruction laws.

In the Senate trial in May 1868, Johnson escaped removal from office by a single vote short of the two-thirds required. A handful of Republicans who held the balance of power hesitated. Some believed that Johnson's political tussling with Congress fell short of the "high crimes and misdemeanors" required by the Constitution. Others distrusted Radical Republican senator Benjamin Wade, who was next in line for the presidency and a crude, combative figure much like Johnson himself.

Johnson remained publicly defiant after his narrow acquittal, granting amnesty to more Confederates and pardons to Jefferson Davis and Robert E. Lee. During the trial, however, Republicans obtained his private promise to accept the Reconstruction Act. The disgrace of impeachment ensured that Johnson would be a one-term president.

14-3b Completion of Congress's Plan

Americans elect Grant and Congress finalizes Reconstruction legislation.

Only six months intervened between Johnson's impeachment trial and the election of 1868. The Republicans turned to Civil War hero Ulysses S. Grant as their nominee. Although he lacked political experience, Grant had won Republicans' respect by eagerly enlisting black soldiers and backing Congress in its dispute with Johnson. The Republican platform, however, placated conservatives by leaving the question of black suffrage in the loyal North to the states. Between 1865 and 1868, white voters in the North had rejected equal suffrage amendments in eight states, passing them only in Iowa and Minnesota.

The Democrats nominated former New York governor Horatio Seymour, who had opposed emancipation and wartime expansion of federal power. The party's platform denounced Congressional Reconstruction as a "military despotism" designed to secure "negro supremacy." The party used openly racist appeals in the North and furtive violence in the South, where the Ku Klux Klan and other white supremacist groups tried to prevent black and white Republicans from voting. Violence succeeded in a few states, including Louisiana, where armed whites negated black voting rights granted by the constitution of 1868 (see this chapter's introduction). But African American votes helped Grant win five southern states, ensuring his strong victory (214 to 80) in the Electoral College.

In February 1869, the Republicans used their large majority in both houses of Congress to impose a new Reconstruction requirement. The **Fifteenth Amendment**, adopted in direct response to voter suppression in the recent election, outlawed denial of the vote "on account of race, color, or previous condition of servitude." The amendment's language left open a loophole for literacy, property, or other restrictions. To boost the amendment's chances, Congress required three as yet unreconstructed states—Mississippi, Texas, and Virginia—to ratify it before readmission.

In February 1870, the Fifteenth Amendment became law. Although its language was not airtight, it was a landmark addition to the Constitution. African American men were guaranteed the vote in states where they had recently been slaves. Ironically, they were also given the vote for the first time in fourteen northern states where racial prejudices remained strong. The amendment's adoption sealed the readmission of all former Confederate states to the Union, almost all with Republican-dominated legislatures. Congressional Republicans had restored the southern states and, they believed, reconstructed southern politics.

In the process, these Republicans expanded the scope and power of the federal government over states in ways that they believed necessary but that many Americans found troubling. Reconstruction continued the nationalizing process begun during the Civil War. In 1870, Democratic politicians and the conservative majority on the Supreme Court began responding by reasserting state prerogatives. Before that, the Court handed congressional Republicans an important victory in *Texas v. White* (1869). The case hinged on the legality of Confederate state war bonds, which the justices invalidated, declaring that the South's unilateral secession had been unconstitutional. It was too late to save seven hundred thousand soldiers' lives, but the ruling codified the Union's victory in law.

14-3c Women's Suffrage and Electoral Reform

Feminists enter voting rights debates in the United States and Great Britain.

The post-Civil War battle in the United States over black voting rights took place at the same time that the British Parliament debated extending suffrage to most male workers. The example of radical Reconstruction influenced Britain's Reform Act of 1867, which lowered property requirements for voting. In both nations, women's rights advocates demanded to be included in electoral reform.

American feminists were angered by the Reconstruction amendments. The Fourteenth Amendment guaranteed voting rights only to male citizens, and the Fifteenth Amendment permitted denial of the vote on grounds of sex. Women's rights advocates, who had actively supported emancipation and the Union, felt betrayed. Elizabeth Cady Stanton vowed to oppose the Fourteenth Amendment unless the word "male" was deleted, but Republican leaders gave priority to racial justice over "the lesser question of sex." Even Frederick Douglass, a longtime women's rights supporter, argued that Reconstruction was "the Negro's hour." Mainstream Republican leaders believed that endorsing female suffrage would jeopardize the immediate task of enfranchising African American men.

Stanton and Susan B. Anthony next opposed the Fifteenth Amendment, whose passage, they claimed, would establish an "aristocracy of sex." By 1869, the dispute over Reconstruction amendments split women's rights advocates into rival organizations. Moderates in the **American Woman Suffrage Association** such as Lucy Stone and Julia Ward Howe cooperated with the Republican Party, supported the Fifteenth Amendment, and focused on winning the vote through state-level campaigns. The more radical **National Woman Suffrage Association**, led by Stanton and Anthony, attacked

Fifteenth Amendment Constitutional addition that became law in 1870, prohibiting states and the federal government from denying the vote on grounds of skin color or prior condition of servitude.

American Woman Suffrage Association Organization formed after women's rights advocates split over the Fifteenth Amendment and that supported black voting rights despite women's exclusion.

National Woman Suffrage Association Organization formed by a splinter group of women's activists who opposed Fourteenth and Fifteenth Amendments and other discriminatory laws.

Women Press Congress for the Vote, 1871 Joined by Susan B. Anthony (second from the right in the foreground), Victoria Woodhull presented a petition to the House Judiciary Committee in January 1871 claiming that the Fourteenth Amendment gave women as citizens the right to vote—an argument that the committee rejected. Woodhull ran for president the following year as the candidate of the Equal Rights Party, becoming the first woman to do so. ◄

discrimination more broadly and pushed for a federal women's suffrage amendment.

Women's suffrage advocates in England watched U.S. developments closely, but they divided over class, not race. Moderates advised winning the vote incrementally beginning with educated and propertied women, whereas radicals pushed immediately for equal rights for all women. Parliament put off the former proposal and roundly rejected the latter in 1867 when the philosopher-politician John Stuart Mill introduced it.

Suffrage advocates won small victories in 1869 and 1870 when two western U.S. territories, Wyoming and Utah, enfranchised women, in part to attract female migrants. Elsewhere the state-by-state strategy met with strong opposition from traditionalists as women's suffrage proposals failed in New York and Kansas. The federal government also proved hostile to gender equality. When Susan B. Anthony voted in the 1872 presidential election, a federal marshal arrested her. Missouri suffragist Virginia Minor, who attempted to follow her example, sued the registrar who had blocked her, claiming that the Fourteenth Amendment's guarantee of citizenship enfranchised women. In ***Minor v. Happersett*** (1875), the Supreme Court ruled that national citizenship did not compel states to grant women the vote. American feminists' defeats during Reconstruction and British feminists' rejection in Parliament indicated that a long struggle would be necessary before the "women's hour" arrived in the Anglo-American world.

14-3d Reconstruction of the Nation's Borders

Union victory expands U.S. territory and influence in North America.

Increased federal power at home under Reconstruction was complemented by reaffirmed U.S. prowess in North America. The Civil War had threatened to remake the continent's borders and reshuffle its deck of players, but U.S. leaders used the Union's victory to restore, and even enhance, the nation's continental preeminence.

Deploying troops freed by the war's end, U.S. officials helped Mexican liberals overthrow the French-imposed regime of Emperor Maximilian (see Chapter 13). Far north of the U.S. border, Americans seized an opportunity to extend the nation's reach into the Pacific by purchasing the vast territory of Alaska from Russia.

The imperial Russian-American Company had attempted to monopolize the fur trade, but it lacked the resources to colonize Alaska or to thwart the westward push of Britain's Hudson's Bay Company across Canada. To keep Alaska out of Britain's hands, Russia offered to sell it to the United States, and Secretary of State William Seward readily agreed. He had long championed a U.S. continental empire, and purchasing Alaska would end one more European power's presence in North America. Confederate attacks on Yankee whaling ships had convinced him that the nation needed advanced outposts in the northern Pacific. In the spring of 1867, the U.S. Senate ratified Seward's treaty, purchasing Alaska for $7.2 million.

Skeptics mocked the **Alaska Purchase** as "Seward's Folly." Although Americans did not organize a territorial government there until 1884, Seward was vindicated when a major gold deposit was discovered in the Yukon in 1896. Meanwhile, Alaska's Aleutian Islands, which stretched twelve hundred miles westward toward Japan, provided a safe harbor for American whaling boats, naval vessels, and merchant ships bound for Asia. For similar reasons, Seward authorized the navy to occupy the uninhabited Midway Islands eleven hundred miles west of Hawai'i in 1867, the nation's first seizure of overseas lands.

Some Americans saw purchasing Alaska as the prelude to annexing British Columbia, which Seward's deal sandwiched between two U.S. landmasses. Officials in

United States Coast Guard

Global Americans One of ten children of Michael Morris Healy, an Irish immigrant planter in Georgia, and his wife, Mary Eliza Smith, a mixed-race African American woman who had been his slave, blue-eyed **Michael Healy** "passed" for white. Because racial intermarriage was illegal in Georgia and the Healy children were technically born into slavery, they were sent to northern states and Canada to be educated in Catholic schools. Most pursued careers in the church, but free-spirited Healy signed aboard a U.S. clipper ship bound for Calcutta. During the Civil War, he entered the U.S. Revenue Marine Service (later the Coast Guard) and in 1868, cruised to the newly purchased Alaska Territory. Soon commanding his own cutter, Healy represented the U.S. government in Alaska for two decades, informally called "king" but acting as policeman, judge, rescuer, and medical officer to whaling crews, merchant seamen, and Alaskan natives. In the 1880s, Healy took the renowned naturalist John Muir on several scientific voyages. When commercial fishermen overhunted seals and whales, Healy steamed to Russia's Siberian coast and returned with herds of reindeer, which became an essential source of food and clothing for Alaska natives. "Hell Roaring Mike" was a hard drinker and larger-than-life figure, beloved and feared by subordinates and recognized as the dominant U.S. authority on the North Pacific rim. Not until Healy died in 1904 did his African American ancestry become public knowledge.

Canada eyed the United States suspiciously, aware of Americans' annexationist dreams and fearing reprisals for Canadian aid to Confederates. British Canadians were alarmed when the **Fenians**, a secret brotherhood pledged to promote Irish nationhood, launched raids in 1866 across the U.S. border intended to dismember Britain's empire. Joined by hundreds of Irish-American Union veterans, the Fenians aspired to conquer Canada and exchange it with England for Ireland's independence.

When Britain captured two Irish-American Fenians and charged them with treason, Congress responded with the Expatriation Act (1868), which denied other countries' claims that naturalized U.S. citizens still owed them allegiance. This law and the **Bancroft treaties** that the United States signed with dozens of foreign countries after 1868 struck a decisive blow for voluntary citizenship against the feudal doctrine of "perpetual allegiance" to monarchs. The same conflict underlay the impressment controversy that had sparked the War of 1812, but increased naval power allowed U.S. naturalization policies to prevail after the Civil War.

In response to threats from Fenians and U.S. annexationists, Britain took steps to unite its Canadian colonies under a single government. The **British North America Act** of 1867 created a federal Dominion of Canada that stretched from the Maritime Provinces to western Ontario, and four years later to British Columbia. Confederation was designed to fortify Canada against U.S. pressure to invade or annex it and to take the Civil War's lesson that a stronger government might prevent internal secessions.

Tensions over Canada added to difficult Anglo-American negotiations over Civil War damages. Americans recalled the wartime attacks on Union ships by the *Alabama* and other Confederate raiders built in Britain, and some demanded Canadian territory as reparation. Claims and counterclaims hummed over the undersea transatlantic cable, which, ironically, had begun operating in 1866 with friendly telegrams between Queen Victoria and President Johnson. Eventually, diplomats moderated their demands, and in 1871, the two nations signed the **Treaty of Washington**. The *Alabama* claims and others were submitted to a five-nation arbitration commission, which awarded the United States $15.5 million and England about half that sum. The treaty also resolved a standoff over the San Juan Islands, which occupied the Puget Sound between Vancouver Island and the Pacific Coast. This final U.S.–Canada boundary settlement fixed the northern U.S. border and put to rest the question of annexation.

Minor v. Happersett Supreme Court decision declaring that citizenship rights were separate from voting rights and used by states to justify outlawing women's suffrage.

Alaska Purchase U.S. acquisition of Alaska Territory from Russia, designed to promote continental expansion and overseas trade.

Fenians Members of an Irish republican organization founded in the United States whose raids into Canada in 1866 aimed to coerce Ireland's independence from Britain.

Bancroft treaties Agreements between the United States and other nations signed after 1868 that recognized naturalized citizens as long as they resided in their new countries.

British North America Act Parliamentary law creating the federal Dominion of Canada from three British colonies to strengthen transcontinental ties and fend off U.S. expansion.

Treaty of Washington Pact that fixed the U.S.–Canadian border and addressed claims for Civil War damages between Britain and the United States.

MOTHER BRITANNIA.—" Take care, my child!"
UNCLE SAM.—" Oh! never mind, if she falls I'll catch her!"

McCord Museum

Canadian Confederation In this British cartoon of 1870, Mother Britannia exults that her child Canada can stand alone, while Uncle Sam urges "Oh! Never mind, if she falls I'll catch her!" The image reflects British anxiety about potential U.S. annexation of Canada after the Civil War, which might be disguised as economic assistance or protection against foreign "interference." ◄

14-4

Reconstruction and Resistance in the South

This lithograph, entitled *The First Vote,* was published in a northern magazine in 1867. It pictures the uniquely American—although temporary—postemancipation enforcement of equal political rights for former slaves under the terms of Congressional Reconstruction.

Whom does the artist portray as representative African American male voters in the South? Which party would they likely support? Why are they under an American flag? What problems might voting in public view create? ►

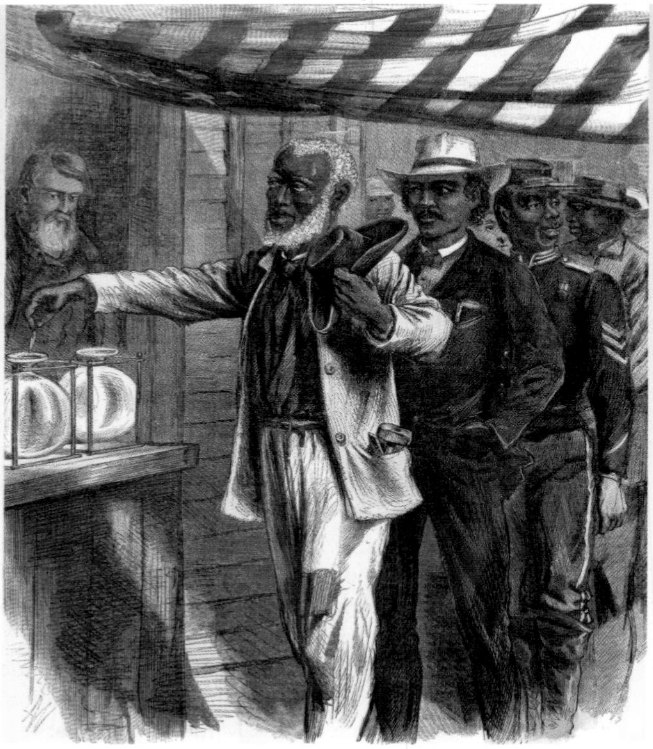

North Wind Picture Archives/Alamy Stock Photo

Many Northerners were confident that with new laws and constitutional amendments, the South was being reconstructed as well as restored to the Union. Southerners, however, knew that a long struggle lay ahead. Ex-slaves and former masters argued over access to land and terms of labor, evolving the compromise system of sharecropping. Relying heavily on black voters, the South's Republican Party built a coalition that formed new state governments and enacted programs for education and economic development. But white Southerners refused to accept the Republican regimes and their challenge to the old order. Mobilizing through the Democratic Party and violent paramilitary groups, angry whites fought to reverse Reconstruction's gains for blacks and retake political control.

☞ As you read, consider the key issues under dispute in the postwar South. What important changes did Reconstruction bring to the South's politics and society? How were these changes contested and eventually reversed?

14-4a Transition to Sharecropping

The majority of the South's freed people aspired to become independent farmers, but this was a dream deferred. By 1867, federal authorities had restored almost all confiscated lands to planters, and several land redistribution bills had died in Congress. The **Southern Homestead Act** of 1866, modeled on the earlier national law, gave African Americans and loyal whites access to public lands in five states in plots of eighty or one hundred sixty acres. The law was not well publicized, however, and the acreage was often unsuitable for tilling. In the end, only a thousand free blacks were granted land certificates.

Postwar land and labor systems limit freed people's rise.

In some areas, the number of black farm workers dwindled to half its prewar total because freedmen migrated elsewhere and freedwomen withdrew from fieldwork. To relieve the shortage, southern states established agencies to encourage immigration. But as the result of local prejudices against Asian and Caribbean immigrants and opposition by the federal government, the effort to import cheap substitutes for the South's former slaves floundered.

Gradually, **sharecropping** and other forms of tenant farming evolved as the most widespread alternative to wage labor for freed people or contracts for imported workers. Landlords divided plantations into parcels of twenty-five to fifty acres, allowing families to settle on the land. In return, the owner received a share of the annual crop, usually half (see Map 14.2). In tenant farming, a variant that involved more poor whites than blacks, households received the crop's proceeds but used them to pay rent and to reimburse the landlord for the outlay of equipment and animals.

Southern Homestead Act Legislation that opened public lands in the South for settlement by free blacks and loyal whites initially, and later all Southerners, but was repealed in 1876.

sharecropping System of tenant farming by which renters worked a plot of land in return for paying half or more of the crop to landlords.

crop-lien system Legal restriction by which landlords and other creditors asserted priority rights to tenant farmers' crops.

In theory, sharecropping and tenant farming represented a reasonable compromise between planters and former slaves. Planters gave up daily supervision of freedmen, who lived in separate cottages and set their own hours. Freed people rented land but hoped to accrue enough crop surpluses to buy their own farm. Both parties avoided outlays of cash, which was in short supply in the South. In practice, sharecroppers and tenants got the short end of the bargain. Unscrupulous landlords raised rents, cheated in weighing the crop, or evicted independent-minded tenants. Rural merchants (often planters themselves) advanced food, clothing, and other supplies to tenants on credit at interest rates as high as 50 percent. Under the **crop-lien system**, the landlord and merchant secured their

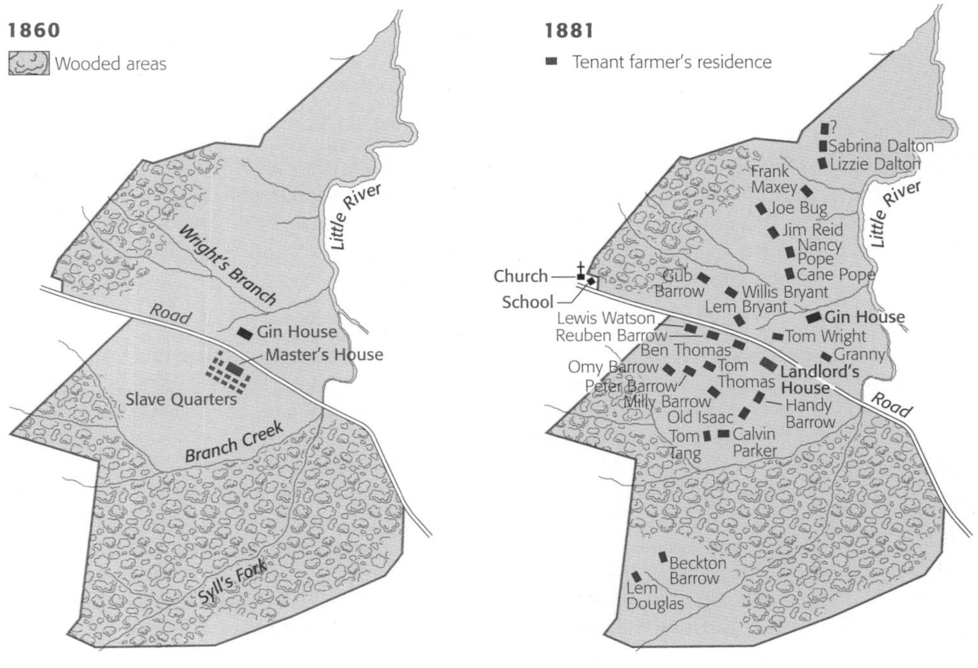

Map 14.2 From Plantation to Sharecropping Maps of the Barrow plantation in Georgia in 1860 and 1881 illustrate the postwar transformation of southern agriculture. In 1860, about one hundred thirty-five slaves lived in quarters behind the master's house. After the Civil War and a brief interlude of growing cotton for wages, freed people moved to cottages on rented farms of twenty-five to thirty acres on plantation lands. The former master had become their landlord. Note the presence of some female-headed households as well as a church and school established by African Americans. ◀

History without Borders

After Slavery: Debt Bondage in Sugar and Cotton

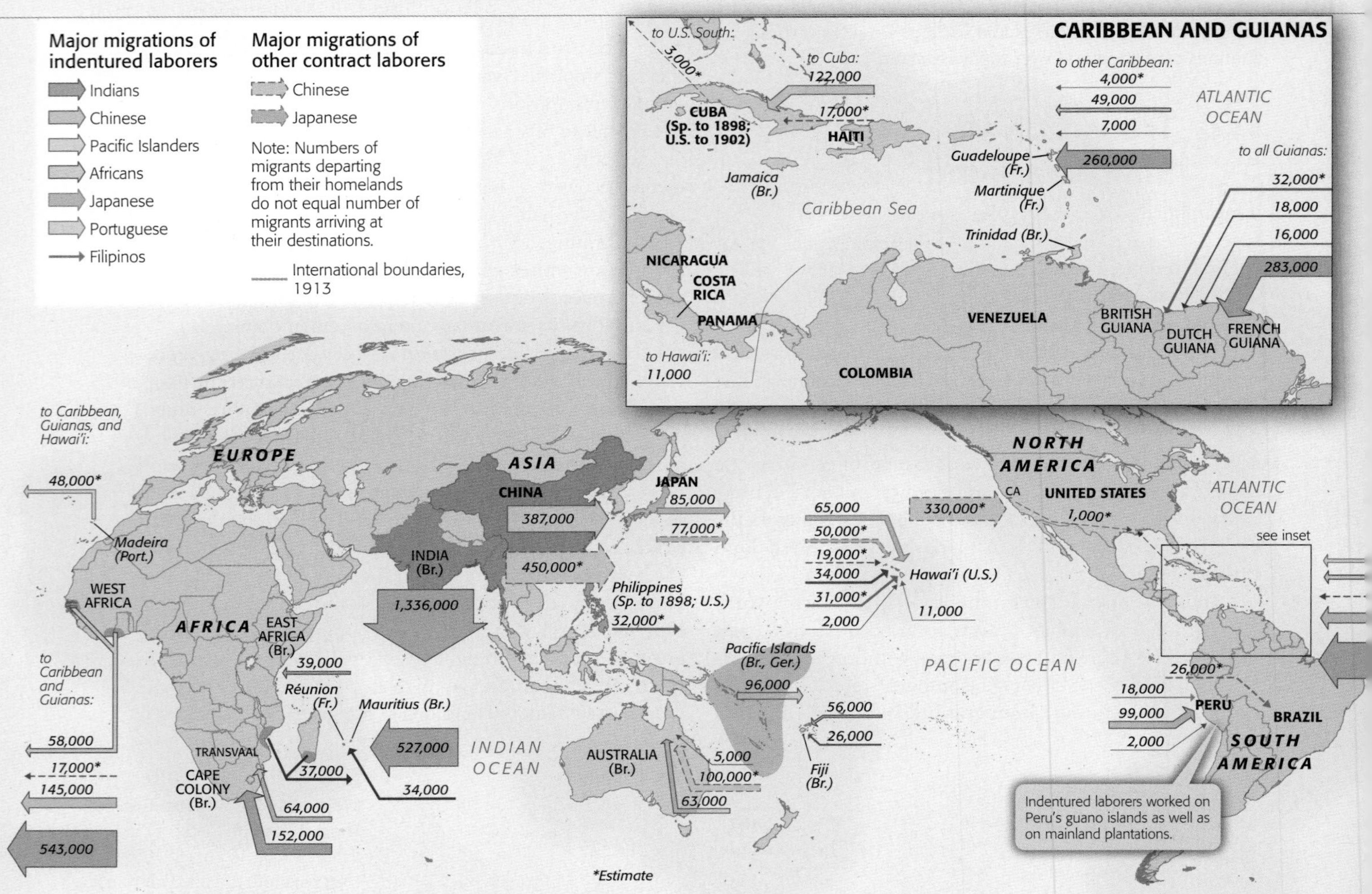

Major Overseas Indentured Migrations, 1834–1919 Millions of workers from Asia, Africa, and the South Pacific were recruited overseas to replace emancipated slaves. Some were bound by strict indenture agreements while others worked under simple wage contracts. Whereas the majority of indentured laborers from Africa and Asia harvested sugar and similar plantation crops, other migrant workers were employed building railroads in the United States, mining gold in South Africa, or shoveling guano (valuable as fertilizer) in Peru. ▲

For millions of agricultural workers across several continents, the abolition of slavery led not to prosperity but to a subtler form of bondage based on indebtedness rather than ownership of persons. Looking for ways to boost production after emancipation, planters and merchants tied to the growing global market for cash crops created new forms of dependent labor.

To replace newly freed slaves, sugar planters worldwide recruited contract laborers from Asia, Africa, and the South Pacific. Great Britain opened the trade for *coolies* (a Tamil-origin term for hirelings) to its Indian Ocean sugar islands in 1834. As slave emancipation spread, Indian laborers were sent to Fiji and South Africa to harvest sugar, and Chinese and Japanese migrants worked in Caribbean sugar fields. The first Chinese contract workers arrived in Hawai'i in 1852, and within thirty years, they made up half of the sugar plantation workforce. Altogether, more than 1 million contract laborers were recruited to harvest sugar between 1865 and 1885.

Customary indenture contracts compelled these workers to work for several years and repay the cost of their voyage. In practice, this arrangement was often brutal, and workers had little legal recourse. Some of them were kidnapped or coerced to sign contracts, and many never earned enough to pay off their debt. Such conditions and planters'

Historic New Orleans Collection

Chinese Contract Laborers in Louisiana
In 1867, hundreds of Chinese laborers were brought from Cuba to Louisiana to harvest sugar cane. Some cotton farmers were eager to follow suit to boost production and reassert white supremacy. "Give us five million Chinese laborers in the valley of the Mississippi," wrote a planter's wife, "and we can furnish the world with cotton and teach the negro his proper place." ◄

Universal History Archive/Getty Images

Cotton Cultivators in Egypt In this 1873 illustration, Egyptian farm workers deliver cotton in bags to a mercantile house, where it is weighed before packing and shipment overseas. By the 1870s, large landowners, small farmers, and tenants expanded Egypt's and India's cotton exports to more than triple their pre-Civil War total. But many peasant cultivators incurred debts to local moneylenders, suffered from declining cotton prices, and lacked access to food crops, resulting in regional food shortages and even famines. ◄

use of impoverished Asian workers to replace African slaves in tropical lands led critics to charge that a new form of racial slavery had emerged. When abuses were publicized and local protests erupted against "coolie labor," Britain and the United States restricted its trade in the 1880s. Latin American governments gradually followed, but the practice continued in modified forms elsewhere into the twentieth century.

Cotton growers chose a different option. During and after the Civil War, production of cotton went global, stimulated initially by the Confederacy's cutoff of shipments. Around the world, farm workers aspired to become growers and shunned picking cotton for wages. In contrast to sugar, cotton was increasingly produced by cultivators who worked their own small farms or rented land using family labor and outside capital.

In the U.S. South, planters and former slaves developed the sharecropping system, which dominated cotton production. In other lands, tenants and small farmers predominated and financial elites encouraged them to abandon subsistence crops to grow cotton for the world market. In India and Brazil, farmers used advances from European capitalists and local merchants to plant cotton. After 1860, cotton exports from India, Brazil, and Egypt increased dramatically. But whether they were landowners, sharecroppers, or tenants, small farmers depended on merchants and landlords, who were backed by harsh lien laws. Vulnerable to price fluctuations, subject to punitive laws, and politically marginalized, small cotton growers were technically free but often trapped in debt.

To indentured sugar workers and small cotton farmers, the postemancipation global economy appeared to offer opportunities for advancement. But the global market's demands for commodities and profits translated into new forms of exploitation. Historians disagree when comparing migrant contract laborers to slaves, but most agree that indentures often led to agricultural "debt bondage." The United Nations Supplementary Convention on the Abolition of Slavery outlawed indentured labor in 1956. The practice continues, however, in South Asia, and the recent wave of globalization has resulted in the rise of other varieties of forced migrant labor.

Critical Thinking Questions

► How did the abolition of slavery transform global sugar and cotton production? What factors led to the establishment of indentured migrants and tenant farmers as dependent farm laborers?

► In what ways was agricultural debt bondage similar to slavery? How was it different?

Carpetbaggers Derisive term for Northerners who moved to the South after the Civil War and became active Republicans and whom southern Democrats saw as interlopers.

Scalawags Derogatory term for white Southerners who backed the Republican Party during Reconstruction and were marked as turncoats by southern Democrats.

advances by placing a legal claim on the farmer's next crop. The system guaranteed payouts for creditors but not their victims, and most tenants and sharecroppers fell into chronic debt.

By 1880, the division of plantations into tenant and sharecropping tracts encompassed the majority of farms in the cotton belt and nearly three-quarters of the South's black farmers. Because lienholders made borrowers grow cotton, which was easy to sell, the South's small farmers turned from diversified or subsistence farming to growing a single crop for the national and global market. Cotton production recovered to surpass prewar levels, but prices declined (see Table 14.1). Caught in a perfect storm of low cotton prices, spiraling debt, and reduced access to food crops, the South's freed people saw their dreams of economic independence fade. By the end of Reconstruction, few black sharecroppers had graduated to owning their own farms.

Table 14.1 U.S. Cotton Production and Exports, 1860–1880

After severe wartime declines and the adjustment to tenant farming and sharecropping, the South's production of cotton recovered in the mid-1870s to surpass prewar levels. U.S. cotton exports gradually approached their pre-Civil War share of the global market. At the same time, prices fell to half the immediate postwar level.

Year	Cotton Produced (Thousands of Bales)	Price (Cents per Pound)	U.S Share of British Cotton Imports (Percentage)
1860	3,841	12	80
1861	4,491	15	65
1862	1,597	30	4
1863	449	51	8
1864	299	53	9
1865	2,094	45	20
1866	2,097	25	38
1867	2,520	20	42
1868	2,366	16	43
1869	3,011	19	38
1870	4,352	18	54
1871	2,974	13	49
1872	3,933	15	35
1873	4,168	14	47
1874	3,836	13	49
1875	4,631	13	50
1876	4,474	12	57
1877	4,773	11	62
1878	5,074	12	73
1879	5,756	11	71
1880	6,606	12	71

14-4b Republican Governments in the South

Fragile Republican Party coalitions bring change to reconstructed southern states.

Freed people's political status improved under Congressional Reconstruction. Between 1867 and 1869, all states in the former Confederacy adopted new constitutions as required by Congress. These charters brought progressive changes to the South's electoral system, but the Republican coalitions that won the first statewide elections found it difficult to forge a common platform and even harder to win acceptance from southern whites.

The coalition was made up of three groups. **Carpetbaggers**, or transplanted Northerners, were caricatured by southern whites as transient opportunists, but most contradicted the stereotype. Their numbers included former Union soldiers who stayed in the South after the war along with businessmen, Freedmen's Bureau agents, and teachers. **Scalawags**, another derisive name invented by political opponents, were southern whites who joined the Republicans. Some were small farmers who had been wartime Unionists, others represented the South's business and financial elites, and a few others were planters who wagered that cooperating with Republicans was the best route to postwar recovery or personal gain.

African Americans were the third and by far the largest component of the South's Republican alliance. Their votes were essential for the party to control state governments. After the ordeal of slavery and years of political mobilization, they were eager to participate. "It is the hardest thing in the world to keep a negro away from the polls," a white Alabamian admitted as he watched former slaves respond to voter registration drives.

White Southerners opposed to Reconstruction stigmatized it as "Negro Rule." Taken literally, this charge was exaggerated. Fourteen blacks served during Reconstruction in the U.S. Congress and two in the Senate. South Carolina had a black majority in its House of Representatives, led by former slave and Union naval hero Robert Smalls. Yet African Americans held no major offices in Alabama, Georgia, North Carolina, or Texas. Despite providing four-fifths of the South's Republican votes, blacks received less than one-fifth of the offices, mostly local positions. Carpetbaggers and scalawags were determined to dominate Reconstruction politics.

If Reconstruction was not "negro rule," it was still a startling reversal of status for blacks and whites. Black mayors, sheriffs, town councilmen, and justices of the peace ran many small southern communities. Perhaps most galling to former Confederates, African Americans dominated the state militias called out to suppress local riots and protect black voting rights. The rise of the Ku Klux Klan and other white supremacist groups created an increasingly militarized environment, and there were not enough federal troops to patrol the entire South.

Beset by violent white opponents, the South's Republican Party also suffered internal tensions. Party supporters had divergent agendas. Moderates courted southern whites by promoting compromise whereas radicals relied on black voters. Yankee carpetbaggers pushed to modernize the South's economy while freedmen concentrated on voting rights, debt relief, and public schools. Poor whites sought economic relief but opposed racial integration. Each group had to make concessions, but all came to realize that most white Southerners would never join the Republicans. The party's continued rule depended on the national government.

While they lobbied for federal support, Republican leaders in the South enacted important changes in civil rights, public welfare, and economic development. New state laws empowered African American men to serve on juries and in police and fire departments. Reorganized southern states built public orphan and insane asylums and enacted laws against child abuse. Continuing the assault on illiteracy begun by freedmen's schools, Republican regimes set up public educational systems in every state in the South. Black leaders accepted segregated schools, often reluctantly, as the price for this improvement. Despite substandard facilities and shortages of funds, the literacy rate in 1875 among southern blacks had risen to more than 30 percent, three times the figure at the war's end. Educational gains were the most notable achievement of Republican rule in the South.

Republicans' economic programs were less successful. Seeking to diversify the South's economy and expand its markets, white Republican leaders chartered hundreds of new banks and encouraged construction of factories. Above all, state leaders promoted railroads, believing them an almost magical key to prosperity. According to one Tennessee Republican, "a free and living Republic [will] spring up in the track of the railroad . . . as surely as grass and flowers follow in the spring." Track mileage increased by 40 percent, a pace that outran farmers' needs and saddled state governments with huge debts.

Generous charters and subsidies for bonds led to a building spree. The construction boom overwhelmed southern state budgets. Republican lawmakers addressed deficits by raising taxes to levels unseen in the tax-hating prewar South. Soaring tax bills alienated landowners already reeling from the loss of $2.4 billion in slave "property" and spurred charges of waste and corruption. Some southern states had honest governments, but in others, such as South Carolina, Louisiana, and Florida, bribery, embezzlement, and profiteering were rampant. Political corruption was probably no more prevalent in the postwar South than in the North, but it lent a strong impetus to southern Democrats and others determined to end Republican rule.

14-4c Conservative White Resurgence

Using politics and terror, southern Democrats restore white supremacy.

The high taxes and blatant corruption of some Republican regimes gave southern Democrats potent campaign issues. In reality, they had never considered Republicans legitimate participants in the South's politics. Many white Southerners saw Reconstruction as a foreign occupation, with the former slaves controlled by white Republicans who ruled with the backing of nearby federal troops.

Such attitudes sanctioned any form of resistance, from ballots to bullets. If policy differences failed to rouse the white public, racial hatred worked. Just as a shared belief in white supremacy had united prewar slaveholders and nonslaveholding whites, postwar Democrats used race baiting and violence to energize white voters. Violence against African Americans escalated as former slaves entered politics and served in local militias. White paramilitary groups spread spontaneously to punish "uppity" African Americans, sometimes after false accusations that they had raped or dishonored white women. The

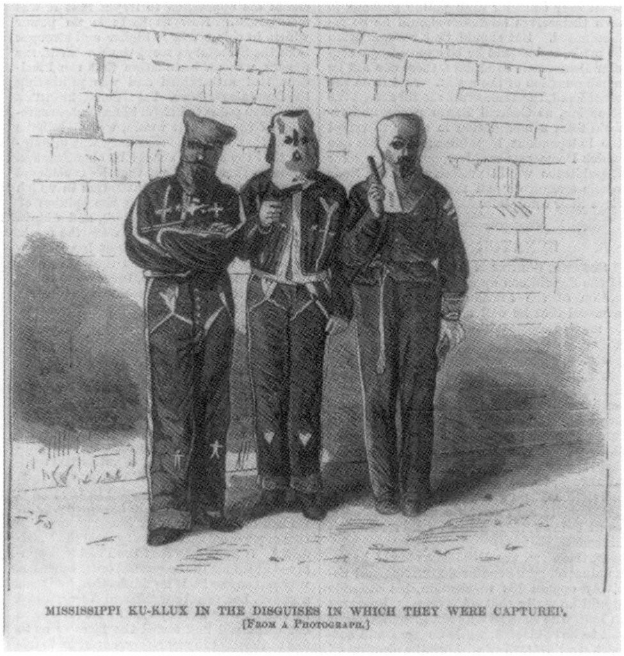

MISSISSIPPI KU-KLUX IN THE DISGUISES IN WHICH THEY WERE CAPTURED.
[FROM A PHOTOGRAPH.]

Library of Congress Prints and Photographs Division

Ku Klux Klan in Mississippi, 1871 Mississippi Klan members pose for a photograph in the disguises they wore when they were arrested by federal authorities for attempted murder. None is wearing a pointed hood or white clothes, regalia that the Klan adopted in the early twentieth century. Enforcement of federal anti-Klan laws in the early 1870s netted hundreds of arrests, but violent resistance to black voting and office holding persisted among a variety of secret white supremacist organizations in the South. ▲

Redeemers Self-description of southern Democrats who rebelled against Reconstruction and restored Democratic rule and white dominance in the 1870s.

convict lease system Legal practice of hiring out convicts to employers for low wages that was combined with vagrancy laws to reduce many black Southerners to semislaves.

Ku Klux Klan, the most notorious of these groups, conducted night raids clad in costumed disguise, murdering dozens of blacks and several white Republican leaders before Congress sanctioned a campaign against it.

The Klan and its imitators served as the terrorist wing of the South's Democratic Party. Other Democrats adopted more subtle means of controlling black voters. In an era before the secret ballot, the party supervised polling places to identify Republican voters as potential targets of intimidation or retaliation. Employers required workers to sign contracts barring participation in political meetings, and landlords threatened politically active tenants with eviction.

One by one, southern states fell to conservative Democrats, who called themselves **Redeemers**. The counterrevolution succeeded first in 1869 in Virginia and Tennessee, upper South states whose black population was too small to sustain Republican electoral victories. In the Deep South, more violence was required to suppress Republican voters. In 1875, the White Line movement in Mississippi mobilized Democratic supporters to break up Republican meetings, patrol voter registration sites, and march in military formation through black neighborhoods. Republican governors hesitated to call out black-dominated state militias to restore order, fearing it would enrage whites further or spark all-out race war. By 1876, the Democrats had toppled Republican regimes in all but three Deep South states.

Redeemer governments wasted no time in their effort to erase Reconstruction. Once in power, southern Democrats slashed taxes on land and state spending on schools and social services. Poll taxes, long-term residency requirements, and other restrictions not expressly forbidden by the Fifteenth Amendment were adopted to curtail black voting. Unable to reverse constitutional emancipation, the South's Democrats employed an arsenal of legal tactics to "re-enslave the colored race," as Texas Republicans charged in 1876. Toughened criminal codes restricted hunting and fishing and meted out prison terms for trespassing or petty theft. Redeemer legislators revived the Black Codes' vagrancy laws to imprison unemployed or loitering blacks. From overcrowded prisons, the **convict lease system** rented black inmates to private contractors for work on chain gangs harvesting crops, mining coal, or building railroads. Conditions were so bad that death tolls among prisoners averaged 15 percent annually and reached 41 percent in Alabama in 1870. Protesting this system, a Tennessee convention of freedmen in 1875 called it a "condition of servitude scarcely less degrading than that endured before the late civil war."

14-5 Abandonment of Reconstruction

Frank Leslie's Illustrated Newspaper. Image courtesy of Wikimedia.

A series of scandals damaged Grant's presidency. In the Crédit Mobilier affair, U.S. lawmakers accepted shares of stock for allowing payments to a phony railroad company. None were charged with crimes. In this cartoon, Uncle Sam, backed by public opinion, directs senators implicated in the scheme to commit hari-kari, or ritual suicide. In Japanese tradition, when a person is condemned to hari-kari, the victim's best friend stands by to complete the work.

Why would the cartoonist suggest suicide as the appropriate fictional punishment for the Crédit Mobilier conspirators? Why is Senator Roscoe Conkling, a spokesman for Grant, shown unsheathing a sword? How might Americans have learned about hari-kari in this era? ▶

White Southerners' violent return to power succeeded in part because Northerners abandoned their commitment to Reconstruction. After a decade of turmoil, many Northerners were impatient to leave the "Southern question" behind. Northern voters were preoccupied by the booms and busts of the national economy, distracted by overseas adventures, and frustrated by the difficulty of transforming southern ways. The Republicans were weakened by corruption and factionalism within their party and joined voters in turning against Reconstruction. The contested presidential election of 1876 completed the process by which the former Confederate states were restored without being truly reconstructed.

☞ As you read, consider the impact that political changes and economic fluctuations had on the federal government's enforcement of Reconstruction. What factors, attitudes, and events led Northerners to abandon Reconstruction?

14-5a "Grantism" and the Gilded Age

Political scandals and unchecked corporate influence herald a new era.

Grant moved into the White House pledging both to uphold Congressional Reconstruction and to restore sectional peace. This agenda was daunting and perhaps contradictory. Grant made a good-faith effort to assist embattled freed people in the South and even to reform federal Indian policy, but his prospects were hurt by the growing taint of fraud and corruption that surrounded his administration.

To sustain black voting rights, Grant worked hard to pass the Fifteenth Amendment, whose adoption he believed "the most important political event since the nation came into life." To protect Native Americans from further dispossession and bring peace to federal-Indian relations, Grant overhauled reservation appointments and policies (see Chapter 15). Finally, to atone for his notorious wartime order expelling Jews (whom he stigmatized as cotton speculators) from his military district on the Mississippi River, he appointed several prominent Jews to government positions.

Yet Grant made serious mistakes with other appointments. Although scrupulously honest as a soldier, he had a lower standard concerning civilians. Some of his advisees and cabinet members were mediocre men, bumbling relatives, and wartime cronies to whom Grant remained loyal after their incompetence or deceptions were exposed.

Partly as a result, a string of scandals weakened his administration and fixed the label "Grantism" on political corruption. On "Black Friday" in September 1869, the price of gold plummeted after financier Jay Gould and his partner Jim Fisk tried to corner the market. They had involved Grant's brother-in-law in the scheme. In 1872, Grant's vice president, Schuyler Colfax, was reportedly among the thirty federal officeholders given shares in **Crédit Mobilier**, a phony construction company formed by the directors of the Union Pacific Railroad to multiply profits. Colfax was dropped from the Republican ticket that year, but the scandals continued. Grant's private secretary Orville Babcock was indicted in 1875 for allowing federal agents to accept bribes from whiskey distillers to avoid excise taxes. The next year, a House investigation revealed that Grant's secretary of war, William Belknap, sold rights to trading posts in Indian Territory. He was impeached, but Grant allowed him to resign to avoid conviction. Grant's later cabinet appointees were able men who attacked corruption in the Interior, Treasury, and Justice Departments. But the damage to the president's relationship with Congress and the public had already been done.

The wave of scandals in railroads, finance, and government contracts showed that opportunities for illicit gain were legion during the postwar era's surge of economic growth. Industrial production nearly doubled during Reconstruction as did the number of workers in manufacturing and construction. Railroads, lavishly subsidized by federal and state governments, reached from coast to coast and incorporated new southern lines. The National Mineral Act of 1866 granted mining companies free access to millions of acres of public land.

To gain subsidies, win contracts, and avoid regulation, promoters of railroads and oil and mining corporations wooed politicians with shares of stock, appointments to boards, or outright bribes. Ethical standards were low and conflict of interest laws nonexistent. One wag wrote that John D. Rockefeller of the Standard Oil Company could do everything he wanted with the Pennsylvania legislature except refine it. Republican leaders increasingly catered to big business interests instead of tending to farmers' aspirations or freed peoples' rights.

Republicans were not alone in pocketing cash. The nation's mushrooming cities provided enticing opportunities for politicians who awarded contracts or distributed patronage. Many big-city bosses ran **political machines**. In New York City, Democratic boss William M. Tweed and his ring of operatives stole tens of millions of dollars from the city treasury through embezzlement, inflated contracts, and bribes. Tweed's headquarters, **Tammany Hall**, became a national byword for corrupt city government. One Tammany leader's epitaph, "I seen my opportunities and I took 'em," could serve as a motto for the frenzied speculation and flagrant corruption of an era that novelist Mark Twain and his coauthor Charles Dudley Warner labeled the **Gilded Age**.

Crédit Mobilier Grant administration scandal in which railroad companies generated fraudulent profits and distributed shares of stock to government accomplices.

political machine Powerful political organization in which a party boss or elite rewards loyal supporters with jobs, money, or contracts, often acquired illegally.

Tammany Hall New York City's Democratic Party political machine, named after its headquarters and controlled by Boss William M. Tweed from 1869 to 1873.

Gilded Age Term coined in 1873 to critique an era of political corruption and economic inequality that stretched to 1900.

14-5b Influence and Opportunities Overseas

As postwar business booms, Americans seek influence in Latin America and Asia.

As Reconstruction waned, American policy makers refocused on gaining markets and raw materials in Latin America and strengthening

Virginia Baptist Historical Society.

Global Americans Born into a family of wealthy Virginia planters, **Charlotte "Lottie" Moon** and her sisters were given an unusually fine education. At first a nonbeliever, she underwent a religious awakening at age eighteen through revivals on her college campus. During the Civil War, Moon took teaching positions at various Virginia schools; after the war, she settled into a teaching career but felt called to overseas missionary work. Treaties with China opened the country to foreign missionaries, and in 1872, the Southern Baptists reversed their policy against sending single women abroad. The next year, Moon left for the treaty port of Tengchow, beginning a forty-year ministry in China. In 1885, she gave up teaching and evangelized full-time in China's interior. During her missionary career, Moon faced famine, plague, revolution, and war and responded with practical assistance to natives. (Here she is shown with students in Japan after fleeing China's Boxer Rebellion.) Moon's time in Asia coincided with renewed U.S. overseas expansionism after the Civil War and enlarged public roles for women. By 1900, 60 percent of American overseas missionaries were women. Missionaries spread Western religion and middle-class values, believing them superior to native peoples' ways. Moon advocated a similar paternalism of racial "uplift" for southern blacks. But Moon and other U.S. missionaries also fostered women's education abroad, introduced Americans to other cultures, and sometimes criticized colonial policies.

the nation's position in the Caribbean. Yet the issues of slavery and race continued to influence U.S. policies in complex ways. On the one hand, emancipation hastened the end of bondage in two New World societies where plantation slavery still thrived. In 1866, Emperor Dom Pedro II suggested that Brazil consider abolishing slavery, and five years later, a law declared that the children of slaves born thereafter would be freed. The Thirteenth Amendment also energized abolitionists in Cuba, many of whom sought U.S. assistance in winning the island's independence from Spain. On the other hand, Reconstruction disputes often spilled into foreign affairs, and motives of national interest competed with moral considerations in the struggle to define U.S. diplomacy.

Grant proved an inconsistent champion of both U.S. expansion and local freedom struggles in the Caribbean. Shortly after acquiring Alaska from Russia, Secretary of State Seward negotiated a treaty to purchase for $7.5 million two islands of the Danish West Indies (later called the *Virgin Islands*) to be used as naval stations. But President-elect Grant was hostile and the U.S. Senate, hounded by critics of the Alaska deal and preoccupied with the Johnson impeachment crisis, refused to act.

When Cuban colonists rose up against Spanish rule in 1868, Grant favored assisting them, but he feared war with Spain or a costly diversion from Reconstruction. Guided by cautious Secretary of State Hamilton Fish, Grant called the revolt "premature," accepted Spanish rule, and urged Madrid to adopt reforms. Even when Spain seized a hired American ship that transported supplies to the rebels and executed fifty-three persons aboard, the United States remained a bystander. The Ten Years' War, the Cuban struggle for independence and emancipation, ended in 1878. Spain freed slaves who had fought in the war (but not others) and enacted financial reforms but maintained its colonial rule. Not until 1886 did Spain decree freedom for all of Cuba's slaves. Some Cuban rebels, including the young nationalist writer José Martí, refused to surrender and continued plotting from U.S. soil to free their homeland.

Burlingame Treaty U.S.–China pact promoting cooperation that recognized China's territorial sovereignty and rights of Chinese immigrants except for U.S. citizenship.

Although Grant hesitated over Cuba, he made strenuous efforts to acquire the small Caribbean republic of Santo Domingo (later the Dominican Republic), whose corrupt president, Buenaventura Báez, was willing to exchange annexation for debt relief. The U.S. navy, eager for Caribbean bases, coveted the island's protected Samaná Bay. Grant believed that the tropical land could become a refuge for the South's persecuted freed people, and he convinced Frederick Douglass that this would increase southern blacks' leverage at home. But opposition arose from many sides. U.S. newspapers derided the project as a financial risk, and some warned against "adding to our population nearly a million of creoles and West Indian negroes." Charles Sumner, Republican chair of the Senate Foreign Relations Committee, opposed annexation as the plot of unsavory speculators and a threat to neighboring Haiti. When the annexation treaty came before the Senate in June 1870, it fell short of the necessary two-thirds approval.

Across the Pacific, the reunified United States continued to seek trade concessions similar to those won by aggressive European powers. U.S. diplomacy veered between conciliation and force. The nation's minister to China, Radical Republican Anson Burlingame, saw parallels between Reconstruction's program of racial equality at home and respect for Asian peoples abroad. The **Burlingame Treaty**, ratified in 1868, recognized China's control of its territory and declared discriminatory anti-Chinese legislation in California illegal. But it did not remove the ban on naturalizing Chinese immigrants to the United States, and it reaffirmed the rights of American missionaries to China granted ten years earlier.

In Japan, the United States again sought a leading role, although the Civil War limited its ability to enforce the unequal treaties of the 1850s. Subdued by a flotilla of European ships that included a lone U.S. gunboat, Japan's Shogun agreed in 1864 to pay indemnities and allow Westerners access to local traders. Popular resentment of this national humiliation helped precipitate the Shogun's overthrow in the **Meiji Restoration** of 1868. Asserting power over samurai warriors and regional lords, the young emperor Meiji and his ministers embarked on a crash program to modernize Japan by abolishing feudal privileges, developing industry, and creating an efficient government bureaucracy.

Americans viewed this revolution as a potential bonanza for U.S. producers and traders, but the Japanese were determined to copy modern industrial methods without becoming subject to Western domination. During a seven-month "knowledge-seeking" mission to the United States in 1873, Japanese envoys paid special attention to new technologies and political reforms. Disappointed American political humorist Finley Peter Dunne complained through his Irish alter ego, "Mr. Dooley": "the throuble is whin the gallant Commodore [Perry] kicked open th' door, we didn't go in. They come out."

Still, more than three hundred U.S. experts were recruited in the 1870s to assist Japan's modernization. They taught scientific farming and brought new breeds of livestock to northern Japan. U.S. educators designed a college-level science curriculum and helped draw up Japan's blueprint for universal schooling. In 1873, Horace Wilson, a Union army veteran, introduced baseball at elite schools in Tokyo. Within two decades, the game had captivated the Japanese as it had the Americans.

Americans resorted to violence to pry open the Kingdom of Korea, which strongly resisted foreign trade. In 1866, a heavily armed U.S. merchant vessel, the *General Sherman*, landed at Pyongyang to impose a trade agreement. Angry Koreans set fire to the ship and killed its fleeing crew. In retaliation, the Grant administration sent a squadron of warships in 1871. Fired on as they approached Seoul, the Americans landed a squad of marines who killed some three hundred Koreans before departing. Eventually, the U.S. navy secured China's help to reach a pact with Korea in 1882 that granted concessions to American merchants and missionaries.

14-5c Republicans in Retreat

Despite Grant's reelection, Congress and the courts back away from Reconstruction.

By the time Grant's first term ended, a Republican splinter movement had formed to voice several grievances against party policies. First, congressional expansion of federal power during Reconstruction worried such reformers, who subscribed to the **laissez-faire** doctrines that were gaining traction with transatlantic industrialists and intellectuals. Adopting as a model Britain's Liberal Party, whose leader William Gladstone became prime minister in 1868, the **Liberal Republicans** advocated limited government, free trade, and unfettered enterprise. These policies, they argued, would create prosperity and reduce taxes and corruption. Liberals also called for a **civil service system** to replace appointed spoilsmen with professional managers. Finally, the Liberals opposed continued federal intervention to support black Southerners and prop up the region's Republican governments. Further progress, the Liberals declared, was up to freed people themselves. This retreat from Reconstruction allied them with southern white opponents of Reconstruction. The Liberals proposed a general amnesty for unreconstructed Southerners and a return to self-government by the "best men" among former Confederates.

The rise of the Liberal Republicans temporarily shook up existing party alignments. Unable to convert Republican "regulars," they formed an alliance with Democrats and nominated Horace Greeley, longtime editor of the *New York Tribune*, for president. Greeley, who had earlier supported Congressional Reconstruction, urged Americans to put the Civil War behind them and "clasp hands across the bloody chasm." Grant, running for a second term, defeated Greeley easily. Drawing on his reservoir of goodwill among the northern public and a high turnout among the South's black voters, Grant amassed 56 percent of the popular vote and carried all but six southern states.

The Liberal Republican revolt ended with the election but brought changes. Grant signed the nation's first civil service law in 1871 to select federal employees on merit, not political connections. Responding to Greeley's call for reconciliation, Congress passed the Amnesty Act, which allowed almost all former Confederates to hold office. More generally, the Liberal split forecast increased impatience among Republicans with their party's reconstruction program.

Toward the end of his first term and into his second, Grant remained committed to radical Reconstruction. When the South's Republicans clamored for protection from violent attacks, Congress responded with strong measures. To protect black voters, the **Ku Klux Klan Act** of 1871 and related enforcement acts authorized the government to prosecute members of groups that denied citizens' civil rights. Although these laws did not end racial violence, they resulted in hundreds of convictions of Klan members. Grant sent federal troops to South Carolina to break up the Klan and dispatched army units to North Carolina, Mississippi, and Louisiana to quell white supremacist insurrections. Congress

Meiji Restoration Rise to power of Japan's Emperor Meiji after widespread protests against unequal treaties, leading to modernization program for Japanese government, army, and industry.

laissez-faire Doctrine opposing government regulation or intervention in economic matters beyond a necessary minimum.

Liberal Republicans Party faction that favored limited government, free trade, and conciliation of southern whites and bolted to the Democratic ticket in 1872 under Greeley.

civil service system Arrangement for hiring and promoting government employees by professional merit rather than personal or political connections.

Ku Klux Klan Act Legislation also known as the Third Enforcement Act that allowed the president to impose martial law to combat attacks by the Klan and other white supremacist organizations.

followed with the Civil Rights Act of 1875, which banned racial discrimination in theaters, hotels, and other public places.

Before long, however, Congress realized that many Northerners had grown tired of southern tumult and the "negro question." Northern businessmen sought order and stability in the South to secure trade and investment. The number of Union soldiers in the South dwindled as they and Civil War generals such as O. O. Howard, the former head of the Freedmen's Bureau, were reassigned to the West to enforce the government's new reservation policy for Native Americans.

White Republicans who had supported African American rights primarily for partisan political advantage never shed their racial prejudice. In the 1870s, many northern Republicans swallowed tales of "black rule" and "barbarism" told by journalists touring the South. Increasingly, former supporters of black suffrage blamed southern violence and Republican losses on black voters, whom they condemned as ignorant and easily corrupted by Democrats.

Republicans who stood firm on African American rights suffered a major defeat when the Supreme Court, uneasy about Reconstruction's expansion of federal powers, restricted the government's authority to enforce civil rights. In its first ruling on the Fourteenth Amendment, the so-called **Slaughterhouse Cases** of 1873, the Court declared that freedom of speech, the right to a fair trial, and most other civil rights derived from state, not national, citizenship and were controlled by state law.

Another damaging decision concerned the **Colfax Massacre**, the bloodiest instance of racial violence during Reconstruction. In 1873, an armed mob of white Louisiana Democrats attacked a courthouse that was held by newly elected Republican officeholders (mostly black) and defended by the state militia. More than one hundred African Americans were killed, many while fleeing or surrendering. Prosecutors secured the conviction of only three men for murder and conspiracy. Reviewing their appeal, the Supreme Court ruled in ***U.S. v. Cruikshank*** (1876) that the Reconstruction amendments gave Congress the power to outlaw acts of discrimination only by state governments, not private individuals. This ruling was solidified in the Civil Rights Cases of 1883, when the Court declared the antidiscrimination strictures of the Civil Rights Act of 1875 unconstitutional. These decisions undermined federal protection of equal rights and gave a tacit go-ahead to white supremacist organizations in the South.

Radical Republicans began to lose in Congress as well as the courts. In the 1874 elections, the Democrats gained control of the House for the first time since the 1850s, proof that support for Reconstruction had dwindled. Grant cared about southern blacks' rights, but he understood which way the political winds were blowing. Responding to a call from South Carolina to suppress a massacre of black militiamen in 1876, Grant deplored the incident but weakly appealed to "the better judgment and co-operation of citizens of the State" to bring the offenders to justice "without aid from the Federal Government."

Slaughterhouse Cases Supreme Court ruling that weakened the Fourteenth Amendment by declaring that state, not federal, laws covered most civil rights.

Colfax Massacre Murderous attack by armed whites on black officeholders and state militia defending a county courthouse in Louisiana.

U.S. v. Cruikshank Supreme Court decision concerning the Colfax Massacre that exempted private individuals from federal prosecution for civil rights violations.

Panic of 1873 International financial crisis that led to U.S. economic depression, weakening Republican control and eroding support for Reconstruction.

14-5d Panic and Compromise

An economic crisis and a contested election end Reconstruction.

The North's shift away from Reconstruction accelerated when the postwar economic boom slid into a deep depression. Like earlier U.S. financial crises, the **Panic of 1873** originated in Europe. After its victory in the Franco-Prussian War (1870–1871), an increasingly powerful Germany demanded payments to it in gold rather than silver. This decree spurred bank failures in Vienna that spread through financial networks to northern Europe and North America. The U.S. economy was especially vulnerable because of speculation and overbuilding of railroads. The influential investment firm Jay Cooke and Company shut down, sparking a chain reaction among

The Library of Congress

Bank Panic, 1873 The run on the Union Trust Company in New York City was among those on hundreds of banks that had to suspend operations in the Panic of 1873. Founded as savings banks, trust companies were virtually unregulated and prone to speculative schemes. Dramatic scenes of bank runs predominated in magazine depictions of the panic and depression. Such male-dominated images overlooked the depression's devastating effects on unemployed women and families. ▲

banks and businesses. Over the next five years, one of four American railroads failed, hundreds of banks folded, and many businesses closed. Unemployment reached 15 percent, and those who hung onto their jobs faced seasonal layoffs and severe wage cuts.

For working-class victims of the depression, the crisis exposed the inadequacy of Republicans' free-labor ideology to the new industrial era. Unemployed workers in New York and other cities demanded that government officials create jobs or at least finance public relief. But Republican spokesmen and business leaders denounced such programs as interfering with the free market and discouraging hard work. According to laissez-faire tenets, workers in the North, like southern blacks, enjoyed mobility and civil rights and had to rise by their own efforts. As Reconstruction evolved, it hardened, rather than tempered, the creed of middle-class individualism that Republicans had fashioned in the 1850s.

The lingering economic depression and the Grant administration's continuing scandals gave the Democrats momentum going into the 1876 presidential campaign. They nominated Governor Samuel J. Tilden of New York, a reformer renowned for prosecuting the Tweed Ring in New York City. In addition to "corrupt centralism" in Washington, Tilden promised to end "carpetbag tyrannies" in the South. The Republicans nominated Rutherford B. Hayes, a former Civil War general with a clean record as governor of Ohio, who promised to crack down on graft and voiced conciliatory sentiments toward southern whites.

Tilden received 250,000 more popular votes than Hayes, but in the Electoral College, his total was 184, one shy of the number required for victory (see Map 14.3). Hayes received 166, but the votes of one Oregon elector and three southern states were disputed. South Carolina, Louisiana, and Florida were the only remaining Republican governments in the South. The contest there was marred by fraud, and both parties claimed victory.

Faced with this unprecedented situation, Congress created a fifteen-member commission composed of senators, representatives, and Supreme Court justices to examine the disputed returns. The commission voted eight to seven along strict party lines to give Hayes all the contested electoral votes and with them the presidency. Outraged Democrats threatened to block Hayes's victory in the House of Representatives. The impasse was broken when Democrats and Republicans appeared to negotiate a series of back-room deals just two days before the inauguration. The arrangement became known as the **Compromise of 1877**. In return for the Democrats' acceptance of Hayes as president, the Republicans agreed (among other concessions) to provide federal subsidies for a southern transcontinental railroad (the northern line had been completed in 1869). Most importantly, the Republicans pledged to withdraw federal troops that bolstered the remaining Republican regimes in the South.

The Compromise of 1877 broke down so rapidly that some historians question whether it was forged at all. The most important feature held, however: Shortly after Hayes was inaugurated, he removed federal troops stationed in the three contested states. Without the army to support them, the South's Republicans ceded control of Louisiana, South Carolina, and Florida to the Democrats. This closed the long sectional struggle over whether the postwar South would simply be restored to the Union or thoroughly reconstructed. Sectional peace returned, but at the price of relinquishing Reconstruction's transformational agenda. By abandoning the pledge of civil and political equality recently inscribed in the Fourteenth and Fifteenth Amendments, the North and South were reunited.

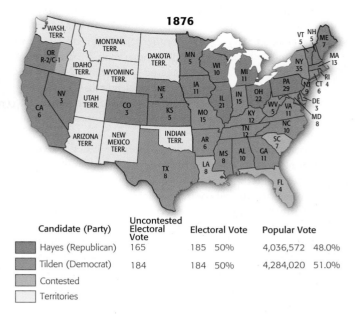

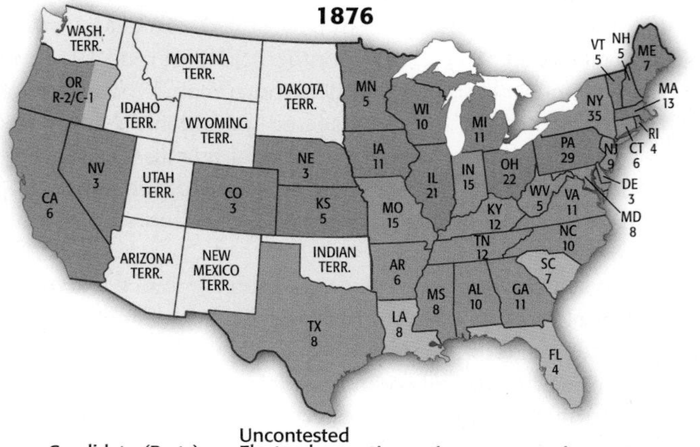

Candidate (Party)	Uncontested Electoral Vote	Electoral Vote		Popular Vote	
Hayes (Republican)	165	185	50%	4,036,572	48.0%
Tilden (Democrat)	184	184	50%	4,284,020	51.0%
Contested					
Territories					

Map 14.3 Election of 1876 and Compromise of 1877 Democratic gains in the North and the collapse of Reconstruction governments in the South gave Samuel Tilden the majority of popular votes. However, Republican Rutherford Hayes captured the presidency after a special commission gave him all the disputed Electoral College votes and a private agreement assured Democrats that Reconstruction was over. ▲

Compromise of 1877 Political deal that resolved the disputed election of 1876 by ceding electoral votes to Republican candidate Hayes in exchange for ending Reconstruction.

14-5e Reconstruction's Troubled Legacy at Home and Abroad

Home rule in the South isolates it politically and entrenches racist practices.

The end of Reconstruction had important consequences for relations between the South and the nation. Relinquishing rule to the South's large landowners enabled them to recapture their regional power and set the terms of southern race relations, but they no longer controlled national politics. Before the Civil War, white Southerners dominated the presidency, Supreme Court, and other federal leadership positions; afterward, the sectional balance of power was reversed. In the next fifty years,

Lost Cause Nostalgic praise of the plantation South and Confederate bravery voiced by white Southerners who were opposed to Reconstruction and racial equality.

only 7 of 31 Supreme Court appointees and 14 of 133 cabinet members were Southerners. Not until 1912 was a southern-born man, Woodrow Wilson, elected president. Nationally, political party allegiances were evenly divided, but the Republicans' economic agenda, including banking, land, tariff, and tax policies that favored the industrial North, prevailed.

Meanwhile, wartime destruction combined with unfavorable conditions in the international market to inflict lasting damage on the South's economy. While mechanized farming made rural communities in the North prosperous, the traditional hand-harvested staples of cotton, tobacco, rice, and sugar still dominated southern agriculture. All these crops suffered from global overproduction and declining prices. Industrialization and diversified farming might ensure future prosperity, but Southerners lacked the home-grown capital to make changes, and many resisted industry as an alien way of life. Southerners emerged from Reconstruction dependent on the North's banks, factories, and corporations to offset diminishing returns from staple crops. The South's subordination in the national government and its lagging economic development resembled the outcome of national consolidation in countries such as Italy and Germany, where north-south disparities continued to divide nations that were unified politically in midcentury.

Shaken by their declining status, southern whites idealized the prewar plantation economy, lamented the Confederacy's **Lost Cause**, and demonized their alleged oppressors during radical Reconstruction. Once the South's Republican regimes were toppled, white politicians launched systematic campaigns to disfranchise, intimidate, and segregate African Americans. To justify discrimination against blacks and nonwhite immigrants, white commentators and academics in both the North and South developed elaborate racial theories based on ideas of Anglo-Saxon superiority, immutable racial traits, or the evolutionary "backwardness" of nonwhite peoples.

By providing fodder for such racial theories, the abandonment of Reconstruction had damaging international repercussions. According to James Bryce, Britain's ambassador to the United States and a respected authority on American society, postwar turmoil in the South showed "the risk a democracy runs when the suffrage is granted to a large mass of half-civilized men." British imperialists in lands such as Australia and South Africa cited Bryce's view that Reconstruction was a mistake as proof that nonwhite peoples were incapable of self-rule. Such views produced segregation laws, racial exclusion from voting, literacy tests, and similar methods of disfranchisement in Britain's so-called white dominions that were based on models from the U.S. South.

Blacks in the American South, like their global counterparts, did not let such views go unchallenged. Beginning in the mid-1870s, emigration movements recruited heavily in the cotton belt. Perhaps 30,000 southern blacks left for Kansas in the so-called Exoduster movement (see Chapter 15) and another 4,000 sought new lives in Liberia. The vast majority remained in their adopted land, struggling to make a living and fighting for their rights. Despite legal restrictions and physical threats, the South's African Americans continued to vote in large numbers into the 1880s. When in the next decade southern states passed laws restricting voting and mandating segregation, people of color, including Louisiana's Rodolphe Desdunes and his friend Homère Plessy, reasserted equal rights against all odds.

Summary

Americans entered the post-Civil War era with conflicting agendas for restoring peace and distributing justice. Emancipated slaves sought political rights and economic independence. Former Confederates insisted on the freedom to retain regional power and racial dominance. Republicans in Congress held the balance of political power and debated plans for the postwar settlement. The contest between revolutionizing the South and restoring the prewar status quo galvanized the nation when the Republicans impeached their renegade president and framed a program to reconstruct southern life as a precondition to reunion. Congressional Reconstruction strengthened the federal government's domestic power at the same time that the purchase of Alaska confirmed the nation's continental dominance. In 1867, the United States became the only postemancipation society in the Americas committed to guaranteeing former slaves full civil and political rights.

Reconstruction shook southern society to its foundations as Republican state governments elected with African American votes enacted sweeping changes in politics, education, and public welfare. But in the South, as in postemancipation societies in Caribbean islands, white planters who had resisted emancipation led determined efforts to maintain their racial and economic supremacy after slavery's end. Using the Democratic Party and secret paramilitary groups, angry white Southerners arose to take control of their states. As political winds shifted, industrial upheavals and overseas expansion drew the public's attention, and the North's Republicans retreated from their commitment to enforce racial equality.

By the time Reconstruction officially ended in 1877, an informal settlement emerged by which Northerners dominated the newly powerful national government and traditional white elites regained control over the postwar South's politics, agriculture, and race relations. As in most nations undergoing unification struggles, sectional integration was incomplete and cultural and ideological rifts lingered. The North returned to peace, prosperity, and expansion, the South assumed a subordinate relationship in national politics, and the Union's promise of full freedom to the former slaves was sacrificed. Instead of serving as a model of political equality for other postemancipation societies, Americans provided examples of racial segregation and political disfranchisement amid glimpses of progress.

Thinking Back, *Looking Forward*

As you review this chapter, think about how Reconstruction transformed American politics, the national economy, and social relations in the South. Which changes endured, and which were temporary? Did the North win the Civil War but lose the postwar peace? Why did Americans retreat from their unique pledge of postemancipation equality between races? How complete was U.S. national unification compared to that of other nations? In the next chapters, look for the lasting consequences of Reconstruction's battles. What did the South's segregationist regime mean for Reconstruction's legacy? What were the consequences of Reconstruction for Native Americans, immigration, and U.S. citizenship?

To make your study concrete, review the timeline and reflect on the entries there. Think about their causes, consequences, and connections. How do they fit with global trends?

Additional Resources

Books

Beckert, Sven. *Empire of Cotton: A Global History*. New York: Knopf, 2014. ▶ Documentation of the worldwide switch to tenancy and small-farm production after the U.S. Civil War.

Cook, Adrian. *The Alabama Claims: American Politics and Anglo-American Relations, 1865–1872*. Ithaca, NY: Cornell University Press, 1975. ▶ Scholarly history of U.S.–Great Britain relations during Reconstruction.

Dubois, Ellen Carol. *Feminism and Suffrage: The Emergence of an Independent Women's Movement in America, 1848–1869*. Ithaca. NY: Cornell University Press, 1978. ▶ Account of the break of women's rights' advocates from their abolitionist roots to focus on the vote.

Foner, Eric. *Reconstruction: America's Unfinished Revolution, 1863–1877*. New York: HarperCollins, 1988. ▶ The best single-volume history of the period.

Hahn, Steven. *A Nation under Our Feet: Black Political Struggles in the Rural South from Slavery to the Great Migration*. Cambridge, MA: Harvard University Press, 2005. ▶ Exploration of the hidden history of black political organizing during and after Reconstruction.

Hunter, Tera W. *To 'Joy My Freedom: Southern Black Women's Lives and Labors after the Civil War*. Cambridge, MA: Harvard University Press, 1997. ▶ Retelling of urban black women's lives and struggles as domestics.

Litwack, Leon. *Been in the Storm So Long: The Aftermath of Slavery*. New York: Vintage Books, 1980. ▶ Classic account, based on participants' testimony, of how blacks experienced freedom.

Scott, Rebecca J. *Degrees of Freedom: Louisiana and Cuba after Slavery*. Cambridge: Belknap Press, 2005. ▶ Comparison and contrast of emancipation and race relations in two sugar plantation societies.

Simpson, Brooks D. *The Reconstruction Presidents*. Lawrence: University Press of Kansas, 1998. ▶ A comparative assessment that rehabilitates Grant's reputation.

Stewart, David O. *Impeached: The Trial of President Andrew Johnson and the Fight for Lincoln's Legacy*. New York: Simon & Schuster, 2009. ▶ A dramatic narrative that criticizes Johnson for squandering Lincoln's hopes for emancipation.

Trelease, Allen. *White Terror: The Ku Klux Klan Conspiracy and Southern Reconstruction*. Baton Rouge: Louisiana State University Press, 1995. ▶ A comprehensive, state-by-state history of Klan activities during Reconstruction.

Go to the MindTap® for **Global Americans** to access the full version of select books from this Additional Resources section.

Websites

Andrew Johnson Impeachment Trial. (http://www.law.umkc.edu/faculty/projects/ftrials/impeach/impeachmt.htm). ▶ A collection of documents, information, and links about the impeachment.

Freedmen and Southern Society Project. (http://www.history.umd.edu/Freedmen/). ▶ Essays and primary source documents related to emancipation, land, and labor.

Freedmen's Bureau Online. (http://www.freedmensbureau.com/) ▶ State-by-state reports and documents, many capturing African American voices.

***Harper's Weekly*. (http://blackhistory.harpweek.com/default.htm).** ▶ Collection of reports on Black America 1857–1874 that includes editorials, news stories, and cartoons on Reconstruction from the popular northern magazine.

Ohio State University Libraries. (http://cartoons.osu.edu/digital_albums/thomasnast/index.htm). ▶ Extensive portfolio of Thomas Nast's political cartoons, which reflect changing Republican attitudes during Reconstruction.

Reconstruction: The Second Civil War. (http://www.pbs.org/wgbh/amex/reconstruction/index.html). ▶ Background information, documents, and access to two PBS documentary films about Reconstruction.

MindTap®

Continue exploring online through MindTap®, where you can:

- **Assess your knowledge with the Chapter Test**
- **Watch historical videos related to the chapter**
- **Further your understanding with interactive maps and timelines**

Reunion and Retreat: Reconstruction

1863

December

Lincoln's Proclamation of Amnesty and Reconstruction outlines lenient plan for restoring rebellious states to the Union.

1864

July

Lincoln pocket vetoes congressional Wade-Davis bill imposing strict terms for readmission to the Union.

1865

March

Congress establishes Freedmen's Bureau to assist former slaves.

April

Lincoln is assassinated and is succeeded by Vice President Andrew Johnson .

May

Johnson announces plan to disfranchise Confederate leaders and quickly restore former Confederate states.

Summer

White governments in restored southern states adopt Black Codes restricting freed people's rights.

October

Morant Bay Rebellion in Jamaica stiffens southern whites' resistance to freedmen's rights.

December

Thirteenth Amendment is ratified, outlawing slavery in United States.

Ku Klux Klan is organized in Tennessee to terrorize freed people.

1866

April

Civil Rights Act extends citizenship and accompanying rights to all persons born in the United States, including former slaves.

May–June

Fenian Brotherhood launches invasion of Canada aimed at securing Irish independence.

July

Armed U.S. merchant ship *General Sherman* is attacked and destroyed in Korea.

1867

March

United States purchases Alaska territory from Russia to promote continental expansion and Pacific trade.

Reconstruction Act returns former Confederate states to military rule and sets congressional requirements for readmission.

British North America Act creates Canadian Confederation in response to threat of U.S. expansion.

August

Reform Act in Britain expands voting rights to double the electorate but rejects women's suffrage.

1868

January

Japan's Meiji Restoration initiates modernization and increases U.S. influence in its industry and educational system.

February

Bancroft Treaties spread recognition of naturalized citizenship, beginning with pact between German states and the United States.

March

Johnson impeached but not convicted by Congress in dispute over Reconstruction policies.

July

Fourteenth Amendment gives citizenship to African Americans and establishes birthright citizenship as U.S. policy.

Burlingame Treaty between U.S. and China proclaims mutual respect and continues Chinese immigration to United States.

October

United States stays neutral as the Ten Years' War erupts in Cuba over abolition and colonial independence from Spain.

November

Republican candidate and Civil War hero Ulysses Grant is elected president.

1869 – 1870

April
In *Texas v. White*, the Supreme Court declares secession unconstitutional without consent of the United States.

May
Debate over Reconstruction amendments splits U.S. women's suffrage activists.

March
Fifteenth Amendment bans denial of vote on grounds of race.

June
U.S. Senate rejects annexation of Santo Domingo.

1871

January
Women's suffrage advocates appear before Congress to press their claims.

May
Treaty of Washington resolves U.S.–Britain disputes over Civil War claims and Canadian border.

June
U.S. expedition to Korea avenges *General Sherman* incident but fails to open trade relations.

September
Brazil, influenced by prior British and U.S emancipation, adopts a gradual emancipation law.

1872

September
Crédit Mobilier scandal rocks Grant administration, eroding support for Republican Party.

November
Grant is reelected president as Liberal Republican revolt fails.

1873

April
White Southerners murder black officeholders in Louisiana's Colfax Massacre.

U.S. Supreme Court weakens Fourteenth Amendment in Slaughterhouse Cases ruling.

September
Bank Panic in Europe triggers U.S. economic crisis and six-year global depression.

1874

November
Democrats win control of House of Representatives for the first time since the Civil War.

1875

March
U.S. Supreme Court rejects women's suffrage in *Minor v. Happersett*.

1876

March
U.S. v. Cruikshank drastically limits federal oversight of freed people's civil rights.

November
Republican Rutherford Hayes and Democrat Samuel Tilden deadlock in disputed presidential election.

1877

March
Electoral College and congressional compromise declare Hayes president and officially end Reconstruction.

Go to MindTap® to engage with an interactive version of the timeline. Analyze events and themes with clickable content, view related videos, and respond to critical thinking questions.

1869 – 1870

April

In *Texas v. White*, the Supreme Court declares secession unconstitutional without consent of the United States.

May

Debate over Reconstruction amendments splits U.S. women's suffrage activists.

March

Fifteenth Amendment bans denial of vote on grounds of race.

June

U.S. Senate rejects annexation of Santo Domingo.

1871

January

Women's suffrage advocates appear before Congress to press their claims.

May

Treaty of Washington resolves U.S.–Britain disputes over Civil War claims and Canadian border.

June

U.S. expedition to Korea avenges *General Sherman* incident but fails to open trade relations.

September

Brazil, influenced by prior British and U.S emancipation, adopts a gradual emancipation law.

1872

September

Crédit Mobilier scandal rocks Grant administration, eroding support for Republican Party.

November

Grant is reelected president as Liberal Republican revolt fails.

1873

April

White Southerners murder black officeholders in Louisiana's Colfax Massacre.

U.S. Supreme Court weakens Fourteenth Amendment in Slaughterhouse Cases ruling.

September

Bank Panic in Europe triggers U.S. economic crisis and six-year global depression.

1874

November

Democrats win control of House of Representatives for the first time since the Civil War.

1875

March

U.S. Supreme Court rejects women's suffrage in *Minor v. Happersett*.

1876

March

U.S. v. Cruikshank drastically limits federal oversight of freed people's civil rights.

November

Republican Rutherford Hayes and Democrat Samuel Tilden deadlock in disputed presidential election.

1877

March

Electoral College and congressional compromise declare Hayes president and officially end Reconstruction.

Go to MindTap® to engage with an interactive version of the timeline. Analyze events and themes with clickable content, view related videos, and respond to critical thinking questions.

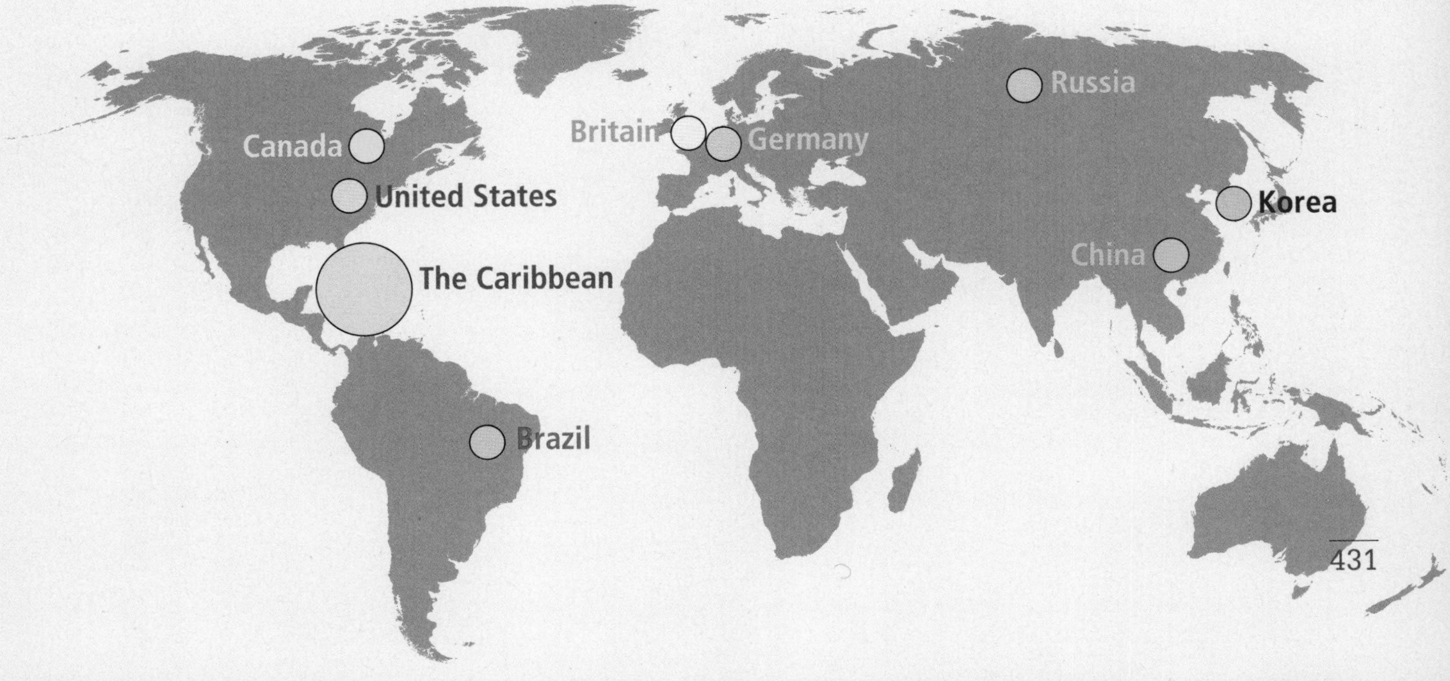

Appendix

The Declaration of Independence

In Congress, July 4, 1776

The Unanimous Declaration of the Thirteen United States of America

When in the Course of human events it becomes necessary for one people to dissolve the political bands which have connected them with another, and to assume among the Powers of the earth, the separate and equal station to which the Laws of Nature and of Nature's God entitle them, a decent respect to the opinions of mankind requires that they should declare the causes which impel them to the separation.

We hold these truths to be self-evident, that all men are created equal, that they are endowed by their Creator with certain unalienable Rights, that among these are Life, Liberty and the pursuit of Happiness. That to secure these rights, Governments are instituted among Men, deriving their just Powers from the consent of the governed. That whenever any Form of Government becomes destructive of these ends, it is the Right of the People to alter or to abolish it, and to institute new Government, laying its foundation on such principles and organizing its Powers in such form, as to them shall seem most likely to effect their Safety and Happiness. Prudence, indeed, will dictate that Governments long established should not be changed for light and transient causes; and accordingly all experience hath shewn, that mankind are more disposed to suffer, while evils are sufferable, than to right themselves by abolishing the forms to which they are accustomed. But when a long train of abuses and usurpations, pursuing invariably the same Object evinces a design to reduce them under absolute Despotism, it is their right, it is their duty, to throw off such Government, and to provide new Guards for their future security. Such has been the patient sufferance of these Colonies; and such is now the necessity which constrains them to alter their former Systems of Government. The history of the present King of Great Britain is a history of repeated injuries and usurpations, all having in direct object the establishment of an absolute Tyranny over these States. To prove this, let Facts be submitted to a candid world.

He has refused his Assent to Laws, the most wholesome and necessary for the public good.

He has forbidden his Governors to pass Laws of immediate and pressing importance, unless suspended in their operation till his Assent should be obtained; and when so suspended, he has utterly neglected to attend to them.

He has refused to pass other Laws for the accommodation of large districts of people, unless those people would relinquish the right of Representation in the Legislature, a right inestimable to them and formidable to tyrants only.

He has called together legislative bodies at places unusual, uncomfortable, and distant from the depository of their Public Records, for the sole Purpose of fatiguing them into compliance with his measures.

Text is reprinted from the facsimile of the engrossed copy in the National Archives. The original spelling, capitalization, and punctuation have been retained. Paragraphing has been added.

He has dissolved Representative Houses repeatedly, for opposing with manly firmness his invasions on the rights of the People.

He has refused for a long time, after such dissolutions, to cause others to be elected; whereby the Legislative Powers, incapable of Annihilation, have returned to the People at large for their exercise; the State remaining in the mean time exposed to all the dangers of invasion from without, and convulsions within.

He has endeavoured to prevent the Population of these States; for that purpose obstructing the Laws for Naturalization of Foreigners; refusing to pass others to encourage their migrations hither, and raising the conditions of new Appropriations of Lands.

He has obstructed the Administration of Justice, by refusing his Assent to Laws for establishing Judiciary Powers.

He has made Judges dependent on his Will alone, for the tenure of their offices, and the amount and payment of their salaries.

He has erected a multitude of New Offices, and sent hither swarms of Officers to harass our People, and eat out their substance.

He has kept among us, in times of peace, Standing Armies without the Consent of our legislatures.

He has affected to render the Military independent of and superior to the Civil Power.

He has combined with others to subject us to a jurisdiction foreign to our constitution, and unacknowledged by our laws; giving his Assent to their Acts of pretended Legislation: For Quartering large bodies of armed troops among us: For protecting them, by a mock Trial, from Punishment for any Murders which they should commit on the Inhabitants of these States: For cutting off our Trade with all parts of the world: For imposing Taxes on us without our Consent: For depriving us in many cases, of the benefits of Trial by Jury: For transporting us beyond Seas to be tried for pretended offences: For abolishing the free System of English Laws in a neighbouring Province, establishing therein an Arbitrary government, and enlarging its Boundaries so as to render it at once an example and fit instrument for introducing the same absolute rule into these Colonies: For taking away our Charters, abolishing our most valuable Laws, and altering fundamentally the Forms of our Governments: For suspending our own Legislatures, and declaring themselves invested with Power to legislate for us in all cases whatsoever.

He has abdicated Government here, by declaring us out of his Protection, and waging War against us.

He has plundered our seas, ravaged our Coasts, burnt our towns, and destroyed the lives of our people.

He is at this time transporting large Armies of foreign Mercenaries to compleat the works of death, desolation and tyranny, already begun with circumstances of Cruelty and perfidy scarcely paralleled in the most barbarous ages, and totally unworthy the Head of a civilized nation.

He has constrained our fellow Citizens taken Captive on the high Seas to bear Arms against their Country, to become the executioners of their friends and Brethren, or to fall themselves by their Hands.

He has excited domestic insurrections amongst us, and has endeavoured to bring on the inhabitants of our frontiers, the merciless Indian Savages, whose known rule of warfare, is an undistinguished destruction of all ages, sexes and conditions.

In every stage of these Oppressions We have Petitioned for Redress in the most humble terms: Our repeated Petitions have been answered only by repeated injury. A Prince, whose character is thus marked by every act which may define a Tyrant, is unfit to be the ruler of a free People.

Nor have We been wanting in attentions to our British brethren. We have warned them from time to time of attempts by their legislature to extend an unwarrantable jurisdiction over us. We have reminded them of the circumstances of our emigration and settlement here. We have appealed to their native justice and magnanimity, and we have conjured them by the ties of our common kindred to disavow these usurpations, which, would inevitably interrupt our connections and correspondence. They too have been deaf to the voice of justice and of consanguinity. We must, therefore, acquiesce in the necessity, which denounces our Separation, and hold them, as we hold the rest of mankind, Enemies in War, in Peace Friends.

We, therefore, the Representatives of the United States of America, in General Congress, Assembled, appealing to the Supreme Judge of the world for the rectitude of our intentions, do, in the Name, and by Authority of the good People of these Colonies, solemnly publish and declare, That these United Colonies are, and of Right ought to be Free and Independent States; that they are Absolved from all Allegiance to the British Crown, and that all political connection between them and the State of Great Britain, is and ought to be totally dissolved; and that, as Free and Independent States, they have full Power to levy War, conclude Peace, contract Alliances, establish Commerce, and to do all other Acts and Things which Independent States may of right do. And for the support of this Declaration, with a firm reliance on the protection of divine Providence, we mutually pledge to each other our Lives, our Fortunes and our sacred Honor.

The Constitution of the United States of America

We the People of the United States, in Order to form a more perfect Union, establish Justice, insure domestic Tranquility, provide for the common defence, promote the general Welfare, and secure the Blessings of Liberty to ourselves and our Posterity, do ordain and establish this Constitution for the United States of America.

Article I

SECTION 1. All legislative Powers herein granted shall be vested in a Congress of the United States, which shall consist of a Senate and House of Representatives.

SECTION 2. The House of Representatives shall be composed of Members chosen every second Year by the People of the several States, and the Electors in each State shall have the Qualifications requisite for Electors of the most numerous Branch of the State Legislature.

No Person shall be a Representative who shall not have attained to the Age of twenty five Years, and been seven Years a Citizen of the United States, and who shall not, when elected, be an Inhabitant of that State in which he shall be chosen.

Representatives and direct Taxes[1] shall be apportioned among the several States which may be included within this Union, according to their respective Numbers, which shall be determined by adding to the whole Number of free Persons, including those bound to Service for a Term of Years, and excluding Indians not taxed, three fifths of all other Persons.[2]

The actual Enumeration shall be made within three Years after the first Meeting of the Congress of the United States, and within every subsequent Term of ten Years, in such Manner as they shall by Law direct. The Number of Representatives shall not exceed one for every thirty Thousand, but each State shall have at Least one Representative; and until such enumeration shall be made, the State of New Hampshire shall be entitled to chuse three; Massachusetts eight; Rhode Island and Providence Plantations one; Connecticut five; New York six; New Jersey four; Pennsylvania eight; Delaware one; Maryland six; Virginia ten; North Carolina five; South Carolina five; and Georgia three.

When vacancies happen in the Representation from any State, the Executive Authority thereof shall issue Writs of Election to fill such Vacancies.

The House of Representatives shall chuse their Speaker and other Officers; and shall have the sole Power of Impeachment.

SECTION 3. The Senate of the United States shall be composed of two Senators from each State, chosen by the Legislature thereof, for six Years; and each Senator shall have one Vote.[3]

Immediately after they shall be assembled in Consequence of the first Election, they shall be divided as equally as may be into three Classes. The Seats of the Senators of the first Class shall be vacated at the Expiration of the second Year, of the second Class at the Expiration of the fourth Year, and of the third Class at the Expiration of the sixth Year, so that one third may be chosen every second Year; and if Vacancies happen by Resignation, or otherwise, during the

---

Text is from the engrossed copy in the National Archives. Original spelling, capitalization, and punctuation have been retained.

[1] Modified by the Sixteenth Amendment.

[2] Replaced by the Fourteenth Amendment.

[3] Superseded by the Seventeenth Amendment.

Recess of the Legislature of any State, the Executive thereof may make temporary Appointments until the next Meeting of the Legislature, which shall then fill such Vacancies.[4]

No Person shall be a Senator who shall not have attained to the Age of thirty Years, and been nine Years a Citizen of the United States, and who shall not, when elected, be an Inhabitant of that State for which he shall be chosen.

The Vice President of the United States shall be President of the Senate, but shall have no Vote, unless they be equally divided.

The Senate shall chuse their other Officers, and also a President pro tempore, in the Absence of the Vice President, or when he shall exercise the Office of President of the United States.

The Senate shall have the sole Power to try all Impeachments. When sitting for that Purpose, they shall be on Oath or Affirmation. When the President of the United States is tried, the Chief Justice shall preside: And no Person shall be convicted without the Concurrence of two thirds of the Members present.

Judgment in Cases of Impeachment shall not extend further than to removal from Office, and disqualification to hold and enjoy any Office of honor, Trust or Profit under the United States: but the Party convicted shall nevertheless be liable and subject to Indictment, Trial, Judgment and Punishment, according to Law.

SECTION 4. The Times, Places and Manner of holding Elections for Senators and Representatives, shall be prescribed in each State by the Legislature thereof, but the Congress may at any time by Law make or alter such Regulation, except as to the Places of chusing Senators.

The Congress shall assemble at least once in every Year, and such Meeting shall be on the first Monday in December, unless they shall by Law appoint a different Day.[5]

SECTION 5. Each House shall be the Judge of the Elections, Returns and Qualifications of its own Members, and a Majority of each shall constitute a Quorum to do Business; but a smaller Number may adjourn from day to day, and may be authorized to compel the Attendance of absent Members, in such Manner, and under such Penalties as each House may provide.

Each House may determine the Rules of its Proceedings, punish its Members for disorderly Behaviour, and, with the Concurrence of two thirds, expel a Member.

Each House shall keep a Journal of its Proceedings, and from time to time publish the same, excepting such Parts as may in their Judgment require Secrecy; and the Yeas and Nays of the Members of either House on any question shall, at the Desire of one fifth of those Present, be entered on the Journal.

Neither House, during the Session of Congress, shall, without the Consent of the other, adjourn for more than three days, nor to any other Place than that in which the two Houses shall be sitting.

SECTION 6. The Senators and Representatives shall receive a Compensation for their Services, to be ascertained by Law, and paid out of the Treasury of the United States. They shall in all Cases, except Treason, Felony and Breach of the Peace, be privileged from Arrest during their Attendance at the Session of their respective Houses, and in going to and returning from the same; and for any Speech or Debate in either House, they shall not be questioned in any other Place.

No Senator or Representative shall, during the Time for which he was elected, be appointed to any civil Office under the Authority of the United States, which shall have been created, or the Emoluments whereof shall have been encreased during such time; and no Person holding any Office under the United States, shall be a Member of either House during his Continuance in Office.

---

[4] Modified by the Seventeenth Amendment.

[5] Superseded by the Twentieth Amendment.

SECTION 7. All Bills for raising Revenue shall originate in the House of Representatives; but the Senate may propose or concur with Amendments as on other Bills.

Every Bill which shall have passed the House of Representatives and the Senate shall, before it become a Law, be presented to the President of the United States; If he approve he shall sign it, but if not he shall return it, with his Objections to that House in which it shall have originated, who shall enter the Objections at large on their Journal, and proceed to reconsider it. If after such Reconsideration two thirds of that House shall agree to pass the Bill, it shall be sent, together with the Objections, to the other House, by which it shall likewise be reconsidered, and if approved by two thirds of that House, it shall become a Law. But in all such Cases the Votes of both Houses shall be determined by yeas and Nays, and the Names of the Persons voting for and against the Bill shall be entered on the Journal of each House respectively. If any Bill shall not be returned by the President within ten Days (Sundays excepted) after it shall have been presented to him, the Same shall be a Law, in like Manner as if he had signed it, unless the Congress by their Adjournment prevent its Return, in which Case it shall not be a Law.

Every Order, Resolution, or Vote to which the Concurrence of the Senate and House of Representatives may be necessary (except on a question of Adjournment) shall be presented to the President of the United States; and before the Same shall take Effect, shall be approved by him, or being disapproved by him shall be repassed by two thirds of the Senate and House of Representatives, according to the Rules and Limitations prescribed in the Case of a Bill.

SECTION 8. The Congress shall have power To lay and collect Taxes, Duties, Imposts and Excises, to pay the Debts and provide for the common Defence and general Welfare of the United States; but all Duties, Imposts and Excises shall be uniform throughout the United States; To borrow Money on the credit of the United States; To regulate Commerce with foreign Nations, and among the several States, and with the Indian Tribes; To establish an uniform Rule of Naturalization, and uniform Laws on the subject of Bankruptcies throughout the United States; To coin Money, regulate the Value thereof, and of foreign Coin, and fix the Standard of Weights and Measures; To provide for the Punishment of counterfeiting the Securities and current Coin of the United States; To establish Post Offices and post Roads; To promote the Progress of Science and useful Arts, by securing for limited Times to Authors and Inventors the exclusive Right to their respective Writings and Discoveries; To constitute Tribunals inferior to the supreme Court; To define and punish Piracies and Felonies committed on the high Seas, and Offences against the Law of Nations;

To declare War, grant Letters of Marque and Reprisal, and make Rules concerning Captures on Land and Water; To raise and support Armies, but no Appropriation of Money to that Use shall be for a longer Term than two Years; To provide and maintain a Navy; To make Rules for the Government and Regulation of the land and naval Forces; To provide for calling forth the Militia to execute the Laws of the Union, suppress Insurrections and repel Invasions; To provide for organizing, arming, and disciplining, the Militia, and for governing such Part of them as may be employed in the Service of the United States, reserving to the States respectively, the Appointment of the Officers, and the Authority of training the Militia according to the discipline prescribed by Congress; To exercise exclusive Legislation in all Cases whatsoever, over such District (not exceeding ten Miles square) as may, by Cession of particular States, and the Acceptance of Congress, become the Seat of the Government of the United States, and to exercise like Authority over all Places purchased by the Consent of the Legislature of the State in which the Same shall be, for the Erection of Forts, Magazines, Arsenals, dock-Yards, and other needful Buildings;—And To make all Laws which shall be necessary and proper for carrying into Execution the foregoing Powers, and all other Powers vested by this Constitution in the Government of the United States, or in any Department or Officer thereof.

SECTION 9. The Migration or Importation of such Persons as any of the States now existing shall think proper to admit, shall not be prohibited by the Congress prior to the Year one thousand eight hundred and eight, but a Tax or duty may be imposed on such Importation, not exceeding ten dollars for each Person.

The Privilege of the Writ of Habeas Corpus shall not be suspended, unless when in Cases of Rebellion or Invasion the public Safety may require it.

No Bill of Attainder or ex post facto Law shall be passed.

No Capitation, or other direct, Tax shall be laid, unless in Proportion to the Census or Enumeration herein before directed to be taken.

No Tax or Duty shall be laid on Articles exported from any State.

No Preference shall be given by any Regulation of Commerce or Revenue to the Ports of one State over those of another: nor shall Vessels bound to, or from, one State, be obliged to enter, clear, or pay Duties in another.

No Money shall be drawn from the Treasury, but in Consequence of Appropriations made by Law, and a regular Statement and Account of the Receipts and Expenditures of all public Money shall be published from time to time.

No Title of Nobility shall be granted by the United States: And no Person holding any Office of Profit or Trust under them, shall, without the Consent of the Congress, accept of any present, Emolument, Office, or Title, of any kind whatever, from any King, Prince, or foreign State.

SECTION 10. No State shall enter into any Treaty, Alliance, or Confederation; grant Letters of Marque and Reprisal; coin Money; emit Bills of Credit; make any Thing but gold and silver Coin a Tender in Payment of Debts; pass any Bill of Attainder, ex post facto Law, or Law impairing the Obligation of Contracts, or grant any Title of Nobility.

No State shall, without the Consent of the Congress, lay any Imposts or Duties on Imports or Exports, except what may be absolutely necessary for executing its inspection Laws: and the net Produce of all Duties and Imposts, laid by any State on Imports or Exports, shall be for the Use of the Treasury of the United States; and all such Laws shall be subject to the Revision and Controul of the Congress.

No State shall, without the Consent of Congress, lay any Duty of Tonnage, keep Troops, or Ships of War in time of Peace, enter into any Agreement or Compact with another State, or with a foreign Power, or engage in War, unless actually invaded, or in such imminent Danger as will not admit of delay.

Article II

SECTION 1. The executive Power shall be vested in a President of the United States of America. He shall hold his Office during the Term of four Years, and, together with the Vice President, chosen for the same Term, be elected, as follows: Each State shall appoint, in such Manner as the Legislature thereof may direct, a Number of Electors, equal to the whole Number of Senators and Representatives to which the State may be entitled in the Congress: but no Senator or Representative, or Person holding an Office of Trust or Profit under the United States, shall be appointed an Elector.

The Electors shall meet in their respective States, and vote by Ballot for two Persons, of whom one at least shall not be an Inhabitant of the same State with themselves. And they shall make a List of all the Persons voted for, and of the Number of Votes for each; which List they shall sign and certify, and transmit sealed to the Seat of the Government of the United States, directed to the President of the Senate. The President of the Senate shall, in the Presence of the Senate and House of Representatives, open all the Certificates, and the Votes shall then be counted. The Person having the greatest Number of Votes shall be the President, if such Number be a Majority of the whole Number of Electors appointed; and if there be more than one who have such Majority, and have an equal Number of Votes, then the House of Representatives shall immediately chuse by Ballot one of them for President; and if no Person have a Majority, then from the five highest on the List the said House shall in like Manner chuse the President. But in chusing the President, the Votes shall be taken by States, the Representation from each State having one Vote; A quorum for this Purpose shall consist of a Member or Members from two thirds of the States, and a Majority of all the States shall be necessary to a Choice. In every Case, after the Choice of the

President, the Person having the greatest Number of Votes of the Electors shall be the Vice President. But if there should remain two or more who have equal Votes, the Senate shall chuse from them by Ballot the Vice President.[6]

The Congress may determine the Time of chusing the Electors, and the Day on which they shall give their Votes; which Day shall be the same throughout the United States.

No Person except a natural born Citizen, or a Citizen of the United States, at the time of the Adoption of this Constitution, shall be eligible to the Office of President, neither shall any Person be eligible to that Office who shall not have attained to the Age of thirty five Years, and been fourteen Years a Resident within the United States.

In Case of the Removal of the President from Office, or of his Death, Resignation, or Inability to discharge the Powers and Duties of the said Office, the Same shall devolve on the Vice President, and the Congress may by Law provide for the Case of Removal, Death, Resignation or Inability, both of the President and Vice President, declaring what Officer shall then act as President, and such Officer shall act accordingly, until the Disability be removed, or a President shall be elected.[7]

The President shall, at stated Times, receive for his Services, a Compensation, which shall neither be encreased nor diminished during the Period for which he shall have been elected, and he shall not receive within that Period any other Emolument from the United States, or any of them.

Before he enter on the Execution of his Office, he shall take the following Oath or Affirmation:—"I do solemnly swear (or affirm) that I will faithfully execute the Office of President of the United States, and will to the best of my Ability, preserve, protect and defend the Constitution of the United States."

SECTION 2. The President shall be Commander in Chief of the Army and Navy of the United States, and of the Militia of the several States, when called into the actual Service of the United States; he may require the Opinion, in writing, of the principal Officer in each of the executive Departments, upon any Subject relating to the Duties of their respective Offices, and he shall have Power to grant Reprieves and Pardons for Offences against the United States, except in Cases of Impeachment.

He shall have Power, by and with the Advice and Consent of the Senate, to make Treaties, provided two thirds of the Senators present concur; and he shall nominate, and by and with the Advice and Consent of the Senate, shall appoint Ambassadors, other public Ministers and Consuls, Judges of the supreme Court, and all other Officers of the United States, whose Appointments are not herein otherwise provided for, and which shall be established by Law; but the Congress may by Law vest the Appointment of such inferior Officers, as they think proper, in the President alone, in the Courts of Law, or in the Heads of Departments.

The President shall have Power to fill up all Vacancies that may happen during the Recess of the Senate, by granting Commissions which shall expire at the End of their next Session.

SECTION 3. He shall from time to time give the Congress Information of the State of the Union, and recommend to their Consideration such Measures as he shall judge necessary and expedient; he may, on extraordinary Occasions, convene both Houses, or either of them, and in Case of Disagreement between them, with Respect to the Time of Adjournment, he may adjourn them to such Time as he shall think proper; he shall receive Ambassadors and other public Ministers; he shall take Care that the Laws be faithfully executed, and shall Commission all the Officers of the United States.

SECTION 4. The President, Vice President and all civil Officers of the United States, shall be removed from Office on Impeachment for, and Conviction of, Treason, Bribery, or other high Crimes and Misdemeanors.

[6] Superseded by the Twelfth Amendment.

[7] Modified by the Twenty-fifth Amendment.

Article III

SECTION 1. The judicial Power of the United States, shall be vested in one supreme Court, and in such inferior Courts as the Congress may from time to time ordain and establish.

The Judges, both of the supreme and inferior Courts, shall hold their Offices during good Behaviour, and shall, at stated Times, receive for their Services, a Compensation, which shall not be diminished during their Continuance in Office.

SECTION 2. The judicial Power shall extend to all Cases, in Law and Equity, arising under this Constitution, the Laws of the United States, and Treaties made, or which shall be made, under their Authority;—to all Cases affecting Ambassadors, other public Ministers and Consuls;—to all Cases of admiralty and maritime Jurisdiction;—to Controversies to which the United States shall be a Party;—to Controversies between two or more States;—between a State and Citizens of another State;[8]—between Citizens of different States,—between Citizens of the same State claiming Lands under Grants of different States, and between a State, or the Citizens thereof, and foreign States, Citizens or Subjects.

In all Cases affecting Ambassadors, other public Ministers and Consuls, and those in which a State shall be Party, the supreme Court shall have original Jurisdiction. In all the other Cases beforementioned, the supreme Court shall have appellate Jurisdiction, both as to Law and Fact, with such Exceptions, and under such Regulations as the Congress shall make.

The Trial of all Crimes, except in Cases of Impeachment, shall be by Jury; and such Trial shall be held in the State where the said Crimes shall have been committed; but when not committed within any State, the Trial shall be at such Place or Places as the Congress may by Law have directed.

SECTION 3. Treason against the United States, shall consist only in levying War against them, or in adhering to their Enemies, giving them Aid and Comfort. No Person shall be convicted of Treason unless on the Testimony of two Witnesses to the same overt Act, or on Confession in open Court.

The Congress shall have Power to declare the Punishment of Treason, but no Attainder of Treason shall work Corruption of Blood, or Forfeiture except during the Life of the Person attainted.

Article IV

SECTION 1. Full Faith and Credit shall be given in each State to the public Acts, Records, and judicial Proceedings of every other State. And the Congress may by general Laws prescribe the Manner in which such Acts, Records and Proceedings shall be proved, and the Effect thereof.

SECTION 2. The Citizens of each State shall be entitled to all Privileges and Immunities of Citizens in the several States.

A Person charged in any State with Treason, Felony, or other Crime, who shall flee from Justice, and be found in another State, shall on Demand of the executive Authority of the State from which he fled, be delivered up, to be removed to the State having Jurisdiction of the Crime.

No Person held to Service or Labour in one State, under the Laws thereof, escaping into another, shall, in Consequence of any Law or Regulation therein, be discharged from such Service or Labour, but shall be delivered up on Claim of the Party to whom such Service or Labour may be due.

SECTION 3. New States may be admitted by the Congress into this Union; but no new State shall be formed or erected within the Jurisdiction of any other State, nor any State be formed by the Junction of two or more States, or Parts of States, without the Consent of the Legislatures of the States concerned as well as of the Congress.

---

[8] Modified by the Eleventh Amendment.

The Congress shall have Power to dispose of and make all needful Rules and Regulations respecting the Territory or other Property belonging to the United States; and nothing in this Constitution shall be so construed as to Prejudice any Claims of the United States, or of any particular State.

SECTION 4. The United States shall guarantee to every State in this Union a Republican Form of Government, and shall protect each of them against Invasion; and on Application of the Legislature, or of the Executive (when the Legislature cannot be convened) against domestic Violence.

Article V

The Congress, whenever two thirds of both Houses shall deem it necessary, shall propose Amendments to this Constitution, or, on the Application of the Legislatures of two thirds of the several States, shall call a Convention for proposing Amendments, which, in either Case, shall be valid to all Intents and Purposes, as Part of this Constitution, when ratified by the Legislatures of three fourths of the several States, or by Conventions in three fourths thereof, as the one or the other Mode of Ratification may be proposed by the Congress; Provided that no Amendment which may be made prior to the Year One thousand eight hundred and eight shall in any Manner affect the first and fourth Clauses in the Ninth Section of the first Article; and that no State, without its Consent, shall be deprived of its equal Suffrage in the Senate.

Article VI

All Debts contracted and Engagements entered into, before the Adoption of this Constitution, shall be as valid against the United States under this Constitution, as under the Confederation.

This Constitution, and the Laws of the United States which shall be made in Pursuance thereof; and all Treaties made, or which shall be made, under the Authority of the United States, shall be the supreme Law of the Land; and the Judges in every State shall be bound thereby, any Thing in the Constitution or Laws of any State to the Contrary notwithstanding.

The Senators and Representatives before mentioned, and the Members of the several State Legislatures, and all executive and judicial Officers, both of the United States and of the several States, shall be bound by Oath or Affirmation, to support this Constitution; but no religious Test shall ever be required as a Qualification to any Office or public Trust under the United States.

Article VII

The Ratification of the Conventions of nine States, shall be sufficient for the Establishment of this Constitution between the States so ratifying the Same.

Done in Convention by the Unanimous Consent of the States present the Seventeenth Day of September in the Year of our Lord one thousand seven hundred and Eighty seven and of the Independence of the United States of America the Twelfth. In witness whereof We have hereunto subscribed our Names,

Articles in Addition to, and Amendment of, the Constitution of the United States of America, Proposed by Congress, and Ratified by the Legislatures of the Several States, Pursuant to the Fifth Article of the Original Constitution.

Amendment I[9]

Congress shall make no law respecting an establishment of religion, or prohibiting the free exercise thereof; or abridging the freedom of speech, or of the press; or the right of the people peaceably to assemble, and to petition the Government for a redress of grievances.

[9] The first ten amendments were passed by Congress September 25, 1789. They were ratified by three-fourths of the states December 15, 1791.

Amendment II

A well regulated Militia, being necessary to the security of a free State, the right of the people to keep and bear Arms shall not be infringed.

Amendment III

No Soldier shall, in time of peace, be quartered in any house, without the consent of the Owner, nor in time of war, but in a manner to be prescribed by law.

Amendment IV

The right of the people to be secure in their persons, houses, papers, and effects, against unreasonable searches and seizures, shall not be violated, and no Warrants shall issue, but upon probable cause, supported by Oath or affirmation, and particularly describing the place to be searched, and the persons or things to be seized.

Amendment V

No person shall be held to answer for a capital or otherwise infamous crime, unless on a presentment or indictment of a Grand Jury, except in cases arising in the land or naval forces, or in the Militia, when in actual service in time of War or public danger; nor shall any person be subject for the same offence to be twice put in jeopardy of life or limb; nor shall be compelled in any criminal case to be a witness against himself, nor be deprived of life, liberty, or property, without due process of law; nor shall private property be taken for public use, without just compensation.

Amendment VI

In all criminal prosecutions, the accused shall enjoy the right to a speedy and public trial, by an impartial jury of the State and district wherein the crime shall have been committed, which district shall have been previously ascertained by law, and to be informed of the nature and cause of the accusation; to be confronted with the witnesses against him; to have compulsory process for obtaining witnesses in his favor, and to have the Assistance of Counsel for his defence.

Amendment VII

In suits at common law, where the value in controversy shall exceed twenty dollars, the right of trial by jury shall be preserved, and no fact tried by a jury, shall be otherwise reexamined in any Court of the United States, than according to the rules of the common law.

Amendment VIII

Excessive bail shall not be required, nor excessive fines imposed, nor cruel and unusual punishments inflicted.

Amendment IX

The enumeration in the Constitution, of certain rights, shall not be construed to deny or disparage others retained by the people.

Amendment X

The powers not delegated to the United States by the Constitution; nor prohibited by it to the States, are reserved to the States respectively, or to the people.

Amendment XI[10]

The Judicial power of the United States shall not be construed to extend to any suit in law or equity, commenced or prosecuted against one of the United States by Citizens of another State, or by Citizens or Subjects of any Foreign State.

Amendment XII[11]

The Electors shall meet in their respective States and vote by ballot for President and Vice-President, one of whom, at least, shall not be an inhabitant of the same State with themselves; they shall name in their ballots the person voted for as President, and in distinct ballots the person voted for as Vice-President, and they shall make distinct lists of all persons voted for as President, and of all persons voted for as Vice-President, and of the number of votes for each, which lists they shall sign and certify, and transmit sealed to the seat of the government of the United States, directed to the President of the Senate;—The President of the Senate shall, in the presence of the Senate and House of Representatives, open all the certificates and the votes shall then be counted;—The person having the greatest number of votes for President, shall be the President, if such number be a majority of the whole number of Electors appointed; and if no person have such majority, then from the persons having the highest numbers not exceeding three on the list of those voted for as President, the House of Representatives shall choose immediately, by ballot, the President.

But in choosing the President, the votes shall be taken by states, the representation from each state having one vote; a quorum for this purpose shall consist of a member or members from two-thirds of the states, and a majority of all the states shall be necessary to a choice. And if the House of Representatives shall not choose a President whenever the right of choice shall devolve upon them, before the fourth day of March next following, then the Vice-President shall act as President, as in the case of the death or other constitutional disability of the President.—The person having the greatest number of votes as Vice-President, shall be the Vice-President, if such number be a majority of the whole number of Electors appointed, and if no person have a majority, then from the two highest numbers on the list, the Senate shall choose the Vice-President; a quorum for the purpose shall consist of two-thirds of the whole number of Senators, and a majority of the whole number shall be necessary to a choice. But no person constitutionally ineligible to the office of President shall be eligible to that of Vice-President of the United States.

Amendment XIII[12]

SECTION 1. Neither slavery nor involuntary servitude, except as a punishment for crime whereof the party shall have been duly convicted, shall exist within the United States, or any place subject to their jurisdiction.

SECTION 2. Congress shall have power to enforce this article by appropriate legislation.

Amendment XIV[13]

SECTION 1. All persons born or naturalized in the United States, and subject to the jurisdiction thereof, are citizens of the United States and of the State wherein they reside. No State shall make or enforce any law which shall abridge the privileges or immunities of citizens of the United States; nor shall any State deprive any person of life, liberty, or property, without due process of law; nor deny to any person within its jurisdiction the equal protection of the laws.

---

[10] Passed March 4, 1794. Ratified January 23, 1795.

[11] Passed December 9, 1803. Ratified June 15, 1804.

[12] Passed January 31, 1865. Ratified December 6, 1865.

[13] Passed June 13, 1866. Ratified July 9, 1868.

SECTION 2. Representatives shall be apportioned among the several States according to their respective numbers, counting the whole number of persons in each State, excluding Indians not taxed. But when the right to vote at any election for the choice of electors for President and Vice-President of the United States, Representatives in Congress, the Executive and Judicial officers of a State, or the members of the Legislature thereof, is denied to any of the male inhabitants of such State, being twenty-one years of age, and citizens of the United States, or in any way abridged, except for participation in rebellion, or other crime, the basis of representation therein shall be reduced in the proportion which the number of such male citizens shall bear to the whole number of male citizens twenty-one years of age in such State.

SECTION 3. No person shall be a Senator or Representative in Congress, or elector of President and Vice-President, or hold any office, civil or military, under the United States, or under any State, who, having previously taken an oath, as a member of Congress, or as an officer of the United States, or as a member of any State legislature, or as an executive or judicial officer of any State, to support the Constitution of the United States, shall have engaged in insurrection or rebellion against the same, or given aid or comfort to the enemies thereof. But Congress may by a vote of two-thirds of each House, remove such disability.

SECTION 4. The validity of the public debt of the United States, authorized by law, including debts incurred for payment of pensions and bounties for services in suppressing insurrection or rebellion, shall not be questioned. But neither the United States nor any State shall assume or pay any debt or obligation incurred in aid of insurrection or rebellion against the United States, or any claim for the loss or emancipation of any slave; but all such debts, obligations, and claims shall be held illegal and void.

SECTION 5. The Congress shall have the power to enforce, by appropriate legislation, the provisions of this article.

Amendment XV[14]

SECTION 1. The right of citizens of the United States to vote shall not be denied or abridged by the United States or by any State on account of race, color, or previous conditions of servitude—

SECTION 2. The Congress shall have power to enforce this article by appropriate legislation.

Amendment XVI[15]

The Congress shall have power to lay and collect taxes on incomes, from whatever source derived, without apportionment among the several States, and without regard to any census or enumeration.

Amendment XVII[16]

The Senate of the United States shall be composed of two Senators from each State, elected by the people thereof, for six years; and each Senator shall have one vote. The electors in each State shall have the qualifications requisite for electors of the most numerous branch of the State legislatures.

When vacancies happen in the representation of any State in the Senate, the executive authority of such State shall issue writs of election to fill such vacancies: Provided, That the legislature of any State may empower the executive thereof to make temporary appointments until the people fill the vacancies by election as the legislature may direct.

---

[14] Passed February 26, 1869. Ratified February 2, 1870.

[15] Passed July 12, 1909. Ratified February 3, 1913.

[16] Passed May 13, 1912. Ratified April 8, 1913.

This amendment shall not be so construed as to affect the election or term of any Senator chosen before it becomes valid as part of the Constitution.

Amendment XVIII[17]

SECTION 1. After one year from the ratification of this article the manufacture, sale, or transportation of intoxicating liquors within, the importation thereof into, or the exportation thereof from the United States and all territory subject to the jurisdiction thereof for beverage purposes is hereby prohibited.

SECTION 2. The Congress and the several States shall have concurrent power to enforce this article by appropriate legislation.

SECTION 3. This article shall be inoperative unless it shall have been ratified as an amendment to the Constitution by the legislatures of the several States, as provided in the Constitution, within seven years from the date of the submission hereof to the States by the Congress.

Amendment XIX[18]

The right of citizens of the United States to vote shall not be denied or abridged by the United States or by any State on account of sex.

Congress shall have power to enforce this article by appropriate legislation.

Amendment XX[19]

SECTION 1. The terms of the President and Vice-President shall end at noon on the 20th day of January, and the terms of Senators and Representatives at noon on the 3d day of January, of the years in which such terms would have ended if this article had not been ratified; and the terms of their successors shall then begin.

SECTION 2. The Congress shall assemble at least once in every year, and such meeting shall begin at noon on the 3d day of January, unless they shall by law appoint a different day.

SECTION 3. If, at the time fixed for the beginning of the term of the President, the President elect shall have died, the Vice-President elect shall become President. If a President shall not have been chosen before the time fixed for the beginning of his term, or if the President elect shall have failed to qualify, then the Vice-President elect shall act as President until a President shall have qualified; and the Congress may by law provide for the case wherein neither a President elect nor a Vice-President elect shall have qualified, declaring who shall then act as President, or the manner in which one who is to act shall be selected, and such person shall act accordingly until a President or Vice-President shall have qualified.

SECTION 4. The Congress may by law provide for the case of the death of any of the persons from whom the House of Representatives may choose a President whenever the right of choice shall have devolved upon them, and for the case of the death of any of the persons from whom the Senate may choose a Vice-President whenever the right of choice shall have devolved upon them.

SECTION 5. Sections 1 and 2 shall take effect on the 15th day of October following the ratification of this article.

SECTION 6. This article shall be inoperative unless it shall have been ratified as an amendment to the Constitution by the legislatures of three-fourths of the several States within seven years from the date of its submission.

[17] Passed December 18, 1917. Ratified January 16, 1919.

[18] Passed June 4, 1919. Ratified August 18, 1920.

[19] Passed March 2, 1932. Ratified January 23, 1933.

Amendment XXI[20]

SECTION 1. The eighteenth article of amendment to the Constitution of the United States is hereby repealed.

SECTION 2. The transportation or importation into any State, Territory, or possession of the United States for delivery or use therein of intoxicating liquors, in violation of the laws thereof, is hereby prohibited.

SECTION 3. This article shall be inoperative unless it shall have been ratified as an amendment to the Constitution by conventions in the several States, as provided in the Constitution, within seven years from the date of the submission hereof to the States by the Congress.

Amendment XXII[21]

No person shall be elected to the office of the President more than twice, and no person who has held the office of President, or acted as President, for more than two years of a term to which some other person was elected President shall be elected to the office of the President more than once.

But this Article shall not apply to any person holding the office of President when this Article was proposed by the Congress, and shall not prevent any person who may be holding the office of President, or acting as President, during the term within which this Article becomes operative from holding the office of President or acting as President during the remainder of such term.

Amendment XXIII[22]

SECTION 1. The District constituting the seat of Government of the United States shall appoint in such manner as the Congress may direct: A number of electors of President and Vice President equal to the whole number of Senators and Representatives in Congress to which the District would be entitled if it were a State, but in no event more than the least populous State; they shall be in addition to those appointed by the States, but they shall be considered, for the purposes of the election of President and Vice President, to be electors appointed by the State; and they shall meet in the District and perform such duties as provided by the twelfth article of amendment.

SECTION 2. The Congress shall have power to enforce this article by appropriate legislation.

Amendment XXIV[23]

SECTION 1. The right of citizens of the United States to vote in any primary or other election for President or Vice President, or for Senator or Representative in Congress, shall not be denied or abridged by the United States or any State by reason of failure to pay any poll tax or other tax.

SECTION 2. The Congress shall have power to enforce this article by appropriate legislation.

Amendment XXV[24]

SECTION 1. In case of the removal of the President from office or of his death or resignation, the Vice President shall become President.

SECTION 2. Whenever there is a vacancy in the office of the Vice President, the President shall nominate a Vice President who shall take office upon confirmation by a majority vote of both Houses of Congress.

---

[20] Passed February 20, 1933. Ratified December 5, 1933.

[21] Passed March 12, 1947. Ratified March 1, 1951.

[22] Passed June 16, 1960. Ratified April 3, 1961.

[23] Passed August 27, 1962. Ratified January 23, 1964.

[24] Passed July 6, 1965. Ratified February 11, 1967.

SECTION 3. Whenever the President transmits to the President pro tempore of the Senate and the Speaker of the House of Representatives his written declaration that he is unable to discharge the powers and duties of his office, and until he transmits them a written declaration to the contrary, such powers and duties shall be discharged by the Vice President as Acting President.

SECTION 4. Whenever the Vice President and a majority of either the principal officers of the executive department or of such other body as Congress may by law provide, transmit to the President pro tempore of the Senate and the Speaker of the House of Representatives their written declaration that the President is unable to discharge the powers and duties of his office, the Vice President shall immediately assume the powers and duties of the office of Acting President.

Thereafter, when the President transmits to the President pro tempore of the Senate and the Speaker of the House of Representatives his written declaration that no inability exists, he shall resume the powers and duties of his office unless the Vice President and a majority of either the principal officers of the executive department or of such other body as Congress may by law provide, transmit within four days to the President pro tempore of the Senate and the Speaker of the House of Representatives their written declaration that the President is unable to discharge the powers and duties of his office. Thereupon Congress shall decide the issue, assembling within forty-eight hours for that purpose if not in session. If the Congress, within twenty-one days after receipt of the latter written declaration, or, if Congress is not in session, within twenty-one days after Congress is required to assemble, determines by two-thirds vote of both Houses that the President is unable to discharge the powers and duties of his office, the Vice President shall continue to discharge the same as Acting President; otherwise, the President shall resume the powers and duties of his office.

Amendment XXVI[25]

SECTION 1 The right of citizens of theUnited States,who are eighteen years of age or older, to vote shall not be denied or abridged by the United States or by any State on account of age.

SECTION 2. The Congress shall have power to enforce this article by appropriate legislation.

Amendment XXVII[26]

No law, varying the compensation for the service of the Senators and Representatives, shall take effect, until an election of Representatives shall have intervened.

[25] Passed March 23, 1971. Ratified July 5, 1971.

[26] Passed September 25, 1789. Ratified May 7, 1992.

Admission of States

Order of admission	State	Date of admission	Order of admission	State	Date of admission
1	Delaware	December 7, 1787	26	Michigan	January 26, 1837
2	Pennsylvania	December 12, 1787	27	Florida	March 3, 1845
3	New Jersey	December 18, 1787	28	Texas	December 29, 1845
4	Georgia	January 2, 1788	29	Iowa	December 28, 1846
5	Connecticut	January 9, 1788	30	Wisconsin	May 29, 1848
6	Massachusetts	February 6, 1788	31	California	September 9, 1850
7	Maryland	April 28, 1788	32	Minnesota	May 11, 1858
8	South Carolina	May 23, 1788	33	Oregon	February 14, 1859
9	New Hampshire	June 21, 1788	34	Kansas	January 29, 1861
10	Virginia	June 25, 1788	35	West Virginia	June 20, 1863
11	New York	July 26, 1788	36	Nevada	October 31, 1864
12	North Carolina	November 21, 1789	37	Nebraska	March 1, 1867
13	Rhode Island	May 29, 1790	38	Colorado	August 1, 1876
14	Vermont	March 4, 1791	39	North Dakota	November 2, 1889
15	Kentucky	June 1, 1792	40	South Dakota	November 2, 1889
16	Tennessee	June 1, 1796	41	Montana	November 8, 1889
17	Ohio	March 1, 1803	42	Washington	November 11, 1889
18	Louisiana	April 30, 1812	43	Idaho	July 3, 1890
19	Indiana	December 11, 1816	44	Wyoming	July 10, 1890
20	Mississippi	December 10, 1817	45	Utah	January 4, 1896
21	Illinois	December 3, 1818	46	Oklahoma	November 16, 1907
22	Alabama	December 14, 1819	47	New Mexico	January 6, 1912
23	Maine	March 15, 1820	48	Arizona	February 14, 1912
24	Missouri	August 10, 1821	49	Alaska	January 3, 1959
25	Arkansas	June 15, 1836	50	Hawai'i	August 21, 1959

Population of the United States

Year	Total population	Number per square mile	Year	Total population	Number per square mile	Year	Total population	Number per square mile
1790	3,929	4.5	1828	12,237		1866	36,538	
1791	4,056		1829	12,565		1867	37,376	
1792	4,194		1830	12,901	7.4	1868	38,213	
1793	4,332		1831	13,321		1869	39,051	
1794	4,469		1832	13,742		1870	39,905	13.4
1795	4,607		1833	14,162		1871	40,938	
1796	4,745		1834	14,582		1872	41,972	
1797	4,883		1835	15,003		1873	43,006	
1798	5,021		1836	15,423		1874	44,040	
1799	5,159		1837	15,843		1875	45,073	
1800	5,297	6.1	1838	16,264		1876	46,107	
1801	5,486		1839	16,684		1877	47,141	
1802	5,679		1840	17,120	9.8	1878	48,174	
1803	5,872		1841	17,733		1879	49,208	
1804	5,065		1842	18,345		1880	50,262	16.9
1805	6,258		1843	18,957		1881	51,542	
1806	6,451		1844	19,569		1882	52,821	
1807	6,644		1845	20,182		1883	54,100	
1808	6,838		1846	20,794		1884	55,379	
1809	7,031		1847	21,406		1885	56,658	
1810	7,224	4.3	1848	22,018		1886	57,938	
1811	7,460		1849	22,631		1887	59,217	
1812	7,700		1850	23,261	7.9	1888	60,496	
1813	7,939		1851	24,086		1889	61,775	
1814	8,179		1852	24,911		1890[1]	63,056	21.2
1815	8,419		1853	25,736		1891	64,361	
1816	8,659		1854	26,561		1892	65,666	
1817	8,899		1855	27,386		1893	66,970	
1818	9,139		1856	28,212		1894	68,275	
1819	9,379		1857	29,037		1895	69,580	
1820	9,618	5.6	1858	29,862		1896	70,885	
1821	9,939		1859	30,687		1897	72,189	
1822	10,268		1860	31,513	10.6	1898	73,494	
1823	10,596		1861	32,351		1899	74,799	
1824	10,924		1862	33,188		1900	76,094	25.6
1825	11,252		1863	34,026		1901	77,585	
1826	11,580		1864	34,863		1902	79,160	
1827	11,909		1865	35,701		1903	80,632	

Figures are from *Historical Statistics of the United States, Colonial Times to 1957* (1961), pp. 7, 8; *Statistical Abstract of the United States: 1974*, p. 5, Census Bureau for 1974 and 1975; and *Statistical Abstract of the United States: 1988*, p. 7.

Note: Population figures are in thousands. Density figures are for land area of continental United States.

[1] Indians living in Indian Territory or on reservations were not included in the population count until 1890.

Population of the United States *(continued)*

Year	Total population	Number per square mile	Year	Total population[1]	Number per square mile	Year	Total population[1]	Number per square mile
1904	82,165		1941	133,894		1978	218,717	
1905	83,820		1942	135,361		1979	220,584	
1906	85,437		1943	137,250		1980	226,546	64.0
1907	87,000		1944	138,916		1981	230,138	
1908	88,709		1945	140,468		1982	232,520	
1909	90,492		1946	141,936		1983	234,799	
1910	92,407	31.0	1947	144,698		1984	237,001	
1911	93,868		1948	147,208		1985	239,283	
1912	95,331		1949	149,767		1986	241,596	
1913	97,227		1950	150,697	50.7	1987	234,773	
1914	99,118		1951	154,878		1988	245,051	
1915	100,549		1952	157,553		1989	247,350	
1916	101,966		1953	160,184		1990	250,122	70.3
1917	103,414		1954	163,026		1991	254,521	
1918	104,550		1955	165,931		1992	245,908	
1919	105,063		1956	168,903		1993	257,908	
1920	106,466	35.6	1957	171,984		1994	261,875	
1921	108,541		1958	174,882		1995	263,434	
1922	110,055		1959	177,830		1996	266,096	
1923	111,950		1960	178,464	60.1	1997	267,901	
1924	114,113		1961	183,642		1998	269,501	
1925	115,832		1962	186,504		1999	272,700	
1926	117,399		1963	189,197		2000	282,172	80.0
1927	119,038		1964	191,833		2001	285,082	
1928	120,501		1965	194,237		2002	287,804	
1929	121,700		1966	196,485		2003	290,326	
1930	122,775	41.2	1967	198,629		2004	293,046	
1931	124,040		1968	200,619		2005	295,753	
1932	124,840		1969	202,599		2006	298,593	
1933	125,579		1970	203,875	57.5[2]	2007	301,580	
1934	126,374		1971	207,045		2008	304,375	
1935	127,250		1972	208,842		2009	307,007	
1936	128,053		1973	210,396		2010	308,746	87.4
1937	128,825		1974	211,894		2011	311,588	
1938	129,825		1975	213,631		2012	313,914	
1939	130,880		1976	215,152		2013	316,439	
1940	131,669	44.2	1977	216,880				

[1] Figures after 1940 represent total population including armed forces abroad, except in official census years.

[2] Figure includes Alaska and Hawai'i, were territories through 1950, and were first included in the United States in the 1960 census.

Presidential Elections

Year	Number of states	Candidates[1]	Parties	Popular vote	Electoral vote	Percentage of popular vote[2]
1789	11	**George Washington**	No party designations		69	
		John Adams			34	
		Minor Candidates			35	
1792	15	**George Washington**	No party designations		132	
		John Adams			77	
		George Clinton			50	
		Minor Candidates			5	
1796	16	**John Adams**	Federalist		71	
		Thomas Jefferson	Democratic-Republican		68	
		Thomas Pinckney	Federalist		59	
		Aaron Burr	Democratic-Republican		30	
		Minor Candidates			48	
1800	16	**Thomas Jefferson**	Democratic-Republican		73	
		Aaron Burr	Democratic-Republican		73	
		John Adams	Federalist		65	
		Charles C. Pinckney	Federalist		64	
		John Jay	Federalist		1	
1804	17	**Thomas Jefferson**	Democratic-Republican		162	
		Charles C. Pinckney	Federalist		14	
1808	17	**James Madison**	Democratic-Republican		122	
		Charles C. Pinckney	Federalist		47	
		George Clinton	Democratic-Republican		6	
1812	18	**James Madison**	Democratic-Republican		128	
		DeWitt Clinton	Federalist		89	
1816	19	**James Monroe**	Democratic-Republican		183	
		Rufus King	Federalist		34	
1820	24	**James Monroe**	Democratic-Republican		231	
		John Quincy Adams	Independent Republican		1	
1824	24	**John Quincy Adams**	Democratic-Republican	108,740	84	30.5
		Andrew Jackson	Democratic-Republican	153,544	99	43.1
		William H. Crawford	Democratic-Republican	46,618	41	13.1
		Henry Clay	Democratic-Republican	47,136	37	13.2
1828	24	**Andrew Jackson**	Democratic	647,286	178	56.0
		John Quincy Adams	National Republican	508,064	83	44.0

[1]Before the passage of the Twelfth Amendment in 1804, the Electoral College voted for two presidential candidates; the runner-up became vice president. Figures are from *Historical Statistics of the United States, Colonial Times to 1957* (1961), pp. 682–83; and the U.S. Department of Justice.

[2]Candidates receiving less than 1 percent of the popular vote have been omitted. For that reason the percentage of popular vote given for any election year may not total 100 percent.

Presidential Elections *(continued)*

Year	Number of states	Candidates	Parties	Popular vote	Electoral vote	Percentage of popular vote[1]
1832	24	**Andrew Jackson**	Democratic	687,502	219	55.0
		Henry Clay	National Republican	530,189	49	42.4
		William Wirt	Anti-Masonic		7	
		John Floyd	National Republican	33,108	11	2.6
1836	26	**Martin Van Buren**	Democratic	765,483	170	50.9
		William H. Harrison	Whig		73	
		Hugh L. White	Whig	739,795	26	
		Daniel Webster	Whig		14	
		W. P. Mangum	Whig		11	
1840	26	**William H. Harrison**	Whig	1,274,624	234	53.1
		Martin Van Buren	Democratic	1,127,781	60	46.9
1844	26	**James K. Polk**	Democratic	1,338,464	170	49.6
		Henry Clay	Whig	1,300,097	105	48.1
		James G. Birney	Liberty	62,300		2.3
1848	30	**Zachary Taylor**	Whig	1,360,967	163	47.4
		Lewis Cass	Democratic	1,222,342	127	42.5
		Martin Van Buren	Free Soil	291,263		10.1
1852	31	**Franklin Pierce**	Democratic	1,601,117	254	50.9
		Winfield Scott	Whig	1,385,453	42	44.1
		John P. Hale	Free Soil	155,825		5.0
1856	31	**James Buchanan**	Democratic	1,832,955	174	45.3
		John C. Frémont	Republican	1,339,932	114	33.1
		Millard Fillmore	American	871,731	8	21.6
1860	33	**Abraham Lincoln**	Republican	1,865,593	180	39.8
		Stephen A. Douglas	Democratic	1,382,713	12	29.5
		John C. Breckinridge	Democratic	848,356	72	18.1
		John Bell	Constitutional Union	592,906	39	12.6
1864	36	**Abraham Lincoln**	Republican	2,206,938	212	55.0
		George B. McClellan	Democratic	1,803,787	21	45.0
1868	37	**Ulysses S. Grant**	Republican	3,013,421	214	52.7
		Horatio Seymour	Democratic	2,706,829	80	47.3
1872	37	**Ulysses S. Grant**	Republican	3,596,745	286	55.6
		Horace Greeley	Democratic	2,843,446	[2]	43.9
1876	38	**Rutherford B. Hayes**	Republican	4,036,572	185	48.0
		Samuel J. Tilden	Democratic	4,284,020	184	51.0

[1] Candidates receiving less than 1 percent of the popular vote have been omitted. For that reason the percentage of popular vote given for any election year may not total 100 percent.

Presidential Elections *(continued)*

Year	Number of states	Candidates	Parties	Popular vote	Electoral vote	Percentage of popular vote[1]
1880	38	**James A. Garfield**	Republican	4,453,295	214	48.5
		Winfield S. Hancock	Democratic	4,414,082	155	48.1
		James B. Weaver	Greenback-Labor	308,578		3.4
1884	38	**Grover Cleveland**	Democratic	4,879,507	219	48.5
		James G. Blaine	Republican	4,850,293	182	48.2
		Benjamin F. Butler	Greenback-Labor	175,370		1.8
		John P. St. John	Prohibition	150,369		1.5
1888	38	**Benjamin Harrison**	Republican	5,477,129	233	47.9
		Grover Cleveland	Democratic	5,537,857	168	48.6
		Clinton B. Fisk	Prohibition	249,506		2.2
		Anson J. Streeter	Union Labor	146,935		1.3
1892	44	**Grover Cleveland**	Democratic	5,555,426	277	46.1
		Benjamin Harrison	Republican	5,182,690	145	43.0
		James B. Weaver	People's	1,029,846	22	8.5
		John Bidwell	Prohibition	264,133		2.2
1896	45	**William McKinley**	Republican	7,102,246	271	51.1
		William J. Bryan	Democratic	6,492,559	176	47.7
1900	45	**William McKinley**	Republican	7,218,491	292	51.7
		William J. Bryan	Democratic; Populist	6,356,734	155	45.5
		John C. Wooley	Prohibition	208,914		1.5
1904	45	**Theodore Roosevelt**	Republican	7,628,461	336	57.4
		Alton B. Parker	Democratic	5,084,223	140	37.6
		Eugene V. Debs	Socialist	402,283		3.0
		Silas C. Swallow	Prohibition	258,536		1.9
1908	46	**William H. Taft**	Republican	7,675,320	321	51.6
		William J. Bryan	Democratic	6,412,294	162	43.1
		Eugene V. Debs	Socialist	420,793		2.8
		Eugene W. Chafin	Prohibition	253,840		1.7
1912	48	**Woodrow Wilson**	Democratic	6,296,547	435	41.9
		Theodore Roosevelt	Progressive	4,118,571	88	27.4
		William H. Taft	Republican	3,486,720	8	23.2
		Eugene V. Debs	Socialist	900,672		6.0
		Eugene W. Chafin	Prohibition	206,275		1.4
1916	48	**Woodrow Wilson**	Democratic	9,127,695	277	49.4
		Charles E. Hughes	Republican	8,533,507	254	46.2
		A. L. Benson	Socialist	585,113		3.2
		J. Frank Hanly	Prohibition	220,506		1.2

[1] Candidates receiving less than 1 percent of the popular vote have been omitted. For that reason the percentage of popular vote given for any election year may not total 100 percent.

[2] Greeley died shortly after the election; the electors supporting him then divided their votes among minor candidates.

Year	Number of states	Candidates	Parties	Popular vote	Electoral vote	Percentage of popular vote[1]
1920	48	**Warren G. Harding**	Republican	16,143,407	404	60.4
		James N. Cox	Democratic	9,130,328	127	34.2
		Eugene V. Debs	Socialist	919,799		3.4
		P. P. Christensen	Farmer-Labor	265,411		1.0
1924	48	**Calvin Coolidge**	Republican	15,718,211	382	54.0
		John W. Davis	Democratic	8,385,283	136	28.8
		Robert M. La Follette	Progressive	4,831,289	13	16.6
1928	48	**Herbert C. Hoover**	Republican	21,391,993	444	58.2
		Alfred E. Smith	Democratic	15,016,169	87	40.9
1932	48	**Franklin D. Roosevelt**	Democratic	22,809,638	472	57.4
		Herbert C. Hoover	Republican	15,758,901	59	39.7
		Norman Thomas	Socialist	881,951		2.2
1936	48	**Franklin D. Roosevelt**	Democratic	27,752,869	523	60.8
		Alfred M. Landon	Republican	16,674,665	8	36.5
		William Lemke	Union	882,479		1.9
1940	48	**Franklin D. Roosevelt**	Democratic	27,307,819	449	54.8
		Wendell L. Willkie	Republican	22,321,018	82	44.8
1944	48	**Franklin D. Roosevelt**	Democratic	25,606,585	432	53.5
		Thomas E. Dewey	Republican	22,014,745	99	46.0
1948	48	**Harry S. Truman**	Democratic	24,105,812	303	49.5
		Thomas E. Dewey	Republican	21,970,065	189	45.1
		J. Strom Thurmond	States' Rights	1,169,063	39	2.4
		Henry A. Wallace	Progressive	1,157,172		2.4
1952	48	**Dwight D. Eisenhower**	Republican	33,936,234	442	55.1
		Adlai E. Stevenson	Democratic	27,314,992	89	44.4
1956	48	**Dwight D. Eisenhower**	Republican	35,590,472	457	57.6
		Adlai E. Stevenson	Democratic	26,022,752	73	42.1
1960	50	**John F. Kennedy**	Democratic	34,227,096	303	49.9
		Richard M. Nixon	Republican	34,108,546	219	49.6
1964	50	**Lyndon B. Johnson**	Democratic	43,126,506	486	61.1
		Barry M. Goldwater	Republican	27,176,799	52	38.5
1968	50	**Richard M. Nixon**	Republican	31,785,480	301	43.4
		Hubert H. Humphrey	Democratic	31,275,165	191	42.7
		George C. Wallace	American Independent	9,906,473	46	13.5
1972	50	**Richard M. Nixon**	Republican	47,169,911	520	60.7
		George S. McGovern	Democratic	29,170,383	17	37.5
1976	50	**Jimmy Carter**	Democratic	40,827,394	297	50.0
		Gerald R. Ford	Republican	39,145,977	240	47.9

[1] Candidates receiving less than 1 percent of the popular vote have been omitted. For that reason the percentage of popular vote given for any election year may not total 100 percent.

Presidential Elections *(continued)*

Year	Number of states	Candidates	Parties	Popular vote	Electoral vote	Percentage of popular vote[1]
1980	50	**Ronald W. Reagan**	Republican	43,899,248	489	50.8
		Jimmy Carter	Democratic	35,481,435	49	41.0
		John B. Anderson	Independent	5,719,437		6.6
		Ed Clark	Libertarian	920,859		1.0
1984	50	**Ronald W. Reagan**	Republican	54,281,858	525	59.2
		Walter F. Mondale	Democratic	37,457,215	13	40.8
1988	50	**George H. Bush**	Republican	47,917,341	426	54
		Michael Dukakis	Democratic	41,013,030	112	46
1992	50	**William Clinton**	Democratic	44,908,254	370	43.0
		George H. Bush	Republican	39,102,343	168	37.4
		Ross Perot	Independent	19,741,065		18.9
1996	50	**William Clinton**	Democratic	45,628,667	379	49.2
		Robert Dole	Republican	37,869,435	159	40.8
		Ross Perot	Reform	7,874,283		8.5
2000	50	**George W. Bush**	Republican	50,456,062	271	47.9
		Albert Gore	Democratic	50,996,582	266	48.4
		Ralph Nader	Green	2,858,843		2.7
2004	50	**George W. Bush**	Republican	62,040,606	286	51
		John F. Kerry	Democratic	59,028,109	252	48
		Ralph Nader	Green/Independent	411,304		1
2008	50	**Barack Obama**	Democratic	66,882,230	365	53
		John McCain	Republican	58,343,671	173	46
2012	50	**Barack Obama**	Democratic	65,917,258	332	51
		Mitt Romney	Republican	60,932,235	206	47

[1]Candidates receiving less than 1 percent of the popular vote have been omitted. For that reason the percentage of popular vote given for any election year may not total 100 percent.

Presidents and Vice Presidents

Term	President	Vice President
1789–1793	George Washington	John Adams
1793–1797	George Washington	John Adams
1797–1801	John Adams	Thomas Jefferson
1801–1805	Thomas Jefferson	Aaron Burr
1805–1809	Thomas Jefferson	George Clinton
1809–1813	James Madison	George Clinton (d. 1812)
1813–1817	James Madison	Elbridge Gerry (d. 1814)
1817–1821	James Monroe	Daniel D. Tompkins
1821–1825	James Monroe	Daniel D. Tompkins
1825–1829	John Quincy Adams	John C. Calhoun
1829–1833	Andrew Jackson	John C. Calhoun (resigned 1832)
1833–1837	Andrew Jackson	Martin Van Buren
1837–1841	Martin Van Buren	Richard M. Johnson
1841–1845	William H. Harrison (d. 1841) John Tyler	John Tyler
1845–1849	James K. Polk	George M. Dallas
1849–1853	Zachary Taylor (d. 1850) Millard Fillmore	Millard Fillmore
1853–1857	Franklin Pierce	William R. D. King (d. 1853)
1857–1861	James Buchanan	John C. Breckinridge
1861–1865	Abraham Lincoln	Hannibal Hamlin
1865–1869	Abraham Lincoln (d. 1865) Andrew Johnson	Andrew Johnson
1869–1873	Ulysses S. Grant	Schuyler Colfax
1873–1877	Ulysses S. Grant	Henry Wilson (d. 1875)
1877–1881	Rutherford B. Hayes	William A. Wheeler
1881–1885	James A. Garfield (d. 1881) Chester A. Arthur	Chester A. Arthur
1885–1889	Grover Cleveland	Thomas A. Hendricks (d. 1885)
1889–1893	Benjamin Harrison	Levi P. Morton
1893–1897	Grover Cleveland	Adlai E. Stevenson
1897–1901	William McKinley	Garret A. Hobart (d. 1899)
1901–1905	William McKinley (d. 1901) Theodore Roosevelt	Theodore Roosevelt
1905–1909	Theodore Roosevelt	Charles W. Fairbanks
1909–1913	William H. Taft	James S. Sherman (d.1912)
1913–1917	Woodrow Wilson	Thomas R. Marshall
1917–1921	Woodrow Wilson	Thomas R. Marshall
1921–1925	Warren G. Harding (d. 1923) Calvin Coolidge	Calvin Coolidge
1925–1929	Calvin Coolidge	Charles G. Dawes
1929–1933	Herbert Hoover	Charles Curtis
1933–1937	Franklin D. Roosevelt	John N. Garner
1937–1941	Franklin D. Roosevelt	John N. Garner
1941–1945	Franklin D. Roosevelt	Henry A. Wallace
1945–1949	Franklin D. Roosevelt (d. 1945) Harry S Truman	Harry S Truman
1949–1953	Harry S Truman	Alben W. Barkley
1953–1957	Dwight D. Eisenhower	Richard M. Nixon
1957–1961	Dwight D. Eisenhower	Richard M. Nixon
1961–1965	John F. Kennedy (d. 1963) Lyndon B. Johnson	Lyndon B. Johnson
1965–1969	Lyndon B. Johnson	Hubert H. Humphrey, Jr.
1969–1974	Richard M. Nixon	Spiro T. Agnew (resigned 1973); Gerald R. Ford
1974–1977	Gerald R. Ford	Nelson A. Rockefeller
1977–1981	Jimmy Carter	Walter F. Mondale
1981–1985	Ronald Reagan	George Bush
1985–1989	Ronald Reagan	George Bush
1993–1993	George Bush	J. Danforth Quayle III
1993–2001	William Clinton	Albert Gore, Jr.
2001–2005	George W. Bush	Richard Cheney
2005–2009	George W. Bush	Richard Cheney
2009–	Barack Obama	Joseph Biden

Justices of the U.S. Supreme Court

Name	Term of service	Years of service	Appointed by	Name	Term of service	Years of service	Appointed by
John Jay	1789–1795	5	Washington	Robert C. Grier	1846–1870	23	Polk
John Rutledge	1789–1791	1	Washington	Benjamin R. Curtis	1851–1857	6	Fillmore
William Cushing	1789–1810	20	Washington	John A. Campbell	1853–1861	8	Pierce
James Wilson	1789–1798	8	Washington	Nathan Clifford	1858–1881	23	Buchanan
John Blair	1789–1796	6	Washington	Noah H. Swayne	1862–1881	18	Lincoln
Robert H. Harrison	1789–1790	—	Washington	Samuel F. Miller	1862–1890	28	Lincoln
James Iredell	1790–1799	9	Washington	David Davis	1862–1877	14	Lincoln
Thomas Johnson	1791–1793	1	Washington	Stephen J. Field	1863–1897	34	Lincoln
William Paterson	1793–1806	13	Washington	**Salmon P. Chase**	1864–1873	8	Lincoln
John Rutledge[1]	1795	—	Washington	William Strong	1870–1880	10	Grant
Samuel Chase	1796–1811	15	Washington	Joseph P. Bradley	1870–1892	22	Grant
Oliver Ellsworth	1796–1800	4	Washington	Ward Hunt	1873–1882	9	Grant
Bushrod Washington	1798–1829	31	J. Adams	**Morrison R. Waite**	1874–1888	14	Grant
Alfred Moore	1799–1804	4	J. Adams	John M. Harlan	1877–1911	34	Hayes
John Marshall	1801–1835	34	J. Adams	William B. Woods	1880–1887	7	Hayes
William Johnson	1804–1834	30	Jefferson	Stanley Matthews	1881–1889	7	Garfield
H. Brockholst Livingston	1806–1823	16	Jefferson	Horace Gray	1882–1902	20	Arthur
Thomas Todd	1807–1826	18	Jefferson	Samuel Blatchford	1882–1893	11	Arthur
Joseph Story	1811–1845	33	Madison	Lucius Q. C. Lamar	1888–1893	5	Cleveland
Gabriel Duval	1811–1835	24	Madison	**Melville W. Fuller**	1888–1910	21	Cleveland
Smith Thompson	1823–1843	20	Monroe	David J. Brewer	1890–1910	20	B. Harrison
Robert Trimble	1826–1828	2	J. Q. Adams	Henry B. Brown	1890–1906	16	B. Harrison
John McLean	1829–1861	32	Jackson	George Shiras, Jr.	1892–1903	10	B. Harrison
Henry Baldwin	1830–1844	14	Jackson	Howell E. Jackson	1893–1895	2	B. Harrison
James M. Wayne	1835–1867	32	Jackson	Edward D. White	1894–1910	16	Cleveland
Roger B. Taney	1836–1864	28	Jackson	Rufus W. Peckham	1895–1909	14	Cleveland
Philip P. Barbour	1836–1841	4	Jackson	Joseph McKenna	1898–1925	26	McKinley
John Catron	1837–1865	28	Van Buren	Oliver W. Holmes, Jr.	1902–1932	30	T. Roosevelt
John McKinley	1837–1852	15	Van Buren	William R. Day	1903–1922	19	T. Roosevelt
Peter V. Daniel	1841–1860	19	Van Buren	William H. Moody	1906–1910	3	T. Roosevelt
Samuel Nelson	1845–1872	27	Tyler	Horace H. Lurton	1910–1914	4	Taft
Levi Woodbury	1845–1851	5	Polk	Charles E. Hughes	1910–1916	5	Taft

[1] Acting chief justice; Senate refused to confirm appointment.

Note: Chief justices appear in bold type.

Justices of the U.S. Supreme Court *(continued)*

Name	Term of service	Years of service	Appointed by	Name	Term of service	Years of service	Appointed by
Willis Van Devanter	1911–1937	26	Taft	Sherman Minton	1949–1956	7	Truman
Joseph R. Lamar	1911–1916	5	Taft	**Earl Warren**	1953–1969	16	Eisenhower
Edward D. White	1910–1921	11	Taft	John Marshall Harlan	1955–1971	16	Eisenhower
Mahlon Pitney	1912–1922	10	Taft	William J. Brennan, Jr.	1956–1990	34	Eisenhower
James C. McReynolds	1914–1941	26	Wilson	Charles E. Whittaker	1957–1962	5	Eisenhower
Louis D. Brandeis	1916–1939	22	Wilson	Potter Stewart	1958–1981	23	Eisenhower
John H. Clarke	1916–1922	6	Wilson	Byron R. White	1962–1993	31	Kennedy
William H. Taft	1921–1930	8	Harding	Arthur J. Goldberg	1962–1965	3	Kennedy
George Sutherland	1922–1938	15	Harding	Abe Fortas	1965–1969	4	Johnson
Pierce Butler	1922–1939	16	Harding	Thurgood Marshall	1967–1994	24	Johnson
Edward T. Sanford	1923–1930	7	Harding	**Warren E. Burger**	1969–1986	18	Nixon
Harlan F. Stone	1925–1941	16	Coolidge	Harry A. Blackmun	1970–1994	24	Nixon
Charles E. Hughes	1930–1941	11	Hoover	Lewis F. Powell, Jr.	1971–1987	15	Nixon
Owen J. Roberts	1930–1945	15	Hoover	**William H. Rehnquist**	1971–2005	34	Nixon
Benjamin N. Cardozo	1932–1938	6	Hoover	John P. Stevens III	1975–2010	35	Ford
Hugo L. Black	1937–1971	34	F. Roosevelt	Sandra Day O'Connor	1981–2006	25	Reagan
Stanley F. Reed	1938–1957	19	F. Roosevelt	Antonin Scalia	1986–2016	30	Reagan
Felix Frankfurter	1939–1962	23	F. Roosevelt	Anthony M. Kennedy	1988–	—	Reagan
William O. Douglas	1939–1975	36	F. Roosevelt	David Souter	1990–2009	19	Bush
Frank Murphy	1940–1949	9	F. Roosevelt	Clarence Thomas	1991–	—	Bush
Harlan F. Stone	1941–1946	5	F. Roosevelt	Ruth Bader Ginsburg	1993–	—	Clinton
James F. Byrnes	1941–1942	1	F. Roosevelt	Stephen G. Breyer	1994–	—	Clinton
Robert H. Jackson	1941–1954	13	F. Roosevelt	**John G. Roberts, Jr.**	2005–	—	G. W. Bush
Wiley B. Rutledge	1943–1949	6	F. Roosevelt	Samuel Anthony Alito, Jr.	2006–	—	G. W. Bush
Harold H. Burton	1945–1958	13	Truman	Sonia Sotomayor	2009–	—	Obama
Fred M. Vinson	1946–1953	7	Truman	Elena Kagan	2010–	—	Obama
Tom C. Clark	1949–1967	18	Truman				

Note: Chief justices appear in bold type.

Index